INDEPENDENT EVENTS

E and F are independent if $P(E|F) = P(E)$,
$P(F|E) = P(F)$, or $P(E \cap F) = P(E) \cdot P(F)$

BAYES FORMULA

$$P(E_i|F) = \frac{P(E_i) \cdot P(F|E_i)}{P(E_1) \cdot P(F|E_1) + P(E_2) \cdot P(F|E_2) + \cdots + P(E_n) \cdot P(F|E_n)}$$

BERNOULLI EXPERIMENTS

Probability of x successes in n trials $=$
$C(n, x) \cdot p^x \cdot (1 - p)^{n - x}$

$E(X) = np$
$\sigma^2(X) = npq$
$\sigma(X) = \sqrt{npq}$

EXPECTED VALUE

$$E(x) = x_1 p_1 + x_2 p_2 + \cdots + x_n p_n$$

SIMPLE INTE  W9-CTM-814

$I = Prt$
$A = P(1 + rt)$

SIMPLE DISCOUNT

$D = Mdt$
$PR = M(1 - dt)$

COMPOUND INTEREST

$A = P(1 + i)^k$

FUTURE VALUE OF AN ANNUITY

$$A = R\left[\frac{(1 + i)^k - 1}{i}\right]$$

PRESENT VALUE OF AN ANNUITY

$$P = R\left[\frac{(1 + i)^n - 1}{i(1 + i)^n}\right] = R\left[\frac{1 - (1 + i)^{-n}}{i}\right]$$

MATHEMATICS
for Management, Social & Life Sciences

MATHEMATICS
for Management, Social & Life Sciences

Howard L. Rolf
Baylor University

Raymond J. Cannon, Jr.
Baylor University

Gareth Williams
Stetson University

Wm. C. Brown Publishers

Book Team

Editor *Earl McPeek*
Developmental Editor *Janette S. Scotchmer*
Designer *Elise A. Burckhardt*

WCB **Wm. C. Brown Publishers**

President *G. Franklin Lewis*
Vice President, Publisher *George Wm. Bergquist*
Vice President, Publisher *Thomas E. Doran*
Vice President, Operations and Production *Beverly Kolz*
National Sales Manager *Virginia S. Moffat*
Advertising Manager *Ann M. Knepper*
Marketing Manager *John W. Calhoun*
Editor in Chief *Edward G. Jaffe*
Managing Editor, Production *Colleen A. Yonda*
Production Editorial Manager *Julie A. Kennedy*
Production Editorial Manager *Ann Fuerste*
Publishing Services Manager *Karen J. Slaght*
Manager of Visuals and Design *Faye M. Schilling*

Cover photo © Paul Silverman/Fundamental Photographs

Printed in the United States of America by Wm. C. Brown Publishers,
2460 Kerper Boulevard, Dubuque, IA 52001

10 9 8 7 6 5 4 3 2 1

To: *Anita Ward Rolf*
Jo, Catherine, Karen, and Susan
Donna, Brian, and Jeff

Contents

Preface

MATHEMATICS AS WE KNOW it came into existence through an evolutionary process, and that process continues today. Occasionally, a mathematical idea will fade away as it is replaced by a better idea. Old ideas become modified, or new and significant concepts are developed and take their place. Mathematical concepts have been found useful in understanding and applying the ideas of many disciplines. Therefore some mathematical concepts were developed in an attempt to solve problems in a particular discipline. *Mathematics for Management, Social, and Life Sciences* deals with some of the topics that are especially useful in business, the life sciences, and the social sciences. This book assumes at least one year of high school algebra, and Appendix A provides a brief review for those who may need to refresh their memory.

FEATURES

Exposition

The authors have concentrated on writing that is clear, friendly, and considerate of the students. We have avoided a terse, formal style and have included enough detail in the computations that students can follow successive steps. We use over 790 examples both to develop and to illustrate the concepts. Furthermore, while formal proofs of every theorem would be inappropriate for a text like this, we have included explanations to justify some results that are not intuitively obvious (for example, the product rule for derivatives). Students will become more mathematically sophisticated as they proceed through the text, and our writing recognizes and encourages this.

Algebra Review

Appendix A contains a review of algebraic skills needed for the course. This appendix is written in the same expository and pedagogical style as the rest of the text, with worked examples followed by exercises to test understanding of the topics. Thus an instructor may begin a course with Appendix A or begin in Chapter 1, using the appendix to assign review problems for the class or as a source of review for individual students.

Pre-Calculus Review

Instructors might want to review the concept of functions and functional notation found in Sections A–7 and A–8 of Appendix A before beginning Chapter 9.

Flexibility

Mathematics for Management, Social, and Life Sciences was written to provide flexibility in the choice and order of topics. Some topics must, of necessity, be covered in sequence. The finite math chapters that are prerequisites are shown in the following diagram.

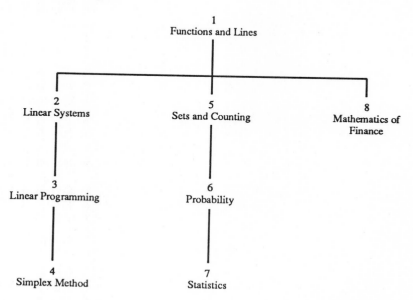

Although a good understanding of most calculus topics depends on a good understanding of preceding topics, we have tried to keep the calculus chapters as flexible as possible. Different instructors will have different tastes, some emphasizing one topic that others may omit; we have attempted to structure the text with this fact in mind.

Pedagogy

The pedagogical system is designed to assist the student in understanding and applying the concepts discussed.

- *Cross-referencing of Examples and Exercises.* The exercise sets form an integral part of any mathematics textbook, but not the only part. Our exercises are structured to encourage students to read the body of the text for explanations and examples. We have done this by cross-referencing examples with exercises. After reading a particular example, students can go directly to the referenced example to test their understanding. Conversely, selected exercises refer to examples that illustrate the concepts needed to work them.

- *Exercises.* Over 4400 exercises provide ample means for the student to apply mathematical concepts to problems and give the instructor a variety of choices in assigning problems. Exercises are also included that illustrate applications of the concepts.

- *Graded Exercises.* The exercises are graded into three levels from routine problems to those that are more challenging.

- Material at the end of each chapter includes important terms referenced to the section in which they are defined and review exercises for the chapter.

- Definitions, key formulas, theorems, procedures, and summaries are boxed to emphasize their importance to the student.

- All figures use two colors to reinforce learning.

- Occasional **Caution** or **Note** statements are included as warnings of typical problem areas or reminders of concepts that were introduced earlier.

- Answers to odd-numbered exercises are located in Appendix B to provide feedback to students.

Applications

Finally, we recognize that while students want to see the relevance of mathematics to real-world problems, a complete and accurate description of such problems may require knowledge beyond a beginning student's expertise. Moreover, the purpose of this text is to teach *mathematics*. While recognizing these facts, we also realize that other disciplines require this course precisely because of the many applications of mathematical concepts. Thus we have included examples and exercises that involve a wide variety of these applications. At the end of this preface is a listing of the chapters in this text, together with a few of the applications that appear in the exercises in each chapter.

Some applications are developed in more depth with discussions that are entirely self-contained; see, for example, Sections 11–6 (Optimization in Applications), 12–1 (Exponential Functions), 12–5 (Applications of Exponential Functions), and 13–5 (Applications of Area).

COMMENTS ON THIS EDITION

This book is the combined version of *Finite Mathematics,* Second Edition, by Rolf and Williams and *Calculus for Management, Social, and Life Sciences,* Second Edition, by Cannon and Williams. A combined version of the first editions of these books was not published, so this combined version is considered a first edition. Even so, comments of students and teachers have been helpful in revising the explanations and exercises. For those who are familiar with the first editions of the separate texts, the following indicate some changes made in the second editions that are incorporated into this book.

1. The number of examples and exercises has increased by 15% to provide more applications and a total of more than 2100 exercises for the finite math chapters and 2300 exercises for the calculus chapters.

2. Section 1–3 introduces the concept of mathematical modeling to help make students aware that the process of modeling occurs in the attempt to solve real-world problems.

3. The exercises in Chapter 3 have been increased to include a larger number and variety of maximization and minimization problems.

4. The big M method in Chapter 4 has been replaced with a unified approach to maximum, minimum, and mixed constraint linear programming problems. The unified approach is easier for students to grasp.

5. A wider choice of counting techniques and their applications has been included in Chapter 5.

6. Limit notation is introduced in Section 9–1, Rate of Change and the Derivative, to help speed the development of the theory.

7. The cut point method for solving inequalities has been moved to Section 9–4, Applications of Continuity, where continuity can be used to explain why the method works. Another application shows how to approximate solutions to equations by using the bisection method.

8. A new section, Section 11–4, Graphing: Putting It All Together, has been added to Chapter 11 in which techniques of graphing that were introduced section by section are put together in a general strategy for graphing.

9. More word problems have been included in Section 11–6, Optimization in Applications, and an example has been added to give students and instructors a choice of methods for some typical applications.

10. Section 12–2 now deals with differentiation of the exponential function and follows directly the introduction of the topic in Section 12–1. Thus instructors may more easily cover the exponential function completely and then move on to the logarithm function if they desire.

11. Chapter 13, The Integral, contains the Fundamental Theorem of Calculus, with accompanying geometric motivation. Exercises have been included to test the geometric understanding of both versions of the fundamental theorem.

12. Section 13–4, The Definite Integral and Area, has been rewritten to allow quicker coverage of applications of area, which now also includes producers' surplus.

13. A new section, Section 14–5, on numerical techniques of integration has been added to Chapter 14, Techniques of Integration.

14. A glossary of all key terms has been added at the end of the text.

15. The front and back endsheets contain useful formulas and illustrations for quick referencing by the student.

USE OF A CALCULATOR

Students are encouraged to use a calculator in working problems. Limited tables are provided for compound interest, annuities, and amortization so that a student can work problems without a calculator. However, students should learn to calculate the entries in the table so that they can see how these entries arise and can solve problems for which the needed calculation is not in a table.

SUPPLEMENTS

The Instructor's Manual contains answers to all exercises, transparency masters, and a printout of the Test Item File in *TestPak 3.0.*

The *Instructor's Solutions Manual* contains solutions to all exercises.

The *Student's Solutions Manual* contains solutions to all odd-numbered exercises.

The *TestPak 3.0* is a computerized test bank of approximately 3000 problems available for test preparation. Problems are organized by section and level of difficulty. *TestPak 3.0* is available to instructors who adopt *Mathematics for Management, Social, and Life Sciences* and is designed to save test preparation time. It is available for Apple, Macintosh, and IBM PC. Its features include formatting options to print the test in the format desired, graphics that can be added to questions, multiple possible versions of a test, and ASCII-formatted questions that can be used with your own word-processing program.

The *QuizPak* contains ten-questions quizzes from any given chapter. Specific questions can be selected for quizzing directly on the computer and consist of true/false and multiple-choice questions. There are approximately 750 problems available for *QuizPak*.

The *GradePak* is a grade file that is available to the instructor. Students' total points, average percentages, letter grades, and GPAs can be calculated, printed, and displayed. Each file holds up to 250 students with 50 test scores. All data can be transferred to Lotus 1-2-3 or Visical.

The *Call-in/Mail-in/Fax Service* allows an instructor to call in and order a test from *TestPak,* and the test will be sent within two working days. Details are available from a Wm. C. Brown representative.

ACKNOWLEDGMENTS

A number of people contributed to the writing of this book. We are most grateful to the reviewers who provided constructive criticism, helping to clarify ideas and to improve the presentation of the concepts.

Jerry Bloomberg, Essex Community College
Michael Simon, Fairfield University
Mary Nelson, George Mason University
Edwina R. Stowe, North Idaho College
Danny W. Turner, Baylor University
William Bonnice, University of New Hampshire

Jere A. DeVilbiss, University of Missouri–Columbia
John D. O'Neill, University of Detroit
Sandy Spears, Jefferson Community College
David A. Ponick, University of Wisconsin–Eau Claire
David P. Nasby, Orange Coast College
Ronald D. Schwartz, University of Michigan–Dearborn
M. D. Tewari, Virginia State University
Louis A. Talman, Metropolitan State College
Charlotte Jarrett Newsom, Tidewater Community College
William H. Richardson, Wichita State University
Fred Bakenhus, Concordia Lutheran College
Elizabeth Bourquin Kennedy, University of Detroit

Many thanks go to the staff of Wm. C. Brown Publishers who supported us with their enthusiasm and expertise. Special thanks go to Earl McPeek, Executive Editor, and Jan Scotchmer, Senior Developmental Editor.

INDEX OF APPLICATIONS

This index provides a list of finite mathematics and calculus topics and indications of where in the book these topics are applied to the disciplines of business, personal finance, and social and life sciences.

The authors wish to emphasize that the purpose of *Mathematics for Management, Social, and Life Sciences* is to teach mathematical concepts and techniques. We realize that the applications of these concepts are the reason for studying them. That is why examples and exercises in the text are designed to point toward these applications. Even so, the application of mathematical concepts requires an understanding of the mathematics and an expertise in the area of application. That expertise must be obtained through other courses or experience. To give you some hints on possible applications, we provide the following list of areas of application for certain topics. As you work the exercises, you will find some that are related to the areas mentioned. We want you to understand that the exercises are simplified versions of what is encountered in actual applications.

Chapter 1: Functions and Lines

Fees and Expenses
Cost and Revenue Functions
Operating Costs
Depreciation
Break-Even Analysis
Production Capacity

Chapter 2: Linear Systems

Supply and Demand Analysis
Diet and Calorie Intake
Competitive Markets
Production Scheduling
Investments
Cost Control
Billing
Energy Consumption
Manufacturing
Industrial Interdependencies
Input-Output Models

Chapter 3 and 4: Linear Programming

Optimum Allocation of Resources
Minimizing Costs
Maximizing Revenues
Purchasing Decisions
Manufacturing Strategies
Transportation Management
Resource Management and Cost Control
Division of Labor
Plant and Space Management

Chapter 5: Sets and Counting

Sampling Populations
Sampling Preferences and Opinions
Product Combinations
Product Selections
Display Planning
Conducting Surveys
Developing Polls

Chapter 6: Probability

Predicting Outcomes
Projecting Results
Evaluating Preferences
Interpreting Surveys
Quality Control
Traffic Control
Medical Evaluations
Advertising

1

Functions and Lines

Functions

Graphs and Lines

Mathematical Models and Applications of Linear Functions

1-1   FUNCTIONS

MATHEMATICS IS A POWERFUL tool used in the design of automobiles, electronic equipment, and buildings. It helps in solving problems of business, industry, environment, science, and social sciences. Mathematics helps to predict sales, population growth, the outcome of elections, and the location of black holes. Some of the techniques of mathematics are straightforward; others are complicated and difficult. Nearly all practical problems involve two or more quantities that are related in some manner. For example, the amount withheld from a paycheck for FICA is related to an employee's salary; the area of a rectangle is related to the length of its sides (area = length × width); the amount charged for sales tax depends on the price of an item; and UPS shipping costs depend on the weight of the package and the distance shipped.

Mathematicians formalize certain kinds of relationships between quantities and call them **functions.** Nearly always in this book, the quantities involved are measured by real numbers.

A function consists of three parts: two sets and a rule. The **rule of a function** describes the relationship between a number in the first set (called the **domain**) and a number in the second set (called the **range**). The rule is often stated in the form of an equation like $A = $ length^2 for the relation between the area of a square and the length of a side.

Definition **Function**	A **function** is a rule that assigns to each number from the first set (domain) exactly one number from the second set (range).

We generally use the letter x to represent a number from the first set and y to represent a letter from the second set. Thus for each value of x there is exactly one value of y assigned to x.

EXAMPLE 1   *(Compare Exercise 1)*

A consultant's fee is $300 for miscellaneous expenses plus $50 per hour. In this instance the domain consists of positive numbers of hours, and the range consists of positive numbers of dollars (fees). The rule that determines the fee that corresponds to a certain number of consulting hours is given by the formula

$$y = 50x + 300$$

where x is the number of hours consulted and y is the total fee in dollars. Notice that the formula gives exactly one fee for each number of consulting hours.

EXAMPLE 2 *(Compare Exercise 3)*

When a family goes to a concert, the amount paid depends on the number attending, that is, the total admission is a function of the number attending. The ticket office usually has a chart giving total admission, so for them the rule is a chart something like this:

NUMBER OF TICKETS	TOTAL ADMISSION
1	$ 6.50
2	$13.00
3	$19.50
4	$26.00
5	$32.50
6	$39.00

From this chart the domain is the set $\{1, 2, 3, 4, 5, 6\}$, and the range is $\{6.50, 13.00, 19.50, 26.00, 32.50, 39.00\}$.

Mathematicians have a standard notation for functions. For example, the equation $y = 50x + 300$ is often written as

$$f(x) = 50x + 300$$

$f(x)$ is read "f of x" indicating "f is a function of x." The $f(x)$ notation is especially useful to indicate a substitution of a number for x. $f(3)$ looks as though 3 has been put in place of x in $f(x)$. This is the correct interpretation. $f(3)$ represents the **value** of the function when 3 is substituted for x in

$$f(x) = 50x + 300$$

that is,

$$f(3) = 50(3) + 300$$
$$= 150 + 300$$
$$= 450$$

EXAMPLE 3 *(Compare Exercise 5)*

(a) If $f(x) = -7x + 22$, then

$$f(2) = -7(2) + 22 = 8$$
$$f(-1) = -7(-1) + 22$$
$$= 7 + 22$$
$$= 29$$

(b) If $f(x) = 4x - 11$, then

$$\begin{aligned}
f(5) &= 4(5) - 11 \\
&= 20 - 11 \\
&= 9 \\
f(0) &= 4(0) - 11 \\
&= 0 - 11 \\
&= -11
\end{aligned}$$

(c) If $f(x) = x(4 - 2x)$, then

$$\begin{aligned}
f(6) &= 6(4 - 2(6)) \\
&= 6(4 - 12) \\
&= 6(-8) \\
&= -48 \\
f(a) &= a(4 - 2a)
\end{aligned}$$

We conclude this section with some applications.

EXAMPLE 4   *(Compare Exercise 9)*

Baked potatoes contain 26 calories per ounce (before adding a topping). Define a function as follows:

x is a positive number representing weight in ounces.

$f(x)$ is a positive number representing the number of calories.

The calorie function is

$$f(x) = 26x$$

(a) What is $f(3)$? $f(1.5)$? $f(2.4)$?
(b) If $f(x) = 143$ calories, how much did the potato weigh?

SOLUTION

(a) $f(3) = 26(3) = 78$
$f(1.5) = 26(1.5) = 39$
$f(2.4) = 62.4$

(b) If $f(x) = 143$, then

$$\begin{aligned}
143 &= 26x \\
x &= \frac{143}{26} = 5.5
\end{aligned}$$

So if the potato contains 143 calories, it weighs 5.5 ounces.

EXAMPLE 5 *(Compare Exercise 23)*

All lots in a new subdivision are 200 feet deep. The area of a lot is given by the function

$$f(x) = 200x$$

where x represents the width of the lot in feet and $f(x)$ the area in square feet.

(a) What is the area of a lot 150 feet wide?
(b) What is $f(275)$?
(c) A family wants an acre lot (44,000 square feet). How wide a lot should they buy?

SOLUTION

(a) If $x = 150$,

$$f(150) = 200(150) = 30,000$$

so the area is 30,000 square feet.

(b) $f(275) = 200(275) = 55,000$ square feet

(c) We are given $f(x) = 44,000$ so $44,000 = 200x$, and

$$x = \frac{44,000}{200} = 220$$

So a lot containing 44,000 square feet is 220 feet wide.

We use letters other than f and x to represent functions and variables. We might refer to the cost of producing x items as $C(x) = 5x + 540$; the price of x pounds of steak as $p(x) = 2.19x$; the area of a circle of radius r as $A(r) = \pi r^2$; and the distance an object falls in t seconds as $d(t) = 16t^2$.

1-1 EXERCISES

I

1. *(See Example 1)* A tree service company charges $20 plus $15 per hour to trim trees. Write the rule relating their fee and hours worked using x for the number of hours worked and y for their fee.

2. An appliance repairman charges $30 plus $20 per hour for house calls. Write the rule that relates hours worked and his fee.

3. *(See Example 2)* The price of movie tickets is given by the following chart:

NUMBER OF TICKETS	TOTAL ADMISSION
1	$4.75
2	$9.50
3	$14.25
4	$19.00
5	$23.75
6	$28.50
7	$33.25

(a) What is $f(5)$?
(b) What is $f(3)$?

4. Tickets to a football game cost $14 each. Make a chart showing the total cost function for the purchase of one, two, three, four, five, and six tickets.

5. (*See Example 3*) $f(x) = 4x - 3$. Determine:
   (a) $f(1)$
   (b) $f(-2)$
   (c) $f\left(\dfrac{1}{2}\right)$
   (d) $f(a)$

6. $f(x) = x(2x - 1)$. Determine:
   (a) $f(3)$
   (b) $f(-2)$
   (c) $f(0)$
   (d) $f(b)$

7. $f(x) = \dfrac{x + 1}{x - 1}$. Determine:
   (a) $f(5)$
   (b) $f(-6)$
   (c) $f(0)$
   (d) $f(2c)$

II

8. $f(x) = -4x + 7$. Determine:
   (a) $f(a)$
   (b) $f(y)$
   (c) $f(a + 1)$
   (d) $f(a + h)$
   (e) $f(3a)$
   (f) $f(2b + 1)$

9. (*See Example 4*) The function for calories in French fried potatoes is given by

   $$f(x) = 78x$$

   where x represents the weight of French fried potatoes in ounces and $f(x)$ is the number of calories.
   (a) Find $f(5)$, $f(2.5)$, and $f(6.4)$.
   (b) If a serving of French fried potatoes contains 741 calories, what is the weight of the serving?

10. A small cheese pizza is cut into four pieces. The calcium content of pizza is given by the function

    $$f(x) = 221x$$

where x is the number of pieces of pizza and $f(x)$ is the quantity of calcium in milligrams.
   (a) How many milligrams of calcium is contained in one pizza?
   (b) The recommended daily requirement for calcium is 750 mg. How many pieces should be eaten to get that amount?

11. Swimming requires 9 calories per minute of energy, so the function for calories used in swimming is given by

    $$f(x) = 9x$$

   where x is the number of minutes and $f(x)$ is the number of calories used.
   (a) How many calories are used in swimming for one hour?
   (b) A swimmer wants to use 750 calories. How long should she swim?

III

Each of the following statements describes a function. Write an equation of the function.

12. The cost of grapes at the Corner Grocery is 49¢ per pound.

13. The cost of catering a hamburger cookout is a $25 service charge plus $1.25 per hamburger.

14. The monthly income of a salesman is $500 plus 5% of sales.

15. The sale price of all items in The Men's Clothing Store is 20% off the regular price.

16. The monthly sales of Pappa's Pizza is $1200 plus $3 for each dollar spent on advertising.

17. Dion hauls sand and gravel. His hauling costs (per load) are overhead costs of $12.00 per load and operating costs of $0.60 per mile.

18. Becky has a lawn-mowing service. She charges a base price of $5 plus $4 per hour.

19. Paloma University found that a good estimate of its operating budget is $5,000,000 plus $3500 per student.

20. Peoples Bank collects a monthly service charge of $2.00 plus $0.10 per check.

21. An automobile dealer's invoice cost is 0.88 of the list price of an automobile.

22. A telephone company provides measured phone service. The rate is $7.60 per month plus $0.05 per call.

23. (*See Example 5*) A street is 30 feet wide. The area of a section of the street is given by

$$f(x) = 30x$$

where x represents the length of that section of the street in feet and $f(x)$ is the area.

(a) What is the area of a section that is 450 feet long?

(b) What is $f(125)$?

(c) A 650-ft-long section of the street is paved at a cost of $0.40 per square foot. How much did the paving cost?

(d) A contractor paved 15,900 square feet of the street. How long was the section?

24. If

$$f(x) = (x + 2)(x - 1) \quad \text{and}$$

$$g(x) = \frac{7x + 4}{x + 1}$$

find $f(3) + g(2)$.

1-2 GRAPHS AND LINES

- *Definition of a Graph*
- *Linear Functions and Straight Lines*
- *Slope and Intercept*
- *Horizontal and Vertical Lines*
- *Slope-Intercept Equation*
- *Point-Slope Equation*
- *Parallel Lines*

DEFINITION OF A GRAPH

"A picture is worth a thousand words" may be an overworked phrase, but it does convey an important idea. You may even occasionally use the expression "Oh, I see!" when you really grasp a difficult concept. A **graph** shows a picture of a function, and can help you to understand the behavior of the function. Imagine how difficult it would be to convey all the information (and the drama!) in the following example without the aid of the graphs.

The 1975 Masters Golf Tournament in Augusta, Georgia, was one of the most dramatic events in the history of golf. In early rounds, several players held or shared the lead, but by the end, all eyes were focused on a battle among three of the finest players in the game: Jack Nicklaus, Tom Weiskopf, and Johnny Miller.

The graphs in Figure 1-1 (one for each player) tell the story. Follow Miller's plunge over the opening holes and his record-breaking six straight birdies later. Follow the slow, descending plateaus of Weiskopf's flawless game over much of the third day. Follow Nicklaus's early dominance and his seesaw battle with Weiskopf. Would Miller have won on a 73rd hole?

FIGURE 1–1

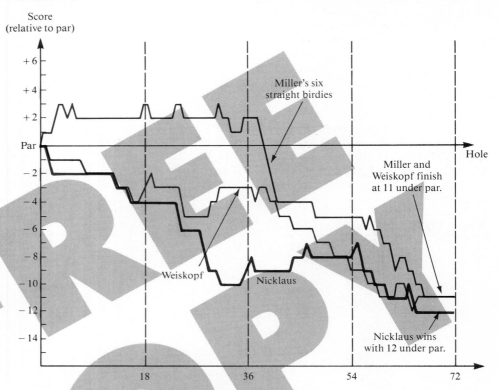

This example makes another important point. The graph seems to indicate that Miller was $2\frac{1}{2}$ over par after $17\frac{1}{2}$ holes; such an interpretation would be silly—golfers never talk about half of a hole. It is much harder to get information from a graph drawn with just dots. Remember those drawings you made when you were a child by connecting the dots? The picture made a lot more sense after you drew in the connecting lines. In Figure 1–1 we sacrificed some technical accuracy by "connecting the dots" but got a better picture of what happened by doing so. Professional users of mathematics do the same thing; an accountant may let $C(x)$ represent the cost of manufacturing x items, or a manager may let $E(x)$ represent an efficiency index when x people are involved in a large project. In reality the domains of these functions involve only positive integers. But many methods of mathematics require the domain of the function to be an interval or intervals, rather than isolated points. These methods have proven so powerful in solving problems that people set up their functions using such domains. They then use some common sense in interpreting their answer. If the manager finds that the most efficient number of people to assign to a project is 54.87, she will probably end up using either 54 or 55 people.

Definition	The **graph of a function** f is the set of points (x, y) in the plane that
Graph of a Function	satisfy the equation $y = f(x)$.

As we develop different mathematical techniques throughout this text, we will use some concrete applications. This in turn will require some familiarity with the functions involved and some idea of the shape of their graphs. We start with the simplest functions and graphs.

LINEAR FUNCTIONS AND STRAIGHT LINES

Definition	A function is called a **linear function** if its rule—its defining equation—
Linear Function	can be written $f(x) = mx + b$. Such a function is called linear because its graph is a straight line.

EXAMPLE 1 *(Compare Exercise 1)*

Draw the graph of $f(x) = 2x + 5$.

SOLUTION The graph will be a straight line, and it takes just two points to determine a straight line. If we let $x = 1$, then we have $f(1) = 7$; if we let

FIGURE 1–2

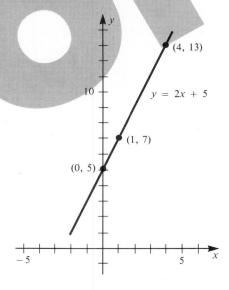

$x = 4$, then $f(4) = 13$. This means that the points $(1, 7)$ and $(4, 13)$ are on the graph of $f(x) = 2x + 5$. Since we also use y for $f(x)$, we could also say that these points are on the line $y = 2x + 5$. By plotting the points $(1, 7)$ and $(4, 13)$ and drawing the line through them, we obtain Figure 1–2. (We can use any pair of x-values to get two points on the line.) It is usually a good idea to plot a third point to help catch any error. Because $f(0) = 5$, the point $(0, 5)$ is also on the graph of f.

SLOPE AND INTERCEPT

When the equation of a line is written in the form $y = 2x + 5$ ($y = mx + b$ is the general form), the constants 2 and 5 (m and b in general) give key information about the line. The constant b (5 in this case) is the value of y when $x = 0$. Thus $(0, b)$ (or $(0, 5)$ in our example) is a point on the line. We refer to b as the **y-intercept** of the line; it determines the point where the line intercepts the y-axis. The constant m gives information about the direction, or slant, of a line. We call m the **slope** of the line. We will give more information about the slope later.

EXAMPLE 2   *(Compare Exercise 7)*

What are the slope and y-intercept of each of the following lines?

(a) $y = 3x - 5$ **(b)** $y = -6x + 15$

SOLUTION

(a) For the line $y = 3x - 5$, the slope $m = 3$ and the y-intercept $b = -5$.
(b) For the line $y = -6x + 15$, the slope is -6 and the y-intercept is 15.

CAUTION The coefficient of x in a general linear equation does not automatically give you the slope of the line. When the equation of the line is in the form $y = mx + b$, the coefficient of x is the slope of the line and the constant term is the y-intercept. If the equation is in another form, it is a good idea to change to this form to determine the slope and y-intercept.

EXAMPLE 3   *(Compare Exercise 11)*

What are the slope and y-intercept of the line $3x + 2y - 4 = 0$?
SOLUTION   We rewrite the equation $3x + 2y - 4 = 0$ in the slope-intercept form, $y = mx + b$, by solving the given equation for y:

$$3x + 2y - 4 = 0$$
$$2y = -3x + 4$$
$$y = -\frac{3}{2}x + 2$$

Thus the slope-intercept form is $y = -\frac{3}{2}x + 2$. Now we can say that the slope is $-\frac{3}{2}$ and the y-intercept is 2.

FIGURE 1–3

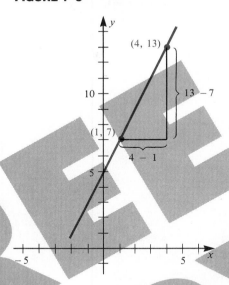

The slope relates to the way the line slants in the following manner. Select two points on the line $y = 2x + 5$, such as (1, 7) and (4, 13). (See Figure 1–3.) Compute the difference in the y-coordinates of the two points: $13 - 7 = 6$. Now compute the difference in x-coordinates: $4 - 1 = 3$. The quotient $\frac{6}{3} = 2$ is m, the slope of the line $y = 2x + 5$. Following this procedure with any other two points on the line $y = 2x + 5$ will also yield the answer 2.

The following general formula shows how to compute the slope of a line.

Slope Formula Choose two points P and Q on the line. Let (x_1, y_1) be the coordinates of P and (x_2, y_2) be the coordinates of Q. The **slope** of the line, m, is given by the equation

$$m = \frac{y_2 - y_1}{x_2 - x_1} = \frac{\text{change in } y}{\text{change in } x} \quad \text{where} \quad x_2 \neq x_1$$

The slope is the difference in the y-coordinates divided by the difference in the x-coordinates.

Figure 1–4 shows the geometric meaning of this quotient.

FIGURE 1–4

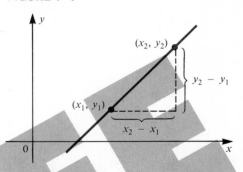

EXAMPLE 4   *(Compare Exercise 15)*

Find the slope of the line through the points $(1, 2)$ and $(5, 6)$.

SOLUTION   We let $(x_1, y_1) = (1, 2)$ and $(x_2, y_2) = (5, 6)$. From the definition for m,

$$m = \frac{6 - 2}{5 - 1} = \frac{4}{4} = 1$$

Figure 1–5 shows the geometry.

NOTE   Notice that it doesn't matter which point we call (x_1, y_1) and which one we call (x_2, y_2); it doesn't affect the computation of m. If we label the points differently in Example 4, the computation becomes

$$m = \frac{2 - 6}{1 - 5} = \frac{-4}{-4} = 1$$

The answer is the same. Just be sure to subtract the x- and y-coordinates in the same order.

FIGURE 1–5

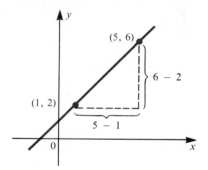

EXAMPLE 5

Determine the slope of the line through the points (4, 5) and (6, 2).

SOLUTION   If we let (x_1, y_1) be (4, 5) and (x_2, y_2) be (6, 2), we get

$$m = \frac{y_2 - y_1}{x_2 - x_1} = \frac{2 - 5}{6 - 4} = \frac{-3}{2} = -\frac{3}{2}$$

The geometry is shown in Figure 1–6.

FIGURE 1–6

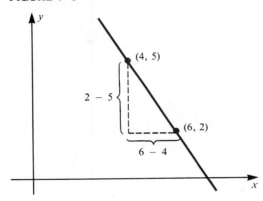

HORIZONTAL AND VERTICAL LINES

EXAMPLE 6   *(Compare Exercise 19)*

Determine the equation of the line through the points (2, 5) and (6, 5).

SOLUTION   The slope of the line is

$$m = \frac{5 - 5}{6 - 2} = \frac{0}{4} = 0$$

Whenever $m = 0$, the equation $f(x) = 0x + b$ is written more simply as $f(x) = b; f$ is called a constant function. The graph of a constant function is a line parallel to the x-axis; such a line has an equation of the form $y = b$ and is called a **horizontal line.** (See Figure 1–7.) Since all points on a horizontal line have the same y-coordinates, the value of b can be determined from the y-coordinate of any point on the line. The equation of the line is $y = 5$.

FIGURE 1–7

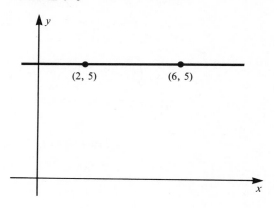

EXAMPLE 7   *(Compare Exercise 27)*

Determine the equation of the line through the points (4, 1) and (4, 3).

SOLUTION   We can try to use the rule for computing the slope, but we obtain the quotient

$$\frac{3 - 1}{4 - 4} = \frac{2}{0}$$

which doesn't make sense because division by zero is not defined. The slope is not defined. When we plot the two points, however, we have no difficulty in drawing the line through them. See Figure 1–8.

The line, parallel to the *y*-axis, is called a **vertical line.** A point lies on this line when the first coordinate of the point is 4, so the equation of the line is *x* = 4.

FIGURE 1–8

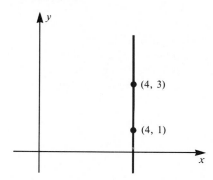

FIGURE 1-9

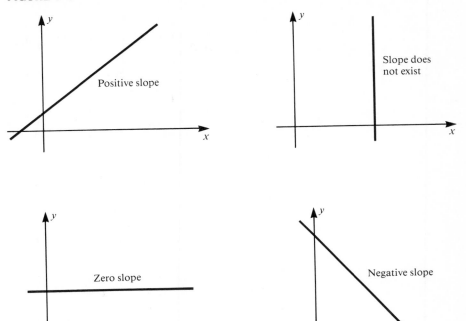

Whenever $x_2 = x_1$, you get a 0 in the denominator when computing the slope, so we say that the *slope does not exist* for such a line.

CAUTION A vertical line does *not* have a slope, but it does have an equation.

The slope of a line can be positive, negative, zero, or even not exist. These situations are depicted in Figure 1-9.

This figure shows the relationship between the slope and the slant of the line. If $m > 0$, the graph slants up as x moves to the right. If $m < 0$, the graph slants down as x moves to the right. If $m = 0$, the graph remains at the same height. If m does not exist, the line is vertical, and the line is *not* the graph of a linear function. The equation of a vertical line cannot be written in form $f(x) = mx + b$ because there is no m.

We conclude this section by showing how to find equations of lines. Linear functions arise in many applied settings. When an application provides the appropriate two pieces of information, you can find an equation of the corresponding line. This information may be given either as:

1. the slope and a point on the line or
2. two points on the line.

We will show each form in a particular application and then give the general method of solving the problem.

SLOPE-INTERCEPT EQUATION

EXAMPLE 8 *(Compare Exercise 35)*

Determine an equation of the line with slope 3 and *y*-intercept 2.

SOLUTION This information gives $m = 3$ and $b = 2$ in the equation $y = mx + b$, so the equation is

$$y = 3x + 2$$

EXAMPLE 9 *(Compare Exercise 41)*

Determine an equation of the line that has slope -2 and passes through the point $(-3, 5)$.

SOLUTION The value of $m = -2$, so the line has an equation of form

$$y = -2x + b$$

To complete the solution, we find the value of *b*. Since the point $(-3, 5)$ lies on the line, $x = -3$ and $y = 5$ must be a solution to $y = -2x + b$. Just substitute those values into $y = -2x + b$ to obtain

$$5 = (-2)(-3) + b$$
$$5 = 6 + b$$
$$5 - 6 = b$$

Thus $b = -1$, and the equation of the line is $y = -2x - 1$.

There is a quicker method to write an equation of the line when the slope and a point are given. This method requires only one step, and it is called the **point-slope equation.**

POINT-SLOPE EQUATION

We will work with the information in Example 9, $m = -2$ and the point $(-3, 5)$. Use the slope formula with $(-3, 5)$ as (x_1, y_1) and use an arbitrary point, (x, y), as (x_2, y_2). Because $m = -2$, we can write

$$-2 = \frac{y - 5}{x - (-3)} = \frac{y - 5}{x + 3}$$

Multiply both sides by $x + 3$ to obtain

$$-2(x + 3) = y - 5$$

The formula is usually written as

$$y - 5 = -2(x + 3)$$

Check that this has the same slope-intercept form as we obtained in Example 9.

Point-Slope Equation	If a line has slope m and passes through (x_1, y_1), an equation of the line is

$$y - y_1 = m(x - x_1)$$

EXAMPLE 10   *(Compare Exercise 45)*

Find an equation of the line with slope 4 that passes through $(-1, 5)$.

SOLUTION $x_1 = -1$ and $y_1 = 5$; $m = 4$, so the point-slope formula gives us

$$y - 5 = 4(x - (-1)) = 4(x + 1)$$

EXAMPLE 11   *(Compare Exercise 74)*

Carlos started a paper route and decided to add $7 each week to his savings account. By the eighth week he had $242 in savings. Write his total savings as a linear function of the number of weeks since he started his paper route.

SOLUTION   Let x be the number of weeks and y be the total in savings. Each time x increases by 1 (one week), y increases by 7 ($7 deposit). Thus the slope equals

$$\frac{\text{change in } y}{\text{change in } x} = \frac{7}{1} = 7$$

At 8 weeks the savings totaled $242, so the point $(8, 242)$ lies on the line. Using the point-slope formula, we have

$$y - 242 = 7(x - 8)$$

Solving for y, we have $y = 7x + 186$.

NOTE   The slope of the line is the rate of change of y per unit change in x.

Just as we have a point-slope formula, we have a formula for finding an equation of a line using the coordinates of two points on the line.

Two-Point Equation	If a line passes through the points (x_1, y_1) and (x_2, y_2), with $x_1 \neq x_2$, an equation of the line is

$$y - y_1 = m(x - x_1)$$

where

$$m = \frac{y_2 - y_1}{x_2 - x_1}$$

EXAMPLE 12   *(Compare Exercise 49)*

Determine an equation of the straight line through the points (1, 3) and (4, 7).
SOLUTION   Let (x_1, y_1) be the point (1, 3) and let (x_2, y_2) be the point (4, 7);
then

$$m = \frac{7 - 3}{4 - 1} = \frac{4}{3}$$

The point-slope formula gives $y - 3 = \frac{4}{3}(x - 1)$ as an equation of this line.

EXAMPLE 13   *(Compare Exercise 76)*

An electric utility computes the monthly electric bill for residential customers
with a linear function of the number of kilowatt hours (KWH) used. One month
a customer used 1560 KWH, and the bill was $118.82. The next month the bill
was $102.26 for 1330 KWH used. Find the equation relating KWH used and
the monthly bill.
SOLUTION   Let $x =$ the number of KWH used and $y =$ the monthly bill. The
information provided gives two points on the line, (1560, 118.82) and (1330,
102.26). The slope of the line is

$$\frac{118.82 - 102.26}{1560 - 1330} = \frac{16.56}{230} = 0.072$$

The equation can now be written as

$$y - 102.26 = 0.072(x - 1330)$$
$$y - 102.26 = 0.072x - 95.76$$
$$y = 0.072x + 6.50$$

We conclude this section with a discussion of parallel lines.

PARALLEL LINES

Definition **Parallel Lines**	Two lines are **parallel** if they have the same slope or if they are both vertical lines.

EXAMPLE 14   *(Compare Exercise 59)*

Is the line through the points (1, 2) and (3, 3) parallel to the line through the
points (−3, 2) and (5, 6)?

SOLUTION Let L_1 be the line through $(1, 2)$ and $(3, 3)$, and let m_1 be its slope:

$$m_1 = \frac{3 - 2}{3 - 1} = \frac{1}{2}$$

Let L_2 be the line through $(-3, 2)$ and $(5, 6)$, and let m_2 be its slope:

$$m_2 = \frac{6 - 2}{5 - (-3)} = \frac{4}{8} = \frac{1}{2}$$

The slopes are identical; thus the lines are parallel. (See Figure 1–10.)

FIGURE 1–10

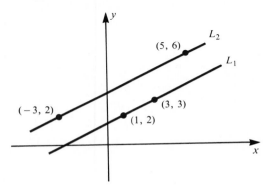

EXAMPLE 15 *(Compare Exercise 61)*

Is the line through $(5, 4)$ and $(-1, 2)$ parallel to the line through $(3, -2)$ and $(6, 4)$?

SOLUTION The slope of the first line is

$$m_1 = \frac{4 - 2}{5 - (-1)} = \frac{2}{6} = \frac{1}{3}$$

The slope of the second line is

$$m_2 = \frac{-2 - 4}{3 - 6} = \frac{-6}{-3} = 2$$

Since the slopes are not equal, the lines are not parallel.

Summary of Equations of a Linear Function

Slope: $m = \dfrac{y_2 - y_1}{x_2 - x_1}$, where (x_1, y_1) and (x_2, y_2) are points on the line with $x_1 \neq x_2$.

Standard Equation: $Ax + By = C$ where (x, y) is any point on the line and at least one of A, B is not zero.

Slope-Intercept Equation: $y = mx + b$, where m is the slope and b is the y-intercept.

Point-Slope Equation: $y - y_1 = m(x - x_1)$, where m is the slope and (x_1, y_1) is a given point on the line.

Horizontal Line: $y = k$, where (h, k) is a point on the line.

Vertical Line: $x = h$, where (h, k) is a point on the line.

1-2 EXERCISES

I

Draw the graphs of the lines in Exercises 1 through 6.

1. (*See Example 1*)
$f(x) = 3x + 8$

2. $f(x) = 4x - 2$

3. $f(x) = x + 7$

4. $f(x) = -2x + 5$

5. $f(x) = -3x - 1$

6. $f(x) = \dfrac{2}{3}x + 4$

Find the slope and y-intercept of the lines in Exercises 7 through 10.

7. (*See Example 2*)
$y = 7x + 22$

8. $y = 13x - 4$

9. $y = \dfrac{-2}{5}x + 6$

10. $y = \dfrac{-1}{4}x - \dfrac{1}{3}$

Find the slope and y-intercept of the lines in Exercises 11 through 14.

11. (*See Example 3*)
$2x + 5y - 3 = 0$

12. $4x + y - 3 = 0$

13. $x - 3y + 6 = 0$

14. $5x - 2y = 7$

Determine the slopes of the straight lines through the pairs of points in Exercises 15 through 18.

15. (*See Example 4*)
$(1, 2), (3, 4)$

16. $(2, 3), (-3, 1)$

17. $(-4, -1), (-1, -5)$

18. $(2, -4), (6, -3)$

Find the equations of the lines in Exercises 19 through 22 through the given points.

19. (*See Example 6*)
$(5, -2), (-3, -2)$

20. $(8, 3), (1, 3)$

21. $(-1, 0), (-4, 0)$

22. $(0, 0), (17, 0)$

Graph the lines in Exercises 23 through 26.

23. $y = 6$

24. $y = -2$

25. $y = 4.5$

26. $y = -3.5$

Find an equation of the line through the given points in Exercises 27 through 30.

27. (*See Example 7*)
$(3, 2), (3, 5)$

28. $(-4, 6), (-4, 9)$

29. $(10, 0), (10, 7)$

30. $(-6, -1), (-6, 13)$

Graph the lines in Exercises 31 through 34.

31. $x = 8$

32. $x = -1$

33. $x = 1.5$

34. $x = -4.25$

Find the equations of the lines in Exercises 35 through 40 with the given slope and y-intercept.

35. (*See Example 8*) Slope 4 and y-intercept 3

36. Slope -2 and y-intercept 5

37. $m = -1, b = 6$

38. $m = \dfrac{-3}{4}, b = 7$

39. $m = \dfrac{1}{2}, b = 0$

40. $m = 3.5, b = -1.5$

Find the equations of the lines in Exercises 41 through 44 with the given slope and passing through the given point.

41. (*See Example 9*) Slope -4 and point $(2, 1)$

42. Slope 6 and point $(-1, -1)$

43. Slope $\dfrac{1}{2}$ and point $(5, 4)$

44. Slope -1.5 and point $(2.6, 5.2)$

Use the point-slope formula to find the equations of the lines with given point and slope in Exercises 45 through 48.

45. (*See Example 10*) Slope 7 and point $(1, 5)$

46. Slope -2 and point $(3, 1)$

47. Slope $\dfrac{1}{5}$ and point $(9, 6)$

48. Slope $\dfrac{-2}{3}$ and passing through $(-1, 4)$

In Exercises 49 through 54, determine the equations of the straight lines through the pairs of points, and sketch the lines.

49. (*See Example 12*) $(-1, 0), (2, 1)$

50. $(3, 0), (1, -1)$

51. $(0, 0), (1, 2)$

52. $(1, 3), (1, 5)$

53. $(2, 4), (5, 4)$

54. $(0, 3), (7, 0)$

The **x-intercept** of a line is similar to the y-intercept. It is the x-coordinate of the point where the line crosses the x-axis. To find the x-intercept, set $y = 0$ in the linear equation and solve for x. Find the x- and y-intercepts of the lines in Exercises 55 through 58 and sketch the graph.

55. $5x - 3y = 15$

56. $6x + 5y = 30$

57. $2x - .5y = 25$

58. $3x + 4y = 15$

59. (*See Example 14*) Is the line through the points $(8, 2)$ and $(3, -3)$ parallel to the line through $(6, -1)$ and $(16, 9)$?

60. Is the line through $(9, -1)$ and $(2, 8)$ parallel to the line through $(3, 5)$ and $(10, -4)$?

61. (*See Example 15*) Is the line through $(5, 4)$ and $(1, -2)$ parallel to the line through $(1, 2)$ and $(6, 8)$?

62. Determine whether the line through $(6, 2)$ and $(-3, 5)$ is parallel to the line through $(4, 1)$ and $(0, 5)$.

II

Determine whether the pairs of lines in Exercises 63 through 66 are parallel.

63. $y = 6x + 22$
    $y = 6x - 17$

64. $3x + 2y = 5$
    $6x + 4y = 15$

65. $x - 2y = 3$
    $2x + y = 1$

66. $3x - 5y = 4$
    $-6x + 10y = -8$

67. Write the equation of the line through $(-1, 5)$ that is parallel to $y = 3x + 4$.

68. Write the equation of the line through $(2, 6)$ that is parallel to $3x + 2y = 17$.

69. Write the equation of the line with y-intercept 8 that is parallel to $5x + 7y = -2$.

70. Write the equation of the line through $(-4, 5)$ that is parallel to the line through $(6, 1)$ and $(2, -3)$.

71. Find an equation of the line passing through the point $(6, -4)$ and parallel to the x-axis.

72. Find an equation of the line passing through the point $(0, 0)$ with slope 2.3.

73. Find the y-intercept of the line passing through $(2, 5)$ and having slope $\dfrac{2}{3}$.

III

74. (*See Example 11*) Jane got a regular job and started adding $9 per week to her savings account. At the end of 11 weeks she has $315 in savings. Write her savings as a linear function of the number of weeks since she started the job.

75. Raul is on a carefully supervised diet that causes a weight loss of 3 pounds per week. After 14 weeks his weight is 196 pounds.
    (a) Write Raul's weight as a linear function of weeks on the diet.
    (b) What was his weight when the diet started?

76. (*See Example 13*) Valley Electric Utility computes the monthly electric bill for residential customers with a linear function of the number of kilowatt hours (KWH) used. One month a customer used 1170 KWH, and the bill was $100.02. Another month the bill was $120.27 for 1420 KWH used. Find the equation relating KWH used and the monthly bill.

77. Robinson Wholesale Company paid $1340 for 500 items. Later they bought 800 items for $1760. Assume that the cost is a linear function of the number of items. Write the equation.

78. The calorie content of four large shrimp is 36 calories, and eleven shrimp contain 99 calories. Write the calorie content as a linear function of the number of shrimp.

79. The slope and one point on a line are given. A coordinate of a second point is missing. Find the missing coordinate so that the second point is on the line.
   (a) $m = 3$, $(2, 3)$, $(-1,\ \ )$
   (b) $m = -4$, $(1, 2)$, $(\ \ , 3)$
   (c) $m = \dfrac{3}{4}$, $(-2, 0)$, $(5,\ \ )$
   (d) $m = -\dfrac{1}{2}$, $(-1, -3)$, $(\ \ , 4)$

80. Brian requires 3000 calories per day to maintain his daily activities and to maintain a constant weight. He wants to gain weight. Each pound of body weight requires an additional 3500 calories. Write his daily calorie intake as a linear function of the number of pounds gained per day.

81. Find an equation of the line passing through the point $(6, 4)$ and with a y-intercept of 9.

82. Temperature measured in degrees Celsius (C) is related to temperature measured in degrees Fahrenheit (F) by a linear equation. Water boils at 100° C and 212° F. Water freezes at 0° C and 32° F. Find the linear equation relating Celsius and Fahrenheit temperatures.

83. In 1980 a certain rare coin was worth $185. In 1990 it was worth $220. Assume that the value of the coin increases linearly as a function of time. Find a linear equation that describes this relation.

84. In 1975 a certain rare coin was worth $340. In 1986 it was worth $395. Assume that the value of the coin increases linearly as a function of time. Find a linear equation that describes this relation.

85. City Electric Company calculates a customer's monthly electricity bill as $5.00 plus 7.8 cents for each KWH of electricity used. Write the linear equation relating KWH used and the monthly bill.

86. An electric company calculates a customer's monthly electricity bill as $7.50 plus 8.2 cents for each KWH of electricity used over 50 KWH. Write the linear equation relating KWH used and the monthly bill. (Assume that at least 50 KWH is used.)

87. The slope of a line is the amount of change in y when x increases by one unit. For $y = 3x + 7$, y increases by 3 when x increases by 1. For $y = -2x + 4$, y decreases by 2 when x increases by 1. (The negative value indicates a decrease in y.) Find the change in y when x increases by 1:
   (a) $y = 4x - 5$
   (b) $y = -3x + 4$
   (c) $y = \dfrac{2}{3}x + 7$
   (d) $y = \dfrac{-1}{2}x + \dfrac{2}{5}$
   (e) $3y + 2x - 4 = 0$
   (f) $y = 17$

88. Linda needs 2100 calories per day to maintain her present weight and daily activities. She wants to lose x pounds per day. Each pound of body weight is equivalent to 3500 calories. Write her daily calorie intake as a linear function of the number of pounds of weight lost per day.

89. Executive Auto Rental charges a fixed daily rate and a mileage charge. One customer rents a car for one day and drives it 125 miles. His bill is $35.75. Another customer rents a car for one day and drives it 265 miles. Her bill is $51.15. Write the linear equation relating miles driven and total cost.

90. One standard form of an equation of a straight line is $Ax + By = C$. In this form show that:
   (a) The slope of the line is $-\dfrac{A}{B}$.
   (b) The y-intercept is $\dfrac{C}{B}$.
   (c) The x-intercept is $\dfrac{C}{A}$.

1–3　MATHEMATICAL MODELS AND APPLICATIONS OF LINEAR FUNCTIONS

- *Mathematical Models*
- *Constructing a Mathematical Model*
- *Applications*
- *Cost-Volume Function*
- *Revenue Function*
- *Break-Even Analysis*
- *Straight-Line Depreciation*
- *Applications of Linear Inequalities*

MATHEMATICAL MODELS

The general idea of a **model** is familiar to all of us. Children like to play with toys such as dolls, trucks, and airplanes that model the real thing in make-believe situations. A model represents the real thing by capturing certain features or characteristics. Some models are quite simple representations (a rough sketch of a person), while others may be quite complex (a finished portrait). A model represents a complex structure in a relatively simple way.

Mathematical models describe scientific phenomena, population growth, sociological trends, economic growth, product costs, and national political opinions using mathematical equations and procedures. The mathematical model attempts to capture the essence of a phenomenon or process by relating important features in a mathematical formula. These key features are usually represented by the **variables** in the equations.

One formula that gives some information about that old phrase "just the tip of the iceberg" relates the amount of ice above the water to the amount below. The relationship is modeled by the equation

$$m_A = 0.08m_B$$

where m_A and m_B represent the mass of the iceberg above and below the surface, respectively. This tells us the tip of the iceberg is about 8% of the part of the iceberg that is below the surface.

The equation $E = mc^2$ was chalked on sidewalks of campuses across the country the day after Albert Einstein died. It was written in tribute to his profound work on the theory of relativity. This simple equation relates energy, $E,$ the mass of a body, $m,$ and the speed of light, $c.$ This equation does not tell us all about energy, but it describes the energy released when matter is transformed into energy. It helps to predict the energy released from a mass of uranium and the energy stored in the sun.

Science has developed numerous mathematical models that accurately describe scientific phenomena. Social sciences and business have also developed many mathematical models. However, these models generally only approximate the real situations. Even so, such models can be useful in making decisions and estimating the consequences of these decisions.

CONSTRUCTING A MATHEMATICAL MODEL

Constructing a mathematical model can be quite complex, but four basic steps are usually involved.

Step 1: Begin with a real-world problem. Study the information and data available to determine the variables and their relationships. Determine which variables are significant and which ones are unimportant.

Step 2: Formulate a mathematical model by describing the relationships of variables using mathematical concepts and equations.

Step 3: Use the mathematical model together with mathematical techniques to draw conclusions and to predict the outcomes of possible strategies.

Step 4: Compare the conclusions and predictions with the real-world problem. If they are unrealistic or contain too much error, the modeling cycle starts all over. (See Figure 1–11.) Study the problem some more and refine the model to give better results.

There is no guarantee of success. Generally, constructing a model is a difficult task, and the process may be repeated many times before a satisfactory model is developed.

FIGURE 1–11

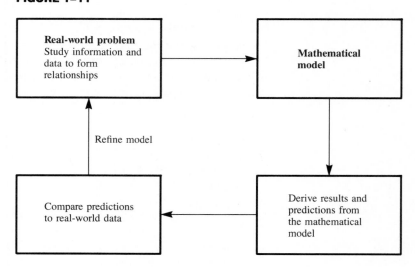

APPLICATIONS

In practical problems the relationship between the variables can be quite complicated. For example, the variables and their relationship that affect the stock market still defy the best analysts. However, many times a linear relationship can be used to provide a reasonable and useful model for solving practical problems. We now look at several applications of the linear function.

COST-VOLUME
FUNCTION

A manufacturer of mopeds conducted a study of production costs and found that fixed costs averaged $5600 per week and material costs averaged $359 per moped. This information can be stated as

$$C = 359x + 5600$$

where x represents the number of mopeds produced per week, also called the **volume,** and C is the total weekly cost of producing x mopeds. A linear function like this is used when:

1. there are **fixed costs** such as rent, utilities, and salaries that are the same each week independent of the number of items produced;
2. there are **variable costs** that depend on the number of items produced, such as the cost of materials for the items, packaging, and shipping costs.

   The moped example illustrates a linear **cost-volume function** (often simply called the cost function). A linear function is appropriate when the general form of the cost function C is given by

$$C(x) = ax + b$$

where

   x is the number of items (volume),

   b is the **fixed cost** in dollars,

   a is the *unit* **cost** (the cost per item) in dollars,

   $C(x)$ is the **total cost** in dollars of producing x items.

Notice the form of the cost function. It is essentially the slope-intercept form of a line where the slope is the unit cost and the intercept is the fixed cost.

EXAMPLE 1   (*Compare Exercise 1*)

If the cost of manufacturing x mopeds per week is given by

$$C(x) = 415x + 5200$$

then:

(a) determine the unit cost and the fixed cost.
(b) determine the cost of producing 700 mopeds per week.
(c) determine how many mopeds were produced if the production cost for one week was $230,130.

SOLUTION

(a) The unit cost is \$415, and the fixed cost is \$5200 per week.

(b) Substitute $x = 700$ into the cost equation to obtain

$$C(700) = 415(700) + 5200$$
$$= 290{,}500 + 5200$$
$$= 295{,}700$$

So the total cost is \$295,700.

(c) This information gives $C(x) = 230{,}130$, so we have

$$230{,}130 = 415x + 5200$$

We need to solve this for x:

$$230{,}130 - 5200 = 415x$$
$$224{,}930 = 415x$$
$$x = \frac{224{,}930}{415} = 542$$

So 542 mopeds were produced that week.

EXAMPLE 2   *(Compare Exercise 13)*

A company made a cost study and found that it cost \$10,170 to produce 800 purses and \$13,810 to produce 1150 purses.

(a) Determine the cost-volume function.

(b) Find the fixed cost and the unit cost.

SOLUTION

(a) Let $x =$ the number of purses. The information gives two points on the cost-volume line: (800, 10170) and (1150, 13810). The slope of the line is

$$m = \frac{13{,}810 - 10{,}170}{1150 - 800} = \frac{3640}{350} = 10.40$$

Using the point (800, 10170) in the point-slope equation, we have

$$y - 10{,}170 = 10.40(x - 800)$$
$$y = 10.40x + 1850$$

Therefore $C(x) = 10.40x + 1850$.

(b) From the equation $C(x) = 10.40x + 1850$ the fixed cost is \$1850 per week, and the unit cost is \$10.40

REVENUE FUNCTION

If a sporting goods store sells mopeds for \$798 each, the total income (**revenue**) in dollars from mopeds is 798 times the number of mopeds sold. This illustrates the general concept of a **revenue function;** it gives the total revenue obtained from the sale of x items. In the moped example the revenue function is given by

$$R(x) = 798x$$

where x represents the number of mopeds sold, 798 is the selling price in dollars for each item, and $R(x)$ is the total revenue in dollars from x items.

EXAMPLE 3   *(Compare Exercise 5)*

The sporting goods store has a sale on mopeds at $725 each.

(a) Give the revenue function.
(b) The store sold 23 mopeds. What was the total revenue?
(c) One salesperson sold $5075 worth of mopeds. How many did she sell?

SOLUTION

(a) The revenue function is given by

$$R(x) = 725x$$

(b) The revenue for 23 mopeds is obtained from the revenue function when $x = 23$:

$$R(23) = 725(23) = 16,675$$

The revenue in this case is $16,675.

(c) This gives $R(x) = 5075$, so

$$725x = 5075$$

$$x = \frac{5075}{725} = 7$$

So she sold 7 mopeds.

BREAK-EVEN ANALYSIS

Break-even analysis answers a common management question: At what sales volume will we break even? When do revenues equal costs? Greater sales will induce a profit while lesser sales will show a loss.

The **break-even point** occurs when the cost equals the revenue, so the cost and revenue functions can be used to determine the break-even point. Using function notation, we write this as $C(x) = R(x)$.

EXAMPLE 4   *(Compare Exercise 9)*

A department store pays $99 each for tape decks. The store's monthly fixed costs are $1250. The store sells the tape decks for $189.95 each.

(a) What is the cost-volume function?
(b) What is the revenue function?
(c) What is the break-even point?

SOLUTION   Let x represent the number of tape decks sold.

(a) The cost function is given by

$$C(x) = 99x + 1250$$

(b) The revenue function is defined by

$$R(x) = 189.95x$$

(c) The break-even point occurs when cost equals revenue,

$$C(x) = R(x)$$

Writing out the function gives

$$99x + 1250 = 189.95x$$

The solution of this equation gives the break-even point:

$$99x + 1250 = 189.95x$$
$$1250 = 189.95x - 99x$$
$$1250 = 90.95x$$
$$x = \frac{1250}{90.95}$$
$$= 13.74$$

Because x represents the number of tape decks, we use the next integer, 14, as the number sold per month to break even. If more than 14 are sold, there will be a profit. If fewer than 14 are sold, there will be a loss.

EXAMPLE 5   *(Compare Exercise 15)*

A temporary secretarial service has a fixed weekly cost of $730. The wages and benefits of the secretaries amount to $5.85 per hour. A firm that employs a secretary pays Temporary Service $8.15 per hour. How many hours per week of secretarial service must Temporary Service place in order to break even?

SOLUTION   First, write the cost and revenue functions. The fixed cost is $730, and the unit cost is $5.85, so the cost function is given by

$$C(x) = 5.85x + 730$$

where x is the number of hours placed each week. The revenue function is given by

$$R(x) = 8.15x$$

Equating cost and revenue, we have

$$5.85x + 730 = 8.15x$$

This equation reduces to

$$8.15x - 5.85x = 730$$
$$2.3x = 730$$
$$x = \frac{730}{2.3}$$
$$= 317.4$$

Temporary Service must place secretaries for a total of 318 hours per week (rounded up) in order to break even.

STRAIGHT-LINE DEPRECIATION

When a corporation buys a fleet of cars, it expects them to decline in value due to wear and tear. For example, if the corporation purchases new cars for $11,500 each, it may expect them to be worth only $2500 three years later. This decline in value is called **depreciation.** The value of an item after deducting depreciation is called its **book value.** In three years, each car depreciated $9000, and its book value at the end of three years was $2500. For tax and accounting purposes a company will report depreciation and book value each year during the life of an item. The Internal Revenue Service allows several methods of depreciation. The simplest is **straight-line depreciation.** This method assumes that the book value is a linear function of time, that is,

$$BV = mx + b$$

where BV is the book value and x is the number of years. For example, each car had a book value of $11,500 when $x = 0$ ("brand new" occurs at zero years). When $x = 3$, its book value declined to $2500. This information is equivalent to giving two points $(0, 11500)$ and $(3, 2500)$ on the straight line representing book value. (See Figure 1–12.)

We obtain the linear equation of the book value by finding the equation of a line through these two points. The slope of the line is

$$m = \frac{y_2 - y_1}{x_2 - x_1} = \frac{2500 - 11,500}{3 - 0}$$
$$= \frac{-9000}{3} = -3000$$

and the y-intercept is 11,500, so the equation is

$$BV = -3000x + 11,500$$

The book value at the end of two years is

$$BV = -3000(2) + 11,500 = -6000 + 11,500 = 5500$$

The *negative value of the slope indicates a decrease* in the book value of $3000 each year. This annual decrease is the **annual depreciation.**

FIGURE 1–12

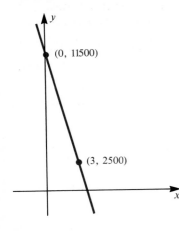

Generally, a company will estimate the number of years of useful life of an item. The value of the item at the end of its useful life is called its **scrap value.** The values of x are restricted to $0 \leq x \leq n$, where n is the number of years of useful life.

EXAMPLE 6   *(Compare Exercise 17)*

Acme Manufacturing Co. purchases a piece of equipment for $28,300 and estimates its useful life as eight years. At the end of its useful life, its scrap value is estimated at $900.

(a) Find the linear equation expressing the relationship between book value and time.
(b) Find the annual depreciation.
(c) Find the book value for the first, fifth, and seventh year.

SOLUTION

(a) The line passes through the two points (0, 28300) and (8, 900). Therefore the slope is

$$m = \frac{900 - 28,300}{8 - 0} = -3425$$

and the y-intercept is 28,300, giving the equation

$$BV = -3425x + 28,300$$

(b) The annual depreciation is obtained from the slope and is $3425.
(c) For year 1, $BV = -3425(1) + 28,300 = 24,875$. For year 5, $BV = -3425(5) + 28,300 = 11,175$. For year 7, $BV = -3425(7) + 28,300 = 4325$. Thus after seven years the book value of the equipment is $4325.

APPLICATIONS OF LINEAR INEQUALITIES

For some applications an interval of values, instead of one specific value, gives an appropriate answer to the problem. These situations can often be represented by inequalities. Here are two examples using linear inequalities. (See Appendix A–4 for a review of the properties of linear inequalities.)

EXAMPLE 7   *(Compare Exercise 21)*

A doughnut shop sells doughnuts for $2.15 per dozen. The shop has fixed weekly costs of $650 and unit costs of $1.05 per dozen. How many dozens of doughnuts must be sold weekly for the shop to make a profit?

SOLUTION   Let $x =$ number of dozens of doughnuts sold per week. The revenue and cost functions are

$$R(x) = 2.15x$$
$$C(x) = 1.05x + 650$$

The shop makes a profit when the revenue exceeds the costs, that is, when $R(x) > C(x)$. Therefore we want to solve

$$2.15x > 1.05x + 650$$
$$2.15x - 1.05x > 650$$
$$1.10x > 650$$
$$x > \frac{650}{1.10} = 590.9$$

Therefore at least 591 dozen doughnuts must be sold in order to make a profit. The interval notation for this solution is $[591, \infty)$.

EXAMPLE 8   (*Compare Exercise 23*)

A quick-copy store can select from two plans to lease a copy machine. Plan A costs $75 per month plus five cents per copy. Plan B costs $200 per month plus two cents per copy. When will it be to the copy shop's advantage to lease under Plan A?

SOLUTION   Let $x =$ number of copies per month. Then the monthly costs are as follows:

$$\text{Plan A:} \quad CA(x) = 75 + 0.05x$$
$$\text{Plan B:} \quad CB(x) = 200 + 0.02x$$

Plan A is better when $CA(x) < CB(x)$. We find the solution by solving

$$75 + 0.05x < 200 + 0.02x$$
$$0.05x - 0.02x < 200 - 75$$
$$0.03x < 125$$
$$x < \frac{125}{0.03} = 4166.7$$

Plan A is better when the number of copies per month is fewer than 4167 copies. The interval notation for this answer is $(0, 4167)$.

1-3 EXERCISES

I

1. (*See Example 1*) The weekly cost function of manufacturing x bicycles is given by

$$C(x) = 43x + 2300$$

(a) Determine the cost of producing 180 bicycles per week.
(b) One week the total production cost was $11,889. How many bicycles were produced that week?
(c) Find the unit cost and fixed cost.

2. A software company produces a home accounting system. The company's cost function for producing x systems per month is

$$C(x) = 16.25x + 28,300$$

(a) Determine the cost of producing 2500 systems per month.
(b) One month the production costs were $63,010. How many systems did the company produce?
(c) Find the company's unit cost and fixed cost.

3. A company has determined that the relationship between daily cost and volume (the cost-volume formula) for T-shirts is $C(x) = 3x + 400$.
   (a) Determine the fixed cost and the unit cost.
   (b) Find the total costs when the production is 600 units per day and 1000 units per day.

4. The cost-volume formula for men's belts is $y = 2.5x + 750$, where x is the number of belts produced per week. Determine the fixed cost and the unit cost. Find the total costs when the weekly production is
   (a) 100 units
   (b) 300 units
   (c) 650 units

5. (*See Example 3*) A store sells jogging shoes for $32 per pair.
   (a) Write the revenue function.
   (b) The store sold 78 pairs. What was the revenue?
   (c) One day the store sold $672 worth of jogging shoes. How many pairs did it sell?

6. Tony's Cassette Warehouse sells cassettes for $6.25 each.
   (a) Write the revenue function.
   (b) What is the revenue from selling 265 cassettes?

7. Cold Pizza sells frozen pizzas for $3.39 each.
   (a) Write the revenue function.
   (b) What is the revenue from selling 834 pizzas?

8. A club sells cookies for 60 cents each.
   (a) Write the rule that gives the revenue function.
   (b) The revenue one day was $343.80. How many cookies were sold?

9. (*See Example 4*) A clothing store pays $57 each for sports coats and has a fixed monthly cost of $780. The store sells the coats for $79 each.
   (a) What is the linear cost-volume function?
   (b) What is the linear revenue function?
   (c) What is the break-even point?

10. Find the linear cost equation if the fixed cost is $700 and the cost per unit volume is $2.50. What are the total costs when the volume produced is 400 units?

11. Find the cost-volume formula if the fixed cost is $500 and the cost per unit volume is $4. What are the total costs when the volume produced is 800 units?

12. A company has a cost function of
$$C(x) = 22x + 870$$
and a revenue function of
$$R(x) = 37.50x$$
Find the break-even point.

13. (*See Example 2*) The Academic T-Shirt Company did a cost study and found that it costs $1400 to produce 600 "I Love Math" T-shirts. The total cost is $1600 for a volume of 700 T-shirts.
   (a) Determine the linear cost-volume function.
   (b) What is the fixed cost?
   (c) What is the unit cost?

14. The monthly expenses of The Campus Copy Shop are given by the cost equation
$$C(x) = 3690 + 0.025x$$
where x is the number of pages copied in a month. The revenue function is
$$R(x) = 0.055x$$
Find the break-even point of The Campus Copy Shop.

15. (*See Example 5*) The Computer Shop sells computers. The shop has fixed costs of $1500 per week. Its average cost per computer is $649 each, and the average selling price is $899 each.
   (a) Write the linear cost function.
   (b) Write the linear revenue function.
   (c) Find the cost of selling 37 computers per week.
   (d) Find the revenue from selling 37 computers.
   (e) Find the break-even point.

16. A Toy Co. estimates that total costs are $1000 when its volume is 500 Fastback cars and $1200 when its volume is 900 Fastback cars.
   (a) Determine the linear cost-volume function.
   (b) Find the fixed cost and unit cost.
   (c) What are the estimated total costs when the volume is 1200 units?

17. (*See Example 6*) A TV costs $425, has a scrap value of $25, and has a useful life of eight years. Find
   (a) the linear equation relating book value and number of years.
   (b) the annual depreciation.
   (c) the book value for year 3.

18. A machine costs $1500 and has a useful life of ten years. If it has a scrap value of $200, find
   (a) the linear equation relating book value and number of years.
   (b) the annual depreciation.
   (c) the book value for year 7.

19. An automobile costs $9750, has a useful life of six years, and has a scrap value of $300. Find
   (a) the linear equation relating book value and number of years.
   (b) the annual depreciation.
   (c) the book value for years 2 and 5.

20. A machine costs $13,500, has a useful life of 12 years, and has no scrap value. Find the linear equation relating book value and number of years.

21. (*See Example 7*) The Cookie Store sells cookies for 45 cents each. The store has monthly fixed costs of $475 per month and units costs of 23 cents per cookie. How many cookies must it sell each month to make a profit?

22. A manufacturing company produces an item that sells for $145 and has a unit cost of $70. If fixed manufacturing costs are $225,000 per year, how many must the company sell to make a profit?

II

23. (*See Example 8*) A family plans to rent a car for a one-week vacation. Company A rents a car for $105 per week plus 14 cents per mile. Company B rents a car for $23 per day plus ten cents per mile. Find the number of miles traveled that makes the car from Company A the better deal.

24. A graduating senior has a choice of two salary plans from a company. The first plan will pay $1000 per month plus 2% of the senior's monthly sales. The second plan will pay a straight 7.5% commission. How much must the senior sell per month to do better under the second plan?

25. The Times-Herald is planning a special-edition magazine. The publishing expenses include fixed costs of $1400 and printing costs of 40 cents per magazine. The magazine will sell for 85 cents each, and advertising revenue is 20 cents per magazine. How many magazines must be sold to make a profit?

26. The Student Center plans to bring a musical group for a concert. It expects a sellout crowd of 1200. The group will come for a flat fee of $3000 or for a fee of $1000 plus 30% of gate receipts. The Student Center decides to pay $1000 plus 30% of the gate receipts.
   (a) What admission prices should the Student Center charge in order for this cost to be less than the other choice of $3000?
   (b) If other costs are $2500, what admission price should the Student Center charge in order to make a profit?

27. Davis Printing finds that the unit cost of printing a book is $12.65. The total cost for printing 2700 books is $36,295. Find the linear cost-volume function.

28. A company makes microwave stands at a cost of $48 each and sells them for $62 each. The company spent $28,000 to begin making the stands. How many stands must it sell to break even?

III

29. The Beta Club plans a dance as a fund raiser. The band costs $650, decorations cost $45, and the refreshments cost $2.20 per person. The admission tickets are $6 each.
   (a) How many tickets must be sold to break even?
   (b) How many tickets must be sold to clear $700?
   (c) If admission tickets are $7.50 each, how many must be sold to clear $700?

30. A store handles a specialty item that has a unit cost of $24 and a fixed cost of $360. The sales required to break even are 75 items.
   (a) Find the linear cost function.
   (b) Find the linear revenue function.

31. A health club membership costs $35 per month. The club has 1238 members.
   (a) What is the linear monthly revenue function?
   (b) What is the monthly revenue?
   (c) One month the revenue increased by $595. What was the increase in membership?

32. A company's records showed that the daily fixed costs for one of its production lines was $1850 and the total cost of one day's production of 320 items was $3178. What is the linear cost-volume function?

33. A company purchased a piece of equipment and used the straight-line depreciation method. The company books showed that the book value was $14,175 at the end of the third year and $8475 at the end of the seventh year.
  (a) Find the linear equation relating book value and number of years.
  (b) Find the annual depreciation.
  (c) Find the purchase price.

34. The Unique Shoppe sells personalized telephones. Its weekly cost function is

$$C(x) = 28x + 650$$

and the break-even point is $x = 65$ phones per week. What is the revenue function?

35. The break-even point for a tanning salon is 260 memberships, which produce $3120 in monthly revenue. If the salon sells only 200 memberships, it will lose $330 per month.
  (a) What is the linear revenue function?
  (b) What is the linear cost function?

36. The profit function is revenue minus cost, that is,

$$P(x) = R(x) - C(x)$$

  (a) The cost and revenue functions for Acme Manufacturing are

$$C(x) = 28x + 465$$
$$R(x) = 52x$$

  (i) Write the profit function.
  (ii) What is the profit from selling 25 items?

  (b) The weekly expenses of selling x bicycles in The Bike Shop are given by the cost function

$$C(x) = 1200 + 130x$$

and revenue is given by

$$R(x) = 210x$$

  (i) Write the profit function.
  (ii) Find the profit from selling 18 bicycles in a week.

  (c) Another Bike Shop has monthly fixed costs of $5200 and unit costs of $145. Its bicycles sell for $225 each.
  (i) Write the linear profit function.
  (ii) What is the profit from selling 75 bicycles per month?

37. A specialty shop owner used a revenue function and a cost-volume function to analyze his monthly sales. One month he found that with a sales volume of 1465 items he had revenues of $32,962.50 and a total cost of $26,405.50. Another month he had total costs of $17,638 on a sales volume of 940 items.
  (a) Find the linear revenue function.
  (b) Find the linear cost function.
  (c) Find the break-even point.

38. Midwest Office Supply sold 27 briefcases for a total revenue of $1134. The cost is a linear function, and the break-even point occurs when 88 briefcases are sold. If the company sells 100 briefcases, it makes a profit of $132. Find the cost and revenue functions.

IMPORTANT TERMS

1-1

Function

Domain

Range

Rule of a Function

1-2

Graph

Linear Function

Slope

y-Intercept

Horizontal Line

Vertical Line

Slope-Intercept Equation

Point-Slope Equation

Two-Point Equation

Parallel Lines

1-3

Mathematical Model

Variables

Cost-Volume Function

Fixed Costs

Variable Costs

Unit Costs

Revenue Function

Break-Even Analysis

Break-Even Point

Depreciation

Book Value

Straight-Line Depreciation

Annual Depreciation

Scrap Value

REVIEW EXERCISES

1. If $f(x) = \dfrac{7x - 3}{2}$, find:

(a) $f(5)$
(b) $f(1)$
(c) $f(4)$
(d) $f(b)$

2. If $f(x) = 8x - 4$, find:

(a) $f(2)$
(b) $f(-3)$
(c) $f\left(\dfrac{1}{2}\right)$
(d) $f(c)$

3. If $f(x) = \dfrac{x + 2}{x - 1}$ and $g(x) = 5x + 3$,
find $f(2) + g(3)$.

4. If $f(x) = (x + 5)(2x - 1)$ find:

(a) $f(1)$
(b) $f(0)$
(c) $f(-5)$
(d) $f(a - 5)$

5. Apples cost \$1.20 per pound, so the price of a bag of apples is $f(x) = 1.20x$, where x is the weight in pounds and $f(x)$ is the purchase price in dollars.
(a) What is $f(3.5)$?
(b) A bag of apples cost \$3.30. How much did it weigh?

6. Tuition and fees charges at a university are given by

$$f(x) = 135x + 450$$

where x is the number of semester hours enrolled and $f(x)$ is the total cost of tuition and fees.
(a) Find $f(15)$.
(b) A student's bill for tuition and fees was \$2205; for how many semester hours was she enrolled?

7. Write an equation of the function described by the following statements.
(a) All the shoes on this table are \$29.95 per pair.
(b) A catering service charges \$40 plus \$1.25 per person to cater a reception.

8. Sketch the graph of:
(a) $f(x) = 2x - 5$
(b) $6x + 10y = 30$

9. Graph the lines:
(a) $y = 3x - 5$
(b) $y = -7$
(c) $x = 5.5$
(d) $y = x$

10. Graph the lines:
(a) $y = 6.5$
(b) $x = -4.75$
(c) $y = -1.3$
(d) $x = 7$

11. Find the slope and y-intercept for the following lines:
(a) $y = -2x + 3$
(b) $y = \dfrac{2}{3}x - 4$
(c) $4y = 5x + 6$
(d) $6x + 7y + 5 = 0$

12. Find the slope of the line through the following pairs of points:
(a) $(2, 7)$ and $(-3, 4)$
(b) $(6, 8)$ and $(-11, 8)$
(c) $(4, 2)$ and $(4, 6)$

13. For the line $6x + 5y = 15$, find:
(a) the slope.
(b) the y-intercept.
(c) the x-intercept.

14. For the line $-2x + 9y = 6$, find:
(a) the slope.
(b) the y-intercept.
(c) the x-intercept.

15. Find an equation of the following lines:
(a) with slope $-\dfrac{3}{4}$ and y-intercept 5
(b) with slope 8 and y-intercept -3
(c) with slope -2 and passing through $(5, -1)$
(d) with slope 0 and passing through $(11, 6)$
(e) passing through $(5, 3)$ and $(-1, 4)$
(f) passing through $(-2, 5)$ and $(-2, -2)$
(g) passing through $(2, 7)$ and parallel to $4x - 3y = 22$

16. Find an equation of the line with the given slope and passing through the given point:
(a) $m = 5$ and point $(2, -1)$
(b) with slope $-\dfrac{2}{3}$ and point $(5, 4)$
(c) with $m = 0$ and point $(7, 6)$
(d) with slope 1 and point $(-2, -2)$

17. Find an equation of the line through the given points:
(a) $(6, 2)$ and $(-3, 2)$
(b) $(-4, 5)$ and $(-4, -2)$
(c) $(5, 0)$ and $(5, 10)$
(d) $(-7, 6)$ and $(7, 6)$

18. Determine whether the following pairs of lines are parallel:
(a) $7x - 4y = 12$ and $-21x + 12y = 17$
(b) $3x + 2y = 13$ and $2x - 3y = 28$

19. Is the line through $(5, 19)$ and $(-2, 7)$ parallel to the line through $(11, 3)$ and $(-1, -5)$?

20. Is the line through $(4, 0)$ and $(7, -2)$ parallel to the line through $(7, 4)$ and $(10, 2)$?

21. Determine whether the line through $(8, 6)$ and $(-3, 14)$ is parallel to the line $8x + 4y = 34$.

22. Determine whether the line through $(-2.5, 0)$ and $(-1, 4.5)$ is parallel to the line $3x - y = 19$.

23. Determine whether the line through $(9, 10)$ and $(5, 6)$ is parallel to the line $3x - 2y = 14$.

24. Determine whether the following pair of lines are parallel:

(a) $y = 5x + 13$ (b) $6x + 2y = 15$
      $y = 5x - 24$ $15x + 5y = -27$
(c) $-8x + 9y = 41$ (d) $12x - 5y = 60$
      $9x - 8y = 13$ $6x + y = 15$

25. A manufacturer has fixed costs of $12,800 per month and a unit cost of $36 per item produced. What is the cost function?

26. The weekly cost function of a manufacturer is

$$C(x) = 83x + 960$$

(a) What are the weekly fixed costs?
(b) What is the unit cost?

27. The cost function of producing x bags of Hi-Gro fertilizer per week is:

$$C(x) = 3.60x + 2850$$

(a) What is the cost of producing 580 bags per week?
(b) If the production costs for one week amounted to $5208, how many bags were produced?

28. A shoe store has a special sale in which all jogging shoes are $28.50 per pair. Write the revenue function for jogging shoes.

29. A T-shirt shop pays $6.50 each for T-shirts. The shop's weekly fixed expenses are $675. It sells the T-shirts for $11.00 each.
(a) What is the revenue function?
(b) What is the cost function?
(c) What is the break-even point?

30. Midstate Manufacturing sells calculators for $17.45 each. The unit cost is $9.30, and the fixed cost is $17,604. Find the quantity that must be sold to break even.

31. The comptroller of Southern Watch Company wants to find the company's break-even point. She has the following information: The company sells the watches for $19.50 each. One week it produced 1840 watches at a production cost of $25,260.00. Another week it produced 2315 watches at a production cost of $31,102.50. Find the weekly volume of watches the company must produce to break even.

32. Find an equation of the line described in the following:
(a) through the point $(5, 7)$ and parallel to
     $6x - y = 15$
(b) through the point $(-2, -5)$ and parallel to the line through $(4, -2)$ and $(9, 5)$
(c) with y-intercept 6 and passing through $(2, -5)$

33. Norton's, Inc. purchases a piece of equipment for $17,500. The useful life is eight years, and the scrap value at the end of 8 years is $900.
(a) Find the equation relating book value and its age using straight-line depreciation.
(b) What is the annual depreciation?
(c) What is the book value for the fifth year?

34. The function for the book value of a truck is

$$f(x) = -2300x + 16,500$$

where x is its age and $f(x)$ is its book value.
(a) What did the truck cost?
(b) If its useful life is seven years, what is its scrap value?

35. An item cost $1540, has a useful life of five years, and has a scrap value of $60. Find the equation relating book value and number of years using straight-line depreciation.

36. Find the x- and y-intercepts of the line $8x + 6y = 24$ and sketch its graph.

37. A line passes through the point $(2, 9)$ and is parallel to $4x - 5y = 10$. Find the value of k so that $(-3, k)$ is on the line.

38. Lawn Care Manufacturing estimates that the material for each lawnmower costs $85. The manufacturer's fixed operating costs are $4250 per week. Find the company's weekly costs.

39. Nguyen's Auto Parts bought a new delivery van for $12,000. Nguyen expects the van to be worth $1500 in five years. Find the value of the van as a linear function of its age.

40. A manufacturer found that it cost \$48,840 to produce 940 items in one week. The next week it cost \$42,535 to produce 810 items. Find the linear cost-volume function.

41. A hamburger place estimates that the materials for each hamburger cost \$0.67. One day it made 1150 hamburgers, and the total operating costs were \$1250.50. Find the cost function.

42. A fast food franchise owner must pay the parent company \$1200 per month plus 4.1% of receipts. Find the monthly franchise cost function.

43. A company offers an inventor two royalty options for her product. The first is a one-time-only payment of \$17,000. The second is a payment of \$2000 plus \$0.75 for each item sold. Determine when the second option is better than the first.

44. A university estimates that 92% of the applicants who pay the admissions deposit will enroll. How many applicants who pay their admissions deposit are required in order to have a class of 2300 students?

45. Find the value of k so that the points (9, 4) and $(-2, k)$ lie on a line with slope -2.

46. A caterer's fee to cater a wedding reception is a linear function based on a fixed fee and an amount per person. Stephanie and Roy's wedding was planned for 350 guests and cost \$1550. Jennifer and Brett's wedding was planned for 290 guests and cost \$1370. Find the cost function.

47. A manufacturer of videotapes uses a linear cost function. One week the company produced 1730 tapes for a total cost of \$12,813.60. The unit cost is known to be \$6.82. Find the fixed cost.

48. Jones established a small business with a reserve of \$12,000 to cover operating expenses in the early stages when a loss is expected. The reserve is reduced \$620 each week to cover operating costs.
(a) Write the function giving the amount remaining in the reserve fund.
(b) How much is in the fund after eight weeks?
(c) How long will it take to deplete the fund?

2
Linear Systems

2-1 SYSTEMS OF TWO EQUATIONS

- *Solution by Graphing*

- *Substitution Method*

- *Elimination Method*

- *Inconsistent Systems*

- *Systems That Have Many Solutions*

- *Application: Supply and Demand Analysis*

*I*N CHAPTER 1 YOU learned some applications of linear equations. While many problems in mathematics, business, engineering, and sciences can be solved by using a linear equation, many problems involve more than one linear equation. We use a simple example to illustrate the concept.

A company makes two kinds of fruit punch from apple juice and pineapple juice. It has 142 gallons of apple juice and 108 gallons of pineapple juice. Each case of Golden Punch requires four gallons of apple juice and six gallons of pineapple juice. Each case of Light Punch requires seven gallons of apple juice and three gallons of pineapple juice. How many cases of each punch should be made in order to use all the apple and pineapple juice?

The above information can be stated by using linear equations in the following manner:

Let x represent the number of cases of Golden Punch, and let y represent the number of cases of Light Punch. The amount of apple juice used totals 142 gallons and is the total of the apple juice used in each punch. Similarly, the pineapple juice used in each punch totals 108 gallons. We state this information as follows:

$$4x + 7y = 142 \qquad \text{(total apple juice)}$$
$$6x + 3y = 108 \qquad \text{(total pineapple juice)}$$

We want to find the number of cases of each kind of punch that makes both equations true.

We will not solve this problem here, but we will discuss some examples and techniques that demonstrate methods of solving a system of equations. You will then be able to solve this problem (Exercise 53).

The pair of equations is called a **system of equations.** A pair of numbers, one a value of x and the other a value of y, that makes *both* equations true is called a **solution of the system of equations.**

SOLUTION BY
GRAPHING

We use the following simple system to illustrate the geometric meaning of solving a system of linear equations.

EXAMPLE 1

Solve the system

$$2x - y = 3$$
$$x + 2y = 4$$

SOLUTION   Geometrically, each of these equations represents a line. When the lines are graphed with the same coordinate axes, they intersect at the point (2,1) (Figure 2–1). The values $x = 2$ and $y = 1$ satisfy both equations (check to be sure). Thus they form a solution to the system.

FIGURE 2–1

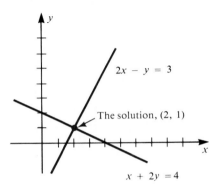

NOTE   Remember that the pair of numbers $x = 2$ and $y = 1$ forms *one* solution.

We can estimate the solution to a system by graphing the lines and noting the intersection of the lines. However, the graph must be accurate, and even so the precision of the solution may be in doubt. Precise solutions may be obtained through algebraic techniques. We will use two algebraic techniques, the **substitution method** and the **elimination method.**

SUBSTITUTION
METHOD

The Substitution Method   The basic approach of the substitution method is

1. Solve for a variable in one of the equations.
2. Substitute for that variable in the other equation.

EXAMPLE 2 *(Compare Exercise 1)*

Solve the system

$$2x - y = 3$$
$$x + 2y = 4$$

by substitution.

SOLUTION   In this case it is easy to solve for x in the second equation because its coefficient is 1. We obtain

$$x = 4 - 2y$$

Substitute this expression for x in the first equation, $2x - y = 3$:

$$2(4 - 2y) - y = 3$$
$$8 - 4y - y = 3$$
$$8 - 5y = 3$$
$$8 = 3 + 5y$$
$$5 = 5y$$
$$y = 1$$

Now substitute 1 for y in $x = 4 - 2y$ to obtain $x = 4 - 2 = 2$. You could also substitute in $2x - y = 3$. Thus the solution to the system is $(2, 1)$. You may also solve for y in the first equation and substitute it in the second equation. This will yield the same solution. (Try it.) To be sure you have made no error, you should check your solution in *both* equations.

EXAMPLE 3 *(Compare Exercise 13)*

Solve the system

$$2x - 3y = -18$$
$$4x + 5y = 8$$

SOLUTION   Solve for x in one equation. From the first equation we obtain

$$2x = -18 + 3y$$

$$x = \frac{1}{2}(-18 + 3y)$$

$$= -9 + \frac{3}{2}y$$

Substitute the expression for x in the second equation:

$$4\left(-9 + \frac{3}{2}y\right) + 5y = 8$$
$$-36 + 6y + 5y = 8$$
$$-36 + 11y = 8$$
$$11y = 44$$
$$y = 4$$

Now substitute $y = 4$ into one of the equations. We use

$$x = -9 + \left(\frac{3}{2}\right)y$$

to obtain

$$x = -9 + \frac{3}{2}(4)$$
$$= -9 + 6$$
$$= -3$$

The pair $x = -3$, $y = 4$ gives the solution to the system. Check it in both equations.

ELIMINATION METHOD

The elimination method finds the solution by systematically modifying the system to simpler systems. It does so in a manner that gives a system with exactly the same solutions as the original system. We call this an **equivalent system.** The elimination method is especially useful because it can be used with systems with several variables and equations. The elimination method produces a series of systems of equations by eliminating a variable from an equation or equations to obtain a simpler system. As you study the examples, observe that the operations used to transform a system (eliminate a variable) into a simpler yet equivalent system are the following

Equivalent Linear Systems

To transform one system of linear equations into an equivalent system, use one or more of the following:

1. Interchange two equations.
2. Multiply or divide one or more equations by a nonzero constant.
3. Multiply one equation by a constant and add it to or subtract it from another equation.

We illustrate this method with the system

$$3x - y = 3$$
$$x + 2y = 8$$

The arithmetic is a little easier if we eliminate a variable that has 1 as a coefficient. It is usually more convenient to use the top equation to eliminate x, so we interchange the two equations to get

$$x + 2y = 8$$
$$3x - y = 3$$

Now eliminate x from the bottom equation as follows:

$$-3x - 6y = -24 \quad \text{(Multiply the top equation by } -3 \text{ because it gives } -3x, \text{ the negative of the } x\text{-term in the bottom equation)}$$

$$\underline{3x - y = 3} \quad \text{(Now add it to the bottom equation)}$$

$$-7y = -21 \quad \text{(The new second equation)}$$

Since the new equation came from equations in the system, it is true whenever the system is true. It replaces the equation $3x - y = 3$ to give the system

$$x + 2y = 8$$
$$-7y = -21$$

Notice that the bottom equation has been modified so that the variable x has been *eliminated* from it. Simplify the bottom equation further by dividing by -7:

$$x + 2y = 8$$
$$y = 3$$

This system has the same solution as the original system, but it has the advantage of giving the value of y at the common solution, namely, 3. Now substitute 3 for y in the top equation to obtain

$$x + 2(3) = 8$$

(Actually, you can substitute y into either of the original equations.) This simplifies to $x = 2$, so the solution to the system is (2, 3).

EXAMPLE 4   *(Compare Exercise 17)*

Solve this system by elimination:

$$2x - 3y = -19$$
$$5x + 7y = 25$$

SOLUTION   We want to eliminate x from the second equation and find the value of y for the common solution. We modify the system of equations as follows:

$$-10x + 15y = 95 \quad \text{(Multiply the top equation by } -5\text{)}$$
$$\underline{10x + 14y = 50} \quad \text{(Multiply the bottom equation by 2)}$$
$$29y = 145 \quad \text{(Now add)}$$
$$y = 5 \quad \text{(Divide through by 29 to find } y\text{)}$$

Replace the bottom equation to obtain the modified, and equivalent, system

$$2x - 3y = -19$$
$$y = 5$$

Now substitute this value of y into one of the equations. We use the first to obtain

$$2x - 3(5) = -19$$
$$2x = -4$$
$$x = -2$$

The solution to the original system is $(-2, 5)$.

NOTE Each of the original equations was multiplied by a number so that the resulting equations have the same coefficients of x, except for the sign. Then it was easy to eliminate x from the second equation by adding.

It is a good practice to check your solutions because errors in arithmetic sometimes occur. To check, substitute your solution into *all* of the equations in the original system. If your solution fails to satisfy one or more of the equations, an error has occurred.

EXAMPLE 5 *(Compare Exercise 43)*

A woman must control her diet carefully. She selects milk and bagels for breakfast. How much of each should she serve in order to consume 700 calories and 28 g of protein. Each cup of milk contains 170 calories and 8 g of protein. Each bagel contains 138 calories and 4 g of protein.

SOLUTION Let x be the number of cups of milk and y the number of bagels. Then the total number of calories is

$$170x + 138y$$

and the total protein is

$$8x + 4y$$

so we need to solve the system

$$8x + 4y = 28$$
$$170x + 138y = 700$$

Divide the top equation by 4 and the bottom equation by 2 to simplify somewhat:

$$2x + y = 7$$
$$85x + 69y = 350$$

Next, multiply the top equation by -69 and add it to the bottom equation in order to eliminate y from the second equation:

$$-138x - 69y = -483$$
$$\underline{85x + 69y = 350}$$
$$-53x = -133$$
$$x = \frac{133}{53} = 2.509 \quad \text{(rounded)}$$

Now substitute and solve for y:

$$2(2.509) + y = 7$$
$$5.018 + y = 7$$
$$y = 1.982$$

It is reasonable to round these answers to 2.5 cups of milk and 2 bagels. ⬛

EXAMPLE 6   *(Compare Exercise 47)*

A silversmith has two alloys, one containing 40% silver and one containing 65% silver. How much of each should be melted and combined to give 100 grams of an alloy containing 50% silver?

SOLUTION   Let x = number of grams of the 40% alloy. Let y = number of grams of the 65% alloy. A total of 100 grams is desired, so

$$x + y = 100$$

The silver content of the first alloy is $0.40x$, and that of the second is $0.65y$. Since the mixture of the two alloys yields a 50% silver content, the silver content totals 50 grams, so

$$0.40x + 0.65y = 50$$

To solve the system

$$x + y = 100$$
$$0.40x + 0.65y = 50$$

we can use the substitution method. Substitute $x = 100 - y$ into the second equation:

$$0.40(100 - y) + 0.65y = 50$$
$$40 - 0.40y + 0.65y = 50$$
$$0.25y = 10$$
$$y = 40$$

It then follows that $x = 60$. The proper mixture is 60 grams of the 40% alloy and 40 grams of the 65% alloy. ⬛

EXAMPLE 7   *(Compare Exercise 49)*

An electronics company manufactures transistor radios at its plants in Jonesboro and Smithville. At the Jonesboro plant the unit cost is $6.40, and the fixed cost is $9360. At the Smithville plant the unit cost is $7.10, and the fixed cost is $8400. The vice-president instructs the two plants to manufacture a total of 1200 radios, but the total cost must be the same at each plant. How many radios should each plant produce?

SOLUTION Let x = number of radios produced at Jonesboro. Let y = number of radios produced at Smithville. The total number of radios produced is

$$x + y = 1200$$

The total cost at Jonesboro is $C_J = 6.40x + 9360$. The total cost at Smithville is $C_S = 7.10y + 8400$. Since the total costs must be the same at each plant,

$$6.40x + 9360 = 7.10y + 8400$$

We seek the solution of the system

$$x + y = 1200$$
$$6.40x + 9360 = 7.10y + 8400$$

This simplifies to

$$x + y = 1200$$
$$6.40x - 7.10y = -960$$

Substitute $x = 1200 - y$ into the second equation:

$$6.40(1200 - y) - 7.10y = -960$$
$$7680 - 6.40y - 7.10y = -960$$
$$-13.5y = -8640$$
$$y = 640$$
$$x = 560$$

If 560 radios are produced at Jonesboro and 640 at Smithville, the total production costs will be the same at each plant.

⎯⎯⎯⎯▌

INCONSISTENT
SYSTEMS

Each system in the preceding examples has exactly one solution. Do not expect this always to be the case. If the equations represent two parallel lines, they have no points in common, and a solution to the system does not exist. We say that this is an **inconsistent system.** Figure 2–2 shows the graph of the two lines

FIGURE 2–2

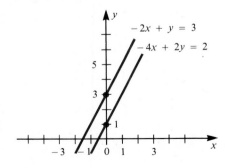

Parallel lines

$$-2x + y = 3$$
$$-4x + 2y = 2$$

Each line has slope 2, and they do not intersect, so no solution exists for the system.

EXAMPLE 8 *(Compare Exercise 29)*

Let's see what happens when we try to solve the system of parallel lines

$$-2x + y = 3$$
$$-4x + 2y = 2$$

To eliminate x from the second equation, multiply the first by -2 and add it to the second. The new system is

$$-2x + y = 3$$
$$0y = -4$$
$$0 = -4$$

The last equation gives an inconsistency, $0 = -4$. When an attempt to solve a system leads to an inconsistency, the system has no solution. This will happen when the system represents two different parallel lines.

SYSTEMS THAT HAVE MANY SOLUTIONS

Suppose you graph the two lines

$$9x - 3y = 6$$
$$6x - 2y = 4$$

You will find their graphs are identical, so they coincide. Furthermore, both have slope 3 with y-intercept 2, so when you put them in the slope-intercept form, $y = mx + b$, you will find that the slopes and intercepts are the same, so their graphs are identical. Every point on this line is a solution to the system (see Figure 2–3). The following example illustrates what happens when we try to solve such a system.

FIGURE 2–3

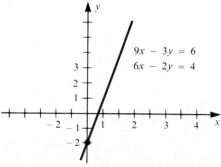

Lines $9x - 3y = 6$ and $6x - 2y = 4$ coincide.

EXAMPLE 9   *(Compare Exercise 31)*

Solve the system

$$9x - 3y = 6$$
$$6x - 2y = 4$$

We eliminate x as follows:

$$-18x + 6y = -12 \qquad \text{(Multiply the first equation by } -2)$$
$$\underline{18x - 6y = \quad 12} \qquad \text{(Multiply the second equation by 3)}$$
$$0 = \quad 0 \qquad \text{(Add the two equations)}$$

The system is transformed into the system

$$9x - 3y = 6$$
$$0 = 0$$

The system reduces to a single equation; any solution to this equation gives a solution to the system. There are an infinite number of solutions to this equation that may be represented by solving for y:

$$y = 3x - 2 \qquad \text{where } x \text{ may be any number}$$

For example, solutions are obtained when

$$x = \quad 3 \quad \text{and} \quad y = 7$$
$$x = -5 \quad \text{and} \quad y = -17$$
$$x = \quad 0 \quad \text{and} \quad y = -2$$

We can also describe the infinity of solutions in **parametric form.** The letter k, called a **parameter,** represents an arbitrary value of x. When substituting $x = k$ into one of the equations, we get the corresponding value of y,

$$y = 3k - 2$$

The point $(k, 3k - 2)$ represents a solution to the system when any real number is used for k.

APPLICATION:
SUPPLY AND
DEMAND ANALYSIS

Department stores are well aware that they can sell large quantities of goods if they advertise a reduction in price. The lower the price, the more they sell. Retailers understand this relationship between the price of a commodity and the consumer **demand** (the amount consumers buy). They also know that there may be more than one relationship between price and demand depending on circumstances. In times of shortages a different psychology takes effect, and prices tend to *increase* when demand *increases*. Real estate is another example in which an increase in demand causes an increase in price. We will analyze one market situation, the perfectly competitive market of supply and demand.

In the competitive situation a decrease in price can cause an increase in demand (when a store has a sale). This suggests that demand is a function of price. On other occasions a store may lower prices because an item is in great demand and it expects to increase profits by a greater volume. This suggests that price is a function of demand. Since the cause-and-effect relationship between price and demand can go either way—a change in price causes a change in demand or a change in demand can cause a change in price—we need to decide how to write the demand equation. The analysis is easier if we write the demand equation (and the supply equation in the next paragraph) so that the price is a function of demand (or supply).

EXAMPLE 10   *(Compare Exercise 41)*

The Bike Shop held an annual sale. The consumer price and demand relationship for the Ten-Speed Special was

$$y = -2x + 179$$

where x is the number of bikes in demand at the price y. The negative slope, -2, indicates that when an *increase* occurs in one of the variables, price or demand, a decrease occurs in the other. This relationship between price and demand is a linear function. Its graph illustrates the decrease in price with an increase in demand (see Figure 2–4). When demand increases from 10 to 40, prices drop from $159 to $99.

FIGURE 2–4

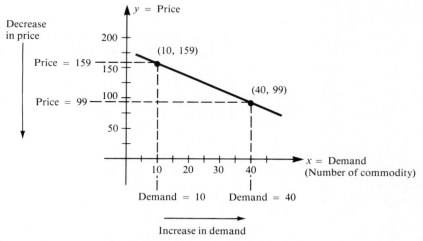

The price-demand function $y = -2x + 179$

FIGURE 2-5

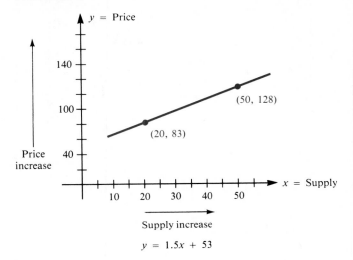

$$y = 1.5x + 53$$

The Bike Shop cannot lower prices indefinitely because the supplier wants to make a profit also. In a competitive situation a price increase gives the supplier incentive to produce more. When prices fall, the supplier tends to produce less. The quantity produced by the supplier is called **supply.** Suppose Bike Manufacturing produces the Ten-Speed Special and the relationship between supply and price is given by the linear function

$$y = 1.5x + 53$$

The graph of this equation illustrates that an increase in price leads to a higher supply (see Figure 2–5). When the price increases from \$83 to \$128, the supply increases from 20 to 50 units.

Supply and demand are two sides of a perfect competitive market. They interact to determine the price of a commodity. The price of a commodity settles down in the market to one at which the amount willingly supplied and the amount willingly demanded are equal. This price is called the **equilibrium price.** The equilibrium price may be determined by solving a system of equations. In our example the system is

$$y = -2x + 179$$
$$y = 1.5x + 53$$

Solve the system to obtain the equilibrium solution by either the substitution method or the elimination method. The solution is $x = 36$ and $y = 107$. (Be sure you can find this solution.) The equilibrium price is \$107 when the supply and demand are 36 bikes. See Figure 2–6.

FIGURE 2–6

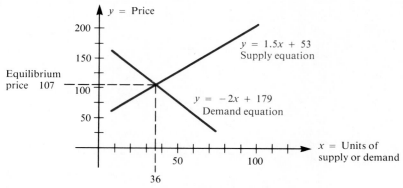

Equilibrium solution of supply and demand equations.

2–1 EXERCISES

I

Solve the systems of equations in Exercises 1 through 16 by substitution.

1. (*See Example 2*)
   $4x - y = 5$
   $x + 2y = 8$

2. $2x + y = 7$
   $x - 3y = 7$

3. $5x - y = -15$
   $x + y = -3$

4. $2x - y = -1$
   $2x + y = -3$

5. $y = 5x$
   $6x - 2y = 12$

6. $x = 5 - 2y$
   $3x - y = 15$

7. $7x - y = 32$
   $2x + 3y = 19$

8. $x - 2y = -16$
   $3x - 4y = -34$

9. $5x + 2y = 14$
   $x - 3y = 30$

10. $4x - y = 13$
    $3x - 5y = 31$

11. $22x + y = 81$
    $8x - 3y = 16$

12. $3x - y = -47$
    $x + 2y = 17$

13. (*See Example 3*)
    $6x - 3y = 9$
    $9x - 15y = 31$

14. $0.06x - y + 1.4 = 0$
    $0.07x - 0.04y - 0.62 = 0$

15. $y = 3x - 5$
    $8x - 4y - 30 = 0$

16. $5x - y = 8$
    $8x - 1.5y = 6.5$

Solve the systems of equations in Exercises 17 through 28 by elimination.

17. (*See Example 4*)
    $3x - 4y = 22$
    $2x + 5y = 7$

18. $2x + y = 13$
    $3x + 5y = 16$

19. $6x - y = 18$
    $2x + y = 2$

20. $2x - 3y = -14$
    $3x + 4y = -4$

21. $-2x + y = 7$
    $6x + 12y = 24$

22. $7x - 2y = 14$
    $-14x + 6y = -18$

23. $2x + y = -9$
    $4x + 3y = 1$

24. $2x + 3y = 237$
    $6x - 2y = 370$

25. $7x + 3y = -1.5$
    $2x - 5y = -30.3$

26. $11x - 2y = 387$
    $3x + 6y = -189$

27. $2x - 3y = -0.27$
    $5x - 2y = 0.04$

28. $49x - 27y + 47 = 0$
    $14x - 45y + 30 = 0$

The systems of equations in Exercises 29 through 34 do not have unique solutions. Determine whether each system has no solution or an infinite number of solutions.

29. (*See Example 8*)
    $6x - 9y = 8$
    $10x - 15y = -20$

30. $8x + 10y = 18$
    $20x + 25y = 45$

31. (*See Example 9*)
$$8x + 10y = 2$$
$$12x + 15y = 3$$

32.
$$3x - 7y = 20$$
$$-6x + 14y = 15$$

33.
$$x - 6y = 4$$
$$5x - 30y = 20$$

34.
$$4x + 14y = 15$$
$$6x + 21y = 26$$

Determine the equilibrium solutions in Exercises 35 through 40. The demand equation is given first and the supply equation second.

35.
$$y = -3x + 15$$
$$y = 2x - 5$$

36.
$$y = -8x + 200$$
$$y = 3x - 20$$

37.
$$y = -4x + 130$$
$$y = x - 20$$

38.
$$y = -6x + 68$$
$$y = 3x - 4$$

39.
$$y = -5x + 83$$
$$y = 4x - 52$$

40.
$$y = -8x + 2000$$
$$y = 6x - 800$$

II

41. (*See Example 10*) The demand equation for portable television sets is $y = -2.5x + 148$, where x is the demand quantity and y is the price. The supply equation is $y = 1.7x + 43$, where x is the supply quantity and y is the price. Find the equilibrium solution.

42. The research department of a major corporation keeps careful records on its product. It finds that the demand equation is

$$y = -18x + 970$$

where x is the demand and y is the price. The supply equation is

$$y = 15x + 640$$

Find the equilibrium solution.

43. (*See Example 5*) An orange contains 50 mg of calcium and 0.5 mg of iron. An apple contains 8 mg of calcium and 0.4 mg of iron. How many of each is required to obtain 151 mg of calcium and 2.55 mg of iron?

44. Jim has $440 in his savings account and adds $12 per week. At the same time, Rhonda has $260 in her savings account and adds $18 per week.
  (a) How long will it take for Rhonda to have the same amount as Jim?
  (b) How much will each have?

III

45. A child has $14.35 worth of nickels and dimes in her piggy bank. There is a total of 165 coins. How many of each does she have?

46. A child has 34 nickels and dimes. Their total value is $2.35. How many of each does he have?

47. (*See Example 6*) Chemical Products Corp. wishes to fill an order of 840 gallons of a solution that is 30% acid. Solutions of 20% acid and 55% acid are available. How many gallons of each should be used to obtain the 30% acid solution?

48. Mrs. Alford invested $5000 in securities. Part of the money was invested at 8% and part at 9%. The total annual income was $415. How much was invested at each rate?

49. (*See Example 7*) An electronics firm manufactures calculators at the McGregor plant and the Ennis plant. At McGregor the unit cost is $8.40, and the fixed cost is $7480. At Ennis the unit cost is $7.80, and the fixed cost is $5419. The company wants the two plants to produce a combined total of 1500 calculators, and the total costs at each plant must be the same. How many should be produced at each plant?

50. Action, Inc. makes videotapes at two locations, Atlanta and Baltimore. At Atlanta the unit cost is $4.30, and the fixed cost is $1840. At Baltimore the unit cost is $4.70, and the fixed cost is $2200. The company wishes to produce a combined total of 900 tapes at the two locations, but the total cost at each location must be the same. How many tapes should be produced at each location?

51. A merchant wants to mix peanuts costing $3 per pound with cashews costing $7 per pound to obtain an 80 pound mixture costing $4 per pound. How many pounds of each should he use?

52. Wholesale Jewelry receives an order for a total of 800 tie tacks and lapel pins. The tie tacks cost $5.65 each, and the lapel pins cost $7.42 each. A check for $4897.01 is enclosed, but the order fails to specify the number of each. Help the distributor determine how to fill the order.

53. Zest Fruit Juices makes two kinds of fruit punch from apple juice and pineapple juice. The company has 142 gallons of apple juice and 108 gallons of pineapple juice. Each case of Golden Punch requires four gallons of apple juice and six gallons of pineapple juice. Each case of Light Punch requires seven gallons of apple juice and three gallons of pineapple juice. How many cases of each punch should be made in order to use all the apple and pineapple juice?

54. Urban Developers has two size lots in its development. One sells for $2500, and the other for $3000. One month the developer sold 22 lots for a total of $61,500. How many of each did it sell?

55. The Beef Pit sells two kinds of sandwiches, chopped beef and smoked sausage. One day it sold 115 sandwiches for a total of $138.90. The chopped beef costs $1.30 each, and the smoked sausage costs $1.10 each. Find the number of each kind sold.

56. Pet Products has two production lines, I and II. Line I can produce 5 tons of regular dog food per hour and 3 tons of premium per hour. Line II can produce 3 tons of regular dog food per hour and 6 tons of premium. How many hours of production should be scheduled in order to produce 360 tons of premium and 460 tons of regular dog food?

57. Mr. Hamilton has $50,000 to invest in a tax-free fund and in a money market fund. The tax-free fund pays 7.4%, and the money market pays 8.8%. How much should he invest in each to get a return of $4071 per year?

58. The Coffee Cup blends two types of coffee that sell for $3.20 and $3.60 per pound to obtain 100 pounds of coffee that sells for $3.50. How much of each kind should be used?

59. Home Service Corp. has taxable income of $198,000. The federal tax is 20% of taxable income after state taxes have been paid. The state tax is 5% of taxable income after federal taxes have been paid. Find the amount of each tax.

2–2 SYSTEMS OF THREE EQUATIONS

- *Elimination Method*
- *Matrices*
- *Matrices and Systems of Equations*
- *Gauss-Jordan Method*
- *Summary*
- *Application*

ELIMINATION METHOD

Some applications of linear equations have more than two variables and may involve more than two equations. Let's make up an example with nice numbers to illustrate the procedure for solving such a system.

EXAMPLE 1   *(Compare Exercise 5)*

A toy store set up some bargain tables in the shopping mall. Three children, Ali, Bob, and Cindy, bought some items. On the basis of the following information determine how many items each child purchased.

(a) The total number of items purchased was 5.
(b) Ali paid $1 for each item he purchased, Bob paid $2 each, and Cindy paid $3 each. The total spent by all three was $10.
(c) The toy store gave balloons when items were purchased. Ali got 2 balloons for each item he purchased; Bob and Cindy got 1 balloon for each item. The children received a total of 6 balloons.

SOLUTION   Let's state this information in mathematical form and determine number of items each child purchased. Let

$$x = \text{number of items purchased by Ali}$$
$$y = \text{number of items purchased by Bob}$$
$$z = \text{number of items purchased by Cindy}$$

The given information may be written as follows

$$
\begin{array}{ll}
x + y + z = 5 & \text{(Total number of items)} \\
x + 2y + 3z = 10 & \text{(Total value of purchases)} \\
2x + y + z = 6 & \text{(Total number of balloons)}
\end{array}
$$

The solution to this system of three equations in three variables gives the number of items sold to each child. Before we solve this system, let's look at some basic ideas.

A set of values for x, y, z that satisfies all three equations is called a **solution** to the system. ***Be sure*** you understand that a solution consists of three numbers, one each for x, y, and z.

You know that a linear equation in two variables represents a line in two-dimensional space. However, a linear equation in three variables does not represent a line, it represents a plane in three-dimensional space. A solution to a system of three equations in three variables corresponds to a point that lies in all three planes. Figure 2–7 illustrates some possible ways in which the planes might intersect. If the three planes have just one point in common, the solution will be unique. If the planes have no points in common, there will be no solution to the system. If the planes have many points in common, the system will have many solutions.

FIGURE 2–7

Unique solution:

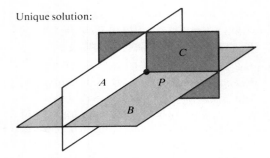

Three planes A, B, C intersect at a single point P;
P corresponds to a unique solution.

No solutions:

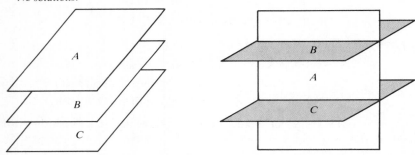

Planes A, B, C have no point of common intersection, no solution.

Many solutions:

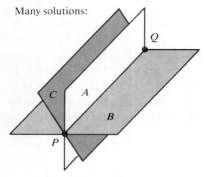
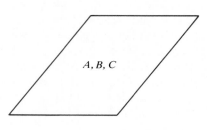

Any point on the
line PQ is a solution.

Three equations represent the same plane;
any point on the plane is a solution.

We need not stop with a system of three variables. There are applications that require larger systems with more variables. While larger systems are more difficult to interpret geometrically and are more tedious to solve, they also can have a unique solution, no solution, or many solutions.

The method of elimination used to solve systems of two equations can be adapted to solve larger systems. Let's rewrite the system of equations from our example and show its method of solution:

$$x_1 + x_2 + x_3 = 5$$
$$x_1 + 2x_2 + 3x_3 = 10$$
$$2x_1 + x_2 + x_3 = 6$$

Notice that we use x_1, x_2, and x_3 instead of x, y, and z for the variables. This notation is better for a system with several variables because we won't run out of letters for a larger number of variables and it provides a standard notation for variables.

Now let's proceed with the solution. First, eliminate x_1 from the second equation by subtracting the first equation from the second equation to obtain a new second equation:

$x_1 + 2x_2 + 3x_3 = 10$	(Equation 2)
$\underline{x_1 + x_2 + x_3 = 5}$	(Equation 1)
$x_2 + 2x_3 = 5$	(This will replace the second equation in the system)

As we work through the example, notice that we usually multiply one equation by a constant before adding it to another. The choice of the multiple is determined by the coefficients of the variable we want to eliminate.

Now eliminate x_1 from the third equation by multiplying the first equation by -2 and adding to the third:

$2x_1 + x_2 + x_3 = 6$	(Equation 3)
$\underline{-2x_1 - 2x_2 - 2x_3 = -10}$	($-2 \times$ Equation 1)
$-x_2 - x_3 = -4$	(This will replace the third equation in the system)

This gives the new and simpler equivalent system

$$x_1 + x_2 + x_3 = 5$$
$$x_2 + 2x_3 = 5$$
$$-x_2 - x_3 = -4$$

Observe that the variable x_1 has been eliminated from both the second and third equations. This system of three equations becomes the current system from which we eliminate another variable.

In order to describe the operations performed in a concise manner, we will use the notation Eq. 2 − Eq. 1 to mean the first equation is subtracted from the second. −2(Eq. 1) + Eq. 3 means to multiply the first equation by −2 and add it to the third. We continue the process by eliminating more variables from the new system.

Now we can eliminate the variable x_2 from the first and third equations of the current system by using the second equation:

CURRENT SYSTEM		NEXT SYSTEM
$x_1 + x_2 + x_3 = 5$	Eq. 1 − Eq. 2 yields	$x_1 \quad - \quad x_3 = 0$
$x_2 + 2x_3 = 5$	remains	$x_2 + 2x_3 = 5$
$-x_2 - x_3 = -4$	Eq. 3 + Eq. 2 yields	$x_3 = 1$

The system on the right is equivalent to the original system and is now the current system. We can complete the solution by eliminating x_3 from the first and second equations of this latest system:

CURRENT SYSTEM		NEXT SYSTEM
$x_1 \quad - \quad x_3 = 0$	Eq. 1 + Eq. 3 yields	$x_1 = 1$
$x_2 + 2x_3 = 5$	Eq. 2 − 2(Eq. 3) yields	$x_2 = 3$
$x_3 = 1$	remains	$x_3 = 1$

The solution to this system and thus the solution to the original system is $x_1 = 1, x_2 = 3, x_3 = 1$, which is also written $(1, 3, 1)$. This solution tells us that Ali bought 1 item, Bob bought 3 items, and Cindy bought 1 item. (Check the solution in the original system.)

MATRICES

The method of elimination may be used to solve larger systems, but it is tedious, and errors are easily made. Let's look at a method that reduces the work and gives a more efficient approach to solving a system. It also is more adaptable to a computer. The method we will learn is called the **Gauss-Jordan method,** and it uses **matrices.** This method uses a shorthand notation that keeps track of the variables but does not write them.

Basically, we make the elimination method more concise by matrix notation. Since the coefficients of the variables determine the multipliers used in the elimination method, some labor can be saved if we can avoid writing the variables and concentrate on the coefficients. Matrices enable us to keep track of the variables without writing them. The formal definition of a matrix is the following.

Definition
Matrix

A **matrix** is a rectangular array of numbers. The numbers in the array are called the **elements of the matrix.** The array is enclosed with brackets.

An array composed of a single row of numbers is called a **row matrix.**

An array composed of a single column of numbers is called a **column matrix.**

Some examples of matrices are

$$\begin{bmatrix} 1 & 2 & 3 \\ 0 & -1 & 1 \end{bmatrix} \quad \begin{bmatrix} 2 & 3 \\ 1 & 1 \\ 4 & 1 \end{bmatrix} \quad \begin{bmatrix} 1 & 2 & 3 \\ 4 & 5 & 6 \\ 0 & 1 & 2 \end{bmatrix}$$

The location of each element in a matrix is described by the row and column in which it lies. Count the rows from the top of the matrix and the columns from the left.

$$\begin{array}{cccc} Col.\ 1 & Col.\ 2 & Col.\ 3 & Col.\ 4 \end{array}$$
$$\begin{matrix} Row\ 1 \\ Row\ 2 \\ Row\ 3 \end{matrix} \begin{bmatrix} 4 & 6 & -3 & 2 \\ 1 & 5 & 9 & -2 \\ 7 & 8 & 3 & 4 \end{bmatrix}$$

The element 9 is in row 2 and column 3 of the matrix. We call this location the (2, 3) location; the row is indicated first and the column second. A standard notation for the number in that location is a_{23} (read as "*a* sub 2, 3"), so $a_{23} = 9$. The element 7, designated $a_{31} = 7$, is in the (3, 1) location; and -3, designated $a_{13} = -3$, is in the (1, 3) location.

EXAMPLE 2 *(Compare Exercise 11)*

For the matrix

$$\begin{bmatrix} 2 & -6 & -5 & -1 & 0 \\ 1 & 7 & 6 & -4 & 4 \\ 9 & 5 & -8 & 3 & -2 \end{bmatrix}$$

find

(a) the (1, 1) element (a_{11}).
(b) the (2, 5) element (a_{25}).
(c) the (3, 3) element (a_{33}).
(d) the location of -4.
(e) the location of 0.

SOLUTION

(a) 2 is the $(1, 1)$ element $(a_{11} = 2)$.

(b) 4 is the $(2, 5)$ element $(a_{25} = 4)$.

(c) The $(3, 3)$ element is -8 $(a_{33} = -8)$.

(d) -4 is in the $(2, 4)$ location $(a_{24} = -4)$.

(e) 0 is in the $(1, 5)$ location $(a_{15} = 0)$.

Let's pause to point out that you encounter matrices more often than you might realize. When you go to a fast food restaurant, the cashier may record your order on a device that resembles Figure 2–8. When you order three Big Burgers, the cashier presses the Big Burger location, the $(1, 2)$ location, to record the number ordered. Your completed order forms a matrix, with some entries zero, which the computer uses to compute your bill. Both the cashier and the company computer understand that a number in a location counts the number of the item represented by the location.

The rows and columns of a matrix often represent categories. A gradebook shows a rectangular array of numbers. Each column represents a test, and each row represents a student.

FIGURE 2–8

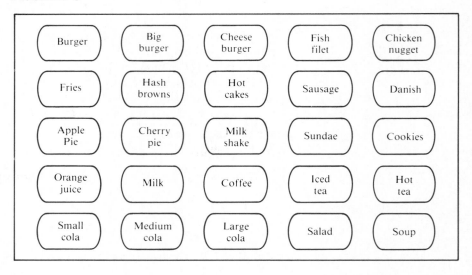

MATRICES AND
SYSTEMS OF
EQUATIONS

Let us use the following system to see how matrices relate to systems of linear equations:

$$x_1 + x_2 + x_3 = 3$$
$$2x_1 + 3x_2 + x_3 = 5$$
$$x_1 - x_2 - 2x_3 = -5$$

One matrix may be formed by using only the coefficients of the system. This gives the **coefficient matrix**

$$\begin{bmatrix} 1 & 1 & 1 \\ 2 & 3 & 1 \\ 1 & -1 & -2 \end{bmatrix}$$

Column 1 lists the coefficients of x_1, column 2 lists the coefficients of x_2, and column 3 lists the coefficients of x_3. Notice that they are listed in the order first, second, and third equations, so the first row represents the left-hand side of the first equation, and so on.

A matrix that also includes the numbers on the right-hand sides of the equations is called the **augmented matrix** of the system

$$\left[\begin{array}{ccc|c} 1 & 1 & 1 & 3 \\ 2 & 3 & 1 & 5 \\ 1 & -1 & -2 & -5 \end{array}\right]$$

The augmented matrix gives complete information about the system of equations, provided that we agree that each row represents an equation and each column, except the last, consists of the coefficients of one variable.

Generally, we place a vertical line between the coefficients and the column of constant terms.

EXAMPLE 3 *(Compare Exercise 13)*

Write the coefficient matrix and the augmented matrix of the system

$$5x_1 - 7x_2 + 2x_3 = 17$$
$$-x_1 + 3x_2 + 8x_3 = 12$$
$$6x_1 + 9x_2 - 4x_3 = -23$$

SOLUTION The coefficient matrix is

$$\begin{bmatrix} 5 & -7 & 2 \\ -1 & 3 & 8 \\ 6 & 9 & -4 \end{bmatrix}$$

and the augmented matrix is

$$\left[\begin{array}{ccc|c} 5 & -7 & 2 & 17 \\ -1 & 3 & 8 & 12 \\ 6 & 9 & -4 & -23 \end{array}\right]$$

EXAMPLE 4   *(Compare Exercise 19)*

Write the system of linear equations represented by the augmented matrix

$$\begin{bmatrix} 3 & 7 & 2 & -3 & | & 8 \\ 4 & 0 & -5 & 7 & | & -2 \end{bmatrix}$$

SOLUTION   The system is

$$3x_1 + 7x_2 + 2x_3 - 3x_4 = 8$$
$$4x_1 \qquad - 5x_3 + 7x_4 = -2$$

We can solve a system of linear equations by using its augmented matrix. Since each row in the matrix represents an equation, we perform the same kinds of operations on rows of the matrix as we do on the equations in the system. These **row operations** are as follows:

Row Operations   **1.** Interchange two rows.
2. Multiply or divide a row by a nonzero constant.
3. Multiply a row by a constant and add it to or subtract it from another row.

Two augmented matrices are **equivalent** if one is obtained from the other by using row operations.

GAUSS-JORDAN METHOD

To illustrate the matrix technique, we solve a system of linear equations using the augmented matrix and row operations. This technique is basically a simplification of the elimination method. You will soon find that even this "simplified" method can be tedious and subject to arithmetic errors. However, a method such as this is widely used on computers to solve systems of equations. While the examples and exercises use equations that yield relatively simple answers, actual applications don't always have nice, neat, unique solutions.

First, we solve a system of two equations in two variables and then a system of three equations in three variables. In each case we show the solutions of the systems by both the elimination method and the method using matrices. They are shown in parallel so that you can see the relationship between the two methods.

EXAMPLE 5   *(Compare Exercise 31)*

Solve the system of equations

$$x + 3y = 11$$
$$2x - 5y = -22$$

SEQUENCE OF EQUIVALENT SYSTEMS OF EQUATIONS	CORRESPONDING EQUIVALENT AUGMENTED MATRICES

Original system:

$$x + 3y = 11$$
$$2x - 5y = -22$$

Eliminate x from the second equation by multiplying the first equation by -2 and adding to the second:

$$x + 3y = 11$$
$$-11y = -44$$

Simplify the second equation by dividing through by -11:

$$x + 3y = 11$$
$$y = 4$$

Eliminate y from the first equation by multiplying the second equation by -3 and adding it to the first:

$$x = -1$$
$$y = 4$$

Original augmented matrix:

$$\begin{bmatrix} 1 & 3 & 11 \\ 2 & -5 & -22 \end{bmatrix}$$

Get a 0 in the second row, first column by multiplying the first row by -2 and adding it to the second row:

$$\begin{bmatrix} 1 & 3 & 11 \\ 0 & -11 & -44 \end{bmatrix}$$

Simplify the second row by dividing through by -11:

$$\begin{bmatrix} 1 & 3 & 11 \\ 0 & 1 & 4 \end{bmatrix}$$

Get a 0 in the first row, second column by multiplying the second row by -3 and adding it to the first:

$$\begin{bmatrix} 1 & 0 & -1 \\ 0 & 1 & 4 \end{bmatrix}$$

Read the solution from this augmented matrix. The first row gives $x = -1$, and the second row gives $y = 4$.

Some of the details that arise in larger systems do not show up in a system of two equations with two variables, so we now solve a system of three equations with three variables.

EXAMPLE 6   *(Compare Exercise 37)*

Solve the system of equations.

$$x_1 + x_2 + x_3 = 5$$
$$x_1 + 2x_2 + 3x_3 = 10$$
$$2x_1 + x_2 + x_3 = 6$$

SOLUTION   This system was solved earlier in Example 1. We use it again so that you can concentrate on the procedure. We show the solution of this system by both the elimination method and the method using matrices. They are shown in parallel so that you can see the relationship between the two methods.

SEQUENCE OF EQUIVALENT SYSTEMS OF EQUATIONS

CORRESPONDING EQUIVALENT AUGMENTED MATRICES

Original system:

$$x_1 + x_2 + x_3 = 5$$
$$x_1 + 2x_2 + 3x_3 = 10$$
$$2x_1 + x_2 + x_3 = 6$$

Original augmented matrix:

$$\begin{bmatrix} 1 & 1 & 1 & 5 \\ 1 & 2 & 3 & 10 \\ 2 & 1 & 1 & 6 \end{bmatrix}$$

Eliminate x_1 from the second equation by multiplying the first equation by -1 and adding to the second.
Eliminate x_1 from the third equation by multiplying the first equation by -2 and adding to the third:

Get 0 in the second row, first column by multiplying the first row by -1 and adding to the second.
Get 0 in the third row, first column by multiplying the first row by -2 and adding to the third:

$$x_1 + x_2 + x_3 = 5$$
$$x_2 + 2x_3 = 5$$
$$-x_2 - x_3 = -4$$

$$\begin{bmatrix} 1 & 1 & 1 & 5 \\ 0 & 1 & 2 & 5 \\ 0 & -1 & -1 & -4 \end{bmatrix}$$

Eliminate x_2 from the first equation by multiplying the second equation by -1 and adding to the first.
Eliminate x_2 from the third equation by adding the second equation to the third:

Get 0 in the first row, second column by multiplying second row by -1 and adding to the first.
Get 0 in the third row, second column by adding the second row to the third:

$$x_1 - x_3 = 0$$
$$x_2 + 2x_3 = 5$$
$$x_3 = 1$$

$$\begin{bmatrix} 1 & 0 & -1 & 0 \\ 0 & 1 & 2 & 5 \\ 0 & 0 & 1 & 1 \end{bmatrix}$$

Eliminate x_3 from the first equation by adding the third equation to the first.
Eliminate x_3 from the second equation by multiplying the third equation by -2 and adding to the second:

$$\begin{aligned} x_1 && = 1 \\ & x_2 & = 3 \\ && x_3 = 1 \end{aligned}$$

Get 0 in the first row, third column by adding the third row to the first.
Get 0 in the second row, third column by multiplying the third row by -2 and adding to the second:

$$\left[\begin{array}{ccc|c} 1 & 0 & 0 & 1 \\ 0 & 1 & 0 & 3 \\ 0 & 0 & 1 & 1 \end{array}\right]$$

Read the solution from this augmented matrix. The first row gives $x_1 = 1$, the second row gives $x_2 = 3$, and the third row gives $x_3 = 1$.   ∎

This technique of using row operations to reduce an augmented matrix to a simple matrix is called the **Gauss-Jordan method.** The form of the final matrix is such that the solution to the original system can easily be read from the matrix. Notice that the final matrix in the example above was

$$\left[\begin{array}{ccc|c} 1 & 0 & 0 & 1 \\ 0 & 1 & 0 & 3 \\ 0 & 0 & 1 & 1 \end{array}\right]$$

For the moment, ignore the last column of the matrix. The remaining columns have zeros everywhere except in the $(1, 1)$, $(2, 2)$, and $(3, 3)$ locations. These are called the **diagonal locations.** The Gauss-Jordan method attempts to reduce the augmented matrix until there are 1's in the diagonal locations and 0's elsewhere (except in the last column).

When a matrix is reduced to this diagonal form, each row easily shows the value of a variable in the solution. In the matrix above, the rows represent

$$\begin{aligned} x_1 &= 1 \\ x_2 &= 3 \\ x_3 &= 1 \end{aligned}$$

which gives the solution.

We now look at another example and focus attention on the procedure for arriving at this desired diagonal form. In this section we will focus our attention on augmented matrices that can be reduced to this diagonal form. The cases in which the diagonal form is not possible are studied in the next section.

A new notation is introduced in the next example to reduce the writing involved. When we are reducing a matrix and you see

$$\frac{1}{4} R1 \quad \text{gives} \quad [1 \quad 2 \quad -3 \quad 11] \rightarrow R1$$

this means that row 1 of the current matrix is divided by 4 and gives the new row $[1 \quad 2 \quad -3 \quad 11]$, which is placed in row 1 of the next matrix. The notation $-2R2 + R3 \rightarrow R3$ means that row 2 of the current matrix is multiplied by -2 and added to row 3. The result becomes row 3 of the next matrix.

EXAMPLE 7   *(Compare Exercise 41)*

Solve this system of equations by reducing the augmented matrix to the diagonal form:

$$4x_1 + 8x_2 - 12x_3 = 44$$
$$3x_1 + 6x_2 - 8x_3 = 32$$
$$-2x_1 - x_2 \qquad = -7$$

The augmented matrix of this system is

$$\begin{bmatrix} 4 & 8 & -12 & 44 \\ 3 & 6 & -8 & 32 \\ -2 & -1 & 0 & -7 \end{bmatrix}$$

We now use row operations to find the solution to the system.

MATRIX	THIS OPERATION ON PRESENT MATRIX	PUT IN NEW ROW

Need
1
here
$$\begin{bmatrix} ④ & 8 & -12 & 44 \\ 3 & 6 & -8 & 32 \\ -2 & -1 & 0 & -7 \end{bmatrix}$$

$(\frac{1}{4})$R1 gives $[1 \quad 2 \quad -3 \quad 11] \rightarrow$ R1

Need
0
here
$$\begin{bmatrix} 1 & 2 & -3 & 11 \\ ③ & 6 & -8 & 32 \\ ⊖2 & -1 & 0 & -7 \end{bmatrix}$$

-3R1 + R2 gives $[0 \quad 0 \quad 1 \quad -1] \rightarrow$ R2
2R1 + R3 gives $[0 \quad 3 \quad -6 \quad 15] \rightarrow$ R3

Need
1
here
$$\begin{bmatrix} 1 & 2 & -3 & 11 \\ 0 & ⓪ & 1 & -1 \\ 0 & 3 & -6 & 15 \end{bmatrix}$$

Interchange row 2 and row 3

$$\begin{bmatrix} 1 & 2 & -3 & 11 \\ 0 & 3 & -6 & 15 \\ 0 & 0 & 1 & -1 \end{bmatrix}$$

$(\frac{1}{3})$R2 gives $[0 \quad 1 \quad -2 \quad 5] \rightarrow$ R2

Need
0
here
$$\begin{bmatrix} 1 & ② & -3 & 11 \\ 0 & 1 & -2 & 5 \\ 0 & 0 & 1 & -1 \end{bmatrix}$$

-2R2 + R1 gives $[1 \quad 0 \quad 1 \quad 1] \rightarrow$ R1

Need
0
here
$$\begin{bmatrix} 1 & 0 & ① & 1 \\ 0 & 1 & ⊖2 & 5 \\ 0 & 0 & 1 & -1 \end{bmatrix}$$

$-$R3 + R1 gives $[1 \quad 0 \quad 0 \quad 2] \rightarrow$ R1
2R3 + R2 gives $[0 \quad 1 \quad 0 \quad 3] \rightarrow$ R2

$$\begin{bmatrix} 1 & 0 & 0 & 2 \\ 0 & 1 & 0 & 3 \\ 0 & 0 & 1 & -1 \end{bmatrix}$$

The last matrix is in a diagonal form and represents the system

$$\begin{aligned} x_1 & = 2 \\ x_2 & = 3 \\ x_3 & = -1 \end{aligned}$$

so the solution is $(2, 3, -1)$.

The next example uses a more abbreviated notation in the solution.

EXAMPLE 8   *(Compare Exercise 49)*

Solve the system

$$
\begin{aligned}
x_1 - x_2 + x_3 + 2x_4 &= 1 \\
2x_1 - x_2 \qquad + 3x_4 &= 0 \\
-x_1 + x_2 + x_3 + x_4 &= -1 \\
x_2 \qquad + x_4 &= 1
\end{aligned}
$$

SOLUTION   The augmented matrix of this system is

$$
\left[\begin{array}{cccc|c}
1 & -1 & 1 & 2 & 1 \\
2 & -1 & 0 & 3 & 0 \\
-1 & 1 & 1 & 1 & -1 \\
0 & 1 & 0 & 1 & 1
\end{array}\right]
$$

Performing the indicated row operations produces the following sequence of equivalent augmented matrices.

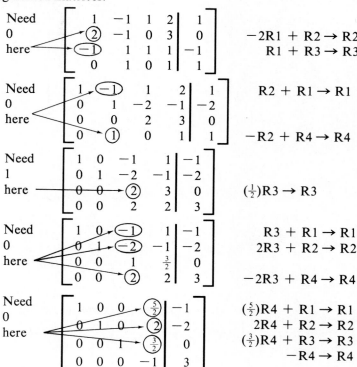

$$\begin{bmatrix} 1 & 0 & 0 & 0 & \frac{13}{2} \\ 0 & 1 & 0 & 0 & 4 \\ 0 & 0 & 1 & 0 & \frac{9}{2} \\ 0 & 0 & 0 & 1 & -3 \end{bmatrix}$$

This matrix is in the reduced diagonal form so we can read the solution to the system:

$$x_1 = \frac{13}{2}, \qquad x_2 = 4, \qquad x_3 = \frac{9}{2}, \qquad x_4 = -3$$

The examples in this section all have unique solutions. In such cases the last column of the diagonal form gives the unique solution.

Summary

Solve a System with Augmented Matrices

Solve a system of n equations in n variables by using row operations on the augmented matrix.

1. Write the augmented matrix of the system.
2. Get a 1 in the (1, 1) position of the matrix by
   (a) rearranging rows or
   (b) dividing row 1 by the (1, 1) entry, a_{11}.
3. Get a zero in the other positions of column 1.
   (a) Take the negative of the number in the position to be made zero and multiply row 1 by it.
   (b) Add this multiple of row 1 to the row where the zero is needed. The result becomes a new row there.
4. Get a 1 in the (2, 2) location by
   (a) rearranging the rows below row 1 or
   (b) dividing row 2 by the (2, 2) entry, a_{22}.
5. Get a zero in all other positions of column 2 (leave 1 in the (2, 2) position).
   (a) Take the negative of the number in the position to be made zero and multiply row 2 by it.
   (b) Add this multiple of row 2 to the row where the zero is needed. The result becomes the new row there.
6. Get a 1 in the (3, 3), (4, 4), . . . positions, and in each case get zeros in the other positions of that column.
7. Each row now gives the value of a variable $x_1 = c_1$, $x_2 = c_2$, etc. in the solution.

NOTE In some systems it might be impossible to get a 1 in some of the diagonal positions. The next section deals with that situation.

APPLICATION

EXAMPLE 9   *(Compare Exercise 59)*

A brokerage firm packaged blocks of blue-chip stocks, bonds, and high-risk stocks into three portfolios, which it offers to its customers. Portfolio I contains one block of blue-chip stocks, four blocks of bonds, and three blocks of high-risk stocks. Portfolio II contains two blocks of blue-chip stocks, one block of bonds, and two blocks of high-risk stocks. Portfolio III contains four blocks of blue-chip stocks, two blocks of bonds, and one block of high-risk stocks. A customer wants eight blocks of blue-chip stocks, 11 blocks of bonds, and nine blocks of high-risk stocks. How many of each portfolio should the customer purchase?

SOLUTION   Let

$$x_1 = \text{number of Portfolio I}$$
$$x_2 = \text{number of Portfolio II}$$
$$x_3 = \text{number of Portfolio III}$$

The number of blocks of each type of investment can be stated by the following equations:

$$
\begin{aligned}
x_1 + 2x_2 + 4x_3 &= 8 &&\text{(blue-chip stocks)}\\
4x_1 + x_2 + 2x_3 &= 11 &&\text{(bonds)}\\
3x_1 + 2x_2 + x_3 &= 9 &&\text{(high-risk stocks)}
\end{aligned}
$$

The solution to this system gives the desired number of each type investment. Find the solution by using augmented matrices. The following sequence of matrix reductions leads to the solution:

Initial matrix:
$$
\left[\begin{array}{ccc|c}
1 & 2 & 4 & 8\\
4 & 1 & 2 & 11\\
3 & 2 & 1 & 9
\end{array}\right]
\quad
\begin{array}{l}
-4\text{R}1 + \text{R}2 \rightarrow \text{R}2\\
-3\text{R}1 + \text{R}3 \rightarrow \text{R}3
\end{array}
$$

$$
\left[\begin{array}{ccc|c}
1 & 2 & 4 & 8\\
0 & -7 & -14 & -21\\
0 & -4 & -11 & -15
\end{array}\right]
\quad
\begin{array}{l}
(-\frac{1}{7})\text{R}2 \rightarrow \text{R}2\\
-\text{R}3 \rightarrow \text{R}3
\end{array}
$$

$$
\left[\begin{array}{ccc|c}
1 & 2 & 4 & 8\\
0 & 1 & 2 & 3\\
0 & 4 & 11 & 15
\end{array}\right]
\quad
\begin{array}{l}
-2\text{R}2 + \text{R}1 \rightarrow \text{R}1\\
-4\text{R}2 + \text{R}3 \rightarrow \text{R}3
\end{array}
$$

$$
\left[\begin{array}{ccc|c}
1 & 0 & 0 & 2\\
0 & 1 & 2 & 3\\
0 & 0 & 3 & 3
\end{array}\right]
\quad
(\tfrac{1}{3})\text{R}3 \rightarrow \text{R}3
$$

$$
\left[\begin{array}{ccc|c}
1 & 0 & 0 & 2\\
0 & 1 & 2 & 3\\
0 & 0 & 1 & 1
\end{array}\right]
\quad
-2\text{R}3 + \text{R}2 \rightarrow \text{R}2
$$

$$\begin{bmatrix} 1 & 0 & 0 & | & 2 \\ 0 & 1 & 0 & | & 1 \\ 0 & 0 & 1 & | & 1 \end{bmatrix}$$

This gives the solution $x_1 = 2$, $x_2 = 1$, $x_3 = 1$, so the customer should purchase two blocks of Portfolio I and one block each of Portfolios II and III.

2-2 EXERCISES

I

Use the elimination method to solve the systems in Exercises 1 through 10.

1. $x + 2y = 7$
$3x + 5y = 19$

2. $x - 4y = 0$
$2x + 6y = 14$

3. $2x + 5y = -1$
$6x - 4y = 16$

4. $3x + 7y = -44$
$12x + 5y = -61$

5. (*See Example 1*)
$x + y - z = -1$
$x - y + z = 5$
$x - y - z = 1$

6. $x + y + 2z = 12$
$2x + 3y - z = -2$
$-3x + 4y + z = -8$

7. $x + 4y - 2z = 21$
$3x - 6y - 3z = -18$
$2x + 4y + z = 37$

8. $x + y + z = 2$
$4x + 3y + 2z = -4$
$-2x + y - z = 2$

9. $2x + 4y - 6z = -2$
$4x - 3y + z = 11$
$3x + 2y - 2z = 7$

10. $x + 2y = 3$
$y + z = 3$
$x + 3z = 2$

11. (*See Example 2*) For the matrix

$$\begin{bmatrix} 2 & 4 & 6 \\ -1 & 3 & 5 \\ 7 & 0 & 6 \\ 9 & 8 & 11 \end{bmatrix}$$

(a) give the (1, 1), (2, 2), (3, 3), and (4, 3) elements;
(b) determine the location of 5;
(c) find a_{12}, a_{32}, and a_{41}.

12. For the matrix

$$\begin{bmatrix} 6 & -2 & 3 & 1 & 9 \\ -7 & 5 & 0 & -5 & 4 \\ 8 & -2 & 12 & -2 & 11 \\ -1 & -9 & 15 & -4 & 0 \end{bmatrix}$$

(a) give the (1, 1), (2, 2), (3, 4), (4, 3), (2, 5) elements;
(b) determine the locations that contain -2;
(c) find a_{35}, a_{24}, and a_{13}.

Determine the matrix of coefficients and the augmented matrix for each of the systems of linear equations in Exercises 13 through 18.

13. (*See Example 3*)
$5x_1 - 2x_2 = 1$
$3x_1 + x_2 = 7$

14. $x_1 + x_2 + x_3 = 9$
$5x_1 + 3x_2 + 6x_3 = 21$
$x_1 - 4x_2 + x_3 = 7$

15. $x_1 + x_2 - x_3 = 14$
$3x_1 + 4x_2 - 2x_3 = 9$
$2x_1 + x_3 = 7$

16. $6x_1 + 4x_2 - x_3 = 0$
$-x_1 - x_2 - x_3 = 7$
$5x_1 = 15$

17. $x_1 + 5x_2 - 2x_3 + x_4 = 12$
$x_1 - x_2 + 2x_3 + 4x_4 = -5$
$6x_1 + 3x_2 - 11x_3 + x_4 = 14$
$5x_1 - 3x_2 - 7x_3 + x_4 = 22$

18. $x_1 - 3x_2 + x_3 + 5x_4 = 10$
$6x_1 - x_2 - x_3 - x_4 = -18$
$x_1 + 7x_2 = -1$
$x_1 + x_2 + x_3 + x_4 = 9$

Write the systems of equations represented by the augmented matrices in Exercises 19 through 23.

19. (*See Example 4*)

$$\begin{bmatrix} 5 & 3 & -2 \\ -1 & 4 & 4 \end{bmatrix}$$

20.
$$\begin{bmatrix} 1 & 4 & -1 & 5 \\ 2 & 1 & 2 & 0 \\ -3 & 5 & 1 & 6 \end{bmatrix}$$

21.
$$\begin{bmatrix} 5 & 2 & -1 & 3 \\ -2 & 7 & 8 & 7 \\ 3 & 0 & 1 & 5 \end{bmatrix}$$

22.
$$\begin{bmatrix} 1 & 3 & 2 & 1 \\ 0 & 1 & 5 & 2 \\ 5 & 4 & 0 & 9 \end{bmatrix}$$

23.
$$\begin{bmatrix} 3 & 0 & 2 & 6 & 4 \\ -4 & 5 & 7 & 2 & 2 \\ 1 & 3 & 2 & 5 & 0 \\ -2 & 6 & -5 & 3 & 4 \end{bmatrix}$$

24. List the diagonal elements of the following matrices:

(a)
$$\begin{bmatrix} 2 & 1 & 7 & -2 \\ 5 & 0 & 1 & 4 \\ 7 & 2 & -3 & 14 \end{bmatrix}$$

(b)
$$\begin{bmatrix} 1 & 2 & 3 & 4 & 5 \\ -2 & -6 & 5 & 9 & 14 \\ 8 & 0 & -7 & 6 & 19 \\ 1 & 1 & -5 & 13 & 21 \end{bmatrix}$$

Perform the row operations indicated beside each matrix in Exercises 25 through 30. Write the matrix obtained.

25.
$$\begin{bmatrix} 3 & 6 & -12 & 18 \\ 4 & 2 & 5 & 7 \\ 1 & -1 & 0 & 4 \end{bmatrix} \quad (\tfrac{1}{3})\, R1 \rightarrow R1$$

26.
$$\begin{bmatrix} 5 & 1 & 4 & 6 \\ 3 & 2 & 1 & 2 \\ 4 & 2 & -3 & 1 \end{bmatrix} \quad -R3 + R1 \rightarrow R1$$

27.
$$\begin{bmatrix} 1 & 3 & 2 & -4 \\ 2 & -1 & 3 & 5 \\ 4 & 6 & -2 & 3 \end{bmatrix} \quad \begin{array}{l} -2R1 + R2 \rightarrow R2 \\ -4R1 + R3 \rightarrow R3 \end{array}$$

28.
$$\begin{bmatrix} 1 & 3 & -2 & 0 \\ 0 & 1 & -1 & 4 \\ 0 & 5 & 2 & 13 \end{bmatrix} \quad \begin{array}{l} -3R2 + R1 \rightarrow R1 \\ -5R2 + R3 \rightarrow R3 \end{array}$$

29.
$$\begin{bmatrix} 1 & -3 & 2 & -6 \\ 0 & 5 & -10 & 20 \\ 0 & 4 & 3 & 8 \end{bmatrix} \quad (\tfrac{1}{5})R2 \rightarrow R2$$

30.
$$\begin{bmatrix} 1 & 0 & 3 & 4 \\ 0 & 1 & -6 & -1 \\ 0 & 0 & 1 & -2 \end{bmatrix} \quad \begin{array}{l} -3R3 + R1 \rightarrow R1 \\ 6R3 + R2 \rightarrow R2 \end{array}$$

Solve the following systems of equations by reducing the augmented matrix.

31. (*See Example 5*)
$$2x + 3y = 5$$
$$x - 2y = -1$$

32.
$$x + 2y = -3$$
$$12x + 4y = -12$$

33.
$$x - 3y = -1$$
$$4x + 5y = 30$$

34.
$$3x + 7y = -10$$
$$15x - 2y = 98$$

35.
$$2x + 4y = -7$$
$$x - 3y = 9$$

36.
$$x + 8y = 13$$
$$-5x + 2y = 19$$

37. (*See Example 6*)
$$x_1 + 2x_2 - x_3 = 3$$
$$x_1 + 3x_2 - x_3 = 4$$
$$x_1 - x_2 + x_3 = 4$$

38.
$$x_1 + x_2 + 2x_3 = 5$$
$$3x_1 + 2x_2 = 4$$
$$2x_1 - x_3 = 2$$

39.
$$2x_1 + 4x_2 + 2x_3 = 6$$
$$2x_1 + x_2 + x_3 = 16$$
$$x_1 + x_2 + 2x_3 = 9$$

40.
$$x_1 + 2x_3 = 5$$
$$x_2 - 30x_3 = -17$$
$$x_1 - 2x_2 + 4x_3 = 10$$

41. (*See Example 7*)
$$x_1 + 2x_2 - x_3 = -1$$
$$2x_1 - 3x_2 + 2x_3 = 15$$
$$x_2 + 4x_3 = -7$$

42.
$$x_1 + 2x_2 + x_3 = 3$$
$$x_2 - x_3 = -1$$
$$x_2 + 5x_3 = 14$$

43.
$$x_1 + 5x_2 - x_3 = 1$$
$$4x_1 - 2x_2 - 3x_3 = 6$$
$$-3x_1 + x_2 + 3x_3 = -3$$

44.
$$x_1 - 2x_2 + x_3 = -4$$
$$3x_2 + 6x_3 = 12$$
$$1.5x_1 + x_2 - 2.5x_3 = -2$$

45.
$$2x_1 + 2x_2 + 4x_3 = 16$$
$$x_1 + 2x_2 - x_3 = 6$$
$$-3x_1 + x_2 - 2x_3 = 0$$

46.
$$x_1 + 5x_2 - 2x_3 = 4$$
$$4x_1 - 2x_2 + 3x_3 = 5$$
$$2x_1 + 5x_3 = 7$$

47.
$$x_1 + 2x_2 - 3x_3 = -6$$
$$x_1 - 3x_2 - 7x_3 = 10$$
$$x_1 - x_2 + x_3 = 10$$

48.
$$x_1 - x_2 + 4x_3 = -3$$
$$2x_1 + x_2 + 2x_3 = 1.5$$
$$4x_1 + 3x_2 + x_3 = 6$$

II

49. (*See Example 8*)
$$x_1 + x_2 + x_3 + x_4 = 4$$
$$x_1 + 2x_2 - x_3 - x_4 = 7$$
$$2x_1 - x_2 - x_3 - x_4 = 8$$
$$x_1 - x_2 + 2x_3 - 2x_4 = -7$$

50.
$$x_1 + x_2 + 2x_3 + x_4 = 3$$
$$x_1 + 2x_2 + x_3 + x_4 = 2$$
$$x_1 + x_2 + x_3 + 2x_4 = 1$$
$$2x_1 + x_2 + x_3 + x_4 = 4$$

51.
$$2x_1 + 6x_2 + 4x_3 - 2x_4 = 18$$
$$x_1 + 4x_2 - 2x_3 - x_4 = -1$$
$$3x_1 - x_2 - x_3 + 2x_4 = 6$$
$$-x_1 - 2x_2 - 5x_3 = -20$$

52.
$$x_1 + 3x_2 - x_3 + 2x_4 = -2$$
$$-3x_1 + x_2 + x_3 + 3x_4 = -1$$
$$2x_1 - 4x_2 - 2x_3 + x_4 = 3$$
$$2x_2 - 4x_4 = -6$$

III

Set up the systems of equations needed to solve Exercises 53 through 58. Do *not* solve the systems.

53. Fruit Products, Inc. makes three kinds of fruit punch, Regular, Premium, and Classic. Each case of Regular punch uses 4 gallons of apple juice, 5 gallons of pineapple juice, and 1 gallon of cranberry juice. Each case of Premium punch uses 4 gallons of apple juice, 4 gallons of pineapple juice, and 2 gallons of cranberry juice. Each case of Classic punch uses 5 gallons of apple juice, 2 gallons of pineapple juice, and 3 gallons of cranberry juice. The firm has 142 gallons of cranberry juice, 292 gallons of pineapple juice, and 316 gallons of apple juice in stock. How many cases of each kind of punch should be made in order to use all the juices?

54. Dealer's Electric makes three kinds of monitors, A, B, and C, which must be manufactured and tested. A requires 3 hours of manufacturing and 1 hour of testing; B requires 4 hours of manufacturing and 2 hours of testing; C requires 6 hours of manufacturing and 2 hours of testing. The company has 285 hours for manufacturing and 115 hours for testing available. How many of each kind should be made so that a total of 70 monitors is produced?

55. A student club sponsored a jazz concert and charged $3 admission for students, $5 for faculty and $8 for the general public. The total ticket sales amounted to $2542. Three times as many students bought tickets as faculty. The general public bought twice as many tickets as did the students. How many tickets were sold to each group?

56. The Snack Shop makes three mixes of nuts in the following proportions:

MIX I: 7 pounds peanuts, 5 pounds cashews, and 1 pound pecans

MIX II: 3 pounds peanuts, 2 pounds cashews, and 2 pounds pecans

MIX III: 4 pounds peanuts, 3 pounds cashews, and 3 pounds pecans

The shop has 67 pounds of peanuts, 48 pounds of cashews, and 32 pounds of pecans in stock. How much of each mix can it produce?

57. An investor owns a portfolio of three stocks, X, Y, and Z. On March 1 the closing prices were: X, $44; Y, $22; and Z, $64. The value of the investor's portfolio amounted to $20,480. Three weeks later the closing prices were: X, $42; Y, $28; and Z, $62. The investor's portfolio was valued at $20,720. Two weeks later the closing prices were: X, $42; Y, $30; and Z, $60 with a total portfolio value of $20,580. How many shares of each stock did the investor hold in the portfolio?

58. Watson Electric has production facilities in Valley Mills, Marlin, and Hillsboro. Each one produces radios, stereos, and TV sets. Their production capacities are:
Valley Mills: 10 radios, 12 stereos, and 6 TV sets per hour
Marlin: 7 radios, 10 stereos, and 8 TV sets per hour
Hillsboro: 5 radios, 4 stereos, and 13 TV sets per hour
   (a) The firm receives an order for 1365 radios, 1530 stereos, and 1890 TV sets. How many hours should each plant be scheduled in order to produce these amounts?
   (b) How many hours should each plant be scheduled to fill an order of 1095 radios, 1230 stereos, and 1490 TV sets?

Solve Exercises 59 through 64.

59. (*See Example 9*)
A brokerage firm packaged blocks of blue-chip stocks, bonds, and high-risk stocks into three portfolios which it offers to its customers. Portfolio I contains one block of blue-chip stocks, three blocks of bonds, and one block of high-risk stocks. Portfolio II contains three blocks of blue-chip stocks, two blocks of bonds, and two blocks of high-risk stocks. Portfolio III contains two blocks of blue-chip stocks, one block of bonds, and four blocks of high-risk stocks. A customer wants to buy 15 blocks of blue-chip stocks, 14 blocks of bonds, and 16 blocks of high-risk stocks. How many of each portfolio should the customer buy?

60. As part of a promotional campaign the T-Shirt Company packaged thousands of cartons of T-shirts for its retail outlets. Each carton contained small, medium, and large sizes. Three types of cartons were packed according to the quantities shown in the table. The entries in the table give the number (in dozens) of each size of T-shirt in the carton:

| | | CARTON | | |
		A	B	C
	SMALL	2	5	4
SIZE	MEDIUM	5	8	6
	LARGE	3	2	10

The promotion was a flop, and the company's warehouse was full of the packed cartons. When the company received an order from T-Shirt Orient for 45 dozen small, 78 dozen medium, and 52 dozen large, it wanted to fill the order with the packed cartons in order to save repacking costs. How many of each carton should it send to fill the order?

61. Ms. Hardin invested $40,000 in three stocks. The first year, stock A paid 6% dividends and increased 3% in value; stock B paid 7% dividends and increased 4% in value; stock C paid 8% dividends and increased 2% in value. If the total dividends were $2730 and the total increase in value was $1080, how much was invested in each stock?

62. Curt has one hour to spend at the athletic club, where he will jog, play handball, and ride a bicycle. Jogging uses 13 calories per minute, handball 11, and cycling 7. He jogs as long as he rides the bicycle. How long should he participate in each of these activities in order to use 640 calories?

63. Concert Special, Inc. has a package deal for three concerts, the Rock Stars, the Smooth Sounds, and the Baroque Band. The customer must buy a ticket to all three concerts in order to get the special prices. This chart shows how ticket prices are divided among the musical groups:

| TICKET PRICES FOR | | | |
	HIGH SCHOOL STUDENTS	COLLEGE STUDENTS	ADULTS
ROCK STARS	$4	$6	$8
SMOOTH SOUNDS	$4	$5	$9
BAROQUE BAND	$2	$7	$7

The total ticket sales were $14,980 for the Rock Stars, $14,430 for the Smooth Sounds, and $14,450 for the Baroque Band. Determine the number of tickets sold to high school students, to college students, and to adults.

64. A study showed that for young women a breakfast containing approximately 23 g protein, 49 g carbohydrate, 20 g fat, and 460 calories is a nutritious breakfast that prevents a hungry feeling before lunch. The following table shows the content of four breakfast foods. How much of each should be served in order to obtain the desired amounts of protein, carbohydrates, fat, and calories?

	PROTEIN	CARBOHYDRATES	FAT	CALORIES
1 cup orange juice	2	24	0	110
1 scrambled egg	8	4	8	120
1 slice bread	2	10	6	100
1 cup skim milk	10	13	0	85

65. Solve Exercise 53.
66. Solve Exercise 54.
67. Solve Exercise 55.
68. Solve Exercise 56.
69. Solve Exercise 57.
70. Solve Exercise 58.

2–3 GAUSS-JORDAN METHOD FOR GENERAL SYSTEMS OF EQUATIONS

- *Reduced Echelon Form*
- *Application*
- *Summary*

The previous section dealt with the Gauss-Jordan method of solving a system of equations. Those systems had the same number of equations as variables and had unique solutions. Generally, a system may have a unique solution, no solution, or many solutions, and the number of equations can be different from the number of variables. Basically, solving these systems starts with the augmented matrix of the system of equations. Then a sequence of row operations eventually gives a simpler matrix, which yields the solution directly. In Section 2–2 the matrices reduced to a diagonal form, which gave a unique solution to the system of equations. Sometimes an augmented matrix cannot be reduced to such a diagonal form. However, a **reduced echelon form** is always possible.

REDUCED ECHELON FORM

We give the general definition of reduced echelon form. The diagonal forms of the preceding section also conform to this definition.

Definition
Reduced Echelon Form

A matrix is in **reduced echelon form** if all the following are true.

1. All rows consisting entirely of zeros are grouped at the bottom of the matrix.
2. The leftmost nonzero number in each row is 1. This element is called the *leading* 1.
3. The leading 1 of a row is to the right of the leading 1 of the previous row.
4. All entries directly above and below a leading 1 are zeros.

The following matrices are all in reduced echelon form. Check the conditions in the definition to make sure you understand why.

$$\left[\begin{array}{ccc|c} 1 & 0 & 0 & 2 \\ 0 & 1 & 0 & 4 \\ 0 & 0 & 1 & -2 \end{array}\right] \qquad \left[\begin{array}{ccc|c} 1 & 4 & 0 & 0 \\ 0 & 0 & 1 & 0 \\ 0 & 0 & 0 & 1 \end{array}\right] \qquad \left[\begin{array}{ccc|c} 1 & 2 & 0 & 4 \\ 0 & 0 & 1 & 3 \\ 0 & 0 & 0 & 0 \end{array}\right]$$

$$\left[\begin{array}{cccccc|c} 1 & 4 & 1 & 0 & 4 & 0 & 2 \\ 0 & 0 & 0 & 1 & 3 & 0 & -2 \\ 0 & 0 & 0 & 0 & 0 & 1 & 3 \end{array}\right]$$

$$\left[\begin{array}{cccccc|c} 1 & 0 & 5 & 0 & 4 & 0 & 5 \\ 0 & 1 & 2 & 0 & -3 & 0 & 0 \\ 0 & 0 & 0 & 1 & 2 & 0 & -2 \\ 0 & 0 & 0 & 0 & 0 & 1 & 3 \end{array}\right]$$

The following matrices are not in reduced echelon form:

$$\left[\begin{array}{cccc|c} 1 & 2 & 0 & 4 & 0 \\ 0 & 0 & 0 & 0 & 0 \\ 0 & 0 & 1 & 3 & 0 \\ 0 & 0 & 0 & 0 & 1 \end{array}\right] \qquad \left[\begin{array}{cccc|c} 1 & 2 & 0 & 3 & 0 \\ 0 & 0 & 3 & 4 & 0 \\ 0 & 0 & 0 & 0 & 1 \end{array}\right]$$

There is a row consisting of zeros that is not at the bottom of the matrix.

The leftmost nonzero element in row 2 is not 1.

$$\left[\begin{array}{ccc|c} 1 & 0 & 0 & 2 \\ 0 & 0 & 1 & 4 \\ 0 & 1 & 0 & 3 \end{array}\right] \qquad \left[\begin{array}{ccc|c} 1 & 2 & 0 & 4 \\ 0 & 1 & 0 & -3 \\ 0 & 0 & 1 & 2 \\ 0 & 0 & 0 & 0 \end{array}\right]$$

The leading 1 in row 3 is not to the right of the leading 1 in row 2.

The element directly above the leading 1 in row 2 is not 0.

We now work through the details of modifying a matrix until we obtain the reduced echelon form. As we work through it, notice how we use row operations to obtain the leading 1 in row 1, row 2, and so on, and then get zeros in the rest of a column with a leading 1.

We use the same row operations that are used in reducing an augmented matrix to obtain a solution to a linear system.

EXAMPLE 1   *(Compare Exercise 19)*

Find the reduced echelon form of the matrix

$$\begin{bmatrix} 0 & 1 & -3 & 2 \\ 2 & 4 & 6 & -4 \\ 3 & 5 & 2 & 2 \end{bmatrix}$$

SOLUTION

MATRICES	ROW OPERATIONS	COMMENTS
Need 1 here $\begin{bmatrix} 0 & 1 & -3 & 2 \\ 2 & 4 & 6 & -4 \\ 3 & 5 & 2 & 2 \end{bmatrix}$	R2 ↔ R1	Interchange row 1 and row 2 to get nonzero number at top of column 1.
Need 1 here $\begin{bmatrix} 2 & 4 & 6 & -4 \\ 0 & 1 & -3 & 2 \\ 3 & 5 & 2 & 2 \end{bmatrix}$	$(\frac{1}{2})$ R1 → R1	Divide row 1 by 2 to get a 1.
Need 0 here $\begin{bmatrix} 1 & 2 & 3 & -2 \\ 0 & 1 & -3 & 2 \\ 3 & 5 & 2 & 2 \end{bmatrix}$	-3R1 + R3 → R3	Get zeros in rest of column 1.
Leading 1 here $\begin{bmatrix} 1 & 2 & 3 & -2 \\ 0 & 1 & -3 & 2 \\ 0 & -1 & -7 & 8 \end{bmatrix}$		Now get leading 1 in row 2. No changes necessary this time.
Need 0 here $\begin{bmatrix} 1 & 2 & 3 & -2 \\ 0 & 1 & -3 & 2 \\ 0 & -1 & -7 & 8 \end{bmatrix}$	-2R2 + R1 → R1 R2 + R3 → R3	Zero entries above and below leading 1 of row 2.
Need leading 1 here $\begin{bmatrix} 1 & 0 & 9 & -6 \\ 0 & 1 & -3 & 2 \\ 0 & 0 & -10 & 10 \end{bmatrix}$	$(-\frac{1}{10})$R3 → R3	Get a leading 1 in the next row.
Need 0 here $\begin{bmatrix} 1 & 0 & 9 & -6 \\ 0 & 1 & -3 & 2 \\ 0 & 0 & 1 & -1 \end{bmatrix}$	-9R3 + R1 → R1 3R3 + R2 → R2	Zero entries above, leading 1 in row 3.
$\begin{bmatrix} 1 & 0 & 0 & 3 \\ 0 & 1 & 0 & -1 \\ 0 & 0 & 1 & -1 \end{bmatrix}$		This is the reduced echelon form.

EXAMPLE 2 *(Compare Exercise 23)*

Find the reduced echelon form of this matrix:

$$\begin{bmatrix} 0 & 0 & 2 & -2 & | & 2 \\ 3 & 3 & -3 & 9 & | & 12 \\ 4 & 4 & -2 & 11 & | & 12 \end{bmatrix}$$

SOLUTION   Again we show much of the detailed row operations.

	MATRICES	ROW OPERATIONS	COMMENTS
Need 1 here	$\begin{bmatrix} ⓪ & 0 & 2 & -2 & \| & 2 \\ 3 & 3 & -3 & 9 & \| & 12 \\ 4 & 4 & -2 & 11 & \| & 12 \end{bmatrix}$	R1 ↔ R2	
Need 1 here	$\begin{bmatrix} ③ & 3 & -3 & 9 & \| & 12 \\ 0 & 0 & 2 & -2 & \| & 2 \\ 4 & 4 & -2 & 11 & \| & 12 \end{bmatrix}$	$(\frac{1}{3})$R1 → R1	
Need 0 here	$\begin{bmatrix} 1 & 1 & -1 & 3 & \| & 4 \\ 0 & 0 & 2 & -2 & \| & 2 \\ ④ & 4 & -2 & 11 & \| & 12 \end{bmatrix}$	$(\frac{1}{2})$R2 → R2 -4R1 + R3 → R3	
Leading 1 row 2	$\begin{bmatrix} 1 & 1 & -1 & 3 & \| & 4 \\ 0 & 0 & ① & -1 & \| & 1 \\ 0 & 0 & 2 & -1 & \| & -4 \end{bmatrix}$		The leading 1 of row 2 must come from row 2 or below. Since all entries in column 2 are zero in row 2 and 3, go to column 3 for leading 1.
Need 0 here	$\begin{bmatrix} 1 & 1 & ⊖1 & 3 & \| & 4 \\ 0 & 0 & 1 & -1 & \| & 1 \\ 0 & 0 & ② & -1 & \| & -4 \end{bmatrix}$	R2 + R1 → R1 -2R2 + R3 → R3	
Need 0 here	$\begin{bmatrix} 1 & 1 & 0 & ② & \| & 5 \\ 0 & 0 & 1 & ⊖1 & \| & 1 \\ 0 & 0 & 0 & 1 & \| & -6 \end{bmatrix}$	-2R3 + R1 → R1 R3 + R2 → R2	
	$\begin{bmatrix} 1 & 1 & 0 & 0 & \| & 17 \\ 0 & 0 & 1 & 0 & \| & -5 \\ 0 & 0 & 0 & 1 & \| & -6 \end{bmatrix}$		This is reduced echelon form.

We now solve various systems of equations to illustrate the Gauss-Jordan method of elimination.

EXAMPLE 3   *(Compare Exercise 33)*

Solve, if possible, the system

$$2x_1 - 4x_2 + 12x_3 = 20$$
$$-x_1 + 3x_2 + 5x_3 = 15$$
$$3x_1 - 7x_2 + 7x_3 = 5$$

SOLUTION   We start with the augmented matrix and convert it to reduced echelon form:

$$\begin{bmatrix} 2 & -4 & 12 & \bigm| & 20 \\ -1 & 3 & 5 & \bigm| & 15 \\ 3 & -7 & 7 & \bigm| & 5 \end{bmatrix} \qquad \tfrac{1}{2}R1 \rightarrow R1$$

$$\begin{bmatrix} 1 & -2 & 6 & \bigm| & 10 \\ -1 & 3 & 5 & \bigm| & 15 \\ 3 & -7 & 7 & \bigm| & 5 \end{bmatrix} \qquad \begin{array}{l} R1 + R2 \rightarrow R2 \\ -3R1 + R3 \rightarrow R3 \end{array}$$

$$\begin{bmatrix} 1 & -2 & 6 & \bigm| & 10 \\ 0 & 1 & 11 & \bigm| & 25 \\ 0 & -1 & -11 & \bigm| & -25 \end{bmatrix} \qquad \begin{array}{l} 2R2 + R1 \rightarrow R1 \\[4pt] R2 + R3 \rightarrow R3 \end{array}$$

$$\begin{bmatrix} 1 & 0 & 28 & \bigm| & 60 \\ 0 & 1 & 11 & \bigm| & 25 \\ 0 & 0 & 0 & \bigm| & 0 \end{bmatrix}$$

This matrix is the reduced echelon form of the augmented matrix. It represents the system of equations

$$x_1 \quad + 28x_3 = 60$$
$$x_2 + 11x_3 = 25$$

When the reduced echelon form gives equations containing more than one variable, such as $x_1 + 28x_3 = 60$, the system has many solutions. Many sets of x_1, x_2, and x_3 satisfy these equations. Usually, we solve the first equation for x_1 and the second for x_2 to get

$$x_1 = 60 - 28x_3$$
$$x_2 = 25 - 11x_3$$

This represents the general solution with x_3 selected arbitrarily then computing x_1 and x_2. For example, one specific solution is found by assigning $x_3 = 1$. Then $x_1 = 60 - 28 = 32$, and $x_2 = 25 - 11 = 14$. In general, we assign the arbitrary value k to x_3 and solve for x_1 and x_2. The arbitrary solution can then be expressed as $x_1 = 60 - 28k$, $x_2 = 25 - 11k$, $x_3 = k$. As k ranges over the real numbers, we get all solutions. In such a case, k is called a parameter. For example, when

$k = 2$, we get $x_1 = 4$, $x_2 = 3$, $x_3 = 2$. When $k = -1$, we get the solution $x_1 = 88$, $x_2 = 36$, $x_3 = -1$. In summary, the solutions to this example may be written in two ways:

$$x_1 = 60 - 28x_3$$
$$x_2 = 25 - 11x_3$$

or

$$x_1 = 60 - 28k$$
$$x_2 = 25 - 11k$$
$$x_3 = k$$

The latter is sometimes written as $(60 - 28k, 25 - 11k, k)$.

The reduction of an augmented matrix can be tedious. However, this method reduces the solution of a system of equations to a routine. This routine can be carried out on a computer. When dozens of variables are involved, a computer is the only practical way to solve such a system. We want you to be able to perform this routine, so we have two more examples to help you.

EXAMPLE 4   *(Compare Exercise 37)*

If possible, solve the system

$$x_1 + 2x_2 - x_3 + 3x_4 + x_5 = 2$$
$$2x_1 + 4x_2 - 2x_3 + 6x_4 + 3x_5 = 6$$
$$-x_1 - 2x_2 + x_3 - x_4 + 3x_5 = 4$$

We get the augmented matrix and start reducing to echelon form:

$$\begin{bmatrix} 1 & 2 & -1 & 3 & 1 & | & 2 \\ 2 & 4 & -2 & 6 & 3 & | & 6 \\ -1 & -2 & 1 & -1 & 3 & | & 4 \end{bmatrix} \quad \begin{array}{l} -2R1 + R2 \to R2 \\ R1 + R3 \to R3 \end{array}$$

$$\begin{bmatrix} 1 & 2 & -1 & 3 & 1 & | & 2 \\ 0 & 0 & 0 & 0 & 1 & | & 2 \\ 0 & 0 & 0 & 2 & 4 & | & 6 \end{bmatrix} \quad R2 \leftrightarrow R3 \text{ (Exchange R2 and R3)}$$

$$\begin{bmatrix} 1 & 2 & -1 & 3 & 1 & | & 2 \\ 0 & 0 & 0 & 2 & 4 & | & 6 \\ 0 & 0 & 0 & 0 & 1 & | & 2 \end{bmatrix} \quad (\tfrac{1}{2})R2 \to R2$$

$$\begin{bmatrix} 1 & 2 & -1 & 3 & 1 & | & 2 \\ 0 & 0 & 0 & 1 & 2 & | & 3 \\ 0 & 0 & 0 & 0 & 1 & | & 2 \end{bmatrix} \quad -3R2 + R1 \to R1$$

$$\begin{bmatrix} 1 & 2 & -1 & 0 & -5 & | & -7 \\ 0 & 0 & 0 & 1 & 2 & | & 3 \\ 0 & 0 & 0 & 0 & 1 & | & 2 \end{bmatrix} \qquad \begin{array}{l} 5R3 + R1 \rightarrow R1 \\ -2R3 + R2 \rightarrow R2 \end{array}$$

$$\begin{bmatrix} 1 & 2 & -1 & 0 & 0 & | & 3 \\ 0 & 0 & 0 & 1 & 0 & | & -1 \\ 0 & 0 & 0 & 0 & 1 & | & 2 \end{bmatrix}$$

This matrix is the reduced echelon form of the augmented matrix. The corresponding system of equations is

$$\begin{array}{rcl} x_1 + 2x_2 - x_3 & = & 3 \\ x_4 & = & -1 \\ x_5 & = & 2 \end{array}$$

Solving for x_1 in terms of the remaining variables, we get

$$x_1 = -2x_2 + x_3 + 3, \qquad x_4 = -1, \qquad x_5 = 2$$

The variable x_1 is expressed in terms of the two variables x_2 and x_3, so we make arbitrary choices of each. Let us assign the arbitrary values k to x_2 and r to x_3. The arbitrary solution then is

$$x_1 = -2k + r + 3, \qquad x_2 = k, \qquad x_3 = r, \qquad x_4 = -1,$$
$$x_5 = 2$$

which may be written $(-2k + r + 3, k, r, -1, 2)$. We get specific solutions by assigning values to k and r. ∎

It is possible for a system to have no solution. We illustrate this in the following example.

EXAMPLE 5 *(Compare Exercise 39)*

The following system has no solution. Let's see what happens when we try to solve it.

$$\begin{array}{rcl} x_1 + 3x_2 - 2x_3 & = & 5 \\ 4x_1 - x_2 + 3x_3 & = & 7 \\ 2x_1 - 7x_2 + 7x_3 & = & 4 \end{array}$$

SOLUTION

$$\begin{bmatrix} 1 & 3 & -2 & | & 5 \\ 4 & -1 & 3 & | & 7 \\ 2 & -7 & 7 & | & 4 \end{bmatrix} \qquad \begin{array}{l} -4R1 + R2 \rightarrow R2 \\ -2R1 + R3 \rightarrow R3 \end{array}$$

$$\begin{bmatrix} 1 & 3 & -2 & | & 5 \\ 0 & -13 & 11 & | & -13 \\ 0 & -13 & 11 & | & -6 \end{bmatrix} \qquad -R2 + R3 \rightarrow R3$$

$$\begin{bmatrix} 1 & 3 & -2 & | & 5 \\ 0 & -13 & 11 & | & -13 \\ 0 & 0 & 0 & | & 7 \end{bmatrix}$$

The last matrix is not yet in reduced echelon form. However, we need proceed no further because the last row represents the equation $0 = 7$. When we reach an inconsistency like this, we know that the system has no solution.

Usually, you cannot look at a system of equations and tell whether there is no solution, just one solution, or many solutions. When a system has fewer equations than variables, we generally expect many solutions. Here is such an example.

EXAMPLE 6   *(Compare Exercise 43)*

Solve the system

$$x_1 + 2x_2 - x_3 = -3$$
$$4x_1 + 3x_2 + x_3 = 13$$

SOLUTION   Set up the augmented matrix and solve:

$$\begin{bmatrix} 1 & 2 & -1 & | & -3 \\ 4 & 3 & 1 & | & 13 \end{bmatrix} \qquad -4R1 + R2 \rightarrow R2$$

$$\begin{bmatrix} 1 & 2 & -1 & | & -3 \\ 0 & -5 & 5 & | & 25 \end{bmatrix} \qquad -\tfrac{1}{5}R2 \rightarrow R2$$

$$\begin{bmatrix} 1 & 2 & -1 & | & -3 \\ 0 & 1 & -1 & | & -5 \end{bmatrix} \qquad -2R2 + R1 \rightarrow R1$$

$$\begin{bmatrix} 1 & 0 & 1 & | & 7 \\ 0 & 1 & -1 & | & -5 \end{bmatrix}$$

This matrix is in reduced echelon form and represents the equations

$$x_1 = 7 - x_3$$
$$x_2 = -5 + x_3$$

Since x_3 can be arbitrarily chosen, this system has many solutions. The parametric form of this solution is

$$x_1 = 7 - k$$
$$x_2 = -5 + k$$
$$x_3 = k$$

which may be written $(7 - k, -5 + k, k)$.

You should not conclude from the preceding example that a system with fewer equations than variables will always yield many solutions. In some cases the system contains an inconsistency and no solution is possible.

EXAMPLE 7   *(Compare Exercise 47)*

Attempt to solve the following system:

$$\begin{aligned} x_1 + x_2 - x_3 + 2x_4 &= 4 \\ -2x_1 + x_2 + 3x_3 + x_4 &= 5 \\ -x_1 + 2x_2 + 2x_3 + 3x_4 &= 6 \end{aligned}$$

SOLUTION

$$\left[\begin{array}{cccc|c} 1 & 1 & -1 & 2 & 4 \\ -2 & 1 & 3 & 1 & 5 \\ -1 & 2 & 2 & 3 & 6 \end{array}\right] \qquad \begin{array}{c} 2R1 + R2 \to R2 \\ R1 + R3 \to R3 \end{array}$$

$$\left[\begin{array}{cccc|c} 1 & 1 & -1 & 2 & 4 \\ 0 & 3 & 1 & 5 & 13 \\ 0 & 3 & 1 & 5 & 10 \end{array}\right] \qquad -R2 + R3 \to R3$$

$$\left[\begin{array}{cccc|c} 1 & 1 & -1 & 2 & 4 \\ 0 & 3 & 1 & 5 & 13 \\ 0 & 0 & 0 & 0 & -3 \end{array}\right]$$

The last row of this matrix represents $0 = -3$, an inconsistency, so the system has no solution.

A system with more equations than variables may have a unique solution, no solution, or many solutions. The following examples illustrate these cases.

EXAMPLE 8   *(Compare Exercise 51)*

If possible solve the system

$$\begin{aligned} x + 3y &= 11 \\ 3x - 4y &= -6 \\ 2x - 7y &= -17 \end{aligned}$$

SOLUTION

$$\left[\begin{array}{cc|c} 1 & 3 & 11 \\ 3 & -4 & -6 \\ 2 & -7 & -17 \end{array}\right] \qquad \begin{array}{c} -3R1 + R2 \to R2 \\ -2R1 + R3 \to R3 \end{array}$$

$$\left[\begin{array}{cc|c} 1 & 3 & 11 \\ 0 & -13 & -39 \\ 0 & -13 & -39 \end{array}\right] \qquad -R2 + R3 \to R3$$

$$\left[\begin{array}{cc|c} 1 & 3 & 11 \\ 0 & -13 & -39 \\ 0 & 0 & 0 \end{array}\right] \qquad (-\tfrac{1}{13})R2 \to R2$$

$$\begin{bmatrix} 1 & 3 & | & 11 \\ 0 & 1 & | & 3 \\ 0 & 0 & | & 0 \end{bmatrix} \qquad -3R2 + R1 \rightarrow R1$$

$$\begin{bmatrix} 1 & 0 & | & 2 \\ 0 & 1 & | & 3 \\ 0 & 0 & | & 0 \end{bmatrix}$$

This reduced echelon matrix gives the solution $x = 2$, $y = 3$, a unique solution. ∎

EXAMPLE 9 *(Compare Exercise 55)*

If possible solve the system

$$\begin{aligned} x_1 - x_2 + 2x_3 &= 2 \\ 2x_1 + 3x_2 - x_3 &= 14 \\ 3x_1 + 2x_2 + x_3 &= 16 \\ x_1 + 4x_2 - 3x_3 &= 12 \end{aligned}$$

SOLUTION

$$\begin{bmatrix} 1 & -1 & 2 & | & 2 \\ 2 & 3 & -1 & | & 14 \\ 3 & 2 & 1 & | & 16 \\ 1 & 4 & -3 & | & 12 \end{bmatrix} \qquad \begin{array}{l} -2R1 + R2 \rightarrow R2 \\ -3R1 + R3 \rightarrow R3 \\ -R1 + R4 \rightarrow R4 \end{array}$$

$$\begin{bmatrix} 1 & -1 & 2 & | & 2 \\ 0 & 5 & -5 & | & 10 \\ 0 & 5 & -5 & | & 10 \\ 0 & 5 & -5 & | & 10 \end{bmatrix} \qquad \begin{array}{l} -R2 + R3 \rightarrow R3 \\ -R2 + R4 \rightarrow R4 \end{array}$$

$$\begin{bmatrix} 1 & -1 & 2 & | & 2 \\ 0 & 5 & -5 & | & 10 \\ 0 & 0 & 0 & | & 0 \\ 0 & 0 & 0 & | & 0 \end{bmatrix} \qquad \tfrac{1}{5}R2 \rightarrow R2$$

$$\begin{bmatrix} 1 & -1 & 2 & | & 2 \\ 0 & 1 & -1 & | & 2 \\ 0 & 0 & 0 & | & 0 \\ 0 & 0 & 0 & | & 0 \end{bmatrix} \qquad R2 + R1 \rightarrow R1$$

$$\begin{bmatrix} 1 & 0 & 1 & | & 4 \\ 0 & 1 & -1 & | & 2 \\ 0 & 0 & 0 & | & 0 \\ 0 & 0 & 0 & | & 0 \end{bmatrix}$$

This matrix represents the system

$$x_1 \quad + x_3 = 4$$
$$x_2 - x_3 = 2$$

so there are an infinite number of solutions of the form

$$x_1 = 4 - x_3$$
$$x_2 = 2 + x_3$$

or $(4 - k, 2 + k, k)$ in parametric form.

EXAMPLE 10 *(Compare Exercise 59)*

This example has no solutions. We attempt to solve the system

$$x_1 - \quad x_2 + 2x_3 = \quad 3$$
$$2x_1 - 2x_2 + 5x_3 = \quad 4$$
$$x_1 + 2x_2 - \quad x_3 = -3$$
$$2x_2 + 2x_3 = \quad 1$$

SOLUTION We get the augmented matrix

$$\left[\begin{array}{ccc|c} 1 & -1 & 2 & 3 \\ 2 & -2 & 5 & 4 \\ 1 & 2 & -1 & -3 \\ 0 & 2 & 2 & 1 \end{array}\right]$$

Now proceed to use row operations to reduce the matrix.

$$\left[\begin{array}{ccc|c} 1 & -1 & 2 & 3 \\ 2 & -2 & 5 & 4 \\ 1 & 2 & -1 & -3 \\ 0 & 2 & 2 & 1 \end{array}\right] \qquad \begin{array}{l} -2R1 + R2 \rightarrow R2 \\ -R1 + R3 \rightarrow R3 \end{array}$$

$$\left[\begin{array}{ccc|c} 1 & -1 & 2 & 3 \\ 0 & 0 & 1 & -2 \\ 0 & 3 & -3 & -6 \\ 0 & 2 & 2 & 1 \end{array}\right] \qquad (\tfrac{1}{3})R3 \text{ and interchange R2 and R3}$$

$$\left[\begin{array}{ccc|c} 1 & -1 & 2 & 3 \\ 0 & 1 & -1 & -2 \\ 0 & 0 & 1 & -2 \\ 0 & 2 & 2 & 1 \end{array}\right] \qquad \begin{array}{l} R2 + R1 \rightarrow R1 \\ \\ \\ -2R2 + R4 \rightarrow R4 \end{array}$$

$$\left[\begin{array}{ccc|c} 1 & 0 & 1 & 1 \\ 0 & 1 & -1 & -2 \\ 0 & 0 & 1 & -2 \\ 0 & 0 & 4 & 5 \end{array}\right] \qquad \begin{array}{l} -R3 + R1 \rightarrow R1 \\ R3 + R2 \rightarrow R2 \\ \\ -4R3 + R4 \rightarrow R4 \end{array}$$

$$\begin{bmatrix} 1 & 0 & 0 & | & 3 \\ 0 & 1 & 0 & | & -4 \\ 0 & 0 & 1 & | & -2 \\ 0 & 0 & 0 & | & 13 \end{bmatrix}$$ $(\tfrac{1}{13})R4 \rightarrow R4$

$$\begin{bmatrix} 1 & 0 & 0 & | & 3 \\ 0 & 1 & 0 & | & -4 \\ 0 & 0 & 1 & | & -2 \\ 0 & 0 & 0 & | & 1 \end{bmatrix}$$

This matrix is not in reduced echelon form; zeros still have to be created above the 1 in the last row. However, in such a situation, when the last nonzero row is of the form $[0 \quad 0 \quad \cdots \quad 0 \quad 1]$, there is no need to proceed further. The system has no solutions. To see this, let us write down the system that corresponds to the above matrix. We get

$$\begin{aligned} x_1 & & & = & 3 \\ & x_2 & & = & -4 \\ & & x_3 & = & -2 \\ & & 0 & = & 1 \end{aligned}$$

Because this last equation is false, this system cannot be satisfied for any values of x_1, x_2, and x_3; therefore the original system has no solutions.

Each nonzero row in the reduced echelon matrix gives the value of one variable—either as a number or expressed in terms of another variable. When the system reduces to fewer equations than variables, there are not enough rows in the matrix to give a row for each variable. This means that you can solve only for some of the variables, and they will be expressed in terms of the remaining variables (parameters). Examples 3, 4, and 6 illustrate the relationship between the number of variables solved in terms of parameters. Notice the following:

Example 3 reduces to two equations and three variables, and two of the variables were solved in terms of one parameter.

In Example 4, which has three equations and five variables, three of the variables were solved in terms of two parameters.

In Example 6, which has two equations and three variables, two variables were solved in terms of one parameter.

The relationship is as follows: If there are k equations with n variables, $n > k$, then k of the variables can be solved in terms of $n - k$ parameters. The system has many solutions.

Whenever a row in a reduced matrix becomes all zeros, then an equation is eliminated from the system, and the number of equations is reduced by one. In the reduced echelon matrix, count the nonzero rows to count the number of equations in the solution.

APPLICATION

EXAMPLE 11 *(Compare Exercise 67)*

A brokerage firm packaged blocks of common stocks, bonds, and preferred stocks into three different portfolios. The portfolios contained the following:

PORTFOLIO	COMMON	BONDS	PREFERRED
I	3 blocks	2 blocks	5 blocks
II	2 blocks	6 blocks	8 blocks
III	5 blocks	8 blocks	13 blocks

A customer wants to buy 110 blocks of common stock, 190 blocks of bonds, and 300 blocks of preferred stock. How many of each portfolio should be purchased to accomplish this?

SOLUTION Let x, y, and z represent the number of portfolios I, II, and III used. The information given can be stated as a system of equations

$$\begin{aligned} \text{Common stock:} \quad & 3x + 2y + 5z = 110 \\ \text{Bonds:} \quad & 2x + 6y + 8z = 190 \\ \text{Preferred stock:} \quad & 5x + 8y + 13z = 300 \end{aligned}$$

The augmented matrix is

$$\begin{bmatrix} 3 & 2 & 5 & | & 110 \\ 2 & 6 & 8 & | & 190 \\ 5 & 8 & 13 & | & 300 \end{bmatrix}$$

This matrix reduces to the following matrix. (Show that it does.)

$$\begin{bmatrix} 1 & 0 & 1 & | & 20 \\ 0 & 1 & 1 & | & 25 \\ 0 & 0 & 0 & | & 0 \end{bmatrix}$$

The system has an infinite number of solutions

$$\begin{aligned} x &= 20 - z \\ y &= 25 - z \end{aligned}$$

Common sense tells us that x, y, and z cannot be negative, so z can be an integer zero through 20. A larger value of z makes x or y negative. To fill the customer's order, the brokerage firm can use the following number of each portfolio:

Portfolio III: From zero through 20

Portfolio II: 25 reduced by the number of III used

Portfolio I: 20 reduced by the number of III used

SUMMARY

The nonzero rows of the reduced echelon matrix give the needed information about the solutions to a system of equations. Three situations are possible.

1. No solution.
At least one row has all zeros in the coefficient portion of the matrix (to the left of the vertical line) and a nonzero entry to the right of the vertical line.

$$\begin{bmatrix} 1 & 0 & 0 & | & 3 \\ 0 & 1 & 0 & | & 2 \\ 0 & 0 & 0 & | & 5 \end{bmatrix} \quad \text{No solution}$$

Two more possibilities arise when a solution exists.

2. The solution is unique.
The number of nonzero rows equals the number of variables in the system.

$$\begin{bmatrix} 1 & 0 & | & 5 \\ 0 & 1 & | & -2 \end{bmatrix} \quad \begin{bmatrix} 1 & 0 & 0 & | & -4 \\ 0 & 1 & 0 & | & 3 \\ 0 & 0 & 1 & | & 2 \\ 0 & 0 & 0 & | & 0 \end{bmatrix} \quad \text{Unique solution}$$

3. Infinite number of solutions.
The number of nonzero rows is less than the number of variables in the system.

$$\begin{bmatrix} 1 & 0 & 0 & 2 & | & 3 \\ 0 & 1 & 0 & 5 & | & 2 \\ 0 & 0 & 1 & 3 & | & 4 \end{bmatrix} \quad \begin{bmatrix} 1 & 0 & 1 & | & 2 \\ 0 & 1 & 2 & | & 4 \\ 0 & 0 & 0 & | & 0 \end{bmatrix} \quad \text{Infinite number of solutions}$$

2-3 EXERCISES

I

State whether or not the matrices in Exercises 1 through 10 are in reduced echelon form. If a matrix is not in reduced echelon form, explain why it is not.

1. $\begin{bmatrix} 1 & 0 & 0 & 0 & | & 0 \\ 0 & 0 & 1 & 2 & | & 3 \\ 0 & 0 & 0 & 0 & | & 0 \end{bmatrix}$

2. $\begin{bmatrix} 1 & 0 & 0 & | & 3 \\ 0 & 1 & 0 & | & 4 \\ 0 & 0 & 2 & | & 1 \end{bmatrix}$

3. $\begin{bmatrix} 1 & 0 & 0 & 3 & | & 2 \\ 0 & 2 & 0 & 6 & | & 1 \\ 0 & 0 & 1 & 2 & | & 3 \end{bmatrix}$

4. $\begin{bmatrix} 1 & 6 & 0 & 0 & 2 & | & -1 \\ 0 & 0 & 1 & 0 & 4 & | & 3 \\ 0 & 0 & 0 & 1 & 3 & | & 1 \end{bmatrix}$

5. $\begin{bmatrix} 1 & 0 & 0 & | & 2 \\ 0 & 0 & 1 & | & 3 \\ 0 & 1 & 0 & | & 4 \end{bmatrix}$

6. $\begin{bmatrix} 1 & 2 & 0 & 0 & | & 4 \\ 0 & 0 & 1 & 0 & | & 6 \\ 0 & 0 & 0 & 1 & | & 5 \end{bmatrix}$

7. $\begin{bmatrix} 1 & 0 & 4 & 2 & 6 \\ 0 & 1 & 2 & 3 & 4 \\ 0 & 0 & 0 & 1 & 2 \\ 0 & 0 & 0 & 0 & 1 \end{bmatrix}$

8. $\begin{bmatrix} 1 & 5 & 4 & 2 & 1 \\ 0 & 0 & 1 & 5 & 3 \\ 0 & 0 & 0 & 0 & 1 \\ 0 & 0 & 0 & 0 & 0 \end{bmatrix}$

9. $\left[\begin{array}{cccc|c} 1 & 5 & 0 & 0 & 0 \\ 0 & 0 & 2 & 0 & 0 \\ 0 & 0 & 0 & 1 & 0 \\ 0 & 0 & 0 & 0 & 1 \end{array}\right]$

10. $\left[\begin{array}{cccccc|c} 1 & 2 & 0 & 2 & 0 & 2 & 0 \\ 0 & 0 & 1 & 3 & 0 & 4 & 0 \\ 0 & 0 & 0 & 0 & 1 & 3 & 0 \\ 0 & 0 & 0 & 0 & 0 & 0 & 1 \end{array}\right]$

Interpret each of the matrices in Exercises 11 through 18 as being a matrix in the sequence that leads to the reduced echelon form of a given system of linear equations. Find the next matrix in the sequence in each case.

11. $\left[\begin{array}{ccc|c} 1 & 0 & 1 & 4 \\ 0 & 1 & 2 & 3 \\ 0 & 0 & 3 & 6 \end{array}\right]$

12. $\left[\begin{array}{cc|c} 1 & 2 & 4 \\ 0 & 3 & 6 \\ 0 & 4 & 2 \end{array}\right]$

13. $\left[\begin{array}{ccc|c} 1 & 3 & 4 & -1 \\ 0 & 0 & 6 & 2 \\ 0 & 4 & 3 & 4 \end{array}\right]$

14. $\left[\begin{array}{ccc|c} 1 & 0 & 0 & -1 & 6 \\ 0 & 1 & 3 & 2 & 4 \\ 0 & 0 & 0 & 1 & 2 \\ 0 & 0 & 0 & 3 & 1 \end{array}\right]$

15. $\left[\begin{array}{cccc|c} 1 & 4 & 2 & 4 & 5 \\ 0 & 0 & 0 & 0 & 6 \\ 0 & 0 & 0 & 2 & 3 \\ 0 & 0 & 3 & 1 & 2 \end{array}\right]$

16. $\left[\begin{array}{cc|c} 0 & 4 & -2 \\ 0 & 6 & 4 \\ 2 & 3 & 6 \\ 1 & 1 & 7 \end{array}\right]$

17. $\left[\begin{array}{ccc|c} 1 & 0 & 2 & 3 \\ 0 & 1 & 4 & 4 \\ 0 & 0 & 0 & 0 \\ 0 & 0 & 0 & 5 \end{array}\right]$

18. $\left[\begin{array}{ccccc|c} 1 & 0 & 0 & 2 & 5 & 1 \\ 0 & 1 & 4 & 6 & 1 & 3 \\ 0 & 0 & 0 & 0 & 0 & 2 \\ 0 & 0 & 0 & 0 & 3 & 4 \end{array}\right]$

In Exercises 19 through 24, reduce each matrix to its reduced echelon form.

19. (*See Example 1*)
$\left[\begin{array}{ccc|c} 1 & -1 & 7 & 1 \\ 1 & -2 & 1 & 4 \\ 2 & 1 & 0 & 1 \end{array}\right]$

20. $\left[\begin{array}{ccc|c} 1 & 3 & 5 & 4 \\ -3 & -4 & 0 & 3 \\ 0 & 2 & 1 & 1 \end{array}\right]$

21. $\left[\begin{array}{ccc|c} 2 & 4 & 8 & -4 \\ 3 & 5 & -1 & 6 \\ 1 & -1 & -9 & 10 \end{array}\right]$

22. $\left[\begin{array}{ccc|c} 3 & -2 & 5 & 1 \\ -6 & 4 & -10 & -2 \\ 12 & -8 & 20 & 4 \end{array}\right]$

23. (*See Example 2*)
$\left[\begin{array}{cccc|c} 1 & 2 & 1 & 0 & 3 \\ 0 & 1 & 4 & 1 & 2 \\ 2 & -1 & 3 & 1 & 4 \end{array}\right]$

24. $\left[\begin{array}{cccc|c} 1 & -1 & 2 & 2 & 4 \\ 2 & 0 & 1 & 3 & 5 \\ 3 & 4 & -2 & 1 & 2 \end{array}\right]$

Each of the matrices in Exercises 25 through 32 is in reduced echelon form. Write down the system of equations that corresponds to each matrix. Solve each system if possible.

25. $\left[\begin{array}{cccc|c} 1 & 0 & 0 & 0 & 2 \\ 0 & 1 & 2 & 0 & 3 \\ 0 & 0 & 0 & 1 & -1 \end{array}\right]$

26. $\left[\begin{array}{cccc|c} 1 & 2 & 0 & 0 & 2 \\ 0 & 0 & 1 & 0 & 3 \\ 0 & 0 & 0 & 1 & 4 \end{array}\right]$

27. $\left[\begin{array}{ccccc|c} 1 & 0 & 2 & 0 & 2 & -1 \\ 0 & 1 & 4 & 0 & 3 & 2 \\ 0 & 0 & 0 & 1 & 4 & 1 \end{array}\right]$

28. $\begin{bmatrix} 1 & 0 & 2 & 0 & | & 0 \\ 0 & 1 & 4 & 0 & | & 0 \\ 0 & 0 & 0 & 1 & | & 0 \\ 0 & 0 & 0 & 0 & | & 1 \end{bmatrix}$

29. $\begin{bmatrix} 1 & 0 & 2 & 0 & | & 2 \\ 0 & 1 & -3 & 0 & | & 1 \\ 0 & 0 & 0 & 1 & | & 3 \\ 0 & 0 & 0 & 0 & | & 0 \end{bmatrix}$

30. $\begin{bmatrix} 1 & 3 & 4 & 0 & 0 & 0 & | & 1 \\ 0 & 0 & 0 & 1 & 0 & 0 & | & 2 \\ 0 & 0 & 0 & 0 & 1 & 0 & | & 4 \\ 0 & 0 & 0 & 0 & 0 & 1 & | & 3 \end{bmatrix}$

31. $\begin{bmatrix} 1 & 2 & 0 & 1 & 0 & 0 & | & 4 \\ 0 & 0 & 1 & 3 & 0 & 0 & | & -1 \\ 0 & 0 & 0 & 0 & 1 & 0 & | & 3 \\ 0 & 0 & 0 & 0 & 0 & 1 & | & 2 \end{bmatrix}$

32. $\begin{bmatrix} 1 & 0 & 0 & | & 0 \\ 0 & 1 & 0 & | & 0 \\ 0 & 0 & 1 & | & 0 \\ 0 & 0 & 0 & | & 1 \end{bmatrix}$

Solve each system of equations in Exercises 33 through 65 (if possible).

33. (*See Example 3*)
$$\begin{aligned} x_1 + 4x_2 - 2x_3 &= 13 \\ 3x_1 - x_2 + 4x_3 &= 6 \\ 2x_1 - 5x_2 + 6x_3 &= -4 \end{aligned}$$

34. $\begin{aligned} 2x_1 + 4x_2 - x_3 &= -4 \\ x_1 + 3x_2 + 6x_3 &= -15 \\ 3x_1 + 5x_2 - 8x_3 &= 7 \end{aligned}$

35. $\begin{aligned} 3x_1 - 2x_2 + 2x_3 &= 10 \\ 2x_1 + x_2 + 3x_3 &= 3 \\ x_1 + x_2 - x_3 &= 5 \end{aligned}$

36. $\begin{aligned} x_1 + 3x_2 + 6x_3 - 2x_4 &= -7 \\ -2x_1 - 5x_2 - 10x_3 + 3x_4 &= 10 \\ x_1 + 2x_2 + 4x_3 \phantom{{}- 3x_4} &= 0 \\ x_2 + 2x_3 - 3x_4 &= -10 \end{aligned}$

37. (*See Example 4*)
$$\begin{aligned} x_1 + x_2 + x_3 - x_4 &= -3 \\ 2x_1 + 3x_2 + x_3 - 5x_4 &= -9 \\ x_1 + 3x_2 - x_3 - 6x_4 &= 7 \end{aligned}$$

38. $\begin{aligned} x_1 + 6x_2 - x_3 - 4x_4 &= 0 \\ -2x_1 - 12x_2 + 5x_3 + 17x_4 &= 0 \\ 3x_1 + 18x_2 - x_3 - 6x_4 &= 0 \end{aligned}$

39. (*See Example 5*)
$$\begin{aligned} x_1 - x_2 + x_3 &= 3 \\ -2x_1 + 3x_2 + x_3 &= -8 \\ 4x_1 - 2x_2 + 10x_3 &= 10 \end{aligned}$$

40. $\begin{aligned} x_1 + 4x_2 - 2x_3 &= 10 \\ 3x_1 - x_2 + 4x_3 &= 6 \\ 2x_1 - 5x_2 + 6x_3 &= 7 \end{aligned}$

41. $\begin{aligned} x_1 + x_2 + x_3 &= 6 \\ x_1 - 3x_2 + 2x_3 &= 1 \\ 3x_1 - x_2 + 4x_3 &= 5 \end{aligned}$

42. $\begin{aligned} 2x_1 + 4x_2 + 2x_3 &= 4 \\ 6x_1 + 3x_2 - x_3 &= -5 \\ 7x_1 + 5x_2 \phantom{{}- x_3} &= 8 \end{aligned}$

43. (*See Example 6*)
$$\begin{aligned} x_1 + 2x_2 - x_3 &= -13 \\ 2x_1 + 5x_2 + 3x_3 &= -3 \end{aligned}$$

44. $\begin{aligned} 2x_1 + 3x_2 - 4x_3 &= 1 \\ 4x_1 + x_2 + 2x_3 &= -3 \end{aligned}$

45. $\begin{aligned} x_1 - 2x_2 + x_3 + x_4 - 2x_5 &= -9 \\ 5x_1 + x_2 - 6x_3 - 6x_4 + x_5 &= 21 \end{aligned}$

46. $\begin{aligned} x_1 - 3x_2 + 4x_3 &= 6 \\ 2x_1 - 5x_2 - 6x_3 &= 11 \end{aligned}$

47. (*See Example 7*)
$$\begin{aligned} x_1 + x_2 - 3x_3 + x_4 &= 4 \\ -2x_1 - 2x_2 + 6x_3 - 2x_4 &= 3 \end{aligned}$$

48. $\begin{aligned} 2x_1 - 4x_2 + 16x_3 - 14x_4 &= 12 \\ -x_1 + 5x_2 - 17x_3 + 19x_4 &= -2 \\ x_1 - 3x_2 + 11x_3 - 11x_4 &= 4 \end{aligned}$

49. $\begin{aligned} x_1 + x_2 - x_3 - x_4 &= -1 \\ 3x_1 - 2x_2 - 4x_3 + 2x_4 &= 1 \\ 4x_1 - x_2 - 5x_3 + x_4 &= 5 \end{aligned}$

50. $\begin{aligned} 2x_1 - 3x_2 + x_3 &= 5 \\ -4x_1 + 6x_2 - 2x_3 &= 4 \end{aligned}$

51. (*See Example 8*)
$$\begin{aligned} x + 4y &= -10 \\ -2x + 3y &= -13 \\ 5x - 2y &= 16 \end{aligned}$$

52. $\begin{aligned} x + y &= -5 \\ 4x + 5y &= 2 \\ 3x + y &= 7 \end{aligned}$

53. $\begin{aligned} x - y &= -7 \\ x + y &= -3 \\ 3x - y &= -17 \end{aligned}$

54. $\begin{aligned} 3x + 4y &= 14 \\ 6x - y &= 10 \\ 3x - 5y &= -4 \end{aligned}$

II

55. (*See Example 9*)

$$x_2 + 2x_3 = 7$$
$$x_1 - 2x_2 - 6x_3 = -18$$
$$x_1 - x_2 - 2x_3 = -5$$
$$2x_1 - 5x_2 - 15x_3 = -46$$

56.

$$x_1 + x_2 - x_3 = 3$$
$$x_1 + 2x_2 + 2x_3 = 10$$
$$2x_1 + 3x_2 + x_3 = 13$$
$$x_1 \qquad - 4x_3 = -7$$

57.

$$3x_1 - 2x_2 + 4x_3 = 4$$
$$2x_1 + 5x_2 - x_3 = -2$$
$$x_1 - 7x_2 + 5x_3 = 6$$
$$5x_1 + 3x_2 + 3x_3 = 3$$

58.

$$x_1 - x_2 - 5x_3 = 4$$
$$x_1 + 2x_2 - x_3 = 7$$
$$3x_1 + 3x_2 - 7x_3 = 18$$
$$3x_2 + 4x_3 = 3$$

59. (*See Example 10*)

$$2x - 5y = 5$$
$$6x + y = 31$$
$$2x + 11y = 18$$

60.

$$2x_1 - 4x_2 - 14x_3 = 6$$
$$x_1 - x_2 - 5x_3 = 4$$
$$2x_1 - 4x_2 - 17x_3 = 9$$
$$-x_1 + 3x_2 + 10x_3 = -3$$
$$2x_2 + 2x_3 = 4$$

61.

$$x_1 - x_2 + 2x_3 \qquad = 7$$
$$3x_1 - 4x_2 + 18x_3 - 13x_4 = 17$$
$$2x_1 - 2x_2 + 2x_3 - 4x_4 = 12$$
$$-x_1 + x_2 - x_3 + 2x_4 = -6$$
$$-3x_1 + x_2 - 8x_3 - 10x_4 = -21$$

62.

$$4x_1 + 8x_2 - 12x_3 = 28$$
$$-x_1 - 2x_2 + 3x_3 = -7$$
$$2x_1 + 4x_2 - 6x_3 = 14$$
$$-3x_1 - 6x_2 + 9x_3 = 15$$

III

63.

$$x_1 + 2x_2 - x_3 - x_4 = 0$$
$$x_1 + 2x_2 \qquad + x_4 = 4$$
$$-x_1 - 2x_2 + 2x_3 + 4x_4 = 5$$
$$-x_1 - x_2 - x_3 \qquad = 1$$

64.

$$x_1 + 2x_2 - 2x_3 + 7x_4 + 7x_5 = 0$$
$$-x_1 - 2x_2 + 2x_3 - 9x_4 - 11x_5 = 0$$
$$x_3 - 2x_4 - x_5 = 0$$
$$2x_1 + 4x_2 - 3x_3 + 12x_4 + 13x_5 = 0$$

65.

$$x_1 + 2x_2 - 3x_3 + 2x_4 + 5x_5 - x_6 = 0$$
$$-2x_1 - 4x_2 + 6x_3 - x_4 - 4x_5 + 5x_6 = 0$$
$$3x_1 + 6x_2 - 9x_3 + 5x_4 + 13x_5 - 4x_6 = 0$$

66. A brokerage firm packaged blocks of common stocks, bonds, and preferred stocks into three different portfolios. They contained the following

PORTFOLIO I: three blocks of common stock, two blocks of bonds, and one block of preferred stock

PORTFOLIO II: one block of common stock, four blocks of bonds, and one block of preferred stock

PORTFOLIO III: five blocks of common stock, ten blocks of bonds, and three blocks of preferred stock

A customer wants to buy 50 blocks of common stock, 160 blocks of bonds, and 25 blocks of preferred stock. Show that it is impossible to fill this order with the portfolios described.

67. (*See Example 11*)
An investor bought $45,000 in stocks, bonds, and money market funds. The total invested in bonds and money market funds was twice the amount invested in stocks. The return on the stocks, bonds, and money market funds was 10%, 7%, and 7.5%, respectively. The total return was $3660. How much was purchased of each?

68. A contractor builds houses, duplexes, and apartment units. He has financial backing to build 250 units. He makes a profit of $4500 on each house, $4000 on each duplex, and $3000 on each apartment unit. Each house requires 10 man-months of labor, each duplex requires 12 man-months, and each apartment requires 6 man-months. How many of each should the contractor build if he has 2050 man-months of labor available and wishes to make a total profit of $875,000?

69. Celia had one hour to spend at the athletic club, where she will jog, play handball, and ride a bicycle. Jogging uses 13 calories per minute, handball 11, and cycling 7. She jogs twice as long as she rides the bicycle. How long should she participate in each of these activities in order to use 660 calories?

70. Here is a problem that has been making the rounds of offices and stores. It has most employees stumped. Use your skill to solve it.
A farmer has $100 to buy 100 chickens. Roosters cost $5 each, hens $3 each, and baby chicks $0.05 each. How many of each does the farmer buy if he must buy at least one of each and pay exactly $100 for exactly 100 chickens?

2–4 MATRIX OPERATIONS

- *Equal Matrices*
- *Addition of Matrices*
- *Scalar Multiplication*

In Section 2–3 we used an augmented matrix to represent a system of linear equations. We then performed row operations on the augmented matrix to arrive at a solution to the system. This is just one use of matrices. Matrices are also used to summarize information in tabular form. For example, a mathematics teacher records grade information for two sections of a mathematics course in the following matrix:

$$\begin{array}{c} & \text{Section} \\ & \begin{array}{cc} 1 & 2 \end{array} \\ \begin{array}{c} \text{Homework} \\ \text{Quizzes} \\ \text{Exams} \end{array} & \begin{bmatrix} 76 & 79 \\ 71 & 70 \\ 73 & 74 \end{bmatrix} \end{array}$$

Each row represents a different type of grade, and each column represents a section.

Since there is an endless variety of ways in which someone might want to break information into categories and summarize it, matrices come in various shapes and sizes. Independent of the source of information summarized in a matrix, we can classify matrices by the number of rows and columns they have. For example,

$$\begin{bmatrix} 3 & -1 & 4 \\ 2 & 1 & 5 \end{bmatrix}$$

is a 2 × 3 matrix because it has two rows and three columns.

$$\begin{bmatrix} 5 & 0 & 1 \\ 2 & 1 & 4 \\ 3 & 2 & 2 \\ -1 & 6 & -2 \end{bmatrix}$$

is a 4×3 matrix, having four rows and three columns. The convention used in describing the size of a matrix states the number of rows first, followed by the number of columns.

A matrix with the same number of rows as columns is said to be a **square matrix.** Two matrices are of the **same size** if they have the same number of rows and the same number of columns. For example,

$$\begin{bmatrix} -2 & 8 & -3 \\ 1 & 0 & 1 \end{bmatrix} \quad \text{and} \quad \begin{bmatrix} 2 & 5 & 9 \\ 3 & 6 & 7 \end{bmatrix}$$

are matrices of the same size; they are both 2×3 matrices.

EXAMPLE 1 *(Compare Exercise 1)*

The Campus Bookstore carries spirit shirts in white, green, and gold. In September it sold 238 white, 317 green, and 176 gold shirts. In October it sold 149 white, 342 green, and 369 gold shirts. In November it sold 184 white, 164 green, and 201 gold shirts. Summarize this information in a matrix.

SOLUTION   Let each of three columns represent a month and each of three rows represent a color of shirts. Label the columns and rows.

$$\begin{array}{c} \\ \text{White} \\ \text{Green} \\ \text{Gold} \end{array} \begin{array}{ccc} \text{Sept.} & \text{Oct.} & \text{Nov.} \\ \begin{bmatrix} 238 & 149 & 184 \\ 317 & 342 & 164 \\ 176 & 369 & 201 \end{bmatrix} \end{array}$$

EQUAL MATRICES

Two matrices of the same size are **equal matrices** if and only if their corresponding components are equal. If the matrices are not the same size, they are not equal.

EXAMPLE 2 *(Compare Exercise 17)*

$$\begin{bmatrix} 3 & 7 \\ 5 - 1 & 4 \times 4 \end{bmatrix} = \begin{bmatrix} \frac{6}{2} & 7 \\ 4 & 16 \end{bmatrix}$$

because corresponding components are equal.

$$\begin{bmatrix} 1 & 2 & 5 \\ 3 & 6 & 4 \end{bmatrix} \neq \begin{bmatrix} 1 & 2 & 5 \\ 3 & -1 & 4 \end{bmatrix}$$

because the entries in row 2, column 2 are different; that is, the $(2, 2)$ entries are not equal.

EXAMPLE 3 *(Compare Exercise 43)*

Find the value of x such that

$$\begin{bmatrix} 3 & 4x \\ 2.1 & 7 \end{bmatrix} = \begin{bmatrix} 3 & 9 \\ 2.1 & 7 \end{bmatrix}$$

SOLUTION   For the matrices to be equal, the corresponding components must be equal, so $4x = 9$ and $x = \frac{9}{4}$.   ▌

ADDITION OF MATRICES

A businessperson has two stores. She is interested in the daily sales of the regular size and the giant economy size of laundry soap. She can use matrices to record this information. These two matrices show sales for two days.

	STORE 1 2	STORE 1 2
REG. GIANT	$\begin{bmatrix} 8 & 12 \\ 9 & 7 \end{bmatrix}$	$\begin{bmatrix} 6 & 5 \\ 11 & 4 \end{bmatrix}$
	Day 1	Day 2

The position in the matrix identifies the store and package size. For example, store 2 sold 7 giant sizes and 12 regular on day 1, and so on.

The total sales, by store and package size, can be obtained by **addition of matrices.** Doesn't it seem reasonable that the sum of the two sales matrices is

$$\begin{bmatrix} 8 & 12 \\ 9 & 7 \end{bmatrix} + \begin{bmatrix} 6 & 5 \\ 11 & 4 \end{bmatrix} = \begin{bmatrix} 14 & 17 \\ 20 & 11 \end{bmatrix}$$

because we just add the sales in each individual category to get the total in that category? This procedure applies generally to the addition of matrices.

CAUTION   To add two matrices, they must be of the same size.

Definition
Matrix Addition

The **sum** of two matrices of the same size is obtained by adding corresponding elements. If two matrices are not of the same size, they cannot be added; we say that their sum does not exist. Subtraction is performed on matrices of the same size by subtracting corresponding elements.

EXAMPLE 4   *(Compare Exercise 23)*

For the following matrices:

$$A = \begin{bmatrix} -1 & 2 & 3 \\ 0 & 1 & 4 \end{bmatrix}, \quad B = \begin{bmatrix} 3 & -2 & 6 \\ 7 & -1 & 2 \end{bmatrix}, \quad C = \begin{bmatrix} -1 & 2 \\ 0 & 1 \end{bmatrix}$$

determine the sums $A + B$ and $A + C$ if possible.
SOLUTION

$$A + B = \begin{bmatrix} -1 & 2 & 3 \\ 0 & 1 & 4 \end{bmatrix} + \begin{bmatrix} 3 & -2 & 6 \\ 7 & -1 & 2 \end{bmatrix}$$

$$= \begin{bmatrix} -1 + 3 & 2 - 2 & 3 + 6 \\ 0 + 7 & 1 - 1 & 4 + 2 \end{bmatrix} = \begin{bmatrix} 2 & 0 & 9 \\ 7 & 0 & 6 \end{bmatrix}$$

Neither the sum $A + C$ nor $B + C$ exists, since matrices A and C and matrices B and C are not matrices of the same size. (Try adding these matrices using the rule.)

Let us extend our definition to enable us to add more than just two matrices. For example, define the sum of three matrices as

$$\begin{bmatrix} 1 & 2 \\ 0 & -1 \end{bmatrix} + \begin{bmatrix} 3 & 4 \\ 2 & 1 \end{bmatrix} + \begin{bmatrix} 5 & 2 \\ -1 & 0 \end{bmatrix} = \begin{bmatrix} 1+3+5 & 2+4+2 \\ 0+2-1 & -1+1+0 \end{bmatrix}$$

$$= \begin{bmatrix} 9 & 8 \\ 1 & 0 \end{bmatrix}$$

We add a string of matrices that are of the same size by adding corresponding elements. The following example illustrates a use of this rule.

EXAMPLE 5 *(Compare Exercise 41)*

A clinic has three doctors, each with his or her own specialty. Patients attending the clinic may see more than one doctor. The accounts are drawn up monthly and handled systematically through the use of matrices. We illustrate this accounting system with four patients. It can easily be extended to accommodate any number of patients.

	DOCTOR I	II	III
A	10	25	0
B	0	20	40
C	15	0	25
D	10	10	0

PATIENT

The entries in the above matrix are in dollars and represent the bill from each doctor to each patient for a certain month.

For a given quarter, three such matrices represent monthly bills. To determine the quarterly bill to each patient from each doctor, add the three matrices. Assume that the monthly bills are as follows:

FIRST MONTH + SECOND MONTH + THIRD MONTH = QUARTER

$$\begin{bmatrix} 10 & 25 & 0 \\ 0 & 20 & 40 \\ 15 & 0 & 25 \\ 10 & 10 & 0 \end{bmatrix} + \begin{bmatrix} 0 & 0 & 0 \\ 10 & 100 & 0 \\ 10 & 0 & 0 \\ 20 & 0 & 0 \end{bmatrix} + \begin{bmatrix} 20 & 0 & 0 \\ 0 & 0 & 0 \\ 0 & 0 & 20 \\ 15 & 15 & 0 \end{bmatrix} = \begin{bmatrix} 30 & 25 & 0 \\ 10 & 120 & 40 \\ 25 & 0 & 45 \\ 45 & 25 & 0 \end{bmatrix}$$

Thus A's bill from doctor I during the quarter would total $30; B's quarterly bill from doctor III would total $40; and so on.

Although this analysis and others like it can be carried out without the use of matrices, the handling of large quantities of data is often most efficiently done on computers using matrix techniques.

SCALAR MULTIPLICATION

Let us now turn our attention to multiplying matrices by numbers. We are interested in defining the following type of operation:

$$3\begin{bmatrix} 1 & 2 \\ 4 & 1 \end{bmatrix}$$

The product is

$$3\begin{bmatrix} 1 & 2 \\ 4 & 1 \end{bmatrix} = \begin{bmatrix} 3 & 6 \\ 12 & 3 \end{bmatrix}$$

Note that the net effect is that every element in the matrix is multiplied by 3. Let us use this example as a prototype for a definition of **scalar multiplication.** (*Scalar* is a term used by mathematicians for *number*.)

Definition
Scalar Multiplication

The operation of multiplying a matrix by a number is called **scalar multiplication.** It is carried out by multiplying every element in the matrix by the scalar.

EXAMPLE 6   *(Compare Exercise 31)*

$$-2\begin{bmatrix} 1 & 2 \\ 3 & 0 \\ 1 & -4 \end{bmatrix} = \begin{bmatrix} -2 & -4 \\ -6 & 0 \\ -2 & 8 \end{bmatrix}$$

EXAMPLE 7   *(Compare Exercise 47)*

The following matrix represents total trade figures between certain countries for the five-year period. The numbers are values in millions of U.S. dollars. We use this matrix to illustrate a manner in which scalar multiplication of a matrix can arise.

TO:	CANADA	E.C.	JAPAN	U.S.A.
FROM:				
CANADA	0	12,600	4,890	63,690
E.C.	9,230	0	8,280	56,510
JAPAN	4,020	13,230	0	37,170
U.S.A.	54,750	59,690	25,190	0

The annual average over this period is $\frac{1}{5}$ of the five-year figure. We can get the annual figures by scalar multiplying the above matrix by $\frac{1}{5}$:

TO:	CANADA	E.C.	JAPAN	U.S.A.

$$\left(\frac{1}{5}\right)A = \begin{array}{l} \text{FROM:} \\ \text{CANADA} \\ \text{E.C.} \\ \text{JAPAN} \\ \text{U.S.A.} \end{array} \begin{bmatrix} 0 & 2{,}520 & 978 & 12{,}738 \\ 1{,}846 & 0 & 1{,}656 & 11{,}302 \\ 804 & 2{,}646 & 0 & 7{,}434 \\ 10{,}950 & 11{,}938 & 5{,}038 & 0 \end{bmatrix}$$

EXAMPLE 8   *(Compare Exercise 51)*

A class of ten students had five tests during the quarter. A perfect score on each of the tests is 50. The scores are listed in Table 2–1.

We can express these scores as column matrices:

$$\begin{bmatrix} 40 \\ 20 \\ 40 \\ 25 \\ 35 \\ 50 \\ 22 \\ 35 \\ 28 \\ 40 \end{bmatrix} \begin{bmatrix} 45 \\ 15 \\ 35 \\ 40 \\ 35 \\ 46 \\ 24 \\ 27 \\ 31 \\ 35 \end{bmatrix} \begin{bmatrix} 30 \\ 30 \\ 25 \\ 45 \\ 38 \\ 45 \\ 30 \\ 20 \\ 25 \\ 36 \end{bmatrix} \begin{bmatrix} 48 \\ 25 \\ 45 \\ 40 \\ 37 \\ 48 \\ 32 \\ 41 \\ 27 \\ 32 \end{bmatrix} \begin{bmatrix} 42 \\ 10 \\ 46 \\ 38 \\ 39 \\ 47 \\ 29 \\ 30 \\ 31 \\ 38 \end{bmatrix}$$

To obtain each person's average, we use matrix addition to add the matrices and then scalar multiplication to multiply by $\frac{1}{5}$ (dividing by the number of tests). We get

$$\frac{1}{5}\begin{bmatrix} 205 \\ 100 \\ 191 \\ 188 \\ 184 \\ 236 \\ 137 \\ 153 \\ 142 \\ 181 \end{bmatrix} = \begin{bmatrix} 41.0 \\ 20.0 \\ 38.2 \\ 37.6 \\ 36.8 \\ 47.2 \\ 27.4 \\ 30.6 \\ 28.4 \\ 36.2 \end{bmatrix}$$ (Column matrix giving each person's average score)

TABLE 2–1

	TEST 1	TEST 2	TEST 3	TEST 4	TEST 5
Anderson	40	45	30	48	42
Boggs	20	15	30	25	10
Chittar	40	35	25	45	46
Diessner	25	40	45	40	38
Farnam	35	35	38	37	39
Gill	50	46	45	48	47
Homes	22	24	30	32	29
Johnson	35	27	20	41	30
Schomer	28	31	25	27	31
Wong	40	35	36	32	38

Row matrices are also useful; a person's complete set of scores corresponds to a row matrix. For example,

$$[25 \quad 40 \quad 45 \quad 40 \quad 38]$$

is a row matrix giving Diessner's scores.

This approach to analyzing test scores has the advantage of lending itself to implementation on the computer. A computer program can be written that will perform the desired matrix additions and scalar multiplications.

2-4 EXERCISES

I

In Exercises 1 through 4, summarize the given information in matrix form.

1. (*See Example 1*) The Alpha Club and the Beta Club perform service work for the Salvation Army, the Boys Club, and the Girl Scouts. The Alpha Club performs 50 hours at the Salvation Army, 85 hours at the Boy's Club, and 68 hours for the Girl Scouts. The Beta Club performs 65 hours at the Salvation Army, 32 hours at the Boy's Club, and 94 hours for the Girl Scouts.

2. An appliance salesperson sold 15 washers, 8 dryers, and 13 microwave ovens in March. She sold 12 washers, 11 dryers, and 6 microwave ovens in April.

3. Citizens' Bank awards prizes to the employees who sign the largest number of new customers. In October, Joe signed up 12 new checking accounts, 15 savings accounts, and eight safe deposit boxes. Jane signed up 11 new checking accounts, 18 savings accounts, and nine safe deposit boxes. Judy signed up five new checking accounts, eight savings accounts, and 21 safe deposit boxes.

4. Tom scored 78, 82, and 72 on the first three biology exams. Dick scored 62, 71, and 76. Harriet scored 98, 70, and 81.

State the size of each matrix in Exercises 5 through 16.

5. $\begin{bmatrix} 2 & -1 \\ 3 & 6 \end{bmatrix}$

6. $\begin{bmatrix} 1 & 2 \\ -1 & 3 \\ 4 & 6 \end{bmatrix}$

7. $\begin{bmatrix} 1 & 2 & 3 \\ -1 & 4 & 6 \\ 3 & 1 & 2 \end{bmatrix}$

8. $\begin{bmatrix} 1 & 2 & 3 & -1 \\ 4 & 6 & 0 & 1 \end{bmatrix}$

9. $\begin{bmatrix} 3 \\ -1 \\ 2 \end{bmatrix}$

10. $[-1 \quad 0 \quad 4 \quad 6]$

11. $\begin{bmatrix} 1 & 2 & -1 \\ 3 & 4 & 1 \end{bmatrix}$

12. $\begin{bmatrix} 1 & 2 & 3 & 1 \\ 2 & 1 & 6 & 0 \end{bmatrix}$

13. $\begin{bmatrix} 0 \\ 1 \end{bmatrix}$

14. $[0 \quad -3 \quad 2 \quad 6]$

15. $\begin{bmatrix} 1 & 2 \\ -1 & 3 \end{bmatrix}$

16. $\begin{bmatrix} 1 & 4 & 2 \\ 2 & 6 & 1 \\ 3 & -1 & 4 \end{bmatrix}$

In Exercises 17 through 22, determine which of the pairs of matrices are equal.

17. (*See Example 2*)
$\begin{bmatrix} 2 & 1 & 3 \\ 4 & 0 & 2 \end{bmatrix}, \begin{bmatrix} 4 & 0 & 2 \\ 2 & 1 & 3 \end{bmatrix}$

18. $\begin{bmatrix} \frac{3}{4} & 16 \\ 8 & \frac{1}{2} \end{bmatrix}, \begin{bmatrix} 0.75 & 16 \\ 8 & 0.5 \end{bmatrix}$

19. $\begin{bmatrix} 5+2 & 5-2 \\ \frac{5}{2} & \frac{2}{5} \end{bmatrix}, \begin{bmatrix} 7 & 3 \\ 2.5 & 0.4 \end{bmatrix}$

20. $\begin{bmatrix} 2 & 1 & 3 & 6 \\ 5 & 9 & 4 & 1 \end{bmatrix}, \begin{bmatrix} 2 & 3 & 6 \\ 5 & 4 & 1 \end{bmatrix}$

21. $\begin{bmatrix} -1 & 4 & 1 \\ 3 & 2 & 0 \end{bmatrix}, \begin{bmatrix} -1 & 3 \\ 4 & 2 \\ 1 & 0 \end{bmatrix}$

22. $\begin{bmatrix} 1 & 0 \\ 0 & 2 \end{bmatrix}, \begin{bmatrix} 2 & 0 \\ 0 & 1 \end{bmatrix}$

If possible, add the matrices in Exercises 23 through 30. We say that the sum does not exist if the matrices cannot be added.

23. (*See Example 4*)
$\begin{bmatrix} 1 & -1 & 3 \\ 2 & 4 & 1 \end{bmatrix} + \begin{bmatrix} 2 & 4 & -1 \\ 5 & 0 & 2 \end{bmatrix}$

24. $\begin{bmatrix} 0 & 1 \\ 2 & 3 \\ -1 & 4 \end{bmatrix} + \begin{bmatrix} 3 & -1 \\ 2 & 0 \\ 4 & -6 \end{bmatrix}$

25. $\begin{bmatrix} 2 \\ 5 \end{bmatrix} + \begin{bmatrix} -1 \\ 4 \end{bmatrix} + \begin{bmatrix} 1 \\ 49 \end{bmatrix}$

26. $\begin{bmatrix} 5 & 1 \\ -2 & 0 \end{bmatrix} + \begin{bmatrix} 2 & 8 \\ 4 & 6 \end{bmatrix}$

27. $[4 \quad 5 \quad 2] + [7 \quad -1]$

28. $\begin{bmatrix} 4 & 1 & 5 \\ 6 & -3 & 9 \end{bmatrix} + \begin{bmatrix} -1 & 3 \\ 6 & 8 \\ 7 & 2 \end{bmatrix}$

29. $\begin{bmatrix} 1 & 4 & 2 \\ 3 & 0 & 1 \\ 6 & -1 & 5 \end{bmatrix} + \begin{bmatrix} 5 & 1 & 6 \\ 2 & 1 & 2 \\ -1 & -2 & -1 \end{bmatrix}$

30. $\begin{bmatrix} 1 & 0 & 1 & 0 \\ 0 & 1 & 0 & 1 \\ 2 & 1 & 2 & 1 \\ 1 & 2 & 1 & 2 \end{bmatrix} + \begin{bmatrix} 3 & 4 & 3 & 4 \\ 2 & 5 & 2 & 5 \\ 3 & 0 & 3 & 0 \\ 2 & 2 & 3 & 3 \end{bmatrix}$

Perform the scalar multiplications in Exercises 31 through 37.

31. (*See Example 6*)
$3\begin{bmatrix} 4 & 1 \\ 2 & 5 \end{bmatrix}$

32. $2\begin{bmatrix} 3 & -2 & 1 \\ 6 & 0 & -3 \end{bmatrix}$

33. $5\begin{bmatrix} 4 \\ 3 \\ 1 \\ 2 \end{bmatrix}$

34. $-3\begin{bmatrix} 3 & 1 \\ -2 & 4 \end{bmatrix}$

35. $-3[4 \quad -2 \quad 5]$

36. $\frac{1}{2}\begin{bmatrix} 4 & 5 \\ 8 & 6 \end{bmatrix}$

37. $0\begin{bmatrix} 3 & 5 \\ 0 & -2 \end{bmatrix}$

II

38. The Music Store's inventory of recordings is:

POPULAR MUSIC: cassettes, 848; LPs, 145; CDs, 969

CLASSICAL MUSIC: cassettes, 159; LPs, 37; CDs, 246

The Sound Shop's inventory of recordings is:

POPULAR MUSIC: cassettes, 753; LPs, 252; CDs, 639

CLASSICAL MUSIC: cassettes, 342; LPs, 19; CDs, 113

(a) Represent the Music Store's inventory in a matrix *A* and the Sound Shop's inventory in a matrix *B*.

(b) If the stores merge, represent the merged inventory by adding the matrices.

39. If

$$A = \begin{bmatrix} 1 & 2 \\ 3 & 0 \end{bmatrix}, \qquad B = \begin{bmatrix} -1 & 2 \\ 1 & 1 \end{bmatrix},$$

$$C = \begin{bmatrix} 0 & 1 \\ 1 & 4 \end{bmatrix}$$

determine the matrices
(a) $2A$, $3B$, and $-2C$
(b) $A + B$, $B + A$, $A + C$, and $B + C$
(c) $A + 2B$, $3A + C$, and $2A + B - C$

40. If

$$A = \begin{bmatrix} -1 & 4 & 5 \\ 0 & 1 & 2 \end{bmatrix}, \qquad B = \begin{bmatrix} 1 & 1 & 0 \\ 2 & 3 & 1 \end{bmatrix},$$

$$C = \begin{bmatrix} 4 & 5 & 0 \\ 2 & -1 & -1 \end{bmatrix}$$

determine
(a) $A - B$, $B + 3C$, and $2B + C$
(b) $4A$, $-B$, and $3C$
(c) $A + 3B$, $2A - B + C$, and $A + 2B - 2C$

41. (*See Example 5*)
A distributor furnishes PC computers, printers, and diskettes to three customers. He summarizes monthly sales in a matrix.

	Customer								
	I	II	III	I	II	III	I	II	III
PC	5	7	8	8	6	5	10	4	7
Printer	6	4	5	10	9	4	3	9	2
Diskette	45	52	35	52	60	42	54	39	28
	June			July			August		

Find the three-month total by item and by customer.

In Exercises 42 through 46, find the value of x that makes the pairs of matrices equal.

42. $\begin{bmatrix} 3 & x \\ 2 & 1 \end{bmatrix} = \begin{bmatrix} 3 & 9 \\ 2 & 1 \end{bmatrix}$

43. (*See Example 3*)
$$\begin{bmatrix} 5x & 7 \\ 2 & 4 \end{bmatrix} = \begin{bmatrix} 15 & 7 \\ 2 & 4 \end{bmatrix}$$

44. $\begin{bmatrix} 2x + 3 & -2 \\ 6 & 1 \end{bmatrix} = \begin{bmatrix} 3x - 1 & -2 \\ 6 & 1 \end{bmatrix}$

45. $\begin{bmatrix} 17 & 6x + 4 \\ 94 & -39 \end{bmatrix} = \begin{bmatrix} 17 & 14x - 13 \\ 94 & -39 \end{bmatrix}$

46. $\begin{bmatrix} 2x + 1 & 6 \\ 5 & -4 \end{bmatrix} = 2\begin{bmatrix} 3x + 5 & 6 \\ 5 & -4 \end{bmatrix}$

47. (*See Example 7*)
A firm has three plants, all of which produce small, regular, and giant size boxes of detergent. The annual report shows the total production (in thousands of boxes), broken down by plant and size, in the following matrix:

	Plant		
	A	B	C
Small	65	110	80
Regular	90	135	60
Giant	75	112	84

Find the average monthly production by plant and size.

III

48. A cafeteria manager estimates that the amount of food needed to serve one person is

Meat: 4 oz
Peas: 2 oz
Rice: 3 oz
Bread: 1 slice
Milk: 1 cup

Use matrix arithmetic to find the amount needed to serve 114 people.

49. A manufacturer has plants at Fairfield and Tyler that produce the pollutants sulfur dioxide, nitric oxide, and particulate matter in the amounts shown in the matrix. The amounts are in kilograms and represent the average per month.

	Sulfur dioxide	Nitric oxide	Particulate matter
Fairfield	230	90	140
Tyler	260	115	166

Find the annual totals by plants and pollutant.

50. The total sales of regular and giant size detergent at two stores is given for three months.

	1	2	1	2	1	2
REGULAR	85	46	80	61	50	42
GIANT	77	93	93	47	61	38
	March		April		May	

Use matrix arithmetic to find the average monthly sales by store and size.

51. (*See Example 8*)
The test scores for five students are given in the following table.

	TEST 1	TEST 2	TEST 3
A	90	88	91
B	62	69	73
C	76	78	72
D	82	80	84
E	74	76	77

Use matrix arithmetic to find each student's average.

2–5 MULTIPLICATION OF MATRICES

- *Dot Product*

- *Matrix Multiplication*

You have learned to add matrices and multiply a matrix by a number. It is natural to ask whether one can multiply two matrices together and whether this helps to solve problems. Mathematicians have devised a way of multiplying two matrices. It might seem rather complicated, but it has many useful applications. For example, you will learn how to use matrix multiplication to solve a problem like the following.

A manufacturer makes tables and chairs. The time, in hours, required to assemble and finish the items is given by the matrix

$$\begin{array}{c} \\ \text{Assemble} \\ \text{Finish} \end{array} \begin{array}{c} \text{Chair} \quad \text{Table} \\ \begin{bmatrix} 2 & 3 \\ 2.5 & 4.75 \end{bmatrix} \end{array}$$

The total assembly and finishing time required to produce 950 chairs and 635 tables can be obtained by an appropriate matrix multiplication.

Before we show you how to multiply matrices, here's an overview of the process.

1. For two matrices A and B we will find their product AB. Call their product C ($AB = C$).
2. C is a matrix. The problem is to find the entries of C.
3. Each entry in C will depend on a row from matrix A and a column from matrix B.

We call the entry in row i and column j the (i, j) entry of a matrix. The (i, j) entry in C is a number obtained using all entries of row i in A and using all entries of column j in B. For example, the $(2, 3)$ entry in C depends on row 2 of A and column 3 of B. We show you how to find an entry in C by using the **dot product** of a row in A and a column in B.

DOT PRODUCT

We use the two matrices

$$A = \begin{bmatrix} 1 & 3 \\ 2 & -1 \end{bmatrix} \quad \text{and} \quad B = \begin{bmatrix} 4 & -5 \\ 1 & 6 \end{bmatrix}$$

to illustrate matrix multiplication. We use the first row of A, R1 $= [1 \quad 3]$, and the first column of B,

$$C1 = \begin{bmatrix} 4 \\ 1 \end{bmatrix}$$

to find the $(1, 1)$ entry of the product. To do so, we need to find what is called the **dot product,** R1 $\cdot$ C1, of the row and column. It is

$$\text{R1} \cdot \text{C1} = [1 \quad 3] \cdot \begin{bmatrix} 4 \\ 1 \end{bmatrix} = 1(4) + 3(1) = 7$$

Notice the following:

1. The dot product of a row and a column is a single number.
2. Obtain the dot product by multiplying the first numbers from both the row and column, then the second numbers from both, etc., and then adding the results.

There are three other dot products possible using a row from A and a column from B. They are:

$$\text{R1} \cdot \text{C2} = [1 \quad 3] \cdot \begin{bmatrix} -5 \\ 6 \end{bmatrix} = 1(-5) + 3(6) = 13$$

$$\text{R2} \cdot \text{C1} = [2 \quad -1] \cdot \begin{bmatrix} 4 \\ 1 \end{bmatrix} = 2(4) + (-1)(1) = 7$$

$$\text{R2} \cdot \text{C2} = [2 \quad -1] \cdot \begin{bmatrix} -5 \\ 6 \end{bmatrix} = 2(-5) + (-1)(6) = -16$$

The general form of the dot product of a row and column is

$$[a_1 \quad a_2 \quad \cdots \quad a_n] \cdot \begin{bmatrix} b_1 \\ b_2 \\ \vdots \\ b_n \end{bmatrix} = a_1 b_1 + a_2 b_2 + \cdots + a_n b_n$$

NOTE The dot product is defined only when the row and column matrices have the same number of entries.

The total cost of a purchase at the grocery store can be determined by using the dot product of a price matrix and a quantity matrix as illustrated in the next example.

EXAMPLE 1   *(Compare Exercise 7)*

Let the row matrix [.95   1.75   2.15] represent the prices of a loaf of bread, a six-pack of soft drinks, and a package of granola bars, in that order. Let

$$\begin{bmatrix} 5 \\ 3 \\ 4 \end{bmatrix}$$

represent the quantity of bread (5), soft drinks (3), and granola bars (4) purchased in that order. Then

$$[0.95 \quad 1.75 \quad 2.15] \cdot \begin{bmatrix} 5 \\ 3 \\ 4 \end{bmatrix} = 0.95(5) + 1.75(3) + 2.15(4)$$

$$= 4.75 + 5.25 + 8.60 = 18.60$$

gives the total cost of the purchase.

MATRIX MULTIPLICATION

Recall that we said the entries in $C = AB$ depend on a row of A and a column of B. The entries are actually the dot product of a row and column. In the product

$$C = AB = \begin{bmatrix} 1 & 3 \\ 2 & -1 \end{bmatrix} \begin{bmatrix} 4 & -5 \\ 1 & 6 \end{bmatrix}$$

the (1, 2) entry in C is the dot product R1 $\cdot$ C2, for example. In the product AB,

$$C = \begin{bmatrix} R1 \cdot C1 & R1 \cdot C2 \\ R2 \cdot C1 & R2 \cdot C2 \end{bmatrix}$$

$$= \begin{bmatrix} [1 \quad 3] \cdot \begin{bmatrix} 4 \\ 1 \end{bmatrix} & [1 \quad 3] \cdot \begin{bmatrix} -5 \\ 6 \end{bmatrix} \\ [2 \quad -1] \cdot \begin{bmatrix} 4 \\ 1 \end{bmatrix} & [2 \quad -1] \cdot \begin{bmatrix} -5 \\ 6 \end{bmatrix} \end{bmatrix}$$

$$= \begin{bmatrix} 1(4) + 3(1) & 1(-5) + 3(6) \\ 2(4) + (-1)(1) & 2(-5) + (-1)(6) \end{bmatrix}$$

$$= \begin{bmatrix} 7 & 13 \\ 7 & -16 \end{bmatrix}$$

EXAMPLE 2   *(Compare Exercise 11)*

Find the product AB of

$$A = \begin{bmatrix} 1 & 3 & 2 \\ -1 & 0 & 4 \end{bmatrix} \quad \text{and} \quad B = \begin{bmatrix} 7 & 5 \\ -2 & 6 \\ -3 & -4 \end{bmatrix}$$

SOLUTION

$$AB = \begin{bmatrix} R1 \cdot C1 & R1 \cdot C2 \\ R2 \cdot C1 & R2 \cdot C2 \end{bmatrix}$$

$$= \begin{bmatrix} 1(7) + 3(-2) + 2(-3) & 1(5) + 3(6) + 2(-4) \\ (-1)(7) + 0(-2) + 4(-3) & -1(5) + 0(6) + 4(-4) \end{bmatrix}$$

$$= \begin{bmatrix} -5 & 15 \\ -19 & -21 \end{bmatrix} .$$

EXAMPLE 3   *(Compare Exercise 22)*

Multiply the matrices

$$A = \begin{bmatrix} 1 & 3 \\ 5 & 4 \end{bmatrix} \quad \text{and} \quad B = \begin{bmatrix} -1 & 6 \\ 2 & 7 \\ 0 & 8 \end{bmatrix}$$

SOLUTION   The product AB is not possible because a row-column dot product can occur only when the row of A and the column of B have the same number of entries.

This example illustrates that two matrices may or may not have a product. There must be the same number of columns in the first matrix as the number of rows in the second in order for multiplication to be possible.

Multiplication of Matrices   Given matrices A and B, to find $AB = C$ (**matrix multiplication**):

1. Check the number of columns of A and the number of rows of B. If they are equal, the product is possible. If they are not equal, no product is possible.
2. Form all possible dot products using a row from A and a column from B. The dot product of row i with column j gives the entry for the (i, j) position in C.

We now return to the problem at the beginning of the section.

EXAMPLE 4   *(Compare Exercise 53)*

The time, in hours, required to assemble and finish a table and a chair is given by the matrix

$$\begin{array}{c} \\ \text{Assemble} \\ \text{Finish} \end{array} \begin{array}{cc} \text{Chair} & \text{Table} \\ \begin{bmatrix} 2 & 3 \\ 2.5 & 4.75 \end{bmatrix} \end{array}$$

How long will it take to assemble and finish 950 chairs and 635 tables?

SOLUTION   Matrix multiplication gives the answer when we let

$$\begin{bmatrix} 950 \\ 635 \end{bmatrix}$$

be the column matrix that specifies the number of chairs and tables produced. Multiply the matrices:

$$\begin{bmatrix} 2 & 3 \\ 2.5 & 4.75 \end{bmatrix} \begin{bmatrix} 950 \\ 635 \end{bmatrix} = \begin{bmatrix} 2(950) & + \ 3(635) \\ 2.5(950) & + \ 4.75(635) \end{bmatrix} = \begin{bmatrix} 3805 \\ 5391.25 \end{bmatrix}$$

The rows of the result correspond to the rows in the first matrix; the first row in each represents assembly time, and the second represents finishing time. In the final matrix, 3805 is the *total* number of hours of assembly, and 5391.25 is the *total* number of hours for finishing required for 950 chairs and 635 tables.

EXAMPLE 5

Find *AB* and *BA:*

$$A = \begin{bmatrix} 1 & 3 \\ 5 & -2 \end{bmatrix} \quad \text{and} \quad B = \begin{bmatrix} 2 & 1 \\ 3 & -4 \end{bmatrix}$$

SOLUTION

$$AB = \begin{bmatrix} 1 & 3 \\ 5 & -2 \end{bmatrix} \begin{bmatrix} 2 & 1 \\ 3 & -4 \end{bmatrix} = \begin{bmatrix} 11 & -11 \\ 4 & 13 \end{bmatrix}$$

$$BA = \begin{bmatrix} 2 & 1 \\ 3 & -4 \end{bmatrix} \begin{bmatrix} 1 & 3 \\ 5 & -2 \end{bmatrix} = \begin{bmatrix} 7 & 4 \\ -17 & 17 \end{bmatrix}$$

This example shows that *AB* and *BA* are not always equal. In fact, sometimes one of them may exist and the other not. The following example illustrates this.

EXAMPLE 6   *(Compare Exercise 33)*

Find *AB* and *BA,* if possible.

$$A = \begin{bmatrix} 1 & 2 & 3 \\ -4 & 0 & -2 \\ 1 & 1 & 1 \end{bmatrix} \quad \text{and} \quad B = \begin{bmatrix} 5 & -2 \\ 1 & 4 \\ 2 & 3 \end{bmatrix}$$

SOLUTION

$$AB = \begin{bmatrix} 1 & 2 & 3 \\ -4 & 0 & -2 \\ 1 & 1 & 1 \end{bmatrix} \begin{bmatrix} 5 & -2 \\ 1 & 4 \\ 2 & 3 \end{bmatrix} = \begin{bmatrix} 13 & 15 \\ -24 & 2 \\ 8 & 5 \end{bmatrix}$$

$$BA = \begin{bmatrix} 5 & -2 \\ 1 & 4 \\ 2 & 3 \end{bmatrix} \begin{bmatrix} 1 & 2 & 3 \\ -4 & 0 & -2 \\ 1 & 1 & 1 \end{bmatrix} = 5(1) + (-2)(-4) + ?(1)$$

When we attempt to use row 1 from B and column 1 from A to find the $(1, 1)$ entry of BA, we find no entry in row 1 to multiply by the bottom entry, 1, of column 1. Therefore we cannot complete the computation. BA does not exist. ∎

EXAMPLE 7   *(Compare Exercise 55)*

The Kaplans have 150 shares of Acme Corp., 100 shares of High Tech, and 240 shares of ABC in an investment portfolio. The closing prices of these stocks one week were:

Monday: Acme, $56; High Tech, $132; ABC, $19
Tuesday: Acme, $55; High Tech, $133; ABC, $19
Wednesday: Acme, $55; High Tech, $131; ABC, $20
Thursday: Acme, $54; High Tech, $130; ABC, $22
Friday: Acme, $53; High Tech, $128; ABC, $21

Summarize the closing prices in a matrix. Write the number of shares in a matrix and find the value of the Kaplans' portfolio each day by matrix multiplication.

SOLUTION   Set up the matrix of closing prices by letting each column represent a stock and each row a day:

$$
\begin{array}{c}
 \\
 \\
\text{Mon.} \\
\text{Tue.} \\
\text{Wed.} \\
\text{Thur.} \\
\text{Fri.}
\end{array}
\begin{array}{ccc}
\text{Acme} & \text{High Tech} & \text{ABC} \\
\end{array}
\begin{bmatrix}
56 & 132 & 19 \\
55 & 133 & 19 \\
55 & 131 & 20 \\
54 & 130 & 22 \\
53 & 128 & 21
\end{bmatrix}
$$

We point out that using rows to represent stocks and columns to represent days is also acceptable. The matrix showing the number of each share could be either a row matrix or a column matrix. Which of the matrices giving the number of shares,

$$
\begin{bmatrix} 150 & 100 & 240 \end{bmatrix} \qquad \text{or} \qquad \begin{bmatrix} 150 \\ 100 \\ 240 \end{bmatrix}
$$

should be used? First of all, notice that the products

$$
\begin{bmatrix} 150 & 100 & 240 \end{bmatrix}
\begin{bmatrix}
56 & 132 & 19 \\
55 & 133 & 19 \\
55 & 131 & 20 \\
54 & 130 & 22 \\
53 & 128 & 21
\end{bmatrix}
$$

$$\begin{bmatrix} 150 \\ 100 \\ 240 \end{bmatrix} \begin{bmatrix} 56 & 132 & 19 \\ 55 & 133 & 19 \\ 55 & 131 & 20 \\ 54 & 130 & 22 \\ 53 & 128 & 21 \end{bmatrix}$$

$$\begin{bmatrix} 56 & 132 & 19 \\ 55 & 133 & 19 \\ 55 & 131 & 20 \\ 54 & 130 & 22 \\ 53 & 128 & 21 \end{bmatrix} \begin{bmatrix} 150 & 100 & 240 \end{bmatrix}$$

are not possible.

The product

$$\begin{bmatrix} 56 & 132 & 19 \\ 55 & 133 & 19 \\ 55 & 131 & 20 \\ 54 & 130 & 22 \\ 53 & 128 & 21 \end{bmatrix} \begin{bmatrix} 150 \\ 100 \\ 240 \end{bmatrix} = \begin{bmatrix} 26{,}160 \\ 26{,}110 \\ 26{,}150 \\ 26{,}380 \\ 25{,}790 \end{bmatrix}$$

is possible. Does it give the desired result? Notice that the first entry in the answer, 26,160, is obtained by

$$56(150) + 132(100) + 19(240)$$

which is

(price of Acme) $\times$ (no. shares of Acme)
$+$ (price of High Tech) $\times$ (no. shares of High Tech)
$+$ (price of ABC) $\times$ (no. shares of ABC)

This is exactly what is needed to find the total value of the portfolio on Monday. The other entries are correct for the other days.

When you use a matrix product in an application, check to see which order of multiplication makes sense.

2–5 EXERCISES

I

Find the dot products in Exercises 1 through 6.

1. $[1 \quad 3] \cdot \begin{bmatrix} 2 \\ 4 \end{bmatrix}$

2. $[-2 \quad 5] \cdot \begin{bmatrix} 4 \\ 1 \end{bmatrix}$

3. $[6 \quad 5] \cdot \begin{bmatrix} 2 \\ 0 \end{bmatrix}$

4. $[3 \quad -1 \quad 2] \cdot \begin{bmatrix} -2 \\ 5 \\ 3 \end{bmatrix}$

5. $[1 \quad 0 \quad 1] \cdot \begin{bmatrix} 6 \\ 7 \\ 8 \end{bmatrix}$

6. $[2 \quad 1 \quad 3 \quad -2] \cdot \begin{bmatrix} 5 \\ 5 \\ -1 \\ 3 \end{bmatrix}$

7. (*See Example 1*) The price matrix of bread, milk, and cheese is, in that order, [0.90 1.85 0.65]. The quantity of each purchased, in the same order, is given by the column matrix

$$\begin{bmatrix} 2 \\ 1 \\ 4 \end{bmatrix}$$

Find the total bill for the purchases.

8. Find the total bill for the purchase of hamburgers, fries, and drink where the price and quantities are listed in that order in the matrices.

$$\text{Price matrix} = [1.65 \quad 0.80 \quad 0.59],$$

$$\text{quantity matrix} = \begin{bmatrix} 10 \\ 15 \\ 8 \end{bmatrix}$$

Find the products in Exercises 9 through 12.

9. $\begin{bmatrix} 3 & 1 \\ 2 & 4 \end{bmatrix}\begin{bmatrix} -2 & 3 \\ 1 & 2 \end{bmatrix}$ 10. $\begin{bmatrix} -6 & 2 \\ 0 & 4 \end{bmatrix}\begin{bmatrix} 1 & -1 \\ 3 & 5 \end{bmatrix}$

11. (*See Example 2*)

$$\begin{bmatrix} 2 & 1 & 4 \\ 3 & -1 & 5 \end{bmatrix}\begin{bmatrix} 3 & -2 \\ 0 & 2 \\ 6 & 1 \end{bmatrix}$$

12. $\begin{bmatrix} 1 & 2 & 3 \\ 5 & -1 & 2 \end{bmatrix}\begin{bmatrix} 1 & 0 \\ 3 & 2 \\ 4 & 5 \end{bmatrix}$

Compute the products in Exercises 13 through 20, if they exist.

13. $\begin{bmatrix} 1 & 2 \\ -1 & 3 \end{bmatrix}\begin{bmatrix} 2 & 4 \\ 6 & 1 \end{bmatrix}$ 14. $\begin{bmatrix} 2 & 1 \\ 3 & 6 \end{bmatrix}\begin{bmatrix} 0 & -1 \\ 2 & 4 \end{bmatrix}$

15. $\begin{bmatrix} 4 & 1 \\ 2 & 3 \end{bmatrix}\begin{bmatrix} 1 \\ 6 \end{bmatrix}$ 16. $\begin{bmatrix} 1 & 2 & 3 \\ -1 & 4 & 6 \end{bmatrix}\begin{bmatrix} 0 & 1 \\ 2 & 3 \end{bmatrix}$

17. $\begin{bmatrix} 1 & 2 \\ 3 & -1 \\ 4 & 6 \end{bmatrix}\begin{bmatrix} 1 & 2 \\ 3 & 1 \end{bmatrix}$

18. $\begin{bmatrix} 1 & 2 & -1 \\ 0 & 3 & 1 \\ 2 & 4 & 6 \end{bmatrix}\begin{bmatrix} 1 & 2 \\ 2 & 2 \\ 3 & -1 \end{bmatrix}$

19. $\begin{bmatrix} -1 & 2 & 0 \\ 6 & 3 & 1 \\ 4 & 1 & 3 \end{bmatrix}\begin{bmatrix} 0 & 2 & 1 \\ -6 & 3 & -1 \\ 4 & 1 & 2 \end{bmatrix}$

20. $[1 \quad 2 \quad 3]\begin{bmatrix} 1 & 3 \\ 1 & 1 \\ 2 & 1 \end{bmatrix}$

Find the products in Exercises 21 through 28, if possible.

21. $\begin{bmatrix} 0 & 1 \\ 2 & 3 \end{bmatrix}\begin{bmatrix} 1 & -1 \\ 2 & 3 \end{bmatrix}$

22. (*See Example 3*)

$[1 \quad 1 \quad 2]\begin{bmatrix} 1 \\ 3 \end{bmatrix}$

23. $\begin{bmatrix} 1 & 2 & 3 \\ -1 & 4 & 6 \end{bmatrix}\begin{bmatrix} 0 & 1 \\ 2 & 3 \end{bmatrix}$

24. $\begin{bmatrix} 1 & 3 & 1 \\ 2 & 4 & 2 \end{bmatrix}\begin{bmatrix} 1 & 0 & 5 \\ 3 & -1 & 1 \\ 1 & 4 & 3 \end{bmatrix}$

25. $\begin{bmatrix} 1 & 2 \\ 3 & 1 \end{bmatrix}\begin{bmatrix} 1 & 2 \\ 5 & 2 \\ 6 & 3 \end{bmatrix}$

26. $[1 \quad 2 \quad 3]\begin{bmatrix} 1 & 4 \\ 2 & 6 \end{bmatrix}$

27. $\begin{bmatrix} 1 & 2 & 3 \\ -1 & 4 & 6 \\ 2 & 1 & 3 \end{bmatrix}\begin{bmatrix} 1 \\ 2 \end{bmatrix}$

28. $\begin{bmatrix} 1 & 3 \\ 2 & 2 \end{bmatrix}\begin{bmatrix} 6 & 5 & -2 & -1 \\ 3 & 7 & 3 & 1 \end{bmatrix}$

Find *AB* and *BA* in Exercises 29 through 32.

29. $A = \begin{bmatrix} 1 & 2 \\ 0 & 1 \end{bmatrix}, B = \begin{bmatrix} 3 & 4 \\ -1 & 2 \end{bmatrix}$

30. $A = \begin{bmatrix} 1 & 2 & 3 \\ 4 & 0 & -2 \end{bmatrix}, B = \begin{bmatrix} 3 & 5 \\ 1 & -4 \\ 3 & 1 \end{bmatrix}$

31. $A = \begin{bmatrix} 1 & 3 \\ -1 & 2 \end{bmatrix}, B = \begin{bmatrix} 0 & 1 \\ -1 & 3 \end{bmatrix}$

32. $A = [1 \quad 3 \quad 4], B = \begin{bmatrix} 2 \\ 5 \\ 1 \end{bmatrix}$

In Exercises 33 through 36, find AB and BA, if possible.

33. (*See Example 6*)
$$A = \begin{bmatrix} 1 & 2 \\ -3 & 1 \end{bmatrix}, B = \begin{bmatrix} 4 & 2 & 3 \\ 1 & 0 & 5 \end{bmatrix}$$

34. $A = \begin{bmatrix} 1 & 2 & 3 \\ 4 & 1 & 2 \\ 3 & -1 & 0 \end{bmatrix}, B = \begin{bmatrix} 1 \\ 2 \\ 3 \end{bmatrix}$

35. $A = \begin{bmatrix} 1 & 3 & 5 \end{bmatrix}, B = \begin{bmatrix} -1 & 4 \\ 6 & 3 \\ 2 & 5 \end{bmatrix}$

36. $A = \begin{bmatrix} 2 & 4 & 6 \end{bmatrix}, B = \begin{bmatrix} 5 \\ 3 \end{bmatrix}$

II

Perform the indicated matrix operations in Exercises 37 through 52.

37. $\begin{bmatrix} 1 & 2 & 3 \end{bmatrix} \begin{bmatrix} 1 & 2 \\ 0 & 1 \\ 4 & 3 \end{bmatrix} \begin{bmatrix} 1 & 3 \\ 2 & 4 \end{bmatrix}$

38. $\begin{bmatrix} 1 & 2 \\ 0 & 3 \end{bmatrix} \begin{bmatrix} 3 & 0 & -2 \\ 4 & 1 & 1 \end{bmatrix} \begin{bmatrix} 1 \\ 2 \\ 3 \end{bmatrix}$

39. $\begin{bmatrix} 0 & 1 & 2 & 3 \\ 4 & 1 & 2 & 5 \\ -1 & 2 & 3 & 1 \\ 1 & 2 & 9 & 7 \end{bmatrix} \begin{bmatrix} 1 & 2 & 3 & 2 & 6 \\ 2 & 4 & 1 & -9 & 2 \\ 3 & 6 & 0 & 7 & 3 \\ -1 & 7 & \frac{1}{2} & 8 & 4 \end{bmatrix}$

40. $\begin{bmatrix} 1 & 2 \\ 3 & 1 \end{bmatrix} \begin{bmatrix} 3 & 4 \\ -1 & 5 \end{bmatrix} + \begin{bmatrix} 0 & 2 \\ 1 & 1 \end{bmatrix}$

41. $\begin{bmatrix} -1 & 3 & 1 \\ 2 & 1 & 3 \end{bmatrix} \begin{bmatrix} 1 & 3 \\ 1 & 1 \\ 2 & 1 \end{bmatrix} + \begin{bmatrix} 1 & 2 \\ 3 & 1 \end{bmatrix} \begin{bmatrix} -1 & 2 \\ 4 & 3 \end{bmatrix}$

42. $\begin{bmatrix} 1 & 2 & 3 \end{bmatrix} \begin{bmatrix} 1 & 1 \\ 2 & 1 \\ -1 & 2 \end{bmatrix} - \begin{bmatrix} 1 & 2 \end{bmatrix} \begin{bmatrix} 1 & 4 \\ 3 & 1 \end{bmatrix}$

43. $\begin{bmatrix} 1 & 2 \\ 3 & 1 \end{bmatrix} \begin{bmatrix} 1 & 0 \\ 0 & 1 \end{bmatrix}$

44. $\begin{bmatrix} 1 & 0 \\ 0 & 1 \end{bmatrix} \begin{bmatrix} 3 & -1 \\ 2 & 6 \end{bmatrix}$

45. $\begin{bmatrix} 1 & 2 & 3 \\ 4 & -1 & 0 \\ 2 & 1 & 7 \end{bmatrix} \begin{bmatrix} 1 & 0 & 0 \\ 0 & 1 & 0 \\ 0 & 0 & 1 \end{bmatrix}$

46. $\begin{bmatrix} 1 & 2 & 3 & 4 \\ 0 & -1 & 4 & 2 \\ 3 & 1 & 2 & 0 \\ 1 & 2 & 3 & 1 \end{bmatrix} \begin{bmatrix} 1 & 0 & 0 & 0 \\ 0 & 1 & 0 & 0 \\ 0 & 0 & 1 & 0 \\ 0 & 0 & 0 & 1 \end{bmatrix}$

47. $\begin{bmatrix} 3 & 1 \\ 2 & 4 \end{bmatrix} \begin{bmatrix} x \\ y \end{bmatrix}$

48. $\begin{bmatrix} 2 & 1 & 3 \\ 4 & -2 & 6 \\ 1 & 5 & -4 \end{bmatrix} \begin{bmatrix} x \\ y \\ z \end{bmatrix}$

49. $\begin{bmatrix} 1 & 2 & -1 \\ 3 & 1 & 4 \\ 2 & -1 & -1 \end{bmatrix} \begin{bmatrix} x_1 \\ x_2 \\ x_3 \end{bmatrix}$

50. $\begin{bmatrix} 1 & 5 & 9 \\ 2 & 1 & 6 \end{bmatrix} \begin{bmatrix} x_1 \\ x_2 \\ x_3 \end{bmatrix}$

51. $\begin{bmatrix} 1 & 3 & 5 & 6 \\ -2 & 9 & 6 & 1 \\ 8 & 0 & 17 & 5 \end{bmatrix} \begin{bmatrix} x_1 \\ x_2 \\ x_3 \\ x_4 \end{bmatrix}$

52. $\begin{bmatrix} 1 & 0 & 2 & -1 \\ 5 & 4 & 1 & 2 \\ 1 & 6 & -3 & -1 \\ 1 & -1 & 1 & -1 \end{bmatrix} \begin{bmatrix} x_1 \\ x_2 \\ x_3 \\ x_4 \end{bmatrix}$

III

53. (*See Example 4*)
The Home Entertainment Firm makes stereos and TV sets. The matrix below shows the time required for assembly and checking.

	Stereo	TV
Assembly	4	5.5
Check	1	2

Use matrices to determine the total assembly time and total checking time for 300 stereos and 450 TV sets.

54. Speed King Corp. has two production lines, I and II. Both produce ten-speed and three-speed bicycles. The number produced per hour is given by the matrix

	Line I	Line II
Three-speed	10	15
Ten-speed	12	20

Find the number of each type bicycle that is produced if Line I operates 60 hours and Line II 48 hours.

55. (*See Example 7*) An investment portfolio contains 60 shares of SCM and 140 shares of Apex Corp. The closing prices on three days were:

MONDAY: SCM, $114; Apex, $85
WEDNESDAY: SCM, $118; Apex, $84
FRIDAY: SCM, $116; Apex, $86

Use matrix multiplication to find the value of the portfolio on each of the three days.

56. The following matrix gives the vitamin content of a typical breakfast in conveniently chosen units:

	Vitamin A	B_1	B_2	C
Orange juice	500	0.2	0	129
Oatmeal	0	0.2	0	0
Milk	1560	0.32	1.7	6
Biscuit	0	0	0	0
Butter	460	0	0	0

If you have one unit of orange juice, one unit of oatmeal, $\frac{1}{4}$ unit of milk, two units of biscuit, and two units of butter, find the matrix that tells how much of each type vitamin you have consumed. (Notice that you need to multiply a row matrix of the units times the given matrix.)

57. Use the vitamin content from Exercise 56. Two breakfast menus are summarized in the matrix

	Menus I	II
Orange juice	0.5	0
Oatmeal	1.5	1.0
Milk	0.5	1.0
Biscuit	1.0	3.0
Butter	1.0	2.0

Find the matrix that tells the amount of each vitamin consumed in each diet.

58. Data from three supermarkets are summarized in this matrix.

	Store 1	Store 2	Store 3
Sugar (per pound)	64¢	62¢	68¢
Peaches (per can)	63¢	68¢	71¢
Chicken (per pound)	59¢	58¢	57¢
Bread (per loaf)	80¢	82¢	78¢

What is the total grocery bill at each store if the following purchase is made at each store: five pounds of sugar, three cans of peaches, three pounds chicken, and two loaves of bread?

2–6 THE INVERSE OF A MATRIX

- *Identity Matrix*
- *Inverse of a Square Matrix*
- *Matrix Equations*
- *Using A^{-1} to Solve a System*

IDENTITY MATRIX

You are familiar with the number fact

$$1 \cdot a = a \cdot 1 = a$$

where a is any real number. We call 1 the **identity** for multiplication.

We have no similar property for multiplication of matrices; there is no matrix I such that $AI = IA = A$ for all matrices A. However, there is such a matrix for certain sets of matrices. For example, if

$$A = \begin{bmatrix} 4 & 3 \\ 7 & 2 \end{bmatrix} \qquad \text{and} \qquad I = \begin{bmatrix} 1 & 0 \\ 0 & 1 \end{bmatrix}$$

then

$$AI = \begin{bmatrix} 4 & 3 \\ 7 & 2 \end{bmatrix} \begin{bmatrix} 1 & 0 \\ 0 & 1 \end{bmatrix} = \begin{bmatrix} 4 & 3 \\ 7 & 2 \end{bmatrix} = A$$

and

$$IA = \begin{bmatrix} 1 & 0 \\ 0 & 1 \end{bmatrix} \begin{bmatrix} 4 & 3 \\ 7 & 2 \end{bmatrix} = \begin{bmatrix} 4 & 3 \\ 7 & 2 \end{bmatrix} = A$$

Furthermore, for any 2×2 matrix A, the matrix I has the property that $AI = A$ and $IA = A$. This can be justified by using a 2×2 matrix with arbitrary entries

$$A = \begin{bmatrix} a & b \\ c & d \end{bmatrix}$$

Now

$$AI = \begin{bmatrix} a & b \\ c & d \end{bmatrix} \begin{bmatrix} 1 & 0 \\ 0 & 1 \end{bmatrix} \begin{bmatrix} a \times 1 + b \times 0 & a \times 0 + b \times 1 \\ c \times 1 + d \times 0 & c \times 0 + d \times 1 \end{bmatrix}$$

$$= \begin{bmatrix} a & b \\ c & d \end{bmatrix} = A$$

You should now multiply IA to verify that it is indeed A. Thus

$$\begin{bmatrix} 1 & 0 \\ 0 & 1 \end{bmatrix}$$

is the **identity matrix** for all 2×2 matrices. If we try to multiply the 3×3 matrix

$$A = \begin{bmatrix} 1 & 2 & 3 \\ 5 & 7 & 12 \\ 8 & 4 & -2 \end{bmatrix} \qquad \text{by} \qquad \begin{bmatrix} 1 & 0 \\ 0 & 1 \end{bmatrix}$$

we find we are unable to multiply at all because A has 3 columns and I has only two rows. So

$$\begin{bmatrix} 1 & 0 \\ 0 & 1 \end{bmatrix}$$

is not the identity for 3×3 matrices. However, the matrix

$$I = \begin{bmatrix} 1 & 0 & 0 \\ 0 & 1 & 0 \\ 0 & 0 & 1 \end{bmatrix}$$

is an identity matrix for the set of all 3×3 matrices:

$$\begin{bmatrix} a & b & c \\ d & e & f \\ g & h & i \end{bmatrix} \begin{bmatrix} 1 & 0 & 0 \\ 0 & 1 & 0 \\ 0 & 0 & 1 \end{bmatrix} = \begin{bmatrix} a & b & c \\ d & e & f \\ g & h & i \end{bmatrix}$$

$$\begin{bmatrix} 1 & 0 & 0 \\ 0 & 1 & 0 \\ 0 & 0 & 1 \end{bmatrix} \begin{bmatrix} a & b & c \\ d & e & f \\ g & h & i \end{bmatrix} = \begin{bmatrix} a & b & c \\ d & e & f \\ g & h & i \end{bmatrix}$$

In general, if we let I be the $n \times n$ matrix with ones on the **main diagonal** and zeros elsewhere, it is the identity matrix for the class of all $n \times n$ matrices. (The **main diagonal** runs from the upper left to lower right corner.)

INVERSE OF A SQUARE MATRIX

We can extend another number fact to matrices. The simple multiplication facts

$$2 \times \frac{1}{2} = 1$$

$$\frac{3}{4} \times \frac{4}{3} = 1$$

$$1.25 \times 0.8 = 1$$

have a common property. Each of the numbers 2, $\frac{3}{4}$, and 1.25 can be multiplied by another number to obtain 1. In general, for any real number a, except zero, there is a number b such that $a \times b = 1$. We call b the *inverse* of a. The standard notation for the inverse of a is a^{-1}.

EXAMPLE 1   *(Compare Exercise 1)*

$$3^{-1} = \frac{1}{3}, \qquad 2^{-1} = 0.5, \qquad \left(\frac{5}{8}\right)^{-1} = \frac{8}{5},$$

$$0.4^{-1} = 2.5, \qquad 625^{-1} = .0016$$

A similar property exists in terms of matrix multiplication. For example,

$$\begin{bmatrix} 1 & 1 \\ 1 & 2 \end{bmatrix} \begin{bmatrix} 2 & -1 \\ -1 & 1 \end{bmatrix} = \begin{bmatrix} 1 & 0 \\ 0 & 1 \end{bmatrix}$$

We can restate this equation as $AA^{-1} = I$, where

$$A = \begin{bmatrix} 1 & 1 \\ 1 & 2 \end{bmatrix} \qquad \text{and} \qquad A^{-1} = \begin{bmatrix} 2 & -1 \\ -1 & 1 \end{bmatrix}$$

We call A^{-1} the inverse of the matrix A.

Definition
Inverse of a Matrix A

If A and B are square matrices such that $AB = BA = I$, then B is the **inverse matrix** of A. The inverse of A is denoted A^{-1}. If B is found so that $AB = I$, then a theorem from linear algebra states that $BA = I$, so it is sufficient to just check $AB = I$.

EXAMPLE 2   *(Compare Exercise 3)*

(a) For the two matrices

$$A = \begin{bmatrix} 2 & 5 & 4 \\ 1 & 4 & 3 \\ 1 & -3 & -2 \end{bmatrix} \qquad \text{and} \qquad B = \begin{bmatrix} -1 & 2 & 1 \\ -5 & 8 & 2 \\ 7 & -11 & -3 \end{bmatrix}$$

determine whether B is the inverse of A.

(b) For the two matrices

$$A = \begin{bmatrix} 4 & 7 \\ 2 & 1 \end{bmatrix} \qquad \text{and} \qquad B = \begin{bmatrix} -\frac{1}{10} & \frac{7}{10} \\ \frac{1}{5} & -\frac{2}{5} \end{bmatrix}$$

determine whether $B = A^{-1}$.

(c) Determine whether B is the inverse of A for

$$A = \begin{bmatrix} 0 & 1 & 0 \\ 1 & 1 & 0 \\ 0 & 1 & 1 \end{bmatrix} \qquad \text{and} \qquad B = \begin{bmatrix} -1 & 1 & 0 \\ 1 & 0 & 1 \\ -1 & 1 & 0 \end{bmatrix}$$

SOLUTION   In each case it suffices to compute AB. If $AB = I$, then B is the inverse of A. If $AB \neq I$, then B is not the inverse of A.

(a) $AB = \begin{bmatrix} 2 & 5 & 4 \\ 1 & 4 & 3 \\ 1 & -3 & -2 \end{bmatrix} \begin{bmatrix} -1 & 2 & 1 \\ -5 & 8 & 2 \\ 7 & -11 & -3 \end{bmatrix}$

$= \begin{bmatrix} -2 - 25 + 28 & 4 + 40 - 44 & 2 + 10 - 12 \\ -1 - 20 + 21 & 2 + 32 - 33 & 1 + 8 - 9 \\ -1 + 15 - 14 & 2 - 24 + 22 & 1 - 6 + 6 \end{bmatrix}$

$= \begin{bmatrix} 1 & 0 & 0 \\ 0 & 1 & 0 \\ 0 & 0 & 1 \end{bmatrix} = I$

so B is the inverse of A

(b) $AB = \begin{bmatrix} 4 & 7 \\ 2 & 1 \end{bmatrix} \begin{bmatrix} -\frac{1}{10} & \frac{7}{10} \\ \frac{1}{5} & -\frac{2}{5} \end{bmatrix}$

$= \begin{bmatrix} -\frac{4}{10} + \frac{7}{5} & \frac{28}{10} - \frac{14}{5} \\ -\frac{2}{10} + \frac{1}{5} & \frac{14}{10} - \frac{2}{5} \end{bmatrix} = \begin{bmatrix} 1 & 0 \\ 0 & 1 \end{bmatrix}$

so $B = A^{-1}$.

(c) $AB = \begin{bmatrix} 0 & 1 & 0 \\ 1 & 1 & 0 \\ 0 & 1 & 1 \end{bmatrix} \begin{bmatrix} -1 & 1 & 0 \\ 1 & 0 & 1 \\ -1 & 1 & 0 \end{bmatrix} = \begin{bmatrix} 1 & 0 & 1 \\ 0 & 1 & 1 \\ 0 & 1 & 1 \end{bmatrix} \neq I$

so B is not the inverse of A.

In general, a matrix A has an inverse if there is a matrix A^{-1} that fulfills the conditions that $AA^{-1} = A^{-1}A = I$. Not all matrices have inverses. In fact, a matrix must be square in order to have an inverse, and some square matrices have no inverse. We now come to the problem of deciding if a square matrix has an inverse. If it does, how do we find it? Let's approach this problem with a simple 2×2 example.

EXAMPLE 3   (Compare Exercise 9)

If we have the square matrix

$$A = \begin{bmatrix} 2 & 1 \\ 3 & 2 \end{bmatrix}$$

find its inverse if possible.

SOLUTION   We want to find a 2×2 matrix A^{-1} such that $AA^{-1} = I$. Since we don't know the entries in A^{-1}, let's enter variables, x_1, x_2, y_1, and y_2 and attempt to find their values. Write

$$A^{-1} = \begin{bmatrix} x_1 & y_1 \\ x_2 & y_2 \end{bmatrix}$$

The condition $AA^{-1} = I$ can now be written

$$\begin{bmatrix} 2 & 1 \\ 3 & 2 \end{bmatrix} \begin{bmatrix} x_1 & y_1 \\ x_2 & y_2 \end{bmatrix} = \begin{bmatrix} 1 & 0 \\ 0 & 1 \end{bmatrix}$$

We want to find values of x_1, x_2, y_1, and y_2 so that the product on the left equals the identity matrix on the right. First, form the product AA^{-1}. We get

$$\overset{AA^{-1}}{\begin{bmatrix} (2x_1 + x_2) & (2y_1 + y_2) \\ (3x_1 + 2x_2) & (3y_1 + 2y_2) \end{bmatrix}} = \overset{I}{\begin{bmatrix} 1 & 0 \\ 0 & 1 \end{bmatrix}}$$

Recall that two matrices are equal only when they have equal entries in corresponding positions. So the matrix equality reduces to the equations

$$\begin{matrix} 2x_1 + x_2 = 1 \\ 3x_1 + 2x_2 = 0 \end{matrix} \quad \text{and} \quad \begin{matrix} 2y_1 + y_2 = 0 \\ 3y_1 + 2y_2 = 1 \end{matrix}$$

Notice that we have one system of two equations with variables x_1 and x_2:

1. $2x_1 + x_2 = 1$
    $3x_1 + 2x_2 = 0$ with augmented matrix $\begin{bmatrix} 2 & 1 & | & 1 \\ 3 & 2 & | & 0 \end{bmatrix}$

and a system with variables y_1 and y_2:

2. $2y_1 + y_2 = 0$
    $3y_1 + 2y_2 = 1$ with augmented matrix $\begin{bmatrix} 2 & 1 & | & 0 \\ 3 & 2 & | & 1 \end{bmatrix}$

The solution to system 1 gives $x_1 = 2$, $x_2 = -3$. The solution to system 2 gives $y_1 = -1$, $y_2 = 2$, so the inverse of

$$A = \begin{bmatrix} 2 & 1 \\ 3 & 2 \end{bmatrix} \quad \text{is} \quad A^{-1} = \begin{bmatrix} 2 & -1 \\ -3 & 2 \end{bmatrix}$$

We check our results by computing AA^{-1} and $A^{-1}A$:

$$AA^{-1} = \begin{bmatrix} 2 & 1 \\ 3 & 2 \end{bmatrix} \begin{bmatrix} 2 & -1 \\ -3 & 2 \end{bmatrix} = \begin{bmatrix} 1 & 0 \\ 0 & 1 \end{bmatrix}$$

$$A^{-1}A = \begin{bmatrix} 2 & -1 \\ -3 & 2 \end{bmatrix} \begin{bmatrix} 2 & 1 \\ 3 & 2 \end{bmatrix} = \begin{bmatrix} 1 & 0 \\ 0 & 1 \end{bmatrix}$$

It checks. (*Note:* It suffices to check just one of these.)

Look at the two systems we just solved. The two systems have precisely the same coefficients; they differ only in the constant terms. The left-hand portions of the augmented matrices are exactly the same. In fact, each is the matrix A. Combine the two augmented matrices into one using the common coefficient portion on the left, and list both columns from the right sides. This gives the matrix

$$\begin{bmatrix} 2 & 1 & | & 1 & 0 \\ 3 & 2 & | & 0 & 1 \end{bmatrix}$$

Now proceed in the same way you do to solve a system of equations with an augmented matrix, that is, use row operations to reduce the left-hand portion to the identity. This gives the following sequence:

$$\begin{bmatrix} 2 & 1 & 1 & 0 \\ 3 & 2 & 0 & 1 \end{bmatrix} \qquad (\tfrac{1}{2})R1 \to R1$$

$$\begin{bmatrix} 1 & \tfrac{1}{2} & \tfrac{1}{2} & 0 \\ 3 & 2 & 0 & 1 \end{bmatrix} \qquad -3R1 + R2 \to R2$$

$$\begin{bmatrix} 1 & \tfrac{1}{2} & \tfrac{1}{2} & 0 \\ 0 & \tfrac{1}{2} & -\tfrac{3}{2} & 1 \end{bmatrix} \qquad -R2 + R1 \to R1$$

$$\begin{bmatrix} 1 & 0 & 2 & -1 \\ 0 & \tfrac{1}{2} & -\tfrac{3}{2} & 1 \end{bmatrix} \qquad 2R2 \to R2$$

$$\begin{bmatrix} 1 & 0 & 2 & -1 \\ 0 & 1 & -3 & 2 \end{bmatrix}$$

The final matrix has the identity matrix formed by the first two columns and A^{-1} formed by the last two columns. This is no accident; one may find the inverse of a square matrix in this manner.

Method to Find the Inverse of a Square Matrix

1. To find the inverse of a matrix A, form an augmented matrix $[A|I]$ by writing down the matrix A and then writing the identity matrix to the right of A.
2. Perform a sequence of row operations that reduces this matrix to reduced echelon form.
3. If the "A portion" of the reduced echelon form is the identity matrix, then the matrix found in the "I portion" is A^{-1}.
4. If the reduced echelon form produces a row in the A portion that is all zeros, then A has no inverse.

EXAMPLE 4   *(Compare Exercise 13)*

Find the inverse of the matrix

$$A = \begin{bmatrix} 1 & 3 & 2 \\ 2 & 4 & 2 \\ 1 & 2 & -1 \end{bmatrix}$$

SOLUTION   First, set up the augmented matrix $[A \mid I]$:

$$\begin{bmatrix} 1 & 3 & 2 & 1 & 0 & 0 \\ 2 & 4 & 2 & 0 & 1 & 0 \\ 1 & 2 & -1 & 0 & 0 & 1 \end{bmatrix}$$

Next use row operations to get zeros in column 1:

$$\left[\begin{array}{ccc|ccc} 1 & 3 & 2 & 1 & 0 & 0 \\ 0 & -2 & -2 & -2 & 1 & 0 \\ 0 & -1 & -3 & -1 & 0 & 1 \end{array}\right]$$

Now divide row 2 by -2:

$$\left[\begin{array}{ccc|ccc} 1 & 3 & 2 & 1 & 0 & 0 \\ 0 & 1 & 1 & 1 & -\frac{1}{2} & 0 \\ 0 & -1 & -3 & -1 & 0 & 1 \end{array}\right]$$

Next, get zeros in the second column:

$$\left[\begin{array}{ccc|ccc} 1 & 0 & -1 & -2 & \frac{3}{2} & 0 \\ 0 & 1 & 1 & 1 & -\frac{1}{2} & 0 \\ 0 & 0 & -2 & 0 & -\frac{1}{2} & 1 \end{array}\right]$$

Now divide row 3 by -2:

$$\left[\begin{array}{ccc|ccc} 1 & 0 & -1 & -2 & \frac{3}{2} & 0 \\ 0 & 1 & 1 & 1 & -\frac{1}{2} & 0 \\ 0 & 0 & 1 & 0 & \frac{1}{4} & -\frac{1}{2} \end{array}\right]$$

Finally, get zeros in the third column:

$$\left[\begin{array}{ccc|ccc} 1 & 0 & 0 & -2 & \frac{7}{4} & -\frac{1}{2} \\ 0 & 1 & 0 & 1 & -\frac{3}{4} & \frac{1}{2} \\ 0 & 0 & 1 & 0 & \frac{1}{4} & -\frac{1}{2} \end{array}\right]$$

When the left-hand portion of the augmented matrix reduces to the identity matrix, A^{-1} comes from the right-hand portion:

$$A^{-1} = \left[\begin{array}{ccc} -2 & \frac{7}{4} & -\frac{1}{2} \\ 1 & -\frac{3}{4} & \frac{1}{2} \\ 0 & \frac{1}{4} & -\frac{1}{2} \end{array}\right]$$

Now look at a case in which the matrix has no inverse.

EXAMPLE 5   *(Compare Exercise 17)*

Find the inverse of

$$A = \left[\begin{array}{cc} 1 & 3 \\ 3 & 9 \end{array}\right]$$

SOLUTION   Adjoin I to A to obtain

$$\left[\begin{array}{cc|cc} 1 & 3 & 1 & 0 \\ 3 & 9 & 0 & 1 \end{array}\right]$$

Now reduce to echelon form using row operations:

$$\begin{bmatrix} 1 & 3 & | & 1 & 0 \\ 3 & 9 & | & 0 & 1 \end{bmatrix} \qquad -3R1 + R2 \rightarrow R2$$

$$\begin{bmatrix} 1 & 3 & | & 1 & 0 \\ 0 & 0 & | & -3 & 1 \end{bmatrix}$$

The bottom row of the matrix represents two equations $0 = -3$ and $0 = 1$. Both of these are impossible, so in our attempt to find A^{-1} we reached an inconsistency. Whenever we reach an inconsistency in trying to solve a system of equations, we conclude that there is no solution. Therefore, in this case A has no inverse.

In general, when we use an augmented matrix $[A \mid I]$ to find the inverse of A and reach a step where a row of the A portion is all zeros, then A has no inverse.

MATRIX EQUATIONS

We can write systems of equations using matrices and solve some systems using matrix inverses.

The **matrix equation**

$$\begin{bmatrix} 5 & 3 & -4 & 12 \\ 8 & -21 & 7 & -19 \\ 2 & 1 & -15 & 1 \end{bmatrix} \begin{bmatrix} x_1 \\ x_2 \\ x_3 \\ x_4 \end{bmatrix} = \begin{bmatrix} 7 \\ 16 \\ -22 \end{bmatrix}$$

becomes the following when the multiplication on the left is performed:

$$\begin{bmatrix} 5x_1 + 3x_2 - 4x_3 + 12x_4 \\ 8x_1 - 21x_2 + 7x_3 - 19x_4 \\ 2x_1 + x_2 - 15x_3 + x_4 \end{bmatrix} = \begin{bmatrix} 7 \\ 16 \\ -22 \end{bmatrix}$$

These matrices are equal only when corresponding components are equal; that is,

$$5x_1 + 3x_2 - 4x_3 + 12x_4 = 7$$
$$8x_1 - 21x_2 + 7x_3 - 19x_4 = 16$$
$$2x_1 + x_2 - 15x_3 + x_4 = -22$$

In general, we can write a system of equations in the compact matrix form

$$AX = B$$

where A is a matrix formed from the coefficients of the variables, X is a column matrix formed by listing the variables, and B is the column matrix formed from the constants in the system.

EXAMPLE 6   *(Compare Exercise 27)*

Here is a system of equations:

$$4x_1 + 7x_2 - 2x_3 = 5$$
$$3x_1 - x_2 + 7x_3 = 8$$
$$x_1 + 2x_2 - x_3 = 9$$

The coefficient matrix of this system is

$$\begin{bmatrix} 4 & 7 & -2 \\ 3 & -1 & 7 \\ 1 & 2 & -1 \end{bmatrix}$$

and the augmented matrix is

$$\left[\begin{array}{ccc|c} 4 & 7 & -2 & 5 \\ 3 & -1 & 7 & 8 \\ 1 & 2 & -1 & 9 \end{array}\right]$$

The system of equations can be written in the matrix form, $Ax = B$ as

$$\begin{bmatrix} 4 & 7 & -2 \\ 3 & -1 & 7 \\ 1 & 2 & -1 \end{bmatrix} \begin{bmatrix} x_1 \\ x_2 \\ x_3 \end{bmatrix} = \begin{bmatrix} 5 \\ 8 \\ 9 \end{bmatrix}$$

USING A^{-1} TO SOLVE A SYSTEM

Now we can illustrate the use of the inverse in solving a system of equations when the matrix of coefficients has an inverse. Sometimes it helps to be able to solve a system by using the inverse matrix. One such situation occurs when a number of systems need to be solved, and all have the same coefficients. That is, the constant terms change, but the coefficients don't. Here is a simple example.

A doctor treats patients who need adequate calcium and iron in their diet. The doctor has found that two foods, A and B, provide these. Each unit of food A has 0.5 mg iron and 25 mg calcium. Each unit of food B has 0.3 mg iron and 7 mg calcium. Let x = number of units of food A eaten by the patient; let y = number of units of food B eaten by the patient. Then $0.5x + 0.3y$ gives the total mg of iron consumed by the patient and $25x + 7y$ gives the total mg of calcium. Suppose the doctor wants patient Jones to get 6 mg iron and 60 mg calcium. The amount of each food to be consumed is the solution to

$$0.5x + 0.3y = 6$$
$$25x + 7y = 60$$

If patient Smith requires 7 mg iron and 80 mg calcium, the amount of food required is found in the solution of the system

$$0.5x + 0.3y = 7$$
$$25x + 7y = 80$$

These two systems have the same coefficients; they differ only in the constant terms.

The inverse of the coefficient matrix

$$A = \begin{bmatrix} 0.5 & 0.3 \\ 25 & 7 \end{bmatrix}$$

may be used to avoid going through the Gauss-Jordan elimination process with each patient.

Here's how A^{-1} may be used to solve a system. Let $AX = B$ be a system for which A actually has an inverse. When both sides of $AX = B$ are multiplied by A^{-1}, the equation reduces to

$$A^{-1}AX = A^{-1}B$$
$$IX = A^{-1}B$$
$$X = A^{-1}B$$

The product $A^{-1}B$ gives the solution. The solution to such a system exists, and it is unique.

EXAMPLE 7   (*Compare Exercise 37*)

Use an inverse matrix to solve this system of equations:

$$x_1 + 3x_2 + 2x_3 = 3$$
$$2x_1 + 4x_2 + 2x_3 = 8$$
$$x_1 + 2x_2 - x_3 = 10$$

SOLUTION   First, write the system in matrix form, $Ax = B$:

$$\begin{bmatrix} 1 & 3 & 2 \\ 2 & 4 & 2 \\ 1 & 2 & -1 \end{bmatrix} \begin{bmatrix} x_1 \\ x_2 \\ x_3 \end{bmatrix} = \begin{bmatrix} 3 \\ 8 \\ 10 \end{bmatrix}$$

In matrix form the solution is

$$\begin{bmatrix} x_1 \\ x_2 \\ x_3 \end{bmatrix} = \begin{bmatrix} 1 & 3 & 2 \\ 2 & 4 & 2 \\ 1 & 2 & -1 \end{bmatrix}^{-1} \begin{bmatrix} 3 \\ 8 \\ 10 \end{bmatrix}$$

The inverse was found in Example 4. Substitute it and obtain

$$\begin{bmatrix} x_1 \\ x_2 \\ x_3 \end{bmatrix} = \begin{bmatrix} -2 & \frac{7}{4} & -\frac{1}{2} \\ 1 & -\frac{3}{4} & \frac{1}{2} \\ 0 & \frac{1}{4} & -\frac{1}{2} \end{bmatrix} \begin{bmatrix} 3 \\ 8 \\ 10 \end{bmatrix} = \begin{bmatrix} 3 \\ 2 \\ -3 \end{bmatrix}$$

The system has the unique solution $x_1 = 3$, $x_2 = 2$, $x_3 = -3$. (Check this solution in each of the original equations.)

EXAMPLE 8   *(Compare Exercise 41)*

Solve the systems

$$AX = B$$

where

$$A = \begin{bmatrix} 1 & 2 \\ 4 & 3 \end{bmatrix} \quad \text{and} \quad X = \begin{bmatrix} x \\ y \end{bmatrix}$$

Using

$$B = \begin{bmatrix} 6 \\ 3 \end{bmatrix}, \qquad \begin{bmatrix} 10 \\ 15 \end{bmatrix}, \qquad \text{and} \qquad \begin{bmatrix} 2 \\ 11 \end{bmatrix}$$

SOLUTION   First find A^{-1}. Adjoin the identity matrix of A:

$$\begin{bmatrix} 1 & 2 & | & 1 & 0 \\ 4 & 3 & | & 0 & 1 \end{bmatrix}$$

This reduces to

$$\begin{bmatrix} 1 & 0 & | & -\frac{3}{5} & \frac{2}{5} \\ 0 & 1 & | & \frac{4}{5} & -\frac{1}{5} \end{bmatrix}$$

so the inverse of A is

$$\begin{bmatrix} -\frac{3}{5} & \frac{2}{5} \\ \frac{4}{5} & -\frac{1}{5} \end{bmatrix}$$

For $B = \begin{bmatrix} 6 \\ 3 \end{bmatrix}$ the solution is

$$\begin{bmatrix} x \\ y \end{bmatrix} = \begin{bmatrix} -\frac{3}{5} & \frac{2}{5} \\ \frac{4}{5} & -\frac{1}{5} \end{bmatrix} \begin{bmatrix} 6 \\ 3 \end{bmatrix} = \begin{bmatrix} -\frac{12}{5} \\ \frac{21}{5} \end{bmatrix}$$

so $x = -\dfrac{12}{5}$, $y = \dfrac{21}{5}$ is the solution.

For $B = \begin{bmatrix} 10 \\ 15 \end{bmatrix}$,

$$\begin{bmatrix} x \\ y \end{bmatrix} = \begin{bmatrix} -\frac{3}{5} & \frac{2}{5} \\ \frac{4}{5} & -\frac{1}{5} \end{bmatrix} \begin{bmatrix} 10 \\ 15 \end{bmatrix} = \begin{bmatrix} 0 \\ 5 \end{bmatrix}$$

For $B = \begin{bmatrix} 2 \\ 11 \end{bmatrix}$,

$$\begin{bmatrix} x \\ y \end{bmatrix} = \begin{bmatrix} -\frac{3}{5} & \frac{2}{5} \\ \frac{4}{5} & -\frac{1}{5} \end{bmatrix} \begin{bmatrix} 2 \\ 11 \end{bmatrix} = \begin{bmatrix} \frac{16}{5} \\ -\frac{3}{5} \end{bmatrix}$$

EXAMPLE 9   *(Compare Exercise 45)*

Let's return to the earlier example where a doctor prescribed foods containing calcium and iron. Let

$$x = \text{the number of units of food A}$$
$$y = \text{the number of units of food B}$$

where A contains 0.5 mg iron and 25 mg calcium and B contains 0.3 mg iron and 7 mg calcium per unit.

(a) Find the amount of each food for patient Jones, who needs 1.3 mg iron and 49 mg calcium.

(b) Find the amount of each food for patient Smith, who needs 2.6 mg iron and 106 mg calcium.

SOLUTION

(a) We need the solution to

$$0.5x + 0.3y = 1.3$$
$$25x + 7y = 49$$

In matrix form this is

$$\begin{bmatrix} 0.5 & 0.3 \\ 25 & 7 \end{bmatrix} \begin{bmatrix} x \\ y \end{bmatrix} = \begin{bmatrix} 1.3 \\ 49 \end{bmatrix}$$

The inverse of

$$\begin{bmatrix} 0.5 & 0.3 \\ 25 & 7 \end{bmatrix} \quad \text{is} \quad \begin{bmatrix} -1.75 & 0.075 \\ 6.25 & -0.125 \end{bmatrix}$$

The solution to the system is

$$\begin{bmatrix} x \\ y \end{bmatrix} = \begin{bmatrix} -1.75 & 0.075 \\ 6.25 & -0.125 \end{bmatrix} \begin{bmatrix} 1.3 \\ 49 \end{bmatrix} = \begin{bmatrix} -1.75(1.3) + 0.075(49) \\ 6.25(1.3) - 0.125(49) \end{bmatrix}$$

$$= \begin{bmatrix} 1.4 \\ 2.0 \end{bmatrix}$$

so 1.4 units of food A and 2.0 units of food B are required.

(b) In this case the solution is

$$\begin{bmatrix} x \\ y \end{bmatrix} = \begin{bmatrix} -1.75 & 0.075 \\ 6.25 & -0.125 \end{bmatrix} \begin{bmatrix} 2.6 \\ 106.0 \end{bmatrix} = \begin{bmatrix} 3.4 \\ 3.0 \end{bmatrix}$$

2–6 EXERCISES

I

1. (*See Example 1*)

Find 25^{-1}, $\left(\dfrac{2}{3}\right)^{-1}$, $(-5)^{-1}$, 0.75^{-1}, and 11^{-1}.

Determine whether B is the inverse of A in each of Exercises 2 through 8.

2. $A = \begin{bmatrix} 4 & 7 \\ 1 & 2 \end{bmatrix}$, $B = \begin{bmatrix} 2 & -7 \\ -1 & 4 \end{bmatrix}$

3. (*See Example 2*)

$A = \begin{bmatrix} -2 & 1 & 3 \\ 2 & 4 & -1 \\ 3 & 0 & -4 \end{bmatrix}$,

$B = \begin{bmatrix} -16 & 4 & -13 \\ 5 & -1 & 4 \\ -12 & 3 & -10 \end{bmatrix}$

4. $A = \begin{bmatrix} 1 & -2 & 3 \\ -2 & -2 & 0 \\ 4 & -5 & 6 \end{bmatrix}$,

$B = \begin{bmatrix} -\frac{4}{6} & -\frac{1}{6} & \frac{2}{6} \\ \frac{4}{6} & -\frac{2}{6} & -\frac{2}{6} \\ 1 & -\frac{1}{6} & -\frac{2}{6} \end{bmatrix}$

5. $A = \begin{bmatrix} 2 & -1 \\ -6 & 2 \end{bmatrix}$, $B = \begin{bmatrix} -1 & -2 \\ -3 & -1 \end{bmatrix}$

6. $A = \begin{bmatrix} 2 & 1 & -1 \\ 1 & 1 & -1 \\ -1 & -2 & 3 \end{bmatrix}$, $B = \begin{bmatrix} 1 & -1 & 1 \\ -2 & 5 & 1 \\ -1 & 3 & 1 \end{bmatrix}$

7. $A = \begin{bmatrix} 2 & 0 & 0 \\ 0 & 3 & 0 \\ 0 & 0 & 5 \end{bmatrix}$, $B = \begin{bmatrix} \frac{1}{2} & 0 & 0 \\ 0 & \frac{1}{3} & 0 \\ 0 & 0 & \frac{1}{5} \end{bmatrix}$

8. $A = \begin{bmatrix} 3 & 2 \\ 0 & 0 \end{bmatrix}$, $B = \begin{bmatrix} \frac{1}{3} & 0 \\ 0 & \frac{1}{2} \end{bmatrix}$

Find the inverse of the matrices in Exercises 9 through 16.

9. (*See Example 3*) $\begin{bmatrix} 1 & 2 \\ 3 & 5 \end{bmatrix}$

10. $\begin{bmatrix} 9 & 11 \\ 1 & 5 \end{bmatrix}$

11. $\begin{bmatrix} 3 & 2 \\ 4 & 3 \end{bmatrix}$

12. $\begin{bmatrix} 3 & 5 \\ 2 & 4 \end{bmatrix}$

13. (*See Example 4*) $\begin{bmatrix} 1 & 3 & 9 \\ 0 & 1 & 4 \\ 3 & 2 & 3 \end{bmatrix}$

14. $\begin{bmatrix} 1 & 2 & 1 \\ 2 & -1 & 3 \\ 2 & 2 & 1 \end{bmatrix}$

15. $\begin{bmatrix} 0 & 4 & -2 \\ 1 & 3 & 5 \\ 1 & 4 & 2 \end{bmatrix}$

16. $\begin{bmatrix} 1 & 0 & 2 \\ 2 & -4 & 2 \\ 0 & 1 & -1 \end{bmatrix}$

Find the inverse, if possible, of the matrices in Exercises 17 through 19.

17. (*See Example 5*) $\begin{bmatrix} 4 & -2 \\ -2 & 1 \end{bmatrix}$

18. $\begin{bmatrix} 1 & 0 & 1 \\ 1 & -1 & 2 \\ 3 & -1 & 4 \end{bmatrix}$

19. $\begin{bmatrix} 1 & 3 & 1 \\ 2 & 0 & -2 \\ 3 & 3 & -1 \end{bmatrix}$

Determine the inverses (if they exist) of the matrices in Exercises 20 through 26.

20. $\begin{bmatrix} 1 & 2 & -1 \\ 3 & -1 & 0 \\ 2 & -3 & 1 \end{bmatrix}$

21. $\begin{bmatrix} 1 & 2 & 1 \\ 1 & -3 & 2 \\ 2 & -1 & 3 \end{bmatrix}$

22. $\begin{bmatrix} 1 & 0 \\ 2 & 1 \end{bmatrix}$

23. $\begin{bmatrix} 2 & 1 \\ 4 & 3 \end{bmatrix}$

24. $\begin{bmatrix} 0 & 2 \\ -\frac{1}{3} & \frac{1}{3} \end{bmatrix}$

25. $\begin{bmatrix} 1 & 2 & 3 \\ 2 & -1 & 4 \\ 0 & -1 & 1 \end{bmatrix}$

26. $\begin{bmatrix} 1 & 2 & -1 \\ 2 & 4 & -3 \\ 1 & -2 & 0 \end{bmatrix}$

For each of the systems of equations in Exercises 27 through 30, write (a) the augmented matrix; (b) the coefficient matrix; and (c) the system in the form $AX = B$.

27. (*See Example 6*)

$$\begin{aligned} 3x_1 + 4x_2 - 5x_3 &= 4 \\ 2x_1 - x_2 + 3x_3 &= -1 \\ x_1 + x_2 - x_3 &= 2 \end{aligned}$$

28.

$$\begin{aligned} x_1 - 4x_2 + 3x_3 &= 6 \\ x_1 \quad\quad + x_3 &= 2 \\ 2x_1 + 5x_2 - 6x_3 &= 1 \end{aligned}$$

29.

$$\begin{aligned} 4x + 5y &= 2 \\ 3x - 2y &= 7 \end{aligned}$$

30.

$$\begin{aligned} 7x_1 + 9x_2 - 5x_3 + x_4 &= 14 \\ 3x_1 + 5x_2 + 6x_3 - 8x_4 &= 23 \\ -2x_1 + x_2 \quad\quad + 17x_4 &= 12 \end{aligned}$$

II

Express each of the systems in Exercises 31 through 34 as a single matrix equation, $AX = B$.

31.

$$\begin{aligned} x_1 + 3x_2 &= 5 \\ 2x_1 - x_2 &= 6 \end{aligned}$$

32.

$$\begin{aligned} 2x_1 - 3x_2 + x_3 &= 4 \\ 4x_1 - x_2 + 2x_3 &= -1 \\ x_1 + x_2 - x_3 &= 2 \end{aligned}$$

33.

$$\begin{aligned} x_1 + 2x_2 - 3x_3 + 4x_4 &= 0 \\ x_1 + x_2 \quad\quad + x_4 &= 5 \\ 3x_1 + 2x_2 + x_3 + 2x_4 &= 4 \end{aligned}$$

34.

$$\begin{aligned} x_1 + 5x_2 - x_3 &= 7 \\ 4x_1 + 3x_2 + 6x_3 &= 15 \end{aligned}$$

Find the inverse of the matrices in Exercises 35 and 36.

35.
$$\begin{bmatrix} 1 & 1 & 0 & 0 \\ 0 & 1 & 1 & 0 \\ 1 & 0 & 0 & 1 \\ 0 & 0 & 1 & 1 \end{bmatrix}$$

36.
$$\begin{bmatrix} -3 & -1 & 1 & -2 \\ -1 & 3 & 2 & 1 \\ 1 & 2 & 3 & -1 \\ -2 & 1 & -1 & -3 \end{bmatrix}$$

Solve the systems of equations in Exercises 37 through 40 by determining the inverse of the matrix of coefficients and then using matrix multiplication.

37. (*See Example 7*)

$$\begin{aligned} x_1 + 2x_2 - x_3 &= 2 \\ x_1 + x_2 + 2x_3 &= 0 \\ x_1 - x_2 - x_3 &= 1 \end{aligned}$$

38.

$$\begin{aligned} x_1 + 3x_2 &= 5 \\ 2x_1 + x_2 &= 10 \end{aligned}$$

39.

$$\begin{aligned} x_1 + x_2 + 2x_3 + x_4 &= 4 \\ 2x_1 \quad\quad - x_3 + x_4 &= 6 \\ x_2 + 3x_3 - x_4 &= 3 \\ 3x_1 + 2x_2 \quad\quad + x_4 &= 9 \end{aligned}$$

40.

$$\begin{aligned} x_1 - x_2 \quad\quad &= 1 \\ x_1 + x_2 + 2x_3 &= 2 \\ x_1 + 2x_2 + x_3 &= 0 \end{aligned}$$

Using the matrix inverse method, solve the system of equations in Exercises 41 through 44 for each of the B matrices.

41. (*See Example 8*)

$$\begin{aligned} -2x_1 + x_2 + 3x_3 &= b_1 \\ 2x_1 + 4x_2 - x_3 &= b_2 \\ 3x_1 \quad\quad - 4x_3 &= b_3 \end{aligned} \quad \begin{bmatrix} b_1 \\ b_2 \\ b_3 \end{bmatrix} = \begin{bmatrix} 1 \\ 5 \\ 2 \end{bmatrix}, \begin{bmatrix} -1 \\ 3 \\ 1 \end{bmatrix}, \begin{bmatrix} 0 \\ 1 \\ 2 \end{bmatrix}$$

42.

$$\begin{aligned} x_1 + x_2 &= b_1 \\ 2x_1 + 3x_2 &= b_2 \end{aligned} \quad \begin{bmatrix} b_1 \\ b_2 \end{bmatrix} = \begin{bmatrix} 0 \\ 1 \end{bmatrix}, \begin{bmatrix} 5 \\ 13 \end{bmatrix}, \begin{bmatrix} 1 \\ 2 \end{bmatrix}$$

43.

$$\begin{aligned} x_1 + 2x_2 &= b_1 \\ 3x_1 + 5x_2 &= b_2 \end{aligned} \quad \begin{bmatrix} b_1 \\ b_2 \end{bmatrix} = \begin{bmatrix} 3 \\ 8 \end{bmatrix}, \begin{bmatrix} 4 \\ 9 \end{bmatrix}, \begin{bmatrix} 3 \\ 7 \end{bmatrix}$$

44.

$$\begin{aligned} x_1 + 3x_2 - x_3 &= b_1 \\ x_1 + x_2 + x_3 &= b_2 \\ 2x_1 + 5x_2 - 2x_3 &= b_3 \end{aligned} \quad \begin{bmatrix} b_1 \\ b_2 \\ b_3 \end{bmatrix} = \begin{bmatrix} 2 \\ 0 \\ 2 \end{bmatrix}, \begin{bmatrix} 3 \\ 1 \\ -5 \end{bmatrix}, \begin{bmatrix} 4 \\ 6 \\ 0 \end{bmatrix}$$

III

45. (*See Example 9*) A doctor advises his patients to eat two foods for vitamins A and C. The contents per unit of food are given as follows:

$$\text{Food}$$

$$\begin{array}{c} \text{Vitamin C (mg)} \\ \text{Vitamin A (iu)} \end{array} \begin{array}{cc} A & B \end{array} \begin{bmatrix} 32 & 24 \\ 900 & 425 \end{bmatrix} = M$$

It turns out that

$$M^{-1} = \begin{bmatrix} -0.053125 & 0.003 \\ 0.1125 & -0.004 \end{bmatrix}$$

Let

$x =$ number of units of food A
$y =$ number of units of food B
$b_1 =$ desired intake of vitamin C
$b_2 =$ desired intake of vitamin A

(a) Show that the $MX = B$ describes the relationship between units of food consumed and desired intake of vitamins.
(b) If a patient eats 3.2 units of food A and 2.5 units of food B, what is the vitamin C and vitamin A intake?
(c) If a patient eats 1.5 units of food A and 3.0 units of B, what is the vitamin A and vitamin C intake?
(d) The doctor wants a patient to consume 107.2 mg of vitamin C and 2315 iu of vitamin A. How many units of each food should be eaten?
(e) The doctor wants a patient to consume 104 mg vitamin C and 2575 iu vitamin A. How many units of each food should be eaten?

46. The Restaurant Association sponsored a Taster's Choice evening in which restaurants set up booths and served food samples to attendees. The number of shrimp, steak bits, and cheese chunks given to each man, woman, and child by the Elite Cafe is summarized as follows.

	MAN	WOMAN	CHILD
SHRIMP	1	2	1
STEAK	1	1	1
CHEESE	3	1	1

Use

$$\begin{bmatrix} 0 & -\frac{1}{2} & \frac{1}{2} \\ 1 & -1 & 0 \\ -1 & \frac{5}{2} & -\frac{1}{2} \end{bmatrix} = \begin{bmatrix} 1 & 2 & 1 \\ 1 & 1 & 1 \\ 3 & 1 & 1 \end{bmatrix}^{-1}$$

(a) If the Elite Cafe served 614 shrimp, 404 steak bits, and 684 cheese chunks, how many men, women, and children were served?
(b) If the Elite Cafe served 740 shrimp, 510 steak bits, and 940 cheese chunks, how many men, women, and children were served?
(c) If the Elite Cafe served 409 shrimp, 278 steak bits, and 488 cheese chunks, how many men, women, and children were served?

47. A theater charges $4 for children and $8 for adults. One weekend, 900 people attended the theater, and the admission receipts totaled $5840. These can be represented by

$$\begin{bmatrix} 1 & 1 \\ 4 & 8 \end{bmatrix} \begin{bmatrix} x \\ y \end{bmatrix} = \begin{bmatrix} 900 \\ 5840 \end{bmatrix}$$

where $x =$ number of children and $y =$ number of adults. It is true that

$$\begin{bmatrix} 1 & 1 \\ 4 & 8 \end{bmatrix}^{-1} = \begin{bmatrix} 2 & -0.25 \\ -1 & 0.25 \end{bmatrix}$$

(a) Find the number of children and adults attending.
(b) If the total attendance is 1000 and the admission receipts total $6260, find the number of children and adults attending.
(c) If the attendance totals 750 and receipts total $5560, find the number of children and adults attending.

2–7 LEONTIEF INPUT-OUTPUT MODEL IN ECONOMICS (OPTIONAL)

- *The Leontief Closed Model*
- *Leontief Production Model*

The economic health of our country affects each of us in some way. You want a good job upon graduation. The availability of a good job depends on the ability of an economic system to deal with problems that arise. Some problems are challenging indeed. How do we control inflation? How do we avoid a depression? How will a change in interest rates affect my options in buying a house or a car?

A better understanding of the interrelationships between prices, production, interest rates, consumer demand, and the like could improve our ability to deal with economic problems. Matrix theory has been successful in describing mathematical models used to analyze how industries depend on one another in an economic system. Wassily Leontief of Harvard University pioneered work in this area with a massive analysis of the U.S. economic system. As a result of the mathematical models he developed, he received the Nobel Prize in Economics in 1973. Since that time we have seen the applications of the **Leontief input-output model** mushroom. The model is widely used to study the economic structure of businesses, corporations, and political units like cities, states, and countries. In practice, a large number of variables are required to describe an economic situation. Thus the problems are quite complicated, so they can best be handled with computers using matrix techniques. In this section we study some simple examples of the **closed model** and the **production model.**

THE LEONTIEF CLOSED MODEL

In an input-output **closed model** we have an economic system consisting of a number of "industries" that produce and use goods. In a closed system the industries in the system produce and use all items among themselves. There are no imports and exports. All industries pay the same price for a specific product. In a closed model the prices for the goods are such that the total expenditures for each industry equals their total income. In this state of equilibrium, no one makes money or loses money. We illustrate the closed model with a simple example.

EXAMPLE 1   *(Compare Exercise 1)*

A society has three industries that produce its basic requirements of food, clothing, and shelter. A farmer, tailor, and carpenter produce one commodity each, and each one uses a share of the commodities produced by himself or herself and by the other two. The following table shows the portion of a commodity used by each.

(OUTPUT) PORTION OF GOODS CONSUMED BY:		(INPUT) COMMODITIES PRODUCED BY		
		Farmer	Carpenter	Tailor
	Farmer	0.2	0.1	0.6
	Carpenter	0.4	0.5	0.1
	Tailor	0.4	0.4	0.3

Each column tells how the commodity of that industry is divided among the others. For example, the first column indicates that of the food produced by the farmer: two-tenths is consumed by the farmer, four-tenths by the carpenter, and four-tenths by the tailor. Of the carpenter's input, 0.1 is consumed by the farmer, 0.5 by the carpenter, and 0.4 by the tailor. Each row indicates the portion of each industry used by the one industry represented by the row. For example, row 3 tells that the tailor used 0.4 of the farmer's products, 0.4 of the carpenter's, and 0.3 of the tailor's.

Everyone pays the same price for a given commodity, even the one he or she produces. The farmer pays himself the same price for the food he uses as that paid by the tailor and carpenter. However, the total income (and expense) of each industry need not be the same. We want to find the total income (and expense) for each industry so that income equals expense for each one.

Let x_1, x_2, and x_3 be the total income received by the farmer, carpenter, and tailor, respectively. Then the expenditure of each one is as follows:

$$0.2x_1 + 0.1x_2 + 0.6x_3 \quad \text{(Farmer)}$$
$$0.4x_1 + 0.5x_2 + 0.1x_3 \quad \text{(Carpenter)}$$
$$0.4x_1 + 0.4x_2 + 0.3x_3 \quad \text{(Tailor)}$$

Since each one's expenditures must equal income, we have

$$0.2x_1 + 0.1x_2 + 0.6x_3 = x_1 \quad \text{(Farmer)}$$
$$0.4x_1 + 0.5x_2 + 0.1x_3 = x_2 \quad \text{(Carpenter)}$$
$$0.4x_1 + 0.4x_2 + 0.3x_3 = x_3 \quad \text{(Tailor)}$$

Notice we can write this system of equations as $AX = X$, where

$$A = \begin{bmatrix} 0.2 & 0.1 & 0.6 \\ 0.4 & 0.5 & 0.1 \\ 0.4 & 0.4 & 0.3 \end{bmatrix} \quad \text{and} \quad X = \begin{bmatrix} x_1 \\ x_2 \\ x_3 \end{bmatrix}$$

This system reduces to

$$-0.8x_1 + 0.1x_2 + 0.6x_3 = 0$$
$$0.4x_1 - 0.5x_2 + 0.1x_3 = 0$$
$$0.4x_1 + 0.4x_2 - 0.7x_3 = 0$$

The augmented matrix of this system,

$$\begin{bmatrix} -0.8 & 0.1 & 0.6 & 0 \\ 0.4 & -0.5 & 0.1 & 0 \\ 0.4 & 0.4 & -0.7 & 0 \end{bmatrix}$$

can be used to solve the system. The usual process of row operations reduces it to

$$
\begin{bmatrix}
1 & 0 & -\frac{31}{36} & 0 \\
0 & 1 & -\frac{8}{9} & 0 \\
0 & 0 & 0 & 0
\end{bmatrix}
$$

From this matrix we obtain the solution to the original system: $x_1 = \frac{31}{36}x_3$ and $x_2 = \frac{8}{9}x_3$. Thus there are an infinite number of solutions, depending on the choice of x_3. However, the values of x_1, x_2, and x_3 maintain the same relative proportions regardless of the choice of x_3. If we choose $x_3 = 3600$ (the tailor's income), then $x_1 = 3100$ (the farmer's income) and $x_2 = 3200$ (the carpenter's income). If the farmer receives \$3100 for food, the carpenter \$3200 for work, and the tailor \$3600 for clothing, then each one's income balances expenses. ∎

In the situation in which there are a number of industries, the solution to the closed input-output model may be written $AX = X$, where each column of A represents the production of an industry and the entries of the column represent the fraction of that product used by the industries (the ith entry in a column is the fraction of that commodity used by the ith industry).

The matrix A is called the **input-output matrix** because it gives information on the products put into the system by each industry and the commodities taken out (consumed).

EXAMPLE 2

In a closed model, three industries, I, II, and III, produce goods used by themselves and others. The fraction of goods used by each industry is given in an input-output matrix as follows:

$$
\begin{array}{c}
\text{Goods produced by} \\
\begin{array}{ccc}
\text{I} & \text{II} & \text{III}
\end{array}
\end{array}
$$

$$
\begin{array}{cc}
\begin{array}{l}
\text{Goods} \\
\text{consumed} \\
\text{by}
\end{array}
&
\begin{array}{c}
\text{I} \\
\text{II} \\
\text{III}
\end{array}
\begin{bmatrix}
0.2 & 0.3 & 0.1 \\
0.4 & 0.5 & 0.3 \\
0.4 & 0.2 & 0.6
\end{bmatrix}
\end{array}
$$

Find the total amount each industry receives for its goods so an equilibrium will occur.

SOLUTION   Let x_1, x_2, and x_3 represent the total income of each industry. The problem now is to find the solution to

$$
\begin{bmatrix}
0.2 & 0.3 & 0.1 \\
0.4 & 0.5 & 0.3 \\
0.4 & 0.2 & 0.6
\end{bmatrix}
\begin{bmatrix}
x_1 \\
x_2 \\
x_3
\end{bmatrix}
=
\begin{bmatrix}
x_1 \\
x_2 \\
x_3
\end{bmatrix}
$$

This is equivalent to

$$\begin{bmatrix} -0.8 & 0.3 & 0.1 \\ 0.4 & -0.5 & 0.3 \\ 0.4 & 0.2 & -0.4 \end{bmatrix} \begin{bmatrix} x_1 \\ x_2 \\ x_3 \end{bmatrix} = \begin{bmatrix} 0 \\ 0 \\ 0 \end{bmatrix}$$

The augmented matrix is

$$\left[\begin{array}{ccc|c} -0.8 & 0.3 & 0.1 & 0 \\ 0.4 & -0.5 & 0.3 & 0 \\ 0.4 & 0.2 & -0.4 & 0 \end{array}\right]$$

which reduces to

$$\left[\begin{array}{ccc|c} 4 & 0 & -2 & 0 \\ 0 & 1 & -1 & 0 \\ 0 & 0 & 0 & 0 \end{array}\right]$$

From this we have the solution

$$4x_1 = 2x_3$$
$$x_2 = x_3$$

or $(0.5k, k, k)$. If we let $k = 1000$, then $x_1 = 500$ and $x_2 = 1000$, so Industry I receives \$500, Industry II receives \$1000, and Industry III receives \$1000 for an economic equilibrium.

———————∎

LEONTIEF PRODUCTION MODEL

The **production model** differs from the closed model in that the industries produce greater quantities of commodities than they use among themselves; the economic system exports its products. Our general economy depends on industries that produce goods (like electricity) that are available to outsiders, the consumers. This model is also called an **open model.**

To illustrate the production model, imagine a simple economy with just two industries: electricity and steel. These industries exist to produce electricity and steel for the consumers. However, both production processes themselves use electricity and steel. The electricity industry uses steel in the generating equipment and uses electricity to light the plant and to heat and cool the buildings. The steel industry uses electricity to run some of its equipment, and that equipment in turn contains steel components.

In the production model we will describe the quantities in the input-output matrix in terms of dollar values. We are interested in the quantities of each product that are needed to provide for the consumers (their demand) and to provide for that consumed internally.

EXAMPLE 3

The amount of electricity and steel consumed by the electric company and the steel company in producing their own products depends on the amount they produce. For example, an electric company may find that whatever the value of electricity produced, 15% of that goes to pay for the electricity used internally and 5% goes to pay for the steel used in production. Thus if the electric company produces $200,000 worth of electricity, then $30,000 worth (15%) of electricity and $10,000 worth (5%) of steel are consumed by the electric company. Now let's state this concept in a more general form and bring in the cost of producing steel as well.

Let x be the value of electricity produced and y the value of steel produced. The cost of producing electricity includes the following: Of the value of the electricity produced, x, 15% of it, $0.15x$, pays for the electricity, and 5%, $0.05x$, pays for the steel consumed internally. The cost of producing steel includes the following: Of the value of the steel produced, y, 40% of it, $0.40y$, pays for the electricity, and 10% of it, $0.10y$, pays for the steel consumed internally. We can express this information as

$$\text{total electricity consumed internally} = 0.15x + 0.40y$$
$$\text{total steel consumed internally} = 0.05x + 0.10y$$

Now note that this can also be expressed as

$$\begin{bmatrix} 0.15 & 0.40 \\ 0.05 & 0.10 \end{bmatrix} \begin{bmatrix} x \\ y \end{bmatrix}$$

The coefficient matrix used here is just the input-output matrix of the production model.

		Production	
		Electricity	Steel
Fraction	Electricity	$\begin{bmatrix} 0.15$	$0.40 \end{bmatrix}$ = A
used by	Steel	0.05	0.10

There is one row for each industry. The row labeled electricity gives the value of the electricity ($0.15) needed to produce $1 worth of electricity and the value of the electricity ($0.40) needed to produce $1 worth of steel. The second row shows the value of the steel ($0.05) needed to produce $1 worth of electricity and value of the steel ($0.10) needed to produce $1 worth of steel.

You might be wondering why this information is presented in matrix form. It makes it easier to answer questions such as:

1. "The production capacity of industry is $9 million worth of electricity and $7 million worth of steel. How much of each is consumed internally by the production processes?"

2. "The consumers want $6 million worth of electricity and $8 million worth of steel for their use. How much of each should be produced in order to satisfy their demands and also to provide for the amounts consumed internally?"

Before we learn how to answer these two questions, let's make some observations that will help set up the problems.

Recall that we let x = the dollar value of electricity produced and y = the dollar value of steel produced. These values include that used internally for production and that available to the consumers. Then the total amounts consumed internally are

$$\text{electricity consumed internally} = 0.15x + 0.40y$$
$$\text{steel consumed internally} = 0.05x + 0.10y$$

which we expressed in matrix form as

$$\begin{bmatrix} \text{electricity consumed internally} \\ \text{steel consumed internally} \end{bmatrix} = \begin{bmatrix} 0.15 & 0.40 \\ 0.05 & 0.10 \end{bmatrix} \begin{bmatrix} x \\ y \end{bmatrix} = A \begin{bmatrix} x \\ y \end{bmatrix}$$

If production capacities are $9 million worth of electricity ($x = 9$) and $7 million worth of steel ($y = 7$), the amount consumed internally is

$$\begin{bmatrix} 0.15 & 0.40 \\ 0.05 & 0.10 \end{bmatrix} \begin{bmatrix} 9 \\ 7 \end{bmatrix} = \begin{bmatrix} 4.15 \\ 1.15 \end{bmatrix}$$

$4.15 million and $1.15 million worth of electricity and steel.

Another fact relates the amount of electricity and steel produced to that available to the consumer

$$[\text{amount produced}] = \begin{bmatrix} \text{amount consumed} \\ \text{internally} \end{bmatrix} + \begin{bmatrix} \text{amount available} \\ \text{to consumer} \end{bmatrix}$$

We call these matrices *output, internal demand,* and *consumer demand* matrices, respectively.

In the case in which $9 million and $7 million worth of electricity were produced with $4.15 and $1.15 million consumed internally,

Output	Internal Demand		Consumer Demand
$\begin{bmatrix} 9 \\ 7 \end{bmatrix}$	=	$\begin{bmatrix} 4.15 \\ 1.15 \end{bmatrix}$	+ $\begin{bmatrix} \text{electricity available to consumer} \\ \text{steel available to consumer} \end{bmatrix}$

we get $4.85 million and $5.85 million worth of electricity and steel available to the consumers.

If we call the output matrix X, the consumer demand matrix D, and the input-output matrix A, then the internal demand matrix is AX and

$$X = AX + D$$

expresses the relation between output, internal demand, and consumer demand.

The question, "What total output is necessary to supply consumers with $6 million worth of electricity and $8 million worth of steel?" asks for the output X when consumer demand D is given. Using the same input-output matrix, we want to find x and y (output) so that

$$
\begin{array}{ccccc}
X & = & & A\ X & + & D \\[4pt]
\begin{bmatrix} x \\ y \end{bmatrix} & = & \begin{bmatrix} 0.15 & 0.40 \\ 0.05 & 0.10 \end{bmatrix} & \begin{bmatrix} x \\ y \end{bmatrix} & + & \begin{bmatrix} 6 \\ 8 \end{bmatrix}
\end{array}
$$

Notice that the variables x and y appear in two matrices.

Let's use the general form $X = AX + D$ and apply some matrix algebra to find the matrix X.

You need to solve for the matrix X in

$$X = AX + D$$

This is equivalent to solving for X in the following:

$$
\begin{aligned}
X - AX &= D \\
IX - AX &= D \\
(I - A)X &= D \\
X &= (I - A)^{-1}D
\end{aligned}
$$

The last equation is the most helpful. To find the total production X that meets the final demand D and also provides the quantities needed to carry out the internal production processes, find the inverse of the matrix $I - A$ (as you did in Section 2–5) and multiply it by the matrix D. Using

$$A = \begin{bmatrix} 0.15 & 0.40 \\ 0.05 & 0.10 \end{bmatrix}$$

$$I - A = \begin{bmatrix} 0.85 & -0.40 \\ -0.05 & 0.90 \end{bmatrix}$$

and

$$(I - A)^{-1} = \begin{bmatrix} 1.208 & 0.537 \\ 0.0671 & 1.141 \end{bmatrix}$$

where the entries in $(I - A)^{-1}$ are rounded. For the demand matrix

$$D = \begin{bmatrix} 6 \\ 8 \end{bmatrix}$$

$$X = \begin{bmatrix} 1.208 & 0.537 \\ 0.0671 & 1.141 \end{bmatrix} \begin{bmatrix} 6 \\ 8 \end{bmatrix} = \begin{bmatrix} 11.544 \\ 9.531 \end{bmatrix}$$

so $11.544 million worth of electricity and $9.531 million worth of steel must be produced in order to provide $6 million worth of electricity and $8 million worth of steel to the consumers and to provide for the electricity and steel used internally in production.

We just found X by solving $X = (I - A)^{-1}D$. We could also find X by using the Gauss-Jordan method to solve $(I - A)X = D$.

EXAMPLE 4   *(Compare Exercises 6, 11)*

An input-output matrix for electricity and steel is

$$A = \begin{bmatrix} 0.25 & 0.20 \\ 0.50 & 0.20 \end{bmatrix}$$

(a) If the production capacity of electricity is $15 million and the production capacity for steel is $20 million, how much of each is consumed internally for capacity production?

(b) How much electricity and steel must be produced to have $5 million worth of electricity and $8 million worth of steel available for consumer use?

SOLUTION

(a) We are given

$$A = \begin{bmatrix} 0.25 & 0.20 \\ 0.50 & 0.20 \end{bmatrix} \quad \text{and} \quad X = \begin{bmatrix} 15 \\ 20 \end{bmatrix}$$

We want to find AX:

$$AX = \begin{bmatrix} 0.25 & 0.20 \\ 0.50 & 0.20 \end{bmatrix} \begin{bmatrix} 15 \\ 20 \end{bmatrix} = \begin{bmatrix} 7.75 \\ 11.50 \end{bmatrix}$$

so $7.75 million worth of electricity and $11.50 million worth of steel are consumed internally.

(b) We are given

$$A = \begin{bmatrix} 0.25 & 0.20 \\ 0.50 & 0.20 \end{bmatrix} \quad \text{and} \quad D = \begin{bmatrix} 5 \\ 8 \end{bmatrix}$$

and we need to solve for X in $(I - A)^{-1}D = X$ or in $(I - A)X = D$. We will use the latter this time:

$$I - A = \begin{bmatrix} 0.75 & -0.20 \\ -0.50 & 0.80 \end{bmatrix}$$

Then the augmented matrix for $(I - A)X = D$ is

$$\left[\begin{array}{cc|c} 0.75 & -0.20 & 5 \\ -0.50 & 0.80 & 8 \end{array} \right]$$

which reduces to

$$\left[\begin{array}{cc|c} 1 & 0 & 11.2 \\ 0 & 1 & 17.0 \end{array} \right] \qquad \text{(Check it)}$$

The two industries must produce $11.2 million worth of electricity and $17.0 million worth of steel to have $5 million worth of electricity and $8 million worth of steel available to the consumers.

EXAMPLE 5   *(Compare Exercise 12)*

An economy consists of three industries and has the following input-output matrix A. Compute the output levels required of each industry to meet the demands of the other industries and of the consumers for each of the three given demand levels:

$$A = \begin{bmatrix} \frac{1}{5} & \frac{1}{5} & \frac{3}{10} \\ \frac{1}{2} & \frac{1}{2} & 0 \\ 0 & 0 & \frac{1}{5} \end{bmatrix} \qquad D = \begin{bmatrix} 9 \\ 12 \\ 16 \end{bmatrix}, \begin{bmatrix} 6 \\ 9 \\ 8 \end{bmatrix}, \begin{bmatrix} 12 \\ 18 \\ 32 \end{bmatrix}$$

SOLUTION   The units of D are millions of dollars. We wish to compute the X's that correspond to the various D's. We need to find X as follows for each D:

$$X = (I - A)^{-1}D$$

For our matrix A,

$$I - A = \begin{bmatrix} 1 & 0 & 0 \\ 0 & 1 & 0 \\ 0 & 0 & 1 \end{bmatrix} - \begin{bmatrix} \frac{1}{5} & \frac{1}{5} & \frac{3}{10} \\ \frac{1}{2} & \frac{1}{2} & 0 \\ 0 & 0 & \frac{1}{5} \end{bmatrix}$$

$$= \begin{bmatrix} \frac{4}{5} & -\frac{1}{5} & -\frac{3}{10} \\ -\frac{1}{2} & \frac{1}{2} & 0 \\ 0 & 0 & \frac{4}{5} \end{bmatrix}$$

$(I - A)^{-1}$ is computed by using Gauss-Jordan elimination:

$$(I - A)^{-1} = \begin{bmatrix} \frac{5}{3} & \frac{2}{3} & \frac{5}{8} \\ \frac{5}{3} & \frac{8}{3} & \frac{5}{8} \\ 0 & 0 & \frac{5}{4} \end{bmatrix}$$

We can efficiently compute $X = (I - A)^{-1}D$ for each of the three values of D by forming a matrix having the various values of D as columns:

$$X = \underbrace{\begin{bmatrix} \frac{5}{3} & \frac{2}{3} & \frac{5}{8} \\ \frac{5}{3} & \frac{8}{3} & \frac{5}{8} \\ 0 & 0 & \frac{5}{4} \end{bmatrix}}_{(I - A)^{-1}} \underbrace{\begin{bmatrix} 9 & 6 & 12 \\ 12 & 9 & 18 \\ 16 & 8 & 32 \end{bmatrix}}_{\substack{\text{Various values} \\ \text{of } D}} = \underbrace{\begin{bmatrix} 33 & 21 & 52 \\ 57 & 39 & 88 \\ 20 & 10 & 40 \end{bmatrix}}_{\substack{\text{Corresponding} \\ \text{outputs}}}$$

The output levels of the three industries to meet the demands

$$\begin{bmatrix} 9 \\ 12 \\ 16 \end{bmatrix}, \begin{bmatrix} 6 \\ 9 \\ 8 \end{bmatrix}, \text{ and } \begin{bmatrix} 12 \\ 18 \\ 32 \end{bmatrix}$$

are

$$\begin{bmatrix} 33 \\ 57 \\ 20 \end{bmatrix}, \quad \begin{bmatrix} 21 \\ 39 \\ 10 \end{bmatrix}, \quad \text{and} \quad \begin{bmatrix} 52 \\ 88 \\ 40 \end{bmatrix}$$

respectively, the units being millions of dollars.

Today the concept of a world economy has become a reality. In 1973 the United Nations commissioned an input-output model of the world economy. The aim of the model was to transform the vast collection of economic facts that describe the world economy into an organized system from which economic projections could and have been made. In the model the world is divided into 15 distinct geographic regions, each one described by an individual input-output matrix. The regions are then linked by a larger matrix which is used in an input-output model. Overall, more than 200 variables enter into the model, and the computations are, of course, done on a computer. By feeding in projected values for certain variables, researchers use the model to create scenarios of future world economic possibilities.

2–7 EXERCISES

1. (*See Example 1*)
A farmer, a carpenter, and a tailor use their commodities in a closed model as shown:

		COMMODITIES PRODUCED BY:		
		FARMER	CARPENTER	TAILOR
COMMODITIES	FARMER	$\frac{7}{16}$	$\frac{1}{2}$	$\frac{3}{16}$
CONSUMED	CARPENTER	$\frac{5}{16}$	$\frac{1}{6}$	$\frac{5}{16}$
BY:	TAILOR	$\frac{4}{16}$	$\frac{1}{3}$	$\frac{8}{16}$

Find the income each should receive in order for his or her income to balance expenses. The income for each should be in the $3,000–$15,000 range.

2. In a simple closed economy with the commodities food, shelter, and clothing the farmer consumes $\frac{2}{5}$ of the food, $\frac{1}{3}$ of the shelter, and $\frac{1}{2}$ of the clothing; the carpenter consumes $\frac{2}{5}$ of the food, $\frac{1}{3}$ of the shelter, and $\frac{1}{2}$ of the clothes; the tailor consumes $\frac{1}{5}$ of the food, $\frac{1}{3}$ of the shelter, and none of the clothing.

(a) Find the input-output matrix of this economy.

(b) Find the total income of each industry so that the economy is in equilibrium.

3. Find the total incomes for each of three commodities for a closed economic system with the input-output matrix

$$\begin{bmatrix} 0.6 & 0.2 & 0.5 \\ 0.1 & 0.2 & 0.5 \\ 0.3 & 0.6 & 0 \end{bmatrix}$$

State incomes in the $5,000–$10,000 range.

4. Find total incomes for each of three commodities for a closed economic system with the input-output matrix

$$\begin{bmatrix} \frac{1}{3} & \frac{2}{3} & 0 \\ \frac{1}{3} & 0 & \frac{1}{4} \\ \frac{1}{3} & \frac{1}{3} & \frac{3}{4} \end{bmatrix}$$

Exercises 5 through 8 give the input-output matrix and the output of some industries. Determine the amount consumed internally by the production processes.

5. $A = \begin{bmatrix} 0.15 & 0.08 \\ 0.30 & 0.20 \end{bmatrix}, X = \begin{bmatrix} 8 \\ 12 \end{bmatrix}$

6. (*See Example 4*)
$A = \begin{bmatrix} 0.10 & 0.20 \\ 0.25 & 0.15 \end{bmatrix}, X = \begin{bmatrix} 20 \\ 15 \end{bmatrix}$

7. $A = \begin{bmatrix} 0.06 & 0.12 & 0.09 \\ 0.15 & 0.05 & 0.10 \\ 0.08 & 0.04 & 0.02 \end{bmatrix}, X = \begin{bmatrix} 8 \\ 14 \\ 10 \end{bmatrix}$

8. $A = \begin{bmatrix} 0.03 & 0 & 0.02 & 0.06 \\ 0.08 & 0.02 & 0 & 0.05 \\ 0.07 & 0.10 & 0.01 & 0.04 \\ 0.05 & 0.04 & 0.02 & 0.06 \end{bmatrix}, X = \begin{bmatrix} 10 \\ 30 \\ 20 \\ 40 \end{bmatrix}$

Compute $(I - A)^{-1}$ for the matrices in Exercises 9 and 10.

9. $A = \begin{bmatrix} 0.2 & 0.3 \\ 0.2 & 0.3 \end{bmatrix}$ **10.** $A = \begin{bmatrix} 0.32 & 0.16 \\ 0.22 & 0.36 \end{bmatrix}$

11. (*See Example 4*) Find the output required to meet the consumer demand and internal demand for the following input-output matrix and consumer demand matrix:

$$A = \begin{bmatrix} 0.24 & 0.08 \\ 0.12 & 0.04 \end{bmatrix} \qquad D = \begin{bmatrix} 15 \\ 12 \end{bmatrix}$$

The economies in Exercises 12 through 16 are either two or three industries. Determine the output levels required of each industry to meet the demands of the other industries and of the consumer. The units are millions of dollars.

12. (*See Example 5*)
$A = \begin{bmatrix} 0.20 & 0.60 \\ 0.40 & 0.10 \end{bmatrix}, D = \begin{bmatrix} 24 \\ 12 \end{bmatrix}, \begin{bmatrix} 8 \\ 6 \end{bmatrix}, \text{and} \begin{bmatrix} 0 \\ 12 \end{bmatrix}$

13. $A = \begin{bmatrix} 0.10 & 0.40 \\ 0.30 & 0.20 \end{bmatrix}, D = \begin{bmatrix} 6 \\ 12 \end{bmatrix}, \begin{bmatrix} 18 \\ 6 \end{bmatrix}, \text{and} \begin{bmatrix} 24 \\ 12 \end{bmatrix}$

14. $A = \begin{bmatrix} 0.30 & 0.60 \\ 0.35 & 0.10 \end{bmatrix}, D = \begin{bmatrix} 42 \\ 84 \end{bmatrix}, \begin{bmatrix} 0 \\ 10 \end{bmatrix}, \begin{bmatrix} 14 \\ 7 \end{bmatrix}, \text{and} \begin{bmatrix} 42 \\ 42 \end{bmatrix}$

15. $A = \begin{bmatrix} 0.20 & 0.20 & 0.10 \\ 0 & 0.40 & 0.20 \\ 0 & 0.20 & 0.60 \end{bmatrix}$,
$D = \begin{bmatrix} 4 \\ 8 \\ 8 \end{bmatrix}, \begin{bmatrix} 0 \\ 8 \\ 16 \end{bmatrix}, \text{and} \begin{bmatrix} 8 \\ 24 \\ 8 \end{bmatrix}$

16. $A = \begin{bmatrix} 0.20 & 0.20 & 0 \\ 0.40 & 0.40 & 0.60 \\ 0.40 & 0.10 & 0.40 \end{bmatrix}$,
$D = \begin{bmatrix} 36 \\ 72 \\ 36 \end{bmatrix}, \begin{bmatrix} 36 \\ 0 \\ 18 \end{bmatrix}, \begin{bmatrix} 3 \\ 0 \\ 0 \end{bmatrix} \text{and} \begin{bmatrix} 0 \\ 18 \\ 18 \end{bmatrix}$

The economies in Exercises 17 through 19 are either two or three industries. The output level of each industry is given. Determine the amounts consumed internally and the amounts available for the consumer from each industry.

17. $A = \begin{bmatrix} 0.20 & 0.40 \\ 0.50 & 0.10 \end{bmatrix}, X = \begin{bmatrix} 8 \\ 10 \end{bmatrix}$

18. $A = \begin{bmatrix} 0.10 & 0.20 & 0.30 \\ 0 & 0.10 & 0.40 \\ 0.50 & 0.40 & 0.20 \end{bmatrix}, X = \begin{bmatrix} 10 \\ 10 \\ 20 \end{bmatrix}$

19. $A = \begin{bmatrix} 0.20 & 0.20 & 0 \\ 0.40 & 0.40 & 0.60 \\ 0.40 & 0.10 & 0.40 \end{bmatrix}, D = \begin{bmatrix} 36 \\ 72 \\ 36 \end{bmatrix}$

20. Three contractors—a carpenter, an electrician, and a painter—contract to build homes. When one of them obtains a contract, he or she uses the services of the other two firms. For each $1 worth of work the carpenter contracts, he uses $0.35 of his own work, $0.20 of the electrician's work, and $0.30 of the painter's work. For each $1 worth of the electrician's contract, she uses $0.25 of the carpenter's work, $0.10 of her own work, and $0.25 of the painter's work. For each $1 worth of the painter's contract, she uses $0.25 of the carpenter's work, $0.15 of the electrician's work, and $0.30 of her own work.
   (a) Find the input-output matrix of this production model.
   (b) The carpenter contracts for a $75,000 house, the electrician contracts for a $65,000 home, and the painter contracts for a $70,000 home. Find the dollar value of the work done by each of the contractors to construct the homes.

IMPORTANT TERMS

2-1

System of Equations

Solution of a System

Substitution Method

Elimination Method

Equivalent System

Inconsistent System

Many Solutions to a System

Parametric Form of a Solution

Parameter

Supply and Demand

Equilibrium Price

2-2

Matrix

Elements of the Matrix

Row Matrix

Column Matrix

Coefficient Matrix

Augmented Matrix

Row Operations

Equivalent Augmented Matrices

Gauss-Jordan Method

Diagonal Locations

2-3

Reduced Echelon Form

No Solution

Unique Solution

Many Solutions

2-4

Square Matrix

Size of Matrix

Equal Matrices

Addition of Matrices

Scalar Multiplication

2-5

Dot Product

Matrix Multiplication

2-6

Identity Matrix

Main Diagonal of Matrix

Inverse Matrix

Matrix Equations

2-7

Leontief Input-Output Model

Closed Model

Production Model

Input-Output Matrix

Open Model

Output Matrix

Internal Demand Matrix

Consumer Demand Matrix

REVIEW EXERCISES

Solve the systems in Exercises 1 and 2 by substitution.

1. $3x + 2y = 5$
$\quad 2x + 4y = 9$

2. $x + 5y = 2$
$\quad 3x - 7y = 12$

Solve the systems in Exercises 3 through 6 by elimination.

3. $5x - y = 34$
$\quad 2x + 3y = 0$

4. $x + 3y - 2z = -15$
$\quad 4x - 3y + 5z = 50$
$\quad 3x + 2y - 2z = -4$

5. $\quad x - 2y + 3z = 3$
$\quad 4x + 7y - 6z = 6$
$\quad -2x + 4y + 12z = 0$

6. $2x - 3y + z = -10$
$\quad 3x - 2y + 4z = -5$
$\quad x + y + 3z = 5$

Solve the systems in Exercises 7 through 16 by the Gauss-Jordan method

7. $2x_1 - 4x_2 - 14x_3 = 50$
$\quad x_1 - x_2 - 5x_3 = 17$
$\quad 2x_1 - 4x_2 - 17x_3 = 65$

8. $3x_1 + 2x_2 = 3$
$\quad 6x_1 - 6x_2 = 1$

9. $x - y = 3$
$\quad 4x + 3y = 5$
$\quad 6x + y = 9$

10. $x + y - z = 0$
$\quad 2x - 3y + 3z = 10$
$\quad 5x - 5y + 5z = 20$

11. $x + z = 0$
$\quad 2x - y + z = -1$
$\quad x - y = -1$

12. $x_1 + 2x_2 - x_3 + 3x_4 = 3$
$\quad x_1 + 3x_2 + x_3 - x_4 = 0$
$\quad 2x_1 + x_2 - 6x_3 + 2x_4 = -11$
$\quad 2x_1 - 2x_2 + x_3 = 9$

13. $\begin{aligned} x_1 + 2x_2 - x_3 + 3x_4 &= 3 \\ x_1 + 3x_2 + x_3 - x_4 &= 0 \\ 2x_1 + x_2 - 6x_3 + 2x_4 &= -11 \\ 3x_1 + 7x_2 - x_3 + 5x_4 &= 6 \end{aligned}$

14. $\begin{aligned} x_1 + 2x_2 - x_3 + 3x_4 &= 3 \\ x_1 + 3x_2 + x_3 - x_4 &= 0 \\ 2x_1 + x_2 - 6x_3 + 2x_4 &= -11 \\ 3x_1 + 4x_2 - 5x_3 + x_4 &= 7 \end{aligned}$

15. $\begin{aligned} 2x_1 + 3x_2 - 5x_3 &= 8 \\ 6x_1 - 3x_2 + x_3 &= 16 \end{aligned}$

16. $\begin{aligned} x - 2y &= 12 \\ 3x + 4y &= 16 \\ x + 8y &= -8 \end{aligned}$

17. Find the value of x that makes the matrices equal

$$\begin{bmatrix} 4 & 3 \\ 3x + 2 & 6 \end{bmatrix} = \begin{bmatrix} 4 & 3 \\ 5 - x & 6 \end{bmatrix}$$

Perform the indicated matrix operations in Exercises 18 through 25, if possible.

18. $-3 \begin{bmatrix} 1 & 4 \\ -2 & 7 \end{bmatrix}$

19. $-1 \begin{bmatrix} 3 & 2 \\ -6 & -7 \end{bmatrix}$

20. $\begin{bmatrix} 1 & 5 \\ -2 & 6 \end{bmatrix} + \begin{bmatrix} 3 & 1 \\ 0 & -4 \end{bmatrix}$

21. $\begin{bmatrix} 3 & 2 \\ 6 & -4 \\ 1 & 1 \end{bmatrix} + \begin{bmatrix} 8 & -5 \\ 1 & 3 \\ 2 & -1 \end{bmatrix}$

22. $\begin{bmatrix} 2 & 1 & 5 \\ 3 & 0 & 2 \end{bmatrix} + \begin{bmatrix} 1 & 1 \\ -2 & 4 \\ 3 & 1 \end{bmatrix}$

23. $\begin{bmatrix} 3 & 1 & -2 \end{bmatrix} \begin{bmatrix} 4 \\ 1 \\ 5 \end{bmatrix}$

24. $\begin{bmatrix} 1 & 0 & 2 \\ 3 & 1 & 1 \end{bmatrix} \begin{bmatrix} 6 & 4 & -2 \\ 3 & 5 & -3 \\ -1 & 0 & 1 \end{bmatrix}$

25. $\begin{bmatrix} 5 & 9 & 1 \\ 6 & -2 & 4 \end{bmatrix} \begin{bmatrix} 3 & 5 \\ -7 & 2 \end{bmatrix}$

Find the inverse, when possible, of the matrices in Exercises 26 through 30.

26. $\begin{bmatrix} 5 & -7 \\ -3 & 4 \end{bmatrix}$　　　27. $\begin{bmatrix} 8 & 6 \\ 7 & 5 \end{bmatrix}$

28. $\begin{bmatrix} 5 & -2 \\ -10 & 4 \end{bmatrix}$　　29. $\begin{bmatrix} 1 & 0 & 3 \\ 2 & -5 & 4 \\ 1 & -2 & 2 \end{bmatrix}$

30. $\begin{bmatrix} 1 & 1 & 2 \\ 0 & 1 & -4 \\ 3 & 2 & 10 \end{bmatrix}$

31. Write the augmented matrix of the system

$$\begin{aligned} 6x_1 + 4x_2 - 5x_3 &= 10 \\ 3x_1 - 2x_2 &= 12 \\ x_1 + x_2 - 4x_3 &= -2 \end{aligned}$$

Find the reduced echelon form of the matrices in Exercises 32 through 34.

32. $\begin{bmatrix} 1 & 3 & 2 & 1 \\ 2 & 4 & -2 & 6 \\ 3 & 1 & 4 & -3 \end{bmatrix}$　33. $\begin{bmatrix} 2 & 4 & 6 & -2 \\ 3 & 1 & 0 & 5 \\ -2 & 1 & 3 & -11 \end{bmatrix}$

34. $\begin{bmatrix} 3 & -1 & 2 \\ 1 & 4 & -1 \\ 4 & 3 & 1 \\ 1 & -9 & 4 \end{bmatrix}$

35. A basketball player scored 59 points in a game with a total of 36 field goals and free throws. How many of each did he make? (A field goal is 2 points, and a free throw is 1 point.)

36. Determine the equilibrium solutions of the following. The demand equation is given first and the supply equation second.
    (a) $y = -4x + 241$
    $\quad y = 3x - 158$
    (b) $y = -7x + 1544$
    $\quad y = 5x - 832$

37. An investor wants to earn $5000 per year by investing $50,000. She can earn 7% from bonds and 12% from stocks. How much should she invest in each?

38. A firm makes three mixes of nuts that contain peanuts, cashews, and almonds in the following proportions.
    I. six pounds peanuts, three pounds cashews, and one pound almonds
    II. five pounds peanuts, two pounds cashews, and two pounds almonds

III. eight pounds peanuts, three pounds cashews, and three pounds almonds

The firm has 183 pounds of peanuts, 78 pounds of cashews, and 58 pounds of almonds in stock. How much of each mix can they make?

39. An investor owns High-Tech and Big Burger stock. On Monday the closing prices were $38 for High Tech and $16 for Big Burger, and the value of the portfolio was $5648. On Friday the closing prices were $40\frac{1}{2}$ for High Tech and $15\frac{3}{4}$ for Big Burger and the value of the portfolio was $5931. How many shares of each stock does the investor own?

40. An investor has $25,000 to invest in two funds. One fund pays 6.5%, and the other pays 8.1%. How much should be invested in each so that the yield on the total investment is 7.5%?

41. A toy company makes its best-selling doll at plants A and B. At plant A the unit cost is $3.60, and the fixed cost is $1260. At plant B the unit cost is $3.30, and the fixed cost is $2637. The company wants the two plants to produce a combined total of 900 dolls, but the total cost at each plant must be the same. How many dolls should be produced at each plant?

42. Tank A has 150 gallons of water, and Tank B has 60 gallons. Water is added to Tank A at the rate of 2.5 gallons per minute and to Tank B at the rate of 3.3 gallons per minute.
  (a) How long will it take for the two tanks to contain the same amount of water?
  (b) How much water will they each contain at that time?

43. The population of Laverne is growing linearly. Six years ago the population was 4600. Today it is 5400. What is the expected population 15 years from now?

44. There are 150,000 registered Democrats, Republicans, and Independents in a county. The number of Independents is 20% of the total number of Democrats and Republicans. In an election, 40% of the Democrats voted, 50% of the Republicans, and 70% of the Independents. The votes totaled 72,000. How many Democrats, Republicans, and Independents are registered?

3

Linear Programming

*L*INEAR PROGRAMMING IS AN application of mathematics that was developed to solve problems in several different disciplines. In 1947, George B. Dantzig and his colleagues were working on logistics planning problems for the U.S. Air Force. Dantzig noticed that many of the problems were similar in nature and could be put in a form that we now call a linear programming problem. He found that people working in game theory and models of economic behavior encountered problems of the same general nature. Dantzig realized that there might be an important mathematical structure underlying these problems. Since that time, linear programming techniques have evolved, and applications abound in industry, government, and business.

The Nobel Prize committee recognized the significance of linear programming by awarding the Nobel Prize in Economics to Professors Leonid Kantorovich of the Soviet Union and Tjalling C. Koopmans of the United States in 1975 for their "contributions to the theory of optimum allocation of resources." Kantorovich used linear programming to improve economic planning in the Soviet Union, and Koopmans used it to determine optimal scheduling of ships across the Atlantic in World War II.

Today, linear programming helps to determine best diets, most efficient production scheduling, and most economical transportation of goods. The term **programming** predates computers. **Linear programming** refers to a precise procedure that will solve a certain type of problem that involves linear conditions.

3-1   LINEAR INEQUALITIES IN TWO VARIABLES

The recommended minimum daily requirements of vitamin B_6 for adults is 2.0 mg. A deficiency of vitamin B_6 in men may increase their cholesterol level and lead to a thickening and degeneration in the walls of their arteries. Many meats, breads, and vegetables contain no vitamin B_6. Fruits usually contain this vitamin. For example, one small banana contains 0.45 mg of vitamin B_6, and one ounce of grapes contains 0.02 mg of vitamin B_6. What quantities of bananas and grapes should an adult consume in order to meet or exceed the minimum requirements?

Mathematically, this question is equivalent to asking for solutions of the **linear inequality**

$$0.45x + 0.02y \geq 2.0$$

where $x =$ the number of bananas eaten and $y =$ the number of ounces of grapes eaten.

Let's see how we solve inequalities like this. If a point is selected, say (3, 5), and its coordinates are substituted into the inequality for x and y, we obtain

$$0.45(3) + 0.02(5) = 1.35 + 0.10$$
$$= 1.45 \qquad \text{which is not greater than 2.0}$$

Since (3, 5) makes $0.45x + 0.02y > 2.0$ false, (3, 5) is *not* a solution. However, the point (4, 12) is a solution because

$$0.45(4) + 0.02(12) = 1.80 + 0.24$$
$$= 2.04$$

Thus $x = 4$ and $y = 12$ make the inequality true. Actually, an infinite number of points make the statement true as we shall see.

If an arbitrary point is selected and its coordinates are substituted for x and y in

$$0.45x + 0.02y$$

we can expect one of three different outcomes:

$$0.45x + 0.02y = 2.0$$
$$0.45x + 0.02y < 2.0$$

or

$$0.45x + 0.02y > 2.0$$

You should recognize the first of these, $0.45x + 0.02y = 2.0$, as the equation of a straight line. Any point that makes this statement true lies on that line. This line holds the key to finding the solution to the original inequality. A line divides the plane into two parts. The areas on either side of the line are called **half planes.** (See Figure 3–1.)

FIGURE 3–1

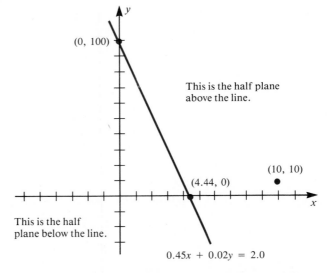

The line $0.45x + 0.02y = 2.0$ divides the plane into two half planes.

One useful fact is that all the points that satisfy

$$0.45x + 0.02y < 2.0$$

lie on one side of the line $0.45x + 0.02y = 2.0$ and all the points that satisfy

$$0.45x + 0.02y > 2.0$$

lie on the other side. We find the solution when we determine which half plane satisfies $0.45x + 0.02y > 2.0$.

There is a simple way to decide. Just pick a point and substitute its coordinates for x and y. For example, the point $(10, 10)$ lies in the half plane above the line. Since $0.45(10) + 0.02(10) = 4.5 + 0.2$, the point $(10, 10)$ satisfies the inequality $0.45x + 0.02y > 2.0$. Consequently, *all* points above the line satisfy the same inequality. The graph of the inequality is the half plane above the line. Indicate this by shading that half plane. (See Figure 3–2.) The line itself is not a part of the solution, so the line is shown dotted.

FIGURE 3–2

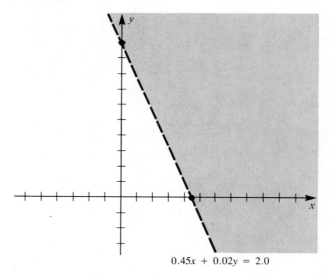

$$0.45x + 0.02y = 2.0$$

The graph of $0.45x + 0.02y > 2.0$

EXAMPLE 1

(a) *(Compare Exercise 3)* Solve $2x + 3y \leq 12$
(b) *(Compare Exercise 7)* Solve $2x + 3y > 12$
SOLUTION   First, replace the inequality by equals and obtain

$$2x + 3y = 12$$

This line divides the plane into two half planes (see Figure 3–3), the part where

$$2x + 3y > 12$$

and the part where

$$2x + 3y < 12$$

FIGURE 3–3

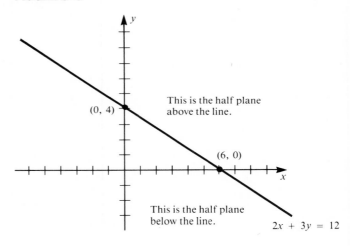

The line $2x + 3y = 12$ divides the plane into two half planes.

(a)   To decide which part satisfies

$$2x + 3y < 12$$

select a point and substitute its coordinates for x and y. For example, the point $(0, 0)$ is in the half plane below the line. Since $2(0) + 3(0) = 0 <$ 12, the point $(0, 0)$ satisfies the inequality $2x + 3y < 12$. Consequently, *all* points below the line satisfy the same inequality. The graph of the inequality consists of the points on the line and the points in the half plane below the line. Indicate this by shading that half plane. (See Figure 3–4.) The line $2x + 3y = 12$ is drawn as a solid line, indicating that it is a part of the solution.

If you select the point $(5, 6)$, a point above the line, you find that

$$2(5) + 3(6) = 28 > 12$$

so the half plane above the line is not the correct one. This is another way to conclude that the correct part is the half plane below the line.

FIGURE 3–4

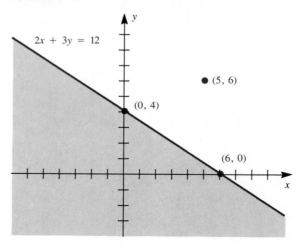

The graph of $2x + 3y \leq 12$

(b) In part (a) we found that $(0, 0)$ satisfies $2x + 3y < 12$. Thus all points in the other half plane, the one opposite $(0, 0)$, satisfy $2x + 3y > 12$. The points on the line are not a part of the solution because the "=" is not a part of the inequality. In such a case the line is drawn as dotted to indicate that it is not a part of the solution. (See Figure 3–5.)

FIGURE 3–5

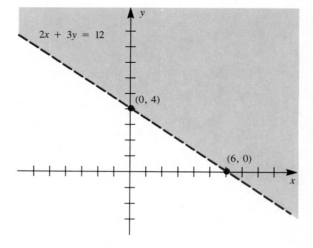

Solution to $2x + 3y > 12$

EXAMPLE 2   *(Compare Exercise 11)*

Graph the inequality $x \leq 5$.

SOLUTION   We use the line $x = 5$ as a boundary and determine the correct half plane by checking the point $(0, 0)$. Since its coordinates satisfy $x \leq 5$, it lies in the half plane forming the solution. (See Figure 3–6.)

FIGURE 3–6

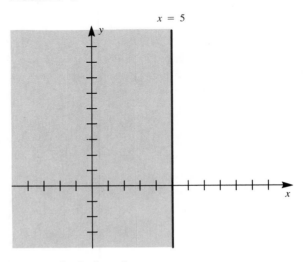

Graph of $x \leq 5$

Procedure for Graphing a Linear Inequality   Graph the inequality of the form $ax + by \leq c$. (The procedure also applies if the inequality symbols are $<$, $>$, or $\geq$.)

1. Graph the line $ax + by = c$. This line is the boundary between two half planes.
2. Select a point that is not on the line from one half plane. The point $(0, 0)$ is usually a good choice when it is not on the line. If $(0, 0)$ is on the line, use a point that is not on the line.
3. Substitute the coordinates of the point for x and y in the inequality.
    (a) If the selected point satisfies the inequality, then shade the half plane where the point lies. These points are on the graph.
    (b) If the selected point does not satisfy the inequality, shade the half plane opposite the point.
    (c) If the inequality symbol is $<$ or $>$, use a dotted line for the graph of $ax + by = c$. This indicates that the points on the line are *not* a part of the graph.
    (d) If the inequality symbol is $\leq$ or $\geq$, use a solid line for the graph of $ax + by = c$. This indicates that the line is a part of the graph.

EXAMPLE 3   *(Compare Exercise 21)*

An automobile assembly plant has an assembly line that produces the Hatchback Special and the Sportster. Each Hatchback requires 2.5 hours of assembly line time, and each Sportster requires 3.5 hours. The assembly line has a maximum operating time of 140 hours per week. Graph the number of cars of each type that can be produced in one week.

SOLUTION   Let x be the number of Hatchback Specials and y be the number of Sportsters produced per week. The total amount of assembly line time required is

$$2.5x + 3.5y$$

Since the total assembly line time is restricted to 140 hours, we need to graph the solution of the inequality

$$2.5x + 3.5y \leq 140$$

Graph the line $2.5x + 3.5y = 140$. Use a solid line. Since the point $(0, 0)$ is a solution to the system, it is in the half plane of the graph. Figure 3–7 shows the graph of the inequality.

FIGURE 3–7

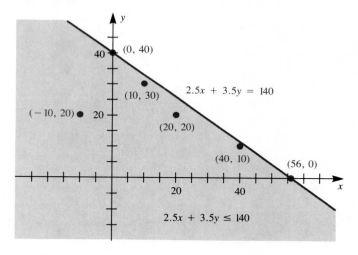

Notice that the points $(20, 20)$, $(10, 30)$, and $(40, 10)$ all lie in the region of solutions. This tells us that the combination 20 Hatchbacks and 20 Sportsters could be produced, or 10 Hatchbacks and 30 Sportsters, or 40 Hatchbacks and 10 Sportsters. The point $(-10, 20)$ also lies in the region of solutions, but it makes no sense to say that negative 10 Hatchbacks and 20 Sportsters could be produced. Thus the nature of the problem requires that neither x nor y can be

FIGURE 3–8

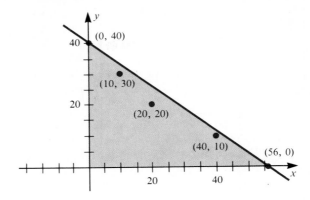

negative. We can state this restriction with $x \geq 0$ and $y \geq 0$. Therefore the inequalities that describe the problem are

$$2.5x + 3.5y \leq 140$$
$$x \geq 0, y \geq 0$$

These conditions restrict the graph to the first quadrant as shown in Figure 3–8. When you set up a problem, you should be careful to include restrictions like this even though they may not be stated explicitly.

   This example illustrates how methods of graphing an inequality are used to find the region that satisfies an inequality, but the context dictates that common sense be used in interpreting the answer. For example, the point (10.3, 5.2) is in the region of solutions, but it doesn't make sense to talk about producing 10.3 Hatchbacks and 5.2 Sportsters. Once the region of solutions is found, only points with whole number coordinates are reasonable.

   If the problem had found the number of acres a farmer should plant with wheat and the number with corn, fractional values would be appropriate.

3–1   EXERCISES

I

In Exercises 1 and 2, determine whether each of the given points is a solution to the inequality.

1. $5x + 2y \leq 17$
   $(1, -1), (4, 1), (3, 1), (4, 4), (2, 3)$

2. $7x - 3y > 24$
   $(5, 1), (3, -3), (2, 2), (4, 1)$

Graph the solution for the inequalities in Exercises 3 through 20.

3. (*See Example 1(a)*)
   $6x + 8y \leq 24$

4. $15x + 55y \leq 1650$

5. $3x - 7y \leq 21$

6. $4x - 5y \leq 20$

7. (*See Example 1(b)*)
   $5x + 4y < 20$

8. $5x + 3y < 15$

9. $6x + 5y < 30$

10. $2x - 10y < 30$

11. (*See Example 2*)
    $x \leq 10$

12. $x > -2$

13. $y \geq -3$

14. $y < 8$

15. $9x - 6y > 30$

16. $4x + 3y \geq 12$

17. $4x - 3y > 12$

18. $9x - 2y < 18$

19. $-2x - 5y > 10$

20. $-12x + 15y < -60$

II

21. (*See Example 3*) Alpine Products produces air conditioners and commercial fans. Each air conditioner requires 3.2 hours of assembly line time, and each fan requires 1.8 hours. The assembly line has a maximum operating time of 144 hours per week. Graph the number of each that can be produced in one week.

22. American Desk Company makes desks and tables. There are 350 hours of labor available each week in the finishing room. Each table requires 2.5 hours in the finishing room, and each desk requires four hours. Graph the number of each that can be produced in one week.

23. A service club agrees to donate at least 500 hours of community service. A full member is to give four hours, and a pledge gives six hours.
    (a) Write the inequality that expresses this information.
    (b) Graph the inequality.

24. Acme Manufacturing has two production lines. Line A can produce 200 gadgets per hour, and line B can produce 350 widgets per hour. Because of warehouse limitations, the total number of gadgets and widgets produced must not exceed 75,000.
    (a) Express this information with an inequality.
    (b) Graph the inequality.

III

25. The Cowley and Associates advertising agency has an advertising budget of $75,000 to advertise a client's product. The agency needs to decide how to schedule the advertising between TV and newspaper ads. Each TV spot costs $900, and each Sunday newspaper ad costs $830. Graph the number of each the agency can schedule.

26. Admission prices for a concert are $8 for adults and $3 for students. The concert will not be booked unless total ticket sales are at least $2500. Write the inequality that expresses this information.

27. Foods Inc. plans to grow strawberries and tomatoes on an 80-acre plot. There will be 750 hours of labor available for the picking. It takes nine hours to pick an acre of strawberries and six hours to pick an acre of tomatoes. Write the inequality that expresses the labor information.

28. Nemecek Bros. makes a single product on two separate production lines, A and B. Its labor force is equivalent to 1000 hours per week, and it has $3000 outlay weekly on operating costs. It takes one hour and four hours to produce a single item on lines A and B, respectively. The cost of producing a single item is $5

on line A and $4 on line B.
    (a) Write the inequality that expresses the labor information.
    (b) Write the inequality that expresses the cost information.

29. Brent Publishing has two plants. The plant on Glen Echo Lane produces 200 paperback books and 300 hardback books per day, and the plant on Speegleville Road produces 300 paperback books and 200 hardback books per day. An order is received for 2400 paperbacks and 2100 hardbacks.
    (a) Write the inequality that expresses the relation between the number of days each plant operates and the number of paperbacks produced.
    (b) Write the inequality that expresses the relation between the number of days each plant operates and the number of hardbacks produced.

30. An investor wants to invest in tax exempt bonds with a 7.5% return and taxable bonds with a 9% return so that the total return will be at least $8100. Write the inequality that expresses this information.

3-2 SYSTEMS OF LINEAR INEQUALITIES

- *Feasible Region*
- *Boundaries and Corners*
- *No Feasible Solution*
- *Graphing a System of Inequalities*

FEASIBLE REGION

Linear programming problems are described mathematically by **systems of linear inequalities** rather than a system of *linear equations*. The solution to a linear programming problem depends on the ability to solve and graph such systems.

EXAMPLE 1   *(Compare Exercise 1)*

Graph the following system of inequalities:

$$x + y \leq 2$$
$$x + 4y < 4$$

SOLUTION   The solution involves three basic steps. The results are drawn in Figure 3–9.

First, graph $x + y \leq 2$.

(a) Graph the line $x + y = 2$. The $\leq$ symbol implies that the line itself is a part of the solution, so use a solid line. (Recall from Section 3–1 that this line divides the plane into two half planes, one of which is included in the solution of the inequality.)

(b) Select a test point not on the line, say $(0, 0)$. (If the point selected satisfies $x + y = 2$, then it lies on the line, and you need to select another one.)

(c) Substitute $x = 0$ and $y = 0$ into $x + y \leq 2$, that is, $0 + 0 \leq 2$. Since this is true, the point $(0, 0)$ is in the correct half plane. Shade that half plane.

FIGURE 3–9

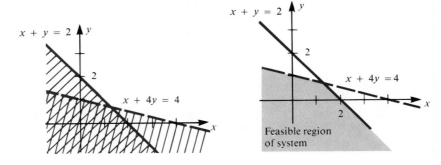

Next, graph $x + 4y < 4$.

(a) Graph the line $x + 4y = 4$. The $<$ symbol implies that the line itself is *not* a part of the solution, so use a dotted line.
(b) Select a test point, say $(2, 2)$.
(c) Substitute $x = 2$ and $y = 2$ into $x + 4y$, that is, $2 + 4(2)$. Since this is not less than 4, the point $(2, 2)$ does *not* make the inequality $x + 4y < 4$ true. Because the inequality is false, the point $(2, 2)$ is not in the correct half plane. The other half plane is correct, so shade it as the solution.

   The points that satisfy both inequalities at once make up the **solution** to the system. These points lie in the region where both half planes overlap. This region of intersection (the solution set of the system) is called the **feasible region** (Figure 3–9(b)).

EXAMPLE 2   *(Compare Exercise 5)*

Graph the solutions to the following system:

$$-x + y \le 1$$
$$x + y \le 3$$
$$x \ge 0$$

SOLUTION   The lines $x = 0$, $-x + y = 1$, and $x + y = 3$ determine half planes that form solutions to the given inequalities. The graphs of the lines and the appropriate half planes are shown in Figure 3–10. The shaded region common to all three half planes forms the solution to the system of inequalities. Just as a check, substitute x and y from the point $(2, 0)$ into each of the original inequalities. You will find that those values satisfy all three inequalities, so the point belongs to the solution set.

FIGURE 3–10

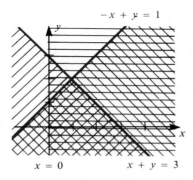

Half plane determined by:
$$-x + y \le 1$$
$$x + y \le 3$$
$$x \ge 0$$

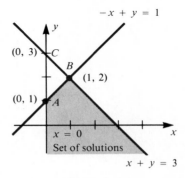

Solution to the system:
$$-x + y \le 1$$
$$x + y \le 3$$
$$x \ge 0$$

BOUNDARIES AND CORNERS

The lines $x = 0$, $-x + y = 1$, and $x + y = 3$ determine the **boundaries** of the solution set in Example 2. The points contained within the boundaries, and the appropriate points on a boundary, form the solution set of the system. In linear programming terminology a point that satisfies all inequalities of the system is called a **feasible solution,** and the solution set is called the **feasible region.** Points A and B in Figure 3–10 are **corners** of the region, points in the feasible region where boundary lines intersect.

In linear programming, you will learn that the corners of the solution set (feasible region) contain the optimal solution. We find the corners by solving pairs of simultaneous equations, using equations of lines forming the boundary.

To find the corner A, the point of intersection of the lines $x = 0$ and $-x + y = 1$, we solve the system

$$x = 0$$
$$-x + y = 1$$

Corner A is the point $(0, 1)$.

Corner B occurs at the point of intersection of the lines $-x + y = 1$ and $x + y = 3$. To determine B, solve the system

$$-x + y = 1$$
$$x + y = 3$$

You should find that corner B is the point $(1, 2)$.

The point C, $(0, 3)$, is the solution of the system

$$x = 0$$
$$x + y = 3$$

and so it is the intersection of two boundary lines. However, C is not a corner point because it lies outside the feasible region. This shows that *you cannot pick two boundary lines arbitrarily* and expect their intersection to form a corner point. You need to determine if the point lies in the feasible region.

EXAMPLE 3 *(Compare Exercise 18)*

Sketch the feasible region (solution set) of the system

$$x + \ y \leq 3$$
$$-x + 2y \leq 3$$
$$x \geq 0, \quad y \geq 0$$

SOLUTION The nonnegative restrictions $x \geq 0$ and $y \geq 0$ often enter into linear programming problems since the variables usually represent quantities of things such as TV sets or hours a production line is available. Other inequalities represent restrictions associated with these quantities, such as capital limitations or available labor. The graph is the shaded region with corners, A, B, C, and O in Figure 3–11.

FIGURE 3–11

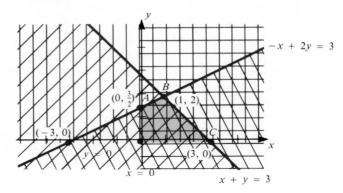

To find the Corner A, solve the system of equations

$$-x + 2y = 3$$
$$x \qquad = 0$$

Corner A is the point $(0, \frac{3}{2})$.
Find B by solving the system

$$x + \ y = 3$$
$$-x + 2y = 3$$

On solving this system we find that B is the point $(1, 2)$.
Corner C is the solution to the system

$$x + y = 3$$
$$y = 0$$

C is the point $(3, 0)$.
The corners of the solution set are

$$A: \left(0, \frac{3}{2}\right), \quad B: (1, 2), \quad C: (3, 0), \quad \text{and} \quad O: (0, 0)$$

**NO FEASIBLE
SOLUTION**

Some systems of inequalities have no solution set, as the following example illustrates.

EXAMPLE 4   *(Compare Exercise 19)*

Find the solution set (feasible region) of the system

$$5x + 7y \geq 35$$
$$3x + 4y \leq 12$$
$$x \geq 0$$
$$y \geq 0$$

FIGURE 3–12

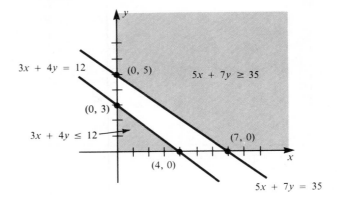

SOLUTION The inequalities $x \geq 0$ and $y \geq 0$ force the solutions to be in the first quadrant. The test point $(0, 0)$ shows that the points that satisfy $5x + 7y > 35$ lie above the line $5x + 7y = 35$ and the points that satisfy $3x + 4y < 12$ lie below the line $3x + 4y = 12$. As shown in Figure 3–12, these two regions do not intersect in the first quadrant. The system then has no solution. We sometimes say that there is **no feasible solution.**

EXAMPLE 5 *(Compare Exercise 26)*

The organizer of a conference has $5000 expense money available to participants. Some participants may receive $25 each for expenses, and others may receive $75 each. Attendance at the conference is limited to 80 participants. State the inequalities that represent this information.

SOLUTION Let x equal the number of participants who may receive $25, and let y equal the number of participants who may receive $75. Then $25x + 75y$ is the total amount of expense money distributed. The inequality $25x + 75y \leq 5000$ states that total expenses are limited to $5000. The inequality $x + y \leq 80$ states that the conference is limited to 80 participants. Since a negative number of participants makes no sense, the restrictions $x \geq 0$ and $y \geq 0$ are also needed.

GRAPHING A SYSTEM OF INEQUALITIES

To graph a system of inequalities:

1. Replace each inequality symbol with an equals sign to obtain a linear equation.
2. Graph each line. Use a solid line if it is a part of the solution. Use a dotted line if it is not a part of the solution. The line is a part of the solution when $\leq$ or $\geq$ is used. The line is not a part of the solution when $<$ or $>$ is used.

3. Select a test point not on the line.
4. If the test point satisfies the original inequality, it is in the correct half plane. If it does not satisfy the inequality, the other half plane is the correct one.
5. Shade the correct half plane.
6. When the above steps are completed for each inequality, determine where the shaded half planes overlap. This region is the graph of the system of inequalities.

3-2 EXERCISES

I

Graph the systems of inequalities in Exercises 1 through 8.

1. (*See Example 1*)
$$x + y \leq 3$$
$$2x - y < -2$$

2. $2x + y \geq 4$
$$4x - y \geq 8$$

3. $x \geq 3$
$$ y \geq 2$$
$$3x + 2y < 18$$

4. $-x + 3y < 6$
$$2x + y < 7$$
$$ y \geq 0$$

5. (*See Example 2*)
$$4x + 6y \leq 18$$
$$x + 3y \leq 6$$
$$x \geq 0$$

6. $2x + y \leq 50$
$$4x + 5y \leq 160$$
$$x \geq 0, y \geq 0$$

7. $2x + y \leq 60$
$$2x + 3y \leq 120$$
$$x \geq 0, y \geq 0$$

8. $4x + 3y \leq 72$
$$4x + 9y \leq 144$$
$$x \geq 2, y \geq 0$$

Find the feasible regions of the systems of inequalities in Exercises 9 through 24. Determine the corners of each feasible region.

9. $x + y > 4$
$$2x - 3y \geq 8$$

10. $-x + y \leq 3$
$$2x + y \leq 6$$
$$x \geq 0, y \geq 0$$

11. $-2x + y < 4$
$$x + y \geq 3$$

12. $-x + 2y \geq 3$
$$2x + y \geq 2$$

13. $x \geq 0$
$$y < 0$$

14. $-x + y \leq 3$
$$x + y \leq 4$$
$$x \geq 0, y \geq 0$$

15. $2x + y \leq 1$
$$-x + y > 4$$
$$y \geq 0$$

16. $x - y \leq 2$
$$2x + y \leq 4$$
$$x + 2y \leq 4$$

II

17. $3x + 4y > 24$
$$4x + 5y < 20$$
$$x > 0$$

18. (*See Example 3*)
$$x + y \leq 2$$
$$3x + y \leq 6$$
$$x \geq 0, y \geq 0$$

19. (*See Example 4*)
$$x + y \leq 2$$
$$2x + y \geq 6$$
$$y \geq 0$$

20. $2x + y \geq 2$
$$x - 3y \leq 6$$
$$-4x + y < -3$$

21. $x + y \geq 1$
$$-x + y \geq 2$$
$$5x - y \leq 4$$

22. $2x + y \leq 3$
$$5x + 2y \leq 7$$
$$x \geq 0, y \geq 0$$

23. $8x + y \geq -10$
$$-2x + y \leq 6$$
$$4x + y \leq 2$$
$$3x - y \leq -1$$

24. $4x - 3y \geq 60$
$$x + y \leq 10$$
$$-x + 2y \geq -50$$

III

25. Determine the feasible region and corners of this system:
$$-2x + y \leq 2$$
$$3x + y \leq 3$$
$$-x + y \geq -4$$
$$x + y \geq -3$$

26. (*See Example 5*) The seating capacity of a theater is 250. Tickets are $3 for children and $5 for adults. The theater must take in at least $1000 per performance. Express this information as a system of inequalities.

27. High Fibre and Corn Bits cereals contain the following amounts of minimum daily requirements of Vitamins A and D for each ounce of cereal.

	VITAMIN A	VITAMIN D
HIGH FIBRE	25%	4%
CORN BITS	2%	10%

Use inequalities to express how much of each Mrs. Smith should eat to obtain at least 40% of her minimum daily requirements of Vitamin A and 25% of that for Vitamin D.

28. High Fibre and Corn Bits cereals contain the following amounts of sodium and calories per ounce.

	CALORIES	SODIUM (mg)
HIGH FIBRE	90	160
CORN BITS	120	200

Mr. Brown's breakfast should provide at least 600 calories but less than 800 mg of sodium. Find the constraints on the amount of each cereal.

29. The Musical Group has two admission prices for its concerts, $8 for adults and $3 for students. They will not book a concert unless they are assured an audience of at least 500 people and total ticket sales of $2500 or more. Write the constraints on the number of each kind of tickets sold.

30. To be eligible for a University Scholarship, a student must score at least 600 on the SAT verbal test and 600 on the SAT mathematics test and must have a combined verbal-mathematics score of 1325 or more. Write this as a system of inequalities.

31. A test is scored by giving 4 points for each correct answer and −1 for each incorrect answer. To obtain an acceptable score, a student must answer at least 60 questions and attain a score of 200 points. Express this information with inequalities.

3–3 LINEAR PROGRAMMING—A GEOMETRICAL APPROACH

- *Constraints and Objective Function*
- *Geometrical Solution*
- *Unusual Linear Programming Situations*

CONSTRAINTS AND OBJECTIVE FUNCTION

Managers in business and industry often make decisions in an effort to maximize or minimize some quantity. For example, a plant manager wants to minimize overtime pay for production workers, a store manager makes an effort to maximize revenue, and a stockbroker tries to maximize the return on investments. Most of these decisions are complicated by restrictions that limit choices. The plant manager might not be able to eliminate all overtime and still meet the contract deadline. A store might be swamped by customers because of its low prices, but the prices might be so low that the store is losing money.

Linear programming is a mathematical technique that solves certain problems of this kind. Let's start with a simple example.

EXAMPLE 1   *(Compare Exercise 1)*

An appliance store manager plans to offer a special on washers and dryers. The storeroom capacity is limited to 50 items. Each washer requires two hours to unpack and set up, and each dryer requires one hour. The manager has 80 hours of employee time available for unpacking and setup. Washers sell for $300 each, and dryers sell for $200 each. How many of each should the manager order to obtain the maximum revenue?

SOLUTION   Convert the given information to mathematical statements:

$$\text{Let } x = \text{the number of washers}$$
$$y = \text{the number of dryers}$$

The total number to be placed in the storeroom is

$$x + y$$

and the total setup time is

$$2x + 1y$$

Since the manager has space for only 50 items and setup time of 80 hours, we have the restrictions

$$x + y \leq 50$$
$$2x + y \leq 80$$

Since x and y cannot be negative, we also have

$$x \geq 0 \qquad \text{and} \qquad y \geq 0$$

Since washers sell for $300 and dryers sell for $200, we want to find values of x and y that maximize the total revenue

$$z = 300x + 200y$$

Here is the problem stated in concise form.
   Maximize z, where

$$z = 300x + 200y$$

subject to

$$x + y \leq 50$$
$$2x + y \leq 80$$
$$x \geq 0$$
$$y \geq 0$$

The inequalities

$$x + y \leq 50 \qquad \text{and} \qquad 2x + y \leq 80$$

impose restrictions on the problem, and we call them **constraints.** The restrictions $x \geq 0, y \geq 0$ are **nonnegative conditions.** We call the function $z = 300x + 200y$ the **objective function.** Find the values of x and y that satisfy the system of con-

FIGURE 3-13

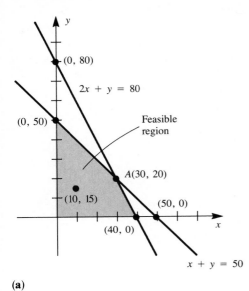

(a)

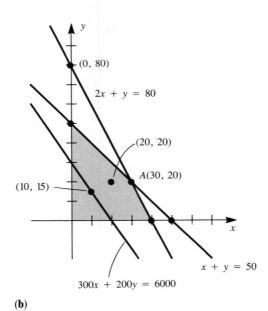

(b)

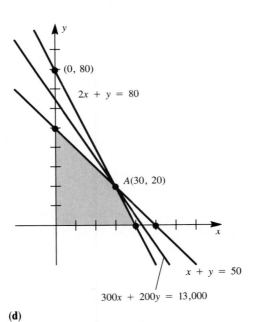

(c)

(d)

straints (inequalities) by the methods from the last section. You should obtain the feasible region as shown in Figure 3–13(a). Corner A is (30, 20).

Each point in the feasible region determines a value for the objective function. We want to find the point in the feasible region that maximizes the objective function. The point (10, 10) gives $z = 300x + 200y$ the value $z = 5000$, while the point (20, 20) gives the value $z = 10,000$. Since the feasible region contains an infinite number of points, we will not easily find the maximum value of z by a haphazard trial-and-error process.

Definition
**Constraints,
Nonnegative Condition**

A linear inequality of the form

$$a_1 x + a_2 y \leq b$$

or

$$a_1 x + a_2 y \geq b$$

is called a **constraint** of a linear programming problem. The restrictions

$$x \geq 0 \qquad \text{and} \qquad y \geq 0$$

are **nonnegative conditions.**

**GEOMETRICAL
SOLUTION**

A basic theorem makes it easier to find a maximum or minimum value of an objective function. The term **optimal** refers to either maximum or minimum.

Theorem 1
Optimal Values

Given a linear objective function subject to linear inequality constraints, if the objective function has an optimal value (maximum or minimum), it must occur at a corner point of the feasible region.

The feasible region of the above example has corner points (0, 0), (0, 50), (30, 20), and (40, 0). The value of the objective function in each case is $z = 0$ at (0, 0), $z = 10,000$ at (0, 50), $z = 13,000$ at (30, 20), and $z = 12,000$ at (40, 0). The maximum value of z within the feasible region is therefore 13,000, and the minimum value is 0.

---

*Graphical Solution to
Linear Programming
Problem*

1. Use each constraint (linear inequality) in turn to sketch the boundary of the feasible region.
2. Determine the corner points of the feasible region by solving pairs of linear equations (equations obtained from the constraints).
3. Evaluate the objective function at each corner point.
4. The maximum (minimum) of the objective function at corner points yields the desired maximum (minimum).

Let's look at Example 1 in order to understand why optimal values of the objective function occur at corner points. The point (10, 15) lies in the feasible region (See Figure 3–13(a).) The value of the objective function $z = 300x + 200y$ at that point is

$$z = 300(10) + 200(15) = 6000$$

This value of z can be obtained at other points in the feasible region; in fact, $z = 6000$ will occur at any point in the feasible region that lies on the line $300x + 200y = 6000$. (See Figure 3–13(b).) Furthermore, for any point (x, y) in the feasible region, one of the following will occur:

$$300x + 200y = 6000$$
$$300x + 200y < 6000$$

or

$$300x + 200y > 6000$$

We have already observed that equality holds for points on the line $300x + 200y = 6000$. The point (0, 0) satisfies $300x + 200y < 6000$, so all points below the line do also. From graphing inequalities we then know that the points in the half plane *above* the line $300x + 200y = 6000$ must satisfy

$$300x + 200y > 6000$$

From Figure 3–13(b) we observe the point (20, 20) lies in the feasible region and lies above $300x + 200y = 6000$, so that point will yield a larger value of the objective function. It yields $z = 300(20) + 200(20) = 10,000$. Is this the largest possible value of the objective function, or do other points in the feasible region yield a larger value of z? Again, we observe that any point on the line $300x + 200y = 10,000$ will satisfy

$$300x + 200y = 10,000$$

Any point below that line will satisfy

$$300x + 200y < 10,000$$

and any point above the line will satisfy

$$300x + 200y > 10,000$$

Figure 3–13(c) shows that there are points in the feasible region above the line, so larger values of z are possible.

If we select the point (30, 20),

$$z = 300(30) + 200(20) = 13,000$$

This gives a larger value of z. Notice in Figure 3–13(d) that there are no points in the feasible region above the line

$$300x + 200y = 13,000$$

so the corner point (30, 20) gives the largest possible value of z. Thus the optimal value of z is 13,000 and occurs at the corner point (30, 20). Points above the line give larger values of z, but the points lie outside the feasible region.

In this example the feasible region is **bounded** because it can be enclosed in a finite rectangle. For a bounded feasible region the objective function will have both a maximum and a minimum.

In some cases the constraints lead to an inconsistency, so there are no points in the feasible region—it is **empty** (see Example 4 of Section 3–2).

Theorem 2 **Bounded Feasible** **Region**	When the feasible region is not empty and is bounded, the objective function has both a maximum and a minimum value, and they must occur at corner points.

EXAMPLE 2   *(Compare Exercise 3)*

Find the maximum value of the objective function

$$z = 10x + 15y$$

subject to the constraints

$$x + 4y \le 360$$
$$2x + y \le 300$$
$$x \ge 0, \quad y \ge 0$$

SOLUTION   Graph the feasible region of the system of inequalities (Figure 3–14). The corner points of the feasible region are (0, 90), (0, 0), (150, 0), and (120, 60). The point (120, 60) is found by solving the system

$$x + 4y = 360$$
$$2x + y = 300$$

FIGURE 3–14

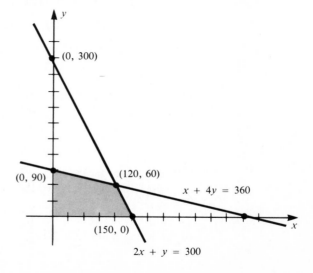

Find the value of z at each corner point.

CORNER	$z = 10x + 15y$
(0, 90)	1350
(0, 0)	0
(150, 0)	1500
(120, 60)	2100

The maximum value of z is 2100 and occurs at the corner (120, 60).

EXAMPLE 3 *(Compare Exercise 7)*

Find the minimum value of $z = 5x + 10y$ subject to the constraints

$$3x + 2y \geq 60$$
$$x + 4y \geq 40$$
$$x \geq 0, \quad y \geq 0$$

SOLUTION   The corner points of the feasible region are (0, 30), (16, 6), and (40, 0). (See Figure 3–15.) The value of z at each of these points is: $z = 300$ at (0, 30); $z = 140$ at (16, 6); and $z = 200$ at (40, 0). Thus the minimum value of z is 140 and occurs at (16, 6).

FIGURE 3–15

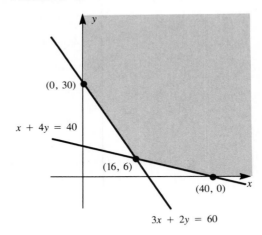

EXAMPLE 4 *(Compare Exercise 11)*

Find the maximum value of $z = 3x + 5y$ subject to the constraints

$$x + y \leq 10$$
$$x + 2y \leq 18$$
$$2x + y \leq 16$$
$$x \geq 0, \quad y \geq 0$$

SOLUTION   The feasible region defined by the constraints is shown in Figure 3–16. Its corner points are $(0, 0)$, $(0, 9)$, $(2, 8)$, $(6, 4)$, and $(8, 0)$. The values of z are: $z = 45$ at $(0, 9)$; $z = 46$ at $(2, 8)$; $z = 38$ at $(6, 4)$; and $z = 24$ at $(8, 0)$. Thus the maximum value of z is 46, and it occurs at $(2, 8)$.   ∎

FIGURE 3–16

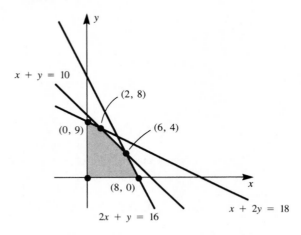

EXAMPLE 5   *(Compare Exercise 15)*

Determine the minimum value of

$$z = 4x + 6y$$

subject to the constraints

$$5x + 2y \geq 220$$
$$x + y \geq 80$$
$$x + 2y \geq 105$$
$$x \geq 0, \quad y \geq 0$$

SOLUTION   The feasible region of this problem is shown in Figure 3–17. The corner points are $(0, 110)$, $(20, 60)$, $(55, 25)$, and $(105, 0)$. The values of z at these corner points are the following:

CORNER	$z = 4x + 6y$
$(0, 110)$	660
$(20, 60)$	440
$(55, 25)$	370
$(105, 0)$	420

The minimum value of z is 370, and it occurs at $(55, 25)$.   ∎

FIGURE 3–17

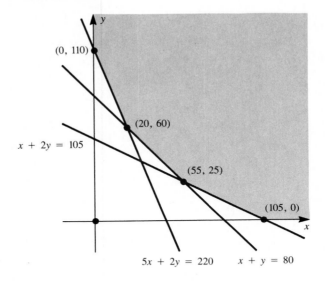

$x + 2y = 105$

$5x + 2y = 220$ $x + y = 80$

EXAMPLE 6 *(Compare Exercise 19)*

Find the maximum and minimum values of

$$z = 4x + 6y$$

subject to the constraints

$$5x + 3y \geq 15$$
$$x + 2y \leq 20$$
$$7x + 9y \leq 105$$
$$x \geq 0, \quad y \geq 0$$

SOLUTION   The feasible region of this system and its corners are shown in Figure 3–18. Compute the value of z at each corner to determine the maximum and minimum values of z.

CORNER	VALUE OF z
(0, 5)	30
(0, 10)	60
(6, 7)	66
(15, 0)	60
(3, 0)	12

The maximum value of z is 66 and occurs at the corner (6, 7). The minimum value of z is 12 and occurs at the corner (3, 0).

FIGURE 3–18

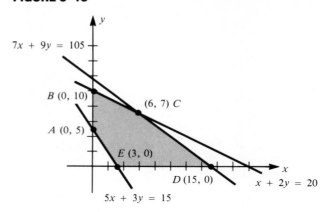

EXAMPLE 7   *(Compare Exercise 35)*

A company makes two products, one on production line A and the other on production line B. Available resources include a labor force equivalent to 900 hours per week and \$2800 for weekly operating costs. It takes five hours labor to produce each item on line A and two hours labor to produce each item on line B. The company requires that line B produce at least 50 items per week. Each item produced on line A costs \$8, and those on line B cost \$10. The company wishes to maximize its profits. If the profit on each item produced on line A is \$3 and the profit for each item produced on line B is \$2, how many of each item should be produced to achieve maximum profit?

SOLUTION   This problem contains two restrictions: time and funds available. The company wants to maximize profit under these restrictions. The problem may be solved in four steps:

1. Specify the variables used.
2. Use mathematical statements to describe the situation.
3. Sketch the graph.
4. Use the graph to determine the solution.

Let

$$x = \text{the number of items produced on line A}$$
$$y = \text{the number of items produced on line B}$$

The time required to produce x items on line A is $5x$, and that required for line B is $2y$, so the total hours labor involved is

$$5x + 2y$$

The inequality

$$5x + 2y \leq 900$$

states that no more than 900 hours of labor is available. The cost of x items on line A is $8x$ and on line B is $10y$, so

$$8x + 10y$$

represents the total weekly operating costs. The inequality

$$8x + 10y \leq 2800$$

describes the restriction on operating costs; $y \geq 50$ states that Line B must produce at least 50 items. The total profit is

$$3x + 2y$$

The objective function is the quantity to be maximized or minimized, so $z = 3x + 2y$ is the objective function. Because x and y represent the number of items produced, they cannot be negative, so we have $x \geq 0$ and $y \geq 0$.

We state this linear programming problem as follows: Maximize the objective function

$$z = 3x + 2y$$

subject to the constraints

$$5x + 2y \leq 900$$
$$8x + 10y \leq 2800$$
$$y \geq 50$$
$$x \geq 0, \quad y \geq 0$$

We want to find the solutions of this system of inequalities that gives the maximum value of $3x + 2y$. Graph this system as shown in Figure 3–19. Its corners are the points where pairs of lines intersect, and are found from the following systems:

$8x + 10y = 2800$	$8x + 10y = 2800$	$5x + 2y = 900$	$x = 0$
$x = 0$	$5x + 2y = 900$	$y = 50$	$y = 50$

giving the corners (0, 280), (100, 200), (160, 50), and (0, 50). The maximum value of z is attained at one of these corner points. Examine each one:

At (0, 280), $z = 3(0) + 2(280) = 560$.
At (100, 200), $z = 3(100) + 2(200) = 700$.
At (160, 50), $z = 3(160) + 2(50) = 580$.
At (0, 50), $z = 100$.

The maximum value of $z = 3x + 2y$, 700, occurs when $x = 100$ and $y = 200$. These results indicate that \$700 is the maximum weekly profit that can be attained under the given constraints and that the company should produce 100 items on line A and 200 items on line B.

FIGURE 3–19

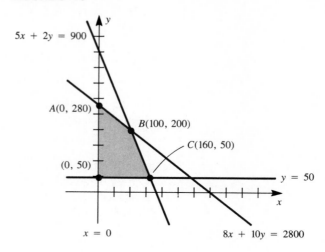

EXAMPLE 8 *(Compare Exercise 45)*

Mom's Old-Fashioned Casseroles produces a luncheon casserole that consists of 50% carbohydrates, 30% protein, and 20% fat. The dinner casserole consists of 75% carbohydrates, 20% protein, and 5% fat. The luncheon casserole costs $2.00 per pound and the dinner casserole costs $2.50 per pound. How much of each type of casserole should be used to provide at least 3 pounds of carbohydrates, 1.50 pounds of protein and 0.50 pound of fat at a minimum cost?

SOLUTION   Let $x =$ the number of pounds of the luncheon casserole and $y =$ the number of pounds of dinner casserole. We wish to minimize the cost, $z = 2x + 2.50y$. The constraints are

$$0.50x + 0.75y \geq 3 \qquad \text{(Total carbohydrates)}$$
$$0.30x + 0.20y \geq 1.50 \qquad \text{(Total protein)}$$
$$0.20x + 0.05y \geq 0.50 \qquad \text{(Total fat)}$$
$$x \geq 0, \quad y \geq 0$$

Figure 3–20 shows the feasible region with corners $(0, 10)$, $(1, 6)$, $(4.2, 1.2)$, and $(6, 0)$. The values of z at each of these corners is: $z = 25$ at $(0, 10)$; $z = 17$ at $(1, 6)$; $z = 11.4$ at $(4.2, 1.2)$; and $z = 12$ at $(6, 0)$. Then the minimum cost is $11.40 when 4.2 pounds of the luncheon casserole and 1.2 pounds of the dinner casserole is used.

FIGURE 3–20

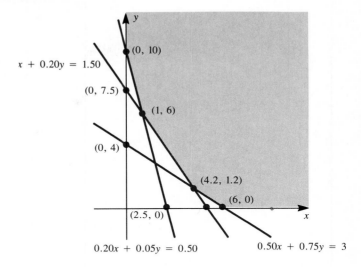

$x + 0.20y = 1.50$

(0, 10)

(0, 7.5)

(1, 6)

(0, 4)

(4.2, 1.2)

(6, 0)

(2.5, 0)

$0.20x + 0.05y = 0.50$

$0.50x + 0.75y = 3$

UNUSUAL LINEAR PROGRAMMING SITUATIONS

Multiple Optimal Solutions. In the preceding example there was just one corner point that gave an optimal solution. It is possible for more than one optimal solution to exist. In other cases there may be no solution at all. First, look at an example with multiple solutions.

EXAMPLE 9 *(Compare Exercise 23)*

Determine the maximum value of

$$z = 8x + 2y$$

subject to the constraints

$$4x + \quad y \le 32$$
$$4x + 3y \le 48$$
$$x \ge 0, \quad y \ge 0$$

SOLUTION The feasible region of these constraints is shown in Figure 3–21. The corners of the feasible region are (0, 16), (6, 8), (8, 0), and (0, 0).

The value of $z = 8x + 2y$ at each of these points is as follows:

At (0, 16), $z = 32$.
At (6, 8), $z = 64$.
At (8, 0), $z = 64$.
At (0, 0), $z = 0$.

Thus the maximum value of $8x + 2y$ is 64, and it occurs at two points, (6, 8) and (8, 0). When this happens in a linear programming problem, the objective function has the same value at every point on the line segment joining the two corners. In this case the objective function has the maximum value of 64

FIGURE 3–21

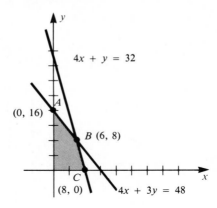

along the boundary line $4x + y = 32$ from the point $(6, 8)$ to the point $(8, 0)$. For example, the point $(7, 4)$ lies on the line $4x + y = 32$ and gives z the value $8(7) + 2(4) = 64$.

Multiple solutions allow a number of choices of x and y that yield the same optimal value for the objective functions. For example, if x and y represent production quantities, then management can achieve optimal production with a variety of production levels. If problems should occur with one production line, management might adjust production on the other line and still achieve optimal production. When there is just one optimal solution, management has no flexibility; there is one choice of x and y by which management can achieve its objective.

You might wonder how to tell whether there are multiple solutions. It turns out that this happens when a boundary line has the same slope as the objective function. (*See Exercise 57.*)

Unbounded Feasible Region. The constraints of a linear programming problem might define an unbounded feasible region for which the objective function has no maximum value. In such a case the problem has no solution. Here is an illustration.

EXAMPLE 10   (*Compare Exercise 29*)

Determine the maximum value of the objective function $z = x + 4y$, subject to the constraints

$$-4x + y \leq 2$$
$$2x - y \leq 1$$
$$x \geq 0, \quad y \geq 0$$

SOLUTION   Figure 3–22 shows the feasible region of these constraints. Observe that the feasible region extends upward indefinitely. Suppose someone claims that

FIGURE 3–22

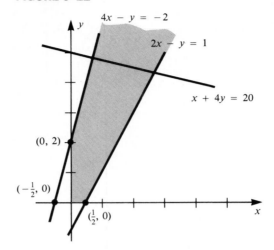

the maximum value of the objective function is 20. This is equivalent to stating that

$$x + 4y = 20$$

and no other values of x and y in the feasible region give larger values. You recognize this as the equation of a straight line. Figure 3–22 shows that this line crosses the feasible region. Next, observe that the test point $(0, 0)$ does *not* satisfy the inequality $x + 4y > 20$, so the points in the half plane above the line *must* satisfy it. Thus every point in the feasible region that lies above the line $x + 4y = 20$ will give a larger value of the objective function. If we substitute larger values, say 100, 5000, and so on, instead of 20 in the equation, we essentially determine lines that are parallel to $x + 4y = 20$ but are farther away from the origin. In each case, points in the feasible region that lie above the line give an even larger value of $x + 4y$. Since the feasible region extends upward indefinitely, we can never find a largest value.

We point out that the objective function $z = x + 4y$ does have a *minimum* value at $(0, 0)$. So an unbounded feasible region does not rule out an optimal solution. It depends on the region and what kind of optimal solution is sought. ∎

No Optimal Solution Because There Is No Feasible Region. The system of inequalities

$$5x + 7y \geq 35$$
$$3x + 4y \leq 12$$
$$x \geq 0, \quad y \geq 0$$

is a system of inequalities that has no solution. (See Example 4 of Section 3–2.) Whenever the constraints of a linear programming problem do not define a feasible region, there can be no optimal solution.

3-3 EXERCISES

1. (*See Example 1*) Set up the constraints and objective function for the following linear programming problem. A discount store is offered two styles of slightly damaged coffee tables. The store has storage space for 80 tables and 110 hours labor for repairing the defects. Each table of style A requires one hour labor to repair, and each table of Style B requires two hours. Style A is priced at $50 each, and style B at $40 each. How many of each style should be ordered to maximize gross sales?

2. The organizer of a day conference has $2000 expense money available for distribution to participants. The participants fall into two categories: those having $30 expenses and those having $10 expenses. Facilities are available to host 100 participants at the conference. Describe the constraints on each type of participant.

3. (*See Example 2*) Find the maximum value of the objective function $z = 20x + 12y$, subject to the constraints

$$3x + 2y \leq 18$$
$$3x + y \leq 15$$
$$x \geq 0, \quad y \geq 0$$

4. Maximize $z = 2x + 3y$, subject to

$$3x + y \leq 24$$
$$3x + 2y \leq 42$$
$$x \geq 0, \quad y \geq 0$$

5. Maximize $z = 9x + 2y$, subject to

$$5x + y \leq 35$$
$$3x + y \leq 27$$
$$x \geq 0, \quad y \geq 0$$

6. Maximize $z = 21x + 10y$, subject to

$$x + 3y \leq 24$$
$$7x + 2y \leq 35$$
$$x \geq 0, \quad y \geq 0$$

7. (*See Example 3*) Minimize $z = 2x + 3y$, subject to

$$4x + y \geq 40$$
$$4x + 3y \geq 64$$
$$x \geq 0, \quad y \geq 0$$

8. Minimize $z = 5x + 4y$, subject to

$$x + y \geq 8$$
$$5x + 3y \geq 30$$
$$x \geq 0, \quad y \geq 0$$

9. Maximize $z = 9x + 13y$, subject to

$$10x + 11y \leq 330$$
$$4x + 6y \leq 156$$
$$x \geq 0, \quad y \geq 0$$

10. Minimize $z = 7x + 5y$, subject to

$$9x + 5y \geq 45$$
$$3x + 10y \geq 60$$
$$x \geq 0, \quad y \geq 0$$

11. (*See Example 4*)
Maximize $z = 20x + 30y$, subject to

$$-x + 2y \leq 40$$
$$x + 4y \leq 54$$
$$3x + y \leq 63$$
$$x \geq 0, \quad y \geq 0$$

12. Maximize $z = 10x + 15y$, subject to

$$x + 5y \leq 60$$
$$5x + y \leq 60$$
$$x + y \leq 16$$
$$x \geq 0, \quad y \geq 0$$

13. Maximize $z = 320x + 140y$, subject to

$$x + 5y \leq 250$$
$$2x + 5y \leq 300$$
$$x \leq 75$$
$$x \geq 0, \quad y \geq 0$$

14. Maximize $z = 8x + 3y$, subject to

$$x + 2y \leq 28$$
$$x + 4y \leq 48$$
$$3x + y \leq 54$$
$$x \geq 0, \quad y \geq 0$$

15. (*See Example 5*)
Minimize $z = 5x + 3y$, subject to

$$6x + y \geq 52$$
$$2x + y \geq 20$$
$$x + 4y \geq 24$$
$$x \geq 0, \quad y \geq 0$$

16. Minimize $z = 6x + 2y$, subject to

$$x + 5y \geq 40$$
$$x + y \geq 16$$
$$4x + 2y \geq 48$$
$$x \geq 0, \quad y \geq 0$$

17. Minimize $z = 5x + 3y$, subject to

$$3x + y \geq 30$$
$$4x + 3y \geq 60$$
$$x + 2y \geq 20$$
$$x \geq 0, \quad y \geq 0$$

18. Minimize $z = 2x + 8y$, subject to

$$x + 3y \geq 29$$
$$x + y \geq 21$$
$$2x + y \geq 26$$
$$x \geq 0, \quad y \geq 0$$

II

19. (*See Example 6*)
Find the maximum and minimum values of
$z = 20x + 30y$, subject to

$$2x + 10y \leq 80$$
$$6x + 2y \leq 72$$
$$3x + 2y \geq 6$$
$$x \geq 0, \quad y \geq 0$$

20. Find the maximum and minimum values of
$z = 5x + 12y$, subject to

$$x + y \leq 20$$
$$2x + 3y \geq 30$$
$$-x + 2y \leq 10$$
$$x \geq 0, \quad y \geq 0$$

21. Find the maximum and minimum values of
$z = 5x + 6y$, subject to

$$6x + 8y \leq 300$$
$$15x + 22y \geq 330$$
$$x \leq 40, \qquad y \leq 21$$
$$x \geq 0, \qquad y \geq 0$$

22. Find the maximum and minimum values of
$z = 10x + 8y$, subject to

$$x + 2y \leq 54$$
$$x + y \geq 28$$
$$4x - 3y \leq 84$$
$$x \geq 0, \quad y \geq 0$$

23. (*See Example 9*)
Maximize $z = 15x + 9y$, subject to

$$5x + 3y \leq 30$$
$$5x + y \leq 20$$
$$x \geq 0, \quad y \geq 0$$

24. Maximize $z = 6x + 3y$, subject to

$$2x + y \leq 11$$
$$3x + 4y \leq 24$$
$$x \geq 0, \quad y \geq 0$$

25. Maximize $z = 3x + 6y$, subject to

$$3x + 2y \geq 60$$
$$10x + 3y \leq 180$$
$$y \leq 24$$
$$x \geq 0, \quad y \geq 0$$

26. Maximize $z = 2x + 6y$, subject to

$$x + y \geq 10$$
$$x + 3y \leq 72$$
$$10x + 3y \leq 180$$
$$x \geq 0, \quad y \geq 5$$

27. Minimize $z = 5x + 10y$, subject to

$$3x + y \geq 150$$
$$x + 2y \geq 100$$
$$y \geq 20$$
$$x \geq 0, \quad y \geq 0$$

28. Maximize $z = 8x + 3y$, subject to

$$2x - 5y \leq 10$$
$$-2x + y \leq 2$$
$$x \geq 0, \quad y \geq 0$$

29. (*See Example 10*)
Maximize $z = 3x + y$, subject to

$$2x - 3y \geq 10$$
$$x \leq 8$$
$$x \geq 0, \quad y \geq 0$$

30. Maximize $z = 4x + 5y$, subject to

$$-3x + y \leq 3$$
$$x - 2y \leq 4$$
$$x \geq 0, \quad y \geq 0$$

31. Minimize $z = x + 2y$, subject to

$$-3x + y \leq 4$$
$$-2x - y \geq 1$$
$$x \geq 0, \quad y \geq 0$$

32. Maximize $z = 5x + 4y$, subject to

$$-5x + y \leq 3$$
$$-2x + y \geq 3$$
$$x \geq 0, \quad y \geq 0$$

33. Maximize $z = 9x + 13y$, subject to

$$3x - y \leq 8$$
$$x - 2y \geq 2$$
$$x \geq 0, \quad y \geq 0$$

Set up the objective function and the constraints for Exercises 34 through 40, but do not solve.

34. Jack has a casserole and salad dinner. Each serving of casserole contains 250 calories, 3 grams of vitamins, and 9 grams of protein. Each serving of salad contains 30 calories, 6 grams of vitamins, and 1 gram of protein. Jack wants to consume at least 23 grams of vitamins and 28 grams of protein but keep the calories at a minimum. How many servings of each food should he eat?

35. (*See Example 7*) Wilson Electronics produces a standard VCR and a deluxe VCR. The company has 2200 hours of labor and $18,000 in operating expenses available each week. It takes eight hours to produce a standard VCR and nine hours to produce a deluxe VCR. Each standard VCR costs $115, and each deluxe VCR costs $136. The company is required to produce at least 35 standard VCRs. The company makes a profit of $39 for each standard VCR and $26 for each deluxe VCR. How many of each type of VCR should be produced to maximize profit.

36. A company has two skill levels of production workers, I and II. A level I worker is paid $8.60 per hour and produces 15 items per hour. The level II worker is paid $12.25 per hour and produces 22 items per hour. The company is required to use at least 2600 employee hours per week, and it must produce at least 45,000 items per week. How many hours per week should the company use each skill level to minimize labor costs?

37. Home Furnishings, Inc. has contracted to make at least 250 sofas per week, which are to be shipped to two distributors, A and B. Distributor A has a maximum capacity of 140 sofas, and distributor B has a maximum capacity of 165 sofas. It costs $13 to ship a sofa to A and $11 to ship to B. If A already has 30 sofas and B has 18, how many sofas should be produced and shipped to each distributor to minimize shipping costs.

38. A company makes a single product on two separate production lines, A and B. The company's labor force is equivalent to 1000 hours per week, and it has $3000 outlay weekly for operating costs. It takes 1 hour and 4 hours to produce a single item on lines A and B, respectively. The cost of producing a single item on A is $5 and on B is $4. How many items should be produced on each line to maximize total output?

39. The maximum production of a soft drink bottling company is 5000 cartons per day. The company produces two kinds of soft drinks, regular and diet. It costs $1.00 to produce each carton of regular and $1.20 to produce each carton of diet. The daily operating budget is $5400. The profit is $0.15 per carton on regular and $0.17 per carton on diet drinks. How much of each type of drink is produced to obtain the maximum profit?

40. Chemical Products makes two insect repellents, Regular and Super. The chemical used for Regular is 15% DEET, and the chemical used for Super is 25% DEET. Each carton of repellent contains 24 ounces of the chemical. In order to justify starting production the company must produce at least 12,000 cartons of insect repellent, and it must produce at least twice as many cartons of Regular as of Super. Labor costs are $8 per carton for Regular and $6 per carton for Super. How many cartons of each repellent should be produced to minimize labor costs if 59,400 ounces of DEET are available?

Solve Exercises 41 through 56.

41. (*See Example 7*) Lamps, Inc. makes desk lamps and floor lamps. The company has 1200 hours of labor and

$4200 to purchase materials each week. It takes 0.8 hour of labor to make a desk lamp and 1.0 hour to make a floor lamp. The materials cost $4 for each desk lamp and $3 for each floor lamp. The company makes a profit of $2.65 on each desk lamp and $3.15 on each floor lamp. How many of each should be made each week to maximize profit?

42. A T-shirt company has three machines, I, II, and III, which can be used to produce two types of T-shirts, standard design and custom design. The following table shows the number of minutes required on each machine to produce the designs.

| | MACHINE | | |
	I	II	III
STANDARD	1	1	1
CUSTOM	1	4	5

For efficient use of equipment the company uses Machine I at least 240 minutes per day, Machine II at least 660 minutes per day, and Machine III at least 1000 minutes per day. Each standard T-shirt costs $3, and each custom T-shirt costs $4. Find the number of each type of T-shirt that should be produced to minimize costs.

III

43. The Circle K Ranch manager wants to graze cattle and sheep on 1000 acres of pasture land. Each acre will support two cows or eight sheep. The manager has enough ranch hands to graze a total of 3200 or fewer animals. The expected profit is $15 per cow and $4 per sheep. How many acres should be allotted to cattle and how many acres to sheep to maximize profit?

44. A sewing machine operator may sew coats or trousers. The trousers require three minutes sewing time, and the operator receives $0.50 each. A coat requires eight minutes sewing time, and the operator receives $1.00 each. The operator must sew at least three coats per hour. How many coats and how many trousers should the operator sew each hour to maximize hourly income?

45. (*See Example 8*) Two foods, I and II, contain the following percentages of carbohydrates, protein, and fat:

I: 40% carbohydrates, 50% protein, 6% fat
II: 60% carbohydrates, 20% protein, 4% fat

Food I costs 3¢ per gram, and food II costs 4¢ per gram. Determine the amount of each that should be served to produce at least 10 grams of carbohydrates, 7.5 grams of protein, and 1.2 grams of fat if cost is to be minimized.

46. The Nut Factory produces a mixture of peanuts and cashews. The company guarantees that at least 40% of the total weight is cashews. It has a contract to produce 1000 pounds or more of the mixture. The peanuts cost $0.80 per pound, and the cashews cost $1.50 per pound. Find the amount of each kind of nut the company should use to minimize the cost:
 (a) if 720 pounds of peanuts are available.
 (b) if 500 pounds of peanuts are available.

47. Precision Machinists makes two grades of gears for industrial machinery, standard and heavy duty. The process requires two steps. Step 1 takes eight minutes for the standard gear and ten minutes for the heavy duty. Step 2 takes three minutes for the standard gear and ten minutes for the heavy duty. The company's labor contract requires that it use at least 200 labor-hours per week on the Step 1 equipment and 140 labor-hours per week on the Step 2 equipment. The materials cost $15 for each standard gear and $22 for each heavy duty. How many of each gear should be made each week to minimize costs?

48. Beauty Products makes two styles of hair dryers, the Petite and the Deluxe. It requires one hour of labor to make the Petite and two hours of labor to make the Deluxe. The materials cost $4 for each Petite and $3 for each Deluxe. The profit is $5 for the Petite and $6 for the Deluxe. The company has 3950 labor-hours available each week and a materials budget of $9575 per week. How many of each dryer should be made each week to maximize profit?

49. A delivery service is considering the purchase of vans. The model SE costs $16,000 with an expected annual operating-maintenance cost of $2700. The model LE costs $20,000 with an expected annual operating-maintenance cost of $2400. The company needs at least 9 vans and has $160,000 available for purchase. How many of each should it purchase to minimize the expected operating maintenance costs?

50. Solve Exercise 38.

51. Solve Exercise 39.

52. Solve Exercise 40.

53. The design of a building calls for at least 4000 square feet of exterior glass. Two types of glass are available. The ability of glass to transfer heat from the warm side to the cooler side is called *conductance*. It is measured in the number of BTU's transferred each hour per square foot and per degree of difference between inside and outside temperature. The glass that conducts the least is the most desirable. The contract allows up to $4500 to be spent on glass. The following holds for each type of glass:

	TYPE A	TYPE B
CONDUCTANCE (BTU per sq ft)	1	0.25
COST (per sq ft)	$0.80	$1.20

 (a) Find the number of square feet of each type of glass that will minimize conductance.
 (b) How many square feet of each type of glass should be used if the total conductance can be no more than 2200 BTU per hour and the cost is to be minimized?

54. Omega Saw and Tool uses two kinds of machines, A and B, in a manufacturing process. The company rates the machines by operating costs per hour and productivity in units produced per hour. It has space for at most 22 machines. The machines are rated as follows:

	A	B
OPERATING COST (per hour)	$16	$24
PRODUCTIVITY (units per hour)	8	10

 (a) If operating costs cannot exceed $600 per hour, find the number of each that should be used to maximize hourly productivity.
 (b) If productivity must be at least 200 units per hour, find the number of each machine that will minimize hourly costs.

55. Brent Publishing has two plants. The plant on Glen Echo Lane produces 200 paperback books and 300 hardback books per day, and the plant on Speegleville Road produces 300 paperback books and 200 hardback books per day. An order is received for 2400 paperbacks and 2100 hardbacks. Find the number of days each plant should operate so that the combined number of days in operation is a minimum.

56. A syrup manufacturer blends 14 gallons of maple syrup and 18 gallons of corn syrup to make two new syrups, Maple-Flavored and Taste-of-Maple. Each gallon of Maple-Flavored contains 0.3 gallon of corn syrup and 0.4 gallon of maple syrup. Each gallon of Taste-of-Maple contains 0.4 gallon of corn syrup and 0.2 gallon of maple syrup. The company makes a profit of $4.50 per gallon on Maple-Flavored and $3.00 per gallon on Taste-of-Maple. How many gallons of each should be produced to maximize profits.

57. The general form of the objective function is $z = Ax + By$. For a given value of z the resulting line has a slope of $-A/B$. Show that each of the following linear programming problems has multiple optimal solutions. Verify in each case that the objective function has the same slope as one of the boundary lines. (The constraint $Cx + Dy \le E$ has the boundary $Cx + Dy = E$, and its slope is $-C/D$)

(a) Maximize $z = 10x + 4y$, subject to

$$5x + 2y \le 50$$
$$x + 4y \le 28$$
$$x \ge 0, \quad y \ge 0$$

(b) Maximize $z = 5x + 6y$, subject to

$$5x + 12y \le 300$$
$$10x + 12y \le 360$$
$$10x + 6y \le 300$$
$$x \ge 0, \quad y \ge 0$$

(c) Minimize $z = 10x + 15y$, subject to

$$3x + 2y \ge 50$$
$$2x + 3y \ge 60$$
$$x + 4y \ge 40$$
$$x \ge 0, \quad y \ge 0$$

(d) Maximize $z = 10x + 24y$, subject to

$$5x + 12y \le 1200$$
$$5x + 4y \le 600$$
$$x \ge 0, \quad y \ge 0$$

IMPORTANT TERMS

3-1
Linear Inequality
Half Plane
Graph of a Linear Inequality

3-2
System of Linear Inequalities
Solutions to a System of Linear Inequalities
Graph of a System of Linear Inequalities

Feasible Solution
Feasible Region
Boundary of a Feasible Region
Corners of a Feasible Region
No Feasible Solution

3-3
Linear Programming
Constraints

Nonnegative Conditions
Objective Function
Maximize Objective Function
Minimize Objective Function
Optimal Solution
Multiple Optimal Solutions
Bounded Feasible Region
Unbounded Feasible Region

REVIEW EXERCISES

1. Graph the solution to the following inequalities.
   (a) $5x + 7y < 70$ (b) $2x - 3y > 18$
   (c) $x + 9y \le 21$ (d) $-2x + 12y \ge 26$
   (e) $y \ge -6$ (f) $x \le 3$

2. Graph the following systems of inequalities.
   (a) $2x + y \le 4$ (b) $x + y \le 5$
        $x + 3y < 9$ $x - y > 3$
                        $x \ge 1, \quad y \le 3$

Find the feasible region and corner points of the systems in Exercises 3 through 7.

3. $x - 3y \ge 6$ 4. $5x + 2y \le 50$
   $x - y \le 4$ $x + 4y \le 28$
        $y \ge -5$ $x \ge 0$

5. $-3x + 4y \le 20$ 6. $3x + 10y \le 150$
   $x + y \ge -2$ $2x + y \le 32$
   $8x + y \le 40$ $x \le 14$
           $y \ge 0$ $x \ge 0, \quad y \ge 0$

7. $x - 2y \le 0$
   $-2x + y \le 2$
   $x \le 2, \quad y \le 2$

8. Maximize $z = x + 2y$, subject to
   $$x + y \le 8$$
   $$x \le 5$$
   $$x \ge 0, \quad y \ge 0$$

9. Maximize $z = 5x + 4y$, subject to
   $$3x + 2y \le 12$$
   $$x + y \le 5$$
   $$x \ge 0, \quad y \ge 0$$

10. Find the maximum and minimum values of
    $$z = 2x + 5y$$
    subject to
    $$2x + y \ge 9$$
    $$4x + 3y \ge 23$$
    $$x \ge 0, \quad y \ge 0$$

11. (a) Find the minimum value of
    $$z = 5x + 4y$$
    subject to
    $$3x + 2y \ge 18$$
    $$x + 2y \ge 10$$
    $$5x + 6y \ge 46$$
    $$x \ge 0, \quad y \ge 0$$

    (b) Find the minimum value of
    $$z = 10x + 12y$$
    subject to the constraints of part (a).

12. Maximize $z = x + 5y$, subject to
    $$x + y \le 10$$
    $$2x + y \ge 10$$
    $$x + 2y \ge 10$$
    $$x \ge 0, \quad y \ge 0$$

13. Maximize $z = 4x + 7y$, subject to
    $$2x + y \le 90$$
    $$x + 2y \le 80$$
    $$x + y \le 50$$
    $$x \ge 0, \quad y \ge 0$$

14. Minimize $z = 7x + 3y$, subject to
    $$x + 2y \ge 16$$
    $$3x + 2y \ge 32$$
    $$5x + 2y \ge 40$$
    $$x \ge 0, \quad y \ge 0$$

15. An assembly plant has two production lines. Line A can produce 65 items per hour, and Line B can produce 105 per hour. The loading dock can ship a maximum of 1500 items per day.
    (a) Express the information with an inequality.
    (b) Graph the inequality.

16. A building supplies truck has a load capacity of 25,000 pounds. A delivery requires at least 12 pallets of brick weighing 950 pounds each and at least 15 pallets of roofing material weighing 700 pounds each. Express these restrictions with a system of inequalities.

17. The Ivy Twin Theater has a seating capacity of 275 seats. Adult tickets sell for $4.50 each, and children's tickets sell for $3.00 each. The theater must have ticket sales of at least $1100 to break even for the night. Write these constraints as a system of inequalities.

18. A tailor makes suits and dresses. A suit requires one yard of polyester and four yards of wool. Each dress requires two yards of polyester and two yards of wool. The tailor has a supply of 80 yards of polyester and 150 yards of wool. What restrictions does this place on the number of suits and dresses she can make?

19. The Hoover Steel Mill produces two grades of stainless steel, which is sold in 100-pound bars. The standard grade is 90% steel and 10% chromium by weight, and the premium grade is 80% steel and 20% chromium. The company has 80,000 pounds of steel and 12,000 pounds of chromium on hand. If the price per bar is $90 for the standard grade and $100 for the premium grade, how much of each grade should it produce to maximize revenue?

20. The Nut Factory produces a mixture of peanuts and cashews. It guarantees that at least one third of the total weight is cashews. A retailer wants 1200 pounds or more of the mixture. The peanuts cost the Nut Factory $0.75 per pound, and the cashews cost $1.40 per pound. Find the amount of each kind of nut the company should use to minimize the cost:
(a) if 600 pounds of peanuts are available.
(b) if 900 pounds of peanuts are available.

4

LINEAR PROGRAMMING: THE SIMPLEX METHOD

*E*VEN THOUGH GEORGE B. DANTZIG and his colleagues observed and defined an important class of problems, linear programming problems, they had no efficient procedure for solving them. In the mid-1940s, Dantzig invented a procedure that became the workhorse in solving linear programming problems. He called it the **simplex method.** It is a procedure for examining corners of a feasible region in an intelligent manner that speeds up the process of finding the optimal solution.

Because the simplex method is a search technique that searches along a boundary from one vertex to another, many mathematicians, including Dantzig, thought there should be a better way. In 1984, 28-year-old Narendra Karmarkar of Bell Laboratories announced that he had developed a better method for large-scale problems (problems involving thousands of variables). His method has attracted a lot of attention and has been analyzed for its strong and weak features. It is considerably more complicated than the simplex method, so we study only the simplex method. Researchers are continuing their efforts to improve the simplex method and to find new methods.

4–1 SETTING UP THE SIMPLEX METHOD

- *Standard Maximum*
- *A Matrix Form of the Standard Maximum Problem*
- *The Geometric Form of the Problem*
- *Slack Variables*
- *Simplex Tableau*

Chapter 3 introduced you to the basic ideas of linear programming. Perhaps you noticed that all the examples and problems involved two variables. In practice, linear programming problems involve dozens of variables. The graphical method is not practical in problems with more than two variables. There is an algebraic technique that applies to any number of variables and enables us to solve larger linear programming problems. It has the added advantage that it is well suited to a computer, thereby making it possible to avoid tedious pencil-and-paper solutions. This technique is called the **simplex method.** Basically, it involves modifying the constraints so that one has a system of linear equations and then finding selected solutions of the system. Remember how we solved a system of linear equations using an augmented matrix and reducing it with row operations? The simplex method follows a similar procedure. We introduce the simplex method in several steps, and we shall refer to the graphical method to illustrate the steps involved.

STANDARD MAXIMUM

The following linear programming problem will be referred to several times.

ILLUSTRATIVE EXAMPLE

Maximize the objective function

$$z = 4x_1 + 12x_2$$

subject to the constraints

$$3x_1 + x_2 \leq 180$$
$$x_1 + 2x_2 \leq 100 \qquad (1)$$
$$-2x_1 + 2x_2 \leq 40$$

and the nonnegative conditions

$$x_1 \geq 0, \quad x_2 \geq 0$$

Notice that we now use the notation x_1 and x_2 for the variables instead of x and y. This notation allows us to use several variables without running out of letters for variables.

In this section we deal only with **standard maximum** linear programming problems. They are problems like the above example which have the following properties.

Standard Maximum Problem

1. The objective function is to be maximized.
2. All of the constraint inequalities are $\leq$ (excluding the nonnegative conditions).
3. The constants in the constraints to the right of $\leq$ are never negative (180, 100, and 40 in the example).
4. The variables are restricted to nonnegative values (nonnegative conditions).

A MATRIX FORM OF THE STANDARD MAXIMUM PROBLEM

In Chapter 2 we wrote a system of equations as a matrix equation of the form $AX = B$. Similarly, the standard maximum can be expressed by using matrices. We use an illustrative example to show how.

EXAMPLE 1 *(Compare Exercise 1)*

Maximize $z = 4x_1 + 12x_2$, subject to the constraints

$$3x_1 + x_2 \leq 180$$
$$x_1 + 2x_2 \leq 100$$
$$-2x_1 + 2x_2 \leq 40$$
$$x_1 \geq 0, \quad x_2 \geq 0$$

SOLUTION   This problem can be expressed in matrix form as follows.
The objective function $z = 4x_1 + 12x_2$ can be written as

$$z = [4 \quad 12]\begin{bmatrix} x_1 \\ x_2 \end{bmatrix}$$

The constraints

$$3x_1 + x_2 \leq 180$$
$$x_1 + 2x_2 \leq 100$$
$$-2x_1 + 2x_2 \leq 40$$

can be written as

$$\begin{bmatrix} 3 & 1 \\ 1 & 2 \\ -2 & 2 \end{bmatrix}\begin{bmatrix} x_1 \\ x_2 \end{bmatrix} \leq \begin{bmatrix} 180 \\ 100 \\ 40 \end{bmatrix}$$

and the nonnegative conditions $x_1 \geq 0$, $x_2 \geq 0$ can be written as

$$\begin{bmatrix} x_1 \\ x_2 \end{bmatrix} \geq \begin{bmatrix} 0 \\ 0 \end{bmatrix}$$

The notation $A \leq B$ means that every element of A is less than or equal to the corresponding element of B.

If we let X be the column matrix of variables

$$\begin{bmatrix} x_1 \\ x_2 \end{bmatrix}$$

let A be the coefficient matrix of the constraints

$$\begin{bmatrix} 3 & 1 \\ 1 & 2 \\ -2 & 2 \end{bmatrix}$$

let B be the column matrix of constant terms of the constraints

$$\begin{bmatrix} 180 \\ 100 \\ 40 \end{bmatrix}$$

and let $C = [4 \quad 12]$ be the row matrix of the coefficients of the objective function, then we can state the standard maximum problem as: Maximize CX subject to $AX \leq B$, where $X \geq 0$.

THE GEOMETRIC FORM OF THE PROBLEM

We now show the graph of the feasible region of the illustrative example to help us see the steps of the simplex method. The problem is as follows:

Maximize $z = 4x_1 + 12x_2$, subject to

$$3x_1 + x_2 \leq 180$$
$$x_1 + 2x_2 \leq 100$$
$$-2x_1 + 2x_2 \leq 40$$
$$x_1 \geq 0, \quad x_2 \geq 0$$

Recall that the boundary to the feasible region is formed by the lines

$$3x_1 + x_2 = 180$$
$$x_1 + 2x_2 = 100$$
$$-2x_1 + 2x_2 = 40$$
$$x_1 = 0, \quad x_2 = 0$$

The feasible region is shown in Figure 4–1.

FIGURE 4–1

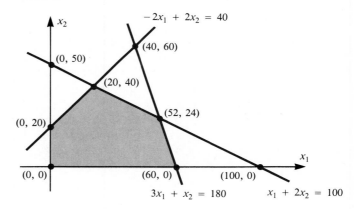

In the geometric approach we look at the corners of the feasible region for optimal values. A corner point occurs at the intersection of a pair of boundary lines such as (52, 24) and (60, 0). Not all pairs of boundary lines intersect at a corner point. Notice the point (40, 60) is not a corner point; it lies outside the feasible region.

The equation of the boundary lines can give us only points on the boundaries. To represent points in the interior of the feasible region, we must introduce some new variables called *slack variables*.

SLACK VARIABLES

The first step in the simplex method converts the constraints to linear equations. We do this by introducing additional variables called **slack variables.** The first constraint, $3x_1 + x_2 \leq 180$, is true for pairs of numbers such as $x_1 = 10$ and $x_2 = 20$ because $3(10) + 20 \leq 180$. Observe that $3x_1 + x_2 + 130 = 180$ when $x_1 = 10$ and $x_2 = 20$. In general, for any pair of values for x_1 and x_2 that make $3x_1 + x_2 \leq 180$ true, there is a number s_1 such that $3x_1 + x_2 + s_1 = 180$. We call s_1 the slack variable because it takes up the slack between $3x_1 + x_2$ and 180. The value of s_1 is never negative. We can add a nonnegative slack variable to each constraint to obtain a set of linear equations.

EXAMPLE 2

With the addition of slack variables, the constraints (1) become

$$
\begin{aligned}
3x_1 + x_2 + s_1 \quad\quad\quad\quad\quad &= 180 \\
x_1 + 2x_2 \quad\quad + s_2 \quad\quad &= 100 \quad\quad (2) \\
-2x_1 + 2x_2 \quad\quad\quad\quad + s_3 &= 40 \\
x_1 \geq 0, \quad x_2 \geq 0, \quad s_1 \geq 0, \quad s_2 \geq 0, \quad s_3 \geq 0&
\end{aligned}
$$

The last line gives the nonnegative conditions that apply to the variables.   ∎

You might wonder how this system of equations will help. Here's how. When nonnegative values of x_1, x_2, and s_1 are chosen to satisfy $3x_1 + x_2 + s_1 = 180$, then the point obtained from the values of x_1 and x_2 will satisfy the constraint $3x_1 + x_2 \leq 180$. Furthermore, x_1 and x_2 from an interior point such as (20, 30), for example, with $s_1 = 90$, $s_2 = 20$, and $s_3 = 20$ satisfy the system of equations (2).

In general, the points in the feasible region are determined from the solutions to a system of equations like (2), provided that we use only those solutions in which *all* the variables (x_1, x_2, s_1, s_2, s_3 in this case) are nonnegative.

EXAMPLE 3   *(Compare Exercise 6)*

Write the following constraints as a system of equations using slack variables:

$$
\begin{aligned}
5x_1 + 3x_2 + 17x_3 &\leq 140 \\
7x_1 + 2x_2 + 4x_3 &\leq 256 \\
3x_1 + 9x_2 + 11x_3 &\leq 540 \\
2x_1 + 16x_2 + 8x_3 &\leq 99
\end{aligned}
$$

SOLUTION   Introduce a slack variable for each equation:

$$
\begin{aligned}
5x_1 + 3x_2 + 17x_3 + s_1 \quad\quad\quad\quad\quad &= 140 \\
7x_1 + 2x_2 + 4x_3 \quad\quad + s_2 \quad\quad\quad &= 256 \\
3x_1 + 9x_2 + 11x_3 \quad\quad\quad\quad + s_3 \quad &= 540 \\
2x_1 + 16x_2 + 8x_3 \quad\quad\quad\quad\quad + s_4 &= 99
\end{aligned}
$$

∎

The objective function needs to be included in the system of equations because we want to find the value of z that comes from the solution of the above system. Its form might need to be modified by writing all terms on the left-hand side. For example,

$$z = 3x_1 + 5x_2$$

is modified to

$$-3x_1 - 5x_2 + z = 0$$

and

$$z = 6x_1 + 7x_2 + 15x_3 + 2x_4$$

is modified to

$$-6x_1 - 7x_2 - 15x_3 - 2x_4 + z = 0$$

EXAMPLE 4

Include the objective function

$$z = 20x_1 + 35x_2 + 40x_3$$

with the constraints of Example 3 and write them as a system of equations.

SOLUTION

$$
\begin{aligned}
5x_1 + \;\; 3x_2 + 17x_3 + s_1 &= 140 \\
7x_1 + \;\; 2x_2 + \;\; 4x_3 + s_2 &= 256 \\
3x_1 + \;\; 9x_2 + 11x_3 + s_3 &= 540 \\
2x_1 + 16x_2 + \;\; 8x_3 + s_4 &= \;\; 99 \\
-20x_1 - 35x_2 - 40x_3 + z &= \;\;\; 0
\end{aligned}
$$

EXAMPLE 5 *(Compare Exercise 9)*

Write the following as a system of equations. Maximize $z = 4x_1 + 12x_2$, subject to

$$
\begin{aligned}
3x_1 + \;\; x_2 &\le 180 \\
x_1 + 2x_2 &\le 100 \\
-2x_1 + 2x_2 &\le \;\; 40 \\
x_1 \ge 0, \quad x_2 &\ge 0
\end{aligned}
$$

SOLUTION

$$
\begin{aligned}
3x_1 + \;\; x_2 + s_1 \qquad\qquad\qquad &= 180 \\
x_1 + 2x_2 \qquad + s_2 \qquad\qquad &= 100 \\
-2x_1 + 2x_2 \qquad\qquad + s_3 \qquad &= \;\; 40 \\
-4x_1 - 12x_2 \qquad\qquad\qquad + z &= \;\;\; 0
\end{aligned}
$$

Let's pause to make some observations about the systems of equations that we obtain.

1. One slack variable is introduced for each constraint (four in Example 4 and three in Example 5).
2. The total number of variables in the system is the number of original variables (number of x's) plus the number of constraints (number of slack variables) plus one for z. (The total is $3 + 4 + 1 = 8$ in Example 4 and $2 + 3 + 1 = 6$ in Example 5.)
3. The introduction of slack variables always results in fewer equations than variables. Recall from the summary in Chapter 2 that this situation generally yields an infinite number of solutions. In fact, one variable for each equation can be written in terms of some other variables.

Look back at the system of equations in Example 5. One general form of the solution occurs when we solve for s_1, s_2, s_3, and z in terms of x_1 and x_2:

$$
\begin{aligned}
s_1 &= 180 - 3x_1 - x_2 \\
s_2 &= 100 - x_1 - 2x_2 \\
s_3 &= 40 + 2x_1 - 2x_2 \\
z &= 4x_1 + 12x_2
\end{aligned}
$$

You find a particular solution when you substitute values for x_1 and x_2. The first step of the simplex method always uses zero for that substitution because it gives corner points. So when $x_1 = 0$ and $x_2 = 0$, we obtain $s_1 = 180$, $s_2 = 100$, $s_3 = 40$, and $z = 0$.

SIMPLEX TABLEAU

The simplex method uses matrices and row operations on matrices to determine an optimal solution. Let's use the problem from Example 5 to set up the matrix that is called the simplex tableau.

EXAMPLE 6   *(Compare Exercise 13)*

Maximize $z = 4x_1 + 12x_2$, subject to

$$
\begin{aligned}
3x_1 + x_2 &\leq 180 \\
x_1 + 2x_2 &\leq 100 \\
-2x_1 + 2x_2 &\leq 40 \\
x_1 \geq 0, \quad x_2 &\geq 0
\end{aligned}
$$

SOLUTION   First, write the problem as a system of equations using slack variables:

$$
\begin{aligned}
3x_1 + x_2 + s_1 &= 180 \\
x_1 + 2x_2 + s_2 &= 100 \\
-2x_1 + 2x_2 + s_3 &= 40 \\
-4x_1 - 12x_2 + z &= 0
\end{aligned}
$$

Next, form the augmented matrix of this system:

$$
\begin{array}{c}
\begin{array}{cccccc} x_1 & x_2 & s_1 & s_2 & s_3 & z \end{array} \\
\left[
\begin{array}{cccccc|c}
3 & 1 & 1 & 0 & 0 & 0 & 180 \\
1 & 2 & 0 & 1 & 0 & 0 & 100 \\
-2 & 2 & 0 & 0 & 1 & 0 & 40 \\
\hline
-4 & -12 & 0 & 0 & 0 & 1 & 0
\end{array}
\right]
\end{array}
$$

This is the initial simplex tableau.

The line drawn above the bottom row emphasizes that the bottom row is the objective function and each **pivot element** will be chosen from above the line. (You will learn to find the pivot element in the next section.)

EXAMPLE 7 *(Compare Exercise 17)*

Set up the initial simplex tableau for the following problem.

A company manufactures three items: hoes, rakes, and shovels. It takes three minutes of labor to produce each hoe, five minutes of labor to produce each rake, and four minutes of labor to produce each shovel. Each hoe costs $2.50 to produce, each rake costs $3.15, and each shovel costs $3.35. The profit is $3.20 per hoe, $3.35 per rake, and $4.10 per shovel. If the company has 108,000 minutes of labor and $6800 in operating funds available per week, how many of each item should it produce to maximize profit?

SOLUTION First, observe that we want to find the number of hoes, rakes, and shovels, so the variables are x_1 = number of hoes, x_2 = number of rakes, and x_3 = number of shovels.

It often helps to summarize the given information in a chart before writing the constraints. In this problem there are three variables and three types of information: labor time, cost, and profit. Look at the information and observe that it can be summarized as follows:

	x_1 (HOES)	x_2 (RAKES)	x_3 (SHOVELS)	MAX. AVAILABLE
LABOR (minutes)	3	5	4	108,000
COST	$2.50	$3.15	$3.35	$6800
PROFIT	$3.20	$3.35	$4.10	

The information on labor requirements, operating costs, and profit can be written as follows:

$$3x_1 + 5x_2 + 4x_3 \leq 108,000 \quad \text{(labor)}$$
$$2.50x_1 + 3.15x_2 + 3.35x_3 \leq 6800 \quad \text{(operating cost)}$$
$$\text{Maximize:} \quad 3.20x_1 + 3.35x_2 + 4.10x_3 = z \quad \text{(profit)}$$

We introduce slack variables into the constraints to form equations and re-write the objective function (profit) as follows:

$$3x_1 + 5x_2 + 4x_3 + s_1 = 108{,}000$$
$$2.50x_1 + 3.15x_2 + 3.35x_3 + s_2 = 6800$$
$$-3.20x_1 - 3.35x_2 - 4.10x_3 + z = 0$$

The simplex tableau is

$$\begin{array}{cccccc}
x_1 & x_2 & x_3 & s_1 & s_2 & z \\
\end{array}$$

$$\left[\begin{array}{ccccccc}
3 & 5 & 4 & 1 & 0 & 0 & 108{,}000 \\
2.50 & 3.15 & 3.35 & 0 & 1 & 0 & 6800 \\
\hline
-3.20 & -3.35 & -4.10 & 0 & 0 & 1 & 0
\end{array}\right]$$

4–1 EXERCISES

I

In Exercises 1 through 4, write the standard maximum problems in matrix form, $AX \geq B$, etc.

1. (*See Example 1*) Maximize $z = 50x_1 + 80x_2$, subject to

$$7x_1 + 15x_2 \leq 30$$
$$3x_1 + 14x_2 \leq 56$$
$$x_1 \geq 0, \quad x_2 \geq 0$$

2. Maximize $z = 130x_1 + 210x_2 + 110x_3$, subject to

$$5x_1 + x_2 + 17x_3 \leq 48$$
$$6x_1 + 7x_2 + 22x_3 \leq 94$$
$$12x_1 + 8x_2 + x_3 \leq 66$$
$$x_1 \geq 0, \quad x_2 \geq 0, \quad x_3 \geq 0$$

3. Maximize $z = 42x_1 + 26x_2 + 5x_3$, subject to

$$13x_1 + 4x_2 + 23x_3 \leq 88$$
$$4x_1 + 15x_2 + 7x_3 \leq 92$$
$$3x_1 - 2x_2 + 32x_3 \leq 155$$
$$x_1 \geq 0, \quad x_2 \geq 0, \quad x_3 \geq 0$$

4. Maximize $z = 500x_1 + 340x_2 + 675x_3 + 525x_4$, subject to

$$12x_1 + 5x_2 + 9x_3 + 21x_4 \leq 85$$
$$31x_1 + 14x_2 + 2x_3 \leq 65$$
$$x_1 + 43x_2 + 4x_3 + 17x_4 \leq 90$$
$$x_1 \geq 0, \quad x_2 \geq 0, \quad x_3 \geq 0 \quad x_4 \geq 0$$

In Exercises 5 through 8, convert the systems of inequalities to systems of equations, using slack variables.

5. $2x_1 + 3x_2 \leq 9$
$x_1 + 5x_2 \leq 16$

6. (*See Example 3*)
$3x_1 - 4x_2 \leq 24$
$9x_1 + 5x_2 \leq 16$
$-x_1 + x_2 \leq 5$

7. $x_1 + 7x_2 - 4x_3 \leq 150$
$5x_1 + 9x_2 + 2x_3 \leq 435$
$8x_1 - 3x_2 + 16x_3 \leq 345$

8. $x_1 + x_2 + x_3 + x_4 \leq 78$
$3x_1 + 2x_2 + x_3 - x_4 \leq 109$

In Exercises 9 through 12, express the problems as a system of equations.

9. (*See Example 5*)
Maximize $z = 3x_1 + 7x_2$, subject to

$$2x_1 + 6x_2 \leq 9$$
$$x_1 - 5x_2 \leq 14$$
$$-3x_1 + x_2 \leq 8$$
$$x_1 \geq 0, \quad x_2 \geq 0$$

10. Maximize $z = 150x_1 + 280x_2$, subject to

$$12x_1 + 15x_2 \leq 50$$
$$8x_1 + 22x_2 \leq 65$$
$$x_1 \geq 0, \quad x_2 \geq 0$$

11. Maximize $z = 420x_1 + 260x_2 + 50x_3$, subject to

$$6x_1 + 7x_2 + 12x_3 \leq 50$$
$$4x_1 + 18x_2 + 9x_3 \leq 85$$
$$x_1 - 2x_2 + 14x_3 \leq 66$$
$$x_1 \geq 0, \quad x_2 \geq 0, \quad x_3 \geq 0$$

12. Maximize $z = 3x_1 + 4x_2 + 7x_3 + 2x_4$, subject to

$$x_1 + 5x_2 + 7x_3 + x_4 \leq 82$$
$$3x_1 + 6x_2 + 12x_3 \leq 50$$
$$2x_1 + 15x_3 + 19x_4 \leq 240$$
$$x_1 \geq 0, \quad x_2 \geq 0, \quad x_3 \geq 0, \quad x_4 \geq 0$$

II

In Exercises 13 through 16, set up the simplex tableau. Do not solve.

13. (*See Example 6*) Maximize $z = 3x_1 + 17x_2$, subject to

$$4x_1 + 5x_2 \leq 10$$
$$3x_1 + x_2 \leq 25$$
$$x_1 \geq 0, \quad x_2 \geq 0$$

14. Maximize $z = 140x_1 + 245x_2$, subject to

$$85x_1 + 64x_2 \leq 560$$
$$75x_1 + 37x_2 \leq 135$$
$$24x_1 + 12x_2 \leq 94$$
$$x_1 \geq 0, \quad x_2 \geq 0$$

15. Maximize $z = 20x_1 + 45x_2 + 40x_3$, subject to

$$16x_1 - 4x_2 + 9x_3 \leq 128$$
$$8x_1 + 13x_2 + 22x_3 \leq 144$$
$$5x_1 + 6x_2 - 15x_3 \leq 225$$
$$x_1 \geq 0, \quad x_2 \geq 0, \quad x_3 \geq 0$$

16. Maximize $z = 18x_1 + 24x_2 + 95x_3 + 50x_4$, subject to

$$x_1 + 2x_2 + 5x_3 + 6x_4 \leq 48$$
$$4x_1 + 8x_2 - 15x_3 + 9x_4 \leq 65$$
$$3x_1 - 2x_2 + x_3 - 8x_4 \leq 50$$
$$x_1 \geq 0, \quad x_2 \geq 0, \quad x_3 \geq 0, \quad x_4 \geq 0$$

III

Set up the simplex tableau for each of Exercises 17 through 25. Do not solve.

17. (*See Example 7*) Hardware Supplies manufactures three items: screwdrivers, chisels, and putty knives. It takes three hours of labor per carton to produce screwdrivers, four hours of labor per carton of chisels, and five hours of labor per carton of putty knives. Each carton of screwdrivers costs $15 to produce, each carton of chisels costs $12, and each carton of putty knives costs $11. The profit per carton is $5 for screwdrivers, $6 for chisels, and $5 for putty knives. If the company has 2200 hours of labor and $8500 in operating funds available per week, how many cartons of each item should it produce to maximize profit?

18. The maximum daily production of an oil refinery is 1900 barrels. The refinery can produce three types of fuel: gasoline, diesel, and heating oil. The production cost per barrel is $6 for gasoline, $5 for diesel, and $8 for heating oil. The daily production budget is $13,400. The profit is $7.00 per barrel on gasoline, $6.00 on diesel, and $9.00 for heating oil. How much of each should be produced to maximize profit?

19. Gina eats a meal of steak, baked potato with butter, and salad with dressing. One ounce of each contains the indicated calories, protein, and fat.

	CALORIES	PROTEIN (mg)	FAT (mg)
SALAD (oz)	20	0.5	1.5
POTATO (oz)	50	1.0	3.0
STEAK (oz)	56	9.0	2.0

She is to consume no more than 1000 calories and 35 mg of fat. How much of each should she eat to maximize the protein consumed?

20. Paper Products, Inc. uses three machines, I, II, and III, to produce three products: notepads, loose-leaf paper, and spiral notebooks. It takes two, four, and zero minutes of time on each of the machines, respectively, to manufacture a carton of notepads. It takes three, zero, and six minutes on the machines, respectively, to produce a carton of loose-leaf paper. To manufacture a carton of spiral notebooks involves one, two, and three minutes, respectively, on each machine.

The total time available on each machine per day is six hours. The profits are $10, $8, and $12 on each carton of notepads, loose-leaf paper, and spiral notebooks, respectively. How many of each item should be produced to maximize total profit?

21. The Health Fare Cereal Company makes three cereals using wheat, oats, and raisins. The computation and profit of each cereal are shown in the following chart:

| CEREAL | PORTION OF EACH POUND OF CEREAL | | | |
	WHEAT	OATS	RAISINS	PROFIT/POUND
Lite	0.75	0.25	0	$0.25
Trim	0.50	0.25	0.25	$0.25
Health Fare	0.15	0.60	0.25	$0.32

The company has 2320 pounds of wheat, 1380 pounds of oats, and 700 pounds of raisins available. How many pounds of each cereal should it produce to maximize profit?

22. The Humidor blends regular coffee, High Mountain coffee, and chocolate to obtain three kinds of coffee: Early Riser, After Dinner and Deluxe. The blends and profit for each blend are given in the following chart:

| | BLEND | | |
	EARLY RISER	AFTER DINNER	DELUXE
Regular	80%	75%	50%
High Mountain	20%	20%	0%
Chocolate	0%	5%	10%
Profit/Pound	$1.00	$1.10	$1.20

The shop has 255 pounds of regular coffee, 80 pounds of High Mountain coffee, and 15 pounds of chocolate. How many pounds of each blend should be produced to maximize profit?

23. The Williams Trunk Company makes trunks for the military, for commercial use, and for decorative pieces. Each military trunk requires four hours for assembly, one hour for finishing, and 0.1 hour for packaging. Each commercial trunk requires three hours for

assembly, two hours for finishing, and 0.2 hour for packaging. Each decorative trunk requires two hours for assembly, four hours for finishing, and 0.3 hour for packaging. The profit on each trunk is $6 for military, $7 for commercial, and $9 for decorative. If 4900 hours are available for assembly work, 2200 for finishing, and 210 for packaging, how many of each type of trunk should be made to maximize profit?

24. The Snack Shop makes three nut mixes from peanuts, cashews, and pecans in 1-kilogram packages. (1 kilogram = 1000 grams.) The composition of each mix is as follows:

TV MIX: 600 grams of peanuts, 300 grams of cashews, and 100 grams of pecans

PARTY MIX: 500 grams of peanuts, 300 grams of cashews, and 200 grams of pecans

DINNER MIX: 300 grams of peanuts, 200 grams of cashews, and 400 grams of pecans

The shop has 39,500 grams of peanuts, 22,500 grams of cashews, and 16,500 grams of pecans. The selling price per package of each mix is $4.40 for TV mix, $4.80 for Party mix, and $5.20 for Dinner mix. How many packages of each should be made to maximize revenue?

25. The Clock Works produces three clock kits for amateur woodworkers: the Majestic Grandfather Clock, the Traditional Clock, and the Wall Clock. The following chart shows the times required for cutting, sanding, and packing each kit and the price of each kit:

PROCESS	MAJESTIC	TRADITIONAL	WALL
Cutting	4 hours	2 hours	1 hour
Sanding	3 hours	2 hours	1 hour
Packing	1 hour	1 hour	0.5 hour
Price	$400	$250	$160

The cutting machines are available 120 hours per week, the sanding machines 80 hours, and the packing machines 40 hours. How many of each type of kit should be produced each week to maximize revenue?

4-2 THE SIMPLEX METHOD

- *System of Equations: Many Solutions*
- *Basic Solution*
- *Pivot Column, Row, and Element*
- *Final Tableau*

SYSTEM OF EQUATIONS: MANY SOLUTIONS

You will see that the simplex method involves a system of equations in which the number of variables is greater than the number of equations. In such a case the system generally has an infinite number of solutions. Recall that when the solutions of a system are represented by an augmented matrix such as

$$
\begin{array}{cccc}
x_1 & x_2 & x_3 & x_4 \\
\end{array}
$$
$$
\left[
\begin{array}{cccc|c}
1 & 0 & 0 & 2 & 3 \\
0 & 1 & 0 & -1 & 5 \\
0 & 0 & 1 & 4 & 7 \\
\end{array}
\right]
$$

then the solutions can be written as

$$
\begin{aligned}
x_1 &= 3 - 2x_4 \\
x_2 &= 5 + x_4 \\
x_3 &= 7 - 4x_4
\end{aligned}
$$

where any value may be assigned to x_4, thereby determining values of x_1, x_2, and x_3. We solve for x_1, x_2, and x_3 in terms of x_4 because x_1 occurs in only one row. (All entries in the x_1 column are zero except for one entry.) Similarly, x_2 and x_3 occur only once. The variable x_4 occurs in all rows, so it appears in each equation of the solution. Observe that the entries in the x_1, x_2, and x_3 columns form a column from the identity matrix (call these **unit columns**). The x_4 column is not like a column from an identity matrix. In general, we solve for variables corresponding to unit columns in terms of variables whose columns are not unit columns. For example, in the augmented matrix

$$
\begin{array}{ccccc}
x_1 & x_2 & x_3 & x_4 & x_5 \\
\end{array}
$$
$$
\left[
\begin{array}{ccccc|c}
3 & 0 & -1 & 0 & 1 & 4 \\
1 & 1 & 0 & 0 & 0 & -6 \\
2 & 0 & 5 & 1 & 0 & 10 \\
\end{array}
\right]
$$

the unit columns are the x_2, x_4, and x_5 columns, so we solve for x_2, x_4, and x_5 in terms of x_1 and x_3, giving

$$
\begin{aligned}
x_2 &= -6 - x_1 && \text{(From Row 2)} \\
x_4 &= 10 - 2x_1 - 5x_3 && \text{(From Row 3)} \\
x_5 &= 4 - 3x_1 + x_3 && \text{(From Row 1)}
\end{aligned}
$$

Specific solutions are obtained by assigning arbitrary values to x_1 and x_3.

We will see how the simplex method selects certain solutions to a system by assigning zeros to the arbitrary variables.

BASIC SOLUTION

The simplex method is a process of finding a sequence of selected solutions to a system of equations. The selections are made so that the optimal solution is found in a relatively small number of steps.

Let's look at the illustrative example in Section 4–1 again. It is the following. Maximize the objective function $z = 4x_1 + 12x_2$, subject to the constraints

$$
\begin{aligned}
3x_1 + x_2 &\le 180 \\
x_1 + 2x_2 &\le 100 \qquad (1) \\
-2x_1 + 2x_2 &\le 40 \\
x_1 \ge 0, \quad x_2 &\ge 0
\end{aligned}
$$

We introduce slack variables to obtain the following. Maximize $z = 4x_1 + 12x_2$, subject to

$$
\begin{aligned}
3x_1 + x_2 + s_1 &= 180 \\
x_1 + 2x_2 + s_2 &= 100 \qquad (2) \\
-2x_1 + 2x_2 + s_3 &= 40
\end{aligned}
$$

where x_1, x_2, s_1, s_2, and s_3 are all nonnegative.

The simplex tableau is

$$
\begin{array}{ccccccc}
x_1 & x_2 & s_1 & s_2 & s_3 & z & \\
\left[\begin{array}{cccccc|c}
3 & 1 & 1 & 0 & 0 & 0 & 180 \\
1 & 2 & 0 & 1 & 0 & 0 & 100 \\
-2 & 2 & 0 & 0 & 1 & 0 & 40 \\
\hline
-4 & -12 & 0 & 0 & 0 & 1 & 0
\end{array}\right]
\end{array}
$$

Notice that unit columns occur in the s_1, s_2, and s_3 columns. Since the feasible region is determined by the constraints, we will leave out the bottom row (objective function) and the z column. Thus we can solve for s_1, s_2, and s_3 as

$$
\begin{aligned}
s_1 &= 180 - 3x_1 - x_2 \\
s_2 &= 100 - x_1 - 2x_2 \\
s_3 &= 40 + 2x_1 - 2x_2
\end{aligned}
$$

We can substitute any values whatever for x_1 and x_2 to obtain s_1, s_2, and s_3. Those five numbers will form a solution to the system of equations. However, only those nonnegative values of x_1 and x_2 that also yield nonnegative values for s_1, s_2, and s_3 give **feasible solutions**. The simplest choices are $x_1 = 0$ and $x_2 = 0$. This gives $s_1 = 180$, $s_2 = 100$, and $s_3 = 40$. Solutions like this where the arbitrary variables are set to zero are called **basic solutions**. The number of variables set to zero in this case was two, which happens to be the number of x's involved. In general, the number of x's determines the number of arbitrary variables set to zero.

We chose zero for the values of x_1 and x_2, not just for simplicity, but also because that gives a corner point $(0, 0)$ of the feasible region.

Definition
Basic Solution

If a linear programming problem has k x's in the constraints, then a **basic solution** is obtained by setting k variables (except z) to zero and solving for the others.

Actually, we can find a basic solution by setting any two variables to zero and solving for the others.

If we set $s_1 = 0$ and $s_3 = 0$, we can obtain another basic solution by solving for the other variables from the simplex tableau. If $s_1 = 0$ and $s_3 = 0$, the system (2) reduces to

$$\begin{aligned}
3x_1 + x_2 \phantom{{}+ s_2 + z} &= 180 \\
x_1 + 2x_2 + s_2 \phantom{{}+ z} &= 100 \\
-2x_1 + 2x_2 \phantom{{}+ s_2 + z} &= 40 \\
-4x_1 - 12x_2 \phantom{{}+ s_2} + z &= 0
\end{aligned}$$

We have four equations in four unknowns, x_1, x_2, s_2, and z, to solve. This system has the solution (we omit the details)

$$x_1 = 40, \quad x_2 = 60, \quad s_2 = -60, \quad z = 880$$

Notice that s_2 is *negative*. This violates the nonnegative conditions on the x's and slack variables. While the solution

$$x_1 = 40, \quad x_2 = 60, \quad s_1 = 0, \quad s_2 = -60, \quad s_3 = 0, \quad z = 880$$

is a basic solution, it is not feasible.

If you look at Figure 4–1, you will see that $(40, 60)$ is a point where two boundary lines intersect, but it lies outside the feasible region. Properly carried out, the simplex method finds only basic *feasible* solutions that are corner points of the feasible region.

Definition	Call the number of x variables in a linear programming problem k. A
Basic Feasible Solution	**basic feasible solution** of the system of equations is a solution with k variables (except z) set to zero and with none of the slack variables or x's negative.

The variables set to zero are called **nonbasic variables.** The others are called **basic variables.**

With this background, let us proceed to solve this example by finding the appropriate basic feasible solution.

Solve by the simplex method:

Maximize $z = 4x_1 + 12x_2$, subject to

$$3x_1 + x_2 \leq 180$$
$$x_1 + 2x_2 \leq 100$$
$$-2x_1 + 2x_2 \leq 40$$
$$x_1 \geq 0, \quad x_2 \geq 0$$

Step 1. (*Compare Exercise 1*) Begin with the initial tableau:

$$\begin{array}{cccccc}
x_1 & x_2 & s_1 & s_2 & s_3 & z \\
\end{array}$$
$$\left[\begin{array}{cccccc|c}
3 & 1 & 1 & 0 & 0 & 0 & 180 \\
1 & 2 & 0 & 1 & 0 & 0 & 100 \\
-2 & 2 & 0 & 0 & 1 & 0 & 40 \\
\hline
-4 & -12 & 0 & 0 & 0 & 1 & 0
\end{array}\right]$$

We find the first basic feasible solutions. Notice that the unit columns are for s_1, s_2, and s_3, so we can solve for them in terms of the x's. Now we can set the x's to zero to obtain $s_1 = 180$, $s_2 = 100$, and $s_3 = 40$. (You can read these from the tableau.) Since this basic feasible solution is the first found, we call it the **initial basic feasible solution.** It always occurs at the origin of the feasible region.

In this case the unit columns give s_1, s_2, and s_3 as the basic variables. The nonbasic variables are x_1 and x_2.

PIVOT COLUMN, ROW, AND ELEMENT

Step 2. (*Compare Exercise 5*) Next we want to modify the tableau so that the new tableau has a basic feasible solution that increases the value of z. This step requires the selection of a **pivot element** from the tableau as follows:

(a) To select the column containing the pivot element, do the following. Select the *most negative* entry from the bottom row:

$$\begin{array}{cccccc}
x_1 & x_2 & s_1 & s_2 & s_3 & z \\
\end{array}$$
$$\left[\begin{array}{cccccc|c}
3 & 1 & 1 & 0 & 0 & 0 & 180 \\
1 & 2 & 0 & 1 & 0 & 0 & 100 \\
-2 & 2 & 0 & 0 & 1 & 0 & 40 \\
\hline
-4 & \boxed{-12} & 0 & 0 & 0 & 1 & 0
\end{array}\right]$$

└─Most negative entry gives pivot column

This selects the **pivot column** containing the pivot element. The pivot element itself is an entry in this column *above* the line. We must now determine which row contains the pivot element.

(b) To select the row, called the **pivot row,** containing the pivot element, do the following. Divide each constant above the line in the last column by the corresponding entries in the pivot column. The ratios are written to the right of the tableau. In this example, all ratios are positive. However, negative or zero ratios can occur.

   (i) If a negative ratio occurs, do *not* use that row for the pivot row.

  (ii) If all ratios are positive (they will be in most cases), select the *smallest positive ratio* (20 in this case). The row containing this ratio is the pivot row.

 (iii) If a zero ratio occurs, check to see whether it was obtained by dividing zero by a *positive* number. If so, use that row for the pivot row. If the zero was obtained by dividing zero by a *negative* number, that row is *not* the pivot row.

Now look at the ratios on the right of the tableau.

$$
\begin{array}{c}
\quad \\
\quad \\
\text{Pivot} \\
\text{row}\rightarrow \\
\quad
\end{array}
\begin{array}{cccccc}
x_1 & x_2 & s_1 & s_2 & s_3 & z \\
\end{array}
$$

$$
\left[
\begin{array}{cccccc|c}
3 & 1 & 1 & 0 & 0 & 0 & 180 \\
1 & 2 & 0 & 1 & 0 & 0 & 100 \\
-2 & ② & 0 & 0 & 1 & 0 & 40 \\
\hline
-4 & -12 & 0 & 0 & 0 & 1 & 0
\end{array}
\right]
\quad
\begin{array}{l}
\frac{180}{1} = 180 \\
\frac{100}{2} = 50 \\
\frac{40}{2} = 20
\end{array}
$$

Pivot element

Since all ratios are positive, the smallest, 20, determines the pivot row. The entry 2 in the pivot row and pivot column is the **pivot element.**

    Step 3. (Compare Exercise 15) Move to the next basic feasible solution. We call this process **pivoting** on the pivot element. In this case we pivot on 2 in Row 3, Column 2.

    To pivot on 2, use row operations to modify the tableau so that the pivot element becomes a 1 and the rest of the pivot column contains 0's. (You recognize that this is part of the Gauss-Jordan method for solving systems.)

    Multiply each entry in the third row (pivot row) by $\frac{1}{2}$ so that the pivot entry becomes 1. The third row becomes

$$[-1 \quad 1 \quad 0 \quad 0 \quad \tfrac{1}{2} \quad 0 \quad 20]$$

giving the tableau

$$
\begin{array}{cccccc}
x_1 & x_2 & s_1 & s_2 & s_3 & z \\
\end{array}
$$

$$
\left[
\begin{array}{cccccc|c}
3 & ① & 1 & 0 & 0 & 0 & 180 \\
1 & ② & 0 & 1 & 0 & 0 & 100 \\
-1 & 1 & 0 & 0 & \tfrac{1}{2} & 0 & 20 \\
\hline
-4 & -12 & 0 & 0 & 0 & 1 & 0
\end{array}
\right]
$$

We now need zeros in the circled locations of the pivot column.

Each of the rows where zeros are needed is replaced by multiplying Row 3 by a constant and adding it to the row to be replaced. The constant used each time is the one that gives a zero in the pivot column. This is accomplished as follows.

Replace Row 1 with (Row 1 − Row 3):

$$= [4 \quad 0 \quad 1 \quad 0 \quad -\tfrac{1}{2} \quad 0 \quad 160]$$

Replace Row 2 with (Row 2 + (−2)Row 3):

$$= [3 \quad 0 \quad 0 \quad 1 \quad -1 \quad 0 \quad 60]$$

Replace Row 4 with (Row 4 + (12)Row 3):

$$= [-16 \quad 0 \quad 0 \quad 0 \quad 6 \quad 1 \quad 240]$$

This gives the tableau

$$
\begin{array}{ccccccc}
x_1 & x_2 & s_1 & s_2 & s_3 & z & \\
\end{array}
$$

$$
\left[
\begin{array}{cccccc|c}
4 & 0 & 1 & 0 & -\tfrac{1}{2} & 0 & 160 \\
3 & 0 & 0 & 1 & -1 & 0 & 60 \\
-1 & 1 & 0 & 0 & \tfrac{1}{2} & 0 & 20 \\
\hline
-16 & 0 & 0 & 0 & 6 & 1 & 240
\end{array}
\right]
$$

To determine the basic feasible solution from this tableau, observe that the columns under x_2, s_1, and s_2 are unit columns. These variables are the *basic variables*, the ones we solve for. The other two variables, x_1 and s_3, are nonbasic variables, the ones we set to zero.

The basic feasible solution from this tableau is

$$x_1 = 0, \quad x_2 = 20, \quad s_1 = 160, \quad s_2 = 60, \quad s_3 = 0, \quad z = 240$$

The initial solution gave $z = 0$, and this solution gave $z = 240$, so we do indeed have a larger value of the objective function.

We need to know when we have reached the optimal solution, the maximum value of z. We can tell when the maximum has been achieved from the simplex tableau.

Step 4. Is z maximum?

If the last row contains any negative coefficients, z is not maximum. Since −16 is a coefficient from the last row, 240 is not the maximum value of z, so we proceed to move to another basic feasible solution.

FINAL TABLEAU

Step 5. Find another basic feasible solution.
Proceed as in Steps 2 and 3 with the most recent tableau:

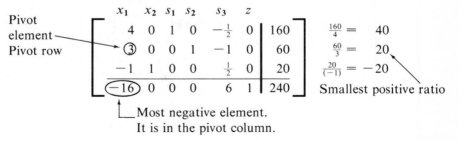

Since there are no zero ratios, the smallest positive ratio determines the pivot row, Row 2 in this case, and 3 is the pivot element.

We now use row operations to obtain a 1 in the pivot element position and zeros in the rest of the pivot column. Replace Row 2 with $(\frac{1}{3})$Row 2 = $[1 \quad 0 \quad 0 \quad \frac{1}{3} \quad -\frac{1}{3} \quad 0 \quad 20]$ to obtain a 1 in the pivot position:

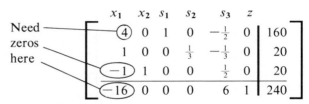

We obtain the desired zeros by replacing the rows as follows:
Replace Row 1 with (Row 1 + (−4)Row 2):

$$= [0 \quad 0 \quad 1 \quad -\tfrac{4}{3} \quad \tfrac{5}{6} \quad 0 \quad 80]$$

Replace Row 3 with (Row 3 + Row 2):

$$= [0 \quad 1 \quad 0 \quad \tfrac{1}{3} \quad \tfrac{1}{6} \quad 0 \quad 40]$$

Replace Row 4 with (Row 4 + (16)Row 2):

$$= [0 \quad 0 \quad 0 \quad \tfrac{16}{3} \quad \tfrac{2}{3} \quad 1 \quad 560]$$

giving the tableau

$$
\begin{array}{ccccccc}
x_1 & x_2 & s_1 & s_2 & s_3 & z & \\
\end{array}
$$

$$
\begin{bmatrix}
0 & 0 & 1 & -\frac{4}{3} & \frac{5}{6} & 0 & 80 \\
1 & 0 & 0 & \frac{1}{3} & -\frac{1}{3} & 0 & 20 \\
0 & 1 & 0 & \frac{1}{3} & \frac{1}{6} & 0 & 40 \\
\hline
0 & 0 & 0 & \frac{16}{3} & \frac{2}{3} & 1 & 560 \\
\end{bmatrix}
$$

The basic variables are x_1, x_2, s_1, and z because those columns are unit columns. The basic feasible solution is obtained by setting s_2 and $s_3 = 0$ and solving for the others. The solution is

$$x_1 = 20, \quad x_2 = 40, \quad s_1 = 80, \quad s_2 = 0, \quad s_3 = 0, \quad z = 560$$

with x_1, x_2, and s_1 the basic variables and s_2 and s_3 nonbasic.

The value of z can be increased by going to another tableau only when there is a negative number in the bottom row. The last tableau, the **final tableau**, has no negative numbers in the last row, so $z = 560$ is the maximum value of z.

EXAMPLE 1　(Compare Exercise 19)

Use the simplex method to maximize $z = 2x_1 + 3x_2 + 2x_3$, subject to

$$2x_1 + x_2 + 2x_3 \le 13$$
$$x_1 + x_2 - 3x_3 \le 8$$
$$x_1 \ge 0, \quad x_2 \ge 0, \quad x_3 \ge 0$$

SOLUTION　We first write the problem as a system of equations:

$$2x_1 + \ x_2 + 2x_3 + s_1 \qquad\qquad = 13$$
$$x_1 + \ x_2 - 3x_3 \qquad + s_2 \qquad = 8$$
$$-2x_1 - 3x_2 - 2x_3 \qquad\qquad + z = 0$$

The initial simplex tableau is

$$
\begin{array}{cccccc}
x_1 & x_2 & x_3 & s_1 & s_2 & z \\
\end{array}
$$
$$
\left[
\begin{array}{cccccc|c}
2 & 1 & 2 & 1 & 0 & 0 & 13 \\
1 & 1 & -3 & 0 & 1 & 0 & 8 \\
\hline
-2 & -3 & -2 & 0 & 0 & 1 & 0 \\
\end{array}
\right]
$$

Since there are three x's, all basic solutions will have three variables set to zero. From the initial tableau the initial basic feasible solution is

$$x_1 = 0, \quad x_2 = 0, \quad x_3 = 0, \quad s_1 = 13, \quad s_2 = 8, \quad z = 0$$

Since there are negative entries in the last row, the solution is not optimal.

Find the pivot element:

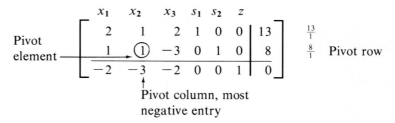

Since all ratios are positive, the smallest, 8, determines the pivot row. Use Row 2 to pivot on 1 in Row 2, Column 2 to find the next tableau. Use the following row operations.
Replace Row 1 with (Row 1 − Row 2):

$$= [1 \quad 0 \quad 5 \quad 1 \quad -1 \quad 0 \quad 5]$$

Replace Row 3 with (Row 3 + (3)Row 2):

$$= [1 \quad 0 \quad -11 \quad 0 \quad 3 \quad 1 \quad 24]$$

giving

$$\begin{array}{ccccccc} x_1 & x_2 & x_3 & s_1 & s_2 & z & \\ \end{array}$$
$$\begin{bmatrix} 1 & 0 & 5 & 1 & -1 & 0 & 5 \\ 1 & 1 & -3 & 0 & 1 & 0 & 8 \\ 1 & 0 & -11 & 0 & 3 & 1 & 24 \end{bmatrix}$$

Again the solution is not optimal since a negative entry, −11, occurs in the last row. Find the new pivot element:

$$\begin{array}{ccccccc} x_1 & x_2 & x_3 & s_1 & s_2 & z & \\ \end{array}$$

Pivot element
$$\begin{bmatrix} 1 & 0 & ⑤ & 1 & -1 & 0 & 5 \\ 1 & 1 & -3 & 0 & 1 & 0 & 8 \\ 1 & 0 & -11 & 0 & 3 & 1 & 24 \end{bmatrix}$$

$\frac{5}{5} = 1$ (smallest positive ratio)
$\frac{8}{-3} = -2.67$

Pivot column

This tableau has no zero ratios, so choose the smallest positive, 1, which gives Row 1 as the pivot row. Now use Row 1 to pivot on 5 in Row 1, Column 3. First divide Row 1 by 5:

$$\begin{array}{ccccccc} x_1 & x_2 & x_3 & s_1 & s_2 & z & \\ \end{array}$$
$$\begin{bmatrix} \frac{1}{5} & 0 & 1 & \frac{1}{5} & -\frac{1}{5} & 0 & 1 \\ 1 & 1 & -3 & 0 & 1 & 0 & 8 \\ 1 & 0 & -11 & 0 & 3 & 1 & 24 \end{bmatrix}$$

Next, use the following row operations.
Replace Row 2 with (Row 2 + (3)Row 1):

$$= [\tfrac{8}{5} \quad 1 \quad 0 \quad \tfrac{3}{5} \quad \tfrac{2}{5} \quad 0 \quad 11]$$

Replace Row 3 with (Row 3 + (11)Row 1):

$$= [\tfrac{16}{5} \quad 0 \quad 0 \quad \tfrac{11}{5} \quad \tfrac{4}{5} \quad 1 \quad 35]$$

giving the tableau

$$
\begin{array}{c}
\begin{array}{cccccc} x_1 & x_2 & x_3 & s_1 & s_2 & z \end{array} \\
\left[\begin{array}{cccccc|c}
\frac{1}{5} & 0 & 1 & \frac{1}{5} & -\frac{1}{5} & 0 & 1 \\
\frac{8}{5} & 1 & 0 & \frac{3}{5} & \frac{2}{5} & 0 & 11 \\
\hline
\frac{16}{5} & 0 & 0 & \frac{11}{5} & \frac{4}{5} & 1 & 35
\end{array} \right]
\end{array}
$$

The basic feasible solution from the tableau is

$$x_1 = 0, \quad x_2 = 11, \quad x_3 = 1, \quad s_1 = 0, \quad s_2 = 0, \quad z = 35$$

Since there are no negative entries in the last row, $z = 35$ is a maximum. ∎

Summary of the Simplex Method

Standard Maximization Problem

1. Convert the problem to a system of equations:
   (a) Convert each inequality to an equation by adding a slack variable.
   (b) Write the objective function

   $$z = ax_1 + bx_2 + \cdots + kx_n$$

   as

   $$-ax_1 - bx_2 - \cdots - kx_n + z = 0$$

2. Form the initial simplex tableau from the equations.
3. Locate the pivot element of the tableau:
   (a) Locate the most negative entry in the bottom row. It is in the pivot column. If there is a tie for most negative, choose either.
   (b) Divide each entry in the last column (above the line) by the corresponding entry in the pivot column.
      (i) If there are *no* zero ratios, choose the smallest positive one. It is in the pivot row.
      (ii) If there is a zero ratio, choose one with a positive divisor. It is in the pivot row. If all zero ratios have negative divisors, use the smallest positive ratio.
      In case of a tie for pivot row, choose either.
   (c) The element where the pivot column and pivot row intersect is the pivot element.
4. Modify the simplex tableau by using row operations to obtain a new basic feasible solution.
   (a) Divide each entry in the pivot row by the pivot element to obtain a 1 in the pivot position.
   (b) Use the pivot row and row operations to obtain zeros in the other entries of the pivot column.

5. Determine whether z has reached its maximum.
 (a) If there is a negative entry in the last row of the tableau, z is not maximum. Repeat the process in Steps 3 and 4.
 (b) If the bottom row contains no negative entries, z is maximum and the solution is available from the final tableau.
6. Determine the solution from the final tableau.
 (a) Set k variables to 0, where k is the number of x's used in the constraints. These are the nonbasic variables. They correspond to the columns that contain more than one nonzero entry.
 (b) Determine the values of the basic variables. They correspond to unit columns.

EXAMPLE 2 *(Compare Exercise 27)*

Maximize $z = 9x_1 + 5x_2 + 9x_3$, subject to

$$6x_1 + x_2 + 4x_3 \le 72$$
$$3x_1 + 4x_2 + 2x_3 \le 30$$
$$x_1 \ge 0, \quad x_2 \ge 0, \quad x_3 \ge 0$$

SOLUTION Form the system of equations

$$6x_1 + x_2 + 4x_3 + s_1 \qquad\qquad = 72$$
$$3x_1 + 4x_2 + 2x_3 \qquad + s_2 \qquad = 30$$
$$-9x_1 - 5x_2 - 9x_3 \qquad\qquad + z = 0$$

From this system we write the initial tableau:

$$\begin{array}{cccccc}
x_1 & x_2 & x_3 & s_1 & s_2 & z \\
\left[\begin{array}{ccccc|c}
6 & 1 & 4 & 1 & 0 & 0 \\
3 & 4 & 2 & 0 & 1 & 0 \\
\hline
-9 & -5 & -9 & 0 & 0 & 1
\end{array}\right. & & & & & \left.\begin{array}{c} 72 \\ 30 \\ \hline 0 \end{array}\right]
\end{array}$$

Since there is a tie in the last row for the most negative entry, we have two choices for the pivot column. We use the first one.

$$\begin{array}{cccccc}
x_1 & x_2 & x_3 & s_1 & s_2 & z \\
\end{array}$$

Pivot element →

$$\left[\begin{array}{ccccc|c}
6 & 1 & 4 & 1 & 0 & 0 & 72 \\
\textcircled{3} & 4 & 2 & 0 & 1 & 0 & 30 \\
\hline
-9 & -5 & -9 & 0 & 0 & 1 & 0
\end{array}\right]$$

$\frac{72}{6} = 12$
$\frac{30}{3} = 10$

We give the sequence of tableaux to find the optimal solution but leave out some of the details. Be sure you follow each step.

$$\begin{bmatrix} 6 & 1 & 4 & 1 & 0 & 0 & 72 \\ 1 & \frac{4}{3} & \frac{2}{3} & 0 & \frac{1}{3} & 0 & 10 \\ \hline -9 & -5 & -9 & 0 & 0 & 1 & 0 \end{bmatrix}$$

$$\begin{bmatrix} 0 & -7 & 0 & 1 & -2 & 0 & 12 \\ 1 & \frac{4}{3} & \frac{2}{3} & 0 & \frac{1}{3} & 0 & 10 \\ \hline 0 & 7 & -3 & 0 & 3 & 1 & 90 \end{bmatrix}$$

Not a maximum yet

New pivot element

$$\begin{bmatrix} 0 & -7 & 0 & 1 & -2 & 0 & 12 \\ \frac{3}{2} & 2 & 1 & 0 & \frac{1}{2} & 0 & 15 \\ \hline 0 & 7 & -3 & 0 & 3 & 1 & 90 \end{bmatrix}$$

$$\begin{bmatrix} 0 & -7 & 0 & 1 & -2 & 0 & 12 \\ \frac{3}{2} & 2 & 1 & 0 & \frac{1}{2} & 0 & 15 \\ \hline \frac{9}{2} & 13 & 0 & 0 & \frac{9}{2} & 1 & 135 \end{bmatrix}$$

This is the final tableau with the solution

$$x_1 = 0, \quad x_2 = 0, \quad x_3 = 15, \quad s_1 = 12, \quad s_2 = 0, \quad z = 135$$

In case of a tie for the most negative entry in the last row, each one will lead to the same answer. However, one might lead to the answer in fewer steps. You have no way of knowing which choice is shorter.

Now let's look at an example that has a tie for pivot row.

EXAMPLE 3   *(Compare Exercise 31)*

Maximize $z = 3x_1 + 8x_2$, subject to

$$x_1 + 2x_2 \leq 80$$
$$4x_1 + x_2 \leq 68$$
$$5x_1 + 3x_2 \leq 120$$
$$x_1 \geq 0, \quad x_2 \geq 0$$

SOLUTION   The initial tableau is

$$\begin{bmatrix} 1 & 2 & 1 & 0 & 0 & 0 & 80 \\ 4 & 1 & 0 & 1 & 0 & 0 & 68 \\ 5 & 3 & 0 & 0 & 1 & 0 & 120 \\ \hline -3 & -8 & 0 & 0 & 0 & 1 & 0 \end{bmatrix} \quad \begin{array}{l} \frac{80}{2} = 40 \\ \frac{68}{1} = 68 \\ \frac{120}{3} = 40 \end{array}$$

Pivot column

Since there are two ratios of 40 each, either Row 1 or Row 3 may be selected as the pivot row. If we select Row 1, then 2 is the pivot element, and our sequence of tableaux is the following. You should work the row operations so that you see that each tableau is correct.

$$\begin{bmatrix} \frac{1}{2} & 1 & \frac{1}{2} & 0 & 0 & 0 & | & 40 \\ 4 & 1 & 0 & 1 & 0 & 0 & | & 68 \\ 5 & 3 & 0 & 0 & 1 & 0 & | & 120 \\ -3 & -8 & 0 & 0 & 0 & 1 & | & 0 \end{bmatrix}$$

$$\begin{bmatrix} \frac{1}{2} & 1 & \frac{1}{2} & 0 & 0 & 0 & | & 40 \\ \frac{7}{2} & 0 & -\frac{1}{2} & 1 & 0 & 0 & | & 28 \\ \frac{7}{2} & 0 & -\frac{3}{2} & 0 & 1 & 0 & | & 0 \\ 1 & 0 & 4 & 0 & 0 & 1 & | & 320 \end{bmatrix}$$

This final tableau gives the optimal solution

$$x_1 = 0, \quad x_2 = 40, \quad s_1 = 0, \quad s_2 = 28, \quad s_3 = 0, \quad z = 320$$

4-2 EXERCISES

I

Write the basic feasible solution from the tableau given in Exercises 1 through 4. Indicate which variables are basic and which are nonbasic.

1. (*See Step 1*)

x_1	x_2	s_1	s_2	z		
1	3	2	0	0		8
0	−1	1	1	0		10
0	−4	2	0	1		14

2.

x_1	x_2	s_1	s_2	s_3	z		
0	0	3	$\frac{1}{2}$	1	0		8
0	1	1	$-\frac{3}{2}$	0	0		15
1	0	4	$\frac{5}{2}$	0	0		2
0	0	−8	$\frac{1}{2}$	0	1		19

3.

x_1	x_2	x_3	s_1	s_2	s_3	z		
5	0	−3	1	6	0	0		54
8	1	5	0	14	0	0		86
−2	0	1	0	−8	1	0		39
−4	0	3	0	−2	0	1		148

4.

x_1	x_2	x_3	s_1	s_2	z		
8	6	−1	1	0	0		160
5	2	4	0	1	0		148
−6	−10	−5	0	0	1		0

Determine the pivot element in each of the simplex tableaux in Exercises 5 through 14.

5. (*See Step 2*)

5	4	3	1	0	0	0		8
2	7	1	0	1	0	0		15
6	8	5	0	0	1	0		24
−8	−10	−4	0	0	0	1		0

6.

3	4	2	1	0	0		15
5	2	6	0	1	0		10
−8	−3	10	0	0	1		0

7.

2	5	3	1	0	0	0		15
4	1	4	0	1	0	0		12
7	3	−5	0	0	1	0		10
−25	−30	−50	0	0	0	1		0

8.

6	8	1	0	0		75
−2	5	0	1	0		20
−20	−5	0	0	1		0

9.

2	1	1	0	0	0		7
3	4	0	1	0	0		12
2	5	0	0	1	0		15
−5	−8	0	0	0	1		0

10.
$$\begin{bmatrix} 2 & 5 & 1 & 0 & 0 & 0 & | & 8 \\ 1 & 9 & 0 & 1 & 0 & 0 & | & 4 \\ 3 & 4 & 0 & 0 & 1 & 0 & | & 20 \\ \hline -9 & -4 & 0 & 0 & 0 & 1 & | & 0 \end{bmatrix}$$

11.
$$\begin{bmatrix} 3 & 5 & 6 & 1 & 0 & 0 & 0 & | & 9 \\ 2 & 8 & 2 & 0 & 1 & 0 & 0 & | & 6 \\ 5 & 4 & 3 & 0 & 0 & 1 & 0 & | & 15 \\ \hline -6 & -12 & -12 & 0 & 0 & 0 & 1 & | & 0 \end{bmatrix}$$

12.
$$\begin{bmatrix} 8 & 4 & 3 & 2 & 1 & 0 & 0 & | & 50 \\ 5 & 6 & 1 & 7 & 0 & 1 & 0 & | & 65 \\ \hline -6 & -20 & 5 & -20 & 0 & 0 & 1 & | & 0 \end{bmatrix}$$

13.
$$\begin{bmatrix} 6 & 2 & 1 & 0 & 0 & 0 & | & 3 \\ 4 & 3 & 0 & 1 & 0 & 0 & | & 0 \\ 3 & 5 & 0 & 0 & 1 & 0 & | & 8 \\ \hline -12 & -3 & 0 & 0 & 0 & 1 & | & 0 \end{bmatrix}$$

14.
$$\begin{bmatrix} 1 & 6 & 1 & 0 & 0 & 0 & | & 16 \\ 3 & -1 & 0 & 1 & 0 & 0 & | & 0 \\ 5 & 4 & 0 & 0 & 1 & 0 & | & 16 \\ \hline -3 & -8 & 0 & 0 & 0 & 1 & | & 0 \end{bmatrix}$$

In each tableau in Exercises 15 through 18, pivot on the circled entry.

15. (*See Step 3*)
$$\begin{bmatrix} 2 & 3 & 1 & 0 & 0 & 0 & | & 12 \\ ① & 2 & 0 & 1 & 0 & 0 & | & 6 \\ 2 & 5 & 0 & 0 & 1 & 0 & | & 20 \\ \hline -4 & -3 & 0 & 0 & 0 & 1 & | & 0 \end{bmatrix}$$

16.
$$\begin{bmatrix} \frac{1}{2} & \frac{1}{4} & 1 & \frac{1}{4} & 0 & 0 & 0 & | & 85 \\ -3 & ⑤\frac{5}{2} & 0 & -\frac{5}{2} & 1 & 0 & 0 & | & 50 \\ \frac{7}{2} & \frac{11}{4} & 0 & -\frac{1}{4} & 0 & 1 & 0 & | & 425 \\ \hline -\frac{1}{2} & -\frac{21}{4} & 0 & \frac{15}{4} & 0 & 0 & 1 & | & 1275 \end{bmatrix}$$

17.
$$\begin{bmatrix} 6 & 11 & 4 & 1 & 0 & 0 & 0 & | & 250 \\ -5 & -14 & -8 & 0 & 1 & 0 & 0 & | & -460 \\ -1 & -1 & ⊖-3 & 0 & 0 & 1 & 0 & | & -390 \\ \hline -10 & -50 & -30 & 0 & 0 & 0 & 1 & | & 0 \end{bmatrix}$$

18.
$$\begin{bmatrix} ⑩\frac{10}{3} & 0 & \frac{25}{3} & 1 & \frac{4}{3} & 0 & | & \frac{86}{3} \\ -\frac{1}{3} & 1 & -\frac{1}{3} & 0 & -\frac{1}{3} & 0 & | & \frac{10}{3} \\ -\frac{16}{3} & 0 & -\frac{1}{3} & 0 & 0 & 1 & | & \frac{10}{3} \end{bmatrix}$$

II

Use the simplex method to solve Exercises 19 through 36.

19. (*See Example 1*)

Maximize $z = 2x_1 + x_2$, subject to
$$3x_1 + x_2 \le 22$$
$$3x_1 + 4x_2 \le 34$$
$$x_1 \ge 0, \quad x_2 \ge 0$$

20. Maximize $z = x_1 - 3x_2$, subject to
$$x_1 + x_2 \le 5$$
$$x_1 + 5x_2 \le 13$$
$$x_1 \ge 0, \quad x_2 \ge 0$$

21. Maximize $z = 4x_1 + 5x_2$, subject to
$$x_1 + 4x_2 \le 9$$
$$4x_1 + x_2 \le 6$$
$$x_1 \ge 0, \quad x_2 \ge 0$$

22. Maximize $z = 3x_1 + 2x_2$, subject to
$$-3x_1 + 2x_2 \le 8$$
$$5x_1 + 2x_2 \le 16$$
$$x_1 \ge 0, \quad x_2 \ge 0$$

23. Maximize $z = 8x_1 + 4x_2$, subject to
$$x_1 + x_2 \le 240$$
$$4x_1 + 3x_2 \le 720$$
$$x_1 \ge 0, \quad x_2 \ge 0$$

24. Maximize $z = 2x_1 + x_2 + x_3$, subject to
$$4x_1 + 12x_2 - x_3 \le 124$$
$$8x_1 + x_2 - 5x_3 \le 152$$
$$x_1 \ge 0, \quad x_2 \ge 0, \quad x_3 \ge 0$$

25. Maximize $z = 100x_1 + 200x_2 + 50x_3$, subject to
$$5x_1 + 5x_2 + 10x_3 \le 1000$$
$$10x_1 + 8x_2 + 5x_3 \le 2000$$
$$10x_1 + 5x_2 \le 500$$
$$x_1 \ge 0, \quad x_2 \ge 0, \quad x_3 \ge 0$$

26. Maximize $z = 10x_1 + 24x_2 + 13x_3$, subject to
$$x_1 + 6x_2 + 3x_3 \le 36$$
$$3x_1 + 6x_2 + 6x_3 \le 45$$
$$5x_1 + 6x_2 + x_3 \le 46$$
$$x_1 \ge 0, \quad x_2 \ge 0, \quad x_3 \ge 0$$

27. (*See Example 2*)
Maximize $z = 3x_1 + 5x_2 + 5x_3$, subject to

$$x_1 + x_2 + x_3 \le 100$$
$$3x_1 + 2x_2 + 4x_3 \le 210$$
$$x_1 + 2x_2 \le 150$$
$$x_1 \ge 0, \quad x_2 \ge 0, \quad x_3 \ge 0$$

28. Maximize $z = 8x_1 + 8x_2$, subject to

$$4x_1 + x_2 \le 32$$
$$4x_1 + 3x_2 \le 48$$
$$x_1 \ge 0, \quad x_2 \ge 0$$

29. Maximize $z = 15x_1 + 9x_2 + 15x_3$, subject to

$$2x_1 + x_2 + 4x_3 \le 360$$
$$2x_1 + 5x_2 + 10x_3 \le 850$$
$$3x_1 + 3x_2 + x_3 \le 510$$
$$x_1 \ge 0, \quad x_2 \ge 0, \quad x_3 \ge 0$$

30. Maximize $z = 8x_1 + 6x_2 + 8x_3$, subject to

$$x_1 - 3x_2 + 5x_3 \le 50$$
$$2x_1 + 4x_2 \le 40$$
$$x_1 \ge 0, \quad x_2 \ge 0, \quad x_3 \ge 0$$

31. (*See Example 3*)
Maximize $z = 33x_1 + 9x_2$, subject to

$$x_1 + 8x_2 \le 66$$
$$3x_1 + 9x_2 \le 72$$
$$2x_1 + 6x_2 \le 48$$
$$x_1 \ge 0, \quad x_2 \ge 0$$

32. Maximize $z = 4x_1 + 3x_2$, subject to

$$2x_1 + 3x_2 \le 12$$
$$x_1 + 2x_2 \le 6$$
$$2x_1 + 5x_2 \le 20$$
$$x_1 \ge 0, \quad x_2 \ge 0$$

33. Maximize $z = 22x_1 + 20x_2 + 18x_3$, subject to

$$2x_1 + x_2 + 2x_3 \le 100$$
$$x_1 + 2x_2 + 2x_3 \le 100$$
$$2x_1 + 2x_2 + x_3 \le 100$$
$$x_1 \ge 0, \quad x_2 \ge 0, \quad x_3 \ge 0$$

34. Maximize $z = x_1 + 2x_2 + 3x_3$, subject to

$$2x_1 + x_2 + 2x_3 \le 330$$
$$x_1 + 2x_2 + 2x_3 \le 330$$
$$-2x_1 - 2x_2 + x_3 \le 132$$
$$x_1 \ge 0, \quad x_2 \ge 0, \quad x_3 \ge 0$$

35. Maximize $z = 8x_1 + 9x_2 + 15x_3$, subject to

$$2x_1 + x_2 + 4x_3 \le 340$$
$$2x_1 + 5x_2 + 10x_3 \le 850$$
$$4x_1 + 3x_2 + x_3 \le 510$$
$$x_1 \ge 0, \quad x_2 \ge 0, \quad x_3 \ge 0$$

36. Maximize $z = x_1 + 2x_2 + 4x_3 - x_4$, subject to

$$5x_1 + 4x_3 + 6x_4 \le 20$$
$$4x_1 + 2x_2 + 2x_3 + 8x_4 \le 40$$
$$x_1 \ge 0, \quad x_2 \ge 0, \quad x_3 \ge 0, \quad x_4 \ge 0$$

III

37. A hardware manufacturing company makes three items: screwdrivers, chisels, and putty knives. It takes three hours of labor per carton to produce screwdrivers, four hours of labor per carton to produce chisels, and five hours of labor per carton to produce putty knives. Each carton of screwdrivers costs $15 to produce, each carton of chisels costs $12, and each carton of putty knives costs $11. The profit per carton is $5 for screwdrivers, $6 for chisels, and $5 for putty knives. If the company has 2200 hours of labor and $8500 in operating funds available per week, how many cartons of each item should it produce to maximize profit?

38. The maximum daily production of an oil refinery is 1900 barrels. The refinery can produce three types of fuel: gasoline, diesel, and heating oil. The production cost per barrel is $6 for gasoline, $5 for diesel, and $8 for heating oil. The daily production budget is $13,400. The profit is $8.00 per barrel on gasoline, $6.00 on diesel, and $9.00 for heating oil. How much of each should be produced to maximize profit?

39. A manufacturing company uses three machines, I, II, and III, to produce three products: notepads, loose-leaf paper, and spiral notebooks. It takes two, four, and zero minutes of time on each of the machines, respectively, to manufacture a carton of notepads. It takes three, zero, and six minutes on the machines, respectively, to produce a carton of loose-leaf paper. To manufacture a carton of spiral notebooks involves one, two, and three minutes, respectively, on each machine. The total time available on each machine per day is six hours. The profits are $10, $8, and $12 on each carton of notepads, loose-leaf paper, and spiral notebooks, respectively. How many of each item should be produced to maximize total profit?

40. The Health Fare Cereal Company makes three cereals using wheat, oats, and raisins. The computation and profit of each cereal are shown in the following chart:

| CEREAL | PORTION OF EACH POUND OF CEREAL | | | PROFIT/POUND |
	WHEAT	OATS	RAISINS	
Lite	0.75	0.25	0	$0.25
Trim	0.50	0.25	0.25	$0.25
Health Fare	0.15	0.60	0.25	$0.32

The company has 2320 pounds of wheat, 1380 pounds of oats, and 700 pounds of raisins available. How many pounds of each cereal should it produce to maximize profit?

41. The Humidor blends regular coffee, High Mountain coffee, and chocolate to obtain three kinds of coffee: Early Riser, After Dinner, and Deluxe. The blends and profit for each blend are given in the following chart:

| | BLEND | | |
	EARLY RISER	AFTER DINNER	DELUXE
Regular	80%	75%	50%
High Mountain	20%	20%	40%
Chocolate	0%	5%	10%
Profit/Pound	$1.00	$1.10	$1.20

The shop has 255 pounds of regular coffee, 80 pounds of High Mountain coffee, and 15 pounds of chocolate. How many pounds of each blend should be produced to maximize profit?

42. The Williams Trunk Company makes trunks for the military, for commercial use, and for decorative pieces. Each military trunk requires four hours for assembly, one hour for finishing, and 0.1 hour for packaging. Each commercial trunk requires three hours for assembly, two hours for finishing, and 0.2 hour for packaging. Each decorative trunk requires two hours for assembly, four hours for finishing and 0.3 hour for packaging. The profit on each trunk is $6 for military,

$7 for commercial, and $9 for decorative. If 4900 hours are available for assembly work, 2200 for finishing, and 210 for packaging, how many of each type of trunk should be made to maximize profit?

43. The Snack Shop makes three nut mixes from peanuts, cashews, and pecans in 1-kilogram packages. (1 kilogram = 1000 grams.) The composition of each mix is as follows:

TV MIX: 600 grams of peanuts, 300 grams of cashews, and 100 grams of pecans

PARTY MIX: 500 grams of peanuts, 300 grams of cashews, and 200 grams of pecans

DINNER MIX: 300 grams of peanuts, 200 grams of cashews, and 400 grams of pecans

The shop has 39,500 grams of peanuts, 22,500 grams of cashews, and 16,500 grams of pecans. The selling price per package of each mix is $4.40 for TV mix, $4.80 for Party mix, and $5.20 for Dinner mix. How many packages of each should be made to maximize revenue?

44. A craftsman makes two kinds of jewelry boxes for craft shows. The oval box requires 30 minutes of machine work and 20 minutes of finishing. The square box requires 20 minutes of machine work and 40 minutes of finishing. Machine work is limited to 600 minutes per day, and finishing to 800 minutes. If there is $3 profit on the oval box and $4 profit on the square box, how many of each should be produced to maximize profit?

45. The Clock Works produces three clock kits for amateur woodworkers: the Majestic Grandfather Clock, the Traditional Clock, and the Wall Clock. The following chart shows the times required for cutting, sanding, and packing each kit and the price of each kit:

PROCESS	MAJESTIC	TRADITIONAL	WALL
Cutting	4 hours	2 hours	1 hour
Sanding	3 hours	1 hour	1 hour
Packing	1 hour	1 hour	0.5 hour
Price	$400	$250	$160

The cutting machines are available 124 hours per week, the sanding machines 81 hours, and the packing machines 46 hours. How many of each type of kit should be produced each week to maximize revenue?

4–3   WHAT'S HAPPENING IN THE SIMPLEX METHOD?

Let's look at what is happening in the simplex method. We will outline the steps of the simplex method and explain why we perform these steps. We will use Example 5 from Section 4–1 again.

Maximize $z = 4x_1 + 12x_2$, subject to

$$3x_1 + x_2 \leq 180$$
$$x_1 + 2x_2 \leq 100$$
$$-2x_1 + 2x_2 \leq 40$$
$$x_1 \geq 0, \quad x_2 \geq 0$$

The graph of the feasible region and the lines forming its boundary is shown in Figure 4–2.

1. We convert the problem to a system of equations by adding a nonnegative slack variable to each inequality

$$3x_1 + x_2 + s_1 \qquad\qquad = 180$$
$$x_1 + 2x_2 \qquad + s_2 \qquad\qquad = 100$$
$$-2x_1 + 2x_2 \qquad\qquad + s_3 \qquad = 40$$
$$-4x_1 - 12x_2 \qquad\qquad\qquad + z = 0$$

where x_1, x_2, s_1, s_2, and s_3 are all nonnegative.

2. The simplex method searches for solutions to this system of equations. Each simplex tableau gives a basic feasible solution. Recall that we set a variable to zero for each x in the system. This gives points where two of the boundary lines of the feasible region intersect.

FIGURE 4–2

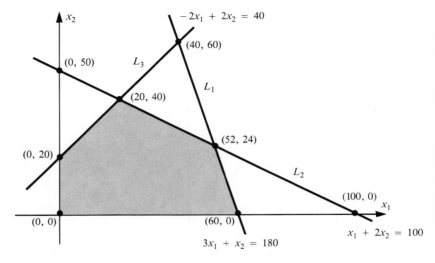

Look at Figure 4–2 to illustrate this. The boundary lines are

$$L_1: \qquad 3x_1 + x_2 = 180$$
$$L_2: \qquad x_1 + 2x_2 = 100$$
$$L_3: \quad -2x_1 + 2x_2 = 40$$

$$x_1\text{-axis:} \quad x_2 = 0$$
$$x_2\text{-axis:} \quad x_1 = 0$$

Now, look at points where two of these boundary lines intersect. Find the points (0, 0), (0, 20), (0, 50), (20, 40), (40, 60), (52, 24), (60, 0), and (100, 0).

We want to observe how these points relate to the system of equations

$$3x_1 + x_2 + s_1 = 180$$
$$x_1 + 2x_2 + s_2 = 100$$
$$-2x_1 + 2x_2 + s_3 = 40$$

(The objective function is not included because it does not enter into determining the feasible region.)

This system has three equations and five variables. When there are more variables than equations, some of the variables can be chosen in any manner whatever. In this case, two variables are arbitrary (two = number of variables minus number of equations). Let us choose the two variables x_1 and x_2. Now we must decide what values we will use for each. We use x_1 and x_2 that come from points of intersection of boundary lines. For each point of intersection we substitute those values of x_1 and x_2 into each equation of the system. Then we find the corresponding values of the s_1, s_2, and s_3 that form a solution to the system. We omit these computations, but show the results in Table 4–1.

Now let's observe some properties of Table 4–1 and see how they relate to Figure 4–2.

TABLE 4–1

POINT	x_1	x_2	s_1	s_2	s_3
(0, 0)	0	0	180	100	40
(0, 20)	0	20	160	60	0
(0, 50)	0	50	130	0	−60
(20, 40)	20	40	80	0	0
(40, 60)	40	60	0	−60	0
(52, 24)	52	24	0	0	96
(60, 0)	60	0	0	40	160
(100, 0)	100	0	−120	0	240

Observation 1. Notice that $s_1 = 0$ for points $(40, 60)$, $(52, 24)$, and $(60, 0)$. Look at Figure 4–2. All of these points are on L_1. Similarly, $s_2 = 0$ for all points on L_2 $((0, 50)$, $(20, 40)$, $(52, 24)$, and $(100, 0))$; and $s_3 = 0$ for all points on L_3.

In general, when a point lies on a boundary line of the feasible region, that slack variable is zero. For a point not on a boundary line, that slack variable is *not* zero.

Since the point $(52, 24)$ is on both L_1 and L_2, $s_1 = 0$ and $s_2 = 0$.

Observation 2. For each of the points in the table, two of the five variables are zero. Remember that we set two variables to zero to get basic solutions in the simplex method. This was done so that we would be using corner points. If we set two variables to zero in an arbitrary fashion, we will get a point where two boundary lines meet, but it might not be a corner because the point might not be in the feasible region.

Observation 3. Some points listed in Table 4–1 are not corner points of the feasible region, namely, $(0, 50)$, $(40, 60)$, and $(100, 0)$. We can observe this by looking at Figure 4–2. However, the table can be used to distinguish a point that is a corner point from one that is not. Look at each point that is not a corner; one of the slack variables is negative. A negative slack variable violates the basic condition that none of the variables are negative. So negative slack variables for the points $(0, 50)$, $(40, 60)$, and $(100, 0)$ indicate that they all lie outside the feasible region. The other points listed are in the feasible region.

Now let's put this information together.

(a) When we set two (in general, it is the number of x's) variables to zero, we get a basic solution, a point where two boundaries intersect.

(b) If the basic solution is *feasible,* it is a corner point.

(c) Since the maximum value of the objective function occurs at a corner point, we want the simplex method to give only basic feasible solutions (corner points).

3. The procedure for choosing the pivot element actually accomplishes two things.

   (a) It increases z as much as possible; and

   (b) it restricts basic solutions to corner points.

   Let's look at the initial tableau to illustrate this:

$$\begin{bmatrix} x_1 & x_2 & s_1 & s_2 & s_3 & z & \\ 3 & 1 & 1 & 0 & 0 & 0 & 180 \\ 1 & 2 & 0 & 1 & 0 & 0 & 100 \\ -2 & 2 & 0 & 0 & 1 & 0 & 40 \\ \hline -4 & -12 & 0 & 0 & 0 & 1 & 0 \end{bmatrix}$$

(a) Let's see how the choice of the pivot column increases z as much as possible. The objective function in this problem is

$$z = 4x_1 + 12x_2$$

If values of x_1 and x_2 are given, and if you are allowed to increase either one of them by a specified amount, say 1, which one would you change to increase z the most? The coefficients of x_1 and x_2 hold the key to your response. If x_1 is increased by 1, then the coefficient 4 causes z to increase by 4. Similarly, an increase of 1 in x_2 causes z to increase by 12. The greatest increase in z is gained by increasing the variable with the largest positive coefficient, 12 in this case. In the tableau, $z = 4x_1 + 12x_2$ is written as $-4x_1 - 12x_2 + z = 0$. In this form the choice of the *most negative* coefficient is equivalent to choosing the variable that will increase z the most. So in the simplex method the pivot column is chosen by the most negative entry in the bottom row because this gives the variable that will increase z the most.

(b) Let's see how the choice of the pivot row restricts basic solutions to corner points.

In the initial tableau the basic solution assumes that both x_1 and x_2 are zero. Then the x_2 column becomes the pivot column to obtain the next tableau because that column contains the most negative entry of the last row. Since this means that we want to increase x_2, x_1 remains zero. Using $x_1 = 0$, let's write each row of the initial tableau in equation form:

$$[3 \quad 1 \quad 1 \quad 0 \quad 0 \quad 0 \quad 180] \quad \text{becomes}$$
$$x_2 + s_1 = 180$$
$$[1 \quad 2 \quad 0 \quad 1 \quad 0 \quad 0 \quad 100] \quad \text{becomes}$$
$$2x_2 + s_2 = 100$$

and

$$[-2 \quad 2 \quad 0 \quad 0 \quad 1 \quad 0 \quad 40] \quad \text{becomes}$$
$$2x_2 + s_3 = 40$$

(The first number in each row doesn't appear in the equation because it is the coefficient of x_1, which we are using as 0.)

We can write these three equations in the following form:

$$s_1 = 180 - x_2$$
$$s_2 = 100 - 2x_2$$
$$s_3 = 40 - 2x_2$$

Keep in mind that we are going to increase x_2 to achieve the largest increase in z. The larger the increase in x_2, the more z increases; but be careful: We must remain in the feasible region. Since s_1, s_2, and s_3 must not be negative, x_2 must be chosen to avoid making any one of them negative.

The equations

$$s_1 = 180 - x_2$$
$$s_2 = 100 - 2x_2$$
$$s_3 = 40 - 2x_2$$

and the nonnegative condition $s_1 \geq 0$, $s_2 \geq 0$, and $s_3 \geq 0$ indicate that

$$180 - x_2 \geq 0$$
$$100 - 2x_2 \geq 0$$

and

$$40 - 2x_2 \geq 0$$

must all be true. Solving each of these inequalities for x_2 gives

$$\frac{180}{1} \geq x_2$$

$$\frac{100}{2} \geq x_2$$

$$\frac{40}{2} \geq x_2$$

In order for *all three* of s_1, s_2, and s_3 to be nonnegative, the smallest value of x_2, 20, must be used. The ratios

$$\frac{180}{1}, \frac{100}{2}, \frac{40}{2}$$

are exactly the ratios that are used in the simplex method to determine the pivot row. The selection of the smallest nonnegative ratio makes a basic solution a feasible basic solution, that is, a corner point is chosen.

4. Recall that the maximum value of z occurs when the last row of the simplex tableau contains no negative entries. The final tableau of this problem was

$$\begin{array}{cccccc} x_1 & x_2 & s_1 & s_2 & s_3 & z \\ \left[\begin{array}{cccccc|c} 0 & 0 & 1 & -\frac{4}{3} & \frac{5}{6} & 0 & 80 \\ 1 & 0 & 0 & \frac{1}{3} & -\frac{1}{3} & 0 & 20 \\ 0 & 1 & 0 & \frac{1}{3} & \frac{1}{6} & 0 & 40 \\ \hline 0 & 0 & 0 & \frac{16}{3} & \frac{2}{3} & 1 & 560 \end{array}\right] \end{array}$$

This tableau tells us that s_2 and s_3 are set to zero (their columns are not unit columns) in the optimal solution; and since the last row contains no negative entries, we know that we cannot increase z further. Here's why: Write the last row of this tableau in equation form. It is

$$\frac{16}{3}s_2 + \frac{2}{3}s_3 + z = 560$$

which can be written as

$$z = 560 - \frac{16}{3}s_2 - \frac{2}{3}s_3$$

This form tells us that if we use any positive number for s_2 or s_3, we will subtract something from 560, thereby making z smaller. So we stop because another tableau will move us to another corner point, and s_2 or s_3 will become positive and therefore reduce z.

Let's compare this situation with the next to the last tableau. Its last row was

$$[-16 \quad 0 \quad 0 \quad 0 \quad 6 \quad 1 \quad 240]$$

This row represents the equation

$$-16x_1 + 6s_3 + z = 240$$

which may be written

$$z = 240 + 16x_1 - 6s_3$$

If x_1 is increased from 0 to a positive number, then a positive quantity will be added to z, thereby increasing it. If you look back at this step in the solution, you will find that x_1 was increased from 0 to 10.

The value of z can be increased as long as there is a negative entry in the last row. It can be increased no further when no entry is negative.

On the basis of the preceding discussion, the simplex method can be summarized this way.

The simplex method maximizes the objective function by computing the objective function at selected corner points of the feasible region until the optimal solution is reached. The method begins at the origin and moves at each stage to a corner point determined by the variable that yields the largest increase in z.

4–3 EXERCISES

I

1. The constraint $4x_1 + 3x_2 \leq 17$ is written as

$$4x_1 + 3x_2 + s_1 = 17$$

using a slack variable.
(a) Find the value of s_1 for each of the points $(0, 0)$, $(2, 2)$, $(5, 10)$, $(2, 1)$, and $(2, 3)$
(b) Which points are in the feasible region?
(c) Which points lie on the line $4x_1 + 3x_2 = 17$?

2. The constraint $6x_1 + 5x_2 \leq 25$ is written as

$$6x_1 + 5x_2 + s_1 = 25$$

using a slack variable. Find the value of s_1 for each of the points $(0, 5)$, $(2, 2)$, $(1.5, 3)$, and $(2.5, 2)$.

3. Find the values of the slack variable s_1 in the constraint

$$3x_1 + 4x_2 + x_3 \le 40$$

for the points $(0, 0, 0)$, $(1, 2, 3)$, $(0, 10, 0)$, and $(4, 2, 7)$.

4. Find the values of the slack variables s_1 and s_2 in the constraints

$$2x_1 + x_2 + 5x_3 + s_1 = 30$$
$$x_1 + 6x_2 + 4x_3 + s_2 = 28$$

for the points $(1, 1, 1)$, $(2, 1, 5)$, $(0, 4, 1)$, and $(5, 10, 2)$.

5. The constraints of a linear programming problem are

$$x_1 + 5x_2 \le 70$$
$$6x_1 + x_2 \le 72$$
$$7x_1 + 6x_2 \le 113$$

Using slack variables, this reduces to

$$x_1 + 5x_2 + s_1 \qquad = 70$$
$$6x_1 + x_2 \qquad + s_2 \qquad = 72$$
$$7x_1 + 6x_2 \qquad + s_3 = 113$$

For each point listed in the table below, find the missing entries.

POINT	s_1	s_2	s_3	IS POINT ON BOUNDARY?	IS POINT IN FEASIBLE REGION?
(5, 10)					
(8, 10)					
(5, 13)					
(11, 13)					
(10, 12)					
(15, 11)					

6. Which single variable contributes the most to increasing z in the following objective functions?
   (a) $z = 6x_1 + 5x_2 + 14x_3$
   (b) $z = 8x_1 - 12x_2 + 3x_3$
   (c) $z = 8x_1 + 4x_2 - 7x_3 + 5x_4$

7. The linear programming problem
   Maximize $z = 3x_1 + 2x_2$, subject to

$$5x_1 + 2x_2 \le 900$$
$$8x_1 + 10x_2 \le 2800$$
$$x_1 \ge 0, \quad x_2 \ge 0$$

has a feasible region bounded by

$$5x_1 + 2x_2 = 900$$
$$8x_1 + 10x_2 = 2800$$
$$x_1 = 0, \quad x_2 = 0$$

The simplex method solution to this problem includes the following tableaux:

$$(\text{i}) \quad \begin{array}{ccccc|c} x_1 & x_2 & s_1 & s_2 & z & \\ 5 & 2 & 1 & 0 & 0 & 900 \\ 8 & 10 & 0 & 1 & 0 & 2800 \\ -3 & -2 & 0 & 0 & 1 & 0 \end{array}$$

$$(\text{ii}) \quad \begin{bmatrix} 1 & \frac{2}{5} & \frac{1}{5} & 0 & 0 & 180 \\ 0 & \frac{34}{5} & -\frac{8}{5} & 1 & 0 & 1360 \\ 0 & -\frac{4}{5} & \frac{3}{5} & 0 & 1 & 540 \end{bmatrix}$$

$$(\text{iii}) \quad \begin{bmatrix} 1 & 0 & \frac{25}{85} & -\frac{1}{17} & 0 & 100 \\ 0 & 1 & -\frac{4}{17} & \frac{5}{34} & 0 & 200 \\ 0 & 0 & \frac{7}{17} & \frac{2}{17} & 1 & 700 \end{bmatrix}$$

(a) Write the basic solution from each tableau.
(b) Determine the two boundary lines whose intersection gives the basic solution.

II

8. Given the constraint

$$x_1 + 5x_2 + s_1 = 48$$

(a) When $x_1 = 0$, what is the largest value x_2 can have so that s_1 meets the nonnegative condition?
(b) When $x_1 = 6$, what is the largest value x_2 can have so that s_1 meets the nonnegative condition?
(c) When $x_2 = 0$, what is the largest possible value of x_1 so that the point is in the feasible region?

III

9. Given the constraints

$$6x_1 + 7x_2 + s_1 \qquad = 36$$
$$2x_1 + 5x_2 \qquad + s_2 = 32$$

   (a) When $x_1 = 0$, what is the largest possible value of x_2 so that the point is in the feasible region?
   (b) When $x_2 = 0$, what is the largest possible value of x_1 so that the point is in the feasible region?

10. Given the constraint

$$4x_1 + 5x_2 + x_3 + s_1 = 45$$

When $x_1 = 0$, what is the largest possible value of x_2 so that s_1 is nonnegative?

4–4 MIXED CONSTRAINTS

- *Minimizing a Function*
- *Negative Constant in $\leq$ Constraint*
- *Problems with $\geq$ Constraints*
- *Minimization Problems*
- *Equality Constraints*
- *Examples and Applications*

The simplex method has been used to solve standard maximum problems (all constraints have $\leq$ inequalities and nonnegative constant terms).

In this section we study more general problems. The constraints may be a mixture of $\leq$, $\geq$, or $=$, and we may wish to either maximize or minimize the objective function. Because such problems contain a mixture of $\leq$, $\geq$, or $=$, they are referred to as having **mixed constraints.**

MINIMIZING A FUNCTION

Because the simplex method solves problems in which the objective function is to be maximized, it is not used directly to solve minimization problems. We can make an adjustment that converts a minimization problem to a maximization problem whose solution enables us to find the solution to the minimization problem.

The adjustment is simple. If z is the objective function to be minimized, then solve the maximization problem using $w = -z$ as the objective function. This works because if k is the maximum value of w, then $-k$ is the minimum value of z. For example, when you multiply a set of numbers by -1, you reverse the order. The set of numbers $\{1, 5, 7, 16\}$ has 1 as the smallest number and 16 as the largest number. The set made of the negatives of these numbers is $\{-1, -5, -7, -16\}$. It has -1 as the *largest* number and -16 as the *smallest*.

EXAMPLE 1 *(Compare Exercise 1)*

Here is an example that illustrates the simplex solution of a minimization problem.

Minimize $z = 2x_1 - 3x_2$, subject to

$$x_1 + 2x_2 \leq 10$$
$$2x_1 + x_2 \leq 11$$
$$x_1 \geq 0, \quad x_2 \geq 0$$

SOLUTION Convert the objective function to $w = -2x_1 + 3x_2$.

The tableaux for the solution are as follows:

$$
\begin{array}{ccccc}
x_1 & x_2 & s_1 & s_2 & w \\
\end{array}
$$

$$
\left[\begin{array}{ccccc|c}
1 & 2 & 1 & 0 & 0 & 10 \\
2 & 1 & 0 & 1 & 0 & 11 \\
\hline
2 & -3 & 0 & 0 & 1 & 0
\end{array}\right] \quad \tfrac{1}{2}R1 \to R1
$$

$$
\left[\begin{array}{ccccc|c}
\tfrac{1}{2} & 1 & \tfrac{1}{2} & 0 & 0 & 5 \\
2 & 1 & 0 & 1 & 0 & 11 \\
\hline
2 & -3 & 0 & 0 & 1 & 0
\end{array}\right] \quad \begin{array}{c} -R1 + R2 \to R2 \\ 3R1 + R3 \to R3 \end{array}
$$

$$
\left[\begin{array}{ccccc|c}
\tfrac{1}{2} & 1 & \tfrac{1}{2} & 0 & 0 & 5 \\
\tfrac{3}{2} & 0 & -\tfrac{1}{2} & 1 & 0 & 6 \\
\hline
\tfrac{7}{2} & 0 & \tfrac{3}{2} & 0 & 1 & 15
\end{array}\right]
$$

The optimal solution (maximum) is $w = 15$ when $x_1 = 0$, $x_2 = 5$. The original problem then has as its optimal (minimum) solution $z = -15$ at $x_1 = 0$, $x_2 = 5$. ∎

NEGATIVE CONSTANT IN ≤ CONSTRAINT

Whenever a maximization problem has a $\leq$ constraint with a negative constant term, the simplex method does not apply directly. We can set up the initial tableau in the usual manner and then make some modifications that allow us to find a solution using the simplex method. We illustrate with a simple example.

EXAMPLE 2 *(Compare Exercise 5)*

Maximize $z = 20x + 50y$, subject to

$$3x + 4y \leq 72$$
$$-5x + 2y \leq -16$$
$$x \geq 0, \quad y \geq 0$$

SOLUTION The graph of the feasible region is shown in Figure 4–3. Notice that the corners of the feasible region are $(\tfrac{16}{5}, 0)$, $(24, 0)$, and $(8, 12)$.

If we set up the initial tableau for this problem in the usual way, we obtain

$$
\left[\begin{array}{ccccc|c}
3 & 4 & 1 & 0 & 0 & 72 \\
-5 & 2 & 0 & 1 & 0 & -16 \\
\hline
-20 & -50 & 0 & 0 & 1 & 0
\end{array}\right]
$$

FIGURE 4-3

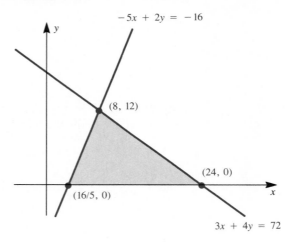

The basic solution from this tableau is $x = 0$, $y = 0$, $s_1 = 72$, and $s_2 = -16$. This solution is *not feasible* because s_2 is negative. Because the basic solution is not feasible, we need to adjust the tableau so that the simplex procedure can be used. Here's how.

In the initial tableau, select the row with a negative constant in the last column (Row 2 because of -16). Next select another negative entry in that row (-5 in the first column). This entry becomes a pivot element. Divide the second row by -5 to obtain the following tableau:

$$\begin{bmatrix} 3 & 4 & 1 & 0 & 0 & 72 \\ 1 & -\frac{2}{5} & 0 & -\frac{1}{5} & 0 & \frac{16}{5} \\ \hline -20 & -50 & 0 & 0 & 1 & 0 \end{bmatrix}$$

After pivoting on 1 in Row 2, Column 1, we have the following tableau:

$$\begin{bmatrix} 0 & \frac{26}{5} & 1 & \frac{3}{5} & 0 & \frac{312}{5} \\ 1 & -\frac{2}{5} & 0 & -\frac{1}{5} & 0 & \frac{16}{5} \\ \hline 0 & -58 & 0 & -4 & 1 & 64 \end{bmatrix}$$

This tableau yields the basic feasible solution $x = \frac{16}{5}$, $y = 0$, $s_1 = \frac{312}{5}$, and $s_2 = 0$. Because the basic solution is feasible, we can apply the simplex method to this tableau in the usual manner. The next pivot element is $\frac{26}{5}$ in row 1. Pivoting gives

$$\begin{bmatrix} 0 & 1 & \frac{5}{26} & \frac{3}{26} & 0 & 12 \\ 1 & 0 & \frac{1}{13} & -\frac{2}{13} & 0 & 8 \\ \hline 0 & 0 & \frac{145}{13} & \frac{35}{13} & 1 & 760 \end{bmatrix}$$

This tableau gives the optimal solution of $z = 760$ at $x = 8$, $y = 12$. ▬

Look back over the solution to the problem and observe two phases that generally apply to problems of this type.

Phase I. Set up the initial tableau. When a negative constant appears in the rightmost column of the tableau and the basic solution is not feasible, the tableau must be modified so that the basic solution is feasible. This is done by selecting a row with a negative entry in the last column and using another negative entry in that row as a pivot element. It might be necessary to pivot more than once in Phase I in order to remove all negative entries in the last column.

Phase II. When the modifications in Phase I produce a tableau with feasible basic solutions, then proceed with the usual simplex method.

Now look back at Figure 4-3 to see what happened in Phase I. The initial tableau gives the basic solution with $x = 0$, $y = 0$. In this case this point, $(0, 0)$, lies outside the feasible region. (That's why we got an infeasible solution.) When we pivot on -5, the next basic solution has $x = \frac{16}{5}$, $y = 0$ with both slack variables nonnegative. This solution is feasible and represents the corner $(\frac{16}{5}, 0)$ of the feasible region.

When a feasible solution is reached in Phase I, we enter Phase II and follow the simplex procedure. In this example the optimal solution is reached in one more pivot. Notice that the pivot takes us from the corner $(\frac{16}{5}, 0)$ to the corner $(8, 12)$, the optimal solution.

Here is another example to be sure that you understand the procedure followed in Phase I and Phase II.

EXAMPLE 3

Maximize $3x_1 + 8x_2 + 4x_3$, subject to

$$
\begin{aligned}
x_1 + x_2 + x_3 &\leq 12 \\
2x_1 + 6x_2 + 3x_3 &\leq 42 \\
-x_1 + 2x_2 &\leq -6 \\
x_1 \geq 0, \quad x_2 \geq 0, \quad x_3 &\geq 0
\end{aligned}
$$

SOLUTION *Phase I.* The initial tableau is

$$
\begin{bmatrix}
1 & 1 & 1 & 1 & 0 & 0 & 0 & 12 \\
2 & 6 & 3 & 0 & 1 & 0 & 0 & 42 \\
-1 & 2 & 0 & 0 & 0 & 1 & 0 & -6 \\
-3 & -8 & -4 & 0 & 0 & 0 & 1 & 0
\end{bmatrix}
$$

Pivot on -1 in Row 3:

$$
\begin{bmatrix}
0 & 3 & 1 & 1 & 0 & 1 & 0 & 6 \\
0 & 10 & 3 & 0 & 1 & 2 & 0 & 30 \\
1 & -2 & 0 & 0 & 0 & -1 & 0 & 6 \\
0 & -14 & -4 & 0 & 0 & -3 & 1 & 18
\end{bmatrix}
$$

This tableau gives a feasible basic solution, $x_1 = 6$, $x_2 = 0$, $x_3 = 0$, $s_1 = 6$, $s_2 = 30$, $s_3 = 0$, so proceed to Phase II.

Phase II. Pivot on 3 in Row 1:

$$\begin{bmatrix} 0 & 1 & \frac{1}{3} & \frac{1}{3} & 0 & \frac{1}{3} & 0 & 2 \\ 0 & 0 & -\frac{1}{3} & -\frac{10}{3} & 1 & -\frac{4}{3} & 0 & 10 \\ 1 & 0 & \frac{2}{3} & \frac{2}{3} & 0 & -\frac{1}{3} & 0 & 10 \\ 0 & 0 & \frac{2}{3} & \frac{14}{3} & 0 & \frac{5}{3} & 1 & 46 \end{bmatrix}$$

The optimal solution is $z = 46$ at $(10, 2, 0)$.

PROBLEMS WITH $\geq$ CONSTRAINTS

Whenever a constraint is written as

$$a_1x_1 + a_1x_1 + \cdots + a_1x_1 \geq b$$

we need to adjust the constraint so that the simplex method can be used. We modify the problem by multiplying the $\geq$ constraint by -1, which reverses the sign, giving a $\leq$ constraint. This may introduce a negative constant in the new constraint, but we handle that situation as described earlier.

EXAMPLE 4   *(Compare Exercise 9)*

Modify the following problem and set up the initial tableau.
Maximize $20x_1 + 70x_2$, subject to

$$2x_1 + 5x_2 \leq 58$$
$$x_1 - x_2 \geq 15$$
$$x_1 \geq 0, \quad x_2 \geq 0$$

SOLUTION   We convert $x_1 - x_2 \geq 15$ to a $\leq$ constraint by multiplying through by -1 to obtain

$$-x_1 + x_2 \leq -15$$

We can now state the problem as follows:

Maximize $20x_1 + 70x_2$, subject to

$$2x_1 + 5x_2 \leq 58$$
$$-x_1 + x_2 \leq -15$$
$$x_1 \geq 0, \quad x_2 \geq 0$$

The initial tableau is

x_1	x_2	s_1	s_2	z	
2	5	1	0	0	58
-1	1	0	1	0	-15
-20	-70	0	0	1	0

Here is another example.

EXAMPLE 5 *(Compare Exercises 11 and 15)*

Maximize $z = 8x_1 + 2x_2 + 6x_3$, subject to

$$6x_1 + 4x_2 + 5x_3 \le 68$$
$$4x_1 + 3x_2 + x_3 \ge 32$$
$$2x_1 + 4x_2 + 3x_3 \ge 36$$
$$x_1 \ge 0, \quad x_2 \ge 0, \quad x_3 \ge 0$$

SOLUTION Write all the constraints, other than the nonnegative conditions, as $\le$ constraints. The problem then becomes

Maximize $z = 8x_1 + 2x_2 + 6x_3$, subject to

$$6x_1 + 4x_2 + 5x_3 \le 68$$
$$-4x_1 - 3x_2 - x_3 \le -32$$
$$-2x_1 - 4x_2 - 3x_3 \le -36$$
$$x_1 \ge 0, \quad x_2 \ge 0, \quad x_3 \ge 0$$

The initial simplex tableau is

$$\left[\begin{array}{ccccccc|c}
6 & 4 & 5 & 1 & 0 & 0 & 0 & 68 \\
-4 & -3 & -1 & 0 & 1 & 0 & 0 & -32 \\
-2 & -4 & -3 & 0 & 0 & 1 & 0 & -36 \\
\hline
-8 & -2 & -6 & 0 & 0 & 0 & 1 & 0
\end{array}\right]$$

Since this tableau has negative entries in the last column, we enter Phase I.

Phase I. Select a negative entry in the last column, -36 in row 3 in this case. Find the most negative entry in that row that is to the left of -36. The entry is -4 in column 2 in this case. Use it for the pivot element to obtain the tableau

$$\left[\begin{array}{ccccccc|c}
4 & 0 & 2 & 1 & 0 & 1 & 0 & 32 \\
-\frac{5}{2} & 0 & \frac{5}{4} & 0 & 1 & -\frac{3}{4} & 0 & -5 \\
\frac{1}{2} & 1 & \frac{3}{4} & 0 & 0 & -\frac{1}{4} & 0 & 9 \\
\hline
-7 & 0 & -\frac{9}{2} & 0 & 0 & -\frac{1}{2} & 1 & 18
\end{array}\right]$$

Since a negative entry, -5, remains in the last column, we repeat the process with row 2 and use $-\frac{5}{2}$ in row 2, column 1 for the pivot element to obtain

$$\left[\begin{array}{ccccccc|c}
0 & 0 & 4 & 1 & \frac{8}{5} & -\frac{1}{5} & 0 & 24 \\
1 & 0 & -\frac{1}{2} & 0 & -\frac{2}{5} & \frac{3}{10} & 0 & 2 \\
0 & 1 & 1 & 0 & \frac{1}{5} & -\frac{2}{5} & 0 & 8 \\
\hline
0 & 0 & -8 & 0 & -\frac{14}{5} & \frac{8}{5} & 1 & 32
\end{array}\right]$$

This tableau has the basic solution $x_1 = 2$, $x_2 = 8$, $x_3 = 0$, $s_1 = 24$, $s_2 = 0$, $s_3 = 0$, and $z = 32$, which is a feasible solution. We now go to Phase II.

Phase II. We proceed with the simplex method until there are no negative entries in the bottom row. The most negative entry, -8, indicates that we use column 3 for the pivot column. The ratios of the entries in the last column and column 3 are 6, -4, and 8, so row 1 is the pivot row. Using 4 as the pivot element, we obtain

$$\left[\begin{array}{ccccccc|c} 0 & 0 & 1 & \frac{1}{4} & \frac{2}{5} & -\frac{1}{20} & 0 & 6 \\ 1 & 0 & 0 & \frac{1}{8} & -\frac{1}{5} & \frac{11}{40} & 0 & 5 \\ 0 & 1 & 0 & -\frac{1}{4} & -\frac{1}{5} & -\frac{7}{20} & 0 & 2 \\ \hline 0 & 0 & 0 & 2 & \frac{2}{5} & \frac{6}{5} & 1 & 80 \end{array}\right]$$

This solution is optimal with $z = 80$ when $x_1 = 5$, $x_2 = 2$, and $x_3 = 6$.

MINIMIZATION PROBLEMS

A minimization problem may have $\geq$ constraints. Such problems can be solved by using methods already studied: Replace the objective function "Minimize z" with "Maximize $w = -z$" and multiply each $\geq$ constraint with -1 to convert it to a $\leq$ constraint. Then apply Phase I and Phase II as necessary. We illustrate with a simple example.

EXAMPLE 6

Minimize $z = 10x_1 - 25x_2$, subject to

$$x_1 + 3x_2 \leq 30$$
$$2x_1 - 4x_2 \geq 30$$
$$x_1 \geq 0, \quad x_2 \geq 0$$

(a) (*Compare Exercise 17*) Set up the initial tableau.
(b) (*Compare Exercise 19*) Solve by the simplex method.

SOLUTION

(a) Set up the initial tableau.

Modify the problem to a maximization problem by using the objective function

$$w = -z = -10x_1 + 25x_2$$

and replace the $\geq$ constraint with

$$-2x_1 + 4x_2 \leq -30$$

The modified problem becomes

Maximize $w = -10x_1 + 25x_2$, subject to

$$x_1 + 3x_2 \leq 30$$
$$-2x_1 + 4x_2 \leq -30$$
$$x_1 \geq 0, \quad x_2 \geq 0$$

The introduction of slack variables gives the system of equations

$$
\begin{aligned}
x_1 + 3x_2 + s_1   &= 30 \\
-2x_1 + 4x_2 + s_2 &= -30 \\
10x_1 - 25x_2   + w &= 0
\end{aligned}
$$

The initial tableau is then

$$
\begin{array}{ccccc}
x_1 & x_2 & s_1 & s_2 & w \\
\end{array}
$$

$$
\left[
\begin{array}{ccccc|c}
1 & 3 & 1 & 0 & 0 & 30 \\
-2 & 4 & 0 & 1 & 0 & -30 \\
\hline
10 & -25 & 0 & 0 & 1 & 0
\end{array}
\right]
$$

(b) Solve the problem.

Phase I. The -30 in the last column indicates that we enter Phase I to reduce the tableau to one with a feasible basic solution. The row 2, column 1 entry, -2, is the pivot element. The tableau obtained by pivoting there is

$$
\begin{array}{ccccc}
x_1 & x_2 & s_1 & s_2 & w \\
\end{array}
$$

$$
\left[
\begin{array}{ccccc|c}
0 & 5 & 1 & \frac{1}{2} & 0 & 15 \\
1 & -2 & 0 & -\frac{1}{2} & 0 & 15 \\
\hline
0 & -5 & 0 & 5 & 1 & -150
\end{array}
\right]
$$

This tableau has a feasible solution, so we proceed to Phase II.

Phase II. Next pivot on 5 in row 1 to obtain this tableau:

$$
\begin{array}{ccccc}
x_1 & x_2 & s_1 & s_2 & w \\
\end{array}
$$

$$
\left[
\begin{array}{ccccc|c}
0 & 1 & \frac{1}{5} & \frac{1}{10} & 0 & 3 \\
1 & 0 & \frac{2}{5} & -\frac{3}{10} & 0 & 21 \\
\hline
0 & 0 & 1 & \frac{11}{2} & 1 & -135
\end{array}
\right]
$$

This solution is optimal with maximum $w = -135$ at $x_1 = 21$, $x_2 = 3$. Thus the original problem has minimum $z = 135$ at $x_1 = 21$, $x_2 = 3$.

EQUALITY CONSTRAINTS

In some cases a linear programming program may have a constraint in the form of an equation, not an inequality. This type of constraint is called an **equality constraint.** We can still use the simplex method after an appropriate adjustment. The adjustment simply replaces the $=$ constraint with two constraints, a $\geq$ and a $\leq$ constraint. Then we apply Phase I and Phase II as appropriate. This works because the two inequalities $a \geq b$ and $b \geq a$ are equivalent to $a = b$. We illustrate with an example.

EXAMPLE 7

Maximize $z = 4x_1 + 12x_2$, subject to

$$3x_1 + x_2 \leq 180$$
$$x_1 + 2x_2 = 100$$
$$-2x_1 + 2x_2 \leq 40$$
$$x_1 \geq 0, \quad x_2 \geq 0$$

(a) (*Compare Exercise 23*) Obtain the initial simplex tableau.

(b) (*Compare Exercise 25*) Apply Phase I and Phase II to find an optimal solution.

SOLUTION

(a) Initial tableau.

Replace the constraint $x_1 + 2x_2 = 100$ with the two constraints

$$x_1 + 2x_2 \leq 100$$
$$x_1 + 2x_2 \geq 100$$

and thereby modify the problem to the following:

Maximize $z = 4x_1 + 12x_2$, subject to

$$3x_1 + x_2 \leq 180$$
$$x_1 + 2x_2 \leq 100$$
$$x_1 + 2x_2 \geq 100$$
$$-2x_1 + 2x_2 \leq 40$$
$$x_1 \geq 0, \quad x_2 \geq 0$$

Since these constraints contain a $\geq$ constraint, multiply it by -1 so that the problem is modified to the following:

Maximize $z = 4x_1 + 12x_2$, subject to

$$3x_1 + x_2 \leq 180$$
$$x_1 + 2x_2 \leq 100$$
$$-x_1 - 2x_2 \leq -100$$
$$-2x_1 + 2x_2 \leq 40$$
$$x_1 \geq 0, \quad x_2 \geq 0$$

This problem has the initial tableau

x_1	x_2	s_1	s_2	s_3	s_4	z	
3	1	1	0	0	0	0	180
1	2	0	1	0	0	0	100
-1	-2	0	0	1	0	0	-100
-2	2	0	0	0	1	0	40
-4	-12	0	0	0	0	1	0

(b) Find the solution. Because of the -100 entry in the last column, this tableau yields a nonfeasible basic solution. Therefore we enter Phase I.

Phase I. The row with -100 in the last column is the pivot row. Except for the last column, the most negative entry in this row is the -2 in column 2. Thus column 2 is the pivot column, and -2 in row 3, column 2 is the pivot element. After pivoting we obtain the tableau

$$
\begin{array}{ccccccc|c}
x_1 & x_2 & s_1 & s_2 & s_3 & s_4 & z & \\
\frac{5}{2} & 0 & 1 & 0 & \frac{1}{2} & 0 & 0 & 130 \\
0 & 0 & 0 & 1 & 1 & 0 & 0 & 0 \\
\frac{1}{2} & 1 & 0 & 0 & -\frac{1}{2} & 0 & 0 & 50 \\
-3 & 0 & 0 & 0 & 1 & 1 & 0 & -60 \\
\hline
2 & 0 & 0 & 0 & -6 & 0 & 1 & 600
\end{array}
$$

Since this tableau has a negative entry in the last column, we must pivot again, using -3 as the pivot element:

$$
\begin{array}{ccccccc|c}
x_1 & x_2 & s_1 & s_2 & s_3 & s_4 & z & \\
0 & 0 & 1 & 0 & \frac{4}{3} & \frac{5}{6} & 0 & 80 \\
0 & 0 & 0 & 1 & 1 & 0 & 0 & 0 \\
0 & 1 & 0 & 0 & -\frac{1}{3} & \frac{1}{6} & 0 & 40 \\
1 & 0 & 0 & 0 & -\frac{1}{3} & -\frac{1}{3} & 0 & 20 \\
\hline
0 & 0 & 0 & 0 & -\frac{16}{3} & \frac{2}{3} & 1 & 560
\end{array}
$$

This tableau has a feasible basic solution, so we proceed with Phase II.

Phase II. The most negative entry in the bottom row of the last tableau is $-\frac{16}{3}$, so the s_3 column is the pivot column. The ratios obtained from the entries in the last column and the pivot column are 60, $\frac{0}{1}$, -120, and -60. Since the second ratio is zero divided by a *positive* number, it determines the pivot row, row 2. Pivoting with the 1 in row 2, column 5, we obtain

$$
\begin{array}{ccccccc|c}
x_1 & x_2 & s_1 & s_2 & s_3 & s_4 & z & \\
0 & 0 & 1 & -\frac{4}{3} & 0 & \frac{5}{6} & 0 & 80 \\
0 & 0 & 0 & 1 & 1 & 0 & 0 & 0 \\
0 & 1 & 0 & \frac{1}{3} & 0 & \frac{1}{6} & 0 & 40 \\
1 & 0 & 0 & \frac{1}{3} & 0 & -\frac{1}{3} & 0 & 20 \\
\hline
0 & 0 & 0 & \frac{16}{3} & 0 & \frac{2}{3} & 1 & 560
\end{array}
$$

This tableau yields the optimal solution $z = 560$ when $x_1 = 20$ and $x_2 = 40$.

A minimization problem with an equality constraint can be modified to be solved by the simplex method.

EXAMPLE 8   *(Compare Exercise 29)*

Minimize $z = 8x_1 + 5x_2$, subject to

$$x_1 + x_2 \le 24$$
$$2x_1 + x_2 \le 48$$
$$4x_1 + 3x_2 = 84$$
$$x_1 \ge 0, \quad x_2 \ge 0$$

SOLUTION   We make two modifications to this problem. First, replace "Minimize $z = 8x_1 + 5x_2$" with "Maximize $w = -z = -8x_1 - 5x_2$." Second, replace $4x_1 + 3x_2 = 84$ with $4x_1 + 3x_2 \le 84$ and $-4x_1 - 3x_2 \le -84$. This gives the following statement of the problem:

Maximize $w = -8x_1 - 5x_2$, subject to

$$x_1 + x_2 \le 24$$
$$2x_1 + x_2 \le 48$$
$$4x_1 + 3x_2 \le 84$$
$$-4x_1 - 3x_2 \le -84$$
$$x_1 \ge 0, \quad x_2 \ge 0$$

The initial simplex tableau is

$$
\begin{array}{ccccccc}
x_1 & x_2 & s_1 & s_2 & s_3 & s_4 & w \\
\end{array}
$$

$$
\left[
\begin{array}{ccccccc|c}
1 & 1 & 1 & 0 & 0 & 0 & 0 & 24 \\
2 & 1 & 0 & 1 & 0 & 0 & 0 & 48 \\
4 & 3 & 0 & 0 & 1 & 0 & 0 & 84 \\
-4 & -3 & 0 & 0 & 0 & 1 & 0 & -84 \\
\hline
8 & 5 & 0 & 0 & 0 & 0 & 1 & 0 \\
\end{array}
\right]
$$

Because of the -84 in the last column the basic solution is not feasible, so we enter Phase I.

Phase I. Pivot on the -4 entry in row 4. This gives the tableau

$$
\left[
\begin{array}{ccccccc|c}
0 & \frac{1}{4} & 1 & 0 & 0 & \frac{1}{4} & 0 & 3 \\
0 & -\frac{1}{2} & 0 & 1 & 0 & \frac{1}{2} & 0 & 6 \\
0 & 0 & 0 & 0 & 1 & 1 & 0 & 0 \\
1 & \frac{3}{4} & 0 & 0 & 0 & -\frac{1}{4} & 0 & 21 \\
\hline
0 & -1 & 0 & 0 & 0 & 2 & 1 & -168 \\
\end{array}
\right]
$$

The last tableau has a basic feasible solution, so we proceed to Phase II.

Phase II. The pivot element in the above matrix is $\frac{1}{4}$ in row 1, column 2. Pivoting there yields

$$
\begin{bmatrix}
0 & 1 & 4 & 0 & 0 & 1 & 0 & 12 \\
0 & 0 & 2 & 1 & 0 & 1 & 0 & 12 \\
0 & 0 & 0 & 0 & 1 & 1 & 0 & 0 \\
1 & 0 & -3 & 0 & 0 & -1 & 0 & 12 \\
\hline
0 & 0 & 4 & 0 & 0 & 3 & 1 & -156
\end{bmatrix}
$$

This tableau has the optimal solution maximum $w = -156$ at $x_1 = 12$, $x_2 = 12$, so the original problem has the solution minimum $z = 156$ at $x_1 = 12$, $x_2 = 12$.

⎯⎯⎯⎯⎯⎯ ∎

EXAMPLES AND APPLICATIONS

We now work through some examples that use all the procedures of this section.

EXAMPLE 9 *(Compare Exercises 33 and 35)*

Maximize $z = 7x_1 + 2x_2 + 3x_3$, subject to

$$
\begin{aligned}
5x_1 + 4x_2 + 6x_3 &\le 282 \\
3x_1 + 8x_2 + 2x_3 &= 210 \\
x_1 + 10x_2 + 5x_3 &\ge 297 \\
x_1 \ge 0, \quad x_2 \ge 0, \quad x_3 &\ge 0
\end{aligned}
$$

SOLUTION We adjust the $\ge$ and $=$ constraints, so the problem is modified to

Maximize $z = 7x_1 + 2x_2 + 3x_3$, subject to

$$
\begin{aligned}
5x_1 + 4x_2 + 6x_3 &\le 282 \\
3x_1 + 8x_2 + 2x_3 &\le 210 \\
-3x_1 - 8x_2 - 2x_3 &\le -210 \\
-x_1 - 10x_2 - 5x_3 &\le -297 \\
x_1 \ge 0, \quad x_2 \ge 0, \quad x_3 &\ge 0
\end{aligned}
$$

The initial tableau is then

$$
\begin{bmatrix}
5 & 4 & 6 & 1 & 0 & 0 & 0 & 0 & 282 \\
3 & 8 & 2 & 0 & 1 & 0 & 0 & 0 & 210 \\
-3 & -8 & -2 & 0 & 0 & 1 & 0 & 0 & -210 \\
-1 & -10 & -5 & 0 & 0 & 0 & 1 & 0 & -297 \\
\hline
-7 & -2 & -3 & 0 & 0 & 0 & 0 & 1 & 0
\end{bmatrix}
$$

The following sequence of tableaux in Phase I and Phase II lead to the optimal solution. Some details are left out, so be sure you can go from each tableau to the next.

Phase I.

$$\begin{bmatrix} 5 & 4 & 6 & 1 & 0 & 0 & 0 & 0 & | & 282 \\ 3 & 8 & 2 & 0 & 1 & 0 & 0 & 0 & | & 210 \\ -3 & -8 & -2 & 0 & 0 & 1 & 0 & 0 & | & -210 \\ -1 & -10 & -5 & 0 & 0 & 0 & 1 & 0 & | & -297 \\ \hline -7 & -2 & -3 & 0 & 0 & 0 & 0 & 1 & | & 0 \end{bmatrix}$$

Pivot on -10 in row 4 to obtain

$$\begin{bmatrix} \frac{23}{5} & 0 & 4 & 1 & 0 & 0 & \frac{2}{5} & 0 & | & \frac{816}{5} \\ \frac{11}{5} & 0 & -2 & 0 & 1 & 0 & \frac{4}{5} & 0 & | & -\frac{138}{5} \\ -\frac{11}{5} & 0 & 2 & 0 & 0 & 1 & -\frac{4}{5} & 0 & | & \frac{138}{5} \\ \frac{1}{10} & 1 & \frac{1}{2} & 0 & 0 & 0 & -\frac{1}{10} & 0 & | & \frac{297}{10} \\ \hline -\frac{34}{5} & 0 & -2 & 0 & 0 & 0 & -\frac{1}{5} & 1 & | & \frac{297}{5} \end{bmatrix}$$

Pivot on -2 in row 2 to obtain

$$\begin{bmatrix} 9 & 0 & 0 & 1 & 2 & 0 & 2 & 0 & | & 108 \\ -\frac{11}{10} & 0 & 1 & 0 & -\frac{1}{2} & 0 & -\frac{2}{5} & 0 & | & \frac{69}{5} \\ 0 & 0 & 0 & 0 & 1 & 1 & 0 & 0 & | & 0 \\ \frac{13}{20} & 1 & 0 & 0 & \frac{1}{4} & 0 & \frac{1}{10} & 0 & | & \frac{114}{5} \\ \hline -9 & 0 & 0 & 1 & -1 & 0 & -1 & 1 & | & 87 \end{bmatrix}$$

We now proceed to Phase II because the tableau has a feasible basic solution.

Phase II. Pivot on 9 in row 1 to obtain

$$\begin{bmatrix} 1 & 0 & 0 & \frac{1}{9} & \frac{2}{9} & 0 & \frac{2}{9} & 0 & | & 12 \\ 0 & 0 & 1 & \frac{11}{90} & -\frac{23}{90} & 0 & -\frac{7}{45} & 0 & | & 27 \\ 0 & 0 & 0 & 0 & 1 & 1 & 0 & 0 & | & 0 \\ 0 & 1 & 0 & -\frac{13}{180} & \frac{19}{180} & 0 & -\frac{2}{45} & 0 & | & 15 \\ \hline 0 & 0 & 0 & 1 & 1 & 0 & 1 & 1 & | & 195 \end{bmatrix}$$

This yields the optimal solution of maximum $z = 195$ at $x_1 = 12$, $x_2 = 15$, $x_3 = 27$

EXAMPLE 10   *(Compare Exercise 39)*

Minimize $3x_1 + 5x_2 + 2x_3$, subject to

$$\begin{aligned} 6x_1 + 9x_2 + 12x_3 &\le 672 \\ x_1 - x_2 + 2x_3 &= 92 \\ 5x_1 + 10x_2 + 10x_3 &\ge 480 \\ x_1 \ge 0, \quad x_2 \ge 0, \quad x_3 &\ge 0 \end{aligned}$$

SOLUTION To use the simplex method, we modify this problem to the following:
Maximize $w = -z = -3x_1 - 5x_2 - 2x_3$, subject to

$$6x_1 + 9x_2 + 12x_3 \le 672$$
$$x_1 - x_2 + 2x_3 \le 92$$
$$x_1 - x_2 + 2x_3 \ge 92$$
$$-5x_1 - 10x_2 - 10x_3 \le -480$$
$$x_1 \ge 0, \quad x_2 \ge 0, \quad x_3 \ge 0$$

The following sequence of tableaux begins with the initial tableau and ends with
the tableau having the optimal solution.

Phase I. The initial tableau is

$$
\begin{bmatrix}
6 & 9 & 12 & 1 & 0 & 0 & 0 & 0 & 672 \\
1 & -1 & 2 & 0 & 1 & 0 & 0 & 0 & 92 \\
-1 & 1 & -2 & 0 & 0 & 1 & 0 & 0 & -92 \\
-5 & -10 & -10 & 0 & 0 & 0 & 1 & 0 & -480 \\
3 & 5 & 2 & 0 & 0 & 0 & 0 & 1 & 0
\end{bmatrix}
$$

Pivot on -10 in Row 4, Column 2 to obtain

$$
\begin{bmatrix}
\frac{3}{2} & 0 & 3 & 1 & 0 & 0 & \frac{9}{10} & 0 & 240 \\
\frac{3}{2} & 0 & 3 & 0 & 1 & 0 & -\frac{1}{10} & 0 & 140 \\
-\frac{3}{2} & 0 & -3 & 0 & 0 & 1 & \frac{1}{10} & 0 & -140 \\
\frac{1}{2} & 1 & 1 & 0 & 0 & 0 & -\frac{1}{10} & 0 & 48 \\
\frac{1}{2} & 0 & -3 & 0 & 0 & 0 & \frac{1}{2} & 1 & -240
\end{bmatrix}
$$

Pivot on -3 in row 3 to obtain

$$
\begin{bmatrix}
0 & 0 & 0 & 1 & 0 & 1 & 1 & 0 & 100 \\
0 & 0 & 0 & 0 & 1 & 1 & 0 & 0 & 0 \\
\frac{1}{2} & 0 & 1 & 0 & 0 & -\frac{1}{3} & -\frac{1}{30} & 0 & \frac{140}{3} \\
0 & 1 & 0 & 0 & 0 & \frac{1}{3} & -\frac{1}{15} & 0 & \frac{4}{3} \\
2 & 0 & 0 & 0 & 0 & -1 & \frac{2}{5} & 1 & -100
\end{bmatrix}
$$

Phase II. Pivot on the 1 in row 2, column 6 to obtain

$$
\begin{bmatrix}
0 & 0 & 0 & 1 & -1 & 0 & 1 & 0 & 100 \\
0 & 0 & 0 & 0 & 1 & 1 & 0 & 0 & 0 \\
\frac{1}{2} & 0 & 1 & 0 & \frac{1}{3} & 0 & -\frac{1}{30} & 0 & \frac{140}{3} \\
0 & 1 & 0 & 0 & -\frac{1}{3} & 0 & -\frac{1}{15} & 0 & \frac{4}{3} \\
2 & 0 & 0 & 0 & 1 & 0 & \frac{2}{5} & 1 & -100
\end{bmatrix}
$$

The optimal solution is maximum $w = -100$ at $x_1 = 0$, $x_2 = \frac{4}{3}$, $x_3 = \frac{140}{3}$. Thus
the original problem has the optimal solution $z = -w = 100$ at $x_1 = 0$,
$x_2 = \frac{4}{3}$, $x_3 = \frac{140}{3}$.

EXAMPLE 11   *(Compare Exercise 47)*

An investment firm offers three types of investments to its clients. To help a client make a better-informed decision, each investment is assigned a risk factor. The risk factor and expected return of each investment are the following:

Investment A: 12% return per year, risk factor = 0.50
Investment B: 15% return per year, risk factor = 0.75
Investment C: 9% return per year, risk factor = 0.40

A client wishes to invest up to \$50,000. He wants an annual return of at least \$6300 and at least \$10,000 invested in type C investments. How much should be invested in each type to minimize his total risk? *Note:* If \$20,000 is invested in A, that risk totals $0.50 \times 20,000 = 10,000$.

SOLUTION   Let x_1 = amount invested in A, x_2 = amount invested in B, and x_3 = amount invested in C. The total risk is to be minimized, so the objective function is

$$\text{Minimize}\quad z = 0.50x_1 + 0.75x_2 + 0.40x_3$$

The constraints are

$$
\begin{aligned}
x_1 + x_2 + x_3 &\le 50,000 \quad \text{(Total investment)}\\
0.12x_1 + 0.15x_2 + 0.09x_3 &\ge 6,300 \quad \text{(Total annual return)}\\
x_3 &\ge 10,000 \quad \text{(At least \$10,000 in C)}
\end{aligned}
$$

$$x_1 \ge 0,\quad x_2 \ge 0,\quad x_3 \ge 0$$

Modify the objective function to a maximum and the $\ge$ constraints to $\le$ and obtain

$$\text{Maximize}\quad w = -0.50x_1 - 0.75x_2 - 0.40x_3 \text{ subject to}$$

$$
\begin{aligned}
x_1 + x_2 + x_3 &\le 50,000\\
-0.12x_1 - 0.15x_2 - 0.09x_3 &\le -6300\\
-x_3 &\le -10,000
\end{aligned}
$$

$$x_1 \ge 0,\quad x_2 \ge 0,\quad x_3 \ge 0$$

The sequence of tableaux that lead to the optimal solution follows.
   Phase I.

$$
\left[\begin{array}{ccccccc|c}
1 & 1 & 1 & 1 & 0 & 0 & 0 & 50,000\\
-0.12 & -0.15 & -0.09 & 0 & 1 & 0 & 0 & -6300\\
0 & 0 & -1 & 0 & 0 & 1 & 0 & -10,000\\
\hline
0.50 & 0.75 & 0.40 & 0 & 0 & 0 & 1 & 0
\end{array}\right]
$$

Pivot on -1 in row 3 to obtain

$$
\left[\begin{array}{ccccccc|c}
1 & 1 & 0 & 0 & 1 & 1 & 0 & 40,000\\
-0.12 & -0.15 & 0 & 1 & 0 & -0.09 & 0 & -5400\\
0 & 0 & 1 & 0 & 0 & -1 & 0 & 10,000\\
\hline
0.5 & 0.75 & 0 & 0 & 0 & \frac{2}{5} & 1 & -4,000
\end{array}\right]
$$

Pivot on -0.15 in row 2 to obtain

$$
\begin{bmatrix}
\frac{1}{5} & 0 & 0 & 1 & \frac{20}{3} & \frac{2}{5} & 0 & 4000 \\
\frac{4}{5} & 1 & 0 & 0 & -\frac{20}{3} & \frac{3}{5} & 0 & 36{,}000 \\
0 & 0 & 1 & 0 & 0 & -1 & 0 & 10{,}000 \\
-\frac{1}{10} & 0 & 0 & 0 & 5 & -\frac{1}{20} & 1 & -31{,}000
\end{bmatrix}
$$

Phase II. Pivot on $\frac{1}{5}$ in row 1 to obtain

$$
\begin{bmatrix}
1 & 0 & 0 & 5 & \frac{100}{3} & 2 & 0 & 20{,}000 \\
0 & 1 & 0 & -4 & -\frac{100}{3} & -1 & 0 & 20{,}000 \\
0 & 0 & 1 & 0 & 0 & -1 & 0 & 10{,}000 \\
0 & 0 & 0 & \frac{1}{2} & \frac{25}{3} & \frac{3}{20} & 1 & -29{,}000
\end{bmatrix}
$$

This tableau gives the optimal solution maximum $w = -29{,}000$ when $x_1 = 20{,}000$, $x_2 = 20{,}000$, $x_3 = 10{,}000$. Therefore the original problem has the optimal solution minimum $z = 29{,}000$ when $x_1 = 20{,}000$, $x_2 = 20{,}000$, $x_3 = 10{,}000$. The minimum risk occurs when \$20,000 is invested in A, \$20,000 in B, and \$10,000 in C.

EXAMPLE 12 *(Compare Exercise 49)*

A convenience store has to order three items, A, B, and C. The following table summarizes information about the items.

ITEM	COST	SELLING PRICE	STORAGE SPACE REQUIRED	WEIGHT
A	\$10	\$19	0.6 cu ft	2 lb
B	\$12	\$22	0.4 cu ft	3 lb
C	\$ 8	\$13	0.2 cu ft	4 lb

The purchasing agent must abide by the following guidelines:

(a) The order must provide at least 3700 items.
(b) The total cost of the order must not exceed \$36,000.
(c) The total storage space available is 1420 cubic feet.
(d) The total weight must not exceed 11,400 pounds.

How many of each item should be ordered to maximize profit?
SOLUTION Let $x_1 =$ number of items A, $x_2 =$ number of items B, and

x_3 = number of items C. The objective function and constraints described by the given information are the following:

Maximize $z = 9x_1 + 10x_2 + 5x_3$ (profit = selling price − cost), subject to

$$
\begin{array}{rllll}
x_1 + & x_2 + & x_3 \geq & 3700 & \text{(Total number of items)} \\
10x_1 + & 12x_2 + & 8x_3 \leq & 36{,}000 & \text{(Total cost)} \\
0.6x_1 + & 0.4x_2 + & 0.2x_3 \leq & 1420 & \text{(Storage space)} \\
2x_1 + & 3x_2 + & 4x_3 \leq & 11{,}400 & \text{(Total weight)} \\
x_1 \geq 0, & x_2 \geq 0, & x_3 \geq 0 & & \text{(Nonnegative conditions)}
\end{array}
$$

The initial tableau and subsequent tableaux that lead to the optimal solution are as follows.

The initial tableau is

$$
\begin{bmatrix}
-1 & -1 & -1 & 1 & 0 & 0 & 0 & 0 & -3700 \\
10 & 12 & 8 & 0 & 1 & 0 & 0 & 0 & 36{,}000 \\
0.6 & 0.4 & 0.2 & 0 & 0 & 1 & 0 & 0 & 1420 \\
2 & 3 & 4 & 0 & 0 & 0 & 1 & 0 & 11{,}400 \\
\hline
-9 & -10 & -5 & 0 & 0 & 0 & 0 & 1 & 0
\end{bmatrix}
$$

Phase I. Since a negative number occurs in the last column, pivot on a -1 in that row to obtain

$$
\begin{bmatrix}
1 & 1 & 1 & -1 & 0 & 0 & 0 & 0 & 3700 \\
2 & 4 & 0 & 8 & 1 & 0 & 0 & 0 & 6400 \\
0.4 & 0.2 & 0 & 0.2 & 0 & 1 & 0 & 0 & 680 \\
-2 & -1 & 0 & 4 & 0 & 0 & 1 & 0 & -3400 \\
\hline
-4 & -5 & 0 & -5 & 0 & 0 & 0 & 1 & 18{,}500
\end{bmatrix}
$$

Pivot on -2 in row 4 to obtain

$$
\begin{bmatrix}
0 & \frac{1}{2} & 1 & 1 & 0 & 0 & \frac{1}{2} & 0 & 2000 \\
0 & 3 & 0 & 12 & 1 & 0 & 1 & 0 & 3000 \\
0 & 0 & 0 & 1 & 0 & 1 & 0.2 & 0 & 0 \\
1 & \frac{1}{2} & 0 & -2 & 0 & 0 & -\frac{1}{2} & 0 & 1700 \\
\hline
0 & -3 & 0 & -13 & 0 & 0 & -2 & 1 & 25{,}300
\end{bmatrix}
$$

Phase II. Column 4 is the pivot column. The ratio $0/1$ determines the pivot row, so the 1 in Row 3, Column 4 is the pivot element:

$$
\begin{bmatrix}
0 & \frac{1}{2} & 1 & 0 & 0 & -1 & \frac{3}{10} & 0 & 2000 \\
0 & 3 & 0 & 0 & 1 & -12 & -\frac{7}{5} & 0 & 3000 \\
0 & 0 & 0 & 1 & 0 & 1 & 0.2 & 0 & 0 \\
1 & \frac{1}{2} & 0 & 0 & 0 & 2 & -\frac{1}{10} & 0 & 1700 \\
\hline
0 & -3 & 0 & 0 & 0 & 13 & \frac{3}{5} & 1 & 25{,}300
\end{bmatrix}
$$

The next pivot element is the 3 in Column 2:

$$
\begin{bmatrix}
0 & 0 & 1 & 0 & -\frac{1}{6} & 1 & \frac{8}{15} & 0 & 1500 \\
0 & 1 & 0 & 0 & \frac{1}{3} & -4 & -\frac{7}{15} & 0 & 1000 \\
0 & 0 & 0 & 1 & 0 & 1 & 0.2 & 0 & 0 \\
1 & 0 & 0 & 0 & -\frac{1}{6} & 4 & \frac{2}{15} & 0 & 1200 \\
\hline
0 & 0 & 0 & 0 & 1 & 1 & -\frac{4}{5} & 1 & 28{,}300
\end{bmatrix}
$$

Finally, pivot on 0.2 in Column 7 to obtain the optimal solution:

$$
\begin{bmatrix}
0 & 0 & 1 & -\frac{8}{3} & -\frac{1}{6} & -\frac{5}{3} & 0 & 0 & 1500 \\
0 & 1 & 0 & \frac{7}{3} & \frac{1}{3} & -\frac{5}{3} & 0 & 0 & 1000 \\
0 & 0 & 0 & 5 & 0 & 5 & 1 & 0 & 0 \\
1 & 0 & 0 & -\frac{2}{3} & -\frac{1}{6} & \frac{10}{3} & 0 & 0 & 1200 \\
\hline
0 & 0 & 0 & 4 & 1 & 5 & 0 & 1 & 28{,}300
\end{bmatrix}
$$

The optimal solution is maximum $z = 28{,}300$ when $x_1 = 1200$, $x_2 = 1000$, and $x_3 = 1500$. The purchasing agent should order 1200 of item A, 1000 of item B, and 1500 of item C to provide a maximum profit of $28,300.

Summary of the Simplex Method for Problems with Mixed Constraints

1. For minimization problems, maximize $w = -z$.
2. ($\geq$ constraint) For each constraint of the form

$$a_1x_1 + a_2x_2 + \cdots + a_nx_n \geq b$$

multiply the inequality by -1 to obtain

$$-a_1x_1 - a_2x_2 - \cdots - a_nx_n \leq -b$$

3. ($=$ constraint) Replace each constraint of the form

$$a_1x_1 + a_2x_2 + \cdots + a_nx_n = b$$

with

$$a_1x_1 + a_2x_2 + \cdots + a_nx_n \leq b$$

and

$$a_1x_1 + a_2x_2 + \cdots + a_nx_n \geq b$$

The latter is written

$$-a_1x_1 - a_2x_2 - \cdots - a_nx_n \leq -b$$

4. Form the initial simplex tableau.
5. If no negative entry appears in the last column of the initial tableau, proceed to Phase II.

6. (Phase I) If there is a negative entry in the last column, change it to a positive entry by pivoting in the following manner. (Ignore a negative entry in the objective function (last row) for this step.)
   (a) The pivot row is the row containing the negative entry in the last column.
   (b) Select the most negative entry in the pivot row (to the left of the last column). This entry is the pivot element.
   (c) Reduce the pivot element to 1 and the other entries of the pivot column to 0 using row operations.
7. Repeat the parts of Step 6 as long as a negative entry occurs in the last column. When no negative entries remain in the last column (except possibly in the last row), proceed to Phase II.
8. (Phase II) The basic solution to the tableau is now feasible. Use the standard simplex procedure to obtain the optimal solution.

4-4 EXERCISES

I

1. (*See Example 1*)
   Minimize $z = 2x_1 - 5x_2$, subject to

$$4x_1 + 3x_2 \leq 120$$
$$2x_1 + x_2 \leq 50$$
$$x_1 \geq 0, \quad x_2 \geq 0$$

2. Minimize $z = 15x_1 + 40x_2$, subject to

$$-7x_1 + 3x_2 \geq 138$$
$$5x_1 + 3x_2 \leq 210$$

3. Minimize $z = 4x_1 + 5x_2 - 9x_3$, subject to

$$3x_1 + 2x_2 - 12x_3 \leq 120$$
$$2x_1 + 4x_2 + 6x_3 \leq 120$$
$$x_1 - 2x_2 + 3x_3 \leq 52$$
$$x_1 \geq 0, \quad x_2 \geq 0, \quad x_3 \geq 0$$

4. Minimize $z = -15x_1 - 20x_2 + 5x_3$, subject to

$$72x_1 - 48x_2 + 94x_3 \leq 2360$$
$$5x_1 + 4x_2 - 2x_3 \leq 30$$
$$-2x_1 + 8x_2 + x_3 \leq 40$$
$$x_1 \geq 0, \quad x_2 \geq 0, \quad x_3 \geq 0$$

5. (*See Example 2*)
   Maximize $5x_1 + 2x_2$, subject to

$$3x_1 + 2x_2 \leq 36$$
$$-2x_1 + x_2 \leq -3$$
$$x_1 \geq 0, \quad x_2 \geq 0$$

6. Maximize $11x_1 + 15x_2$, subject to

$$x_1 + 3x_2 \leq 6$$
$$x_1 - 3x_2 \leq -3$$
$$x_1 \geq 0, \quad x_2 \geq 0$$

7. (*See Example 3*)
   Maximize $z = 3x_1 - 2x_2 + 9x_3$, subject to

$$2x_1 + 4x_2 + 7x_3 \leq 42$$
$$x_1 - 3x_2 + x_3 \leq -14$$
$$x_1 \geq 0, \quad x_2 \geq 0, \quad x_3 \geq 0$$

8. Maximize $z = 35x_1 + 60x_2$, subject to

$$8x_1 - 15x_2 \leq -20$$
$$5x_1 + 9x_2 \leq 40$$
$$x_1 \geq 0, \quad x_2 \geq 0$$

Write the initial tableau for Exercises 9 and 10. Do not solve.

9. (*See Example 4*)
Maximize $z = 20x_1 + 35x_2 + 28x_3$, subject to

$$8x_1 + 12x_2 + 7x_3 \leq 171$$
$$5x_1 + 14x_2 + 8x_3 \geq 172$$
$$2x_1 + 9x_2 + 13x_3 \leq 174$$
$$x_1 \geq 0, \quad x_2 \geq 0, \quad x_3 \geq 0$$

10. Maximize $z = 7x_1 + 31x_2 + 8x_3 + 16x_4$, subject to

$$x_1 + 7x_2 + 2x_3 + 4x_4 \geq 53$$
$$2x_1 + 5x_2 + x_3 + 2x_4 \leq 40$$
$$x_1 \geq 0, \quad x_2 \geq 0, \quad x_3 \geq 0, \quad x_4 \geq 0$$

Solve Exercises 11 through 16.

11. (*See Example 5*)
Maximize $z = 15x_1 + 22x_2$, subject to

$$5x_1 + 11x_2 \leq 350$$
$$15x_1 + 8x_2 \geq 300$$
$$x_1 \geq 0, \quad x_2 \geq 0$$

12. Maximize $z = x_1 - 2x_2$, subject to

$$x_1 + x_2 \geq 10$$
$$2x_1 + 5x_2 \leq 60$$
$$x_1 \geq 0, \quad x_2 \geq 0$$

13. Maximize $2x_1 + 3x_2$, subject to

$$-x_1 + 3x_2 \leq 12$$
$$-x_1 + x_2 \geq 2$$
$$x_1 \geq 0, \quad x_2 \geq 0$$

14. Maximize $x_1 + x_2$, subject to

$$-x_1 + 4x_2 \leq 16$$
$$-5x_1 + 8x_2 \geq 8$$
$$x_1 \geq 0, \quad x_2 \geq 0$$

15. (*See Example 5*)
Maximize $z = 10x_1 + 50x_2 + 30x_3$, subject to

$$6x_1 + 12x_2 + 4x_3 \leq 900$$
$$5x_1 + 16x_2 + 8x_3 \geq 120$$
$$3x_1 + x_2 + x_3 \geq 300$$
$$x_1 \geq 0, \quad x_2 \geq 0, \quad x_3 \geq 0$$

16. Maximize $z = 14x_1 + 24x_2 + 26x_3$, subject to

$$7x_1 + 12x_2 + 12x_3 \leq 312$$
$$13x_1 + 20x_2 + 12x_3 \geq 384$$
$$5x_1 + 4x_2 + 12x_3 \geq 192$$
$$x_1 \geq 0, \quad x_2 \geq 0, \quad x_3 \geq 0$$

Set up the initial tableau for Exercises 17 and 18. Do not solve.

17. (*See Example 6(a)*)
Minimize $z = 11x_1 + 20x_2$, subject to

$$5x_1 + 8x_2 \leq 180$$
$$3x_1 + 6x_2 \geq 127$$
$$x_1 \geq 0, \quad x_2 \geq 0$$

18. Minimize $z = 7x_1 + 7x_2 + 3x_3$, subject to

$$x_1 + 4x_2 + 3x_3 \leq 125$$
$$2x_1 + 10x_2 + 5x_3 \geq 295$$
$$6x_1 + x_2 + x_3 \leq 90$$
$$x_1 \geq 0, \quad x_2 \geq 0, \quad x_3 \geq 0$$

Solve Exercises 19 through 22.

19. (*See Example 6(b)*)
Minimize $z = -3x_1 + 4x_2$, subject to

$$x_1 + 3x_2 \leq 75$$
$$-2x_1 + 3x_2 \geq 30$$
$$x_1 \geq 0, \quad x_2 \geq 0$$

20. Minimize $z = 15x_1 + 8x_2$, subject to

$$-x_1 + 2x_2 \leq 20$$
$$3x_1 + 2x_2 \geq 36$$
$$x_1 \geq 0, \quad x_2 \geq 0$$

21. Minimize $z = 4x_1 + 5x_2 + x_3$, subject to

$$10x_1 + 12x_2 + 5x_3 \geq 100$$
$$5x_1 + 7x_2 + 5x_3 \leq 75$$
$$x_1 \geq 0, \quad x_2 \geq 0, \quad x_3 \geq 0$$

22. Minimize $z = 12x_1 + 6x_2 + 3x_3$, subject to

$$8x_1 + 2x_2 + 3x_3 \geq 144$$
$$6x_1 + x_2 + 3x_3 \leq 120$$
$$x_1 \geq 0, \quad x_2 \geq 0, \quad x_3 \geq 0$$

Set up the initial tableau for Exercises 23 and 24. Do not solve.

23. (*See Example 7(a)*)
Maximize $3x_1 - x_2$, subject to

$$8x_1 + 10x_2 \leq 80$$
$$-2x_1 + 5x_2 = 10$$
$$x_1 \geq 0, \quad x_2 \geq 0$$

24. Maximize $z = 7x_1 + 7x_2 + 3x_3$, subject to

$$x_1 + 4x_2 + 3x_3 \leq 125$$
$$2x_1 + 10x_2 + 5x_3 \leq 295$$
$$6x_1 + x_2 + 3x_3 = 100$$
$$x_1 \geq 0, \quad x_2 \geq 0, \quad x_3 \geq 0$$

Solve Exercises 25 through 32.

25. (*See Example 7(b)*)
Maximize $z = 5x_1 + 20x_2$, subject to

$$3x_1 + 2x_2 \leq 48$$
$$2x_1 + 4x_2 \leq 64$$
$$5x_1 + 6x_2 = 104$$
$$x_1 \geq 0, \quad x_2 \geq 0$$

26. Maximize $3x_1 + 4x_2$, subject to

$$5x_1 + 2x_2 \leq 10$$
$$x_1 + 2x_2 = 6$$
$$x_1 \geq 0, \quad x_2 \geq 0$$

27. Maximize $z = 5x_1 + 5x_2 + 9x_3$, subject to

$$2x_1 + x_2 + 4x_3 \leq 86$$
$$x_1 + 3x_2 + 2x_3 \leq 103$$
$$3x_1 + x_2 + 3x_3 = 90$$
$$x_1 \geq 0, \quad x_2 \geq 0, \quad x_3 \geq 0$$

28. Maximize $z = 6x_1 + 5x_2 + 3x_3$, subject to

$$3x_1 + x_2 + 3x_3 \leq 9$$
$$2x_1 + 3x_2 + x_3 \leq 12$$
$$x_1 + x_2 - x_3 = 3$$
$$x_1 \geq 0, \quad x_2 \geq 0, \quad x_3 \geq 0$$

29. (*See Example 8*)
Minimize $z = 30x_1 + 10x_2$, subject to

$$3x_1 + 8x_2 \leq 120$$
$$2x_1 + x_2 \leq 50$$
$$x_1 + x_2 = 20$$
$$x_1 \geq 0, \quad x_2 \geq 0$$

30. Minimize $z = 5x_1 + 8x_2$, subject to

$$-x_1 + 4x_2 \leq 48$$
$$2x_1 + 2x_2 \leq 60$$
$$x_1 + 2x_2 = 36$$
$$x_1 \geq 0, \quad x_2 \geq 0$$

31. Minimize $z = 10x_1 + 10x_2 + 10x_3$, subject to

$$20x_1 + 3x_2 + 25x_3 \leq 620$$
$$20x_1 + 11x_2 + 10x_3 \leq 440$$
$$120x_1 + 94x_2 + 105x_3 = 2820$$
$$x_1 \geq 0, \quad x_2 \geq 0, \quad x_3 \geq 0$$

32. Minimize $z = 20x_1 + 30x_2 + 10x_3$, subject to

$$2x_2 + x_3 = 18$$
$$7x_1 + 65x_2 + 10x_3 \leq 390$$
$$-21x_1 + 55x_2 + 30x_3 \leq 330$$
$$x_1 \geq 0, \quad x_2 \geq 0, \quad x_3 \geq 0$$

Set up the initial tableau for Exercises 33 and 34. Do not solve.

33. (*See Example 9*)
Maximize $z = 7x_1 + 7x_2 + 3x_3$, subject to

$$x_1 + 4x_2 + 3x_3 \leq 124$$
$$2x_1 + 10x_2 + 5x_3 \geq 295$$
$$6x_1 + x_2 + 3x_3 = 100$$
$$x_1 \geq 0, \quad x_2 \geq 0, \quad x_3 \geq 0$$

34. Minimize $z = 2x_1 + 11x_2 + 12x_3$, subject to

$$2x_1 + 3x_2 + 4x_3 = 39$$
$$5x_1 + 2x_2 + x_3 \leq 52$$
$$x_1 + 4x_2 + x_3 \geq 30$$
$$x_1 \geq 0, \quad x_2 \geq 0, \quad x_3 \geq 0$$

II

Solve Exercises 35 through 46.

35. (*See Example 9*)
Maximize $z = 6x_1 + 4x_2$, subject to

$$3x_1 + 2x_2 \le 60$$
$$2x_1 + 3x_2 \ge 24$$
$$x_1 + x_2 = 25$$
$$x_1 \ge 0, \quad x_2 \ge 0$$

36. Maximize $z = 21x_1 + 72x_2$, subject to

$$10x_1 + 8x_2 \le 440$$
$$5x_1 + 8x_2 \ge 83$$
$$-2x_1 + 8x_2 = 48$$
$$x_1 \ge 0, \quad x_2 \ge 0$$

37. Maximize $z = 10x_1 + 24x_2 + 26x_3$, subject to

$$7x_1 + 12x_2 + 12x_3 \le 312$$
$$13x_1 + 20x_2 + 12x_3 \ge 384$$
$$5x_1 + 4x_2 + 12x_3 = 168$$
$$x_1 \ge 0, \quad x_2 \ge 0, \quad x_3 \ge 0$$

38. Maximize $z = 7x_1 + 7x_2 + 3x_3$, subject to

$$x_1 + 4x_2 + 3x_3 \le 134$$
$$2x_1 + 10x_2 + 5x_3 \ge 280$$
$$5x_1 + x_2 + 3x_3 = 100$$
$$x_1 \ge 0, \quad x_2 \ge 0, \quad x_3 \ge 0$$

39. (*See Example 10*)
Minimize $z = 9x_1 + 5x_2$, subject to

$$-2x_1 + 5x_2 \le 90$$
$$4x_1 + 3x_2 = 80$$
$$2x_1 - x_2 \ge 20$$
$$x_1 \ge 0, \quad x_2 \ge 0$$

40. Minimize $z = 15x_1 + 15x_2$, subject to

$$-4x_1 + 3x_2 = 6$$
$$10x_1 + 3x_2 \le 300$$
$$x_1 + 5x_2 \ge 125$$
$$x_1 \ge 0, \quad x_2 \ge 0$$

41. Minimize $z = 8x_1 + 10x_2 + 2x_3$, subject to

$$10x_1 + 12x_2 + 5x_3 \ge 100$$
$$5x_1 + 7x_2 + 5x_3 \le 75$$
$$10x_1 + 2x_2 + 10x_3 = 120$$
$$x_1 \ge 0, \quad x_2 \ge 0, \quad x_3 \ge 0$$

42. Minimize $z = 8x_1 + 10x_2 + 2x_3$, subject to

$$8x_1 + 12x_2 + 5x_3 \ge 96$$
$$5x_1 + 7x_2 + 5x_3 \le 75$$
$$28x_1 + 28x_2 - 21x_3 = 28$$
$$x_1 \ge 0, \quad x_2 \ge 0, \quad x_3 \ge 0$$

43. Minimize $z = 8x_1 + 5x_2 + 12x_3$, subject to

$$x_1 + x_2 + x_3 \ge 37$$
$$3x_1 + x_2 + 3x_3 \le 81$$
$$3x_1 + 6x_2 + 8x_3 = 216$$
$$x_1 \ge 0, \quad x_2 \ge 0, \quad x_3 \ge 0$$

44. Minimize $z = 30x_1 + 15x_2 + 16x_3$, subject to

$$5x_1 + 3x_2 + 4x_3 \ge 45$$
$$5x_1 + 6x_2 + 8x_3 \le 120$$
$$20x_1 + 6x_2 + 14x_3 = 300$$
$$x_1 \ge 0, \quad x_2 \ge 0, \quad x_3 \ge 0$$

III

45. Minimize $z = 16x_1 + 20x_2 + 9x_3$, subject to

$$4x_1 + 2x_2 + x_3 \ge 72$$
$$5x_1 + 6x_2 + 2x_3 \ge 138$$
$$8x_1 + 12x_2 + 6x_3 \ge 272$$
$$x_1 \ge 0, \quad x_2 \ge 0, \quad x_3 \ge 0$$

46. Minimize $z = 17x_1 + 17x_2 + 6x_3$, subject to

$$x_1 + 2x_2 - x_3 \ge 20$$
$$4x_1 + 6x_2 + 2x_3 \ge 232$$
$$12x_1 + 9x_2 + 5x_3 \ge 540$$
$$x_1 \ge 0, \quad x_2 \ge 0, \quad x_3 \ge 0$$

47. (*See Example 11*) A distributor offers a store a special on two models of night stands, the Custom and the Executive, if the store buys at least 100. The Custom costs $70 each, and the store will sell them for $90 each. The Executive costs $80 each and sells for $120 each. The store has 800 square feet of storage space available. Each Custom requires 4 square feet, and each Executive requires 5 square feet. The store manager wants gross sales of at least $10,800. How many of each type should be ordered so that the total cost will be minimized?

48. A bricklayers' union agrees to furnish 50 bricklayers to a shopping mall builder. The bricklayers are classified in three categories according to skill: Low, Medium, and High. The union requires that the total number of Medium and High skilled bricklayers be at least four times the number of Low skilled. The average number of bricks laid per hour for each skill level is: Low, 40 per hour; Medium, 60 per hour; High, 75 per hour. The builder knows that the bricklayer crew must lay at least 3100 bricks per hour to stay on schedule. If the wages per hour are $10, $15, and $18 for Low, Medium, and High skills, respectively, how many of each type should be hired to minimize total hourly wages?

49. (*See Example 12*) A store orders three items, A, B, and C. The following table summarizes information about the items.

ITEM	COST	SELLING PRICE	STORAGE SPACE REQUIRED	WEIGHT
A	$20	$26	1 cu ft	8 lb
B	$25	$34	3 cu ft	10 lb
C	$15	$21	2 cu ft	15 lb

The purchasing agent has the following restrictions:
(a) The order must provide at least 6600 items.
(b) The total cost must not exceed $133,000.
(c) The total storage space available is 13,600 cubic feet.
(d) The total weight must not exceed 73,000 pounds.
How many of each item should be ordered to maximize profit?

50. Change the first restriction in Exercise 49 to: The order must provide at least 6800 items. Leave the other information as is and find how many of each item should be ordered to maximize profit.

51. Change the first and fourth restrictions in Exercise 49 to: The order must provide at least 6800 items. Total weight must not exceed 80,000 pounds. Add the restriction that at least 2000 of item B must be ordered. Leave the other information as is and find how many of each item should be ordered to maximize profit.

52. A college wishes to offer admission to exactly 1000 incoming freshmen. The college will give $3000 scholarships based on need and $2000 scholarships based on merit, but the total scholarships cannot exceed $900,000. The college will give at least 100 students scholarships based on need. Past experience indicates that the students who receive merit scholarships will have an average SAT score of 1200, those who receive need scholarships will have an average SAT score of 1000, and those receiving no scholarships will have an average SAT score of 900. How many need, merit, and other freshmen should the college admit to maximize the total SAT scores of all entering freshmen?

53. Roseanne jogs, plays handball, and swims, at the athletic club. Jogging uses 13 calories per minute, handball 11, and swimming 7. She spends equal amounts of time jogging and swimming. She plays handball at least twice as long as she jogs.
   (a) How long should she participate in each activity to use at least 660 calories in minimum time?
   (b) She has a maximum of 90 minutes to exercise. How long should she participate in each activity to maximize the calories used?

54. Carl jogs, plays handball, and swims at the athletic club. Jogging uses 15 calories per minute, handball 11, and swimming 7. He swims 30 minutes and plays handball at least twice as long as he jogs.
   (a) If he has 90 minutes to exercise, how long should he participate in each activity to maximize calories used?
   (b) How long should he participate in each activity to use at least 715 calories in minimum time?

4–5 MULTIPLE SOLUTIONS, UNBOUNDED SOLUTIONS, AND NO SOLUTIONS

- *Multiple Solutions*
- *Unbounded Solutions*
- *No Feasible Solution*

Generally, the linear programming problems given in the exercises have unique optimal solutions. Recall that the simplex method converts a system of constraints to a system of equations and finds certain kinds of solutions of the system of equations. Therefore it should be no surprise if a linear programming problem has many solutions, no solutions, or a unique solution.

Let us look at some simple examples to show how to tell from a tableau when a solution is not unique.

MULTIPLE SOLUTIONS

Here is a problem with multiple optimal solutions.

EXAMPLE 1 *(Compare Exercise 1)*

Maximize $z = 18x + 24y$, subject to

$$3x + 4y \leq 48$$
$$x + 2y \leq 22$$
$$3x + 2y \leq 42$$
$$x \geq 0, \quad y \geq 0$$

SOLUTION Figure 4–4 shows the graph of the feasible region. Notice that the corners are $(0, 0)$, $(0, 11)$, $(4, 9)$, $(12, 3)$, and $(14, 0)$, so the maximum value occurs at one or more of these corners.

The initial tableau is

$$
\begin{bmatrix}
x & y & s_1 & s_2 & s_3 & z & \\
3 & 4 & 1 & 0 & 0 & 0 & 48 \\
1 & 2 & 0 & 1 & 0 & 0 & 22 \\
3 & 2 & 0 & 0 & 1 & 0 & 42 \\
\hline
-18 & -24 & 0 & 0 & 0 & 1 & 0
\end{bmatrix}
$$

The pivot element is 2 in row 2, column 2. Pivoting these gives this tableau

$$
\begin{bmatrix}
x & y & s_1 & s_2 & s_3 & z & \\
1 & 0 & 1 & -2 & 0 & 0 & 4 \\
\frac{1}{2} & 1 & 0 & \frac{1}{2} & 0 & 0 & 11 \\
2 & 0 & 0 & -1 & 1 & 0 & 20 \\
\hline
-6 & 0 & 0 & 12 & 0 & 1 & 264
\end{bmatrix}
$$

FIGURE 4–4

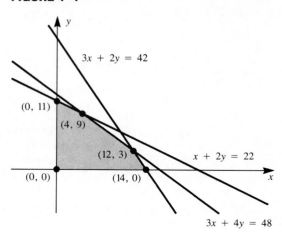

This is not optimal, so we pivot on 1 in row 1, column 1 to obtain the following tableau:

$$
\begin{array}{cccccc}
x & y & s_1 & s_2 & s_3 & z \\
\end{array}
$$

$$
\left[
\begin{array}{cccccc|c}
1 & 0 & 1 & -2 & 0 & 0 & 4 \\
0 & 1 & -\frac{1}{2} & \frac{3}{2} & 0 & 0 & 9 \\
0 & 0 & -2 & 3 & 1 & 0 & 12 \\
\hline
0 & 0 & 6 & 0 & 0 & 1 & 288 \\
\end{array}
\right]
$$

This tableau gives an optimal solution $z = 288$ when $x = 4$, $y = 9$. Recall that we say that x, y, and s_3 are basic variables and s_1 and s_2 are nonbasic variables. Notice that there is a zero in the bottom row of the s_2 column. This zero is the clue that there might be a different optimal solution.

To determine whether there is another optimal solution, use the s_2 column as the pivot column. The ratios of the entries in the last column are -2, 6, and 4. Since 4 is the smallest *nonnegative* ratio, row 3 is the pivot row, and 3 in row 3, column 4 is the pivot element. After pivoting we obtain the tableau

$$
\begin{array}{cccccc}
x & y & s_1 & s_2 & s_3 & z \\
\end{array}
$$

$$
\left[
\begin{array}{cccccc|c}
1 & 0 & -\frac{1}{3} & 0 & \frac{2}{3} & 0 & 12 \\
0 & 1 & \frac{1}{2} & 0 & -\frac{1}{2} & 0 & 3 \\
0 & 0 & -\frac{2}{3} & 1 & \frac{1}{3} & 0 & 4 \\
\hline
0 & 0 & 6 & 0 & 0 & 1 & 288 \\
\end{array}
\right]
$$

This tableau gives an optimal solution $z = 288$ when $x = 12$, $y = 3$. Thus the same maximum value of z, 288, occurs at another point. The optimal solution occurs at the corners (4, 9) and (12, 3) of the feasible region. Actually, all points on the line segment between (4, 9) and (12, 3) also yield the maximum value of $z = 288$.

Multiple Solutions   To determine whether a problem has more than one optimal solution:

1. Find an optimal solution by the usual simplex method.
2. Look at zeros in the bottom row of the final tableau. If a zero appears in the bottom row of a column for a *nonbasic* variable, there might be other optimal solutions.
3. To find another optimal solution, if any, use the column of a nonbasic variable with a zero at the bottom as the pivot column. Find the pivot row in its usual manner, and then pivot on the pivot element.
4. If this new tableau gives the same optimal value of z at another point, then multiple solutions exist.
5. Given the two optimal solutions, all points on the line segment joining them are also optimal solutions.

UNBOUNDED SOLUTIONS

The following example illustrates a problem with an unbounded feasible region. In such a case the objective function has no maximum value because it can be arbitrarily large.

EXAMPLE 2   *(Compare Exercise 5)*

Maximize $x_1 + 4x_2$, subject to

$$x_1 - x_2 \leq 3$$
$$-4x_1 + x_2 \leq 4$$
$$x_1 \geq 0, \quad x_2 \geq 0$$

SOLUTION   The graph of the feasible region is shown in Figure 4–5. This problem converts to the system

$$x_1 - x_2 + s_1 \qquad = 3$$
$$-4x_1 + x_2 \qquad + s_2 \qquad = 4$$
$$-x_1 - 4x_2 \qquad \qquad + z = 0$$

and to the initial simplex tableau

$$
\begin{array}{ccccc}
x_1 & x_2 & s_1 & s_2 & z \\
\end{array}
$$

$$
\left[
\begin{array}{ccccc|c}
1 & -1 & 1 & 0 & 0 & 3 \\
-4 & \textcircled{1} & 0 & 1 & 0 & 4 \\
-1 & -4 & 0 & 0 & 1 & 0 \\
\end{array}
\right]
$$

Pivot element

FIGURE 4–5

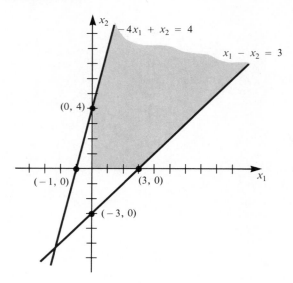

Unbounded feasible region

Except for the pivot element, convert all entries in the pivot column to 0 to obtain the next tableau:

$$\begin{bmatrix} -3 & 0 & 1 & 1 & 0 & 7 \\ -4 & 1 & 0 & 1 & 0 & 4 \\ \hline -17 & 0 & 0 & 4 & 1 & 16 \end{bmatrix}$$

Because of the -17 in the last row, we know that z is not maximal. When we check for the pivot row, we get the ratios $-7/3$ and -1. We cannot proceed with the simplex method because all ratios are negative. When this occurs, there is no maximum. Because the feasible region is unbounded (Figure 4–5), a maximum value of the objective function does not exist.

Unbounded Solutions   When you arrive at a simplex tableau that has no positive entries in the pivot column, the feasible region is unbounded, and the objective function is unbounded. There is no maximum value.

**NO FEASIBLE
SOLUTION**

The following example illustrates what happens in a simplex tableau when the problem has no feasible solution.

EXAMPLE 3   *(Compare Exercise 9)*

Maximize $z = 8x_1 + 24x_2$, subject to

$$x_1 + x_2 \leq 10$$
$$2x_1 + 3x_2 \geq 60$$
$$x_1 \geq 0, \quad x_2 \geq 0$$

SOLUTION   The graph of the constraints (Figure 4–6) shows that the half plane below $x_1 + x_2 = 10$ and the half plane above $2x_1 + 3x_2 = 60$ do not intersect in the first quadrant, so no feasible solution exists. Let's attempt to solve the problem with the simplex method and see what happens.
   Here is the initial tableau:

$$
\begin{array}{c}
\begin{array}{ccccc} x_1 & x_2 & s_1 & s_2 & z \end{array} \\
\left[
\begin{array}{ccccc|c}
1 & 1 & 1 & 0 & 0 & 10 \\
-2 & -3 & 0 & 1 & 0 & -60 \\
\hline
-8 & -24 & 0 & 0 & 1 & 0
\end{array}
\right]
\end{array}
$$

To remove the negative entry in the last column, we pivot on -3 in row 2, column 2 and obtain the next tableau:

$$
\begin{array}{c}
\begin{array}{ccccc} x_1 & x_2 & s_1 & s_2 & z \end{array} \\
\left[
\begin{array}{ccccc|c}
\frac{1}{3} & 0 & 1 & \frac{1}{3} & 0 & -10 \\
\frac{2}{3} & 1 & 0 & -\frac{1}{3} & 0 & 20 \\
\hline
8 & 0 & 0 & -8 & 1 & 480
\end{array}
\right]
\end{array}
$$

FIGURE 4–6

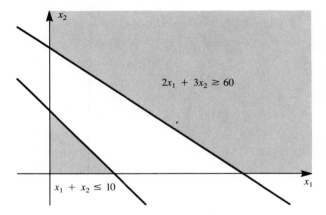

No feasible region

The first row indicates no feasible solution. Here's why. The first row represents the equations $\frac{1}{3}x_1 + s_1 + \frac{1}{3}s_2 = -10$. Since x_1, s_1, and s_2 cannot be negative, there are no values that can be used on the left-hand side that will give a negative number. Therefore there is no feasible solution.

No Feasible Solution	When a simplex tableau has a negative entry in the last column and no other entries in that row are negative, then there is no feasible solution to the problem.

EXAMPLE 4   *(Compare Exercise 26)*

A machine shop makes standard and heavy-duty gears. The process requires two steps. Step 1 takes eight minutes for the standard gear and ten minutes for the heavy-duty gear. Step 2 takes six minutes for the standard gear and ten minutes for the heavy-duty gear. The company's labor contract requires that it use at least 200 labor hours (12,000 minutes) per week on the Step 1 equipment. The maintenance required on the Step 2 machine restricts it to 140 hours per week or less (8,400 minutes). The materials cost $15 for each standard gear and $22 for each heavy-duty gear. How many of each type of gear should be made each week to minimize material costs?

Show that this problem has no solution.

SOLUTION   Let x = number of standard gears and y = number of heavy duty. The problem is:

Minimize $z = 15x + 22y$, subject to

$$8x + 10y \geq 12{,}000$$
$$6x + 10y \leq 8{,}400$$
$$x \geq 0, \quad y \geq 0$$

To use the simplex method, we modify the problem to:

Maximize $w = -15x - 22y$, subject to

$$-8x - 10y \leq -12{,}000$$
$$6x + 10y \leq 8{,}400$$
$$x \geq 0, \quad y \geq 0$$

The initial tableau is

$$\begin{bmatrix} -8 & -10 & 1 & 0 & 0 & | & -12{,}000 \\ 6 & 10 & 0 & 1 & 0 & | & 8400 \\ \hline 15 & 22 & 0 & 0 & 1 & | & 0 \end{bmatrix}$$

Since the basic solution is not feasible, we must apply Phase I and pivot on -10 in Row 1:

$$\begin{bmatrix} \frac{8}{10} & 1 & -\frac{1}{10} & 0 & 0 & | & 1200 \\ 6 & 10 & 0 & 1 & 0 & | & 8400 \\ \hline 15 & 22 & 0 & 0 & 1 & | & 0 \end{bmatrix}$$

$$\begin{bmatrix} \frac{8}{10} & 1 & -\frac{1}{10} & 0 & 0 & | & 1200 \\ -2 & 0 & 1 & 1 & 0 & | & -3600 \\ \hline -\frac{13}{5} & 0 & \frac{11}{5} & 0 & 1 & | & -26{,}400 \end{bmatrix}$$

Now pivot on -2 in Row 2:

$$\begin{bmatrix} 0 & 1 & \frac{3}{10} & \frac{2}{5} & 0 & | & -240 \\ 1 & 0 & -\frac{1}{2} & -\frac{1}{2} & 0 & | & 1800 \\ \hline 0 & 0 & \frac{9}{10} & -\frac{13}{10} & 1 & | & -21{,}720 \end{bmatrix}$$

Row 1 has a negative number in the constant column, and all coefficients to the left of the line are nonnegative. This indicates that there is no feasible region and therefore no solution.

4–5 EXERCISES

I

Find the multiple solutions in Exercises 1 through 4.

1. (*See Example 1*)
Maximize $z = 15x_1 + 15x_2$, subject to

$$3x_1 + 5x_2 \le 60$$
$$x_1 + x_2 \le 14$$
$$2x_1 + x_2 \le 24$$
$$x_1 \ge 0, \quad x_2 \ge 0$$

2. Maximize $z = 15x_1 + 10x_2$, subject to

$$2x_1 + 9x_2 \le 144$$
$$2x_1 + 3x_2 \le 60$$
$$3x_1 + 2x_2 \le 75$$
$$x_1 \ge 0, \quad x_2 \ge 0$$

3. Maximize $z = 3x_1 + 3x_2 + 4x_3$, subject to

$$2x_1 + x_2 + 2x_3 \le 20$$
$$x_1 + 2x_2 + 2x_3 \le 20$$
$$x_1 + x_2 + 4x_3 \le 20$$
$$x_1 \ge 0, \quad x_2 \ge 0, \quad x_3 \ge 0$$

4. Maximize $z = 30x_1 + 70x_2 + 20x_3$, subject to

$$32x_1 + 40x_2 + 63x_3 \le 1600$$
$$2x_1 + 2x_2 + x_3 \le 40$$
$$4x_1 + 12x_2 + 3x_3 \le 120$$
$$x_1 \ge 0, \quad x_2 \ge 0, \quad x_3 \ge 0$$

Show that the feasible regions in Exercises 5 through 8 are unbounded.

5. (*See Example 2*)
Maximize $z = 8x_1 + 3x_2$, subject to

$$2x_1 - 5x_2 \le 10$$
$$-2x_1 + x_2 \ge 2$$
$$x_1 \ge 0, \quad x_2 \ge 0$$

6. Maximize $z = 5x_1 + 4x_2$, subject to

$$-5x_1 + x_2 \le 3$$
$$-2x_1 + x_2 \ge 3$$
$$x_1 \ge 0, \quad x_2 \ge 0$$

7. Maximize $z = 8x_1 + 6x_2 + 2x_3$, subject to

$$x_1 - 3x_2 + 2x_3 \leq 50$$
$$-2x_1 + 4x_2 + 5x_3 \leq 40$$
$$x_1 \geq 0, \quad x_2 \geq 0, \quad x_3 \geq 0$$

8. Maximize $z = 2x_1 + 4x_2 + x_3$, subject to

$$-x_1 + 2x_2 + 3x_3 \leq 6$$
$$-x_1 + 4x_2 + 5x_3 \leq 5$$
$$-x_1 + 5x_2 + 7x_3 \leq 7$$
$$x_1 \geq 0, \quad x_2 \geq 0, \quad x_3 \geq 0$$

Show that Exercises 9 through 12 have no feasible solutions.

9. (*See Example 3*)
Maximize $z = 12x_1 + 20x_2$, subject to

$$-x_1 + x_2 \geq 13$$
$$2x_1 + 9x_2 \leq 72$$
$$x_1 \geq 0, \quad x_2 \geq 0$$

10. Minimize $z = 15x_1 + 9x_2$, subject to

$$3x_1 + 20x_2 \leq 60$$
$$-x_1 + 2x_2 \geq 30$$
$$x_1 \geq 0, \quad x_2 \geq 0$$

11. Maximize $z = 20x_1 + 30x_2 + 15x_3$, subject to

$$6x_1 + 4x_2 + 3x_3 \leq 60$$
$$3x_1 + 6x_2 + 4x_3 \leq 48$$
$$x_1 + x_2 - 2x_3 \leq -60$$
$$x_1 \geq 0, \quad x_2 \geq 0, \quad x_3 \geq 0$$

12. Minimize $z = 8x_1 + 5x_2 + 10x_3$, subject to

$$4x_1 + 6x_2 + 3x_3 \leq 36$$
$$14x_1 + 21x_2 + 12x_3 \geq 168$$
$$2x_1 - 3x_2 + x_3 \leq 12$$
$$x_1 \geq 0, \quad x_2 \geq 0, \quad x_3 \geq 0$$

II

Determine whether each of Exercises 13 through 25 has multiple solutions, unbounded solutions, or no feasible solutions.

13. Maximize $z = x_1 + 4x_2$, subject to

$$-4x_1 + x_2 \leq 2$$
$$2x_1 - x_2 \leq 1$$
$$x_1 \geq 0, \quad x_2 \geq 0$$

14. Maximize $z = 15x_1 + 9x_2$, subject to

$$5x_1 + 3x_2 \leq 30$$
$$5x_1 + x_2 \leq 20$$
$$x_1 \geq 0, \quad x_2 \geq 0$$

15. Maximize $z = 18x_1 + 15x_2 + 8x_3$, subject to

$$-9x_1 + 4x_2 + 6x_3 \geq 36$$
$$4x_1 + 5x_2 + 8x_3 \leq 40$$
$$6x_1 - 2x_2 + x_3 \leq 18$$
$$x_1 \geq 0, \quad x_2 \geq 0, \quad x_3 \geq 0$$

16. Minimize $z = 12x_1 + 3x_2 + 18x_3$, subject to

$$3x_1 + 4x_2 \leq 12$$
$$2x_2 + 5x_3 \leq 10$$
$$-10x_2 + 30x_3 \geq 75$$
$$x_1 \geq 0, \quad x_2 \geq 0, \quad x_3 \geq 0$$

17. Maximize $z = 15x_1 + 9x_2$, subject to

$$5x_1 + 3x_2 \leq 30$$
$$2x_1 + x_2 \geq 20$$
$$x_1 \leq 0, \quad x_2 \leq 0$$

18. Maximize $z = 2x_1 + 3x_2$, subject to

$$-5x_1 + x_2 \leq 5$$
$$x_1 - 4x_2 \leq 8$$
$$x_1 \geq 0, \quad x_2 \geq 0$$

19. Maximize $z = 4x_1 + 12x_2$, subject to

$$10x_1 + 15x_2 \leq 150$$
$$6x_1 + 3x_2 \geq 180$$
$$x_1 \geq 0, \quad x_2 \geq 0$$

20. Maximize $z = 5x_1 + 8x_2$, subject to

$$x_1 + 4x_2 \le 20$$
$$5x_1 + 4x_2 \ge 200$$
$$x_1 \ge 0, \quad x_2 \ge 0$$

21. Maximize $z = 7x_1 + 15x_2 + 5x_3$, subject to

$$3x_1 + 3x_2 + 2x_3 \le 120$$
$$4x_1 + 12x_2 + 3x_3 \le 240$$
$$-25x_1 + 15x_2 + 15x_3 \le 150$$
$$x_1 \ge 0, \quad x_2 \ge 0, \quad x_3 \ge 0$$

22. Maximize $z = 10x_1 + 18x_2 + 7x_3$, subject to

$$2x_1 + 3x_2 - 9x_3 \le 72$$
$$2x_1 + 5x_2 + 10x_3 \ge 100$$
$$x_1 \ge 0, \quad x_2 \ge 0, \quad x_3 \ge 0$$

III

23. Minimize $z = 2x_1 + 3x_2 + x_3$, subject to

$$2x_1 + 3x_2 + 4x_3 \ge 60$$
$$2x_1 + 3x_2 - 6x_3 \ge 30$$
$$6x_2 - 5x_3 \le 30$$
$$x_1 \ge 0, \quad x_2 \ge 0, \quad x_3 \ge 0$$

24. Minimize $z = 6x_1 + 14x_2 + 4x_3$, subject to

$$10x_1 + 12x_2 + 39x_3 \ge 480$$
$$2x_1 + 2x_2 + x_3 \ge 40$$
$$4x_1 + 12x_2 + 3x_3 \ge 120$$
$$x_1 \ge 0, \quad x_2 \ge 0, \quad x_3 \ge 0$$

25. Maximize $z = 8x_1 + 5x_2 + 8x_3$, subject to

$$3x_1 - 10x_2 + 6x_3 \le 60$$
$$-15x_1 + 4x_2 + 6x_3 \le 60$$
$$4x_1 + 5x_2 - 20x_3 \le 100$$
$$x_1 \ge 0, \quad x_2 \ge 0, \quad x_3 \ge 0$$

26. (*See Example 4*) A plant makes Gadgets and Widgets. The materials to make Gadgets cost $0.20 each, and those to make Widgets cost $0.25 each. The plant sells Gadgets for $2.50 each and Widgets for $3.00 each. The operating costs are $0.10 per Gadget and $0.20 per Widget. The plant must make at least a total of 4000 items, must gross at least $12,000, and must keep the materials cost at $900 or less. How many of each should the plant make to minimize operating costs? Show that this problem has no solution.

27. Show that the following problem has no solution. Beauty Products makes two styles of hair dryers, the Petite and the Deluxe. It requires one hour of labor to make the Petite and two hours to make the Deluxe. The materials cost $4 for each Petite and $3 for each Deluxe. The profit is $5 for each Petite and $6 for each Deluxe. The company has 3950 labor hours available each week and a materials budget of $9575 per week and must make at least 2000 Deluxe hair dryers. Find the number of each type that must be made per week to maximize profit.

4–6   THE STANDARD MINIMUM PROBLEM: DUALITY (OPTIONAL)

- *Standard Minimum Problem*
- *Dual Problem*
- *Solve the Minimization Problem via the Dual Problem*

STANDARD MINIMUM PROBLEM

We have used the simplex method to solve a variety of optimization problems: maximization problems and minimizations using a mixture of constraints. All of these except the standard maximum problem require adjustments before the simplex method can be applied directly. Another method, the dual method, can be used to solve a certain kind of minimization problem, the **standard minimum problem.** The dual method converts a standard minimum problem to a standard maximum problem. Before we show you this method, we define a standard minimum problem.

Definition **Standard Minimum**	A linear programming problem is **standard minimum** if
	  1. the objective function is to be minimized,
	  2. all the inequalities are $\geq$, and
	  3. the constants to the right of the inequalities are nonnegative.

DUAL PROBLEM

We can solve the standard minimum problem by converting it to a *dual* maximum problem. Let's look at an example to describe how to set up the **dual problem.**

EXAMPLE 1

A doctor specifies that a patient's diet contain certain minimum amounts of iron and calcium, but calories are to be held to a minimum.

Two foods, A and B, are used in a meal; and the amounts of iron, calcium, and calories are given in the following table.

	AMOUNT PROVIDED BY ONE UNIT OF		AMOUNT REQUIRED
	A	B	
Iron	4	1	12 or more
Calcium	2	3	10 or more
Calories	90	120	

We convert this information into a linear programming form as follows:

$$\text{Let } x_1 = \text{the number of units of A}$$
$$x_2 = \text{the number of units of B}$$

The iron requirement is

$$4x_1 + x_2 \geq 12$$

The calcium requirement is

$$2x_1 + 3x_2 \geq 10$$

and the calorie count is

$$90x_1 + 120x_2$$

where $x_1 \geq 0$ and $x_2 \geq 0$

The problem is

Minimize $z = 90x_1 + 120x_2$, subject to

$$4x_1 + x_2 \geq 12$$
$$2x_1 + 3x_2 \geq 10$$
$$x_1 \geq 0, \quad x_2 \geq 0$$

SOLUTION To form the dual problem, we first write the minimum problem in a matrix form, using an augmented matrix of the constraints and objective function. For this example the matrix takes the following form. Notice its similarity to the augmented matrix of a system of equations.

$$\left[\begin{array}{cc|c} 4 & 1 & 12 \\ 2 & 3 & 10 \\ \hline 90 & 120 & 1 \end{array}\right]$$

CAUTION This is *not* a simplex tableau because it does not contain slack variables, and the objective function has not been rewritten. We wrote the matrix in this form because it is used to obtain a maximization problem first.

Next, we obtain a new matrix by taking each *row* of

$$A = \left[\begin{array}{cc|c} 4 & 1 & 12 \\ 2 & 3 & 10 \\ \hline 90 & 120 & 1 \end{array}\right]$$

and making it the *column* of the new matrix. (The new matrix is called the **transpose of the matrix.**) The new matrix is

$$B = \left[\begin{array}{cc|c} 4 & 2 & 90 \\ 1 & 3 & 120 \\ \hline 12 & 10 & 1 \end{array}\right]$$

From the new matrix, B, set up a standard maximum problem. We introduce new variables, y_1 and y_2, because they play a different role from the original ones. We use the rows above the line to form constraints for the maximum problem.

The row below the line forms the new objective function. Since we want this matrix to give a standard maximum problem, all inequalities are $\leq$. We write the new constraints and objective functions next to their rows:

$$
\begin{array}{cc}
y_1 & y_2 \\
\end{array}
\left[
\begin{array}{cc|c}
4 & 2 & 90 \\
1 & 3 & 120 \\
\hline
12 & 10 & 1
\end{array}
\right]
\qquad
\begin{array}{l}
\text{New constraint } 4y_1 + 2y_2 \leq 90 \\
\text{New constraint } y_1 + 3y_2 \leq 120 \\
\text{New objective function } w = 12y_1 + 10y_2
\end{array}
$$

This gives the dual problem:

Maximize $w = 12y_1 + 10y_2$, subject to

$$4y_1 + 2y_2 \leq 90$$
$$y_1 + 3y_2 \leq 120$$
$$y_1 \geq 0, \quad y_2 \geq 0$$

EXAMPLE 2   *(Compare Exercise 5)*

Set up the dual problem to the following standard minimum problem.

Minimize $z = 30x_1 + 40x_2 + 50x_3$, subject to

$$10x_1 + 14x_2 + 5x_3 \geq 220$$
$$5x_1 + 3x_2 + 9x_3 \geq 340$$
$$x_1 \geq 0, \quad x_2 \geq 0, \quad x_3 \geq 0$$

SOLUTION   Form the augmented matrix of the problem with the objective function written in the last row:

$$
A =
\begin{array}{ccc}
x_1 & x_2 & x_3 \\
\end{array}
\left[
\begin{array}{ccc|c}
10 & 14 & 5 & 220 \\
5 & 3 & 9 & 340 \\
\hline
30 & 40 & 50 & 1
\end{array}
\right]
$$

Form the transpose of A:

$$
B =
\begin{array}{cc}
y_1 & y_2 \\
\end{array}
\left[
\begin{array}{cc|c}
10 & 5 & 30 \\
14 & 3 & 40 \\
5 & 9 & 50 \\
\hline
220 & 340 & 1
\end{array}
\right]
$$

Set up the dual problem from this matrix using $\leq$ on all constraints:

Maximize $w = 220y_1 + 340y_2$, subject to

$$10y_1 + 5y_2 \leq 30$$
$$14y_1 + 3y_2 \leq 40$$
$$5y_1 + 9y_2 \leq 50$$
$$y_1 \geq 0, \quad y_2 \geq 0$$

Set Up the Dual Problem of a Standard Minimum Problem	1. Start with a standard minimum problem. 2. Write the augmented matrix, A, of the minimum problem. Write the objective function in the last row. 3. Write the transpose of the matrix A to obtain matrix B. Each row of A becomes the corresponding column of B. 4. Form a constraint for the dual problem from each row of B (except the last) using the new variables and $\leq$. 5. Form the objective function of the dual problem from the last row. It is to be maximized.

SOLVE THE MINIMIZATION PROBLEM VIA THE DUAL PROBLEM

The theory relating a standard minimum problem and its dual problem is beyond the level of this course. The relationship between the solution of a minimum problem and its dual problem is a fundamental theorem, which we will use.

Theorem 1   A standard minimum problem has a solution if and only if its dual problem has a solution. If a solution exists, the standard minimum problem and its dual problem *have the same* optimal value.

This theorem states that the maximum value of the dual problem objective function is the minimum value of the objective function for the minimum problem. To help see this, let's work through the diet example at the beginning of the section. The problem and its dual are as follows:

STANDARD MINIMUM PROBLEM	DUAL PROBLEM
Minimize $z = 90x_1 + 120x_2$, subject to	Maximize $w = 12y_1 + 10y_2$, subject to
$4x_1 + x_2 \geq 12$	$4y_1 + 2y_2 \leq 90$
$2x_1 + 3x_2 \geq 10$	$y_1 + 3y_2 \leq 120$
$x_1 \geq 0, \quad x_2 \geq 0$	$y_1 \geq 0, \quad y_2 \geq 0$

The procedure is straightforward: Solve the dual problem by the simplex method. We first write the dual problem as a system of equations using slack variables and obtain

$$
\begin{aligned}
4y_1 + 2y_2 + x_1 \qquad\qquad &= 90 \\
y_1 + 3y_2 \qquad + x_2 \qquad &= 120 \\
-12y_1 - 10y_2 \qquad\qquad + w &= 0
\end{aligned}
$$

Notice that x_1 and x_2 are used for slack variables. These are intended to be the same as the variables in the original minimum problem because it turns out that certan values of the slack variables of the dual problem give the desired values of the original variables in the minimum problem. Let's set up the simplex tableau and work through the solution.

The initial tableau is

$$
\begin{array}{ccccc|c}
y_1 & y_2 & x_1 & x_2 & w & \\
4 & 2 & 1 & 0 & 0 & 90 \\
1 & 3 & 0 & 1 & 0 & 120 \\
\hline
-12 & -10 & 0 & 0 & 1 & 0
\end{array}
$$

We now proceed to find the pivot element and perform row operations in the usual manner. You should fill in details that are omitted.

$$
\begin{array}{ccccc|c}
y_1 & y_2 & x_1 & x_2 & w & \\
4 & 2 & 1 & 0 & 0 & 90 \\
1 & 3 & 0 & 1 & 0 & 120 \\
\hline
-12 & -10 & 0 & 0 & 1 & 0
\end{array}
\qquad \tfrac{1}{4}\,\text{R1} \to \text{R1}
$$

$$
\begin{array}{ccccc|c}
y_1 & y_2 & x_1 & x_2 & w & \\
1 & \tfrac{1}{2} & \tfrac{1}{4} & 0 & 0 & \tfrac{90}{4} \\
1 & 3 & 0 & 1 & 0 & 120 \\
\hline
-12 & -10 & 0 & 0 & 1 & 0
\end{array}
\qquad
\begin{array}{l}
-\text{R1} + \text{R2} \to \text{R2} \\
12\text{R1} + \text{R3} \to \text{R3}
\end{array}
$$

$$
\begin{array}{ccccc|c}
y_1 & y_2 & x_1 & x_2 & w & \\
1 & \tfrac{1}{2} & \tfrac{1}{4} & 0 & 0 & \tfrac{90}{4} \\
0 & \tfrac{5}{2} & -\tfrac{1}{4} & 1 & 0 & \tfrac{390}{4} \\
\hline
0 & -4 & 3 & 0 & 1 & 270
\end{array}
\qquad \tfrac{2}{5}\,\text{R2} \to \text{R2}
$$

$$
\begin{array}{ccccc|c}
y_1 & y_2 & x_1 & x_2 & w & \\
1 & \tfrac{1}{2} & \tfrac{1}{4} & 0 & 0 & \tfrac{90}{4} \\
0 & 1 & -\tfrac{1}{10} & \tfrac{2}{5} & 0 & 39 \\
\hline
0 & -4 & 3 & 0 & 1 & 270
\end{array}
\qquad
\begin{array}{l}
-\tfrac{1}{2}\,\text{R2} + \text{R1} \to \text{R1} \\[4pt]
4\text{R2} + \text{R3} \to \text{R3}
\end{array}
$$

$$
\begin{array}{ccccc|c}
y_1 & y_2 & x_1 & x_2 & w & \\
1 & 0 & \tfrac{6}{20} & -\tfrac{1}{5} & 0 & 3 \\
0 & 1 & -\tfrac{1}{10} & \tfrac{2}{5} & 0 & 39 \\
\hline
0 & 0 & \tfrac{26}{10} & \tfrac{8}{5} & 1 & 426
\end{array}
$$

Since no entries of the last row are negative, the solution is optimal, and the maximum value is 426. The maximum value occurs when

$$
y_1 = 3 \quad \text{and} \quad y_2 = 39
$$

By Theorem 1 the *minimum* value of the original objective function, $z = 90x_1 + 120x_2$, is also 426. The values of x_1 and x_2 that yield this minimum value are found in the bottom row of the final tableau of the dual problem. That bottom row is

$$
\begin{array}{ccccccc}
y_1 & y_2 & x_1 & x_2 & w & \\
[0 & 0 & 2.6 & 1.6 & 1 & 426]
\end{array}
$$

The numbers under x_1 and x_2 are the values of x_1 and x_2 that give the optimal value of the original minimization problem. So the objective function $z = 90x_1 + 120x_2$ has the minimum value of 426 at $x_1 = 2.6$, $x_2 = 1.6$.

NOTE   To find the solution of a standard minimum problem, *look at the bottom row of the final tableau of the dual problem.*

EXAMPLE 3   *(Compare Exercise 9)*

Solve the minimization problem by the dual problem method.
   Minimize $z = 8x_1 + 15x_2$, subject to

$$4x_1 + 5x_2 \geq 80$$
$$2x_1 + 5x_2 \geq 60$$
$$x_1 \geq 0, \quad x_2 \geq 0$$

SOLUTION   The augmented matrix of this problem is

$$
A = \left[\begin{array}{cc|c}
4 & 5 & 80 \\
2 & 5 & 60 \\
\hline
8 & 15 & 1
\end{array}\right]
$$

The transpose of A is

$$
B = \left[\begin{array}{cc|c}
4 & 2 & 8 \\
5 & 5 & 15 \\
\hline
80 & 60 & 1
\end{array}\right]
$$

B represents the maximization problem:
   Maximize $w = 80y_1 + 60y_2$, subject to

$$4y_1 + 2y_2 \leq 8$$
$$5y_1 + 5y_2 \leq 15$$
$$y_1 \geq 0, \quad y_2 \geq 0$$

The initial simplex tableau of this problem is

$$
\begin{array}{ccccc}
y_1 & y_2 & x_1 & x_2 & w \\
\end{array}
$$
$$
\left[\begin{array}{ccccc|c}
4 & 2 & 1 & 0 & 0 & 8 \\
5 & 5 & 0 & 1 & 0 & 15 \\
\hline
-80 & -60 & 0 & 0 & 1 & 0
\end{array}\right]
$$

Now proceed with the pivot and row operations to obtain the sequence of tableaux:

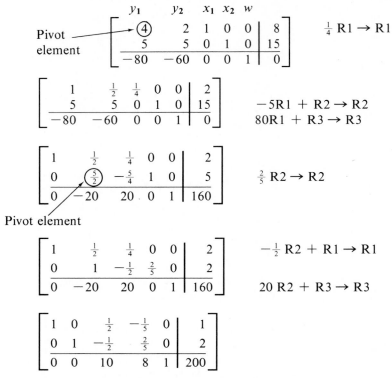

$$\begin{array}{c} \quad y_1 \quad\;\; y_2 \quad x_1 \; x_2 \; w \\ \left[\begin{array}{ccccc|c} \textcircled{4} & 2 & 1 & 0 & 0 & 8 \\ 5 & 5 & 0 & 1 & 0 & 15 \\ \hline -80 & -60 & 0 & 0 & 1 & 0 \end{array}\right] \end{array} \qquad \tfrac{1}{4}\,R1 \rightarrow R1$$

Pivot element (points to 4)

$$\left[\begin{array}{ccccc|c} 1 & \tfrac{1}{2} & \tfrac{1}{4} & 0 & 0 & 2 \\ 5 & 5 & 0 & 1 & 0 & 15 \\ \hline -80 & -60 & 0 & 0 & 1 & 0 \end{array}\right] \qquad \begin{array}{l} -5R1 + R2 \rightarrow R2 \\ 80R1 + R3 \rightarrow R3 \end{array}$$

$$\left[\begin{array}{ccccc|c} 1 & \tfrac{1}{2} & \tfrac{1}{4} & 0 & 0 & 2 \\ 0 & \textcircled{\tfrac{5}{2}} & -\tfrac{5}{4} & 1 & 0 & 5 \\ \hline 0 & -20 & 20 & 0 & 1 & 160 \end{array}\right] \qquad \tfrac{2}{5}\,R2 \rightarrow R2$$

Pivot element

$$\left[\begin{array}{ccccc|c} 1 & \tfrac{1}{2} & \tfrac{1}{4} & 0 & 0 & 2 \\ 0 & 1 & -\tfrac{1}{2} & \tfrac{2}{5} & 0 & 2 \\ \hline 0 & -20 & 20 & 0 & 1 & 160 \end{array}\right] \qquad \begin{array}{l} -\tfrac{1}{2}\,R2 + R1 \rightarrow R1 \\ \\ 20\,R2 + R3 \rightarrow R3 \end{array}$$

$$\left[\begin{array}{ccccc|c} 1 & 0 & \tfrac{1}{2} & -\tfrac{1}{5} & 0 & 1 \\ 0 & 1 & -\tfrac{1}{2} & \tfrac{2}{5} & 0 & 2 \\ \hline 0 & 0 & 10 & 8 & 1 & 200 \end{array}\right]$$

This is the final tableau of the dual problem. The last row gives the solution to the minimum problem:

$$x_1 = 10, \quad x_2 = 8, \quad z = 200$$

EXAMPLE 4   *(Compare Exercise 15)*

A tire company has plants in Chicago and Detroit. The Chicago plant can make 600 radials and 100 standard tires per day. The Detroit plant can make 300 radial and 100 standard tires per day. It costs $20,000 per day to operate the Chicago plant and $15,000 per day to operate the Detroit plant. The company has a contract to make at least 24,000 radial and 5000 standard tires. How many days should each plant be scheduled to minimize operating costs?

SOLUTION   Let

$$x_1 = \text{number of days the Chicago plant operates}$$
$$x_2 = \text{number of days the Detroit plant operates}$$

The number of radial tires produced is $600x_1 + 300x_2$, the number of standard tires produced is $100x_1 + 100x_2$, and the operating expenses are $20,000x_1 + 15,000x_2$. The linear programming problem is as follows:

Minimize $z = 20,000x_1 + 15,000x_2$, subject to

$$600x_1 + 300x_2 \geq 24,000$$
$$100x_1 + 100x_2 \geq 5000$$
$$x_1 \geq 0, \quad x_2 \geq 0$$

This is a standard minimization problem, so we solve it by using its dual problem. The augmented matrix of the problem is

$$A = \begin{bmatrix} 600 & 300 & | & 24,000 \\ 100 & 100 & | & 5000 \\ 20,000 & 15,000 & | & 1 \end{bmatrix}$$

The transpose of A is

$$B = \begin{bmatrix} 600 & 100 & | & 20,000 \\ 300 & 100 & | & 15,000 \\ 24,000 & 5000 & | & 1 \end{bmatrix}$$

This matrix represents the dual problem:

Maximize $w = 24,000y_1 + 5000y_2$, subject to

$$600y_1 + 100y_2 \leq 20,000$$
$$300y_1 + 100y_2 \leq 15,000$$
$$y_1 \geq 0, \quad y_2 \geq 0$$

The tableaux that solve this dual problem follow:
The initial tableau is

$$\begin{array}{ccccc} y_1 & y_2 & x_1\ x_2\ w & \\ \begin{bmatrix} 600 & 100 & 1\ \ 0\ \ 0 & | & 20,000 \\ 300 & 100 & 0\ \ 1\ \ 0 & | & 15,000 \\ -24,000 & -5000 & 0\ \ 0\ \ 1 & | & 0 \end{bmatrix} & \frac{1}{600}\,R1 \to R1 \end{array}$$

$$\begin{bmatrix} 1 & \frac{1}{6} & \frac{1}{600} & 0 & 0 & | & \frac{200}{6} \\ 300 & 100 & 0 & 1 & 0 & | & 15,000 \\ -24,000 & -5000 & 0 & 0 & 1 & | & 0 \end{bmatrix} \quad \begin{array}{l} -300\,R1 + R2 \to R2 \\ 24,000\,R1 + R3 \to R3 \end{array}$$

$$\begin{bmatrix} 1 & \frac{1}{6} & \frac{1}{600} & 0 & 0 & | & \frac{200}{6} \\ 0 & 50 & -\frac{1}{2} & 1 & 0 & | & 5000 \\ 0 & -1000 & 40 & 0 & 1 & | & 800,000 \end{bmatrix} \quad \frac{1}{50}\,R2 \to R2$$

$$\begin{bmatrix} 1 & \frac{1}{6} & \frac{1}{600} & 0 & 0 & | & \frac{200}{6} \\ 0 & 1 & -\frac{1}{100} & \frac{1}{50} & 0 & | & 100 \\ 0 & -1000 & 40 & 0 & 1 & | & 800,000 \end{bmatrix} \quad \begin{array}{l} -\frac{1}{6}\,R2 + R1 \to R1 \\ 1000\,R2 + R3 \to R3 \end{array}$$

$$\left[\begin{array}{ccccc|c} 1 & 0 & \frac{1}{300} & -\frac{1}{300} & 0 & \frac{100}{6} \\ 0 & 1 & -\frac{1}{100} & \frac{1}{50} & 0 & 100 \\ \hline 0 & 0 & 30 & 20 & 1 & 900{,}000 \end{array}\right]$$

The last row gives the solution to the original problem:

$$x_1 = 30, \quad x_2 = 20, \quad z = 900{,}000$$

The minimum operating costs are $900,000 when the Chicago plant operates 30 days and the Detroit plant operates 20 days. ∎

4-6 EXERCISES

I

Write the transpose of the matrices in Exercises 1 through 4.

1. $\begin{bmatrix} 2 & 1 & 3 \\ 4 & 0 & 2 \end{bmatrix}$

2. $\begin{bmatrix} 5 & -1 & 6 \\ 2 & 1 & 2 \\ 3 & -3 & 5 \end{bmatrix}$

3. $\begin{bmatrix} 4 & 3 & 2 \\ 1 & 8 & -2 \\ 6 & -7 & 1 \\ 2 & 4 & 6 \end{bmatrix}$

4. $\begin{bmatrix} 2 & 1 & 5 & 4 & 3 \\ 10 & -2 & 7 & 9 & 14 \\ 8 & 15 & -3 & 6 & 1 \end{bmatrix}$

For each of the minimization problems in Exercises 5 through 8:
(a) set up the augmented matrix for the problem,
(b) find the transpose of the matrix in part (a), and
(c) set up the initial tableau for the dual problem.

5. (*See Example 2*) Minimize $z = 25x_1 + 30x_2$, subject to

$$6x_1 + 5x_2 \geq 30$$
$$8x_1 + 3x_2 \geq 42$$
$$x_1 \geq 0, \quad x_2 \geq 0$$

6. Minimize $z = 14x_1 + 27x_2 + 9x_3$, subject to

$$7x_1 + 9x_2 + 4x_3 \geq 60$$
$$10x_1 + 3x_2 + 6x_3 \geq 80$$
$$4x_1 + 2x_2 + x_3 \geq 48$$
$$x_1 \geq 0, \quad x_2 \geq 0, \quad x_3 \geq 0$$

7. Minimize $z = 500x_1 + 700x_2$, subject to

$$22x_1 + 30x_2 \geq 110$$
$$15x_1 + 40x_2 \geq 95$$
$$20x_1 + 35x_2 \geq 68$$
$$x_1 \geq 0, \quad x_2 \geq 0$$

8. Minimize $z = 40x_1 + 60x_2 + 50x_3 + 35x_4$, subject to

$$7x_1 + 6x_2 - 5x_3 + x_4 \geq 45$$
$$12x_1 + 18x_2 + 4x_3 + 6x_4 \geq 86$$
$$x_1 \geq 0, \quad x_2 \geq 0, \quad x_3 \geq 0, \quad x_4 \geq 0$$

Solve Exercises 9 through 14 by solving the dual problem.

9. (*See Example 3*)
Minimize $z = 4x_1 + 3x_2$, subject to

$$x_1 + x_2 \geq 8$$
$$2x_1 + x_2 \geq 14$$
$$x_1 \geq 0, \quad x_2 \geq 0$$

10. Minimize $z = 42x_1 + 70x_2$, subject to

$$5x_1 + 4x_2 \geq 30$$
$$3x_1 + 4x_2 \geq 22$$
$$x_1 \geq 0, \quad x_2 \geq 0$$

II

11. Minimize $z = 10x_1 + 16x_2 + 20x_3$, subject to

$$3x_1 + x_2 + 6x_3 \geq 9$$
$$x_1 + x_2 \geq 9$$
$$4x_2 + x_3 \geq 12$$
$$x_1 \geq 0, \quad x_2 \geq 0, \quad x_3 \geq 0$$

12. Minimize $z = 20x_1 + 30x_2$, subject to

$$6x_1 + 10x_2 \geq 60$$
$$10x_1 + 6x_2 \geq 60$$
$$x_1 + x_2 \geq 8$$
$$x_1 \geq 0, \quad x_2 \geq 0$$

13. Minimize $z = 8x_1 + 5x_2 + 12x_3$, subject to

$$x_1 + x_2 + x_3 \geq 37$$
$$3x_1 + x_2 + 3x_3 \geq 81$$
$$3x_1 + 6x_2 + 8x_3 \geq 216$$
$$x_1 \geq 0, \quad x_2 \geq 0, \quad x_3 \geq 0$$

14. Minimize $z = 30x_1 + 15x_2 + 28x_3$, subject to

$$5x_1 + 3x_2 + 4x_3 \geq 45$$
$$5x_1 + 6x_2 + 8x_3 \geq 120$$
$$20x_1 + 6x_2 + 14x_3 \geq 300$$
$$x_1 \geq 0, \quad x_2 \geq 0, \quad x_3 \geq 0$$

III

15. (*See Example 4*) A tire company has two plants, one in Dallas and one in New Orleans. The Dallas plant can make 800 radial and 280 standard tires per day. The New Orleans plant can make 500 radial and 150 standard tires per day. It costs $22,000 per day to operate the Dallas plant and $12,000 per day to operate the New Orleans plant. The company has a contract to make at least 28,000 radial and 9000 standard tires. How many days should each plant be scheduled to minimize operating costs?

16. A plant makes two models of an item. Each model A requires three hours of skilled labor and six hours of unskilled labor. Each model B requires five hours of skilled labor and four hours of unskilled labor. The plant's labor contract requires that it employ at least 3000 hours of skilled labor and at least 4200 hours of unskilled labor. Each model A costs $21, and each model B costs $25. How many of each model should be produced to minimize costs if the plant must produce a total of 900 items or more?

IMPORTANT TERMS

4-1
Simplex Method
Standard Maximum Problem
Slack Variable
Simplex Tableau

4-2
Unit Column
Basic Solution
Basic Feasible Solution
Basic Variable
Nonbasic Variable

Initial Basic Feasible Solution
Pivot Column
Pivot Row
Pivot Element
Pivoting
Final Tableau

4-4
Mixed Constraints
Phase I
Phase II
Equality Constraint

4-5
Multiple Solution
Unbounded Solution
No Feasible Solution

4-6
Standard Minimum Problem
Dual Problem
Transpose of a Matrix

REVIEW EXERCISES

In Exercises 1 through 3, write the constraints as a system of equations using slack variables.

1. $6x_1 + 4x_2 + 3x_3 \leq 220$
$\quad x_1 + 5x_2 + \quad x_3 \leq 162$
$\quad 7x_1 + 2x_2 + 5x_3 \leq 139$

2. $5x_1 + 3x_2 \leq 40$
$\quad 7x_1 + 2x_2 \leq 19$
$\quad 6x_1 + 5x_2 \leq 23$

3. $6x_1 + 5x_2 + 3x_3 + 3x_4 \leq 89$
$\quad 7x_1 + 4x_2 + 6x_3 + 2x_4 \leq 72$

In Exercises 4 through 6, write the constraints and objective function as a system of equations.

4. Objective function: $z = 3x_1 + 7x_2$
Constraints:

$$7x_1 + 5x_2 \leq 14$$
$$3x_1 + 6x_2 \leq 25$$
$$4x_1 + 3x_2 \leq 29$$

5. Objective function: $z = 20x_1 + 36x_2 + 19x_3$
Constraints:

$$10x_1 + 12x_2 + 8x_3 \leq 24$$
$$7x_1 + 13x_2 + 5x_3 \leq 35$$

6. Objective function: $z = 5x_1 + 12x_2 + 8x_3 + 2x_4$
Constraints:

$$9x_1 + 7x_2 + \quad x_3 + \quad x_4 \leq 84$$
$$x_1 + 3x_2 + 5x_3 + \quad x_4 \leq 76$$
$$2x_1 + \quad x_2 + 6x_3 + 3x_4 \leq 59$$

Write Exercises 7 through 10 as systems of equations.

7. Maximize $z = 9x_1 + 2x_2$, subject to

$$3x_1 + 7x_2 \leq 14$$
$$9x_1 + 5x_2 \leq 18$$
$$x_1 - \quad x_2 \leq 21$$
$$x_1 \geq 0, \quad x_2 \geq 0$$

8. Maximize $z = x_1 + 5x_2 + 4x_3$, subject to

$$x_1 + \quad x_2 + \quad x_3 \leq 20$$
$$4x_1 + 5x_2 + \quad x_3 \leq 48$$
$$2x_1 - 6x_2 + 5x_3 \leq 38$$
$$x_1 \geq 0, \quad x_2 \geq 0, \quad x_3 \geq 0$$

9. Maximize $z = 6x_1 + 8x_2 + 4x_3$, subject to

$$x_1 + \quad x_2 + x_3 \leq 15$$
$$2x_1 + 4x_2 + x_3 \leq 44$$
$$x_1 \geq 0, \quad x_2 \geq 0, \quad x_3 \geq 0$$

10. Maximize $z = 5x_1 + 5x_2$, subject to

$$5x_1 + 3x_2 \leq 15$$
$$2x_1 + 3x_2 \leq 12$$
$$x_1 \geq 0, \quad x_2 \geq 0$$

11. Find the pivot element in each of the following tableaux.

(a)
$$\begin{bmatrix} 5 & 3 & 2 & 1 & 0 & 0 & 0 & 660 \\ 4 & 6 & 1 & 0 & 1 & 0 & 0 & 900 \\ 1 & 2 & 3 & 0 & 0 & 1 & 0 & 800 \\ -5 & -8 & -4 & 0 & 0 & 0 & 1 & 0 \end{bmatrix}$$

(b)
$$\begin{bmatrix} 1 & 4 & 0 & 3 & 0 & -2 & 0 & 60 \\ 0 & 6 & 1 & 5 & 0 & 4 & 0 & 60 \\ 0 & -3 & 0 & 1 & 1 & 2 & 0 & 60 \\ 0 & -1 & 0 & -2 & 0 & 3 & 1 & 48 \end{bmatrix}$$

(c)
$$\begin{bmatrix} 5 & 0 & 1 & 1 & -6 & 0 & 0 & 75 \\ 4 & 1 & 3 & 0 & 3 & 0 & 0 & 150 \\ 2 & 0 & -2 & 0 & 2 & 1 & 0 & 80 \\ -3 & 0 & -5 & 0 & 4 & 0 & 1 & 98 \end{bmatrix}$$

12. Find the pivot element in each of the following tableaux.

(a)
$$\begin{bmatrix} 3 & 0 & 5 & 1 & 0 & 0 & 20 \\ 2 & 0 & -1 & 0 & 1 & 0 & 6 \\ 1 & 1 & 4 & 0 & 0 & 0 & 0 \\ 4 & 0 & -8 & 0 & 0 & 1 & 145 \end{bmatrix}$$

(b)
$$\begin{bmatrix} 6 & 1 & 0 & -5 & 0 & 2 & 0 & 0 \\ 4 & 0 & 1 & 2 & 0 & -4 & 0 & 10 \\ -2 & 0 & 0 & 7 & 1 & 3 & 0 & 21 \\ -1 & 0 & 0 & -9 & 0 & 6 & 1 & 572 \end{bmatrix}$$

13. Write the basic feasible solution for each of the following tableaux.

(a)
$$\left[\begin{array}{ccccc|c} 6 & 0 & 10 & 1 & 0 & 42 \\ 5 & 1 & 8 & 0 & 0 & 80 \\ \hline -2 & 0 & 5 & 0 & 1 & 98 \end{array}\right]$$

(b)
$$\left[\begin{array}{ccccccc|c} 0 & 1 & 0 & 8 & 6 & 4 & 0 & 42 \\ 1 & 0 & 0 & -2 & 3 & 3 & 0 & 73 \\ 0 & 0 & 1 & 5 & -1 & 6 & 0 & 15 \\ \hline 0 & 0 & 0 & 4 & 2 & 5 & 1 & 138 \end{array}\right]$$

14. Write the initial simplex tableau for each of the following problems. Do not solve.

(a) Minimize $z = 5x_1 - 7x_2$, subject to
$$5x_1 + 4x_2 \le 20$$
$$3x_1 + 7x_2 \le 21$$
$$x_1 \ge 0, \quad x_2 \ge 0$$

(b) Minimize $z = 4x_1 - 5x_2 + 3x_3$, subject to
$$9x_1 + 7x_2 + \quad x_3 \le 45$$
$$3x_1 + 2x_2 + \quad 4x_3 \le 39$$
$$x_1 + 5x_2 + 12x_3 \le 50$$
$$x_1 \ge 0, \quad x_2 \ge 0, \quad x_3 \ge 0$$

(c) Maximize $z = 8x_1 + 13x_2$, subject to
$$9x_1 + 5x_2 \le 45$$
$$6x_1 + 8x_2 \ge 48$$
$$x_1 \ge 0, \quad x_2 \ge 0$$

15. Write the initial simplex tableau for each of the following problems. Do not solve.

(a) Maximize $z = 3x_1 + 5x_2 + 4x_3$, subject to
$$11x_1 + \quad 5x_2 + 3x_3 \le 142$$
$$3x_1 + \quad 4x_2 + 7x_3 \ge \quad 95$$
$$2x_1 + 15x_2 + \quad x_3 \le 124$$
$$x_1 \ge 0, \quad x_2 \ge 0, \quad x_3 \ge 0$$

(b) Minimize $z = 14x_1 + 22x_2$, subject to
$$7x_1 + 4x_2 \le 28$$
$$x_1 + 3x_2 \ge \quad 6$$
$$x_1 \ge 0, \quad x_2 \ge 0$$

(c) Maximize $z = x_1 + 3x_2 + 5x_3$, subject to
$$x_1 + 2x_2 + 7x_3 \le \quad 90$$
$$8x_1 + 4x_2 + 3x_3 \le 100$$
$$5x_1 + \quad x_2 + 6x_3 \ge \quad 75$$
$$x_1 \ge 0, \quad x_2 \ge 0, \quad x_3 \ge 0$$

16. Write the initial simplex tableau for each of the following problems. Do not solve.

(a) Maximize $z = 24x_1 + 36x_2$, subject to
$$2x_1 + 9x_2 \le 18$$
$$5x_1 + 7x_2 \le 35$$
$$x_1 + 8x_2 = \quad 8$$
$$x_1 \ge 0, \quad x_2 \ge 0$$

(b) Maximize $z = x_1 + 2x_2 + 4x_3$, subject to
$$x_1 + 2x_2 + 5x_3 \le 18$$
$$2x_1 + 3x_2 + 6x_3 \le 20$$
$$x_1 + \quad x_2 + 2x_3 = 12$$
$$x_1 \ge 0, \quad x_2 \ge 0, \quad x_3 \ge 0$$

(c) Minimize $z = 6x_2 + 11x_3$, subject to
$$5x_1 + 4x_2 \ge 20$$
$$3x_1 + 8x_2 \ge 24$$
$$x_1 + \quad x_2 = 22$$
$$x_1 \ge 0, \quad x_2 \ge 0$$

17. Write the initial simplex tableau for each of the following problems. Do not solve.

(a) Minimize $z = x_1 + 3x_2 + 9x_3$, subject to
$$6x_1 + 4x_2 + \quad x_3 \ge 40$$
$$x_1 + 2x_2 + 5x_3 \ge 36$$
$$5x_1 + \quad x_2 + 3x_3 = 30$$
$$x_1 \ge 0, \quad x_2 \ge 0, \quad x_3 \ge 0$$

(b) Maximize $z = 5x_1 + 12x_2$, subject to
$$15x_1 + \quad 8x_2 \ge 120$$
$$10x_1 + 12x_2 \le 120$$
$$15x_1 + \quad 5x_2 = \quad 75$$
$$x_1 \ge 0, \quad x_2 \ge 0$$

(c) Minimize $z = 3x_1 + 2x_2$, subject to
$$14x_1 + \quad 9x_2 \le 126$$
$$10x_1 + 11x_2 \ge 110$$
$$-5x_1 + \quad x_2 = \quad 9$$
$$x_1 \ge 0, \quad x_2 \ge 0$$

Solve Exercises 18 through 23.

18. Maximize $z = 4x_1 + 5x_2$, subject to
$$x_1 + 3x_2 \le 12$$
$$2x_1 + 4x_2 \le 16$$
$$x_1 \ge 0, \quad x_2 \ge 0$$

19. Maximize $z = 3x_1 + 5x_2 + 2x_3$, subject to

$$2x_1 + 4x_2 + 2x_3 \le 34$$
$$3x_1 + 6x_2 + 4x_3 \le 57$$
$$2x_1 + 5x_2 + x_3 \le 30$$
$$x_1 \ge 0, \quad x_2 \ge 0, \quad x_3 \ge 0$$

20. Maximize $z = 3x_1 + 4x_2$, subject to

$$x_1 - 3x_2 \le 6$$
$$x_1 + x_2 \le 8$$
$$x_1 \ge 0, \quad x_2 \ge 0$$

21. Maximize $z = 10x_1 + 15x_2$, subject to

$$-4x_1 + x_2 \le 3$$
$$x_1 - 2x_2 \le 12$$
$$x_1 \ge 0, \quad x_2 \ge 0$$

22. Maximize $z = 3x_1 + 6x_2 + x_3$, subject to

$$4x_1 + 4x_2 + 8x_3 \le 800$$
$$8x_1 + 6x_2 + 4x_3 \le 1800$$
$$8x_1 + 4x_2 \le 400$$
$$x_1 \ge 0, \quad x_2 \ge 0, \quad x_3 \ge 0$$

23. Maximize $z = x_1 + 3x_2 + x_3$, subject to

$$4x_1 + x_2 + x_3 \le 372$$
$$x_1 + 8x_2 + 6x_3 \le 1116$$
$$x_1 \ge 0, \quad x_2 \ge 0, \quad x_3 \ge 0$$

24. Find the values of the slack variables in the constraints

$$4x_1 + 3x_2 + 6x_3 + s_1 = 68$$
$$x_1 + 2x_2 + 5x_3 + s_2 = 90$$

for the points (3, 2, 1) and (5, 10, 3).

25. Which variable contributes the most to increasing z in the following objective functions?
   (a) $z = 7x_1 + 2x_2 + 9x_3$
   (b) $z = x_1 + 8x_2 + x_3 + 7x_4$

26. Given the constraint

$$7x_1 + 4x_2 + 17x_3 + s_1 = 56$$

When $x_2 = 0$, what is the largest possible value of x_3 so that s_1 is nonnegative?

27. Write the transpose of the matrices

$$\begin{bmatrix} 3 & 1 & -2 \\ 4 & 0 & 6 \\ 5 & 7 & 8 \end{bmatrix} \quad \text{and} \quad \begin{bmatrix} 4 & 3 & 2 & 1 \\ -5 & 0 & 12 & 9 \end{bmatrix}$$

Solve Exercises 28 through 36.

28. Minimize $z = 3x_1 + 5x_2 + 4x_3$, subject to

$$3x_1 - 3x_2 + x_3 \le 54$$
$$x_1 + x_2 + x_3 \ge 24$$
$$-3x_1 + 2x_3 \le 15$$
$$x_1 \ge 0, \quad x_2 \ge 0, \quad x_3 \ge 0$$

29. Minimize $z = 6x_1 + 8x_2 + 16x_3$, subject to

$$2x_1 + x_2 \ge 6$$
$$x_2 + 2x_3 \ge 8$$
$$x_1 \ge 0, \quad x_2 \ge 0, \quad x_3 \ge 0$$

30. Minimize $z = 10x_1 + 20x_2 + 15x_3$, subject to

$$x_1 + x_2 + x_3 \ge 100$$
$$9x_1 - 4x_3 \le 128$$
$$x_1 + 4x_2 = 48$$
$$x_1 \ge 0, \quad x_2 \ge 0, \quad x_3 \ge 0$$

31. Maximize $z = 6x_1 + 11x_2 + 8x_3$, subject to

$$2x_1 + 5x_2 + 4x_3 \le 40$$
$$40x_1 + 45x_2 + 30x_3 \le 430$$
$$6x_1 + 3x_2 + 4x_3 \ge 48$$
$$x_1 \ge 0, \quad x_2 \ge 0, \quad x_3 \ge 0$$

32. Maximize $z = 3x_1 + 4x_2 + x_3$, subject to

$$x_1 + x_2 + x_3 \le 28$$
$$3x_1 + 4x_2 + 6x_3 \ge 60$$
$$2x_1 + x_2 = 30$$
$$x_1 \ge 0, \quad x_2 \ge 0, \quad x_3 \ge 0$$

33. Maximize $z = 2x_1 + 5x_2 + 3x_3$, subject to

$$x_1 + x_2 + x_3 \ge 6$$
$$2x_1 + x_2 + 3x_3 \le 10$$
$$2x_2 - x_3 \le 5$$
$$x_1 \ge 0, \quad x_2 \ge 0, \quad x_3 \ge 0$$

34. Minimize $z = 18x_1 + 24x_2$, subject to

$$3x_1 + 4x_2 \ge 48$$
$$x_1 + 2x_2 \le 22$$
$$3x_1 + 2x_2 \le 42$$
$$x_1 \ge 0, \quad x_2 \ge 0$$

35. Maximize $z = 20x_1 + 32x_2$, subject to

$$x_1 - 3x_2 \le 24$$
$$-5x_1 + 4x_2 \le 20$$
$$x_1 \ge 0, \quad x_2 \ge 0$$

36. Minimize $z = 8x_1 + 10x_2 + 25x_3$, subject to

$$x_1 \quad + \quad x_3 \geq 30$$
$$2x_1 + 4x_2 + 5x_3 \geq 70$$
$$2x_2 + \quad x_3 \geq 27$$
$$x_1 \geq 0, \quad x_2 \geq 0, \quad x_3 \geq 0$$

Solve Exercises 37 through 41.

37. Minimize $z = 18x_1 + 36x_2$, subject to

$$3x_1 + 2x_2 \geq 24$$
$$5x_1 + 4x_2 \geq 46$$
$$4x_1 + 9x_2 \geq 60$$
$$x_1 \geq 0, \quad x_2 \geq 0$$

38. Maximize $5x_1 + 15x_2$, subject to

$$4x_1 + \quad x_2 \leq 200$$
$$x_1 + 3x_2 \geq 120$$
$$x_1 \geq 0, \quad x_2 \geq 0$$

39. Maximize $5x_1 + 15x_2$, subject to

$$4x_1 + \quad x_2 \leq 180$$
$$x_1 + 3x_2 \geq 120$$
$$-x_1 + 3x_2 = 150$$
$$x_1 \geq 0, \quad x_2 \geq 0$$

40. Minimize $z = 3x_1 - 2x_2$, subject to

$$x_1 + 3x_2 \leq 30$$
$$3x_1 + \quad x_2 \leq 21$$
$$x_1 \geq 0, \quad x_2 \geq 0$$

41. Maximize $z = 2x_1 + x_2$, subject to

$$x_1 + 3x_2 \leq \quad 9$$
$$x_1 - \quad x_2 \leq -2$$
$$x_1 \geq 0, \quad x_2 \geq 0$$

42. For each of the following minimization problems, set up the augmented matrix and the initial tableau for the dual problem. Do not solve.

(a) Minimize $x = 30x_1 + 17x_2$, subject to

$$4x_1 + \quad 5x_2 \geq 52$$
$$7x_1 + 14x_2 \geq 39$$
$$x_1 \geq 0, \quad x_2 \geq 0$$

(b) Minimize $z = 100x_1 + 225x_2 + 145x_3$, subject to

$$20x_1 + 35x_2 + 15x_3 \geq 130$$
$$40x_1 + 10x_2 + \quad 6x_3 \geq 220$$
$$35x_1 + 22x_2 + 18x_3 \geq 176$$
$$x_1 \geq 0, \quad x_2 \geq 0, \quad x_3 \geq 0$$

Set up the initial simplex tableau for Exercises 43 and 44. Do not solve.

43. A company manufactures three items: hunting jackets, all-weather jackets, and ski jackets. It takes three hours of labor per dozen to produce hunting jackets, 2.5 hours per dozen for all-weather jackets, and 3.5 hours per dozen for ski jackets. The cost per dozen is $26 for hunting jackets, $20 for all-weather jackets, and $22 for ski jackets. The profit per dozen is $7.50 for hunting jackets, $9 for all-weather jackets, and $11 for ski jackets. The company has 3200 hours of labor and $18,000 in operating funds available. How many of each jacket should it produce to maximize profits?

44. A fertilizer company produces two kinds of fertilizers, Lawn and Tree. It has orders on hand that call for the production of at least 20,000 bags of Lawn fertilizer and 5000 bags of Tree fertilizer. Plant A can produce 500 bags of Lawn and 100 bags of Tree fertilizer per day. Plant B can produce 250 bags of Lawn and 90 bags of Tree fertilizer per day. It costs $18,000 per day to operate plant A and $12,000 per day to operate plant B. How many days should the company operate each plant to minimize operating costs?

5

Sets and Counting

*A*N UNDERSTANDING OF SET theory is basic to understanding logic, enumeration problems, and probability. Through the centuries, set theory evolved slowly as an element of logic and mathematics. While a number of mathematicians contributed to the development of set theory, an Englishman, George Boole, extended and formalized their ideas into an algebra of set theory and logic that brought a well defined structure of them. His book *Investigation of the Laws of Thought,* published in 1854, was significant in the evolution of mathematics.

The theory of enumeration, permutation, and combinatorics evolved over a wide geographical area and time period. There are traces of it in China during the twelfth century. About the same time the Hindus found rules to determine the number of "changes upon apertures of a building," "the scheme of musical permutations," and "the combination of different savours" in medicine (Bhäskara in *Lilavati*). The early Hebrews and Arabs studied permutations because of their belief in the mysticism of arrangements and the combinations of planets.

The first major publication on the theory of enumeration was the work of a Swiss mathematician, Jacques Bernoulli. *Ars Conjectandi* was published in 1713 after his death.

Today, permutations and combinations have moved out of the realm of mysticism and find applications in the sciences, engineering, social science, statistics, and computer science.

5-1 SETS

- *Set-Builder Notation*
- *Equal Sets*
- *Empty Set*
- *Subset*
- *The Union of Two Sets*
- *The Intersection of Two Sets*
- *Disjoint Sets*

One of the basic concepts in mathematics is that of a **set.** Even in everyday life we talk about sets. We talk about a set of dishes, a set of spark plugs, a reading list (a set of books), the people invited to a party (a set of people), the vegetables served at the cafeteria (a set of vegetables), and the teams in the NFL playoffs (a set of football teams).

The concept of a set is so basic that proposed definitions of it tend to use words that mean essentially the same thing. We may speak of a set as a collection of objects. If we attempt to define a collection, we tend to think of the same words as we use in defining a set. Rather than go in circles trying to define a set, we will not give a definition. However, you should have an intuitive feeling of the meaning of a set.

While we do not define the concept of a set, any particular set should be well defined in the sense that there should be no ambiguity as to the objects that make up the set. For example, the collection of all letters of the English alphabet forms a set of 26 elements. No ambiguity arises as to which elements are in the set and which are not, so the set is well defined. However, the collection of the ten greatest American authors is not well defined; it depends on who makes the selection and what they mean by "great."

Let's look at some of the traditional terminology used in speaking about sets. The objects that form a set may be varied. We can have a set of people, a set of numbers, a set of ideas, or a set of raindrops. In mathematics the general term for an object in a set is **element.** A set may have people, numbers, ideas, or raindrops as elements. So that the contents of a set will be clearly understood, we need to be rather precise in describing a set of elements. One way to describe a set is to list explicitly all its elements. We usually enclose the list with braces. When we write

$$A = \{\text{Tom, Dick, Harry}\}$$

we are stating that we have named the set "A," and its elements are Tom, Dick, and Harry. Customarily, capital letters designate sets, and lowercase letters represent elements in a set. The notation

$$x \in A$$

is read "x is an element of A." We may also say that "x is a member of the set A." The statement "x is not an element of the set A" is written

$$x \notin A$$

For the set

$$B = \{2, 4, 6, 8\}$$

we may write $4 \in B$ to specify that 4 is one of the elements of the set B and $5 \notin B$ to specify that 5 is not one of the elements of B. Here are some examples of other sets:

EXAMPLE 1

The set of positive integers less than 7 is $\{1, 2, 3, 4, 5, 6\}$.

EXAMPLE 2

The vowels of the English alphabet form the set $\{a, e, i, o, u\}$.

EXAMPLE 3

The countries of North America form the set $\{\text{Canada, USA, Mexico}\}$.

EXAMPLE 4

The set of all natural numbers is $\{1, 2, 3, 4, \ldots\}$. Notice that we used three dots to indicate that the natural numbers continue, without ending, beyond 4. This is an infinite set. The three dots are commonly used to indicate that the preceding pattern continues. This notation is the mathematical equivalent of *et cetera*. The context in which the three dots are used determines which elements are missing from the list. The notation $\{20, 22, 24, \ldots, 32\}$ indicates that 26, 28, and 30 are missing from the list. This set is finite because it contains a finite number of elements. When "$\ldots$" is used in representing a finite set, the last element of the set is usually given. An infinite set gives no indication of a last element, as in the set of positive even numbers $\{2, 4, 6, \ldots\}$.

SET-BUILDER NOTATION

Another way of describing a set uses the **implicit** or **set-builder notation.** The set of the vowels of the English alphabet may be described by

$$\{x \mid x \text{ is a vowel of the English alphabet}\}$$

Read this as "The set of all x such that x is a vowel of the English alphabet." Note that the vertical line $|$ is read "such that." The symbol preceding the vertical line, x in this instance, designates a typical element of the set. The statement to the right of the vertical line *describes* a typical element of the set; it tells how to find a specific instance of x.

EXAMPLE 5   *(Compare Exercise 2)*

(a) The elements of the set $A = \{x \mid x \text{ is an odd integer between 10 and 20}\}$ are 11, 13, 15, 17, and 19.
(b) The set $\{x \mid x \text{ is a male student at Community College and } x \text{ is over 6 ft tall}\}$ is the set of all male students at Community College who are over 6 ft tall.
(c) The set $\{x \mid x \text{ is a member of the United States Senate}\}$ is the set of all senators of the United States.
(d) The set $\{x \mid x = 3n - 2 \text{ where } n \text{ is a positive integer}\}$ contains 1, 4, 7, 10, $\ldots$.

EQUAL SETS

Two sets A and B are said to be **equal** if they consist of exactly the same elements; this is denoted by $A = B$. The sets $A = \{2, 4, 6, 8\}$ and $B = \{6, 6, 2, 8, 4\}$ are equal because they consist of the same elements. Listing the elements in a different order or with repetition does not create a different set.

EMPTY SET

Sometimes a set is described and it has no elements. For example, the set of golfers who made nine consecutive holes-in-one at the Richland Golf Course has no elements. Such a set, consisting of no elements, plays an important role in set theory. It is called the **empty set** and is denoted by ∅. A set is called *nonempty* if it contains one or more elements. The set of people who are 10 feet tall is empty. The set of blue-eyed people is not empty. The set of numbers that belong to both $\{1, 3, 5\}$ and $\{2, 4, 6\}$ is empty.

SUBSET

The set B is said to be a **subset** of A if every element of B is also an element of A. This is written $B \subset A$.

EXAMPLE 6 *(Compare Exercise 13)*

$\{2, 5, 9\} \subset \{1, 2, 4, 5, 7, 9\}$ because every element of $\{2, 5, 9\}$ is in the set $\{1, 2, 4, 5, 7, 9\}$. The set $\{3, 5, 9\}$ is not a subset of $\{1, 2, 4, 5, 7, 9\}$ because 3 is in the first set but not in the second.

EXAMPLE 7 *(Compare Exercise 21)*

The subsets of $\{1, 2, 3\}$ are

$$\emptyset, \{1\}, \{2\}, \{3\}, \{1, 2\}, \{1, 3\}, \{2, 3\}, \{1, 2, 3\}$$

Notice that a set is a subset of itself; $\{1, 2, 3\}$ is a subset of $\{1, 2, 3\}$. Because ∅ contains no elements, it is true that every element of ∅ is in $\{1, 2, 3\}$, so $\emptyset \subset \{1, 2, 3\}$. In the same sense, ∅ is a subset of every set. The set $\{1, 2\}$ is a **proper** subset of $\{1, 2, 3\}$ because it is a subset of and not equal to $\{1, 2, 3\}$. We point out that if $A \subset B$ and $B \subset A$, then $A = B$.

THE UNION OF TWO SETS

Sometimes, we wish to construct a set using elements from two given sets. One way to obtain a new set is to combine the two given sets into one.

> *Definition 1*
> **Union of Sets**
>
> The **union** of two sets, A and B, is the set whose elements are from A or from B, or from both. Denote this set by $A \cup B$.
> In set-builder notation this is
> $$A \cup B = \{x \mid x \in A \text{ or } x \in B \text{ or } x \text{ in both}\}$$

If you ask a number of people how they interpret a statement like "It is Joe or it is Jane," some will interpret it as either Joe or Jane, but not both. Others may include the possibility of both. In standard mathematical terminology the phrase "$x \in A$ or $x \in B$" includes the possibility of x existing in both. Therefore the phrase "or x in both" is mathematically redundant.

EXAMPLE 8   *(Compare Exercise 33)*

Given $A = \{2, 4, 6, 8, 10\}$ and $B = \{6, 7, 8, 9, 10\}$. To determine $A \cup B$, list all elements of A and add those from B that are not already listed to obtain

$$A \cup B = \{2, 4, 6, 8, 10, 7, 9\}$$

NOTE The order in which the elements in a set are listed is not important. It might seem more natural to list the elements as $\{2, 4, 6, 7, 8, 9, 10\}$. Notice that an element that appears in both A and B is listed only once in $A \cup B$.

EXAMPLE 9

(a) Given the sets

$$A = \{\text{Tom, Dick, Harry}\} \qquad \text{and}$$
$$B = \{\text{Sue, Ann, Jo, Carmen}\}$$
$$A \cup B = \{\text{Tom, Dick, Harry, Sue, Ann, Jo, Carmen}\}$$

(b) Given the sets

$$A = \{x \mid x \text{ is a letter of the word } radio\}$$

and

$$B = \{x \mid x \text{ is one of the first six letters of the English alphabet}\}$$
$$A \cup B = \{a, b, c, d, e, f, r, i, o\}$$

THE INTERSECTION OF TWO SETS

Another way to construct a set from two sets is by performing the operation called the **intersection** of two sets:

Definition 2
Intersection of Sets

The **intersection** of two sets, A and B, is the set of all elements contained in both sets A and B, that is, those elements which A and B have in common. The intersection of A and B is denoted by

$$A \cap B = \{x \mid x \in A \text{ and } x \in B\}$$

EXAMPLE 10   *(Compare Exercise 37)*

(a) If $A = \{2, 4, 5, 8, 10\}$ and $B = \{3, 4, 5, 6, 7\}$, then

$$A \cap B = \{4, 5\}$$

(b) If $A = \{a, b, c, d, e, f, g, h\}$ and $B = \{b, d, e\}$, then

$$A \cap B = \{b, d, e\}$$

EXAMPLE 11 *(Compare Exercise 57)*

Given the sets

$$A = \text{set of all positive even integers}$$

and

$$B = \text{set of all positive multiples of 3}$$

describe and list the elements of $A \cap B$ and $A \cup B$.

SOLUTION Since an element of $A \cap B$ must be even (a multiple of 2) and a multiple of 3, then each such element must be a multiple of 6. Thus $A \cap B$ is the set of all positive multiples of 6, that is, $\{6, 12, 18, 24, . . .\}$. Since this is an infinite set, only the pattern of numbers can be listed. $A \cup B$ is the set of positive integers that are multiples of 2 or multiples of 3. ∎

In a finite set you can count the elements and finish at a definite number. You can never count all the elements in an infinite set. No matter how high you count, there will be some left uncounted. The set of whole numbers between 10 and 20 is finite; there are 9 of them. The set of fractions between 10 and 20 is infinite; there is no end to them.

DISJOINT SETS

If A and B do not have any elements in common, they are said to be **disjoint,** and $A \cap B = \emptyset$. The sets $A = \{2, 4, 6, 8\}$ and $B = \{1, 3, 5, 7\}$ are disjoint.

5–1 EXERCISES

I

1. Establish whether each of the following statements is true or false for $A = \{1, 2, 3, 4\}$, $B = \{3, 4, 5, 6\}$, $C = \{5, 6, 7, 8\}$, $D = \{1, 3, 5, 7, . . .\}$.
   - **(a)** $2 \in A$
   - **(b)** $5 \in A$
   - **(c)** $8 \in B$
   - **(d)** $5 \notin C$
   - **(e)** $6 \notin A$
   - **(f)** $5 \in D$
   - **(g)** $20 \in D$
   - **(h)** $49 \in D$
   - **(i)** $200 \in D$
   - **(j)** $201 \in D$

List the elements of each of the sets in Exercises 2 through 6.

2. *(See Example 5)*
   $A = \{x|x \text{ is a positive odd integer less than 10}\}$
3. $B = \{x|x \text{ is a letter in the word Mississippi}\}$
4. $A = \{x|x \text{ is an integer larger than 13 and less than 20}\}$
5. $C = \{x|x \text{ is an even integer larger than 15}\}$
6. $A = \{x|x \text{ is a prime less than 20}\}$

Which of the following pairs of sets in Exercises 7 through 12 are equal?

7. $A = \{1, 2, 3, 4\}$, $B = \{3, 1, 2, 5\}$
8. $A = \{1, -1, 0, 4\}$, $B = \{-1, 0, 1, 4\}$
9. $A = \{a, e, i, o, u\}$,
   $B = \{x|x \text{ is a vowel of the English alphabet}\}$
10. $A = \{x|x \text{ is a prime integer less than 20}\}$
    $B = \{2, 3, 5, 7, 11, 13, 17, 19\}$
11. $A = \{5, 10, 15, 20\}$, $B = \{x|x \text{ is a multiple of 5}\}$
12. $A = \{x|x \text{ is a letter in the word REPORTER}\}$
    $B = \{x|x \text{ is a letter in the word POTTER}\}$

In which of Exercises 13 through 20 is A a subset of B?

13. *(See Example 6)*
    $A = \{2, 4, 6, 8\}$, $B = \{1, 2, 3, 4, 5, 6, 7, 8, 9, 10\}$

14. $A = \{1, 2, 3, 5\}$, $B = \{1, 2, 3, 4, 5\}$

15. $A = \{a, b, c\}$, $B = \{a, e, i, o, u\}$

16. $A = \{1, 3, 7, 9, 11, 13\}$, $B = \{1, 9, 13\}$

17. $A = \{3, 8, 2, 5\}$, $B = \{2, 3, 5, 8\}$

18. $A =$ set of male college students,
$B =$ set of college students

19. $A =$ set of even integers, $B =$ set of integers

20. $A = \{x \mid x$ is a prime number less than 15$\}$
$B = \{x \mid x$ is an odd integer less than 15$\}$

21. (*See Example 7*) Determine all the subsets of A, B, and C.
 (a) $A = \{-1, 2, 4\}$ (b) $B = \{4\}$
 (c) $C = \{-3, 5, 6, 8\}$

Which of the sets in Exercises 22 through 32 are empty?

22. Female presidents of the United States

23. A flock of extinct birds

24. The integers larger than 10 and less than 5

25. English words that begin with the letter k and end with the letter e

26. Families with five children

27. Odd integers divisible by 2

28. Integers larger than 0 and less than 37

29. Integers larger than 5 and less than 6

30. Fractions larger than 5 and less than 6

31. $\{2, 4, 6\} \cap \{1, 8, 13\}$

32. $\{5, 9, 27\} \cap \{8, 9, 10\}$

List the elements of the sets in Exercises 33 through 38.

33. (*See Example 8*) $\{2, 1, 7\} \cup \{4, 6, 7\}$

34. $\{h, i, s, t, o, r, y\} \cup \{m, u, s, i, c\}$

35. $\{a, b, c, x, y, z\} \cup \{b, a, d\}$

36. $\{5, 2, 9, 4\} \cup \{3, 0, 8\}$

37. (*See Example 10*)
$\{1, 3, 5, 9, 12\} \cap \{6, 7, 8, 9, 10, 11, 12\}$

38. $\{h, i, s, t, o, r, y\} \cap \{e, n, g, l, i, s, h\}$

To determine the sets indicated in Exercises 39 through 49, use $A = \{1, 2, 3\}$, $B = \{1, 2, 3, 6, 9\}$, and $C = \{-3, -1, 0, 2, 3, 6, 7\}$.

39. $A \cap B$ **40.** $A \cap C$

41. $A \cup B$ **42.** $A \cup C$

43. $A \cap B \cap C$ **44.** $A \cup B \cup C$

45. $A \cap \emptyset$ **46.** $B \cap \emptyset$

47. $(A \cup C) \cap B$ **48.** $A \cup (B \cap C)$

49. $(A \cap C) \cup B$

II

List the first three elements of each of the sets in Exercises 50 through 52.

50. $\{x \mid x = 3n, n$ a positive integer$\}$

51. $\{x \mid x = n^2 - 3, n$ a positive integer greater than 3$\}$

52. $\{x \mid x = n^3, n$ a nonnegative integer$\}$

List all the elements of the sets in Exercises 53 and 54.

53. $\{x \mid x$ is a positive integer less than 5$\}$

54. $\{x \mid (x + 2)(x - 5)(x - 7) = 0\}$

55. Replace the asterisk in each of the following statements with =, ⊂, or "neither," as appropriate.
 (a) $\{2, 4, 6\} * \{1, 2, 3, 4, 5, 6\}$
 (b) $\{2, 4, 8\} * \{1, 3, 5, 9\}$
 (c) $\{2, 5, 17\} * \{17, 5, 2\}$
 (d) $\{8, 10, 12\} * \{8, 10\}$
 (e) $\{2, 4, 6, 8\} * \{x \mid x$ is an even integer$\}$

56. Find $A \cap B$ where
$A = \{x \mid x$ is an integer larger than 12$\}$
$B = \{x \mid x$ is an integer less than 21$\}$

57. (*See Example 11*) Find $A \cap B$ where
$A = \{x \mid x$ is an integer that is a multiple of 5$\}$
$B = \{x \mid x$ is an integer that is a multiple of 7$\}$

Determine which of the pairs of sets in Exercises 58 through 61 are disjoint.

58. $A = \{1, 2, 3, 4, 5, 6\}$, $B = \{2, 4, 6, 8, 10\}$

59. A = the set of prime numbers greater than 100
   B = the set of even integers

60. $A = \{3, 6, 9, 12\}$, $B = \{5, 10, 15, 20\}$

61. A = all multiples of 4
   B = all multiples of 3

62. Sets $A, B, C,$ and D are the following:
$A = \{1, 2, 3, 4\}$, $B = \{-5, 7, 8, 10\}$,
$C = \{1, 2, 3, 4, 5, 9, 10, 11\}$, and $D = \emptyset$. Find the following:
(a) $A \cup B$ (b) $B \cup D$
(c) $A \cup B \cup C$ (d) $A \cap C$
(e) $A \cap D$ (f) $A \cap B \cap D$

III

63. Let A be the set of students at Miami Bay University who are taking finite mathematics. Let B be the set of students at Miami Bay University who are taking American history. Describe $A \cap B$.

64. Let A be the set of students in the Collegiate Choir and let B be the set of students in the University Orchestra.
(a) Describe $A \cup B$.   (b) Describe $A \cap B$.

5–2 VENN DIAGRAMS

- *Venn Diagrams*
- *Complement*
- *Number of Elements in a Subset*
- *Venn Diagrams Using Three Sets*

VENN DIAGRAMS

It usually helps to use a diagram to represent an idea. For sets it is customary to use a rectangular area to represent the **universe** to which a set belongs. We have not used the term *universe* before. The universe is not some all-inclusive set that contains everything. When I talk about a set of students, I am generally thinking of college students, so the elements of my set of students are restricted to college students. In that context the universe is the set of college students. When a student at Midway High speaks of a set of students, she restricts the elements of her set to students at her school, so the set of all students at Midway High School forms her universe. In a given context the sets under discussion have elements that come from some restricted set. We call the set from which the elements come the universe or the **universal set.** We usually represent the universe by a rectangle. A circular area within the rectangle represents a set of elements in the universe. The diagram in Figure 5–1 represents a set A in a universe U. It is called a **Venn diagram.**

FIGURE 5–1

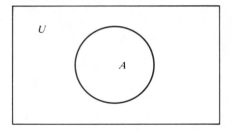

FIGURE 5–2

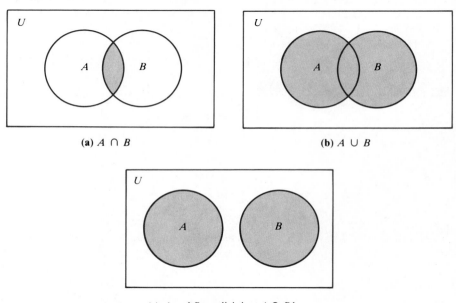

(a) $A \cap B$

(b) $A \cup B$

(c) A and B are disjoint. $A \cap B$ has no elements; it is the empy set.

$$A \cap B = \phi$$

The shaded area is $A \cup B$.

EXAMPLE 1

Figure 5–2(a) shows the Venn diagram of the intersection of two sets. The shaded area is $A \cap B$.

Figure 5–2(b) shows a Venn diagram that represents the union of two sets. The shaded area represents $A \cup B$.

Figure 5–2(c) shows two disjoint sets. While their intersection is empty, their union is not, and it is shown by the shaded area.

EXAMPLE 2

Let

U = set letters of the English alphabet

A = set of vowels

B = set of the first nine letters of the alphabet

Place each of the letters a, c, d, e, i, u, x, y in the appropriate region in a Venn diagram.

SOLUTION The letters $a, e, i,$ and u are elements of $A;$ $a, c, d, e,$ and i are elements of $B;$ and x and y are in neither set. Notice that $a, e,$ and i are in both A and B, so they are in their intersection. We may indicate this as shown in Figure 5–3.

FIGURE 5–3

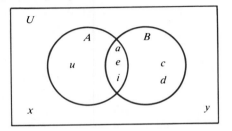

COMPLEMENT

The elements in the universe U that lie outside A form a set called the **complement** of A, denoted by A'. (See Figure 5–4.)

FIGURE 5–4

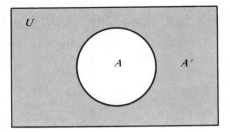

EXAMPLE 3   *(Compare Exercise 1)*

Let $U = \{1, 2, 3, 4, 5, 6, 7, 8\}$ and $A = \{1, 2, 8\}$. Then $A' = \{3, 4, 5, 6, 7\}$.

From the definition of complement it follows that for any set A in a universe U,

$$A \cap A' = \emptyset \qquad \text{and} \qquad A \cup A' = U$$

A set and its complement have no elements in common. The union of a set and its complement is the universal set.

NUMBER OF ELEMENTS IN A SUBSET

We now turn our attention to counting the elements in a set. We want to be able to use information about a set and determine the number of elements in it but avoid actually counting the elements one by one.

We use the notation $n(A)$, read "n of A," to indicate the number of elements in set A. If A contains 23 elements, we write $n(A) = 23$.

Suppose that you count 10 people in a group that like brand X cola and 15 that like brand Y. We denote this by $n(\text{brand X}) = 10$ and $n(\text{brand Y}) = 15$. How many people are involved in the count? The answer depends on the number who like both brands. In set terminology the people who like brand X form one set, and those who like brand Y form another set. The totality of all people involved in the count form the union of the two sets, and those who like both brands form the intersection of the two sets. If we attempt to determine the total count by adding the number who like brand X and the number who like brand Y, then we count those who like both X and Y twice. We need to subtract the number who like both from the sum of those who like X and those who like Y in order to obtain the total number involved. If there are 4 people who like both brands, then the total count is $10 + 15 - 4 = 21$.

In general, the relationship between the number of elements in each of two sets, their union, and their intersection is given by the following theorem.

Theorem 1 **$n(A \cup B)$**	$$n(A \cup B) = n(A) + n(B) - n(A \cap B)$$ where $n(A)$ represents the number of elements in set A, $n(B)$ represents the number of elements in set B, and $n(A \cap B)$ represents the number of elements of $A \cap B$.

EXAMPLE 4   *(Compare Exercise 7)*

$A = \{a, b, c, d, e, f\}$, $B = \{a, e, i, o, u, w, y\}$. Count $n(A)$, $n(B)$, $n(A \cap B)$, and $n(A \cup B)$.

SOLUTION $n(A) = 6$ and $n(B) = 7$. In this case, $A \cap B = \{a, e\}$, so $n(A \cap B) = 2$. $A \cup B = \{a, b, c, d, e, f, i, o, u, w, y\}$, so $n(A \cup B) = 11$. This checks with the formula, $n(A \cup B) = 6 + 7 - 2 = 11$.

EXAMPLE 5   *(Compare Exercise 9)*

Set A is the 9 o'clock English class of 15 students, so A contains 15 elements. Set B is the 11 o'clock history class of 20 students, so B contains 20 elements. $A \cap B$ is the set of students in both classes (there are seven), so $A \cap B$ contains seven elements. The number of elements in $A \cup B$ (a joint meeting of the classes) is

$$n(A \cup B) = n(A) + n(B) - n(A \cap B)$$

so

$$n(A \cup B) = 15 + 20 - 7 = 28$$

Notice where the elements of A and B lie in the Venn diagram in Figure 5–5.

FIGURE 5–5

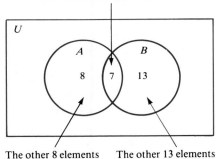

7 elements in the intersection

The other 8 elements of A here

The other 13 elements of B here

EXAMPLE 6   *(Compare Exercise 11)*

The union of two sets, $A \cup B$, has 48 elements. Set A contains 27 elements, and set B contains 30 elements. How many elements are in $A \cap B$?

SOLUTION   Using the relationship of Theorem 1, we have

$$48 = 27 + 30 - n(A \cap B)$$
$$48 - 27 - 30 = -n(A \cap B)$$
$$-9 = -n(A \cap B)$$

So

$$n(A \cap B) = 9$$

EXAMPLE 7   *(Compare Exercise 27)*

One hundred students were asked whether they were taking psychology (P) or biology (B). The responses showed that:

> 61 were taking psychology, that is, $n(P) = 61$;
> 18 were taking both, that is, $n(P \cap B) = 18$;
> 12 were taking neither.

(a) How many were taking biology? (Find $n(B)$)
(b) How many were taking psychology but not biology? (Find $n(P \cap B')$)
(c) How many were not taking biology? (Find $n(B')$)
(d) Find $n(B \cap P)'$.

SOLUTION

(a) Since 12 were taking neither, the rest, 88, were taking at least one of the courses; so $n(P \cup B) = 88$. We can find $n(B)$ from

$$n(P \cup B) = n(P) + n(B) - n(P \cap B)$$
$$88 = 61 + n(B) - 18$$
$$n(B) = 45$$

(b) Since 18 students were taking both psychology and biology, the remainder of the 61 psychology students were taking only psychology. So, $61 - 18 = 43$ students were taking psychology but not biology.

(c) The students not taking biology were those 12 taking neither and the 43 taking only psychology, a total of 55 not taking biology. (See Figure 5–6.)

(d) Figure 5–6 shows the number outside $B \cap P$, that is, $n(B \cap P)'$, is $43 + 27 + 12 = 82$.

FIGURE 5–6

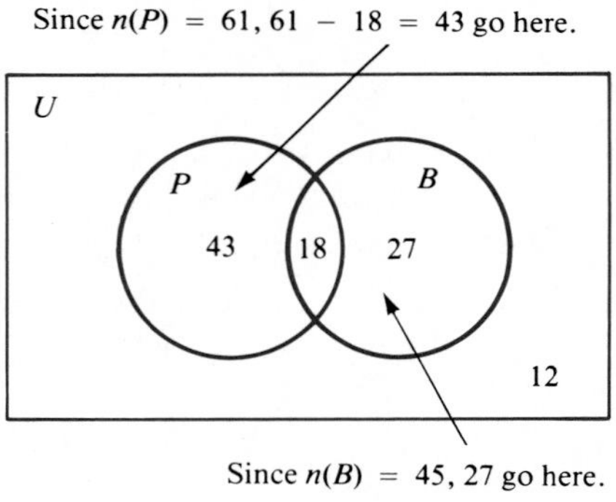

Since $n(P) = 61, 61 - 18 = 43$ go here.

Since $n(B) = 45$, 27 go here.

VENN DIAGRAMS USING THREE SETS

A Venn diagram of three sets divides a universe into as many as eight regions. (See Figure 5–7.) We can use information about the number of elements in some of the regions (subsets) to obtain the number of elements in other subsets.

FIGURE 5–7

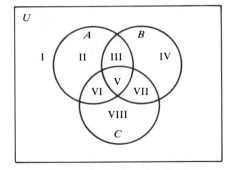

Three sets may divide the Universe into eight regions.

EXAMPLE 8

The sets *A*, *B*, and *C* intersect as shown in Figure 5–8. The numbers in each region indicate the number of elements in that subset.

The number of elements in other subsets may be obtained from this diagram. For example,

$$n(A) = 9 + 2 + 3 + 7 = 21$$
$$n(B) = 2 + 3 + 1 + 4 = 10$$
$$n(A \cap B) = 2 + 3 = 5$$
$$n(A \cap B \cap C) = 3$$
$$n(A \cup B) = 9 + 2 + 3 + 7 + 4 + 1 = 26$$

FIGURE 5–8

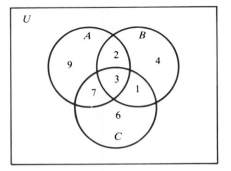

EXAMPLE 9 *(Compare Exercise 31)*

A survey yields the following information about the musical preferences of students:

30 like classical,

24 like country,

31 like jazz,

9 like country and classical,

12 like country and jazz,

10 like classical and jazz,

4 like all three,

6 like none of the three.

Draw a diagram that shows this breakdown of musical tastes. Determine the total number of students interviewed.

SOLUTION Begin by drawing a Venn diagram as shown in Figure 5–9(a).

FIGURE 5–9

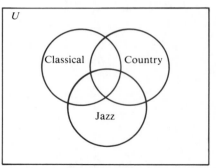

(a) A Venn diagram representing students grouped by musical preferenced.

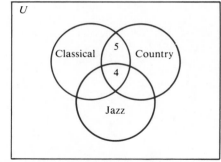

(b) Four students like all 3 types of music. A total of 9 like both classical and country.

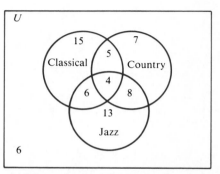

(c) The number in each category of musical preferences.

The universe is the set of college students interviewed. We want to determine the number of students in each region of the diagram. Since some students may like more than one kind of music, these sets may overlap. We begin where the largest number of sets overlap (where the three sets intersect) and work out to fewer intersecting sets. Using the information that four students like all three types of music, place a 4 in the region where all three sets intersect. Of the nine students who like both country and classical, we have already recorded four of them (those who like all three). The other five are in the intersection of classical and country that lies outside jazz (Figure 5–9(b)). In a similar fashion the number who like both jazz and country breaks down into the four who like all three and the eight who like jazz and country but are outside the region of all three. Since these three regions account for 17 of those who like country, the other seven who like country are in the region where country does not intersect the jazz and classical. Fill in the rest of the regions; the results are shown in the diagram in Figure 5–9(c).

Obtain the total number of students interviewed by adding the number in each region of the Venn diagram. The total is 64.

5-2 EXERCISES

I

1. (*See Example 3*) If $U = \{15, 16, 17, 18, 19, 20, 21\}$ and $A = \{15, 16, 20, 21\}$, find A'.

2. If $U = \{-1, 0, 1\}$ and $A = \{-1, 1\}$, find A'.

3. If $U = \{1, 2, 3, 11, 12, 13\}$ and $A = \{1, 2, 3\}$, find A'.

4. If $U = \{a, b, c, d, e, f\}$, $A = \{a, b\}$, and $B = \{b, c, d\}$, find
   (a) A'
   (b) B'
   (c) $(A \cup B)'$
   (d) $(A \cap B)'$

5. If $U = \{-1, 0, 1, 11, 12, 13\}$, $A = \{1, 11, 13\}$, and $B = \{-1, 0, 11\}$, find
   (a) A'
   (b) B'
   (c) $(A \cup B)'$
   (d) $(A \cap B)'$

6. If $U = \{a, b, c, d, e, f, g\}$, $A = \{a, c, f\}$, and $B = \{b, c, d\}$, find
   (a) A'
   (b) B'
   (c) $A' \cup B'$
   (d) $A' \cap B'$

7. (*See Example 4*) $A = \{a, b, c, d, e, f, g, x, y, z\}$, $B = \{c, r, a, z, y\}$. Find
   (a) $n(A)$
   (b) $n(B)$
   (c) $n(A \cap B)$
   (d) $n(A \cup B)$

8. $A = \{1, 3, 5, 7, 9, 11\}$, $B = \{3, 6, 9, 12\}$. Find
   (a) $n(A)$
   (b) $n(B)$
   (c) $n(A \cap B)$
   (d) $n(A \cup B)$

9. (*See Example 5*) Given $n(A) = 120$, $n(B) = 100$, and $n(A \cap B) = 40$. Find $n(A \cup B)$.

10. Given $n(A) = 26$, $n(B) = 14$, and $n(A \cap B) = 6$, determine $n(A \cup B)$.

11. (*See Example 6*) Given $n(A) = 15$, $n(B) = 22$, and $n(A \cup B) = 30$, determine $n(A \cap B)$.

12. Given $n(A) = 21$, $n(A \cup B) = 33$, and $n(A \cap B) = 5$, determine $n(B)$.

13. For two sets A and B, $n(A) = 14$, $n(A \cup B) = 28$, and $n(A \cap B) = 5$. Find $n(B)$.

14. If $n(A \cup B) = 249$, $n(A \cap B) = 36$, and $n(B) = 98$, find $n(A)$.

15. If $U = \{f, g, h, i, j, k, l, m\}$, $A = \{h, k, l\}$, and $B = \emptyset$. Find
   (a) A'
   (b) B'
   (c) $A \cap B$
   (d) $A \cup B$
   (e) $A' \cap B'$

16. If $U = \{-7, -6, -5, 0, 1, 2, 8, 10\}$, $A = \{-7, -5, 2, 8\}$, $B = \{0, 1, 2\}$, and $D = \emptyset$, determine
   (a) A'
   (b) B'
   (c) D'
   (d) $(A \cup B)'$
   (e) $(A \cap B)'$
   (f) $(A \cup D)'$
   (g) $(A \cap D)'$

II

17. Two sets are formed using 100 elements. There are 60 elements in one set and 75 in the other. How many elements are in the intersection of the two sets?

18. Use Figure 5–10 to find the following.
    (a) $n(A')$
    (b) $n(B')$
    (c) $n(A' \cup B')$
    (d) $n(A' \cap B')$

FIGURE 5–10

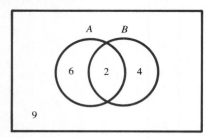

19. Look at Figure 5–11 to find the following.
    (a) $n(A)$
    (b) $n(B)$
    (c) $n(A \cup B)$
    (d) $n(A')$
    (e) $n(B')$
    (f) $n(A \cap B)'$
    (g) $n(A \cup B)'$
    (h) $n(A' \cap B')$
    (i) $n(A' \cup B')$

FIGURE 5–11

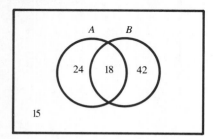

20. Use the Venn diagram in Figure 5–12. The number of elements in each subset is given.

    Compute
    (a) $n(A \cap B)$
    (b) $n(A \cap B \cap C)$
    (c) $n(A \cup B)$
    (d) $n(A \cup B \cup C)$
    (e) $n(A')$

FIGURE 5–12

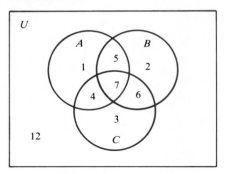

21. Use the Venn diagram in Figure 5–13. The number of elements in each subset is given.

    Compute
    (a) $n(A \cup B)$
    (b) $n(A \cup B)'$
    (c) $n(A \cap B)$
    (d) $n(A \cap B)'$
    (e) $n(A' \cup B')$
    (f) $n(B \cap C')$

FIGURE 5–13

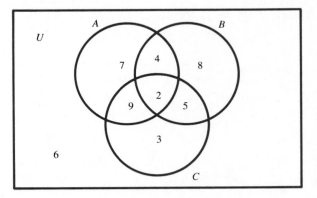

22. The following information gives the number of elements in some subsets of A, B, and C. Represent this information with a Venn diagram.
    $n(A \cap B \cap C) = 2$, $n(A \cap B) = 6$, $n(A \cap C) = 5$, $n(B \cap C) = 3$, $n(A) = 15$, $n(B) = 12$, $n(C) = 15$.

23. The following information gives the number of elements in some subsets of *A, B,* and *C.* Represent this information with a Venn diagram.
$n(A \cup B \cup C) = 33$, $n(A) = 14$, $n(B) = 20$, $n(C) = 23$, $n(A \cap B) = 7$, $n(A \cap C) = 11$, $n(A \cap B \cap C) = 6$.

24. A marketing class polled 150 people at a shopping center to determine how many read the *Daily News* and how many read the *Weekly Gazette*. They found the following:

> 126 read the *Daily News,*
> 31 read both,
> 10 read neither.

How many read the *Weekly Gazette?*

25. If a universal set contains 500 elements, $n(A) = 240$, $n(A \cup B) = 460$, and $n(A \cap B) = 55$, find $n(B')$.

26. If a universal set contains 250 elements, $n(A) = 85$, $n(B) = 130$, and $n(A \cap B) = 35$, find $n(A \cup B)'$.

27. (*See Example 7*) If 20 people belong to the Alpha Club, 30 people belong to the Beta Club, and six belong to both clubs:
   (a) how many belong only to the Alpha Club?
   (b) how many belong only to the Beta Club?
   (c) how many belong to just one club?
   (d) how many belong to one or both clubs?

28. Of the 19 fast food businesses on Valley Mills Drive, the number that have a drive-up window, outside seating, or a pay telephone is summarized as follows:

> 15 have a drive-up window,
> 14 have outside seating,
> 5 have pay telephones,
> 10 have a drive-up window and outside seating,
> 4 have outside seating and a pay telephone,
> 3 have a drive-up window and a pay telephone,
> 2 have all three.

Find the number of businesses that have
   (a) A drive-up window and outside seating
   (b) A drive-up window and outside seating, but no pay telephone
   (c) No pay telephone
   (d) Only a drive-up window
   (e) Outside seating or a pay telephone

29. Of 50 students surveyed, 19 owned a microcomputer, 42 owned a calculator, and 15 owned both.
   (a) How many students did not own a calculator?
   (b) How many students owned a calculator but did not own a microcomputer?
   (c) How many owned neither?
   (d) How many owned one or the other but not both?

30. A business advertised for applicants for secretarial, clerical, and typist positions. Respondents could apply for one or more of the positions. The responses were as follows:

> 12 applied for secretary,
> 10 applied for clerk,
> 14 applied for typist,
> 7 applied for secretary and typist,
> 5 applied for secretary and clerk,
> 3 applied for clerk and typist,
> 2 applied for all three,
> 3 applied for none of the positions.

Draw a Venn diagram and use it to find the following.
   (a) What was the total number of respondents?
   (b) How many applied for the typist position only?
   (c) How many applied for the secretary position but not the clerk position?

31. (*See Example 9*) A survey of 100 students at New England College showed the following:

> 48 take English,
> 49 take history,
> 38 take language,
> 17 take English and history,
> 15 take English and language,
> 18 take history and language,
> 7 take all three.

How many students:
   (a) take history but neither of the other two?
   (b) take English and history but not language?
   (c) take none of the three?
   (d) take just one of the three?
   (e) take exactly two of the three?
   (f) do not take language?

32. A university has three word processors that are available to its computer users, *Word* (W), *Write* (WR), and *Express* (E). A survey of users showed the following:

> Everyone used at least one of the three,
> 42 used only W,
> 58 used WR,
> 25 used only WR,
> 12 used only E,
> 13 used W and E,
> 18 used WR and E,
> 8 used all three.

(a) What was the total number of users?
(b) How many used W and WR but not E?
(c) How many used W?

33. A survey of 75 college students found that of the three student publications, *The Lariat, The Rope,* and *The Roundup:*

> 23 read *The Lariat,*
> 18 read *The Rope,*
> 14 read *The Roundup,*
> 10 read *The Lariat* and *The Rope,*
> 9 read *The Lariat* and *The Roundup,*
> 8 read *The Rope* and *The Roundup,*
> 5 read all three.

(a) How many read none of the publications?
(b) How many read only *The Lariat?*
(c) How many read neither *The Lariat* nor *The Rope?*
(d) How many read *The Rope* or *The Roundup* or both?

III

34. Forty students in a music appreciation class could attend a piano recital or a voice recital for extra points. Twenty students attended the piano recital, 23 attended the voice recital, and six attended neither. How many attended both?

35. A mathematics teacher assigned two homework problems to a class of 35 students. At the next meeting 17 indicated that they had worked the first problem, 19 had worked the second problem, and eight had worked both. Determine the number who:
(a) worked at least one of the problems.
(b) worked only the first problem.
(c) worked exactly one of the problems.
(d) worked neither of the problems.

36. A home economics class surveyed 1100 students about which meals they ate in their dormitory cafeteria. The class found the following information:

> 425 ate breakfast,
> 680 ate lunch,
> 855 ate dinner,
> 275 ate breakfast and lunch,
> 505 ate lunch and dinner,
> 375 ate breakfast and dinner,
> 240 ate all three meals in the cafeteria.

(a) How many ate only breakfast in the cafeteria?
(b) How many ate at least two meals?
(c) How many ate only one meal?
(d) How many ate exactly two meals?
(e) How many did not eat in the cafeteria?

37. Mr. X taught freshman English and Mrs. X taught freshman history. They hosted a party at their home for members of their classes and their dates. Twenty-eight of the students were in Mr. X's class, 33 were in Mrs. X's class, 7 were in both Mr. and Mrs. X's classes, and 15 other students were in neither class. How many students were at the party?

38. A group of 63 music students were comparing notes on their high school activities. They found that:

> 40 played in the band,
> 31 sang in a choral group,
> 9 neither played in the band nor sang in a choral group.

How many played in the band and sang in a choral group?

39. What is inconsistent about the following?
$n(A) = 25,$ $n(B) = 10,$ $n(A \cup B) = 23$

40. In the Rivercrest Apartments the tenants owned answering machines (A), VCR's, or microwave ovens (M) as follows:

ITEM	NUMBER
A	42
VCR	39
M	48
A and VCR	27
A and M	21
VCR and M	19
All three	12
None	8

(a) How many owned only answering machines?

(b) How many did not own a VCR?

(c) How many owned a VCR or answering machine but not a microwave?

41. A marketing class polled 85 faculty members to determine whether they had American Express or Visa cards. The class found that 42 had American Express and 35 had Visa. Of the Visa card holders, 12 also had American Express cards.

(a) How many American Express card holders did not have Visa?

(b) How many had neither?

42. There are 29 elements in sets *A, B,* and *C.* Is the following information consistent?

$$n(A) = 15$$
$$n(B) = 12$$
$$n(C) = 15$$
$$n(A \cap B) = 5$$
$$n(A \cap C) = 6$$
$$n(B \cap C) = 4$$
$$n(A \cap B \cap C) = 2$$

43. Charles Tally gave the following summary of his interviews with 135 students for a sociology project:

65 said they like to go to movies,

77 said they like to go to football games,

61 said they like to go to the theater,

28 said they like to attend movies and football games,

25 said they like to attend movies and the theater,

29 said they like to attend football games and the theater,

8 said they like to attend all three,

4 said they do not like to attend any of these.

The professor refused to accept Charles's paper because the information was inconsistent. Was the professor justified in claiming that the information was inconsistent?

44. A staff member of the news service of Great Lakes University gave out the following information in a news release:

Of a class of 500 students at Great Lakes, 281 are taking English, 196 are taking English and math, 87 are taking math and a foreign language, 143 are taking English and a foreign language, and 36 are taking all three.

The staff member was told that the information must not be released. Why?

45. Given two sets *A* and *B* where $n(A) = 5$, $n(B) = 10$, and $n(A \cup B) = 15$:

(a) Find $n(A \cap B)$. (b) What is $A \cap B$?

46. Use a Venn diagram to establish that if $A \subset B$, then $A \cap B = A$.

5–3 FUNDAMENTAL COUNTING PRINCIPLE

- *Tree Diagrams*
- *Fundamental Counting Principle*

A teenager posed the following problem: How many different outfits can she wear if she has two skirts and three blouses? We can solve this simple counting problem by listing the different outfits in a systematic manner:

1. First skirt with first blouse
2. First skirt with second blouse
3. First skirt with third blouse
4. Second skirt with first blouse
5. Second skirt with second blouse
6. Second skirt with third blouse

Notice the pattern of the list. For each skirt she can obtain three outfits by selecting each of the different blouses, so the total number of outfits is simply three times the number of skirts.

If you are to select one book from a list of five books and a second book from a list of seven books, you can determine the number of selections of the two books by writing the first book from list one with each of the seven books from list two. You will list the seven books five times, one with each of the books from list one, so you will have a list that is $5 \times 7 = 35$ long.

We can list all possible selections in another way using tree diagrams.

TREE DIAGRAMS

Let's look at another problem. Suppose that there are two highways from Spee-gleville to Crawford and three highways from Crawford to McGregor. How many different routes can we choose to go from Speegleville to McGregor through Crawford? A **tree diagram** provides a visual means to list all possible routes (Figure 5–14).

FIGURE 5–14

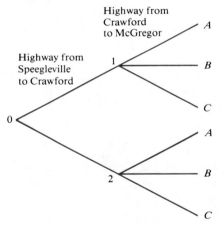

Reading from left to right, starting at 0, draw two branches representing the two highways from Speegleville to Crawford (use 1 and 2 to designate the highways). At the end of each of these two branches, draw three branches representing the three highways from Crawford to McGregor. (Use *A, B,* and *C* to designate the highways). A choice of a first-level branch and a second-level branch determines a route from Speegleville to McGregor. Notice that the total number of possible routes is six because each first-level branch is followed by three second-level branches.

EXAMPLE 1   *(Compare Exercise 1)*

A company has two positions to fill, those of a department manager and an assistant manager. Three people are eligible for the manager position, and four people are eligible for the assistant manager position. Use a tree diagram to show the different ways in which the two positions can be filled.

SOLUTION   Label the candidates for department manager as *A*, *B*, and *C*. Label the candidates for assistant manager as *D*, *E*, *F*, and *G*.

FIGURE 5–15

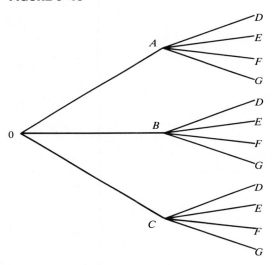

The tree diagram in Figure 5–15 illustrates the 12 possible ways in which the positions can be filled. Reading from left to right, starting at 0, you find three possible "branches" (managers). A branch for each possible assistant manager is attached to the end of each branch representing a manager. In all, 12 paths begin at 0 and go to the end of a branch. For example, the path 0*BD* represents the selection of *B* as the manager and *D* as the assistant manager.

A tree diagram shows all possible ways to make a sequence of selections, and it shows the number of different ways the selections can be made.

The total number of selections is the product of the number of first-level branches and the number of second-level branches, that is, the number of ways in which the first selection can be made times the number of ways in which the second selection can be made.

These three examples are fundamentally the same kind of problem. Let's make a general statement that includes each one.

FUNDAMENTAL COUNTING PRINCIPLE

Suppose that there are two activities, A_1 and A_2. Each activity can be carried out in several ways. Determine in how many different ways the first activity can be performed followed by the second activity.

In the three preceding examples, A_1 and A_2 are the following.

Selections of an outfit: A_1 is the activity of selecting a skirt, and A_2 is the activity of selecting a blouse.

Routes from Speegleville to McGregor: A_1 is the selection of a highway from Speegleville to Crawford, and A_2 is the selection of a highway from Crawford to McGregor.

Filling two positions: A_1 is the selection of a manager, and A_2 is the selection of an assistant manager.

In many cases we do not need a list of all possible selections, but we need their number. In such a case the problem reduces to a question of the number of ways in which we can carry out the activity A_1 followed by the activity A_2. The solution is quite simple: multiply the number of ways in which activity A_1 can be performed by the number of ways in which activity A_2 can be performed. This is often called the **fundamental counting principle.**

Theorem 2
Fundamental Counting Principle

Given two activities, A_1 and A_2, that can be performed in N_1 and N_2 different ways, respectively, the total number of ways in which A_1 followed by A_2 can be performed is

$$N_1 \times N_2$$

EXAMPLE 2   *(Compare Exercise 5)*

A taxpayers' association is to elect a chairman and a secretary. There are four candidates for chairman and five candidates for secretary. In how many different ways can a slate of officers be elected?

SOLUTION   Here, A_1 is the activity of selecting a candidate for chairman, and $N_1 = 4$. A_2 is the activity of selecting a candidate for secretary, and $N_2 = 5$. Therefore $4 \times 5 = 20$ slates can be elected.

EXAMPLE 3   *(Compare Exercise 8)*

The library wishes to display two rare books, one from the history collection and one from the literature collection. If the library has 50 history and 125 literature books to select from, how many different displays are possible?

SOLUTION   The number of displays $= 50 \times 125 = 6250$.

EXAMPLE 4   *(Compare Exercise 13)*

Jane selects one card from a deck of 52 different cards. The first card is *not* replaced before Joe selects the second one. In how many different ways can they select the two cards?

SOLUTION Jane selects from a set of 52 cards, so $N_1 = 52$. Joe selects from the remaining cards, so $N_2 = 51$. Two cards can be drawn in $52 \times 51 = 2652$ ways.

The fundamental counting principle also can be used to apply to several activities.

Corollary Given activities $A_1, A_2, \ldots, A_k$, which can be performed in $N_1, N_2, \ldots, N_k$ different ways, respectively, the number of ways in which one can perform A_1 followed by $A_2 \ldots$ followed by A_k is

$$N_1 \times N_2 \times \cdots \times N_k$$

EXAMPLE 5 *(Compare Exercise 15)*

How many different ways can class officers be selected if there are three candidates for president, four candidates for vice-president, and seven candidates for secretary?

SOLUTION The number of different ways is given by

$$3 \times 4 \times 7 = 84$$

EXAMPLE 6 *(Compare Exercise 19)*

A quiz consists of four multiple-choice questions with five possible responses to each question. In how many different ways can the quiz be answered?

SOLUTION In this case there are four activities, that is, answering each of four questions. Each activity (answering a question) can be performed (choosing a response) in five different ways. The answers can be given in

$$5 \times 5 \times 5 \times 5 = 625$$

different ways.

EXAMPLE 7 *(Compare Exercise 21)*

A university uses nine-digit budget numbers in which the first digit must be a 1 or 2 and each of the following digits is an integer from 0 through 9. How many different budget numbers can be formed?

SOLUTION There are two possibilities for the first digit and ten possibilities for each of the other digits, giving

$$2 \times 10 \times 10 \times 10 \times 10 \times 10 \times 10 \times 10 \times 10$$

different budget numbers.

EXAMPLE 8   *(Compare Exercise 23)*

The digits 0 through 9 are written one per card. Three different cards are drawn, and a three-digit number is formed. How many different three-digit numbers can be formed in this way?

SOLUTION   Since the number is formed from the three cards drawn, the digits must all be different, that is, no repetitions of digits occur in a number. There are ten possibilities for the first digit, then any of the nine remaining digits may be used for the second digit, and finally, the third digit may be any of the remaining eight digits, so

$$10 \times 9 \times 8 = 720$$

different numbers can be formed.

EXAMPLE 9   *(Compare Exercise 31)*

Three couples attend a movie and are seated in a row of six seats. How many different seating arrangements are possible if couples are seated together?

SOLUTION   Think of this as a sequence of six activities, that of assigning a person to sit in each of seats 1 through 6. The fundamental counting principle states that the number of ways in which this can be done is the product of the numbers of ways in which each selection can be made.

> First seat: Any one of the six people may be chosen, so there are six choices.
> Second seat: Only the spouse of the person in the first seat may be chosen, so there is one choice.
> Third seat: One couple is seated, so any one of the remaining four people may be chosen. Thus there are four choices.
> Fourth seat: There is one choice only because it must be the spouse of the person in the third seat.
> Fifth seat: There are two choices because either of the two remaining people may be seated.
> Sixth seat: The one remaining person is the only choice.

By the fundamental counting principle the number of possible arrangements is the product of the number of choices for each seat, $6 \times 1 \times 4 \times 1 \times 2 \times 1 = 48$.

EXAMPLE 10   *(Compare Exercise 35)*

An art gallery has several paintings by each of five artists. A wall has space to hang four paintings in a row. How many different arrangements by artists are possible if:

(a) the paintings are by different artists?
(b) more than one painting by an artist may be displayed but may not be hung next to each other?

SOLUTION   These problems may be viewed as a sequence of four activities, choosing an artist for each of the four spaces. The total number of ways is the product of the number of choices for each space.

(a) Since all artists must be different, there are five choices for the artist in the first space, four for the second, three for the third, and two for the fourth. The number of arrangements is $5 \times 4 \times 3 \times 2 = 120$

(b) There are 5 choices for the first artist. A painting by that artist may not be used in the second space, but a painting by any of the remaining 4 artists may be used. The artist chosen for the second space may not be chosen for the third space, but the artist chosen for the first space may be used. (The first and third paintings are not hung next to each other.) Thus there are four choices for the third space. Likewise, there are four choices for the fourth space. The total number of arrangements is $5 \times 4 \times 4 \times 4 = 320$.

EXAMPLE 11   *(Compare Exercise 37)*

In how many different ways can three science and two history books be arranged on a shelf if books on each subject are kept together?

SOLUTION   First, observe that the subjects can be arranged in two ways, science on the left and history on the right or vice versa.

Next, count the number of ways in which the books can be arranged within the subject arrangements.

Science-history: There are five positions to be filled, science first and history second. The number of possible arrangements is $3 \times 2 \times 1 \times 2 \times 1 = 12$.

History-science: Again there are five positions to be filled, but history books are placed first and science books second. The number of possible arrangements is $2 \times 1 \times 3 \times 2 \times 1 = 12$.

The total number of arrangements from these two cases is $12 + 12 = 24$.

5-3 EXERCISES

I

1. (*See Example 1*) A student has a red tie and a green tie. He has a white shirt, a blue shirt, and a yellow shirt. Draw a tree diagram that shows all possible ways in which a tie and shirt can be selected.

2. Draw a tree diagram to show the different ways in which a boy and then a girl can be selected from the following set of children:

   {Anita, Bobby, Carl, Debbie, Enrique, Flo}

3. Draw a tree diagram showing all sequences of heads and tails in two tosses of a coin.

4. For her breakfast, Susan always selects one item from each of the following:

   orange juice or tomato juice,
   cereal or eggs,
   toast or muffins.

   Draw a tree diagram to show all her possible menus.

5. (*See Example 2*) Each day a teacher has a boy and a girl summarize the assignment for the day. There are 12 boys and 15 girls in class. In how many different ways can the teacher select the two students?

6. A woman has six necklaces and eight pairs of earrings. In how many different ways can she select a necklace and a pair of earrings to wear?

7. A grocery store has five brands of crackers and nine different varieties of cheese. How many different combinations of one brand of cheese and one brand of crackers can a shopper buy?

8. (*See Example 3*) A reading list for American history contains two groups of books. There are 16 books in the first group and 21 in the second. A student is to read 1 book from each group. In how many ways can the choice of books be made?

9. A man has six suits and seven shirts. How many different outfits can he form?

10. A house has four doors and 18 windows. In how many ways can a burglar pass through the house by entering through a window and leaving through a door?

11. The cafeteria has a selection of four meats and seven vegetables. How many different selections of one meat and one vegetable are possible?

12. A traveling salesperson may take one of five different routes from Brent to Centreville and three different routes from Centreville to Moundville. How many different routes are possible from Brent to Moundville through Centreville?

13. (*See Example 4*)
   (a) In how many different ways can a player select a diamond and a club from a deck of 52 bridge cards?
   (b) In how many different ways can a player select one card of each suit from a bridge deck?

14. A manufacturer of disks for microcomputers packs them 10 to a box. If a box contains four defective disks, in how many different ways can one defective and one good disk be selected from the box?

15. (*See Example 5*) A cafeteria offers a selection of two meats, four vegetables, and three desserts. In how many different ways can a diner select a meal of one meat, one vegetable, and one dessert?

16. An interior decorator has a choice of three different carpets, six different wall coverings, and three different upholstery fabrics. How many interiors can she design?

17. A car manufacturer provides six exterior colors, five interior colors, and three different trims. How many different color-trim schemes are available?

18. A builder developing a subdivision may choose from four different roofing subcontractors, five different electrical subcontractors, three different plumbing subcontractors, two different carpenters, and six different painters. In how many ways can he select one of each?

II

19. (*See Example 6*) A quiz consists of six multiple-choice questions with four possible responses to each one. In how many different ways can the quiz be answered?

20. A coin is flipped three times. How many different sequences of heads and tails are possible?

21. (*See Example 7*) A telephone number consists of seven digits. How many phone numbers are possible if the first digit is neither 1 nor 0?

22. How many different radio call letters beginning with K and consisting of four letters can be assigned to radio stations?

23. (*See Example 8*) How many four-digit numbers can be formed from the digits {1, 2, 3, 4, 5}:
   (a) if a digit can be repeated?
   (b) if a digit cannot be repeated?

24. How many different three-digit numbers can be formed from the digits {0, 1, 2, 3, 4, 5}:
   (a) if a digit cannot be repeated?
   (b) if a digit can be repeated?

25. A license plate number consists of three letters followed by three digits.
   (a) How many different license numbers can be formed if repetition of letters and digits is allowed?
   (b) How many different license numbers can be formed if repetition of letters and digits is not allowed?

26. Draw a tree diagram showing all sequences of heads and tails that are possible in three tosses of a coin.

27. Use a tree diagram to show the different ways in which first, second, and third prizes can be awarded to three different contestants, Jones, Allen, and Cooper.

III

28. A three-digit number is formed using digits from {1, 2, 3, 4, 5}.
   (a) How many numbers can be formed using three different digits?
   (b) How many numbers can be formed if digits may be repeated?
   (c) How many even numbers can be formed using three different digits?
   (d) How many even numbers can be formed if digits may be repeated?
   (e) How many multiples of 5 can be formed if digits may be repeated?

29. A child forms three-letter "words" using three different letters from HISTORY. A three-letter "word" is any arrangement of three letters, whether it is in the dictionary or not.
   (a) How many three-letter "words" are possible?
   (b) How many three-letter "words" beginning with H are possible?
   (c) How many three-letter "words" beginning with a vowel are possible?
   (d) How many three-letter "words" with a vowel for the middle letter are possible?
   (e) How many three-letter "words" with exactly one vowel are possible?

30. A child forms three-letter "words" using letters from INVOKED. A letter may be repeated within a "word."
   (a) How many different three-letter "words" are possible?
   (b) How many different three-letter "words" beginning with K are possible?
   (c) How many different three-letter "words" beginning with a vowel are possible?
   (d) How many different three-letter "words" with a vowel for a middle letter are possible?
   (e) How many different three-letter "words" containing exactly one vowel are possible?

31. (*See Example 9*) Four couples attend a play and are seated in a row of eight chairs. How many different arrangements are possible if couples are seated together?

32. In how many different ways can three men and three women be seated in a row if no one sits next to a member of the same sex?

33. In how many different ways can four men and three women be seated in a row if no one sits next to a member of the same sex?

34. In how many different ways can five people be seated in a row if two certain people must be seated together?

35. (*See Example 10*) An art gallery has several paintings by each of six artists. A wall has space to hang four paintings in a row. How many different arrangements by artists are possible if:
   (a) the paintings are by different artists?
   (b) more than one painting by an artist may be displayed but they may not be hung next to each other?

36. Jones starts a chain letter by sending letters to ten people the first week. The second week, each person who received a letter sends ten letters to other people. This continues each week. Assume that no one receives two letters.
   (a) How many people receive letters the second week?
   (b) How many people receive letters the third week?
   (c) How many people receive letters the fourth week?

37. (*See Example 11*) In how many different ways can five art and three music books be arranged on a shelf if books on the same subject are kept together?

38. A portion of a test contains six multiple-choice questions. If for each question a student may leave the answer blank or select one of the four answers given, in how many different ways can the student respond to the questions?

39. A customer who orders a hamburger at the Burger Place has the choice of "with or without" for each of the following: lettuce, tomato, onion, catsup, mustard, mayonnaise, and cheese. In how many different ways can a hamburger be ordered?

40. A group of 12 people likes to share rumors with one another. One person calls another, that person calls another, and so on. A person can pass the rumor on to anyone in the group except the one who just called.
   (a) How many paths can the rumor take in three calls if the individuals involved are all different? (*Note:* Three calls will involve four people, one to start the rumor and three to receive calls.)
   (b) How many paths can the rumor take in three calls if the individuals involved need not be different?
   (c) How many paths can the rumor take if the person who starts the rumor receives the third call?

41. In a group of 750 people, at least two have the same first and last initials. Explain why this is true.

42. Each parent has two genes for a given trait, AA, Aa, or aa. A child will inherit one gene from each parent. Draw a tree diagram to show the possibilities for a child if one parent has AA and the other has Aa.

43. The Panthers and Lions baseball teams play a championship series. The first team to win two games (best two out of three) is the winner. Use a tree diagram to show the possible outcomes of the series.

44. A Boy Scout troop hikes from the mall to their camping area at Hilltop Farm. They have three possible routes from the mall to the farm; the highway access road, a gravel road, or through a subdivision. At the farm they can continue to the camping area by way of a trail through the woods, a lane across the pasture, or along a stream. Show all possible routes from the mall to their camping area with a tree diagram.

5–4 PERMUTATIONS

- *Permutations*
- *Notation for Number of Permutations*
- *Permutations of Objects with Some Alike*

PERMUTATIONS

The fundamental counting principle is but one of a number of counting techniques, so we will look at some others. The first of these deals with **permutations.** We illustrate this type of counting technique with the following example.

EXAMPLE 1 *(Compare Exercise 17)*

A jewelry store has a collection of five silver service sets. It plans to display them three at a time, arranged in a row of display windows. How many different arrangements are possible?

SOLUTION   First, we point out that there are two ways to obtain different arrangements:

(a) One or more silver service sets may be replaced by another that is not in the display.

(b) The location of two or more of the silver service sets on display may be exchanged.

This problem may be viewed as a fundamental counting problem with three activities.

Activity 1: Select a silver service for the first location. This can be done in five ways because any of the five sets can be selected.

Activity 2: Select a silver service for the second location. This can be done in four ways because any one of the four remaining sets can be selected.

Activity 3: Select a silver service for the third location. This can be done in three ways because two sets are already displayed and any one of the three remaining can be selected.

Therefore there are $5 \times 4 \times 3$ possible arrangements.

This example has three characteristics that determine a permutation.

Permutations	1. A permutation is an arrangement of elements from a single set.
	2. Repetitions are not allowed.
	3. The order in which the elements are arranged is significant.

The statement "order is significant" may be interpreted in a number of ways. Order is significant in situations such as the following:

(a) Different positions are to be filled, and the exchange of objects in two positions is considered a different way to fill the positions.
(b) Objects are arranged in a row or in specified locations.
(c) People are selected to fill different offices in an organization. (Each office is a position.)
(d) Prizes are given for first place, second place, and so on. (Each prize is a position.)
(e) Items are distributed among several people. (Each person may be considered a position.)

EXAMPLE 2 *(Compare Exercise 21)*

Ten students each submit one essay for competition. In how many ways can first, second, and third prizes be awarded?

SOLUTION This is a permutation problem because:

1. each essay selected is from the same set;
2. no essay can be submitted more than once; that is, an essay cannot be awarded two prizes (no repetition);
3. the order (prize given) of the essays is important.

Any of the ten essays may be chosen for first prize. Then any of the remaining nine may be chosen for the second prize, and any of the other eight may be chosen for third prize. According to the fundamental counting principle, the three prizes may be awarded in

$$10 \times 9 \times 8 = 720$$

different ways.

EXAMPLE 3   *(Compare Exercise 25)*

In how many different ways can a penny, a nickel, a dime, and a quarter be given to four children if one coin is given to each child?

SOLUTION   Each child may be considered a "position" that receives a coin. The number of ways a coin may be given to each child is:

First child: four possibilities of a coin
Second child: three possibilities of a coin
Third child: two possibilities of a coin
Fourth child: one possibility of a coin

Therefore the coins may be distributed in

$$4 \times 3 \times 2 \times 1 = 24$$

different ways.

EXAMPLE 4   *(Compare Exercise 29)*

At the Cumberland River Festival, four Cumberland "belles" are stationed at historic Fort House; one stands at the entrance, one in the living room, one in the dining room, and one on the back veranda. If there are ten Cumberland belles, in how many different ways can four be selected for stations?

SOLUTION   This is a permutation, since a woman can be selected for, at most, one station, and the order (place stationed) is significant. The permutation can be made in

$$10 \times 9 \times 8 \times 7 = 5040$$

different ways.

If the problem in Example 4 had been to select four belles to be present in the living room with no particular station for each one, then Example 4 would not have been a permutation problem, since the belles would not be arranged in any particular order. (The number of selections in this case uses a technique that we will discuss later.)

NOTATION FOR NUMBER OF PERMUTATIONS

The notation commonly used to represent the number of permutations for a set is written like $P(8, 3)$, which is read "permutation of eight things taken three at a time." This notation represents the number of permutations of three elements from a set of eight elements. $P(10, 4)$ represents the number of permutations of four elements selected from a set of ten elements. ($P(5, 3)$ is the answer to Example 1, and $P(10, 4)$ is the answer to Example 4.)

We want you to understand the pattern for calculating numbers like $P(10, 4)$ so that you can do it routinely. Let's look at some examples.

$P(10, 4) = 10 \times 9 \times 8 \times 7$ permutations of four elements taken from a set of ten elements.

$P(5, 3) = 5 \times 4 \times 3$

$P(7, 2) = 7 \times 6$ permutations of two elements selected from a set of seven elements.

$P(21, 3) = 21 \times 20 \times 19$

In each case the calculation begins with the first number in the parentheses, 21 in $P(21, 3)$ and 7 in $P(7, 2)$. The second number in $P(21, 3)$, $P(7, 2)$, and so on determines the number of terms in the product. Since the terms decrease by one to the next term, you need to know only the first term and how many are needed to calculate the answer.

This reasoning lets us know that $P(30, 5)$ is a product of five terms beginning with 30, each term thereafter decreasing by one, so

$$P(30, 5) = 30 \times 29 \times 28 \times 27 \times 26$$
$$P(105, 4) = 105 \times 104 \times 103 \times 102$$

and

$$P(4, 4) = 4 \times 3 \times 2 \times 1$$

Can you give the last term in $P(52, 14)$ without writing out all the terms? The preceding examples give a pattern that helps. The last term of

$P(5, 3)$ is $5 - 2 = 3$	(Also written $5 - 3 + 1$)
$P(10, 4)$ is $10 - 3 = 7$	(Also written $10 - 4 + 1$)
$P(105, 4)$ is $105 - 3 = 102$	(Also written $105 - 4 + 1$)

so we expect the last term of

$P(52, 14)$ to be $52 - 13 = 39$	(Also written $52 - 14 + 1$)

The numbers in parentheses above are another way of calculating the last terms. That form is more useful in calculating the general case.

In general, $P(n, k)$ indicates the number of arrangements that can be formed by selecting k elements from a set of n elements. Following the observed pattern, it may be written

$$P(n, k) = n(n - 1)(n - 2) \cdots (n - k + 1)$$

There is a special notation for the case when a permutation uses all elements of a set. Notice that $P(4, 4)$ is just the product of the integers 4 through 1— $4 \times 3 \times 2 \times 1$. In general, $P(n, n)$ is the product of the integers n through 1. The following notation is used.

Definition 3	The product of the integers n through one is denoted by $n!$ (called n
$n!$	**factorial**).

$$n! = n(n-1)(n-2) \times \cdots \times 2 \times 1$$

EXAMPLE 5   *(Compare Exercise 1)*

$$7! = 7 \times 6 \times 5 \times 4 \times 3 \times 2 \times 1$$
$$2! = 2 \times 1$$
$$6! = 6 \times 5 \times 4 \times 3 \times 2 \times 1$$

Notice that $6! = 6 \times 5!$ and $4! = 4 \times 3!$, and so on.

$$1! = 1$$

$0!$ is defined to be 1

Arithmetic involving factorials can be carried out easily if you are careful to use the factorial as defined.

$$\frac{5!}{3!} = \frac{5 \times 4 \times 3 \times 2 \times 1}{3 \times 2 \times 1}$$
$$= 5 \times 4$$
$$= 20$$
$$3!\, 4! = 3 \times 2 \times 1 \times 4 \times 3 \times 2 \times 1 = 144$$

EXAMPLE 6   *(Compare Exercise 33)*

How many different ways can six people be seated in a row of six chairs?

SOLUTION   This is a permutation with six positions to be filled from a set of six, so the number of arrangements is

$$P(6, 6) = 6! = 6 \times 5 \times 4 \times 3 \times 2 \times 1 = 720$$

Factorials allow us to write the expression for the number of permutations in another form that is sometimes useful. For example,

$$P(8, 3) = 8 \times 7 \times 6$$
$$= \frac{8 \times 7 \times 6 \times 5!}{5!}$$

Since $8 \times 7 \times 6 \times 5! = 8 \times 7 \times 6 \times 5 \times 4 \times 3 \times 2 \times 1 = 8!$, we can write

$$P(8, 3) = \frac{8!}{5!}$$

Be sure you understand that

$$P(6, 4) = \frac{6!}{2!} \qquad (2! \text{ came from } (6 - 4)!)$$

In general, we can write

$$P(n, k) = \frac{n!}{(n - k)!}$$

EXAMPLE 7 *(Compare Exercise 37)*

Many auto license plates have three letters followed by three digits. How many different license plates are possible if

(a) letters and digits are not repeated on a license plate?
(b) repetitions of letters and digits are allowed?

SOLUTION

(a) First of all, this is a fundamental counting problem with two activities. The first activity is the selection and arrangement of letters; the second activity is the selection and arrangement of digits. The number of license plates is found by multiplying the number of selections of letters and the number of selections of digits. The selection of letters is a permutation, $P(26, 3)$ in number, and the selection of digits is a permutation, $P(10, 3)$ in number. The number of license plates is then $P(26, 3) \times P(10, 3) = 15{,}600 \times 720 = 11{,}232{,}000$.

(b) This is not a permutation, since a letter or digit may appear more than once on a license plate. This is a fundamental counting problem with six activities, the selection of three letters followed by the selection of three digits. This can be done in $26 \times 26 \times 26 \times 10 \times 10 \times 10 = 17{,}576{,}000$ ways.

PERMUTATIONS OF OBJECTS WITH SOME ALIKE

So far the permutation problems have involved objects that are all different. Sometimes we arrange objects when some are alike. For example, we may ask for all arrangements of the letters of the word AGREE. Generally, we have said that we can arrange five objects in $P(5, 5) = 5! = 120$ ways. However, when we interchange the two E's in a word, we obtain the same word. Each time we "spell" a word, the E's are placed in certain positions. We can arrange the E's in those positions in 2! ways and still have the same "word." Therefore the number of different "words" (arrangements) is 120/2!.

For example, in the word EAGER we can think of the two E's as E_1 and E_2 to distinguish them momentarily. One spelling is E_1AGE_2R, and another is E_2AGE_1R. The number of "different" spellings that give the same words depends on the number of arrangements of the identical letters. In this case the two E's can be arranged in 2! ways. In general, k identical objects can be arranged in $k!$ ways that leave the overall arrangement unchanged.

EXAMPLE 8   *(Compare Exercise 41)*

How many different words can be formed using all the letters of DEEPEN?

SOLUTION   Because three of the six letters (E's) are identical, the number of permutations is $\dfrac{6!}{3!} = 120$

Theorem **Permutation of** **Identical Objects**	**(a)** The number of permutations of n objects with r of the objects identical is $\dfrac{n!}{r!}$. **(b)** If a set of n objects contains k subsets of objects in which the objects in each subset are identical and objects in different subsets are not identical, the number of different permutations of all n objects is $$\frac{n!}{r_1!r_2! \cdots r_k!}$$ where r_1 is the number of identical objects in the first subset, r_2 is the number of identical objects in the second subset, and so on.

Part (b) of the theorem tells how to compute the number of permutations when there are two or more categories of identical objects.

EXAMPLE 9   *(Compare Exercise 45)*

In how many ways can the letters of REARRANGE be permuted?

SOLUTION   There are nine letters with three R's, two A's, and two E's. The number of permutations is

$$\frac{9!}{3!2!2!} = \frac{9 \cdot 8 \cdot 7 \cdot 6 \cdot 5 \cdot 4 \cdot 3 \cdot 2 \cdot 1}{3 \cdot 2 \cdot 1 \cdot 2 \cdot 1 \cdot 2 \cdot 1} = 15,120$$

EXAMPLE 10   *(Compare Exercise 47)*

A coin is tossed five times, giving a sequence of heads and tails. How many sequences of three heads and two tails are possible?

SOLUTION   This is equivalent to finding the permutations of three H's and two T's. This is

$$\frac{5!}{3!2!} = 10$$

EXAMPLE 11 *(Compare Exercise 49)*

Basketball teams X and Y are in a playoff. The team that wins three out of a possible five games is the winner. Denote the sequence of winners by a sequence of letters such as XXYYY. This indicates that X won the first two games and Y won the last three. How many different sequences are possible if X wins the playoff?

SOLUTION This is equivalent to arranging sequences of three X's and two Y's. This can be done in

$$\frac{5!}{3!2!} = 10$$

different ways.

5–4 EXERCISES

I

Perform the computations in Exercises 1 through 15.

1. *(See Example 5)* 3!
2. 7!
3. 5!
4. 3!2!
5. 5!3!
6. $\dfrac{5!}{6!}$
7. $\dfrac{7!}{3!}$
8. $\dfrac{10!}{4!6!}$
9. $\dfrac{12!}{7!}$
10. $P(12, 3)$
11. $P(6, 4)$
12. $P(6, 2)$
13. $P(100, 3)$
14. $P(5, 5)$
15. $P(7, 4)$
16. The number of permutations of eight objects taken three at a time.

II

17. *(See Example 1)* An artist selects three paintings from a collection of six to display in a row. How many different arrangements of the display are possible?

18. How many arrangements of three people seated along one side of a table are possible if there are eight people to select from?

19. The program committee of a music festival must arrange five numbers for an evening performance. Seven numbers are available. How many different arrangements of the evening performance are possible?

20. Five people are to be seated in a row. How many different arrangements of all five people are possible?

21. *(See Example 2)* Eight fellows are candidates for Mr. Ugly. In how many different ways can first, second, and third places be awarded?

22. In how many ways can five essays be ranked in a contest?

23. Seven paintings are exhibited by art students.
    (a) An art appreciation class is asked to rank the paintings 1 through 7. How many different rankings are possible?
    (b) If the students are asked to rank only the top three, how many rankings are possible?

24. Six runners are competing in a 100-meter race. In how many different ways can runners finish in first, second, and third place?

25. (*See Example 3*) A father bought three different gifts. In how many different ways can he give one to each of his three children?

26. The bookstore gives four different books, one to each of four students. In how many different ways can this be done?

27. Three different door prizes are given at a club meeting at which 22 people are present. A person may receive at most one prize. In how many different ways can the prizes be awarded?

28. Three women are selected from the audience of a style show to receive a purse, a pair of gloves, and a scarf. If 30 women are present, in how many different ways may the gifts be given?

29. (*See Example 4*) There are four Pizza Places in Lorena, and the management must assign a manager to each place.
    (a) If four people are available, in how many ways can they be assigned?
    (b) If seven people are available, in how many ways can a manager be assigned?

30. An organization is to select a president and a vice-president from a group of five people. Find the total number of selections possible.

31. Seven firms are competing for three different contracts. In how many ways can the contracts be awarded if no firm gets more than one contract?

32. In how many ways can a president, a vice-president, and a secretary be selected from an organization of 32 members?

33. (*See Example 6*) In how many ways can five people be seated in a row of five chairs?

34. Six horses are running in a race. In how many different orders can the horses finish?

35. How many different "words" can be made using all the letters of MATH? A "word" is any arrangement of letters, not just arrangements that give words in a dictionary.

36. In how many ways can five children line up in a row to have their picture taken?

37. (*See Example 7*) How many three-digit numbers can be formed using the digits from {2, 4, 6, 8} if:
    (a) repetitions are not allowed?
    (b) repetitions are allowed?

38. A music teacher selects four boys and five girls to sing at a PTA meeting. The children stand in a row with the boys on the left and the girls on the right. How many such arrangements of children are possible if the teacher can select from seven boys and nine girls?

39. A voice teacher selects 9 students from the class to sing for the trustees. The class has 11 men and 12 women. In how many ways can nine students be selected and arranged in a row with five men in the middle and two women on each end?

40. A club has 25 members and 12 pledges. A president, vice-president, and secretary are selected from the members, and a pledge chairman and pledge vice-chairman are selected from the pledges. In how many ways can these five officers be selected?

41. (*See Example 8*) How many different "words" are possible using all letters of POSSIBLE?

42. How many different "words" are possible using all the letters of POPPER?

43. How many different color arrangements are possible by placing three green balls, one red ball, one yellow ball, and one tan ball in a row?

44. How many different "words" can be formed using all letters of FALLEN?

45. (*See Example 9*) How many different "words" are possible using all the letters of
    (a) MISSOURI   (b) MISSISSIPPI
    (c) BOOKKEEPER   (d) REARRANGED

46. How many color arrangements are possible by placing four red balls, three green balls, and two yellow balls in a row?

47. (*See Example 10*) A coin is tossed seven times:
    (a) How many sequences of four heads and three tails are possible?
    (b) How many sequences of five heads and two tails are possible?

48. Codes to identify entries in a computer file are formed by using sequences of four zeros and six ones. How many such sequences are possible?

49. (*See Example 11*) Teams A and B play in the World Series. The team that wins four of seven games is the winner.
    (a) How many sequences of games are possible if A wins the series?
    (b) How many sequences of games are possible if B wins the series?
    (c) How many different sequences of games are possible?

50. A student did not study for a test, so he has no idea of the correct answers to ten true–false questions. He decides to answer five true and five false. How many sequences of five true and five false answers are possible?

51. Ten students apply for the position of grader in mathematics. One grader is to be assigned to each of four teachers. In how many different ways can the teachers be assigned a grader if no student grades for two teachers?

52. Three children go to the ice cream store that serves 31 flavors. In how many different ways can the children be served one dip of ice cream each:
    (a) if each child receives a different flavor?
    (b) if the same flavor can be served to more than one child?

53. A recreation center has 28 video games. Mia has time to play three. In how many different orders can she play three different games?

54. How many four-digit numbers can be formed using the digits 1 through 9 if no digit can appear twice in a number?

III

55. Write out the following as expressions in n:
    (a) $P(n, 2)$ (b) $P(n, 3)$
    (c) $P(n, 1)$ (d) $P(n, 5)$

56. If $P(7, k) = 210$, what is k?

57. A password to a computer consists of five characters: a letter, a digit, a letter, a digit, and a letter in that order, where the numbers from 1 through 9 are allowed for digits. How many different passwords are possible?

58. Three pairs of shoes are displayed in a row.
    (a) In how many ways can the six shoes be arranged with no restriction on their positions?
    (b) In how many ways can the shoes be arranged if mates must be kept together but mates can be placed in either order?
    (c) In how many ways can the shoes be arranged if mates must be kept together and left and right mates are placed in order, left shoe then right?

59. Fifteen students are competing for four Rotary scholarships, one in England, one in Germany, one in Brazil, and one in Japan. In how many ways can the scholarships be awarded to different students?

60. The Student Foundation has 120 members, of whom 80 are seniors, 25 are juniors, and 15 are sophomores. They select a Publicity Chair, a Financial Chair, a Solicitation Chair, and a Coordinator. The Coordinator and Solicitation Chair must be seniors, and the Publicity Chair and Financial Chair must be juniors. In how many different ways can the officers be selected?

61. The permutation of objects arranged in a circle differs from arrangements in a line because there is no first or last position in a circle. To compute permutations of circular arrangements, fix one object in the circle as the start and arrange the others. Then the number of permutations of n objects arranged in a circle is $(n - 1)!$.
    (a) In how many ways can six people be seated around a circular table?
    (b) In how many ways can ten children stand in a circle?
    (c) In how many ways can five different jewels be arranged on a necklace?

62. At a family reunion, three adult males, three adult females, and four children line up for their picture to be taken.

(a) In how many different ways can they be arranged in a row?

(b) In how many ways can they be arranged in a row if the adult males are together, the adult females are together, and the children are together?

63. Use the grids shown at right. In each case, find the number of paths from *A* to *B* traveling along grid lines. At any given intersection you may proceed only to the right (R) or down (D). (*Hint:* A path is a sequence of R's and D's.)

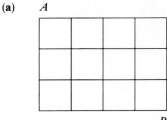

(a)

(b)

5–5 COMBINATIONS

- *Combinations*
- *Problems Involving More Than One Counting Technique*
- *Special Cases*

COMBINATIONS

When you pay your bill at the Pizza Place, the cashier is interested in the collection of coins and bills you give her, not the order in which you present them. When you are asked to answer six out of eight test questions, the collection of questions is important, not the arrangement. Therefore if the professor wishes to compute the number of different ways in which students can choose six questions from eight, she is not dealing with permutations. She wants the number of ways in which a subset of six elements can be obtained.

> *Definition 1*
> **Combination**
> A subset of elements chosen from a given set without regard to their arrangement is called a **combination.**

The notation $C(n, k)$, read "combinations of *n* things taken *k* at a time," represents the number of subsets consisting of *k* elements taken from a set of *n* elements.

$C(8, 3)$ denotes the number of ways in which three elements can be selected from a set of eight. $C(52, 6)$ denotes the number of ways in which six elements can be selected from a set of 52.

The keys to recognizing a combination are given in the following box.

Combinations	**1.** A combination selects elements from a single set.
	2. Repetitions are not allowed.
	3. The order in which the elements are arranged is *not* significant.

Notice that a combination differs from a permutation only in that order is not significant in a combination, whereas it is important in a permutation.

EXAMPLE 1

Given the set $A = \{a, b, c, d, e, f\}$, the subset $\{b, d, f\}$ is a combination of three elements taken from a set of six elements.

Since the elements of the subset $\{b, d, f\}$ can be arranged in several ways, we expect there to be several permutations for each subset. This indicates that you should expect more permutations than combinations in a given set.

EXAMPLE 2   *(Compare Exercise 9)*

List all combinations of two elements taken from the set $\{a, b, c\}$.

SOLUTION   Because of the small number of elements involved, it is rather easy to list all subsets consisting of two elements. They are $\{a, b\}$, $\{a, c\}$, and $\{b, c\}$. Therefore $C(3, 2) = 3$.

It is much more difficult to list all five element subsets from a set of 26 elements. If we are interested only in the number of such subsets, not their listing, the problem becomes easier. Let's look at an example that illustrates how we can determine the number of combinations.

EXAMPLE 3

Let's determine $C(6, 3)$, the number of different ways in which we can select a subset of three elements from a set of six elements. Let's look at the subset $\{a, b, c\}$. From the material on permutations you know that we can arrange these three elements from one combination in $3! = 6$ different ways. They are

$$abc, \quad acb, \quad bac, \quad bca, \quad cab, \quad \text{and} \quad cba$$

Each of these six permutations is made of the same set of three elements; that is, they are made from the same **combination** of elements. In fact, if you take any combination of three elements, they can be arranged in 3! different ways (permutations). This gives us a relationship between combinations and permutations. Since each combination of three elements can be arranged in 3! ways, we can obtain all permutations by taking the elements from a combination and finding all six arrangements of those three elements. Therefore

$$P(6, 3) = 3!C(6, 3)$$

Be sure you understand this relationship. To obtain all permutations of three elements, you first select one combination of those three elements and form all permutations of those elements. Then select a combination of three other elements and form all permutations. Each time you select a combination of three elements, you can form 3! permutations.

By dividing both sides of

$$P(6, 3) = 3!C(6, 3)$$

by 3! we get

$$C(6, 3) = \frac{P(6, 3)}{3!}$$

Similarly,

$$C(12, 4) = \frac{P(12, 4)}{4!}$$

$$C(5, 2) = \frac{P(5, 2)}{2!}$$

$$C(101, 14) = \frac{P(101, 14)}{14!}$$

In general we have the following theorem.

Theorem 1 $P(n, k) = k!\, C(n, k)$

or $C(n, k) = \dfrac{P(n, k)}{k!}$

Because $P(n, k)$ can be written as

$$\frac{n!}{(n - k)!}$$

$C(n, k)$ can also be written as

$$\frac{n!}{k!(n - k)!}$$

We now have a convenient way of calculating the number of combinations.

EXAMPLE 4 *(Compare Exercise 1)*

$$C(5, 2) = \frac{P(5, 2)}{2!} = \frac{5 \times 4}{2 \times 1} = 10$$

$$C(5, 3) = \frac{P(5, 3)}{3!} = \frac{5 \times 4 \times 3}{3 \times 2 \times 1} = 10$$

$$C(10, 3) = \frac{P(10, 3)}{3!} = \frac{10 \times 9 \times 8}{3 \times 2 \times 1} = 120$$

$$C(30, 4) = \frac{P(30, 4)}{4!} = \frac{30 \times 29 \times 28 \times 27}{4 \times 3 \times 2 \times 1}$$

$$= 27,405$$

$$C(8, 6) = \frac{8!}{6!2!} = 28$$

$$C(15, 3) = \frac{15!}{3!12!}$$

EXAMPLE 5 *(Compare Exercise 13)*

A student has seven books on his desk. In how many different ways can he select a set of three?

SOLUTION Since the order is not important, this is a combination problem:

$$C(7, 3) = \frac{P(7, 3)}{3!} = \frac{7 \times 6 \times 5}{3 \times 2 \times 1} = 35$$

EXAMPLE 6 *(Compare Exercise 17)*

(a) In how many ways can a committee of four be selected from a group of ten people?

(b) In how many ways can a slate of officers consisting of a president, vice-president, and secretary be selected from a group of ten people?

SOLUTION

(a) The order of selection is not important in the selection of a committee, so this is a combination problem of taking four elements from a set of ten:

$$C(10, 4) = \frac{P(10, 4)}{4!} = 210$$

(b) In selecting a slate of officers, President Jones, Vice-President Smith, and Secretary Allen is a different slate than President Allen, Vice-President Smith, and Secretary Jones. Each office is a position to be filled, so order is significant. The number of slates is $P(10, 3)$.

Notice the pattern used in computing combinations. To compute $C(10, 4)$, begin with 10 and write four integers in decreasing order. Then divide by 4!. This is true in general. To compute $C(15, 5)$, form the numerator using the five integers beginning with 15 and decreasing by 1. The denominator is 5!. In general, we can write $C(n, k)$ by forming the numerator from the product of k integers that begin with n and decrease by 1. The denominator is $k!$.

PROBLEMS INVOLVING MORE THAN ONE COUNTING TECHNIQUE

The solution to a problem may involve more than one counting technique. Often the first level is fundamental counting with two or more activities involved. To count the number of ways in which each of these activities can occur may require permutations, combinations, or fundamental counting again. The examples that follow involve more than one counting technique.

EXAMPLE 7   *(Compare Exercise 19)*

A cafeteria offers a selection of four meats, six vegetables, and five desserts. In how many ways can you select a meal consisting of two different meats, three different vegetables, and two different desserts?

SOLUTION   Basically, this is a problem that can be solved by using the fundamental counting principle. We obtain the possible number of meals by multiplying the number of ways in which you can select two meats, the number of ways in which you can select three vegetables, and the number of ways in which you can select two desserts.

Each of the numbers of ways in which you can select meats, vegetables, and desserts forms a combination problem. Therefore we obtain the number of meals as

$$(\text{number of meat selections}) \times (\text{number of vegetable selections})$$
$$\times (\text{number of dessert selections}) = C(4, 2) \times C(6, 3) \times C(5, 2)$$
$$= \frac{4 \times 3}{2 \times 1} \times \frac{6 \times 5 \times 4}{3 \times 2 \times 1} \times \frac{5 \times 4}{2 \times 1}$$
$$= 6 \times 20 \times 10 = 1200$$

EXAMPLE 8   *(Compare Exercise 21)*

A club has 14 male and 16 female members. A committee composed of three men and three women is formed. In how many ways can this be done?

SOLUTION   The male members can be chosen in

$$C(14, 3) = \frac{14 \times 13 \times 12}{3 \times 2 \times 1} = 364$$

different ways. The female members can be chosen in

$$C(16, 3) = \frac{16 \times 15 \times 14}{3 \times 2 \times 1} = 560$$

different ways. By the fundamental counting principle the committee can be chosen in $364 \times 560 = 203,840$ ways.

∎

Instead of counting the number of outcomes for a sequence of activities, some counting problems seek the number of possible outcomes when the outcome selected is from one activity *or* another.

EXAMPLE 9

How many different committees can be selected from eight men and ten women if a committee is composed of three men *or* three women?

SOLUTION   For a moment, think of listing all possible selections of a committee. The list has two parts, a list of committees composed of three women and a list of committees composed of three men. The total number of possible committees can be obtained by adding the number of all-female to the number of all-male committees. We get each of these by the following:

$$\begin{aligned}
\text{Number of all-female committees} &= C(10, 3) = 120 \\
\text{Number of all-male committees} &= C(8, 3) \; = \underline{\; 56} \\
\text{Total number of committees} &\qquad\qquad\; = 176
\end{aligned}$$

Do not confuse this problem with the number of ways in which a committee of three men *and* a committee of three women can be chosen. That calls for the selection of a *pair* of committees. This example calls for the selection of *one* committee.

∎

EXAMPLE 10   *(Compare Exercise 27)*

One freshman, three sophomores, four juniors, and six seniors apply for five positions on an Honor Council. If the council must have at least two seniors, in how many different ways can the council be selected?

SOLUTION   The council has at least two seniors when it has two, three, four, or five seniors. We must compute the number of councils possible with two, with three, and so on, and add:

2 seniors and 3 others: $C(6, 2) \times C(8, 3) = 15 \times 56 = 840$
3 seniors and 2 others: $C(6, 3) \times C(8, 2) = 20 \times 28 = 560$
4 seniors and 1 other: $C(6, 4) \times C(8, 1) = 15 \times 8 = 120$
5 seniors: $C(6, 5) = 6$

The total is $840 + 560 + 120 + 6 = 1526$.

∎

EXAMPLE 11   *(Compare Exercise 31)*

A manufacturing firm forms a six-person advisory committee. The committee is composed of a chair, vice-chair, and secretary from the administrative staff and three members from the plant workers. Seven members from the administrative staff and eight plant workers are eligible for the committee positions. In how many different ways can the committee be formed?

SOLUTION   At the first level this is a fundamental counting problem because two activities are involved: selecting officers from the administrative staff and selecting committee members from the plant workers. We compute the number of ways in which each can occur and then we multiply. The selection of officers is a permutation because repetitions are not allowed (a person may not hold two offices) and the different offices impose an order. The number of slates of officers is $P(7, 3)$. The selection of committee members from the plant workers is a combination because no distinction is made between those positions, and repetitions are not allowed. The number of selections is $C(8, 3)$.

The total number of ways in which the administrative committee can be selected is $P(7, 3) \times C(8, 3) = 11,760$.

SPECIAL CASES

The other form,

$$C(n, k) = \frac{n!}{(n - k)!k!}$$

is also a useful form. Let's use it to look at some special cases.

1. In how many ways can one element be selected from a set? $C(6, 1)$ is the number of ways one element can be selected from a set of six. It is

$$C(6, 1) = \frac{6!}{1!5!} = \frac{6 \cdot 5!}{1!5!} = 6$$

In general,

$$C(n, 1) = \frac{n!}{1!(n - 1)!}$$

$$= \frac{n(n - 1)!}{1!(n - 1)!} = n$$

So one item can be selected from a set of n items in n ways.

2. In how many ways can zero items be selected from a set? We write $C(6, 0)$ to represent the number of ways in which no elements can be selected from a set of six. The formula gives

$$C(6, 0) = \frac{6!}{0!6!}$$

Since $0! = 1$, this reduces to $C(6, 0) = 1$. In general,

$$C(n, 0) = \frac{n!}{0!n!} = 1$$

Does your intuition tell you that there is just one way to select zero elements from a set? The one way is to take none.

3. In how many ways can all the elements be selected from a set? Our intuition tells us there is just one way, namely, take all of them. The formula agrees.

$$C(6, 6) = \frac{6!}{6!0!} = 1$$

and

$$C(n, n) = \frac{n!}{n!0!} = 1$$

4. For positive integers, n, $P(n, 1) = n$, so when one element is selected from a set, the number of permutations equals the number of combinations, n.

5–5 EXERCISES

I

Perform the computations in Exercises 1 through 7.

1. (*See Example 4*)
   $C(6, 2)$

2. $C(4, 3)$

3. $C(13, 3)$

4. $C(9, 4)$

5. $C(9, 5)$

6. $C(20, 3)$

7. $C(4, 4)$

8. Verify the following.
   (a) $C(7, 3) = C(7, 4)$ (b) $C(7, 2) = C(7, 5)$
   (c) $C(6, 4) = C(6, 2)$ (d) $C(9, 6) = C(9, 3)$
   (e) $C(8, 3) = C(8, 5)$
   These are examples of a general fact that $C(n, k) = C(n, n - k)$.

9. (*See Example 2*) List all combinations of two different elements taken from $\{a, b, c, d\}$.

10. List all combinations of three different elements taken from $\{$Tom, Dick, Harriet, Jane$\}$.

11. List all combinations of four elements taken from $\{a, b, c, d, e\}$.

12. List all combinations of two elements taken from $\{$penny, nickel, dime, quarter$\}$.

II

13. (*See Example 5*) The Pizza Place must hire two employees from six applicants. In how many ways can this be done?

14. Students are to answer four out of five exam questions. In how many different ways can the questions be selected?

15. A Boy Scout troop has 15 members. In how many different ways can the scoutmaster appoint three members to clean up camp?

16. Blackhawk Tech gives four presidential scholarships. If there are 50 nominees, in how many ways can the scholarships be awarded?

17. (*See Example 6*)
    (a) In how many ways can a committee of four be selected from a group of seven people?
    (b) In how many ways can a slate of officers consisting of a chair, vice-chair, secretary, and treasurer be selected from a group of seven people?

18. An executive hires three office workers from six applicants.
    (a) In how many ways can the selection be made?
    (b) In how many ways can the selection be made if one worker is to be a receptionist, one a secretary, and one a technical typist?

19. (*See Example 7*) A cafeteria offers a selection of five meats, six vegetables, and eight desserts. In how many ways can you select a meal of two different meats, three different vegetables, and two different desserts?

20. From a set of seven math books, nine science books, and five literature books, in how many ways can a student select two from each set?

21. (*See Example 8*) A company must hire three truck drivers and four clerks. There are six applicants for truck driver and ten for clerk. In how many ways can the seven employees be chosen?

22. A candy manufacturer makes five kinds of brown chocolate candies and three kinds of white chocolate candies. A sample package contains two kinds of brown and two kinds of white chocolate candies. How many different sample packages can be prepared?

23. (*See Example 9*) How many different committees can be formed from a group of nine women and eleven men if a committee is composed of three women or three men?

24. A child has three pennies, five nickels, and four dimes. In how many ways can two coins of the same denomination be selected?

25. A couple is considering the purchases of three paintings for their home. Their decorator advises that the selection be made from a collection of seven landscapes or from a collection of six historical paintings. In how many different ways can they select three paintings from one collection or the other?

26. A desk holder contains eight pens and five pencils. In how many ways can four pens or four pencils be selected?

III

27. (*See Example 10*) A committee of five is selected from five men and six women. How many committees are possible if there must be at least three men on the committee?

28. Five freshmen, four sophomores, and two juniors are present at a meeting of students.
    (a) In how many ways can a six-member committee of three freshmen, two sophomores, and one junior be formed?
    (b) In how many ways can a committee be selected with no more than two freshmen members?

29. An English reading list has eight American novels and six English novels. A student must read four from the list, and at least two must be American novels. In how many different ways can the four books be selected?

30. A professor assigns five students to work on a project. The group is to have no more than one freshman. In how many ways can the group be selected if there are five freshmen and ten sophomores in the class?

31. (*See Example 11*) A club has 40 members and 10 pledges. The club selects an executive committee composed of a chair and vice-chair, who must be members, and an advisory committee of three pledges. In how many ways can the executive committee be formed?

32. A scout troop has 22 members. The scoutmaster appoints a five-member campout crew composed of a leader, a cook, and a cleanup crew (three scouts). How many different campout crews are possible?

33. A Presidential Task Force is selected from eight executives and twelve staff positions. The task force has a chair and secretary chosen from the executives and four members chosen from the staff positions. In how many different ways can the task force be selected?

34. The Chamber of Commerce forms a five-person committee to attract industry to the city. The committee consists of an arrangements chair and a spokesperson from the Chamber office and three people from the business community. If four people from the Chamber office and seven people from business volunteer, in how many ways can the committee be formed?

35. In how many different ways can you select three different letters from the word HISTORY?

36. In how many ways can three aces be selected from a bridge deck?

37. A teacher has a collection of 20 questions. How many different tests of five questions each can be made from the set of questions?

38. In how many ways can one select three different letters from the word HISTORY and two different letters from the word ENGLISH?

39. A set contains four people. Denote it by $A = \{$Alice, Bianca, Cal, Dewayne$\}$.
    (a) List all subsets of one person each.
    (b) List all subsets of two people.
    (c) List all subsets of three people.
    (d) List all subsets of four people.
    (e) List all subsets containing no people.
    (f) Find the total number of subsets.
    (*Note:* You should obtain a total of 2^4. In general, a set of n elements has 2^n subsets.)

40. From a penny, a nickel, a dime, a quarter, a half dollar, how many sums of money can be formed:
    (a) using three coins?
    (b) using four coins?

41. In how many ways can a five-card hand containing exactly two queens and three kings be dealt from a 52-card bridge deck?

42. A quiz team of five children is to be selected from a class of 25 children. There are 15 girls and 10 boys in the class.
    (a) How many teams, made up of three girls and two boys, can be selected?
    (b) How many teams can be selected with at least three girls?

43. A test consists of ten true–false and eight multiple-choice questions.
    (a) In how many ways can a student select six true–false and five multiple-choice questions to answer?
    (b) In how many ways can a student select ten questions, at least six of which are multiple-choice?

44. A club has nine seniors, 16 juniors, 14 sophomores, and ten freshmen. In how many ways can two representatives be selected if the selection must be composed of a senior and a freshman or a junior and a sophomore?

45. From a set of five light fiction, six biography, and four science books, in how many ways can a student select two of the same kind of books?

46. A literature class is given a reading list of 12 short stories, seven by twentieth century authors and five by nineteenth century authors. Students are required to read eight of the 12 stories.
    (a) In how many ways can the selections be made?
    (b) How many ways can the selections be made if they are to read three nineteenth century authors and five twentieth century authors?

5–6 PARTITIONS (OPTIONAL)

- *Ordered Partitions*
- *Number of Ordered Partitions*
- *Special Case: Partition into Two Subsets*
- *Unordered Partitions*
- *Number of Unordered Partitions*

In this section we discuss an idea called the **partitioning** of a set. We want to determine the number of ways in which a set can be partitioned. We will look at two kinds of partitions, **ordered** and **unordered** partitions. Let's begin with an example to lead us into the ideas.

EXAMPLE 1   *(Compare Exercise 9)*

A group of 15 students is to be divided into three groups to be transported to a game. The three vehicles will carry four, five, and six students, respectively. In how many different ways can the three groups be formed?

SOLUTION   Select the four students that ride in the first vehicle. This can be done in

$$C(15, 4) = \frac{15!}{4!11!}$$

different ways. (Notice the form we use for $C(15, 4)$. It is more useful in this case.) After this selection, five students may be selected for the second vehicle in

$$C(11, 5) = \frac{11!}{5!6!}$$

different ways. (There are 11 students left after the first vehicle is filled.) There are six students left for the last vehicle, and they can be chosen in

$$C(6, 6) = \frac{6!}{6!0!}$$

different ways.

By the fundamental counting principle the total number of different ways is

$$C(15, 4) \times C(11, 5) \times C(6, 6) = \frac{15!}{4!11!} \times \frac{11!}{5!6!} \times \frac{6!}{6!0!}$$

$$= \frac{15!}{4!5!6!} = 630,630$$

This partition problem has the following properties that make it a partition.

1. The set is divided into disjoint subsets (no two subsets intersect).
2. Each member of the set is in one of the subsets.

The following is a more formal definition of a partition.

Definition 1 Partition	A set S is **partitioned** into k nonempty subsets $A_1, A_2, \ldots, A_k$ if:
	1. Every pair of subsets is disjoint: that is, $A_i \cap A_j = \emptyset$ when $i \neq j$.
	2. $A_1 \cup A_2 \cup \cdots \cup A_k = S$.

ORDERED PARTITIONS

We first discuss ordered partitions.

Definition Ordered Partition	A partition is **ordered** if different subsets of the partition have characteristics that distinguish one from the other.

The characteristics that distinguish subsets may vary widely. For example, one subset may be males, another females; one subset may be A students, another C students; one subset is awarded a million dollar contract, another a \$1000 contract; one subset is the first team, another the second team, another the third team; one subset contains ten elements, another eight elements.

NUMBER OF ORDERED PARTITIONS

We now determine the number of ways in which a set can be partitioned.

From Example 1 we see that the number of ways in which a set of 15 elements can be partitioned into subsets of four, five, and six elements may be expressed as

$$\frac{15!}{4!5!6!}$$

A commonly used notation for this quantity is

$$\binom{15}{4,\ 5,\ 6}$$

This is generalized in the following theorem.

Theorem 1 Ordered Partitions	A set with n elements can be partitioned into k ordered subsets of $r_1, r_2, \ldots, r_k$ elements $(r_1 + r_2 + r_k = n)$ in the following number of ways:
	$$\binom{n}{r_1,\ r_2,\ \ldots,\ r_k} = \frac{n!}{r_1!r_2!\ldots r_k!}$$

EXAMPLE 2   *(Compare Exercise 11)*

A set of 12 people ($n = 12$) can be divided into three groups of three, four, and five (r_1, r_2, and r_3) in

$$\binom{12}{3,\,4,\,5} = \frac{12!}{3!4!5!} = 27{,}720$$

different ways.

EXAMPLE 3   *(Compare Exercise 15)*

The United Way Allocations Committee has 14 members. In how many ways can they be divided into the following subcommittees so that no member serves on two subcommittees?

Scouting subcommittee: two members

Salvation Army subcommittee: four members

Health Services subcommittee: five members

Summer Recreational Program subcommittee: three members

SOLUTION   The subcommittees form a partition, since no one is on two subcommittees and all 14 members are used. The partitions are ordered for two reasons: The subcommittees are of different sizes, and they have different functions. The number of partitions is

$$\binom{14}{2,\,4,\,5,\,3} = \frac{14!}{2!4!5!3!} = 2{,}522{,}520$$

EXAMPLE 4   *(Compare Exercise 19)*

A college basketball squad has 15 players. In how many ways can the coach form a first, second, and third team of five players each?

SOLUTION   This is an ordered partition because there is a distinction between teams. The number of partitions is

$$\binom{15}{5,\,5,\,5} = \frac{15!}{5!5!5!} = 756{,}756$$

SPECIAL CASE: PARTITION INTO TWO SUBSETS

Let's look at a special case of partitions. Suppose a set of eight objects is partitioned into two subsets of three and five objects. The formula for partitions gives

$$\binom{8}{3,\,5} = \frac{8!}{3!5!}$$

Notice that the formula for $C(8, 3)$ and $C(8, 5)$ both give

$$C(8, 3) = \frac{8!}{5!3!} = C(8, 5)$$

so the number of partitions into two subsets is just the number of ways in which a subset of one size can be selected. This result occurs because when one subset of three objects is selected, the remaining five objects automatically form the other subset in the partition.

In general the following is true.

> The number of partitions of a set into two ordered subsets is the number of ways in which one of the subsets can be formed.

UNORDERED PARTITIONS

We now look at partitions that are not ordered.

Definition
Unordered Partition

A partition is **unordered** when no distinction is made between subsets.

For a partition to be unordered, all subsets must be the same size; otherwise, the different sizes would distinguish between subsets. When a teacher partitions a class into four equal groups, all groups working on the same problem, an **unordered partition** has been formed. If the four equal groups work on different problems, the partition is **ordered.** If eight members of a traveling squad are paired to room together on the trip, an unordered partition is formed. If the pairs are assigned to rooms 516, 517, 518, and 519, an ordered partition is formed.

NUMBER OF UNORDERED PARTITIONS

A basketball squad of 15 members can be divided into first, second, and third teams of five players each in $\frac{15!}{5!5!5!}$ ways. Because a distinction is made between teams, this is an ordered partition. We ask in how many ways an unordered partition can be made; that is, no distinction is made between teams. We can find the number by relating the number of ordered and unordered partitions.

First, divide the 15 players into three teams of five each with no distinction made between teams. Call these teams A, B, and C. These teams can be ordered into first, second, and third teams in six ways: ABC, ACB, BAC, BCA, CAB, and CBA. You recognize this as the 3! permutations of the three groups. In general, the ordered partitions can be obtained by forming three groups (an unordered partition) and then arranging them in 3! ways. If we let N be the number of unordered partitions, then

$$3!N = \text{number of ordered partitions} = \binom{15}{5, 5, 5}$$

This gives

$$N = \frac{1}{3!} \begin{pmatrix} 15 \\ 5, 5, 5 \end{pmatrix} = \frac{15!}{3!5!5!5!}$$

This generalizes to the following theorem.

Theorem 2   A set of n elements can be partitioned into k **unordered subsets** of r elements each $(kr = n)$ in the following number of ways:

$$\frac{1}{k!} \begin{pmatrix} n \\ r, r, r \end{pmatrix} = \frac{n!}{k!r!r! \ldots r!} = \frac{n!}{k!(r!)^k}$$

EXAMPLE 5   *(Compare Exercise 23)*

A set of 12 elements can be partitioned into three unordered subsets of four each in

$$\frac{12!}{3!4!4!4!} = 5775 \text{ ways}$$

Here is an example of partitioning a set when no distinction is made between some subsets and a distinction is made between others.

EXAMPLE 6   *(Compare Exercise 27)*

Find the number of partitions of a set of 12 elements into subsets of three, three, four, and two elements. No distinction is to be made between subsets except for their size.

SOLUTION   Because the two subsets of three elements are the same size, no distinction is made between them. Because they are of different sizes, a distinction is made between subsets of size 2 and 4 (or 2 and 3). The number of ordered partitions is $\frac{12!}{3!3!4!2!}$. The number of unordered partitions is found by dividing by 2! because two sets (of size 3) are indistinct. Thus there are $\frac{12!}{2!3!3!4!2!}$ unordered partitions.

EXAMPLE 7   *(Compare Exercise 31)*

Find the number of unordered partitions of a set of 23 elements that is partitioned into two subsets of four elements and three sets of five elements.

SOLUTION Since there are two indistinct subsets of four elements and three indistinct subsets of five elements, we divide the number of *unordered* subsets by 2! and 3! to obtain $\dfrac{23!}{2!3!4!4!5!5!5!}$.

⎯⎯⎯⎯▌

In general the number of unordered partitions is given by the following theorem.

Theorem 3   A set of *n* elements is partitioned into unordered subsets with *k* subsets of *r* elements each and *j* subsets of *t* each ($kr + jt = n$). The number of such partition is

$$\frac{\text{number of ordered partitions}}{k!j!} = \frac{n!}{k!j!(r!)^k(t!)^j}$$

5-6 EXERCISES

I

Perform the computations in Exercises 1 through 8.

1. $\dbinom{12}{3,\,3,\,3,\,3}$

2. $\dbinom{8}{2,\,2,\,4}$

3. $\dbinom{7}{3,\,4}$

4. $\dbinom{10}{4,\,6}$

5. $\dbinom{9}{2,\,3,\,4}$

6. $\dbinom{8}{4,\,4}$

7. $\dbinom{6}{2,\,4}$

8. $\dbinom{7}{2,\,2,\,2,\,1}$

II

9. (*See Example 1*) In how many ways can a lab instructor assign nine students so that three perform experiment A, three perform experiment B, and three perform experiment C?

10. In how many ways can a set of nine objects be divided into subsets of two, three, and four objects?

11. (*See Example 2*) In how many ways can 14 people be divided into three groups of three, five, and six?

12. In how many ways can 16 different books be divided into stacks of four, five, and seven books?

13. An accounting instructor separates her 18 students into three groups of six each. Each group is assigned a different problem. In how many ways can the class be divided into these groups?

14. A store has 12 items to be displayed in three display windows. In how many ways can they be displayed if six are placed in one window, four in the second window, and two in the third window?

15. (*See Example 3*) In how many different ways can a 15-person committee be subdivided into subcommittees having six, four, and five members?

16. The State University football team plays 11 games. In how many ways can they complete the season with four wins, six losses, and one tie?

17. A scholarship committee will award four $5000 scholarships, four $8000 scholarships, and two $10,000 scholarships. Ten students are selected to receive scholarships. In how many ways can the scholarships be awarded?

18. A high school dance committee of 17 members is divided into the following subcommittees

    Decorations: four members
    Music: two members
    Refreshments: three members
    Publicity: five members
    Ticket sales: three members.

    In how many different ways can the subcommittees be assigned?

19. (*See Example 4*) In how many ways can ten players be divided into first and second teams of five members each?

20. In how many different ways can 12 directors of a corporation be divided into four equal groups to discuss new products, sales forecasts, implications of recent legislation, and benefit programs, respectively?

21. A drama class of 18 students is divided into three equal groups to work on costumes, lighting, and backdrops, respectively. In how many ways can this be done?

22. A magazine has 20 articles that need to be evaluated. Four assistant editors are given five articles each to evaluate. In how many ways can this distribution of articles be made?

23. (*See Example 5*) In how many ways can a set of nine elements be partitioned into three unordered subsets of three elements each?

24. In how many ways can a set of eight elements be partitioned into four unordered subsets of two elements each?

25. In how many ways can a set of 12 elements be partitioned into three subsets of equal size?

26. (a) A teacher assigns six students to three groups of two each to work on three different homework problems. Each group has a different problem. In how many ways can this be done?
    (b) A teacher assigns six students to three groups of two each to work on a homework problem. In how many different ways can this be done?

27. (*See Example 6*) Find the number of partitions of a set of 15 elements into subsets of five, five, three, and two elements. No distinction is made between subsets except for their size.

28. Find the number of partitions of a set of 17 elements into subsets of five, five, five, and two elements.

29. An antique shop has 16 dining chairs; no two are alike. They plan to offer them at a reduced price in groups of six, six, and four chairs. In how many ways can the chairs be divided that way?

30. A group of 21 executives is divided into four groups of five, five, five, and six each for a brainstorming session. In how many ways can the division be made? Leave your answer in factorial form.

31. (*See Example 7*) Find the number of unordered partitions of a set of 22 objects that is partitioned into three subsets of two each and four subsets of four each. Leave your answer in factorial form.

32. A bookstore displays 16 different books in groups of three, three, four, two, two, and two books. In how many ways can this be done?

33. A university scholarship committee wishes to award three $5000 scholarships, four $3500 scholarships, and two $8000 scholarships. It selects nine students to receive scholarships. In how many different ways can they be awarded?

III

34. A party of 24 students goes to a restaurant for a study break. They are seated at tables seating two, two, two, four, four, four, and six people. In how many different ways can they be seated? Leave your answer in factorial form.

35. During a mixer for 50 students the students are divided into ten groups of five students each. In how many different ways can this be done? Leave your answer in factorial form.

36. In the game of bridge the deck of cards contains 52 cards. Each of the four players receives 13 cards. In how many different ways can this be done? Leave your answer in factorial form.

IMPORTANT TERMS

5-1
Set
Element of a Set
Set-Builder Notation
Equal Sets
Empty Set
Subset
Union
Intersection
Disjoint Sets

5-2
Universe
Venn Diagram
Complement

5-3
Tree Diagram
Fundamental Counting Principle

5-4
Permutation
Factorial
Permutation with Identical Objects

5-5
Combination

5-6
Partition
Ordered Partition
Unordered Partition

REVIEW EXERCISES

1. Let $A = \{6, 10, 15, 21, 30\}$, $B = \{6, 12, 24, 48\}$, $C = \{x|x$ is an integer divisible by 3$\}$. Identify the following as true or false.
   (a) $21 \in A$ (b) $21 \in B$
   (c) $25 \in C$ (d) $30 \notin A$
   (e) $16 \notin B$ (f) $24 \notin C$
   (g) $6 \in A \cap B \cap C$ (h) $12 \in A \cap B$
   (i) $10 \in A \cup B$ (j) $A \subset B$
   (k) $B \subset C$ (l) $C \subset A$
   (m) $\emptyset \subset B$ (n) $A \subset C$
   (o) A and B are disjoint

2. Let the universe set $U = \{-2, -1, 0, 1, 2, 3, 4\}$, $A = \{-2, 0, 2, 4\}$, $B = \{-2, -1, 1, 2\}$. Find the following.
   (a) A' (b) B' (c) $(A \cap B)'$
   (d) $A' \cap B'$ (e) $A' \cup B'$ (f) $A \cup A'$

3. Which of the following pairs of sets are equal?
   (a) $A = \{x|x$ is a digit in the number 25102351$\}$
       $B = \{x|x$ is a digit in the number 5111023$\}$
   (b) $A = \{x|x$ is a letter in the word PATTERN$\}$
       $B = \{x|x$ is a letter in the word REPEAT$\}$
   (c) $A = \{2, 4, 9, 8\} \cap \{6, 7, 20, 22, 23\}$
       $B = \{x|x$ is a letter in both words STRESS and HAPPY$\}$

4. $n(A) = 27$, $n(B) = 30$, and $n(A \cap B) = 8$. Find $n(A \cup B)$.

5. $n(A \cup B) = 58$, $n(A) = 32$, and $n(B) = 40$. Find $n(A \cap B)$.

6. A and B are sets in a universe U with $n(U) = 42$, $n(A) = 15$, $n(B) = 24$, and $n(A \cup B)' = 8$. Find $n(A \cup B)$ and $n(A \cap B)$.

7. Draw a tree diagram showing the ways in which you can select a meat and then a vegetable from roast, fish, chicken, peas, beans, and squash.

8. The freshman class traditionally guards the school mascot the night before homecoming. There are five key locations where a freshman is posted. Nine freshmen volunteer for the 2:00 A.M. assignment. In how many different ways can they be assigned?

9. How many different license plates can be made using four digits followed by two letters:
   (a) If repetitions of digits and letters are allowed?
   (b) If repetitions are not allowed?

10. A museum has a display case with four display compartments. Eight antique vases are available for display. How many ways can the display be arranged with one vase in each compartment?

11. A medical research team selects five patients at random from a group of 15 patients for special treatment. In how many different ways can the patients be selected?

12. In how many different ways can a medical research team assign 15 patients to three groups of five each?

13. One student representative is selected from each of four clubs. In how many different ways can the four students be selected, given the following number of members in each club: Rodeo Club, 40 members; Kite Club, 27 members; Frisbee Club, 85 members; Canoeing Club, 34 members.

14. In the finale of the University Sing, there are ten people on the first row. Club A has three members on the left end, club B has four members in the center, and Club C has three members on the right end. In how many different ways can the line be arranged?

15. A program consists of four musical numbers and three speeches. In how many ways can the program be arranged so that it begins and ends with a musical number?

16. Students take four exams in Sociology 101. On each exam the possible grades are A, B, C, D, and F. How many sequences of grades can a student receive?

17. An advertising agency designs 11 full-page ads for Uncle Dan's Barbecue. In how many ways can one ad be selected for each of three different magazines:
    (a) if the three ads are different?
    (b) if the ads need not be different?

18. A computer password is composed of six alphabetic characters. How many different passwords are possible?

19. In how many different ways can a chairman, a secretary, and four other committee members be formed from a group of ten people?

20. A club has 12 pledges. On a club work day, four pledges are assigned to the Red Cross, six are assigned to the Salvation Army, and two are not assigned. In how many ways can the groups be selected?

21. Compute
    (a) $P(15, 3)$
    (b) $C(15, 3)$
    (c) $P(101, 2)$
    (d) $P(22, 4)$
    (e) $3!$
    (f) $\dfrac{10!}{3!7!}$
    (g) $\begin{pmatrix} 8 \\ 3, 2, 3 \end{pmatrix}$
    (h) $\begin{pmatrix} 11 \\ 3, 2, 2, 4 \end{pmatrix}$

22. The Venn diagram in Figure 5–16 represents the number of auto mechanic students at State Technical Institute studying diesel engines (D), gasoline engines (G), and automatic transmissions (AT).

FIGURE 5–16

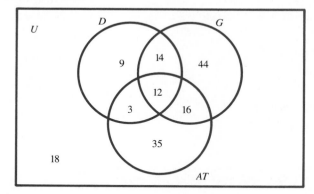

Find:
(a) the number of students studying gasoline engines only.
(b) the number of students studying gasoline and diesel engines.
(c) the number of students studying gasoline engines, diesel engines, and automatic transmissions.
(d) the number of students studying automatic transmissions but not diesel engines.
(e) the number of students studying gasoline engines or automatic transmissions.

23. A survey of 60 people gave the following information:
    25 jog regularly,
    26 ride a bicycle regularly,
    26 swim regularly,
    10 both jog and swim,
    6 both swim and ride a bicycle,
    7 both jog and ride a bicycle,
    1 does all three,
    3 do none of the three.

    Show that there is an error in this information.

24. The bookstore had a sale on records, books, and T-shirts. A cashier observed the purchases of 38 people and found that:

>   16 bought records,
>   15 bought books,
>   19 bought T-shirts,
>   5 bought books and records,
>   7 bought books and T-shirts,
>   6 bought records and T-shirts,
>   3 bought all three.

(a) How many bought records and T-shirts but no books?

(b) How many bought records but no books?

(c) How many bought T-shirts but no books and no records?

(d) How many bought none of the three?

25. A poll was conducted among a group of teenagers to see how many have televisions, radios, and microcomputers. The results were as follows: T denotes television, R denotes radio, and M denotes microcomputer.

ITEM	NUMBER OF TEENAGERS HAVING THIS ITEM
T	39
R	73
M	10
T and R	22
M and R	3
T and M	4
T and R and M	2

Determine the following.

(a) How many had a radio and TV but no microcomputer?

(b) How many had a microcomputer and had no TV?

(c) How many had exactly two of the three items?

26. During the summer, 110 students toured Europe. Their language skills were as follows: 46 spoke German, 56 spoke French, eight spoke Italian, 16 spoke French and German, three spoke French and Italian, two spoke German and Italian, one spoke all three, and 20 spoke none of the three.

(a) How many spoke only French?

(b) How many spoke French or German?

(c) How many spoke French or Italian but not both?

(d) How many spoke none of the languages?

27. A woman has five bracelets, eight necklaces, and seven sets of earrings. In how many ways can she select one of each to wear?

28. The Labor Day Raft Race has 110 entries. In how many ways is it possible to award prizes for the fastest raft, the slowest raft, and the most original raft?

29. From a group of five people, two are to be selected to be delegates to a conference. How many selections are possible?

30. In how many different ways can a group of 15 people select a president, vice-president, and secretary?

31. Twenty people attend a meeting at which three different door prizes are awarded by drawing names.

(a) If a name is drawn and replaced for the next drawing, in how many ways can the door prizes be awarded?

(b) If a name is drawn and not replaced, in how many ways can the door prizes be awarded?

32. A bag contains six white balls, four red balls, and three green balls. In how many ways can a person draw out two white balls, three red balls, and two green balls?

33. An Honor Council consists of four seniors, four juniors, three sophomores, and one freshman. Fifteen seniors, 20 juniors, 25 sophomores, and 11 freshmen apply. In how many ways can the Honor Council be selected? Leave your answer in symbolic form.

34. An art gallery has eight oil paintings and four watercolors. A display of five oil paintings and two watercolors arranged in a row is planned. How many different displays are possible with a watercolor at each end and the oils in the center?

35. A club agrees to provide five students to work at the school carnival. One sells balloons, one sells popcorn, one sells cotton candy, one sells candied apples, and one sells soft drinks. Nine students agree to help. In how many ways can the assignments be made?

36. A professor gives a reading list of six books. A student is to read three. In how many ways can the selection be made?

37. Five students are to be chosen from a high school government class of 22 students to meet the governor when he visits the school. In how many ways can this be done?

38. How many different five-card hands can be obtained from a deck of 52 cards?

39. Compute
    (a) $P(8, 4)$ (b) $C(9, 5)$ (c) $P(7, 7)$
    (d) $C(5, 5)$ (e) $4!$ (f) $\dfrac{7!}{3!4!}$
    (g) $\dfrac{8!}{4!}$

40. One day a machine produced 50 good circuit boards and eight defective ones.
    (a) In how many ways can two defective circuit boards be selected?
    (b) In how many ways can three good circuit boards be selected?
    (c) In how many ways can two defective and three good circuit boards be selected?

41. A club has 80 members of whom 20 are seniors, 15 are juniors, 25 are sophomores, and 20 are freshmen. A chair, vice-chair, secretary, and treasurer are to be selected. The chair and vice-chair must be seniors, the treasurer must be a junior, and the secretary must be a sophomore. How many different slates of officers can be formed?

42. A bookstore has three copies of a Finite Mathematics text, five copies of a Business Calculus text, and two copies of a College Algebra text. In how many different ways can the books be arranged on a shelf?

43. A social organization and a service club held a joint meeting. Of the 83 people present, 46 belonged to the social organization and 51 belonged to the service club. How many belonged to both?

44. The digits $\{2, 3, 4, 5, 6, 7\}$ are used to form three-digit numbers.
    (a) How many can be formed if repetitions are allowed?
    (b) How many can be formed if repetitions are not allowed?
    (c) How many larger than 500 can be formed with repetitions allowed?

45. A department store has ten sportswear outfits for display purposes. In how many ways can a group of four outfits be selected for display?

46. A business has 16 female employees and 14 male employees. How many different advisory committees consisting of two males and two females are possible?

47. List all the subsets of $\{$red, white, blue$\}$.

48. A panel of four is selected from eight businessmen and seated in a row behind a table. In how many different orders can they be seated?

49. A club has ten freshmen and eight sophomore members. At a club picnic the cook and entertainment leader are freshmen, and the cleanup crew consists of three sophomores. In how many different ways can these five be selected?

50. Draw a tree diagram showing the ways a girl and then a boy can be selected from Carlos, Betty, Darla, Gary, and Natasha.

51. A student is allowed to check out four books from the reserve room. All the books must come from one collection of six books or from another collection of eight books. In how many different ways can the selection be made?

52. Three married couples are seated in a row. How many different seating arrangements are possible:
    (a) if there is no restriction of seating order?
    (b) if the men sit together and the women sit together?
    (c) if a husband and wife sit together?

53. How many different words are possible using all the letters of:
    (a) RELAX?   (b) PUPPY?   (c) OFFICIAL?

54. In how many different ways can seven chairs be arranged in a circle?

55. Find the number of unordered partitions of 18 objects into subsets of three, three, six, and six objects.

56. Nine students are to be divided into three groups of three each to work on a math problem. In how many ways can this be done:
    (a) if each group has the same problem?
    (b) if each group has a different problem?

57. Twelve students are divided into four groups of three each. Two groups are to work on Problem 15 and two groups are to work on Problem 18. In how many ways can this be done?

58. Fifteen children are going to pick up aluminum cans along the roadway. In how many ways can they be divided into groups of three, three, four, and five children?

6
Probability

6–1 INTRODUCTION TO PROBABILITY

- *Terminology*
- *Probability Assignment*
- *Empirical Probability*

*W*HEN THE WEATHERMAN PREDICTS the weather, when a coach evaluates the team's chances of winning, or when a businessman projects the success of the big clearance sale, an element of uncertainty exists. The weatherman knows he is often wrong, the coach knows there is no such thing as a sure win, and the businessman knows the best advertised sale sometimes flops. Often in our daily lives we would like to measure the likelihood of an outcome of an event or activity. An area of mathematics known as **probability theory** provides a measure of the likelihood of the outcome of phenomena and events. The government uses it to determine fiscal and economic policies, theoretical physicists use it to understand the nature of atomic-sized systems in quantum mechanics, and public-opinion polls, such as the Harris Poll, have their theoretical acceptability based on probability theory.

The theory of probability is said to have originated from the following gambling question. Two gamblers are playing for a stake that goes to the player who first wins a specified number of points. The game is interrupted before either player has won enough points to win the stake. (We don't know whether the game was raided.) The question is to determine a fair division of the stakes based on the number of points won by each player at the time of the interruption.

This problem was mentioned from time to time in the mathematical literature for a period of 150 years but received no widespread attention until it was proposed to the French mathematician Blaise Pascal about 1654. Pascal communicated the problem to another French mathematician, Pierre Fermat, who also became quite interested in it. The two mathematicians arrived at the same answer by different methods. Their discussions aroused quite a bit of interest in that type of problem. Pascal and Fermat are generally considered the founders of probability theory.

Probability turned out to have applications far beyond interrupted gambling games. J. C. Maxwell used probability theory to derive his famous gas laws in 1860. Edmund Halley, the first astronomer to predict the return of a comet, applied probability to actuarial science in 1693. Today, insurance companies depend on probability to determine competitive and profitable rates for their policies. Quality control in manufacturing and product development decisions are based on probability. The military uses it in the theory of search for enemy submarines. We will learn some elementary applications in this chapter.

TERMINOLOGY

In order to discuss and use probability theory we need to understand some terminology used: **experiment, trials, outcomes, sample space,** and **event.**

Definition 1
Experiment, Outcome, Trial

An activity or phenomenon that is under consideration is called an **experiment.** The experiment can produce a variety of results, called **outcomes.** We study activities that can be repeated or phenomena that can be observed a number of times. We call each observation or repetition of the experiment a **trial.**

EXAMPLE 1

(a) Predicting the weather is an experiment with "fair," "cooler," "warmer," "snow," "rain," and so on as possible outcomes. Each prediction is a trial.

(b) Drawing a number out of a hat is an experiment with the number drawn as an outcome. Each draw of a number is a trial.

(c) Tossing a coin is an experiment with "heads" and "tails" as possible outcomes. A trial occurs each time the coin is tossed.

(d) A test to determine the germination of flower seeds is an experiment with "germinated" and "not germinated" as possible outcomes. Each test conducted is a trial.

In general, experiments involve chance or random results. This means that the outcomes do not occur in a set pattern but vary depending on impartial chance, and the outcome cannot be determined in advance. The selection of a card from a well-shuffled deck, the order in which leaves fall off a tree, and the number of cars that pass a checkpoint on the freeway are examples of experiments that have random outcomes.

An experiment need not classify outcomes in a unique way. It depends on how the results are interpreted. When a multiple-choice test of 100 questions is given, the instructor wants to know the number of correct answers given by each student. For this purpose an outcome can be any of the numbers 0 through 100. When the tests are returned to the students, they tend to ask, "What is an A?" They are interested in the outcomes A, B, C, D, and F. Then there might be the student who only asks, "What is passing?" To that student there are just two outcomes of interest, pass and fail.

When asked "What is today?" a person may respond in several ways, such as "It is April 1," "It is Friday," "It is payday," or any one of numerous responses. Depending on the focus of the individual, the set of possible responses may be all the days in a year; all the days of the week; or the two outcomes payday and not payday.

Since the outcomes of an experiment can be classified in a variety of ways, it is important that everyone understand which set of outcomes is used. We call the set of outcomes used a **sample space.**

Definition 2
Sample Space

A **sample space** is the set of all possible outcomes of an experiment. Each element of the sample space is called a **sample point** or **simple outcome.**

EXAMPLE 2   *(Compare Exercise 1)*

(a) If the experiment is tossing a coin, the sample space is {heads, tails}.

(b) If the experiment is drawing a card from a bridge deck, one sample space is the set of 52 cards.

(c) If the experiment is drawing a number from the numbers 1 through 10, the sample space can be {1, 2, 3, 4, 5, 6, 7, 8, 9, 10}. If the numbers are drawn to randomly divide ten people into two groups, the set {even, odd} is an appropriate sample space.

(d) If the experiment is tossing a coin twice, a sample space is {HH, HT, TH, TT}.

We do not insist on just one correct sample space for an experiment because the situation dictates how to interpret the results. However, we do insist that a sample space conform to two properties.

Properties of a Sample Space

Let S be the sample space of an experiment.

1. Each element in the set S is an outcome of the experiment.
2. Each outcome of the experiment corresponds to exactly one element in S.

If a student is selected from a group of university students, and the class standing of the student is the outcome of interest, then {freshman, sophomore, junior, senior} is a valid sample space. If the sex of the student is the outcome of interest, then {male, female} is a valid sample space. You can form other sample spaces using age, GPA, and so on as the outcomes of interest.

In some instances our interest lies in a collection of outcomes in the sample space, not just one outcome. If I toss a coin twice, I may be interested in the likelihood that the coin will land with the same face up both times. I am interested in the subset of outcomes {HH, TT}, not just one of the possible outcomes. We call such a collection of simple outcomes an **event.**

Definition 3
Event

An **event** is a subset of a sample space.
An event can be a subset with a single outcome, so a simple outcome is a special case of an event.

EXAMPLE 3

(a) In the experiment of drawing a number from the numbers 1 through 10 the sample space is

$$S = \{1, 2, 3, 4, 5, 6, 7, 8, 9, 10\}$$

The event of drawing an odd number is the subset {1, 3, 5, 7, 9}. The event of drawing an even number is the subset {2, 4, 6, 8, 10}. The event of drawing a prime number is the subset {2, 3, 5, 7}.

(b) A teacher selects one student from a group of six students. The sample space is {Scott, Jane, Mary, Kaye, Ray, Randy}. The event of selecting a student with first initial R is {Ray, Randy}. The event of selecting a student with first initial J is {Jane}. The event of selecting a student with first initial A is the empty set.

An Event Occurs   We say that an *event occurs* when any of the simple outcomes of the event occurs.

PROBABILITY ASSIGNMENT

How do we measure the likelihood of an event? What is the likelihood of getting a prime number when selecting a number from the set 1 through 10? How does that compare to the likelihood of getting an even number? We call the measure of the likelihood of an event the **probability** of the event. The probability of an event is a number assigned to that event. We use 0 for the probability that an event cannot occur (like the probability of a coin standing on edge), and use 1 for the probability of an event that is bound to occur (such as the probability of the sun rising in the east). Other probabilities range from 0 to 1. A larger number indicates a higher likelihood of the event occurring. If we call an event E, we designate the probability of the event by $P(E)$ (called "P of E").

There is no single, predetermined way of assigning probability. It depends on the situation, the features that we want to emphasize, and the features that we consider unimportant. However, we use some standard properties of probability to assign probabilities to the outcomes in any sample space.

Properties of Probability   Let a sample space be $S = \{e_1, e_2, \ldots, e_n\}$.

1. Each outcome in the sample space, e_i, is assigned a probability denoted by $P(e_i)$.
2. Each probability is a number that is not negative and is no larger than 1 ($0 \leq P(e_i) \leq 1$).
3. If an event E is a set of simple outcomes, then $P(E)$ is the sum of the probabilities of all simple outcomes that make up the event, for example, $P(\{e_1, e_2, e_3\}) = P(e_1) + P(e_2) + P(e_3)$.
4. The sum of probabilities of all the simple outcomes in a sample space is 1, that is, $P(e_1) + P(e_2) + \cdots + P(e_n) = 1$.

EXAMPLE 4   *(Compare Exercise 3)*

(a) If an experiment has five possible outcomes, and we assign the following probabilities to the outcomes:

$$P_1 = .20, \quad P_2 = .10, \quad P_3 = .15, \quad P_4 = .30, \quad P_5 = .25$$

we have a valid probability assignment because:
1. Each outcome is assigned a probability.
2. Each probability is nonnegative and not larger than 1.
3. The sum of all the probabilities is 1.

(b) Suppose we assign the following probabilities to a five-point sample space:

$$P_1 = .2, \quad P_2 = .2, \quad P_3 = .3, \quad P_4 = .25, \quad P_5 = .4$$

This is not a valid probability assignment because the sum of all probabilities is 1.35.

(c) The assignment of probabilities

$$P_1 = .3, \quad P_2 = -.1, \quad P_3 = .2, \quad P_4 = .3, \quad P_5 = .3$$

is not valid because a negative probability is assigned.

EXAMPLE 5   *(Compare Exercise 5)*

The sample space of an experiment is $\{A, B, C, D\}$, where $P(A) = .35$, $P(B) = .15$, $P(C) = .22$, $P(D) = .28$.

$$P(\{A, B\}) = .35 + .15 = .50$$
$$P(\{A, C\}) = .35 + .22 = .57$$
$$P(\{B, C, D\}) = .15 + .22 + .28 = .65$$
$$P(\{A, B, C, D\}) = .35 + .15 + .22 + .28 = 1.00$$

EXAMPLE 6   *(Compare Exercise 9)*

A bag contains six balls that are colored red, white, or blue. There are heavy balls and light balls. The experiment is to draw one ball from the bag. Assign individual probabilities according to the following table:

	RED	WHITE	BLUE
Heavy	.05	.15	.23
Light	.10	.17	.30

(a) The probability of drawing a heavy blue ball is .23. Using the $P(E)$ notation, this is written $P(\text{heavy blue}) = .23$.

(b) What is the probability of drawing a white ball? Here the event is the subset {heavy white, light white}. We are interested in the probability that the ball drawn is in that subset. According to the third probability property, the probability of drawing a white ball is .15 + .17 = .32, the sum of the probabilities of the individual outcomes making up the event.

In a similar fashion we obtain the probability of the following events:

(c) The probability of drawing a light ball is

$$.10 + .17 + .30 = .57 \; (P(\text{light}) = .57)$$

(d) The probability of drawing a heavy red ball or a light blue ball is .05 + .30 = .35.

(e) The probability of drawing a ball that is not blue is

$$.05 + .15 + .10 + .17 = .47$$

$(P(\text{not blue}) = .47)$.

EXAMPLE 7 *(Compare Exercise 11)*

A football coach responds to a question about the team's chances of winning the big game with the following statement: "The probability of winning is twice that of losing, and the probability of a tie is half that of losing." Find the probability of each outcome: win, lose, or tie.

SOLUTION   Let x = probability of losing. Then $P(\text{win}) = 2x$ and $P(\text{tie}) = 0.5x$. Since these probabilities must add to 1, we have

$$x + 2x + 0.5x = 1$$
$$3.5x = 1$$

so

$$x = \frac{1}{3.5} = .286 \quad \text{(rounded)}$$

From this we have $P(\text{win}) = .572$, $P(\text{lose}) = .286$, and $P(\text{tie}) = .143$. (Because we rounded to three decimal places, these add to 1.001.)

Two Important Special Cases

1. If an event is the empty set, the probability that an outcome is in the event is zero, that is, $P(\emptyset) = 0$.
2. If an event is the entire sample space, then $E = S$ and $P(E) = P(S) = 1$.

EMPIRICAL PROBABILITY

Probabilities may be assigned by observing a number of trials and using the frequency of outcomes to estimate probability. For example, the operator of a concession stand at a park keeps a record of the kinds of drinks children buy. Her records show the following:

DRINK	FREQUENCY
Cola	150
Lemonade	275
Fruit juice	75
	500

To estimate the probability that a child will buy a certain kind of drink, we compute the **relative frequency** of each drink. We do this by dividing the frequency of each drink by the total number of drinks.

DRINK	FREQUENCY	RELATIVE FREQUENCY
Cola	150	$\frac{150}{500} = .30$
Lemonade	275	$\frac{275}{500} = .55$
Fruit juice	$\frac{75}{500}$	$\frac{75}{500} = .15$

Notice that the relative frequency has all the properties of a probability assignment, so we use it to estimate probability. The probability that a child will buy lemonade is .55, $P(\text{cola}) = .30$, and $P(\text{fruit juice}) = .15$. We call probability based on relative frequency **empirical probability.**

EXAMPLE 8 *(Compare Exercise 15)*

A college has an enrollment of 1210 students. The number in each class is as shown in the following table:

CLASS	NUMBER OF STUDENTS
Freshman	420
Sophomore	315
Junior	260
Senior	215
	1210

A student is selected at random. Estimate the probability that the student is:

(a) a freshman,
(b) a sophomore,
(c) a junior,
(d) a senior.

SOLUTION Estimate the probability of each as the relative frequency.

CLASS	NUMBER OF STUDENTS	RELATIVE FREQUENCY
Freshman	420	$\dfrac{420}{1210} = .35$
Sophomore	315	$\dfrac{315}{1210} = .26$
Junior	260	$\dfrac{260}{1210} = .21$
Senior	215	$\dfrac{215}{1210} = .18$

This gives $P(\text{freshman}) = .35$, $P(\text{sophomore}) = .26$, $P(\text{junior}) = .21$, and $P(\text{senior}) = 18$.

6-1 EXERCISES

I

1. (*See Example 2*) Give a sample space for each of the following experiments:
   (a) Answering a true-false question
   (b) Selecting a letter at random from the English alphabet
   (c) Tossing a single die (six-sided)
   (d) Tossing a coin three times
   (e) Selecting a day of the week
   (f) Predicting the outcome of a football game between Grand Canyon College and Bosque College (Give two different ways in which you could describe the outcome of a game, that is, give two sample spaces.)
   (g) The grade received in a course (Give two ways in which the space might be formed.)
   (h) Selecting two students from {Susan, Leah, Dana, Julie}.
   (i) Selecting a day from the month of January (Give two ways in which the sample space can be formed.)

   (j) Selecting a person from a speech class (Give two sample spaces.)

2. Consider the experiment of tossing a coin. Give the sample space and list all the events associated with this experiment. Indicate the simple events.

3. (*See Example 4*) Which of the following probability assignments are valid? Give reasons for your answer.
   (a) Sample space = {A, B, C, D}
       $P(A) = .3$, $P(B) = .2$, $P(C) = .1$, $P(D) = .4$
   (b) Sample space = {A, B, C}
       $P(A) = .4$, $P(B) = 0$, $P(C) = .6$
   (c) Sample space = {Tom, Dick, Harry}
       $P(\text{Tom}) = .35$, $P(\text{Dick}) = .40$, $P(\text{Harry}) = .20$
   (d) Sample space = {2, 4, 6, 8, 10}
       $P(2) = .2$, $P(4) = .3$, $P(6) = .25$, $P(8) = .25$, $P(10) = .15$

(e) Sample space = $\{A, B, C, D, E\}$

$$P(A) = \frac{1}{5}, P(B) = \frac{1}{5}, P(C) = \frac{1}{5},$$

$$P(D) = \frac{1}{5}, P(E) = \frac{1}{5}$$

(f) Sample space = $\{$Oklahoma, Utah, Maine, Alabama$\}$

$P($Oklahoma$) = .3$, $P($Utah$) = -.4$, $P($Maine$) = .5$, $P($Alabama$) = .6$

(g) Sample space = $\{$True, False$\}$

$P($True$) = 1$, $P($False$) = 0$

(h) Sample space = $\{$Yes, No, Maybe$\}$

$P($Yes$) = .8$, $P($No$) = .3$, $P($Maybe$) = 1.1$

(i) Sample space = $\{$True, False$\}$

$P($True$) = 0$, $P($False$) = 0$

4. Sample space = $\{A, B, C, D\}$

$P(A) = .12$, $P(B) = .26$, $P(C) = .34$

Find $P(D)$.

5. (*See Example 5*) The sample space of an experiment is $\{A, B, C, D\}$, where $P(A) = .1$, $P(B) = .2$, $P(C) = .3$, and $P(D) = .4$.

(a) Find $P(\{A, B\})$. ·
(b) Find $P(\{B, D\})$.
(c) Find $P(\{A, C, D\})$.
(d) Find $P(\{A, B, C, D\})$.

6. For the sample space $\{A, B, C\}$ the points A and B are assigned probabilities $P(A) = .2$ and $P(B) = .4$. What is $P(C)$?

7. The sample space of an experiment is $\{$Ford, Saab, VW, Plymouth, Honda$\}$, where $P($Ford$) = .05$, $P($Saab$) = .18$, $P($Plymouth$) = .30$, $P($VW$) = .10$, and $P($Honda$) = .37$.

(a) Find $P(\{$VW, Honda$\})$.
(b) Find $P(\{$Ford, Saab, Plymouth$\})$.

8. For the sample space $\{w, x, y, z\}$, $P(x) = .25$, $P(y) = .15$, $P\{w, y\} = .65$, and $P\{x, z\} = .35$. Find $P(w)$ and $P(z)$.

9. (*See Example 6*) A sales table is piled with a jumble of sweaters. The sweaters are wool, dacron, or dacron-wool, and their sizes are small, medium, or large. For a random selection the probability of each kind of sweater (material and size) being selected is given in the following table:

	SMALL	MEDIUM	LARGE
Wool	.05	.10	.06
Dacron	.12	.15	.09
Dacron-wool	.11	.18	.14

A sweater is selected at random. Find the probability that it is:

(a) wool.
(b) medium.
(c) wool or dacron-wool.
(d) small or medium dacron.

II

10. A student is to be selected from a group of six students. For each classification of freshman and sophomore there is a math major, an art major, and a biology major. The probability of each individual being selected is given in the following table:

	MATH	ART	BIOLOGY
Freshman	.10	.08	.17
Sophomore	.22	.30	.13

(a) Find the probability that a freshman is selected.
(b) Find the probability that an art major is chosen.
(c) Find the probability that a freshman math major or a sophomore biology major is chosen.

11. (*See Example 7*) A sample space has four simple outcomes, A, B, C, and D. Find the probability of each if $P(A) = 2 P(D)$, $P(B) = 3 P(D)$, and $P(C) = 4 P(D)$.

12. A sample space of an experiment is $\{A, B, C\}$. Find the probability of each simple outcome if $P(A) = P(B)$ and $P(C) = 2 P(A)$.

13. The sample space of an experiment is $\{A, B, C\}$, where $P(A) + P(B) = .75$, $P(B) + P(C) = .45$. Find $P(A)$, $P(B)$, and $P(C)$.

14. The sample space of an experiment is $\{a, b, c\}$ with $P(b) = .25$. If $P(\{a, b\}) = .375$ and $P(\{b, c\}) = .875$, find $P(a)$ and $P(c)$.

15. (*See Example 8*) The owner of a hamburger stand found that 800 people bought hamburgers as follows:

KIND OF BURGER	FREQUENCY
Miniburger	140
Burger	345
Big Burger	315

Find the probability of a customer purchasing each kind of hamburger.

16. An auto dealer sold 120 minivans. His records show that the following repairs were required during the first year:

REPAIRS	FREQUENCY
Minor	70
Major	28
No repairs	22

A customer purchases a minivan from the dealer. Find the probability that she will return during the first year for:
- (a) minor repairs.
- (b) major repairs.
- (c) no repairs.

17. A radar unit clocked 1800 vehicles on the interstate highway. The unit's report showed the following information:

SPEED	FREQUENCY
Below 40	160
40–49	270
50–55	1025
Over 55	345

On the basis of this report, estimate the probability of a vehicle driving within each of the speed categories.

18. Customers at a shopping center are given a taste test to determine their preference for coffee. On the basis of the following information, estimate $P(A)$, $P(B)$, and $P(C)$:

BRAND	NUMBER PREFERRING THIS BRAND
A	88
B	62
C	17

19. For the sample space $\{1, 2, 3, 4, 5\}$ the following probabilities are assigned: $P(1) = .15$, $P(2) = .16$, $P(3) = .19$, $P(4) = .30$, and $P(5) = .20$.
- (a) Find the probability of $\{2, 4\}$.
- (b) Find the probability of $\{1, 3, 5\}$.
- (c) Find the probability of selecting a prime.

III

20. A fellow has some change in his pocket: two pennies, four nickels, three dimes, four quarters, and two half dollars. He draws out a coin at random. The probability of drawing any one of the coins is:

.05 for each penny,
.02 for each dime,
.04 for each nickel,
.07 for each quarter,
.20 for each half dollar.

- (a) Find the probability that the coin drawn is a dime.
- (b) Find the probability that the coin drawn is a quarter or a half dollar.
- (c) Find the probability that the coin drawn is a nickel.
- (d) Find the probability that the value of the coin drawn is less than 10 cents.

21. An experiment consists of drawing one card from a bridge deck. The sample space contains 52 outcomes, one for each of the 52 cards. Suppose we assign a probability of $\frac{1}{52}$ to each of the cards.
- (a) Find the probability that an ace is drawn.
- (b) Find the probability that the card drawn is a king or a queen.
- (c) Find the probability that the card drawn is a diamond.
- (d) Find the probability that the card drawn is a red card.

6–2 EQUALLY LIKELY EVENTS

In general, no unique method exists for assigning probabilities to the outcomes of an experiment. However, there exists a class of experiments in which the assignments are straightforward. Such experiments have the characteristic that the individual outcomes are **equally likely.** That is, each outcome has the same chance, or probability, of occurring as any other outcome. Generally, we say that a tossed coin is just as likely to turn up a head as a tail, so heads and tails are equally likely to happen. If a coin is altered so that it comes up heads two thirds of the time, then heads and tails are not equally likely. Unless stated otherwise, we assume that a tossed coin is fair; that is, heads and tails are equally likely. All cards drawn from a well-shuffled deck have an equal chance of being drawn. We say that the outcomes are equally likely.

If a coin is drawn from a purse with coins of different denominations, it doesn't seem reasonable to say that the outcomes are equally likely because of the variations of size. The small size of a dime makes it less likely to be drawn than a half dollar, for example.

For experiments with a finite number of equally likely outcomes, the probability of each simple outcome is $\frac{1}{n}$, where n is the number of outcomes in the sample space.

If we toss a coin, the sample space is $\{H, T\}$. We intuitively agree that heads and tails are equally likely, so

$$P(H) = \frac{1}{2} \qquad \text{and} \qquad P(T) = \frac{1}{2}$$

because the sample space has two elements. If we select a name at random from 25 different names, then each name has $\frac{1}{25}$ probability of being drawn.

Since the probability of an event is the sum of probabilities of all simple outcomes in the event, we can compute probabilities of events like the following.

Select a number at random from the set

$$S = \{1, 2, 3, 4, 5, 6, 7, 8, 9\}$$

Determine the probability that it is even, that is, the number is in the event

$$E = \{2, 4, 6, 8\}$$

We assume equally likely outcomes, so the probability of each number is $\frac{1}{9}$. Then

$$P(E) = P(2) + P(4) + P(6) + P(8)$$
$$= \frac{1}{9} + \frac{1}{9} + \frac{1}{9} + \frac{1}{9}$$
$$= \frac{4}{9}$$

It is no accident that

$$\frac{4}{9} = \frac{\text{number of elements in } E}{\text{number of elements in } S}$$

For an experiment with equally likely outcomes, compute the probability of an event by counting the number of elements in the event and then dividing by the number of elements in the sample space. We sometimes call the outcomes in the event **successes** and outcomes not in the event **failures.**

Theorem 1   For an event E where (a) E contains s simple outcomes (successes), (b) the sample space S contains n simple outcomes, and (c) the simple outcomes are equally likely (have the same probabilities), then the probability of E is

$$P(E) = \frac{s}{n} = \frac{\text{number of outcomes of interest (success)}}{\text{total number of outcomes possible}}$$

$$= \frac{n(E)}{n(S)}$$

NOTE   The event E occurs when any of the simple outcomes in E occurs.

If the event can fail in f ways, the probability of failure is

$$q = \frac{f}{n}$$

Since we admit only success or failure, $n = s + f$. We can conclude from this that

$$P(\text{success}) + P(\text{failure}) = \frac{s}{n} + \frac{f}{n} = \frac{s+f}{n} = \frac{n}{n} = 1$$

so the probability of success and the probability of failure always add to 1.

EXAMPLE 1   *(Compare Exercise 1)*

Draw a number at random from the integers 1 through 10. What is the probability that a prime is drawn?

SOLUTION   In this case, $n = 10$ and $E = \{2, 3, 5, 7\}$, so $s = 4$. This gives $P(\text{prime}) = \frac{4}{10}$.

EXAMPLE 2   *(Compare Exercise 3)*

An urn contains four red balls, three green balls, and five white balls. If a single ball is drawn, what is the probability that it is green?

SOLUTION   Since there are a total of 12 balls, $n = 12$. An outcome is successful in three ways, the drawing of any one of the three green balls, so $s = 3$. Therefore

$$P(\text{green}) = \frac{3}{12} = \frac{1}{4}$$

EXAMPLE 3   *(Compare Exercise 5)*

A pair of dice is rolled. What is the probability of rolling an 8 (the two numbers that turn up add to 8)? Of rolling a 3 (the two numbers add to 3)?

SOLUTION   According to the fundamental counting principle, there are $6 \times 6 = 36$ ways the two dice can turn up, so $n = 36$.

Each outcome in the sample space may be thought of as a pair of numbers like (3, 2); the number showing on the first die is 3, and the number showing on the second die is 2. The sample space is composed of the following pairs:

(1, 1),   (1, 2),   (2, 1),   (1, 3),   (3, 1),   (1, 4),   (4, 1),
(1, 5),   (5, 1),   (1, 6),   (6, 1),   (2, 2),   (2, 3),   (3, 2),
(2, 4),   (4, 2),   (2, 5),   (5, 2),   (2, 6),   (6, 2),   (3, 3),
(3, 4),   (4, 3),   (3, 5),   (5, 3),   (3, 6),   (6, 3),   (4, 4),
(4, 5),   (5, 4),   (4, 6),   (6, 4),   (5, 5),   (5, 6),   (6, 5),
(6, 6)

We say that an 8 is rolled when the two numbers showing add to 8. An 8 may be obtained in five different ways:

first die 2, second die 6, that is, (2, 6);
first die 6, second die 2, that is, (6, 2);
first die 3, second die 5, that is, (3, 5);
first die 5, second die 3, that is, (5, 3);
first die 4, second die 4, that is, (4, 4).

Therefore

$$P(8) = \frac{5}{36}$$

Since there are just two ways to roll a 3,

$$P(3) = \frac{2}{36} = \frac{1}{18}$$

Random Selection   **Random selection** or **random outcomes** imply that outcomes are equally likely.

EXAMPLE 4   *(Compare Exercise 7)*

Two students are selected at random from a class of eight boys and nine girls. What is the probability that both students selected are girls?

SOLUTION   Determine the number of outcomes in the event of interest by the number of different ways in which two girls can be selected from a group of nine. This is

$$C(9, 2) = \frac{9 \times 8}{2 \times 1} = 36$$

The number of outcomes, n, in the sample space is the number of different ways two students can be selected from the whole group of 17. This is

$$C(17, 2) = \frac{17 \times 16}{2 \times 1} = 136$$

Thus

$$P(\text{two girls}) = \frac{36}{136} = \frac{9}{34}$$

EXAMPLE 5   *(Compare Exercise 13)*

Find the probability of at least two heads appearing on three tosses of a coin.

SOLUTION   We use a tree diagram to obtain the necessary information. (See Figure 6–1.)

We observe that there are a total of eight possible outcomes with four of them showing two or more heads. Thus

$$P(\text{at least 2 heads}) = \frac{4}{8} = \frac{1}{2}$$

EXAMPLE 6   *(Compare Exercise 15)*

A grocery store stocks eight different sugar-coated cereals and twelve that are not sugar-coated. A child is allowed to select some cereal. He grabs three different cereals. What is the probability that two are sugar-coated and one is not?

FIGURE 6–1

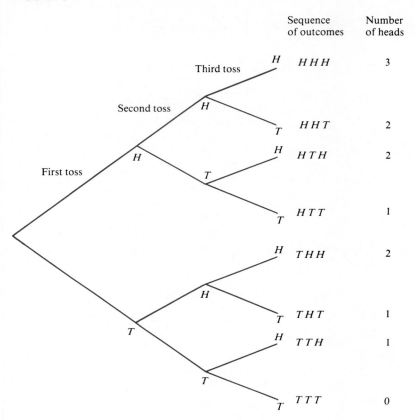

	Sequence of outcomes	Number of heads
HHH	HHH	3
HHT	HHT	2
HTH	HTH	2
HTT	HTT	1
THH	THH	2
THT	THT	1
TTH	TTH	1
TTT	TTT	0

Sequence of heads and tails
on three tosses of a coin

SOLUTION   The total number of outcomes, n, is $C(20, 3)$, since there are 20 different cereals. A success is the selection of two cereals that are sugar-coated and one that is not. These can be selected in $C(8, 2) \times C(12, 1)$ different ways. The probability is

$$P = \frac{C(8, 2) \times C(12, 1)}{C(20, 3)} = \frac{28 \times 12}{1140} = \frac{28}{95}$$

Here is an example using permutations.

EXAMPLE 7 *(Compare Exercise 19)*

A corporation has eight men and six women on its board of directors. At a stock-holders' meeting, seven directors are seated in a row on the platform. The directors are chosen and assigned a seat in a random manner.

(a) What is the probability that the directors are arranged so that there are men in seats 1 through 3 and women in seats 4 through 7?
(b) What is the probability that the directors are arranged so that men and women alternate seats with a man in seat 1, a women in seat 2, and so on?
(c) Find the probability that three men are seated together and four women are seated together.

SOLUTION Since the directors are arranged in a row, the order of arrangement is significant.

(a) The number of possible ways to arrange any seven directors in a row is $P(14, 7)$. (This is the total number of outcomes possible.) The number of successes is the number of arrangements with three men first and four women next in the row. This can be done in $P(8, 3) \times P(6, 4)$ ways. Thus the probability of men in seats 1 through 3 and women in seats 4 through 7 is

$$\frac{P(8, 3) \times P(6, 4)}{P(14, 7)} = \frac{8 \times 7 \times 6 \times 6 \times 5 \times 4 \times 3}{14 \times 13 \times 12 \times 11 \times 10 \times 9 \times 8} = \frac{1}{143}$$

(b) Again the total number of outcomes is $P(14, 7)$. To find the number of successes, we need to find the number of ways in which seven people can be arranged with a man first, a woman second, a man third, and so on. To do so, we multiply the number of choices for seat 1, for seat 2, . . . , for seat 7. That product is

$$\frac{8 \times 6 \times 7 \times 5 \times 6 \times 4 \times 5}{14 \times 13 \times 12 \times 11 \times 10 \times 9 \times 8} = \frac{5}{429}$$

(c) This arrangement can succeed in two ways: men in seats 1 through 3 and women in seats 4 through 7 or women in seats 1 through 4 and men in seats 5 through 7. We compute the number of each and add to obtain the total number of successes, that is,

$$P(8, 3)P(6, 4) + P(6, 4)P(8, 3) = 2P(8, 3)P(6, 4)$$

The probability is

$$\frac{2P(8, 3)P(6, 4)}{P(14, 7)} = \frac{2}{143}$$

6-2 EXERCISES

I

1. (*See Example 1*) Fifteen names are written, one per card. Two of the names begin with a C, four begin with a T, five begin with a B, and four begin with a P. If a name is drawn at random, what is the probability that it begins with a T?

2. A number is drawn at random from the numbers 1 through 24.
   (a) What is the probability that the number is a multiple of 5?
   (b) What is the probability that the number is a multiple of 6?

3. (*See Example 2*) An urn contains five red balls and three green balls. If one ball is drawn, what is the probability that it is red?

4. An urn contains three red balls, four white balls, and seven green balls.
   (a) If one ball is drawn, find the probability that it is white.
   (b) Find the probability that it is not white.

5. (*See Example 3*) A pair of dice is rolled. Find the probability of rolling a 7.

6. Find the probability of rolling a 12 with a pair of dice.

7. (*See Example 4*) Two students are selected at random from a class of ten males and seven females. Find the probability that both students are males.

8. An urn contains four red balls and five white balls. Two balls are drawn. Find the probability that both are red.

9. Two cards are drawn from a deck of cards. Find the probability that both are aces.

10. A card is drawn at random from a deck of bridge cards. Find the probability that it is:
    (a) a three.
    (b) a 10 or a jack.
    (c) not a diamond.

11. A bag contains four black marbles and five white marbles that are all exactly alike except in color. If one marble is drawn, find the probability that it will be:
    (a) white.
    (b) red.
    (c) black or white.

12. Five red books and three green books are placed at random on a shelf. Without looking, a person takes a book. Find the probability that it is a red book.

13. (*See Example 5*) Find the probability of at least one head appearing on two tosses of a coin.

14. Find the probability of at most one head appearing on three tosses of a coin.

15. (*See Example 6*) There are twelve freshmen and nine sophomores in a class. If three students are selected at random, find the probability that two are freshmen and one is a sophomore.

16. A box contains seven red balls and ten green balls. Three balls are drawn from the box. Find the probability that two are red and one is green.

II

17. A tray of electronic components contains 15 components, four of which are defective. If four components are selected, what is the probability that:
    (a) all four are defective?
    (b) three are defective and one is good?
    (c) exactly two are defective?
    (d) none are defective?

18. Two people are selected at random from a group of twelve Republicans and ten Democrats. Find the probability that:
    (a) both are Democrats.
    (b) one is a Republican and one is a Democrat.

19. (*See Example 7*) A club has ten members and six pledges. Five of them are arranged in a row for a club meeting. The five are selected and seated at random.
    (a) Find the probability that members are in seats 1 through 2 and pledges in seats 3 through 5.
    (b) Find the probability that members and pledges alternate seats with members in seats 1, 3, 5 and pledges in seats 2 and 4.

20. A speech class has eight freshmen and five sophomores. Three people are selected at random to give speeches.
   (a) Find the probability that the first is a sophomore, the second is a freshman, and the third is a sophomore.
   (b) Find the probability that all three are freshmen.
   (c) Find the probability that the first is a sophomore and the other two are freshmen.

21. A child has eight cans of soft drinks, four different brands with one regular and one diet drink for each brand. The child arranges four of the cans in a row in a random manner.
   (a) Find the probability that the arrangement consists of all diet drinks.
   (b) Find the probability that the first two are diet drinks and the second two are regular.

22. A contestant draws three cards, one question per card, and tries to answer the three questions. There are four cards with history questions, five cards with literature questions, and six cards with science questions.
   (a) Find the probability that the questions are history, literature, and science, in that order.
   (b) Find the probability that all three are literature questions.
   (c) Find the probability that the first is science, the second is history, and the third is science.

23. The probability that the university football team will win is .6, and the probability that it will lose is .3. What is the probability of a tie?

III

24. A teacher writes 15 problems on cards, one per card. The problems include six easy problems, five medium problems, and four hard problems. A student draws three problems for a quiz. Find the probability that all three are hard problems.

25. A child has nine cards numbered 1 through 9. The child places three cards in a row to form a three-digit number. Find the probability that the number is larger than 500.

26. Six children are selected from a group of ten boys and twelve girls. Find the probability that half are boys and half are girls.

27. A secretary types a letter and envelope addressed to each of five people. A temporary worker inserts a letter in each envelope without looking.
   (a) Find the probability that all letters are placed in the correct envelopes.
   (b) If two letters are addressed out-of-state and three are addressed in-state, find the probability that the in-state letters are put into in-state envelopes and the out-of-state letters are put into out-of-state envelopes.

28. A door to a restricted area has a combination lock with six buttons. Access is gained by pressing three buttons in the correct sequence. (The correct sequence might require a button to be pushed more than once.) If a person who doesn't know the correct sequence pushes a sequence of three buttons, what is the probability of gaining access?

29. A shipment of 14 televisions contains six regular and eight deluxe models. The manufacturer failed to mark the model designation on the cartons. If four cartons are selected at random, what is the probability that exactly three of them are the deluxe model?

30. Two bad light bulbs get mixed up with seven good ones. If you take two of the bulbs, what is the probability that both are bad?

31. A mathematics class is composed of twelve freshmen, ten sophomores, and six juniors. Three of the freshmen, two of the sophomores, and one junior receive A grades in the course. If a student is selected at random from the class, find the probability that:
   (a) the student is an A student.
   (b) the student is an A freshman student.
   (c) the student is a sophomore.

32. Five thousand lottery tickets are sold. Jones buys five tickets. If one ticket is drawn for a $100 prize, what is the probability that Jones wins?

33. An urn contains six blue balls, five yellow balls, and three white balls. If a ball is drawn at random, find the probability that:
   (a) it is yellow.
   (b) it is not yellow.

34. In a roll of 50 pennies there are 15 dated 1977, 18 with a Denver mint mark, and six with the Denver mint mark dated 1977. If a penny is drawn at random, what is the probability that it is dated 1977 or has a Denver mint mark?

35. A coin is bent, so heads and tails are not equally likely. The coin is tossed 500 times, and heads occur 400 times.
 (a) Estimate the probability of a toss of the coin coming up heads.
 (b) Estimate the probability of tails.

36. A die is loaded (weighted on one side so that it is not fair). It is rolled 300 times, and the following outcomes are observed:

> 1 occurs 21 times,
> 2 occurs 35 times,
> 3 occurs 67 times,
> 4 occurs 51 times,
> 5 occurs 54 times,
> 6 occurs 72 times.

Estimate the probability of rolling:
 (a) 2
 (b) 5
 (c) 6

37. Fifteen cards are numbered 1 through 15. The cards are shuffled, and three cards are drawn and arranged in a row.
 (a) Find the probability that all three are odd.
 (b) Find the probability that the first two are odd and the third is even.
 (c) Find the probability that the arrangement consists of three cards larger than 10.

38. A box contains eight red balls and six green balls. Two different balls are drawn.
 (a) Find the probability that the first is red and the second is green.
 (b) Find the probability that both are green.

39. For several years a mathematics teacher studied the relationship between ACT scores in mathematics and performance in calculus. He observed that of the students who scored above 28 on ACT mathematics test, 324 made an A grade in calculus and 246 made below an A in calculus. If an entering freshman with a score above 28 on the ACT mathematics test is chosen at random, what is the probability that the student will make an A grade in calculus?

40. A coin is flipped twice in succession. Use a tree diagram to determine the probability of its landing on heads the first time and tails the second time.

41. A coin is flipped four times in succession. Find the probability of:
 (a) three heads and one tail, order being unimportant.
 (b) heads on the first three tosses and tails on the fourth toss.

42. A die is tossed twice. Using a sample space, find the probability of:
 (a) a 4 and a 5, order being unimportant.
 (b) a 4 the first time and a 5 the second time.
 (c) the sum of the numbers obtained being 6.
 (d) the same number on both dice.

43. A box contains two black balls and two white balls. Three balls are drawn in succession without replacement. Determine the probability of drawing:
 (a) two black balls and then a white ball.
 (b) two black balls and a white ball, order being unimportant.

44. The probability of randomly selecting a female from a group of 50 people is .4. How many females are in the group?

45. Tanya has a jar containing 250 dimes. If she selects a dime at random, the probability of drawing a dime dated before 1960 is .2. How many dimes are dated before 1960?

46. An urn contains six green balls and balls of other colors. If a ball is selected at random, the probability of drawing a green ball is .3. How many balls are in the urn?

47. A car has six spark plugs, two of which are malfunctioning. If two of the plugs are replaced at random, what is the probability that both malfunctioning plugs are replaced?

48. Two children are selected in succession from a group of five children. Three of them are girls: Ayesha, Beth, and Cindy. Two of them are boys: Dan and Esteban. Draw a tree diagram and use it to compute the probability of:
 (a) selecting a girl first, then a boy.
 (b) selecting a girl and a boy, order being unimportant.

49. A box contains five yellow balls, three green balls, and two red balls. A sequence of three different balls is drawn.

(a) Find the probability a green, a yellow, and a red ball are drawn in that order.

(b) Find the probability the first two are yellow and the third is red.

(c) Find the probability that a green, then a red, then a green are drawn.

50. Leave your answer to this problem in terms of factorials. A bridge deck is shuffled.

(a) Find the probability that the cards are arranged with all 13 clubs first, all 13 diamonds second, all 13 hearts third, and all 13 spades last.

(b) Find the probability that all the red cards are first and all the black cards are next.

(c) Find the probability that the red cards are together and the black cards are together.

6–3 COMPOUND EVENTS: UNION, INTERSECTION, AND COMPLEMENT

- *Keys to Recognizing Compound Events*

- *Probability of Compound Events*

- *Probability of E′*

- *Probability of E ∪ F*

- *Mutually Exclusive Events*

Since events are subsets of a sample space, we can use set operations to form other events. In particular, we may form the union or intersection of two events E and F to form another event. We may also take the complement of an event to form another event. We will see how the probabilities of events E and F relate to the probabilities of their union, intersection, and complement. An understanding of these relationships often helps to analyze a complex problem by breaking it down into simpler problems. An event that can be described in terms of union, intersection, or complements of some events is called a **compound event.**

Compound Events   Let E and F be events in a sample space S.

1. The event $E \cup F$ is the event consisting of those outcomes that are in E or F or both (**union**).

2. The event $E \cap F$ is the event consisting of those outcomes that are in both E and F (**intersection**).

3. The event $E′$ (**complement** of E) is the event consisting of those elements in the sample space that are not in E.

344   Chapter 6   Probability

EXAMPLE 1   *(Compare Exercise 1)*

Let the sample space $S = \{1, 2, 3, 4, 5, 6, 7, 8, 9, 10\}$. Let the event E be "the number is even." Then $E = \{2, 4, 6, 8, 10\}$. Let the event F be "the number is prime." Then $F = \{2, 3, 5, 7\}$. From these,

$$E \cup F = \{2, 3, 4, 5, 6, 7, 8, 10\}$$
$$E \cap F = \{2\}$$
$$F' = \{1, 4, 6, 8, 9, 10\}$$
$$E' = \{1, 3, 5, 7, 9\}$$

See Figure 6–2.

EXAMPLE 2   *(Compare Exercise 3)*

For the experiment of selecting a student at random, let E be the event "the student is taking art," and let F be the event "the student is taking history." Then

$E \cup F$ is the event "the student is taking art or history or both."

$E \cap F$ is the event "the student is taking both art and history."

E' is the event "the student is not taking art."

F' is the event "the student is not taking history."

KEYS TO RECOGNIZING COMPOUND EVENTS

Let's emphasize the key words and phrases that describe compound events. They will help in recognizing the approach to take in solving those problems.

$E \cup F$. An outcome is in $E \cup F$ if it is in E or in F or in both. The key word for describing and recognizing $E \cup F$ is "or." When the word "or" is used in mathematics, it means E or F or both unless stated otherwise. Another way to state that an event is in E or F is to state that the event is in *at least one* of them.

The statements

"Find the probability of $E \cup F$."

"Find the probability that an outcome is in E or F."

"Find the probability that an outcome is in at least one of E and F."

are equivalent statements.

FIGURE 6–2

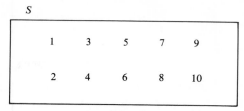

Sample space S

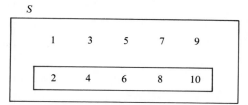

$E =$ Set of even numbers in S

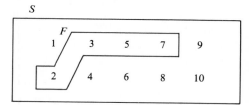

$F =$ Set of prime numbers in S

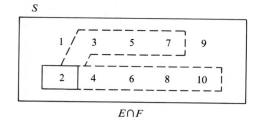

$E \cap F$

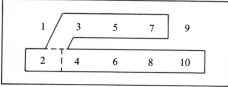

$E \cup F$

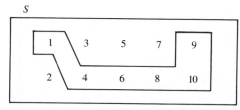

$\overline{F}$

E ∩ F. An outcome is in *E ∩ F* if it is in both *E* and *F.* A key word for recognizing and describing *E ∩ F* is "and."

The statements

"Find $P(E \cap F)$."
"Find the probability that an outcome is in *E* and *F.*"
"Find the probability of both *E* and *F.*"

are equivalent statements.

E′. An outcome is in *E′* if it is not in *E.* A key word for recognizing and describing *E′* is "not."

The statements

"Find $P(E')$."
"Find the probability that an outcome is not in *E.*"
"Find the probability that *E* fails."

are equivalent statements.

PROBABILITY OF COMPOUND EVENTS

It is often helpful to determine the probability of a compound event by using the probabilities of the individual events making up the compound event.

PROBABILITY OF *E′*

You recognize that if 10% of a class receives an A grade, then $100\% - 10\% = 90\%$ do not receive an A grade. If $\frac{2}{3}$ of a store's customers prefer brand A, then $1 - \frac{2}{3} = \frac{1}{3}$ of the customers do not prefer brand A. These statements are similar to the probability statement in Theorem 1.

Theorem 1
Failure Theorem

For an event *E,*

$$P(E') = 1 - P(E)$$
$$P(E) = 1 - P(E')$$

where *E′* is the complement of *E* in the sample space *S.*

EXAMPLE 3   *(Compare Exercise 5)*

If the probability that Smith wins the door prize at a club meeting is 0.1, then the probability that Smith does not win is $1 - 0.1 = 0.9$.

If the probability that a part is defective is 0.08, then the probability that it is not defective is $1 - .08 = 0.92$.

If the probability that Jones fails to get a promotion is 0.35, then the probability that Jones does get a promotion is 0.65.

You will encounter problems in which it may be difficult to find the probability of an event, but rather easy to find the probability of the event failing. If so, Theorem 1 enables us to easily find the probability of the event. The following example illustrates this idea.

EXAMPLE 4   *(Compare Exercise 21)*

A branch office of a corporation employs six women and five men. If four employees are selected at random to help open a new branch office, find the probability that at least one is a woman.

SOLUTION   Selection of at least one woman occurs when one woman or two women or three women or four women are selected.

We count the number of successes by counting the number of ways in which we can select:

one woman and three men,

two women and two men,

three women and one man,

four women,

and adding these four results. (*See Examples 9 and 10 in Section 5–5.*) The number of successes is

$$C(6, 1)C(5, 3) + C(6, 2)C(5, 2) + C(6, 3)C(5, 1) + C(6, 4)$$

This quantity is divided by $C(11, 4)$ to obtain the probability of at least one woman being selected. You can carry out the above computation if you like, but let's look at an easier way.

The only way the company can *fail* to select at least one woman is to select *all* men. That probability is

$$\frac{C(5, 4)}{C(11,4)} = \frac{1}{66}$$

By Theorem 1 the probability of success is 1 minus the probability of failure. So the probability of at least one woman being selected is $1 - \frac{1}{66} = \frac{65}{66}$. (See Figure 6–3.)

FIGURE 6–3

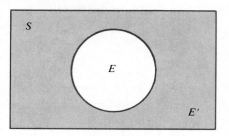

E' is the complement of E in S

PROBABILITY
OF $E \cup F$

EXAMPLE 5   *(Compare Exercise 25)*

In a group of 200 students, 40 take English, 50 take math, and 10 take both. If a student is selected at random, the following probabilities hold:

$$P(\text{English}) = \frac{\text{number taking English}}{\text{number in the group}} = \frac{40}{200}$$

$$P(\text{math}) = \frac{\text{number taking math}}{\text{number in the group}} = \frac{50}{200}$$

$$P(\text{English and math}) = \frac{\text{number taking English and math}}{\text{number in the group}} = \frac{10}{200}$$

$$P(\text{English or math}) = \frac{\text{number taking English or math}}{\text{number in the group}} = \frac{80}{200}$$

The number 80 in the last equation was obtained by using the formula from Section 5–2 on sets:

$$n(E \cup F) = n(E) + n(E) - n(E \cap F)$$

If we let S be the group of 200 students, let E be those taking English, and let F be those taking math, then the above equations may be written as

$$P(\text{English}) = \frac{n(E)}{n(S)} = \frac{40}{200}$$

$$P(\text{math}) = \frac{n(F)}{n(S)} = \frac{50}{200}$$

$$P(\text{English and math}) = \frac{n(E \cap F)}{n(S)} = \frac{10}{200}$$

$$P(\text{English or math}) = \frac{n(E \cup F)}{n(S)}$$

$$= \frac{n(E) + n(F) - n(E \cap F)}{n(S)}$$

FIGURE 6–4

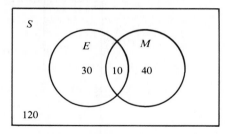

$n(S) = 200, n(E) = 40, n(M) = 50, n(E \cap M) = 10,$
$n(E \cup M) = 80$

$$= \frac{40 + 50 - 10}{200} = \frac{80}{200}$$

(See Figure 6–4.)

You might wonder why we seem to have complicated the last equation. We want to illustrate a basic property of probability, so we need to carry the last equation a little further. We may write

$$P(E \cup F) = \frac{40 + 50 - 10}{200}$$

as

$$P(E \cup F) = \frac{40}{200} + \frac{50}{200} - \frac{10}{200}$$

The right-hand side of the last equation is

$$P(E) + P(F) - P(E \cap F)$$

This holds in general.

Theorem 2 (a) $P(E \cup F) = P(E) + P(F) - P(E \cap F)$
(b) If the outcomes are equally likely, then

$$P(E \cup F) = \frac{n(E) + n(F) - n(E \cap F)}{n(S)}$$

We point out that the above example assumes equally likely outcomes. However, Theorem 2(a) is true in other cases as well.

EXAMPLE 6   *(Compare Exercise 29)*

In a remote jungle village the probability of a child contracting malaria is .45, the probability of contracting measles is .65, and the probability of contracting both is .20. What is the probability of a child contracting malaria or measles?

SOLUTION   By Theorem 2,

$$P(\text{malaria or measles}) = P(\text{malaria}) + P(\text{measles}) - P(\text{malaria and measles})$$
$$= .45 + .65 - .20 = .90$$

EXAMPLE 7   *(Compare Exercise 33)*

A survey of couples in a certain country found the following:

> The probability that the husband has a college degree is .65.
> The probability that the wife has a college degree is .70.
> The probability that both have a college degree is .50.

A couple is selected at random.

(a) Find the probability that at least one has a college degree.
(b) Find the probability that neither has a college degree.

SOLUTION   Let M represent the event that the husband has a college degree and F the event that the wife has a college degree.

(a) Then $M \cup F$ represents the event that at least one of them has a college degree, and $P(M \cup F) = .65 + .70 - .50 = .85$.

(b) The event that "neither has a college degree" is the failure of "at least one has a college degree," so

$$P(\text{neither has a degree}) = 1 - P(\text{at least one has a degree})$$
$$= 1 - .85 = .15$$

MUTUALLY EXCLUSIVE EVENTS

Theorem 2 might not be helpful in some problems because we might not know how to compute $P(E \cap F)$. That will come in the next section. However, the special situation in which E and F have no outcomes in common can be solved.

Definition 1
Mutually Exclusive

Two events E and F are said to be **mutually exclusive** if they have no outcomes in common.

When two events are mutually exclusive, an outcome in one is excluded from the other. As sets, E and F are **disjoint**.

See Figure 6–5.

FIGURE 6–5

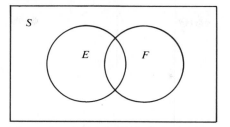

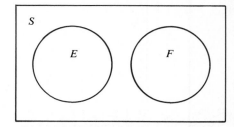

E and *F* are not
mutually exclusive.

E and *F* are
mutually exclusive.

EXAMPLE 8   *(Compare Exercises 11–15)*

When a coin is tossed, "heads" and "tails" are mutually exclusive because each one excludes the other.

Rolling a 7 with a pair of dice is mutually exclusive with rolling a 9 because they cannot occur at the same time.

Taking English and taking art are not mutually exclusive because both courses can be taken if the classes meet at different times.

When two events are mutually exclusive, the computation of the probability of *E* or *F* simplifies because $E \cap F = \emptyset$. Recall that $P(\emptyset) = 0$, so when *E* and *F* are mutually exclusive,

$$P(E \cup F) = P(E) + P(F) - P(E \cap F)$$

becomes

$$P(E \cup F) = P(E) + P(F)$$

Theorem 3   If *E* and *F* are mutually exclusive events, then
$$P(E \cup F) = P(E) + P(F)$$

EXAMPLE 9   *(Compare Exercise 16)*

Two people are selected at random from a group of seven men and five women. Find the probability that both are men or both are women.

SOLUTION   The events "both men" and "both women" are mutually exclusive because the existence of one excludes the other. Thus

$$P(\text{both men or both women}) = P(\text{both men}) + P(\text{both women})$$

$$= \frac{C(7, 2)}{C(12, 2)} + \frac{C(5, 2)}{C(12, 2)}$$

$$= \frac{21}{66} + \frac{10}{66} = \frac{31}{66}$$

6-3 EXERCISES

I

In Exercises 1 through 4, describe $E \cup F$, $E \cap F$, and E'.

1. (*See Example 1*) $S = \{1, 2, 3, 4, 5, 6, 7, 8, 9, 10\}$, $E = \{1, 3, 5, 7, 9\}$, $F = \{1, 2, 3, 4\}$.

2. S is the set of customers who shop at Harvey's Department Store. E is the set of customers who shop in the bargain basement. F is the set of customers who shop in the jewelry department.

3. (*See Example 2*) S is the set of students at State U. E is the set of students passing English. F is the set of students not passing chemistry.

4. S is the set of employees of a major corporation. E is the set of executives. F is the set of women employees.

5. (*See Example 3*) The probability that Jack can work a problem is $\frac{3}{5}$. Find the probability that Jack cannot work the problem.

6. $P(E) = .6$. Find $P(E')$.

7. $P(E') = .7$. Find $P(E)$.

8. $P(E) = 0$. Find $P(E')$.

9. The probability that a person selected at random likes hamburgers at a local hamburger stand is 0.3. Find the probability that a person selected at random does not like the hamburgers.

10. The Doomsday Life Insurance Company conducted a study that indicated that a person who reaches 50 years of age has a probability of .23 of eventually dying of cancer. Find the probability of that person dying of some other cause.

Are events described in Exercises 11 through 15 mutually exclusive? (*See Example 8*)

11. E: selecting a boy from a group of students
    F: selecting a girl from a group of students

12. E: drawing a king from a deck of cards
    F: drawing a face card from a deck of cards

13. E: selecting a student who is taking English
    F: selecting a student who is taking math

14. E: selecting a number that is a multiple of 5
    F: selecting a number that is a multiple of 7

15. E: a person having a birthday in February
    F: a person having a birthday on the 30th of a month

16. (*See Example 9*) Two people are selected at random from a group of eight women and ten men. Find the probability that both are men or both are women.

17. Four cards are drawn at random from a deck of 52 playing cards.
    (a) Find the probability that they are all aces.
    (b) Find the probability that they are all aces or all jacks.

18. A bag contains six black marbles, three white marbles, and two red marbles. One marble is drawn. Find the probability of drawing:
    (a) a black marble.
    (b) a white marble.
    (c) a red marble.
    (d) a white or a red marble.

19. An urn contains two red balls, one white ball, three black balls, and four green balls. One ball is drawn. Find the probability that it is white or black.

20. A bag contains ten balls, four of which are white, five black, and one red. Find the probability of getting, in one drawing:
    (a) a white ball.
    (b) a black ball.
    (c) a red ball.
    (d) a black or white ball.
    (e) a white or red ball.

21. (*See Example 4*) Three people are selected at random from five females and seven males.
    (a) Find the probability that at least one is a male.
    (b) Find the probability that at most two are male.

22. A coin is tossed four times. Find the probability that heads turns up at least once.

23. A new apartment complex advertises that it will give away three mopeds by a drawing from the first 50 students that sign a lease. Four friends are among the first 50 to sign. What is the probability that at least one of them will win a moped?

24. A pen holder holds ten pens, three of which do not write. If three pens are selected at random, find the probability that:
    (a) at least one writes.
    (b) at least one does not write.

II

25. (*See Example 5*) Of 400 college students, 120 are enrolled in math, 220 are enrolled in English, and 55 are enrolled in both. If a student is selected at random, find the probability that:
    (a) the student is enrolled in mathematics.
    (b) the student is enrolled in English.
    (c) the student is enrolled in both.
    (d) the student is enrolled in mathematics or English.

26. A survey of 100 college faculty shows that 70 own a car, 30 own a bicycle, and 10 own both. Find the probability that a faculty member chosen at random owns a car or a bicycle.

27. In a group of 35 children, ten have blonde hair, 14 have brown eyes, and four have both blonde hair and brown eyes. If a child is selected at random:
    (a) find the probability that the child has blonde hair and brown eyes.
    (b) find the probability that the child has blonde hair or brown eyes.

28. In a group of 100 children, 28 have the first initial R, 11 have the last initial R, and six have both first and last initial R. If a child is selected at random, find the probability that the child has a first or last initial R.

29. (*See Example 6*) The probability of a preschool child contracting chicken pox is .75, the probability of contracting measles is .24, and the probability of contracting both is .18. Find the probability of a preschool child contracting measles or chicken pox.

30. A senior interviews with Acme Corp. and Mills, Inc. The probability of receiving an offer from Acme is .35, from Mills is .48, and from both is .15. Find the probability of receiving an offer from Acme Corp. or Mills, Inc.

31. For a certain model car the probability of the air conditioner failing before the warranty expires is .36, the probability of the alternator failing is .26, and the probability of both failing is .11. Find the probability of the air conditioner or the alternator failing before the warranty expires.

32. Cammy and Valerie enter different beauty pageants. The probability of Cammy winning in her pageant is .55, the probability of Valerie winning in her pageant is .60, and the probability of both winning is .22. Find the probability that Cammy or Valerie wins.

33. (*See Example 7*) A survey of couples in a city found the following probabilities:

    The probability that the husband is employed is .85.
    The probability that the wife is employed is .60.
    The probability that both are employed is .55.

    A couple is selected at random.
    (a) Find the probability that at least one of them is employed.
    (b) Find the probability that neither is employed.

34. Studies on the side effects of a new antihistamine found that it produces headaches in 3% of users, drowsiness in 35%, and both in 1.5%. If a user is selected at random:
    (a) find the probability that at least one of the side effects is produced.
    (b) find the probability that neither side effect is produced.

35. Two tollbooths are located at the entrance of an airport. At any given time the probability of a line at Booth 1 is .75, the probability of a line at Booth 2 is .63, and the probability of a line at both booths at the same time is .54.
   (a) Find the probability of a line at least at one booth.
   (b) Find the probability of a line at neither booth.

36. An inspection of desks made at a furniture plant reveals that 2% of the desks have structural defects, 3% have finish defects, and 1% have both. A desk is selected at random.
   (a) Find the probability that the desk has at least one kind of defect.
   (b) Find the probability that the desk has neither kind of defect.

37. A jeweler's bag contains six rings. One is plain gold, one is plain silver, one is gold with emeralds and rubies, one is silver with diamonds, one is gold with diamonds and emeralds, and one is silver with rubies. If a ring is selected at random, find the probability that:
   (a) it is a gold ring.
   (b) it is a ring with diamonds.
   (c) it is a ring with diamonds or emeralds.
   (d) it does not have rubies.

Determine whether or not the events given in Exercise 38 through 41 are mutually exclusive.

38. A person is selected from the customers at Fast Foods. *F* is the event that a female is selected, and *G* is the event that a child is selected.

39. Consider the experiment of selecting a student from a college. *F* is the event of a foreign student attending on a student visa, and *G* is the event of a U.S. student.

40. A child is selected from a group of children who were born prematurely. *F* is the event that the child suffers some loss of hearing, and *G* is the event that the child suffers some loss of vision.

41. A coin is tossed three times. *F* is the event that it lands heads up on the second toss, and *G* is the event that it lands tails up on the second toss.

42. A single card is drawn from a deck of 52 bridge cards. Find the probability that it is:
   (a) a 5.
   (b) a club.
   (c) a red spade.
   (d) an even number.
   (e) a 9 or a 10.
   (f) a heart, diamond, or black card.

43. On a single toss of one die, find the probability of tossing:
   (a) a number less than 6.
   (b) the number 4.
   (c) 2, 4, or 5.
   (d) an odd number less than 5.
   (e) 1 or 3.

44. A card is drawn at random from a deck of 52 playing cards. Find the probability of drawing:
   (a) an ace or a 7.
   (b) a 6, a 7, or an 8.

45. A box contains ten balls numbered 1 through 10. One ball is selected at random. Find the probability of getting:
   (a) number 10.
   (b) number 1.
   (c) an even number.
   (d) an odd number.
   (e) a number greater than 5.
   (f) an even number or a number greater than 4.
   (g) an even number or a number less than 8.

46. Two dice are thrown. What is the probability that the same number appears on both dice?

47. A card is drawn from a deck of 52 playing cards. Find the probability that it is an ace or a spade.

III

48. A person is selected at random from a pool of ten people consisting of six men and four women for a psychology study. Find the probability that the person selected is:
   (a) a man.
   (b) a woman.

49. For a proposed piece of legislation the probability of its passing the House is .76, the probability of its passing the Senate is .62, and the probability of its passing at least one is .89. Find the probability of its passing both.

50. A person's birthday is known to be in April.
    (a) What is the probability that it is April 15?
    (b) What is the probability that it is in the first seven days of April?
    (c) What is the probability that it is in the first half of April?

51. In a corporation, 65% of the employees are female, executives, or both. Furthermore, 55% of the employees are female, and 5% are female executives. Find the percent of employees who are male executives.

52. The professor reveals only the following information about a class: There are 21 seniors, 14 English majors, eight students who are neither seniors nor English majors, and a total of 34 students.
    (a) Determine the number who are both seniors and English majors.
    (b) Determine the number who are English majors but are not seniors.
    (c) If a student is selected at random, find the probability that the student is a senior.

53. A die is rolled. What is the probability that the number is odd or is a 2?

54. A die is rolled. Use a tree diagram to find the probability of rolling:
    (a) an even number less than 6.
    (b) an odd number less than 5.

55. In a certain state there are three large state universities, two large private universities, one small state university and four small private universities. A student plans to attend one of these institutions. Let E be the event that the student attends a state university, F that the student attends a private university, G that he goes to a large university, and H that he goes to a small university. Compute and interpret the following probabilities:
    (a) $P(E)$, $P(F)$, $P(G)$, $P(H)$
    (b) $P(E')$
    (c) $P(E \cup G)$
    (d) $P(F' \cap H)$

56. Three numbers are drawn from $\{1, 2, 3, 4, 5, 6, 7\}$ and placed in a row in the order drawn to form a three-digit number.
    (a) What is the probability that the number is 456?
    (b) What is the probability that the first digit is 2, 4, or 6?
    (c) What is the probability that it is larger than 600?
    (d) What is the probability that it is less than 326?

57. A plumber needs a certain part to complete a repair job. The probability that one part supplier has the part is .85, the probability that the other part supplier has the part is .93, and the probability that both have the part is .81. Find the probability that the plumber will be able to complete the repair.

6–4 CONDITIONAL PROBABILITY

- *Conditional Probability*
- *Multiplication Rule*

CONDITIONAL PROBABILITY

We have seen ways to compute the probability of an event E based on the outcomes in the sample space and in the event E. Sometimes a related event F occurs that provides additional information that allows us to adjust the probability of E.

For example, suppose you are taking a test with multiple-choice questions. A question has four possible answers listed, and you have no idea of the correct answer. If you make a wild guess at the answer, the probability of guessing the correct answer is $\frac{1}{4}$. However. suppose you know that one of the given answers cannot be correct. This improves your chances of guessing the right answer, and the probability becomes $\frac{1}{3}$.

In general terms this example is described as follows. The probability of an event E is sought. In case a related event F has occurred, giving reason to change the sample space and consequently the probability of E, we determine the **conditional probability** of E given that the event F has occurred. We denote this by $P(E|F)$, which we read "the probability of E given F."

We can state the above example as: "The probability of guessing the correct answer given that one answer is known to be incorrect is $\frac{1}{3}$."

If a student guesses wildly at the correct answer from the four given ones, the sample space consists of the four possible answers. When one answer is ruled out, the sample space reduces to three possible answers. Sometimes it helps to look at a conditional probability problem as one in which the sample space changes when certain conditions exist or related information is given. Let's look at the following from that viewpoint.

A student has a job testing microcomputer chips. The chips are produced by two machines, I and II. It is known that 5% of the chips produced by machine I are defective and 15% of the chips produced by machine II are defective. The student has a batch of chips that she assumes is a mixture from both machines. If she selects one at random, what is the probability that it is defective? You cannot give a precise answer to this question unless you know the proportion of chips from each machine. It does seem reasonable to say that the probability lies in the interval from 0.05 through 0.15.

Now suppose that the student obtains more information: The chips are all from machine II. This certainly changes her estimate of the probability of a defective chip; she knows that the probability is 0.15. The sample space changes from a set of chips from both machines to a set of chips from machine II. This illustrates the point that when you gain information about the state of the experiment, you may be able to change the probabilities assigned to the outcomes.

Here's how we write some of the information from the above examples.

EXAMPLE 1   *(Compare Exercise 1)*

(a) Machines I and II produce microchips, with 5% of those from machine I being defective and 15% of those from Machine II being defective. This can be stated as

$$P(\text{defective chip} \mid \text{machine I}) = .05$$
$$P(\text{defective chip} \mid \text{machine II}) = .15$$

(b) There are four possible answers to a multiple-choice question, one of which is correct. The probability of guessing the right answer is $\frac{1}{4}$. However, if one incorrect answer can be eliminated, the sample space is reduced from four to three answers, and the probability of guessing correctly becomes $\frac{1}{3}$. This is stated as

$$P(\text{guessing correct answer}) = \frac{1}{4}$$

$$P(\text{guessing correct answer} \mid \text{one incorrect answer eliminated}) = \frac{1}{3}$$

Let's look at an example of how to compute $P(E|F)$.

EXAMPLE 2   *(Compare Exercise 3)*

Professor X teaches two sections of philosophy. The regular section has 35 students, and the honors section has 25 students. The professor gives both sections the same test, and 14 students make an A, five in the regular section and nine in the honors section.

(a) If a test paper is selected at random, what is the probability that it is an A paper?

(b) A test paper is selected at random. If it is known that the paper is from the honors section, what is the probability that it is an A paper?

SOLUTION   The sample space S is the collection of all 60 papers, the event E is the set of all A papers, and F is the set of papers from the honors class.

(a) $P(E) = \dfrac{14}{60}$

(b) The knowledge that the paper is from the honors section reduces the sample space to those 25 papers, the event F. The problem is to find the probability of an A paper, given that it is from the honors section, that is, find $P(E|F)$. Since the honors section contains nine A papers and 25 papers total,

$$P(E|F) = \frac{9}{25}$$

See Figure 6–6.

FIGURE 6–6

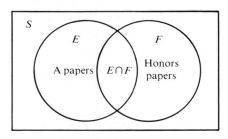

S = All of the exams, 60 total
E = All A exam papers, 14 total
F = Papers from Honors section, 25 total
$E \cap F$ = A papers from Honors section, 9 total

We now express the above results in a different form to make a general statement about conditional probability. The conditional probability from this example can be written

$$P(E|F) = \frac{9}{25} = \frac{n(E \cap F)}{n(F)}$$

If we divide the numerator and the denominator of the last fraction by $n(S)$, we have

$$P(E|F) = \frac{\dfrac{n(E \cap F)}{n(S)}}{\dfrac{n(F)}{n(S)}} = \frac{P(E \cap F)}{P(F)}$$

Be sure you understand that, in essence, F becomes the sample space when we compute $P(E|F)$, and we focus our attention on the contents of F. F is sometimes called the **reduced sample space**. Then $E \cap F$ becomes the set of successful outcomes. The definition of conditional probability is similar to the results of the last example.

Rule for Computing $P(E|F)$

E and F are events in a sample space S, with $P(F) \neq 0$. The conditional probability of E given F, denoted by $P(E|F)$, is

(a) $P(E|F) = \dfrac{P(E \cap F)}{P(F)}$

This holds whether or not the outcomes of S are equally likely.

(b) If the outcomes of S are equally likely, $P(E|F)$ may be written as

$$P(E|F) = \frac{n(E \cap F)}{n(F)}$$

EXAMPLE 3   *(Compare Exercise 9)*

In a group of 200 students, 40 are taking English, 50 are taking mathematics, and 12 are taking both.

(a) If a student is selected at random, what is the probability that the student is taking English?

(b) A student is selected at random from those taking mathematics. What is the probability that the student is taking English?

(c) A student is selected at random from those taking English. What is the probability that the student is taking mathematics?

SOLUTION

(a) $P(\text{English}) = \dfrac{40}{200} = \dfrac{1}{5}$

(b) This problem is that of finding $P(\text{English}|\text{math})$, so

$$P(\text{English}|\text{math}) = \frac{n(\text{English and math})}{n(\text{math})} = \frac{12}{50} = \frac{6}{25} = .24$$

This may also be expressed in terms of probability:

$$P(\text{English}|\text{math}) = \frac{P(\text{English and math})}{P(\text{math})} = \frac{\frac{12}{200}}{\frac{50}{200}} = \frac{.06}{.25} = .24$$

(c) This asks for

$$P(\text{math}|\text{English}) = \frac{n(\text{math and English})}{n(\text{English})} = \frac{12}{40} = \frac{3}{10}$$

Parts (b) and (c) illustrate that $P(E|F)$ and $P(F|E)$ might not be equal. ∎

MULTIPLICATION RULE

We obtain a useful formula for the probability of E and F by multiplying the equation for conditional probability throughout by $P(F)$.

Theorem 1
Multiplication Rule

E and F are events in a sample space S.

$$P(E \cap F) = P(F)P(E|F)$$

This may also be written as

$$P(E \cap F) = P(E)P(F|E)$$

This theorem states that we can find the probability of E and F by multiplying the probability of E by the conditional probability of F given E.

EXAMPLE 4   *(Compare Exercise 19)*

Two cards are drawn from a bridge deck, without replacement. What is the probability that the first is an ace and the second is a king?

SOLUTION   According to Theorem 3, we want to find

$$P(\text{ace first and king second}) = P(\text{ace first}) \times P(\text{king second}|\text{ace first})$$

Since the first card is drawn from the full deck of 52 cards,

$$P(\text{ace first}) = \frac{4}{52}$$

This first card is not replaced, so the sample space for the second card is reduced to 51 cards. Since we are assuming that the first card was an ace, there are still four kings in the deck. Then

$$P(\text{king second}|\text{ace first}) = \frac{4}{51}$$

It then follows that

$$P(\text{ace first and king second}) = \left(\frac{4}{52}\right) \times \left(\frac{4}{51}\right) = \frac{4}{663}$$

EXAMPLE 5 *(Compare Exercise 23)*

A box contains 12 light bulbs, three of which are defective. If three bulbs are selected at random, what is the probability that all three are defective?

SOLUTION According to the multiplication rule, applied twice,

$$P(\text{first defective and second defective and third defective})$$
$$= \left(\frac{3}{12}\right)\left(\frac{2}{11}\right)\left(\frac{1}{10}\right) = \frac{1}{220}$$

Here are two examples in which selections are made *with replacement*.

EXAMPLE 6 *(Compare Exercise 27)*

Two cards are drawn from a bridge deck. The first card is drawn, the outcome is observed, and the card is replaced and the deck shuffled before the second card is drawn. Find the probability that the first is an ace and the second is a king.

SOLUTION The fact that the first card is replaced before the second card is drawn makes this example different from Example 4. We still use the multiplication rule, but notice the difference when we compute

$$P(\text{ace first and king second})$$
$$= P(\text{ace first}) \times P(\text{king second}|\text{ace first})$$

When we compute $P(\text{ace first})$, we get $\frac{4}{52}$, just as we did in Example 4.

When the second card is drawn, the deck still contains 52 cards because the first card drawn was replaced. This gives

$$P(\text{king second}|\text{ace first}) = \frac{4}{52}$$

We now have

$$P(\text{ace first and king second})$$
$$= P(\text{ace first}) \times P(\text{king second}|\text{ace first})$$
$$= \frac{4}{52} \times \frac{4}{52} = \frac{1}{169}$$

Be sure you understand how this example differs from Example 4. They both use the basic property that

$$P(E \cap F) = P(E)P(F|E)$$

but replacing the first card in this example makes the sample space for the second draw different from the sample space in Example 4. In Example 4 the sample space for the second draw contains 51 cards, an ace having been removed. In this example the sample space for the second draw contains 52 cards because the ace drawn first was replaced before the second draw occurred.

These two examples illustrate that you need to be sure you understand what effect the first action has on the second when you compute conditional probability.

EXAMPLE 7   *(Compare Exercise 31)*

A box contains five red balls, six green balls, and two white balls. Three balls are drawn, but each one is replaced before the next one is drawn. Find the probability the first is red, the second is green, and the third is white.

SOLUTION

$$P(\text{red first and green second and white third})$$
$$= P(\text{red first}) \times P(\text{green second}|\text{red first})$$
$$\times P(\text{white third}|\text{red first and green second})$$
$$= \frac{5}{13} \times \frac{6}{13} \times \frac{2}{13} = \frac{60}{2197}$$

Notice that the sample space has 13 elements for each draw because the balls are replaced. If the balls are not replaced after each draw, the probability is

$$\frac{5}{13} \times \frac{6}{12} \times \frac{2}{11}$$

EXAMPLE 8   *(Compare Exercise 33)*

A large corporation has 1500 male and 1200 female employees. In a fitness survey it was found that 40% of the men and 30% of the women are overweight. An employee is selected at random. Find the probability that:
(a) the person is a male.
(b) the person is overweight, given that the person is a male.
(c) the person is overweight, given that the person is a female.
(d) the person is overweight.
(e) the person is a male, given that the person is overweight.

SOLUTION   Let O represent the event of an overweight person, let F represent the event of a female, and let M represent the event of a male.

(a) We want $P(M)$, which is $\dfrac{1500}{2700} = \dfrac{5}{9}$.

(b) $P(O|M)$ is given by the statement that 40% of the males are overweight, so $P(O|M) = .40$.

(c) Since 30% of the females are overweight, $P(O|F) = .30$.

(d) The given information tells us that 600 males are overweight (40% of 1500) and 360 females are overweight (30% of 1200), giving a total of 960 overweight persons. Then

$$P(O) = \frac{960}{2700} = \frac{32}{90}$$

(e) $P(M \cap O) = \frac{600}{2700} = \frac{2}{9}$, so

$$P(M|O) = \frac{P(M \cap O)}{P(O)} = \frac{\frac{2}{9}}{\frac{32}{90}} = \frac{10}{16} = .625$$

6-4 EXERCISES

I

1. (*See Example 1*) The probability that Jane will solve a problem is $\frac{3}{4}$, and the probability that Jill will solve the problem is $\frac{1}{2}$.
   (a) What is P(problem will be solved|Jane)?
   (b) What is P(problem will be solved|Jill)?

2. A plant manufactures TV sets on two assembly lines, A and B. Quality control studies found 1% of TV sets assembled on line A are defective and 2.5% of those on line B are defective. State this information in terms of conditional probability.

3. (*See Example 2*) A French professor gives Sections 1 and 2 of a French course the same passage to translate. Section 1 has 24 students, and seven translate the passage correctly. Section 2 has 21 students, and nine translate the passage correctly.
   (a) If one of the papers is selected at random, what is the probability that it is a correct translation?
   (b) One of the papers is selected and is known to be from Section 1. What is the probability that it is a correct translation?
   (c) A paper is selected and is known to be a correct translation. What is the probability that it is from Section 2?

4. A letter is drawn at random from the 26 letters of the alphabet. Find the probability that it is:
   (a) an *a*, given that it is a vowel.
   (b) an *x*, given that it is not a vowel.
   (c) an *x, y,* or *z*, given that it is not a vowel.

5. A wallet contains seven $1 bills, three $5 bills, and five $10 bills. A bill is selected at random from the wallet. Find the probability that the bill is:
   (a) a $5 bill, given that it is not a $1 bill.
   (b) a $1 bill, given that it is smaller than $10.

6. A creative writing class has 30 students, of whom 16 are seniors, 12 are juniors, and four are sophomores. Nine of the seniors, five of the juniors, and two of the sophomores are journalism majors. A student is selected at random. Find the probability that:
   (a) the student is a journalism major, given that the student is a junior.
   (b) the student is not a senior, given that the student is a journalism major.

7. A class has 15 boys and 10 girls. One student is selected. *F* is the event of selecting a girl, and *K* is the event of selecting Kate, one of the girls in the class. Determine $P(K|F)$ and $P(F|K)$.

8. A card is drawn from a pack of 52 playing cards. Find the probability that the card will be a king, given that it is a face card. (The face cards are the jacks, queens, and kings.)

9. (*See Example 3*) In a group of 60 children, 28 are enrolled in a summer swimming program, 20 signed up for soccer, and six are in both.
   (a) If a child is selected at random, find the probability that the child is enrolled in swimming.
   (b) If a child is selected from those signed up for soccer, what is the probability that the child is enrolled in swimming?
   (c) If a child is selected from those enrolled in swimming, what is the probability that the child is signed up for soccer?

10. A furniture factory makes desks. Inspectors find that the probability that a desk has a structural defect is .04, the probability that it has a defect in finish is .09, and the probability of both kinds of defect is .02.
   (a) A desk is randomly selected. Find the probability that it has a structural defect, given that it has a defect in finish.
   (b) A desk is randomly selected. Find the probability that it has a defect in finish, given that it has a structural defect.

Compute $P(E|F)$ and $P(F|E)$ in Exercises 11 through 14.

11. $P(E) = .6, P(F) = .7, P(E \cap F) = .3$

12. $P(E) = \frac{4}{5}, P(F) = \frac{3}{5}, P(E \cap F) = \frac{1}{5}$

13. $P(E) = .60, P(F) = .40, P(E \cap F) = .24$

14. $P(E) = \frac{3}{7}, P(F) = \frac{2}{7}, P(E \cap F) = \frac{1}{7}$

15. A mathematics professor assigns two problems for homework and knows that the probability of a student solving the first problem is .75, the probability of solving the second is .45, and the probability of solving both is .20.
   (a) What is the probability that a student solves the first problem, given that he has solved the second?
   (b) What is the probability that a student solves the second problem, given that she has solved the first?

16. The following table summarizes the graduating class of Old Main University:

	B.A.	B.S.	B.B.A.	TOTAL
Male	180	60	240	480
Female	159	23	194	376
Total	339	83	434	856

A student is selected at random from the graduation class. Find the probability that the student:
(a) is male.
(b) is receiving a B.A. degree.
(c) is a female receiving a B.B.A. degree.
(d) is a female, given that the student is receiving a B.S. degree.
(e) is receiving a B.A. degree, given that the student is a female.
(f) is a male, given that the student is receiving a B.A. or B.S. degree.

17. A university cafeteria surveyed its customers for their coffee preferences. The findings are summarized as follows:

	DO NOT DRINK COFFEE	PREFER REGULAR COFFEE	PREFER DECAFFEINATED COFFEE	TOTAL
Female	23	145	69	237
Male	18	196	46	260
Total	41	341	115	497

A student is selected at random from this group. Find the probability that:
(a) the student does not drink coffee.
(b) the student is male.
(c) the student is a female who prefers regular coffee.
(d) the student prefers decaffeinated coffee, given that the student is male.
(e) the student is male, given that the student prefers decaffeinated coffee.
(f) the student is female, given that the student prefers regular coffee or does not drink coffee.

18. A standardized reading test was given to fourth and fifth grade classes at an elementary school. A summary of the results is the following:

	SCORING BELOW GRADE LEVEL	SCORING AT GRADE LEVEL	SCORING ABOVE GRADE LEVEL	TOTAL
Fourth grade	120	342	216	678
Fifth grade	105	324	98	527
Total	225	666	314	1205

A student is selected at random. Find the probability that the student is:

(a) a fourth grade student.
(b) a fourth grade student scoring above grade level.
(c) a fifth grade student scoring at or above grade level.
(d) a fourth grade student, given that the student scores below grade level.
(e) a student scoring below grade level, given that the student is in the fourth grade.

19. (*See Example 4*) Two cards are drawn from a bridge deck without replacement. Find the probability that the first is a 4 and the second is a 5.

20. Two people are selected at random from eight men and six women. Find the probability that the first is a woman and the second is a man.

21. A card is drawn at random from a deck of playing cards. It is replaced, and another card is drawn.
(a) Find the probability that the first card is an 8 and the second is a 10.
(b) Find the probability that both are clubs.
(c) Find the probability that both are red cards.

22. The letters of the word BETTER appear on a child's blocks, one letter per block. The child arbitrarily selects two of the blocks. Find the probability that the child selects a T followed by R.

23. (*See Example 5*) A person draws three balls in succession from a box containing four red balls, two white balls, and six blue balls. Find the probability that the balls drawn are red, white, and blue, in that order.

24. Three people are selected from a group of seven men and five women.
(a) Find the probability that all three are men.
(b) Find the probability that the first two are women and the third is a man.

25. A company motor pool contains six Dodge and eight Ford cars. Each of two salespeople is randomly assigned a car. Find the probability that both are assigned Dodges.

26. A random selection of four books is made from a shelf containing six novels, five chemistry books, and three history books. Find the probability that all four are novels.

27. (*See Example 6*) The name of each person attending a club meeting is written on a card and placed in a box for a drawing of two door prizes. A name is drawn for one prize, and the name is replaced before the second one is drawn. If 32 people are present, find the probability that both prizes go to the Rosen family. Three members of the Rosen family are present.

28. A box contains three black balls and two white balls. Two balls are drawn in succession; the ball is replaced after each drawing. Determine the probability of first drawing a black ball and then a white ball.

29. Fifteen cards are numbered 1 through 15. Two cards are drawn with replacement.
(a) Find the probability that both are less than 5.
(b) Find the probability that the first is less than 5 and the second is greater than 12.

30. A pen holder contains 12 identical pens, four of which do not write. A child randomly selects a pen, replaces it, and selects again. Find the probability that both pens do not write.

31. (*See Example 7*) A box contains four black balls, six red balls, and five green balls. Three balls are drawn, and each one is replaced before the next one is drawn.
(a) Find the probability that the balls drawn are red, black, and red in that order.
(b) Find the probability that all three balls are green.

32. A die is rolled three times. Find the probability that the numbers rolled are 2, 6, and 3 in that order.

33. (*See Example 8*) In a group of college students, 60 males and 75 females, 35% of the males and 40% of the females are from out of state. A student is randomly selected. Find the probability that:
(a) the person is a female.
(b) the person is from out of state, given that the person is a male.
(c) the person is from out of state, given that the person is a female.
(d) the person is from out of state.
(e) the person is a female, given that the person is from out of state.

34. In a group of professional people, 25 are accountants, 15 are engineers, 30 are teachers, and 10 are nurses. The number of females within each profession is 11 accountants, six engineers, 24 teachers, and nine nurses. A person is selected at random from the group. Find the probability that the selection is:
   (a) a female.
   (b) an engineer.
   (c) a female engineer.
   (d) a female, given that the person is an engineer.
   (e) an engineer, given that the person is a female.
   (f) a female, given that the person is an accountant or engineer.
   (g) a teacher or nurse, given that the person is a female.

35. Two dice are tossed. What is the probability that their sum will be 6, given that one face shows 2?

36. Two cards are drawn at random from a deck of playing cards without replacement. Find the probability that the first is a king and the second is a queen.

II

37. A university planning committee is composed of 24 faculty members and 16 administrative staff members. A group of 12 people is selected at random from the committee. Find the probability that the group consists of nine faculty members and three staff members.

38. A seminar has ten students, one of whom is a National Merit Scholar. If five students are selected at random from the seminar, find the probability that one of them will be the National Merit Scholar.

39. In a class of 28 freshmen, eight receive financial aid and 20 do not. If six students are selected at random from the class, find the probability that three receive financial aid and three do not.

40. Find the probability of a person being dealt all spades in a bridge hand (13 cards).

41. In a club with 15 seniors, 20 juniors, ten sophomores, and five freshmen, a committee of eight members is chosen at random. Find the probability that the committee selected consists of two seniors, two juniors, two sophomores, and two freshmen.

42. A subcommittee consisting of eight students is to be selected from a committee of 22 students: seven seniors, six juniors, five sophomores, and four freshmen. Find the probability that the committee will consist of three seniors, two juniors, two sophomores, and one freshman.

43. A hand of 13 cards is dealt from a pack of 52 bridge cards. Determine the probability of:
   (a) getting only one ace.
   (b) getting all four aces.
   (c) getting no aces.

III

44. The winning ticket of a lottery is a sequence of three numbers chosen from the numbers 1 through 100.
   (a) If a number may repeat in the sequence, find the probability that a player guesses the winning sequence.
   (b) If a number may not repeat in the winning sequence, find the probability that a player guesses the winning sequence.

45. If one check in 10,000 is forged, 5% of all checks are postdated, and 80% of forged checks are postdated, find the probability that a postdated check is forged.

46. In a corporation, 30% of the employees hold college degrees, and 85% of those holding college degrees earn over $30,000. If an employee is selected at random, what is the probability that the employee has a college degree and earns over $30,000?

47. Thirty percent of a freshman class are awarded scholarships, and the probability that a scholarship will continue to the sophomore year is .90. If a freshman is selected at random, what is the probability that it is a student who holds a scholarship that will be continued the next year?

48. At a college, 32% of the freshmen score above 550 on the SAT mathematics test. Of those scoring above 550, 87% make a grade of C or higher in their mathematics course. A freshman is selected at random. What is the probability that the student selected at random scored above 550 and makes a C or above in mathematics?

49. A box contains two white balls and one red ball. Two balls are drawn in succession without replacement. Find the probability of drawing:
(a) two white balls.
(b) a white ball followed by a red ball.
(c) a red ball and a white ball, order being unimportant.

50. A store has 50 boxes of Goodies cereal on the shelf, and five of the boxes contain special prizes. A family purchases four boxes of the cereal. Find the probability that two boxes contain special prizes and two do not.

51. A box contains five balls numbered 1 through 5. Three balls are selected in succession without replacement. Find the probability of getting:
(a) numbers 1, 2, and 3 in that order.
(b) numbers 1, 2, and 3 in any order.
(c) three balls, the sum of whose numbers is 4.
(d) three balls, the sum of whose numbers is 6.
(e) three odd-numbered balls.
(f) two odd-numbered balls and one even-numbered ball.

52. Of a group of children, .4 are boys and .6 are girls. Of the boys, .5 have brown eyes; of the girls, .3 have brown eyes. A child is selected at random from the group.
(a) Find the probability that the child is a girl.
(b) Find $P(\text{brown eyes}|\text{boy})$.
(c) Find the probability that the child is a boy with brown eyes.
(d) Find the probability that the child is a girl with brown eyes.
(e) Find the probability that the child has brown eyes.
(f) Find the probability that the child is a girl, given that the child has brown eyes.

53. Professor X stimulates interest in homework by requiring two students each to draw a problem at random and solve the problem drawn. On a certain day, ten problems were assigned. Anita is to draw first and Al second. They had solved nine problems but had not solved one.
(a) Find the probability that Anita draws the unsolved problem.
(b) Find the probability that neither Anita nor Al draws the unsolved problem.
(c) Find the probability that Al does not draw the unsolved problem.

54. Box A contains six red balls and four green balls, and Box B contains two red balls and eight green balls. A box is selected, and a ball is drawn. The probability of selecting Box A is $\frac{1}{3}$, and the probability of selecting Box B is $\frac{2}{3}$.
(a) Find the probability that the ball is a red ball from Box B.
(b) Find the probability that the ball is green.

55. Mr. Wing has 18 ties, three of which clash with the suit he plans to wear. If he selects four ties at random, find the probability that one of the four clashes with his suit.

56. A senior citizens organization has twice as many women as men. Sixty percent of the men are bald. What is the probability that a randomly selected person is a bald male?

57. Show that if $E \subset F$ and $P(F) \neq 0$, then
$$P(E|F) = \frac{P(E)}{P(F)}$$

58. Show that $P(E|E) = 1$ when $P(E) \neq 0$.
59. Show that if $E \subset F$ and $P(E) \neq 0$, then $P(F|E) = 1$.

6–5   INDEPENDENT EVENTS

- *Independent Events*
- *Mutually Exclusive and Independent Events*

INDEPENDENT EVENTS

Sometimes two events E and F are related in such a way that the occurrence of one event in no way affects the chance of the occurrence or nonoccurrence of the other event. For example, the first toss of a coin has no influence on the outcome of the second toss. If one person selects a card from one deck and another person selects a card from a second deck, then an ace (or any other card) drawn from the first deck has no effect on whether or not a king is drawn from the second deck, and vice versa.

If neither of two events E and F affects the probability of the occurrence of the other, we say that they are **independent,** and we intuitively expect $P(E|F) = P(E)$, since the probability of E is unchanged whether or not we are given F. Similarly, $P(F|E) = P(F)$. This leads to the following definition of independence.

Definition 1
Independent Events

The events E and F are **independent** if

$$P(E|F) = P(E) \text{ or } P(F|E) = P(F).$$

Otherwise, E and F are *dependent.*
   Note: If $P(E|F) = P(E)$, then $P(F|E) = P(F)$ also holds, and vice versa.

Let's check $P(E|F)$ and $P(E)$ for two situations, one in which intuition suggests that the events are dependent and one in which intuition suggests that the events are independent.

EXAMPLE 1

A bag contains nine red and six green balls. Look at two situations:

(a) Two balls are drawn, and the first ball is *not* replaced before the second is drawn.

(b) Two balls are drawn, and the first ball is replaced before the second ball is drawn.

In each situation, determine the probability that the second ball is red, given that the first ball is red.

SOLUTION   First, what does your intuition tell you about the chances of drawing a red ball the second time? Does the fact that a red ball was drawn the first time affect the chances?

In situation (a) the number of red balls available for the second draw depends on whether or not a red ball was drawn first. If a red ball is drawn first, eight of the 14 balls available for the second draw are red. If a green ball is drawn first, then nine of the 14 balls available for the second draw are red. Therefore it intuitively seems that a red ball being drawn first has an effect on the chances of drawing a red ball second. It is reasonable to say the events of drawing a red ball first and drawing a red ball second are dependent.

In situation (b) 15 balls are available for the second draw, nine of which are red, regardless of whether a red or a green ball was drawn first. Therefore it intuitively seems that a red ball being drawn first has no effect on the chances of a red ball being drawn second. It is reasonable to say the events of drawing a red ball first and of drawing a red ball second are independent.

Now let's compute the probability of drawing a red ball second, given that a red ball is drawn first for each situation.

(a) The first ball is not replaced. Let's compute both

$$P(\text{second ball red}) \quad \text{and} \quad P(\text{second ball red}|\text{first ball red})$$

and compare. Compute P(second ball red).

The event "second ball red" occurs in two ways:

(i) the first ball is red and the second red. This occurs in $9 \times 8 = 72$ ways.

(ii) the first ball is green and the second red. This occurs in $6 \times 9 = 54$ ways.

Therefore there are $72 + 54 = 126$ ways in which a red ball can occur second. The total number of ways to draw two balls is $15 \times 14 = 210$ ways. Then

$$P(\text{second ball red}) = \frac{126}{210} = \frac{3}{5}$$

Now compute $P(\text{second ball red}|\text{first ball red})$.

Assuming that a red ball is drawn first, eight of the 14 balls remaining are red, so

$$P(\text{second ball red}|\text{first ball red}) = \frac{8}{14} = \frac{4}{7}$$

We now conclude that "second ball red" and "first ball red" are dependent because

$$P(\text{second ball red}|\text{first ball red}) = \frac{4}{7} \neq \frac{3}{5}$$
$$= P(\text{second ball red})$$

(b) The first ball is replaced before the second draw. Again we compute $P(\text{red second})$ and $P(\text{red second}|\text{red first})$. Compute $P(\text{red second})$.

Since the first ball is replaced before the second draw, nine of the 15 balls are red, so

$$P(\text{red second}) = \frac{9}{15} = \frac{3}{5}$$

Compute $P(\text{red second}|\text{red first})$.

Since the first ball was replaced, the fact that a red ball was drawn first does not change that nine of the 15 balls available for the second draw are red giving

$$P(\text{red second}|\text{red first}) = \frac{9}{15} = \frac{3}{5}$$

Since $P(\text{red second}) = \frac{3}{5} = P(\text{red second}|\text{red first})$, the events "red first" and "red second" are independent.

In Example 1 our intuition and the probabilities behaved in a way that was consistent with Definition 1. Now we go to an extreme and look at an example in which our intuition gives no indication of whether or not two events are independent.

EXAMPLE 2   *(Compare Exercise 1)*

A survey of 100 psychology majors revealed that 25 had taken an economics course (E), 35 had taken a French course (F), and five had taken both economics and French ($E \cap F$). Are the events "had taken economics" and "had taken French" independent or dependent?

SOLUTION   It is helpful to draw a Venn diagram of this information (see Figure 6–7). The sample space contains 100 elements, E contains 25, F contains 35, and $E \cap F$ contains 5. From the Venn diagram we get the following probabilities:

$$P(E) = \frac{25}{100} = .25$$

$$P(F) = \frac{35}{100} = .35$$

$$P(E|F) = \frac{5}{35} = .1429$$

$$P(F|E) = \frac{5}{25} = .20$$

Since $P(E) \neq P(E|F)$, E and F are dependent. We could reach the same conclusion by the observation that $P(F) \neq P(F|E)$.

FIGURE 6–7

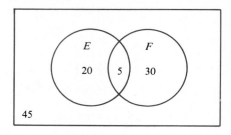

These two examples illustrate that sometimes our intuition correctly tells us whether or not two events are independent and sometimes it does not tell us. The best way to tell is to compute $P(E)$ and $P(E|F)$ and see whether they are equal or not.

When E and F are independent events, the multiplication rule $P(E \cap F) = P(E)P(F|E)$ simplifies to the following.

Theorem 2 **Multiplication Rule for** **Independent Events**	If E and F are **independent** events, then $$P(E \cap F) = P(E)P(F)$$

We can also use Theorem 2 to determine whether two events are independent. For the events in Example 2,

$$P(E \cap F) = \frac{5}{100} = .05$$
$$P(E)P(F) = (.25)(.35) = .0875$$

Since $P(E \cap F) \neq P(E)P(F)$, E and F are not independent—the same conclusion we reached by using Definition 1.

While it may be intuitively clear that two tosses of a coin are independent, in other situations independence may be determined only by using Definition 1 or Theorem 2 (as in Example 2). Actually, any one of the three conditions provides a test for independence.

Test for Independence *of Events*	If any one of the following holds, then events E and F are independent. **1.** $P(E\|F) = P(E)$ **2.** $P(F\|E) = P(F)$ **3.** $P(E \cap F) = P(E)P(F)$

EXAMPLE 3 *(Compare Exercise 7)*

A card is selected at random from the following four cards: 10 of diamonds, 10 of spades, 8 of hearts, and 6 of clubs. Let E be the event "select a red card," and let F be the event "select a 10."

(a) Are E and F mutually exclusive?
(b) Are E and F independent?

SOLUTION

(a) E and F are not mutually exclusive because selecting a red card and selecting a 10 can occur at the same time—for example, selecting the 10 of diamonds.

(b) From the information given,

$$P(E) = P(\text{red card}) = \frac{1}{2}$$

$$P(F) = P(10) = \frac{1}{2}$$

$$P(E \cap F) = P(\text{red 10}) = \frac{1}{4}$$

Since $P(E \cap F) = P(E)P(F) = \frac{1}{4}$, E and F are independent.

This example illustrates two points.

1. Two independent events need not be mutually exclusive. In fact, mutually exclusive events are generally dependent. (*See Exercise 37.*)
2. Sometimes the only way to determine whether events are independent is to perform the computation in the tests for independence.

We can now compute the compound probability, $P(E \cap F)$, by using Theorem 1 of Section 6–4 and Theorem 2 of this section; use Theorem 1 for dependent events and Theorem 2 for independent events.

EXAMPLE 4 *(Compare Exercise 11)*

One bag contains four red balls and five white balls. A second bag contains three green balls and seven yellow balls. If a ball is drawn from each bag, what is the probability that the first is white and the second is green?

SOLUTION Since the balls are drawn from different bags, the two events are independent, so

$$P(\text{first white and second green}) = \left(\frac{5}{9}\right) \times \left(\frac{3}{10}\right) = \frac{1}{6}$$

EXAMPLE 5   *(Compare Exercise 15)*

Jack and Jill work on a problem independently. The probability that Jack solves it is $\frac{2}{3}$, and the probability that Jill solves it is $\frac{4}{5}$.

(a) What is the probability that both solve it?
(b) What is the probability that neither solves it?
(c) What is the probability that exactly one of them solves it?

SOLUTION

(a) The probability that both solve the problem is

$$P(\text{Jack solves it and Jill solves it}) = \left(\frac{2}{3}\right) \times \left(\frac{4}{5}\right)$$

$$= \frac{8}{15}$$

(b) The probability that Jack does not solve the problem is $1 - \frac{2}{3} = \frac{1}{3}$, and the probability that Jill does not is $1 - \frac{4}{5} = \frac{1}{5}$. Then

$$P(\text{Jack doesn't and Jill doesn't}) = \left(\frac{1}{3}\right) \times \left(\frac{1}{5}\right) = \frac{1}{15}$$

(c) There are two ways in which one of them will solve the problem, namely, Jack does and Jill doesn't or Jack doesn't and Jill does. These two ways are mutually exclusive events, so we need to compute the probability of each of these outcomes and then add.

$$P(\text{Jack does and Jill doesn't}) = \left(\frac{2}{3}\right) \times \left(\frac{1}{5}\right) = \frac{2}{15}$$

$$P(\text{Jack doesn't and Jill does}) = \left(\frac{1}{3}\right) \times \left(\frac{4}{5}\right) = \frac{4}{15}$$

Then

$$P(\text{one of them solves the problem}) = \frac{2}{15} + \frac{4}{15} = \frac{6}{15} = \frac{2}{5}$$

Recall that $P(E \cup F) = P(E) + P(F) - P(E \cap F)$. When E and F are independent, $P(E \cap F) = P(E)P(F)$, so we can substitute for $P(E \cap F)$ to obtain the following theorem.

Theorem 3   When E and F are independent,

$$P(E \cup F) = P(E) + P(F) - P(E)P(F)$$

EXAMPLE 6   *(Compare Exercise 21)*

Jack and Jill work on a problem independently. The probability that Jack solves it is $\frac{2}{3}$, and the probability that Jill solves it is $\frac{4}{5}$. What is the probability that at least one of them solves it?

SOLUTION   We will show you three ways to work this problem:

Case I:	Using mutually exclusive events.
Case II:	Using Theorem 3.
Case III:	Using the failure theorem (Theorem 1, Section 6–3).

Case I: At least one of them solving the problem is equivalent to exactly one of them solving the problem (E) or both of them solving the problem (F). These events, E and F, are mutually exclusive, so

$$P(E \cup F) = P(E) + P(F)$$

$$P(E) = \frac{2}{5} \qquad \text{from part (c) of Example 5}$$

$$P(F) = \frac{8}{15} \qquad \text{from part (a) of Example 5}$$

so

$$P(\text{at least one}) = P(E \cup F) = \frac{2}{5} + \frac{8}{15} = \frac{14}{15}$$

Case II: If we let A = the event that Jack solves the problem and B = the event that Jill solves the problem, then $A \cup B$ is one or both (at least one) solves the problem. From Theorem 3 of this section,

$$P(A \cup B) = P(A) + P(B) - P(A)P(B)$$

$$= \frac{2}{3} + \frac{4}{5} - \frac{2}{3} \times \frac{4}{5}$$

$$= \frac{10 + 12 - 8}{15} = \frac{14}{15}$$

Case III: The failure of "at least one solves the problem" is "neither solves the problem," so

$$P(\text{at least one solves}) = 1 - P(\text{neither solves})$$

by the failure theorem (Section 6–3). This is

$$1 - \frac{1}{3} \times \frac{1}{5} = 1 - \frac{1}{15} = \frac{14}{15}$$

Let's illustrate some of these concepts using a tree diagram.

EXAMPLE 7   *(Compare Exercise 29)*

The city council has money for one public service project: a recreation-sports complex, a performing arts center, or a branch library. The council polled 200 citizens for their preference, 120 men and 80 women. The men responded as follows: 45% preferred the recreation-sports complex, 20% the performing arts center, and 35% the branch library. The women responded as follows: 15% favored the recreation-sports complex, 40% the performing arts center, and 45% the branch library.

(a) Represent this information on a tree diagram.
(b) What is the probability that a person selected at random prefers the performing arts center?
(c) What is the probability that a person selected at random is a woman who prefers the performing arts center or the branch library?
(d) Are the events "male" and "prefers the recreation-sports complex" independent?

SOLUTION   Use the following abbreviations: M for male and F for female; RS, PA, and BL for recreation-sports complex, performing arts center, and branch library, respectively.

The information provided gives the following probabilities:

$$P(M) = .6, \qquad P(E) = .4$$
$$P(RS|M) = .45, \qquad P(PA|M) = .20, \qquad P(BL|M) = .35$$
$$P(RS|F) = .15, \qquad P(PA|F) = .40, \qquad P(BL|F) = .45$$

(a) Figure 6–8 shows the tree diagram with this information.

FIGURE 6–8

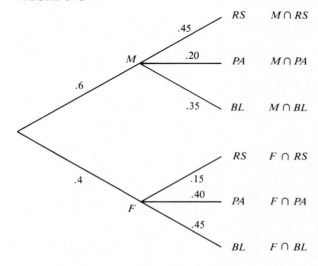

(b) The two branches that terminate at *PA* are $M \cap PA$ and $F \cap PA$, so

$$P(PA) = .12 + .16 = .28$$

(c) The branches $F \cap PA$ and $F \cap BL$ are the two outcomes in this event, so

$$P(F \text{ who prefers } PA \text{ or } BL) = .16 + .18 = .34$$

(d) If the events "male" and "prefers the recreation-sports complex" are independent, then $P(RS|M)$ must equal $P(RS)$. Since $P(RS|M) = .45$ and $P(RS) = .27 + .06 = .33$, the events are not independent. _____ ∎

MUTUALLY EXCLUSIVE AND INDEPENDENT EVENTS

Sometimes students find it difficult to understand the concepts of independent, dependent, and mutually exclusive events. If you determine two events to be dependent, you still might not know whether they are mutually exclusive or not because two dependent events may or may not be mutually exclusive. Let's look at some examples to get a feeling of the concepts.

EXAMPLE 8

Nikki and Alice are two students at the University who do not know each other and have no contacts with each other. In such a case it seems reasonable that Nikki's decision to take Art History or not has no influence on whether or not Alice takes Art History. We say the events "Nikki takes Art History" and "Alice takes Art History" are independent because the probability that one of them takes the course has no influence on the probability that the other takes it. On the other hand, both could take the course, so the events are *not* mutually exclusive. To be mutually exclusive, the occurrence of one event must exclude the possibility of the other occurring.

Under different circumstances, as when Nikki and Alice are roommates, it seems reasonable to think that whether Nikki takes Art History or not might influence whether or not Alice takes it; that is, the events "Nikki takes Art History" and "Alice takes Art History" might be dependent. Even if they are roommates, their decisions might still be independent, but we need information on the probability of each person's decision before we can say.

Even if their decisions are dependent, the events are not mutually exclusive because both could take Art History. _____ ∎

Keep in mind that the test for mutually exclusive events is to determine whether or not the two events can occur at the same time. The test for the independence or dependence of two events depends on how their probabilities are related.

EXAMPLE 9

Some people's eyes become irritated and water when the pollen count rises above a certain threshold value. A similar reaction occurs when the ozone pollution rises above a threshold value. The city's Air Quality Board monitors the pollution levels and knows that 30% of the days the ozone will be above threshold value, 20% of the days pollen will be above threshold, and 6% of the days both will be above threshold.

(a) Are the events "ozone above threshold" and "pollen above threshold" mutually exclusive?

(b) Are the events "ozone above threshold" and "pollen above threshold" independent?

SOLUTION

(a) Both events can occur at the same time. In fact, it is stated that they occur at the same time 6% of the time, so the occurrence of one does not exclude the possibility of the other. They are not mutually exclusive.

(b) To determine independence or dependence, we need to check the probabilities of the events. One test given earlier in this section is to determine whether

$$P(\text{ozone pollution}) \times P(\text{pollen pollution})$$

is equal to

$$P(\text{both ozone and pollen pollution})$$

From the given information we have

$$P(\text{ozone pollution}) \times P(\text{pollen pollution}) = .30 \times .20 = .06$$

and

$$P(\text{both ozone and pollen pollution}) = .06$$

Since these computations are equal, the events are independent.

EXAMPLE 10

Look at the three situations in Figure 6–9 and determine whether the events are mutually exclusive and whether they are independent or dependent.

(a) Since E and F overlap, they have outcomes in common, which tells us that they are not mutually exclusive.

To check for independence, we must compute the probabilities

$$P(E) \times P(F) = \frac{48}{132} \times \frac{22}{132} = \frac{8}{132}$$

and

$$P(E \cap F) = \frac{8}{132}$$

E and F are independent because $P(E) \times P(F) = P(E \cap F)$.

(b) The events E and F are not mutually exclusive because they have events in common.

Now compute

$$P(E) \times P(F) = \frac{45}{320} \times \frac{65}{320} = \frac{117}{4096}$$

and

$$P(E \cap F) = \frac{5}{320} = \frac{1}{64}$$

E and F are dependent because $P(E) \times P(F) \neq P(E \cap F)$.

(c) The events E and F are mutually exclusive because they have no outcomes in common. E and F are dependent because $P(E) \times P(F) \neq P(E \cap F)$ as the following computations show:

$$P(E) \times P(F) = \frac{30}{200} \times \frac{50}{200} = \frac{3}{80}$$

and

$$P(E \cap F) = \frac{0}{200} = 0$$

FIGURE 6–9

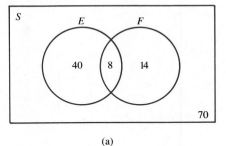

(a)

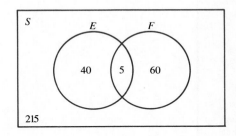

(b)

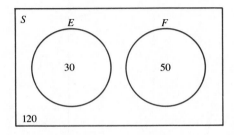

(c)

6-5 EXERCISES

1. (*See Example 2*) Each of the Venn diagrams in Figure 6–10 shows the number of elements in each region determined by the two events E and F and the sample space S. In each case, determine (i) whether the events are mutually exclusive and (ii) whether the events are independent.

Determine whether or not E and F are independent or dependent in Exercises 2 through 5.

2. $P(E) = .6$, $P(F) = .4$, $P(E \cap F) = .10$
3. $P(E) = .3$, $P(F) = .5$, $P(E \cap F) = .15$
4. $P(E) = .4$, $P(F) = .4$, $P(E \cap F) = .16$
5. $P(E) = .3$, $P(F) = .7$, $P(E \cap F) = .20$

FIGURE 6–10

(a)

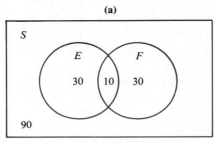

160 elements in S

(b)

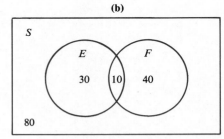

160 elements in S

(c)

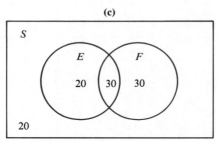

100 elements in S

(d)

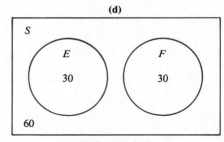

120 elements in S

(e)

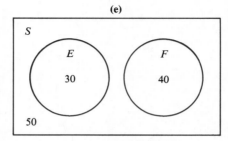

120 elements in S

(f)

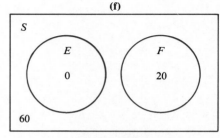

80 elements in S

6. Let E and F be events such that $P(E) = .4$, $P(F) = .6$, and $P(E \cap F) = .3$.
   (a) Find $P(E|F)$ and $P(E \cup F)$.
   (b) Are E and F independent?

7. (*See Example 3*)
   A jewel box contains four rings:

   > one has a diamond and an emerald,
   > one has a diamond and ruby,
   > one has a ruby and emerald,
   > one has pearls.

   A ring is selected at random from the box. Let the event E be "a ring has a diamond" and let the event F be "a ring has a ruby."
   (a) Are the events E and F mutually exclusive?
   (b) Are the events E and F independent?

8. A kennel raises purebred dogs. Several litters from one dog produced 16 puppies with the following markings:

   > six had a white mark on the head only,
   > two had a white mark on the forelegs only,
   > two had a white mark on both head and forelegs,
   > six had neither mark.

   Determine whether the events "white mark on the head" and "white mark on the forelegs" are independent or not.

9. A study of 100 students who took a certain mathematics course revealed that 15 received a grade of A, 20 had SAT mathematics scores above 550, and 10 received a grade of A and had SAT mathematics scores above 550. Determine whether the events "received a grade of A" and "SAT mathematics score above 550" are independent or not.

10. An advertising class conducted a taste test in a shopping mall. Passersby were asked their preference of Brands X and Y coffee and Brands A and B doughnuts. Of 500 people, 320 preferred Brand X coffee, 240 preferred Brand A doughnuts, and 110 preferred both Brand X coffee and Brand A doughnuts. Are the events "prefer Brand X coffee" and "prefer Brand A doughnuts" independent?

11. (*See Example 4*) One bag contains six red balls and eight green balls. The second bag contains nine yellow balls and twelve white balls. If one ball is drawn from each bag, what is the probability that the ball from the first bag is red and the ball from the second bag is white?

12. Box A contains eight $1 bills and two $10 bills. Box B contains five $1 bills, four $5 bills, and one $10 bill. If a bill is drawn at random from each box, find the probability that:
    (a) no $10 bills are drawn.
    (b) exactly one $10 bill is drawn.
    (c) at least one $10 bill is drawn.

13. In a programmed learning module, if a student answers a question correctly, she proceeds to the next question; otherwise, more study is required. Question 1 is a multiple-choice question with four possible responses, and Question 2 is a multiple-choice question with five possible responses. There is one correct response to each question. A student has not studied but tries to proceed through the questions by guessing. Find the probability that she answers both questions correctly.

14. On a Friday night the McClintock and Dietze families independently decide to eat out. The probability that the McClintock family chooses the Elite Cafe is .15, and the probability that the Dietze family chooses the Elite Cafe is .22. Find the probability that:
    (a) only the McClintock family chooses the Elite Cafe.
    (b) both families choose the Elite Cafe.
    (c) neither family chooses the Elite Cafe.

15. (*See Example 5*) The probabilities that two students will not show up for class on a beautiful spring day are .2 and .3, respectively. It is a beautiful spring day.
    (a) Find the probability that neither will show up for class.
    (b) Find the probability that both will show up for class.
    (c) Find the probability that exactly one will show up for class.

16. The probabilities that Jack and Jill can solve a homework problem are $\frac{3}{5}$ and $\frac{2}{3}$, respectively. Find the probability that:
    (a) both will solve the problem.
    (b) neither will solve the problem.
    (c) Jack will and Jill won't solve the problem.
    (d) Jack won't and Jill will solve the problem.
    (e) exactly one of them will solve the problem.

17. Three people are shooting at a target. The probabilities that they hit the target are .5, .6, and .8.
    (a) Find the probability that all three hit the target.
    (b) Find the probability that all three miss the target.

18. The probabilities that three students will not show up for class on a cold winter day are .1, .2, and .4. On a cold winter day, what is the probability that:
    (a) none of the three will show up for class?
    (b) all three will show up for class?
    (c) exactly one of the three will show up for class?

19. In each of the following, E and F are independent. Find $P(E \cup F)$. (*See Theorem 3.*)
    (a) $P(E) = .3$, $P(F) = .5$
    (b) $P(E) = .2$, $P(F) = .6$
    (c) $P(E) = .4$, $P(F) = .6$

20. A sample space has 56 outcomes. E and F are independent events in the sample space. E contains 24 outcomes, and F contains 21 outcomes. Find $P(E \cup F)$.

Assume that events are independent in Exercises 21 through 24.

21. (*See Example 6*) The probabilities that two students will show up for class are .6 and .8.
    (a) Find the probability that at least one shows up for class.
    (b) Find the probability that at least one does not show up for class.

22. The probabilities that Zack and Zelda can solve a homework problem are .4 and .7, respectively. Find the probability that at least one solves the problem.

23. Two people are shooting at a target. The probabilities that they hit the target are .3, and .9. Find the probability that at least one hits the target.

24. A private plane has two engines. The probability that the left one fails in flight is .01, and the probability that the right one fails is .03. Find the probability that at least one fails in flight.

25. Let F be the event of selecting a face card from a pack of 52 playing cards and let G be that of selecting a king. Determine $P(F)$, $P(G)$, $P(G|F)$, and $P(F|G)$. Are F and G independent events?

26. A coin is tossed six times. Find the probability that all six tosses will land on heads.

27. A die is tossed five times. Find the probability of its landing on 4 the first three times and on an even number the last two times.

28. Streams near industrial plants may suffer chemical pollution or thermal pollution from wastewater released in the stream. An environmental task force estimates that 6% of the streams suffer both types of pollution, 40% suffer chemical pollution, and 30% suffer thermal pollution. Determine whether chemical pollution and thermal pollution are independent.

29. (*See Example 7*) The Mall polled 300 customers—180 women and 120 men—about their preference of the use of an open area. The choices were a driftwood display, a fountain, and an abstract sculpture. The men responded as follows: 44% preferred the driftwood display, 36% preferred the fountain, and 20% preferred the abstract sculpture. The women responded as follows: 32% preferred the driftwood display, 52% preferred the fountain, and 16% preferred the abstract sculpture.
    (a) Represent this information with a tree diagram.
    (b) What is the probability that a person selected at random prefers the fountain?
    (c) What is the probability that a person selected at random is a male who prefers the driftwood display?
    (d) Are the events "female" and "prefers the fountain" independent?

30. A record shop surveyed 250 customers—90 high school students, 80 college students and 80 college graduates—about their preference of the musical groups The Swingers and The Top Brass. They responded as follows:
    High school students   65% preferred The Swingers, 35% preferred The Top Brass.
    College students   54% preferred The Swingers, 46% preferred The Top Brass.
    College graduates   48% preferred The Swingers, 52% preferred The Top Brass.

    (a) Represent this information with a tree diagram.
    (b) If a person is selected at random, what is the probability that the person is a college student who prefers The Top Brass?
    (c) What is the probability that a person selected at random prefers The Swingers?
    (d) Are the events "high school student" and "prefers The Top Brass" independent?

31. A card is picked from a pack of 52 playing cards. Let *F* be the event of selecting a red card and let *G* be that of selecting a face card. Are *F* and *G* independent events?

32. A summary of the number of graduating seniors who received job offers is given in the following table:

	YES	JOB OFFER NO	TOTAL
MALE	112	72	184
FEMALE	168	108	276
TOTALS	280	180	460

A graduating senior is selected at random.
(a) Find the probability that the student is a male.
(b) Find the probability that the student has a job offer.
(c) Find the probability that the student is a male with a job offer.
(d) Show that the events "male" and "has a job offer" are independent.

33. A bowler makes a strike if all ten pins are knocked down with the first ball of a frame. A perfect game consists of 12 consecutive strikes.
(a) Whenever Hoffman rolls a first ball of a frame, the probability of making a strike is .5. Find the probability that Hoffman rolls a perfect game.
(b) Whenever McKay rolls a first ball of a frame, the probability of a strike is .90. Find the probability that McKay rolls a perfect game.

34. Let *E* and *F* be events such that $P(E) = .6$, $P(F) = .5$, and $P(E \cup F) = .8$.
(a) Find $P(E \cap F)$.
(b) Find $P(E|F)$.
(c) Are *E* and *F* independent?

35. Tim has two irregular coins. The nickel comes up heads three fifths of the time, and the quarter comes up heads two thirds of the time. The nickel is tossed.
(a) If the nickel comes up heads, then the quarter is tossed twice.
(b) If the nickel comes up tails, the quarter is tossed once.
Find the probability that exactly two tails come up.

36. Professors Harris and Bryant have unusually good mathematics classes with no grades below C. Their grade distributions are as follows:

	HARRIS	BRYANT	TOTAL
A	10	7	17
B	6	4	10
C	8	5	13
Totals	24	16	40

A student is selected at random from the 40 students.
(a) Find the probability that the student is in Bryant's class.
(b) Find the probability that the student is in Harris's class.
(c) Find the probability that the student is an A student.
(d) Find the probability that the student is an A student from Bryant's class.
(e) Find the probability that the student is an A student, given that the student is from Bryant's class.
(f) Find the probability that the student is a B student, given that the student is from Bryant's class.
(g) Show that the events "A student" and "student from Bryant's class" are dependent.
(h) Show that the events "B student" and "student from Bryant's class" are independent.

37. Show that if *E* and *F* are mutually exclusive events, neither with probability zero, then they are dependent. (*Hint:* Consider $P(E \cap F)$ and $P(E)P(F)$.)

6–6 BAYES' RULE

Conditional probability deals with the probability of an event when you have information about something that happened earlier. Let's look at a situation that reverses the information. Imagine the following.

A club separates a stack of bills and places some in box A and the rest in box B for a drawing. Each box contains some $50 bills and other bills. At the drawing, a person selects one box and draws a bill from that box. Conditional probability answers questions such as "If box A is selected, what is the probability that a $50 bill is drawn?" Symbolically, this is "What is $P(\$50$ bill, given that box A is selected)?" This question assumes that the first event (selecting a box) is known and asks for the probability of the second event.

Bayes' rule deals with a reverse situation. It answers a question such as "If the person ends up with a $50 bill, what is the probability that it came from box A?" This assumes that the second event is known and asks for the probability of the first event. Bayes' rule determines the probability of an earlier event based on information about an event that happened later.

Let's look at an example with some probabilities given to see when and how to use Bayes' rule. We will then make a formal statement of the rule.

The student body at a college is 60% male and 40% female. The registrar's records show that 30% of the men attended private high schools and 70% attended public high schools. Further, 80% of the women attended private high schools, and 20% attended public schools.

Before we go further, let's summarize this information in probability notation. We use M and F for male and female, and we abbreviate private and public with PRI and PUB. Then, for a student selected at random,

$$P(M) = .6, \qquad P(F) = .4$$
$$P(PRI|M) = .3, \qquad P(PUB|M) = .7$$
$$P(PRI|F) = .8, \qquad P(PUB|F) = .2$$

Figure 6–11 is a tree diagram of this information, with its four branches terminating at $M \cap PRI$, $M \cap PUB$, $F \cap PRI$, and $F \cap PUB$. Their respective probabilities are

$$P(M \cap PRI) = P(M)P(PRI|M) = .6 \times .3 = .18$$
$$P(M \cap PUB) = P(M)P(PUB|M) = .6 \times .7 = .42$$
$$P(F \cap PRI) = P(F)P(PRI|F) = .4 \times .8 = .32$$
$$P(F \cap PUB) = P(F)P(PUB|F) = .4 \times .2 = .08$$

We can find the probability that a randomly selected student attended a private school by locating all branches that terminate in PRI and adding the probabilities. Thus

$$P(PRI) = .18 + .32 = .50$$
$$P(PUB) = .42 + .08 = .50$$

FIGURE 6–11

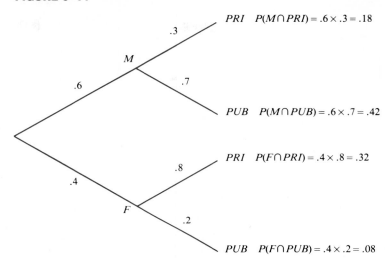

Notice that in symbolic notation,

$$P(PRI) = P(M \cap PRI) + P(F \cap PRI)$$

and

$$P(PUB) = P(M \cap PUB) + P(F \cap PUB)$$

All the above information was developed for reference throughout the example. Now let's look at a problem in which Bayes' rule is helpful.

Suppose a student selected at random is known to have attended a private school. What is the probability that the student selected is female, that is, what is $P(F|PRI)$? Notice that this information is missing from above. The definition of conditional probability gives

$$P(F|PRI) = \frac{P(F \cap PRI)}{P(PRI)}$$

You will find both $P(F \cap PRI)$ and $P(PRI)$ listed above. They were computed, not given originally. We obtained $P(PRI)$ from

$$P(PRI) = P(M \cap PRI) + P(F \cap PRI)$$

so we can write

$$P(F|PRI) = \frac{P(F \cap PRI)}{P(M \cap PRI) + P(F \cap PRI)}$$

This is one form of Bayes' rule. We get a more complicated-looking form, but one that uses the given information more directly, when we substitute

$$P(M \cap PRI) = P(M)P(PRI|M)$$

and

$$P(F \cap PRI) = P(F)P(PRI|F)$$

to get

$$P(F|PRI) = \frac{P(F)P(PRI|F)}{P(M)P(PRI|M) + P(F)P(PRI|F)}$$

$$= \frac{.4 \times .8}{.6 \times .3 + .4 \times .8} = \frac{.32}{.18 + .32} = \frac{.32}{.50} = .64$$

This last form has the advantage of using information that was given directly in the problem.

We need to observe one more fact before making a general statement. We used $P(PRI) = P(M \cap PRI) + P(F \cap PRI)$. The events M and F make up *all* the branches in the first stage of the tree diagram, so $M \cup F$ gives all of the sample space ($M \cup F = S$). Furthermore, M and F are mutually exclusive. These two conditions on M and F are needed for Bayes' rule.

NOTE This means that M and F form a partition of S.

Now we are ready for the general statement.

Bayes' Rule Let E_1 and E_2 be mutually exclusive events whose union is the sample space ($E_1 \cup E_2 = S$). Let F be an event in S, $P(F) \neq 0$. Then

(a) $P(E_1|F) = \dfrac{P(E_1 \cap F)}{P(F)}$

(b) $P(E_1|F) = \dfrac{P(E_1 \cap F)}{P(E_1 \cap F) + P(E_2 \cap F)}$

(c) $P(E_1|F) = \dfrac{P(E_1)P(F|E_1)}{P(E_1)P(F|E_1) + P(E_2)P(F|E_2)}$

EXAMPLE 1   *(Compare Exercise 7)*

A microchip company has two machines that produce the chips. Machine I produces 65% of the chips, but 5% of its chips are defective. Machine II produces 35% of the chips and 15% of its chips are defective.

A chip is selected at random and found to be defective. What is the probability that it came from machine I?

SOLUTION Let I be the set of chips produced by machine I and II be those produced by machine II. We want to find $P(\text{I}|\text{defective})$. We are given $P(\text{I}) = 0.65$, $P(\text{II}) = 0.35$, $P(\text{defective}|\text{I}) = 0.05$, and $P(\text{defective}|\text{II}) = 0.15$. We may use the second form of Bayes' rule directly:

$$P(\text{I}|\text{defective}) = \frac{P(\text{I})P(\text{defective}|\text{I})}{P(\text{I})P(\text{defective}|\text{I}) + P(\text{II})P(\text{defective}|\text{II})}$$

$$= \frac{.65 \times .05}{.65 \times .05 + .35 \times .15}$$

$$= \frac{.0325}{.085} = .38$$

FIGURE 6–12

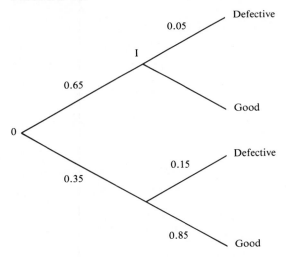

Tree diagram showing the possible situations of defective and good chips from machines I and II.

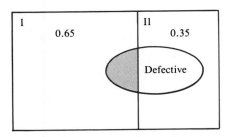

The shaded area represents those chips from machine I that are defective.

Locate all of these computations on the tree diagram in Figure 6–12.

Bayes' rule is not restricted to the situation in which just two mutually exclusive events form all of S. There can be any finite number of mutually exclusive events as long as their union is the sample space. A more general form of Bayes' rule is the following.

Bayes' Rule (General)   Let $E_1, E_2, \ldots, E_n$ be mutually exclusive events whose union is the sample space S (they partition S), and let F be any event where $P(F) \neq 0$. Then

(a) $P(E_i|F) = \dfrac{P(E_i \cap F)}{P(F)}$

(b) $P(E_i|F) = \dfrac{P(E_i \cap F)}{P(E_1 \cap F) + P(E_2 \cap F) + \cdots + P(E_n \cap F)}$

(c) $P(E_i|F) = \dfrac{P(E_i)P(F|E_i)}{P(E_1)P(F|E_1) + P(E_2)P(F|E_2) + \cdots + P(E_n)P(F|E_n)}$

EXAMPLE 2   *(Compare Exercise 10)*

A manufacturer buys an item from three subcontractors, A, B, and C. A has the better quality control; only 2% of its items are defective. A furnishes the manufacturer with 50% of the items. B furnishes 30% of the items, and 5% of its items are defective. C furnishes 20% of the items, and 6% of its items are defective. The manufacturer finds an item defective (D).

(a) What is the probability that it came from A? (Find $P(A|D)$.)

(b) What is the probability that it came from B? (Find $P(B|D)$.)

(c) What is the probability that it came from C? (Find $P(C|D)$.)

SOLUTION   Let

A represent the set of items produced by A,
B represent the set of items produced by B,
C represent the set of items produced by C,
D represent the set of defective items.

The following probabilities are given:

$$P(A) = .50, \qquad P(B) = .30, \qquad P(C) = .20$$
$$P(D|A) = .02, \qquad P(D|B) = .05, \qquad P(D|C) = .06$$

Let's use the first form of Bayes' rule to solve the problem. We need the following probabilities, which are computed by using the multiplication rule:

$$P(D \cap A) = P(A)P(D|A) = .50 \times .02 = .010$$
$$P(D \cap B) = P(B)P(D|B) = .30 \times .05 = .015$$
$$P(D \cap C) = P(C)P(D|C) = .20 \times .06 = .012$$

FIGURE 6–13

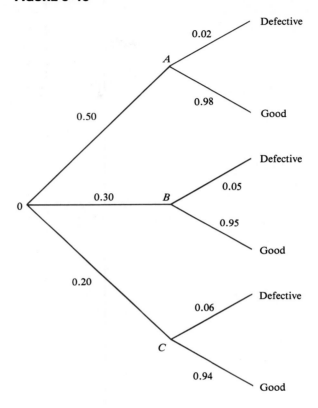

Then

(a) $P(A|D) = \dfrac{.010}{.010 + .015 + .012} = \dfrac{.010}{.037} = .27$

(b) $P(B|D) = \dfrac{.015}{.010 + .015 + .012} = \dfrac{.015}{.037} = .41$

(c) $P(C|D) = \dfrac{.012}{.010 + .015 + .012} = \dfrac{.012}{.037} = .32$

Trace the computations on the tree diagram in Figure 6–13.

EXAMPLE 3 *(Compare Exercise 14)*

Studies show that a pregnant woman who contracts German measles is more likely to produce a child with certain birth defects. In a certain county the probability that a pregnant woman contracts German measles is .2. If a pregnant woman contracts the disease, the probability that her child will have the defect

FIGURE 6-14

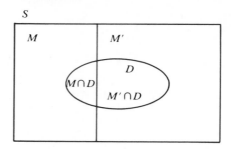

is .1. If a pregnant woman does not contract German measles, the probability that her child will have the defect is .01. A child is born with this defect. What is the probability that the child's mother contracted German measles while pregnant? Restrict the analysis to pregnant women.

SOLUTION   Let

M = the set of pregnant women who contracted measles
M' = the set of pregnant women who did not contract measles
S = the sample space of pregnant women ($M \cup M'$)
D = the set of mothers who bear a child with this defect

The Venn diagram of these events is shown in Figure 6–14.

We are given $P(M) = .2$, $P(M') = .8$, $P(D|M) = .1$, and $P(D|M') = .01$; and we are to find $P(M|D)$:

$$P(M|D) = \frac{P(M \cap D)}{P(M \cap D) + P(M' \cap D)}$$

$$= \frac{P(M)P(D|M)}{P(M)P(D|M) + P(M')P(D|M')}$$

$$= \frac{.2 \times .1}{.2 \times .1 + .8 \times .01} = \frac{.02}{.028} = .71$$

6-6 EXERCISES

I

1. Draw the tree diagram that shows the following information. A class is composed of 30 girls and 20 boys. On the final exam, 12% of the girls and 9% of the boys made an A.

2. Draw the tree diagram that shows the following information. A psychology class checked a group of students for personality types. The students fell into three categories: science, humanities, and social sciences. Of the group, 25% were in science, 35% in humanities, and 40% in social sciences. The findings are summarized as follows.

GROUP	PERSONALITY TYPE	
	A	B
Science	72%	28%
Humanities	61%	39%
Social Sciences	48%	52%

3. Compute $P(E_1|F)$ for the following:
   (a) $E_1 \cup E_2 = S$, $P(E_1 \cap F) = .7$, $P(F) = .9$
   (b) $E_1 \cup E_2 = S$, $P(E_1) = .75$, $P(E_2) = .25$,
       $P(F|E_1) = .40$, $P(F|E_2) = .10$

4. E_1 and E_2 partition the sample space S, and F is an event.

$$P(E_1) = .3, \qquad P(E_2) = .7$$
$$P(F|E_1) = .25, \qquad P(F|E_2) = .15$$

   Find $P(E_1|F)$.

5. F is an event, and E_1, E_2, and E_3 partition S.

$$P(E_1) = \frac{5}{12}, \qquad P(E_2) = \frac{4}{12}, \qquad P(E_3) = \frac{3}{12},$$
$$P(F|E_1) = \frac{2}{5}, \qquad P(F|E_2) = \frac{1}{4}, \qquad P(F|E_3) = \frac{1}{3}$$

   (a) Find $P(E_1 \cap F)$, $P(E_2 \cap F)$, and $P(E_3 \cap F)$.
   (b) Find $P(F)$.
   (c) Find $P(E_1|F)$ and $P(E_3|F)$.

6. F is an event, and E_1, E_2, and E_3 partition S.

$$P(E_1) = .20, \qquad P(E_2) = .35, \qquad P(E_3) = .45$$
$$P(F|E_1) = .40, \qquad P(F|E_2) = .10, \qquad P(F|E_3) = .25$$

   (a) Find $P(E_1 \cap F)$, $P(E_2 \cap F)$, and $P(E_3 \cap F)$.
   (b) Find $P(F)$.
   (c) Find $P(E_2|F)$.

7. (*See Example 1*) A manufacturer has two machines that produce television picture tubes. Machine I products 55% of the tubes, and 3% of its tubes are defective. Machine II produces 45% of the tubes, and 4% of its tubes are defective.
   A picture tube is found to be defective. Find the probability that it was produced by machine II.

8. A refrigerator is found to be defective. It could have been manufactured at either of two plants, I or II. Plant I manufactures 40% of the refrigerators, and plant II manufactures 60% of the refrigerators. Of those refrigerators manufactured at plant I, 3% are defective; of those manufactured at plant II, 2% are defective. Find the probability that the refrigerator came from plant I.

9. A football team plays 60% of its games at home and 40% away. It typically wins 80% of its home games and 55% of its away games. If the team wins on a certain Saturday, what is the probability that it played at home?

II

10. (*See Example 2*). A distributor receives 100 boxes of transistor radios. Factory A shipped 35 boxes, factory B shipped 40 boxes, and factory C shipped 25 boxes. The probability of a radio being defective is .04 from factory A, .02 from factory B, and .06 from factory C. A box and a radio from that box are both selected at random. The radio is found to be defective. Find the probability that it came from factory B.

11. A certain pocket calculator is found to be defective. It could have been manufactured at any one of three factories: I, II, or III. Of all such calculators produced, 15% came from factory I, 45% came from factory II, and 40% came from factory III. Further, it is known that 1% of all calculators produced at factory I are defective, 2% of those produced at factory II are

defective, and 4% of those produced at factory III are defective.
   (a) Find the probability that the defective calculator came from factory I.
   (b) Find the probability that it came from factory II.
   (c) Find the probability that it came from factory III.

12. The durations of the traffic light colors at a major intersection are as follows: green, 90 seconds; yellow, 4 seconds; red, 40 seconds. A car has just passed legally through the intersection (either a green or yellow light was showing). Find the probability that a green light was showing.

13. Box I contains four red balls and six green balls. Box II contains five red balls and seven green balls. A box is selected, and then a ball is drawn from the selected box. The probability of selecting box I is $\frac{3}{5}$.
    (a) Show all possible outcomes and their probabilities by a tree diagram.
    (b) Find $P(\text{red}|\text{box I})$, $P(\text{red and box I})$, and $P(\text{red})$.
    (c) Find $P(\text{box I}|\text{red})$.

14. (*See Example 3*) If a patient is allergic to penicillin, the probability of a reaction to a new drug X is .4. If the patient is not allergic to penicillin, the probability of a reaction to drug X is .1. Eight percent of the population is allergic to penicillin. A patient is given drug X and has a reaction. Find the probability that the patient is allergic to penicillin.

15. It is estimated that 12% of all adults are college graduates, while 88% are not. If 60% of all graduates earn more than $20,000 per annum, and only 20% of nongraduates earn more than $20,000, what proportion of those people who earn more than $20,000 are college graduates?

16. During the hour 9:00 P.M. to 10:00 P.M., the following times were devoted to programs and commercials on the three major networks:

	COMMERCIALS	PROGRAMS
Channel 2	10 min	50 min
Channel 6	12 min	48 min
Channel 9	$11\frac{1}{2}$ min	$48\frac{1}{2}$ min

The three channels are equally likely to be selected. If someone comes into a room between 9:00 and 10:00, and a television is on and showing a commercial, find the probability that the television is tuned to Channel 2.

17. Urn I has five white balls and four black balls. Urn II has three white balls and six black balls. A ball is taken from urn I and put into urn II. A ball is then drawn from urn II and is found to be white.
    (a) Draw a tree diagram.
    (b) What is the probability that the white ball drawn originally came from urn I?

18. At a certain clinic a test for strep has been found to be 90% accurate in that 90% of those with strep will have a positive reaction. However, 1% of those without strep also have a positive reaction. Suppose that 80% of those examined have strep. Find the probability that a child who has a positive reaction has strep.

19. At a clinic a preliminary test for hepatitis has been found to be 95% accurate in that 95% of those with hepatitis have a positive reaction. However, 2% of those without hepatitis also have a positive reaction. Suppose 70% of those examined have hepatitis. Find the probability that a person who has a positive reaction has hepatitis.

20. Authorities testing schoolchildren for hearing deficiency have determined that the test is successful 85% of the time; that is, 85% of those with a hearing deficiency will have a positive reaction, while 5% without a hearing deficiency have a positive reaction. Suppose that 10% of those examined have a hearing deficiency. Find the probability that a child who has a positive reaction does not have a hearing deficiency.

III

21. The following driving-accident statistics have been compiled by an insurance company:

AGE GROUP	PERCENT OF TOTAL ACCIDENTS	PERCENT OF TOTAL POPULATION
Under 25	18	12
25–35	22	24
36–50	30	32
51–70	25	25
Over 70	5	7

Of the total population, 15% are involved in accidents while driving.
    (a) Find the probability that a driver who is involved in an accident is under 25 years of age.
    (b) Find the probability that a driver who is involved in an accident is over 50 years of age.
    (c) Given that a person is under 25, find the probability that the person is involved in an accident.

22. In a major city, 70% of the drivers are over 25 years old, and 12% of them will have a traffic violation during a 12-month period. The drivers 25 years and under comprise 30% of the drivers, and 28% of them will have a traffic violation in a 12-month period. A driver is charged with a traffic violation. Find the probability that the driver is over 25.

23. The IRS checks the deduction for contributions to identify fraudulent tax returns. They believe that if a taxpayer claims more than a certain standard amount, there is a .20 probability that the return is fraudulent. If the deduction does not exceed the IRS standard, the probability of a fraudulent return reduces to .03. About 11% of the returns exceed the IRS standard.
    (a) Estimate the percentage of returns that are fraudulent.
    (b) A concerned citizen informs the IRS that a certain return is fraudulent. Find the probability that its deductions exceed the IRS standard.

24. A chain has three stores in Knoxville, A, B, and C. The stores have 60, 80, and 110 employees, respectively, of whom 40%, 55%, and 50% are women. Economic conditions force the chain to lay off some employees. They decide to do this by random selection. The first person selected is a woman. Find the probability that she works at store C.

25. A certain television set is found to be defective. It could have been manufactured at any one of four factories: A, B, C, or D. Of all such television sets, 10% are produced at A, 15% at B, 55% at C, and 20% at D. It is determined that 3% of the sets produced at A, 1% of those produced at B, 2% of those produced at C, and 1% of those produced at D are defective. For each factory, find the probability that the defective set came from that factory.

26. At a certain university it has been estimated that the probability that a male freshman will major in mathematics is $\frac{1}{10}$, and the probability that a female freshman will major in mathematics is $\frac{1}{15}$. The freshman class is 55% male. If a student chosen at random from the freshman class is a mathematics major, find the probability that the student is male.

27. A certain disease can be detected by a blood test in 95% of those who have it. Unfortunately, the test also has a .02 probability of showing that a person has the disease when in fact he or she does not. It has been estimated that 1% of those people who are routinely tested actually have the disease. If the test shows that a certain person has the disease, find the probability that the person actually has it.

28. The voters in a certain state are registered 30% Republican, 60% Democrat, and 10% independent. In a certain election involving three candidates—a Republican, a Democrat, and an independent—the Republican candidate was elected. It was estimated that she gained 85% of the Republican vote, 40% of the Democrat vote, and 8% of the independent vote. What percentage of those who voted Republican were registered Democrats?

29. A company manufactures integrated circuits on silicon chips at three different plants, X, Y, and Z. Out of every 1000 chips produced, 400 come from X, 350 come from Y, and 250 come from Z. It has been estimated that of the 400 from X, ten are defective, whereas five of those from Y are defective, and only two of those from Z are defective. Determine the probability that a defective chip came from plant Y.

6–7 BERNOULLI EXPERIMENTS

- *Bernoulli Trials*
- *Probability of a Bernoulli Experiment*
- *Justification of the Bernoulli Experiment Formula*

BERNOULLI TRIALS   Suppose that you toss a coin ten times. What is the probability that heads appears seven out of the ten times?

If you guess at the answers of ten multiple-choice questions, what are your chances for a passing grade?

These problems are examples of a certain type of probability problem, **Bernoulli trials.** Such problems involved **repeated trials** of an experiment with only two possible outcomes: heads or tails, right or wrong, yes or no, win or lose, and so on. We classify the two outcomes as **success** or **failure.**

To classify an experiment as a Bernoulli trial experiment, several properties must hold.

Bernoulli Experiment
1. The experiment is repeated a fixed number of times (n times).
2. Each trial has only two possible outcomes: success and failure. The outcomes are exactly the same for each trial.
3. The probability of success remains the same for each trial. (We use p for the probability of success and $q = 1 - p$ for the probability of failure.)
4. The trials are independent. (The outcome of one trial has no influence on later trials.)
5. We are interested in the total number of successes, not the order in which they occur.
      There may be 0, 1, 2, 3, . . . , or n successes in n trials.

EXAMPLE 1

(a) We are interested in the number of times heads occurs when a coin is tossed eight times. Each toss of the coin is a trial, so there are eight repeated trials ($n = 8$). We consider the outcome heads a success and tails a failure. The probability of success (heads) on each trial is $p = \frac{1}{2}$, and the probability of failure (tails) is $1 - \frac{1}{2} = \frac{1}{2}$. This is an example of a Bernoulli trial.

(b) A student guesses at all the answers on a ten-question multiple-choice quiz (four choices of an answer on each question). This fulfills the properties of a Bernoulli trial because

   1. each guess is a trial ($n = 10$);
   2. there are two possible outcomes: correct and incorrect;
   3. the probability of a correct answer is $\frac{1}{4}$ ($p = \frac{1}{4}$), and the probability of an incorrect answer is $\frac{3}{4}$ ($q = \frac{3}{4}$) on each trial; and
   4. the guesses are independent because guessing an answer on one question gives no information on other questions.

(c) Suppose eight cards are drawn from a deck and none are replaced. We are interested in the number of spades drawn. This is not a Bernoulli trial because the trials (selecting a card) are not independent (the first card drawn affects the possible choices of the second card; consequently, the probability of drawing a spade changes each time a card is removed).

(d) Suppose a card is drawn from a deck, the card is noted and placed back in the deck, and the deck is shuffled. This is repeated eight times. We are interested in the number of times a spade is drawn.

   This experiment is a Bernoulli trial because each trial is the same, the trials are independent, and the probability of obtaining a spade remains the same for each trial.

   Technically, each trial has 52 outcomes, each card in the deck. However, we reduce the outcomes to the two possible outcomes "success" or "failure" when we collect all spades into the event defined as success and all other cards into the event defined as failure. Then $p = \frac{13}{52}$ and $q = \frac{39}{52}$.

The following example illustrates how a tree diagram may be used to count the number of successes when the number of trials is small.

EXAMPLE 2   *(Compare Exercise 15)*

A coin is tossed three times. What is the probability of exactly two heads in the three tosses?

SOLUTION   Look at the paths of Figure 6–15 that begin at 0 and terminate at the end of a branch. There are a total of eight paths, and three of them contain exactly two heads. The probability of terminating at the end of those branches is $\frac{1}{8}$ for each one. (Since the probability of each branch is $\frac{1}{2}$, the probability of taking a sequences of three paths is $\frac{1}{2} \cdot \frac{1}{2} \cdot \frac{1}{2} = \frac{1}{8}$.) So the probability of exactly two heads in three tosses of a coin is $\frac{3}{8}$.

FIGURE 6–15

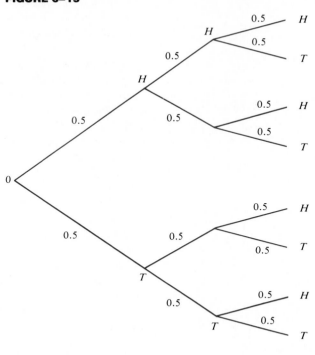

PROBABILITY OF A BERNOULLI EXPERIMENT

The tree diagram of a Bernoulli trial problem can become unwieldy with a large number of trials; so an algebraic formula is useful for computing the probability of a specified number of successes. Let's start with a simple example.

EXAMPLE 3   *(Compare Exercise 18)*

A quiz has five multiple-choice questions with four possible answers to each. A student wildly guesses the answers. What is the probability that he guesses exactly three correctly?

SOLUTION   As a Bernoulli trial problem, $n = 5$, $p = \frac{1}{4}$, and $q = \frac{3}{4}$. We are about to give a formula that calculates the desired probability, but you need to be aware that you have no reason, at this point, to know why it is true. That will be explained later. We want you to understand the quantities used in the formula so that you can more easily follow the justification. Now for the formula. The probability of exactly three correct answers is

$$P(3 \text{ correct}) = C(5, 3)\left(\frac{1}{4}\right)^3\left(\frac{3}{4}\right)^2$$

$$= 10\left(\frac{1}{64}\right)\left(\frac{9}{16}\right)$$

$$= .088 \qquad \text{(Rounded to three decimals)}$$

Let's make some observations about the computation, because they will hold for the general formula.

1. In $C(5, 3)$, 5 is the number of trials, and 3 is the number of successes.
2. In $(\frac{1}{4})^3$, $\frac{1}{4}$ is the probability of success in a single trial, and 3 is the number of successes in the five trials.
3. In $(\frac{3}{4})^2$, $\frac{3}{4}$ is the probability of failure in a single trial, and 2 is the number of failures in five trials. It may seem trivial, but note that $2 = 5 - 3$; the number of failures equals the number of trials minus the number of successes.

We now give you the general formula.

Probability of a Bernoulli Experiment

Given a Bernoulli experiment and

n independent repeated trials,
p is the probability of success in a single trial,
$q = 1 - p$ is the probability of failure in a single trial,
x is the number of successes ($x \leq n$).

Then the probability of x successes in n trials is

$$P(x \text{ successes in } n \text{ trials}) = C(n, x)p^x q^{n-x}$$

$P(k$ successes in n trials) may be written $P(x = k)$.

EXAMPLE 4   *(Compare Experiment 21)*

A single die is rolled three times. Find the probability that a 5 turns up exactly twice.

SOLUTION

$$n = 3, \qquad x = 2, \qquad p = \frac{1}{6}, \qquad q = \frac{5}{6}$$

so

$$P(x = 2) = C(3, 2)\left(\frac{1}{6}\right)^2\left(\frac{5}{6}\right)^1$$

$$= 3\left(\frac{1}{36}\right)\left(\frac{5}{6}\right)$$

$$= .0694$$

Notice that in the tree diagram (Figure 6–16) there are three branches with exactly two 5's. This number is $C(3, 2)$. The probability of termination at the end of one such branch is

$$\left(\frac{1}{6}\right)^2\left(\frac{5}{6}\right)$$

The notation $P(x = 2)$ is used to indicate the probability of two successes.

FIGURE 6–16

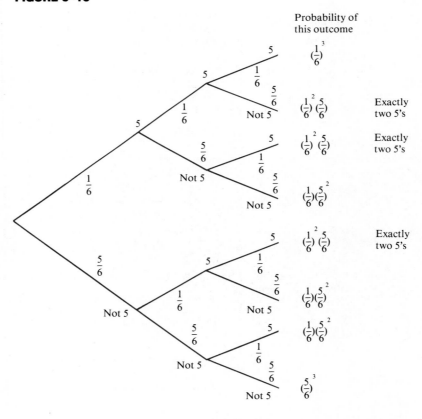

Exactly two 5's occurs three times in three tosses of a die.

EXAMPLE 5 *(Compare Exercise 24)*

A coin is tossed ten times. What is the probability that heads occurs six times?

SOLUTION In this case, $n = 10$, $x = 6$, $p = \frac{1}{2}$, and $q = \frac{1}{2}$.

$$P(x = 6) = C(10, 6)\left(\frac{1}{2}\right)^6\left(\frac{1}{2}\right)^4$$

$$= 210\left(\frac{1}{64}\right)\left(\frac{1}{16}\right)$$

$$= .205$$

JUSTIFICATION OF THE BERNOULLI EXPERIMENT FORMULA

Now let's go back to Example 3 and explain how to obtain the expression used to compute the probability of a Bernoulli trial.

Recall the problem: A multiple-choice quiz has five questions with four possible answers to each, one of which is correct. A student guesses the answers. What is the probability that three of the five are correct?

Let's look at how the student succeeds in answering three of the five questions. There are several ways, and the exact number plays a key role in the solution. First, let's list some ways. We will list the sequence of successes (correct answers) and failures (incorrect answers). One sequence is

SSSFF

which indicates that the first three were correct and the last two were incorrect. Some other sequences of three correct and two incorrect are

SSFSF

FSSSF

and so on. Rather than list all the ways in which three correct and two incorrect answers can be given, let's compute the number.

The basic procedure for forming a sequence of three S's and two F's amounts to selecting the three questions with correct answers. The other two answers are automatically incorrect.

In how many different ways can three questions be selected from the five questions? You should recognize this as $C(5, 3)$. Since $C(5, 3) = 10$, there are ten possible sequences of three S's and 2 F's. The student succeeds in passing if his sequence of guesses is any one of the ten sequences.

NOTE From compound probability the probability that his sequence of answers is one of the ten is obtained by adding the probabilities of each of the ten sequences.

It helps that the probabilities of all ten sequences are exactly the same. Notice that the probability of SSSFF is

$$\left(\frac{1}{4}\right)\left(\frac{1}{4}\right)\left(\frac{1}{4}\right)\left(\frac{3}{4}\right)\left(\frac{3}{4}\right)$$

by the multiplication rule. Also, the probability of SSFSF is

$$\left(\frac{1}{4}\right)\left(\frac{1}{4}\right)\left(\frac{3}{4}\right)\left(\frac{1}{4}\right)\left(\frac{3}{4}\right)$$

Both of these are simply

$$\left(\frac{1}{4}\right)^3\left(\frac{3}{4}\right)^2$$

each written in different order. In fact, the probability of any sequence of three S's and two F's will contain $\frac{1}{4}$ three times and $\frac{3}{4}$ twice, which gives $(\frac{1}{4})^3(\frac{3}{4})^2$.

When we add up the probabilities of the ten sequences, we are adding $(\frac{1}{4})^3(\frac{3}{4})^2$ ten times, which is

$$10\left(\frac{1}{4}\right)^3\left(\frac{3}{4}\right)^2$$

This is the probability obtained in Example 3. A similar situation holds in general for other values of n, x, p, and q.

EXAMPLE 6   *(Compare Exercise 38)*

The cycle of a traffic light on Main Street is green, 50 seconds; yellow, 5 seconds; and red, 25 seconds. What is the probability of getting a green three out of four times you approach the intersection?

SOLUTION   This is an experiment with four repeated trials. A green light is considered a success. A complete cycle requires 80 seconds, so the probability of green is $\frac{50}{80} = .625$.

Then

$$\begin{aligned}
P(x = 3) &= C(4, 3)(.625)^3(.375)^1 \\
&= 4(.244)(.375) \\
&= .366
\end{aligned}$$

EXAMPLE 7   *(Compare Exercise 35)*

A multiple-choice quiz with five questions is given. Each question has four possible answers. A student guesses all answers. What is the probability that she passes the test if at least three correct answers are needed to pass.

SOLUTION   In this case, $n = 5$, $p = \frac{1}{4}$, and $q = \frac{3}{4}$. The student passes if she gets three, four, or five correct answers. We must find the probability of each of these outcomes and add them:

$$\begin{aligned}
P(x = 3) &= C(5, 3)(.25)^3(.75)^2 \\
&= 10(.015625)(.5625) \\
&= .0879
\end{aligned}$$

$$P(x = 4) = C(5, 4)(.25)^4(.75)^1$$
$$= 5(.0039062)(.75)$$
$$= .0146$$
$$P(x = 5) = C(5, 5)(.25)^5(.75)^0$$
$$= 1(.0009765)(1)$$
$$= .00098 \qquad \text{(Rounded)}$$

Then the probability of three or more correct, which we indicate by $p(x \geq 3)$, is

$$P(x \geq 3) = .0879 + .0146 + .00098 = .10348$$

6-7 EXERCISES

I

Compute the Bernoulli trial probabilities in Exercises 1 through 14.

1. $C(6, 4)(.20)^4(.80)^2$
2. $C(7, 3)(.95)^3(.05)^4$
3. $C(4, 2)(.1)^2(.9)^2$
4. $C(5, 2)(.3)^2(.7)^3$
5. $C(8, 7)(.3)^7(.7)$
6. $C(9, 2)(.8)^2(.2)^7$
7. $C(11, 4)(.6)^4(.4)^7$
8. $C(12, 3)(.5)^3(.5)^9$
9. $n = 6, p = 0.5, x = 2$
10. $n = 7, p = \frac{1}{3}, x = 4$
11. $n = 5, p = 0.1, x = 4$
12. $n = 10, p = \frac{1}{5}, x = 6$
13. $P(x = 3)$ for $n = 5, p = \frac{1}{4}$
14. $P(x = 4)$ for $n = 8, p = \frac{2}{3}$

15. (*See Example 2*) The probability that a marksman will hit a moving target is 0.7. Use a tree diagram to determine the probability that he will hit the target in two out of three attempts.

16. The probability that an instructor will give a quiz is 0.4. Use a tree diagram to determine the probability that she will give a quiz in two out of four class meetings.

17. A check of autos passing an intersection reveals that 80% of the drivers are wearing seat belts. Find the probability that three of the next five drivers are wearing seat belts.

18. (*See Example 3*) A multiple-choice quiz of four questions is given. Each question has five possible answers. If a student guesses at all the answers, find the probability that three out of four are correct.

19. If a couple, each with genes for both brown and blue eyes, parent a child, the probability that the child has blue eyes is $\frac{1}{4}$. Find the probability that two of the couple's three children will have blue eyes.

20. A certain drug was developed, tested, and found to be effective 70% of the time. Find the probability of successfully administering the drug to nine out of ten patients.

21. (*See Example 4*) A single die is rolled six times. Find the probability of a 3 turning up four times.

22. A die is tossed three times. Find the probability of throwing two 6's.

23. A die is thrown four times. Determine the probability of throwing: (a) zero 6's. (b) one 6. (c) two 6's. (d) three 6's. (e) four 6's.

24. (*See Example 5*) A coin is tossed seven times. Find the probability of its turning up tails five times.

25. A coin is tossed six times. Determine the probability of its landing heads up four times.

26. A coin is tossed four times. Find the probability of its landing on tails:
    (a) zero times.
    (b) once.
    (c) twice.
    (d) three times.
    (e) four times.

II

27. A certain antibiotic developed in a research lab was tested on patients. It was found to be successful with 80% of the patients. A hospital has six patients with the disease that the antibiotic treats. Find the probability of curing four of these patients with the antibiotic.

28. Five door prizes are to be awarded at a club meeting. There are 100 tickets in the box, and one of them is yours. A ticket is drawn, the prize is awarded, and the ticket is placed back in the box. This continues until all five prizes are awarded.
   (a) Find the probability that your ticket is drawn once.
   (b) Find the probability that your ticket is drawn twice.

29. At State U, 40% of the students are from out of state. Six students are selected at random. Find the probability that half of them are from out of state.

30. The probability of success in drilling for oil is .2. If the company sinks ten wells, find the probability that five wells will strike oil.

31. A certain telephone line is busy 60% of the time. Find the probability of getting through seven times if ten calls are made.

32. A drug was developed, tested, and found to be effective 80% of the time. It is administered to 12 patients. Find the probability that the drug is effective on eight out of 12 patients.

33. The pass completion statistic of a certain quarterback is .6. Find the probability that he will complete eight out of the next ten passes that he attempts.

34. A certain tennis player who has a devastating first serve has been getting 70% of her first serves in. She is due to serve. Find the probability that she will get all of her next four first serves in.

III

35. (*See Example 7*) A single die is rolled five times. Find the probability that a four turns up at least three times.

36. It is estimated that the probability is .8 that an oak tree 10 to 12 feet tall can be transplanted and will survive, given that it is well cared for. Find the probability of transplanting five such oak trees and having at least three live.

37. A coin is tossed eight times. Find the probability that it will land on tails at least five times.

38. (*See Example 6*) A certain traffic light is green 60% of the time. What is the probability of getting the green light nine out of ten times one approaches the intersection?

39. A true-false quiz has ten questions. A student guesses all the answers.
   (a) Find the probability of getting eight correct.
   (b) Find the probability of getting at least eight correct.
   (c) Find the probability of getting no more than two correct.

40. The manufacturer of flash bulbs observes that defective bulbs are produced with a probability of .05. A package contains eight flash bulbs.
   (a) Find the probability that the package contains no defective bulbs.
   (b) Find the probability that the package contains at most one defective bulb.

41. A box contains two red balls and four green balls. Four draws are made, with the ball replaced after each draw. Find the probability that:
   (a) a red ball is never drawn.
   (b) a red ball is drawn once.
   (c) a red ball is drawn twice.
   (d) a red ball is drawn three times.
   (e) a red ball is drawn all four times.

42. A coin is tossed four times. Is it true or false that the probability that it turns up heads twice is $\frac{1}{2}$?

43. A psychology student conducts an ESP experiment in which the subject attempts to identify the number that turns up when an unseen die is rolled. The die is rolled six times. On the basis of chance alone, find the probability that the subject identifies the number correctly four of the six times.

44. Find the probability that in a family of eight children:
  (a) three are girls.
  (b) there are at least two girls.

45. A baseball player has a .360 batting average. Find the probability that he will have at least two hits in five times at bat.

46. It is estimated that a certain brand of automobile tire has a .8 probability of lasting 25,000 miles. Out of four such tires put on a car, find the probability that one will have to be replaced before 25,000 miles.

47. Suppose that 60% of voters were against the repeal of a certain local law. If ten people were chosen at random from the community, what would be the probability that six or more of these people were in favor of the repeal? (Such a selection would make it appear that the majority favored the repeal.)

6–8 MARKOV CHAINS

- *Transition Matrix*
- *Markov Chain*
- *Steady State*
- *Finding the Steady-State Matrix*

TRANSITION MATRIX

Markov chains provide a means to analyze certain kinds of problems. The techniques use matrix operations and systems of equations. You might wish to review those topics.

The alumni office of a university knows that generally 80% of the alumni who contribute one year will contribute the next year. They also know that 30% of those who do not contribute one year will contribute the next. We want to answer the following kinds of questions:

If 40% of a graduating class contributes the first year, how many will contribute the second year? The fifth year? The tenth year?

Before we solve this problem, let's define some terminology and basic concepts.

First, the alumni can be placed in exactly one of two possible categories; they either contribute or do not contribute. These categories are called **states.**

Definition A **state** is a category, situation, outcome, or position that a process can occupy at any given time. The states are disjoint and cover all possible outcomes.

For example, the alumni are either in the state of contributors or in the state of noncontributors. A patient is ill or well. A person's emotional state may be happy, angry, or sad. In a Markov process the system may move from one state to another at any given time. When the process moves from one state to the next, we say that a transition is made from the **present state** to the **next state.** An alumnus can make a transition from the noncontributor state to the contributor state or vice versa.

The information on the proportion of alumni who do or do not contribute can be represented by a **transition matrix.** Let C represent those who contribute and NC represent those who do not.

| | | NEXT STATE | |
		C	NC
Present	C	.8	.2
State	NC	.3	.7

The entries in the transition matrix are probabilities that a person will move from one state (present) to another state (next) the following year. For example, the probability that a person who now contributes will contribute again next year is .8. We get this from the statement "80% of the alumni who contribute one year will contribute the next year."

The headings to the left of the matrix identify the present state, and the headings above the matrix identify the next state. Each entry in the matrix is interpreted as follows:

.8 is the probability that a person passes from present state C to next state C; that is, a contributor remains a contributor.

.2 is the probability that a person passes from present state C to next state NC; a contributor becomes a noncontributor.

.3 is the probability that a person passes from present state NC to next state C; that is, a noncontributor becomes a contributor.

.7 is the probability that a person passes from present state NC to next state NC, that is, a noncontributor remains a noncontributor.

Because each row lists the probabilities of going from that state to each of all possible states, the entries in a row always add to 1.

Transition Matrix   A transition matrix is a square matrix with each entry a number from the interval 0 through 1. The entries in each row add to 1.

In the alumni example a row matrix may be used to represent the proportion of people in each state. For example, the matrix [.40   .60] indicates that 40% are in state C and 60% are in state NC.

The same row matrix may also be interpreted to indicate that the probability of a person being in state C is .40, and the probability of being in state NC is .60.

These row matrices are called **state matrices,** or **probability-state matrices.** For each state it shows the probability that a person is in that state.

Why do we put the information in this form? Because we can use matrix operations to provide useful information. Here's how.

Multiply the state matrix and the transition matrix:

$$\begin{array}{cc} C & NC \end{array}$$
$$[.40 \quad .60] \begin{bmatrix} .8 & .2 \\ .3 & .7 \end{bmatrix}$$

and the result is

$$[(.40)(.8) + (.60)(.3) \quad (.40)(.2) + (.60)(.7)]$$
$$\begin{array}{cc} C & NC \end{array}$$
$$= [.50 \quad .50] \qquad \text{(The next-state matrix)}$$

You should interpret this as follows: In one year the alumni moved from 40% in C and 60% in NC to 50% in each.

Let's look at the tree diagram in Figure 6–17 to help justify this.

FIGURE 6–17

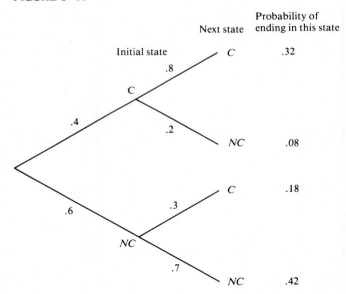

The first stage shows the two possible states, C and NC, with the probability of each. The second stage shows the next states and the probability of entering those states. At the end of each branch is the probability of terminating there. There are two branches that terminate in C. We simply add the two probabilities there to obtain the probability of ending in state C. That probability is

$$(.40)(.8) + (.60)(.3) = .32 + .18 = .50$$

Notice that this is exactly the computation used in the matrix product that gave the first entry in the next-state matrix. The second entry in the next-state matrix is

$$(.40)(.2) + (.60)(.7)$$

which is the probability for entering state *NC*, as obtained from the tree diagram.

This illustrates how the state matrix and transition matrix can be used to get the next-state matrix.

EXAMPLE 1   *(Compare Exercises 9 through 11)*

Using [.40   .60] as the first year's state matrix (sometimes called the **initial-state matrix**) and

$$\begin{bmatrix} .8 & .2 \\ .3 & .7 \end{bmatrix}$$

as the transition matrix for the alumni problem, find the percent of alumni in each category for the second, third, and fourth years.

SOLUTION   As illustrated above, the second-year breakdown is

$$\begin{matrix} C & NC \\ [.40 & .60] \end{matrix} \begin{bmatrix} .8 & .2 \\ .3 & .7 \end{bmatrix} = \begin{matrix} C & NC \\ [.50 & .50] \end{matrix}$$

1st Year   **2nd Year**

The third-year state matrix is obtained by multiplying the second-year state matrix (it is now the present matrix) by the transition matrix:

$$[.50 \quad .50] \begin{bmatrix} .8 & .2 \\ .3 & .7 \end{bmatrix} = [(.50)(.8) + (.50)(.3) \quad (.50)(.2) + (.50)(.7)]$$

$$= [.40 + .15 \quad .10 + .35]$$

$$= [.55 \quad .45]$$

The fourth-year state matrix is

$$[.55 \quad .45] \begin{bmatrix} .8 & .2 \\ .3 & .7 \end{bmatrix} = [(.55)(.8) + (.45)(.3) \quad (.55)(.2) + (.45)(.7)]$$

$$= [.575 \quad .425]$$

This process may be continued for years five, six, and so on.

EXAMPLE 2   *(Compare Exercise 22)*

A rental firm has three locations. A truck rented at one location may be returned to any of the locations. The company's records show the probability of a truck rented at one location being returned to another. From these records the transition matrix is formed. Each location is considered to be a state.

		RETURNED TO		
		I	II	III
RENTED	I	.8	.1	.1
FROM	II	.3	.6	.1
	III	.1	.2	.7

Assume that all the trucks are rented daily.

(a) If the trucks are initially distributed with 40% at location I, 25% at location II, and 35% at location III, find the distribution on the second and third days.

(b) If a truck is rented at location II, for each location, find the probability that it will be at that location after three days.

SOLUTION

(a) The initial-state matrix is [.40 .25 .35]. The distribution for day 2 is

$$[.40 \quad .25 \quad .35] \begin{matrix} I & II & III \end{matrix} \begin{bmatrix} .8 & .1 & .1 \\ .3 & .6 & .1 \\ .1 & .2 & .7 \end{bmatrix} = [.43 \quad .26 \quad .31] \begin{matrix} I & II & III \end{matrix}$$

$$\textbf{Day 1} \qquad\qquad\qquad\qquad \textbf{Day 2}$$

The distribution for day 3 is

$$[.43 \quad .26 \quad .31] \begin{bmatrix} .8 & .1 & .1 \\ .3 & .6 & .1 \\ .1 & .2 & .7 \end{bmatrix} = [.453 \quad .261 \quad .286]$$

$$\textbf{Day 2} \qquad\qquad\qquad\qquad \textbf{Day 3}$$

Thus 45.3% are at location I, 26.1% are at location II, and 28.6% are at location III on the third day.

(b) Since we are interested in the fate of only those trucks originating at location II, we ignore the trucks at the other locations and use [0 1 0] as the initial-state probability matrix.

The probability that a truck is at each location on the second day is given by

$$[0 \quad 1 \quad 0] \begin{bmatrix} .8 & .1 & .1 \\ .3 & .6 & .1 \\ .1 & .2 & .7 \end{bmatrix} = [.3 \quad .6 \quad .1]$$

that is, the probability of being at location I is .3; at location II the probability is .6; and at location III the probability is .1.

For the third day the state probability matrix is

$$[.3 \quad .6 \quad .1] \begin{bmatrix} .8 & .1 & .1 \\ .3 & .6 & .1 \\ .1 & .2 & .7 \end{bmatrix} = [.43 \quad .41 \quad .16]$$

The probability that a truck is at location II on the third day is .41.

MARKOV CHAIN

Let's summarize the ideas of a Markov chain.

> A **Markov chain,** or **Markov process,** is a sequence of experiments with the following properties.
>
> 1. An experiment has a finite number of discrete outcomes, called **states.** The process, or experiment, is always in one of these states.
> 2. With each additional trial the experiment can move from its present state to any other state or remain in the same state.
> 3. The probability of going from one state to another on the next trial depends only on the present state and not on past states.
> 4. The probability of moving from any one state to another in one step is represented in a transition matrix.
>   (a) The transition matrix is square, since all possible states are used for rows and columns.
>   (b) Each entry is between 0 and 1, inclusive.
>   (c) The entries in each row add to 1.
> 5. The state matrix times the transition matrix gives the next-state matrix.

STEADY STATE

A study of Markov processes enables us to determine the probability state matrix for a sequence of trials. Sometimes it helps to know the long-term trends of a population, of the market of a product, or of political processes. A Markov chain may provide some useful long-term information because some Markov processes will tend toward a **steady state,** or **equilibrium.** Here is a simple example.

EXAMPLE 3 *(Compare Exercises 12 and 23)*

The transition matrix of a Markov process is

$$T = \begin{bmatrix} .6 & .4 \\ .1 & .9 \end{bmatrix}$$

and an initial-state matrix is [.50   .50].

If we compute a sequence of next-state matrices, we obtain the following information:

STEP	STATE MATRIX
Initial	[.50 .50]
1	[.35 .65] = [.50 .50]T
2	[.275 .725] = [.35 .65]T = [.50 .50]T^2
3	[.238 .762] = [.275 .725]T = [.50 .50]T^3
4	[.219 .781] = [.238 .762]T = [.50 .50]T^4
5	[.209 .791] = [.219 .781]T = [.50 .50]T^5
6	[.204 .796] = [.209 .791]T = [.50 .50]T^6
7	[.202 .798] = [.204 .796]T = [.50 .50]T^7
8	[.201 .799] = [.202 .798]T = [.50 .50]T^8

It appears that the state matrix is approaching [.20 .80] as the sequence of trials progresses. In fact, that is the case. Furthermore, the state matrix [.20 .80] has an interesting property, which we can observe when we find the next-state matrix:

$$[.20 \quad .80]\begin{bmatrix} .6 & .4 \\ .1 & .9 \end{bmatrix} = [(.20)(.6) + (.80)(.1) \quad (.20)(.4) + (.80)(.9)]$$

$$= [.12 + .08 \quad .08 + .72]$$

$$= [.20 \quad .80]$$

There is no change in the next state matrix. The process has reached a **steady,** or **equilibrium,** state.

Definition   A state matrix $X = [p_1 \quad p_2 \quad \ldots \quad p_n]$ is a **steady-state** or **equilibrium** matrix for a transition matrix T if $XT = X$.

EXAMPLE 4

The steady-state matrix for the alumni problem is [.6 .4] because an initial-state matrix will eventually approach [.6 .4] and

$$[.6 \quad .4]\begin{bmatrix} .8 & .2 \\ .3 & .7 \end{bmatrix} = [.48 + .12 \quad .12 + .28]$$

$$= [.60 \quad .40]$$

This indicates that as long as the transition matrix represents the giving practices of the alumni, they will stabilize at 60% contributing and 40% not contributing.

FINDING THE STEADY-STATE MATRIX

Let's show how to find the steady-state matrix for the alumni problem. Let $X = [x \quad y]$ be the desired, but unknown, steady-state matrix. We want to find x and y so that

$$[x \quad y]\begin{bmatrix} .8 & .2 \\ .3 & .7 \end{bmatrix} = [x \quad y]$$

The matrix product on the left gives

$$[.8x + .3y \quad .2x + .7y] = [x \quad y]$$

so

$$.8x + .3y = x$$
$$.2x + .7y = y$$

which is equivalent to

$$-.2x + .3y = 0$$
$$.2x - .3y = 0$$

Since these two equations are equivalent, we can drop one of them.

Since $[x \quad y]$ is a probability matrix, we must have $x + y = 1$. This, with the equation above, gives the system

$$
\begin{aligned}
.x + y &= 1 \\
-.2x + .3y &= 0
\end{aligned}
$$

If we use an augmented matrix to solve this system, we have

$$
\left[\begin{array}{cc|c}
1 & 1 & 1 \\
-.2 & .3 & 0
\end{array}\right]
$$

which eventually reduces to

$$
\left[\begin{array}{cc|c}
1 & 0 & .6 \\
0 & 1 & .4
\end{array}\right]
$$

so $x = .6$, $y = .4$ gives $[.6 \quad .4]$ as the steady-state matrix. This approach will work in general.

EXAMPLE 5 *(Compare Exercise 25)*

Find the steady-state matrix of the transition matrix

$$
T = \begin{bmatrix}
.3 & .2 & .5 \\
.1 & .4 & .5 \\
.4 & .0 & .6
\end{bmatrix}
$$

SOLUTION Solve the equation

$$
[x \quad y \quad z]\begin{bmatrix}
.3 & .2 & .5 \\
.1 & .4 & .5 \\
.4 & 0 & .6
\end{bmatrix} = [x \quad y \quad z]
$$

for a probability matrix $[x \quad y \quad z]$, which is the system

$$
\begin{aligned}
.3x + .1y + .4z &= x \\
.2x + .4y \phantom{{}+ .4z} &= y \\
.5x + .5y + .6z &= z
\end{aligned}
$$

plus the equation $x + y + z + 1$. Write this as

$$
\begin{aligned}
x + y + z &= 1 \\
-.7x + .1y + .4z &= 0 \\
.2x - .6y \phantom{{}+ .4z} &= 0 \\
.5x + .5y - .4z &= 0
\end{aligned}
$$

Use the Gauss-Jordan method to solve. It gives the following sequence of augmented matrices.

$$\begin{bmatrix} 1 & 1 & 1 & | & 1 \\ -.7 & .1 & .4 & | & 0 \\ .2 & -.6 & 0 & | & 0 \\ .5 & .5 & -.4 & | & 0 \end{bmatrix}$$

Multiply the last three equations through by 10, and use row operations to obtain 0's in column 1 below row 1:

$$\begin{bmatrix} 1 & 1 & 1 & | & 1 \\ 0 & 8 & 11 & | & 7 \\ 0 & -8 & -2 & | & -2 \\ 0 & 0 & -9 & | & -5 \end{bmatrix}$$

$$\begin{bmatrix} 1 & 1 & 1 & | & 1 \\ 0 & 8 & 11 & | & 7 \\ 0 & 0 & 9 & | & 5 \\ 0 & 0 & -9 & | & -5 \end{bmatrix}$$

$$\begin{bmatrix} 1 & 1 & 1 & | & 1 \\ 0 & 8 & 11 & | & 7 \\ 0 & 0 & 9 & | & 5 \\ 0 & 0 & 0 & | & 0 \end{bmatrix}$$

$$\begin{bmatrix} 1 & 1 & 1 & | & 1 \\ 0 & 1 & \frac{11}{8} & | & \frac{7}{8} \\ 0 & 0 & 1 & | & \frac{5}{9} \\ 0 & 0 & 0 & | & 0 \end{bmatrix}$$

$$\begin{bmatrix} 1 & 1 & 0 & | & \frac{4}{9} \\ 0 & 1 & 0 & | & \frac{1}{9} \\ 0 & 0 & 1 & | & \frac{5}{9} \\ 0 & 0 & 0 & | & 0 \end{bmatrix}$$

$$\begin{bmatrix} 1 & 0 & 0 & | & \frac{3}{9} \\ 0 & 1 & 0 & | & \frac{1}{9} \\ 0 & 0 & 1 & | & \frac{5}{9} \\ 0 & 0 & 0 & | & 0 \end{bmatrix}$$

This gives $x = \frac{3}{9}$, $y = \frac{1}{9}$, $z = \frac{5}{9}$, and the steady-state matrix $[\frac{3}{9} \quad \frac{1}{9} \quad \frac{5}{9}]$.

EXAMPLE 6   *(Compare Exercise 26)*

A sociologist made a regional study of the shift of population between rural and urban areas. The transition matrix of the annual shift from one area to another was found to be

		TO	
		R	U
FROM	R	$\begin{bmatrix} .76 & .24 \\ .08 & .92 \end{bmatrix}$	
	U		

indicating that 76% of rural residents remain in rural areas, 24% move from rural to urban areas; 8% of urban residents move from urban to rural areas, and 92% remain in the urban areas. Find the percentage of the population in rural and urban areas when the population stabilizes.

SOLUTION   Let $[x \quad y]$ be the state matrix of the population, with x the proportion in rural areas and y the proportion in urban areas. We want to find the steady-state matrix, that is, the solution to

$$[x \quad y]\begin{bmatrix} .76 & .24 \\ .08 & .92 \end{bmatrix} = [x \quad y]$$

This condition, with $x + y = 1$, gives the system

$$\begin{aligned} x + \quad y &= 1 \\ -.24x + .08y &= 0 \\ .24x - .08y &= 0 \end{aligned}$$

The solution to the system is $x = .25$ and $y = .75$, so the steady-state matrix is $[.25 \quad .75]$ indicating that the population will stabilize at 25% in rural areas and 75% in urban areas.

It is sometimes important to know whether a Markov process will eventually reach equilibrium. In Examples 4 and 5 we found the steady-state matrix. It happens to be true in those cases that we will eventually reach the steady-state matrix after a sequence of trials, regardless of the initial-state matrix. While this is not true for all transition matrices, there is a rather reasonable property that ensures that a Markov process will reach equilibrium. We call transition matrices with this property **regular.** A regular Markov process will eventually reach a steady state, and its transition matrix has the following property.

Definition   A transition matrix T of a Markov process is called **regular** if some power of T has only positive entries.

EXAMPLE 7   *(Compare Exercise 34)*

$$T = \begin{bmatrix} .3 & .7 \\ .25 & .75 \end{bmatrix}$$

is regular because its first power contains all positive entries.

$$T = \begin{bmatrix} 0 & 1 \\ .6 & .4 \end{bmatrix}$$

is regular because

$$\begin{bmatrix} 0 & 1 \\ .6 & .4 \end{bmatrix}^2 = \begin{bmatrix} .6 & .4 \\ .24 & .76 \end{bmatrix}$$

has all positive entries.

EXAMPLE 8   *(Compare Exercise 30)*

Find the steady-state matrix of the regular transition matrix

$$T = \begin{bmatrix} 0 & .5 & .5 \\ .5 & .5 & 0 \\ .5 & 0 & .5 \end{bmatrix}$$

(It is regular.)

SOLUTION   The condition

$$[x \quad y \quad z] \begin{bmatrix} 0 & .5 & .5 \\ .5 & .5 & 0 \\ .5 & 0 & .5 \end{bmatrix} = [x \quad y \quad z]$$

with $x + y + z = 1$ yields a system of four equations whose augmented matrix is

$$\begin{bmatrix} 1 & 1 & 1 & | & 1 \\ -1 & .5 & .5 & | & 0 \\ .5 & -.5 & 0 & | & 0 \\ .5 & 0 & -.5 & | & 0 \end{bmatrix}$$

(Be sure that you can get this matrix.)

We will not show all the row operations that lead to the solution, but the final matrix is

$$\begin{bmatrix} 1 & 0 & 0 & | & \frac{1}{3} \\ 0 & 1 & 0 & | & \frac{1}{3} \\ 0 & 0 & 1 & | & \frac{1}{3} \\ 0 & 0 & 0 & | & 0 \end{bmatrix}$$

so the steady-state matrix is $[\frac{1}{3} \quad \frac{1}{3} \quad \frac{1}{3}]$.

6-8 EXERCISES

I

1. Which of the following are transition matrices?

    (a) $\begin{bmatrix} .6 & .4 \\ .3 & .7 \end{bmatrix}$

    (b) $\begin{bmatrix} .6 & 0 & .4 \\ .2 & .1 & .5 \\ .3 & .4 & .3 \end{bmatrix}$

    (c) $\begin{bmatrix} .5 & .5 \\ .3 & .7 \\ .2 & .8 \end{bmatrix}$

    (d) $\begin{bmatrix} .1 & 0 & .3 & .6 \\ .2 & .3 & 0 & .5 \\ .4 & .2 & .1 & .3 \\ 0 & .25 & .35 & .4 \end{bmatrix}$

2. Which of the following are probability-state matrices?

    (a) $[.4 \quad .3 \quad .3]$

    (b) $[.3 \quad .3 \quad .3]$

    (c) $[.1 \quad .2 \quad .3 \quad .4]$

    (d) $[.6 \quad .7]$

    (e) $[.1 \quad .2 \quad 0 \quad .3 \quad .4]$

3. The matrix T represents the transition of college students between dorms (D) and apartments (A) at the end of a semester.

		TO
		A $\quad$ D
FROM	A	$\begin{bmatrix} .9 & .1 \\ .4 & .6 \end{bmatrix}$
	D	

    (a) What percent of those living in apartments move to a dorm?
    (b) What is the probability that a student will remain in a dorm the next semester?
    (c) What is the probability that an apartment-dwelling student will remain in an apartment?
    (d) What percent of dorm residents move to an apartment?

4. An investment firm invests in stocks, bonds, and mortgages for its clients. One of the partners in the firm analyzed the investment patterns of her clients. She found that during a year they change between types of investments according to the following transition matrix:

			TO	
		S	B	M
FROM	S	$\begin{bmatrix} .88 & .09 & .03 \\ .15 & .75 & .10 \\ .19 & .17 & .64 \end{bmatrix}$		
	B			
	M			

    (a) What percent of those investing in bonds move to mortgages?
    (b) What percent move their investments from stocks to bonds?
    (c) What is the probability that a bond investor will leave his or her investment in bonds?
    (d) What is the probability that a mortgage investor will change to stocks or bonds?

5.

	A	B	C
A	.3	.2	.5
B	.4	.6	0
C	.1	.8	.1

    $= T$

    From the transition matrix T, find:
    (a) the probability of moving from state B to state A.
    (b) the probability of moving from state C to state B.
    (c) the probability of remaining in state A.

For Exercises 6 through 8, find the next-state matrix from the given present-state and transition matrices.

6. $S = [.2 \quad .8]$, $T = \begin{bmatrix} .5 & .5 \\ .8 & .2 \end{bmatrix}$

7. $S = [.45 \quad .55]$, $T = \begin{bmatrix} .4 & .6 \\ .9 & .1 \end{bmatrix}$

8. $S = [.2 \quad .5 \quad .3]$, $T = \begin{bmatrix} .3 & .5 & .2 \\ .2 & .2 & .6 \\ .1 & .8 & .1 \end{bmatrix}$

Initial-state and transition matrices are given in Exercises 9 through 11. Find the following two next-state matrices. (*See Example 1*)

9. $M_0 = [.65 \quad .35]$, $T = \begin{bmatrix} .24 & .76 \\ .36 & .64 \end{bmatrix}$

10. $M_0 = [.3 \quad .7]$, $T = \begin{bmatrix} .8 & .2 \\ .2 & .8 \end{bmatrix}$

11. $M_0 = [.25 \quad .50 \quad .25]$, $T = \begin{bmatrix} .3 & .4 & .3 \\ .1 & .3 & .6 \\ .2 & .5 & .3 \end{bmatrix}$

For Exercises 12 through 15, show that the given state matrix S is the steady-state matrix for the transition matrix T.

12. (*See Example 3*)

$$S = [.375 \quad .625], \quad T = \begin{bmatrix} .5 & .5 \\ .3 & .7 \end{bmatrix}$$

13. $S = \begin{bmatrix} \dfrac{2}{3} & \dfrac{1}{3} \end{bmatrix}, \quad T = \begin{bmatrix} .6 & .4 \\ .8 & .2 \end{bmatrix}$

14. $S = [.625 \quad .375], \quad T = \begin{bmatrix} .58 & .42 \\ .7 & .3 \end{bmatrix}$

15. $S = \begin{bmatrix} \dfrac{13}{28} & \dfrac{15}{28} \end{bmatrix}, \quad T = \begin{bmatrix} .25 & .75 \\ .65 & .35 \end{bmatrix}$

16. Let T be the transition matrix

$$T = \begin{bmatrix} .25 & .75 \\ .40 & .60 \end{bmatrix}$$

and $M_0 = [.2 \quad .8]$ be an initial-state matrix.
(a) Compute the next-state matrix $M_1 = M_0 T$. Then complete the next-state matrix from M_1, that is, $M_2 = M_1 T$.
(b) Compute T^2.
(c) Compute $M_0 T^2$. Verify that it equals $M_1 T$.

17. For $M = [.3 \quad .3 \quad .4]$ and

$$T = \begin{bmatrix} .1 & .5 & .4 \\ .2 & .6 & .2 \\ .4 & .0 & .6 \end{bmatrix}$$

compute MT, $(MT)T$, $((MT)T)T$, and MT^3.

II

18. A department store's charge accounts are either currently paid up or in arrears. The store's records show that
    (i) 90% of accounts that are paid up this month will be paid up next month also.
    (ii) 40% of those in arrears this month will be in arrears next month also.
    (iii) Current accounts are 85% paid up and 15% in arrears.
    (a) Represent this information with a tree diagram.
    (b) Represent this information with a state matrix and a transition matrix.

19. Find x so that $[.2 \quad x \quad .4]$ is a probability-state matrix.

20. Find x, y, z so that

$$\begin{bmatrix} .1 & x & 0 \\ y & .3 & .5 \\ .2 & .7 & z \end{bmatrix}$$

is a transition matrix.

21. The alumni of State University generally contribute (C) or do not contribute (NC) according to the following pattern: 75% of those who contribute one year will contribute the next year; 15% of those who do not contribute one year will contribute the next. The transition matrix is the following:

		NEXT YEAR	
		C	NC
PRESENT	C	$\begin{bmatrix} .75 \\ .15 \end{bmatrix}$	$\begin{bmatrix} .25 \\ .85 \end{bmatrix}$
YEAR	NC		

Forty-five percent of last year's graduating class contributed this year. What percent will contribute next year? In two years?

22. (*See Example 2*) A rental firm has three locations. A truck rented at one location may be returned to any of the three locations. The transition matrix of where the trucks are returned is the following:

		RETURNED TO		
		I	II	III
RENTED	I	$\begin{bmatrix} .6 \\ .1 \\ .2 \end{bmatrix}$	$\begin{bmatrix} .2 \\ .8 \\ .3 \end{bmatrix}$	$\begin{bmatrix} .2 \\ .1 \\ .5 \end{bmatrix}$
FROM	II			
	III			

(a) If all the trucks are rented daily, and they are initially distributed with 50% at location I, 25% at location II, and 25% at location III, how will they be distributed the next day? Two days later?
(b) A truck is rented at location I. Find, for each location, the probability that the truck will be at that location after three days.

23. (*See Example 3*) For the initial-state matrix [.6   .4] and the transition matrix

$$T = \begin{bmatrix} .5 & .5 \\ .2 & .8 \end{bmatrix}$$

find the sequence of the following six next-state matrices. What appears to be the steady-state matrix?

24. Find the steady-state matrix of

$$\begin{bmatrix} .6 & .4 \\ .2 & .8 \end{bmatrix}$$

25. (*See Example 5*) Find the steady-state matrix of the transition matrix

$$T = \begin{bmatrix} .6 & .2 & .2 \\ .1 & .8 & .1 \\ .2 & .4 & .4 \end{bmatrix}$$

26. (*See Example 6*) The transition of college students between dorms and apartments at the end of a semester is given by the following:

		TO	
		D	A
FROM	D	.9	.1
	A	.4	.6

Find the percent of the population in dorms and apartments when the population stabilizes.

27. Find the steady-state matrix of the transition matrix given in Exercise 5.

28. Use the transition matrix of Exercise 21 to find the steady-state distribution of State University Alumni who contribute and who do not contribute.

29. Use the transition matrix of Exercise 22 to find the proportion of trucks at each rental location when equilibrium is reached.

Find the steady-state matrix of the regular matrices in Exercises 30 through 33.

30. (*See Example 8*)

$$\begin{bmatrix} \frac{1}{3} & \frac{2}{3} \\ \frac{3}{4} & \frac{1}{4} \end{bmatrix}$$

31. $\begin{bmatrix} .9 & .1 \\ 1 & 0 \end{bmatrix}$

32. $\begin{bmatrix} .3 & .2 & .5 \\ 0 & .5 & .5 \\ .7 & .2 & .1 \end{bmatrix}$

33. $\begin{bmatrix} \frac{1}{3} & \frac{1}{3} & \frac{1}{3} \\ \frac{1}{2} & \frac{1}{2} & 0 \\ 0 & \frac{1}{4} & \frac{3}{4} \end{bmatrix}$

34. (*See Example 7*) Show that

$$T = \begin{bmatrix} 0 & 0 & 1 \\ .2 & .3 & .5 \\ 0 & .3 & .7 \end{bmatrix}$$

is regular.

35. There are five points on a circle as shown in Figure 6–18. A particle is on one of the points and moves to an adjacent point in either direction. The probability is $\frac{1}{2}$ that it will move clockwise and $\frac{1}{2}$ that it will move counterclockwise. Write the transition matrix for this process.

FIGURE 6–18

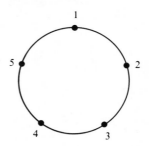

36. A security guard must check three locations periodically. They are located in a triangle. To relieve the monotony, after arriving at one location, he tosses a coin to determine which of the other two he will check next.
(a) Form the transition matrix of this process.
(b) Find the steady-state matrix.

37. A plant with genotype *RW* can produce red (*R*), pink (*P*), or white (*W*) flowers. When two plants of this genotype are crossed, they produce the three colors according to the following transition matrix:

		FLOWERS OF OFFSPRING		
		R	P	W
FLOWERS OF PARENT	R	.50	.50	.0
	P	.25	.50	.25
	W	.0	.50	.50

Flowers of this genotype are crossed for successive generations. When the process reaches a steady state, what percent of the flowers will be red, pink, and white.

38. Assume that a person's profession can be classified as professional, skilled, or unskilled. Sociology studies give the following information about a child's profession as related to his or her parents:

PROFESSIONAL: Of their children, 80% are professional, 10% are skilled, and 10% are unskilled.

SKILLED: Of their children, 60% are skilled, 20% are unskilled, and 20% are professional.

UNSKILLED: Of their children, 35% are skilled, 15% are professional, and 50% are unskilled.

(a) Set up the transition matrix of this process.
(b) Find the probability of an unskilled parent having a grandchild who is a professional.
(c) The population will eventually stabilize into fixed proportions of these professions. Find those proportions, that is, find the steady-state population distribution.

39. A country is divided into three geographic regions: I, II, and III. The matrix T is the transition matrix that shows the probabilities of moving from one region to another.

		TO		
		I	II	III
FROM	I	.9	.06	.04
	II	.15	.8	.05
	III	.3	.1	.6

What is the probability of:
(a) moving from region I to region II?
(b) moving from region II to region III?
(c) remaining in region II?
(d) moving from region I to region III?

40. A country is divided into three geographic regions. It is found that each year 5% of the residents move from region I to region II and 5% move from region I to region III. In region II, 15% move to region I, and 10% move to region III. In region III, 10% move to region I, and 5% to region II.

    Find the steady-state population distribution.

IMPORTANT TERMS

6-1
Experiment
Outcome
Trial
Sample Space
Event
Simple Outcome
Probability Assignment
Empirical Probability

6-2
Equally Likely
Successes
Failures
Random Selection

6-3
Compound Event
Union
Intersection
Complement
Mutually Exclusive Events
Disjoint Events

6-4
Conditional Probability
Reduced Sample Space
Multiplication Rule

6-5
Independent Events

6-6
Bayes' Rule

6-7
Bernoulli Trials
Repeated Trials

6-8
Markov Chain
State
Present State
Next State
Transition Matrix
Probability-State Matrix
Initial-State Matrix
Steady State
Equilibrium
Regular Matrix

REVIEW EXERCISES

1. An experiment has six possible outcomes with the following probabilities:

   $$P_1 = .02, \quad P_2 = 0.3, \quad P_3 = 0.1,$$
   $$P_4 = 0.0, \quad P_5 = 0.2, \quad P_6 = 0.3$$

   Is this a valid probability assignment?

2. An experiment has the sample space $S = \{a, b, c, d\}$. Find the probability of each simple outcome in S if

   $$P(a) = P(b), \quad P(c) = 2P(b), \quad P(d) = 3P(c)$$

3. A refreshment stand kept a tally of the number of soft drinks sold. One day its records showed the following:

	SOFT DRINKS
SIZE	NUMBER SOLD
Small	94
Medium	146
Large	120

   Find the probability that a person selected at random will buy a medium-sized soft drink.

4. Three people are selected at random from a group of five men and two women.
   (a) Find the probability that all three selected are men.
   (b) Find the probability that two men and one woman are selected.
   (c) Find the probability that all three selected are women.

5. In a class of 30 students, ten participate in sports, 12 participate in band, and five participate in both. If a student is selected at random, find the probability that the student participates in sports or band.

6. In a group of 30 school children, 15 are eight-year-olds, 12 are nine-year-olds, and three are ten-year-olds. Of the eight-year-olds, ten are boys; of the nine-year-olds, five are boys; and of the ten-year-olds, two are boys. One child is selected at random from the group. Find the probability that the child is:
   (a) an eight-year-old
   (b) a boy.
   (c) a nine-year-old.
   (d) a twelve-year-old.
   (e) a nine-year-old girl.
   (f) a ten-year-old girl.

7. Three delegates for a conference are to be selected from 12 people. Find the probability that Mrs. Thomas and Ms. Ramirez, two of the group, will be selected.

8. A die is rolled. Find the probability that an even number or a number greater than 4 will be rolled.

9. A single card is picked from a deck of 52 playing cards. Find the probability that it will be a king or a spade.

10. A coin and a die are tossed. Find the probability of throwing:
    (a) a head and a number less than 3.
    (b) a tail and an even number.
    (c) a head and a 6.

11. A coin is tossed five times. Find the probability that all five tosses will land heads up.

12. A card is selected from a deck of 52 playing cards. Find the probability that it will be:
    (a) a red card or a 10.
    (b) a face card or a spade.
    (c) a face card or a 10.

13. A bag contains five red balls, four white balls, and three black balls. Find the probability of drawing:
    (a) a red or a white ball if one ball is drawn.
    (b) two black or two red balls if two balls are drawn without replacement.

14. A card is selected at random from a deck of bridge cards. Find the probability that:
    (a) it is not an ace.
    (b) it is not a face card.

15. A bargain table has 40 books; ten are romance, ten are biographies, ten are crafts, and ten are historical fiction. If two books are selected at random, what is the probability that:
    (a) they are the same kind?
    (b) they are different kinds?

16. A load of lumber contains 40 pieces of birch and 50 pieces of pine. Of the lumber, five pieces of birch and three pieces of pine are warped. Let F, G, and H be the events of selecting birch, pine, and a warped piece of wood, respectively. Compute and interpret the following probabilities.
    (a) $P(F)$, $P(G)$, $P(H)$ (b) $P(F \cap H)$
    (c) $P(F \cup H)$ (d) $P(F' \cup H)$
    (e) $P((F \cup H)')$

17. Compute $C(4, 2)(.4)^2(.6)^2$.

18. Find $P(X = 5)$ for a Bernoulli trial in which $n = 6$ and $p = 0.2$.

19. A card is picked from a deck of 52 playing cards. Let F be the event of selecting an even number, and let G be that of selecting a ten. Are G and F independent events?

20. A card is picked from a deck of 52 playing cards. Let R be the event of selecting a red card, and let Q be the event of selecting a queen. Are R and Q independent?

21. A die is tossed four times. Find the probability of obtaining:
    (a) 1, 2, 3, 4, in that order.
    (b) 1, 2, 3, 4, in any order.
    (c) two even numbers, then a 5, then a number less than 3.

22. Two dice are rolled. Find the probability that:
    (a) the sum of the numbers on the dice is 6.
    (b) the same number is obtained on each die.

23. A student has four examinations to take. She has determined that the probability of her passing the mathematics examination is 0.8, that of passing English is 0.5, that of passing history is 0.3, and that of passing chemistry is 0.7. Assuming independence of examinations, find the probability of her:
    (a) passing mathematics, history, and English but failing chemistry.
    (b) passing mathematics and chemistry but failing history and English.
    (c) passing all four subjects.

24. A study of juvenile delinquents shows that 60% come from low-income families (LI), 45% come from broken homes (BH), and 35% come from both ($LI \cap BH$). A juvenile delinquent is selected at random.
    (a) Find the probability that the juvenile is not from a low-income family.
    (b) Find the probability that the juvenile comes from a broken home or a low-income family.
    (c) Find the probability that the juvenile comes from a low-income family, given that the juvenile comes from a broken home.
    (d) Are LI and BH independent?
    (e) Are LI and BH mutually exclusive?

25. A study of the adult population in a midwestern state found the following information on drinking habits.

	MEN	WOMEN
Abstain	20%	40%
Infrequent	10%	20%
Moderate	50%	35%
Heavy	20%	5%

The adult population of the state is 55% female and 45% male.
    (a) An individual selected at random is found to be an abstainer. Find the probability that the person is male.
    (b) An individual selected at random is found to be a heavy drinker. Find the probability that the individual is female.

26. A stock analyst classifies stocks as either blue chip (BC) or not (NBC). The analyst also classifies stock by whether it goes up (UP), remains unchanged (UC), or goes down (D) at the end of a day's trading. One percent of the stocks are blue chip. The analyst summarizes the performance of stocks as follows:

	PROBABILITY OF		
	UP	UC	D
BC	.45	.35	.20
NBC	.35	.25	.40

    (a) Show this information with a tree diagram.
    (b) A customer selects a stock at random and asks the analyst to buy. Find the probability that the stock is a blue chip stock that goes up the next day.

27. A two-digit number is to be constructed at random from the numbers 1, 2, 3, 4, 5, and 6, repetition not allowed. Find the probability of getting:
    (a) the number 33.
    (b) the number 35.
    (c) a number the sum of whose digits is 10.
    (d) a number whose first digit is greater than its second.
    (e) a number less than 24.

28. A finite mathematics professor observed that 90% of the students who do the homework regularly pass the course. He also observed that only 20% of those who do not do the homework regularly pass the course. One semester, he estimated that 70% of the students did the homework regularly. Given a student who passed the course, find the probability that the student did the homework regularly.

29. A sociology class is composed of ten juniors, 34 seniors, and six graduate students. Two juniors, eight seniors, and three graduate students received an A in the course. A student is selected at random and is found to have received an A. What is the probability that the student is a junior?

30. In a certain population, 5% of the men are colorblind and 3% of the women are colorblind. The population is made up of 55% men and 45% women. If a person chosen at random is colorblind, what is the probability that the person is a man?

31. The probability of having blood type A$^+$ is $\frac{1}{3}$. In a group of eight people, what is the probability that six of them will have this blood type?

32. A survey of working couples in Davidson County revealed the following information: The probability that the husband is happy with his job is .72. The probability that the wife is happy with her job is .55. The probability that both are happy with their jobs is .35.

  A working couple is selected at random.
  (a) Find the probability at least one is happy with his or her job.
  (b) Find the probability that neither is happy with his or her job.

33. Two National Merit finalists and three semifinalists are seated in a row of five chairs on the stage.
  (a) In how many ways can they be seated if the finalists are in the first two chairs and the semifinalists are seated in the last three?
  (b) In how many ways can they be seated if the finalists and semifinalists alternate seats?

34. A box contains six red balls, five yellow balls, and three green balls. Two balls are drawn, without replacement.
  (a) Find the probability that the first is red and the second is green.
  (b) Find the probability that both are yellow.

35. Ten cards are numbered 1 through 10. A card is drawn. It is then replaced in the deck, and the cards are shuffled. A second card is drawn.
  (a) Find the probability that the first card is less than 3 and the second greater than 7.
  (b) Find the probability that both cards are less than 4.

36. A college has 1650 female students and 1460 males. The financial aid office reports that 35% of the males and 40% of the females receive financial aid. A student is selected at random. Find the probability that:
  (a) the student is female.
  (b) the student receives financial aid.
  (c) the student receives financial aid, given that the student is male.
  (d) the student is female, given that the student receives financial aid.

37. A mathematics placement exam is scored High, Middle, and Low. The performance of these students in calculus is summarized as follows.

GRADE	SCORE HIGH	MIDDLE	LOW	TOTAL
C or above	98	124	3	225
Below C	12	118	65	195
Totals	110	242	68	420

One of the 420 students is selected at random. Find the probability that:
  (a) the student makes a grade of C or above.
  (b) the student scored Low on the placement exam.
  (c) the student made a grade below C, given that the student scored Middle on the placement exam.
  (d) the student scored high on the placement exam, given that the student made C or above.

38. A mathematics department compares SAT mathematics scores to performance in calculus. The findings are summarized in the following table:

GRADE	SAT SCORE BELOW 550	550–650	ABOVE 650	TOTAL
A or B	1	55	28	84
C	21	69	25	115
Below C	43	56	2	101
Totals	65	180	55	300

A student is selected at random. Find the probability that:

(a) the student scored above 650.

(b) the student made an A or a B.

(c) the student scored above 650 and made an A or a B.

(d) the student's SAT score was in the 550–650 range.

(e) the student made a C.

(f) Show that "SAT above 650" and "grade of A or B" are dependent.

(g) Show that "SAT is 550–650" and "grade of C" are independent.

39. Reports on 192 accidents showed the following relationship between injuries and using a seat belt:

	INJURIES	NO INJURIES
Seat belt not used	66	28
Seat belt used	14	84

Determine whether the events "seat belt not used" and "injuries" are dependent or independent.

40. A professor gave two forms of an exam to an economics class. The grades by exam form are given in the following table:

GRADE	EXAM	
	FORM A	FORM B
A or B	15	20
Below B	24	32

Show that the events "student took Form A" and "student made an A or a B" are independent.

7
Statistics

*W*HEN THE PRESIDENT OF the United States submits an annual budget to Congress in the trillion-dollar range, many taxpayers ask, "Where is all that money going?" But few of them wish to be handed a detailed budget a foot thick. They want the information summarized in a few broad categories such as defense, social security, education, agriculture, interest on the debt, and so on. Meanwhile, the President might want to know how the voters react to specific budget items such as defense and social security budgets. To poll all voters regarding their opinion of, for instance, the defense budget is impractical. However, the President can obtain valuable, although incomplete, information on voter opinion by a **sample** opinion poll.

The President's budget summary is an example of applying **descriptive statistics.** Descriptive statistics summarize a mass of data and describe its more prominent features.

The sample poll, on the other hand, falls into the category of **inferential statistics.** Inferential statistics make generalizations or draw conclusions from representative information. This chapter presents some methods used in descriptive and inferential statistics. Sections 7–1 through 7–3 deal with descriptive statistics, and Sections 7–4 through 7–8 deal with inferential statistics.

7–1 FREQUENCY DISTRIBUTIONS

- *Frequency Table*
- *Construction of a Frequency Table*
- *Visual Representations of Frequency Distributions*
- *Histogram*
- *Pie Chart*

FREQUENCY TABLE

Opinion polls and population studies use random samples to obtain information. Quite often it helps to organize the information in a tabular or visual form. One tabular form may be obtained by grouping similar observations into categories and reporting the number of observations in each category. For example, a complete list of the size of each class at State University might be too unorganized to help a building-use committee determine classroom needs. A summary like the following table provides more useful information:

SIZE OF CLASSES	NUMBER OF CLASSES
Fewer than 5	9
5–10	37
11–20	52
21–50	213
51–100	91
101–200	5
201–500	2
Total	409

We call this kind of summary a **frequency table** or **frequency distribution.** We call the number of observations in a category the *frequency* of that category. This frequency table gives the number of classes for each class size category at the university. A *range*, or *interval*, of numbers like 5 to 10 or 11 to 20 determines each category.

In some summaries the categories might not be numerical. For example, we may summarize the students' majors by subject category at the university with a frequency table like the following:

MAJOR	NUMBER OF STUDENTS
Science	429
Arts	132
Languages	41
Social sciences	631
Engineering	344
Total	1577

Notice that a frequency table does not present all available information. The frequency table of the size of university courses does not tell the number of students in the smallest or the largest classes. In fact, it does not tell the number of students in any class. It does give general information from which a decision may be made about the number and size of classrooms needed.

EXAMPLE 1

A mathematics quiz consists of five questions. The professor summarizes the performance of the class of 75 students with the following frequency distribution. Each quiz question determines a different category.

QUESTION	NUMBER OF CORRECT ANSWERS (FREQUENCY)
1	36
2	41
3	22
4	54
5	30

EXAMPLE 2 (*Compare Exercise 1*)

A survey of students reveals that they spent the following amounts of money on books for three courses during a semester:

$ 78	$123	$136	$162	$ 96	$145
$115	$183	$150	$110	$191	$ 88
$157	$137	$122	$172	$165	$119
$105	$127	$148	$170	$131	$118

Make a frequency table to summarize the students' book expenses.

SOLUTION   We form five categories with $25 intervals, starting at $75, and obtain the following:

BOOK EXPENSES	NUMBER OF STUDENTS (FREQUENCY)
$75–99	3
$100–124	7
$125–149	6
$150–174	6
$175–199	2

NOTE   The choice of the number of categories and the dollar range for each category could be made in several different ways.

Construction of a Frequency Table

Construct a frequency table in three steps, as follows:

Step 1. Choose the categories by which the information will be grouped, for example, size of classes at State University.

Step 2. Place each piece of information in the appropriate category; for example, sort the classes by size and place them in the appropriate category.

Step 3. Count the data in each category. This is the frequency of the category, for example, State University has two classes in the 201–500 range.

The category decisions in Step 1 make the other two steps mechanical. The determination of categories can be a two-step decision. First, determine the number of categories (e.g., seven) and then the range of values each category covers (e.g., fewer than 5, 5–10, etc). No magic formula exists to make these decisions. They depend on the nature of the data and the message you wish to convey. However, some generally accepted rules of thumb might help. Just remember, exceptions are appropriate at times.

Hints on Setting up Category Intervals

1. Number of categories. Generally, we use five to 15 categories. More categories might be unwieldy, and fewer categories might not distinguish between important features. Be sensible about applying this rule. Don't use five categories to summarize a two-category situation, such as male-female breakdown in enrollment. Fifteen categories are not appropriate when you have only a few observations. Generally, use a larger number of categories for larger amounts of data and fewer categories for smaller amounts of data.

2. Range of values covered by the categories.

(a) Choose each category so that each piece of information is in some category. Be sure to include the largest and smallest values in some category, and be sure you leave no gaps between categories when they might include some of the data. Don't use intervals like $2.00 to $4.00 and $5.00 to $7.00 when $4.75 is a valid data point.

(b) Assign each observation to only one category. If one category has a range of values 300 to 400 and the next category has a range of 400 to 500, it is not clear where to place 400. The category designations 300 to 399 and 400 to 499 clearly indicate where to place 400.

(c) Try to make the category intervals the same length, and use intervals that make sense for the situation. For example, if you summarize traffic speeds for the city traffic department, your boss probably will not be impressed with category intervals such as 33 to 38, and 39 to 42. It is more natural and sensible to use intervals such as 31 to 35 and 36 to 40. On the other hand, don't force equal intervals when different lengths make sense. We summarize class performance on a test with intervals of 0 to 59, 60 to 69, 70 to 79, 80 to 89, 90 to 100 because these intervals represent letter grades. Notice that the example of class sizes also uses intervals of different lengths.

VISUAL REPRESENTATIONS OF FREQUENCY DISTRIBUTIONS

Because a picture conveys a more forceful message than a column of numbers, a visual presentation of a frequency table sometimes provides a better understanding of the data. We will study two common visual methods: the **histogram** and the **pie chart.** In each case the graph shows information obtained from a frequency table.

HISTOGRAM

A **histogram** is a bar chart in which each bar represents a category and its height represents the frequency of the category. Figure 7–1 is the histogram of Example 1.

Mark the categories on a horizontal scale and the frequencies on a vertical scale. The bars are of equal width and are centered above the point that designates the category. In this case a single number forms the category interval. The bars should be of equal width because two bars with the same height and different widths have different areas. This gives an impression of different frequencies.

FIGURE 7–1

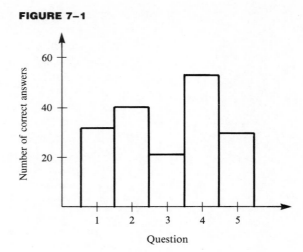

Thus the area, not just the height of the bar, customarily represents the frequency when different bar widths are used. Sometimes a space is left between bars when using a discrete variable. If the category is defined by an interval (such as 1–5, 6–10), the bar is located between the end points of the interval.

The categories in the first two examples are **discrete,** that is, the values in one category are separated from those in another category by a "gap." A summary of the number of correct answers on a quiz uses the possible values 0, 1, 2, 3, 4, and 5 as categories. There is a jump from 3 to 4; a value of 2.65 is not valid. On the other hand, GPA scores are not discrete. Any GPA from 0 through 4.0 is valid. There is no jump from one category to another. In such a case the data is said to be **continuous.** When continuous data are represented by a histogram, the categories are determined by a range of values like 0–0.49, 0.50–1.0, and so on. The next example illustrates the use of a histogram with continuous data.

EXAMPLE 3   *(Compare Exercise 8)*

The university registrar selects 100 transcripts at random and records the GPA for each. The frequency distribution follows:

GPA	FREQUENCY
0–0.49	5
0.5–0.99	9
1.00–1.49	17
1.50–1.99	10
2.00–2.49	18
2.50–2.99	22
3.00–3.49	11
3.50–4.00	8

FIGURE 7–2

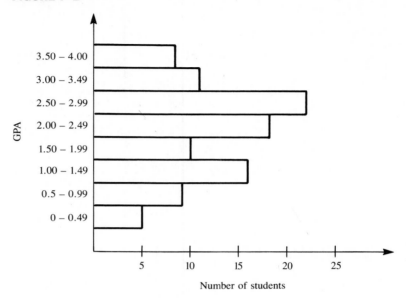

The histogram representing this information appears in Figure 7–2. Notice that we have rotated the histogram so that the bars are horizontal. We did this because the category labels were too long to fit under a bar.

Sometimes a frequency table is summarized with a histogram that uses relative frequency instead of frequency for the vertical scale. **Relative frequency** counts the fractional part of the data that belong to a category.

EXAMPLE 4   *(Compare Exercise 11)*

A question on an Economics exam has five possible responses: A, B, C, D, and E. The number of students who gave each response is the following:

RESPONSE	FREQUENCY
A	6
B	14
C	8
D	22
E	10

Draw a histogram that shows the relative frequency of each response.
SOLUTION   Sixty students answered the question, so the relative frequency is the number responding divided by 60.

RESPONSE	RELATIVE FREQUENCY
A	$\frac{6}{60} = 0.10$
B	$\frac{14}{60} = 0.23$
C	$\frac{8}{60} = 0.13$
D	$\frac{22}{60} = 0.37$
E	$\frac{10}{60} = 0.17$

The histogram is shown in Figure 7–3.

FIGURE 7–3

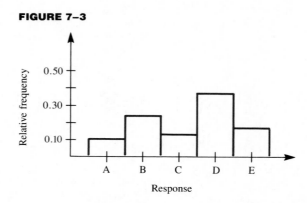

Relative frequency of responses to question

A histogram sometimes conveys the impression that there is a natural break between categories. When continuous data are represented (such as the heights of 18-year-old males) it may be difficult to tell in which category a measurement should be placed. For example, if 5′9″ divides two height categories, it may be difficult to tell whether a person is slightly above or slightly below 5′9″. A smooth curve conveys the impression of continuous data better than a histogram. You can sketch a smooth curve based on a histogram by drawing it through the midpoint at the top of the bars. (See Figure 7–4.)

FIGURE 7–4

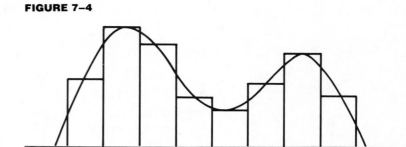

A curve that "smooths" a histogram

EXAMPLE 5

A frequency table of the heights of male high school seniors in Ponca City is the following:

HEIGHT (INCHES)	FREQUENCY
61–62.9	10
63–64.9	51
65–66.9	115
67–68.9	200
69–70.9	240
71–72.9	195
73–74.9	104
75–76.9	42
77–78.9	15

Draw a histogram and a smooth curve representing the data. (See Figure 7–5.)

FIGURE 7–5

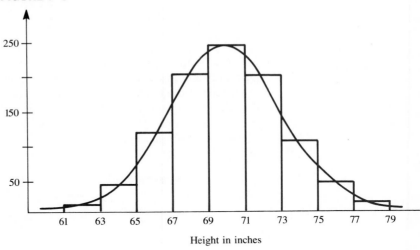

Height in inches

PIE CHART

The second visual representation of data, the **pie chart,** emphasizes the proportion of data that falls into each category. You sometimes see a pie chart in the newspaper that represents the division of a budget into parts. The parts are frequently reported as percentages of the total. You may obtain the percentage of the data that falls into each category from a frequency table.

EXAMPLE 6   *(Compare Exercise 15)*

Jim Dandy has $200 for spending money this month. He carefully prepares the following budget:

CATEGORY	AMOUNT
Dates	$70
Books and records	$20
Laundry	$10
Bicycle repairs	$48
Miscellaneous	$52

Construct a pie chart that represents this budget.

SOLUTION   First, compute the amount in each category as a percentage of the total by dividing the amount in the category by the total, $200.

CATEGORY	PERCENTAGE OF TOTAL AMOUNT
Dates	35
Books and records	10
Laundry	5
Bicycle repair	24
Miscellaneous	26

We "cut the pie" into pieces that have areas in the same proportion as the percentages representing the categories. (See Figure 7–6.) A glance at this pie chart tells us the relative share of each category. The angle at the center of each slice determines the size of the slice. The simplest way to determine the size of the angle is to multiply each percentage by 360°. Then use a protractor to mark off the required angle.

FIGURE 7–6

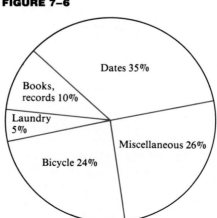

For example, the bicycle repair category in Figure 7–6 accounts for 24% of the budget. The angle used for this category is $0.24 \times 360° = 86°$.

EXAMPLE 7

An advertising firm asked 150 children their favorite flavor of ice cream. Here is a frequency table of their findings:

FLAVOR OF ICE CREAM	NUMBER WHO FAVOR
Vanilla	60
Chocolate	33
Strawberry	18
Peach	24
Other	15
Total	150

Summarize this information with a pie chart.

SOLUTION Compute the percentages of each category and the size of the angle to be used.

FLAVOR OF ICE CREAM	PERCENTAGE	ANGLE IN DEGREES
Vanilla	40 $\left(\frac{60}{150}\right)$	144 (0.40×360)
Chocolate	22 $\left(\frac{33}{150}\right)$	79 (0.22×360)
Strawberry	12 $\left(\frac{18}{150}\right)$	43 (0.12×360)
Peach	16 $\left(\frac{24}{150}\right)$	58 (0.16×360)
Other	10 $\left(\frac{15}{150}\right)$	36 (0.10×360)

(See Figure 7–7.)

FIGURE 7–7

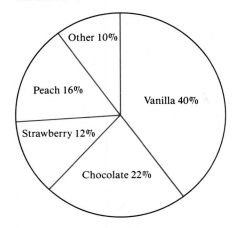

You might wonder why we have two ways to represent a frequency distribution. The histogram and pie chart give visual representations of the same information. The histogram shows the size of each category in reports on monthly sales, annual gross national product growth for several years, or enrollment in accounting courses. Use the pie chart when you wish to show the proportion of data that falls in each category in cases such as a breakdown of students by home state, a summary of family incomes, and a percentage breakdown of letter grades in a course.

7-1 EXERCISES

1. (*See Example 2*) For the given set of data,

$$-1, 2, 2, 4, 6, 2, -1, 4, 4, 4, 6, 8$$

find the frequency of the following numbers:
(**a**) -1 (**b**) 2   (**c**) 4   (**d**) 6   (**e**) 8

2. An experiment is repeated 12 times. The results are

$$-3, 2, 4, -3, 4, 8, -3, 2, 8, 8, 8, 9$$

Give the frequency of each result.

3. The daily total number of students who used the state university swimming pool on 40 days during the summer is as follows:

90	98	137	108	128	115	152	122
110	132	149	131	102	109	118	126
121	145	89	149	86	120	97	118
142	139	128	110	105	104	131	159
93	119	107	129	132	129	98	116

Form a frequency table with the classes 85–99, 100–114, 115–129, 130–144, and 145–159.

4. A city police department radar unit recorded the following speeds one afternoon on 17th Street:

30	46	53	28	52	39	34	29
42	27	48	33	37	29	44	42
38	47	31	51	40	31	36	49
41	26	50	39	35	30	45	43
38	41	36	28	52	34	37	43
35	44	49					

Form a frequency table representing these data. Use category intervals of 5 miles per hour.

5. The following table shows the distribution of grades on a mathematics exam:

Grade	Number of Students
0–59	7
60–69	12
70–79	26
80–89	14
90–100	8

Which of the following quantities can be determined from this distribution? If the quantity can be determined, find it.
(**a**) The number of students who took the test
(**b**) The number of students who scored below 70
(**c**) The number of students who scored at least 80
(**d**) The number of students who scored below 75
(**e**) The number of students who scored between 69 and 90
(**f**) The number of students who scored 95

6. The daily totals of students who rode the campus shuttle bus are as follows:

166	172	184	176	181	84	170	198
182	203	210	141	77	93	147	205
164	122	211	137				

Summarize these totals with a frequency table with five categories.

7. A quiz consists of six questions. The following tabulation shows the number of students who received each possible score of 0 through 6:

Score	Number of Students
0	3
1	5
2	12
3	21
4	15
5	8
6	5

Draw a histogram of the data.

8. (*See Example 3*) The student employment office surveyed 150 working students to determine how many hours they worked each week. They found the following information:

Hours per Week	Number of Students
0–4.9	21
5–9.9	34
10–14.9	29
15–19.9	17
20–24.9	27
25–30	22

Draw the histogram of this summary.

9. Professor X polled his students to determine the number of hours per week they spent on homework for his course. Here are his findings:

3.50	7.50	9.00	2.25	3.50	5.25
4.00	2.75	4.75	1.50	4.50	3.50
3.25	8.50	2.75	5.50	0.25	5.75
2.25	6.25	5.00	6.00	3.50	4.00
0.75	2.25	3.50	3.75	4.00	6.50

Summarize this information with a histogram with five category intervals.

10. A sampling of State University freshmen reveals the following data for mathematics ACT scores:

ACT Score	Number of Students
18	10
19	8
20	15
21	21
22	26
23	30
24	44
25	38
26	50
27	28
28	16
29	12

Using two consecutive scores to form category intervals (18–19, 20–21, and so forth), represent this information with a histogram.

11. (*See Example 4*) Students in Professor Anderson's class evaluate her on several items. For the item "Stimulated students' thinking" they selected one response from: 1—Strongly Agree, 2—Agree, 3—Neutral, 4—Disagree, 5—Strongly Disagree. The following table summarizes the responses:

Response	Frequency
1	9
2	19
3	21
4	8
5	7

Draw a histogram that shows the relative frequency of each response.

12. Students in Professor Baker's class evaluate him on several items. For the item "Instructor was well prepared" they selected one response from: 1—Strongly Agree, 2—Agree, 3—Neutral, 4—Disagree, 5—Strongly Disagree. The following table summarizes the responses:

Response	Frequency
1	22
2	20
3	5
4	3
5	0

Draw a histogram that shows the relative frequency of each response.

13. In the Wild West Bicycle Ride the cyclists choose from five distances. The number choosing each distance is summarized as follows:

Distance	Frequency
10 miles	160
25 miles	750
50 miles	980
62 miles	1120
100 miles	190
	3200

Draw a histogram that shows the relative frequency of each distance category.

14. The grades on a departmental exam in Mathematics 1304 are as follows:

Grade	Frequency
95–100	15
90–94	19
85–89	60
80–84	30
75–79	38
70–74	82
65–69	68
60–64	45
Below 60	18
	375

Draw a histogram that shows the relative frequency of each grade category.

15. (*See Example 6*) Draw the pie chart that represents the following frequency distribution:

Brand of Coffee	Number Who Prefer this Brand
Brand X	28
Brand Y	34
Brand Z	18

16. Graph the following information with the most appropriate graph:

Items in Family Budget	Percentage of Income
Food	25
Housing	35
Utilities	22
Clothing	12
Recreation	6

Draw the pie charts for the frequency distributions in Exercises 17 through 23.

17.
Concentration of Ozone in Air of Large City (in parts per billion)	Number of Days
0–40	8
41–80	22
81–120	18
121–160	12

18.
Budget Items of Old Main University	Amount in Budget (dollars)
Instructional	10,500,000
Administrative	1,500,000
Buildings and grounds	2,000,000
Student services	10,100,000
Other	5,700,000

19.
Income of Old Main University	Amount (dollars)
Tuition and fees	11,800,000
Endowment	2,200,000
Gifts	1,500,000
Auxiliary enterprises	10,100,000
Other	2,400,000

20.
Educational Level of Acme Manufacturing Employees	Number of Employees
Less than high school	45
High school graduate	180
College graduate	60
Graduate work	15

21.
GPA of Tech Students	Number of Students
0–0.99	21
1.00–1.99	72
2.00–2.99	98
3.00–4.00	46

22.
Favorite Vacation Spot of State University Students	Number of Students
Beach	340
Mountains	420
A big city	220
Visiting relatives	130

23. The Census Bureau tabulates the income of Dogpatch families as follows:

Income (dollars)	Number of Families
0–4,999	7
5,000–9,999	32
10,000–16,999	19
17,000–30,000	4

7-2 MEASURES OF CENTRAL TENDENCY

- *The Mean*
- *The Median*
- *The Mode*
- *Which Measure of Central Tendency Is Best?*

We have used histograms and pie charts to summarize a set of data. These devices sometimes make it easier to understand the data.

At times, however, we want to be more concise in reporting information so that comparisons can be easily made or so that some important aspect can be described. You often hear questions like:

"What was the class average on the exam?"

"What kind of gas mileage do you get on your car?"

"What happened to the price of homes from 1977 to 1984?"

You generally expect a response to questions like these to be a single number that is somehow "typical" or at the "center" of the exam grades, distance a car is driven on a certain amount of gas, or price of homes. We will study three ways to obtain a "central number," which is called a **measure of central tendency.**

THE MEAN

When we talk about "averages" like test averages, the average price of gasoline, or a basketball player's scoring average, we usually refer to one particular measure of central tendency, the arithmetic **mean.** To compute the mean of a set of numbers, simply add the numbers and divide by how many numbers were used.

Definition
Mean

The **mean** of the n numbers $x_1, x_2, \ldots, x_n$ is sometimes denoted by μ (the Greek letter *mu*) and is computed as follows:

$$\mu = \frac{x_1 + x_2 + \cdots + x_n}{n}$$

The Convenience Chain wants to compare sales in its 56 stores during July with sales a year ago when it had 49 stores. A comparison of total sales for each July may be misleading because the number of stores differs. Sales can be down from a year ago in each of the 49 stores, but total sales can still be up because there are seven additional stores. The mean sales of all stores in each year should better indicate whether sales are improving.

EXAMPLE 1 *(Compare Exercise 1)*

The mean of the test grades 82, 75, 96, 74 is

$$\frac{82 + 75 + 96 + 74}{4} = \frac{327}{4} = 81.75$$

EXAMPLE 2

Find the mean of the annual salaries $25,000, $14,000, $18,000, $14,000, $20,000, $14,000, $18,000, $14,000.

SOLUTION   Add the salaries:

$$
\begin{array}{r}
25,000 \\
14,000 \\
18,000 \\
14,000 \\
20,000 \\
14,000 \\
18,000 \\
\underline{14,000} \\
137,000
\end{array}
$$

Divide this total by eight, the number of salaries, to obtain the mean:

$$\text{Mean} = \frac{137,000}{8} = \$17,125$$

This mean can be written in this more compact form:

$$\frac{25,000 + 4 \times 14,000 + 2 \times 18,000 + 20,000}{8}$$

where 4 is the frequency of the value 14,000, 2 is the frequency of 18,000, and 25,000 and 20,000 each have a frequency of 1. The divisor, 8, is the sum of the frequencies. This form is useful in cases like the following where the scores are summarized in a frequency table.

EXAMPLE 3   *(Compare Exercise 27)*

Scores are summarized in the following frequency table:

SCORE (X)	FREQUENCY (f)
3	2
4	1
5	8
6	4
	15

The mean is given by

$$\text{Mean} = \frac{2 \times 3 + 1 \times 4 + 8 \times 5 + 4 \times 6}{15} = \frac{74}{15} = 4.93$$

The general formula for the mean of a frequency distribution is as follows:

Formula for the Mean of a Frequency Distribution	Given the scores $x_1, x_2, \ldots, x_k$, which occur with frequency $f_1, f_2, \ldots, f_k$, respectively, the mean is $$\text{Mean} = \frac{f_1 x_1 + f_2 x_2 + \cdots + f_k x_k}{n}$$ where $n = f_1 + f_2 + \cdots + f_k$, the sum of the frequencies.

The next example deals with **grouped data.** Scores are combined into categories and the frequency of that category is given.

EXAMPLE 4 *(Compare Exercise 32)*

Professor Tuff gave a 20-question quiz. She summarized the class performance with the following frequency table:

NUMBER OF CORRECT ANSWERS	NUMBER OF STUDENTS
0–5	8
6–10	14
11–15	23
16–20	10

Estimate the class mean for these grouped data.

SOLUTION   We do not have specific values of the data, only the number in the indicated category. To obtain an *estimate* of the mean, we use the midpoint of each category as the representative value and compute the mean by

$$\text{Mean} = \frac{8 \times 2.5 + 14 \times 8.0 + 23 \times 13.0 + 10 \times 18.0}{55}$$

$$= 11.11$$

where 55 is the sum of the frequencies.

   Note: The midpoint of an interval is the mean of the first and last numbers in the interval.

Formula for the Mean of Grouped Data

Let $x_1, x_2, \ldots, x_k$ be the midpoints of each category interval, and let $f_1, f_2, \ldots, f_k$ be the frequency of each interval, respectively. Then an estimate of the mean is

$$\text{Mean} = \frac{f_1 x_1 + f_2 x_2 + \cdots + f_k x_k}{n}$$

where n is the sum of frequencies, $f_1 + f_2 + \cdots + f_k$.

Notice that the formula for the mean of grouped data looks like the formula for the mean of a frequency distribution. Why is it repeated? Be sure to notice the difference. First, we can only estimate the mean of grouped data. Second, the x's used in the formula for grouped data are midpoints of the categories. Thus one number is selected to represent a range of numbers in the category. In a frequency distribution the x's represent the actual scores.

The mean is a useful measure of central tendency because:

1. it is familiar to most people;
2. it is easy to compute;
3. it can be computed for any set of numerical data; and
4. each set has just one mean.

EXAMPLE 5

The salaries of the Acme Manufacturing Company are

President,	$200,000
Vice-president,	25,000
Production workers,	18,000

The company has 15 production workers. They complain to the president that company salaries are too low. Mr. President responds that the average company salary is about $29,117. He maintains that this is a good salary. The production workers and the vice-president remain unimpressed with this information because not a single one of them makes this much money. Although the president computed the mean correctly, he failed to mention that a single salary—his—was so large that the mean was in no way typical of all the salaries. This illustrates one of the disadvantages of the mean as a number that summarizes data. One or two extreme values can shift the mean, making it a poor representative of the data.

⎯⎯⎯■

THE MEDIAN

Another measure of central tendency, this one not so easily affected by a few extreme values, is the **median.** When data from an experiment are listed according to size, people tend to focus on the middle of the list. Thus, the median is a useful measure of central tendency.

Definition	The **median** is the middle number after the data have been arranged in
Median	order. When there is an even number of data items, the median is the mean of the two middle data items.

Basically, the median divides the data into two parts. One part contains the lower half of the data, and the other part contains the upper half of the data.

EXAMPLE 6   *(Compare Exercise 13)*

The median of the numbers 3, 5, 8, 13, 19, 22, and 37 is the middle number, 13. Three terms lie below 13, and three lie above.

EXAMPLE 7   *(Compare Exercise 15)*

The median of the numbers 1, 5, 8, 11, 14, and 27 is the mean of the two middle numbers, 8 and 11. The median is

$$\frac{8 + 11}{2} = 9.5$$

Three terms lie below 9.5, and three lie above.

EXAMPLE 8   *(Compare Exercise 17)*

Find the median of the set of numbers 8, 5, 2, 17, 28, 4, 3, and 2.
SOLUTION   First, the numbers must be placed in ascending order: 2, 2, 3, 4, 5, 8, 17, 28. Since there are eight numbers, an even number, there is no middle number. We find the mean of the two middle numbers, 4 and 5, to obtain 4.5 as the median.

EXAMPLE 9

The set of numbers 2, 5, 9, 10, and 15 has a mean of 8.2 and a median of 9. If 15 is replaced by 140, the mean changes to 33.2, but the median remains 9. A change in one score of a set may make a significant change in the mean and yet leave the median unchanged.

The median is often used to report income, price of homes, and SAT scores.

THE MODE

The **mode** is used less often as a measure of central tendency. It is used to indicate which observation or observations dominate the data because of the frequency of their occurrence.

Definition
Mode

The **mode** of a set of data is the value that occurs the largest number of times. If more than one value occurs this largest number of times, those values are also modes. When no value occurs more than once, we say that there is no mode. Thus a distribution may have one mode, several modes, or no mode.

EXAMPLE 10   *(Compare Exercise 21)*

The mode of the numbers 1, 3, 2, 5, 4, 3, 2, 6, 8, 2, and 9 is 2 because 2 appears more often than any other value.

∎

EXAMPLE 11   *(Compare Exercise 23)*

The set of numbers 2, 4, 8, 3, 2, 5, 3, 6, 4, 3, and 2 has two modes, 2 and 3, because they both appear three times, more than any other value. The set of numbers 2, 5, 17, 3, and 4 has no mode because each number appears just once.

∎

The mode provides useful information about the most frequently occurring categories. The clothing store does not want to know that the mean size of men's shirts is 15.289. However, the store likes to know that it sells more size $15\frac{1}{2}$ shirts than any other size. The mode best represents summaries where the most frequent response is desired such as the most popular brand of coffee.

WHICH MEASURE OF CENTRAL TENDENCY IS BEST?

With three different measures of central tendency, you probably are curious about which is best. The answer is: "It all depends." It all depends on the nature of the data and the information you wish to summarize.

The mean is a good summary for values that represent magnitudes, like exam scores and price of shoes, if extreme values do not distort the mean. The mean is the best measure when equal distances between scores represent equal differences between the things being measured. For example, the difference between $15 and $20 is $5; the same amount of money is the difference between $85 and $90.

The median is a positional average. It is best used when ranking people or things. In a ranking, an increase or decrease by a fixed amount might not represent the same amount of change at one end of the scale as it does at the other. The difference between the number one ranked tennis player and the number two ranked player at Wimbledon may be small indeed. The difference between the tenth and eleventh ranked players may be significantly greater. In contests, in student standings in class, and in taste tests, numbers are assigned for ranking purposes. However, this does not imply that the people or things ranked all differ by equal amounts. In such cases the median better measures central tendency.

The mode is best when summarizing dress sizes or the brands of bread preferred by families. The information desired is the most typical category, the one that occurs most frequently.

EXAMPLE 12

What is the most appropriate measure of central tendency for the price of hamburgers in town? Since the price is a quantity, not a rank, and since prices tend to occur in a fairly limited price range, the mean is the best measure to use. However, if Joe's Greasy Spoon has a super $39.95 hamburger, this extreme value could distort the mean. In such a case the median may be more appropriate.

EXAMPLE 13

A marketing class runs a taste test on hamburgers in town to determine the typical hamburger. What measure of central tendency is most appropriate? The students are evaluating taste, a quality, not a quantity. The mean is not appropriate in this case. It makes sense to use the median because half the hamburgers taste better and half taste worse or to use the mode to indicate the most popular hamburger in town.

When you summarize a set of data with a histogram, you can visualize the mean in the following way. Think of the histogram as being constructed from material of uniform weight, a thickness of plastic or cardboard. If you try to balance the histogram on a point, you will need to position it at the mean. (See Figure 7–8.)

FIGURE 7–8

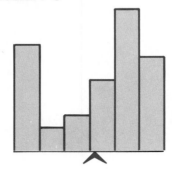

The mean is where the histogram balances.

7–2 EXERCISES

I

Find the mean of the sets of data in Exercises 1 through 8.

1. (*See Example 1*) 2, 4, 6, 8, 10

2. 3, 8, 2, 14, 21

3. 2.1, 3.7, 5.9

4. 150, 225, 345, 86, 176, 410, 330

5. 6, −4, 3, 5, −8, 2

6. 3, 3, 3, 3, 5, 5, 5, 5

7. 5.9, 2.1, 6.6, 4.7

8. 1525, 1640, 1776, 1492, 2000

9. Find the mean grade of the following exam grades: 80, 76, 92, 64, 93, 81, 57, and 77.

10. Six women have the following weights: 106 lb, 115 lb, 130 lb, 110 lb, 120 lb, and 118 lb. What is their mean weight?

11. A radar gun recorded the speeds (in miles per hour) of seven pitches of a baseball pitcher. They were

$$90.5, \quad 89.2, \quad 78.4, \quad 91.0, \quad 84.2, \quad 73.5, \quad 88.7$$

Find the average speed of the pitches.

12. One year the rainfall in Central Texas for each month January through May was

$$1.70 \text{ in.}, \quad 2.05 \text{ in.}, \quad 2.00 \text{ in.}, \quad 3.75 \text{ in.}, \quad 4.70 \text{ in.}$$

Find the average monthly rainfall.

In Exercises 13 through 20, find the median of the given set of numbers.

13. (*See Example 6*) 1, 3, 9, 17, 22

14. (a) 36, 41, 55, 88, 121, 140, 162
    (b) 12, 4, 8, 3, 1, 10, 6

15. (*See Example 7*) 12, 14, 21, 25, 30, 37

16. 1, 3, 9, 10, 14, 17, 18, 19

17. (*See Example 8*) 6, 8, 1, 29, 15, 9, 14, 22

18. 101, 59, 216, 448, 92, 31

19. 72, 86, 65, 90, 72, 98, 81, 72, 68

20. 379, 421, 202, 598, 148

In Exercises 21 through 26, find the mode(s) of the given set of numbers.

21. (*See Example 10*) 1, 5, 8, 3, 2, 5, 6, 11, 5

22. 3, 2, 4, 6, 5, 4, 1, 6, 8, 4, 1, 6, 8, 4, 4, 13, 6

23. (*See Example 11*) 1, 5, 9, 1, 5, 9, 1, 5, 9, 1, 5

24. 10, 14, 10, 16, 10, 14, 16, 14, 21

25. 5, 4, 9, 13, 12, 1, 2

26. 2, 3, 2, 3, 2, 3, 2, 5, 9

II

27. (*See Example 3*) Professor Y had the following grade distribution in her class:

Grade	Frequency
96	2
91	3
85	7
80	13
75	12
70	10
60	8
50	5

What is the class average (mean)?

28. The attendance in a class for a 20-day period was the following:

Attendance	Frequency
19	1
20	2
21	1
22	5
23	8
24	3

Find the average (mean) daily attendance

29. An inspector of PC computer disks records the number of defective disks found per box (ten disks per box). Here is the summary for 1000 boxes inspected:

Number Defective	Frequency
0	430
1	395
2	145
3	25
4	5

Find the mean number of defective disks per box

30. An avid golf fan recorded the scores of 75 golfers on the ninth hole of the Cottonwood Golf Course as follows:

Score	Frequency
1	1
2	1
3	32
4	27
5	8
6	6

Find the average score.

31. A personnel office gave a typing test to all secretarial applicants. The number of errors for 150 applicants is summarized as follows:

Number of Errors	Frequency
0–5	28
6–10	47
11–20	68
21–30	7

Estimate the mean number of errors.

32. (*See Example 4*)
Estimate the mean for the grouped data:

Score	Frequency
0–5	6
6–10	4
11–19	12
20–30	7

33. Professor Z posted the following summary of test grades:

Grade	Number of Grades
90–100	8
80–89	15
70–79	22
60–69	11
45–59	5

Estimate the class average.

34. The advertising department of *Food Today* magazine ran a survey to determine the number of ads read by its subscribers. The survey found the following:

Number of Ads Read	Frequency
0–2	45
3–5	75
6–10	35
10–20	15

Estimate the average number of ads read by a subscriber.

35. The daily stock prices of Acme Corporation for one business week were $139.50, $141.25, $140.75, $138.50, and $132.00. What was the average price (mean) for the week?

36. Henry scored 80, 72, 84, and 68 on four exams. What must he make on the fifth exam to have an average of 80?

37. Throughout the 1989 wheat harvest, a farmer sold his wheat each day as it was harvested. The prices he received per bushel were $3.60, $3.57, $3.90, $3.85, $4.00, $4.15, $4.25, and $4.40. Find the mean and median prices.

38. The family income in a depressed area is reported as follows:

Family Income (Dollars)	Number of Families
0–1999	3
2000–3999	8
4000–7999	15
8000–11,999	6
12,000–14,000	4

Estimate the average (mean) family income by using the midpoint of each category as the actual income.

III

39. The scores of 18 players on the eighth hole of the Putt-Putt course are summarized with the following histogram:

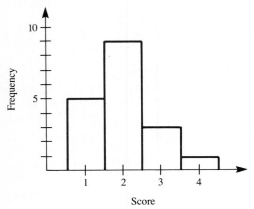

(a) How many made a hole-in-one?
(b) What was the mode score?
(c) What was the mean score?
(d) What was the median score?

40. The results of a five-point quiz are summarized in the following histogram:

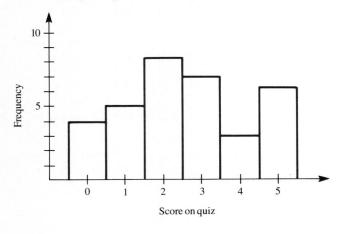

(a) How many scored above 3?
(b) How many scored a 1, 2, or 3?
(c) What is the mode score?
(d) Find the median score.
(e) Find the mean score.

41. Professor X gave a quiz to five students. He remembered four of the grades—72, 88, 81, and 67—and the mean, 78. What was the other grade?

42. Seven cash registers at a supermarket averaged sales of $2946.38 one day. What were the total sales?

43. A vice-president of a company asked the personnel department for a summary of staff salaries. Personnel provided the following:

21 employees at $18,000,
9 employees at $22,000,
14 employees at $25,000,
26 employees at $28,000,
13 employees at $30,000,
8 employees at $35,000.

The vice-president then decided that she wanted the mean salary. Find it for her.

44. The women taking a physical education course were weighed. The results are summarized below:

Weight (pounds)	Number of Women
105–115	9
116–125	13
126–135	15
136–145	21
146–155	14
156–165	14
166–175	11
176–185	2
186–195	1

In which category does the median fall?

45. The mean salary of eight employees is $27,450, and the mean salary of ten others is $31,400. Find the mean salary of the 18 employees.

46. The class average on a test was 73.25. The average of the 16 males in the class was 71.75. There were 20 females tested. What was their average?

47. The median of five test scores is 82. If four of the grades are 65, 93, 77, and 82, what can you determine about the fifth score?

48. If the mean of ten scores is 13.4, and the mean of five other scores is 6.2, find the mean of the 15 scores.

49. The mean price of three sugar-coated cereals is $1.27, and the mean price of two sugar-free cereals is $1.34. Find the mean price of all five cereals.

50. Honest Joe's used car lot sold an average of 23 cars per month over a twelve-month period. Sales for the last seven months of this period averaged 26 cars per month. What was the average for the first five months?

51. The mean of the numbers 6, -2, 4, 9, and 5 is 4.4.
   (a) Add 3 to each of the given numbers and find their mean. How is it related to 4.4?
   (b) Add 10 to each of the given numbers and find their mean. How is it related to 4.4?
   (c) Multiply each of the given numbers by 2 and find their mean. How is it related to 4.4?
   (d) Multiply each of the given numbers by 6 and find their mean. How is it related to 4.4?
   (e) Make a general statement about the effect on the mean when a constant is added to each number or when each number is multiplied by a constant.

52. Determine which measure of central tendency best represents each of the following sets of data:
   (a) The weight of lab rats used in a diet experiment
   (b) SAT scores
   (c) The favorite movie at a video rental shop

(d) Rank on the state bar exam
(e) The number of books read per month by female adults in McLennan County
(f) The number of pages in finite mathematics textbooks
(g) The salaries of janitors at State University
(h) The salaries of 75 janitors, the president, and the vice-president of Ford Tractor Co.
(i) The waist sizes of jeans sold to junior high school boys
(j) The ages of college students

53. The 155 golfers playing in the second round of the 1989 U.S. Open Golf Tournament made the following scores on the sixth hole:

Score	Number of Players
1	4
2	28
3	95
4	24
5	4

Find the mean score for that hole. (Notice that there were four players who made a hole-in-one. This remarkable feat was accomplished by Doug Weaver, Jerry Pate, Nick Price, and Mark Wiebe, all using a 7-iron and all within a period of one hour and 50 minutes.)

7-3 MEASURES OF DISPERSION: RANGE, VARIANCE, AND STANDARD DEVIATION

- *Range*
- *Variance and Standard Deviation*
- *Measurements of Position*
- *Application*

A score often has little meaning unless it is compared with other scores. We have used the mean as one comparison. If you know your test score and the class average, you can compare how far you are above or below the class average. However, the average alone does not tell you how many in the class had grades closer to the average than you.

If two bowlers have the same average, do they have the same ability? If two students have the same average in a course, did they learn the same amount?

While the mean is a rather simple representation of a set of data, sometimes more information is needed about how the scores are clustered about the mean in order to make valid comparisons. Let's use students' class averages to illustrate **measures of dispersion.**

STUDENT A	STUDENT B
80	65
87	92
82	95
92	75
84	98

Each student's mean is 85. However, student A is more consistent. Student B's scores vary more widely. The mean does not distinguish between these two sets of data. As this example shows, two data sets may have the same mean, but in one set the values may be clustered close to the mean, and in the other set the values may be widely scattered. To say something about the amount of cluster as well as the average, we need more information.

RANGE

One way to measure the dispersion of a set of scores is to find the **range,** the distance between the largest and smallest scores. The range is 12 for student A and 33 for student B, so the range suggests that A's scores are clustered closer to the mean, and the mean is thereby a better representation of A's scores than of B's scores. For grouped data, like a frequency table or histogram, the range is the difference between the smaller boundary of the lowest category and the larger boundary of the highest category.

Here are two frequency tables.

I.	CATEGORY	FREQUENCY
	1–2	10
	3–4	5
	5–6	3
	7–8	6
	9–10	16

II.	CATEGORY	FREQUENCY
	1–2	1
	3–4	8
	5–6	11
	7–8	17
	9–10	3

The mean for each is 6.15 (using the grouped data mean), and the range for each is 9. Clearly, the scores in Table II are clustered near the mean, whereas they tend to be more remote in Table I. The range gives information only about the extreme scores and gives no information on their cluster near the mean.

The range is a simple measure of dispersion, but sometimes it helps to know whether the numbers are scattered rather uniformly throughout the range or whether most of them are clustered close together and a few are near the extremes of the range. For example, suppose a company manufactures ball bearings for an automobile company. The automobile company specifies that the bearings should be 0.35 inch in diameter. However, the automobile company and the bearing manufacturer both know that it is impossible to consistently make bearings that are exactly 0.35 inch in diameter. Slight variations in the material, limitations on the precision of equipment, and human error will create deviations from the desired diameter. So the automobile company specifies that the bearings must be 0.35 ± 0.001 inch in diameter. The diameter may deviate as much as 0.001 inch from the desired diameter; that is, the acceptable range of diameters is 0.349 to 0.351. If the manufacturer produces a batch of bearings with all diameters in the range 0.3495 to 0.3508 inch, then there is no problem because all of them are acceptable. However, if the range of diameters is 0.347 to 0.353, there may or may not be a problem. Generally, they expect a few unacceptable bearings. If 90% of the bearings are unacceptable, then major problems exist in the manufacturing process. If fewer than one half of 1 percent are unacceptable, then the process may be considered satisfactory.

In this situation a measure of how a batch of bearings varies from the desired diameter, 0.35 inch, is more useful than the largest and smallest diameters. We now look at two other useful indicators of variation.

VARIANCE AND STANDARD DEVIATION

A widely used measure of variation is the **standard deviation.** A related indicator, the **variance,** is another. These indicators measure the degree to which the scores tend to cluster about a central value, the mean in this case. The variance and standard deviation give measures of the distance of observations from the mean. They are large if the observations tend to be far from the mean and small if they tend to be near. Even when all scores remain within a certain range, the variance and standard deviation will increase or decrease as a score is moved away from or closer to the mean.

Because computation of the standard deviation is more complicated than the mean and the range, we will use the example of student A and student B to go through the steps to compute the variation and standard deviation.

Step 1. Determine the **deviation** of each score from the mean. Compute these deviations by subtracting the mean from each score. The computations below show the deviations for student A and student B using the mean of 85 in each case. Notice that the deviations give the distance of the score from the mean, a positive value for scores greater than the mean and a negative value for those less than the mean. You should also notice that the deviations add to zero for both students. This always holds. The deviations will always add to zero. For this reason we cannot accumulate the deviations to measure the overall deviation from the mean.

Computation of Standard Deviation

	STUDENT A				STUDENT B	
GRADE	DEVIATION	SQUARED DEVIATION	GRADE	DEVIATION	SQUARED DEVIATION
80	$80 - 85 = -5$	25	65	$65 - 85 = -20$	400
87	$87 - 85 = 2$	4	92	$92 - 85 = 7$	49
82	$82 - 85 = -3$	9	95	$95 - 85 = 10$	100
92	$92 - 85 = 7$	49	75	$75 - 85 = -10$	100
84	$84 - 85 = -1$	1	98	$98 - 85 = 13$	169
425	0	88	425	0	818

Step 2. Square each of the deviations. These are shown under the heading "squared deviation."

This process of squaring the deviations allows us to accumulate a sum that is large when the scores tend to be far away from the mean. To adjust for cases in which two sets of data have different numbers of scores, we find a mean as in the next step.

Step 3. Find the mean of the squared deviations. For student A the sum of the squared deviations is 88, and their mean is $\frac{88}{5}$, which equals 17.6. For student B the sum of the squared deviations is 818, and their mean is $\frac{818}{5}$, which equals 163.6. The number 17.6 is the **variance** for student A, and 163.6 is the **variance** for student B.

Step 4. Find the square root of the means just obtained. For student A we have $\sqrt{17.6} = 4.20$. For student B we have $\sqrt{163.6} = 12.79$. These numbers are **standard deviations.** By tradition the symbol σ (sigma) denotes standard deviation, and σ^2 denotes variance. Thus for student A, $\sigma = 4.20$; and for student B, $\sigma = 12.79$. The standard deviation measures the spread of the values about their mean. Student B has the larger standard deviation, so her grades are more widely scattered. The grades of student A cluster closer to the mean.

A formal statement of the formula for variance and standard deviation is the following:

Formula for Variance and Standard Deviation   Given the n numbers $x_1, x_2, \ldots, x_n$ whose mean is μ. The variance, denoted σ^2, and standard deviation, σ, of these numbers is given by

$$\sigma^2 = \frac{(x_1 - \mu)^2 + (x_2 - \mu)^2 + \cdots + (x_n - \mu)^2}{n}$$

$$\sigma = \sqrt{\sigma^2}$$

NOTE: In some applications the divisor in computing variance and standard deviation is $n - 1$ instead of n. If you use a calculator with a standard deviation button, be sure that it uses n for the divisor.

Both the variance and the standard deviation measure the dispersion of data. The variance is measured in the **square** of the units of the original data. The standard deviation is measured in the units of the data, so it is usually preferred as a measure of dispersion.

EXAMPLE 1   *(Compare Exercise 1)*

Compute the mean and standard deviation of the numbers 8, 18, 7, and 10.

SOLUTION   The mean is

$$\frac{8 + 18 + 7 + 10}{4} = \frac{43}{4} = 10.75$$

SCORES	DEVIATION	SQUARED DEVIATION
8	8 − 10.75 = −2.75	7.56 (rounded)
18	18 − 10.75 = 7.25	52.56
7	7 − 10.75 = −3.75	14.06
10	10 − 10.75 = −0.75	0.56
	0	74.74

$$\sigma = \sqrt{\frac{74.74}{4}} = \sqrt{18.69} = 4.32$$

You might have noticed that the sum of the deviations is zero in each of the cases shown. This is no accident. The deviations will always add to zero. Thus the sum of deviations gives no information about the dispersion of scores. We need to use something more complicated, like standard deviation, to determine dispersion.

Let's summarize the procedure for obtaining standard deviation.

Procedure for Computing Standard Deviation

Step 1. Compute the mean of the scores.
Step 2. Subtract the mean from each value to obtain the deviation.
Step 3. Square each deviation.
Step 4. Find the mean of the squared deviations. This is the variance.
Step 5. Take the square root of the variance. This is the standard deviation.

EXAMPLE 2

Find the standard deviation of the scores 8, 10, 19, 23, 28, 31, 32, and 41.

SOLUTION   *Step 1.* Find the mean of the scores:

$$\frac{8 + 10 + 19 + 23 + 28 + 31 + 32 + 41}{8} = \frac{192}{8} = 24$$

Step 2. Compute the deviation from the mean:

$$8 - 24 = -16$$
$$10 - 24 = -14$$
$$19 - 24 = -5$$
$$23 - 24 = -1$$
$$28 - 24 = 4$$
$$31 - 24 = 7$$
$$32 - 24 = 8$$
$$41 - 24 = 17$$

Step 3. Square each deviation:

$$(-16)^2 = 256$$
$$(-14)^2 = 196$$
$$(-5)^2 = 25$$
$$(-1)^2 = 1$$
$$4^2 = 16$$
$$7^2 = 49$$
$$8^2 = 64$$
$$17^2 = 289$$

Step 4. Find the mean of the squared deviations:

$$\frac{256 + 196 + 25 + 1 + 16 + 49 + 64 + 289}{8} = 112$$

Step 5. Take the square root of the result in Step 4. (Use a calculator.)

$$\sigma = \sqrt{112} = 10.6$$

EXAMPLE 3   *(Compare Exercise 11)*

Find the mean and standard deviation for the following frequency distribution:

SCORE	FREQUENCY
10	8
15	3
16	13
20	6

SOLUTION The total of the frequencies is 30, so we have 30 scores. First, compute the mean:

$$\mu = \frac{8 \times 10 + 3 \times 15 + 13 \times 16 + 6 \times 20}{30} = \frac{453}{30} = 15.1$$

Next, compute the variance, using the squares of deviations:

$$\text{Variance} = \frac{8 \times (10 - 15.1)^2 + 3 \times (15 - 15.1)^2 + 13 \times (16 - 15.1)^2 + 6 \times (20 - 15.1)^2}{30}$$

$$= \frac{8(5.1)^2 + 3(0.1)^2 + 13(0.9)^2 + 6(4.9)^2}{30}$$

$$= \frac{362.7}{30} = 12.09$$

The standard deviation is $\sigma = \sqrt{12.09} = 3.48$.

EXAMPLE 4 *(Compare Exercise 15)*

Estimate the standard deviation for the following grouped data:

SCORE	FREQUENCY
0–5	6
6–10	3
11–19	13
20–25	8

SOLUTION Use the midpoint of each category to compute the mean:

$$\text{Mean} = \frac{2.5 \times 6 + 8.0 \times 3 + 15.0 \times 13 + 22.5 \times 8}{30} = 13.8$$

The deviations are computed by using the mean and the midpoints of each category.

DEVIATION	SQUARED DEVIATION
$2.5 - 13.8 = -11.3$	$(-11.3)^2 = 127.69$
$8.0 - 13.8 = -5.8$	$(-5.8)^2 = 33.64$
$15.0 - 13.8 = 1.2$	$(1.2)^2 = 1.44$
$22.5 - 13.8 = 8.7$	$(8.7)^2 = 75.69$

To obtain the variance, we need to use each squared deviation multiplied by the frequency of the corresponding category:

$$\text{Variance} = \frac{127.69 \times 6 + 33.64 \times 3 + 1.44 \times 13 + 75.69 \times 8}{30}$$

$$= \frac{1491.30}{30}$$

$$= 49.71$$

$$\text{Standard deviation} = \sqrt{49.71} = 7.05$$

You do not expect to compute a standard deviation during your daily activities. Yet, on an intuitive level, all of us are interested in standard deviation. For example, you can recall a trip to the grocery store when you selected the shortest checkout line only to find that it took longer than someone who got in a longer line at the same time. Let's look at the situation from the store's viewpoint. The store's managers are interested in customer satisfaction, so they work to reduce waiting time. They proudly announce that, on the average, they check out a customer in 3.5 minutes. The customer might agree that 3.5 minutes is good service, but an occasional long wait might make the customer question the store's claim. Basically, the customer wants the store to have a small standard deviation. A small standard deviation indicates that you expect the waiting time to be near 3.5 minutes per customer.

A restaurant uses a different system of waiting lines. Customers do not choose a table and line up beside it. All customers wait in a single line and are directed to a table as it becomes available—and for a good reason. Diners do not want someone standing over them waiting for them to finish eating.

If we ignore the psychology of lining up at someone's table, which of these two systems is better? Is it better to let the customer choose one of several lines or to have a single line and allow a customer to go to a station as it becomes available? Both systems are reasonable in a bank. One bank may use the system where the customer chooses the teller, and a line forms at each teller. Another bank may use the system where the customers wait in a single line, and the customer at the head of the line goes to the next available teller. It turns out that the average waiting time is the same under both systems. Thus, from the bank's viewpoint, both systems allow it to be equally efficient. But it also turns out that the single-line concept tends to decrease the standard deviation and thereby reduce the extremes in waiting times. More customers will be served near the average waiting time than under the multiple line system. Thus from the customer's viewpoint the single-line concept is better because it helps reduce an occasional long delay. Since the bank's efficiency is the same in both cases, management would do well to adopt the single-line concept.

MEASUREMENTS OF POSITION

Scores are generally meaningless by themselves. "We scored ten runs in our softball game" gives no information about the outcome of the game unless the score of the opponent is known. A grade of 85 is not very impressive if everyone else scored 100.

The mean, median, and mode give a central point of reference for a score. You can compare your score to the mean or median and determine on which side of the central point your score lies.

One familiar measurement of position is the **rank.** A student ranks 15th in a class of 119; a runner places 38th in a field of 420 in the ten-kilometer run; a girl is the fourth runner-up in a beauty contest. Your rank simply gives the position of your score relative to all other scores. It gives no information on the location of the central point and on how closely scores are clustered around it.

If you took the SAT test, you received a numerical score and a **percentile** score, another positional score. A score at the 84th percentile states that 84% of people taking the test scored the same or lower and 16% scored higher. A score at the 50th percentile is a median score: 50% score higher and 50% score the same or lower. The percentile score is used as a positional score when a large number of scores is involved.

EXAMPLE 5 *(Compare Exercise 26)*

(a) A golfer is ranked 22nd in a field of 114 players. What is his percentile?
(b) A golfer is at the 76th percentile in a field of 88. What is her rank?

SOLUTION

(a) Since the golfer is ranked 22nd, there are $114 - 22 = 92$ players ranked lower. Counting the golfer, there are 93 ranked the same or lower. The percentile is $\frac{93}{114} \times 100\% = 81.6\%$, which we round down to 81st percentile.

(b) Since 76% are ranked the same or lower, there are $0.76 \times 88 = 66.88$ or 67 players ranked the same or lower. We say that she is ranked 22nd.

Another standard score is the **z-score.** It is more sophisticated than rank or percentile because it uses a central point of the scores (the mean) and a measure of dispersion (the standard deviation). It is useful in comparing scores when two different reference groups are involved. The z-score is

$$z = \frac{\text{score} - \text{mean}}{\text{standard deviation}}$$

EXAMPLE 6 *(Compare Exercise 21)*

If the mean $= 85$ and $\sigma = 5$, then the z-score for a raw score of 92 is

$$z = \frac{92 - 85}{5} = \frac{7}{5} = 1.4$$

For a score of 70,

$$z = \frac{70 - 85}{5} = \frac{-15}{5} = -3$$

A negative z-score indicates that the score is below the mean. $z = 1.4$ indicates that the score is 1.4 standard deviations above the mean. A z-score of 0 corresponds to the mean.

APPLICATION

EXAMPLE 7 *(Compare Exercise 31)*

A student took both the SAT and ACT tests and made a 480 on the SAT verbal portion and a 22 on the ACT verbal. Which was the better score? *Note:* You need to know that for the SAT verbal test, mean $= 431$ and $\sigma = 111$; and for the ACT verbal, mean $= 17.8$ and $\sigma = 5.5$.

SOLUTION   The z-score for each test is

$$\text{SAT } z = \frac{480 - 431}{111} = \frac{49}{111} = 0.44$$

$$\text{ACT } z = \frac{22 - 17.8}{5.5} = \frac{4.2}{5.5} = 0.76$$

The higher z-score, 0.76, indicates that the student performed better on the ACT because the ACT score was higher above the mean. ____

7-3 EXERCISES

I

Determine the mean, variance, and standard deviation for the sets of data in Exercises 1 through 10.

1. (*See Example 1*) 19, 10, 15, 20

2. 0, 3, 5, 9, 10, 12

3. 4, 8, 9, 10, 14

4. 10, 14, 20, 24

5. 17, 39, 54, 22, 16, 46, 25, 19, 62, 50

6. 1.1, 1.3, 1.5, 1.7

7. $-8, -4, -3, 0, 1, 2$

8. $-5, 4, 8, 10, 15$

9. $-3, 0, 1, 4, 5, 8, 10, 11$

10. $-8, -6, 0, 4, 7, 12$

II

11. (*See Example 3*) Find the mean, variance and standard deviation of the following frequency distribution:

x	Frequency
1	2
2	5
3	2
4	3
5	8

12. Find the mean and standard deviation of the following exam grades:

Grade	Frequency
65	1
70	2
75	5
78	3
80	7
84	4
85	6
90	2

13. Find the mean and standard deviation of the following student summer wages:

Wage (per hour)	Frequency
3.35	10
3.60	12
3.75	8
4.00	5

14. Find the mean and standard deviation of the following frequency distribution:

x	Frequency
12	3
15	4
20	5
22	4

15. (*See Example 4*) Estimate the mean and standard deviation of the following grouped data:

Score	Frequency
0–10	5
11–20	12
21–30	8

16. The following is a summary of test grades for a class. Estimate the mean and standard deviation.

Grades	Frequency
91–100	3
81–90	4
71–80	10
61–70	4
51–60	3

17. Estimate the mean and standard deviation of the following grouped data:

Score	Frequency
10–15	14
16–20	18
21–25	18

18. Estimate the mean and standard deviation of the following ACT scores:

Score	Frequency
17–19	25
20–22	35
23–25	45
26–28	25
29–31	10
32–34	10

19. The daily high temperatures (in degrees Fahrenheit) one week in January were 32, 35, 28, 34, 29, 33, and 26. Find the mean and standard deviation of the temperature.

20. (a) Calculate the standard deviation of the set 6, 6, 6, 6, 6, and 6.
(b) What are the mean and the standard deviation of a set in which all scores are the same?
(c) What are the median and mode of a set in which all scores are the same?

21. (*See Example 6*) Let the mean $= 160$ and $\sigma = 16$.
(a) Find the z-score for the score 180.
(b) Find the z-score for the score 150.
(c) Find the z-score for the score 160.
(d) Find the score X if the z-score $= 1$.
(e) Find the score X if the z-score $= -0.875$.

22. The following statements give a single-number model of situations. Discuss how our view of the situation might change if we also knew the standard deviation.
(a) The mean monthly rainfall in Waco is 2.51 inches.
(b) The average grade on the last test was 82.
(c) The mean of the temperature on July 11, 1987 was 80 degrees.
(d) "But, Dad, I averaged 50 miles per hour."

III

23. A machine shop uses two lathes to make shafts for electric motors. A sample of five shafts from each lathe are checked for quality-control purposes. The diameter of each shaft (in inches) is given as follows:

Lathe I	Lathe II
0.501	0.502
0.503	0.497
0.495	0.498
0.504	0.501
0.497	0.502

The mean diameter in each case is 0.500.
(a) Find the standard deviation for each lathe.
(b) Which lathe is more consistent?

24. (a) Calculate the mean and the standard deviation of the scores 1, 3, 8, and 12.
(b) Add 2 to each of the scores in part (a) and compute the mean and the standard deviation. How are the mean and the standard deviation related to those in part (a)? Would the same kind of relationship exist if you added another constant instead of 2?

25. A set has 8 numbers. Each one is either 2, 3, or 4. The mean of the set is 3.
(a) If $\sigma = 0.5$, what is the set of numbers?
(b) If $\sigma = 1$, what is the set of numbers?
(c) Can σ be larger than 1?

26. (*See Example 5*) A golfer finished 15th in a field of 90 golfers in a tournament. What was his percentile?

27. A student scored at the 70th percentile on a test taken by 110 students. What was her rank?

28. A student learned that 105 students scored higher and 481 scored the same or lower on a standardized test.
    (a) What is the student's rank on the test?
    (b) What is the student's percentile on the test?

29. A student scored at the 98th percentile on a verbal test given to 1545 students. How many scored higher?

30. Suppose that the mean = 140 and $\sigma = 15$. Find the score 2.2 standard deviations above the mean.

31. (*See Example* 7) Leon took an admission's test at two different universities. At one, where the mean was 72 and the standard deviation 8, he scored 86. At the other, with mean 62 and standard deviation 12, he scored 82. Which one was the better performance?

32. Joe scored 114 on a standardized test that had a mean of 120 and a standard deviation of 8. Josephine scored 230 on a test that had a mean of 250 and a standard deviation of 14. Which one preformed better?

33. A runner ran a three-kilometer race in 19 minutes. The average time of all who finished was 18 minutes with $\sigma = 1$ minute. A cyclist rode a 25 mile race in 64 minutes. The average time of all who finished was 59 minutes with $\sigma = 3$. Which athlete had the better performance?

7–4 RANDOM VARIABLES AND PROBABILITY DISTRIBUTIONS OF DISCRETE RANDOM VARIABLES

- *Random Variables*
- *Probability Distributions of Discrete Random Variables*

RANDOM VARIABLES

We routinely use numbers to convey information, to help express an opinion or an emotion, to help evaluate a situation, and to clarify our thoughts. Think how many times you have used phrases such as "On a scale from 1 to 10, what do you think of . . . ?"; "What is your GPA?"; "The chance of rain this weekend is 40%."; "Which team is first in the American League?"; "How many A's did Professor X give?"; and "What did you make on your math test?".

All of these statements use numbers in some form. Notice that the numbers are not the heart of the statement, they represent a key facet of the message. When he says she is an 8 and she says he is a 3, the numbers are not the emotions that are evoked; the numbers indicate something about the strength of the emotions. The product of an examination is an exam paper, but a grade is assigned to the paper to indicate something about the quality of the paper. A trip to the grocery store results in bags of grocery items, but a number—the cost—is usually associated with the purchase.

We associate numbers with outcomes of activities and phenomena because it is easier to compare and analyze numbers. To summarize grades with a GPA is easier than averaging letter grades. The auto driver and the highway patrolman can more nearly agree on the meaning of "drive at 55 mph or less" than they can on "drive at a safe and reasonable speed."

This idea of assigning a number to outcomes of an experiment (activity or process) is an important and useful statistical concept. We call this assignment of numbers a **random variable.**

Definition **Random Variable**	A **random variable** is a rule that assigns a number to each outcome of an experiment.

It is customary to denote the random variable by a capital letter such as X or Y.

When many outcomes are possible, we might find it difficult to understand the implications of the results because of the length of the list. A summary of the results quite often helps our understanding of the outcome (like summarizing test results). This chapter discusses some ways to summarize data. The purpose of a summary is to condense the data into a form that conveys the essence of the data in a simple way.

Before we discuss techniques of summarizing data, let's look at some examples of random variables.

EXAMPLE 1   *(Compare Exercise 1)*

If a coin is tossed twice, there are four possible outcomes: HH, HT, TH, and TT. We can assign a number to each outcome by simply giving the number of heads that appear in each case. The values of X are assigned as follows.

OUTCOME	X
HH	2
HT	1
TH	1
TT	0

EXAMPLE 2   *(Compare Exercise 5)*

A true–false quiz consists of 15 questions. A random variable may be defined by assigning the total number of correct answers to each quiz.

EXAMPLE 3   *(Compare Exercise 7)*

The Hardware Store has a box of Super-Special items. Selecting an item from the box is an experiment with each of the items as an outcome. Two possible ways to define a random variable are to:

(a) assign the original price to each item (outcome) or
(b) assign the sale price to each item.

EXAMPLE 4

(a) Each judge of an Olympic diving contest assigns a number from 1 to 10 to each outcome (dive). We can think of each judge's assignment as a way of defining a random variable.

(b) The housing office gives a congeniality test to incoming students in order to better assign dormitory roommates. The tests are scored 1 through 5 with a higher number indicating more congeniality. The scores are values of a random variable assigned to levels of congeniality.

(c) An airline baggage claim office records the number of bags claimed by each passenger. The number of bags is a random variable associated with each passenger.

EXAMPLE 5 *(Compare Exercise 25)*

Three people are selected from a group of five men and four women. A random variable X is the number of women selected. List the possible values of X and the number of different outcomes that can be associated with each value.

SOLUTION X can assume the value 0, 1, 2, or 3. The number of different outcomes associated with each value is the following:

X	OUTCOME	NUMBER OF POSSIBLE OUTCOMES
0	three men	$C(5, 3) = 10$
1	one woman, two men	$C(4, 1)C(5, 2) = 40$
2	two women, one man	$C(4, 2)C(5, 1) = 30$
3	three women	$C(4, 3) = 4$

In one sense you may be quite arbitrary in the way you define a random variable for an experiment. It depends on what is most useful for the problem at hand. Here are several examples:

EXPERIMENT	RANDOM VARIABLE, *X*
A survey of cars entering mall parking lot	Number of passengers in a car: 1, 2, . . . , 8
Rolling a pair of dice	Sum of numbers that turn up: 2, 3, . . . , 12
Tossing a coin three times	Number of times tails occurs
Selecting a sample of five widgets from an assembly line	Number of defective widgets in the sample
Measuring the height of a student selected at random	Observed height
Finding the average life of a Brand *X* tire	Number of miles driven
Selecting a box of Crunchies cereal	Weight of the box of cereal
Checking the fuel economy of a compact car	Distance *X* the car travels on a gallon of gas

The first four random variables are **discrete variables** because the values assigned come from a set of distinct numbers and the values between are not permitted as outcomes. For example, the number of auto passengers can take on only the values 1, 2, 3, and so on. The number 2.63 is not a valid assignment for the number of passengers. On the other hand, the last four examples are **continuous variables.** Assuming an accurate measuring device, 5 feet 4.274 inches is a valid height. There are no distinct gaps that must be excluded as a valid height. Similarly, even though one might expect a car to travel about 23 miles on a gallon of gas, 22.64 miles cannot be excluded as a valid distance. Any distance in a reasonable interval is a valid possibility.

PROBABILITY DISTRIBUTION OF A DISCRETE RANDOM VARIABLE

We now merge two concepts that we studied earlier. We have used the concept of probability to give a measure of the likelihood of a certain outcome or outcomes occurring in an experiment (Section 6–1). At the beginning of this section we introduced the concept of a random variable, the assigning of a number to each outcome of an experiment. The value assigned to the random variable depends on the outcome that actually occurs. Some outcomes may have a small likelihood of occurring, while others may be quite likely to occur. Thus the associated values of the random variable usually have different levels of likelihood.

We sometimes ask about the chance of observing a certain value of a random variable X (that is, find the probability that a certain value occurs). It is no surprise that such a probability is closely related to the probabilities of the outcomes. Rather than look at the probability of just one value of X, we find the probability of each of the possible values of X. We call this assignment of a probability to each value of a discrete random variable a **probability distribution.** Let's look at a simple example.

EXAMPLE 6   *(Compare Exercise 21)*

A children's game has 15 cards with two different numbers on each card. The two numbers are from the set {1, 2, 3, 4, 5, 6}, and the cards contain all possible pairs from this set. A child draws a card and scores a 5 or a 10 when the two numbers add to 5 or 10, respectively. Otherwise, the score is the smaller of the two numbers. Since a number (the score) is assigned to each outcome (card drawn), this determines a random variable X with outcomes and numbers related as follows:

OUTCOME	VALUE OF X (SCORE)	OUTCOME	VALUE OF X (SCORE)
1, 2	1	2, 6	2
1, 3	1	3, 4	3
1, 4	5	3, 5	3
1, 5	1	3, 6	3
1, 6	1	4, 5	4
2, 3	5	4, 6	10
2, 4	2	5, 6	5
2, 5	2		

The probability of each value of X (probability distribution) is as follows:

X	$P(X)$
1	$\frac{4}{15}$
2	$\frac{3}{15}$
3	$\frac{3}{15}$
4	$\frac{1}{15}$
5	$\frac{3}{15}$
10	$\frac{1}{15}$

Definition
Probability Distribution

If a discrete random variable has the values

$$x_1, x_2, x_1, \ldots, x_k$$

then a **probability distribution** $P(X)$ is a rule that assigns a probability $P(x_i)$ to each value x_i. More specifically,

(a) $0 \leq x_i \leq 1$ for each x_i.
(b) $P(x_1) + P(x_2) + \cdots + P(x_k) = 1$.

EXAMPLE 7   *(Compare Exercise 15)*

A coin is tossed twice. Define a random variable as the number of times heads appears. Compute the probability of zero, one, or two heads in the usual manner to get

$$P(0) = P(\text{TT}) = \frac{1}{4}$$

$$P(1) = P(\text{HT or TH}) = \frac{1}{2}$$

$$P(2) = P(\text{HH}) = \frac{1}{4}$$

We can represent a probability distribution graphically using a histogram. Form a category for each value of the random variable. The probability of each value of X determines the height of that bar.

The graph of this probability distribution is Figure 7–9.

FIGURE 7–9

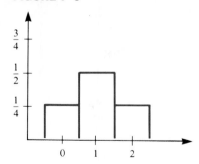

Probability graph of the number of
heads in two tosses of a coin

EXAMPLE 8   *(Compare Exercise 17)*

Each word of the phrase "Now is the time for all good men" is written on a card.
An experiment is conducted by selecting a card at random. The sample space is
the set of words in the phrase. Define a random variable X as the number of letters
in the word selected. The values of X range over the number of letters possible:
2, 3, and 4. What is the probability of each value of X?

SOLUTION $P(2)$ is the probability of selecting a two-letter word. Since the selection is from eight words, and one is a two letter word, $P(2) = \frac{1}{8}$. $P(3)$ is the
probability of selecting a three-letter word, and $P(3) = \frac{5}{8}$. $P(4)$, the probability
of a four-letter word is $\frac{2}{8}$.

A probability distribution of X and its graph are shown in Figure 7–10.

FIGURE 7–10

X	$P(X)$
2	$\frac{1}{8}$
3	$\frac{5}{8}$
4	$\frac{2}{8}$

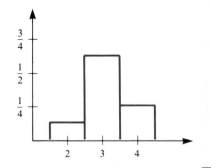

EXAMPLE 9   *(Compare Exercise 27)*

An experiment randomly selects two people from a group of five men and four women. A random variable X is the number of women selected. Find the probability distribution of X.

SOLUTION   The values of X range over the set $\{0, 1, 2\}$, since 0, 1, or 2 women can be selected. The probability of each value is computed in the usual manner.

$$P(0) = \frac{C(5, 2)}{C(9, 2)} = \frac{10}{36} \qquad \text{(Probability both are men)}$$

$$P(1) = \frac{C(5, 1) \times C(4, 1)}{C(9, 2)} = \frac{20}{36} \qquad \text{(Probability of 1 man and 1 woman)}$$

$$P(2) = \frac{C(4, 2)}{C(9, 2)} = \frac{6}{36} \qquad \text{(Probability of 2 women)}$$

The probability distribution and its graph are shown in Figure 7–11.

FIGURE 7–11

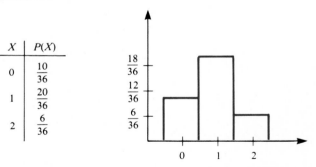

X	$P(X)$
0	$\frac{10}{36}$
1	$\frac{20}{36}$
2	$\frac{6}{36}$

Probability distribution   Graph of probability distribution

EXAMPLE 10   *(Compare Exercise 33)*

The probability of guessing a correct answer on a multiple-choice question is $\frac{1}{4}$. Let X be the number of answers guessed correctly on a four-question quiz. Find the probability distribution of X and draw its graph.

SOLUTION   This is a Bernoulli trial problem with $p = \frac{1}{4}$ and the number of trials, $n = 4$. X takes on the values 0, 1, 2, 3, and 4.

$$P(X = 0) = C(4, 0)\left(\frac{1}{4}\right)^0\left(\frac{3}{4}\right)^4 = .316 \qquad \text{(Rounded)}$$

$$P(X = 1) = C(4, 1)\left(\frac{1}{4}\right)^1\left(\frac{3}{4}\right)^3 = .422$$

$$P(X = 2) = C(4, 2)\left(\frac{1}{4}\right)^2\left(\frac{3}{4}\right)^2 = .211$$

$$P(X = 3) = C(4, 3)\left(\frac{1}{4}\right)^3\left(\frac{3}{4}\right) = .047$$

$$P(X = 4) = C(4, 4)\left(\frac{1}{4}\right)^4\left(\frac{3}{4}\right)^0 = .004$$

The probability distribution table and graph are given in Figure 7–12.

FIGURE 7–12

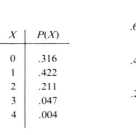

X	P(X)
0	.316
1	.422
2	.211
3	.047
4	.004

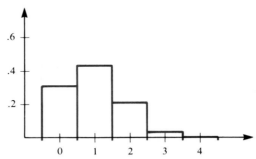

EXAMPLE 11   *(Compare Exercise 43)*

Five red cards are numbered through 1 through 5, and five black cards are numbered 1 through 5. Cards are drawn, without replacement, until a card is drawn that matches the color of the first card. Let the number of cards drawn be the random variable X. Find the probability distribution of X.

SOLUTION   The possible values of X are 2, 3, 4, 5, 6, and 7 because at least two cards must be drawn in order to have a match. There are five cards that are different from the first color, so the sixth card is the last time a card that is different from the first can be drawn. The seventh card must then be a match. To compute probabilities, designate the color of the first card by C, a different color by D, and the color matching the first card by S. Then the possible outcomes of the sequence of colors are the following:

$$X = 2: \text{CS}$$
$$X = 3: \text{CDS}$$
$$X = 4: \text{CDDS}$$
$$X = 5: \text{CDDDS}$$
$$X = 6: \text{CDDDDS}$$
$$X = 7: \text{CDDDDDS}$$

We now compute the probability of each sequence.

Note that it doesn't matter which color is drawn first, so the probability the first card is some color equals 1.

CS: $P(X = 2) = 1 \times \dfrac{4}{9} = \dfrac{4}{9}$

CDS: $P(X = 3) = 1 \times \dfrac{5}{9} \times \dfrac{4}{8} = \dfrac{5}{18}$

CDDS: $P(X = 4) = 1 \times \dfrac{5}{9} \times \dfrac{4}{8} \times \dfrac{4}{7} = \dfrac{10}{63}$

CDDDS: $P(X = 5) = 1 \times \dfrac{5}{9} \times \dfrac{4}{8} \times \dfrac{3}{7} \times \dfrac{4}{6} = \dfrac{5}{63}$

CDDDDS: $P(X = 6) = 1 \times \dfrac{5}{9} \times \dfrac{4}{8} \times \dfrac{3}{7} \times \dfrac{2}{6} \times \dfrac{4}{5} = \dfrac{2}{63}$

CDDDDDS: $P(X = 7) = 1 \times \dfrac{5}{9} \times \dfrac{4}{8} \times \dfrac{3}{7} \times \dfrac{2}{6} \times \dfrac{1}{5} \times \dfrac{4}{4} = \dfrac{1}{126}$

7-4 EXERCISES

I

1. (*See Example 1*) A coin is tossed three times, and the number of heads that occur, X, is assigned to each outcome. List all possible outcomes and the corresponding value of X.

2. A word is selected from the phrase "A stitch in time saves nine." A random variable counts the number of letters in the word selected. List all possible outcomes and the corresponding value of X.

3. Two people are selected from {Ann, Betty, Jason, Tom}, and the number of females selected, X, is assigned to each outcome. List all possible outcomes and the value of X assigned to each.

4. A nickel is tossed. If it turns up heads, a quarter is tossed once. If the nickel turns up tails, the quarter is tossed twice. The number of heads that turns up (on both coins) is the random variable X. List all possible outcomes and the corresponding value of X.

Give all possible values of the random variable in each of Exercises 5 through 7.

5. (*See Example 2*) Three people are selected at random from eight men and six women. The random variable is the number of men selected.

6. Four people are selected at random from five women and three men. The random variable is the number of men selected.

7. (*See Example 3*) An urn contains four red balls, six yellow balls, and three green balls. Four balls are drawn.
   (a) The random variable is the number of yellow balls drawn.
   (b) The random variable is the number of green balls drawn.

8. As a class project, students in the Student Center are asked to report the amount of sleep they had in the previous 24 hours. Then the fraction of the day (time sleeping/24) spent in sleep is recorded for X. What are the possible values for X?

Identify the random variables in Exercises 9 through 12 as discrete or continuous.

9. (a) Number of squirrels in a tree
   (b) Height of a tree
   (c) Volume of water in Lake Belton
   (d) Number of passengers in a car that enters the parking garage

10. **(a)** Number of students in each classroom at 9:00 A.M. on Monday
    (b) The weight of each person enrolling in a diet clinic
    (c) The runs scored by the home team in a baseball game
    (d) The speed of a moped passing a certain point on the street

11. **(a)** The diameter X of a golf ball
    (b) From a random selection of ten students, the number X who have type O blood
    (c) Sixty families live in a remote village. The random variable X is:
       (i) the number of children in a family.
       (ii) the amount of electricity used in a month by a family.
       (iii) the monthly income of a family.

12. **(a)** The number of building permits issued each year in Augusta, Georgia
    (b) The length of time to play a tennis match
    (c) The number of cartons of Blue Bell ice cream sold each week in the Food Mart
    (d) The number of pounds of apples sold each day at Joe's Roadside Fruit Stand

13. Fifty students are polled on the courses they are taking, and X is the number of courses a student takes. The number of courses range from 2 to 6. Is the following a probability distribution of X?

X (Number of Courses)	Fraction Taking X Courses
2	0.08
3	0.12
4	0.48
5	0.30
6	0.02

14. Customers at Lake Air Mall were asked to state which of three brands of coffee tasted the best. The brands were numbered 1, 2, and 3. The results are summarized as follows:

Brand	Fraction Preferring Brand
1	0.25
2	0.40
3	0.20

If the brand number is a random variable, does this define a probability distribution?

15. (*See Example 7*) A coin is tossed three times. X is the number of heads that appear. Find the probability distribution of X and its graph.

16. A pair of dice is tossed. The random variable X is the sum of the numbers that turn up. Find the probability distribution of X.

17. (*See Example 8*) Each word of the slogan "Get ahead, learn finite math" is written on a card, and a card is drawn at random. The random variable X is the number of letters in the word drawn. Find the probability distribution of X.

18. A class of 30 students took a five-point quiz. The results are summarized as follows:

Score	Frequency
0	2
1	4
2	8
3	3
4	12
5	1

Let the random variable X be the score on the quiz. Find the probability distribution of X, and draw its graph.

19. A survey of 75 households revealed the following information on the number of television sets they owned:

Number of TV Sets	Frequency
0	8
1	49
2	13
3	4
4	1

Let the random variable X be the number of television sets owned. Find the probability distribution of X, and sketch its graph.

20. When Luv That Balloon opened, a record of the daily number of phone calls was kept. The records showed the following data:

Number of Calls Per Day	Frequency
1	1
2	3
3	1
4	2
5	14
6	9

Let the number of calls be the random variable X. Use this summary to determine a probability distribution of X.

21. (*See Example 6*) Ten cards of a children's game are numbered with two different numbers from the set {1, 2, 3, 4, 5}. A child draws a card. A random variable X is the score of the card drawn. The score is 5 if the two numbers on the card add to 5; otherwise, the score is the smaller number on the card. Find the probability distribution of X.

22. In a card game a player selects two cards in succession from a 52-card bridge deck. The player receives a score of 10 if the second card is the same suit as the first, a score of 5 if the second card is the same color and different suit, and a score of 0 if the second card is a different color. Let the random variable X be the score and find the probability distribution of X.

II

23. A word is selected from a newspaper article. A random variable X is defined as the number of letters in that word.
    (a) What are the possible values of X?
    (b) Is X discrete or continuous?

24. An experiment consists of selecting a whole number and finding the remainder after division by 3. What are the possible outcomes?

25. (*See Example 5*) Two people are selected from a group of six men and five women. A random variable X is the number of women selected. List the possible values of X and the number of different outcomes that can be associated with each value.

26. A box contains six green balls, four red balls, and eight yellow balls. Three balls are randomly selected. Let the random variable X be the number of green balls. List the possible values of X and the number of different outcomes that can be associated with each value.

27. (*See Example 9*) Two people are selected from a group of four men and four women. A random variable X is the number of men selected. Find the probability distribution for X and its graph.

28. Three people are selected from a group of five men and six women. A random variable X is the number of women selected. Find the probability distribution of X.

29. In a collection of ten electronic components, three are defective. Two are selected at random, and the number of defective components is noted. Let X be the number of defective components, and draw the graph of the probability distribution of X.

30. A number is selected at random from the numbers 1, 2, 3, 4, 5, 6, 7, 8, 9, 10. A random variable X is the remainder when the selected number is divided by 3. Find the probability distribution of X.

31. An urn contains three red balls, two green balls, and one yellow ball. Two balls are selected at random.
    (a) A random variable X is the number of green balls drawn. Find the probability distribution of X.
    (b) A random variable X is the number of yellow balls drawn. Find the probability distribution of X.

32. At each meeting of a club, one person is selected to draw a "lucky number." That person gets the amount in dollars of the number drawn. The box contains 30 cards with the number 1, 14 cards with the number 5, three cards with the number 10, two cards with the number 20, and one card with the number 50. Let the random variable X be the numbers on the cards. Determine the probability distribution of X, and draw its graph.

33. (*See Example 10*) The probability of getting the correct answer on a multiple-choice question is $\frac{1}{5}$. Let X be the number of answers guessed correctly on a four-question quiz. Find the probability distribution of X and its graph.

34. The probability of a baseball player getting a hit in his turn at bat is .300. Let X be the number of hits in three times at bat. Find the probability distribution of X and its graph.

35. A box contains five red balls and seven green balls. Three balls are drawn one at a time, and each ball is replaced before the next one is drawn. Let the random variable X be the number of red balls drawn. Find the probability distribution of X.

III

36. Gloria is one of five people who are arranged in five positions 1 through 5. Let the random variable X be the position number where Gloria is placed. List the possible values of X and determine the number of different arrangements associated with each value.

37. The Green and Gold teams meet in a playoff. When a team wins two games, that team wins the playoff. Let the random variable X be the number of games won by the Green team. List the possible values of X and determine the possible number of sequences of games associated with each value.

38. Lindstrom follows the price of Solartech stock each day to see whether it goes up in price or not.
   (a) Let the random variable X be the number of days the price goes up in a certain three-day period. For each value of X, determine the number of different outcomes that are associated with that value.
   (b) Let the random variable X be the number of days the price goes up in a certain five-day period. For each possible value of X, find the number of different outcomes associated with that value.

39. A shopping mall contains a number of stores appealing to a variety of customers. The manager of a store views each shopper in terms of what the shopper might buy. The manager of a pet shop might view a shopper in terms of the kind of pet he or she might buy. The manager of a bookstore thinks of the number of books a shopper might buy. You ask the manager of each store in the mall to define a random variable that assigns a number to each shopper. How might the manager of each of the following stores assign a number that reflects the kind of store managed?
   (a) A diet clinic
   (b) A men's clothing store
   (c) A women's shoe shop
   (d) A dental clinic

40. A box contains six green balls and four red balls. A ball is drawn. If it is a red ball, the process stops. If the ball is green, it is replaced and another ball is drawn. The process continues until a red ball is drawn. Let the random variable X be the number of balls drawn. Give the possible values of X.

41. A coin is tossed repeatedly until a head turns up, and then the process stops. Let the random variable X be the number of tosses. Give the possible values of X.

42. The probability that a patient with a thyroid deficiency responds to a medication is .8. The medication is given to three patients. Let the number of patients that respond be a random variable X. Find the probability distribution of X.

43. (*See Example 11*) A deck contains four red cards and four black cards. Cards are drawn, without replacement, until a card drawn matches the color of the first card. Let the random variable X be the number of cards drawn. Find the probability distribution of X.

44. Cards are drawn from a deck of five red and five black cards until two cards of the same color are drawn. The number of cards drawn is the random variable X. Find the probability distribution of X.

45. A coin is tossed repeatedly up to three times until a head appears. Even though a head might not appear in the first three times, the process ends with the third toss. Let the number of tosses be the random variable X. Determine the probability distribution of X.

46. A coin is tossed repeatedly until a tail appears. Let the number of tosses be the random variable X. Find the probability distribution of X.

47. Teams A and B meet in a playoff. The first team that wins two games wins the playoff. Let X be the number of games won by team A. For any given game the probability that team A wins is .6. Find the probability distribution of X.

48. On any given day the stock of Hightech Corp. has a probability $\frac{2}{3}$ of going up in price. Three days are selected at random, and the prices are observed. Let the random variable X be the number of days the stock went up. Find the probability distribution of X.

7–5 EXPECTED VALUE

- *Expected Value*
- *Variance and Standard Deviation of a Random Variable*

EXPECTED VALUE

Each day a student puts 50¢ in a candy machine to buy a 35¢ candy bar. She observes three possible outcomes.

1. She gets a candy bar and 15¢ change. This happens 80% of the time.
2. She gets a candy bar and no change. This happens 16% of the time.
3. She gets a candy bar and the machine returns her 50¢. This happens 4% of the time.

Over a period of time, what is the average cost of a candy bar?

The three possible costs, 35¢, 50¢, and 0¢, have a mean of 28.3¢. This is not the average cost because it assumes that 35¢, 50¢, and 0¢ occur equally often; whereas, in fact, 35¢ occurs more often than the other two. If the machine behaved this way for 500 purchases, we would expect the following.

COST (X)	FREQUENCY (PER 500)	PROBABILITY ($P(X)$)
35¢	400	0.80
50¢	80	0.16
0¢	20	0.04
	500	1.00

This presents the information as a frequency table, so we can compute the mean as we have before with a frequency table (Section 7–3). The mean is

$$\frac{400 \times 35 + 80 \times 50 + 20 \times 0}{500} = \frac{14{,}000 + 4{,}000 + 0}{500} = 36$$

so the average cost is 36¢.

Let's write the mean in another way:

$$\frac{400 \times 35 + 80 \times 50 + 20 \times 0}{500} = \frac{400}{500} \times 35 + \frac{80}{500} \times 50 + \frac{20}{500} \times 0$$
$$= .80 \times 35 + .16 \times 50 + .04 \times 0$$

This last expression is simply the sum obtained by adding each cost of a candy bar times the probability that cost occurred, that is,

$$P(35) \times 35 + P(50) \times 50 + P(0) \times 0$$

This illustrates the procedure used to compute the mean when each value occurs with a specified probability. This mean is called the **expected value;** it represents the long-term mean of numerous trials. While a few trials likely would not average to the expected value, a larger and larger number of trials will tend to give a mean closer to the expected value.

We emphasize that the term "expected value" does not mean the value we expect in an everyday sense. In the candy bar example the amount paid for a candy bar is either 0¢, 35¢, or 50¢, while the expected value is 36¢. Since 36¢ is never the amount paid, you never expect to pay that. However, 36¢ is the average amount paid over a large number of purchases. This long-term average is what is called the expected value.

We now make a formal definition of expected value in terms of a random variable and probability distribution.

Definition If X is a random variable with values $x_1, x_2, \ldots, x_n$ and corresponding probabilities $p_1, p_2, \ldots, p_n$, then the **expected value** of X, $E(X)$, is

$$E(X) = p_1x_1 + \cdots + p_nx_n$$

EXAMPLE 1 *(Compare Exercise 1)*

Find the expected value of X, where the values of X and their corresponding probabilities are given by the following table:

x_i	2	5	9	24
p_i	.4	.2	.3	.1

SOLUTION

$$\begin{aligned} E(X) &= .4 \times 2 + .2 \times 5 + .3 \times 9 + .1 \times 24 \\ &= .8 + 1.0 + 2.7 + 2.4 \\ &= 6.9 \end{aligned}$$

EXAMPLE 2 *(Compare Exercise 5)*

(a) A contestant tosses a coin and receives $5 if heads appears and $1 if tails appears. What is the expected value of a trial?
(b) A contestant receives $4.00 if a coin turns up heads and pays $3.00 if it turns up tails. What is the expected value?

SOLUTION

(a) The probability of heads is $\frac{1}{2}$, and the probability of tails is $\frac{1}{2}$. Then

$$E(X) = \frac{1}{2}(5) + \frac{1}{2}(1) = \$3.00$$

(b) Again, the probability of heads is $\frac{1}{2}$, and the probability of tails is $\frac{1}{2}$. So

$$E(X) = \frac{1}{2}(4) + \frac{1}{2}(-3) = \$2.00 - \$1.50 = \$0.50$$

Notice that a negative $3.00 value is used to indicate that the contestant pays $3.00. The $0.50 expected value indicates a long-term gain that averages $0.50 per trial.

_____▮

EXAMPLE 3   *(Compare Exercise 9)*

An IRS study shows that 60% of all income tax returns audited have no errors; 6% have errors that cause overpayments averaging $25; 20% have minor errors that cause underpayments averaging $35; 13% have more serious errors averaging $500 underpayments; and 1% have flagrant errors averaging $7000 underpayment. If the IRS selects returns at random:

(a) What is the average amount per return that is owed to the IRS, that is, what is the expected value of a return selected at random?
(b) How much should the IRS expect to collect if one million returns are audited at random?
(c) If the budget for the Audit Department is $15 million, how many returns must they examine to collect enough to cover their budget expenses?

SOLUTION
(a) Since an underpayment error eventually results in additional money paid to the IRS, and a taxpayer overpayment is money paid back by the IRS, we use positive values for underpayment and negative for overpayment. The probability in each case is the fraction of returns with that type of error.

$$E(X) = 0.60(0) + 0.06(-25) + 0.20(35) + 0.13(500)$$
$$+ 0.01(7000)$$
$$= 140.5$$

Thus, the IRS expects to collect $140.50 for each return selected.
(b) If one million returns are selected at random, they may expect to collect 140.50×1 million $= \$140.5$ million.
(c) Since they expect to collect an average of $140.50 for each return audited, they must examine

$$15,000,000/140.50 = 106,762 \quad \text{returns}$$

_____▮

The next example illustrates that expected value need not be an amount of money. It can be any "payoff" associated with each outcome.

EXAMPLE 4   *(Compare Exercise 15)*

A tray of electronic components contains nine good components and three defective components. If two components are selected at random, what is the expected number of defective components?

SOLUTION   Let a random variable X be the number of defective components selected. X can have the value 0, 1, or 2. We need the probability of each of those numbers:

$$P(0) = \text{probability of no defective (both good)}$$
$$= \frac{C(9, 2)}{C(12, 2)} = \frac{36}{66} = \frac{12}{22}$$
$$P(1) = \text{probability of 1 good and 1 defective}$$
$$= \frac{C(9, 1)C(3, 1)}{C(12, 2)} = \frac{27}{66} = \frac{9}{22}$$
$$P(2) = \text{probability of two defective}$$
$$= \frac{C(3, 2)}{C(12, 2)} = \frac{3}{66} = \frac{1}{22}$$

The expected value is

$$E(X) = \frac{12}{22}(0) + \frac{9}{22}(1) + \frac{1}{22}(2) = \frac{11}{22} = \frac{1}{2}$$

so the expected number of components is $\frac{1}{2}$. Clearly, you don't expect to get half of a component. The value $\frac{1}{2}$ simply says that if a large number of selections are made, you will *average* one-half each time. You expect to get no defectives a little less than half the time and either one or two the rest of the time, but the average will be one half.

VARIANCE AND STANDARD DEVIATION OF A RANDOM VARIABLE

The expected value is the "central tendency," or mean, of the values of a random variable, taking the probability of their occurrence into consideration. Think back on the mean and median; we shouldn't be surprised that sometimes the dispersion, or spread, of a random variable is needed to give more information. We can find the variance of a random variable, and it too measures the dispersion, or spread, of a random variable from the mean (expected value). The greater dispersion gives a greater variance. The histogram of a probability distribution shown in Figure 7–13(a) has a smaller variance than that shown in Figure 7–13(b).

FIGURE 7–13

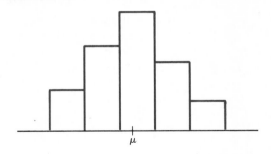

These scores are clustered closer to the mean than those in (b).

(a)

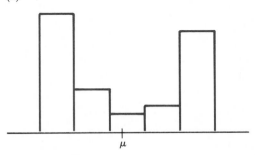

These scores have greater dispersion than those in (a).

(b)

Let's use the candy bar example to illustrate variance and standard deviation. The information is given in the form of a frequency distribution:

AMOUNT PAID	FREQUENCY
35¢	400
50¢	80
0¢	20
	500

We compute the standard deviation using the method shown in Example 3 of Section 7–3 for frequency distributions:

$$\text{Variance} = \frac{400(35-36)^2 + 80(50-36)^2 + 20(0-36)^2}{500}$$

We rewrite this expression as

$$\text{Variance} = \frac{400(35 - 36)^2}{500} + \frac{80(50 - 36)^2}{500} + \frac{20(0 - 36)^2}{500}$$

$$= \frac{400}{500}(35 - 36)^2 + \frac{80}{500}(50 - 36)^2 + \frac{20}{500}(0 - 36)^2$$

$$= .80(35 - 36)^2 + .16(50 - 36)^2 + .04(0 - 36)^2$$

This last expression is of the form

$$\text{Variance} = P(35)(35 - \mu)^2 + P(50)(50 - \mu)^2 + P(0)(0 - \mu)^2$$

where μ is 36. Let's complete the computations for variance and standard deviation:

$$\text{Variance} = .80(-1)^2 + .16(14)^2 + .04(-36)^2$$
$$= .80 + 31.36 + 51.84$$
$$= 84.$$
$$\text{Standard deviation} = \sigma = \sqrt{84} = 9.165$$

Let's give the formal definition of variance and standard deviation of a random variable and then give an example showing the computation. We denote the variance by $\sigma^2(X)$ and let the Greek letter μ (mu) represent the mean (expected value).

Definition
Variance, Standard Deviation

If X is a random variable with values $x_1, x_2, \ldots, x_n$, corresponding probabilities $p_1, p_2, \ldots, p_n$, and expected value $E(X) = \mu$, then

$$\text{Variance} = \sigma^2(X) = p_1(x_1 - \mu)^2 + p_2(x_2 - \mu)^2 + \cdots + p_n(x_n - \mu)^2$$

The standard deviation, $\sigma(X) = \sqrt{\text{variance}}$

EXAMPLE 5 *(Compare Exercise 11)*

Find the variance and standard deviation for the random variable defined by the following table:

x_i	4	7	10	8
p_i	.2	.2	.5	.1

SOLUTION   Set up the computations in the following way:

x_i	p_i	p_ix_i	$x_i - \mu$	$(x_i - \mu)^2$	$p_i(x_i - \mu)^2$
4	.2	.8	-4	16	3.2
7	.2	1.4	-1	1	.2
10	.5	5.0	2	4	2.0
8	.1	.8	0	0	0
		$\mu = 8.0$			$\sigma^2(X) = 5.4$

The variance $\sigma^2(X) = 5.4$. So the standard deviation is

$$\sigma(X) = \sqrt{5.4} = 2.32$$

7-5 EXERCISES

I

1. (*See Example 1*) Find the expected value of X for the following probability distribution:

x_i	3	8	15	22
p_i	.3	.2	.1	.4

2. Find $E(X)$ for the following probability distribution:

x_i	2	4	-1	6	10
p_i	.15	.08	.17	.35	.25

3. Find $E(X)$ for the following probability distribution:

x_i	150	235	350	410	480
p_i	.2	.2	.2	.2	.2

4. Find $E(X)$ for the following probability distribution:

x_i	0	10
p_i	.7	.3

5. (*See Example 2*) A contestant receives $8 if a coin turns up heads and $2 if it turns up tails. What is the expected value of a trial?

6. A contestant rolls a die and receives $5 if it is a 1 or 2, receives $15 if it is a 3, and pays $2 if it is a 4, 5, or 6. What is the expected value of each trial?

7. A game consists of tossing a coin twice. A player who throws the same face, heads or tails, twice wins $1. How much should the organizers charge to enter the game:
(**a**) if they want to break even?
(**b**) if they want to average $1 per person profit?

8. A game involves throwing a pair of dice. The player will win, in dollars, the sum of the numbers thrown. How much should the organizers charge to enter the game if they want to break even?

9. (*See Example 3*) An auto repair shop's records show that 15% of the cars serviced need minor repairs averaging $20, 65% need moderate repairs averaging $130, and 20% need major repairs averaging $700.
(**a**) What is the expected cost of repair of a car selected at random?
(**b**) The shop has 125 cars scheduled for repair. What is the total expected repair cost of these cars?

10. The Chamber of Commerce estimates that of the visitors who come to the West Fest, 35% will spend an average of $150, 25% will spend $250, 30% will spend $350, and 10% will spend $500.
(**a**) Find the expected expenditure of a visitor.
(**b**) If 30,000 visitors attend the West Fest, what is their expected total expenditure?

11. (*See Example 5*) Compute μ, $\sigma^2(X)$, and $\sigma(X)$ for the random variable defined as follows:

x_i	100	140	210
p_i	.4	.5	.1

12. Compute μ and $\sigma(X)$ for the following random variable:

x_i	−1	2	3	4	10
p_i	.1	.2	.1	.3	.3

13. Compute μ and $\sigma(X)$ for the following random variable:

x_i	10	30	50	90
p_i	.4	.2	.3	.1

14. Compute the expected value (μ), the variance ($\sigma^2(X)$), and standard deviation ($\sigma(X)$), for the random variable defined by the following table:

x_i	5	10	14	20
p_i	.1	.1	.5	.3

II

15. (*See Example 4*) Of 15 windup toys on a sale table, four are defective. If two toys are selected at random, find the expected number of defective toys.

16. A lawyer finds that 60% of the wills she prepares for clients are routine and require an average of one hour each. The moderately complex wills require an average of three hours each and account for 30% of her clients. The other 10% are complex and require an average of ten hours each.
    (a) What is the expected time of each will?
    (b) How much time should she schedule to prepare 45 wills?

III

17. A company considers two business ventures. The executives believe that venture A has a .60 probability of a $50,000 profit, a .30 probability of breaking even, and a .10 probability of a $70,000 loss. Venture B has a .55 probability of $100,000 profit and .45 probability of a $60,000 loss. Determine the expected value of each venture. Which is the better risk?

18. A football team can expect 20,000 fans to attend a game if it rains. If it is fair, 50,000 attend. The weather forecast is that there is a 70% chance of rain at kickoff time. What is the expected attendance?

19. Air South overbooks as many as five passengers per flight because some passengers with reservations do not show up for the flight. The airline's records indicate the following probabilities that it will be overbooked at flight time:

Number Over at Flight Time	0	1	2	3	4	5
Probability of Number Over	.75	.10	.06	.04	.04	.01

Find the expected number over for each flight.

20. A departmental mathematics exam consists of six problems. The probability of a student working each problem is known from records kept on similar problems given previously. The point value and probability of working each problem are as follows:

Problem	Points	Probability of Working Problem
1	10	.90
2	10	.85
3	15	.70
4	20	.75
5	20	.55
6	25	.65

Find the expected number of points on the exam.

21. Ten cards of a children's game are numbered with two different numbers from the set $\{1, 2, 3, 4, 5\}$. A child draws a card, and a random variable is the score of the card drawn. The score is 5 if the two numbers on the card add to 5; otherwise, the score is the smaller number on the card. (See Exercise 21 in Section 7–4.)
    (a) Find the expected score of a card.
    (b) Find the standard deviation of X.

22. In a game you toss a coin until a head turns up, but you get four tosses at most. When the first head occurs, you stop and receive payment as follows:

Toss When First Head Occurs	Payoff
1	$ 2
2	$ 4
3	$ 8
4	$16

If no head occurs in four tosses, you receive nothing.
(a) Find the expected value of the game.
(b) If you pay $5 to play this game, what are your expected winnings or losses?

23. Each time a certain Little League baseball player comes to bat, the probability of his getting a hit is .4. His dad promises to pay him $2 if he gets one hit in a game, $4 for two hits, $6 for three hits, and $8 for four hits. What are his expected earnings in a game:
(a) if he bats three times?
(b) if he bats four times?

24. The Pizza Place plans to run an "off-the-wall" TV ad that tends to create a strong reaction from the viewers, sometimes positive and sometimes negative reactions. Past experience indicates that 55% of the time this ad increases sales by $15,000 per week, 25% of the time the sales increase by $5000 and 20% of the time the sales decrease by $4000 per week. Find the expected increase in sales.

25. A plant manufactures microchips, 5% of which are defective. The plant makes a profit of $18 on each good microchip and loses $23 on each defective one.
(a) What is the expected profit on a microchip?
(b) The plant plans a production run of 150,000 microchips. What is the expected profit for the run?

7–6 NORMAL DISTRIBUTION

- *Normal Curve*
- *Area Under a Normal Curve*
- *The z-Score*
- *Probability and a Normal Distribution*

NORMAL CURVE

One of the more important representations of data is the **normal curve.** It is a valid representation of data sets such as heights of adult males, IQ of 18-year-olds, and scores on SAT tests. When a data set can be represented by a normal curve, we say that the data form a **normal distribution.** Just what is a normal distribution? Actually, a rather complicated formula defines a normal distribution. We leave that formula to advanced statistics courses and look at the graph of a normal distribution to observe some of its basic properties. Many histograms that model continuous data can be smoothed to normal curves. It is known that the height of 18-year-old males has a mean of 68 inches and a standard deviation of 3 inches and is well represented by a normal curve. Figure 7–14 shows a histogram and a bell-shaped curve obtained by smoothing the histogram.

Normal curves vary in size and shape depending on the mean and standard deviation of the data. However, all normal curves have "bell shapes" similar to that shown in Figure 7–15. The horizontal base line represents the scores in the

FIGURE 7–14

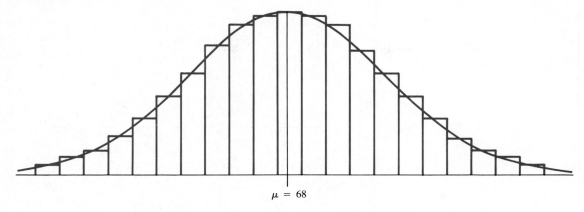

$\mu = 68$

Smooth histogram of heights of 18-year-old males

FIGURE 7–15

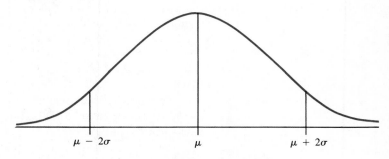

$\mu - 2\sigma$ μ $\mu + 2\sigma$

A normal curve with mean μ

data set, and the height of the curve tells something about the frequency of the score. In fact, we use the area under the curve to represent the fraction of the data that lies between two scores.

The normal curve is a smooth curve that peaks at the mean and is perfectly symmetric about the mean. This symmetry means that one half of the area under the curve lies to the left of the mean, and the other half lies to the right. Since an area under the curve represents a fraction of scores, the total area is taken as 1, representing 100% of the scores. Notice that the curve approaches the base line but never touches it. This indicates that fewer and fewer scores are found as you move away from the mean.

The normal curve represents **continuous data,** that for which the values could be arbitrarily close together. For example, when we measure the heights of male college freshmen, two men could be of different, but nearly the same, height. When we have **discrete data,** like counting the number of heads in five tosses of a coin, two different values must be at least one unit apart. When dealing with

FIGURE 7–16

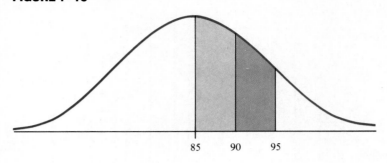

continuous data, we usually do not ask how many men are exactly 5′10″ tall. We may ask how many are between 5′9″ and 5′11″ or within one fourth of an inch of 5′10″, and so on.

AREA UNDER A NORMAL CURVE

The ability to find area under a portion of the normal curve is important because it gives the proportion of scores in a specified category or interval. For example, suppose that a normal distribution has a mean of 85. (See Figure 7–16.) The area under the curve between 90 and 95 represents the fraction of scores, not the number of scores that lies between 90 and 95. (Since the total area under the curve is 1, the area also represents the probability that the score is between 90 and 95.)

Notice that the area under the curve between 85 and 90 is larger than the area between 90 and 95. This indicates a proportionally larger frequency of values between 85 and 90.

The normal curve has the unusual property of being completely determined by the mean and standard deviation. The normal curve can be standardized in a way that allows us to find the area under a portion of a normal curve from one table of values. The distance from the mean, measured in standard deviations, determines the area under the curve in that interval. For example, for all normal curves, about 68% of the scores will lie within one standard deviation of the mean, 34% on one side and 34% on the other. Approximately 95% of the scores will lie within two standard deviations, and over 99% will lie within three standard deviations. (See Figure 7–17.)

We can use the **standard normal curve** to answer questions about normal curves in general. The standard normal curve has mean $\mu = 0$ and $\sigma = 1$. In the standard normal curve, a score is also the number of standard deviations from the mean. Several examples will help you to understand the use of a normal curve.

FIGURE 7–17

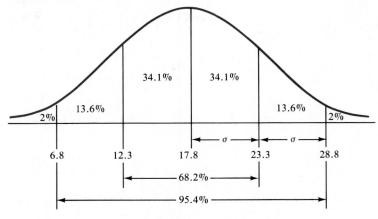

Normal curve with $\mu = 17.8$ and $\sigma = 5.5$

Let's apply this idea to the following.

EXAMPLE 1

One year the ACT English test had a mean $\mu = 17.8$ and a standard deviation $\sigma = 5.5$.

(a) The scores 12.3 and 23.3 are both one standard deviation from the mean, so 34% of the ACT English scores lie between 12.3 and 17.8, and 34% lie between 17.8 and 23.3.

(b) About 95% of the scores lie between 6.8 and 28.8, that is, within two standard deviations of the mean.

(c) Because over 99% of the scores lie within three standard deviations of the mean (a distance of 16.5 or less from the mean), you expect less than 1% to lie *more* than three standard deviations away. So less than 1% of the ACT English scores lie above 34.3 or below 1.3.

Since the mean and standard deviation of a normal distribution completely determine the shape of a normal curve, two normal distributions that have the same mean but different standard deviations will have different shapes. The one with the smaller standard deviation will have a sharper peak, and the one with the larger standard deviation will have a flatter normal curve (See Figure 7–18.). For a normal distribution the mean, the median, and the mode are all the same.

FIGURE 7–18

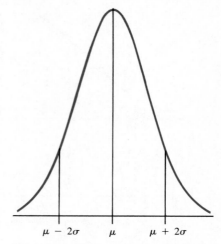

Normal curve with a smaller standard deviation

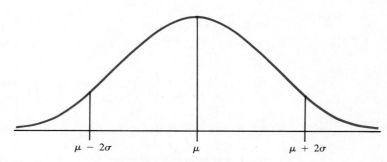

Normal curve with larger standard deviation

THE z-SCORE

We have already discussed the fraction of test scores that lie within 1, 2, or 3 standard deviations of the mean in a normal distribution. How do we determine the number of scores that lie within 1.25, 0.63, or 2.50 standard deviations of the mean? Tables such as Table 7–1 (a table for the standard normal curve) enable you to find the area between the mean and a score. The key is to locate the score according to the number of standard deviations it lies from the mean. Traditionally, the z-score represents the number of standard deviations a score lies from the mean.

Whatever scale is used for scores on a normal curve, we can associate a value of z with each score.

TABLE 7–1. Area Under the Standard Normal Curve

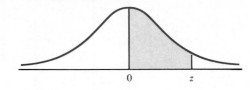

z	A	z	A	z	A	z	A
0.00	0.0000	0.40	0.1554	0.80	0.2881	1.20	0.3849
0.01	0.0040	0.41	0.1591	0.81	0.2910	1.21	0.3869
0.02	0.0080	0.42	0.1628	0.82	0.2939	1.22	0.3888
0.03	0.0120	0.43	0.1664	0.83	0.2967	1.23	0.3907
0.04	0.0160	0.44	0.1700	0.84	0.2996	1.24	0.3925
0.05	0.0199	0.45	0.1736	0.85	0.3023	1.25	0.3944
0.06	0.0239	0.46	0.1772	0.86	0.3051	1.26	0.3962
0.07	0.0279	0.47	0.1808	0.87	0.3079	1.27	0.3980
0.08	0.0319	0.48	0.1844	0.88	0.3106	1.28	0.3997
0.09	0.0359	0.49	0.1879	0.89	0.3133	1.29	0.4015
0.10	0.0398	0.50	0.1915	0.90	0.3159	1.30	0.4032
0.11	0.0438	0.51	0.1950	0.91	0.3186	1.31	0.4049
0.12	0.0478	0.52	0.1985	0.92	0.3212	1.32	0.4066
0.13	0.0517	0.53	0.2019	0.93	0.3238	1.33	0.4082
0.14	0.0557	0.54	0.2054	0.94	0.3264	1.34	0.4099
0.15	0.0596	0.55	0.2088	0.95	0.3289	1.35	0.4115
0.16	0.0636	0.56	0.2123	0.96	0.3315	1.36	0.4131
0.17	0.0675	0.57	0.2157	0.97	0.3340	1.37	0.4147
0.18	0.0714	0.58	0.2190	0.98	0.3365	1.38	0.4162
0.19	0.0754	0.59	0.2224	0.99	0.3389	1.39	0.4177
0.20	0.0793	0.60	0.2258	1.00	0.3413	1.40	0.4192
0.21	0.0832	0.61	0.2291	1.01	0.3438	1.41	0.4207
0.22	0.0871	0.62	0.2324	1.02	0.3461	1.42	0.4222
0.23	0.0910	0.63	0.2357	1.03	0.3485	1.43	0.4236
0.24	0.0948	0.64	0.2389	1.04	0.3508	1.44	0.4251
0.25	0.0987	0.65	0.2422	1.05	0.3531	1.45	0.4265
0.26	0.1026	0.66	0.2454	1.06	0.3554	1.46	0.4279
0.27	0.1064	0.67	0.2486	1.07	0.3577	1.47	0.4292
0.28	0.1103	0.68	0.2518	1.08	0.3599	1.48	0.4306
0.29	0.1141	0.69	0.2549	1.09	0.3621	1.49	0.4319
0.30	0.1179	0.70	0.2580	1.10	0.3643	1.50	0.4332
0.31	0.1217	0.71	0.2612	1.11	0.3665	1.51	0.4345
0.32	0.1255	0.72	0.2642	1.12	0.3686	1.52	0.4357
0.33	0.1293	0.73	0.2673	1.13	0.3708	1.53	0.4370
0.34	0.1331	0.74	0.2704	1.14	0.3729	1.54	0.4382
0.35	0.1368	0.75	0.2734	1.15	0.3749	1.55	0.4394
0.36	0.1406	0.76	0.2764	1.16	0.3770	1.56	0.4406
0.37	0.1443	0.77	0.2794	1.17	0.3790	1.57	0.4418
0.38	0.1480	0.78	0.2823	1.18	0.3810	1.58	0.4430
0.39	0.1517	0.79	0.2852	1.19	0.3830	1.59	0.4441

TABLE 7–1 *(continued)*

z	A	z	A	z	A	z	A
1.60	0.4452	2.00	0.4773	2.40	0.4918	2.80	0.4974
1.61	0.4463	2.01	0.4778	2.41	0.4920	2.81	0.4975
1.62	0.4474	2.02	0.4783	2.42	0.4922	2.82	0.4976
1.63	0.4485	2.03	0.4788	2.43	0.4925	2.83	0.4977
1.64	0.4495	2.04	0.4793	2.44	0.4927	2.84	0.4977
1.65	0.4505	2.05	0.4798	2.45	0.4929	2.85	043978
1.66	0.4515	2.06	0.4803	2.46	0.4931	2.86	0.4979
1.67	0.4525	2.07	0.4808	2.47	0.4932	2.87	0.4980
1.68	0.4535	2.08	0.4812	2.48	0.4934	2.88	0.4980
1.69	0.4545	2.09	0.4817	2.49	0.4936	2.89	0.4981
1.70	0.4554	2.10	0.4821	2.50	0.4938	2.90	0.4981
1.71	0.4564	2.11	0.4826	2.51	0.4940	2.91	0.4982
1.72	0.4573	2.12	0.4830	2.52	0.4941	2.92	0.4983
1.73	0.4582	2.13	0.4834	2.53	0.4943	2.93	0.4983
1.74	0.4591	2.14	0.4838	2.54	0.4945	2.94	0.4984
1.75	0.4599	2.15	0.4842	2.55	0.4946	2.95	0.4984
1.76	0.4608	2.16	0.4846	2.56	0.4948	2.96	0.4985
1.77	0.4616	2.17	0.4850	2.57	0.4949	2.97	0.4985
1.78	0.4625	2.18	0.4854	2.58	0.4951	2.98	0.4986
1.79	0.4633	2.19	0.4857	2.59	0.4952	2.99	0.4986
1.80	0.4641	2.20	0.4861	2.60	0.4953	3.00	0.4987
1.81	0.4649	2.21	0.4865	2.61	0.4955	3.01	0.4987
1.82	0.4656	2.22	0.4868	2.62	0.4956	3.02	0.4987
1.83	0.4664	2.23	0.4871	2.63	0.4957	3.03	0.4988
1.84	0.4671	2.24	0.4875	2.64	0.4959	3.04	0.4988
1.85	0.4678	2.25	0.4878	2.65	0.4960	3.05	0.4989
1.86	0.4686	2.26	0.4881	2.66	0.4961	3.06	0.4989
1.87	0.4693	2.27	0.4884	2.67	0.4962	3.07	0.4989
1.88	0.4700	2.28	0.4887	2.68	0.4963	3.08	0.4990
1.89	0.4706	2.29	0.4890	2.69	0.4964	3.09	0.4990
1.90	0.4713	2.30	0.4893	2.70	0.4965	3.10	0.4990
1.91	0.4719	2.31	0.4896	2.71	0.4966	3.11	0.4991
1.92	0.4726	2.32	0.4898	2.72	0.4967	3.12	0.4991
1.93	0.4732	2.33	0.4901	2.73	0.4968	3.13	0.4991
1.94	0.4738	2.34	0.4904	2.74	0.4969	3.14	0.4992
1.95	0.4744	2.35	0.4906	2.75	0.4970	3.15	0.4992
1.96	0.4750	2.36	0.4909	2.76	0.4971	3.16	0.4992
1.97	0.4756	2.37	0.4911	2.77	0.4972	3.17	0.4992
1.98	0.4762	2.38	0.4913	2.78	0.4973	3.18	0.4993
1.99	0.4767	2.39	0.4916	2.79	0.4974	3.19	0.4993

Here's how we determine a value of z that corresponds with a given score x. Since z represents the number of standard deviations between the mean and the score x, find z by

$$z = \frac{\text{difference between score and mean}}{\text{standard deviation}}$$

$$= \frac{\text{score} - \text{mean}}{\text{standard deviation}} = \frac{x - \mu}{\sigma}$$

We use z to find the area under the normal curve between two scores. To do so, we use Table 7–1. The table does not give area between any two scores; that would require a prohibitively lengthy, cumbersome table. You must understand that the table gives area *between the mean and a z-score* for selected z-scores.

EXAMPLE 2   *(Compare Exercise 1)*

Compute z for each of the following values of the mean, the standard deviation, and a given score:

(a) Mean = 25, standard deviation = 2, score = 31
(b) Mean = 25, standard deviation = 2, score = 19
(c) Mean = 7.5, standard deviation = 1.2, score = 10.5
(d) Mean = 16.85, standard deviation = 2.1, score = 14.12

SOLUTION
(a) Using the formula

$$z = \frac{\text{score} - \text{mean}}{\text{standard deviation}}$$

we obtain

$$z = \frac{31 - 25}{2} = \frac{6}{2} = 3$$

(b) $z = \dfrac{19 - 25}{2} = \dfrac{-6}{2} = -3$

A negative value of z indicates that the score is less than the mean.

(c) $z = \dfrac{10.5 - 7.5}{1.2} = \dfrac{3}{1.2} = 2.5$

(d) $z = \dfrac{14.12 - 16.85}{2.1} = \dfrac{-2.73}{2.1} = -1.3$

EXAMPLE 3   *(Compare Exercise 7)*

Use Table 7–1 to find the fraction of scores between the mean and
(a) $z = 0.75$
(b) $z = -0.75$
(c) $z = 2.58$
(d) $z = -1.92$

SOLUTION

(a) The value for A that corresponds to $z = 0.75$ is 0.2734, the fraction of the area between the mean and $z = 0.75$. (See Figure 7–19.)

FIGURE 7–19

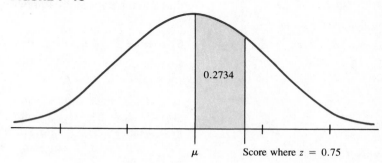

(b) Since the curve is symmetric about the mean, the area between the mean and $z = -0.75$ equals the area between the mean and $z = 0.75$, which is 0.2734. (See Figure 7–20.)

FIGURE 7–20

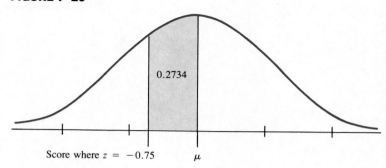

(c) From the table at $z = 2.58$ we find $A = 0.4951$.
(d) We use $z = 1.92$ to find $A = 0.4726$.

EXAMPLE 4 *(Compare Exercise 23)*

Find the fraction of scores between $z = 1.15$ and $z = -1.15$ under the normal curve. (We may also say that we find the area *within* 1.15 standard deviations of the mean.)

SOLUTION We obtain this area by combining the area between the mean and $z = 1.15$ with the area between the mean and $z = -1.15$ because the table gives only the area between the mean and a score, not between two scores. For the area between the mean and $z = 1.15$, look for the area corresponding to $z = 1.15$. It is 0.3749. The area between the mean and $z = -1.15$ is the same, 0.3749, so the total area is $0.3749 + 0.3749 = 0.7498$. (See Figure 7–21.)

FIGURE 7–21

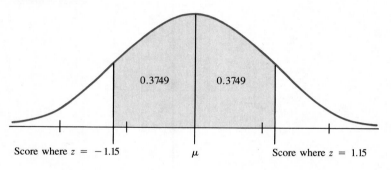

Score where $z = -1.15$ μ Score where $z = 1.15$

EXAMPLE 5 *(Compare Exercise 31)*

Find the area under the normal curve between $z = -0.46$ and $z = 2.32$.

SOLUTION The point where $z = -0.46$ lies below the mean, so the area between the mean and where $z = -0.46$ is 0.1772 (look up A for $z = 0.46$). The point where $z = 2.32$ lies above the mean and the area between the mean and where $z = 2.32$ is 0.4898. Since the two points lie on opposite sides of the mean, add the two areas found, $0.1772 + 0.4898 = 0.6670$, to find the total area. (See Figure 7–22.)

FIGURE 7–22

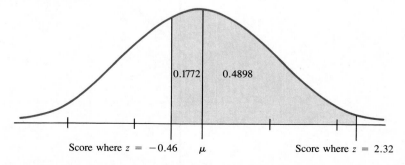

Score where $z = -0.46$ μ Score where $z = 2.32$

EXAMPLE 6   (*Compare Exercise 35*)

Find the fraction of the area under the normal curve that lies to the right of $z = 0.80$.

SOLUTION   Figure 7–23 shows the desired area. Table 7–1 gives $A = 0.2881$ for $z = 0.80$. However, this is the area *below* $z = 0.80$ and above the mean, and we want to know the area *above z*. Remember that all the area above the mean is 0.5000 of the area under the curve. Therefore the area *above* $z = 0.80$ is $0.5000 - 0.2881 = 0.2119$ of the total area.

FIGURE 7–23

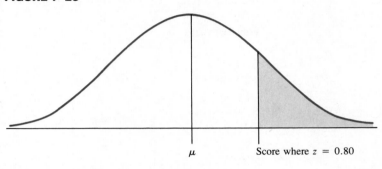

μ   Score where $z = 0.80$

EXAMPLE 7

Find the fraction of scores that are more than 1.40 standard deviations away from the mean.

SOLUTION   This asks for the area to the right of the score where $z = 1.40$ and the area to the left of the score where $z = -1.40$. (See Figure 7–24.) The area between the mean and a score where $z = 1.40$ is 0.4192, so the area to the right of the score is $0.5000 - 0.4192 = 0.0808$. By symmetry the area to the left of the score where $z = -1.40$ is also 0.0808. The total area more than 1.40 standard deviations away from the mean is 0.1616, or about 16.2%.

FIGURE 7–24

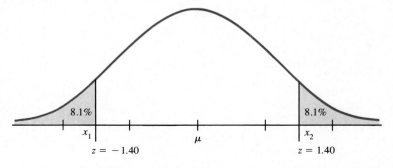

8.1%   8.1%

x_1 x_2

$z = -1.40$ μ $z = 1.40$

Generally, you will be given the mean and scores, not values of z. The following examples show how to find the area between two scores.

EXAMPLE 8   *(Compare Exercise 43)*

A normal distribution has a mean of 30 and a standard deviation of 7. Find the fraction of scores between 30 and 42.

SOLUTION   To use Table 7–1, we must find the z-score that corresponds to a score of 42. It is

$$z = \frac{42 - 30}{7} = \frac{12}{7} = 1.71$$

From Table 7–1 we obtain $A = 0.4564$ when $z = 1.71$. Thus 45.64% of the scores lie between 30 and 42. See Figure 7–25.

FIGURE 7–25

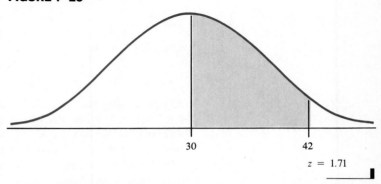

30   42

$z = 1.71$

When two scores are on opposite sides of the mean and are different distances from the mean, we add areas to find the area between the scores.

EXAMPLE 9   *(Compare Exercise 47)*

A normal distribution has a mean $\mu = 50$ and a standard deviation $\sigma = 6$. Find the fraction of scores between 47 and 58.

SOLUTION   Since the mean is between 47 and 58, we need to find the area under the curve in two steps; that is, we need to find the area from the mean to each score.

1. The area between 47 and 50:

$$z_1 = \frac{47 - 50}{6} = \frac{-3}{6} = -0.50$$

From Table 7–1 this area is $A = 0.1915$.

2. The area between 50 and 58:

$$z_2 = \frac{58 - 50}{6} = \frac{8}{6} = 1.33$$

$$A = 0.4082$$

The total area between 47 and 58 is $0.1915 + 0.4082 = 0.5997$, so 0.5997, or 59.97%, of the scores lie between 47 and 58. See Figure 7–26.

FIGURE 7–26

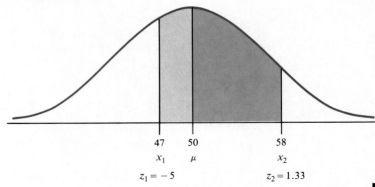

Sometimes, we want to find an area between two scores that lie on the same side of the mean.

EXAMPLE 10   *(Compare Exercise 51)*

A normal distribution has a mean $\mu = 100$ and a standard deviation $\sigma = 8$. Find the fraction of scores that lie between 110 and 120.

SOLUTION   Since all areas are measured from the mean to a score, we can find the area between 100 and 110 and the area between 100 and 120. To find the area between 110 and 120, subtract the area between 100 and 110 from the area between 110 and 120.

For $x_1 = 110$,

$$z_1 = \frac{110 - 100}{8} = \frac{10}{8} = 1.25$$

and $A_1 = 0.3944$

For $X_2 = 120$,

$$z_2 = \frac{120 - 100}{8} = \frac{20}{8} = 2.5$$

and $A_2 = 0.4938$.

The area between 110 and 120 is then $0.4938 - 0.3944 = 0.0994$, so 9.94% of the scores lie between 110 and 120. See Figure 7–27.

FIGURE 7–27

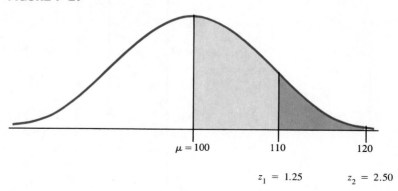

$$\mu = 100 \qquad 110 \qquad 120$$

$$z_1 = 1.25 \qquad z_2 = 2.50$$

PROBABILITY AND A NORMAL DISTRIBUTION

Because the total area under the normal curve is 1, and because the area between two scores gives the fraction of the data that lie between the two scores, an experiment whose data forms a normal distribution is connected to its related normal curve in the following way.

> The probability that an outcome is between two scores x_1 and x_2 is just the area under the normal curve between x_1 and x_2.

EXAMPLE 11   *(Compare Exercise 75)*

Students at Flatland University spend an average of 24.3 hours per week on homework, with a standard deviation of 1.4 hours. Assume a normal distribution.

(a) What percentage of the students spend more than 28 hours per week on homework?

(b) What is the probability that a student spends more than 28 hours per week on homework?

SOLUTION

(a) The value of z corresponding to 28 hours is

$$z = \frac{28 - 24.3}{1.4} = \frac{3.7}{1.4} = 2.64$$

From Table 7–1 we have $A = 0.4959$ when $z = 2.64$. The value $A = 0.4959$ represents the area from the mean, 24.3, to 28 ($z = 2.64$). All of the area under the curve to the right of the mean is one half of the total area. The area to the right of $z = 2.64$ is $0.5000 - 0.4959 = 0.0041$. Therefore 0.41% of the students study more than 28 hours.

(b) The probability that a student studies more than 28 hours is the fraction of the area that is to the right of 28, that is, 0.0041.

EXAMPLE 12   (*Compare Exercise 69*)

(a) Find a value of z such that 4% of the scores are to the right of z.
(b) Find the value of z such that 0.04 is the probability that a score lies to the right of z.

SOLUTION

(a) If 4% of the scores are to the right of z, then the other 46% of the scores to the right of the mean are between the mean and z. (Remember that 50% of the scores are to the right of the mean.) Look for $A = 0.4600$ in Table 7–1. It occurs at $z = 1.75$. This is the desired value of z.
(b) This also occurs at $z = 1.75$.

These examples ask for the probability that a score lies in a certain interval (such as $P(50 \leq X \leq 60)$) or greater than a certain score (such as $P(X \geq 75)$). A natural question is "How do you find the probability of a certain score, such as $P(X = 65)$?" The answer is "The probability is zero." In general, $P(X = c) = 0$ for any value c in a normal distribution. (*See Exercise 89.*) For example, this states that the probability of randomly selecting an 18-year-old male who is *exactly* 5 feet 10 inches tall is zero.

Since the normal curve is symmetric, Table 7–1 gives A only for positive values of z. For negative values of z, when the score is to the left of the mean, simply use the value of A for the corresponding positive z. Keep in mind that each z value determines an area *from the mean* to the z position.

We can find a variety of areas by adding or subtracting areas given from the table. (See Figure 7–28.)

Procedure to Determine the Fraction of Scores Between Two Scores of a Normal Distribution

Step 1. Determine the z-value for each score.
Step 2. From Table 7–1, determine A corresponding to z.
Step 3.
(a) If the two scores are on opposite sides of the mean (z_1 and z_2 have opposite signs), add the values of A corresponding to z_1 and z_2.
(b) If the two scores are on the same side of the mean (z_1 and z_2 have the same signs), subtract the smaller value of A from the larger value.

Procedure to Determine the Fraction of Scores Above (or Below) a Given Score in a Normal Distribution

Step 1. Determine the z-value for the score.
Step 2. From Table 7–1, determine A corresponding to z.
Step 3. If the score is to the right of the mean:
(a) subtract A from 0.5000 to obtain the fraction above.
(b) add A to 0.5000 to obtain the fraction below.
Step 4. If the score is to the left of the mean:
(a) add A to 0.5000 to obtain the fraction above.
(b) subtract A from 0.5000 to obtain the fraction below.

FIGURE 7–28

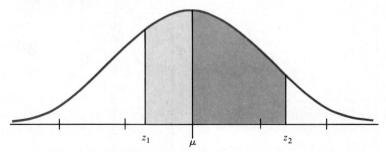

(a) Add the areas for z_1 and z_2 to get the area between z_1 and z_2.

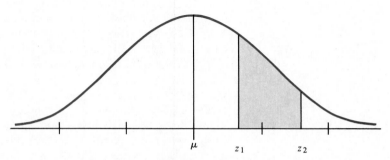

(b) Subtract z_1 area from z_2 area to get the area between z_1 and z_2.

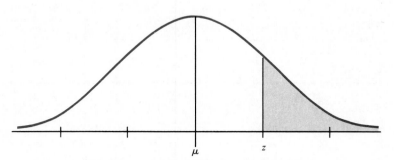

(c) Subtract the z area from 0.500 to get the area beyond z.

EXAMPLE 13 *(Compare Exercise 77)*

A standardized test is given to several hundred thousand junior high students. The mean is 100, and the standard deviation is 10. If a student is selected at random, what is the probability that the student scores in the 114 to 120 interval?

SOLUTION This question may be answered by using the properties of the normal curve, since it represents standardized test scores well. Because the area under the normal curve is 1, we can use the area between 114 and 120 as the probability that the student scores in the 114 to 120 interval.

The values of z corresponding to 114 and 120 are $z = 1.4$ and $z = 2.0$, respectively. For $z = 1.4$, $A = 0.4192$; and for $z = 2.0$, $A = 0.4773$. So the area between 114 and 120 is $0.4773 - 0.4192 = 0.0581$. The probability that the student's score is in the 114 to 120 interval is 0.0581.

Summary of Properties of a Normal Curve	1. All normal curves have the same general bell shape.
	2. It is symmetric with respect to a vertical line that passes through the peak of the curve.
	3. The vertical line through the peak occurs where the mean, median, and mode coincide.
	4. The area under any normal curve is always 1.
	5. The mean and standard deviation completely determine a normal curve. For the same mean a smaller standard deviation gives a taller and narrower peak. A larger standard deviation gives a flatter curve.
	6. The area to the right of the mean is 0.5; the area to the left of the mean is 0.5.
	7. About 68.26% of the area under a normal curve is enclosed in the interval formed by the score one standard deviation to the left of the mean and the score one standard deviation to the right of the mean.
	8. If a random variable X has a normal probability distribution, the probability that a score lies between x_1 and x_2 is the area under the normal curve between x_1 and x_2.
	9. The probability that a score is less than x_1 equals the probability that a score is less than, or equal to x_1, that is, $P(x < x_1) = P(x \le x_1)$.

7-6 EXERCISES

I

Find the value of z in Exercises 1 through 6.

1. (*See Example 2*) Score $= 3.1$, mean $= 4.0$, $\sigma = 0.3$
2. Score $= 38.0$, mean $= 22.5$, $\sigma = 6.2$
3. Score $= 10.1$, mean $= 10.0$, $\sigma = 2.0$
4. Score $= 31$, mean $= 31$, $\sigma = 5$
5. Score $= 2.65$, mean $= 0$, $\sigma = 1.0$
6. Score $= 192$, mean $= 150$, $\sigma = 7$

In Exercises 7 through 14, find the fraction of the area under the normal curve that lies between the mean and the given z-score.

7. (*See Example 3*) $z = 0.50$
8. $z = 1.90$
9. $z = 0.25$
10. $z = 2.50$
11. $z = 1.10$
12. $z = -0.10$
13. $z = -0.75$
14. $z = -2.25$

In Exercises 15 through 18, find the percent of the area under the normal curve that lies between the mean and the given number of standard deviations above the mean.

15. 0.46   **16.** 2.17

17. 0.38   **18.** 1.30

In Exercises 19 through 22, find the percent of the area under the normal curve that lies between the mean and the given number of standard deviations below the mean.

19. 1.24   **20.** 0.24

21. 2.90   **22.** 0.54

In Exercises 23 through 26, find the fraction of the area under the normal curve between the given values of z.

23. (*See Example 4*) $z = 1.25$ and $z = -1.25$

24. $z = 0.40$ and $z = -0.40$

25. $z = 2.20$ and $z = -2.20$

26. $z = 1.80$ and $z = -1.80$

In Exercises 27 through 30, find the percent of the area under the normal curve that lies within the given number of standard deviations of the mean.

27. 0.65   **28.** 1.34

29. 0.38   **30.** 2.73

In Exercises 31 through 34, find the fraction of the area under the normal curve that lies between the given z-scores.

31. (*See Example 5*) $z = -0.60$ and $z = 1.28$

32. $z = -1.75$ and $z = 1.20$

33. $z = -0.80$ and $z = 2.80$

34. $z = -0.20$ and $z = 2.65$

In Exercises 35 through 38, find the fraction of the area under the normal curve that lies above the given value z.

35. (*See Example 6*)   **36.** $z = 0.65$
     $z = 1.30$

37. $z = 2.40$ **38.** $z = 0.15$

Find the percentage of the area under the normal curve that lies more than the given number of standard deviations away from the mean in Exercises 39 through 42.

39. 0.86   **40.** 1.70

41. 1.50   **42.** 2.50

A normal distribution has a mean of 85 and a standard deviation of 5. Find the fraction of scores in the intervals given in Exercises 43 through 46.

43. (*See Example 8*) Between 85 and 98

44. Between 85 and 89

45. Between 85 and 80

46. Between 85 and 73

A normal distribution has a mean of 226 and a standard deviation of 12. Find the fraction of scores in the intervals given in Exercises 47 through 50.

47. (*See Example 9*) Between 220 and 235

48. Between 208 and 240

49. Between 211 and 241

50. Between 222 and 234

A normal distribution has a mean of 140 and a standard deviation of 8. Find the fraction of scores in the intervals given in Exercises 51 through 54.

51. (*See Example 10*) Between 144 and 152

52. Between 142 and 156

53. Between 146 and 156

54. Between 148 and 154

A normal distribution has a mean of 75 and a standard deviation of 5. Find the fraction of scores in the intervals indicated in Exercises 55 through 59.

55. Between 80 and 85

56. Between 77 and 83

57. Above 76

58. Between 68 and 79

59. Either below 70 or above 80

A normal distribution has a mean of 168 and a standard deviation of 10. Find the percent of scores in the intervals indicated in Exercises 60 through 68.

60. Between 168 and 175

61. Between 155 and 169

62. Between 170 and 180

63. Less than 172

64. Less than 150

65. Larger than 173

66. Larger than 170

67. Less than 184

68. Less than 160

Find the value of z in Exercises 69 through 74.

69. (*See Example 12*) 8% of the scores are to the right of z.

70. 15% of the scores are to the right of z.

71. 86% of the scores are to the left of z.

72. 96% of the scores are to the left of z.

73. 91% of the scores are between z and −z.

74. 82% of the scores are between z and −z.

II

Assume a normal distribution in the following problems.

75. (*See Example 11*) Customers at Big Burger spend an average of $3.15 with a standard deviation of $0.75.
  (a) What percent of the customers spend more than $3.75?
  (b) What is the probability that a customer spends more than $3.75?

76. At Montevallo College the students from Harper County have an average GPA of 2.95 with a standard deviation of 0.50.
  (a) What percent have a GPA below 2.50?
  (b) What is the probability that a student from Harper County has a GPA below 2.50?

77. (*See Example 13*) One year the freshmen of all U.S. colleges had a mean average IQ of 110 and a standard deviation of 12. The IQ scores form a normal distribution. If a student is selected at random, find the probability that:
  (a) the student has an IQ between 120 and 125.
  (b) the student has an IQ below 100.
  (c) the student has an IQ between 105 and 115.

78. A standardized test has a mean of 80 and a standard deviation of 5. A test is selected at random. Find the probability that:
  (a) the score is between 84 and 90.
  (b) the score is above 88.
  (c) the score is below 74.
  (d) the score is between 75 and 83.

III

79. The weights of college students at a particular college is a normal distribution with a mean of 126 pounds and a standard deviation of 6 pounds. The college has 700 students.
  (a) How many students weigh between 120 and 132 pounds?
  (b) How many students weigh less than 114 pounds?
  (c) How many students weigh more than 134 pounds?

80. The IQs of individuals form a normal distribution with mean = 100 and σ = 15.
  (a) What percentage of the population have IQs below 85?
  (b) What percentage have IQs over 130?
  (c) A college requires an IQ of 120 or more for entrance. From what percentage of the population must it draw its students?
  (d) In a state with 400,000 high school seniors, how many meet the IQ requirement?
  (e) What is the probability that a student has an IQ below 90?

81. The grades in a large history class fall reasonably close to a normal curve with a mean of 66 and a standard deviation of 17. The professor curves the grades.
   (a) If the top 12% receive A's, what is the cutoff score for an A?
   (b) If the top 6% receive A's, what is the cutoff score for an A?

82. The batteries used for a calculator have an average life of 2000 hours and a standard deviation of 200 hours. The normal distribution closely represents the life of the battery. Find the fraction of batteries that can be expected to last the following lengths of time:
   (a) Between 1800 and 2200 hours
   (b) Between 1900 and 2100 hours
   (c) At least 2500 hours
   (d) No more than 2200 hours
   (e) Less than 1500 hours
   (f) Between 1600 and 2300 hours
   (g) Less than 1900 or more than 2100 hours
   (h) Between 2200 and 2400 hours
   (i) What is the probability that a battery lasts longer than 2244 hours?

83. The scores of students on a standardized test form a normal distribution with a mean of 300 and a standard deviation of 40.
   (a) What fraction of the students scored between 270 and 330?
   (b) What fraction of the students scored between 312 and 330?
   (c) What fraction of the students scored less than 300? Less than 326?
   (d) What must a student score to be in the upper 10%?
   (e) A student is selected at random. What is the probability that the student scored between 312 and 324?

84. An automatic lathe makes shafts for a high-speed machine. The specifications call for a shaft with a diameter of 1.800 inches. An inspector closely monitors production for a week and finds that the actual diameters form a normal distribution with a mean of 1.800 inches and a standard deviation of 0.00033 inch. The design engineer will accept a shaft

that is within 0.001 inch of the specified diameter of 1.800. If a shaft is selected at random, what is the probability that it is within the specified tolerance, that is, that the diameter is in the interval 1.799 to 1.801 inches?

85. A standardized test has a mean of 120 and a standard deviation of 10. If two students are selected at random, what is the probability that both score below 128?

86. Grades on a sociology test are reasonably close to a normal curve and have a mean of 74 and a standard deviation of 10. The professor wants to curve the grades so that the highest 10% receive A and the lowest 5% receive F. The next 25% below an A receive B, and the next 10% above F receive D. The remainder between the B's and D's receive C. Find the cutoff scores for each letter grade.

87. The manufacturer of an electronics device knows that the length of life of the device is a normal distribution with a mean of 1050 hours and a standard deviation of 50 hours. Find the probability that a device will last at least 1140 hours.

88. The average rainfall for September in Hillsboro is 4.65 inches with a standard deviation of 1.10 inches. Find the percentage of the time that the September rainfall is below 5.2 inches.

89. A set of scores is a normal distribution with a mean of 0 ($\mu = 0$) and a standard deviation of 1 ($\sigma = 1$). This is a standard normal distribution, and so a score equals its z-value.
   (a) Find the probability that a score is between 0.5 and 1.5; that is, find $P(0.5 \leq X \leq 1.5)$.
   (b) Find the probability that a score is between 0.6 and 1.4; that is, find $P(0.6 \leq X \leq 1.4)$.
   (c) Find $P(0.7 \leq X \leq 1.3)$.
   (d) Find $P(0.8 \leq X \leq 1.2)$.
   (e) Find $P(0.9 \leq X \leq 1.1)$.
   (f) Find $P(0.95 \leq X \leq 1.05)$.
   (g) Find $P(0.99 \leq X \leq 1.01)$.
   (h) Notice that as the interval squeezes in on $X = 1$, the probabilities get smaller. Does it then seem reasonable to say that $P(X = 1) = 0$? In fact, $P(X = c) = 0$ for any value c in a continuous normal distribution.

7–7 BINOMIAL DISTRIBUTION

- *Binomial Distribution*
- *Normal Approximation to a Binomial Distribution*
- *Application*

BINOMIAL DISTRIBUTION

Recall from Section 6–7 that a Bernoulli experiment meets the following requirements:

1. It consists of a sequence of independent trials.
2. It has two possible outcomes: success and failure.
3. The probability of success remains fixed for each trial.
4. The trials are independent.
5. The probability of x successes in n trials is

$$C(n, x)p^x q^{n-x}$$

We can use **Bernoulli trials** to form an important probability distribution. This distribution is called a **binomial distribution.** Define it in the following way.

Binomial Distribution   For a Bernoulli experiment of n repeated independent trials, define a random variable X as the number of successes in n trials. For each integer value of x, $0 \leq x \leq n$, find the probability of x successes in n trials. The probability distribution obtained is the **binomial distribution.**

EXAMPLE 1   *(Compare Exercise 5)*

Form the binomial distribution for the experiment of rolling a die three times and counting the times a 4 appears.

SOLUTION   The random variable X takes on the values 0, 1, 2, and 3, the possible number of successes in three trials. The probability of each value occurring is computed by using Bernoulli trials with $p = \frac{1}{6}$ and $q = \frac{5}{6}$. ($\frac{1}{6}$ is the probability of rolling a 4 in a single trial.)

X	$P(X)$
0	$C(3, 0)(\frac{5}{6})^3 = .5787$
1	$C(3, 1)(\frac{1}{6})(\frac{5}{6})^2 = .3472$
2	$C(3, 2)(\frac{1}{6})^2(\frac{5}{6}) = .0694$
3	$C(3, 3)(\frac{1}{6})^3 = .0046$

The binomial distribution got its name from the binomial $(p + q)^n$. Each term of the expansion of the binomial gives one of the probabilities in the binomial distribution. Notice that

$$(p + q)^3 = p^3 + 3p^2q + 3pq^2 + q^3$$

which can be written

$$C(3, 3)p^3q^0 + C(3, 2)p^2q + C(3, 1)pq^2 + C(3, 0)q^3$$

where each term represents the probability of 3, 2, 1, or 0 successes, respectively, in a binomial experiment with three trials.

EXAMPLE 2 *(Compare Exercise 7)*

Form the binomial distribution of the experiment of tossing a coin six times and counting the number of heads.

SOLUTION The random variable X takes on the values 0, 1, 2, 3, 4, 5, and 6, the possible number of successes in six tosses. Both p and q are $\frac{1}{2}$. The values of X and the corresponding probabilities computed using Bernoulli trials are the following:

X	$P(X)$
0	$C(6, 0)(\frac{1}{2})^6 = 0.0156$
1	$C(6, 1)(\frac{1}{2})^1(\frac{1}{2})^5 = 0.0938$
2	$C(6, 2)(\frac{1}{2})^2(\frac{1}{2})^4 = 0.2344$
3	$C(6, 3)(\frac{1}{2})^3(\frac{1}{2})^3 = 0.3125$
4	$C(6, 4)(\frac{1}{2})^4(\frac{1}{2})^2 = 0.2344$
5	$C(6, 5)(\frac{1}{2})^5(\frac{1}{2}) = 0.0938$
6	$C(6, 6)(\frac{1}{2})^6 = 0.0156$

The histogram of the distribution is given in Figure 7–29.

FIGURE 7–29

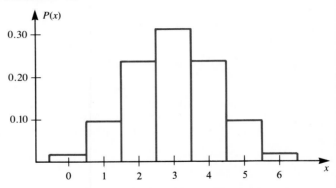

Probability distribution of the number of heads
in 6 tosses of a coin

EXAMPLE 3 *(Compare Exercise 1)*

Find the binomial distribution for $n = 4$ and $p = 0.3$.

SOLUTION The random variable X may take on the values 0, 1, 2, 3, and 4. The probability distribution is the following.

X	$P(X)$
0	$C(4, 0)(0.7)^4 = 0.2401$
1	$C(4, 1)(0.3)(0.7)^3 = 0.4116$
2	$C(4, 2)(0.3)^2(0.7)^2 = 0.2646$
3	$C(4, 3)(0.3)^3(0.7) = .0756$
4	$C(4, 4)(0.3)^4 = .0081$

EXAMPLE 4 *(Compare Exercise 10)*

The probability that a new drug will cure a certain blood disease is 0.7. If it is administered to 100 patients with the disease, what is the probability that 60 of them will be cured?

SOLUTION You should set up

$$P(X = 60) = C(100, 60)(0.7)^{60}(0.3)^{40}$$

with little difficulty. You then may find it tedious to compute the probability and even more tedious to form the binomial distribution of this experiment. Some calculators have functions that make the computations relatively easy.

The normal distribution provides a means to avoid this wearisome computation. It can be used to estimate the binomial distribution for large values of n. Let's see how to do this.

NORMAL APPROXIMATION TO A BINOMIAL DISTRIBUTION

Recall from Section 7–5 that the computation of the mean (or expected value), the variance, and the standard deviation of a probability distribution can be time consuming for a random variable with many values.

In Example 3, $n = 4$ and $p = 0.3$. The expected value of the random variable X is

$$E(X) = .2401(0) + .4116(1) + .2646(2) + .0756(3) + .0081(4)$$
$$= 0 + .4116 + .5292 + .2268 + .0324$$
$$= 1.20$$

The significance of this result is that $1.20 = 4(0.3)$, which is np for this example. This result holds for all binomial distributions, $E(X) = np$. Likewise, the variance and standard deviation can be expressed in rather simple terms of $n, p,$ and $q,$ as follows.

Mean, Variance, and Standard Deviation of a Binomial Distribution

Let X be the random variable for a binomial distribution with n repeated trials, with p the probability of success, q the probability of failure, and

$$P(X = x) = C(n, x)p^x(1 - p)^{n-x}$$

Then the mean (expected value), variance, and standard deviation of X are given by

Mean: $\mu = np$

Variance: $\sigma^2(X) = np(1 - p) = npq$

Standard Deviation: $\sigma(X) = \sqrt{np(1 - p)} = \sqrt{npq}$

EXAMPLE 5   *(Compare Exercise 15)*

(a) For the binomial distribution with $n = 20$, $p = 0.35$:

$$\text{Mean} = \mu = 20(0.35) = 7$$
$$\sigma^2(X) = 20(0.35)(0.65) = 4.55$$
$$\sigma(X) = \sqrt{4.55} = 2.133$$

(b) If $n = 160$, $p = 0.21$,

$$\mu = 160(0.21) = 33.6$$
$$\sigma^2(X) = 160(0.21)(0.79) = 26.544$$
$$\sigma(X) = \sqrt{26.544} = 5.152$$

To illustrate how the normal curve is used to estimate binomial probabilities, we use the following simple example.

EXAMPLE 6   *(Compare Exercise 27)*

Use the normal curve to estimate the probability of:

(a) three heads in six tosses of a coin.
(b) three or four heads in six tosses of a coin.

SOLUTION

(a) We first point out that the binomial distribution of this problem, and its histogram, are given in Example 2. From it, for example, we see that $P(X = 3) = 0.3125$.

For the binomial distribution with $n = 6$ and $p = 0.5$ the mean and standard deviation are

$$\mu = 6(0.5) = 3$$
$$\sigma = \sqrt{6(0.5)(0.5)} = \sqrt{1.5} = 1.225$$

FIGURE 7–30

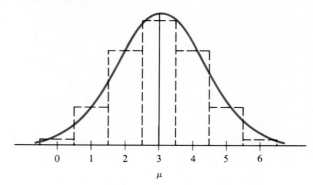

A normal curve superimposed on
a binomial distribution

Figure 7–30 shows a normal curve with $\mu = 3$ and $\sigma = 1.225$ superimposed on the binomial distribution for $n = 6$ and $p = 0.5$. Notice that a portion of the histogram lies above the curve, while some space under the curve is not filled by the rectangles. It appears that if the portions of the rectangle outside were moved into the empty spaces below the curve, then the area under the curve would pretty well be filled. This states that the total area enclosed by the histogram is "close" to the area under the normal curve.

Let's make another observation. Each bar in the histogram is of width 1, and its height is equal to the probability it represents. The bar for $P(X = 3)$ is located between 2.5 and 3.5, with height 0.3125. The area of that bar (1×0.3125) represents the probability that $X = 3$. We mention this because it holds the key to using the normal distribution. To find $P(X = 3)$, find the area under the normal curve between 2.5 and 3.5. Here's how:

Use $\mu = 3$, $\sigma = 1.225$, $x_1 = 2.5$, and $x_2 = 3.5$. Then

$$z_1 = \frac{2.5 - 3}{1.225} = \frac{-0.5}{1.225} = -0.41$$

$$z_2 = \frac{3.5 - 3}{1.225} = \frac{0.5}{1.225} = 0.41$$

Table 7–1 shows that the area under the normal curve between the mean and $z = 0.41$ is $A = 0.1591$. Then the area between $z_1 = -0.41$ and $z_2 = 0.41$ is $0.1591 + 0.1591 = 0.3182$. This estimates $P(X = 3)$ as 0.3182. This compares to the actual probability of 0.3125. Notice that we approximated the binomial probability $P(X = 3)$ by the normal probability $P(2.5 \le X \le 3.5)$.

(b) To find the probability of three or four heads in six tosses of a coin, $P(3 \leq X \leq 4)$, we find the total area of the bars for three and four. This amounts to finding the area in the histogram between 2.5 and 4.5. The normal approximation is the area between

$$z_1 = \frac{2.5 - 3}{1.225} \qquad \text{and} \qquad z_2 = \frac{4.5 - 3}{1.225}$$

that is,

$$z_1 = -0.41 \qquad \text{and} \qquad z_2 = 1.22$$

The corresponding areas are

$$A_1 = 0.1591 \qquad \text{and} \qquad A_2 = 0.3888$$

so the desired probability estimate is $0.1591 + 0.3888 = 0.5479$. The actual probability, from Example 2, is $0.3125 + 0.2344 = .5469$. Notice that we approximated the binomial probability $P(3 \leq X \leq 4)$ by the normal probability $P(2.5 \leq X \leq 4.5)$.

At this point we must confess that the normal approximation worked rather well in the preceding example because p and q were both $\frac{1}{2}$. Had we used $p = \frac{1}{6}$ and $q = \frac{5}{6}$, the normal approximation would not have worked very well. However, if n is 50 instead of 6, the normal approximation is reasonable. So when is it reasonable to use the normal distribution to approximate the binomial distribution? The answer is: "It depends." It depends on the values of n and p. Several rules of thumb are used by statisticians to judge when the normal approximation is reasonable. We use the following.

Rule   The normal distribution provides a good estimate of the binomial distribution when both np and nq are greater than or equal to 5.

In the next three examples we will estimate some binomial probabilities using the normal distribution. In each of the three examples we will use the binomial distribution with

$$n = 14, \quad p = 0.4, \quad \text{and} \quad q = 0.6$$

On the basis of these values we then have

$$\mu = 14(0.4) = 5.6 \qquad \text{and} \qquad \sigma = \sqrt{14(0.4)\,(0.6)} = 1.83$$

These values will be used in the following examples.

EXAMPLE 7   *(Compare Exercise 29)*

For the binomial distribution with $n = 14$, $p = 0.4$, and $q = 0.6$, find

(a) $P(3 \leq X \leq 7)$
(b) $P(3 < X < 7)$

SOLUTION

(a) Figure 7–31(a) shows the graph of the binomial probability with the bars representing $3 \leq X \leq 7$ shaded and a normal curve superimposed. It shows that the area under the normal curve between $X = 2.5$ and 7.5 approximates the desired probability. To find the area, we need the corresponding z-scores.

At $X = 2.5$, $z = \dfrac{2.5 - 5.6}{1.83} = -1.69$, and $A = 0.4545$ (from Table 7–1).

At $X = 7.5$, $z = \dfrac{7.5 - 5.6}{1.83} = 1.04$, and $A = 0.3508$ (from Table 7–1).

The area under the normal curve between 2.5 and 7.5 is then $0.4545 + 0.3508 = 0.8053$, so $P(3 \leq X \leq 7) = 0.8053$.

FIGURE 7–31(a)

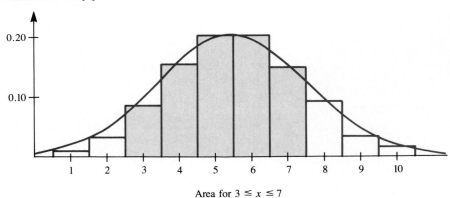

Area for $3 \leq x \leq 7$

(b) To find $P(3 < X < 7)$, we need to find the area under the normal curve between 3.5 and 6.5. (See Figure 7–31(b).)

At $X = 3.5$, $z = \dfrac{3.5 - 5.6}{1.83} = -1.15$, and $A = 0.3749$ (from Table 7–1).

At $X = 6.5$, $z = \dfrac{6.5 - 5.6}{1.83} = 0.49$, and $A = 0.1879$ (from Table 7–1).

The area under the normal curve between $X = 3.5$ and $X = 6.5$ is then $0.3749 + 0.1879 = 0.5628$, so $P(3 < X < 7) = 0.5628$.

FIGURE 7–31(b)

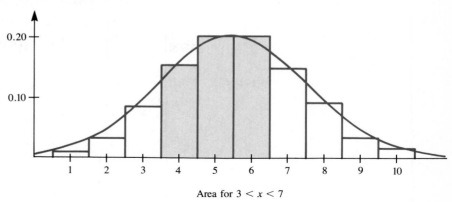

Area for $3 < x < 7$

EXAMPLE 8 *(Compare Exercise 31)*

For the binomial distribution with $n = 14$, $p = 0.4$, and $q = 0.6$, find

(a) $P(X > 3)$

(b) $P(X \geq 3)$

SOLUTION

(a) To approximate $P(X > 3)$, we need to find the area under the normal curve to the right of 3.5. (See Figure 7–32(a).) From Example 7 we have at $X = 3.5$, $z = -1.15$, and the area from $X = 3.5$ to the mean, 5.6, is 0.3749. Since the area to the right of the mean is 0.5000, $P(X > 3) = 0.3749 + 0.5000 = 0.8749$.

FIGURE 7–32(a)

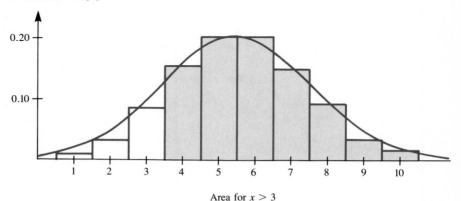

Area for $x > 3$

(b) To approximate $P(X \geq 3)$, we need to find the area under the normal curve to the right of 2.5. (See Figure 7–32(b).) From Example 7 we have at $X = 2.5$, $z = -1.69$, and the area from $X = 2.5$ to the mean, 5.6, is 0.4545. Since the area to the right of the mean is 0.5000, $P(X \geq 3) = 0.4545 + 0.5000 = 0.9545$.

FIGURE 7–32(b)

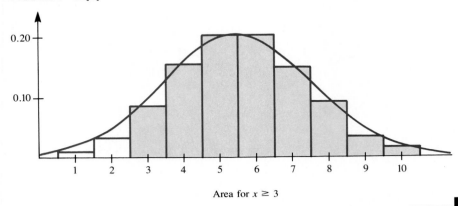

Area for $x \geq 3$

EXAMPLE 9 *(Compare Exercise 33)*

For the binomial distribution with $n = 14$, $p = 0.4$, and $q = 0.6$, find
(a) $P(X < 7)$
(b) $P(X \leq 7)$

SOLUTION

(a) To approximate $P(X < 7)$, we need to find the area under the normal curve to the left of 6.5. (See Figure 7–33(a).) From Example 7 we have at $X = 6.5$, $z = 0.49$, and the area from the mean, 5.6, to $X = 6.5$ is 0.1879. Since the area to the left of the mean is 0.5000, $P(X < 7) = 0.1879 + 0.5000 = 0.6879$.

FIGURE 7–33(a)

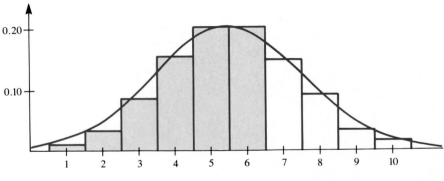

Area for $x < 7$

(b) To approximate $P(X \leq 7)$, we need to find the area under the normal curve to the left of 7.5. (See Figure 7–33(b).) From Example 7 we have at $X = 7.5$, $z = 1.04$, and the area from the mean, 5.6, to $X = 7.5$ is 0.3508. Since the area to the left of the mean is 0.5000, $P(X \leq 7) = 0.3508 + 0.5000 = 0.8508$.

FIGURE 7–33(b)

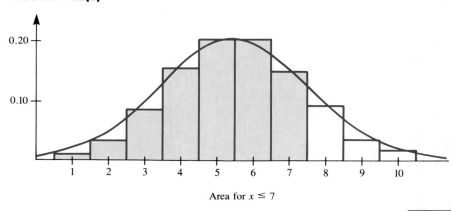

Area for $x \leq 7$

In summary, estimate a binomial probability with a normal distribution as follows.

Procedure for Estimating a Binomial Probability

1. If np and nq are both greater than or equal to 5, you may assume that the normal distribution provides a good estimate.
2. Compute $\mu = np$ and $\sigma = \sqrt{npq}$.
3. To estimate $P(X = c)$, find the area under the normal curve between $c - 0.5$ and $c + 0.5$. To do so, find the area between the z-scores

$$z_1 = \frac{c - 0.5 - \mu}{\sigma} \quad \text{and} \quad z_2 = \frac{c + 0.5 - \mu}{\sigma}$$

4. To estimate $P(c \leq X \leq d)$, $c < d$, find the area under the normal curve between $c - 0.5$ and $d + 0.5$. To do so, find the area between

$$z_1 = \frac{c - 0.5 - \mu}{\sigma} \quad \text{and} \quad z_2 = \frac{d + 0.5 - \mu}{\sigma}$$

5. To estimate $P(c < X < d)$, $c < d$, find the area under the normal curve between $c + 0.5$ and $d - 0.5$. To do so, find the area between

$$z_1 = \frac{c + 0.5 - \mu}{\sigma} \quad \text{and} \quad z_2 = \frac{d - 0.5 - \mu}{\sigma}$$

6. To estimate $P(X > c)$, find the area under the normal curve to the right of $c + 0.5$. To do so, find the area to the right of

$$z = \frac{c + 0.5 - \mu}{\sigma}$$

7. To estimate $P(X \geq c)$, find the area under the normal curve to the right of $c - 0.5$. To do so, find the area to the right of

$$z = \frac{c - 0.5 - \mu}{\sigma}$$

8. To estimate $P(X < c)$, find the area under the normal curve to the left of $c - 0.5$. To do so, find the area to the left of

$$z = \frac{c - 0.5 - \mu}{\sigma}$$

9. To estimate $P(X \leq c)$, find the area under the normal curve to the left of $c + 0.5$. To do so, find the area to the left of

$$z = \frac{c + 0.5 - \mu}{\sigma}$$

APPLICATION

EXAMPLE 10   *(Compare Exercise 35)*

The probability that a new drug will cure a certain blood disease is .7. If it is administered to 100 patients:

(a) what is the probability that 60 of them will be cured?
(b) what is the probability that 60 to 75 of them will be cured?
(c) what is the probability that more than 75 will be cured?

SOLUTION   Since $n = 100$, $p = 0.7$, and $q = 0.3$, we know that $np = 70$ and $nq = 30$. Since both values are greater than 5, a normal curve provides a good estimate, and

$$\mu = 100(0.7) = 70$$
$$\sigma = \sqrt{100(0.7)(0.3)} = \sqrt{21} = 4.583$$

(a) Find the area under the normal curve between 59.5 and 60.5 that is between

$$z_1 = \frac{59.5 - 70}{4.583} = \frac{-10.5}{4.583} = -2.29$$

and

$$z_2 = \frac{60.5 - 70}{4.583} = \frac{-9.5}{4.583} = -2.07$$

The corresponding areas are $A_1 = 0.4890$ and $A_2 = 0.4808$. Since the z-scores lie on the same side of the mean, we must subtract areas, $0.4890 - 0.4808 = .0082$. So $P(X = 60) = .0082$.

(b) To find $P(60 \leq X \leq 75)$, we find the area between 59.5 and 75.5. The corresponding z-values and areas are

$$z_1 = \frac{59.5 - 70}{4.583} = -2.29 \quad \text{and} \quad z_2 = \frac{75.5 - 70}{4.583} = 1.20$$

$A_1 = 0.4890$, and $A_2 = 0.3849$. Since the scores lie on opposite sides of the mean, we add areas to obtain the probability:

$$P(60 \leq X \leq 75) = 0.4890 + 0.3849 = 0.8739$$

(c) To find the probability that more than 75 patients will be cured, $P(X > 75)$, find the area under the normal curve that lies to the right of 75.5. (*Note:* To find the probability of 75 or more, $P(X \geq 75)$, find the area to the right of 74.5.)

For a score of 75.5, $z = 1.20$ and $A = 0.3849$. (See part (b).) Since we want the area above $z = 1.20$, we need to subtract $0.5000 - 0.3849 = 0.1151$ to get $P(X > 75) = 0.1151$.

7-7 EXERCISES

I

1. (*See Example 3*) Find the binomial distribution for $n = 5$ and $p = 0.3$.

2. Find the binomial distribution for $n = 4$ and $p = 0.6$.

3. Form the binomial distribution of an experiment with $n = 5$ and $p = 0.4$.

4. Draw the probability histogram for the binomial distribution for $n = 4$ and $p = 0.2$.

5. (*See Example 1*) Form the binomial distribution for the experiment of rolling a die four times and counting the number of times a 2 appears.

6. Form the binomial distribution of rolling a die three times and counting the number of times a 6 appears.

7. (*See Example 2*) Form the binomial distribution of the experiment of tossing a coin four times and counting the number of heads. Draw the probability histogram.

8. A coin is tossed seven times, and the number of heads is counted. Determine the binomial distribution of the experiment.

9. Five cards are numbered 1 through 5. The cards are shuffled, and a card is drawn. The number drawn is noted. This is done four times, and a count is made of the number of times an odd number appears. Find the probability distribution and draw its histogram.

10. (*See Example 4*) The probability that a new drug will cure a skin rash is .85. If the drug is administered to 500 patients with the skin rash, what is the probability that it will cure 400 of them. Set up but do not compute this probability.

Set up but do not compute the probability for each of the problems in Exercises 11 through 14.

11. The probability of 40 successes, where $n = 90$ and $p = 0.4$

12. The probability of 100 successes, where $n = 500$ and $p = 0.7$

13. $P(X = 35)$, where $n = 75$ and $p = 0.25$

14. $P(40 \leq X \leq 42)$, where $n = 100$ and $p = 0.35$

For each of the binomial distributions in Exercises 15 through 19, compute the mean, variance, and standard deviation.

15. (*See Example 5*)
    $n = 50, p = 0.4$

16. $n = 210, p = 0.3$

17. $n = 600, p = 0.52$

18. $n = 1850, p = 0.24$

19. $n = 470, p = 0.08$

The normal distribution is a good estimate for which of the binomial distributions in Exercises 20 through 26?

20. $n = 30, p = 0.4$

21. $n = 50, p = 0.7$

22. $n = 40, p = 0.1$

23. $n = 40, p = 0.9$

24. $n = 200, p = 0.08$

25. $n = 25, p = 0.5$

26. $n = 15, p = 0.3$

27. (*See Example 6*) Given the binomial experiment with $n = 50$ and $p = 0.7$, use the normal distribution to estimate:
    (a) $P(X = 40)$ (b) $P(X = 28)$ (c) $P(X = 32)$

28. Given the binomial experiment with $n = 12$ and $p = 0.5$, use the normal distribution to estimate:
    (a) $P(X = 6)$ (b) $P(X = 7)$ (c) $P(X = 8)$

29. (*See Example 7*) Given the binomial experiment with $n = 15$ and $p = 0.4$, use the normal distribution to estimate:
    (a) $P(4 < X < 8)$ (b) $P(4 \leq X \leq 8)$
    (c) $P(7 \leq X \leq 8)$

30. Given the binomial experiment with $n = 25$ and $p = 0.3$, use the normal distribution to estimate:
    (a) $P(6 < X < 10)$ (b) $P(6 \leq X \leq 10)$
    (c) $P(5 \leq X \leq 7)$

31. (*See Example 8*) Given the binomial experiment with $n = 16$ and $p = 0.5$, use the normal distribution to estimate:
    (a) $P(X > 5)$ (b) $P(X \geq 5)$ (c) $P(X > 9)$

32. Given the binomial experiment with $n = 30$ and $p = 0.4$, use the normal distribution to estimate:
    (a) $P(X > 14)$ (b) $P(X \geq 14)$ (c) $P(X \geq 9)$

33. (*See Example 9*) Given the binomial experiment with $n = 24$ and $p = 0.3$, use the normal distribution to estimate:
    (a) $P(X < 10)$ (b) $P(X \leq 10)$ (c) $P(X < 6)$

34. Given the binomial experiment with $n = 18$ and $p = 0.35$, use the normal distribution to estimate:
    (a) $P(X < 4)$ (b) $P(X \leq 4)$ (c) $P(X < 9)$

II

35. (*See Example 10*) The probability that a new drug will cure a certain disease is .6. It is administered to 100 patients.
    (a) Find the probability that it will cure 50 to 75 of them.
    (b) Find the probability that it will cure more than 75.
    (c) Find the probability that it will cure fewer than 50.

36. A coin is tossed 30 times. Find the probability that it will land heads up at least 20 times.

37. A die is rolled 20 times. What is the probability that it turns up a 1 or a 3 six, seven, or eight times?

38. A coin is tossed 100 times. Find the probability of 55 through 60 heads.

39. A coin is tossed 100 times. Find the probability of tossing 50 through 55 heads.

40. A die is tossed 36 times. Find the probability of throwing six through eight 4's.

41. A certain Bernoulli trial is repeated 64 times. The probability of success in a single trial is $\frac{1}{4}$. Find the probability of success in 20 through 24 of the trials.

III

42. In a certain city of 30,000 people the probability of a person being involved in a motor accident in any one year is .01. Find the probability of more than 250 people having accidents in a year.

43. An airline knows that 10% of its reservations result in no-shows. It books 270 passengers on a flight that has 250 seats. Find the probability that all passengers who show will have a seat.

44. A drug company has developed a new drug that it believes is 90% effective. It tests the drug on 500 people. Find the probability that at least 90% of the people respond favorably to the drug.

45. A college report states that 30% of its students commute to school. If a random sample of 250 students is taken, find the probability that at least 65 commute.

46. An insurance company estimates that 5% of automobile owners do not carry liability insurance. If 120 cars are stopped at random, what is the probability that fewer than 5% of them have no liability insurance?

47. A true-false test consists of 90 questions. Three points are given for each correct answer, and one point is deducted for each incorrect answer. A student must score at least 98 points to pass.
  (a) How many correct answers are required to pass if a student answers all questions?
  (b) If a student guesses all answers, find the probability of a passing grade.

7–8 ESTIMATING BOUNDS ON A PROPORTION

- *Standard Error of a Proportion*
- *Computing Error Bounds for a Proportion*

Mr. Alexander Quality, President of Quality Cola Company, grew tired of Quality Cola. He wanted a cola with more zest and a new taste. Like his father before him, he had vowed never to drink his competitor's cola. Therefore, he must develop a new Quality Cola or resign himself to the traditional taste. He discussed the problem with his division heads. The head of the research division agreed that it could develop a new formula, but it would cost thousands of dollars. The chief accountant insisted that they should recover the development cost and make a profit. The marketing manager hesitated to put a new product on the market unless she was confident that it would succeed.

Mr. Quality, an astute executive, agreed that his managers had valid points, so he instructed them to develop a new formula, find out if the public preferred it to the old cola, and if so, pour money into advertising it. After weeks of work, the research division developed a formula that it liked and Mr. Quality liked. Now the marketing manager wanted to know if the public liked it. She quickly determined that it would be quite unrealistic and prohibitively expensive to give everyone in the country a taste test. So she asked the company statistician to help her. She told the statistician that she was confident that the new cola would be successful if 40% or more of the population liked it. The statistician outlined the following plan:

1. Select, by a random means, 500 people throughout the country.
2. Give each person a taste test.
3. Find the proportion of the sample that like the new cola.
4. Use the sample proportion as an estimate of the proportion of the total population that like the new cola.

It took the statistician several weeks to select and survey the sample. When the information was in and tabulated, it showed that 43% of the people in the sample test liked the new cola. At first the marketing manager was elated. Enough people liked the new product to make it successful. Then she had second thoughts. What about the millions of people who did not participate in the taste test? They were the ones who would determine the success of the new cola, so she called the statistician.

"Can I depend on 43% of everyone liking the new cola? Perhaps you just happened to pick the few people who like it."

"I cannot guarantee that precisely 43% of the general public will like it. I told you this was an estimate."

"How good is the estimate? If the estimate is off by two or three percentage points, we are O.K. If the proportion for the entire population is actually only 20%, we are in real trouble. Can you put some bounds on how much the estimate might be in error?"

"We can compute what is called the **standard error of a proportion** and use it to put **error bounds** on the proportion. It is similar to the standard deviation used in describing the dispersion of data around the mean."

Here is how the statistician determined the standard error.

STANDARD ERROR OF A PROPORTION

Let n be the number of people in the sample. In our example, $n = 500$.

Let p be the proportion of the sample who like the cola. In our sample, $p = 0.43$. The standard error is defined as

$$SE = \sqrt{\frac{p(1 - p)}{n}}$$

In our case,

$$SE = \sqrt{\frac{(0.43)(0.57)}{500}}$$

$$= \sqrt{\frac{0.2451}{500}}$$

$$= \sqrt{0.000490} = 0.0221$$

We must emphasize that we cannot find absolute bounds. We determine bounds on the basis of a **level of confidence.** Some concepts of a normal distribution can be used. For example, suppose that we are willing to accept bounds on the sample proportion that will enclose the true proportion with a probability of .90. Think of $p = 0.43$ as the mean in a normal distribution, and find the scores positioned equal distances above and below $p = 0.43$ that enclose 90% of the area under the curve. We first find the z-score from the normal distribution that corresponds to $A = 0.45$ (the 90% is divided equally, 45% on each side of p). Find the z-score in Table 7–1 that corresponds to $A = 0.45$. In this case, $z = 1.65$. The number $E = z \times SE = (1.65)(0.0221) = 0.036$ is the maximum error and gives the distance above and below p that encloses the true proportion at the 90% confidence level:

$$p + z \times SE = 0.43 + 1.65 \times 0.0221 = 0.43 + 0.036 = 0.466$$
$$p - z \times SE = 0.43 - 1.65 \times 0.0221 = 0.43 - 0.036 = 0.394$$

Therefore, when we say that about 40% to 47% of the total population likes the new Quality Cola, the probability that we are correct is .90. If we want the error bounds at a higher probability level, say 0.98, we use $A = 0.49$ ($0.49 = \frac{0.98}{2}$) and get $z = 2.33$. Then $p + z \times SE$ and $P - z \times SE$ are the error bounds at the 0.98 probability level. The bounds are

$$0.43 + 2.33(0.0221) = 0.43 + 0.051 = 0.481$$

and

$$0.43 - 2.33(0.0221) = 0.43 - 0.051 = 0.379$$

Thus we state that from 38% to 48% of the general public like the new Quality Cola, and we are 98% confident of the bounds. If we take a number of samples, we will be in error about 2% of the time.

Notice that the higher confidence level gives a wider spread of the error bounds. In order to obtain a higher level of confidence, we must widen the bounds on the error.

Procedure for Computing
Error Bounds
for a Proportion

Let n be the sample size and p the proportion of the sample that respond favorably.

1. Decide on the confidence level to be used, and write it as a decimal c.
2. Compute $A = \frac{c}{2}$. This corresponds to the area under the normal curve between $z = 0$ and the z-score that corresponds to an area equal to A. (A is the same as that found in the normal distribution table.)
3. Find the value of z in Table 7–1 that corresponds to A.
4. Compute the standard error:

$$SE = \sqrt{\frac{p(1 - p)}{n}}$$

5. Compute the maximum error:

$$E = z \times SE = z \times \sqrt{\frac{p(1-p)}{n}}$$

6. Compute the upper and lower limits:

$$p + E \qquad \text{and} \qquad p - E$$

7. Then c, the confidence level, is the probability that the true proportion of the *total* population lies in the interval

$$p - E < x < p + E$$

EXAMPLE 1   *(Compare Exercise 1)*

Compute the error bounds for the proportion $p = 0.55$ obtained from a sample of size $n = 120$. Use the 95% confidence level.

SOLUTION   The steps for the procedure give:

1. $n = 120$, $p = 0.55$, and $c = 0.95$;

2. $A = \dfrac{0.95}{2} = 0.475$;

3. The value of z that corresponds to $A = 0.475$ is $z = 1.96$;

4. $SE = \sqrt{\dfrac{(0.55)(0.45)}{120}} = \sqrt{0.0020625} = 0.045$;

5. $E = z \times SE = 1.96 \times 0.045 = 0.0882$;

6. The upper and lower bounds of the proportion are

$$0.55 + 0.0882 = 0.6382$$
$$0.55 - 0.0882 = 0.4618$$

and the confidence interval is

$$0.4618 < x < 0.6382$$

EXAMPLE 2   *(Compare Exercise 9)*

A marketing class made a random selection of 150 shoppers at a shopping mall to participate in a taste test of different brands of coffee. The class found that 54 shoppers preferred Brand X. Find, at the 95% confidence level, the error bounds of the proportion of shoppers who prefer Brand X.

SOLUTION   For this problem, $n = 150$, $p = \frac{54}{150} = 0.36$, and $c = 0.95$. Then

$$A = \frac{0.95}{2} = 0.475$$

$z = 1.96$ corresponds to $A = 0.475$ in Table 7–1

$$SE = \sqrt{\frac{(0.36)(0.64)}{150}} = \sqrt{0.001536} = 0.0392$$

$$E = 1.96(0.0392) = 0.0768$$

The bounds are

$$0.36 + 0.0768 = 0.4368$$

and

$$0.36 - 0.0768 = 0.2832$$

The confidence interval is $0.2832 < x < 0.4368$.

The marketing class is 95% confident that between 28.32% and 43.68% of all shoppers prefer Brand X. (Or we may say that the probability is .95 that the proportion of the population who prefer Brand X is in the interval $0.2832 < x < 0.4368$.)

EXAMPLE 3   *(Compare Exercise 11)*

Suppose that the sample in Example 2 was $n = 500$ in size but the proportion remained the same. Compute the error bounds of the proportion.

SOLUTION   Now $n = 500$, $p = 0.36$, and $c = 0.95$. We still have $z = 1.96$, but

$$SE = \sqrt{\frac{(0.36)(0.64)}{500}} = \sqrt{0.0004608} = 0.0215$$

Then $E = 1.96 \times (0.0215) = 0.0421$, and the upper and lower bounds are

$$0.36 + 0.0421 = 0.4021 \qquad \text{and} \qquad 0.36 - 0.0421 = 0.3179$$

and the confidence interval is

$$0.3179 < x < 0.4021$$

Notice that this confidence interval is smaller, so the sample proportion is a better estimate of the total population. It is generally true that a larger sample size reduces the maximum error. The sample size that will keep the maximum error to a specified level can be determined.

EXAMPLE 4

A random sample of 200 people shows that 46 of them use No-Plaque toothpaste. On the basis of a 98% confidence level, estimate the proportion of the general population that uses the toothpaste.

SOLUTION   For this sample,

$$n = 200, \quad p = \frac{46}{200} = 0.23, \quad c = 0.98, \quad A = 0.49, \quad z = 2.33$$

$$SE = \sqrt{\frac{(0.23)(0.77)}{200}} = 0.02976$$

$$E = 2.33(0.02976) = 0.0693$$

Then the interval that contains the proportion of the general population is from $0.23 - 0.0693 = 0.1607$ to $0.23 + 0.0693 = 0.2993$. We conclude, with 98% confidence, that about 16% to 30% of the population use No-Plaque toothpaste.

EXAMPLE 5   (Compare Exercise 15)

A random sample of 25 shoppers showed that 24% shopped at Cox's Department store. Find a 90% confidence interval of the proportion of the general population that shop there.

SOLUTION

$$n = 25, \quad p = 0.24, \quad c = 0.90, \quad A = 0.45, \quad z = 1.65$$

$SE = \sqrt{0.007296} = 0.0854$, and $E = 0.1409$. (Be sure that you check these computations.) So the upper and lower bounds are

$$0.24 + 0.1409 = 0.3809$$

and

$$0.24 - 0.1409 = 0.0991$$

So the 90% confidence interval is $0.0991 < x < 0.3809$. Notice that this small sample yields a wide confidence interval.

EXAMPLE 6   (Compare Exercise 16)

KWTX television station wants an estimate of the proportion of the population that watches its late movie. The station wants the estimate to be correct within 5% at the 95% confidence level. How big a sample should it select?

SOLUTION   Basically, the television station wants a maximum error of 5%, written 0.05 in our computations, at the 95% confidence level.

Look at the computations to obtain E. They are

$$E = z\sqrt{\frac{p(1 - p)}{n}}$$

We are given $E = 0.05$, and we know that $z = 1.96$ for the 95% confidence level. We need to find n so that

$$0.05 = 1.96 \sqrt{\frac{p(1 - p)}{n}}$$

We face a dilemma. We need to know the value p so that we can solve for n. However, we find p from the sample. Thus it appears that we need p before we know the size of the sample, and we need the sample to find p. There is a way out of this vicious circle. It can be shown that the largest possible value of $p(1 - p)$ is 0.25 and occurs when $p = 0.5$. (*See Exercise 25.*) So if we use 0.25 for $p(1 - p)$, the value of E may be a little large and the resulting confidence interval a little larger than necessary, but we have erred on the safe side. We proceed using 0.25. Then

$$0.05 = 1.96 \sqrt{\frac{0.25}{n}}$$

Squaring both sides, we get

$$0.0025 = (1.96)^2 \frac{0.25}{n} = \frac{0.9604}{n}$$

Then

$$0.0025n = 0.9604$$

$$n = \frac{0.9604}{0.0025} = 384.16$$

A sample size of 385 will be sufficient to provide the desired maximum error. ∎

7–8 EXERCISES

I

Find the error bounds for the proportion given in Exercises 1 through 8.

1. (*See Example 1*) $p = 0.64$, $n = 140$, 95% confidence level

2. $p = 0.22$, sample size $= 60$, 90% confidence level

3. $p = 0.30$, sample size $= 50$, 90% confidence level

4. $p = 0.30$, sample size $= 50$, 95% confidence level

5. $p = 0.30$, sample size $= 50$, 98% confidence level

6. $p = 0.40$, $n = 300$, 95% confidence level

7. $p = 0.5$, $n = 400$, 95% confidence level

8. $p = 0.1$, $n = 1000$, 95% confidence level

II

9. (*See Example 2*) A survey of 300 people showed that 45% preferred Brand X cola. Find error bounds on the proportion of the population who prefer Brand X:
   (a) using the 90% confidence level.
   (b) using the 95% confidence level.

10. A survey of 450 people showed that 35% thought that inflation would decrease the next year. Find error bounds on the proportion of the population who think that inflation will decrease:
   (a) using the 95% confidence level.
   (b) using the 98% confidence level.

11. (*See Example 3*) A radar unit on an interstate found that 28% of the vehicles exceeded 60 mph. Find the error bounds on the proportion at the 95% confidence level if:
   (a) the number of vehicles checked was 200.
   (b) the number of vehicles checked was 400.

III

12. A random sample of freshmen transcripts revealed that 21% made lower than a C average their first semester. Find error bounds on the proportion at the 95% confidence level if:
   (a) the sample consisted of 275 freshmen.
   (b) the sample consisted of 500 freshmen.

13. (*See Example 4*) The Hillsboro High school paper reported that 243 students out of 300 surveyed cruise Main Street on Saturday nights. On the basis of a 98% confidence level, estimate the proportion of the high school population that cruise Main Street.

14. A health class found that 144 of 320 people surveyed were overweight by 5 pounds or more. On the basis of a 95% confidence level, estimate the proportion of the population that is overweight by 5 pounds or more.

15. (*See Example 5*) A random sample of 60 shoppers showed that 54% shopped at Nate Chadrow's Department Store. Find a 90% confidence interval of the proportion of the general population that shop there.

16. (*See Example 6*) A university food service wants to estimate the proportion of students who like its food. It wants the estimate to be correct within 6% at the 95% confidence level. How big a sample should it select?

17. A candidate for public office wants an estimate of the proportion of voters who will vote for her. She wants the estimate to be accurate within 1% (0.01) at the 95% confidence level.
   (a) How big a sample should be used?
   (b) If a 99% confidence level is desired, how big should the sample be?

18. A state highway department needs an estimate of the percentage of vehicles that exceed 60 mph on an interstate. How large a sample is needed if the maximum error of the estimate is no more than 2% at the 95% confidence level?

19. How big a sample should be taken to ensure a maximum error of 0.0785 in the estimate of the proportion of adults who smoke? Use a 95% confidence level.

20. A random check of 90 students at Classic College revealed that 40 of them did not know the location of the Reserve Room in the Library. Find error bounds on the proportion of Classic students who do not know where the Reserve Room is located. Use a 98% confidence level.

21. A survey of 100 adults showed that 60 of them drank coffee daily. Estimate the proportion of the adult population that drink coffee daily, and find error bounds at the 95% confidence level.

22. The manufacturer of Brand Y coffee wants to estimate the proportion of adults who prefer its coffee. How large a sample should it survey to estimate the proportion with an error of 5% or less. The manufacturer wants a 95% confidence level.

23. A Harris Poll taken in November 1986 showed that confidence in President Reagan slid sharply in the wake of the discovery of an arms deal with Iran. Based on 1252 telephone interviews, the poll showed that 43% gave Reagan a positive rating. Using a 95% confidence level, find the error bounds of this proportion.

24. A 1986 survey of 2000 families showed that 18% owned at least one handgun. Find the error bounds of this proportion using a 95% confidence level.

25. Show that $\frac{1}{4} \geq p(1 - p)$ and the largest value occurs when $p = \frac{1}{2}$. The steps that follow are an outline to the proof. Fill in the details and be sure that you understand the steps.
    1. $(1 - 2p)^2 \geq 0$
    2. $1 - 4p + 4p^2 \geq 0$
    3. $\frac{1}{4} \geq p - p^2$
    4. $\frac{1}{4} \geq p(1 - p)$
    5. When $p = \frac{1}{2}$, $p(1 - p) = \frac{1}{4}$

IMPORTANT TERMS

7-1
Frequency Table
Frequency Distribution
Histogram
Pie Chart
Discrete Data
Continuous Data
Relative Frequency

7-2
Measure of Central Tendency
Mean
Grouped Data
Median
Mode

7-3
Measures of Dispersion
Range
Standard Deviation

Variance
Deviation
Squared Deviation
Rank
Percentile

7-4
Random Variable
Discrete Variable
Continuous Variable
Probability Distribution

7-5
Expected Value
Variance of a Random Variable
Standard Deviation of a Random Variable

7-6
Normal Curve
Normal Distribution
Continuous Data

Discrete Data
Standard Normal Curve
z-Score
Probability and a Normal Distribution

7-7
Bernoulli Trials
Binomial Distribution
Mean of a Binomial Distribution
Variance of a Binomial Distribution
Standard Deviation of a Binomial Distribution
Estimating a Binomial Probability

7-8
Standard Error of a Proportion
Error Bounds
Confidence Level

REVIEW EXERCISES

1. Draw a histogram and a pie chart based on the following frequency table:

New Accounts Opened	Frequency
Monday	17
Tuesday	31
Wednesday	20
Thursday	14
Friday	8

2. Find the mean of 4, 6, -5, 12, 3, 2, and 9.

3. Find the median of:
   (a) 8, 12, 3, 5, 6, 3, and 9.
   (b) 4, 9, 16, 12, 3, 22, 1, and 95.
   (c) 3, -2, 6, 1, 4, and -3.

4. Find the mean for the following quiz data:

Score on Quiz	Frequency
0	2
1	3
2	6
3	9
4	2
5	4

5. Find the mean for the number of passengers in cars arriving at a play.

Number of Passengers in a Car	Frequency
1–2	54
3–4	32
5–6	12

6. Find the mean, median, and mode for the numbers 2, 8, 4, 3, 2, 9, 6, 2, and 7.

7. A shopper paid a total of $90.22 for his purchases. The mean price was $3.47. How many items did he purchase?

8. Find the variance and standard deviation for the numbers 8, 18, 10, 16, 3, and 11.

9. A professor selects three students each day. Let X be the random variable that represents the number who completed their homework. Give all possible values of X.

10. Professor Y asked her students to evaluate her teaching at the end of the semester. Their response to the statement "The tests were a good measure of my knowledge" were marked on a scale of 1 to 5 as follows.

Outcome	Random Variable X	Responses
Strongly agree	1	10
Agree	2	35
Neutral	3	30
Disagree	4	20
Strongly disagree	5	15

Find the probability distribution of X, and sketch its graph.

11. A store has a special on bread with a five-loaf limit. The probability distribution for sales is listed in the following table. Find the average number of loaves per customer.

Number of Loaves per Customer	Probability
0	0.05
1	0.20
2	0.15
3	0.20
4	0.25
5	0.15

12. Find the expected value and variance for the following probability distribution:

X	$P(X)$
1	.14
2	.06
3	.22
4	.15
5	.36
6	.07

13. An instructor summarized his student ratings (scale of 1 to 5) in the following probability distribution:

Response	X	Probability
Excellent	1	.20
Good	2	.32
Average	3	.21
Fair	4	.15
Poor	5	.12

What is his expected average rating?

14. A normal distribution has a mean of 80 and a standard deviation of 6. Find the fraction of scores:
    (a) between 80 and 88.
    (b) between 70 and 84.
    (c) greater than 90.

15. A distributor averages sales of 350 mopeds per month with a standard deviation of 25. Assume that sales follow a normal distribution. What is the probability that sales will exceed 400 during the next month?

16. A construction company contracts to build an apartment complex. The total construction time follows a normal distribution with an average time of 120 days and a standard deviation of 15 days.
    (a) The company will suffer a penalty if construction is not completed within 140 days. What is the probability that it will be assessed the penalty?
    (b) The company will be given a nice bonus if it completes construction in less than 112 days. What is the probability that it will receive the bonus?
    (c) What is the probability that the construction will be completed in 115 to 130 days?

17. Find the binomial distribution for $n = 4$ and $p = 0.25$.

18. A binomial distribution has $n = 22$ and $p = 0.35$. Find the mean and standard deviation of the distribution.

19. The probability that a new drug will cure a certain disease is .65. If it is administered to 80 patients, estimate:
    (a) the probability that it will cure more than 50 patients.
    (b) the probability that it will cure 65 patients.
    (c) the probability that it will cure more than 55 and fewer than 60 patients.

20. For a set of scores, the mean = 240 and $\sigma = 10$.
    (a) Find z for the score 252.
    (b) Find z for the score 230.
    (c) Find the score corresponding to $z = -2.3$.

21. In a cross-country ski race, a skier came in 43rd in a field of 216 skiers. What was her percentile?

22. A brother and sister took two different standardized tests. He scored 114 on a test that had a mean of 100 and a standard deviation of 18. She scored 85 on a test that had a mean of 72 and a standard deviation of 12. Which one had the better score?

23. The housing office measures the congeniality of incoming students with a test scored 1–5. A higher score indicates a higher level of congeniality. A summary of 800 tests is the following:

X (score)	Number Receiving Score
1	20
2	160
3	370
4	215
5	35

On the basis of this information determine a probability distribution of X.

24. A number is drawn at random from $\{1, 2, 3, 4, 5, 6, 7\}$.
    (a) A random variable X has the value $X = 0$ when the number drawn is even and $X = 1$ when the number is odd. Find the probability distribution of X.
    (b) The number drawn is divided by 3 and the remainder is a value of a random variable X. Find the probability distribution of X.

25. Three papers in a creative writing class were graded A and five graded B. The professor selects three of them to read to the class. Let the random variable, X, be the number of A papers selected. List the possible values of X and give the number of possible outcomes that can be associated with each value.

26. A chemistry teacher gives a challenge problem for each meeting of a class of 19 students. A random variable, X, is the number of students who work the challenge problem. What are the possible values of X?

27. A die is rolled, and the player receives, in dollars, the number rolled on the die or $3, whichever is smaller. Let X be the number of dollars received. Determine the number of different ways in which each can occur.

28. A store ran a special on six-pack cartons of Cola, with a maximum of four allowed. A Cola representative recorded the number purchased by each customer. The results are summarized as follows:

Number of Cartons	Frequency
0	85
1	146
2	268
3	204
4	122

Find the mean number of cartons purchased.

29. Find the mean score of the following grouped data:

Score	Frequency
0–6	8
7–10	13
11–14	6
15–20	15

30. Roy bought four textbooks for a mean price of $34.60, and Rhonda bought three textbooks for a mean price of $29.70. Find the mean price of the seven books.

31. Compute the standard error for the given sample sizes and proportions:
   (a) $n = 50$, $p = 0.45$
   (b) $n = 100$, $p = 0.32$
   (c) $n = 400$, $p = 0.20$

32. Compute the error bounds for the following:
   (a) $n = 50$, $p = 0.45$, 95% confidence level
   (b) $n = 100$, $p = 0.30$, 98% confidence level

33. A survey of 30 individuals revealed that 22 watched Monday Night Football. Find, at the 95% confidence level, the error bounds of the proportion who watch Monday Night Football.

34. A manufacturer wants an estimate of the proportion of customers who will respond favorably to its new product. The manufacturer wants the estimate to be correct within 3% at the 95% confidence level. How big a sample should it select?

8

Mathematics of Finance

Simple Interest
Compound Interest
Annuities and Sinking Funds
Present Value of an Annuity and Amortization

*O*UR MODERN ECONOMY DEPENDS on borrowed money. Very few families would own a house, and many would not have a car, if it were not for credit. Business depends on borrowed money for day-to-day operations and for long-term expansion. Government at all levels borrows money. Banks depend on loans for a major source of their income.

"Rented money" is more accurate than "borrowed money" because you pay **interest** on borrowed money. Interest is the fee you pay to use, or "rent" money for a period of time.

When you place money in a savings account, you are in effect renting, or loaning, your money to the bank, and they pay you interest for the use of the money. In turn, they loan the money to someone who pays them interest for the use of the money.

8–1 SIMPLE INTEREST

- *Simple Interest*
- *Future Value*
- *Simple Discount*
- *Treasury Bills*

SIMPLE INTEREST

The fee charged for use of money may be determined in a number of ways. We first look at **simple interest.** It is most often used for loans of shorter duration.

The money borrowed in a loan is called the **principal.** The number of dollars received by the borrower is the **present value.** In a simple interest loan, the principal and present value are the same. The fee for a simple interest loan is usually expressed as a percent of the principal per year and is called the **interest rate.** If the interest rate is 10% per year, then each year the borrower pays 10% of the amount borrowed. The total fee, interest, paid for a simple interest loan is given by the following formula.

Simple Interest $I = Prt$

where

P = principal (amount borrowed)
r = interest rate per time period (expressed in decimal form)
t = number of time periods

An interest rate may be stated as 10% per year, 1% per month, or in terms of other time units. Sometimes no time units are specified. In such cases it is understood that the time unit is years. A statement that the interest rate is 12% should be interpreted as 12% *per year*. The time period will be stated when it is not annual.

EXAMPLE 1   *(Compare Exercise 1)*

Compute the interest paid on a loan of $1400 at a 9% interest rate for 18 months.

SOLUTION

$$P = \$1400$$

$$r = 9\% = 0.09 \text{ in decimal form}$$

$$t = 18 \text{ months} = \frac{18}{12} \text{ years} = 1.5 \text{ years}$$

$$I = 1400 \times 0.09 \times 1.5 = 189$$

So the interest paid is $189.

CAUTION   The time units for r and t must be consistent, so the number of months was converted to years.

EXAMPLE 2   *(Compare Exercise 11)*

An individual borrows $300 for six months at 1% simple interest per month. How much interest is paid?

SOLUTION   Notice that the interest rate is given as 1% *per month*. We can still use the $I = Prt$ formula provided that r and t are consistent in time units, in this case months.

$$I = 300 \times 0.01 \times 6 = \$18$$

EXAMPLE 3   *(Compare Exercise 14)*

Jose borrows money at 8% for two years. He paid $124 interest. How much did he borrow?

SOLUTION   In this case, $I = 124$, $r = 0.08$, and $t = 2$, so

$$124 = P(0.08)(2) = 0.16P$$

$$P = \frac{124}{0.16} = 775$$

The loan was $775.

EXAMPLE 4   *(Compare Exercise 18)*

Jane borrowed $950 for 15 months. The interest was $83.13. Find the interest rate.

SOLUTION   We are given $P = 950$, $t = \frac{15}{12} = 1.25$ years, and $I = 83.13$, so

$$83.13 = 950r(1.25)$$
$$= 1187.5r$$
$$r = \frac{83.13}{1187.5} = 0.07$$

So the interest rate was 7% per year.

FUTURE VALUE

A loan made at simple interest requires the borrower to pay back the sum borrowed (principal) plus the interest. This total, $P + I$, is called the **future value** or **amount** of the loan.

Amount or Future Value of a Loan

$$A = P + I$$
$$= P + Prt$$
$$= P(1 + rt)$$

where

$P =$ principal, or present value
$r =$ annual interest rate
$t =$ time in years
$A =$ amount, or future value

EXAMPLE 5   *(Compare Exercise 22)*

Find the amount (future value) of a $2400 loan for nine months at 11% interest rate.

SOLUTION   We know that $P = 2400$, $r = 0.11$, and $t = \frac{9}{12} = 0.75$ years, so

$$I = 2400(0.11)(0.75) = 198$$

and

$$A = 2400 + 198 = 2598$$

We can also use the formula for $A = P(1 + rt)$ and compute A as

$$A = 2400(1 + 0.11(0.75))$$
$$= 2400(1 + 0.0825)$$
$$= 2400(1.0825)$$
$$= 2598$$

The total of principal and interest is $2598.

EXAMPLE 6   *(Compare Exercise 26)*

How much should you invest at 12% for 21 months to have $3000 at the end of the 21 months?

SOLUTION   In this example you are given the future value, $3000, and are asked to find the present value, P. We know that $r = 0.12$, $t = \frac{21}{12} = 1.75$ years, and $A = 3000$. Then

$$3000 = P(1 + 0.12(1.75))$$
$$= P(1 + 0.21)$$
$$= 1.21P$$

so $P = \frac{3000}{1.21} = \$2479.34$ (rounded to nearest cent).

EXAMPLE 7   *(Compare Exercise 47)*

Your friend loaned some money. The debtor is scheduled to pay him $560 in four months. (The future value is $560.) Your friend needs the money now, so you agree to pay him $525 for the note, and the debtor will pay you the $560 in four months. What annual interest rate will you earn?

SOLUTION   For the purposes of this problem, $A = 560$, $P = 525$, and $t = 4$ months $= \frac{1}{3}$ year. Using the formula $A = P + Prt$, we have

$$560 = 525 + 525r\left(\frac{1}{3}\right)$$
$$= 525 + 175r$$
$$35 = 175r$$
$$r = \frac{35}{175} = .20$$

You will earn 20% annual interest.

SIMPLE DISCOUNT

The borrower of a simple interest loan receives the full amount of the principal and pays the interest at the end of the loan. Some loans deduct the interest from the principal at the time the loan is made, so the borrower receives less than the principal. This type of loan is a **simple discount** note. For example, if someone borrows $600 for one year at 9% interest, the lender will retain 9% of $600, $54, as the **discount** and give the borrower $546, the **proceeds.** The borrower is required to repay $600, the **maturity value,** at the end of the year.

This differs from simple interest in that the principal is the future value (maturity value) and the present value (proceeds) is less than the principal. The **discount rate** plays the same role as the interest rate except that the discount rate is applied to the maturity value. Let's compare a 12% simple interest loan and a 12% discount loan.

On a $1000 simple interest loan at 12%, the borrower receives $1000 and pays $1120 at the end of one year ($1000 principal plus $120 interest).

On a $1000 simple discount loan at 12%, the borrower receives $880 and pays $1000 at the end of one year. The $120 interest is deducted from $1000 before the borrower receives the money. The interest is computed on the principal (what the borrower receives) on a simple interest loan. For a simple discount loan, the interest is computed on the maturity value (what the borrower pays back).

Simple Discount	$$D = Mdt$$
	$$PR = M - D$$
	$$= M - Mdt$$
	$$= M(1 - dt)$$

where

$$M = \text{maturity value (principal)}$$
$$d = \text{discount rate, written decimal form}$$
$$t = \text{time}$$
$$D = \text{discount}$$
$$PR = \text{proceeds, the amount the borrower receives}$$

EXAMPLE 8   *(Compare Exercise 29)*

Find the discount and the amount a borrower receives (proceeds) on a $1500 simple discount loan at 8% discount rate for 1.5 years.

SOLUTION   In this case, $M = 1500$, $d = 0.08$, and $t = 1.5$ years. Then

$$d = 1500(0.08)(1.5)$$
$$= 180$$
$$PR = 1500 - 180$$
$$= 1320$$

so the bank keeps the discount, $180, and the borrower receives $1320.

EXAMPLE 9

A customer borrows money from a bank that gives simple discount loans. The customer needs $4500. How much should he borrow (maturity value) at 11% for two years so that the proceeds will be $4500?

SOLUTION The information gives $PR = 4500$, $d = 0.11$, and $t = 2$, so using the formula

$$PR = M(1 - dt)$$

we get

$$4500 = M(1 - 0.11(2))$$
$$= M(1 - 0.22)$$
$$= 0.78M$$

so

$$M = \frac{4500}{0.78} = 5769.23 \qquad \text{(Rounded to two decimals)}$$

The customer should borrow $5769.23.

If a customer has the choice between a simple interest and a simple discount loan, which is better? The following example gives an answer.

EXAMPLE 10 *(Compare Exercise 52)*

A discount note for $800 is made at a 10% discount rate for three months. The discount is

$$D = 800(0.10)\frac{3}{12}$$
$$= 20$$

so the borrower gets $780.

If the borrower had obtained $780 at simple interest, how much interest would be paid?

SOLUTION The simple interest is

$$I = 780(0.10)\left(\frac{3}{12}\right) = 19.50$$

This illustrates a general fact that, for the same amount received by the borrower, the simple interest paid is less than the discount paid.

TREASURY BILLS

Treasury bills are short-term securities issued by the federal government. The bills do not specify a rate of interest. They are sold at weekly public auctions with financial institutions making competitive bids. For example, a bank may bid $978,300 for a 90-day $1 million treasury bill. At the end of 90 days the bank receives $1 million, which covers the cost of the bill and interest earned on the bill. This is basically a simple discount transaction.

EXAMPLE 11

A bank wants to earn 7.5% simple discount interest on a 90-day $1 million treasury bill. How much should it bid?

SOLUTION   We are given the maturity value, $M = 1,000,000$, the discount rate, $d = 0.075$, and the time, $t = \frac{90}{360}$. (Banks often use 360 days per year when computing daily interest.) We want to find the proceeds, PR.

Substituting these in the simple discount formula, we get

$$PR = 1,000,000\left(1 - (0.075)\frac{90}{360}\right)$$
$$= 1,000,000(1 - 0.01875)$$
$$= 1,000,000(0.98125)$$
$$= 981,250$$

So the bank should bid $981,250.

EXAMPLE 12

A bank paid $983,000 for a 90-day $1 million treasury bill. Find the simple discount rate.

SOLUTION   We are given $M = 1,000,000$, $PR = 983,000$, and $t = \frac{90}{360}$. We want to find d.

$$983,000 = 1,000,000\left(1 - d\left(\frac{90}{360}\right)\right)$$
$$= 1,000,000 - 250,000d$$
$$-17,000 = -250,000d$$
$$d = \frac{17,000}{250,000} = 0.068$$

So the annual discount rate was 6.8%.

8-1 EXERCISES

I

1. (*See Example 1*) Compute the interest on a loan of $1100 at 8% interest rate for nine months.

Compute *I* for Exercises 2 through 5.

2. $P = \$2300, r = 9\%, t = 1.25$ years
3. $P = \$600, r = 10\%, t = 18$ months
4. $P = \$4200, r = 8\%, t = 16$ months
5. $P = \$745, r = 8.5\%, t = 6$ months

6. Compute the simple interest on $500 for one year at 7%.

7. Compute the simple interest and the amount for $300 at 6% for one year.

8. Compute the simple interest on $400 at 6% for three months.

9. Jones borrows $500 for three years at 8% simple interest (annual rate). How much interest will be paid?

10. Smith borrows $250 at 9% (annual rate) for three months. How much interest will be paid?

11. (*See Example 2*) Mrs. Witkowski borrows $700 for five months at 1.5% simple interest per month. How much interest will she pay?

12. $1450 is borrowed for three months at a 1.5% monthly rate. How much interest is paid?

13. How much interest is paid on a $950 loan for seven months at a 1.75% monthly rate?

How much was borrowed for the loans in Exercises 14 through 17?

14. (*See Example 3*) $I = \$24.19, r = 7.5\%, t = 9$ months
15. $I = \$42.90, r = 13\%, t = 6$ months

16. $I = \$38.00, r = 10\%, t = 10$ months
17. Matt paid $116.10 interest on a loan at 9% simple interest for 1.5 years. How much did he borrow?

Find the interest rate in Exercises 18 through 21.

18. (*See Example 4*) $P = \$650, I = \$91.00, t = 2$ years
19. $P = \$1140, I = \$49.40, t = 8$ months
20. $P = \$75, I = \$1.50, t = 2$ months
21. $P = \$5800, I = \$616.25, t = 1.25$ years

Find the amount (future value) of the loans in Exercises 22 through 25.

22. (*See Example 5*) $P = \$1800, r = 10.5\%, t = 7$ months
23. $P = \$2700, r = 8\%, t = 1.5$ years
24. $P = \$240, r = 12\%, t = 10$ months
25. $P = \$6500, r = 8.6\%, t = 1.75$ years

26. (*See Example 6*) How much should you invest at 11% for 16 months to have $3000 at the end of that period?

27. How much should be invested at 8% to have $1800 at the end of 1.5 years?

28. Sandi wants to buy a $400 television set in six months. How much should she invest at 7% simple interest now to have the money then?

Find the discount and the amount the borrower receives (proceeds) for the following discount loans.

29. (*See Example 8*) $M = \$1850, d = 7.5\%, t = 1$ year
30. $M = \$960, d = 10.25\%, t = 10$ months
31. $M = \$485, d = 13\%, t = 1.5$ years
32. $M = \$9540, d = 16.5\%, t = 8$ months

II

33. A sum of $5000 is borrowed for a period of three years at simple interest of 7%. Determine the total interest paid over this period.

34. A sum of $2000 is borrowed for a period of two years at simple interest of $5\frac{3}{4}\%$. Determine the total interest paid.

35. Determine the total simple interest paid on $50,000 over six years at the rate of 7.5%. The interest is to be paid back annually. Find the amount of each annual payment.

36. A sum of $4000 is borrowed for a period of three years at simple interest. The rate is 8% per annum to be paid semiannually (twice a year).
  (a) Determine the interest that is to be paid semiannually.
  (b) Compute the total interest that will be paid over the three-year period.

37. A sum of $100,000 is borrowed for a period of six years at 9% simple interest. The interest is to be paid monthly.
  (a) Determine the monthly interest payments.
  (b) Compute the total interest to be paid over the six-year period.

38. Joe borrowed $150 from a loan company. At the end of one month he paid off the loan with $163.50. What annual interest rate did he pay?

39. Kathy borrowed $800 at 6% interest. The amount of interest paid was $144. What was the length of the loan?

40. For how long did Amy borrow $1200 if she paid $112 in interest at a 7% interest rate?

41. How long will it take $800 to earn $18 at 9% simple interest?

42. A student borrows $200 at 6% simple interest (annual rate). When the loan is repaid, the amount of the principal and interest is $218. What was the length of the loan?

43. A boy borrowed some money from the bank at 7.5% simple interest for a year. He paid $48.75 in interest. How much money was loaned?

44. The Yeager family borrowed some money for 15 months (1.25 years). The interest rate was 9%, and they paid $9.90 in interest. How much did they borrow?

45. A family borrows $20,000 to buy a home. The interest rate is 9%, and each monthly payment is $179.95. How much of the first payment goes for interest and how much for principal?

46. Mr. O'Neill borrows $750 for four months at 12% interest. How much interest does he pay?

47. (*See Example 7*) You pay $860 for a loan that has a future value of $900 in six months. What annual interest rate will you earn?

48. How much should you pay for a loan that has a future value of $320 in three months to earn 9% simple interest?

49. (*See Example 9*) A grocer needs $6500 to stock her store. What should the amount of a simple discount loan be for her to receive proceeds of $6500 at 14% discount rate for one month?

50. A contractor needs to buy $16,000 worth of materials. He receives a simple discount loan for two months at 15% discount rate. What should be the principal of the loan so that he will receive the amount he needs?

51. A car dealer goes to the bank to obtain $38,000 to purchase some autos. The bank will give her a simple discount loan at 12% discount rate for three months. What maturity value should be used so that the dealer will receive $38,000?

52. (*See Example 10*) A discount note for $1000 is made at a 12% discount rate for six months.
  (a) What are the discount and proceeds?
  (b) How much interest would be paid on a simple interest loan for the amount of the proceeds for the same rate and time?

53. A woman goes to the bank to borrow $650 to pay some obligations. She may get either a simple interest or a simple discount loan at 8% for two months. What is the fee (interest or discount) paid in each case?

54. A mechanic borrowed $320 from a loan company and at the end of one month paid off the loan with $324.80. What simple interest rate did he pay?

55. A man borrowed $950. Six months later, he repaid the loan (principal and interest) with $1000. What simple interest rate did he pay?

56. Find the future value of a $1300 loan for 14 months at 9.5% simple interest.

III

57. A jeweler wants to obtain $3000 for four months. She has the choice of a simple interest loan at 10.3% or a discount loan at 10.1%. Which one will result in the lower fee for use of the money?

58. The low point in gross public debt was $38,000 in 1836. If the government paid 6% simple interest, how much were the annual interest payments?

59. The total government debt (federal, state, and local) in 1970 was $450 billion. How much interest was paid for one year if the interest rate averaged 11%?

60. In 1984 the estimated debts of the United States were:

> Government, $1780.7 billion
> Business and corporations, $3206.5 billion
> Individuals, $2133.8 billion

Find the interest paid for one year:
(a) for government loans, assuming a 9% interest rate.
(b) for business and corporations, assuming a 10.5% interest rate.
(c) for individuals, assuming a 12% interest rate.
(d) for the total of all the above.

61. A city has raised $500,000 for the purpose of putting in a new sewer system. This money was raised by issuing bonds that mature after five years. The interest on the bonds is 9% per annum. Determine the total interest paid.

62. A city has sold $750,000 in bonds for the purpose of raising money to develop a transportation system. The interest on the bonds is to be paid annually at 7% simple interest over a period of five years. Determine the annual interest payments that will be made to the bondholders and the total interest that will have been paid over the five-year period.

63. A company has issued $400,000 in ten-year bonds that pay 8% simple interest. The interest is payable semiannually. Determine the amount of each semiannual payment and the total interest that will have been paid on the bonds.

64. An investment company bought $50,000 of three-year bonds at 7% in simple interest payable quarterly. Find the quarterly interest payment and the total interest paid over the three-year period.

65. (*See Example 11*) A bank wants to earn 7% simple discount interest on a 90-day $1 million treasury bill. How much should it pay?

66. How much should a bank pay for a 90-day $1 million treasury bill to earn 6.5% simple discount?

67. (*See Example 12*) A bank paid $982,000 for a 90-day $1 million treasury bill. What was the simple discount rate?

68. A bank paid $987,410 for a 90-day $1 million treasury bill. What was the simple discount rate?

69. How much should a bank bid on a 30-day $2 million treasury bill to receive 7.125% interest?

8–2 COMPOUND INTEREST

- *Compound Interest*
- *Present Value*
- *Doubling an Investment*
- *Effective Rate*

COMPOUND INTEREST   When you deposit money into a savings account, the bank will pay for the use of your money. Normally, the bank pays interest at specified periods of time, such as every three months. Unless instructed otherwise, the bank credits your account with the interest, and for the next time period the bank pays interest on the new total. This is called **compound interest.** Let's look at a simple example.

EXAMPLE 1   *(Compare Exercise 10)*

You put $1000 into an account that pays 8% annual interest. The bank will compute interest and add it to your account at the end of each year. This is called **compounding interest annually.** Here's how your account builds up. We use the formula $A = P(1 + rt)$, where $r = 0.08$ and $t = 1$.

END OF YEAR	BALANCE IN YOUR ACCOUNT
0 (start)	$1000.00
1	$1000(1.08) = 1080.00$
2	$1080(1.08) = 1166.40 = 1000(1.08)^2$
3	$1166.40(1.08) = 1259.71 = 1000(1.08)^3$
4	$1259.71(1.08) = 1360.49 = 1000(1.08)^4$
5	$1360.49(1.08) = 1469.33 = 1000(1.08)^5$

So at the end of five years the account has grown to $1469.33.

Notice how the pattern of growth involves powers of 1.08. This same pattern can be used to obtain the amount in the account after 10 years, 15 years, and so on. For example, the amount in the account at the end of ten years is $1000(1.08)^{10} = 1000(2.15892) = 2158.92$. In general,

Amount of Compound Interest   When P dollars is invested at an annual interest rate r, and the interest is compounded annually, the amount at the end of t years is

$$A = P(1 + r)^t$$

EXAMPLE 2   *(Compare Exercise 12)*

$800 is invested at 6%, and it is compounded annually. What is the amount in the account at the end of four years?
SOLUTION   Here, $P = 800$, $r = 0.06$, and $t = 4$, so

$$A = 800(1.06)^4 = 800(1.26248) = 1009.98$$

In the preceding examples, interest was compounded annually. Interest is often calculated and added to the principal at other regular intervals. The most common intervals are semiannually, quarterly, monthly, and daily.

The **interest rate per compound period** is the annual rate divided by the number of compound periods per year. An 8% annual rate becomes $8\%/4 = 2\%$ quarterly rate. Let's repeat Example 1 but compound the interest quarterly.

EXAMPLE 3

$1000 is invested at 8% annual rate. The interest is compounded quarterly. Find the amount in the account at the end of five years.

SOLUTION   Since interest is compounded quarterly, it must be computed every three months and added to the principal. The quarterly interest rate is 2%, so the computations are the following.

END OF QUARTER	AMOUNT IN ACCOUNT
0	1000.00
1	$1000(1.02) = 1020.00$
2	$1020(1.02) = 1040.40 = 1000(1.02)^2$
3	$1040.40(1.02) = 1061.21 = 1000(1.02)^3$
4	$1061.21(1.02) = 1082.43 = 1000(1.02)^4$

At this stage we have the amount at the end of one year. We will not continue for another 16 computations, but observe the pattern. At th end of ten quarters we correctly expect the amount to be $A = 1000(1.02)^{10}$. Since five years is 20 quarters, the amount at the end of five years is

$$A = 1000(1.02)^{20} = 1000(1.48595) = 1485.95$$

The number $(1.02)^{20} = 1.48595$ may be computed on a scientific calculator or obtained from a table. Notice that compounding quarterly gives an amount of $1485.95, which is larger than the amount $1469.33 obtained from compounding annually. The general formula for finding the amount after a specified number of compound periods is the following.

Compound Interest—
Amount (Future Value)

$$A = P(1 + i)^n$$

where

r = annual interest rate
m = number of times compounded per year
$i = r/m$ = the interest rate per period
n = the number of periods ($n = mt$, where t is the number of years)
A = amount (**future value**) at the end of n compound periods
P = principal (present value)

EXAMPLE 4   *(Compare Exercise 14)*

$800 is invested at 12% for two years. Find the amount at the end of two years if the interest is compounded:

(**a**) annually.   (**b**) semiannually.   (**c**) quarterly.

SOLUTION   In this example, $P = 800$, $r = 0.12$, and $t = 2$ years.

(a) $m = 1$, so $i = 0.12$, $n = 2$:

$$A = 800(1 + 0.12)^2 = 800(1.12)^2 = 800(1.2544) = 1003.52$$

(b) $m = 2$, so $i = \dfrac{0.12}{2} = 0.06$, $n = 4$:

$$A = 800(1 + 0.06)^4 = 800(1.06)^4 = 800(1.26248) = 1009.98$$

(c) $m = 4$, so $i = \dfrac{0.12}{4} = 0.03$, $n = 8$:

$$A = 800(1 + 0.03)^8 = 800(1.03)^8 = 800(1.26677) = 1013.42$$

The computation of numbers like $(1.03)^8$ and $(1.02)^{20}$ can be tedious if you don't have a scientific calculator. Table 8–1 is provided to ease the arithmetic. It lists the answers to the computations needed for a limited number of interest rates. Here's how you use it.

To compute $(1 + i)^n$, you need the values of i and n. Different values of i and n give different results. Table 8–1 has columns of answers for various values of i and n. The value of $(1.03)^8$ is found in the column headed $i = 0.03$. Look under the n heading until you find 8. Adjacent to 8 you will find 1.26677. This number is the answer to $(1.03)^8$. Find $(1.02)^{20}$ by looking under the $i = 0.02$ column to the entry where n is 20. There you should see 1.48595, the value of $(1.02)^{20}$.

Check the table to make sure that you find $(1.01)^{15} = 1.16097$, $(1.04)^{12} = 1.60103$, and $(1.025)^{24} = 1.80873$.

EXAMPLE 5   *(Compare Exercise 16)*

$2500 is invested at 10%, compounded quarterly. Find the amount at the end of eight years.

SOLUTION $P = 2500$, $m = 4$, $r = 0.10$, $i = \dfrac{0.10}{4} = .025$, $t = 8$, and $n = 4 \times 8 = 32$.

$$\begin{aligned} A &= 2500(1.025)^{32} \\ &= 2500(2.20376) \quad \text{(From Table 8–1)} \\ &= 5509.40 \end{aligned}$$

EXAMPLE 6   *(Compare Exercise 21)*

A department store charges 1% per month on the unpaid balance of a charge account. This means that 1% of the bill is added to the account each month it is unpaid. This makes it compound interest. A customer owes $135.00, and the bill is unpaid for four months. What is the amount of the bill at the end of four months?

TABLE 8–1. Compound Interest $A = (1 + i)^n$

Number of Periods n	.01	.015	.02	.025	.03	.04	.05	.06	.07	.075
1	1.01000	1.01500	1.02000	1.02500	1.03000	1.04000	1.05000	1.06000	1.07000	1.07500
2	1.02010	1.03022	1.04040	1.05063	1.06090	1.08160	1.10250	1.12360	1.14490	1.15563
3	1.03030	1.04568	1.06121	1.07689	1.09273	1.12486	1.15762	1.19102	1.22504	1.24230
4	1.04060	1.06136	1.08243	1.10381	1.12551	1.16986	1.21551	1.26248	1.31080	1.33547
5	1.05101	1.07728	1.10408	1.13141	1.15927	1.21665	1.27628	1.33823	1.40255	1.43563
6	1.06152	1.09344	1.12616	1.15969	1.19405	1.26532	1.34010	1.41852	1.50073	1.54330
7	1.07214	1.10984	1.14869	1.18869	1.22987	1.31593	1.40710	1.50363	1.60578	1.65905
8	1.08286	1.12649	1.17166	1.21840	1.26677	1.36857	1.47746	1.59385	1.71819	1.78348
9	1.09369	1.14339	1.19509	1.24886	1.30477	1.42331	1.55133	1.68948	1.83846	1.91724
10	1.10462	1.16054	1.21899	1.28008	1.34392	1.48024	1.62889	1.79085	1.96715	2.06103
11	1.11567	1.17795	1.24337	1.31209	1.38423	1.53945	1.71034	1.89830	2.10485	2.21561
12	1.12683	1.19562	1.26824	1.34489	1.42576	1.60103	1.79586	2.01220	2.25219	2.38178
13	1.13809	1.21355	1.29361	1.37851	1.46853	1.66507	1.88565	2.13293	2.40985	2.56041
14	1.14947	1.23176	1.31948	1.41297	1.51259	1.73168	1.97993	2.26090	2.57853	2.75244
15	1.16097	1.25023	1.34587	1.44830	1.55797	1.80094	2.07893	2.39656	2.75903	2.95888
16	1.17258	1.26899	1.37279	1.48451	1.60471	1.87298	2.18287	2.54035	2.95216	3.18079
17	1.18430	1.28802	1.40024	1.52162	1.65285	1.94790	2.29202	2.69277	3.15882	3.41935
18	1.19615	1.30734	1.42825	1.55966	1.70243	2.02582	2.40662	2.85434	3.37993	3.67580
19	1.20811	1.32695	1.45681	1.59865	1.75351	2.10685	2.52695	3.02560	3.61653	3.95149
20	1.22019	1.34686	1.48595	1.63862	1.80611	2.19112	2.65330	3.20714	3.86968	4.24785

Interest per period i

TABLE 8–1 *(continued)*

21	1.23239	1.36706	1.51567	1.67958	1.86029	2.27877	2.78596	3.39956	4.14056	4.56644
22	1.24472	1.38756	1.54598	1.72157	1.91610	2.36992	2.92526	3.60354	4.43040	4.90892
23	1.25716	1.40838	1.57690	1.76461	1.97359	2.46472	3.07152	3.81975	4.74053	5.27709
24	1.26973	1.42950	1.60844	1.80873	2.03279	2.56330	3.22510	4.04893	5.07237	5.67287
25	1.28243	1.45095	1.64061	1.85394	2.09378	2.66584	3.38635	4.29187	5.42743	6.09834
26	1.29526	1.47271	1.67342	1.90029	2.15659	2.77247	3.55567	4.54938	5.80735	6.55571
27	1.30821	1.49480	1.70689	1.94780	2.22129	2.88337	3.73346	4.82234	6.21387	7.04739
28	1.32129	1.51722	1.74102	1.99650	2.28793	2.99870	3.92013	5.11168	6.64884	7.57594
29	1.33450	1.53998	1.77584	2.04641	2.35657	3.11865	4.11614	5.41839	7.11426	8.14414
30	1.34785	1.56308	1.81136	2.09757	2.42726	3.24340	4.32194	5.74349	7.61225	8.75495
31	1.36133	1.58653	1.84759	2.15001	2.50008	3.37313	4.53804	6.08810	8.14511	9.41157
32	1.37494	1.61032	1.88454	2.20376	2.57508	3.50806	4.76494	6.45338	8.71527	10.11744
33	1.38869	1.63448	1.92223	2.25885	2.65234	3.64838	5.00319	6.84059	9.32534	10.87625
34	1.40258	1.65900	1.96068	2.31532	2.73191	3.79432	5.25335	7.25102	9.97811	11.69196
35	1.41660	1.68388	1.99989	2.37321	2.81386	3.94609	5.51602	7.68608	10.67658	12.56886
36	1.43077	1.70914	2.03989	2.43254	2.89828	4.10393	5.79182	8.14725	11.42394	13.51153
37	1.44508	1.73478	2.08068	2.49335	2.98523	4.26809	6.08141	8.63608	12.22361	14.52489
38	1.45953	1.76080	2.12230	2.55568	3.07478	4.43881	6.33548	9.15425	13.07927	15.61426
39	1.47412	1.78721	2.16474	2.61958	3.16703	4.61637	6.70475	9.70350	13.99481	16.78532
40	1.48886	1.81402	2.20804	2.68506	3.26204	4.80102	7.03999	10.28571	14.97445	18.04422

SOLUTION The interest rate is 1% per month and is compounded monthly. The value of i is then 0.01, and the number of periods is four. The amount of the bill is

$$A = 135(1.01)^4$$
$$= 135(1.04060)$$
$$= 140.48$$

Notice that i and n were given in this example, so they can be substituted directly into the formula.

PRESENT VALUE

The **present value** of an amount due at a specified time is the principal that must be invested now to accumulate the amount due.

EXAMPLE 7 *(Compare Exercise 25)*

How much should Josh invest at 8%, compounded quarterly, so that he will have $5000 at the end of seven years?

SOLUTION In this case we are given $A = 5000$, $r = 0.08$, $m = 4$, and $t = 7$. Then, $i = \dfrac{0.08}{4} = 0.02$ and $n = 4(7) = 28$. Using the compound interest formula, we have

$$5000 = P(1.02)^{28}$$
$$= 1.74102P$$

Solve the equation for P:

$$P = \frac{5000}{1.74102} = 2871.88$$

Josh should invest $2871.88 to have $5000 in seven years. In other words, the present value of $5000 due in seven years is $2871.88.

DOUBLING AN INVESTMENT

If you invest $1000 at 8% interest, compounded quarterly, how long will it be before your investment has doubled in value?

This is a compound interest problem with $P = 1000$, $A = 2000$, $r = 0.08$, and $m = 4$. The value of n is unknown. Use the compound interest formula with $i = 0.08/4 = 0.02$. We know all parts of the formula except the exponent n, so we can write

$$2000 = 1000(1.02)^n$$
$$2 = (1.02)^n$$

We want the value of n that makes this true, that is, the power of 1.02 that gives 2. We can find this in Table 8–1. Since we know that the answer to $(1.02)^n$ is 2, look for 2 in the *answer part* under the $i = 0.02$ column. The nearest numbers that you find are 1.99989 and 2.03989. These correspond to $n = 35$ and $n = 36$. Thus the value will certainly double when $n = 36$ time periods. Since the interest is compounded quarterly, $n = 36$ represents 36 quarters, or nine years.

Actually, the amount invested is irrelevant. If we use P and $2P$ in the formula, we have

$$2P = P(1.02)^n$$

and

$$2 = (1.02)^n$$

the same as for $P = 1000$. So any investment will double in value in nine years if the interest rate is 8% and is compounded quarterly.

EXAMPLE 8 *(Compare Exercise 35)*

An investor has visions of doubling his money in six years. What interest rate is required for him to do so if the investment draws interest compounded quarterly?

SOLUTION P dollars are invested in order to have $2P$ dollars in six years. The future value formula for interest compounded quarterly becomes

$$2P = P(1 + i)^{24}$$

where we wish to find i. We do not need to know the value of P because we can divide both sides by P and have $2 = (1 + i)^{24}$.

Again, we know the answer, 2, in Table 8–1, and we know that we look in the row for $n = 24$. We don't know which column, but we can look for 2 in the row for $n = 24$. The column for $i = 0.03$ gives 2.03279, so we conclude that 3% quarterly interest (12% annual interest) will double an investor's money in six years.

———∎

EFFECTIVE RATE

For a given annual rate, a more frequent compounding of interest gives a larger value of an investment at the end of the year. A 10% annual rate, compounded monthly, gives a larger amount at the end of the year than does 10%, compounded semiannually. However, a lower rate, compounded more frequently, may or may not give a larger return. For example, which yields the better return, 9% compounded semiannually or 8.9% compounded quarterly? To answer this, let's assume that $1000 is invested in each case and compute the amount at the end of one year.

1. $r = 9\%$ compounded semiannually.

Let $P = 1000$, $t = 1$ year, $m = 2$, and $i = \dfrac{0.09}{2} = 0.045$. Then

$$A = 1000(1.045)^2 = 1000(1.09203)$$
$$= 1092.03$$

(Use your calculator to find $(1.045)^2$; it isn't in the table.)

2. $r = 8.9\%$ compounded quarterly.

Let $P = 1000$, $t = 1$ year, $m = 4$, and $i = \dfrac{0.089}{4} = 0.02225$. Then

$$A = 1000(1.02225)^4 \qquad \text{(Use your calculator for } (1.02225)^4.\text{)}$$
$$= 1000(1.09201)$$
$$= 1092.01$$

Thus 9% compounded semiannually is a slightly better investment, but there is no significant difference.

Another way to put different rates and frequency of compounding on a comparable basis is to find the **effective rate.**

Definition **Effective Rate**	The **effective rate** of an annual interest rate r compounded m times per year is the simple interest rate that produces the same total value of the investment per year as the compound interest.

EXAMPLE 9   *(Compare Exercise 28)*

Find the effective rate of 8% compounded quarterly.

SOLUTION   If we invest P dollars, the amount of the investment at the end of the year is

$$A = P(1.02)^4$$

If we invest the same amount, P, at a simple interest rate, r, the amount of the investment at the end of the year is $A = P + Pr(1)$.

Now r is the unknown simple interest rate that gives the same amount A as does compound interest, so

$$P + Pr = P(1.02)^4$$

We can divide throughout by P to get

$$1 + r = (1.02)^4$$

and so

$$r = (1.02)^4 - 1$$
$$= 1.08243 - 1$$
$$= 0.08243$$

In percent form, $r = 8.243\%$ is the effective rate of 8% compounded quarterly.

This method works generally, so we can make the following statement.

Effective Rate   For money invested at an annual rate r and compounded m times per year, the effective rate x, in decimal form, is

$$x = (1 + i)^m - 1 \qquad \text{where} \qquad i = \frac{r}{m}$$

8-2 EXERCISES

I

1. Use a calculator to find the following:
   (a) $(1.07)^3$ (b) $(1.02)^5$ (c) $(1.015)^4$
   (d) $(1.035)^2$ (e) $(1.045)^4$ (f) $(1.025)^5$

2. Use Table 8–1 to find the following:
   (a) $(1.02)^{15}$ (b) $(1.03)^{25}$ (c) $(1.04)^8$
   (d) $(1.01)^{30}$ (e) $(1.025)^{18}$ (f) $(1.02)^5$

3. The annual interest rate is 15%. Find:
   (a) the semiannual interest rate.
   (b) the quarterly interest rate.
   (c) the monthly interest rate.

4. The annual interest rate is 9%. Find:
   (a) the semiannual interest rate.
   (b) the quarterly interest rate.
   (c) the monthly interest rate.

In Exercises 5 through 9, find (a) the final amounts and (b) the total interest earned on the original investment.

5. $4500 is invested at 7.5% compounded annually for six years.

6. $14,500 is invested at 8% compounded semiannually for three years.

7. $31,000 is invested at 7.5% compounded annually for eight years.

8. $3200 is invested at 10% compounded semiannually for five years.

9. $5000 is invested at 7% compounded annually for four years.

10. (*See Example 1*) A family deposits $1500 into an account that pays 6% compounded quarterly. Find the amount in the family's account at the end of each year for four years.

11. $800 is invested at 12% compounded quarterly. Find the amount at the end of the first four quarters.

12. (*See Example 2*) $2600 is invested at 7% compounded annually. What is the amount of the account at the end of three years?

13. $1800 is invested at 9% compounded semiannually. How much is in the account at the end of one year?

14. (*See Example 4*) $4500 is invested at 8% annual rate. Find the amount at the end of two years if the interest is compounded:
   (a) annually   (b) semiannually   (c) quarterly

15. $12,000 is invested at 10% interest. Find the amount at the end of three years if the interest is compounded:
   (a) annually   (b) semiannually   (c) quarterly

Find the amount at the end of the specified time in Exercises 16 through 19.

16. (*See Example 5*) $P = \$7000$, $r = 10\%$, $t = 4$ years, $m = 4$ (compounded quarterly)

17. $P = \$10,000$, $r = 12\%$, $t = 5$ years, $m = 4$

18. $P = \$550$, $r = 8\%$, $t = 4$ years, $m = 2$ (compounded semiannually)

19. $P = \$460$, $r = 10\%$, $t = 6$ months, $m = 12$ (compounded monthly)

II

20. $3500 is invested at 12% compounded quarterly. Find the amount at the end of six years.

21. (*See Example 6*) A loan shark charges 2% per month on the unpaid balance of a loan. A student's loan was for $640. He was unable to pay for six months. What was his loan balance at the end of six months?

22. A store has an interest rate of 1.5% per month on the unpaid balance of charge accounts. (Interest is compounded monthly.) A customer charges $60 but allows it to become four months overdue. What is the bill at that time?

23. Your bookstore charges 1% per month on your unpaid balance. You charge $32.75 for books. You do not pay the bill until four months have passed after the first billing. What is the bill that you owe after four months of accumulated interest?

24. The Brunners fail to pay a bill for items they charged. If the original bill was $140 and the store charges 1.5% interest per month on the unpaid balance, what does the bill total when it is eight months overdue? (Interest is compounded monthly.)

25. (*See Example 7*) A woman buys an investment that pays 6% compounded semiannually. She wants $25,000 when she retires in 15 years. How much should she invest? (Find the present value.)

26. Hank and Gretel want to put money in a savings account now so that they will have $1800 in five years. The savings bank pays 6% interest compounded quarterly. How much should Hank and Gretel invest?

27. Alex wishes to have $3000 available to buy a car in four years. How much should he invest in a savings account now so that he will be able to do this? The bank pays 10% interest compounded quarterly.

28. (*See Example 9*) A savings company pays 8% interest compounded semiannually. What is the effective rate of interest?

29. What is the effective interest rate of 6% interest compounded semiannually?

30. What is the effective interest rate of 6% interest compounded quarterly?

How long does it take an investment to double for the interest rates given in Exercises 31 through 34?

31. 6% compounded semiannually

32. 10% compounded quarterly

33. 12% compounded quarterly

34. 8% compounded semiannually

35. (*See Example 8*) An investor wants to double her money in seven years. What interest rate, compounded quarterly, will enable her to do so?

36. How long will it take to increase an investment by 50% if it is invested at 1.5% per month, compounded monthly?

37. How long does it take to triple an investment if it draws 10% interest per annum and is compounded semiannually?

Exercises 38 through 41 require the use of a calculator.

38. $2400 is invested at 8.5% compounded quarterly. Find the amount at the end of 2.5 years.

39. A store charges 1.6% per month on the unpaid balance of a charge account. A bill of $260 is unpaid for five months. Find the amount of the bill at the end of five months.

40. How much should be invested at 7.6% compounded quarterly in order to have $12,000 at the end of five years?

41. Ken invested $1000 at 9.2% compounded quarterly, and Barb invested $1000 at 9.12% compounded monthly. Which one had the largest amount at the end of five years?

III

42. What interest rate enables an investor to obtain a 60% increase in an investment in three years if the interest is compounded quarterly?

In Exercises 43 through 45 determine which is the better investment.

43. 8.8% compounded semiannually or 8.6% compounded quarterly?

44. 7.2% compounded semiannually or 6.8% compounded quarterly?

45. 9.4% compounded annually or 9.2% compounded quarterly?

46. A credit union pays interest at 6% compounded semiannually on accounts totaling $275,000. It is considering compounding quarterly. How much would this increase the interest the credit union will pay in the period of one year?

47. Which is the better investment, 10.2% compounded annually or 10% compounded quarterly?

48. A loan company charges 36% a year compounded monthly for small loans. How long will it take to triple an amount of money?

49. A town increased in population 2% per year for ten years. If the population was 35,000 at the beginning, how much was it at the end of ten years?

50. The Acme Company's sales have been increasing 4% per year. If sales in the latest year were $600,000, what are they expected to be in five years if the trend continues?

51. On her 58th birthday a woman invests $15,000 in an account that pays 8% compounded quarterly. How much will be in her account when she retires on her 65th birthday?

52. An investment company advertises that an investment with them will yield 12% annual rate compounded monthly. Another firm advertises that its investments will yield 15% compounded semiannually. Which of these gives the better yield?

53. Daniel received a $1000 gift that he deposited in a savings bank that compounded interest quarterly. After five years of accumulating interest, the account had grown to $1485.95. What was the annual interest rate of the bank?

54. The cost of an average family house increased from $32,500 in 1975 to $52,950 in 1984. Determine approximately the average annual inflation in house prices over this ten-year period.

55. Jerri placed $500 in a credit union that compounded interest semiannually. Her account had grown to $633.39 after four years. What was the annual interest rate of the credit union?

56. The Martinelli family sells some property obtained from an inheritance. How much should they invest at 7% compounded annually in order to have $28,000 in six years?

57. Which should you choose—a savings account that starts with $6000 and earns interest at 10% compounded semiannually for ten years or a lump sum of $16,000 at the end of ten years?

58. On graduating from college, a student gets a job that pays $15,000 a year. If inflation is averaging 10%, what will he have to be making five years after graduation to keep pace with inflation? What will he have to make five years after graduation to increase his standard of living by 4%.

59. How long will it take $8000 to increase to $18,000 in an account that pays 6% compounded semiannually?

60. A company acquires an asset and signs an agreement to pay $10,000 for it in three years time. The interest rate is to be 10% compounded semiannually. What is the current market value of the asset to the company?

61. A company will need $240,000 cash to modernize machinery in five years time. A financial institution will invest the company's money in a fund at 8% interest compounded semiannually. Determine the cash that must be deposited at present to meet this need.

8–3 ANNUITIES AND SINKING FUNDS

- *Ordinary Annuity*
- *Sinking Funds*

ORDINARY ANNUITY

A series of equal payments like monthly house payments, installment payments, premiums on life insurance, and regular monthly deposits in a credit union are examples of **annuities.** In general, equal payments paid at equal time intervals form an **annuity.** The time between successive payments is the **payment period** and the amount of each payment is the **periodic payment.** Interest on an annuity is compound interest. Payments may be paid annually, quarterly, monthly, or at any specified time interval. We will study the **ordinary annuity.**

Ordinary Annuity	An **ordinary annuity** is an annuity with periodic payments made at the *end* of each period.

EXAMPLE 1   *(Compare Exercise 1)*

A family enters a savings plan whereby they will invest $1000 at the end of each year for five years. The annuity will pay 7% interest, compounded annually. Find the value of the annuity at the end of the five years.

SOLUTION   Since $1000 is deposited each year, the first deposit will draw interest longer than subsequent deposits. The value of each deposit at the end of five years is the original $1000 plus the compound interest for the time it draws interest. Use the formula for the amount at compound interest. Here is a summary of how payments of $1000 deposited at the end of each year grow over a five-year period. The interest rate, $r = 0.07$, is compounded annually.

YEAR DEPOSITED	LENGTH OF TIME DEPOSIT DRAWS INTEREST	VALUE OF DEPOSIT AT END OF FIVE YEARS
1	4 years	$1000(1.07)^4 = 1310.80$
2	3 years	$1000(1.07)^3 = 1225.04$
3	2 years	$1000(1.07)^2 = 1144.90$
4	1 year	$1000(1.07) = 1070.00$
5	0 year	$1000(1) = \underline{1000.00}$
		Final value: 5750.74

The final value is obtained by adding the five payments and the interest accumulated on each one. The final value is called the **amount** or **future value** of the annuity.

Clearly, computing this total period-by-period can be tedious if the annuity runs for a number of periods. A formula for computing the future value of an annuity helps to ease the computations.

Future Value (Amount) of an Ordinary Annuity (Payments Are Made at the End of Each Period)

$$A = RS$$

where

$$S = \frac{(1 + i)^n - 1}{i}$$

i = interest rate per period

n = number of periods

R = amount of each periodic payment

A = future value or amount

Historical note: The number S is traditionally denoted by $s_{\overline{n}|i}$ (read s sub n angle i). For simplicity we use S. You should be aware that the value of S depends on the interest rate and number of periods. See Appendix C for a derivation of S.

Applying this formula to Example 1, we have

$$S = \frac{(1 + 0.07)^5 - 1}{0.07} = \frac{(1.07)^5 - 1}{0.07} = \frac{1.4025517 - 1}{0.07}$$

$$= \frac{0.4025517}{0.07}$$

$$= 5.75074$$

So $A = 1000(5.75074) = \$5750.74$.

Just as we have a table for computing values of compound interest, we have a table for computing future values of annuities. Table 8–2 gives values of S for selected values of n and i.

EXAMPLE 2

(a) To locate S for $i = 0.04$ and $n = 10$, look down the n column to 10 and then across to the 0.04 column. There you see 12.00611. This is the desired value of S.

(b) Deposits are made quarterly to an annuity for three years. The annual interest rate is 8%. In this case the periodic rate is $i = \frac{0.08}{4} = 0.02$, and the number of periods (quarters) is 12. So $S = 13.41209$ is found in the 0.02 column across from $n = 12$.

TABLE 8–2. Amount of an Ordinary Annuity $S = \dfrac{(1+i)^n - 1}{i}$

Interest per Period i

Number of Periods n	.01	.015	.02	.025	.03	.04	.05	.06	.07	.08	.09	.10
1	1.00000	1.00000	1.00000	1.00000	1.00000	1.00000	1.00000	1.00000	1.00000	1.00000	1.00000	1.00000
2	2.01000	2.01500	2.02000	2.02500	2.03000	2.04000	2.05000	2.06000	2.07000	2.08000	2.09000	2.10000
3	3.03010	3.04523	3.06040	3.07562	3.09090	3.12160	3.15250	3.18360	3.21490	3.24640	3.27810	3.31000
4	4.06040	4.09090	4.12161	4.15252	4.18363	4.24646	4.31012	4.37462	4.43994	4.50611	4.57313	4.64100
5	5.10100	5.15227	5.20404	5.25633	5.30914	5.41632	5.52563	5.63709	5.75074	5.86660	5.98471	6.10510
6	6.15201	6.22955	6.30812	6.38774	6.46841	6.63298	6.80191	6.97532	7.15329	7.33593	7.52333	7.71561
7	7.21354	7.32299	7.43428	7.54743	7.66246	7.89829	8.14201	8.39384	8.65402	8.92280	9.20043	9.48717
8	8.28567	8.43284	8.58297	8.73612	8.89234	9.21423	9.54911	9.89747	10.25980	10.63663	11.02847	11.43589
9	9.36853	9.55933	9.75463	9.95452	10.15911	10.58280	11.02656	11.49132	11.97799	12.48756	13.02104	13.57948
10	10.46221	10.70272	10.94972	11.20338	11.46388	12.00611	12.57789	13.18079	13.81645	14.48656	15.19293	15.93742
11	11.56683	11.86326	12.16872	12.48347	12.80780	13.48635	14.20679	14.97164	15.78360	16.64549	17.56029	18.53117
12	12.68250	13.04121	13.41209	13.79555	14.19203	15.02581	15.91713	16.86994	17.88845	18.97713	20.14072	21.38428
13	13.80933	14.23683	14.68033	15.14044	15.61779	16.62684	17.71298	18.88214	20.14064	21.49530	22.95338	24.52271
14	14.94742	15.45038	15.97394	16.51895	17.08632	18.29191	19.59863	21.01507	22.55049	24.21492	26.01919	27.97498
15	16.09690	16.68214	17.29342	17.93193	18.59891	20.02359	21.57856	23.27597	25.12902	27.15211	29.36092	31.77248
16	17.25786	17.93237	18.63929	19.38022	20.15688	21.82453	23.65749	25.67253	27.88805	30.32428	33.00340	35.94973
17	18.43044	19.20136	20.01207	20.86473	21.76159	23.69751	25.84037	28.21288	30.84022	33.75023	36.97370	40.54470
18	19.61475	20.48938	21.41231	22.38635	23.41444	25.64541	28.13238	30.90565	33.99903	37.45024	41.30134	45.59917
19	20.81090	21.79671	22.84056	23.94601	25.11687	27.67123	30.53900	33.75999	37.37896	41.44626	46.01846	51.15909
20	22.01900	23.12367	24.29737	25.54466	26.87037	29.77808	33.06595	36.78559	40.99549	45.76196	51.16012	57.27500
21	23.23919	24.47052	25.78332	27.18327	28.67649	31.96920	35.71925	39.99273	44.86518	50.42292	56.76453	64.00250
22	24.47159	25.83758	27.29898	28.86286	30.53678	34.24797	38.50521	43.39229	49.00574	55.45676	62.87334	71.40275
23	25.71630	27.22514	28.84496	30.58443	32.45288	36.61789	41.43048	46.99583	53.43614	60.89330	69.53194	79.54302
24	26.97346	28.63352	30.42186	32.34904	34.42647	39.08260	44.50200	50.81558	58.17667	66.76476	76.78981	88.49733
25	28.24320	30.06302	32.03030	34.15776	36.45926	41.64591	47.72710	54.86451	63.24904	73.10594	84.70090	98.34706

EXAMPLE 3   *(Compare Exercise 4)*

A family pays $800 at the end of each six months for seven years into an ordinary annuity paying 10%, compounded semiannually. Find the future value (amount) at the end of seven years.

SOLUTION   Since the payments are made semiannually, the periodic rate $i = \frac{0.10}{2} = 0.05$, the number of periods is 14, and the periodic payments are $R = 800$. Then the future value is $A = 800(19.59863) = \$15,678.90$, where S is obtained from Table 8–2.

SINKING FUNDS

When an amount of money will be needed at some future date, you can systematically accumulate a fund that will build to the desired amount at the time needed. Money accumulated in this way is called a **sinking fund.** A sinking fund is an annuity with the future value specified and the periodic payments unknown. The formula for future value still applies.

EXAMPLE 4   *(Compare Exercise 14)*

Susie wants to deposit her savings at the end of every three months so that she will have $7500 available in four years. The account will pay 8% interest per annum, compounded quarterly. How much should she deposit every quarter?

SOLUTION   Susie is accumulating a sinking fund with a future value of $7500, periodic rate $i = \frac{0.08}{4} = 0.02$, and $n = 16$ time periods. The formula for future value of an annuity can be used to find R, the periodic payments:

$$7500 = R(18.63929)$$
$$R = \frac{7500}{18.63929}$$
$$= 402.38$$

Susie should deposit $402.38 every quarter to accumulate the desired $7500.

The formula for periodic payments into a sinking fund is a variation of the future value formula for an annuity.

Formula for Periodic Payments of a Sinking Fund	$R = \dfrac{A}{S}$

where

A = value of the annuity after n payments

n = number of payments

i = periodic interest rate

S is obtained from Table 8–2 using i and n

R = amount of each periodic payment

EXAMPLE 5 (*Compare Exercise 20*)

A company expects to replace a $65,000 piece of equipment in ten years. The company establishes a sinking fund with annual payments. The fund draws 7% interest, compounded annually. What are these periodic payments?

SOLUTION $A = 65,000$, $i = 0.07$, and $n = 10$, so $S = 13.81645$.

$$R = \frac{65000}{13.81645}$$
$$= \$4704.54$$

8-3 EXERCISES

I

1. (*See Example 1*) $600 is deposited into an account at the end of each year for four years. The money earns 10% compounded annually. Determine the value of each deposit at the end of four years and the total in this account at that time.

2. A boy deposits $500 into an account at the end of each year for three years. The money earns 6% compounded annually. Determine the value of each deposit at the end of three years and the total amount in the account.

3. (*See Example 2*) Locate the value of S in Table 8–2 for the following:
   (a) $n = 15$, $i = 0.03$
   (b) $n = 20$, $i = 0.04$
   (c) 12% compounded quarterly for three years
   (d) 10% compounded semiannually for seven years
   (e) 12% compounded monthly for one year

In Exercises 4 through 13, determine the amount of the ordinary annuities at the end of the given periods.

4. (*See Example 3*) $1500 deposited annually at 8% for six years

5. $16,000 deposited annually at 7% for 15 years

6. $500 deposited annually at 10% for ten years

7. $250 deposited quarterly at 8% for five years

8. $300 deposited quarterly at 10% for six years

9. $200 deposited monthly at 1% per month for 20 months

10. $50 deposited per month at 1.5% per month for 15 months

11. $4,000 deposited semiannually at 8% for ten years

12. $800 deposited semiannually at 10% for eight years

13. $750 deposited quarterly at 12% for four years

In Exercises 14 through 19 the amount (future value) of an ordinary annuity is given. Find the periodic payments.

14. (*See Example 4*) $A = \$8000$, and the annuity earns 7% compounded annually for 15 years.

15. $A = \$2500$, and the annuity earns 9% compounded annually for four years.

16. $A = \$25,000$, and the annuity earns 8% compounded quarterly for four years.

17. $A = \$14,500$, and the annuity earns 10% compounded semiannually for ten years.

18. $A = \$50,000$, and the annuity earns 8% compounded semiannually for eight years.

19. $A = \$10,000$, and the annuity earns 10% compounded quarterly for three years.

In Exercises 20 through 23 the amount desired in a sinking fund is given. Find the periodic payments required to obtain the desired amount.

20. (*See Example 5*) $A = \$12,000$, the interest rate is 8%, and payments are made semiannually for five years.

21. $A = \$75,000$, the interest rate is 10%, and payments are made quarterly for four years.

22. $A = \$40,000$, the interest rate is 6%, and payments are made annually for eight years.

23. $A = \$15,000$, the interest rate is 12%, and payments are made monthly for 18 months.

II

24. An executive prepares for retirement by depositing $2500 into an annuity each year for ten years. The annuity earns 7% per year. Find the future value of the annuity at the end of ten years.

25. A young couple saves for a down payment on a house by depositing $100 each month into an annuity that pays a 12% annual rate. Find the amount in the annuity at the end of two years.

26. The Cooper Foundation contributes $25,000 per year into an annuity fund for building a new zoo. The fund earns 9% interest. Find the amount in the fund at the end of 15 years.

27. A couple pays $400 at the end of each six months for five years into an ordinary annuity paying 8% compounded semiannually. What is the future value at the end of five years?

28. A woman invests $2000 a year in a mutual fund for 20 years. If the market value of the fund increases 6% per year, what will be the value of her shares when she makes the twentieth payment?

29. Sam wants to invest the same amount at the end of every three months so that he will have $4000 in three years. The account will pay 6% compounded quarterly. How much should he deposit each quarter?

30. How much should a family deposit at the end of every six months in order to have $8000 at the end of five years? The account pays 6% interest compounded semiannually.

31. A 13-year-old child received an inheritance of $5000 per year. This was to be invested and allowed to accumulate until the child reached 21 years of age. The first payment was made on the child's thirteenth birthday and the last on the twenty-first birthday. If the money was invested at 7% compounded annually, what did the child receive at age 21?

32. A condominium association decided to set up a sinking fund to accumulate $50,000 by the end of four years to build a new sauna and swimming pool. What quarterly deposits are required if the annual interest rate is 8% and it is compounded quarterly?

33. A company projects that it will need to expand its plant in six years. It expects the expansion to cost $150,000. How much should it put into a sinking fund each year at 7% compounded annually?

III

34. The Citizen's Bank sets up a scholarship fund by making deposits of $1000 every six months into an annuity earning 8% interest. Find the amount of the annuity at the end of eleven years.

35. A city has issued bonds to finance a new convention center. The bonds have a total face value of $750,000 and are payable in eight years. A sinking fund has been opened to meet this obligation. If the interest rate on the fund is 8% compounded semiannually what will the semiannual payments be?

36. A couple plans to start a business of their own in six years. They plan to have $10,000 cash available at the time for this purpose. To raise the $10,000, a fund has been started that earns interest at 8% compounded quarterly. What would the quarterly payments into this fund have to be to raise the $10,000?

37. Electronic Instruments plans to establish a debt retirement fund. The company wants at least $23,800 in five years. Deposits of $4000 are to be made to a trustee each year. Compute an approximate interest rate for the fund on an annual compounding basis to meet these requirements.

38. A company requires each of two subsidiaries to make deposits into a debt retirement fund over the next three years. One subsidiary is to contribute $2000 quarterly, and the other is to contribute $6000 semiannually. Interest at 8% compounded quarterly and semiannually will be paid on the fund. Determine the amount of the fund at the end of three years.

39. A savings institution advertised "Invest $1000 a year for 10 years with us and we will pay you $1000 a year forever." (The institution pays an 8% interest rate compounded annually.)
    (a) What is the value of the investment at the end of ten years?
    (b) The investor ceases payments at the end of ten years, and the investment firm pays him 8% of his investment at the end of each year. How much interest will he receive at the end of each year?

40. (a) A young woman invested $2000 per year in an IRA each year for ten years. The interest rate was 7% compounded annually. At the end of ten years she ceased the IRA payments but left the total of her investment at 7% compounded annually for the next 25 years.
       (i) What was the value of her IRA investments at the end of ten years?
       (ii) What was the value of her investment at the end of the next 25 years? *Note:* $(1.07)^{25} = 5.42743$.
    (b) A friend of the young woman started his IRA investments the tenth year and invested $2000 per year for the next 25 years at 7% compounded annually. What was the value of his investment at the end of the 25 years?
    (c) Which of the two investments had the greater value at the end of the period?

Use your calculator and the amount of an annuity formula

$$A = RS = R\left[\frac{(1 + i)^n - 1}{i}\right]$$

to work Exercises 41 through 43.

41. $100 is deposited monthly into an annuity that earns 1.6% per month compounded monthly. Find the amount at the end of 30 months.

42. $500 is deposited quarterly into an annuity that earns 8.6% compounded quarterly. Find the amount of the annuity at the end of ten years.

43. Mr. Nakamura wants to make monthly deposits into an annuity for his grandchild so that $15,000 will be available in five years. If the interest rate is 9% compounded monthly, find the monthly deposit.

44. The Otwell Company puts $14,000 per year into a sinking fund to purchase major equipment. The fund earns 7.8% interest compounded annually. Find the amount in the fund after eight years.

45. The Hargis Company makes annual deposits into a sinking fund to expand facilities. If the fund pays 8.1% compounded annually, find the annual payments so that $100,000 is accumulated in six years.

8–4   PRESENT VALUE OF AN ANNUITY AND AMORTIZATION

- *Present Value*
- *Amortization*

PRESENT VALUE

We have presented an annuity as a sequence of payments made at regular intervals into an account. The object of an annuity is to accumulate an amount of money at a future date.

Let's look at two variations of this problem.

1. How much should be put into a savings account in one lump sum at compound interest so that the amount accumulated at the end of five years is the same as the amount accumulated by putting in $25 per month into a savings account?

   This lump sum payment that yields the same total amount as equal periodic payments made over the same period of time is called the **present value of the annuity.**

2. How much should be invested so that $100 can be withdrawn each month for five years and the account will be depleted at the end of five years?

Similar problems seek to find how much should be placed in a college fund so that a certain amount will be available each year or how much should be in a retirement fund to provide a monthly retirement benefit for 15 years.

The first problem, finding the present value of an annuity, is solved as follows.

Recall that the amount of an annuity is

$$A = RS = \frac{R((1 + i)^n - 1)}{i}$$

and the amount of compound interest is

$$A = P(1 + i)^n$$

where i is the periodic interest rate, n is the number of periods, R is the periodic payment for the annuity, and P is the lump sum invested at compound interest. We want to find P so that the amount of compound interest equals the amount of the annuity, that is,

$$P(1 + i)^n = \frac{R((1 + i)^n - 1)}{i}$$

Solving for P gives

$$P = \frac{R((1 + i)^n - 1)}{i(1 + i)^n}$$

We let

$$K = \frac{(1 + i)^n - 1}{i(1 + i)^n}$$

to obtain the formula for present value.

Present Value of an Annuity	$P = RK$

where

$$K = \frac{(1 + i)^n - 1}{i(1 + i)^n}$$

i = periodic rate

n = number of periods

R = periodic payments

P = present value of the annuity

Historical note: A common notation for K is $a_{\overline{n}|i}$; we use K for simplicity. In any given problem, K depends on the value of n and i. You may find the value K with a scientific calculator or from Table 8–3.

TABLE 8–3. Present Value of an Ordinary Annuity $K = \dfrac{(1+i)^n - 1}{i(1+i)^n}$

Interest per period i

Number of Periods n	.01	.015	.02	.025	.03	.04	.05	.06	.07	.08	.09	.10
1	.99010	.98522	.98039	.97561	.97087	.96154	.95238	.94340	.93458	.92593	.91743	.90909
2	1.97040	1.95588	1.94156	1.92742	1.91347	1.88609	1.85941	1.83339	1.87802	1.80802	1.75911	1.73554
3	2.94099	2.91220	2.88388	2.85602	2.82861	2.77509	2.72325	2.67301	2.62432	2.57710	2.53129	2.48685
4	3.90197	3.85438	3.80773	3.76197	3.71710	3.62990	3.54595	3.46511	3.38721	3.31213	3.23972	3.16987
5	4.85343	4.78264	4.71346	4.64583	4.57971	4.45182	4.32948	4.21236	4.10020	3.99271	3.88965	3.79079
6	5.79548	5.69719	5.60143	5.50813	5.41719	5.24214	5.07569	4.91732	4.76654	4.62288	4.48592	4.35526
7	6.72819	6.59821	6.47199	6.34939	6.23028	6.00205	5.78637	5.58238	5.38929	5.20637	5.03295	4.86842
8	7.65168	7.48593	7.32548	7.17014	7.01969	6.73274	6.46321	6.20979	5.97130	5.74664	5.53482	5.33493
9	8.56602	8.36052	8.16224	7.97087	7.78611	7.43533	7.10782	6.80169	6.51523	6.24689	5.99525	5.75902
10	9.47130	9.22218	8.98259	8.75206	8.53020	8.11090	7.72173	7.36009	7.02358	6.71008	6.41766	6.14457
11	10.36763	10.07112	9.78685	9.51421	9.25262	8.76048	8.30641	7.88687	7.49867	7.13896	6.80519	6.49508
12	11.25508	10.90750	10.57534	10.25776	9.95400	9.38507	8.86325	8.38384	7.94269	7.53608	7.16073	6.81369
13	12.13374	11.73153	11.34837	10.98318	10.63496	9.98565	9.39357	8.85268	8.35765	7.90378	7.48690	7.10336
14	13.00370	12.54338	12.10625	11.69091	11.29607	10.56312	9.89864	9.29498	8.74547	8.24424	7.78615	7.36669
15	13.86505	13.34323	12.84926	12.38138	11.93794	11.11839	10.37966	9.71225	9.10791	8.55948	8.06069	7.60608
16	14.71787	14.13126	13.57771	13.05500	12.56110	11.65230	10.83777	10.10590	9.44665	8.85137	8.31256	7.82371
17	15.56225	14.90765	14.29187	13.71220	13.16612	12.16567	11.27407	10.47726	9.76322	9.12164	8.54363	8.02155
18	16.39827	15.67256	14.99203	14.35336	13.75351	12.65930	11.68959	10.82760	10.05909	9.37189	8.75563	8.20141
19	17.22601	16.42617	15.67846	14.97889	14.32380	13.13394	12.08532	11.15812	10.33560	9.60360	8.95011	8.36492
20	18.04555	17.16864	16.35143	15.58916	14.87747	13.59033	12.46221	11.46992	10.59401	9.81815	9.12855	8.51356
21	18.85698	17.90014	17.01121	16.18455	15.41502	14.02916	12.82115	11.76408	10.83553	10.01680	9.29224	8.64869
22	19.66038	18.62082	17.65805	16.76541	15.93692	14.45112	13.16300	12.04158	11.06124	10.20074	9.44243	8.77154
23	20.45582	19.33086	18.29220	17.33211	16.44361	14.85684	13.48857	12.30338	11.27219	10.37106	9.58021	8.88322
24	21.24339	20.03041	18.91393	17.88499	16.93554	15.24696	13.79864	12.55036	11.46933	10.52876	9.70661	8.98474
25	22.02316	20.71961	19.52346	18.42438	17.41315	15.62208	14.09394	12.78336	11.65358	10.67478	9.82258	9.07704

EXAMPLE 1   *(Compare Exercise 1)*

Find K for $n = 7$ and $i = 0.04$ by looking in the $i = 0.04$ column across from $n = 7$. You find 6.00205.

For $r = 12\%$ compounded semiannually for eight years, find K. In this case, $i = 0.12/2 = 0.06$ and $n = 16$. The table shows that $K = 10.10590$.

EXAMPLE 2   *(Compare Exercise 5)*

Find the present value of an annuity with periodic payments of $2000, semiannually, for a period of ten years at an interest rate of 6%, compounded semiannually.

SOLUTION   Here, $R = 2000$, $i = 0.06/2 = 0.03$, and $n = 20$. The formula for present value gives

$$P = 2000(14.87747)$$
$$= 29754.94$$

where Table 8–3 gives $K = 14.87747$ for $i = 0.03$ and $n = 20$.

The present value of the annuity is $29,754.94. This lump sum will accumulate the same amount in ten years as $2000 semiannually for ten years.

The second problem, finding the amount to be invested so that equal amounts will be paid out periodically, is an "annuity in reverse." The periodic payments will use up the original investment and any interest accumulated. For example, a lump sum is invested at 8%, compounded quarterly, so that quarterly payments of $500 can be made for ten years. In such a case the amount invested is the present value of $500 invested quarterly at 8% for ten years. So the formula for present value applies to this problem.

EXAMPLE 3   *(Compare Exercise 36)*

Find the present value of an annuity (lump sum investment) that will pay $1000 per quarter for four years. The interest rate is 10%.

SOLUTION   Since $R = 1000$, $i = 2.5\%$, and $n = 16$,

$$P = 1000(13.05500) = 13,055.00$$

where 13.05500 is obtained from Table 8–3 at $i = 0.025$ and $n = 16$. A lump sum investment of $13,055 will yield $1000 per quarter for four years.

AMORTIZATION

The **amortization** method is a way to repay an interest-bearing debt. The amortization method makes a series of equal periodic payments. Each payment pays all the interest for that time period and repays part of the principal. As the principal is gradually reduced, the interest on the unpaid balance decreases. Thus a larger portion of each payment becomes available to apply to the debt.

The last payment pays interest for that period and completes the repayment of the loan. Most of us have personally encountered an amortization, or will someday. When you borrow money to buy a car or home, the repayment of the debt is an amortization.

When a debt is amortized (repaid) by equal payments at equal time intervals, the amount borrowed is just the present value of an annuity. This method usually applies to car payments and house payments. We can use the present value formula for an annuity to find the periodic payments.

EXAMPLE 4   *(Compare Exercise 17)*

An employee borrows $8000 from the company credit union to purchase a car. The interest rate is 12%, compounded quarterly, with payments due every quarter. The employee wants to pay off the loan in three years. (The loan is amortized over three years.) How much are the quarterly payments?

SOLUTION   W have $P = 8000$, $i = 0.12/4 = 0.03$, $n = 12$ quarters, and $K = 9.95400$ (from Table 8–3).

From the present value formula we have

$$8000 = R(9.95400)$$

Solving for R, we have

$$R = \frac{8000}{9.95400} = 803.697$$

The quarterly payments on the car are $803.70 each.

In general, when we solve for R in the present value formula, we have the amortization payment formula.

Amortization Payments

$$R = \frac{P}{K}$$

where

P = amount of the debt (the present value)

K is found in Table 8–3 and depends on the periodic rate, i, and number of time periods, n

R = amount of each periodic payment

You should be aware that the amount of the periodic payment may involve a fraction of a cent. In that case the bank rounds up to the next cent. Consequently, the final payment may be a little less than the other payments.

EXAMPLE 5   *(Compare Exercise 13)*

A student obtained a 24-month loan on a car. The monthly payments are $395.42 and are based on a 12% interest rate. What was the amount borrowed?

SOLUTION   The amount borrowed is just the present value of the annuity. We then have

$$R = 395.42$$

$$i = \frac{0.12}{12} = 0.01 \qquad \text{(Monthly rate)}$$

$$N = 24 \qquad \text{(Number of months)}$$

$$K = 21.24339 \qquad \text{(From Table 8–3)}$$

So

$$P = 395.42(21.24339) = 8400.06$$

It is reasonable to round this to $8400, the amount borrowed.

EXAMPLE 6   *(Compare Exercise 24)*

A family borrows $75,000 to buy a house. The family is to repay the debt in 20 years with equal monthly payments. The interest rate is 14%. How much are the monthly payments?

SOLUTION   This is an amortization problem with $P = 75,000$, $i = \frac{14\%}{12}$, and $n = 12 \times 20 = 240$ months.

Table 8–4 is a special table giving values of K for 20, 25, and 30 years of monthly payments. In it, for $n = 240$ and $i = 0.14/12$ we find $K = 80.41683$. Then

$$R = \frac{75,000}{80.41683}$$

$$= 932.64$$

The monthly payments are $932.64.

TABLE 8–4. $K = \dfrac{(1 + i)^n - 1}{i(1 + i)^n}$

NUMBER OF PERIODS, n	PERIODIC INTEREST RATE, i					
	$\frac{2}{3}\%$	$\frac{3}{4}\%$	$\frac{10}{12}\%$	1%	$\frac{14}{12}\%$	1.25%
240	119.55429	111.14495	103.62460	90.81942	80.41683	75.94228
300	129.56452	119.16162	110.04723	94.94655	83.07297	78.07434
360	136.28349	124.28187	113.95082	97.21833	84.39732	79.08614

EXAMPLE 7   *(Compare Exercise 29)*

A family borrowed $60,000 to buy a house. The loan was for 30 years at 12% interest rate. The monthly payments were $617.17.

(a) How much of the first month's payment was interest and how much was principal?
(b) What total amount did the family pay over the 30 years?

SOLUTION

(a) The monthly interest rate was $1\% = 0.01$, so the first month's interest was $60,000(0.01) = 600.00$.

The family paid $600 interest the first month. The rest of the payment, $17.17, went to repay part of the principal.

(b) The family paid $617.17 each month for 360 months, so the total amount paid was $617.17(360) = \$222,181.20$. You may be surprised at this figure, but it is true. Notice that the total amount paid for interest was

$$\$222,181.20 - 60,000 = \$162,181.20$$

When a family makes monthly payments on a house mortgage, some of each month's payment goes to reduce the loan. In Example 7 the first payment reduced the loan by $17.17. To find the balance of the loan after a period of time, say five years, you can find the amount repaid each month for five years and deduct these from the loan. For example, here is an amortization schedule for the first 12 months of the loan.

$60,000 Loan for 30 Years at 12%

MONTH	MONTHLY PAYMENT	INTEREST PAID	PRINCIPAL PAID	BALANCE
0				$60,000.00
1	617.17	$600.00	$17.17	59,982.83
2	617.17	599.83	17.34	59,965.49
3	617.17	599.65	17.52	59,947.97
4	617.17	599.48	17.69	59,930.28
5	617.17	599.30	17.87	59,912.41
6	617.17	599.12	18.05	59,894.36
7	617.17	598.94	18.23	59,876.13
8	617.17	598.76	18.41	59,857.72
9	617.17	598.58	18.59	59,839.13
10	617.17	598.39	18.78	59,820.35
11	617.17	598.20	18.97	59,801.38
12	617.17	598.01	19.16	59,782.22

This approach is too tedious. There is a formula that helps considerably.

The Balance of an Amortization

$$\text{Bal} = P(1 + i)^n - \frac{M[(1 + i)^n - 1]}{i}$$

where

P = amount borrowed
i = periodic interest rate
n = number of time periods
M = monthly payments

Note that this formula can also be written

$$\text{Bal} = P(1 + i)^n - MS$$

where S is obtained from Table 8–2. In this form,

Bal = future value of compound interest − future value of an annuity

See Appendix C for a derivation of the formula for balance.

EXAMPLE 8   *(Compare Exercise 30)*

What is the balance of the loan in Example 7 after two years?

SOLUTION   In Example 7,

$P = 60,000$
$i = 1\% = 0.01$ per month
$M = 617.17$
$n = 24$ months   (The balance after 24 months is desired)
$S = 26.97346$ (From Table 8–2, using $i = 0.1$ and $n = 24$)

$$
\begin{aligned}
\text{Bal} &= 60,000(1.01)^{24} - 617.17(26.97346) \\
&= 60,000(1.26973) - 617.17(26.97346) \\
&= 76,183.80 - 16,647.21 \\
&= 59,536.59
\end{aligned}
$$

So the balance owed after two years is \$59,536.59. The part of the loan repaid is the **equity:**

Equity = loan − balance

In this case the equity after two years is

Equity = 60,000 − 59,536.59 = \$463.41

The results of these computations might seem wrong. Hardly any principal is repaid each month. In two years the 24 payments total \$14,812.08, but only \$463.41 of the \$60,000 loan has been repaid. However, the amount repaid increases a little each month (about 19¢; see the amortization table for this loan on p. 555). While a 19¢ per month increase hardly seems worthwhile, it eventually becomes a significant increase, and the loan is paid off. Notice from Example 7 that the total interest on the loan of that example is over $160,000.

Now let's look at a situation that combines the future value and present value of an annuity.

EXAMPLE 9   *(Compare Exercise 41)*

The parents of a new baby want to provide for the child's college education. How much should be deposited on each of the child's first 17 birthdays to be able to withdraw $10,000 on each of the next four birthdays? Assume an interest rate of 8%.

SOLUTION   First, compute the amount that must be in the account on the child's seventeenth birthday to withdraw $10,000 per year for four years. This is the present value of an annuity where

> P is to be found
> $i = 0.08$
> $n = 4$
> $R = 10,000$
> $K = 3.31213$ (From Table 8–3)

So $P = RK = 10,000(3.31213) = \$33,121.30$, the total necessary on the seventeenth birthday.

Next, find the annual payments that will yield a future value of $33,121.30 in 17 years at 8%. This is $A = RS$, where

> $A = 33,121.30$
> $i = 0.08$
> $n = 17$
> $S = 33.75023$ (From Table 8–2 using $i = 0.08$ and $n = 17$)
>
> $33,121.30 = 33.75023R$
>
> $$R = \frac{33,121.30}{33.75023}$$
>
> $= 981.37$

So $981.37 should be deposited every birthday for 17 years to provide $10,000 per year for four years.

8–4 EXERCISES

I

Find K from Table 8–3 for Exercises 1 through 4.

1. (*See Example 1*) $n = 15$ and $i = 0.02$
2. $n = 6$ and $i = 0.05$
3. 10% compounded semiannually for eight years
4. 5% compounded annually for ten years

In Exercises 5 through 12, determine the present values of the annuities that will pay the given periodic payments.

5. (*See Example 2*) Periodic payments of $4000 annually for eight years. The interest is 7% compounded annually.
6. Periodic payments of $2300 annually for 15 years. The interest is 9% compounded annually.
7. Periodic payments of $750 quarterly for five years. The interest is 8% compounded quarterly.
8. Periodic payments of $150 monthly for 18 months. The interest is 1.5% compounded monthly.
9. Periodic payments of $500 semiannually for ten years. The interest is 12% compounded semiannually.
10. Periodic payments of $2500 semiannually for five years. The interest is 10% compounded semiannually.
11. Periodic payments of $300 per quarter for 5.5 years. The interest is 10% compounded quarterly.
12. Periodic payments of $75 per month for two years. The interest is 1% compounded monthly.

For Exercises 13 through 16, find the amount borrowed for each loan described.

13. (*See Example 5*) $R = \$226.94$, the interest rate is 8%, and payments are made quarterly for three years.
14. $R = \$1071.84$, the interest rate is 10%, and payments are made semiannually for six years.
15. $R = \$2135.66$, the interest rate is 7%, and payments are made annually for ten years.
16. $R = \$3993.63$, the interest rate is 10%, and payments are made annually for 20 years.

In Exercises 17 through 23 the present value of an annuity is given, and you are asked to compute the periodic payments.

17. (*See Example 4*) $5000; the interest rate is 7% compounded annually for four years.
18. $10,000; the interest rate is 8% compounded semiannually for 12 years.
19. $50,000; the interest rate is 10% compounded quarterly for five years.
20. $4000; the interest rate is 6% compounded annually for three years.
21. $150,000; the interest rate is 12% compounded semiannually for ten years.
22. $3000; the interest rate is 12% compounded quarterly for four years.
23. $2000; the interest rate is 10% compounded quarterly for three years.

II

24. (*See Example 6*) A family borrows $92,000 to buy a house. They are to repay the debt in 25 years with equal monthly payments and at 10% interest. How much are the monthly payments?
25. Determine the monthly payments on a 20-year loan of $20,000 at 8% interest.
26. The monthly payments on a 20-year loan of $25,000 at 8.50% interest are $216.95.
    (a) What is the total amount paid over the 20 years?
    (b) What is the total amount of interest paid?

27. A family obtains a $75,000 house loan for 30 years at 12% interest. The monthly payments are $825.75 each.
    (a) What is the total amount paid over the 30 years?
    (b) What is the total interest paid?
28. A house loan of $30,000 is made for 30 years at 9% interest. For each of the first two monthly payments, find the amount that is paid for interest and the amount that is paid toward the principal.

29. (*See Example 7*) A family borrowed $68,000 to buy a house. The loan was at 15% and for 25 years. The monthly payments were $870.96 each.
    (a) How much of the first month's payment was interest, and how much was principal?
    (b) What was the total amount paid over the 25 years?

30. (*See Example 8*) A family has obtained a house loan of $48,000 for 25 years at 12% interest. The monthly payments are $505.54. What is the balance of their loan after:
    (a) one year?
    (b) two years?
    (c) What is their equity after two years?

31. A company amortizes a $75,000 loan, at 10% interest, with quarterly payments of $2987.72 for ten years. What is the balance of the loan after five years?

32. Find the present value of an annuity that will pay $1500 every six months for nine years from an account paying interest at a rate of 8% compounded semiannually.

33. Ms. Greenberg obtained an 18-month loan on a car. The monthly payments are $484.92 and are based on 18% interest rate. How much did Ms. Greenberg borrow?

34. A druggist borrows $4500 from a bank to stock her drugstore. The interest rate is 8% compounded semiannually with payments due every six months. She wants to repay the loan in 18 months. How much are the semiannual payments?

35. A mechanic borrows $7500 to expand his garage. The interest rate is 10% compounded quarterly with payments due every quarter. What are the quarterly payments if the loan is to be paid off in four years?

36. (*See Example 3*) An executive wants to invest a lump sum that will provide $7500 per year for 15 years for his wife. If the investment earns 8% compounded annually, how much should he invest?

37. A donor wants to establish a fund that will pay the Marlin Public Library $10,000 per year for 20 years. If the fund earns 9% interest compounded annually, how much should be put into the fund?

III

38. Raul wins $1 million in a lottery. He is paid the winnings at $50,000 for 20 years. The lottery establishes an annuity that makes the annual payments. How much should the lottery place in the annuity if it earns 8% compounded annually?

39. Alice borrows $12,000 to buy a car. She pays 12% interest compounded monthly and the loan is for two years. Find the monthly payments.

40. Rachel can amortize a $1400 music center with monthly payments at 1% per month for two years. Find the monthly payments.

41. (*See Example 9*) How much should parents invest on each of their child's first 18 birthdays in order to provide $15,000 per year for the next four years if the investment pays 8% interest?

42. How much should be invested each year for ten years to provide you with $5000 per year for the next 25 years? Assume a 10% interest rate.

Use a calculator to work Exercises 43 through 47.

43. Find the present value of an annuity that will pay $200 each month for five years from an account that pays 9% annual rate compounded monthly.

44. Brett borrowed $13,000 at 6% interest to buy a car. It is a four-year loan. Find the monthly payments.

45. Shelley borrowed $9700 to buy a car at 9% interest. If the loan is for five years, find the monthly payments.

46. How much should be placed in an annuity that earns 7.5% compounded annually in order to provide college expenses of $10,000 per year for four years?

47. A family borrows $85,000 to buy a house. The loan is for ten years at 9% interest. Find the monthly payments.

IMPORTANT TERMS

8-1

Simple Interest

Principal

Present Value

Interest Rate

Future Value

Amount

Simple Discount

Proceeds

Maturity Value

Discount Rate

8-2

Compound Interest

Periodic Interest Rate

Future Value of Compound Interest

Amount

Present Value

Effective Rate

8-3

Annuity

Payment Period

Periodic Payment

Ordinary Annuity

Amount

Future Value

Sinking Fund

8-4

Present Value of an Annuity

Amortization

REVIEW EXERCISES

1. A loan is made for $500 at 9% simple interest for two years. How much interest is paid?

2. How much simple interest was paid on a $1100 loan at 6% for ten months?

3. A loan, principal and interest, was paid with $1190.40. The loan was made at 8% simple interest for three years. How much was borrowed?

4. The interest on a loan was $94.50, the interest rate was 7.5%, and the loan was for 1.5 years. What was the amount borrowed?

5. A sum of $3000 is borrowed for a period of five years at simple interest of 9% per annum. Compute the total interest paid over this period.

6. Find the future value of a $6500 loan at 7.5% for 18 months.

7. A simple discount note at 9% discount rate for two years has a maturity value of $8500. What are the discount and the proceeds?

8. How much should be borrowed on a discount note with 11% discount rate for 1.5 years so that the borrower obtains $900?

9. Compute the interest earned on $5000 in three years if the interest is 7% compounded annually.

10. Compute the interest and the amount of $500 after two years if the interest is 10% compounded semiannually.

11. If money is invested at 8% interest compounded quarterly, how long will it take to double in value?

12. A sum of $1000 is deposited in a savings account that pays interest of 5%, compounded annually. Determine the amount in the account after four years.

13. Find the effective rate of 6% compounded semiannually.

14. Find the effective rate of 5% compounded semiannually.

15. Find the effective rate of 24% compounded monthly.

16. Which is the better investment, one that pays 8% compounded quarterly or one that pays 8.3% compounded annually?

17. Which account gives the better interest, one that gives 18% per annum compounded quarterly or one that gives 19% compounded annually?

18. The price of an automobile is now $5000. What would be the anticipated price of that automobile in two years time if prices are expected to increase at an annual rate of 8%?

Find (a) future values and (b) the total interest earned on the amounts in Exercises 19 through 21.

19. $8000 at 6% compounded annually for four years

20. $3000 at 5% compounded annually for two years

21. $5000 at 10% compounded quarterly for six years

22. A company sets aside $120,000 cash in a special building fund to be used at the end of five years to construct a new building. The fund will earn 6% compounded semiannually. How much money will be in the fund at the end of the period?

23. On January 1, 1988 a Chicago firm purchased a new machine to be used in the plant. The list price of the machine was $15,000, payable at the end of two years with interest of 8% compounded annually. How much was due on the machine on January 1, 1990?

24. Anticipating college tuition for their child in ten years, the Heggens want to deposit a lump sum of money into an account that will provide $16,000 at the end of that ten-year period. The account selected pays 10%, compounded semiannually. How much should they deposit?

25. An executive thinks that it is a good time to sell a certain stock. She wants to take a leave of absence in five years. How much stock should she sell and invest at 8% compounded quarterly so that $50,000 will be available in five years?

26. How long will it take $1000 to increase to $3000 in an account that pays 10% compounded semiannually?

27. A sum of $2000 is invested into an account that pays 12% compounded quarterly. It is to be left in the account until it has grown to $3500. How long will this take?

28. Find S for each of the following:
    (a) $i = 0.02, n = 20$ **(b)** $i = 0.04, n = 20$
    (c) $i = 0.05, n = 15$

Find the future value of each of the ordinary annuities in Exercises 29 through 32.

29. $R = \$200, i = 0.02, n = 10$

30. $R = \$500, i = 0.05, n = 8$

31. $R = \$1000, r = 0.06, n = 5$

32. $R = \$300, i = 0.025, n = 20$

33. Find the future value of $600 paid into an annuity at the end of every six months for five years. The annual interest rate is 10%.

34. Find the future value of $1000 paid into an annuity at the end of every year for six years. The interest rate is 8%.

35. $250 is invested in an annuity at the end of every three months at 8%. Find the value of the annuity at the end of six years.

36. An annuity consists of payments of $1000 at the end of each year for a period of five years. Interest is paid at 6% per year compounded annually. Determine the amount of the annuity at the end of five years.

37. Midway School District sold $2 million of bonds to construct an elementary school. The bonds must be paid in ten years. The district establishes a sinking fund that pays 8% interest. Find the annual payments into the sinking fund that will provide the necessary funds at the end of ten years.

38. A couple wants to start a fund with annual payments that will give them $20,000 cash on retirement in ten years. The proposed fund will give interest of 7% compounded annually. What will the annual payments be?

In Exercises 39 through 42, determine the present value of the given amounts using the given interest rate and length of time.

39. $5000 over five years at 6% compounded annually

40. $4750 over four years at 5% compounded semiannually

41. $6000 over five years at 8% compounded quarterly

42. $1000 over eight years at 10% compounded semiannually

43. A company wants to deposit a certain sum at the present time into an account that pays compound interest at 8% compounded quarterly in order to meet an expected expense of $50,000 in five years time. How much should it deposit?

44. A corporation is planning plant expansion as soon as adequate funds can be accumulated. The corporation has estimated that the additions will cost approximately $105,000. At the present time it has $70,935 cash on hand that will not be needed in the near future. A local savings institution will pay 8% compounded semiannually. How many years will be required for the $70,935 to accumulate to approximately $105,000?

45. A medical supplier is making plans to issue $200,000 in bonds to finance plant modernization. The interest rate on the bonds will be 8% compounded quarterly. The company estimates that it can pay up to a maximum of $97,000 in total interest on the bonds. The company wants to stretch out the period of payment as long as possible. What should be the planned term of the bonds?

46. A corporation owed a $40,000 debt. Its creditor agreed to let the corporation pay the debt in five equal annual payments at 8% interest. Compute the annual payments.

47. A student borrowed $3000 from a credit union toward purchasing a car. The interest rate on such loans is 12% compounded quarterly with payments due every quarter. The student wants to pay off the loan in three years. Find the quarterly payments.

48. The interest on a house mortgage of $53,000 for 30 years is 14%, compounded monthly, with payments made monthly. Compute the monthly payments.

49. Andrew borrows $4800 at 9% interest. It is to be paid in five annual payments. Find the annual payments.

50. Holt's Clothing Store borrowed $125,000 to be repaid in semiannual payments. Find the semiannual payments if the loan is for four years and the interest rate is 10% compounded semiannually.

51. The city of McGregor borrowed $7.8 million to build a zoo. The interest rate is 7% compounded annually, and the loan is to be paid in 20 years. Find the annual payments.

52. The Thaxton family purchased a franchise with a loan of $25,000 at 8% compounded quarterly for six years. Find the quarterly payments.

53. The Bar X Ranch purchased additional land with a loan of $98,000 at 9% compounded annually for eight years. Find the annual payments.

54. Fashion Floors borrowed $65,000 at 10% compounded semiannually for three years. Find the semiannual payments.

55. An investor invests $1000 at 8% compounded quarterly for five years. At the end of the five years the total amount in the account is reinvested at 10% compounded quarterly for another five years. How much is in the account at the end of ten years?

56. A family borrowed $65,000 at 12% for 30 years to buy a house. Their payments are $668.59 per month. How much of the first month's payment is interest? How much of the first month's payment is principal? What is the total amount they will pay over the 30 years?

Use your calculator to solve Exercises 57 through 61.

57. If $1700 is invested at 7.8% compounded quarterly, find the amount at the end of ten years.

58. Find the amount of $20,000 invested at 8% compounded quarterly for 50 years.

59. How much should be invested at 10% compounded quarterly in order to have $500,000 at the end of 40 years?

60. If $100 per month is deposited in an annuity earning 9% interest, find the amount at the end of ten years.

61. How much should be deposited monthly into an annuity paying 12% in order to have $100,000 at the end of six years?

9

The Derivative

9–1 RATES OF CHANGE AND THE DERIVATIVE

- *Introduction*
- *Average Rate of Change*
- *Instantaneous Rate of Change*
- *The Derivative*

INTRODUCTION

*T*HE TWO MAIN CONCEPTS in calculus are the derivative and the integral. We will start our study of calculus with the derivative and will introduce the integral later, in Chapter 13.

Western civilization's view of the universe changed dramatically during the sixteenth and seventeenth centuries. People began to make careful observations of the physical world and to describe what they observed. They developed new mathematics to help with these descriptions and then used this new mathematics to make accurate predictions of physical phenomena. The scientific and technological revolution had begun. The last half of the twentieth century has seen rapid growth in the use of mathematics by what are called the social and behavioral sciences and by business. As in the physical sciences, mathematics is used both to describe and to predict. Mathematics has become especially important in economics. In fact, since the Nobel Prize in Economics was established in 1968, many of the awards have been given to individuals for their application of mathematics or their invention of new mathematical methods. The idea we are about to study, the derivative, is the mathematical tool for talking about rate of change. "Rate of change" may be described by a special word within a particular application. As examples, physicists use "velocity" for the rate of change of position, and economists use "marginal profit" for the rate of change of profit. Not only does the derivative provide the mathematical language for describing rate of change, but we will also see later how the derivative can be used to decide what production strategy will maximize profit, to estimate how a small change in price will affect sales, and to describe how various rates of change are related.

AVERAGE RATE OF CHANGE

One way of describing change is the average rate of change over an interval. For example, if a particular stock sold for $40 a share on Monday morning and for $43.50 the following Friday, then the average daily rate of change of the price of the stock can be computed as follows:

$$\frac{\text{difference in price}}{\text{number of days}} = \frac{3.50}{5} = 0.70$$

Therefore, the average rate of change of the stock is $0.70, or 70¢, per day. If the stock sold for $40 on Monday and $38 on Friday, the average rate of change would be

$$\frac{38 - 40}{5} = -\frac{2}{5} = -0.40$$

for an average rate of change of $-$$0.40 per day.

When the price of the stock increases in value, the average rate of change is positive; when the price of the stock decreases, the average rate of change is negative.

For describing the average rate of change of an arbitrary function, we use the following definition.

Definition
Average Rate of Change

The **average rate of change** of the function f on the interval $[a, b]$ is

$$\frac{f(b) - f(a)}{b - a}$$

the "change in y" divided by the corresponding "change in x."

EXAMPLE 1   *(Compare Exercise 1)*

If $f(x) = 3x + 5$, what is the average rate of change of f on:

(a) the interval $[2, 6]$?
(b) the interval $[1, 8]$?

SOLUTION
(a) Here $a = 2$ and $b = 6$:

$$\frac{f(6) - f(2)}{6 - 2} = \frac{23 - 11}{4} = \frac{12}{4} = 3$$

The average rate of change of f on $[2, 6]$ is 3.
(b) Apply the same formula with $a = 1$ and $b = 8$:

$$\frac{f(8) - f(1)}{8 - 1} = \frac{29 - 8}{7} = \frac{21}{7} = 3$$

The average rate of change of f on $[1, 8]$ is also 3.

NOTE Both answers are the slope of the graph of the function! This example shows an important principle. For a linear function the change in y divided by the change in x is independent of the interval.

Theorem   If the graph of f is a straight line, the average rate of change of f on any interval is the same number—the slope of the straight line.

EXAMPLE 2   *(Compare Exercise 5)*

The revenue R of the X-Cell Company can be expressed as a function of the price p by $R = 50p - 3p^2$.

(a) What is the average change in R if p increases from 4 to 6?
(b) What is the average change in the company's revenue as the price increases from 10 to 12?

SOLUTION

(a) The wording is slightly different from the previous example, but the question is asking for the average rate of change of R on the interval $[4, 6]$:

$$\frac{R(b) - R(a)}{b - a} = \frac{R(6) - R(4)}{6 - 4}$$

$$= \frac{192 - 152}{2} = \frac{40}{2} = 20$$

The average change in R as p increases from 4 to 6 is 20.

(b) Now we compute

$$\frac{R(12) - R(10)}{12 - 10} = \frac{168 - 200}{2} = -\frac{32}{2} = -16$$

The average rate of change of the revenue on the interval $[10, 12]$ is -16.

CAUTION The graph of the revenue function in Example 2 is not a straight line, and so the function has different average rates of change on different intervals. Only linear functions have a constant average rate of change.

Sometimes important information is lost by looking at the average rate of change, as the following examples show.

One measure of inflation (the change in purchasing power of money) in the United States is provided by the Consumer Price Index (CPI) which is issued each month by the Bureau of Labor Statistics. The CPI uses 1967 as its base. For example, the CPI for 1983 was 298.4. This means that in 1983 it cost $298.40 to purchase the same goods that cost $100 in 1967. Similarly, the CPI in 1920 was 60.0, so the goods that cost $100 in 1967 would have cost only $60 in 1920. Figure 9–1 is the graph of the CPI from 1913 (the year it was first issued) to 1980, along with a table of actual values of the CPI for selected years.

EXAMPLE 3   *(Compare Exercise 11)*

Use the table in Figure 9–1 to answer the following questions.

(a) What was the average change in the CPI from 1920 to 1960?
(b) What was the average change in the CPI from 1920 to 1940?
(c) What was the average change in the CPI from 1940 to 1960?

FIGURE 9–1

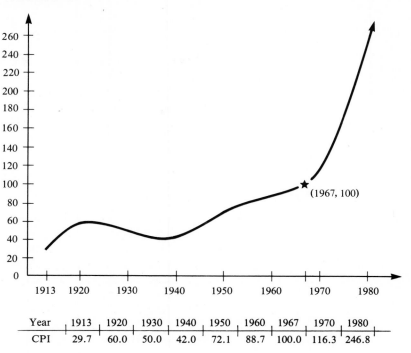

Year	1913	1920	1930	1940	1950	1960	1967	1970	1980
CPI	29.7	60.0	50.0	42.0	72.1	88.7	100.0	116.3	246.8

SOLUTION

(a) The average change from 1920 to 1960 was

$$\frac{\text{CPI}(1960) - \text{CPI}(1920)}{60 - 20} = \frac{88.7 - 60}{40}$$

$$= \frac{28.7}{40}$$

$$\approx 0.72 \quad \text{(dollars per year)}$$

(b) $\dfrac{\text{CPI}(1940) - \text{CPI}(1920)}{40 - 20} = \dfrac{42 - 60}{20} = -0.9 \quad$ (dollars per year)

The CPI declined an average of $0.90 per year for these 20 years.

(c) $\dfrac{\text{CPI}(1960) - \text{CPI}(1940)}{60 - 40} = \dfrac{88.7 - 42.0}{20} \approx 2.34 \quad$ (dollars per year)

The CPI rose an average of approximately $2.34 per year for these 20 years.

The answers to parts (b) and (c) of Example 3 give us more information than did just the answer to part (a). In fact, we would get an even better picture of inflation over these 40 years if we were given several averages, each taken over small time intervals.

Let's look at another example that is probably more familiar to you—the speed of an automobile. One of the authors (Cannon) lives about seven miles from work, and his trip to the office in the morning usually takes about 15 minutes, or 1/4 hour. Cannon's average speed on this trip is

$$\frac{7 \text{ miles}}{1/4 \text{ hr}} = 28 \text{ mph}$$

This average again hides a lot of information. The last two miles are on an interstate highway, where Cannon's speed is 55 mph. The middle of the trip is on a heavily used road that has a speed limit of 40 mph but also has nine traffic lights in a three-mile stretch. Cannon spends a good portion of the 15 minutes at red lights. You would get a better idea of this trip if you were given his average speed in three intervals of 5 minutes each. You would get an even better idea of this trip if you were given his average speed for 15 intervals of 1 minute each. But even with these 15 averages, it would be hard for you to distinguish a minute during which his speed was low the whole time, say, because of heavy traffic, from a minute which had a short period at a light followed by rapid return to 40 mph.

But we've been asking you to consider speed by only using the odometer (to measure distance traveled) and the clock (to measure time intervals). This is a good way to talk about average velocity, but if you wanted to know how Cannon's speed varied on this trip, you would have to read the speedometer during the trip. The speedometer gives the speed, the **rate of change** in the position, of the car *at every instant*. The derivative of a function is like the speedometer of a car—the derivative gives us the rate of change of the function at every point.

Later sections in the text will give you rules to follow to compute the derivative of a function; but to understand how to apply derivatives, you should know what it is you are computing.

EXAMPLE 4   (*Compare Exercise 13*)

Measurements have shown that t seconds after a rock has been dropped, it will have fallen $16t^2$ feet. This means that 3 seconds after the rock is dropped, it has traveled $16 \cdot 9 = 144$ feet. How fast is it traveling 3 seconds after it is dropped?

SOLUTION   The information given is about the distance traveled and the time, so we proceed as with the odometer information—we compute some average speeds. After 3 seconds the rock has dropped 144 feet, and after 4 seconds it has dropped 256 feet. The distance the rock travels in the one second from time $t = 3$ to time $t = 4$ is $256 - 144$. Therefore the average speed as t increases from 3 to 4 is

$$\frac{(16 \cdot 4^2) - (16 \cdot 3^2)}{4 - 3} = \frac{256 - 144}{1} = 112 \quad \text{(ft/sec)}$$

From 3 to 3.5 seconds, the average speed is

$$\frac{16(3.5)^2 - 16(3)^2}{0.5} = 104 \quad \text{(ft/sec)}$$

For $3 \le t \le 3.1$ the average speed is 97.6 ft/sec. For $3 \le t \le 3.01$ the average speed is 96.16 ft/sec. On the other side of 3, for $2.9 \le t \le 3$ the average speed is 94.4 ft/sec. For $2.99 \le t \le 3$ the average speed is 95.84 ft/sec. You might now guess that the speed of the rock when $t = 3$ is about 96 ft/sec. Some algebra will remove the guesswork.

First we introduce some notation that is useful when discussing rates of change. The symbol Δ is the Greek letter "delta"; it means "the change in" and is immediately followed by a variable. Thus Δt means "the change in t," Δy means "the change in y," Δx means "the change in x," and so on. When dealing with linear functions, we have seen in Example 1 that the change in y divided by the change in x is the slope of the line; $\Delta y / \Delta x = m$.

Now back to the falling rock. The length of the interval between the two moments $t = 3$ and $t = 3 + \Delta t$ is Δt. The distance fallen $3 + \Delta t$ seconds after the rock is dropped is

$$16(3 + \Delta t)^2 = 16(9 + 6\Delta t + (\Delta t)^2) = 144 + 96\Delta t + 16(\Delta t)^2 \quad \text{(feet)}$$

The rock has fallen 144 feet after 3 seconds. So the distance traveled in the time interval from 3 to $3 + \Delta t$ is

$$144 + 96\Delta t + 16(\Delta t)^2 - 144 = 96\Delta t + 16(\Delta t)^2 \quad \text{(feet)}$$

To find the average speed over this interval, we divide this distance by the change in time, Δt:

$$\text{Average velocity} = \frac{96\Delta t + 16(\Delta t)^2}{\Delta t}$$

$$= 96 + 16\Delta t \quad \text{(ft/sec)}$$

CAUTION Remember that Δt is one term—it does not mean Δ multiplied by t. For the interval $3 \le t \le 3.1$, $\Delta t = 0.1$; using $\Delta t = 0.1$ in the expression $96 + 16\Delta t$ gives us the average velocity of $96 + 16(0.1) = 96 + 1.6 = 97.6$ (ft/sec) just as we computed above.

For the interval $3 \le t \le 3.001$, Δt is $\frac{1}{1000}$th of a second, and the average velocity on this interval is

$$96 + 16(0.001) = 96.016 \quad \text{(ft/sec)}$$

If Δt is close to 0, then $16 \cdot \Delta t$ is also close to 0, so the average velocity, $(96 + 16 \cdot \Delta t)$ ft/sec, is close to 96 ft/sec. We call 96 ft/sec the *instantaneous velocity* of the rock when $t = 3$. Three seconds after it is dropped, the rock is traveling 96 feet per second.

We can condense these computations now that we have gone through one detailed example.

EXAMPLE 5   *(Compare Exercise 13)*

Use the falling rock from Example 4 to answer the following questions:

(a) What is the rock's average velocity on the interval $[2, 2 + \Delta t]$?
(b) How fast is the rock going when $t = 2$?

SOLUTION   After 2 seconds the rock has dropped $16 \cdot 2^2 = 64$ (feet). After $2 + \Delta t$ seconds the rock has dropped

$$16(2 + \Delta t)^2 = 16(4 + 4\Delta t + (\Delta t)^2) = 64 + 64\Delta t + 16(\Delta t)^2 \quad \text{(feet)}$$

In the interval $[2, 2 + \Delta t]$ the rock has traveled

$$64 + 64\Delta t + 16(\Delta t)^2 - 64 = 64\Delta t + 16(\Delta t)^2 \quad \text{(feet)}$$

(a) The average velocity is

$$\frac{64\Delta t + 16(\Delta t)^2}{\Delta t} = 64 + 16\Delta t \quad \text{(ft/sec)}$$

(b) When Δt is close to 0, $64 + 16\Delta t$ is close to 64. The rock is traveling at 64 ft/sec when $t = 2$.

We have been led to a definition of instantaneous velocity by computing the average velocity over very small intervals. Velocity is the special case of the rate of change of a distance-traveled function. We define the instantaneous rate of change of an arbitrary function in an analogous manner.

INSTANTANEOUS RATE OF CHANGE

To define the rate of change of a function f at the "instant" when $x = a$, we compute the average rate of change of f on the interval $[a, a + \Delta x]$ if $\Delta x > 0$, or $[a + \Delta x, a]$ if $\Delta x < 0$. In either case the average rate of change of the function f on the interval with endpoints a and $a + \Delta x$ is given by the expression

$$\frac{f(a + \Delta x) - f(a)}{\Delta x}$$

If, when Δx is close to 0, the numbers we get as average rates of change are all close to one fixed number, we call that fixed number the **instantaneous rate of change** of f when $x = a$. In Example 4, for instance, when Δt was close to 0, the numbers we obtained as average rates of change were close to the one fixed number 96, so 96 is the instantaneous rate of change of f when $t = 3$. The process of computing the instantaneous rate of change of f at $x = a$ can be broken down into three steps, as shown in the next example.

EXAMPLE 6   (*Compare Exercise 17*)

Find the instantaneous rate of change of $f(x) = 5x^2$ when $x = 3$.

SOLUTION

Step 1. Compute and simplify $f(a + \Delta x) - f(a)$:

$$f(a) = f(3) = 45$$
$$f(a + \Delta x) = f(3 + \Delta x) = 5(3 + \Delta x)^2$$
$$= 5(9 + 6\Delta x + (\Delta x)^2)$$
$$= 45 + 30\Delta x + 5(\Delta x)^2 \qquad \text{(Remember that } \Delta x \text{ is one number)}$$
$$f(a + \Delta x) - f(a) = f(3 + \Delta x) - f(3)$$
$$= 45 + 30\Delta x + 5(\Delta x)^2 - 45$$
$$= 30\Delta x + 5(\Delta x)^2$$

Step 2. Divide the result of Step 1 by Δx:

$$\frac{30\Delta x + 5(\Delta x)^2}{\Delta x} = \frac{(30 + 5\Delta x)\Delta x}{\Delta x} = 30 + 5\Delta x$$

Step 3. Compute the instantaneous rate of change of f at $x = 3$ by letting Δx be close to 0 in the result from Step 2. If Δx is close to 0, then $30 + 5\Delta x$ is close to 30.

Answer: The instantaneous rate of change of $f(x) = 5x^2$ when $x = 3$ is 30.

THE DERIVATIVE

The language in Step 3 is somewhat awkward. We introduce two new words to make Step 3 easier to deal with. First, we summarize the notion of "close to" by saying the instantaneous rate of change of f at $x = a$ is the **limit** as Δx goes to 0 of the average rates of change. We write this as

$$\lim_{\Delta x \to 0} \frac{f(a + \Delta x) - f(a)}{\Delta x}$$

"The instantaneous rate of change of f at $x = a$" is called the **derivative** of f at a, which is written $f'(a)$, where $f'(a)$ is read "f prime of a".

In summary, we now have the following definition.

Definition   **Derivative**   The **derivative** of f at a, written $f'(a)$, is the instantaneous rate of change of f at a:

$$f'(a) = \lim_{\Delta x \to 0} \frac{f(a + \Delta x) - f(a)}{\Delta x}$$

EXAMPLE 7   *(Compare Exercise 31)*

If $f(x) = 10x + 6$, compute the instantaneous rate of change of f when $x = 7$.

SOLUTION   We wish to compute $f'(7)$.

Step 1. Compute and simplify $f(7 + \Delta x) - f(7)$:

$$f(7 + \Delta x) = 10(7 + \Delta x) + 6 = 76 + 10\Delta x$$
$$f(7) = 76$$
$$f(7 + \Delta x) - f(7) = 10\Delta x$$

Step 2. Divide the result of Step 1 by Δx. Here $\frac{10\Delta x}{\Delta x} = 10$.

Step 3. Compute the limit of the result of Step 2 as Δx approaches 0. Here 10 is not affected by Δx, so the limit is the number 10: $\lim_{\Delta x \to 0} 10 = 10$.

Answer: $f'(7) = 10$, the instantaneous rate of change of f when $x = 7$ is 10.

In this example, f is a linear function. There is nothing special about the numbers in Example 7; we can make the following general statement.

Theorem **Instantaneous Rate of Change for a Linear Function**	If $f(x) = mx + b$, then the instantaneous rate of change of f when $x = a$ is the slope m, regardless of the value of a.

We restate this theorem using derivative notation.

Theorem **The Derivative of a Linear Function**	If $f(x) = mx + b$, then $f'(a) = m$ for all values of a.

EXAMPLE 8   *(Compare Exercise 21)*

If $f(x) = 5x^2$, find $f'(-2)$.

SOLUTION   The function is the same as in Example 6, but the value of a is different. Here, $a = -2$.

Step 1. Compute and simplify $f(-2 + \Delta x) - f(-2)$:

$$f(-2) = 20$$
$$f(-2 + \Delta x) = 5(-2 + \Delta x)^2$$
$$= 5(4 - 4\Delta x + (\Delta x)^2)$$
$$= 20 - 20\Delta x + 5(\Delta x)^2$$
$$f(-2 + \Delta x) - f(-2) = 20 - 20\Delta x + 5(\Delta x)^2 - 20$$
$$= -20\Delta x + 5(\Delta x)^2$$

Step 2. Divide the result of Step 1 by Δx:

$$\frac{-20\Delta x + 5(\Delta x)^2}{\Delta x} = \frac{(-20 + 5\Delta x)\Delta x}{\Delta x}$$
$$= -20 + 5\Delta x$$

Step 3. Compute the limit of the result from Step 2 as Δx approaches 0:

$$\lim_{\Delta x \to 0} (-20 + 5\Delta x) = -20$$

Answer: $f'(-2) = -20$

Combining the results of Examples 6 and 8, we see that for $f(x) = 5x^2$, $f'(3) = 30$, but $f'(-2) = -20$. The value of $f'(a)$ depends on a.

NOTE The only functions with a constant derivative are linear functions.

The last two examples in this section show how to handle some algebra that is more complicated than we have seen thus far.

EXAMPLE 9 *(Compare Exercise 23)*

If $f(x) = 3x^2 - 4x$, find $f'(2)$.

SOLUTION

Step 1. Compute $f(a)$, $f(a + \Delta x)$ and then simplify $f(a + \Delta x) - f(a)$. Here, $a = 2$, so $f(2) = 4$:

$$f(2 + \Delta x) = 3(2 + \Delta x)^2 - 4(2 + \Delta x)$$
$$= 3(4 + 4\Delta x + (\Delta x)^2) - 8 - 4\Delta x$$
$$= 12 + 12\Delta x + 3(\Delta x)^2 - 8 - 4\Delta x$$
$$= 4 + 8\Delta x + 3(\Delta x)^2$$
$$f(2 + \Delta x) - f(2) = 4 + 8\Delta x + 3(\Delta x)^2 - 4$$
$$= 8\Delta x + 3(\Delta x)^2$$

Step 2. Divide the result of Step 1 by Δx:

$$\frac{8\Delta x + 3(\Delta x)^2}{\Delta x} = \frac{(8 + 3\Delta x)\Delta x}{\Delta x}$$
$$= 8 + 3\Delta x$$

Step 3. Compute $\lim_{\Delta x \to 0}$ (the result from Step 2):

$$\lim_{\Delta x \to 0} (8 + 3\Delta x) = 8$$

Answer: $f'(2) = 8$

EXAMPLE 10 *(Compare Exercise 25)*

If $f(x) = 36/x$, find $f'(3)$.

SOLUTION

Step 1. Compute and simplify $f(3 + \Delta x) - f(3)$:

$$f(3) = 12$$

$$f(3 + \Delta x) = \frac{36}{3 + \Delta x}$$

$$f(3 + \Delta x) - f(3) = \frac{36}{3 + \Delta x} - 12$$

In this case, "simplify" means to combine terms into one fraction:

$$\frac{36}{3 + \Delta x} - 12 = \frac{36}{3 + \Delta x} - \frac{12(3 + \Delta x)}{3 + \Delta x}$$

$$= \frac{36 - 12(3 + \Delta x)}{3 + \Delta x}$$

$$= \frac{-12\Delta x}{3 + \Delta x}$$

Step 2. Divide the result of Step 1 by Δx. Dividing by Δx is the same as multiplying $1/\Delta x$, which is often an easier way to do this step when Step 1 leaves you with a fraction. We get

$$\frac{-12\Delta x}{3 + \Delta x} \cdot \frac{1}{\Delta x} = \frac{-12}{3 + \Delta x}$$

Step 3. Compute $\lim_{\Delta x \to 0}$ (the result from Step 2):

$$\lim_{\Delta x \to 0} \left(\frac{-12}{3 + \Delta x} \right) = \frac{-12}{3} = -4$$

Answer: $f'(3) = -4$

9-1 EXERCISES

I

For each of the functions in Exercises 1 through 10, find the average rate of change of f on the indicated interval or intervals.

Function   **Interval or Intervals**

1. *(See Example 1)*
$f(x) = -7x + 5$ **(a)** $[2, 6]$ **(b)** $[-1, 3]$

2. $f(x) = 3x - 8$ **(a)** $[0, 7]$ **(b)** $[-2, 3]$

Function	Interval or Intervals

3. $f(x) = \dfrac{1}{2}x + 9$ **(a)** $[2, 6]$ **(b)** $[-4, 4]$ **(c)** $[2, 2 + \Delta x]$

4. $f(x) = -\dfrac{2}{3}x - 5$ **(a)** $[-3, 9]$ **(b)** $[-6, 6]$ **(c)** $[a, a + \Delta x]$

5. (*See Example 2*)
$f(x) = x^2 + 2x$ **(a)** $[1, 3]$ **(b)** $[0, 2]$ **(c)** $[1, 1 + \Delta x]$

6. $f(x) = x^2 - 2x + 5$ **(a)** $[0, 4]$ **(b)** $[1, 5]$ **(c)** $[3, 3 + \Delta x]$

7. $f(x) = x^2 - 4x + 6$ **(a)** $[0, 4]$ **(b)** $[-1, 5]$ **(c)** $[a, a + \Delta x]$

8. $f(x) = x^2 - x - 2$ **(a)** $[-1, 2]$ **(b)** $[1, 4]$ **(c)** $[a, a + \Delta x]$

9. $f(x) = \sqrt{x + 16}$ **(a)** $[0, 9]$ **(b)** $[-12, -7]$

10. $f(x) = \sqrt{x^2 + 9}$ **(a)** $[0, 4]$ **(b)** $[-4, 4]$

II

Use the table in Figure 9-1 to get the values of the CPI for Exercises 11 and 12.

11. (*See Example 3*) What was the average rate of change in the CPI: **(a)** from 1920 to 1940? **(b)** From 1920 to 1930? **(c)** From 1930 to 1940?

12. What was the average rate of change in the CPI: **(a)** from 1950 to 1960? **(b)** From 1960 to 1970? **(c)** From 1950 to 1970?

13. (*See Examples 4 and 5*)
  (a) What is the average velocity of a dropped rock on the interval $[4, 4 + \Delta t]$?
  (b) How fast is the rock moving 4 seconds after it is dropped?

14. **(a)** What is the average velocity of a dropped rock for the interval $1 \le t \le 1 + \Delta t$?
  (b) How fast is the rock moving 1 second after it is dropped?

15. An automobile has traveled $40t^2 + 10t$ feet after t seconds.
  (a) How far has the auto traveled after 3 seconds?
  (b) How far has the auto traveled after $3 + \Delta t$ seconds?
  (c) What is its average velocity on the interval $[3, 3 + \Delta t]$?
  (d) How fast is it going when $t = 3$?

16. Use the same automobile as in Exercise 15.
  (a) How far has the auto traveled after 2 seconds?
  (b) How far has the auto traveled after $2 + \Delta t$ seconds?
  (c) What is its average velocity on the interval $[2, 2 + \Delta t]$?
  (d) How fast is it going when $t = 2$?

III

In Exercises 17 through 20, find the instantaneous rate of change of each function at the indicated value of a.

17. (*See Example 6*)   **18.** $f(x) = -x^2$, $a = 5$
  $f(x) = 4x^2$, $a = 3$

19. $f(x) = x^2 - 3$, $a = 1$ **20.** $f(x) = 4 - x^2$, $a = 3$

21. (*See Example 8*)
  If $f(x) = -x^2$, compute $f'(-1)$.

22. If $f(x) = 6x^2$, compute $f'(-2)$.

23. (*See Example 9*)
  If $f(x) = x^2 - 7x$, compute $f'(3)$.

24. If $f(x) = 2x^2 + 5x + 1$, compute $f'(0)$.

25. (*See Example 10*)
  If $f(x) = \dfrac{3}{x}$, compute $f'(2)$.

26. If $f(x) = \dfrac{4}{x}$, compute $f'(5)$.

27. If $f(x) = mx + b$, compute $f'(a)$.

28. If a company's daily revenue function is given by $R(x) = 100x - x^2$, where x is the number of items produced each day, what is the instantaneous rate of change of revenue when $x = 20$?

29. Use the revenue function from Exercise 28 to compute the instantaneous rate of change of revenue when 50 items are produced each day.

30. Use the revenue function from Exercise 28 to compute the instantaneous rate of change of revenue when 80 items are produced each day.

31. (*See Example 7*) If a company's weekly cost function is given by $C(x) = 17x + 2800$, where x is the number of items produced each week, what is the instantaneous rate of change of cost when
    (a) $x = 10$?   (b) $x = 30$?
    (c) 60 items are produced each week?

32. The height of a thrown ball is given by $h(t) = -16t^2 + 100t + 5$, where t is measured in seconds. How fast is the ball traveling after 2 seconds?

33. An investment company predicts that the net worth of a pizza-by-the-slice franchise in a local mall will be given by $W(t) = \frac{1}{50}t^2 + 0.06t + 20$, where $W(t)$ is in tens of thousands of dollars and t is in years. How fast is the worth of the franchise growing after one year?

9-2 LIMITS

- *Introduction*
- *Definition of Limit*
- *Graphical Interpretation of Limits*
- *Rules for Computing Limits*
- *Quotients Involving Zero Limits*

INTRODUCTION

In the previous section we saw that $f'(a)$, the derivative of f at a, which gives the instantaneous rate of change of f at a, is defined as the limit as Δx approaches 0 of the average rates of change of f over intervals of length Δx:

$$f'(a) = \lim_{\Delta x \to 0} \frac{f(a + \Delta x) - f(a)}{\Delta x}$$

Thus, the derivative is defined in terms of a limit. We now begin a more general discussion of limit. The limit concept turns out to be important in other contexts as well and, in fact, is central to the major topics of calculus.

DEFINITION OF LIMIT

Definition
Limit of a Function
We say that the **limit of a function** f as x approaches c is the number L if the values of $f(x)$ are close to L whenever x is close to, but not equal to, c. The mathematical notation is

$$\lim_{x \to c} f(x) = L$$

which is read "the limit of $f(x)$ as x approaches c is L."

FIGURE 9–2

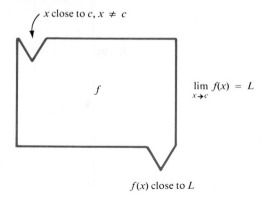

x close to c, $x \neq c$

f

$\lim_{x \to c} f(x) = L$

$f(x)$ close to L

Another way to express the idea of limit is to say that $f(x)$ approaches L as x approaches c.

The description of a function as a machine may help. The picture is shown in Figure 9–2.

CAUTION When determining a limit L, notice that L has nothing to do with $f(c)$, the value of the function at $x = c$. The condition that $x \neq c$ specifically excludes considering $f(c)$ in deciding what L is. The reason to exclude the value $x = c$ comes from the definition of derivative; the quotient

$$\frac{f(a + \Delta x) - f(a)}{\Delta x}$$

isn't defined if $\Delta x = 0$.

GRAPHICAL INTERPRETATION OF LIMITS

We would like to help you develop some geometric intuition for the meaning of the statement " $\lim_{x \to c} f(x) = L$." (There is a lot of symbolism used in that statement. Practice saying the statement in words whenever you come across it: $\lim_{x \to c} f(x) = L$ is read "the limit of $f(x)$ at c equals L." You are learning new words in a "foreign language"; not many people can master this language completely on one reading. And don't be afraid to stumble with these terms; almost everybody feels a bit awkward when first using unfamiliar words, but nobody becomes good at anything without practicing.)

EXAMPLE 1 *(Compare Exercise 1)*

What is $\lim_{x \to 3} x^2$? That is, what is the limit of $f(x) = x^2$ as x approaches 3?

SOLUTION We apply the definition, with $f(x) = x^2$ and $c = 3$.
If x is near 3, x^2 is near 9, so $L = 9$:

$$\lim_{x \to 3} x^2 = 9$$

FIGURE 9–3

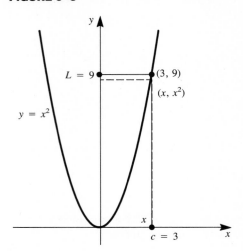

This is shown graphically in Figure 9–3. (*Compare Exercise 21*)

Remember that points on the graph are of the form $(x, f(x))$—the second coordinate represents $f(x)$. Graphically, if x is close to 3, then (x, x^2) is close to the point $(3, 9)$, and x^2 is close to 9.

FIGURE 9–4

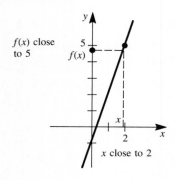

EXAMPLE 2   (*Compare Exercise 5*)

What is $\lim\limits_{x \to 2} (3x - 1)$?

SOLUTION   Applying the definition of limit, we know that if x is close to 2, then $3x$ is close to 6, so $3x - 1$ is close to 5:

$$\lim_{x \to 2} (3x - 1) = 5$$

See Figure 9–4.

In these two examples we were able to find the limit by using the definition and "common sense." That is, if x is near 2, "common sense" leads us to believe that $3x - 1$ is near 5.

Now let's look at an example in which the answer isn't as clear.

EXAMPLE 3 *(Compare Exercise 35)*

Find $\lim\limits_{x \to 3} \dfrac{x^2 - 9}{x - 3}$.

SOLUTION Now we are looking at a quotient, and when x is near 3, both the numerator and the denominator are close to 0. It is not immediately obvious what number

$$\frac{x^2 - 9}{x - 3}$$

is near if x is near 3. In fact, the expression

$$\frac{x^2 - 9}{x - 3}$$

makes no sense at all when $x = 3$. Since we can't tell what's going on just by looking, we rewrite this expression by factoring the numerator and trying to simplify:

$$\frac{x^2 - 9}{x - 3} = \frac{(x - 3)(x + 3)}{x - 3} = x + 3, \qquad \text{if } x \neq 3$$

Therefore, if $x \neq 3$, then

$$\frac{x^2 - 9}{x - 3} = x + 3$$

and when x is close to 3, $x + 3$ is close to 6. We can conclude that

$$\lim_{x \to 3} \frac{x^2 - 9}{x - 3} = \lim_{x \to 3} (x + 3) = 6$$

CAUTION When trying to evaluate

$$\lim_{x \to 3} \frac{x^2 - 9}{x - 3}$$

you do *not* substitute $x = 3$. Again, examples like this are the reason that $x \neq c$ is part of the definition of limit.

The graph of

$$f(x) = \frac{x^2 - 9}{x - 3}$$

FIGURE 9–5

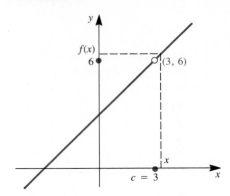

gives a picture of what is going on here. We saw above that $f(x) = x + 3$ whenever $x \neq 3$. The graph of $y = x + 3$ is a straight line; but since x can't be 3, then we must remove the point $(3, 6)$ from the line. Therefore, the graph of

$$f(x) = \frac{x^2 - 9}{x - 3}$$

is a line with a "hole" in it—the point $(3, 6)$ is missing from the line. See Figure 9–5.

The graph shows that if x is near 3, $f(x)$ is near 6, and that's what $\lim_{x \to 3} f(x) = 6$ means, even if $f(3)$ itself doesn't make sense. (*Compare Exercise 17*)

RULES FOR COMPUTING LIMITS

Notice that what we did in Example 3 was to replace a complicated expression,

$$\frac{x^2 - 9}{x - 3}$$

by a simpler expression, $x + 3$, which still gave the values of $f(x)$ whenever $x \neq 3$. This important technique is often used in computing limits and is justified by the following theorem.

Theorem
Replacement Principle

If f and g are two functions with $f(x) = g(x)$ for all x near c, $x \neq c$, and if $\lim_{x \to c} g(x) = L$, then $\lim_{x \to c} f(x) = L$ also.

You will use this theorem whenever you replace one expression for $f(x)$ by a simpler one. In Example 3 we used this theorem with

$$f(x) = \frac{x^2 - 9}{x - 3}$$

$g(x) = x + 3$, $c = 3$, and $L = 6$.

NOTE   The replacement principle corresponds to the simplifying step in computing derivatives in the previous section. See the next example.

EXAMPLE 4   *(Compare Exercise 45)*

If $f(x) = 3x^2$, compute $f'(2)$:

SOLUTION

$$f'(2) = \lim_{\Delta x \to 0} \frac{f(2 + \Delta x) - f(2)}{\Delta x}$$

$$= \lim_{\Delta x \to 0} \frac{3(2 + \Delta x)^2 - 3(2)^2}{\Delta x}$$

$$= \lim_{\Delta x \to 0} \frac{3(4 + 4\Delta x + (\Delta x)^2) - 12}{\Delta x}$$

$$= \lim_{\Delta x \to 0} \frac{12\Delta x + 3(\Delta x)^2}{\Delta x}$$

Next, replace $\dfrac{12\Delta x + 3(\Delta x)^2}{\Delta x}$ by $12 + 3\Delta x$; they are equal if $\Delta x \neq 0$:

$$f'(2) = \lim_{\Delta x \to 0} (12 + 3\Delta x)$$

$$= 12$$

So $f'(2) = 12$.

We look more closely now at some computational principles that we can use when evaluating limits. We state these principles formally as a theorem, which shows that the familiar operations of arithmetic carry over to operating with limits. For example, if f and g are two functions, and x near c means both that $f(x)$ is close to some number L and that $g(x)$ is close to some number K, then we can conclude that $f(x) + g(x)$ is near $L + K$.

That sentence is awkward; using the limit notation, we have

$$\lim_{x \to c} (f(x) + g(x)) = \lim_{x \to c} f(x) + \lim_{x \to c} g(x)$$

A more informal way to remember this is "*the limit of the sum is the sum of the limits.*"

The other arithmetic operations of subtraction, multiplication, and division also carry over to limits in a natural way. For example, "*the limit of the product is the product of the limits.*" We summarize this discussion in the following theorem.

Theorem
Arithmetic with Limits

If $\lim\limits_{x \to c} f(x) = L$ and $\lim\limits_{x \to c} g(x) = K$, then

1. (Sum)

$$\lim\limits_{x \to c} [f(x) + g(x)] = \lim\limits_{x \to c} f(x) + \lim\limits_{x \to c} g(x) = L + K$$

The limit of the sum is the sum of the limits.

2. (Difference)

$$\lim\limits_{x \to c} [f(x) - g(x)] = \lim\limits_{x \to c} f(x) - \lim\limits_{x \to c} g(x) = L - K$$

The limit of the difference is the difference of the limits.

3. (Product)

$$\lim\limits_{x \to c} [f(x) \cdot g(x)] = \lim\limits_{x \to c} f(x) \cdot \lim\limits_{x \to c} g(x) = L \cdot K$$

The limit of the product is the product of the limits.

4. (Quotient) If $K \neq 0$,

$$\lim\limits_{x \to c} \frac{f(x)}{g(x)} = \frac{\lim\limits_{x \to c} f(x)}{\lim\limits_{x \to c} g(x)} = \frac{L}{K}$$

The limit of the quotient is the quotient of the limits if the limit of the denominator is not zero.

Two more observations about limits provide what we need for most computations.

Theorem
Two Special Limits

1. If K is a constant, then $\lim\limits_{x \to c} K = K$.

2. $\lim\limits_{x \to c} x = c$.

See Figure 9–6.

FIGURE 9–6

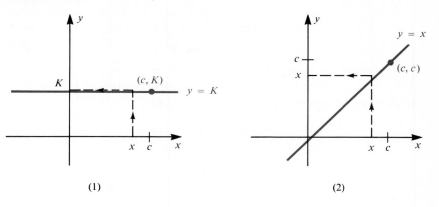

(1)   (2)

(Compare Exercise 25)

If $\lim\limits_{x \to 8} f(x) = 2$, what is $\lim\limits_{x \to 8} (xf(x))$?

$$\lim_{x \to 8} (xf(x)) = \left(\lim_{x \to 8} x \right)\left(\lim_{x \to 8} f(x) \right) = 8 \cdot 2 = 16$$

EXAMPLE 6 *(Compare Exercise 27)*

If $\lim\limits_{x \to 3} f(x) = 5$ and $\lim\limits_{x \to 3} g(x) = 4$, what are:

(a) $\lim\limits_{x \to 3} (f(x) \cdot g(x))$?

(b) $\lim\limits_{x \to 3} \dfrac{f(x)}{g(x)}$?

(c) $\lim\limits_{x \to 3} (2f(x) - 6g(x))$?

SOLUTION

(a) $\lim\limits_{x \to 3} (f(x) \cdot g(x)) = \lim\limits_{x \to 3} f(x) \cdot \lim\limits_{x \to 3} g(x) = 5 \cdot 4 = 20$

(b) $\lim\limits_{x \to 3} \dfrac{f(x)}{g(x)} = \dfrac{\lim\limits_{x \to 3} f(x)}{\lim\limits_{x \to 3} g(x)} = \dfrac{5}{4}$

(c) $\lim\limits_{x \to 3} (2f(x) - 6g(x)) = \lim\limits_{x \to 3} (2f(x)) - \lim\limits_{x \to 3} (6g(x))$

$$= 2 \lim_{x \to 3} f(x) - 6 \lim_{x \to 3} g(x)$$

$$= 2 \cdot 5 - 6 \cdot 4 = -14$$

These examples are special cases of a more general theorem that simplifies the computation of limits when the function is a polynomial. By applying the arithmetic theorem many times we can derive the following result, which lets us quickly compute limits of polynomial functions.

Theorem
Limit of a Polynomial

If f is a polynomial function, that is, if

$$f(x) = a_n x^n + a_{n-1}x^{n-1} + \cdots + a_1 x + a_0$$

then, for any number c,

$$\lim_{x \to c} f(x) = f(c)$$

In short, if $f(x)$ is a polynomial, then $\lim_{x \to c} f(x) = f(c)$.

EXAMPLE 7   *(Compare Exercise 11)*

Compute $\lim_{x \to -1} (3x^4 - 7x^2 + 2x + 3)$.

SOLUTION   The function is the polynomial

$$f(x) = 3x^4 - 7x^2 + 2x + 3$$

The value of the function at $x = -1$ is

$$f(-1) = 3(-1)^4 - 7(-1)^2 + 2(-1) + 3$$
$$= -3$$

Thus $\lim_{x \to -1} (3x^4 - 7x^2 + 2x + 3) = -3$.

We have a similar theorem if $f(x)$ is the quotient of polynomials.

Theorem
Limit of a Quotient of Polynomials

If $f(x) = \dfrac{P(x)}{Q(x)}$ and P and Q are polynomials with $Q(c) \neq 0$, then

$$\lim_{x \to c} f(x) = f(c)$$

EXAMPLE 8   *(Compare Exercise 7)*

Compute $\lim_{x \to 3} \dfrac{2x^2 + 3x - 1}{x^3 - 7}$.

SOLUTION   Interpret

$$\frac{2x^2 + 3x - 1}{x^3 - 7}$$

as the quotient of the polynomial $2x^2 + 3x - 1$ by the polynomial $x^3 - 7$. Since $\lim_{x \to 3} (x^3 - 7) = 3^3 - 7 = 20$, the limit of the denominator is nonzero. Thus, we can apply the result

$$\lim_{x \to c} \frac{f(x)}{g(x)} = \frac{\lim_{x \to c} f(x)}{\lim_{x \to c} g(x)}$$

We get

$$\lim_{x \to 3} \frac{2x^2 + 3x - 1}{x^3 - 7} = \frac{\lim_{x \to 3} (2x^2 + 3x - 1)}{\lim_{x \to 3} (x^3 - 7)} = \frac{2 \cdot 9 + 3 \cdot 3 - 1}{27 - 7}$$

$$= \frac{26}{20}$$

CAUTION It is important to realize the implication of the condition $\lim_{x \to c} g(x) \neq 0$ when applying the rule

$$\lim_{x \to c} \frac{f(x)}{g(x)} = \frac{\lim_{x \to c} f(x)}{\lim_{x \to c} g(x)}$$

If the limit of the denominator is zero, this method cannot be used; however, the limit of the quotient may or may not exist. We have to resort to alternative approaches to discuss the limit. Such quotient functions do play a fundamental role in calculus, so we now look at some examples to illustrate some of the concepts involved. *You must check that $Q(c) \neq 0$.*

EXAMPLE 9   *(Compare Exercise 37)*

FIGURE 9–7

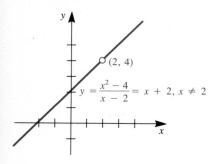

$y = \dfrac{x^2 - 4}{x - 2} = x + 2, x \neq 2$

Compute $\lim_{x \to 2} \dfrac{x^2 - 4}{x - 2}$.

SOLUTION   We cannot just let $x = 2$ and get an answer. Nor is it legitimate to say that the limit in the denominator is 0 and, since division by 0 is impossible, the limit of the quotient doesn't exist. Remember the definition of derivative, which is one of the most important applications of limits. This theorem tells you what happens if $Q(c) \neq 0$; it doesn't tell you what happens if $Q(c) = 0$. In fact here,

$$\lim_{x \to 2} \frac{x^2 - 4}{x - 2} = \lim_{x \to 2} \frac{(x - 2)(x + 2)}{x - 2} = \lim_{x \to 2} (x + 2) = 4$$

See Figure 9–7.

We had to rewrite the problem and simplify $\dfrac{x^2 - 4}{x - 2}$ to see what was really going on. The graph of

$$f(x) = \frac{x^2 - 4}{x - 2}$$

is given in Figure 9–7.

It is also true that limits behave the way you'd like them to when exponents are involved.

EXAMPLE 10

Find $\lim\limits_{x \to 3} (x + 5)^2$.

SOLUTION   If x is near 3, $x + 5$ is near 8, and so $(x + 5)^2$ is near 8^2, or 64. We conclude that $\lim\limits_{x \to 3} (x + 5)^2 = 64$.

EXAMPLE 11

Find $\lim\limits_{x \to 11} \sqrt{x + 14}$.

SOLUTION   If x is near 11, $x + 14$ is near 25, so $\sqrt{x + 14}$ is near $\sqrt{25}$, or 5. We have $\lim\limits_{x \to 11} \sqrt{x + 14} = 5$.

The general property is stated as follows.

Theorem
Limit of a Power

If k is a real number, then

$$\lim_{x \to c} (f(x))^k = \left(\lim_{x \to c} f(x) \right)^k$$

whenever the expressions make sense. (That qualifying remark is included because, for instance, we can't take square roots of negative numbers.) The limit of a power is the power of the limit.

EXAMPLE 12   *(Compare Exercise 29)*

If $\lim\limits_{x \to 5} f(x) = 4$, what are:

(a) $\lim\limits_{x \to 5} (f(x))^2$?

(b) $\lim\limits_{x \to 5} \sqrt{f(x)}$?

SOLUTION

(a) $\lim_{x \to 5} (f(x))^2 = \left(\lim_{x \to 5} f(x) \right)^2 = 4^2 = 16$

(b) $\lim_{x \to 5} \sqrt{f(x)} = \sqrt{\lim_{x \to 5} f(x)} = \sqrt{4} = 2$

Sometimes we can have limits involving square roots that require some algebra to help us compute the answer.

EXAMPLE 13 (*Compare Exercise 41*)

Find $\lim_{x \to 4} \dfrac{\sqrt{x} - 2}{x - 4}$.

SOLUTION Here again the individual limits in the numerator and denominator are both 0. In previous courses you may have had to rationalize the denominator to simplify an expression involving square roots. Here, the square root is in the numerator, but the procedure is the same. Multiply numerator and denominator by $\sqrt{x} + 2$:

$$\lim_{x \to 4} \frac{\sqrt{x} - 2}{x - 4} = \lim_{x \to 4} \frac{(\sqrt{x} - 2)(\sqrt{x} + 2)}{(x - 4)(\sqrt{x} + 2)}$$

$$= \lim_{x \to 4} \frac{x - 4}{(x - 4)(\sqrt{x} + 2)} \quad \text{(Divide numerator and denominator by } x - 4)$$

$$= \lim_{x \to 4} \frac{1}{\sqrt{x} + 2} = \frac{1}{2 + 2} = \frac{1}{4}$$

Therefore,

$$\lim_{x \to 4} \frac{\sqrt{x} - 2}{x - 4} = \frac{1}{4}$$

QUOTIENTS INVOLVING ZERO LIMITS

Suppose that $f(x)$ is a quotient, that the limit of the numerator is L, and that the limit of the denominator is K. That is, suppose

$$f(x) = \frac{h(x)}{g(x)}$$

with $\lim_{x \to c} h(x) = L$ and $\lim_{x \to c} g(x) = K$.

1. If $K \neq 0$, we can evaluate $\lim_{x \to c} f(x)$ as $\dfrac{L}{K}$.

2. If $K = 0$ and $L = 0$, we must try to simplify the quotient and use the replacement principle to compute $\lim_{x \to c} f(x)$.

3. If $K = 0$ and $L \neq 0$, then $\lim\limits_{x \to c} f(x)$ is not a real number. We will treat this case more extensively in Chapter 11, but for now we will just say "$\lim\limits_{x \to c} f(x)$ is not a number."

EXAMPLE 14   *(Compare Exercise 49)*

Find $\lim\limits_{x \to 0} \dfrac{1}{x}$.

SOLUTION   If x is slightly bigger than 0, then $\frac{1}{x}$ is a very large positive number. The closer x is to 0, the larger $\frac{1}{x}$ is. There is no single number we can call the limit of $\frac{1}{x}$ as x approaches 0. We say that $\lim\limits_{x \to 0} \frac{1}{x}$ is not a number.

EXAMPLE 15   *(Compare Exercise 51)*

Find $\lim\limits_{x \to 1} \dfrac{x^2 - 1}{x + 3}$.

SOLUTION   We can use the quotient theorem, and say that the limit is $\frac{0}{4} = 0$. It's only when the *denominator* is 0 that we can't apply the theorem.

9-2 EXERCISES

I

Use the definition of limit to find the limits in Exercises 1 through 10.

1. *(See Example 1)*
   $\lim\limits_{x \to 2} x^2$

2. $\lim\limits_{x \to 2} 3x$

3. $\lim\limits_{x \to 7} (2x - 8)$

4. $\lim\limits_{x \to -2} (5x - 3)$

5. *(See Example 2)*
   $\lim\limits_{x \to 2} (x^2 - 9)$

6. $\lim\limits_{x \to 3} (2x + 5)$

7. *(See Example 8)*
   $\lim\limits_{x \to -1} \dfrac{x^2 + 3}{2x - 1}$

8. $\lim\limits_{x \to -2} \dfrac{x^2 + 4}{x + 7}$

9. $\lim\limits_{x \to 3} 5$

10. $\lim\limits_{x \to 1} -2$

Use the theorems on arithmetic with limits to compute the limits in Exercises 11 through 14.

11. *(See Example 7)*
    $\lim\limits_{x \to -3} (2x^2 - x - 4)$

12. $\lim\limits_{x \to 1} \dfrac{5x^2 - 2x}{3x + 1}$

13. $\lim\limits_{x \to 4} \sqrt{6x + 1}$

14. $\lim\limits_{x \to 3} \sqrt{10 - 2x}$

FIGURE 9–8

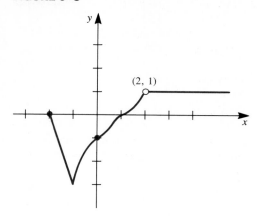

FIGURE 9–9

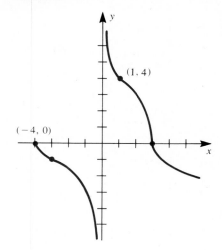

Use Figure 9–8 to find the limits in Exercises 15 through 18.

15. $\lim_{x \to -1} f(x)$

16. $\lim_{x \to 0} f(x)$

17. (*See Figure 9–5*)
$\lim_{x \to 2} f(x)$

18. $\lim_{x \to 3} f(x)$

Use Figure 9–9 to find the limits in Exercises 19 through 22.

19. $\lim_{x \to 0} f(x)$

20. $\lim_{x \to 1} f(x)$

21. (*See Example 1*)
$\lim_{x \to 3} f(x)$

22. $\lim_{x \to -3} f(x)$

II

23. Find $\lim_{x \to 3} f(x)$ if $f(x) = \begin{cases} 2x + 1 & x \le 4 \\ 7 - 2x & x > 4 \end{cases}$

24. Find $\lim_{x \to 2} g(t)$ if $g(t) = \begin{cases} t^2 - 5 & t \le 1 \\ 4t + 1 & t > 1 \end{cases}$

25. (*See Example 5*) If $\lim_{x \to 3} f(x) = 5$, what is

$\lim_{x \to 3} (6f(x))$?

26. If $\lim_{x \to 3} f(x) = 6$ and $\lim_{x \to 3} g(x) = 9$, what are:
(**a**) $\lim_{x \to 3} (f(x) + g(x))$?   (**b**) $\lim_{x \to 3} (f(x) \cdot g(x))$?

27. (*See Example 6*) If $\lim_{x \to 2} f(x) = -1$ and

$\lim_{x \to 2} g(x) = 7$, what are:

(**a**) $\lim_{x \to 2} (3g(x) - f(x))$?   (**b**) $\lim_{x \to 2} \dfrac{g(x)}{f(x)}$?

28. If $\lim_{x \to 2} f(x) = -3$ and $\lim_{x \to 2} g(x) = 8$, what are:
(**a**) $\lim_{x \to 2} (5f(x) + 2g(x))$?
(**b**) $\lim_{x \to 2} (f(x) + x)$?

29. (*See Example 12*) If $\lim_{x \to 4} f(x) = 9$ what are:
(**a**) $\lim_{x \to 4} \sqrt{f(x)}$?   (**b**) $\lim_{x \to 4} (f(x))^2$?

30. If $\lim_{x \to 3} f(x) = 2$ what are:
(**a**) $\lim_{x \to 3} (4x + (f(x))^2)$? (**b**) $\lim_{x \to 3} (f(x))^{-5}$?

31. If $\lim_{x \to 2} f(x) = 5$, what is $\lim_{x \to 2} (xf(x))$?

32. If $\lim_{x \to 3} f(x) = 12$, what is $\lim_{x \to 3} \dfrac{f(x)}{x}$?

33. What is $\lim_{\Delta x \to 0} (6 + \Delta x)^2$?

34. What is $\lim_{\Delta x \to 0} (a + \Delta x)^2$?

III

Compute each of the limits in Exercises 35 through 44.

35. (*See Example 3*)

$$\lim_{x \to 1} \frac{x^2 - 1}{x - 1}$$

36. $\lim_{x \to 2} \dfrac{x^2 + x - 6}{x - 2}$

37. (*See Example 9*)

$$\lim_{x \to 0} \frac{x^2 + 5x}{x}$$

38. $\lim_{\Delta x \to 0} \dfrac{3\Delta x - 7(\Delta x)^2}{\Delta x}$

39. $\lim_{\Delta x \to 0} \dfrac{6\Delta x + (\Delta x)^2 - 4(\Delta x)^3}{\Delta x}$

40. $\lim_{\Delta x \to 0} \dfrac{\sqrt{4 + \Delta x} - 2}{\Delta x}$

41. (*See Example 13*)

$$\lim_{x \to 9} \frac{\sqrt{x} - 3}{x - 9}$$

42. $\lim_{x \to 25} \dfrac{\sqrt{x} - 5}{x - 25}$

43. $\lim_{x \to 4} \dfrac{\dfrac{1}{x} - \dfrac{1}{4}}{x - 4}$

44. $\lim_{x \to 3} \dfrac{\dfrac{1}{x} - \dfrac{1}{3}}{x - 3}$

Use the limit definition of derivative to find $f'(a)$ for the given function and the given value of a in Exercises 45 through 48.

45. (*See Example 4*)
$f(x) = 5x^2, a = 1$

46. $f(x) = x^2, a = -1$

47. $f(x) = \sqrt{x}, a = 4$

48. $f(x) = 1 - x^2, a = 3$

Find the limit or state that the limit is not a number in Exercises 49 through 58.

49. (*See Example 14*)

$\lim_{x \to 0} \dfrac{1}{x^2}$

50. $\lim_{x \to 3} \dfrac{1}{x - 3}$

51. (*See Example 15*)

$\lim_{x \to 1} \dfrac{x - 1}{x}$

52. $\lim_{x \to 2} \dfrac{x - 1}{x^2}$

53. $\lim_{x \to 0} \dfrac{x^2 + 5x}{x + 3}$

54. $\lim_{x \to 0} \dfrac{x^2 + 5x}{x(x + 3)}$

55. $\lim_{x \to 0} \dfrac{x^2 + 5x}{x^2(x + 3)}$

56. $\lim_{x \to 4} \dfrac{(x - 4)^2}{x - 4}$

57. $\lim_{x \to 4} \dfrac{(x - 4)^2}{(x - 4)^2}$

58. $\lim_{x \to 4} \dfrac{(x - 4)^2}{(x - 4)^3}$

9–3 ONE-SIDED LIMITS AND CONTINUITY

- *One-Sided Limits*
- *Continuity*

ONE-SIDED LIMITS

We have seen that, although the formula

$$f(x) = \frac{x^2 - 9}{x - 3}$$

looks complicated, the graph of f is simply a straight line with a hole in it. How does the idea of limit apply to a function whose graph jumps around? A consumer awareness function is such a function. (For further discussion of this function, see Appendix A, Section A–8.) The rule for evaluating this function was as follows:

FIGURE 9–10

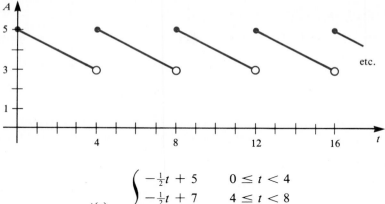

$$A(t) = \begin{cases} -\tfrac{1}{2}t + 5 & 0 \le t < 4 \\ -\tfrac{1}{2}t + 7 & 4 \le t < 8 \\ -\tfrac{1}{2}t + 9 & 8 \le t < 11 \\ \text{etc.} \end{cases}$$

Its graph is shown in Figure 9–10.

What is happening to the function near $t = 4$? What is $\lim\limits_{t \to 4} A(t)$?

The function now is called A, not f, and we are using t (for time) instead of x, but the idea is the same—if t is near 4, what is $A(t)$ near? In this example, knowing that t is near 4 doesn't tell us what $A(t)$ is near. If t is near 4 and a little bit *less than 4*, then $A(t) = -\tfrac{1}{2}t + 5$, so $A(t)$ is near 3. Look at the graph a little bit to the left of $t = 4$.

On the other hand, if t is near 4 and a little bit *greater than 4*, then $A(t) = -\tfrac{1}{2}t + 7$ is close to 5. Now look at the section of the graph just to the right of $t = 4$.

In an attempt to preserve this geometric flavor, mathematicians use the words "left-hand limit" and "right-hand limit." The notation for left-hand limit uses the symbol "$x \to c^-$" in place of "$x \to c$." The minus sign to the right and above c means that x is just a little bit *less* than c.

Definition **Left-hand Limit**	The number L is called **the left-hand limit** of f at c if $f(x)$ is near L whenever x is near c and less than c; we write $\lim\limits_{x \to c^-} f(x) = L$.

To return to the consumer-awareness example, we can now write

$$\lim_{t \to 4^-} A(t) = \lim_{t \to 4^-} (-\tfrac{1}{2}t + 5) = 3$$

The right-hand limit is defined in an analogous manner, using $x \to c^+$ to mean that x is just a little bit more than c.

Definition	The number L is called **the right-hand limit** of f at c if $f(x)$ is near L
Right-hand Limit	whenever x is near c and greater than c; we write $\lim\limits_{x \to c^+} f(x) = L$.

In our consumer-awareness example we can now say

$$\lim_{t \to 4^+} A(t) = \lim_{t \to 4^+} (-\tfrac{1}{2}t + 7) = 5$$

All the rules from the previous section that we used to compute limits are valid for one-sided limits, and we will use them without repeating them here.

Because $A(t)$ is close to 5 if t is close to and greater than 4, but $A(t)$ is close to 3 if t is close to and less than 4, there is not a single number we can say $A(t)$ is close to if t is close to 4. Because there is no such single number, we say that $\lim\limits_{t \to 4} A(t)$ doesn't exist. This example is one instance of a general statement that can help us in computing the limit or in deciding that the limit doesn't exist.

Theorem	$\lim\limits_{x \to c} f(x) = L$ if and only if both $\lim\limits_{x \to c^-} f(x) = L$ *and* $\lim\limits_{x \to c^+} f(x) = L$.
Existence of the Limit	

EXAMPLE 1   *(Compare Exercise 7)*

Using the consumer-awareness function above, what are:

(a) $\lim\limits_{t \to 8^-} A(t)$?   (b) $\lim\limits_{t \to 8^+} A(t)$?   (c) $\lim\limits_{t \to 8} A(t)$?

SOLUTION

(a) $\lim\limits_{t \to 8^-} A(t) = \lim\limits_{t \to 8^-} (-\tfrac{1}{2}t + 7) = -4 + 7 = 3$

(b) $\lim\limits_{t \to 8^+} A(t) = \lim\limits_{t \to 8^+} (-\tfrac{1}{2}t + 9) = -4 + 9 = 5$

(c) Because the answers to parts (a) and (b) are not equal, $\lim\limits_{t \to 8} A(t)$ does not exist.

EXAMPLE 2   *(Compare Exercise 13)*

What is $\lim\limits_{x \to 0} \dfrac{|x|}{x}$?

SOLUTION   (This is a particularly important example, and we will look at it again in a slightly different setting in Section 9–5. Remember that $|x|$ means the absolute value of x, and the rule for evaluating $|x|$ depends on the sign of x. If x is positive, $|x| = x$; but if x is negative, $|x|$ has the opposite sign from x, so $|x| = -x$. Let $f(x) = |x|/x$.

If $x > 0$,

$$f(x) = \frac{|x|}{x} = \frac{x}{x} = 1$$

On the other hand, if $x < 0$,

$$f(x) = \frac{|x|}{x} = \frac{-x}{x} = -1$$

We can rewrite the rule for $f(x)$ as follows:

$$f(x) = \frac{|x|}{x} = \begin{cases} 1 & \text{if } x > 0 \\ -1 & \text{if } x < 0 \end{cases}$$

The graph of $f(x) = |x|/x$ is given in Figure 9–11.

FIGURE 9–11

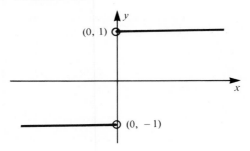

NOTE The empty dots at the points $(0, 1)$ and $(0, -1)$ indicate that these points are not on the graph of f. Furthermore, although the number 0 is not in the domain of f, we can still ask about $\lim_{x \to 0} f(x)$.

The value of $f(x)$ depends on which side of 0 that x comes from; this is a hint to us that we should consider the one-sided limits. Moreover, the geometry of the graph indicates a **jump in the graph** when $x = 0$ and suggests that we should examine limits from each side of 0. For the right-hand limit,

$$\lim_{x \to 0^+} f(x) = \lim_{x \to 0^+} \frac{|x|}{x} = \lim_{x \to 0^+} \frac{x}{x} = \lim_{x \to 0^+} 1 = 1$$

For the left-hand limit,

$$\lim_{x \to 0^-} f(x) = \lim_{x \to 0^-} \frac{|x|}{x} = \lim_{x \to 0^-} \frac{-x}{x} = \lim_{x \to 0^-} -1 = -1$$

Because we get two different numbers, we say that $\lim_{x \to 0} |x|/x$ doesn't exist.

CAUTION It would be a mistake to conclude that a change in the rule for evaluating a function means that the function doesn't have a limit where the rule changes. A change in the evaluation formula suggests the use of one-sided limits; be sure to *use* them before making any conclusions.

EXAMPLE 3   *(Compare Exercise 19)*

Palmer Manufacturing Company has noticed that for the first 50 lawnmowers it produces each day, the cost per mower is a constant $20, and then the cost per mower starts decreasing. A term sometimes used for the cost of the next item is **marginal cost,** written $MC(x)$. This particular company has estimated that its daily marginal cost (in dollars) is given by

$$MC(x) = \begin{cases} 20 & 0 \le x \le 50 \\ 1000/x & x > 50 \end{cases}$$

where x is the number of mowers manufactured on a given day. What is $\lim_{x \to 50} MC(x)$?

SOLUTION   Because the rule for evaluating $MC(x)$ changes at $x = 50$, we will decide about $\lim_{x \to 50} MC(x)$ by examining left-hand and right-hand limits:

$$\text{(Right)} \quad \lim_{x \to 50^+} MC(x) = \lim_{x \to 50^+} \frac{1000}{x} = \frac{1000}{50} = 20$$

$$\text{(Left)} \quad \lim_{x \to 50^-} MC(x) = \lim_{x \to 50^-} 20 = 20$$

Comparing the two limits, we find that

$$\lim_{x \to 50^+} MC(x) = \lim_{x \to 50^-} MC(x) = 20$$

so we conclude that

$$\lim_{x \to 50} MC(x) = 20$$

If the right-hand limit equals the left-hand limit, then their common value is the value of the limit. The graph of this function is shown in Figure 9–12.

A change in the computational rule does not necessarily mean a jump in the graph!

FIGURE 9–12

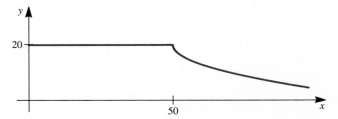

FIGURE 9-13

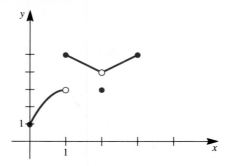

EXAMPLE 4   *(Compare Exercise 1)*

Use the graph in Figure 9–13 to find the following limits:

(a) $\lim\limits_{x \to 1^+} f(x)$ (b) $\lim\limits_{x \to 1^-} f(x)$ (c) $\lim\limits_{x \to 1} f(x)$

(d) $\lim\limits_{x \to 2^+} f(x)$ (e) $\lim\limits_{x \to 2^-} f(x)$ (f) $\lim\limits_{x \to 2} f(x)$

SOLUTION   The rule for evaluating $f(x)$ is not given, so all we can do is look at the graph. Remember the distinction between the number $\lim\limits_{x \to c} f(x)$ and the number $f(c)$. Here, the heavy dots on the graph indicate that $f(1) = 5$ and $f(2) = 3$, but this doesn't tell us anything about the limits.

(a) $\lim\limits_{x \to 1^+} f(x) = 5$ (b) $\lim\limits_{x \to 1^-} f(x) = 3$ (c) $\lim\limits_{x \to 1} f(x)$ doesn't exist

The answer to part (c) follows because the answers to parts (a) and (b) are different. Remember not to look at $f(1)$ in deciding about $\lim\limits_{x \to 1} f(x)$.

(d) $\lim\limits_{x \to 2^+} f(x) = 4$ (e) $\lim\limits_{x \to 2^-} f(x) = 4$ (f) $\lim\limits_{x \to 2} f(x) = 4$

The answer to part (f) follows because the answers to parts (d) and (e) are the same. The fact that $f(2) = 3$ has nothing to do with deciding that $\lim\limits_{x \to 2} f(x) = 4$.

CONTINUITY

If someone said to you, "The water flowed out of the faucet continuously for an hour," you would know that the flow of water was uninterrupted—the stream of water was unbroken. Mathematicians use the word **continuous** in a similar way; they say that a function is continuous if its graph is not broken, that is, if the graph just has one piece. Let's look at two examples of functions that are not continuous and see whether we can discover what causes the graph to have a break in it. We will use what we discover to give the mathematical definition for a continuous function.

FIGURE 9-14

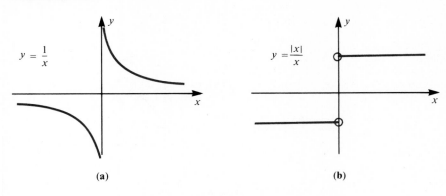

$y = \dfrac{1}{x}$

$y = \dfrac{|x|}{x}$

(a)

(b)

FIGURE 9-15

$f(x) = y = \dfrac{x^2 - 9}{x - 3}$

(3, 6)

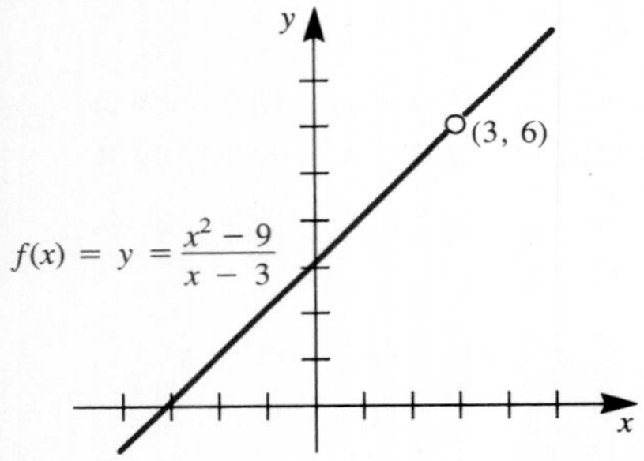

EXAMPLE 5   *(Compare Exercise 4)*

Give examples of graphs that are "broken"; the function is **not continuous**.

SOLUTION

1. The graph can have a jump (see Figure 9–14(a) and 9–14(b)). In both these cases $\lim\limits_{x \to 0} f(x)$ does not exist.

2. The graph can have a **hole** in it (see Figure 9–15). When the graph has a hole in it, there is a point "missing" from the graph. Here, $\lim\limits_{x \to 3} f(x) = 6$, but $f(3)$ is not defined.

These examples are important because they show everything that can produce a break: Either the two pieces of the graph don't match up—the limit of $f(x)$ as $x \to c$ doesn't exist—or they do match up, but the graph has a hole in it—$f(c)$ is not what it should be.

So if we require (1) that the two pieces match up and (2) that the graph doesn't have a hole, then the graph can't have a break, and the function will be continuous.

Mathematicians have discovered that these geometric properties (1) and (2) will hold if $f(c)$ and $\lim\limits_{x \to c} f(x)$ are the same number.

Definition
Continuous at a Point

f is **continuous at** $x = c$ if $\lim\limits_{x \to c} f(x) = f(c)$.

Continuous functions are those that behave nicely; their limits can be found by "plugging in."

NOTE You must go through three steps to see whether a function is continuous at the number c:

1. Check that $f(c)$ is defined.
2. Check that $\lim\limits_{x \to c} f(x)$ exists.
3. Finally, check that the numbers you found in (1) and (2) are the same; $f(c) = \lim\limits_{x \to c} f(x)$.

EXAMPLE 6   (*Compare Exercise 9*)

If $f(x) = \dfrac{x^2 - 9}{x - 3}$:

(a) is f continuous at $x = 3$?
(b) is f continuous at $x = 5$?

SOLUTION

(a) We get this answer quickly; in the first step, we see that $f(3)$ is not defined. Thus f is not continuous at $x = 3$.

(b) First note that

$$f(5) = \frac{25 - 9}{5 - 3} = 8$$

(More simply, $f(x) = x + 3$ whenever $x \neq 3$, so $f(5) = 5 + 3 = 8$.)
Second,

$$\lim_{x \to 5} f(x) = \lim_{x \to 5} \frac{x^2 - 9}{x - 3} = \frac{16}{2} = 8$$

(the limit of a quotient equals the quotient of the limits if the limit in the denominator is not 0). The first and second steps both had 8 as their answer. Thus $\lim\limits_{x \to 5} f(x) = f(5)$, and so f is continuous at $x = 5$.

The statements we had in the previous section about computing limits of polynomials and quotients of polynomials show us that the above example is a special case of a general theorem:

Theorem **Continuity of Polynomials and Their Quotients**	If $f(x) = P(x)$ is a polynomial, then f is continuous at all numbers. If $f(x) = P(x)/Q(x)$ where P and Q are polynomials, then f is continuous at c if and only if $Q(c) \neq 0$.

We can now give fast answers to the previous example: If

$$f(x) = \frac{x^2 - 9}{x - 3}$$

then f is not continuous at $x = 3$ but is continuous at $x = 5$. Here, $P(x) = x^2 - 9$, $Q(x) = x - 3$, and $Q(3) = 0$, but $Q(5) = 2 \neq 0$. This example shows that a function can be continuous at one number and not continuous at another number.

> *Definition*
> **Continuous on an Interval**
>
> We will say that a function is **continuous on an interval I** if the function is continuous at all numbers in the interval I.

As an example, if

$$f(x) = \frac{x^2 - 9}{x - 3}$$

then f is continuous on $(3, 7)$ and on $[1, 2]$ but is not continuous on $(0, 10)$. In fact this function is continuous on any interval that doesn't contain the number 3. Actually, for a function to be continuous at the endpoints of the interval $[a, b]$ all that is required is that $\lim_{x \to a^+} f(x) = f(a)$ and $\lim_{x \to b^-} f(x) = f(b)$. You do not have to consider $\lim_{x \to a^-} f(x)$ or $\lim_{x \to b^+} f(x)$. Remember that a function is continuous on an interval I if the graph of the function over I has just one piece. In this text we will not get involved in many subtle distinctions. For the sake of completeness, however, we do point out that the consumer-awareness function with which we started this section is continuous on $[0, 4)$ and on $[4, 8)$ but is not continuous on $[0, 8)$.

EXAMPLE 7   *(Compare Exercise 11)*

Let

$$f(x) = \begin{cases} \dfrac{x^2 + x - 2}{x - 1} & x \neq 1 \\ 3 & x = 1 \end{cases}$$

Discuss the continuity of f.
SOLUTION   If $x \neq 1$,

$$f(x) = \frac{x^2 + x - 2}{x - 1}$$

is the quotient of polynomials and the denominator is not 0, so f is continuous at all numbers $x \neq 1$.

What about $x = 1$?

First, we check that $f(1)$ is defined. Here, $f(1) = 3$. Careful—don't use the same rule for $x = 1$ that you use for $x \neq 1$.

Second, we must check $\lim\limits_{x \to 1} f(x)$. (If this limit is 3, f is continuous at $x = 1$; if this limit is not 3, f is not continuous at $x = 1$.)

$$\lim_{x \to 1} f(x) = \lim_{x \to 1} \frac{x^2 + x - 2}{x - 1}$$

$$= \lim_{x \to 1} \frac{(x + 2)(x - 1)}{x - 1}$$

$$= \lim_{x \to 1} (x + 2) = 3$$

Third, $f(1) = \lim\limits_{x \to 1} f(x)$, so f is continuous at $x = 1$. We summarize by saying that f is continuous for all x.

Let us look more closely at the function given in Example 7. We draw the graph of f in Figure 9–16. If $x \neq 1$,

$$\frac{x^2 + x - 2}{x - 1} = x + 2$$

FIGURE 9–16

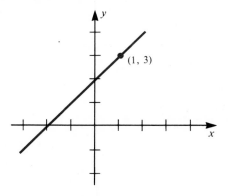

so the graph is the straight line $y = x + 2$ except for point $(1, 3)$. But now, $f(1) = 3$ means that the point $(1, 3)$ *is* on the graph. In fact, the function is $f(x) = x + 2$ but was just in disguise.

CAUTION The rule for computing $f(x)$ may depend upon x, but the graph of f may still be connected. Odd-looking evaluations can still give a continuous function.

9–3 EXERCISES

I

Use Figure 9–17 to complete the equations in Exercises 1 through 3.

1. (*See Example 4*)
   (a) $\lim_{x \to 0^+} f(x) =$ (b) $\lim_{x \to 0^-} f(x) =$
   (c) $\lim_{x \to 0} f(x) =$ (d) $f(0) =$
   (e) Is the function continuous at $x = 0$?

2. (a) $\lim_{x \to 2^-} f(x) =$ (b) $\lim_{x \to 2^+} f(x) =$
   (c) $\lim_{x \to 2} f(x) =$ (d) $f(2) =$
   (e) Is the function continuous at $x = 2$?

3. (a) $\lim_{x \to 3^-} f(x) =$ (b) $\lim_{x \to 3^+} f(x) =$
   (c) $\lim_{x \to 3} f(x) =$ (d) $f(3) =$
   (e) Is the function continuous at $x = 3$?

Use Figure 9–18 to complete the equations in Exercises 4 through 6.

4. (*See Example 5*)
   (a) $\lim_{x \to 0^-} g(x) =$ (b) $\lim_{x \to 0^+} g(x) =$
   (c) $\lim_{x \to 0} g(x) =$ (d) $g(0) =$
   (e) Is the function continuous at $x = 0$?

5. (a) $\lim_{x \to 3^-} g(x) =$ (b) $\lim_{x \to 3^+} g(x) =$
   (c) $\lim_{x \to 3} g(x) =$ (d) $g(3) =$
   (e) Is the function continuous at $x = 3$?

6. (a) $\lim_{x \to 5^-} g(x) =$ (b) $\lim_{x \to 5^+} g(x) =$
   (c) $\lim_{x \to 5} g(x) =$ (d) $g(5) =$
   (e) Is the function continuous at $x = 5$?

FIGURE 9–17

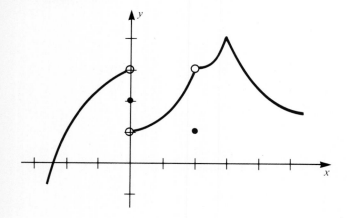

FIGURE 9–18

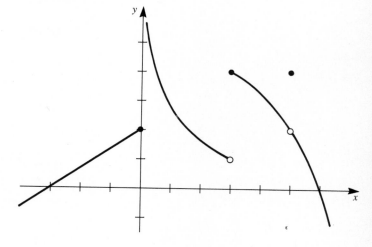

II

7. (*See Example 1*)

Let f be defined by

$$f(x) = \begin{cases} 3x + 2 & x \le 1 \\ x^2 + 5 & x > 1 \end{cases}$$

What is:

(a) $\lim\limits_{x \to 1^-} f(x)$? **(b)** $\lim\limits_{x \to 1^+} f(x)$?

(c) $\lim\limits_{x \to 1} f(x)$? **(d)** $f(1)$?

(e) Is f continuous at $x = 1$?

(f) $\lim\limits_{x \to 2^+} f(x)$? **(g)** $\lim\limits_{x \to 2^-} f(x)$?

(h) $\lim\limits_{x \to 2} f(x)$? **(i)** $f(2)$?

(j) Is f continuous at $x = 2$?

8. Let g be defined by

$$g(x) = \begin{cases} 16 - x^2 & x < 2 \\ 8 & x = 2 \\ 3x + 6 & x > 2 \end{cases}$$

What is:

(a) $\lim\limits_{x \to 2^-} g(x)$? **(b)** $\lim\limits_{x \to 2^+} g(x)$?

(c) $\lim\limits_{x \to 2} g(x)$? **(d)** $g(2)$?

(e) Is g continuous at $x = 2$?

(f) $\lim\limits_{x \to 1^-} g(x)$? **(g)** $\lim\limits_{x \to 1^+} g(x)$?

(h) $\lim\limits_{x \to 1} g(x)$? **(i)** $g(1)$?

(j) Is g continuous at $x = 1$?

9. (*See Example 6*)

Let f be defined by

$$f(x) = \begin{cases} \dfrac{x^2 + x - 6}{x - 2} & x \ne 2 \\ 7 & x = 2 \end{cases}$$

What is:

(a) $\lim\limits_{x \to 2} f(x)$? **(b)** $f(2)$?

(c) Is f continuous at $x = 2$?

10. Let h be defined by

$$h(t) = \begin{cases} \dfrac{t^2 - t - 2}{t - 2} & t \ne 3 \\ 8 & t = 3 \end{cases}$$

What is:

(a) $\lim\limits_{t \to 3} h(t)$? **(b)** $h(3)$?

(c) Is h continuous at $t = 3$?

III

11. (*See Example 7*)

Let f be defined by

$$f(x) = \begin{cases} \dfrac{x^2 - 3x}{x} & x \ne 0 \\ B & x = 0 \end{cases}$$

Is there a value of B such that f is continuous at $x = 0$? If so, what is it?

12. Let f be defined by

$$f(x) = \begin{cases} 2x + 3 & x \le 2 \\ Ax - 9 & x > 2 \end{cases}$$

Is there a value of A such that f is continuous at $x = 2$? If so, what is it?

13. (*See Example 2*)

Let $f(x) = \dfrac{|x - 3|}{x - 3}$. Remember that

$$|x - 3| = \begin{cases} x - 3 & \text{if } x \ge 3 \\ -(x - 3) & \text{if } x < 3 \end{cases}$$

What is:

(a) $\lim\limits_{x \to 3^-} f(x)$? **(b)** $\lim\limits_{x \to 3^+} f(x)$?

(c) $\lim\limits_{x \to 3} f(x)$? **(d)** $\lim\limits_{x \to 4^-} f(x)$?

(e) $\lim\limits_{x \to 4^+} f(x)$? **(f)** $\lim\limits_{x \to 4} f(x)$?

14. Let $g(x) = \dfrac{|4 - x|}{4 - x}$.

What is:

(a) $\lim\limits_{x \to 4^+} g(x)$?   **(b)** $\lim\limits_{x \to 4^-} g(x)$?

(c) $\lim\limits_{x \to 4} g(x)$?   **(d)** $\lim\limits_{x \to 5^+} g(x)$?

(e) $\lim\limits_{x \to 5^-} g(x)$?   **(f)** $\lim\limits_{x \to 5} g(x)$?

15. Graph the function

$$f(x) = \begin{cases} 2x + 1 & x \le 1 \\ 4 - x & x > 1 \end{cases}$$

16. Graph the function

$$f(x) = \begin{cases} x^2 & x < 3 \\ 12 - x & x \ge 3 \end{cases}$$

17. Graph the function

$$f(x) = \begin{cases} \dfrac{x^2 - 3x + 2}{x - 1} & x \ne 1 \\ 4 & x = 1 \end{cases}$$

18. Graph the function

$$f(x) = \begin{cases} \dfrac{x^2 - 2x - 3}{x - 3} & x \ne 3 \\ 4 & x = 3 \end{cases}$$

19. (*See Example 3*)
A company has found that its marginal cost function follows the rule

$$MC(x) = \begin{cases} 50 - 0.5x & 0 \le x \le 60 \\ 20 + 0.01x^2 & x > 60 \end{cases}$$

Is the company's marginal cost function continuous at $x = 60$?

20. The management of Neff's Department Store has found that the employees' general alertness (alertness is measured on a scale of 0–10) after being on the job for t hours follows the pattern given by

$$A(t) = \begin{cases} 5 + 2t - \dfrac{1}{3}t^2 & 0 \le t \le 6 \\ 8 - \dfrac{t}{2} & 6 < t \le 8 \end{cases}$$

Is this alertness function continuous on the interval $[0, 8]$?

21. The Adams Propane Gas Company charges 80¢ per gallon for orders up to ten gallons and 75¢ per gallon for every gallon over ten gallons. Let $C(x)$ be the cost of buying x gallons of propane gas.
(a) Find the rule for evaluating $C(x)$.
(b) Is C continuous at $x = 10$?

22. Schell's Candy Store sells its fudge for 50¢ per ounce for orders of two pounds or less and 45¢ per pound for orders over two pounds. Let x be the number of ounces purchased and $C(x)$ the cost of the purchase.
(a) Find the rule for evaluating $C(x)$.
(b) Is C continuous at $x = 32$?

9–4 APPLICATIONS OF CONTINUITY

- *The Intermediate Theorem*
- *The Bisection Method for Estimating Roots*
- *Solving Inequalities*

THE INTERMEDIATE VALUE THEOREM

In the previous section we discovered that if a function is continuous, then there are no "jumps" or "holes" in its graph. The graph of a continuous function is connected. We state this property more precisely now in the form of a theorem.

Theorem **The Intermediate Value Theorem**	If f is continuous on an interval $[a, b]$ and if M is any number between $f(a)$ and $f(b)$, then the equation $f(x) = M$ has a solution in (a, b); that is, there is some number c in (a, b) with $f(c) = M$.

NOTE There may be more than one solution to $f(x) = M$ between a and b; this theorem guarantees that there is at least one solution.

Geometrically, this theorem says that if you fill in Figure 9–19 with the graph of a continuous function that contains the points $(a, f(a))$ and $(b, f(b))$, then the graph that you draw must intersect the line $y = M$.

The applications in this section use a special case of the intermediate value theorem, which is called a corollary to the theorem. Before stating this corollary we make a preliminary definition.

FIGURE 9–19

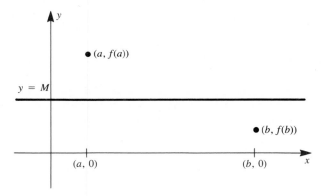

Definition **f Changes Sign**	If f is defined on an interval I and there are two numbers x_1 and x_2 in I with $f(x_1) > 0$ and $f(x_2) < 0$, then we say that f **changes sign** on I.

Corollary	If f is continuous and changes sign on $[a, b]$, then the equation $f(x) = 0$ has a solution between a and b.

First we see how to use this corollary to find an approximate solution to an equation.

THE BISECTION METHOD FOR ESTIMATING ROOTS

We develop the procedure by example.

EXAMPLE 1   *(Compare Exercise 11)*

Approximate to within 0.1 a solution to the equation

$$x^3 - 2x^2 - 1 = 0$$

SOLUTION   We define a function f by $f(x) = x^3 - 2x^2 - 1$. Our problem is now equivalent to approximating a solution to $f(x) = 0$. First note that f is continuous for all x. Next we find two numbers a and b such that $f(a)$ and $f(b)$ have opposite signs. The simplest evaluation is $f(0)$, so we start there.

$$f(0) = -1$$

The important feature to note is that $f(0)$ is negative. We continue by evaluating f at some other integers until we find one for which f is positive.

$$f(1) = -2, \qquad f(2) = -1, \qquad f(3) = 8$$

Now we know that $f(x) = 0$ somewhere in the interval $[2, 3]$ because f changes sign on $[2, 3]$. In particular, $f(2) < 0$ and $f(3) > 0$. *(Compare Exercise 1)* The next step is to determine the sign of f at the midpoint of the interval $[2, 3]$. We evaluate $f(2.5)$: $f(2.5) = 2.125$, which is positive. Since $f(2)$ and $f(2.5)$ have opposite signs, there must be a solution to $f(x) = 0$ in the interval $[2, 2.5]$. Again test the midpoint of the interval, which in this case is 2.25: $f(2.25) = 0.265625$, which is positive. There is a solution to $f(x) = 0$ in $[2, 2.25]$. The midpoint of $[2, 2.25]$ is 2.125. Next, $f(2.125) = -0.43 \ldots < 0$, so now we know that there is a solution in $[2.125, 2.25]$. The midpoint of this interval is 2.1875. Finally, notice that 2.1875 is within 0.1 of all the points in the interval $[2.125, 2.25]$ and so must be within 0.1 of the solution contained in this interval.

Answer: 2.1875 is within 0.1 of a solution to $x^3 - 2x^2 - 1 = 0$.   ∎

We can now summarize the **bisection method.** First, find two numbers a and b such that f is continuous on $[a, b]$ with $f(a)$ and $f(b)$ having opposite signs. Now we know we have a solution to $f(x) = 0$ between a and b. Next we evaluate $f(\frac{a+b}{2})$ and see whether $f(x) = 0$ has a solution in $[a, \frac{a+b}{2}]$ or $[\frac{a+b}{2}, b]$. We continue this process, halving the length of the interval with each step until we have an interval whose length is less than or equal to twice the desired accuracy. The midpoint of that interval is our answer.

In the next example we show how a line chart can help us to keep track of the sign of f.

EXAMPLE 2 *(Compare Exercise 23)*

Find a solution to the equation $2x^3 - 2x = 3x - 2$ that is correct to within 0.05.

SOLUTION The given equation is equivalent to $2x^3 - 5x + 2 = 0$, so we want to approximate a solution to $f(x) = 0$, with $f(x) = 2x^3 - 5x + 2$. Again, we start by noticing that f is continuous on the whole line, and again we start the evaluations with $x = 0$. Here, $f(0) = 2$ is positive; next, $f(1) = -1$ is negative. Therefore, $f(x) = 0$ has a solution in the interval $[0, 1]$. We construct a line chart showing the **sign of $f(x)$** at the various points on the chart:

Sign-of-*f*

$$
\begin{array}{c}
+ \\
\underset{0}{|} \qquad\qquad\qquad\qquad\qquad\qquad\qquad \underset{1}{\overset{-}{|}}
\end{array}
$$

$f(0.5) = -0.25 < 0$. We use this to modify the previous chart:

Sign-of-*f*

$$
\begin{array}{c}
+ \qquad\qquad\qquad - \qquad\qquad\qquad - \\
\underset{0}{|} \qquad\qquad \underset{0.5}{|} \qquad\qquad \underset{1}{|}
\end{array}
$$

The new chart shows us the solution we want is in the interval $[0, 0.5]$, so our new test point is 0.25:

$$f(0.25) = 0.78125 > 0$$

We now have

Sign-of-*f*

$$
\begin{array}{c}
+ \qquad + \qquad\qquad - \qquad\qquad\qquad - \\
\underset{0}{|} \quad \underset{0.25}{|} \quad \underset{0.5}{|} \qquad\qquad \underset{1}{|}
\end{array}
$$

which shows us that our new test point should be halfway between 0.25 and 0.5:

$$\frac{0.25 + 0.5}{2} = 0.375 \qquad f(0.375) = 0.23 \ldots > 0$$

We now have

Sign-of-*f*

$$
\begin{array}{c}
+ \qquad + \quad + \quad - \qquad\qquad\qquad - \\
\underset{0}{|} \quad \underset{0.25}{|}\ \underset{0.375}{|}\ \underset{0.5}{|} \qquad\qquad \underset{1}{|}
\end{array}
$$

Our new test point is $\dfrac{0.375 + 0.5}{2} = 0.4375$:

$$f(0.4375) = -0.02 \ldots < 0$$

The old chart is getting cluttered, so we draw a fresh one.

Sign-of-f

How do we know when to stop? The example asks us to approximate a solution to within 0.05, so we can stop whenever we get an interval with a plus sign on one endpoint and a minus sign on the other endpoint if the total length of the interval is less than or equal to $2 \cdot 0.05 = 0.1$. Then, as in Example 1, the midpoint of that interval will be within the desired distance of a zero. The length of the interval $[0.375, 0.4375] = 0.0625 < 0.1$, so we can say that its midpoint,

$$\frac{0.375 + 0.4375}{2} = 0.40625$$

is within 0.05 of a solution to the given equation.

Answer: 0.40625 is within 0.05 of a solution to $2x^2 - 2x = 3x - 2$.

SOLVING INEQUALITIES

In later work it will be especially important for us to know when certain functions are positive and when they are negative; that is, we will need to solve inequalities of the form $f(x) > 0$ and $f(x) < 0$. The corollary to the intermediate value theorem states that if f changes sign on an interval, then either $f(x) = 0$ on that interval or else f is not continuous on that interval. We restate the corollary in the form that we will use.

Corollary If f is continuous on an interval I and $f(x) = 0$ has no solutions in I, then f does not change sign on I.

We use this corollary to solve the inequality $x^2 + 5x - 6 \le 0$ in the next example.

EXAMPLE 3   *(Compare Exercise 9)*

Solve the inequality $x^2 + 5x - 6 \le 0$.

SOLUTION   Here our function is $f(x) = x^2 + 5x - 6$. First, we solve the equation $f(x) = 0$:

$$x^2 + 5x - 6 = 0$$
$$(x + 6)(x - 1) = 0$$

There are two solutions: $x = -6$ and $x = 1$.

Second, we see whether f has any points of discontinuity. This f is continuous for all x.

Third, we draw a number line and plot all the points we found in the first two steps.

Fourth, using the corollary, we now know that the sign of f cannot change on the intervals between the points we just plotted. That is, the sign of f is constant on each of the intervals $(-\infty, -6)$, $(-6, 1)$, and $(1, \infty)$. To find out what the sign of f is on one of these intervals, we simply pick a point from that interval and evaluate f at that point.

From $(-\infty, -6)$ we can choose -10, and $f(-10) = 44$, which is positive. Therefore, $f(x)$ is positive on $(-\infty, -6)$.

From $(-6, 1)$ we can choose 0; $f(0) = -6$, which is negative, so $f(x)$ is negative on the whole interval $(-6, 1)$.

From the last interval $(1, \infty)$ we choose 2; $f(2) = 8$, and $f(x)$ is positive on $(1, \infty)$.

We summarize these results with a number line:

Sign-of-f
$$\begin{array}{ccc} + & - & + \\ \hline & -6 & \quad 1 \end{array}$$

From this chart we can read that the solution to $f(x) < 0$ is the open interval $(-6, 1)$.

Next, we must check the inequality at the points we plotted on the number line, -6 and 1. We know that these points satisfy $f(x) = 0$, and since we need to solve $f(x) \leq 0$, these points are in the solution.

Finally, we combine the solutions of the inequality with the solution of the equality to get the final answer.

Answer: The solution to $x^2 + 5x - 6 \leq 0$ is all x in $[-6, 1]$.

We will summarize the above procedure, but first we need a definition. Because the points we plot in the first two steps cut the line into intervals on which the sign of f is constant, we call these points **cut points.**

Definition **Cut Point of an** **Inequality**	A point c is called a **cut point** of the inequality $f(x) \leq 0$ if $f(c) = 0$ or if f is not continuous at c.

We will also use the term **cut point** if the inequality is of the form $f(x) < 0$, $f(x) > 0$, or $f(x) \geq 0$.

The procedure can now be summarized in five steps:

1. Find the cut points of the inequality.
2. Plot the cut points on a number line.
3. Determine the sign of f on each of the intervals between successive cut points.

4. Test each cut point in the original inequality.
5. Write the answer using the information from Steps 3 and 4.

NOTE Any inequality is equivalent to one of the type $f(x) \leq 0, f(x) < 0,$ $f(x) > 0,$ or $f(x) \geq 0,$ as shown in the next example.

EXAMPLE 4   *(Compare Exercise 29)*

Solve $\frac{1}{x} + 6 \leq 9$.

SOLUTION   We subtract 9 from both sides to obtain the equivalent inequality

$$\frac{1}{x} - 3 \leq 0$$

We want to solve $f(x) \leq 0$ with

$$f(x) = \frac{1}{x} - 3$$

Step 1. Find the cut points of this inequality.

(a) *Set f(x) = 0 and solve:*

$$\frac{1}{x} - 3 = 0$$
$$1 - 3x = 0$$
$$x = \frac{1}{3}$$

Therefore, $x = \frac{1}{3}$ is a cut point.

(b) *Find the points of discontinuity of f.*
Here, f is not defined when $x = 0$, so $x = 0$ is a cut point.

Step 2. Plot the cut points on a number line:

Step 3. Determine the sign of f on the intervals between successive cut points.
Here, there are three such intervals:

(a) From $(-\infty, 0)$ we pick $x = -1$; $f(-1) = -4$, which is negative, so $f(x) < 0$ on $(-\infty, 0)$.

(b) From $(0, \frac{1}{3})$ we choose $x = \frac{1}{5}$; $f(\frac{1}{5}) = 2$, which is positive, so $f(x) > 0$ on $(0, \frac{1}{3})$.

(c) From $(\frac{1}{3}, \infty)$ we choose $x = 1$, and $f(1) = -2$, which is negative, so $f(x) < 0$ on $(\frac{1}{3}, \infty)$.

We can fill in the sign-of-f chart:

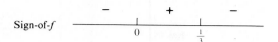

Sign-of-f

Step 4. **Test each cut point in the original inequality.**
The inequality is satisfied when $x = \frac{1}{3}$ but not when $x = 0$.
Step 5. **Write the answer using the information from Steps 3 and 4.**
The answer is the union of the interval $(-\infty, 0)$ and the interval $[\frac{1}{3}, \infty)$.

CAUTION: Solving the inequality $\frac{1}{x} - 3 \leq 0$ may seem simpler than it is. However, the inequality $\frac{1}{x} - 3 \leq 0$ is not the same as the inequality $1 - 3x \leq 0$. For example, $x = -1$ satisfies $\frac{1}{x} - 3 \leq 0$, but $x = -1$ is not a solution to $1 - 3x \leq 0$. Solving inequalities may require some care.

We conclude with an example similar to one that you will see later.

EXAMPLE 5   *(Compare Exercise 35)*
Solve

$$\sqrt{2x + 12} + \frac{x}{\sqrt{2x + 12}} \leq 0$$

SOLUTION
Step 1.

(a) Set

$$\sqrt{2x + 12} + \frac{x}{\sqrt{2x + 12}} = 0$$

and solve. Multiplying through by $\sqrt{2x + 12}$ gives

$$2x + 12 + x = 0$$
$$3x + 12 = 0$$
$$x = -4$$

(b) $f(x) = \sqrt{2x + 12} + \dfrac{x}{\sqrt{2x + 12}}$

is not defined for $2x + 12 \leq 0$. Therefore, f is not continuous on $(-\infty, -6]$, which means that we have a whole interval of cut points; f is continuous on $(-6, \infty)$.

Step 2.

All cut -6 -4
points

Step 3. The only intervals that we have to test are $(-6, -4)$ and $(-4, \infty)$.

(a) From $(-6, -4)$ we choose $x = -5$:

$$f(-5) = \sqrt{2} + \frac{-5}{\sqrt{2}} = -2.12 \ldots$$

which is negative. Therefore, $f(x) < 0$ on the interval $(-6, -4)$.

(b) From $(-4, \infty)$ we choose $x = 0$; $f(0) = \sqrt{12}$, which is positive, and so $f(x) > 0$ on the interval $(-4, \infty)$.

Our chart is as follows:

Sign-of-f

Step 4. The only cut point for which $f(x)$ is defined is $x = -4$, which satisfies the inequality $f(x) \leq 0$.

Step 5. The answer is the interval $(-6, -4]$.

9–4 EXERCISES

I

In Exercises 1 through 4, find an interval of the form $[a, b]$ on which f changes sign.

1. (*See Example 1*) $f(x) = x^2 - 5x - 7$

2. $f(x) = 3x^2 + 8x - 10$

3. $f(x) = -2x^2 + 4x + 8$

4. $f(x) = x^3 + x - 6$

Solve the inequalities in Exercises 5 through 8 using the cut point method. Then solve them without using the cut point method and compare your answers.

5. $6 - 2x < 0$ 6. $15 - 3x > 0$

7. $8x + 3 \leq 2x - 9$ 8. $2x - 18 \leq 5x + 8$

Solve the inequalities in Exercises 9 and 10 using the cut point method.

9. (*See Example 3*)   10. $x^2 + 2x - 3 \geq 0$
$x^2 - x - 6 \leq 0$

II

In Exercises 11 through 16, use the bisection method to find a number that is within 0.2 of a solution to the given equation.

11. (*See Example 1*)   12. $x^2 + 2x - 7 = 0$
$5x^2 - 4\sqrt{x} - 10 = 0$

13. $2x^3 = 8x^2 + 13$ 14. $x^3 - 6x = x^2 - 10$

15. $4x + 3 = 5\sqrt{x} + 11$

16. $2x^3 - 5x^2 = x^3 - 9x + 15$

Solve the inequalities in Exercises 17 through 22 using the cut point method.

17. $2x^2 - 7x - 4 > 0$ 18. $2x^2 - 3x - 5 < 0$

19. $x^2 + 2x \leq 8$ 20. $x^2 + x > 12$

21. $x^2 - 4x \leq 8$ 22. $2x^2 + x \leq 10$

III

In Exercises 23 through 28, approximate to within 0.1 a solution to each of the equations.

23. (*See Example 2*) $3x - \sqrt{x} - 5 = 0$

24. $x^3 - x^2 - 6x + 4 = 0$

25. $x^3 - 3x^2 + 5 = x^2 - 5x + 2$

26. $x^3 + 15 = 0$

27. $x - \dfrac{20}{x^2} = 7$ 28. $3x - \dfrac{50}{x^2} = 12$

Solve the inequalities in Exercises 29 through 38.

29. (*See Example 4*) $\dfrac{2}{x + 5} \leq 6$

30. $\dfrac{1}{x + 7} \leq 9$

31. $\dfrac{1}{3x - 6} \leq \dfrac{1}{x + 2}$

32. $\dfrac{1}{5x - 15} \leq \dfrac{1}{2x - 12}$

33. $\dfrac{4}{x} + 1 \leq 0$

34. $\dfrac{5}{x - 3} \leq x + 1$

35. (*See Example 5*) $\sqrt{x + 9} + \dfrac{x}{2\sqrt{x + 9}} \leq 0$

36. $\sqrt{2x - 12} + \dfrac{x}{\sqrt{2x - 12}} > 0$

37. $(x - 8)^{1/3} + \dfrac{x}{3(x - 8)^{2/3}} < 0$

38. $(x - 1)^{1/3} + \dfrac{x}{3(x - 1)^{2/3}} \leq 0$

39. Evans Refrigeration Company has a weekly cost function given by

$$C(x) = \dfrac{x^3}{100} - 3x^2 + 300x + 81,760$$

where $C(x)$ is in dollars and x is the number of refrigeration units the company produces each week. The weekly revenue function is given by $R(x) = -x^2 + 800x$. What is the company's smallest break-even point? (*Hint:* First try $x = 100$ and then $x = 200$. The answer is a whole number.)

40. Major Electronics has found that its cost for manufacturing x hundred calculators per week is given by

$$C(x) = \dfrac{x^3}{10} - 4x^2 + 500x + 23,600$$

The weekly revenue is $x^2 + 1200x$. What is the company's smallest break-even point?

41. A trucking company has found that the driver's alertness is a function of how long it has been since the last stop. On a scale the company has devised, the alertness can be described by

$$A(t) = 10 - \dfrac{t}{19 - 2t}$$

where t is the number of hours since the driver's last stop. For safety's sake the company demands that $A(t)$ should be greater than or equal to 1. What are the allowable hours a driver can go between stops?

42. A blood-testing laboratory has found that its efficiency depends on the number of blood samples that it batch-tests at one time. If the batch is too small, the company will have to do too many batches; if the batch is too large, the company will have to do too many individual tests later. If x is the number of samples tested in one batch, the company has found that its efficiency, E, can be given by

$$E(x) = \dfrac{x^2 - 110x + 21}{x^2 - 100x}$$

For what values of x is $E(x) \geq 1$?

43. A ball is thrown so that t seconds after it is released, its height in feet, h, is given by $h(t) = -16t^2 + 96t$, $0 \leq t \leq 6$.
    (a) What is the ball's height after 3 seconds?
    (b) What is the ball's height after 5 seconds?
    (c) What are the physical reasons for restricting the domain to the interval $0 \leq t \leq 6$?

44. A ball is thrown so that t seconds after it is released, its height in feet, h, is given by $h(t) = -16t^2 + 112t$, which is valid for t until the ball hits the ground ($h = 0$). What is the domain of h?

45. A ball is thrown so that t seconds after it is released, its height in feet, h, is given by $h(t) = -16t^2 + 100t + 6$, which is valid for all t until the ball hits the ground ($h = 0$). What is the domain of h?

9-5 DERIVATIVES AND TANGENT LINES

- *Introduction*
- *Slope of Tangent Lines*
- *Formulas for Some Derivatives*
- *The Derivative as a Function*
- *Examples in Which the Derivative Does Not Exist*
- *Other Notation for Derivatives*

INTRODUCTION

We do not live in a static world, but one that is always changing; the derivative is the mathematical tool used to quantify and describe rates of change. Recall that the instantaneous rate of change of f when $x = a$ is given by the derivative of f at a, written $f'(a)$, and is defined by the equation

$$f'(a) = \lim_{\Delta x \to 0} \frac{f(a + \Delta x) - f(a)}{\Delta x}$$

This same limit is also important geometrically because there is a connection between $f'(a)$ and the graph of f. Understanding this relation will enable us to graph complicated functions by plotting only a few points. These graphs can then be used to give us a picture of the behavior of a function without burying us in a mass of data. The geometric interpretation of derivative paves the way to seeing how the derivative can be used to find optimal solutions to problems and to shed light on certain principles of economics. For example, one such principle that we shall investigate later states: The biggest profit occurs when the marginal cost and marginal revenue are the same.

SLOPE OF TANGENT LINES

We turn now to a geometric interpretation of $[f(a + \Delta x) - f(a)]/\Delta x$. This quotient represents the change in functional values divided by the change in x. Remember that we use the Greek letter Δ to mean "the change in," so with $y = f(x)$ we can write

$$f(a + \Delta x) - f(a) = \text{the change in } y = \Delta y$$

Now we can rewrite the quotient

$$\frac{f(a + \Delta x) - f(a)}{\Delta x} \quad \text{as} \quad \frac{\Delta y}{\Delta x}$$

The symbols $\Delta y/\Delta x$ can be read literally as "delta y over delta x" or by translating to "the change in y divided by the change in x." For a straight line, $\Delta y/\Delta x$ gives the slope of the line. Let's look at a picture to see what this all means; please refer to Figure 9–20.

FIGURE 9-20

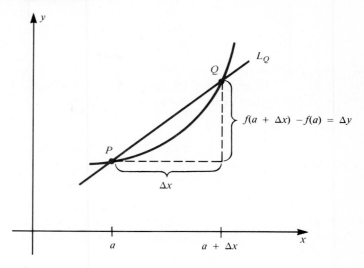

FIGURE 9-21

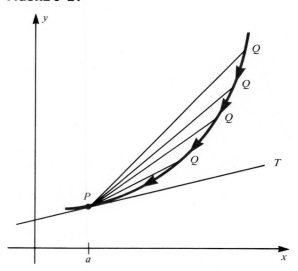

We have labeled the point $(a, f(a))$ with the letter P and used Q to label the point $(a + \Delta x, f(a + \Delta x))$. Then we have drawn the straight line L_Q through P and Q. The slope of L_Q is $\Delta y / \Delta x$. Now as Δx gets smaller, the point Q slides along the graph $y = f(x)$ and approaches the point P, as is shown in Figure 9-21. The figure also shows the line tangent to the curve at the point $(a, f(a))$. Let's call this tangent line T and let m denote the slope of T. If Δx is close to 0, then the line through P and Q has a slope that is close to the slope of T. That is, if Δx is close to 0, then $\Delta y / \Delta x$ is close to m. We have already defined $f'(a)$ to represent the number that $\Delta y/\Delta x$ approaches as Δx approaches 0, so we must have $f'(a) = m$. The derivative of f at a is the slope of the line tangent to the graph of f at the point $(a, f(a))$. We use this to give a formal definition of tangent line.

Definition **Tangent Line**	The **line tangent** to the graph of f at the point $(a, f(a))$ is the line through $(a, f(a))$ with slope $f'(a)$.

EXAMPLE 1   *(Compare Exercises 3 and 9)*

Given the graph $y = x^2 + 3$:

(a) find the slope of the line tangent to the graph at the point $(2, 7)$;

(b) find an equation of this tangent line.

FIGURE 9–22

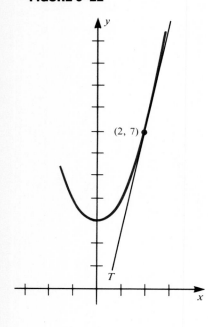

SOLUTION   The graph of f is shown in Figure 9–22, and the tangent line T has also been drawn. We want the slope of T.

(a) The slope of T is

$$f'(2) = \lim_{\Delta x \to 0} \frac{f(2 + \Delta x) - f(2)}{\Delta x}$$

We now compute this limit using our three-step process for computing derivatives.

Step 1. Compute (and simplify) $f(2 + \Delta x) - f(2)$:

$$f(2) = 2^2 + 3 = 7$$
$$f(2 + \Delta x) = (2 + \Delta x)^2 + 3 = 4 + 4\Delta x + (\Delta x)^2 + 3$$
$$= 7 + 4\Delta x + (\Delta x)^2$$

So $f(2 + \Delta x) - f(2) = 4\Delta x + (\Delta x)^2$.

Step 2. Divide the result in Step 1 by Δx:

$$\frac{4\Delta x + (\Delta x)^2}{\Delta x} = \frac{(4 + \Delta x)(\Delta x)}{\Delta x} = 4 + \Delta x$$

Step 3. Compute the limit as $\Delta x \to 0$:

$$\lim_{\Delta x \to 0} (4 + \Delta x) = 4$$

Thus $f'(2) = 4$, and the slope of T is 4.

(b) The line T goes through the point $(2, 7)$, and now we also know the slope of T is 4. We can use the point-slope form to find an equation for T; we have $y - 7 = 4(x - 2)$.

CAUTION Remember to use parentheses; do not write $y - 7 = 4x - 2$.

You will want to compute the derivative to understand the geometry of the graph; sometimes the geometry of the graph helps you to understand the derivative.

EXAMPLE 2   *(Compare Exercise 15)*

Given $f(x) = x^2 + 3$, find $f'(0)$.

SOLUTION   Refer again to the graph in Figure 9–22. $f'(0)$ is the slope of the line tangent to the graph at $(0, 3)$. To the left of $(0, 3)$ the tangent lines will have negative slope; to the right of $(0, 3)$ the tangent lines will have positive slope. The line tangent to the curve at $(0, 3)$ is a horizontal line; the slope of a horizontal line is 0. Thus $f'(0) = 0$.

FORMULAS FOR SOME DERIVATIVES

EXAMPLE 3   *(Compare Exercise 21)*

If $f(x) = x^2 - 2x - 3$, find the slope of the tangent lines when $x = 0$, when $x = 1$, and when $x = 4$.

SOLUTION   Rather than going through three computations to find $f'(0)$, $f'(1)$, and $f'(4)$ separately, let's discover the formula for $f'(a)$ in terms of a. We go through the three-step process for computing

$$\lim_{\Delta x \to 0} \frac{f(a + \Delta x) - f(a)}{\Delta x}$$

Step 1. Compute $f(a + \Delta x) - f(a)$:

$$f(a) = a^2 - 2a - 3$$
$$f(a + \Delta x) = (a + \Delta x)^2 - 2(a + \Delta x) - 3$$
$$= a^2 + 2a\Delta x + (\Delta x)^2 - 2a - 2\Delta x - 3$$

So

$$f(a + \Delta x) - f(a) = a^2 + 2a\Delta x + (\Delta x)^2 - 2a - 2\Delta x - 3 - (a^2 - 2a - 3)$$
$$= a^2 + 2a\Delta x + (\Delta x)^2 - 2a - 2\Delta x - 3 - a^2 + 2a + 3$$
$$= 2a\Delta x + (\Delta x)^2 - 2\Delta x$$

Step 2. Divide the result from Step 1 by Δx.
Note that Δx is a factor of $2a\Delta x + (\Delta x)^2 - 2\Delta x$, so

$$\frac{2a\Delta x + (\Delta x)^2 - 2\Delta x}{\Delta x} = \frac{(2a + \Delta x - 2)\Delta x}{\Delta x}$$
$$= 2a + \Delta x - 2$$

Step 3. Compute the limit as $\Delta x \to 0$:

$$\lim_{\Delta x \to 0} (2a + \Delta x - 2) = 2a - 2$$

There was some messy algebra in Step 1, but now we do have a formula for $f'(a)$: $f'(a) = 2a - 2$.

Substituting the three numbers 0, 1, and 4 into the formula, we have

$$f'(0) = 2 \cdot 0 - 2 = -2$$
$$f'(1) = 0$$
$$f'(4) = 6$$

Geometrically, Figure 9–23 shows what the tangent lines look like: T_0, T_1, and T_4 are the respective tangent lines. The slope of T_0 is -2; the slope of T_1 is 0 (T_1 is a horizontal line); the slope of T_4 is 6.

FIGURE 9–23

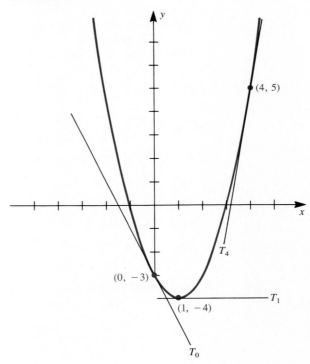

EXAMPLE 4 *(Compare Exercise 23)*

If $f(x) = 1/x$, find a formula for $f'(a)$.

SOLUTION   We use the three-step process for computing

$$\lim_{\Delta x \to 0} \frac{f(a + \Delta x) - f(a)}{\Delta x}$$

Step 1. $f(a) = \dfrac{1}{a}$:

$$f(a + \Delta x) = \frac{1}{(a + \Delta x)}$$

$$f(a + \Delta x) - f(a) = \frac{1}{(a + \Delta x)} - \frac{1}{a}$$

To simplify, we combine into one fraction; the common denominator is $(a + \Delta x)a$. Combining, we have

$$= \frac{a}{(a + \Delta x)a} - \frac{a + \Delta x}{(a + \Delta x)a}$$

$$= \frac{a - a - \Delta x}{(a + \Delta x)a}$$

$$= \frac{-\Delta x}{(a + \Delta x)a}$$

Again note that Δx is a factor of the result of Step 1.

Step 2. Divide the result from Step 1 by Δx. Dividing by Δx is the same as multiplying by $1/\Delta x$.

$$\frac{-\Delta x}{(a + \Delta x)a} \cdot \frac{1}{\Delta x} = \frac{-1}{(a + \Delta x)a}$$

Step 3. Compute the limit as $\Delta x \to 0$ of the result of Step 2:

$$\lim_{\Delta x \to 0} \frac{-1}{(a + \Delta x)a} = \frac{-1}{(a)a} = \frac{-1}{a^2}$$

Thus $f'(a) = \dfrac{-1}{a^2}$.

EXAMPLE 5   *(Compare Exercise 11)*

Find an equation of the line tangent to the graph $f(x) = 1/x$ at the point $(2, \frac{1}{2})$.

SOLUTION   In Example 4 we computed

$$f'(a) = \frac{-1}{a^2}$$

If $a = 2$, then $f'(2) = -\frac{1}{4}$. The tangent line has slope $-\frac{1}{4}$ and goes through $(2, \frac{1}{2})$, so its point-slope equation is

$$y - \frac{1}{2} = -\frac{1}{4}(x - 2)$$

The graph of $f(x) = 1/x$ and the line tangent to the graph at $(2, \frac{1}{2})$ have been drawn in Figure 9–24.

FIGURE 9–24

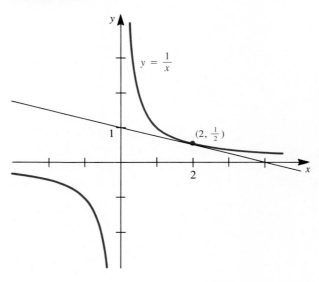

Notice that if you were to draw any line tangent to this graph, the slope of the tangent line would be negative. This geometric fact is confirmed in the formula for $f'(a)$, the slope. We found in Example 4 that

$$f'(a) = -\frac{1}{a^2}$$

which is always negative.

**THE DERIVATIVE
AS A FUNCTION**

The rule for evaluating the derivative doesn't have to use the letter a. For example, if

$$f(x) = \frac{1}{x}$$

we now know that

$$f'(a) = -\frac{1}{a^2}$$

We could just as well write this derivative as

$$f'(x) = -\frac{1}{x^2}$$

Using the result from Example 3, we could also write

If $f(x) = x^2 - 2x - 3,$ then $f'(x) = 2x - 2$

In previous sections we saw that if $f(x) = mx + b$, then $f'(a) = m$. Thus we can write

If $f(x) = mx + b,$ then $f'(x) = m$

EXAMPLE 6 *(Compare Exercise 2)*

If $f(x) = 7x - 4$, find $f'(x)$.
SOLUTION $f'(x) = 7$.

---

*The Derivative
as a Function*

Given a function f, the derivative f' is an associated function whose domain is a subset of the domain of f; the number $f'(x)$ has two interpretations:

1. $f'(x)$ is the instantaneous rate of change of f at x;
2. $f'(x)$ is the slope of the line tangent to the graph of f at the point $(x, f(x))$.

In the next chapter we will show how, given $f(x)$, you can use some computational formulas to write the expression for $f'(x)$ without always having to compute a limit; we did this in Example 6. Right now we present some examples to show that the derivative f' is not always defined at every point in the domain of the original function f.

**EXAMPLES IN WHICH
THE DERIVATIVE
DOES NOT EXIST**

We look at the geometry of tangent lines once again to see what happens when the graph does not have a tangent line at a particular point.

EXAMPLE 7   *(Compare Exercise 17)*

Let $f(x) = |x|$. What is $f'(0)$?

SOLUTION   We repeat the three-step process for computing $f'(0)$.

Step 1. $f(0) = 0; f(0 + \Delta x) = f(\Delta x) = |\Delta x|$

so

$$f(0 + \Delta x) - f(0) = |\Delta x|$$

Step 2. Dividing the result of Step 1 by Δx, we get $|\Delta x|/\Delta x$. We encountered an expression like this in Example 2 of Section 9–3. $|\Delta x|/\Delta x = 1$ if $\Delta x > 0$, but

$$\frac{|\Delta x|}{\Delta x} = -1 \qquad \text{if } \Delta x < 0$$

Step 3. As we saw in Example 2 of Section 9–3, we should use the left-hand and right-hand limits in this case:

$$\lim_{\Delta x \to 0^+} \frac{|\Delta x|}{\Delta x} = \lim_{\Delta x \to 0^+} 1 = 1$$

but

$$\lim_{\Delta x \to 0^-} \frac{|\Delta x|}{\Delta x} = \lim_{\Delta x \to 0^-} -1 = -1$$

Therefore,

$$\lim_{\Delta x \to 0} \frac{|\Delta x|}{\Delta x} \qquad \text{does not exist.}$$

$f'(0)$ does not exist, and the graph does not have a tangent line at $(0, 0)$. The graph of $f(x) = |x|$ has a "corner" at $(0, 0)$ and so differs, for example, from the graph of $f(x) = x^2$ which is "smooth" at $(0, 0)$. See Figure 9–25.

FIGURE 9–25

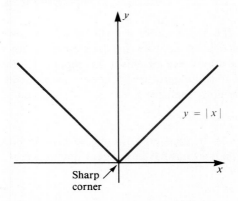
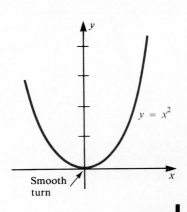

FIGURE 9–26

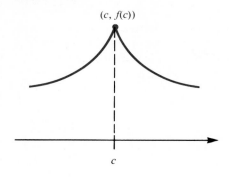

$(c, f(c))$

c

FIGURE 9–27

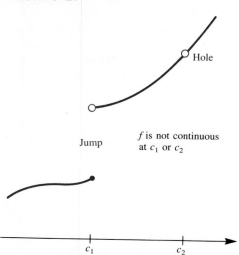

Hole

Jump

f is not continuous
at c_1 or c_2

c_1 c_2

FIGURE 9–28

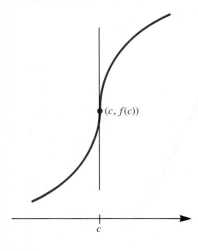

$(c, f(c))$

c

In general, the geometric interpretation of $f'(c)$ as the slope of the line tangent to the graph of f at $(c, f(c))$ leads us to three situations in which $f'(c)$ is not defined.

NOTE There are three cases in which $f'(c)$ is not defined.

1. The graph has a corner—a sharp change of direction. See Figure 9–26.
2. The graph has a jump or hole; the function is not continuous. See Figure 9–27.
3. The graph has a tangent line, but the line is the vertical line $x = c$. See Figure 9–28.

In the first two cases the graph doesn't even have a tangent line, and you can't talk about the slope of something that doesn't even exist! In the third case, remember that a vertical line is the one case of a straight line that doesn't have a slope.

Figure 9–27 gives the geometrical insight into an important theorem connecting the concepts of differentiability and continuity.

Theorem
**Differentiable Implies
Continuous**

If $f'(c)$ exists, then f is continuous at c.

CAUTION Continuous does *not* imply differentiable. Figures 9–26 and 9–28 together with Example 7 give examples to show that f can be continuous at c with f *not* differentiable at c.

OTHER NOTATION FOR DERIVATIVES

The derivative is a very important and useful concept in both pure and applied mathematics. During the 300 years since it was first developed it has been represented by several different notations. Up to now we have used $f'(x)$ to represent the derivative of $f(x)$. Another common notation that we will use is dy/dx (read "the derivative of y with respect to x"). This notation is used to remind us that the derivative is related to slope, and the slope of a line is $\Delta y/\Delta x$. Thus,

$$\frac{dy}{dx} = \lim_{\Delta x \to 0} \frac{\Delta y}{\Delta x}$$

Because we write $y = f(x)$, we also use the notation

$$\frac{d}{dx} f(x)$$

which means the derivative of $f(x)$ with respect to x.

The process of starting with $f(x)$ and then computing the derivative $f'(x)$ is called **differentiation,** or **finding the derivative** of f. Using the result of Example 3 again, we show this terminology in some examples.

EXAMPLE 8   *(Compare Exercise 1)*

If $y = x^2 - 2x - 3$, what is $\dfrac{dy}{dx}$?

SOLUTION $\dfrac{dy}{dx} = 2x - 2$

EXAMPLE 9   *(Compare Exercise 1)*

If $f(x) = x^2 - 2x - 3$, find $\dfrac{d}{dx} f(x)$.

SOLUTION $\dfrac{d}{dx} f(x) = 2x - 2$

EXAMPLE 10   *(Compare Exercise 1)*

Differentiate $f(x) = x^2 - 2x - 3$.

SOLUTION $f'(x) = 2x - 2$ or $\dfrac{dy}{dx} = 2x - 2$ or

$$\frac{d}{dx} f(x) = 2x - 2$$

9-5   EXERCISES

I

1. (*See Examples 4 and 8–10*) If $y = f(x) = \dfrac{1}{x}$:

   (a) what is $f'(x)$?

   (b) what is $\dfrac{d}{dx} f(x)$?

   (c) what is $\dfrac{dy}{dx}$?

   (d) what is the derivative of $f(x)$?

2. (*See Example 6*) If $y = f(x) = 3x + 6$:

   (a) what is $f'(x)$?

   (b) what is $\dfrac{d}{dx} f(x)$?

   (c) what is $\dfrac{dy}{dx}$?

   (d) what is the derivative of $f(x)$?

3. (*See Example 1*) If $y = x^2 + 1$, then $f'(3) = 6$. Use this information to find an equation of the line tangent to the graph of $f(x)$ at the point $(3, 10)$.

4. If $f(x) = \sqrt{x + 3}$, then $f'(1) = \frac{1}{4}$. Use this information to find an equation of the line tangent to the graph of $f(x)$ at the point $(1, 2)$.

5. If $f(x) = 1/(x + 9)$, then $f'(1) = -\frac{1}{100}$. Use this information to find an equation of the line tangent to the curve $y = 1/(x + 9)$ at the point $(1, \frac{1}{10})$.

6. If $f(x) = x^3 - 8x$, then $f'(2) = 4$. Use this information to find an equation of the line tangent to the curve $y = x^3 - 8x$ at the point $(2, -8)$.

7. If $f(x) = x^2 - 8x + 6$, then $f'(a) = 2a - 8$.

   (a) What is $f'(x)$?

   (b) What is $\dfrac{dy}{dx}$ if $y = x^2 - 8x + 6$?

8. If $f(x) = x^3$, then $f'(a) = 3a^2$.

   (a) What is $f'(x)$?

   (b) If $y = x^3$, what is $\dfrac{dy}{dx}$?

II

9. (*See Example 1*) If $y = x^2 - 5$, find the slope of the line tangent to the graph at the point $(2, -1)$.

10. If $f(x) = x^2 + 8$, find the slope of the line tangent to the graph at the point $(3, 17)$.

Use formulas established in this section to answer Exercises 11 through 14.

11. (*See Example 5*) Find an equation of the line tangent to the curve $y = 1/x$ at the point whose first coordinate is -2.

12. Find an equation of the line tangent to the curve $y = 1/x$ at the point whose first coordinate is $1/3$.

13. Find an equation of the line tangent to the curve $y = x^2 - 2x - 3$ at the point whose first coordinate is 3.

14. Find an equation of the line tangent to the curve $y = x^2 - 2x - 3$ at the point whose first coordinate is -2.

15. (*See Example 2*) Use the graph in Figure 9–29 to answer the following questions.

    (a) For what values of x in the interval $(-3, 6)$ does $f'(x)$ fail to exist?

    (b) At what points on the graph for $-3 < x < 6$ does the graph not have a tangent line?

    (c) What is $f(4)$?

    (d) What is $f'(4)$?

    (e) What is $f(1)$?

    (f) What is $f'(1)$?

    (g) For what x is $f'(x) = 0$?

FIGURE 9–29

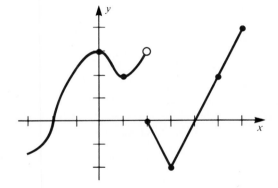

16. Use the graph in Figure 9–30 to answer the following questions.
    (a) For what values of x in the interval $(0, 10)$ does $f'(x)$ fail to exist?
    (b) At what points on the graph for $0 < x < 10$ does the graph not have a tangent line?
    (c) What is $f(1)$?
    (d) What is $f'(1)$?
    (e) What is $f(9)$?
    (f) What is $f'(9)$?

FIGURE 9–30

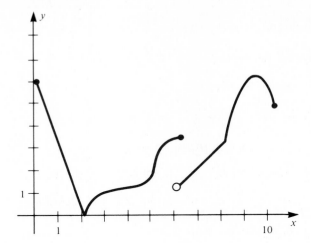

III

17. (*See Example 7*) Use the definition of derivative to show that the curve $y = |x - 3|$ does not have a tangent line at the point $(3, 0)$. Is f continuous at $x = 3$?

18. Use the definition to show that the curve $y = |x - 2| + 4$ does not have a tangent line at the point $(2, 4)$. Is f continuous at $x = 2$?

19. Use the definition of derivative to find the slope of the line tangent to $y = \sqrt{x}$ at the point $(9, 3)$.

20. Use the definition of derivative to find the slope of the line tangent to the curve $y = 1/x^2$ at the point $(4, \frac{1}{16})$.

21. (*See Example 3*) Use the definition of derivative to find the slope of the line tangent to the curve $y = x^2$ at the point (a, a^2).

22. Use the definition of derivative to find the slope of the line tangent to the curve $y = x^2 + 4$ at the point $(a, a^2 + 4)$.

23. (*See Example 4*) Use the definition of derivative to find a formula for $f'(a)$ if $f(x) = 1/(x + 4)$.

24. Use the definition of derivative to find a formula for $f'(a)$ if $f(x) = 3/(5x)$.

25. Use the definition of derivative to show that $f'(0)$ does not exist if $f(x) = x^{1/3}$. Is f continuous at $x = 0$? Draw the graph of f. Does the graph resemble Figure 9–26, 9–27, or 9–28 near $(0, 0)$?

26. Let
$$f(x) = \begin{cases} 2x + 1 & x \le 3 \\ 4 - x & x > 3 \end{cases}$$
Use the definition of derivative to show that $f'(3)$ does not exist. Is f continuous at $x = 3$? Does the graph of f resemble Figure 9–26, 9–27, or 9–28 near $(3, 7)$?

27. Let
$$f(x) = \begin{cases} 2x + 1 & x \le 3 \\ 10 - x & x > 3 \end{cases}$$
Use the definition of derivative to show that $f'(3)$ does not exist. Is f continuous at $x = 3$? Does the graph of f resemble Figure 9–26, 9–27, or 9–28 near $(3, 7)$?

28. Let
$$f(x) = \begin{cases} 2x + 1 & x \le 3 \\ x^2 - 2 & x > 3 \end{cases}$$
Use the definition of derivative to show that $f'(3)$ does not exist. Is f continuous at $x = 3$?

29. Let
$$f(x) = \begin{cases} 2x - 3 & x \le 1 \\ x^2 - 4 & x > 1 \end{cases}$$
Use the definition of derivative to show that $f'(1)$ exists.

30. Let

$$f(x) = \begin{cases} x^2 + 3 & x \le 3 \\ 6x - 6 & x > 3 \end{cases}$$

Use the definition of derivative to show that $f'(3)$ exists.

IMPORTANT TERMS

9-1

Average Rate of Change

Δx

Instantaneous Rate of Change

Three-Step Process for Computing the Instantaneous Rate of Change

Derivative

Derivative of a Linear Function

f'(a)

$$\lim_{\Delta x \to 0} \frac{f(a + \Delta x) - f(a)}{\Delta x}$$

9-2

Limit of a Function

Replacement Principle

9-3

Left-Hand Limit

Right-Hand Limit

Existence of the Limit

Jump in the Graph

Marginal Cost

Hole in the Graph

Continuous at a Point

Continuous on an Interval

9-4

Intermediate Value Theorem

Change of Sign

Bisection Method

Sign-of-f

Cut Point

9-5

Tangent Line

Slope of Tangent Line

Equation of Tangent Line

f'(x)

Nonexistence of Derivative

Differentiation

$$\frac{dy}{dx}, \frac{d}{dx} f(x)$$

REVIEW EXERCISES

Compute each of the limits in Exercises 1 through 14 or state that it does not exist.

1. $\lim_{x \to 3} \dfrac{x - 3}{x + 2}$

2. $\lim_{x \to 3} \dfrac{x + 2}{x - 3}$

3. $\lim_{x \to 5} \sqrt{31 + x}$

4. $\lim_{x \to 5} \dfrac{x^2 - 9x}{x + 4}$

5. $\lim_{x \to 2^+} |x|$

6. $\lim_{x \to 2^-} |x|$

7. $\lim_{x \to 0^-} |x|$

8. $\lim_{x \to -3^-} |x|$

9. $\lim_{x \to 2} \dfrac{x^2 - x - 2}{x - 2}$

10. $\lim_{x \to -1} \dfrac{x^2 + 4x + 3}{x + 1}$

11. $\lim_{x \to 0} \dfrac{x^3 + 4x^2 - 5x}{x^2 + 2x}$

12. $\lim_{x \to 2} \dfrac{x^2 - 7x + 10}{x^2 - 5x + 6}$

13. $\lim_{\Delta x \to 0} \dfrac{\sqrt{4 + \Delta x} - 2}{\Delta x}$

14. $\lim_{\Delta x \to 0} \dfrac{(6 + \Delta x)^2 - 36}{\Delta x}$

15. If $\dfrac{dy}{dx} = 5x + 8$, what is $f'(x)$?

16. If $y = f(x)$ and $f'(x) = 2x - 2$, what is $\dfrac{dy}{dx}$?

17. If $f(x) = x^2 - 3x + 2$, what is the average rate of change of $f(x)$:

   (a) on the interval $[-1, 4]$?

   (b) on the interval $[-1, 2]$?

   (c) on the interval $[2, 4]$?

18. If a new store's daily revenue is given by $R(t) = \sqrt{t + 9}$ in hundreds of dollars t days after it has opened, what is the average change in daily revenue as t increases from 7 to 27?

Use the definition of derivative to compute $f'(a)$ in Exercises 19 through 22.

19. $f(x) = 3x^2 - 4$, $a = 1$ **20.** $f(x) = \sqrt{x}$, $a = 9$

21. $f(x) = \dfrac{x}{2}$, $a = 4$ **22.** $f(x) = \dfrac{2}{x}$, $a = 4$

23. If $f'(4) = 3$ and $f(4) = 6$, what is an equation of the line tangent to the graph $y = f(x)$ at the point whose first coordinate is 4?

24. If $f(7) = -2$ and $f'(7) = 10$, what is an equation of the line tangent to the graph $y = f(x)$ at the point whose first coordinate is 7?

Use the graph in Figure 9–31 to answer Exercises 25 through 40.

25. Is f continuous on the interval: (a) $[-1, 2]$?

   (b) $[3, 4]$?

26. Is f continuous on the interval: (a) $(-3, -1)$?

   (b) $(0, 4)$?

27. What is:

   (a) $\lim\limits_{x \to 1^-} f(x)$?   (b) $\lim\limits_{x \to 1^+} f(x)$?   (c) $\lim\limits_{x \to 1} f(x)$?

28. What is:

   (a) $\lim\limits_{x \to 0^-} f(x)$?   (b) $\lim\limits_{x \to 0^+} f(x)$?   (c) $\lim\limits_{x \to 0} f(x)$?

29. What is:

   (a) $\lim\limits_{x \to 2^-} f(x)$?   (b) $\lim\limits_{x \to 2^+} f(x)$?   (c) $\lim\limits_{x \to 2} f(x)$?

30. What is:

   (a) $\lim\limits_{x \to -1^-} f(x)$? (b) $\lim\limits_{x \to -1^+} f(x)$? (c) $\lim\limits_{x \to -1} f(x)$?

31. Is the function continuous at:

   (a) $x = 0$?   (b) $x = 1$?   (c) $x = 2$?

32. Is the function continuous at:

   (a) $x = -1$?   (b) $x = 4$?   (c) $x = 5$?

33. Is the function continuous at:

   (a) $x = -2$?   (b) $x = 3$?   (c) $x = -3$?

FIGURE 9–31

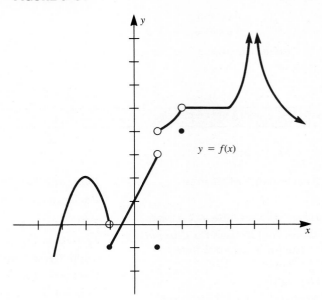

$y = f(x)$

34. What is:

   (a) $f(3)$?   (b) $f'(3)$?

35. What is:

   (a) $f(0)$?   (b) $f'(0)$?

36. What is:

   (a) $f(-2)$?   (b) $f'(-2)$?

37. What is:

   (a) $f(1)$?   (b) $f'(1)$?

38. What is:

   (a) $f(2)$?   (b) $f'(2)$?

39. For what x does $f'(x)$ fail to exist?

40. For what x is $f'(x) = 0$?

41. A delivery service charges \$6 to deliver any package weighing less than four pounds. If the package weighs four pounds or more, the service charges \$2x where x is the package's weight in pounds. If $C(x)$ is the cost in dollars of delivering a package weighing x pounds, what are:

   (a) $\lim\limits_{x \to 4^-} C(x)$ (b) $\lim\limits_{x \to 4^+} C(x)$

   (c) $C(4)$ (d) Is C continuous at $x = 4$? Explain.

42. Let

$$f(x) = \begin{cases} 2x + 1 & x \le 3 \\ x^2 - 2 & x > 3 \end{cases}$$

Is f continuous at $x = 3$?

43. Let

$$f(x) = \begin{cases} \dfrac{x^2 - 9}{x - 3} & x \ne 3 \\ M & x = 3 \end{cases}$$

Is there a value of M such that f is continuous at $x = 3$? If so, what is M?

44. If

$$f(x) = \begin{cases} x^2 + 5 & x < 2 \\ -3x + A & x \ge 2 \end{cases}$$

is there a value of A such that f is continuous at $x = 2$? If so, what is it?

45. If

$$f(x) = \begin{cases} 3x + 9 & x < 1 \\ Bx - 6 & x \ge 1 \end{cases}$$

is there a value of B such that f is continuous at $x = 1$? If so, what is it?

46. If the height in feet of a baseball is given by $h(t) = -16t^2 + 90t + 4$, where t is time in seconds:
  (a) how is the height changing after 2 seconds? (Tell how fast the ball is moving and whether it is rising or falling.)
  (b) how is the height changing after 3 seconds?

47. Use the definition of derivative to find $f'(a)$ if $f(x) = \sqrt{x}$.

48. Use the definition of derivative to find $f'(a)$ if $f(x) = x^3$.

49. Use the definition of derivative to find $f'(x)$ if $f(x) = x^2 + 3x + 1$.

50. Use the definition of derivative to find $f'(x)$ if $f(x) = 3x - x^2$.

Solve the inequalities in Exercises 51 through 58.

51. $\dfrac{1}{x} - 3 \le 2$

52. $\dfrac{6}{x} + 7 \le 10$

53. $x^2 - 4x - 4 \ge 0$

54. $x^2 + 4x \le 10$

55. $\dfrac{9}{\sqrt{x}} - \sqrt{x} > 0$

56. $\sqrt{36 - x^2} - \dfrac{x^2}{\sqrt{36 - x^2}} \le 0$

57. $\dfrac{3}{x + 1} \le \dfrac{5}{x - 2}$

58. $x + 4 \ge \dfrac{x + 11}{x - 1}$

Find an approximate solution, to within 0.1, for the equations in Exercises 59 through 62.

59. $x^3 + 7x - 40 = 0$

60. $x^2 = 3\sqrt{x} + 5$

61. $\dfrac{x^3}{40} - 7x^2 + 1000x = 48{,}000$

62. $4x - \dfrac{50}{x^2} = 20$

63. If a firm's weekly revenue for producing x units per week is given by

$$R(x) = \frac{1}{10}x^2 + 30x$$

and its weekly cost is $C(x) = 24x + 50$, for what values of x does the company make a profit?

64. The concentration of a pollutant in a lake t hours after the pollutant is discharged is given by

$$C(t) = \frac{2t + 30}{t^2 + 50}$$

The lake is unsafe for swimming as long as $C(t) \ge \frac{1}{5}$. How long after the discharge will the lake become safe for swimming again?

65. The Hastings Metal Company has a weekly cost function of

$$C(x) = \frac{x^3}{60} - 3x^2 + 1200x + 20250$$

where x is the number of tons of aluminum produced. The company's revenue function is $R(x) = -x^2 + 1800x$. For what values of x does the company make a profit, to the nearest integer?

66. Fred's Cafeteria has a weekly cost function given by

$$C(x) = \frac{x^3}{125} - 0.8x^2 + 260x + 3276$$

where x is the number (in hundreds) of meals served each week. The revenue function is $R(x) = -0.6x^2 + 340x$. How many meals must the cafeteria serve each week to break even?

10

Techniques of
Differentiation

10–1 SOME RULES FOR COMPUTING DERIVATIVES

IN THE PRECEDING CHAPTER we showed how we could use the definition of derivative,

$$\lim_{\Delta x \to 0} \frac{f(x + \Delta x) - f(x)}{\Delta x}$$

to compute $f'(x)$ for some particular functions. We did this to emphasize both the definition of the derivative and the reason that $f'(x)$ can be called **the instantaneous rate of change of** $f(x)$. But we need to find ways to compute $f'(x)$ without going back to the definition each time.

For example, suppose Moore's Record Store finds that x, its monthly total revenue from selling compact disks, and y, its revenue from selling compact disk players, are related by the equation $x^2 + xy - y^2 = 17$, where the units are thousands of dollars. The store's management wants to start an advertising campaign to boost sales of the compact disk players. How will this affect the sales of compact disks?

Using the definition of derivative in this case would be difficult. Furthermore, it would be very time-consuming to repeat these computations in order to compare the effects of various different advertising campaigns. Indeed, calculus would not have become a powerful problem-solving tool in so many varied fields without an easier method of computing the derivative. Mathematicians have developed some theorems that will allow us to compute derivatives by following certain rules, and we will show you some of these rules in this and the next two sections.

We found a few special formulas in the examples and exercises of the last chapter. For example, we found that

If $\quad f(x) = mx + b,$ then $\quad f'(x) = m.$

The derivative of a linear function is the slope of its graph. The derivative gives the instantaneous rate of change (slope) of a function at a point, and a line of the from $y = mx + b$ has the same rate of change (slope) everywhere.

There are two special cases of this formula that we would like to emphasize. We present the first case as our first rule.

Rule 1 **The Derivative of a Constant Rule**	If $\quad f(x) = c,$ then $\quad f'(x) = 0$ In other notation, If $\quad y = c,$ then $\quad \dfrac{dy}{dx} = 0$

In words, *the derivative of a constant is 0.*

To see that this is a special case of the formula for the derivative of a linear function, we point out that if $f(x) = c$ is a constant function, then its graph is a horizontal line. The slope of a horizontal line is zero, and the derivative of a linear function is the slope of the line, so $f'(x) = 0$.

For the second special case we let $b = 0$ and $m = 1$.

If $f(x) = x$, then $f'(x) = 1$.

We discovered three other similar formulas in Chapter 9:

If $f(x) = x^2$, then $f'(x) = 2x$.
If $f(x) = x^3$, then $f'(x) = 3x^2$.
If $f(x) = x^{-1}$, then $f'(x) = -1x^{-2}$.

These results are all special cases of a theorem called the power rule, which we list as our second rule.

Rule 2
The Power Rule

Let k be a real number, $k \neq 0$.

$$\text{If} \qquad f(x) = x^k, \qquad \text{then} \qquad f'(x) = kx^{k-1}$$

In other notation,

$$\text{If} \qquad y = x^k, \qquad \text{then} \qquad \frac{dy}{dx} = kx^{k-1}$$

NOTE Notice how all four of the examples above follow this pattern; in these examples we had $k = 1, 2, 3,$ and -1, respectively.

We continue with more examples showing how to use the power rule.

EXAMPLE 1   *(Compare Exercise 1)*

If $f(x) = x^7$, what is $f'(x)$?
SOLUTION   Here $k = 7$, so $k - 1 = 6$ and $f'(x) = 7x^6$.

EXAMPLE 2   *(Compare Exercise 7)*

If $f(x) = \sqrt{x^3}$, what is $f'(x)$?
SOLUTION   To express the function in the form needed to apply the power rule, we first rewrite $\sqrt{x^3}$ as $(x^3)^{1/2} = x^{3/2}$. We now have $f(x) = x^{3/2}$, and so we can apply the power rule with $k = \frac{3}{2}$. Then

$$k - 1 = \frac{3}{2} - 1 = \frac{1}{2}$$

Therefore

$$f'(x) = \frac{3}{2}x^{1/2}$$

EXAMPLE 3   *(Compare Exercise 13)*

If $f(x) = \dfrac{1}{x^3}$, what is $f'(x)$?

SOLUTION   Again, we must rewrite the function. Rewriting $1/x^3$ as x^{-3}, we see that $f(x) = x^{-3}$, so $k = -3$, $k - 1 = -4$, and finally, $f'(x) = -3x^{-4} = -3/x^4$.

CAUTION   Remember that you are subtracting 1 from the exponent; the correct computation in this example is $-3 - 1 = -4$. Do not subtract 1 from 3 and then just put a minus sign in front of the result, getting -2 instead of -4.

The power rule alone will not get us $f'(x)$ if $f(x) = 6x^3$; the power rule and the remaining computational rules must be followed very literally. The power rule can't be used directly on $f(x) = 6x^3$ because of the constant factor 6. For this function we need a rule that tells us how to find the derivative of a function of the form $f(x) = cx^k$, for any constant c. The next rule that we consider says, more generally, that if a function f has a derivative, and c is a constant, then c times f, written $c \cdot f$, also has a derivative. In fact, the theorem also tells us how to compute that derivative. That formula is our third rule.

Rule 3 **The Constant-Times Rule**	If f is differentiable, then so is $c \cdot f$. The rule for computing the derivative is $$\frac{d}{dx}(c \cdot f(x)) = c \cdot \frac{d}{dx}f(x)$$ In other notation, $$\text{If} \quad h(x) = c \cdot f(x), \quad \text{then} \quad h'(x) = c \cdot f'(x).$$

In words, *the derivative of a constant times a differentiable function is the constant times the derivative of the function.*

EXAMPLE 4   *(Compare Exercise 9)*

If $f(x) = 6x^3$, what is $f'(x)$?
SOLUTION

$$f'(x) = \frac{d}{dx}f(x) = \frac{d}{dx}(6x^3) = 6\frac{d}{dx}x^3 = 6 \cdot 3x^2 = 18x^2$$

EXAMPLE 5

Find $\dfrac{dy}{dx}$ if $y = \dfrac{7}{x^4}$.

SOLUTION As before, we rewrite the function so we can use the power rule.

$$y = 7x^{-4}$$

so

$$\frac{dy}{dx} = \frac{d}{dx}\,(7x^{-4}) = 7\frac{d}{dx}\,x^{-4}$$

$$= 7(-4x^{-5}) = -28x^{-5} = \frac{-28}{x^5}$$

We won't give the following a special name, but we would like to point out to you that we can combine the constant-times rule and the power rule.

NOTE If $f(x) = cx^k$. then $f'(x) = (c \cdot k)x^{k-1}$.

EXAMPLE 6 *(Compare Exercise 15)*

If $f(x) = 8\sqrt{x}$, what is $f'(x)$?

SOLUTION Rewriting $f(x)$ as $8x^{1/2}$, we have $c = 8$ and $k = \frac{1}{2}$, so

$$f'(x) = 8 \cdot \frac{1}{2}x^{-1/2} = 4x^{-1/2} = \frac{4}{\sqrt{x}}$$

You do not need to memorize these rules by number, Rule 3 for example, but remember the idea:

"The derivative of a constant times a differentiable function is the constant times the derivative of the function."

The following example is to convince you of the reasonableness of this rule.

EXAMPLE 7

If a company has a fleet of 12 identical cars and is depreciating each of them at a rate of $3000 per year, what is the rate of depreciation of the whole fleet?

SOLUTION You do not need calculus to figure out what the answer is; simple arithmetic shows that the answer is $(3000) \cdot 12 = 36,000$ dollars per year. What we want to do here is show how Rule 3 works in a setting in which you already know the answer. Let $f(t)$ stand for the value of each car when it is t years old. Let $g(t)$ be the value of the entire fleet, so $g(t) = 12 \cdot f(t)$. Because depreciation is the rate of change in value and the derivative is also the rate of change, the depreciation is the derivative. The word depreciation means that the fleet's value is decreasing, so the derivative is negative. The problem gives us $f'(t) = -3000$; applying Rule 3 to get the derivative of $g(t) = 12f(t)$, we have $g'(t) = 12 \cdot f'(t)$. Finally,

$$g'(t) = 12(-3000) = -36,000$$

Again, the total depreciation is $36,000 per year.

NOTE   Note the interpretation of the negative derivative. The value of the function is decreasing; this is signified by a negative derivative.

Next, what do we do when $f(x)$ is of the form $f(x) = 5x^3 + 9x$? We know how to compute both the derivative of $5x^3$ and the derivative of $9x$. What happens when we add two functions and we already know the derivative of each one? Our fourth rule, the sum rule, answers this question.

Rule 4
The Sum Rule

If f and g are differentiable, then so is $f + g$. You compute the derivative of $f + g$ by the following rule:

$$\frac{d}{dx}(f(x) + g(x)) = \frac{d}{dx}f(x) + \frac{d}{dx}g(x)$$

In other notation,

If $h(x) = f(x) + g(x)$,   then
$h'(x) = f'(x) + g'(x)$.

In words, *the derivative of the sum of differentiable functions is the sum of the derivatives.*

EXAMPLE 8   *(Compare Exercise 15)*

If $f(x) = 5x^3 + 9x$, what is $f'(x)$?

SOLUTION

$$f'(x) = \frac{d}{dx}f(x) = \frac{d}{dx}(5x^3 + 9x)$$

$$= \frac{d}{dx}(5x^3) + \frac{d}{dx}(9x)$$

$$= 15x^2 + 9$$

The sum rule extends to more than two summands.

EXAMPLE 9   *(Compare Exercise 25)*

If $f(x) = 9x^2 + 5 + \dfrac{4}{x^2}$, then compute $f'(x)$.

SOLUTION   First, rewriting $f(x)$ so that we can apply the power rule to $4/x^2$, we have $f(x) = 9x^2 + 5 + 4x^{-2}$. Now take the derivative of each summand and then add:

$$f'(x) = \frac{d}{dx}(9x^2) + \frac{d}{dx}5 + \frac{d}{dx}(4x^{-2})$$
$$= 18x + 0 + -8x^{-3}$$
$$= 18x - \frac{8}{x^3}$$

EXAMPLE 10   *(Compare Exercise 19)*

What is $f'(x)$ if $f(x) = 6x^3 - 5x^2$?

SOLUTION   Rule 4 deals only with the sum of two functions, and here f is the difference of two functions. However, we can rewrite $f(x)$ as $f(x) = 6x^3 + (-5)x^2$ and now apply the sum rule:

$$f'(x) = 18x^2 + (-10)x$$
$$= 18x^2 - 10x$$

Notice that

$$f'(x) = \frac{d}{dx}(6x^3) - \frac{d}{dx}(5x^2)$$

There was nothing special about this particular example. Because $f(x) - g(x)$ is the same as $f(x) + (-1)g(x)$, we can compute the derivative of the difference of two functions as follows:

$$\frac{d}{dx}[f(x) - g(x)] = \frac{d}{dx}[f(x) + (-1)g(x)]$$

Next, use the sum rule:

$$= \frac{d}{dx}f(x) + \frac{d}{dx}[(-1)g(x)]$$

Then, use the constant-times rule:

$$= \frac{d}{dx}f(x) + (-1)\frac{d}{dx}g(x)$$
$$= \frac{d}{dx}f(x) - \frac{d}{dx}g(x)$$

We have the following rule.

Rule 5 **The Difference Rule**	If f and g are differentiable, then so is $f - g$. The rule for computing the derivative is

$$\frac{d}{dx}(f(x) - g(x)) = \frac{d}{dx}f(x) - \frac{d}{dx}g(x)$$

In other notation,

$$\text{If} \quad h(x) = f(x) - g(x), \quad \text{then} \quad h'(x) = f'(x) - g'(x).$$

In words, *the derivative of the difference of two differentiable functions is the difference of the derivatives.*

Now we can compute the derivative of the difference of two functions directly.

EXAMPLE 11

Compute $f'(x)$ if $f(x) = 7x^3 - 14x$.

SOLUTION

$$f'(x) = \frac{d}{dx}(7x^3) - \frac{d}{dx}(14x) = 21x^2 - 14$$

The difference rule also extends to more than two differences.

EXAMPLE 12   *(Compare Exercise 23)*

If $g(x) = 7x^4 - 9x^2 - 10$, find $g'(x)$.

SOLUTION

$$\begin{aligned} g'(x) &= \frac{d}{dx}(7x^4) - \frac{d}{dx}(9x^2) - \frac{d}{dx}10 \\ &= 28x^3 - 18x - 0 \\ &= 28x^3 - 18x \end{aligned}$$

NOTE We still must rewrite the function so that each term is in the form cx^k. Watch for this in the next two examples.

EXAMPLE 13   *(Compare Exercise 29)*

If $g(t) = 9t^4 - 6\sqrt{t}$, find $g'(t)$.

SOLUTION   We must rewrite $\sqrt{t}$ as $t^{1/2}$ to apply the power rule. Thus

$$g(t) = 9t^4 - 6\sqrt{t} = 9t^4 - 6t^{1/2}$$

Now we can apply the rules:

$$g'(t) = \frac{d}{dt}(9t^4) - \frac{d}{dt}(6t^{1/2})$$

$$= 9 \cdot 4t^3 - 6 \cdot \frac{1}{2}t^{-1/2}$$

$$= 36t^3 - 3t^{-1/2}$$

$$= 36t^3 - \frac{3}{\sqrt{t}}$$

The next example is to remind you of the other kind of exponents you must rewrite—namely, negative exponents.

CAUTION Remember that the exponent goes only with the variable. $8x^2 = 8 \cdot x \cdot x$; the eight is not squared. So when you see something like $\frac{1}{3x}$, be careful.

$$\frac{1}{3x} = \frac{1}{3} \cdot \frac{1}{x} = \frac{1}{3}x^{-1} \qquad \left[\frac{1}{3x} \neq 3x^{-1}\right]$$

The exponent -1 goes only with the x, just as the exponent 2 goes only with the x in $8x^2$.

***

EXAMPLE 14   *(Compare Exercise 37)*

If $f(x) = 16x^3 - 4x^2 - \frac{1}{3x}$, find $f'(x)$.

SOLUTION   Rewrite $f(x)$ as $f(x) = 16x^3 - 4x^2 - \frac{1}{3}x^{-1}$. We have

$$f'(x) = 48x^2 - 8x - \frac{1}{3}(-1x^{-2})$$

$$= 48x^2 - 8x + \frac{1}{3x^2}$$

NOTE The word "marginal" is commonly used in economics to mean "rate of change of." For example, the *marginal revenue* is the *rate of change of the revenue*. Thus, mathematically speaking, the marginal revenue function is the derivative of the revenue function (and the marginal cost function is the derivative of the cost function, and so on). If R denotes the revenue function, then MR denotes the marginal revenue function, and $MR = R'$. Similar notation is used for the other functions. Thus, if C is the cost function, then MC is the marginal cost function and $MC = C'$.

EXAMPLE 15   *(Compare Exercise 51)*

The revenue R (in dollars) a company earns by producing x personal computers per week is given by $R(x) = 1150x - \frac{1}{2}x^2$. The weekly cost function is given by $C(x) = 850x + 20,000$. If the current production level is 200 computers per week, compute the current values of the (a) marginal revenue, (b) marginal cost, and (c) marginal profit functions and interpret each of these values.

SOLUTION

(a) $R(x) = 1150x - \frac{1}{2}x^2$, so $MR(x) = R'(x) = 1150 - x$. Therefore $MR(200) = 1150 - 200 = 950$.
   Interpretation: The weekly revenue is increasing at a rate of \$950 per computer.

(b) $C(x) = 850x + 20,000$, so $MC(x) = 850$. The marginal cost function is constant, so $MC(200) = 850$.
   Interpretation: The weekly cost is increasing at a rate of \$850 per computer produced.

(c) The profit is equal to the revenue minus the cost; symbolically, $P = R - C$. Thus, $MP = P' = (R - C)' = R' - C' = MR - MC$. We have used "the derivative of the difference is the difference of the derivatives" to see that *the marginal profit is the marginal revenue minus the marginal cost.* Thus, $MP(x) = MR(x) - MC(x)$, and $MP(200) = MR(200) - MC(200) = 950 - 850 = 100$.
   Interpretation: The weekly profit is increasing at the rate of \$100 per computer.

We will continue with further discussion of marginal functions throughout the text.

10-1   EXERCISES

I

Find $f'(x)$ for Exercises 1 through 10.

1. *(See Example 1)*
$f(x) = x^5$

2. $f(x) = x^8$

3. $f(x) = x^{-4}$

4. $f(x) = x^{-7}$

5. $f(x) = x^{4/3}$

6. $f(x) = x^{5/2}$

7. *(See Example 2)*
$f(x) = \sqrt{x^5}$

8. $f(x) = \sqrt{x^7}$

9. *(See Example 4)*
$f(x) = 10x^4$

10. $f(x) = 7x^{-2}$

Find $\dfrac{dy}{dx}$ for Exercises 11 through 20.

11. $y = 3x^2$

12. $y = 15x^{1/3}$

13. *(See Example 3)*
$y = \dfrac{9}{x}$

14. $y = \dfrac{4}{x^2}$

15. *(See Examples 6 and 8)*
$y = 10x^3 + 5\sqrt{x}$

16. $y = 8x^2 + 9\sqrt{x}$

17. $y = 15x^{-2} + x^2$

18. $y = 21x + 5x^{-3}$

19. *(See Example 10)*
$y = 10x^2 - 4x$

20. $y = 15x - x^{-3}$

II

Find $f'(x)$ for Exercises 21 through 28.

21. $f(x) = 4x^3 + 5x + 9$

22. $f(x) = 12x^3 + 8 + 4x^{-3}$

23. (*See Example 12*)

$f(x) = 6x^2 - 4x + 5$

24. $f(x) = 8x^{3/2} - 3x^2 + 5x - 9$

25. (*See Example 9*)

$f(x) = 9x^3 - 8 + \dfrac{2}{x^3}$

26. $f(x) = 14 - \dfrac{4}{x}$

27. $f(x) = 14\sqrt{x} - 9 + \dfrac{12}{x^4}$

28. $f(x) = 3\sqrt{x} + \dfrac{5}{x^2}$

Find $\dfrac{dy}{dx}$ for Exercises 29 through 36.

29. (*See Example 13*)   **30.** $y = \dfrac{8}{x} + 7x^2$

$y = 3x^3 - 10\sqrt{x}$

31. $y = 10x^2 - 5 + \dfrac{8}{x^2}$ **32.** $y = 6x - 9 + \dfrac{10}{x^5}$

33. $y = 8\sqrt{x} + 16x - \dfrac{1}{2}$

34. $y = \dfrac{8}{x} - \dfrac{4}{x^2} + \dfrac{2}{3}$

35. $y = 9\sqrt{x} - \dfrac{5}{x^2}$

36. $y = \dfrac{4}{\sqrt{x}} + 8x$

III

Find the derivative in Exercises 37 through 44.

37. (*See Example 14*)   **38.** $f(x) = \dfrac{1}{6x} - \dfrac{8}{\sqrt{x}}$

$f(x) = \dfrac{1}{4x^2} - \sqrt{x}$

39. $f(x) = \dfrac{3}{5x} + \dfrac{6}{7x^2}$ **40.** $f(x) = \dfrac{3}{4x^2} - 8x$

41. $g(t) = \dfrac{4}{5t^2} - \dfrac{5t}{3}$ **42.** $g(t) = \dfrac{6}{7t^3} - \dfrac{7}{4t}$

43. $g(x) = 9x - 4\sqrt{x} + \dfrac{3}{5x^3}$

44. $g(x) = \sqrt{x^3} - \dfrac{9}{\sqrt{x^3}}$

In Exercises 45 through 50, do the algebra to rewrite each function so that you can use the rules of this section; then compute the derivative.

45. $f(x) = \sqrt{9x}$ **46.** $f(x) = \dfrac{1}{\sqrt{16x}}$

47. $f(x) = \left(x + \dfrac{1}{x}\right)^2$ **48.** $g(x) = 3x(x^2 + 4)$

49. $g(t) = \dfrac{t^2 + 6}{3t}$ **50.** $f(x) = \dfrac{x + 5}{\sqrt{x}}$

51. (*See Example 15*) The revenue (in dollars) that a company gets from installing x sprinkler systems a month is given by $R(x) = 2000x - \frac{1}{4}x^2$. The cost (in dollars) of installing x sprinkler systems per month is given by $C(x) = 720x + 3500$. (**a**) Compute the marginal revenue, marginal cost, and marginal profit functions. (**b**) The company is currently installing 600 systems per month. Evaluate the current value of the three marginal functions from part (**a**) and interpret each evaluation.

52. The revenue (in dollars) from producing x clock-radios per week is given by $R(x) = 40x - \frac{1}{10}x^2$, and the cost (in dollars) is given by $C(x) = 25x + 6300$. (**a**) Compute the marginal revenue, marginal cost, and marginal profit functions. (**b**) The company is currently producing 70 clock-radios per week. Evaluate the current value of the three marginal functions from part (**a**), and interpret each evaluation.

53. What is an equation of the line tangent to the graph $y = x^2 - 4x + 3$ at the point $(-1, 8)$?

54. What is an equation of the line tangent to the graph $y = \sqrt{x}$ at the point $(9, 3)$?

10–2 THE PRODUCT AND QUOTIENT RULES

- *The Product Rule*
- *The Quotient Rule*

THE PRODUCT RULE

We have just seen how to compute the derivative of $f(x) = 9x^2 + 5x$ by recognizing that f is the sum of two simpler functions: $f(x)$ is $9x^2$ plus $5x$.

Just as you can form new functions by adding and subtracting functions, you can combine functions by multiplying or dividing them. We can recognize that

$$f(x) = (8x^2 - 9)(x^3 - 5x + 6)$$

is the product of $(8x^2 - 9)$ times $(x^3 - 5x + 6)$. Similarly,

$$g(x) = \frac{2x^3}{x^2 + 5}$$

is the quotient of $2x^3$ divided by $(x^2 + 5)$. Mathematicians have developed rules to show how to differentiate products and quotients as well as sums and differences.

First, we show you the rule for the product of two functions. You won't be surprised to learn that this rule is called **the product rule.**

Rule 6
The Product Rule

If f and g are both differentiable, then so is $f \cdot g$. The rule for computing the derivative is

$$\frac{d}{dx}[f(x) \cdot g(x)] = g(x) \cdot \frac{d}{dx}f(x) + f(x) \cdot \frac{d}{dx}g(x)$$

In other notation.

$$\text{If} \quad h(x) = f(x) \cdot g(x), \quad \text{then}$$
$$h'(x) = g(x) \cdot f'(x) + f(x) \cdot g'(x).$$

The rule in words is a little complicated; it is *"the derivative of the product of two differentiable functions is the second function times the derivative of the first plus the first function times the derivative of the second."*

EXAMPLE 1   *(Compare Exercise 15)*

Find $h'(x)$ if $h(x) = (8x^2 - 9)(x^3 - 5x + 6)$.

SOLUTION   We apply the product rule with $f(x) = 8x^2 - 9$ and $g(x) = x^3 - 5x + 6$:

$$h'(x) = \frac{d}{dx}[(8x^2 - 9)(x^3 - 5x + 6)]$$

$$= (x^3 - 5x + 6)\frac{d}{dx}(8x^2 - 9) + (8x^2 - 9)\frac{d}{dx}(x^3 - 5x + 6)$$

$$= (x^3 - 5x + 6)(16x) + (8x^2 - 9)(3x^2 - 5)$$

Our purpose in this example was to show the mechanics of the product rule, and so we leave the answer in the form the product rule gives us. You might want to check the answer to this example by first multiplying out $(8x^2 - 9)(x^2 - 5x + 6)$ and then computing the derivative.

CAUTION   The product rule generally gives students more difficulty than the preceding rules. You might be tempted to compute the product of the derivatives instead of following this rule. Resist the temptation!

Our next two examples show the importance of this warning. Each gives a function whose derivative you can compute using the rules from Section 10–1, so you know what the derivative is. Note how failure to use the product rule correctly gives the wrong answer in each case.

EXAMPLE 2   *(Compare Exercise 3)*

If $h(x) = 6x^3$, find $h'(x)$.

SOLUTION   From previous rules we know that the answer is $h'(x) = 18x^2$.

If we treat 6 as $f(x)$ and x^3 as $g(x)$ and use the product rule on 6 times x^3, we get

$$h'(x) = \frac{d}{dx}(6x^3) = x^3\frac{d}{dx}6 + 6\frac{d}{dx}x^3$$

$$= x^3 \cdot 0 + 6 \cdot 3x^2 = 0 + 18x^2$$

$$= 18x^2$$

You ordinarily would not use the product rule to compute this derivative, but its correct use does give the correct answer.

Now notice what happens if we compute the product of the derivatives:

$$\left(\frac{d}{dx}6\right) \cdot \left(\frac{d}{dx}x^3\right) = 0 \cdot 3x^2 = 0$$

The wrong procedure gives the wrong answer.

EXAMPLE 3   *(Compare Exercise 1)*

If $f(x) = (3x^2)(4x^3)$, what is $f'(x)$?

SOLUTION   Ordinarily, you would probably find $f'(x)$ by doing the multiplication first and then computing the derivative. Again, our goal here is to give an example that lets you check the result of using the product rule correctly.

$$f'(x) = \frac{d}{dx}[(3x^2)(4x^3)] = (4x^3)\frac{d}{dx}(3x^2) + 3x^2\frac{d}{dx}(4x^3)$$

$$= (4x^3)(6x) + (3x^2)(12x^2)$$

$$= 24x^4 + 36x^4$$

$$= 60x^4$$

To see that this answer agrees with our previous rule, let's do the multiplication before computing the derivative:

$$f(x) = (3x^2)(4x^3) = 12x^5$$

so

$$f'(x) = 60x^4$$

Again, the correct answer is *not* simply the product of the derivatives; that computation would give $(6x)(12x^2) = 72x^3$ rather than $60x^4$. ▌

Products of functions often arise in certain applications. For example, the total sales revenue of a company is the product obtained as (the number of items it sells) times (the selling price per item).

EXAMPLE 4   *(Compare Exercise 47)*

A student service organization wants to sell special sweatshirts for homecoming. The group does some sampling of student opinion and as a result estimates that if it charges $\$p$ per shirt, it can sell $3600 - 100p$ shirts. If R is the total revenue:
(a) express R as a function of p; (b) find $MR(p)$, the marginal revenue;
(c) compute and interpret $MR(12)$; and (d) compute and interpret $MR(20)$.

SOLUTION

(a) Revenue = (price per shirt)(number of shirts sold)

$$= (p)(3600 - 100p)$$

$$R(p) = p(3600 - 100p)$$

(b) Using the product rule, and recalling that $MR(p) = R'(p)$,

$$R'(p) = (3600 - 100p) \cdot 1 + p(-100) = 3600 - 100p - 100p$$

$$= 3600 - 200p$$

(Check this answer by doing the multiplication first and then computing the derivative of $R(p)$.)

(c) $MR(12) = 3600 - (200)(12) = 1200$. When $p = 12$, the revenue is increasing at the rate of \$1200 per dollar increase in price.

(d) $MR(20) = 3600 - (200)(20) = -400$. When $p = 20$, the marginal revenue is negative, which means that the revenue is decreasing at the rate of \$400 per dollar increase in price.

In these examples it might have seemed easier to do the multiplication first and then find the derivative. This is not always true. In fact, for some functions we will encounter later you *must* use the product rule. For now we just look at Example 5, for which it's easier to use the product rule first.

EXAMPLE 5   *(Compare Exercise 15)*

If $f(x) = (x^3 - 4x^2 + 7x - 23)(x^5 + 9x - 10)$, find $f'(x)$.

SOLUTION

$$f'(x) = \frac{d}{dx}f(x)$$

$$= (x^5 + 9x - 10)\frac{d}{dx}(x^3 - 4x^2 + 7x - 23) +$$

$$(x^3 - 4x^2 + 7x - 23)\frac{d}{dx}(x^5 + 9x - 10)$$

$$= (x^5 + 9x - 10)(3x^2 - 8x + 7) +$$
$$(x^3 - 4x^2 + 7x - 23)(5x^4 + 9)$$

Again, we leave the answer in the form given to us by the product rule.

Reason for the Product Rule. We are presenting these differentiation formulas to you as "rules," but you should not interpret that word to mean that these rules are just made up and can be changed, like the rules of basketball, for example. People cannot agree to change the rules for computing derivatives; they are in fact theorems and represent the way different rates of change interact in the "real world." For example, let's look at the product rule and the way that a rectangle grows.

For purposes of this application we suppose that both $f(x)$ and $g(x)$ are positive and that both are increasing as x increases. Let $f(x)$ be the width of a rectangle, and let $g(x)$ be the height. Thus $f(x) \cdot g(x)$ represents the area of the rectangle, and this rectangle is growing as x increases. See Figure 10-1.

Imagine the left and lower boundaries as anchored, so the rectangle is growing only in the direction of the arrows. Let S_1 be the right-hand edge of the rectangle. As S_1 moves to the right, the rate of growth of the area depends on both how long S_1 is and how fast S_1 is moving. The length of S_1 is $g(x)$, the height of the

FIGURE 10–1

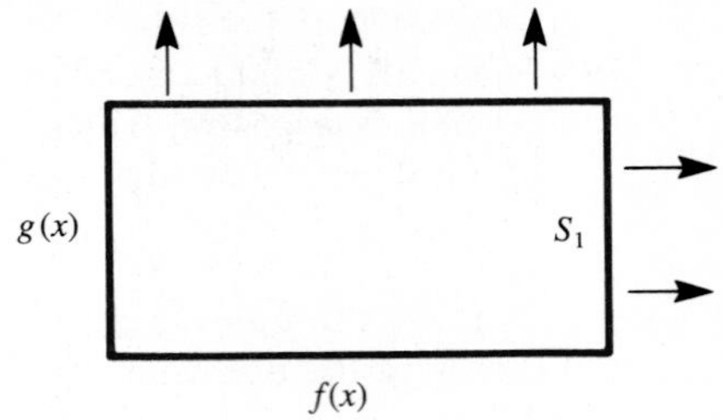

rectangle; how fast S_1 is moving to the right is $f'(x)$, the rate of change of the width. The rate at which the rectangle is growing just by expanding to the right is $g(x) \cdot f'(x)$. A similar discussion shows that the rate at which the rectangle is expanding in the upward direction is $f(x) \cdot g'(x)$. The total rate of expansion is the sum of these two individual rates.

The total rate of change of the area $= g(x) \cdot f'(x) + f(x) \cdot g'(x)$. Also, remember that the area is $f(x) \cdot g(x)$, so that the rate of change of the area is the derivative of $f(x) \cdot g(x)$.

The rate of change of the area $= (d/dx)[f(x) \cdot g(x)]$.

Setting the two expressions for the rate of change of the area equal to each other gives the product rule:

$$\frac{d}{dx}[f(x) \cdot g(x)] = g(x) \cdot f'(x) + f(x) \cdot g'(x)$$

This discussion does not prove the product rule but is intended to give you some geometric feeling for why the product rule is what it is. (*Compare Exercise 37*)

THE QUOTIENT RULE

You will probably not be surprised that the rule following the product rule is the **quotient rule.** As in all the rules regarding combination of functions, we assume that we are starting with two functions that have derivatives.

Rule 7
The Quotient Rule

If f and g are differentiable, and if $h(x) = \dfrac{f(x)}{g(x)}$ with $g(x) \neq 0$, then h is differentiable. The rule is

$$\frac{d}{dx}\left[\frac{f(x)}{g(x)}\right] = \frac{g(x)\dfrac{d}{dx}f(x) - f(x)\dfrac{d}{dx}g(x)}{[g(x)]^2}$$

In other notation,

$$h'(x) = \frac{g(x) \cdot f'(x) - f(x) \cdot g'(x)}{[g(x)]^2}$$

The requirement that $g(x) \neq 0$ ensures that $f(x)/g(x)$ makes sense.

When expressed in words, the quotient rule is even more complicated than the product rule:

"The derivative of a quotient of two differentiable functions is equal to the denominator times the derivative of the numerator minus the numerator times the derivative of the denominator all divided by the square of the denominator."

We would like to give you three special cautions about using the quotient rule.

CAUTION 1 The derivative of the quotient is *not* the quotient of the derivatives. (*See Example 6*)

EXAMPLE 6   (*Compare Exercise 7*)

If $h(x) = \dfrac{8x^4}{2x}$, find $h'(x)$.

SOLUTION   As with our first example following the product rule, if you were to encounter a function like this, the first thing you would probably do is to simplify and write $h(x) = 4x^3$. Thus we know that the answer is $h'(x) = 12x^2$. Let's use the quotient rule and see what happens. Here, the numerator $f(x) = 8x^4$, and the denominator $g(x) = 2x$. Therefore

$$\frac{d}{dx}\left(\frac{8x^4}{2x}\right) = \frac{2x\left(\dfrac{d}{dx}8x^4\right) - 8x^4\left(\dfrac{d}{dx}2x\right)}{(2x)^2}$$

$$= \frac{(2x)(32x^3) - 8x^4(2)}{4x^2}$$

(Note that the new denominator is $(2x)^2$, not $2x^2$.)

$$= \frac{64x^4 - 16x^4}{4x^2} = \frac{48x^4}{4x^2} = 12x^2$$

as we expected.

Note that the quotient of the derivatives is $32x^3/2$ or $16x^3$, rather than the correct answer of $12x^2$.

          ■

CAUTION 2 The roles of f and g in the *product* rule are interchangeable—it doesn't matter which comes first because $f(x) \cdot g(x)$ is the same as $g(x) \cdot f(x)$. You have to be more careful with the *quotient* rule; $f(x)/g(x)$ and $g(x)/f(x)$ are generally different expressions; the order in the quotient rule is important. (*See Example 7*)

EXAMPLE 7   *(Compare Exercise 11)*

If $f(x) = \dfrac{5}{x^3}$, find $f'(x)$.

SOLUTION   We can find $f'(x)$ by writing $f(x)$ as $5x^{-3}$; using the power rule, we get

$$f'(x) = -15x^{-4} = \frac{-15}{x^4}$$

Let's look at what happens if we use the quotient rule:

$$f'(x) = \frac{d}{dx}\left(\frac{5}{x^3}\right) = \frac{x^3\left(\dfrac{d}{dx}5\right) - 5\left(\dfrac{d}{dx}x^3\right)}{(x^3)^2}$$

$$= \frac{x^3(0) - 5(3x^2)}{x^6}$$

$$= \frac{-15x^2}{x^6} = \frac{-15}{x^4}$$

Caution 1 tells us that the derivative is not the quotient of the derivatives, which is $0/3x^2 = 0$. Caution 2 tells us that if we are not careful about subtracting in the right order, we could come up with $15/x^4$ instead of $-15/x^4$.   ∎

EXAMPLE 8   *(Compare Exercise 25)*

Compute $h'(x)$ if $h(x) = \dfrac{x^3 - 2x}{x^2 + 4}$.

SOLUTION $h(x)$ is in the form $\dfrac{f(x)}{g(x)}$, where $f(x) = x^3 - 2x$ and $g(x) = x^2 + 4$. Therefore

$$h'(x) = \frac{(x^2 + 4)\dfrac{d}{dx}(x^3 - 2x) - (x^3 - 2x)\dfrac{d}{dx}(x^2 + 4)}{(x^2 + 4)^2}$$

$$= \frac{(x^2 + 4)(3x^2 - 2) - (x^3 - 2x)(2x)}{(x^2 + 4)^2}$$

As we did with the product rule, we leave the answer in the form given to us by the quotient rule.   ∎

EXAMPLE 9   *(Compare Exercise 21)*

If $h(x) = \dfrac{x^2}{2x^3 + 9x}$, compute $h'(x)$.

SOLUTION   Here $h(x) = \dfrac{f(x)}{g(x)}$, where $f(x) = x^2$, and $g(x) = 2x^3 + 9x$, so

$$h'(x) = \frac{(2x^3 + 9x)(2x) - x^2(6x^2 + 9)}{(2x^3 + 9x)^2} = \frac{4x^4 + 18x^2 - 6x^4 - 9x^2}{(2x^3 + 9x)^2}$$

$$= \frac{-2x^4 + 9x^2}{(2x^3 + 9x)^2}$$

Here we were able to simplify the numerator without too many complications, which leads us to our third caution.

CAUTION 3   When simplifying the numerator of the derivative, remember that the minus sign goes in front of the whole quantity $f(x) \cdot g'(x)$. For instance, in Example 9, when we simplified $-x^2(6x^2 + 9)$, we obtained $-6x^4 - 9x^2$. Note the second minus sign. It can be very frustrating to remember to use the quotient rule correctly and then get into trouble by making an arithmetic error. Be careful.

Definition
Average Cost

The average cost of producing a certain number of items is the total cost of producing these items divided by the number of items produced. Symbolically, if $C(x)$ is the cost of producing x items, the average cost of producing x items, $AC(x)$, is given by

$$AC(x) = \frac{C(x)}{x}$$

EXAMPLE 10   *(Compare Exercise 49)*

If the cost C in dollars of producing x clock-radios per week is given by $C(x) = \frac{1}{20}x^2 + 15x + 3000$:

(a) what is the average cost per radio?
(b) how is the average cost per radio changing at the production level of 200 radios per week?

SOLUTION

(a) The average cost per radio is obtained by dividing the total cost of production by the number of radios. If $AC(x)$ stands for the average cost of producing x radios, we have

$$AC(x) = \frac{C(x)}{x}$$

The average cost is

$$AC(x) = \frac{\frac{1}{20}x^2 + 15x + 3000}{x}$$

(b) Next, the rate of change of the average cost is the derivative of the average cost ("rate of change" = "derivative"). We compute $(AC)'(x)$ by using the quotient rule.

$$(AC)'(x) = \frac{x\left(\frac{2}{20}x + 15\right) - 1\left(\frac{1}{20}x^2 + 15x + 3000\right)}{(x)^2}$$

$$= \frac{\frac{2}{20}x^2 + 15x - \frac{1}{20}x^2 - 15x - 3000}{x^2} \qquad \text{(Notice all the sign changes)}$$

$$= \frac{\frac{1}{20}x^2 - 3000}{x^2}$$

Now let $x = 200$:

$$(AC)'(200) = \frac{\left(\frac{1}{20}\right)(200)(200) - 3000}{(200)^2} = \frac{-1000}{40000} = \frac{-1}{40}$$

The average cost is decreasing at the rate of $0.025 per radio when the production level is 200 radios per week.

Perhaps you would like to rework the solution to Example 10 by doing the division in $AC(x)$ before computing derivatives. The answer is the same, but which way did you find to be easier?

The Reason for the Quotient Rule. Why is the quotient rule what it is? To see one way to arrive at this formula, let us start with $h(x) = f(x)/g(x)$. (We will assume that $h'(x)$ does exist.) Multiplying both sides of this equation by $g(x)$, we get $h(x) \cdot g(x) = f(x)$. Now we take the derivative of both sides of the equation

$$h(x) \cdot g(x) = f(x)$$

using the product rule on the left-hand side:

$$g(x) \cdot h'(x) + h(x) \cdot g'(x) = f'(x)$$

To solve for $h'(x)$, first subtract $h(x) \cdot g'(x)$ from both sides, obtaining

$$g(x) \cdot h'(x) = f'(x) - h(x) \cdot g'(x)$$

Because by assumption $g(x) \neq 0$, we can divide both sides by $g(x)$:

$$h'(x) = \frac{f'(x) - h(x) \cdot g'(x)}{g(x)}$$

Replace $h(x)$ by its equivalent expression $\dfrac{f(x)}{g(x)}$:

$$h'(x) = \frac{f'(x) - \left[\dfrac{f(x)}{g(x)}\right] \cdot g'(x)}{g(x)}$$

Finally, to simplify, multiply numerator and denominator by $g(x)$:

$$h'(x) = \frac{g(x) \cdot f'(x) - f(x) \cdot g'(x)}{(g(x))^2}$$

Again, we emphasize that we have not proven the quotient rule because we haven't proven that $h'(x)$ exists. We have, however, shown what rule must be used to compute $h'(x)$.

10-2 EXERCISES

I

Use the product rule to compute each derivative in Exercises 1 through 6; then simplify the answer. Check your answer by doing the multiplication first and then computing each derivative.

1. (*See Example 3*)
$f(x) = (3x)(7x)$

2. $f(x) = (2x^3)(5x^2)$

3. (*See Example 2*)
$f(x) = (9)(x^3)$

4. $f(x) = (x^2 + 3)(x)$

5. $f(x) = x\sqrt{x}$

6. $f(x) = x^2 x^{3/2}$

Use the quotient rule to compute each derivative in Exercises 7 through 10; then simplify the answer. Check your answer by doing the division first and then computing each derivative.

7. (*See Example 6*)
$f(x) = \dfrac{3x}{x^2}$

8. $f(x) = \dfrac{9x^3}{3x^2}$

9. $f(x) = \dfrac{6x}{2\sqrt{x}}$

10. $f(x) = \dfrac{\sqrt{x}}{x}$

Use the quotient rule to compute each derivative in Exercises 11 through 14; then simplify the answer. Check your answer by computing the derivative, using the alternate form of the function.

11. (*See Example 7*)
$f(x) = \dfrac{1}{x} = x^{-1}$

12. $f(x) = \dfrac{6}{x^4} = 6x^{-4}$

13. $f(x) = \dfrac{x^2}{8} = \dfrac{1}{8}x^2$

14. $f(x) = \dfrac{2x^3}{3} = \dfrac{2}{3}x^3$

II

Compute the derivative in Exercises 15 through 26, using the product rule or the quotient rule.

15. (*See Examples 1 and 5*)
$$f(x) = (x^3 - 4x + 1)(x^2 + 9)$$

16. $f(x) = (x + 1)(x^2 + x - 10)$

17. $f(x) = \left(x + \dfrac{1}{x}\right)\left(x - \dfrac{1}{x}\right)$

18. $f(x) = (x^3 - 9x + 5)(x^4 - 7x + 8)$

19. $f(x) = (x^2 + 3x)\left(x^4 - 7x + \dfrac{1}{x}\right)$

20. $f(x) = \left(x^2 - \dfrac{6}{x^2}\right)(x^3 + 8x - 11)$

21. (*See Example 9*)
$$f(x) = \dfrac{3x + 1}{x - 2}$$

22. $f(x) = \dfrac{9x + 5}{x^2 - 8}$

23. $f(x) = \dfrac{x^2 + 4x}{x^3 - 7x}$

24. $f(x) = \dfrac{x^3 - 4x}{\sqrt{x}}$

25. (*See Example 8*)
$$f(x) = \dfrac{3x^2 - 9x + 2}{x^3 - 5}$$

26. $f(x) = \dfrac{7 - 4x^2}{9x^3 + 8x}$

III

Compute the derivative in Exercises 27 through 30.

27. $f(x) = \dfrac{(x^2 - 8x)(x + 2)}{x^3 - 9}$

28. $f(x) = \dfrac{(x^3 - 5)(6x^2 + 9x)}{x^2 + 1}$

29. $f(x) = \dfrac{3x + 7}{(x + 2)(x^2 + 7)}$

30. $f(x) = \dfrac{7x^2 - 8x}{(14x - 3)(12x^3 - 9x)}$

31. Find an equation of the line tangent to the graph of
$$y = \dfrac{3x + 6}{x - 7}$$
at the point $(4, -6)$.

32. Find an equation of the line tangent to the graph of
$$y = \dfrac{4x}{x^2 + 1}$$
at the point $(1, 2)$.

33. Find an equation of the line tangent to the graph of
$$y = \dfrac{6}{3x + 2}$$
at the point whose first coordinate is -1.

34. Find an equation of the line tangent to the graph of
$$y = \dfrac{7x + 1}{x^3 - 5}$$
at the point whose first coordinate is 2.

35. Find an equation of the line tangent to the graph of
$$y = (x^2 + 2x + 1)(x^3 - 4x + 9)$$
at the point $(1, 24)$.

36. Find an equation of the line tangent to the graph of $y = (x - \sqrt{x})(x^2 + \sqrt{x})$ at the point whose first coordinate is 4.

37. (*See Figure 10–1 and discussion.*) The dimensions of a rectangle are changing. The height is increasing at the rate of 3 inches per minute, and the width is increasing at the rate of 2 inches per minute. What is the rate of change of the area of the rectangle at the moment when its height is 16 inches and its width is 25 inches?

38. The dimensions of a rectangle are changing. The height is increasing at the rate of $\frac{1}{2}$ inch per second, and the width is increasing at the rate of 2 inches per second. How fast is the area of the rectangle changing when the height is 10 inches and the width is 18 inches? (The answer should be in the form of a sentence; indicate whether the rectangle's area is increasing or decreasing.)

39. How is the area of a rectangle changing at the moment when its height is 6 inches and its width is 7 inches if the height is *decreasing* at the rate of 1 inch per minute and its width is increasing at the rate of $\frac{1}{2}$ inch per minute?

40. At a certain moment, a rectangle has height 5 feet and base 10 feet. At this moment the height is increasing at the rate of 3 feet per minute, and the base is *decreasing* at the rate of 2 feet per minute. What is the rate of change of the area of the rectangle at this moment?

41. At the instant when a certain triangle has a base of 16 inches and a height of 9 inches its base is increasing at the rate of 2 inches per minute, and its height is increasing at the rate of 6 inches per minute. What is the rate of change of the area of the triangle at this instant?

42. The dimensions of a triangle are changing. How is the area of the triangle changing at the moment when its height is 8 inches and increasing at the rate of 2 inches per minute and its base is 15 inches and decreasing at a rate of 5 inches per minute?

43. If $f(2) = 7, f'(2) = 3, g(2) = 6$, and $g'(2) = 4$, what is $(f \cdot g)'(2)$?

44. Find an equation of the line tangent to the graph of $f \cdot g$ at the point whose first coordinate is 3 if $f(3) = 2, f'(3) = -1, g(3) = 4$, and $g'(3) = 5$.

45. If $f(1) = 7, f'(1) = 4, g(1) = 2$, and $g'(1) = 3$, what is $\left(\dfrac{f}{g}\right)'(1)$?

46. What is the slope of the line tangent to the graph of $\dfrac{f}{g}$ at the point $(2, -2)$ if $f(2) = 6, f'(2) = 4$, $g(2) = -3$, and $g'(2) = 5$?

47. (*See Example 4*) John wants to mow lawns this summer. After talking to friends he estimates that if he charges $\$p$ per lawn, then he can mow x lawns per week, where $x = \frac{-4}{3}p + 40$.
(a) Express R, his weekly revenue, as a function of p.
(b) Compute the marginal revenue, $MR(p)$.
(c) Find and interpret $MR(12)$.
(d) Find and interpret $MR(21)$.

48. A rock group is going to sell T-shirts at its concert. The price p and demand x are related by the equation $x = 2400 - 120p$.
(a) Express the revenue R as a function of the price p.
(b) What is $MR(p)$, the marginal revenue as a function of p?
(c) Find and interpret $MR(8)$.
(d) Find and interpret $MR(13)$.

49. (*See Example 10*) A company's monthly cost of producing x storm doors is

$$C(x) = \frac{1}{30}x^3 + x^2 + 100x + 9500$$

(a) What is the company's marginal cost function, $MC(x)$?
(b) What is the company's average cost function, $AC(x)$?
(c) What is the company's marginal average cost function, $MAC(x)$?

50. A company's weekly cost of producing x hundred gallons of milk is given by

$$C(x) = \frac{1}{50}x^2 + 40x + 6200$$

(a) What is the company's marginal cost function, $MC(x)$?
(b) What is the company's average cost function, $AC(x)$?
(c) What is the marginal average cost function, $MAC(x)$?

10–3 THE CHAIN RULE

- *Composition of Functions*
- *The Chain Rule*
- *The Generalized Power Rule*

We have seen various ways that functions can be combined to build a new function—functions can be added, subtracted, multiplied, or divided. The previous two sections have shown the rules for computing the derivative of the new function in terms of the functions that were combined. We will now look at another way of combining two functions to form a new function. This new method is called the **composition of functions.**

COMPOSITION OF FUNCTIONS

A function can be compared to a machine, and we shall use that analogy to explain composition. Imagine two function machines, f and g, set up as in Figure 10–2.

The functions are set up in a sequence, or chain, of evaluations. Given the input x, first evaluate $g(x)$ and then use $g(x)$ as the input for f. The final result of this sequence, or chain, of computations is $f(g(x))$.

Let us look at some specific examples.

FIGURE 10–2

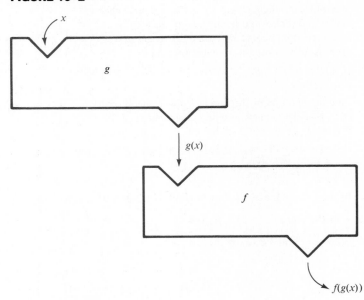

EXAMPLE 1   *(Compare Exercise 1)*

If $g(x) = x^2 + 1$ and $f(x) = 2x + 3$, what is $f(g(x))$?

SOLUTION   Remember that $f(x) = 2x + 3$ means that f multiplies any input by 2 and then adds 3 to that result. Any letter can be used to represent the variable. Thus $f(u) = 2u + 3$ gives the same function as $f(x) = 2x + 3$. If we replace $g(x)$ with the single letter u by setting $u = g(x) = x^2 + 1$, then we can write

$$f(g(x)) = f(u) = 2u + 3$$

To give the final output $f(g(x))$ in terms of the initial input x, simply use the fact that $u = x^2 + 1$:

$$2u + 3 = 2(x^2 + 1) + 3 = 2x^2 + 5$$

Therefore,

$$f(g(x)) = 2x^2 + 5$$

CAUTION   As in most sequences, the order in which things are done is important. Compare Example 1 with Example 2.

EXAMPLE 2

If $g(x) = x^2 + 1$ and $f(x) = 2x + 3$, what is $g(f(x))$?

SOLUTION   This time, $f(x)$ is the first evaluation, so we let the intermediate variable $u = f(x) = 2x + 3$. Then

$$g(f(x)) = g(u) = u^2 + 1 = (2x + 3)^2 + 1$$
$$= 4x^2 + 12x + 10$$

Notice that the answers to Examples 1 and 2 are different. Almost always,

$$f(g(x)) \neq g(f(x))$$

The order of the composition makes a difference.

EXAMPLE 3

If $f(x) = x^2 + 9x$ and $g(x) = \sqrt{x}$, compute:

(a) $f(g(x))$. **(b)** $g(f(x))$.

SOLUTION

(a)   To evaluate $f(g(x))$, let $u = g(x) = \sqrt{x}$:

$$f(u) = u^2 + 9u$$

Therefore,

$$f(g(x)) = (\sqrt{x})^2 + 9\sqrt{x} = x + 9\sqrt{x}$$

(b) On the other hand, to evaluate $g(f(x))$ we first treat $f(x)$ as a single variable; let $u = x^2 + 9x$. Then

$$g(f(x)) = g(u) = \sqrt{u} = \sqrt{x^2 + 9x}$$

THE CHAIN RULE

The function $h(x) = \sqrt{x^2 + 9x}$ is an example of a function whose derivative cannot be computed by using only the rules given in the first two sections of this chapter because $h(x)$ cannot be written as the arithmetic combination of functions of the form x^k. Instead, h involves the composition of functions. The rule used to compute the derivative of the composition of functions is called the chain rule. Let us show how to compute the derivative of $y = \sqrt{x^2 + 9x}$, the function from Example 10(b). The first function evaluated in the composition is $f(x) = x^2 + 9x$. As in Example 10(b), we introduce a new letter that stands for the output of the f machine. (This letter therefore also stands for the input to the g machine.) Let $u = x^2 + 9x$; u forms the link in the chain between y and x. With this link we can now state the **chain rule.**

Rule 8
The Chain Rule

If f and g are differentiable functions, then the function h given by $h(x) = g(f(x))$ is also differentiable, and $h'(x) = g'(f(x)) \cdot f'(x)$. In other notation, if $y = g(u)$ and $u = f(x)$, then

$$\frac{dy}{dx} = \frac{dy}{du} \cdot \frac{du}{dx}$$

Continuing with our example, note that $u = x^2 + 9x$ means that

$$y = \sqrt{u} = u^{1/2} \qquad \text{so} \qquad \frac{dy}{du} = \frac{1}{2}u^{-1/2} = \frac{1}{2\sqrt{u}}$$

Also, $u = x^2 + 9x$ means that $du/dx = 2x + 9$. Substituting these expressions into the chain rule gives

$$\frac{dy}{du} \cdot \frac{du}{dx} = \frac{1}{2\sqrt{u}} \cdot (2x + 9)$$

The last step of the computation is to rewrite dy/dx in terms of only x by substituting back the expression for u in terms of x. Doing this, we obtain

$$\frac{dy}{dx} = \frac{1}{2\sqrt{x^2 + 9x}} \cdot (2x + 9) = \frac{2x + 9}{2\sqrt{x^2 + 9x}}$$

EXAMPLE 4   *(Compare Exercise 5)*

If $y = 4(x^2 - 8)^3$, find $\dfrac{dy}{dx}$.

SOLUTION   Usually, as in this example, the individual functions forming the composition won't be singled out; you must identify them as you identified the individual functions when learning the sum rule or product rule. To help you identify these functions, be on the lookout for parentheses, or polynomials raised to some power, or radical signs. In this example the polynomial $x^2 - 8$ is cubed. We replace the entire polynomial $x^2 - 8$ by a single letter u. Let $u = x^2 - 8$, and $y = 4(x^2 - 8)^3$ becomes $y = 4u^3$. When we express y in terms of u, you notice that we have a single letter raised to a power, and our previous rules can handle that case.

$$y = 4u^3, \qquad \text{so} \qquad \frac{dy}{du} = 12u^2$$

Also, because $u = x^2 - 8$,

$$\frac{du}{dx} = 2x$$

The chain rule requires both $\dfrac{dy}{du}$ and $\dfrac{du}{dx}$.

$$\frac{dy}{dx} = \frac{dy}{du} \cdot \frac{du}{dx} = 12u^2 \cdot 2x$$

The last step is the substitution to get rid of the u. Replace u by $x^2 - 8$:

$$\frac{dy}{dx} = 12(x^2 - 8)^2 \cdot 2x = 24x(x^2 - 8)^2$$

EXAMPLE 5

If $f(x) = (x^2 - 8x + 9)^4$, find $f'(x)$.

SOLUTION   Let $y = (x^2 - 8x + 9)^4$ and $u = x^2 - 8x + 9$. Then $y = u^4$, so

$$\frac{dy}{du} = 4u^3 \qquad \text{and} \qquad \frac{du}{dx} = 2x - 8$$

Then,

$$\frac{dy}{dx} = \frac{dy}{du} \cdot \frac{du}{dx}$$
$$= (4u^3)(2x - 8)$$
$$= 4(x^2 - 8x + 9)^3(2x - 8)$$

EXAMPLE 6   *(Compare Exercise 13)*

If $f(x) = (x^3 - 8x + 5)^{2/3}$, find $f'(x)$.

SOLUTION   Let $y = f(x) = (x^3 - 8x + 5)^{2/3}$ and use the substitution

$$u = x^3 - 8x + 5 \qquad \text{so} \qquad y = u^{2/3}$$

Then

$$\frac{du}{dx} = 3x^2 - 8 \qquad \text{and} \qquad \frac{dy}{du} = \frac{2}{3}u^{-1/3}$$

Therefore

$$\frac{dy}{dx} = \frac{dy}{du} \cdot \frac{du}{dx} = \left(\frac{2}{3}u^{-1/3}\right)(3x^2 - 8)$$

Obtain the final answer by replacing the u by $x^3 - 8x + 5$:

$$= \frac{2}{3}(x^3 - 8x + 5)^{-1/3}(3x^2 - 8)$$

$$f'(x) = \frac{2(3x^2 - 8)}{3(x^3 - 8x + 5)^{1/3}}$$

EXAMPLE 7

If $y = \dfrac{3}{x^2 - 4x + 1}$, find $\dfrac{dy}{dx}$.

SOLUTION   You already know how to find dy/dx using the quotient rule, but in fact you might find it easier to compute dy/dx using the chain rule. Rewrite the equation as $y = 3(x^2 - 4x + 1)^{-1}$, and let $u = x^2 - 4x + 1$, so $y = 3u^{-1}$. Then

$$\frac{dy}{du} = -3u^{-2} = \frac{-3}{u^2} \qquad \text{and} \qquad \frac{du}{dx} = 2x - 4$$

Thus

$$\frac{dy}{dx} = \frac{dy}{du} \cdot \frac{du}{dx}$$

$$\frac{dy}{dx} = \frac{-3}{u^2} \cdot (2x - 4) = \frac{-3(2x - 4)}{u^2}$$

$$= \frac{-3(2x - 4)}{(x^2 - 4x + 1)^2}$$

Compute dy/dx using the quotient rule and compare the two procedures.

THE GENERALIZED POWER RULE

For a function that is the power of another function the chain rule takes on a special form called the **generalized power rule.** This rule enables us to compute the derivative more quickly without actually doing the u substitution. To emphasize that this is a particular case of the chain rule, we do not give this rule a new number; instead we call it Rule 8A.

Rule 8A **The Generalized Power Rule**	If f is differentiable, and if $$y = (f(x))^k, \qquad \text{then} \qquad \frac{dy}{dx} = k(f(x))^{k-1}f'(x)$$

To see that this is a special case of the chain rule, let $u = f(x)$, so $du/dx = f'(x)$. Further, $y = u^k$, so $dy/du = ku^{k-1}$. Thus

$$\frac{dy}{dx} = \frac{dy}{du} \cdot \frac{du}{dx}$$

$$= (ku^{k-1})f'(x) = k(f(x))^{k-1}f'(x)$$

EXAMPLE 8   *(Compare Exercise 9)*

If $y = (5x^4 + 3x)^9$, find $\dfrac{dy}{dx}$.

SOLUTION y is of the form $(f(x))^k$, where $f(x) = 5x^4 + 3x$ and $k = 9$. Computing the derivative of $f(x)$, we have $f'(x) = 20x^3 + 3$. Now we put the pieces together to form dy/dx:

$$\frac{dy}{dx} = 9(5x^4 + 3x)^8(20x^3 + 3)$$

EXAMPLE 9   *(Compare Exercise 17)*

If $y = \dfrac{4}{(x^3 + 1)^2}$, find $\dfrac{dy}{dx}$.

SOLUTION   Rewrite the function as $y = 4(x^3 + 1)^{-2}$. Then

$$\frac{dy}{dx} = -8(x^3 + 1)^{-3}(3x^2) = \frac{-24x^2}{(x^3 + 1)^3}$$

Sometimes you have to use the chain rule together with another rule, such as the product rule or quotient rule.

EXAMPLE 10   *(Compare Exercise 21)*

If $f(x) = x\sqrt{x^3 + 5x}$, find $f'(x)$.

SOLUTION   To find $f'(x)$, we must use the product rule because $f(x)$ is x times $\sqrt{x^3 + 5x}$:

$$f'(x) = \sqrt{x^3 + 5x}\left(\frac{d}{dx}x\right) + x\left(\frac{d}{dx}\sqrt{x^3 + 5x}\right)$$

We have to use the chain rule to compute

$$\frac{d}{dx}\sqrt{x^3 + 5x} = \frac{d}{dx}(x^3 + 5x)^{1/2}$$

Using the generalized power rule with $k = \frac{1}{2}$, we have

$$\frac{d}{dx}(x^3 + 5x)^{1/2} = \frac{1}{2}(x^3 + 5x)^{-1/2}(3x^2 + 5)$$

$$= \frac{3x^2 + 5}{2\sqrt{x^3 + 5x}}$$

Because $\frac{d}{dx}x = 1$, we have

$$f'(x) = \sqrt{x^3 + 5x} \cdot 1 + \frac{x(3x^2 + 5)}{2\sqrt{x^3 + 5x}}$$

$$= \sqrt{x^3 + 5x} + \frac{x(3x^2 + 5)}{2\sqrt{x^3 + 5x}}$$

EXAMPLE 11   *(Compare Exercise 25)*

Compute $g'(x)$ if $g(x) = \dfrac{(x^2 + 1)^3}{x^4 - 9x}$.

SOLUTION   We must use the quotient rule. While using the quotient rule, we must use the chain rule to compute the derivative of the numerator, $(x^2 + 1)^3$.

$$\frac{d}{dx}(x^2 + 1)^3 = 3(x^2 + 1)^2 2x$$

$$= 6x(x^2 + 1)^2$$

Therefore,

$$g'(x) = \frac{(x^4 - 9x)[6x(x^2 + 1)^2] - (x^2 + 1)^3(4x^3 - 9)}{(x^4 - 9x)^2}$$

Sometimes the chain rule must be used more than once.

EXAMPLE 12   (*Compare Exercise 29*)

If $f(x) = [4x + (3x + 1)^6]^{10}$, find $f'(x)$.

SOLUTION

$$f'(x) = 10[4x + (3x + 1)^6]^9 \cdot \frac{d}{dx}[4x + (3x + 1)^6]$$

$$= 10[4x + (3x + 1)^6]^9 \cdot [4 + 6(3x + 1)^5 \cdot 3]$$

Notice the use of the chain rule in computing the derivative of $(3x + 1)^6$.

10–3 EXERCISES

I

1. (*See Example 1*) If $f(x) = x^2 + 3x$ and $g(x) = 2x + 1$, evaluate:
   (a) $f(g(x))$ (b) $g(f(x))$

2. If $f(x) = 3x - 7$ and $g(x) = 6 - 2x$, evaluate:
   (a) $f(g(x))$ (b) $g(f(x))$

3. If $f(x) = \sqrt{x}$ and $g(x) = 9x + 25$, evaluate:
   (a) $f(g(x))$ (b) $g(f(x))$

4. If $f(x) = x^2 + \sqrt{x}$ and $g(x) = 4x$, evaluate:
   (a) $f(g(x))$ (b) $g(f(x))$

Use the given substitution and the chain rule to compute dy/dx in Exercises 5 through 8.

5. (*See Example 4*)
$y = (x^3 - 4x)^5; u = x^3 - 4x$

6. $y = (4x^2 - 9x + 3)^3; u = 4x^2 - 9x + 3$

7. $y = \sqrt{9x + 16}; u = 9x + 16$

8. $y = (25x - 9)^{-1/2}; u = 25x - 9$

II

Find dy/dx in Exercises 9 through 12.

9. (*See Example 8*)
$y = (3x^2 + 8)^3$

10. $y = (5x - 3)^4$

11. $y = \sqrt{4x + 9}$

12. $y = (6x - 8)^{-1}$

Find $f'(x)$ in Exercises 13 through 16.

13. (*See Example 6*)
$f(x) = (x^2 - 9x + 5)^3$

14. $f(x) = (x^3 - 8)^{1/2}$

15. $f(x) = \sqrt{16x - 4}$

16. $f(x) = 3(x^2 + 4)^{-2}$

Find dy/dx in Exercises 17 through 20.

17. (*See Example 9*)
$y = \dfrac{10}{(4x + 1)^3}$

18. $y = \dfrac{1}{(x^2 + 1)^2}$

19. $y = \dfrac{4}{(3x + 1)^3}$

20. $y = \dfrac{6}{(2x^2 + 3)^2}$

III

Find $f'(x)$ in Exercises 21 through 32.

21. (*See Example 10*)
$f(x) = x\sqrt{4x + 9}$

22. $f(x) = (3x + 1)(5x^2 + 1)^4$

23. $f(x) = (7x - 8)^3(6x - 4)^2$

24. $f(x) = (x^2 + 1)\sqrt{x^3 - 4x}$

25. (*See Example 11*)
$f(x) = \dfrac{(x^2 + 1)^3}{8x + 10}$

26. $f(x) = \dfrac{(6x - 8)^4}{3x + 9}$

27. $f(x) = \dfrac{3x + 1}{(x^2 - 4)^2}$

28. $f(x) = \dfrac{2x + 9}{(3x - 5)^3}$

29. (*See Example 12*)
$f(x) = (3x + (2x + 1)^3)^5$

30. $f(x) = \sqrt{6x^2 + (5x + 1)^3}$

31. $f(x) = (7x + \sqrt{3x + 1})^3$

32. $f(x) = ((3x + 4)^2 - \sqrt{9x + 4})^3$

33. What is an equation of the line tangent to the graph of $y = \sqrt{2x + 17}$ at the point $(4, 5)$?

34. What is an equation of the line tangent to the graph of $y = (2x - 6)^5$ at the point $(2, -32)$?

35. What is an equation of the line tangent to the graph of $f(x) = 4x^2\sqrt{x^3 - 2}$ at the point whose first coordinate is 3?

36. What is an equation of the line tangent to the curve

$$y = \frac{5x}{(3x + 1)^2}$$

at the point whose first coordinate is 2?

37. A company hopes that t weeks after a new advertising campaign begins, the weekly demand for its product will be given by $D(t) = (3t + 100)^{3/2}$. Compute and interpret both $D(7)$ and $D'(7)$.

38. The Chamber of Commerce predicts that t years after the opening of a new industrial park, the community will have $30{,}000 + 250t\sqrt{4t + 1}$ jobs. When $t = 2$, how many jobs will the community have, and how will the number of jobs be changing?

39. A company projects that its yearly sales revenue, in millions of dollars, t years after introducing a new model computer will be given by $R(t) = \sqrt{t^2 + 6t}$. What is the yearly revenue and what is the rate of change of revenue after two years?

40. Management has found that the attentiveness of a new trainee can be measured by

$$A(t) = \frac{5t^3 + 9}{(t^2 + 3)^2}$$

after t hours of instruction. What is the rate of change of attentiveness after two hours? Is the trainee's attentiveness increasing or decreasing?

10–4 HIGHER-ORDER DERIVATIVES

INFLATION SLOWDOWN SPEEDS UP

This headline appeared in the first column on the front page of the *Waco Tribune-Herald* on April 21, 1982, and succinctly sums up the first paragraph, which said:

> The unrelenting recession, driving down some prices for the first time in six years, is dampening inflation at a faster rate than most economists had expected.

"INFLATION" is a measure of the change in the value of the dollar. The word "SLOWDOWN" in the headline then is talking about the rate of change of inflation, while "SPEEDS UP" refers to the rate of change in the slowdown.

The mathematical tool for talking about rate of change is the derivative; the rate of change of the rate of change becomes the derivative of the derivative. If we use f' to denote the derivative of f, then $(f')'$ is the derivative of f'. We can (and will from now on) omit the parentheses and write f'' instead of $(f')'$ We call f'' the **second derivative** of f.

Once we have made this step, we see that we can continue this process (as does the headline). The third derivative of f is the derivative of f'' and is written f''', and so on.

EXAMPLE 1 *(Compare Exercise 1)*

If $f(x) = x^3$, compute the fourth derivative of f.

SOLUTION

$$
\begin{array}{ll}
f(x) = x^3 & \text{the function } f \\
f'(x) = 3x^2 & \text{the first derivative of } f \\
f''(x) = 6x & \text{the second derivative of } f \\
f'''(x) = 6 & \text{the third derivative of } f \\
f^{(4)}(x) = 0 & \text{the fourth derivative of } f
\end{array}
$$

Observe the notational change for f''''. The notation of repeating the $'$ symbol becomes awkward after a while; it's easy to lose count of the number of marks. We use the symbol $f^{(n)}$ to mean the nth derivative of f when $n \geq 4$.

The alternative notations of dy/dx and y' are also used for $f'(x)$. Using these notations, **higher-order derivatives** of f are expressed as

$$\frac{d^2y}{dx^2}, \qquad \text{and} \qquad y'' \text{ for } f''(x)$$

$$\frac{d^3y}{dx^3} \qquad \text{and} \qquad y''' \text{ for } f'''(x)$$

$$\begin{array}{cc} . & . \\ . & . \\ . & . \end{array}$$

etc.

EXAMPLE 2 *(Compare Exercise 5)*

If $y = \dfrac{1}{x}$, find $\dfrac{d^3y}{dx^3}$.

SOLUTION We write $y = x^{-1}$ in order to use the power rule:

$$\frac{dy}{dx} = -x^{-2}$$

$$\frac{d^2y}{dx^2} = 2x^{-3}$$

$$\frac{d^3y}{dx^3} = -6x^{-4} = -\frac{6}{x^4}$$

EXAMPLE 3   *(Compare Exercise 7)*

If $y = (5x + 3)^4$, compute $\dfrac{d^3y}{dx^3}$.

SOLUTION   Notice that y is the composition of functions, and so we have to use the chain rule to compute dy/dx. We can use the generalized power rule form of the chain rule with $f(x) = 5x + 3$ and $k = 4$:

$$\frac{dy}{dx} = 4(5x + 3)^3 \cdot 5$$
$$= 20(5x + 3)^3$$
$$\frac{d^2y}{dx^2} = 60(5x + 3)^2 \cdot 5 \qquad \text{(Chain rule again!)}$$
$$= 300(5x + 3)^2$$
$$\frac{d^3y}{dx^3} = 600(5x + 3) \cdot 5$$
$$= 3000(5x + 3)$$

In applications you generally won't have to compute more than the first and second derivatives. But when the first derivative involves the chain rule, the computation of the second derivative may require the product rule, as the next example shows.

EXAMPLE 4   *(Compare Exercise 15)*

If $y = \sqrt{x^4 + 9}$, find y''.

SOLUTION $y = (x^4 + 9)^{1/2}$, so

$$y' = \frac{1}{2}(x^4 + 9)^{-1/2} \cdot 4x^3 \qquad \text{(Chain rule)}$$
$$= 2x^3(x^4 + 9)^{-1/2}$$

We had to be careful to use the chain rule when computing y', and we have to continue to use it to compute y''. But something else has snuck in. The chain rule produced a factor, $4x^3$, that is not constant, and so y' is the product of two functions. We must use the product rule as well as the chain rule when computing y''.

$$y'' = (x^4 + 9)^{-1/2}\left[\frac{d}{dx}2x^3\right] + 2x^3\left[\frac{d}{dx}(x^4 + 9)^{-1/2}\right] \qquad \text{(Used the product rule)}$$
$$= (x^4 + 9)^{-1/2}[6x^2] + 2x^3\left[-\frac{1}{2}(x^4 + 9)^{-3/2} \cdot 4x^3\right] \qquad \text{(Used the chain rule)}$$
$$= \frac{6x^2}{\sqrt{x^4 + 9}} - \frac{4x^6}{(\sqrt{x^4 + 9})^3}$$

When computing a particular derivative, you may be called upon to use more than one rule. Be careful and be patient; don't try to rush to the answer.

EXAMPLE 5   *(Compare Exercise 13)*

Find $f''(x)$ if $f(x) = (5x^2 - 9)^4$.

SOLUTION   The generalized power rule gives

$$f'(x) = 4(5x^2 - 9)^3 \cdot 10x$$
$$= 40x(5x^2 - 9)^3$$
$$f''(x) = (5x^2 - 9)^3 \cdot 40 + 40x \cdot 3(5x^2 - 9)^2 \cdot 10x$$

Don't forget the chain rule at the very end!

$$f''(x) = 40(5x^2 - 9)^3 + 1200x^2(5x^2 - 9)^2$$

EXAMPLE 6   *(Compare Exercise 17)*

Find y'' if $y = \dfrac{3}{(x^2 + 1)^2}$.

SOLUTION   Rewrite y as

$$y = 3(x^2 + 1)^{-2}$$

Then

$$y' = 3[-2(x^2 + 1)^{-3} \cdot 2x]$$
$$= -12x(x^2 + 1)^{-3}$$
$$y'' = (x^2 + 1)^{-3}(-12) + (-12x)[-3(x^2 + 1)^{-4} \cdot 2x]$$
$$= -12(x^2 + 1)^{-3} + 72x^2(x^2 + 1)^{-4}$$

CAUTION   Remember, the second derivative is the rate of change of the rate of change. Be careful with the units when interpreting the significance of the second derivative. (*See Example 7*)

EXAMPLE 7   *(Compare Exercise 23)*

A company has found that its weekly cost C in dollars for producing x thousand ball-point pens is given by

$$C(x) = \frac{1}{100}x^3 + \frac{1}{20}x^2 + 65x + 1200$$

Assume that the company is currently producing 10,000 pens per week.

(a) What is the current weekly cost?
(b) Compute and interpret the current marginal cost.
(c) Compute and interpret the current rate of change of the marginal cost.

SOLUTION

(a) Currently, $x = 10$. (Remember that the thousand units are built into the definition of x.)

$$C(10) = \frac{1}{100}10^3 + \frac{1}{20}10^2 + 65 \cdot 10 + 1200 = 1865$$

The current weekly cost is $1865.

(b) $MC(x) = C'(x) = \frac{3}{100}x^2 + \frac{2}{20}x + 65$. With $x = 10$ the marginal cost is given by

$$MC(10) = \frac{3}{100}10^2 + \frac{1}{10}10 + 65 = 3 + 1 + 65 = 69$$

Currently, costs are increasing at the rate of $69 per thousand pens. (Note that the units of $MC = \dfrac{dC}{dx}$ are dollars per unit of x.) In other words, increasing production another 1000 pens would increase the total costs from $1865 to approximately $1865 + $69 = $1934.

(c) $(MC)'(x) = \dfrac{6}{100}x + \dfrac{2}{20}$. With $x = 10$ we have

$$(MC)'(10) = \frac{60}{100} + \frac{1}{10} = \frac{7}{10} = 0.7$$

The marginal cost is increasing at a rate of 70¢ per thousand. At this rate an increase in production of 1000 pens would boost the marginal cost to $69.70 per thousand. Another way of saying this is "The total cost is **accelerating** at the rate of 70¢ per thousand per thousand."

Note that the units involved in $\dfrac{dMC}{dx}$ are units of MC per unit of x. The units of MC are cost per unit of x. Consequently, the units of $\dfrac{dMC}{dx}$ are cost per unit of x per unit of x. The word acceleration is often used in the interpretation of the second derivative.

10-4 EXERCISES

I

Find the third derivative in Exercises 1 through 6.

1. (*See Example 1*)
$f(x) = 6x + 7$

2. $f(x) = 4x^2 - 9x + 2$

3. $g(t) = t^3 - 8t^2 + 4t - 7$

4. $y = t^4 - 4t^3 + 8t + 1$

5. (*See Example 2*)
$f(x) = \dfrac{5}{x^2}$

6. $f(x) = \dfrac{6}{x^4}$

II

Compute the third derivative in Exercises 7 through 12.

7. (*See Example 3*)
$f(x) = (3x + 1)^5$

8. $f(x) = (6x - 4)^3$

9. $f(x) = \sqrt{8x + 4}$

10. $f(x) = (3x - 6)^2$

11. $g(x) = \dfrac{5}{2x + 1}$

12. $h(t) = \dfrac{6}{(3t + 2)^2}$

III

Compute y'' in Exercises 13 through 20.

13. (*See Example 5*)
$y = (x^2 + 1)^3$

14. $y = (3x^2 - 4)^5$

15. (*See Example 4*)
$y = \sqrt{6x^2 - 8}$

16. $y = \sqrt[3]{27x^3 - 8}$

17. (*See Example 6*)
$y = \dfrac{3}{(x^2 + 1)^3}$

18. $y = -\dfrac{8}{(4x^3 + 8)^2}$

19. $y = \dfrac{4}{(3x^2 + 9)^5}$

20. $y = (4x^2 + 8)^3$

21. If $f(x) = \sqrt{2x^2 + 1}$, find $f''(2)$

22. If $g(t) = (t^3 - 4t)^4$, what is $g''(t)$?

23. (*See Example 7*) A company's daily cost function (in dollars) for producing x units is given by

$$C(x) = \frac{1}{60}x^3 + 5x^2 + 115x + 6200$$

The company is currently producing 150 units.
(a) What is the current daily cost?
(b) Find and interpret the current marginal cost.
(c) Find and interpret $(MC)'(150)$.

24. A sandwich company's weekly cost function (in dollars) for producing x hundred sandwiches per week is given by

$$C(x) = \frac{1}{90}x^3 + x^2 + 84x + 2100$$

When the weekly production level is 3000 sandwiches, find: (a) the company's weekly cost, (b) the company's marginal cost, and (c) the rate of change of the marginal cost.

25. A falling rock is $-16t^2 + 200$ feet above the ground t seconds after it is dropped.
(a) Where is the rock when $t = 3$?
(b) What is the velocity of the rock when $t = 3$?
(c) What is the acceleration of the rock when $t = 3$? (Acceleration is the rate of change of velocity.)

26. An automobile covers

$$\frac{1}{12}t^3 + 15t^2 + 10t \text{ feet}$$

t seconds after it starts.
(a) How far has it gone after four seconds?
(b) How fast is it moving after four seconds?
(c) How is it accelerating after four seconds?

10-5 IMPLICIT DIFFERENTIATION

- *Implicitly Defined Functions*
- *Implicit Differentiation*

IMPLICITLY DEFINED FUNCTIONS

When we write an equation such as $y = 2x^3 - 5x + 7$, we are giving a rule that shows how the value of y depends upon the value of x. For example, if $x = -1$, then we have an explicit formula for computing y: $y = 2(-1)^3 - 5(-1) + 7 = 10$. We say that y is a function of x and write $y = f(x)$ to show that y depends on x. Now the equation $y = 2x^3 - 5x + 7$ can be written in other equivalent forms, such as $y - 2x^3 + 5x - 7 = 0$. Remember that a particular line can have several equivalent equations. For example, $2y - 16x + 10 = 0$ is equivalent to $y = 8x - 5$; both equations define the same line. That is, both equations define the same function but in different forms. When the equation is of the form $y = f(x)$, we say that the function f is given **explicitly;** in any other form we say that the function is given **implicitly.** Thus the equation $2y + 16x - 10 = 0$ implicitly defines y as a function of x.

EXAMPLE 1   *(Compare Exercise 1)*

Each of the following four equations does define y as a function of x. State whether each equation defines y as a function of x *implicitly* or *explicitly.*

(a) $xy = 3x + 2y$
(b) $y = \sqrt{x^4 - 9}$
(c) $y + 6 = 8x$
(d) $y = 4x - y^3$

SOLUTION
(a) Implicitly; the y is not isolated.
(b) Explicitly; the y is isolated.
(c) Implicitly.
(d) Implicitly; note that there is a y-term on both sides of the equation.

Sometimes, when an equation implicitly defines y as a function of x, you can write an equivalent equation that gives the function explicitly. The basic idea is to isolate the single term y on one side of the equation and have an expression on the other side that involves only numbers and the variable x. Let's go back to the equations from Example 1 and see what this means in specific cases. We begin with the easiest.

EXAMPLE 2   *(Compare Exercise 7)*

Given the equation $y + 6 = 8x$, express y explicitly as a function of x.
SOLUTION   We can isolate y by subtracting 6 from both sides of the equation: $y = 8x - 6; f(x) = 8x - 6$.

EXAMPLE 3   *(Compare Exercise 11)*

Find the function $y = f(x)$ defined implicitly by the equation $xy = 3x + 2y$.
SOLUTION   First, get all the terms that involve y on one side of the equal sign and all the remaining terms on the other side:

$$xy - 2y = 3x$$

Next, factor out y on the left-hand side:

$$y(x - 2) = 3x$$

Now isolate y by dividing both sides by $x - 2$:

$$y = \frac{3x}{x - 2}$$

                                                        ■

Sometimes, you cannot isolate the y-term, as with the equation in part (d) of Example 1. We can rewrite that equation in several forms:

$$y^3 + y = 4x$$
$$y(y^2 + 1) = 4x$$

or

$$y = \frac{4x}{y^2 + 1}$$

but notice even this last form does not isolate y because y also appears on the right-hand side of the equation. Still, the equation $y^3 + y = 4x$ does define y as a function of x even if we cannot write down an explicit formula $y = f(x)$ for this function.

The value of y depends on the value of x, and as the value of x changes, the value of y will change also. The derivative of y with respect to x, dy/dx, gives the rate of change of y with respect to x. Knowing this rate of change may be important in an application, but how can you find it if the equation you start with (like $y^3 + y = 4x$) is so complicated that you cannot solve for y explicitly? The technique for finding dy/dx when y and x are related by such complicated equations is called **implicit differentiation.**

IMPLICIT DIFFERENTIATION

We use the equation $y = 4x - y^3$ from Example 1. We begin the process of computing dy/dx by taking the derivative (with respect to x) of both sides of this equation:

$$\frac{d}{dx}y = \frac{d}{dx}(4x - y^3)$$

$$= \frac{d}{dx}(4x) - \frac{d}{dx}y^3$$

On the right-hand side we used "the derivative of the difference is the difference of the derivatives."

Now remember that $\frac{d}{dx}$ means to take the derivative with respect to x of the function that follows. Thus on the left, $\frac{d}{dx}y$ is the derivative of y with respect to x, which we can rewrite as $\frac{dy}{dx}$. Remember that $\frac{dy}{dx}$ is the quantity we are trying to find. Next, $\frac{d}{dx}(4x)$ is the derivative of $4x$ with respect to x, so $\frac{d}{dx}(4x) = 4$.

Finally, we have to compute $\frac{d}{dx}y^3$. To do this, remember that we are assuming that $y = f(x)$ even though we don't know the explicit formula for $f(x)$. If we replace y by $f(x)$, we have

$$\frac{d}{dx}y^3 = \frac{d}{dx}(f(x))^3$$

Now we can use the generalized power rule:

$$\frac{d}{dx}(f(x))^3 = 3(f(x))^2 \cdot \frac{d}{dx}f(x)$$

If we substitute back the y for $f(x)$, we have

$$\frac{d}{dx}y^3 = 3y^2\frac{d}{dx}y$$

Since

$$\frac{d}{dx}y = \frac{dy}{dx}$$

we can write

$$\frac{d}{dx}y^3 = 3y^2\frac{dy}{dx}$$

We can now rewrite our equation

$$\frac{d}{dx}y = \frac{d}{dx}4x - \frac{d}{dx}y^3$$

as

$$\frac{dy}{dx} = 4 - 3y^2\frac{dy}{dx}$$

We use the same method to solve for dy/dx as we used earlier to solve for y. Move all the terms that involve dy/dx to one side of the equal sign and all the other terms to the other side of the equal sign:

$$\frac{dy}{dx} + 3y^2\frac{dy}{dx} = 4$$

Next, factor out dy/dx:

$$(1 + 3y^2)\frac{dy}{dx} = 4$$

Finally, divide by the other factor:

$$\frac{dy}{dx} = \frac{4}{1 + 3y^2}$$

We could not solve explicitly for y as a function of x, so we can not hope to express dy/dx as a function of x. Generally, we will have dy/dx as a function of both x and y.

EXAMPLE 4 *(Compare Exercises 15 and 21)*

Given the equation $3y^2 - 2x^3 = y + 5$, find y' in terms of x and y.

SOLUTION   We differentiate both sides of the original equation with respect to x:

$$\frac{d}{dx}(3y^2 - 2x^3) = \frac{d}{dx}(y + 5)$$

$$\frac{d}{dx}(3y^2) - \frac{d}{dx}(2x^3) = \frac{d}{dx}y + \frac{d}{dx}5$$

$$6y\frac{dy}{dx} - 6x^2 = \frac{dy}{dx} + 0$$

$$6y\frac{dy}{dx} - 6x^2 = \frac{dy}{dx}$$

Again, we use the same technique to solve for dy/dx. Get all the terms that involve dy/dx on one side of the equation and all the remaining terms on the other side:

$$6y\frac{dy}{dx} - \frac{dy}{dx} = 6x^2$$

Factor out dy/dx:

$$(6y - 1)\frac{dy}{dx} = 6x^2$$

Divide by $6y - 1$:

$$\frac{dy}{dx} = \frac{6x^2}{6y - 1}$$

We warn you about some common errors in the following cautions.

CAUTION Remember that y is being used for some unknown function f, and we are trying to find dy/dx, which is the same as $f'(x)$. *Do not* begin the computation by writing $f'(x)$ to indicate that you are taking the derivative. Study the beginning of the solution of Example 4. Sometimes students begin by writing $f'(x) = 6y - 6x^2 = 1$. *Do not start by writing $f'(x) = \ldots$*

CAUTION Remember that

$$\frac{d}{dx}y^2 = 2y\frac{dy}{dx}$$

Do not "just take the derivative" and write $2y$. For every occurrence of y in the original equation there will be a $\dfrac{dy}{dx}$ that appears in the differentiated equation. For instance, in Example 4 the original equation

$$3y^2 - 2x^3 = y + 5$$

has two terms that involve y, and each one leads to a term involving $\dfrac{dy}{dx}$ in the differentiated equation

$$6y\frac{dy}{dx} - 6x^2 = \frac{dy}{dx}$$

Do not forget the chain rule.

Because we have been able to express y' in terms of x and y, we can find an equation of the line tangent to the curve at a given point, as the next example shows.

EXAMPLE 5   *(Compare Exercise 29)*

Find an equation of the line tangent to the graph of $y^3 - 2xy^2 + 6x = 3$ at the point $(2, 3)$.

SOLUTION   First, check that $(2, 3)$ is on the curve.

$$3^3 - 2 \cdot 2 \cdot 3^2 + 6 \cdot 2 = 27 - 36 + 12 = 3$$

so $x = 2$, $y = 3$ satisfies the equation and $(2, 3)$ *is* on the curve. Next, the slope of the tangent line is y', so we use implicit differentiation to find an equation involving y', and then solve for y' in terms of x and y. Differentiate both sides with respect to x.

$$\frac{d}{dx}(y^3 - 2xy^2 + 6x) = \frac{d}{dx}(3)$$

$$\frac{d}{dx}(y^3) - \frac{d}{dx}(2xy^2) + \frac{d}{dx}(6x) = 0$$

$$3y^2 \cdot y' - \left[y^2\left(\frac{d}{dx}2x\right) + 2x\left(\frac{d}{dx}y^2\right) \right] + 6 = 0$$

Notice that to compute $\dfrac{d}{dx}(2xy^2)$, we must use the product rule:

$$3y^2 \cdot y' - [y^2(2) + 2x(2y \cdot y')] + 6 = 0$$
$$3y^2y' - 2y^2 - 4xyy' + 6 = 0$$

Note: The minus sign goes with every term inside the brackets.

Now gather all the terms involving y' on one side and all the remaining terms on the other side:

$$3y^2y' - 4xyy' = 2y^2 - 6$$

Factor out y':

$$y'(3y^2 - 4xy) = 2y^2 - 6$$

Divide by $3y^2 - 4xy$:

$$y' = \frac{2y^2 - 6}{3y^2 - 4xy}$$

Finally, when $x = 2$ and $y = 3$,

$$y' = \frac{2 \cdot 9 - 6}{3 \cdot 9 - 4 \cdot 2 \cdot 3} = \frac{12}{3} = 4$$

The slope of the tangent line is 4.

The point-slope form of the equation of the line tangent to $y^3 - 2xy^2 + 6x = 3$ at the point $(2, 3)$ is $y - 3 = 4(x - 2)$.

Two more cautions are needed; we mentioned the first one in the solution of Example 5.

CAUTION Remember to use the product rule when needed, and be careful with the minus sign when the term is being subtracted.

CAUTION Remember to use the given values of x and y when writing the equation of the tangent line. In Example 5 we had

$$y' = \frac{2y^2 - 6}{3y^2 - 4xy}$$

and used $x = 2$ and $y = 3$ to compute the slope of the tangent line. Note that

$$y - 3 = \frac{2y^2 - 6}{3y^2 - 4xy}(x - 2)$$

is *not* the equation of a line.

10-5   EXERCISES

I

State whether each of the equations in Exercises 1 through 6 defines y as a function of x explicitly or implicitly.

1. (*See Example 1*)
   $x^2 - 3x = y$

2. $3x + 4y = 8$

3. $6y = 5x^2 - 9x + 2$

4. $y = 8x^2 - y^2$

5. $x^2 + y^2 = 25$

6. $x^2 + 3x = y + 2$

Each of the equations in Exercises 7 through 10 implicitly defines y as a function of x. Rewrite the equation so that y is given explicitly in the form $y = f(x)$.

7. (*See Example 2*)
   $3(y - 1) = 2(x + 5)$

8. $y - 9 = x^2 + 4x + 1$

9. $y(x + 1) = 3x - 7$

10. $4y - 2x = 6y + 5x^2 + 7$

II

Rewrite each of the equations in Exercises 11 through 14 so that y is given explicitly as a function of x.

11. (*See Example 3*)
$3y + xy = 10$

12. $y + 5 = x^2y - 9x$

13. $xy + x^2y = 5y - 9x$

14. $y(x^2 + 1) = 6y - 9 + 8x^2$

In Exercises 15 through 20, use implicit differentiation and then solve for y' in terms of x and y.

15. (*See Example 4*)
$x^2 + y^2 = 25$

16. $4y^3 = 5x - 8$

17. $6y^2 + 2y + 5x + 9 = 0$

18. $xy + y^2 = 5$

19. $x^2y + y^3 - 4x^2 = 7$

20. $y^3 - 3x = y + 7$

III

In Exercises 21 through 28, use implicit differentiation and then solve for dy/dx in terms of x and y.

21. (*See Example 4*)
$3x^2 - 6x^2y + y^2 = 9$

22. $5xy + y^3 = 6x - 8$

23. $4y^3 - 6xy^2 + 3y = 9x + 4$

24. $6x^2y^3 + 4y^2 - 4x = 3y + 8$

25. $\dfrac{x}{y} = y^2 + x$ (Use the quotient rule)

26. $(x + y)^2 = 3x + 5$

27. $\dfrac{x}{y} = y^2 + x$ (Multiply both sides by y first; then show that your answer is the same as the answer you obtained to Exercise 25.)

28. $\sqrt{x^2 + y^2} = 3xy$

Find an equation of the line tangent to each of the curves in Exercises 29 through 32 at the indicated point. Check that each point is on the curve.

29. (*See Example 5*)
$y^3 - 2xy + x^2 = 7$; the point is $(2, -1)$

30. $y^3 - x^3 = 28$; the point is $(-1, 3)$

31. $x^2 + y^2 = 25$; the point is $(3, -4)$

32. $x^3 - 4xy + y^3 = 15$; the point is $(-1, 2)$

33. Find a value of C so that $(3, -2)$ is on the curve $10y^2 - 4x^2y^2 + x^3 = C$, and then find an equation of the line tangent to that curve at the point $(3, -2)$.

34. Find the value k so that the curve $x^2 + 2xy^2 - y^3 = k$ contains the point $(-4, 2)$. What is an equation of the line tangent to this curve at $(-4, 2)$?

35. Assume that the demand for wheat, x, is related to the price p by the equation $x^2 + 100p^2 = 4100$.
    (a) What is the demand when $p = 4$? (Remember that $x \geq 0$ because x represents demand.)
    (b) Find $\dfrac{dp}{dx}$ when $p = 4$.
    (c) Find $\dfrac{dx}{dp}$ when $p = 4$.

36. Suppose that the price in dollars, p, and the daily demand, x, for videotapes are related by the equation
$$x^2 + 2xp + p^2 = 41,209$$
    (a) Compute p when $x = 200$. (Since p is price, we know that $p \geq 0$.)
    (b) Find $\dfrac{dp}{dx}$ when $x = 200$.
    (c) Find $\dfrac{dx}{dp}$ when $x = 200$.

10–6 RELATED RATES

In the previous section we saw that the relationship between two variables x and y may be so complicated that we cannot express that relationship explicitly in the form $y = f(x)$. Nevertheless, we can still find dy/dx, the rate of change of y with respect to x.

In applications the two variables x and y frequently depend on a third variable t, usually time. For example, if x is the number of VCRs in use and y is the number of videotapes being produced, then x and y are related. The more people have VCRs, the more videotapes will be produced; conversely, the more videotapes there are on the market, the more likely someone is to invest in a VCR. Thus x and y depend on each other. The numbers x and y can also depend on time, both as the number of VCRs grows and also seasonally (with a heavier demand close to Christmas than during the rest of the year). If we could find an equation relating x and y, can we find an equation relating their *rates of change with respect to time?*

The basic principle is this: If two variables x and y are related to each other by some equation, and if both x and y depend on a third variable t, we can find a new equation that gives a relation between dx/dt and dy/dt by differentiating the original equation *with respect to t.*

Let us look at some examples.

EXAMPLE 1   *(Compare Exercise 1)*

If x and y are related by the equation $x^2 - y^3 = 17$, then find an equation relating x, y, dx/dt, and dy/dt.

SOLUTION   We compute the derivative *with respect to t* of both sides of the equation:

$$\frac{d}{dt}(x^2 - y^3) = \frac{d}{dt}17$$

The procedure is very similar to what we did in the previous section. The derivative of the difference is the difference of the derivatives; we use this fact on the left-hand side:

$$\frac{d}{dt}x^2 - \frac{d}{dt}y^3 = \frac{d}{dt}17$$

Now we must remember to use the generalized power rule *on both members* of the left-hand side:

$$\frac{d}{dt}x^2 = 2x \cdot \frac{dx}{dt} \qquad \text{and} \qquad \frac{d}{dt}y^3 = 3y^2 \cdot \frac{dy}{dt}$$

On the right-hand side, $\dfrac{d}{dt}17 = 0$ because the derivative of a constant is 0, so we have

$$2x\frac{dx}{dt} - 3y^2\frac{dy}{dt} = 0$$

CAUTION Remember to take the derivative of *both* sides of the equation, and remember that the derivative of a constant is always 0.

EXAMPLE 2   *(Compare Exercises 7 and 11)*

Suppose that a runner is jogging on a track and that we can represent the track with the equation $x^2 + 9y^2 = 900$. How is the x-coordinate of the jogger changing when she is at the point $(24, -6)$ if her y-coordinate is decreasing at a rate of 7 feet per second? See Figure 10–3.

FIGURE 10–3

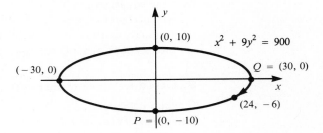

SOLUTION   Before we do the actual computation, let's try to get some geometric feeling for the situation. If the jogger is at the point $(24, -6)$ and her y-coordinate is decreasing, then she must be moving toward P and away from Q. That means that the x-coordinate will be getting smaller; the x-coordinate is decreasing. The rate of change of the x-coordinate is dx/dt; because x is decreasing, we can expect the computation to show that dx/dt is negative. Let's see.

Starting with $x^2 + 9y^2 = 900$, we take the derivative with respect to t of both sides of the equation. Using "the derivative of the sum is the sum of the derivatives," we have

$$\frac{d}{dt}x^2 + \frac{d}{dt}9y^2 = \frac{d}{dt}900$$

Thus

$$2x\frac{dx}{dt} + 18y\frac{dy}{dt} = 0$$

The problem asks for dx/dt when $x = 24$, $y = -6$, and $dy/dt = -7$. (Again, note that if y is decreasing then dy/dt is negative; dy/dt is -7, not 7.) Substituting these values, we have

$$2 \cdot 24 \cdot \frac{dx}{dt} + 18 \cdot -6 \cdot -7 = 0$$

$$48\frac{dx}{dt} + 756 = 0$$

$$\frac{dx}{dt} = -\frac{756}{48} = -\frac{63}{4}$$

(Notice the expected negative sign.) The runner's x-coordinate is decreasing at the rate of $\frac{63}{4}$ feet per second.

EXAMPLE 3   *(Compare Exercise 21)*

Two cars leave a parking lot at the same time. One travels north at 30 mph, and the other goes east at 40 mph.

(a) Determine how far apart they are after 6 minutes.
(b) Describe how the distance between them is changing.

SOLUTION   Let the origin represent the parking lot and, as is usual on maps, let north be up and east to the right. We can say that the car traveling north is going up the positive y-axis; denote its position at a given time by $y(t)$. The other car is moving to the right on the positive x-axis; denote its position by $x(t)$. See Figure 10–4.

FIGURE 10–4

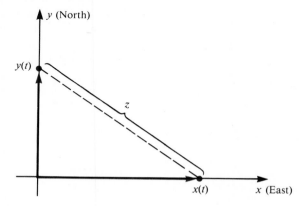

It would be natural to let d (for **distance**) represent the distance between the cars, but we shouldn't use d as a variable in calculus with so many other d's being used to mean derivatives. The next letter after x and y is z, so we use z for the distance between the cars. The relation that we need is given by the Pythagorean theorem, which states that $z^2 = x^2 + y^2$.

One more point about setting up the problem before we start our computations: One reason for stating this problem the way we did is to point out to you the need to *use the right units in your computation.* The speed of the cars is given in miles per hour, but the time is given in minutes. We must either express time in hours or else tell how fast the cars are going per minute. The time is 6 minutes, which is easy to convert to $\frac{1}{10}$ hour, so we will express time in hours. Now we are set up to answer the questions.

(a) To solve this part, we must find z when $t = \frac{1}{10}$.

$$\text{Distance traveled} = (\text{rate}) \cdot (\text{time})$$

so when $t = \dfrac{1}{10}$,

$$x = 40 \cdot \frac{1}{10} = 4$$

and

$$y = 30 \cdot \frac{1}{10} = 3$$

Since $z^2 = x^2 + y^2$, we have $z^2 = 4^2 + 3^2 = 25$; $z = \pm \sqrt{25} = \pm 5$. Since z represents distance, $z \geq 0$, and we choose the positive solution. After 6 minutes the cars are 5 miles apart.

(b) To find the rate of change of the distance between the cars, it is important that we start with the equation $z^2 = x^2 + y^2$, take the derivative with respect to t, and *then* substitute numerical values. If we use $z = 5$, $x = 4$, and $y = 3$ before taking derivatives, we won't get a formula relating dz/dt, dx/dt, and dy/dt. Differentiation of both sides of the equation $z^2 = x^2 + y^2$ with respect to t gives us

$$\frac{d}{dt}z^2 = \frac{d}{dt}x^2 + \frac{d}{dt}y^2$$

$$2z\frac{dz}{dt} = 2x\frac{dx}{dt} + 2y\frac{dy}{dt}$$

Now we substitute the values: $z = 5$, $x = 4$, and $y = 3$. Also, the wording of the problem says that x is increasing at the rate of 40; that is, $dx/dt = 40$. Similarly, we have $dy/dt = 30$ (both x and y are increasing so the derivatives are positive). Using these values, we have

$$2 \cdot 5 \cdot \frac{dz}{dt} = 2 \cdot 4 \cdot 40 + 2 \cdot 3 \cdot 30$$

$$10\frac{dz}{dt} = 320 + 180 = 500$$

$$\frac{dz}{dt} = 50$$

dz/dt is positive, so z is increasing. The distance between the cars is increasing at the rate of 50 mph.

EXAMPLE 4   *(Compare Exercises 17 and 25)*

If x is the number of thousands of running shoes a certain factory manufactures each week and y is the number of thousands of aerobic shoes it manufactures, then x and y satisfy the equation

$$x^2 - xy + 2y^2 = 22 \qquad \text{(Units are in thousands)}$$

If the current levels are $x = 4$ and $y = 3$, and if the production of running shoes is falling off at the rate of 100 per week, what is happening to the production of aerobic shoes?

SOLUTION   Let t be time measured in weeks. The last sentence tells us that $dx/dt = -0.1$. (Remember that units are in thousands; a decrease of 100 shoes means that $\Delta x = -0.1$.) To find dy/dt, we differentiate the equation

$$x^2 - xy + 2y^2 = 22$$

with respect to t:

$$\frac{d}{dt}(x^2 - xy + 2y^2) = \frac{d}{dt}(22)$$

$$\frac{d}{dt}x^2 - \frac{d}{dt}(xy) + \frac{d}{dt}2y^2 = 0$$

$$2x\frac{dx}{dt} - \left[y\frac{dx}{dt} + x\frac{dy}{dt} \right] + 4y\frac{dy}{dt} = 0$$

Now substitute $x = 4$, $y = 3$, and $dx/dt = -0.1$ and then solve for dy/dt:

$$2 \cdot 4(-0.1) - \left[3(-0.1) + 4\frac{dy}{dt}\right] + 4 \cdot 3\frac{dy}{dt} = 0$$

$$-0.8 + 0.3 - 4\frac{dy}{dt} + 12\frac{dy}{dt} = 0$$

$$8\frac{dy}{dt} = 0.5$$

$$\frac{dy}{dt} = 0.0625$$

The production of aerobic shoes is increasing at the rate of $62\frac{1}{2}$ pairs per week. (Remember the units: $0.0625 \times 1000 = 62.5$.)

NOTE When a question asks for a description of what is happening, be sure to answer with a sentence. Notice that the solutions to Examples 2, 3, and 4 end with a sentence.

CAUTION First compute derivatives, then "plug in" the values.

10–6 EXERCISES

I

In Exercises 1 through 6, use the given equation that relates x and y to find another equation that relates x, y, dx/dt, and dy/dt.

1. (*See Example 1*)
$x^2 + y^2 = 25$

2. $3x^2 - 4y^3 = 9$

3. $x + 2y = 10$

4. $3x - 4y = 15$

5. $3x^2 - x + 2y^2 = 18$

6. $5x^2 - 3y + 4y^2 = 22$

Solve for dy/dt in Exercises 7 through 10 by using the given values of x, y, and dx/dt.

7. (*See Example 2*)
$3x\frac{dy}{dt} - 2\frac{dx}{dt} + y\frac{dy}{dt} = 0$; $x = 3$, $y = -1$, and
$\frac{dx}{dt} = 2$

8. $2y^2\frac{dx}{dt} + 4xy\frac{dy}{dt} - 3y^2\frac{dy}{dt} = 0$; $x = -2$, $y = 4$, and
$\frac{dx}{dt} = 6$

9. $y\frac{dy}{dt} - x\frac{dx}{dt} = 4y^2\frac{dy}{dt}$; $x = 1$, $y = 2$, and $\frac{dx}{dt} = 3$

10. $3\frac{dy}{dt} + 5y\frac{dy}{dt} = 7x\frac{dx}{dt}$; $x = -2$, $y = 4$, and $\frac{dx}{dt} = 5$

II

In Exercises 11 through 16, use the given equation to produce another equation that relates x, y, dx/dt, and dy/dt. Then use the given values of x, y, and dx/dt to solve for dy/dt.

11. (*See Example 2*)

$x^2 + y^2 = 25$; $x = 3$, $y = -4$, and $\dfrac{dx}{dt} = 2$

12. $3x - 2y^3 = 17$; $x = 5$, $y = -1$, and $\dfrac{dx}{dt} = -2$

13. $2x + 3y = 3$; $x = 3$, $y = -1$, and $\dfrac{dx}{dt} = 4$

14. $5x - 6y = -17$; $x = -1$, $y = 2$, and $\dfrac{dx}{dt} = -3$

15. $x^2 - \sqrt{y} = 7$; $x = 3$, $y = 4$, and $\dfrac{dx}{dt} = 5$

16. $3x + y^2 - \sqrt{x} = 25$; $x = 9$, $y = -1$, and $\dfrac{dx}{dt} = 2$

III

In Exercises 17 through 20, if x and y are related by the given equation, then find dy/dt for the given values of x, y, and dx/dt.

17. (*See Example 4*)

$6xy = 120$; $x = 2$, $y = 10$, and $\dfrac{dx}{dt} = 3$

18. $x^2 - 2xy + 3y = -34$; $x = 4$, $y = 10$, $\dfrac{dx}{dt} = -2$

19. $3x^2 + 5xy - y^2 = 36$; $x = 2$, $y = 4$, $\dfrac{dx}{dt} = -3$

20. $5x^3y - 6\sqrt{x} + 2y^3 = 20$; $x = 1$, $y = 2$, $\dfrac{dx}{dt} = 10$

21. (*See Example 3*) Two cars leave a parking lot at the same time. One travels north at 20 mph, while the other travels west at 48 mph. How fast is the distance between them changing after 15 minutes?

22. Two cyclists are in a cross-country race. One cyclist is 400 feet from an intersection and is approaching it traveling south. The other cyclist has already gone past the intersection, where the course turns to the east; this cyclist is 300 feet from the intersection. Both cyclists are traveling 30 miles per hour.
   (a) How is the distance between them changing?
   (b) How is the distance measured along the race course between the two cyclists changing?

23. The price and demand for a certain shirt are related by the equation $8x^2 + p^2 = 425$, where p is the price in dollars and x is the demand in thousands of shirts per year. How is the demand changing if the present price is \$15, the current demand is 5000 shirts per year, and the price is increasing at the rate of \$0.75 per year?

24. A store has found that the demand, x, for a certain manufactured product and its price, p, are related by $x^2 + xp + p^2 = 172,900$. How is the demand changing if the present demand is 400 units, the present price is \$30 and the price is increasing at the rate of \$1.50 per year?

25. (*See Example 4*) A video rental store has projected that if x is the number of tapes that it rents in a certain period and y is the number of playback machines it rents in the same period, then

$$x - \sqrt{x}\sqrt{y} - y = 2900$$

If the current values are $x = 3600$ and $y = 100$, and if x is increasing at the rate of 120 rentals per week, what is the rate of change of y?

10-7 THE DIFFERENTIAL AND LINEAR APPROXIMATION

- *Approximation of Change*
- *Approximation of Functional Value*
- *Linear Approximation to f(x)*
- *The Differential*
- *Application to Marginal Analysis*

APPROXIMATION OF CHANGE

The central idea in this section is to take a complicated expression $f(x)$, replace it by a simpler expression $g(x)$, and then use $g(x)$ as an approximation to $f(x)$ near some point a. For example, if $f(x) = \sqrt{x^2 + 7}$, then we can evaluate $f(3)$ easily: $f(3) = \sqrt{9 + 7} = 4$. Now what if x increases a little bit, say to 3.1? Common sense tells us that $f(3.1) = \sqrt{(3.1)^2 + 7}$ is going to be bigger than $f(3)$ because $(3.1)^2 + 7$ is bigger than 16, so $\sqrt{(3.1)^2 + 7}$ is bigger than $f(3) = \sqrt{16} = 4$. But roughly, at least, how much bigger is $f(3.1)$ than $f(3)$? The derivative gives us the rate of change of f, and remembering the analogy between rate of change and speed of a car can help us see how to use the derivative to find an approximate value for $f(3.1)$.

If the speed of a car is a constant, R, then the distance traveled, D, in a given amount of time, T, is given by

$$D = R \cdot T$$

If the rate changes, but not by much, then we can **approximate** the distance traveled by assuming that the rate is constant. For instance, if a car traveled between 59 mph and 61 mph for 1 minute, then we can approximate the distance traveled by assuming a constant speed of 60 mph. The car traveled approximately 1 mile.

Returning to our problem of approximating $f(3.1)$, we will proceed in a similar fashion. The number $f'(3)$ gives the instantaneous rate of change of f when $x = 3$; $f'(x)$, the rate of change of $f(x)$, varies as x goes from 3 to 3.1, but we **approximate** the rate of change by the constant $f'(3)$. (This corresponds to assuming a constant speed.) The interval from 3 to 3.1 has length 0.1. (This corresponds to the length of time T.) Finally, the change in $f(x)$ over this interval is $f(3.1) - f(3)$. (This corresponds to the distance the car traveled.) We use the symbol $\approx$ to mean "**is approximately equal to.**" We have decided that

$$f(3.1) - f(3) \approx f'(3) \cdot (0.1)$$

To carry out these calculations, we first find $f'(x)$:

$$f(x) = (x^2 + 7)^{1/2}$$

Using the generalized power rule, we have

$$f'(x) = \frac{1}{2}(x^2 + 7)^{-1/2} \cdot 2x = \frac{x}{\sqrt{x^2 + 7}}$$

Now we evaluate $f'(3)$:

$$f'(3) = \frac{3}{\sqrt{16}} = \frac{3}{4} = 0.75$$

Finally, we multiply $f'(3)$ by 0.1:

$$f(3.1) - f(3) \approx f'(3) \cdot (0.1) = (0.75)(0.1) = 0.075$$

If x changes from 3 to 3.1, the value of $f(x)$ changes by approximately 0.075. (In this case the actual change is $f(3.1) - f(3) = 0.07553 \ldots$, so our approximation was very good.)

The general statement would be as follows:

If Δx is small, then $f(a + \Delta x) - f(a) \approx f'(a) \cdot \Delta x$.

Using Δy to denote the change in y where $y = f(x)$, we can write

$$\Delta y \approx f'(a) \cdot \Delta x$$

In our example above, $a = 3$ and $\Delta x = 0.1$.

Of course, there is no point in approximating the change in $f(x)$ if you can evaluate both $f(a)$ and $f(a + \Delta x)$ fairly easily. In practice, this technique is reserved for functions which cannot be easily evaluated everywhere.

EXAMPLE 1

If $f(x) = x^{1/3}$, what is the approximate change in $f(x)$ as x increases from 8 to 8.5?

SOLUTION   Here, it is $f(8)$ that we can evaluate easily, so we let $a = 8$. Next,

$$f'(x) = \frac{1}{3}x^{-2/3}$$

so

$$f'(8) = \frac{1}{3}(8)^{-2/3}$$

$$= \frac{1}{3} \cdot ((8)^{1/3})^{-2}$$

$$= \frac{1}{3} \cdot \frac{1}{4} = \frac{1}{12}$$

Compute the change in x (as before, let "the change in x" be denoted by Δx). Here, $\Delta x = 8.5 - 8 = 0.5$, so we have

$$\Delta y \approx f'(a) \cdot \Delta x = \frac{1}{12} \cdot 0.5 = \frac{1}{12} \cdot \frac{1}{2} = \frac{1}{24} = 0.041666 \ldots$$

As x increases from 8 to 8.5, the approximate change in $f(x)$ is 0.041666.

We use the same numbers in the next example because we want to emphasize that the same procedure can be used to answer a different question.

APPROXIMATION OF A FUNCTIONAL VALUE

EXAMPLE 2   *(Compare Exercise 19)*

Approximate $\sqrt[3]{8.5}$.

SOLUTION   The problem asks for the cube root of a number, so we use the cube root function; let $f(x) = x^{1/3}$. Now the problem is to approximate $f(8.5)$. We look for a number a near 8.5 that we know the cube root of; we choose $a = 8$. The procedure of Example 1 gives us the approximate change of $f(x)$:

$$f(8.5) - f(8) \approx f'(8) \cdot (0.5) = 0.041666 \ldots$$

Add $f(8)$ to both sides:

$$f(8.5) \approx f(8) + 0.041666 \ldots = 2 + 0.041666$$

We have

$$\sqrt[3]{8.5} \approx 2.041666 \ldots$$

(The actual decimal expansion of $\sqrt[3]{8.5}$ begins 2.0408 . . .)

Before introducing more notation and looking at a graphical interpretation, we give you one more example in order to show that Δx need not be positive.

EXAMPLE 3   *(Compare Exercise 21)*

Approximate $\sqrt{15.4}$.

SOLUTION   The solution can be broken down into steps.

1. **Choose an appropriate function.** We are asked to approximate the square root of a number, so let $f(x) = \sqrt{x}$.
2. **Choose the number a.** The number a here should be close to 15.4, and we should be able to evaluate $\sqrt{a}$ fairly easily. Here we choose $a = 16$.
3. **Compute Δx.** Remember that Δx is the change in x as x goes from a to $a + \Delta x$. Therefore $\Delta x = (a + \Delta x) - a$ (always subtract a). Here, $a = 16$, so $\Delta x = 15.4 - 16 = -0.6$ (Δx can be negative).
4. **Compute $f'(a)$.** First compute $f'(x)$ and then evaluate $f'(a)$. Here,

$$f'(x) = \frac{1}{2\sqrt{x}} \qquad \text{so} \qquad f'(16) = \frac{1}{2\sqrt{16}} = \frac{1}{8}$$

5. **Approximate Δy.** $\Delta y \approx f'(a) \cdot \Delta x$. Using the results of Steps 3 and 4, we have

$$\Delta y \approx \left(\frac{1}{8}\right)(-0.6) = \left(\frac{1}{8}\right)\left(\frac{-3}{5}\right) = \frac{-3}{40}$$

6. **Approximate $y = f(a + \Delta x)$.** $f(a + \Delta x) \approx f(a) + f'(a)\Delta x$. Here, $f(a) = \sqrt{16} = 4$, so

$$\sqrt{15.4} \approx 4 + \frac{-3}{40} = 3\frac{37}{40} = 3.925$$

(The actual decimal expansion of $\sqrt{15.4}$ begins 3.9242 . . .)

The process will stop with Step 5 if you are asked to approximate the *change in y*. If you are asked to approximate the *value of y*, go on to Step 6.

Now we give the general notation and procedure for approximating functional values.

To Find an Approximate Value of f(b)

1. Write down the general rule for $f(x)$.
2. Look for a number near b for which you can easily evaluate $f(x)$. Call that number a.
3. Let $\Delta x = b - a$.
4. Compute $f'(x)$ and then evaluate $f'(a)$.
5. Approximate the change in y:

$$\Delta y = f(b) - f(a) \approx f'(a) \cdot \Delta x$$

6. Approximate $f(b)$:

$$f(b) \approx f(a) + f'(a) \cdot \Delta x$$

LINEAR APPROXIMATION TO $f(x)$

The quantity $f'(a) \cdot \Delta x$ is the approximate change in $f(x)$ as x goes from a to b; the quantity $f(a) + f'(a) \cdot \Delta x$ is the approximate value of $f(b)$. Since b is any arbitrary number, we could just as well use x in the last approximation formula.

7. $f(x) \approx f(a) + f'(a) \cdot \Delta x = f(a) + f'(a) \cdot (x - a)$

The value of $f(x)$ is on the left-hand side of the equation; the approximating value is on the right-hand side. Let us give a name to the approximating function, say, g. We now have

$$g(x) = f(a) + f'(a)(x - a)$$

In Example 2 we had $f(x) = x^{1/3}$, $a = 8$, $f(a) = 2$, and $f'(a) = \frac{1}{12}$. The function g that approximates $x^{1/3}$ when x is near 8 is given by

$$g(x) = 2 + \frac{1}{12}(x - 8)$$

FIGURE 10–5

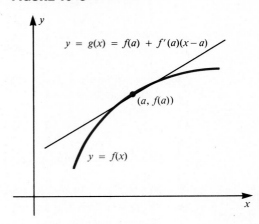

This is the equation of a straight line. In fact, it is the equation of the line tangent to $y = x^{1/3}$ at the point $(8, 2)$. Looking back at the general equation for $g(x)$,

$$g(x) = f(a) + f'(a)(x - a)$$

we see that the graph of g is always the line tangent to the graph of f at the point $(a, f(a))$. See Figure 10–5.

THE DIFFERENTIAL

Because there is such a close connection between the derivative of f and the approximation to the change in $f(x)$, we introduce some notation to emphasize this connection. We have already used Δy to mean the actual change in y; now we introduce the notation dy to mean the approximate change in y; $dy = f'(x)\Delta x \approx \Delta y$. See Figure 10–6.

Figure 10–6 also justifies setting $dx = \Delta x$. We give a name to dy in the following definition.

FIGURE 10–6

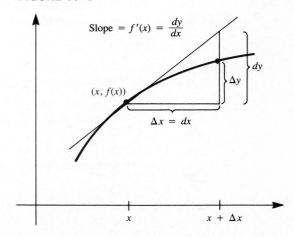

Definition	If $y = f(x)$, then dy is called the **differential** of y and is given by the
Differential	equation

$$dy = f'(x)dx$$

You will see this notation, $dy = f'(x)dx$, used again in Chapter 14. Because the differential is so important, we will give you some examples emphasizing its definition and then show how this notation can shorten the process of computing an approximation. We will end this section with an important application of the differential in economics.

EXAMPLE 4 *(Compare Exercise 1)*

Compute dy if $f(x) = x^3 - 4x$.

SOLUTION

$$dy = f'(x)dx = (3x^2 - 4)dx$$

EXAMPLE 5 *(Compare Exercise 5)*

Compute dy if $y = \dfrac{1}{x}$.

SOLUTION   Here, $f(x) = \dfrac{1}{x}$, so $f'(x) = \dfrac{-1}{x^2}$.

$$dy = \frac{-1}{x^2}dx$$

In applications you will have to do more computations after finding dy, so we give you some examples that show these computations.

EXAMPLE 6 *(Compare Exercise 9)*

Compute dy if $f(x) = \sqrt{x}$, $x = 9$, and $dx = 0.2$.

SOLUTION   Here, $f(x) = x^{1/2}$, so $f'(x) = \dfrac{1}{2\sqrt{x}}$

$$f'(9) = \frac{1}{2\sqrt{9}} = \frac{1}{6}$$

$$dx = 0.2 = \frac{1}{5}$$

so

$$dy = f'(x)dx$$
$$= \left(\frac{1}{6}\right)\left(\frac{1}{5}\right) = \frac{1}{30}$$

EXAMPLE 7   *(Compare Exercise 11)*

Compute dy if $y = x^{1/3}$, $x = 64$, and $dx = -6$.

SOLUTION   We shorten the computations:

$$dy = \frac{1}{3}x^{-2/3}dx$$

$$= \frac{1}{3}[x^{1/3}]^{-2}dx$$

$$= \frac{1}{3}[64^{1/3}]^{-2}(-6)$$

$$= \left(\frac{1}{3}\right)(4)^{-2}(-6)$$

$$= \left(\frac{1}{3}\right)\left(\frac{1}{16}\right)(-6)$$

$$= -\frac{1}{8}$$

EXAMPLE 8   *(Compare Exercise 23)*

Find the approximate value of $\sqrt{22}$.

SOLUTION
1. We have to choose the function; let $f(x) = \sqrt{x}$.
2. We need a number near 22 that we know the square root of; let $x = 25$.
3. Then dx is the change of x as x goes from 25 to 22; $dx = 22 - 25 = -3$. Note the order of subtraction. The dy notation lets us combine Steps 4 and 5.
4. **and 5.** $dy = f'(x)dx = \frac{1}{2\sqrt{x}}dx$. With $x = 25$ and $dx = -3$,

$$dy = \frac{1}{2\sqrt{25}}(-3) = \frac{1}{10}(-3) = -\frac{3}{10} = -0.3$$

6. We have $f(25) = 5$ and $dy = -0.3$, so
$$f(22) \approx f(25) + dy$$
$$f(22) \approx 5 + (-0.3)$$
$$\sqrt{22} \approx 4.7$$

APPLICATION TO MARGINAL ANALYSIS

We introduced the word "marginal" in Section 10–1 to mean "the rate of change of." The word "marginal" in economics is also used to mean the change in the value of a function per unit change in the domain variable. For example, a person's marginal tax rate is the tax on an additional dollar of income for that person.

In this section we see how the rate of change of a function—the derivative—can be used to approximate the change in the value of the function. Similarly, we use the differential to form the link between these two meanings of the word "marginal." The particular function that we will use is the cost function, but our discussion applies to all marginal functions. As usual, we let $C(x)$ be the cost of producing x items, but now we define the marginal cost as the cost of producing the next item. This definition would give us

$$MC(x) = C(x + 1) - C(x)$$

Now, using our approximation techniques of this chapter with $\Delta x = (x + 1) - x = 1$, we can write

$$C(x + 1) - C(x) \approx C'(x) \cdot 1 = C'(x)$$

Thus even with this noncalculus definition of marginal cost, we have $MC(x) \approx C'(x)$.

The next example shows that this approximation can be very close. Indeed, only when $C''(x)$, that is, $MC'(x)$, is very large will this approximation fail to be a good one.

EXAMPLE 9   *(Compare Exercise 27)*

A company's cost for producing x refrigerators per week is

$$C(x) = \frac{1}{100}x^2 + 400x + 3000$$

What is the company's marginal cost if it is producing 50 refrigerators per week?

SOLUTION   Using calculus, we have

$$C'(x) = \frac{1}{50}x + 400$$

$$C'(50) = 1 + 400 = 401$$

The calculus definition gives an answer quickly: The marginal cost is $401. For comparison purposes, computing

$$C(51) - C(50)$$

gives

$$\left[\frac{1}{100}(51)^2 + (400)(51) + 3000\right] - \left[\frac{1}{100}(50)^2 + (400)(50) + 3000\right]$$
$$= [26.01 + 20,400 + 3000] - [25 + 20,000 + 3000]$$
$$= 401.01$$

This lengthier computation gives the answer: The marginal cost is $401.01.
   The difference in the two computations is one penny, or about 0.002%.

Using the derivative as the definition of marginal cost lets us compute the marginal cost more easily. Even more important, it also allows us to determine a rule for evaluating marginal cost and so permits us to talk about and analyze the marginal cost *function* more easily. We will continue therefore to identify the marginal cost function as the derivative of the cost function.

10-7 EXERCISES

I

Find dy in Exercises 1 through 8.

1. (*See Example 4*)
   $f(x) = 5x^3 + 4$

2. $f(x) = 3x^2 + 2x - 1$

3. $f(x) = \sqrt{x^2 + 1}$

4. $f(x) = \dfrac{1}{x^2 + 1}$

5. (*See Example 5*)
   $y = \dfrac{1}{\sqrt{x}}$

6. $y = x^{2/3}$

7. $y = 8x^3 - 4x$

8. $y = (5x + 1)^4$

In Exercises 9 through 14, evaluate dy using the given values of x and dx.

9. (*See Example 6*)
   $y = x^4 - 3x^2;\ x = 2,\ dx = 0.5$

10. $y = \dfrac{1}{x};\ x = 5,\ dx = 0.2$

11. (*See Example 7*)
    $y = \dfrac{1}{x^2 + 1};\ x = 3,\ dx = -0.4$

12. $y = \sqrt{x};\ x = 100,\ dx = -3$

13. $y = (2x + 1)^3;\ x = 2,\ dx = 0.2$

14. $y = \dfrac{1}{\sqrt{x}};\ x = 25,\ dx = -4$

II

In Exercises 15 through 18, find the approximate change in $f(x)$ as x changes from a to b.

15. (*See Example 1*)
    $f(x) = x^2 - 3x;\ a = 4,\ b = 4.2$

16. $f(x) = \dfrac{1}{6}x^3 - 9x;\ a = 10,\ b = 10.3$

17. $f(x) = \dfrac{1}{x};\ a = 20,\ b = 18$

18. $f(x) = \sqrt{x};\ a = 36,\ b = 32$

19. (*See Example 2*) Use $f(x) = x^{1/3}$ and $a = 27$ to approximate $29^{1/3}$.

20. Use $f(x) = \sqrt{x}$ and $a = 100$ to approximate $\sqrt{104}$.

21. (*See Example 3*) Use $f(x) = \sqrt{x}$ and $a = 25$ to approximate $\sqrt{23}$.

22. Use $f(x) = x^2$ and $a = 3$ to approximate $(2.96)^2$.

III

Use the techniques of this section to approximate the numbers given in Exercises 23 through 26.

23. (*See Example 8*) $\sqrt{52}$ **24.** $\sqrt{98}$

25. $\sqrt[3]{61}$ **26.** $\sqrt[3]{1006}$

27. (*See Example 9*) A company's cost (in dollars) for producing x garbage disposals per day is given by

$$C(x) = \frac{1}{100}x^2 + 20x + 300$$

(a) Use differentials to find the approximate cost to the company of producing the 51st garbage disposal.

(b) Compute the actual cost of the 51st disposal, $C(51) - C(50)$.

(c) Compare your answers to parts (a) and (b). Do you think the answer in part (a) is a good approximation to the answer in part (b)?

28. The cost (in dollars) of producing x subcompact automobiles per hour is given by

$$C(x) = \frac{x^3}{10} - 50x^2 + 8000x + 25,000$$

(a) What is the approximate cost of the 101st automobile manufactured?

(b) What is the actual cost of the 101st automobile?

(c) What is the average cost of the first 100 automobiles?

(d) Why should you expect the answer to part (c) to be much larger than the answer to part (a)?

29. A company's revenue (in dollars) from producing x pairs of shoes per hour is given by

$$R(x) = 50x - \frac{1}{4}x^2$$

(a) What is the company's approximate revenue change if production is increased from 40 pairs of shoes per hour to 44 pairs per hour?

(b) Approximate the change in the company's revenue if production is decreased from 40 pairs of shoes per hour to 36 pairs per hour.

30. A company estimates that if it spends x thousand dollars per year on advertising, then its yearly revenue will be (in thousands of dollars)

$$R(x) = 20\sqrt{x^2 + 4x + 1} - 19x$$

The company is currently budgeting $10,000 per year on advertising. Approximate the change in the company's revenue if the advertising budget:

(a) is increased by $1000.

(b) is increased by $3000.

(c) is decreased by $1000.

(d) is decreased by $500.

31. If $f(2) = 6$ and $f'(2) = 3$, what are the approximate values of:

(a) $f(2.15)$?   (b) $f(1.9)$?

32. If $f(3) = 8$ and $f'(3) = -2$, what are the approximate values of:

(a) $f(3.25)$?   (b) $f(2.8)$?

We can also use the linear approximation in another useful manner.

33. If $f(4) = 10$ and $f'(4) = -5$, can you give a reasonable guess at an approximate solution to $f(x) = 0$?

34. If $f(7) = 2$ and $f'(7) = 4$, can you guess at an approximate solution to $f(x) = 0$?

35. The point $(1, 2)$ is on the curve $x^3 + 2xy + y^3 = 13$. Using implicit differentiation, approximate the second coordinate of the point on the curve near $(1, 2)$ whose first coordinate is 1.3.

36. Approximate the second coordinate of the point near $(5, 2)$ on the curve $x^2y - y^2 = 46$ whose first coordinate is 4.6.

IMPORTANT TERMS

10-1

Derivative of a Constant

Power Rule

Constant-Times Rule

Sum Rule

Difference Rule

Marginal

10-2

Product Rule

Quotient Rule

10-3

Composition of Functions

Chain Rule

Generalized Power Rule

10-4

Second Derivative

Acceleration

Higher-Order Derivatives

10-5

Implicitly Defined Functions

Explicitly Defined Functions

Implicit Differentiation

10-6

Related Rates

10-7

Linear Approximation

Differential

REVIEW EXERCISES

Compute $f'(x)$ in Exercises 1 through 8.

1. $f(x) = \sqrt{x^2 + 1}$

2. $f(x) = x\sqrt{x^2 + 1}$

3. $f(x) = \dfrac{x^2 + 1}{x^3 - 4x}$

4. $f(x) = \left(7x^2 - 4 + \dfrac{3}{x}\right)\left(8x^3 - 9x + \dfrac{6}{x^2}\right)$

5. $f(x) = (7x + 4)^2(5x + 1)^3$

6. $f(x) = \dfrac{6x - 4}{9x^2 + 3x}$

7. $f(x) = (3x + \sqrt{5x + 1})^4$

8. $f(x) = [(3x + 1)^2 + (4x - 8)^2]^5$

9. If $y = \dfrac{4}{x^3}$, find y''.

10. If $y = \sqrt{x^3 + 8}$, find $\dfrac{d^2y}{dx^2}$.

11. Find $\dfrac{dy}{dx}$ if $xy + y^2 = 3x$.

12. Find $\dfrac{dy}{dx}$ if $x^3 - 4xy^2 + y^3 = 9$.

13. What is an equation of the line tangent to the graph of $f(x) = 6x\sqrt{5x + 1}$ at the point whose first coordinate is 3?

14. What is an equation of the line tangent to the graph of

$$f(x) = \dfrac{x\sqrt{x}}{x^2 + 1}$$

at the point whose first coordinate is 4?

15. What is an equation of the line tangent to the graph of $x^2 + y^2 = 25$ at the point $(-4, 3)$?

16. What is an equation of the line tangent to the graph of $5xy - y^2 = 21$ at the point $(-2, -3)$?

17. A train has moved $\dfrac{1}{300}t^3 + \dfrac{1}{20}t^2$ miles t minutes after starting from rest.
  (a) How far has the train gone after 3 minutes?
  (b) How fast is the train moving after 3 minutes?
  (c) How fast is the train accelerating after 3 minutes?

18. The height above the ground, in feet, of a thrown ball is given by $h(t) = -16t^2 + 96t + 5$, where time is measured in seconds.
   (a) How high is the ball after 2 seconds?
   (b) How fast is the ball moving after 2 seconds?
   (c) How is the speed of the ball changing after 2 seconds?
   (d) How high is the ball after 4 seconds?
   (e) How fast is the ball moving after 4 seconds?
   (f) How is the speed of the ball changing after 4 seconds?
   (g) Compare the position and motion of the ball after 2 seconds and after 4 seconds. What is the same? What is different?

19. If $x^2 + 5y^2 = 129$, what is dy/dt when $x = -7$, $y = -4$, and $dx/dt = 3$?

20. If $6x^2 - 3xy + y^2 = 16$, how is the x-coordinate changing at the instant $x = 1$ and $y = 5$ if the y-coordinate is decreasing at the rate of 3 units per second?

21. Compute the differential dy if $y = \dfrac{3x + 11}{2x - 5}$.

22. Compute the differential dy if $y = \sqrt{x^3 - 4x^2}$.

23. Use the differential to find an approximate value for $\sqrt[3]{10}$.

24. Use the differential to find an approximate value for $\sqrt{31}$.

25. If a company's marginal cost is $6\sqrt{x} + 5$ when production level is x units per week, and if the marginal revenue is $\sqrt{x^2 + 4x}$, what is the company's marginal profit?

26. If the yearly demand for x hundred items and the price p in dollars are related by the equation $x + xp + 5p = 320$, how is the demand changing if the present demand is 6000 items per year and the current price of $4 is increasing at the rate of 20¢ per year?

27. If $R = x \cdot p$ is the revenue, how is the revenue changing if $x = 10{,}000$, $p = \$4.50$, $dx/dt = -50$ units per week, and $dp/dt = \$0.20$ per week?

28. The cost of producing x items per month is given by
$$C(x) = \frac{1}{1000}x^2 + 12x + 6200$$
   (a) What is the marginal cost?
   (b) What is the average cost per item?
   (c) What is the marginal average cost?

29. If the cost of producing x items per month is
$$C(x) = \frac{1}{600}x^2 + 20x + 5300$$
what is the approximate cost of producing the 101st item?

11
Applications of the Derivative

*O*NE OF THE MAJOR applications of mathematics to real-world problems is to find the best, or optimum, way to achieve a goal. "Best" may mean finding a way to minimize a company's overhead or the time required to complete a project. "Best" may mean finding a way to maximize profit or productivity. Some applications are handled by techniques from finite mathematics—the simplex method, for example. Some applications are handled with techniques from calculus. In this chapter you will see how to use the derivative to find the biggest and smallest values of a function. Further, you will see how to use the derivative to provide a graph of a function showing how the functional values rise and fall and other features of the function that are important in applications.

11–1 THE FIRST DERIVATIVE TEST

- *Increasing and Decreasing Functions*
- *Extreme Values*
- *Relative Extreme Values*
- *Critical Numbers*

INCREASING AND DECREASING FUNCTIONS

The graph in Figure 11–1 gives the temperature in Yourtown, U.S.A. over a period of 24 hours. We will use the temperature function and its graph to establish terminology that will then be used to describe arbitrary functions and graphs.

By reading the graph we can describe how the temperature varied. The temperature fell from midnight until 6 A.M. and started slowly rising. There was a slight period around 9 A.M. when the temperature held steady, but then it continued to increase until 1 P.M. At 1 P.M. the temperature suddenly decreased for a while. Perhaps there was a thunderstorm that ended about 2 P.M. because the temperature started climbing again at 2 P.M. The highest temperature occurred at 5 P.M., and then the temperature decreased for the rest of the day.

FIGURE 11–1

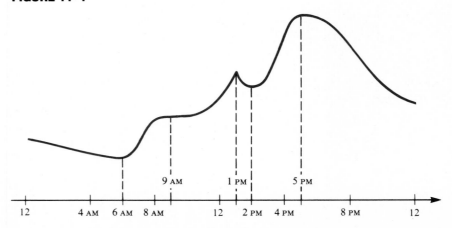

FIGURE 11–2

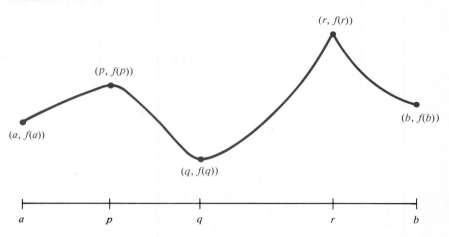

We extend this terminology to arbitrary functions like the one whose graph is given in Figure 11–2.

As x goes from a to p, the graph rises. Said another way, as x moves to the right on (a, p), the values of f increase. We say that the function is **increasing** on the open interval (a, p). The function levels off at p, and as x goes from p to q, the graph falls. We say that f is **decreasing** on the open interval (p, q). Similarly, f is increasing on the open interval (q, r), and f is decreasing on the open interval (r, b).

More formally, we have the following definitions.

Definition **Increasing** **on an Interval**	A function f is said to be **increasing on the interval I** if whenever x_1 and x_2 are numbers in I with $x_1 < x_2$, then $f(x_1) < f(x_2)$. In other words, if x_1 is less than x_2, then $f(x_1)$ is less than $f(x_2)$.

Definition **Decreasing** **on an Interval**	A function f is said to be **decreasing on the interval I** if whenever x_1 and x_2 are numbers in I with $x_1 < x_2$, then $f(x_1) > f(x_2)$. In other words, if x_1 is less than x_2, then $f(x_1)$ is greater than $f(x_2)$.

EXTREME VALUES

From Figure 11–1, we can see that the temperature reached its maximum value for the day at 5 P.M. In Figure 11–2, because $f(r) \geq f(x)$ for all x in (a, b), we say that the function f **has its maximum value on (a, b) when $x = r$** and that $f(r)$ **is the maximum value of f on (a, b).** One of the reasons we started with a graph of the temperature rather than just jumping right into the discussion with Figure 11–2 is to help you with the terminology. "What was the highest temperature?" and "When was the temperature the greatest?" are two different questions.

When a marketing researcher wants to use a mathematical model to predict what price will give the greatest profit, the researcher has to distinguish between two different numbers: the one for price and the one for profit. In applications we will want to know the maximum value of f and what number x produces that maximum value. We must keep straight the distinction between the maximum value of f and the number x that gives the maximum value. A similar distinction must be maintained when talking about least value of the function. The minimum temperature for the day occurred at 6 A.M. In an analogous way we say that f **has its minimum value on (a, b) when $x = q$; the minimum value of f on (a, b) is $f(q)$.** The term **extreme value** of f is used to refer to either a maximum value or a minimum value of f.

For clarity we again state these definitions more formally.

Definition **Maximum Value**	If c is in a set S and $f(c) \geq f(x)$ for all x in S, then $f(c)$ is the **maximum value of f on the set S.**

Definition **Minimum Value**	If c is in the set S and $f(c) \leq f(x)$ for all x in S, then $f(c)$ is the **minimum value of f on the set S.**

Definition **Extreme Value**	If a number $f(c)$ is either the maximum value of f or the minimum value of f, then $f(c)$ is called an **extreme value of f.**

RELATIVE EXTREME VALUES

Something interesting happened at 1 P.M.—the temperature stopped increasing and started decreasing. The same thing happens to the function in Figure 11–2 when $x = p$. The temperature at 1 P.M. was not the maximum temperature for the whole day, but it was the maximum for a while. Referring to Figure 11–2, we say that f has a **relative maximum** at $x = p$ because $f(p)$ is larger than $f(x)$ for all x near p. (The term **local maximum** at $x = p$ is also used; "local" = "relative.") We say that f has a **relative minimum** at $x = q$ because $f(q)$ is smaller than $f(x)$ for all x near q.

Definition **Relative Maximum Value**	If the domain of f contains an open interval (a, b) with c in (a, b) and $f(c) \geq f(x)$ for all x in (a, b), then $f(c)$ is called a **relative maximum** of f.

Definition **Relative Minimum Value**	If the domain of f contains an open interval (a, b) with c in (a, b) and $f(c) \leq f(x)$ for all x in (a, b), then $f(c)$ is called a **relative minimum** of f.

Definition **Relative Extreme Value**	If $f(c)$ is either a relative maximum or a relative minimum value of f, then $f(c)$ is called a **relative extreme value** of f.

CRITICAL NUMBERS

Relative extreme values of a function occur when the graph changes direction, and the figures show how a graph can change direction. In Figure 11–2 the graph has a smooth peak at the point $(p, f(p))$ and a sharp peak at the point $(r, f(r))$. We use the derivative to describe the distinction. The graph has a horizontal tangent line at $(p, f(p))$; that is, $f'(p) = 0$. Similarly, the graph shows that $f'(q) = 0$. The graph does not have a tangent line at $(r, f(r))$; $f'(r)$ does not exist. The graph gives a picture of the following important theorem.

Theorem	If f has a relative extreme value at $x = c$, then either $f'(c) = 0$ or $f'(c)$ does not exist.

This theorem prompts us to make the following definition.

Definition **Critical Number**	A number c in the domain of f is called a **critical number** of f if either $f'(c) = 0$ or $f'(c)$ does not exist.

Critical numbers are defined this way because the theorem tells us that when we are looking for the numbers x that produce the extreme values of f, we need only look at these numbers. They are critical in the search for extreme values.

CAUTION The theorem does *not* say that if $f'(c) = 0$, then $f(c)$ is a relative extreme value. If the graph changes direction when $x = c$, then c is a critical number, but not vice versa; c may be a critical number without the graph changing direction. As the temperature graph in Figure 11–1 shows at 9 A.M., the graph may have a horizontal tangent (corresponding to $f'(c) = 0$) without turning around at that point.

Once we have found all the critical numbers, how do we know which ones correspond to points where the graph changes direction and which ones do not? How do we know whether we have found a relative maximum, a relative minimum, or neither? Critical numbers are defined in terms of the derivative, and the derivative also tells us how the function is changing near c.

Looking at Figures 11–1 and 11–2, you can see geometrically that when the graph is rising, lines tangent to the graph have positive slope, and when the graph is falling, tangent lines have negative slope. From physical applications you know that if the rate of change of a function is positive, the function is increasing; if the rate of change is negative, the function is decreasing.

| *The First Derivative Test for Increasing and Decreasing* | If $f'(x) > 0$ for all x in (a, b), then f is increasing on (a, b) |
| | If $f'(x) < 0$ for all x in (a, b), then f is decreasing on (a, b). |

CAUTION Be careful—the first derivative test refers to two different functions: f and f'. Avoid ambiguous statements like "it's increasing when it's positive." Instead, say "f is increasing because f' is positive."

If f is continuous and f is increasing just to the left of c and decreasing just to the right of c, then f must have a relative maximum value when $x = c$. Furthermore, the sign of the derivative indicates when f is increasing and when f is decreasing. So a change in the sign of the derivative from positive to negative indicates a relative maximum of f.

We summarize this discussion:

The First Derivative Test for Relative Extreme Values	**1.** Find the critical numbers of f.
	2. Determine the sign of f' on the intervals between the critical numbers.
	3. If c is a critical number, then:
	(a) $f(c)$ is a relative maximum if f' changes from positive to negative at c.
	(b) $f(c)$ is a relative minimum if f' changes from negative to positive at c.
	(c) $f(c)$ is not a relative extreme value if f' does not change sign at c.

In determining the sign of f' the critical points play the same role as cut points did in solving inequalities in Chapter 9. We are now interested in the inequalities $f'(x) > 0$ and $f'(x) < 0$.

We will use $f(x) = 2x^3 - 6x^2 - 18x + 7$ in Examples 1 through 4 to analyze the first derivative test step by step.

EXAMPLE 1   *(Compare Exercise 3)*

Find the critical numbers of f if

$$f(x) = 2x^3 - 6x^2 - 18x + 7$$

SOLUTION The function is a polynomial, so $f'(x)$ exists for all x. Therefore, the only critical numbers are solutions to $f'(x) = 0$. Computing $f'(x)$, we have $f'(x) = 6x^2 - 12x - 18$. Next, set $f'(x) = 0$ and solve:

$$6x^2 - 12x - 18 = 0 \qquad \text{(Divide by 6)}$$
$$x^2 - 2x - 3 = 0 \qquad \text{(Factor)}$$
$$(x - 3)(x + 1) = 0 \qquad \text{(Solve)}$$

The critical numbers are $x = -1$ and $x = 3$.

EXAMPLE 2   *(Compare Exercise 7)*

Find the intervals on which f is increasing if

$$f(x) = 2x^3 - 6x^2 - 18x + 7$$

SOLUTION f is increasing if f' is positive, so the problem is equivalent to finding where $f'(x) > 0$. Since $f'(x) = 6x^2 - 12x - 18$, we want to solve $6x^2 - 12x - 18 > 0$. From Example 1 we know that the cut points for this inequality are $x = -1$ and $x = 3$.

We determine the sign of f' on the intervals between critical points by using test numbers.

(a) From the interval $(-\infty, -1)$ we choose $x = -2$ as a test number.

$$f'(-2) = 6(-2)^2 - 12(-2) - 18 = 30 > 0$$

f is positive on $(-\infty, -1)$, so *f is increasing on* $(-\infty, -1)$.
(b) From the interval $(-1, 3)$ we choose $x = 0$ as a test number.

$$f'(0) = -18 < 0$$

f' is negative on $(-1, 3)$, so *f is decreasing on* $(-1, 3)$.
(c) From the interval $(3, \infty)$ we choose $x = 4$ as a test number.

$$f'(4) = 6(4)^2 - 12(4) - 18 = 30 > 0$$

f' is positive on $(3, \infty)$, so *f is increasing on* $(3, \infty)$.

We use the results from parts (a), (b), and (c) to answer the problem.
Answer: f is increasing on the intervals $(-\infty, -1)$ and $(3, \infty)$.

EXAMPLE 3   *(Compare Exercise 11)*

Find and classify the relative extreme values of f if

$$f(x) = 2x^3 - 6x^2 - 18x + 7$$

("Classify" just means to tell whether each relative extreme value is a maximum or a minimum.)
SOLUTION   We use "+" for the sign of f' if f' is positive, and "−" for the sign of f' if f' is negative. Using this notation, we can make the following chart with the results of Example 2:

Sign-of-f' +   −   +
              ———————|—————————|—————————
                    −1   3

Notice that f' changes sign from positive to negative at $x = -1$. Thus the third step in the first derivative test tells us that f has a relative maximum when $x = -1$; the value of the relative maximum is $f(-1) = 17$. Also, because f' changes from negative to positive at $x = 3$, the first derivative test tells us that f has a relative minimum when $x = 3$; the value of the relative minimum is -47.

EXAMPLE 4 *(Compare Exercise 27)*

Sketch the graph of f if $f(x) = 2x^3 - 6x^2 - 18x + 7$.

SOLUTION We plot the points $(c, f(c))$, where c is a critical number, so here we must plot $(-1, 17)$ and $(3, -47)$. f is increasing on $(-\infty, -1)$, so the graph is rising on this interval. $f'(-1) = 0$, so the graph has a horizontal tangent at $(-1, 17)$. The graph then falls over the interval from $x = -1$ to $x = 3$, turns around smoothly $[f'(3) = 0]$, and then continues to rise indefinitely. See Figure 11–3.

FIGURE 11–3

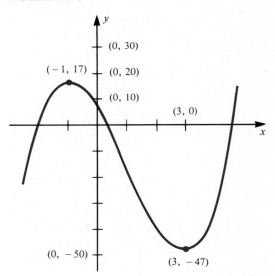

Sometimes you may be asked just to find the critical numbers or the intervals on which a function is increasing, but sometimes you will be asked a question that requires you to put all the steps together.

EXAMPLE 5   *(Compare Exercise 29)*

Sketch the graph of f if $f(x) = x^3 + 3x^2 - 24x + 2$.

SOLUTION

Step 1. Find the critical numbers of f.

The function is a polynomial, so $f'(x)$ exists for all x. The only critical numbers are solutions to the equation $f'(x) = 0$. First compute $f'(x)$:

$$f'(x) = 3x^2 + 6x - 24$$

Next, set $f'(x) = 0$ and solve:

$$3x^2 + 6x - 24 = 0 \qquad \text{(Divide by 3)}$$
$$x^2 + 2x - 8 = 0 \qquad \text{(Factor)}$$
$$(x + 4)(x - 2) = 0$$

The critical numbers are $x = -4$ and $x = 2$.

Step 2. Determine the sign of f' on the intervals between critical numbers.

We begin by drawing the chart.

Sign-of-f' $\underset{\begin{array}{cc} -4 & \quad\; 2 \end{array}}{\rule{8cm}{0.4pt}}$

(a) Use a number less than -4 to test the sign of f' on $(-\infty, -4)$. Using $x = -5$, we have

$$f'(-5) = 3(-5)^2 + 6(-5) - 24 = 21 > 0$$

Now we can start to fill in the chart:

Sign-of-f' $\overset{+}{\underset{\begin{array}{cc} -4 & \quad\; 2 \end{array}}{\rule{8cm}{0.4pt}}}$

(b) Test the sign of f' between -4 and 2. Using $x = 0$, we have

$$f'(0) = 3(0)^2 + 6(0) - 24 = -24 < 0$$

We can continue to fill in the chart:

Sign-of-f' $\overset{+\qquad\quad -}{\underset{\begin{array}{cc} -4 & \quad\; 2 \end{array}}{\rule{8cm}{0.4pt}}}$

(c) Finally, test the sign of f' for some $x > 2$. Using $x = 3$, we have

$$f'(3) = 3(3)^2 + 6(3) - 24 = 21 > 0$$

We can now complete our chart:

Sign-of-f' $\overset{+\qquad\quad -\qquad\quad +}{\underset{\begin{array}{cc} -4 & \quad\; 2 \end{array}}{\rule{8cm}{0.4pt}}}$

FIGURE 11–4

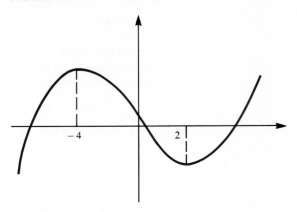

Step 3. Sketch the graph of *f*.

   The sign of f' tells us that f is increasing on $(-\infty, -4)$, decreasing on $(-4, 2)$, and then increasing on $(2, \infty)$. Because f is continuous, its graph is one piece. The graph of f must have a general shape like that in Figure 11–4. We are able to determine the shape of the graph without plotting any points.

   To get a better sketch, we evaluate $f(-4)$ and $f(2)$. Notice that now we are evaluating f; in Step 2 we wanted the sign of f', and we evaluated f' at test points. Now we evaluate f at its critical numbers:

$$f(-4) = (-4)^3 + 3(-4)^2 - 24(-4) + 2 = 82$$
$$f(2) = 2^3 + 3(2)^2 - 24(2) + 2 = -26$$

The graph is shown in Figure 11–5.

FIGURE 11–5

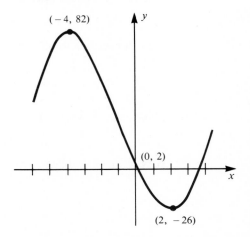

NOTE The general shape of the graph of a function f is completely determined by its derivative f'. If in Example 5 our evaluations had showed $f(-4) < f(2)$, then we would have known that we had made an error somewhere—either in the evaluations or in the analysis of the sign of f'. If your results do not agree, just look for an error.

EXAMPLE 6   *(Compare Exercise 35)*

Sketch the graph of f if $f(x) = x^4 - 4x^3 + 2$.

SOLUTION   First, compute the derivative of f. $f'(x) = 4x^3 - 12x^2$ exists for all x, so the only critical numbers of f are the solutions to $f'(x) = 0$:

$$4x^3 - 12x^2 = 0$$
$$4x^2(x - 3) = 0$$

The critical numbers are $x = 0$ and $x = 3$. Now we fill in the chart for the sign of f'.

Sign-of-f'

$$\underset{\substack{0 \qquad\qquad 3}}{\rule{2in}{0.4pt}}$$

From the interval $(-\infty, 0)$ we choose $x = -1$ as a test number:

$$f'(-1) = 4(-1)^3 - 12(-1)^2 = -16 < 0$$

From the interval $(0, 3)$ we choose $x = 1$:

$$f'(1) = 4(1)^3 - 12(1)^2 = -8 < 0$$

From the interval $(3, \infty)$ we choose $x = 4$:

$$f'(4) = 4(4)^3 - 12(4)^2 = 64 > 0$$

Our completed chart is

Sign-of-f' $\qquad$ $-$ $\qquad$ $-$ $\qquad$ $+$

$$\underset{\substack{0 \qquad\qquad 3}}{\rule{2in}{0.4pt}}$$

Although $x = 0$ is a critical number, f' does not change sign at $x = 0$; therefore $f(0) = 2$ is not a relative extreme value of f. The graph is falling to the left of 0, then levels off at 0 for an instant, and then falls again to the right of 0.

The sign of f' changes from negative to positive when $x = 3$, and so the graph turns around when $x = 3$. f has a relative minimum when $x = 3$, and $f(3) = (3)^4 - 4(3)^3 + 2 = -25$. The graph of f is given in Figure 11–6.

From the graph we can see that -25 is not only a relative minimum but in fact is the minimum value of f.

FIGURE 11-6

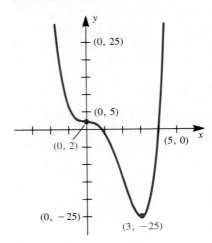

EXAMPLE 7   *(Compare Exercise 33)*

Find the relative extreme values, and sketch the graph of f if

$$f(x) = \frac{x}{4} - 3x^{1/3}$$

SOLUTION   First, note that f is continuous for all x, so its graph will be in one piece. Next, compute the derivative of f:

$$f'(x) = \frac{1}{4} - x^{-2/3} = \frac{1}{4} - \frac{1}{x^{2/3}}$$

f' exists for all x except $x = 0$, so the number $x = 0$ is a critical number. To find the other critical numbers, we need to solve the equation $f'(x) = 0$:

$$\frac{1}{4} - \frac{1}{x^{2/3}} = 0$$

Multiply by $4x^{2/3}$:

$$x^{2/3} - 4 = 0$$
$$x^{2/3} = 4$$
$$x^2 = 64 \qquad \text{(Cube both sides)}$$
$$x = \pm 8 \qquad \text{(Don't forget the negative solution)}$$

There are three critical numbers: -8, 0, and 8. We begin our sign-of-f' chart. Fill in this chart as we go.

Sign-of-f'

$$\begin{array}{c|c|c} & & \\ \hline -8 & 0 & 8 \end{array}$$

We have to evaluate $f'(x) = \dfrac{1}{4} - \dfrac{1}{x^{2/3}}$, so we choose numbers whose cube root we can compute easily. From $(-\infty, -8)$ we choose $x = -27$:

$$f'(-27) = \frac{1}{4} - \frac{1}{(-27)^{2/3}} = \frac{1}{4} - \frac{1}{(-3)^2} = \frac{1}{4} - \frac{1}{9} > 0$$

From $(-8, 0)$ we choose $x = -1$:

$$f'(-1) = \frac{1}{4} - \frac{1}{(-1)^{2/3}} = \frac{1}{4} - \frac{1}{(-1)^2} = \frac{1}{4} - 1 < 0$$

From $(0, 8)$ we choose $x = 1$:

$$f'(1) = \frac{1}{4} - \frac{1}{(1)^{2/3}} = \frac{1}{4} - \frac{1}{1^2} = \frac{1}{4} - 1 < 0$$

From $(8, \infty)$ we choose $x = 27$:

$$f'(27) = \frac{1}{4} - \frac{1}{(27)^{2/3}} = \frac{1}{4} - \frac{1}{(3)^2} = \frac{1}{4} - \frac{1}{9} > 0$$

Your completed chart should look like the following:

Sign-of-f'

$$\begin{array}{c|c|c} + & - & - & + \\ \hline -8 & 0 & 8 \end{array}$$

f is increasing on the intervals $(-\infty, -8)$ and $(8, \infty)$.
f is decreasing on the intervals $(-8, 0)$ and $(0, 8)$.
The values of f at the critical numbers are

$$f(-8) = -\frac{8}{4} - 3(-8)^{1/3} = -2 - 3(-2) = 4$$

$$f(0) = \frac{0}{4} - 3(0)^{1/3} = 0 - 0 = 0$$

$$f(8) = \frac{8}{4} - 3(8)^{1/3} = 2 - 3 \cdot 2 = -4$$

We must be careful filling in the curve because $f'(0)$ doesn't exist. In this case the graph has a vertical tangent at $(0, 0)$, and the graph is shown in Figure 11–7.

FIGURE 11–7

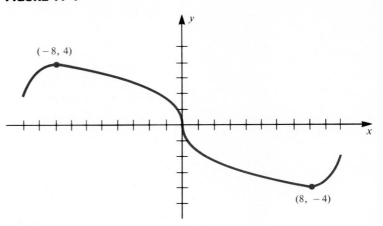

11–1 EXERCISES

I

1. Use Figure 11–8 to complete the following statements:
   (a) The maximum value of f on $[-3, 5]$ is _____ .
   (b) The minimum value of f on $[-3, 5]$ is _____ .
   (c) f has a relative maximum value when $x =$ _____ .
   (d) f has a relative minimum value when $x =$ _____ .
   (e) The numbers _____ are the critical numbers of f.
   (f) f is increasing on the open interval(s) _____ .
   (g) $f'(x) < 0$ on the open interval(s) _____ .
2. Use Figure 11–9 to complete the following statements:
   (a) The maximum value of f on $[-5, 5]$ is _____ .
   (b) The minimum value of f on $[-5, 5]$ is _____ .
   (c) When $x =$ _____ , f has a relative maximum value.
   (d) When $x =$ _____ , f has a relative minimum value.
   (e) The numbers _____ are critical numbers for f.
   (f) f is decreasing on the open interval(s) _____ .
   (g) $f'(x) > 0$ on the open interval(s) _____ .

FIGURE 11–8

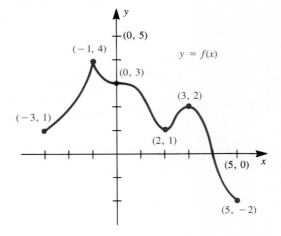

FIGURE 11–9

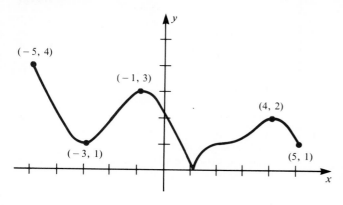

Find all the critical numbers of the functions given in Exercises 3 through 6.

3. (*See Example 1*)
$$f(x) = 6x^2 - 4x + 8$$

4. $f(x) = -3x^2 + 7x - 5$

5. $f(x) = \frac{1}{3}x^3 - \frac{3}{2}x^2 + 2x - 7$

6. $f(x) = x^3 + \frac{11}{2}x^2 - 4x + 3$

In Exercises 7 through 10, find the intervals on which f is increasing.

7. (*See Example 2*)
$$f(x) = -5x^2 + 8x - 9$$

8. $f(x) = x^2 - 6x + 2$

9. $f(x) = \frac{1}{3}x^3 - x^2 - 8x + 6$

10. $f(x) = -\frac{1}{3}x^3 + 2x^2 + 5x + 1$

Find and classify the relative extreme values of f in Exercises 11 through 14.

11. (*See Example 3*)
$$f(x) = -5x^2 + 8x - 9$$

12. $f(x) = x^2 - 6x + 2$

13. $f(x) = \frac{1}{3}x^3 - x^2 - 8x + 6$

14. $f(x) = -\frac{1}{3}x^3 + 2x^2 + 5x + 1$

II

Find all the critical numbers of f in Exercises 15 through 18.

15. $f(x) = 2x^3 - x^2 - 4x + 9$

16. $f(x) = 2x^3 + \frac{13}{2}x^2 - 5x + 8$

17. $f(x) = \sqrt{x^2 + 8x + 20}$

18. $f(x) = \sqrt{x^2 - 4x + 15}$

In Exercises 19 through 22, find the intervals on which f is decreasing.

19. $f(x) = \frac{1}{4}x^4 + \frac{1}{3}x^3 - x^2 + 4$

20. $f(x) = \frac{1}{5}x^5 - \frac{4}{3}x^3 + 6$

21. $f(x) = \sqrt{x^2 - 6x + 10}$

22. $f(x) = \sqrt{x^2 - 10x + 30}$

Find the intervals on which f is increasing and the intervals on which f is decreasing, and sketch a graph of f in Exercises 23 through 26.

23. $f(x) = x^2 - 4x$ **24.** $f(x) = x^2 - 2x - 8$

25. $f(x) = -x^2 + 5x - 4$ **26.** $f(x) = -x^2 + 7x - 6$

III

In Exercises 27 through 44, find the intervals on which f is decreasing and the intervals on which f is increasing. Identify relative extrema. Use this information to sketch a graph of the function.

27. (*See Example 4*)
$f(x) = x^2 + 5x - 6$

28. $f(x) = -x^2 + 3x + 4$

29. (*See Example 5*)
$f(x) = x^3 - 6x^2 + 2$

30. $f(x) = x^3 + 3x^2$

31. $f(x) = x^3 + 12x - 3$

32. $f(x) = -x^3 + 3x^2 + 9x + 1$

33. (*See Example 7*)
$f(x) = (x - 8)^{1/3}$

34. $f(x) = (x - 8)^{2/3}$

35. (*See Example 6*)
$f(x) = x^4 + 4x^3 - 1$

36. $f(x) = -3x^4 + 8x^3 + 5$

37. $f(x) = \sqrt{9 - x^2}$

38. $f(x) = \sqrt{x^2 - 4}$

39. $f(x) = (x^2 - 4x)^{1/3}$

40. $f(x) = (x^2 - 2x - 3)^{1/3}$

41. (*See Example 5 in Section 2–4*)
$f(x) = x\sqrt{2x + 12}$

42. $f(x) = 2x\sqrt{x + 5}$

43. $f(x) = 4x\sqrt{3 - x}$

44. $f(x) = 2x\sqrt{8 - x}$

45. A consulting firm predicted that t days after a certain new stock started to sell, its price P would be given by

$$P(t) = 140 + 10t - \frac{1}{4}t^2, \qquad t \geq 0$$

If the firm is correct:
(a) for what interval(s) will the price of the stock increase?
(b) what will be the largest price of the stock?

46. A book publisher has undertaken market research to arrive at a decision on the number of copies of a certain text to produce. Printing too many copies would mean that many would remain unsold for a long period. Printing too few would imply that the company was not taking full advantage of the available market. The research group arrived at the following equation relating profit P (in dollars) to the number of books published N (in units of one thousand):

$$P = 100(-N^3 + 12N^2 + 60N)$$

(a) For what values of N is the marginal profit positive?
(b) For what values of N is the profit increasing?
(c) For what values of N is the marginal profit increasing?
(d) How many books should be printed to maximize profit?

47. A baseball is thrown upward. The ball is released with an initial velocity of 96 ft/sec from a height of 6 feet above the ground. Its height in feet above the ground t seconds after it is released is given by

$$h(t) = -16t^2 + 96t + 6$$

(a) For what values of t is the height increasing?
(b) What is the maximum height of the ball?
(c) When is the ball at its maximum height?

48. The efficiency E of a person learning a new task was determined to be given by $E(t) = \frac{1}{3}t^3 - 5t^2 + 24t$ for $0 \leq t \leq 8$, where t is the time in hours since starting the new task. For what time periods during the day did the person's efficiency decrease?

49. The cost of manufacturing x items per hour is modeled by $C(x) = \frac{1}{10}x^2 + 13x + 160$, $0 \leq x \leq 100$.
(a) For what values of x is the marginal cost decreasing?
(b) For what values of x is the average cost decreasing?
(c) What is the minimum average cost?
(d) Evaluate $MC(x_1)$, where x_1 minimizes the average cost; compare with the answer to part (c).

50. A company call sell x chairs per week at $150 per chair. The cost of manufacturing x chairs per week is given by $C(x) = \frac{1}{4}x^2 + 50x + 3600$.
(a) For what values of x is the marginal revenue greater than the marginal cost?
(b) For what values of x is the profit an increasing function?
(c) How many chairs per week should the company manufacture to maximize profit?
(d) What is the company's maximum profit?
(e) For what values of x is the average cost per chair decreasing?

51. Suppose that on some interval I a firm's marginal revenue function is greater than its marginal cost function. What, if anything, can you conclude about:
(a) the marginal profit function on the interval I?
(b) the profit function on the interval I?

11–2 CONCAVITY AND THE SECOND DERIVATIVE TEST

- *Concavity*
- *Points of Inflection*

CONCAVITY

Economists typically use a curve like that given in Figure 11–10 to model the cost C as a function of x, where x is the amount of goods produced.

Why do they use a curve with this shape? What features should a cost curve have? First, notice that the y-intercept of the curve is positive. This should always be true because the y-intercept is $C(0)$, which represents the fixed costs. Next, notice that the function is increasing, which represents the fact that costs usually rise as the production level rises.

The next feature of the graph that is important to economists is the way the graph "bends" even while it is rising. For small values of x the slope of the graph is becoming less steep as x increases. For large values of x, however, the slope of the graph is becoming steeper as x increases. This feature of the graph reflects the fact that when x is small, production can be increased efficiently. As production increases, however, there comes a point at which more workers must be added, maintenance of equipment becomes more expensive, or some other factors make increased production inefficient. The quantitative description of "efficient" is based on the geometry of the graph.

FIGURE 11–10

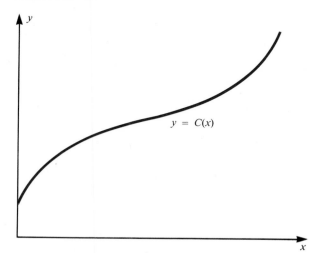

$y = C(x)$

FIGURE 11-11

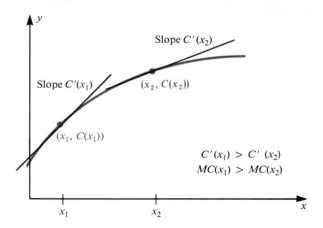

The marginal cost function, MC, is the derivative of the cost function; $MC = C'$. Geometrically, therefore, the marginal cost is the slope of the line tangent to the cost curve at $(x, C(x))$. For small values of x the slopes of these lines decrease as x increases. Said another way, for small values of x the marginal cost decreases as x increases. See Figure 11–11.

Recall that the sign of the derivative of a function indicates whether that function is increasing or decreasing. Thus MC will be decreasing if $(MC)'$ is negative. Furthermore, because $MC = C'$, $(MC)' = C''$. The geometric aspect of the cost curve that we are trying to describe can now be characterized in terms of the sign of the second derivative of the cost function. When x is small, $C''(x) < 0$.

Similarly, for large values of x the increasing steepness of the curve reflects the fact that MC is increasing; $C''(x) > 0$.

The first derivative tells us whether the graph is rising or falling; the second derivative tells us which way the graph is bent. The word **concave** is used to describe the informal notion of "bent."

Definition **Concave Up,** **Concave Down**	**(a)** The graph of f is **concave up** on an interval if $f''(x) > 0$ for each x in the interval. **(b)** The graph of f is **concave down** on an interval if $f''(x) < 0$ for each x in the interval.

CAUTION The concavity of the curve has nothing to do with whether the function is increasing or decreasing. There are four possible ways to pair the sign of f' and the sign of f''. Figure 11–12 shows these possibilities.

FIGURE 11-12

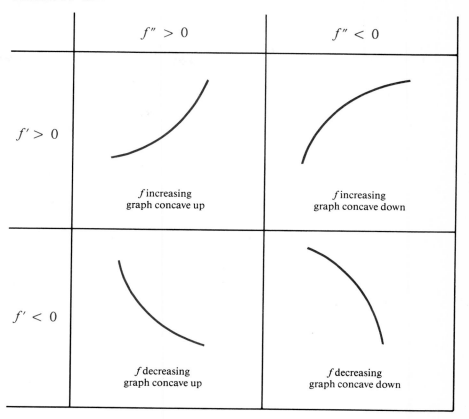

The sign of $f''(c)$ has particular significance if $f'(c) = 0$. Recall that if $f'(c) = 0$, then c is a critical point, and $f(c)$ may be a relative extremum. We saw in the last section that $f(c)$ is a relative extreme value if f' changes sign at c. We now look at the behavior of f'' when f' changes sign. Suppose that $f'(c) = 0$, and f' goes from negative to positive; then the graph of f must look like that in Figure 11-13.

In this situation, as f' goes from negative to positive, f' is increasing. If f' is increasing, then $f''(x) > 0$, and the graph of f is concave up. A similar discussion about what happens at c if $f(c)$ is a relative maximum leads to what is called **the second derivative test.**

FIGURE 11–13

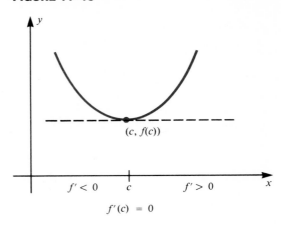

$f'(c) = 0$

The Second Derivative Test for Relative Extreme Values	If $f'(c) = 0$ and

If $f'(c) = 0$ and

(a) $f''(c) > 0$, then f has a relative minimum at $x = c$.
(b) $f''(c) < 0$, then f has a relative maximum at $x = c$.
(c) $f''(c) = 0$, then no conclusion can be drawn.

CAUTION Condition (c) really says that if $f''(c) = 0$, the first derivative test should be used to find out what's going on. It does *not* say that $f(c)$ is not a relative extreme value. See Examples 2 and 3.

CAUTION You cannot use the second derivative test at c unless $f'(c) = 0$. If $f'(c)$ exists and $f'(c) \neq 0$, then $f(c)$ *is not* a relative extreme value.

EXAMPLE 1   *(Compare Exercise 5)*

Let $f(x) = 2x^3 - 6x^2 - 18x + 7$. Use the second derivative test to find the relative extreme values of f. (Compare with Example 1 of the previous section. The graph of f is Figure 11–3.)

SOLUTION $f'(x) = 6x^2 - 12x - 18$; set $f'(x) = 0$ and solve as before:

$$6x^2 - 12x - 18 = 0$$
$$x^2 - 2x - 3 = 0$$
$$(x - 3)(x + 1) = 0$$
$$x = 3 \qquad x = -1$$

The critical numbers are $x = 3$ and $x = -1$.

Next, $f''(x) = 12x - 12$. (Remember to find the derivative of f' this time.) Now evaluate f'' at the critical numbers:

$$f''(3) = 12 \cdot 3 - 12 = 24 > 0$$

The second derivative test tells us that f has a relative minimum when $x = 3$. The value of the relative minimum is $f(3)$, which is -47.

$$f''(-1) = 12(-1) - 12 = -24 < 0$$

The second derivative test tells us that f has a relative maximum when $x = -1$. The value of the relative maximum is $f(-1)$, which is 17.

The next three examples show what to do if $f'(c) = 0$ and $f''(c) = 0$ also.

EXAMPLE 2   *(Compare Exercise 11)*

Find the relative extreme values of f if

$$f(x) = x^4 - 4x^3 + 6x^2 - 4x + 3 = (x - 1)^4 + 2$$

Then sketch the graph of f.

SOLUTION $f'(x)$ exists for all x, so the only critical numbers are the solutions to $f'(x) = 0$. We compute $f'(x)$, using the form $f(x) = (x - 1)^4 + 2$.

$$f'(x) = 4(x - 1)^3(1) + 0 = 4(x - 1)^3 \qquad \text{(Note the use of the chain rule)}$$

Set $f'(x) = 0$; $4(x - 1)^3 = 0$ has only one solution, $x = 1$. Computing $f''(x)$, we have

$$f''(x) = 4 \cdot 3(x - 1)^2 1 = 12(x - 1)^2 \qquad \text{so}$$
$$f''(1) = 12(0)^2 = 0$$

Part **(c)** of the second derivative test tells us to use the first derivative test. The only critical number is $x = 1$. We need to complete the following chart:

Sign-of-f'

FIGURE 11–14

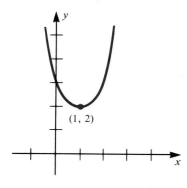

(1, 2)

From $(-\infty, 1)$ we choose $x = 0$; $f'(0) = 4(-1)^3 = -4 < 0$.
From $(1, \infty)$ we choose $x = 2$; $f'(2) = 4(1)^3 = 4 > 0$.
We can now fill in the chart:

Sign-of-f' $-$ $+$

By using the first derivative test we know that f has a relative minimum at $x = 1$; $f(1) = 2$ is the value of the relative minimum. Before drawing the graph of f we check concavity. Because $f''(x) = 12(x - 1)^2$, $f''(x) > 0$ on $(-\infty, 1)$ and $(1, \infty)$. The graph of f is concave up on both these intervals. The graph of f is given in Figure 11–14.

EXAMPLE 3   *(Compare Exercise 11)*

Find the relative extreme values of g if

$$g(x) = -x^4 + 4x^3 - 6x^2 + 4x - 3$$

Then sketch the graph of g.

SOLUTION   Notice that $g(x) = -f(x)$, where $f(x)$ is defined as in Example 2. This means that $g'(x) = -f'(x)$ and $g''(x) = -f''(x)$. Thus $g'(x) = 0$ precisely when $f'(x) = 0$, and $x = 1$ is the only critical number of g. Furthermore, $g''(1) = -f''(1) = 0$, so part **(c)** of the second derivative test again tells us to use the first derivative test. The sign of g' is the opposite of the sign of f', so we have

Sign-of-g' $\underline{\qquad + \qquad | \qquad - \qquad}$
                            1

The first derivative test tells us that g has a relative maximum at $x = 1$. The concavity of the graph of g is determined by the sign of g''. Here, $g''(x) = -12(x - 1)^2$, so $g''(x) < 0$ on $(-\infty, 1)$ and on $(1, \infty)$. The graph of g is concave down on both these intervals. In fact, the graph of g is the reflection in the x-axis of the graph of f and is given in Figure 11–15.

Example 2 shows that when $f''(c) = 0$, $f(c)$ may be a relative minimum; Example 3 shows that when $f''(c) = 0$, $f(c)$ may be a relative maximum. There is even a third possibility, and we look at this case in Example 4.

FIGURE 11–15

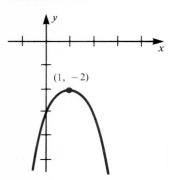

$(1, -2)$

EXAMPLE 4   *(Compare Exercise 11)*

Let $f(x) = x^3 - 3x^2 + 3x + 4$. Find the relative extreme values of f. Then sketch the graph of f.

SOLUTION $f'(x) = 3x^2 - 6x + 3$ for all x, so the only critical numbers of f are those that satisfy $f'(x) = 0$.

Set

$$3x^2 - 6x + 3 = 0$$
$$x^2 - 2x + 1 = 0$$
$$(x - 1)(x - 1) = 0$$

The function has only one critical number, $x = 1$. Compute $f''(x)$: $f''(x) = 6x - 6$. Thus $f''(1) = 6 \cdot 1 - 6 = 0$, and part **(c)** of the second derivative test tells us nothing. We go back to the first derivative test.

Sign-of-f' $\underline{\qquad\qquad | \qquad\qquad}$
                            1

Test $f'(x)$ for $x < 1$. We choose $x = 0$:

$$f'(0) = 3 \cdot 0^2 - 6 \cdot 0 + 3 = 3 > 0$$

so f is increasing on $(-\infty, 1)$.

Next, test $f'(x)$ for $x > 1$. We choose $x = 2$:

$$f'(2) = 3(2)^2 - 6 \cdot 2 + 3 = 3 > 0$$

so f is also increasing on $(1, \infty)$.

Sign-of-f'

f' does not change sign at $x = 1$, so f does not have a relative extreme value at $x = 1$. But $x = 1$ was the only possibility. Therefore f has no relative extreme values.

We now discuss the graph of f. We know that $f'(x) > 0$ for all $x \neq 1$ and that $f'(1) = 0$. Next, we compute $f(1) = 1^3 - 3 \cdot 1^2 + 3 \cdot 1 + 4 = 5$; the point $(1, 5)$ is on the graph. We must draw a graph that rises up to $(1, 5)$, has a horizontal tangent there, and then rises again on the other side of $(1, 5)$.

The graph rises as x increases, but again we face the question of how the graph bends. We look at f'' again, and analyze the sign of f''. The *procedure* is the same as that for analyzing the sign of f'. Set $f''(x) = 0$ and find the cut points for this equation; then the sign of f'' is constant on intervals between cut points. Here, $f''(x) = 6x - 6$, and the only cut point is where $6x - 6 = 0$, or $x = 1$. Now we construct a sign chart for $f''(x)$.

Sign-of-f'' ——————|——————

Test $f''(x)$ for $x < 1$: Choosing $x = 0$, we have

$$f''(0) = 6 \cdot 0 - 6 = -6 < 0$$

Test $f''(x)$ for $x > 1$: Choosing $x = 2$, we have

$$f''(2) = 6 \cdot 2 - 6 = 6 > 0$$

Sign-of-f''

The graph of f is concave down on $(-\infty, 1)$ but concave up on $(1, \infty)$. Such a graph is drawn in Figure 11–16. The line T is the line tangent to the graph at $(1, 5)$.

FIGURE 11-16

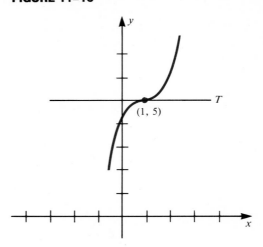

POINTS OF INFLECTION

The graph in Figure 11–16 has a feature at the point (1, 5) that we saw occur in the typical cost curve at the beginning of this section. Now we can describe this feature mathematically; the graph has a change of concavity at (1, 5). In this example and the cost function example the concavity changes from concave down to concave up. We give a special name to the points on the graph where the concavity changes.

Definition **Point of Inflection**	The point $(a, f(a))$ on the graph of f is a **point of inflection** if the graph is concave up on one side of $(a, f(a))$ and concave down on the other side. That is, the point $(a, f(a))$ is a point of inflection if the graph changes concavity at $(a, f(a))$.

We are interested in points of inflection because they enable us to sketch a better graph. Furthermore, points of inflection are very important in understanding "the law of diminishing marginal returns" because they help locate the relative maximum values of f' (see Figure 11–17) and relative minimum values of f' (see Figure 11–18).

CAUTION Remember the definition of a point of inflection; the graph must change concavity at $(a, f(a))$. It is not enough that $f''(a) = 0$. Example 2 shows a function with $f''(1) = 0$, but $(1, f(1))$ is not a point of inflection. Example 6 will show that $(a, f(a))$ may be a point of inflection even if $f''(a)$ doesn't exist.

Points of inflection occur when f'' changes sign, and f'' can change sign at a if either $f''(a) = 0$ or a is not in the domain of f''. Finding the sign of f'' is the same as solving both the inequalities $f''(x) > 0$ and $f''(x) < 0$. We solve these inequalities by using cut points.

FIGURE 11-17

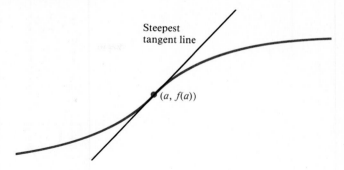

Steepest
tangent line

$(a, f(a))$

FIGURE 11-18

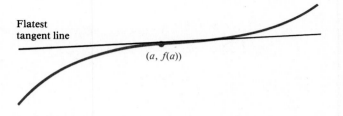

Flatest
tangent line

$(a, f(a))$

EXAMPLE 5   *(Compare Exercise 17)*

Sketch the graph of f if $f(x) = 2 - 9x + 6x^2 - x^3$. Label points corresponding to relative extreme values and inflection points.

SOLUTION $f'(x) = -9 + 12x - 3x^2$ for all x, so the only critical numbers are the solutions to $f'(x) = 0$. Set

$$-9 + 12x - 3x^2 = 0 \qquad \text{(Divide by } -3)$$
$$3 - 4x + x^2 = 0$$
$$(x - 3)(x - 1) = 0$$

The critical numbers of f are $x = 1$ and $x = 3$. The chart

Sign-of-f' $\dfrac{\quad - \qquad\quad + \qquad\quad - \quad}{\qquad\quad\; |\qquad\qquad |}$
                                1   3

tells us that f is decreasing on both $(-\infty, 1)$ and $(3, \infty)$ and that f is increasing on $(1, 3)$. Evaluating $f(x)$ at the critical numbers, we have $f(1) = -2$ and $f(3) = 2$. We plot the points $(1, -2)$ and $(3, 2)$ on the graph.

FIGURE 11-19

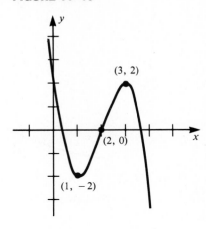

To discuss concavity, we look at f'':

$$f''(x) = 12 - 6x$$

The chart

Sign-of-f'' $\underset{\underset{2}{|}}{\overline{\qquad\quad + \qquad\quad - \qquad\quad}}$

shows that the graph is concave up on $(-\infty, 2)$ and concave down on $(2, \infty)$. The point $(2, f(2)) = (2, 0)$ is an inflection point. The graph of f is given in Figure 11-19.

EXAMPLE 6   *(Compare Exercise 27)*

Sketch the graph of $y = (x + 1)^{1/3} + 2$, and label points of inflection and points corresponding to relative extreme values.

SOLUTION   If $f(x) = (x + 1)^{1/3} + 2$, then f is continuous for all x, so its graph has just one piece:

$$f'(x) = \frac{1}{3}(x + 1)^{-2/3} = \frac{1}{3(x + 1)^{2/3}}$$

Note that $f'(x)$ does not exist for $x = -1$, so -1 is a critical number. There are no solutions to $f'(x) = 0$. Furthermore, $f'(x) > 0$ if $x \neq -1$, so the sign chart for f' is as follows:

Sign-of-f' $\underset{\underset{-1}{|}}{\overline{\qquad\quad + \qquad\quad + \qquad\quad}}$

The function f is increasing on $(-\infty, -1)$ and on $(-1, \infty)$; hence f has no relative extreme values.

To investigate concavity, we turn to the second derivative:

$$f''(x) = \frac{-2}{9}(x + 1)^{-5/3} = \frac{-2}{9(x + 1)^{5/3}}$$

Next, we analyze the sign of f''. We set $f''(x) = 0$, but

$$\frac{-2}{9(x + 1)^{5/3}} = 0$$

has no solution. However, there is a number where $f''(x)$ doesn't exist, namely, $x = -1$. The chart that we must fill in is as follows:

Sign-of-f'' ⊥
                              −1

To test $f''(x)$ with a number less than -1, we choose $x = -2$:

$$f''(-2) = \frac{-2}{9(-1)^{5/3}} = \frac{-2}{9(-1)} = \frac{2}{9} > 0$$

To test $f''(x)$ with a number greater than -1, we choose $x = 0$:

$$f''(0) = \frac{-2}{9(1)^{5/3}} = \frac{-2}{9 \cdot 1} = \frac{-2}{9} < 0$$

The sign chart for f'' is now complete:

Sign-of-f'' +   −
                              −1

Evaluating $f(x)$ at $x = -1$, we obtain $f(-1) = 0^{1/3} + 2 = 2$. The sign chart of f'' tells us that $(-1, 2)$ is a point of inflection because the graph of f changes from concave up to concave down at that point.

The graph of f is concave up over $(-\infty, -1)$ and concave down over $(-1, \infty)$. The graph of f is given in Figure 11–20.

FIGURE 11–20

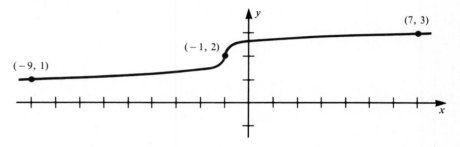

The last example in this section shows that you must be careful about claiming that f has a point of inflection.

EXAMPLE 7   *(Compare Exercise 23)*

Discuss the concavity of the graph of $y = 1/x$.

SOLUTION   First, since $f(x) = 1/x$, the function f is not continuous for all x; the number $x = 0$ is not in the domain of f. Writing $f(x) = x^{-1}$, we find that

$$f'(x) = -1x^{-2} = \frac{-1}{x^2} \qquad \text{and} \qquad f''(x) = 2x^{-3} = \frac{2}{x^3}$$

To analyze the sign of $f''(x) = 2/x^3$, we find the cut points for the equation $2/x^3 = 0$. There are no solutions to this equation, but $x = 0$ is a cut point because 0 is not in the domain of $2/x^3$.

The chart to fill in is as follows:

Sign-of-f'' _____|_____
                        0

To test $f''(x)$ for $x < 0$, we choose $x = -1$:

$$f''(-1) = \frac{2}{(-1)^3} = \frac{2}{-1} < 0$$

To test $f''(x)$ for $x > 0$, we choose $x = 1$:

$$f''(1) = \frac{2}{(1)^3} = \frac{2}{1} > 0$$

The sign chart for f'' now looks like the following:

                      −   +
Sign-of-f'' _____|_____
                        0

The graph is concave down over $(-\infty, 0)$ and concave up on $(0, \infty)$, but the graph has no point of inflection because the function is not even defined at $x = 0$.

For completeness we include the graph of $y = 1/x$.

Because $f'(x)$ is negative for all x in the domain of f, the sign chart for f' looks like the following:

                      −   −
Sign-of-f' _____|_____
                        0

f is decreasing on $(-\infty, 0)$ and on $(0, \infty)$.

We postpone a discussion of the behavior of the graph near the coordinate axes until the next section. The graph of $y = 1/x$ is given in Figure 11–21.

FIGURE 11–21

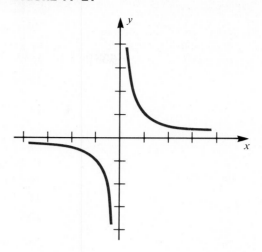

11–2 EXERCISES

I

Use the graph in Figure 11–22 to answer Exercises 1 through 4. (Some tangent lines have been drawn, and the answers involve only integer values of x.)

1. On what open intervals is the graph concave up?
2. On what open intervals is the graph concave down?
3. What are the points of inflection?
4. What are the numbers in the domain where f has a relative extreme value?

FIGURE 11–22

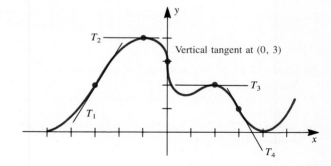

Vertical tangent at (0, 3)

II

In Exercises 5 through 14, use the second derivative test to find the numbers at which f has a relative extreme value, and tell whether f has a relative maximum or minimum at each such number.

5. (*See Example 1*)
$$f(x) = 7x^2 - 4x - 2$$

6. $f(x) = 3x^2 - 6x + 4$

7. $f(x) = -4x^2 + 24x + 5$

8. $f(x) = 6 - 30x - 5x^2$

9. $f(x) = 2x^3 + 9x^2 - 60x + 5$

10. $f(x) = \dfrac{2}{3}x^3 + x^2 - 24x + 7$

11. (*See Examples 2, 3, and 4*)
$$f(x) = 3x^4 - 4x^3 - 12x^2 + 7$$

12. $f(x) = x^4 + 4x^3 - 8x^2 - 10$

13. $f(x) = 9x + \dfrac{1}{x}$

14. $f(x) = 4x + \dfrac{16}{x}$

In Exercises 15 through 28, identify the intervals on which the graph of f is concave up and the intervals on which the graph of f is concave down, and find the points of inflection.

15. $f(x) = 9x^2 - 14x + 1$

16. $f(x) = 8 - 5x - 7x^2$

17. (*See Example 5*)
$$f(x) = x^3 - 6x^2 + 9x - 4$$

18. $f(x) = 2x^3 - 24x^2 + 5x - 9$

19. $f(x) = -5x^3 + 10x^2 + 3x - 8$

20. $f(x) = -10x^3 + 20x^2$

21. $f(x) = x^4 + 2x^3 - 36x^2 + 8x - 4$

22. $f(x) = x^4 - 12x^3 + 9x + 10$

23. (*See Example 7*)   24. $f(x) = x + \dfrac{25}{x}$
$$f(x) = 7 - \dfrac{1}{x}$$

25. $f(x) = 8x^2 + \dfrac{1}{x} + 3$ 26. $f(x) = x^2 - \dfrac{8}{x}$

27. (*See Example 6*)   28. $f(x) = (x + 6)^{2/3} - 4$
$$f(x) = 2 + (x - 5)^{1/3}$$

III

In Exercises 29 through 38:

(a) identify the intervals on which f is increasing or decreasing;

(b) identify the intervals on which f is concave up or concave down; and

(c) sketch the graph of f. Plot the points corresponding to relative extrema and points of inflection.

29. $f(x) = (x - 4)^3 - 3$

30. $f(x) = x^3 - 3x - 2$

31. $f(x) = x^3 + 3x^2 - 9x + 1$

32. $f(x) = \dfrac{1}{4}x^4 + \dfrac{1}{3}x^3 - x^2 + 2$

33. $f(x) = x - 2\sqrt{x}$

34. $f(x) = 4\sqrt{x} - x + 1$

35. $f(x) = 5 - (x - 2)^4$

36. $f(x) = x^3 - \dfrac{3}{2}x^2 - 6x + 4$

37. $f(x) = x^4 - 6x^2 + 1$

38. $f(x) = x^5 - 10x^2 - 3$

39. Using preliminary data, the Davis Company has decided to describe its cost in manufacturing x storm doors per day by
$$C(x) = \dfrac{1}{12}x^3 - 100x^2 + 300x + 610$$

(a) For what value of x is the marginal cost, MC, minimized?

(b) For what values of x is the cost curve concave down?

40. When a company produces x thousand gallons of soft drinks per week, its cost function can be modeled by
$$C(x) = \dfrac{x^3}{180} - 3x^2 + 1305x + 3500$$

(a) What is the first coordinate of each point of inflection of the cost curve?

(b) For what intervals is the graph of C concave down?

(c) What value of x minimizes the marginal cost function?

41. Walker Manufacturing has determined that if it produces x bookcases per week, then its weekly revenue function R can be modeled by

$$R(x) = \frac{-1}{6}x^3 + 70x^2 + 130x$$

(a) On what intervals is the revenue increasing?
(b) Use the second derivative test to classify the relative extreme values of f.
(c) Find the point of diminishing marginal returns, that is, the value of x that maximizes the company's marginal revenue, MR.

42. What is the point of diminishing marginal returns for a company if its revenue function is given by $R(x) = -\frac{1}{10}x^3 + 60x^2 + 210x$?

43. A company has found that a trainee's skill quotient Q is given by the formula

$$Q = 1 - \frac{12}{t^2 + 12}$$

where t is the number of days spent in training.
(a) For what values of t is Q increasing?
(b) The learning rate is defined to be the derivative of Q. For what values of t is the learning rate increasing?
(c) What is the point of diminishing returns for time spent in training?

44. A company's yearly revenue from manufacturing x hundred units is $R(x) = 80x^2 + 500x$; the yearly cost is $\frac{1}{3}x^3 + 25x^2 + 1500x + 50,000$. Find and classify the relative extreme values of the yearly profit function.

45. A company's monthly revenue from manufacturing x thousand units is $R(x) = 34x^2 + 100x$; the monthly cost is $\frac{1}{3}x^3 + 7x^2 + 300x + 12,000$. Find and classify the relative extreme values of the monthly profit function.

Use the graph in Figure 11–23 to answer Exercises 46 through 48. Answers will be in the interval $(-6, 6)$. Note that the graph in Figure 11–23 is the graph of f', the derivative of f, and that the questions refer to f, not to f'.

46. On what intervals is f increasing?

47. On what intervals is the graph of f concave up?

48. What are the x-coordinates of the points of inflection on the graph of f?

FIGURE 11–23

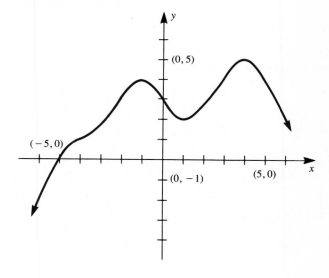

11–3 ASYMPTOTES

- *Average-Cost Function*
- *Geometry of Asymptotes and Limits Involving Infinity*
- *Vertical Asymptotes*
- *Horizontal Asymptotes*

AVERAGE-COST FUNCTION

A certain firm has modeled its cost by a linear function C, where $C(x)$, the cost of producing x items, is given by $C(x) = 1.5x + 4$; as we have seen, the 4 represents fixed costs, and the 1.5 is the cost per item. The firm is assuming that its marginal cost is constant; $MC(x) = C'(x) = 1.5$. Using this model, what does the graph of the average cost function, $AC(x) = \dfrac{C(x)}{x}$, look like? In this particular example,

$$AC(x) = \frac{1.5x + 4}{x} = 1.5 + \frac{4}{x}$$

FIGURE 11–24

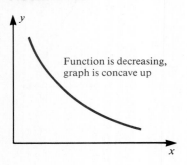

Function is decreasing, graph is concave up

We sketch the graph of $AC(x)$ for $x > 0$, since those are the only values of x that make sense in our application.

$AC(x) = 1.5 + (4/x)$ is continuous for all $x > 0$, so the graph has one piece. Because $(AC)'(x) = -4/x^2$, $(AC)'(x) < 0$ for all x. (Note that x^2, the denominator, is always positive.) The negative derivative indicates that the average cost is always decreasing. The second derivative is $(AC)''(x) = 8/x^3$. $(AC)''(x) > 0$ for all x. (We are assuming that x is positive, so x^3 is positive.) Therefore the graph of the average-cost function is always concave up.

From the first and second derivative we know that the general shape of the graph is like that given in Figure 11–24.

But there are many graphs with this general shape. The question for this function is, "What happens to $AC(x)$ when x is near 0 or when x is very large?"

GEOMETRY OF ASYMPTOTES AND LIMITS INVOLVING INFINITY

What happens to $AC(x) = 1.5 + (4/x)$ if x is a large number? The term $4/x$ is then a number close to 0, so $1.5 + (4/x)$ is close to 1.5. (In fact, because $4/x$ is positive, we can even say that $1.5 + (4/x)$ is a little bit bigger than 1.5.) Furthermore, the larger the value of x, the closer $1.5 + (4/x)$ is to 1.5. We again use the language of limits to describe the notion of "close to." This time, however, there is no number that x is approaching; x is getting arbitrarily large. We introduce a new symbol, ∞, which means "infinity", and we write

$$\lim_{x \to \infty} \left(1.5 + \frac{4}{x}\right) = 1.5$$

FIGURE 11-25

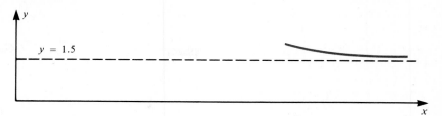

This is the mathematical shorthand for saying "if x is a very large number, then $1.5 + (4/x)$ is close to 1.5." Geometrically, this means the second coordinates of points on the graph are very close to 1.5 when x is big. The points are very close to those of height 1.5. Figure 11-24 gave us the general shape of the graph, and now if we draw the horizontal line $y = 1.5$ with a dotted line, we can see that the tail of the graph on the right must look like Figure 11-25.

The general definition is given below.

Definition
Limit at Infinity

We say the **limit of $f(x)$ as x approaches infinity** is L if $f(x)$ is close to L whenever x is a large number. We write

$$\lim_{x \to \infty} f(x) = L$$

We can also extend this notion to deal with the behavior of a function on the far left-hand side of the line, where x is negative but has a large absolute value.

Definition
Limit at Negative Infinity

We say the **limit of $f(x)$ as x approaches negative infinity** is L if $f(x)$ is close to L whenever x is a negative number with $|x|$ large. We write

$$\lim_{x \to -\infty} f(x) = L$$

CAUTION ∞ and $-\infty$ are special symbols but are not numbers, and the rules of arithmetic are not valid for these symbols. For instance, it is not true that $\frac{\infty}{\infty} = 1$.

We return now to the geometry in Figure 11-25. When x is a large number, the graph is close to the line $y = 1.5$. When this happens, we say that the line $y = 1.5$ is an **asymptote** of the graph. Because the line $y = 1.5$ is horizontal, we call the line $y = 1.5$ a **horizontal asymptote** of the graph.

CAUTION The asymptote is the *line $y = 1.5$*. Asymptotes are lines, not numbers.

FIGURE 11–26

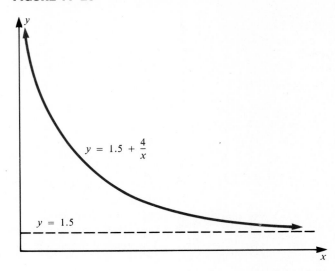

We will investigate limits at infinity and horizontal asymptotes more fully later in this section. We now return to our example of the average cost $AC(x) = 1.5 + (4/x)$. The term $4/x$ is the portion of the fixed cost shared by each of the x items produced; the more items, the smaller this share is for each individual item. Conversely, the fewer items produced, the larger the share per item. We assume that the units are such that x can take on values between 0 and 1 (for example, the item could be gallons of gasoline, and x could be measured in units of 10,000). What happens to $1.5 + (4/x)$ if x is near 0? If x is near 0, then $4/x$ is a large number—if x is 0.00001, then $4/x$ is 400,000.

As x approaches 0 from the right, $4/x$ and hence $1.5 + (4/x)$ grow arbitrarily large. We again use the ∞ symbol and write

$$\lim_{x \to 0^+} \left(1.5 + \frac{4}{x} \right) = \infty$$

The graph of $1.5 + (4/x)$ is given in Figure 11–26.

The definitions of infinite limits follow.

Definition
Infinity as a Limit   We say the limit of $f(x)$ as x approaches c is infinity if $f(x)$ is a large number whenever x is close to c but not equal to c. We write

$$\lim_{x \to c} f(x) = \infty$$

Definition
Negative Infinity as a Limit

We say the limit of $f(x)$ as x approaches c is negative infinity if $f(x)$ is a negative number with $|f(x)|$ large whenever x is close to c but not equal to c. We write

$$\lim_{x \to c} f(x) = -\infty$$

Refer to Figure 11–26 again. When x is close to 0, the graph is nearly vertical; it is very close to the vertical line $x = 0$ (the y-axis). We again use the word asymptote to describe the situation when the graph is close to a line. In this instance, because the line is vertical, we say that the line $x = 0$ is a **vertical asymptote** of the graph of $AC(x)$.

Remember that the general idea behind the definition of asymptote is this: If the graph of f is very close to a line L whenever $|x|$ or $|f(x)|$ is large, then the line L is an asymptote of the graph. We use the language of limits to describe "close to."

We will now examine asymptotes more closely, starting with vertical asymptotes.

VERTICAL ASYMPTOTES

The four graphs in Figure 11–27 show situations that could be described by saying "the line $x = a$ is a vertical asymptote of the graph $y = f(x)$." These pictures involve only one-sided "closeness" of the graph and a line, and the definition of one-sided limits extends to infinite limits just as it did to finite limits. Thus in Figure 11–27(i), the picture is further described by saying

$$\lim_{x \to a^+} f(x) = \infty$$

In Figure 11–27(iii), as x approaches a from the right, the values of f drop off steeply; $f(x)$ is negative but very large in absolute value. We describe this situation by saying $\lim_{x \to a^+} f(x) = -\infty$. Figure 11–27(ii) and Figure 11–27(iv) are described by left-hand limits. We can now give the definition of vertical asymptote.

Definition
Vertical Asymptote

The line $x = a$ is a **vertical asymptote** of the graph of f if at least one of the following four conditions is met:

(i) $\lim_{x \to a^+} f(x) = \infty$,

(ii) $\lim_{x \to a^-} f(x) = \infty$,

(iii) $\lim_{x \to a^+} f(x) = -\infty$, or

(iv) $\lim_{x \to a^-} f(x) = -\infty$.

FIGURE 11–27

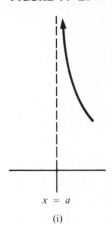

$x = a$

(i)

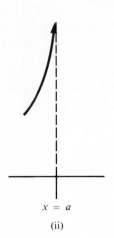

$x = a$

(ii)

$x = a$

(iii)

$x = a$

(iv)

How do you tell whether a graph has a vertical asymptote? Like most general questions, this one doesn't have a quick answer other than "check the definition." The next theorem, however, does describe a situation in which you can be sure that a vertical asymptote exists; you should then use limits to see what the graph looks like near the asymptote.

Theorem
Existence of Vertical Asymptote

If $f(x) = \dfrac{P(x)}{Q(x)}$ where $P(x)$ and $Q(x)$ are polynomials, with $Q(a) = 0$ but $P(a) \neq 0$, then the line $x = a$ is a vertical asymptote of the graph of f.

EXAMPLE 1   *(Compare Exercises 1, 15, and 25)*

Let $f(x) = \dfrac{x + 4}{x - 2}$. Find any vertical asymptote of f and sketch the graph of f near each asymptote.

SOLUTION $f(x) = \dfrac{P(x)}{Q(x)}$, where $P(x) = x + 4$ and $Q(x) = x - 2$. Now $Q(x) = 0$ if $x = 2$. Furthermore, $P(2) = 6 \neq 0$. The theorem quoted above guarantees that *the line $x = 2$ is a vertical asymptote.*

We now use one-sided limits to get a better understanding of the graph. Remember that Figure 11–27 presented four pictures of what the graph can look like near a vertical asymptote.

First, we investigate

$$\lim_{x \to 2^+} \frac{x + 4}{x - 2}$$

If x is close to 2 and greater than 2, then both $x + 4$ and $x - 2$ are positive. Thus

$$f(x) = \frac{x + 4}{x - 2}$$

is the quotient of positive numbers, so $f(x)$ is positive. Just to the right of $x = 2$, the graph must be above the x-axis, and so looks like Figure 11–27(i). Thus

$$\lim_{x \to 2^+} \frac{x + 4}{x - 2} = \infty$$

Next we examine

$$\lim_{x \to 2^-} \frac{x + 4}{x - 2}$$

If x is a little bit less than 2, then $x + 4$ is positive and $x - 2$ is negative. Thus

$$f(x) = \frac{x + 4}{x - 2}$$

is of the form

$$\frac{\text{positive number}}{\text{negative number}}$$

and is therefore negative. Thus $\lim_{x \to 2^-} f(x) = -\infty$, and the graph must look like Figure 11–27(iv). The sketch of the graph of f near its vertical asymptote, the line $x = 2$, is given in Figure 11–28. The asymptote is drawn with a dotted line.

FIGURE 11-28

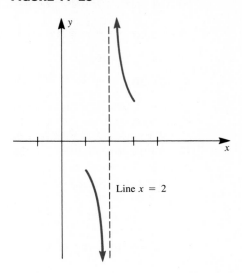

Line $x = 2$

EXAMPLE 2   *(Compare Exercise 29)*

Let

$$f(x) = \frac{x^2 - 6x + 5}{x^2 - 4x + 3}$$

Find all vertical asymptotes of f, and sketch the graph near the points where f is discontinuous.

SOLUTION   Here, $P(x) = x^2 - 6x + 5 = (x - 5)(x - 1)$ and $Q(x) = x^2 - 4x + 3 = (x - 3)(x - 1)$. The denominator of $f(x)$ is zero when $x = 3$ and when $x = 1$. Thus f is discontinuous when $x = 3$ and when $x = 1$, and these give two *possible* lines for vertical asymptotes. Note however that $P(1) = 0$ as well as $Q(1) = 0$. The theorem does not tell us whether or not the line $x = 1$ is a vertical asymptote. We must look at the limit of $f(x)$ at $x = 1$:

$$\lim_{x \to 1} f(x) = \lim_{x \to 1} \frac{(x - 5)(x - 1)}{(x - 3)(x - 1)} = \lim_{x \to 1} \frac{x - 5}{x - 3} = \frac{-4}{-2} = 2$$

FIGURE 11-29

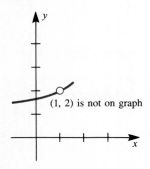

(1, 2) is not on graph

None of the four limit conditions for an asymptote is true, so the line $x = 1$ is *not* a vertical asymptote. Figure 11–29 shows the graph of f for x close to 1.

Next, check the line $x = 3$; $P(3) = -2 \neq 0$, so the line $x = 3$ is a vertical asymptote.

Again, we examine the right- and left-hand limits to see what type of infinite limits we have in this case. We have seen that we can rewrite $f(x)$ as $\dfrac{x - 5}{x - 3}$ if $x \neq 1$. We investigate the right-hand limit, namely,

$$\lim_{x \to 3^+} f(x) = \lim_{x \to 3^+} \frac{x - 5}{x - 3}$$

1. The fact that $\lim_{x \to 3^+} x - 5 = -2 \neq 0$ and $\lim_{x \to 3^+} x - 3 = 0$ tells us that

$$\lim_{x \to 3^+} \frac{x - 5}{x - 3}$$

will be infinite. We must decide on the sign.

2. If x is a little bit larger than 3, then $x - 5$ is close to -2, and so the numerator is negative. Because $x > 3$, $x - 3$ is positive, so the denominator is positive. A negative number divided by a positive number is negative. Thus when x is a little bit larger than 3, $f(x)$ is negative.

3. Putting (1) and (2) together, we have

$$\lim_{x \to 3^+} \frac{x - 5}{x - 3} = -\infty$$

We now know that the line $x = 3$ is a vertical asymptote of the graph of f and that just to the right of $x = 3$, the graph looks like Figure 11–27(iii).

Finally, for the left-hand limit, as above, we know that $\lim_{x \to 3^-} \frac{x - 5}{x - 3}$ is infinite. This time, with x close to 3 but less than 3, both numerator and denominator are negative. Thus their quotient, $f(x)$, is positive, and $\lim_{x \to 3^-} \frac{x - 5}{x - 3} = \infty$.
Just to the left of the line $x = 3$ the graph of f looks like Figure 11–27(ii).

We finish Example 2 with the sketch in Figure 11–30.

FIGURE 11–30

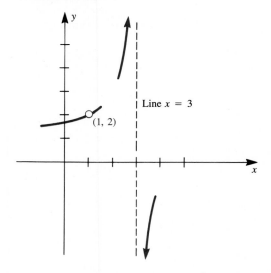

Line $x = 3$

$(1, 2)$

EXAMPLE 3   *(Compare Exercise 33)*

Find the vertical asymptotes of f if

$$f(x) = \frac{6}{(x + 1)(x - 4)}$$

and sketch the graph of f near the points of discontinuity of f.

SOLUTION $f(x)$ is of the form $\dfrac{P(x)}{Q(x)}$, with $P(x) = 6$ and $Q(x) = (x + 1) \cdot$
$(x - 4)$; $Q(x) = 0$ when $x = -1$ and when $x = 4$. So we investigate the behavior of $f(x)$ near $x = -1$ and $x = 4$.

A complete investigation of the situation requires us to look at four one-sided limits: $\lim\limits_{x \to -1^+} f(x)$, $\lim\limits_{x \to -1^-} f(x)$, $\lim\limits_{x \to 4^+} f(x)$, and $\lim\limits_{x \to 4^-} f(x)$.

First,

$$\lim_{x \to -1^+} f(x) = \lim_{x \to -1^+} \frac{6}{(x + 1)(x - 4)}$$

1. The limit of the numerator is not 0, while the limit of the denominator is 0. Therefore the limit of the quotient is infinite, and we must determine the sign.

2. We assume that x is just a little bit larger than -1. The numerator is always 6, which is positive. Now look at the denominator. $x + 1$ is positive, and $x - 4$ is negative, so the denominator, $(x + 1)(x - 4)$, is negative. (Remember that x is a little bit larger than -1.) Thus $f(x)$ is of the form $\dfrac{\text{positive number}}{\text{negative number}}$, and so $f(x)$ is negative.

3. Steps 1 and 2 imply that $\lim\limits_{x \to -1^+} f(x) = -\infty$.

Next, we compute

$$\lim_{x \to -1^-} \frac{6}{(x + 1)(x - 4)}$$

Again Step 1 tells us that this limit is infinite. Now both factors in the denominator are negative, and so the denominator is positive. Thus

$$\lim_{x \to -1^-} \frac{6}{(x + 1)(x - 4)} = \infty$$

We next look at the behavior of f near 4. Both

$$\lim_{x \to 4^-} \frac{6}{(x + 1)(x - 4)} \quad \text{and} \quad \lim_{x \to 4^+} \frac{6}{(x + 1)(x - 4)}$$

are of the form $\dfrac{\text{nonzero limit}}{\text{zero limit}}$, so both limits are infinite. We investigate the sign of each. If x is a little bit less than 4, then $x + 1$ is positive but $x - 4$ is negative.

FIGURE 11–31

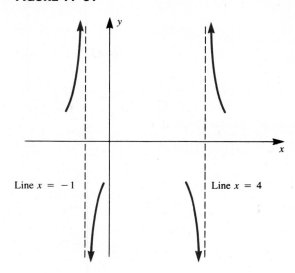

Hence $(x + 1)(x - 4)$ is negative, and so is $\dfrac{6}{(x + 1)(x - 4)}$.

$$\lim_{x \to 4^-} \frac{6}{(x + 1)(x - 4)} = -\infty$$

If x is a little bit larger than 4, then both $x + 1$ and $x - 4$ are positive. Hence $(x + 1)(x - 4)$ is positive, and so

$$\lim_{x \to 4^+} \frac{6}{(x + 1)(x - 4)} = \infty$$

The sketch is given in Figure 11–31.

CAUTION
1. Example 2 shows that you cannot determine whether there is an asymptote just by looking at the denominator.
2. Example 3 shows that you cannot evaluate $\frac{6}{0}$ as ∞. You cannot claim that a positive number divided by 0 is positive infinity. To compute the correct sign, you must look at the sign of $f(x)$ on each side of the asymptote.

HORIZONTAL ASYMPTOTES

Vertical asymptotes describe the behavior of a function near a point in its domain where the function "blows up." That is, vertical asymptotes help us to understand what the graph looks like when $|f(x)|$ is arbitrarily large for values of x near some fixed number. Horizontal asymptotes describe the long-term behavior of the function. That is, horizontal asymptotes help us to understand what the graph looks like when $|x|$ is arbitrarily large and $f(x)$ is near some fixed number. To describe the behavior of f to the far right of its graph, we write $\lim\limits_{x \to \infty} f(x)$; to describe the behavior of f to the far left of its graph, we write $\lim\limits_{x \to -\infty} f(x)$.

Definition
Horizontal Asymptote

The line $y = b$ is called a **horizontal asymptote** of the graph of f if either

$$\lim_{x \to \infty} f(x) = b \qquad \text{or} \qquad \lim_{x \to -\infty} f(x) = b$$

A graph may have no horizontal asymptotes (see Figure 11–32(i)), one horizontal asymptote (see Figure 11–32(ii)), or two horizontal asymptotes (see Figure 11–32(iii)).

Many functions that give rise to horizontal asymptotes in applications are of the form $f(x) = \dfrac{P(x)}{Q(x)}$, where $P(x)$ and $Q(x)$ are polynomials. There is a nice theorem that describes the situation completely in three cases.

Theorem
Existence of Horizontal Asymptotes

Let $P(x) = a_n x^n + \cdots + a_0$, $a_n \neq 0$ (the degree of $P(x)$ is n).
Let $Q(x) = b_m x^m + \cdots + b_0$, $b_m \neq 0$ (the degree of $Q(x)$ is m).

Case 1. If $m > n$,

$$\lim_{x \to \infty} \frac{P(x)}{Q(x)} = 0 \qquad \text{and} \qquad \lim_{x \to -\infty} \frac{P(x)}{Q(x)} = 0$$

Therefore the line $y = 0$ is the horizontal asymptote.
Case 2. If $m = n$,

$$\lim_{x \to \infty} \frac{P(x)}{Q(x)} = \frac{a_n}{b_m} = \lim_{x \to -\infty} \frac{P(x)}{Q(x)}$$

Therefore the line

$$y = \frac{a_n}{b_m}$$

is the horizontal asymptote.
Case 3. If $m < n$, then

$$\lim_{x \to \infty} \frac{P(x)}{Q(x)} \qquad \text{and} \qquad \lim_{x \to -\infty} \frac{P(x)}{Q(x)}$$

are not finite. Therefore the graph does not have a horizontal asymptote.

We will not pursue Case 3 further.

FIGURE 11-32

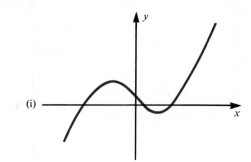

(i)

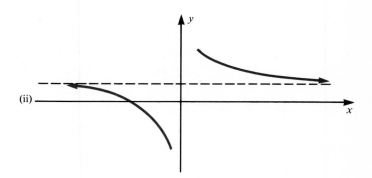

(ii)

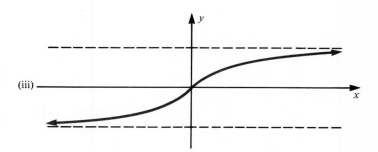

(iii)

EXAMPLE 4 *(Compare Exercise 29)*

Find the horizontal asymptotes of the graph of f if

$$f(x) = \frac{13x + 5}{x^2 + 8}$$

and sketch the asymptotic behavior of the graph of f as $x \to \infty$ and as $x \to -\infty$.

SOLUTION   Here, $f(x) = \dfrac{P(x)}{Q(x)}$, where $P(x) = 13x + 5$ has degree 1 and $Q(x)$ $= x^2 + 8$ has degree 2. [The degree of the denominator] > [the degree of the numerator], so this example falls into Case 1.

$$\lim_{x \to \infty} \frac{13x + 5}{x^2 + 8} = 0$$

and the x-axis is a horizontal asymptote (to the far right).

$$\lim_{x \to -\infty} \frac{13x + 5}{x^2 + 8} = 0$$

and the x-axis is a horizontal asymptote (to the far left).

For large values of x, both $13x + 5$ and $x^2 + 8$ are positive, so $f(x) > 0$, and the graph is close to the x-axis. The graph looks like Figure 11–33. (We could also use the first derivative to show that f is decreasing and the second derivative to show that the graph is concave up. All these approaches will be discussed in the next section on curve sketching.) For x negative but $|x|$ large, $13x + 5$ is negative, and $x^2 + 8$ is positive, so $f(x) < 0$, and the graph is close to the x-axis. The graph looks like Figure 11–34.

FIGURE 11–33

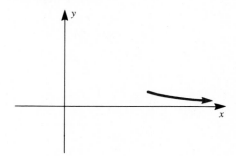

FIGURE 11–34

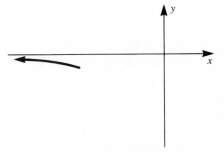

EXAMPLE 5   *(Compare Exercise 21)*

Find the horizontal asymptotes of the graph of f if

$$f(x) = \frac{3x^2 + 9x - 5}{5x^2 - x + 4}$$

Draw a sketch of the asymptotic behavior.

SOLUTION   Here, $f(x) = \dfrac{P(x)}{Q(x)}$, where $P(x) = 3x^2 + 9x - 5$ has degree 2 and $Q(x) = 5x^2 - x + 4$ also has degree 2. [The degree of the denominator] = [the degree of the numerator], so this example falls into Case 2. Thus $\lim\limits_{x \to \infty} \dfrac{P(x)}{Q(x)} =$ the ratio of the coefficients of the highest degree terms $= \dfrac{3}{5}$.

The line $y = \frac{3}{5}$ is a horizontal asymptote (to the far right). Similarly,

$$\lim_{x \to -\infty} \frac{3x^2 + 9x - 5}{5x^2 - x + 4} = \frac{3}{5}$$

so the line $y = \frac{3}{5}$ is a horizontal asymptote (to the far left). Using a hand calculator, you can see that if x is large, $f(x) > \frac{3}{5}$; note that $f(1000) \approx 0.602$. Also, if $|x|$ is large with x negative, then $f(x) < \frac{3}{5}$; note that $f(-1000) \approx 0.598$. The asymptotic behavior is shown in Figure 11–35.

FIGURE 11–35

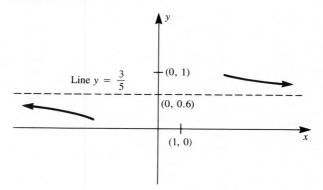

EXAMPLE 6   *(Compare Exercise 13)*

Find the horizontal asymptotes of the graph of f if

$$f(x) = \frac{(x - 3)(x + 1)}{x - 2}$$

and draw a sketch showing the asymptotic behavior.

SOLUTION Here, $f(x) = \dfrac{P(x)}{Q(x)}$, where $P(x) = (x - 3)(x + 1)$ has degree 2 and $Q(x) = x - 2$ has degree 1. This function falls into Case 3, and the graph has no horizontal asymptotes. Hence no sketch is necessary. ∎

11–3 EXERCISES

I

In Exercises 1 through 14, use the theorems from this section on the existence of asymptotes to give the equation of any vertical or horizontal asymptotes that the functions may have. Identify each by type—horizontal or vertical.

1. (*See Example 1*)

$$f(x) = \frac{x + 5}{x - 6}$$

2. $f(x) = \dfrac{2x - 4}{x - 2}$

3. $f(x) = \dfrac{x + 1}{x^2 - 9}$

4. $f(x) = \dfrac{x - 8}{x^2 - 16}$

5. $f(x) = \dfrac{3x + 7}{(2x + 6)(x - 4)}$

6. $f(x) = \dfrac{x + 4}{(2x + 10)(x - 7)}$

7. $f(x) = \dfrac{4x - 7}{5x + 10}$

8. $f(x) = \dfrac{3x^2 + 8}{x^2 + 5}$

9. $f(x) = \dfrac{4x - 9}{x^2 + 1}$

10. $f(x) = \dfrac{x^2 - 9}{x^3 + 8}$

11. $f(x) = \dfrac{x^3 - 2x + 1}{x^2 - 4}$

12. $f(x) = \dfrac{x^2 - x + 5}{x + 6}$

13. (*See Example 6*)

$$f(x) = \frac{x^3 + 4x^2 + 5x}{x^2 + 16}$$

14. $f(x) = \dfrac{x^2 - 9}{x - 6}$

II

In Exercises 15 through 24, compute the limits and draw a sketch interpreting the limit graphically.

15. (*See Example 1*)

$$\lim_{x \to 3^-} \frac{x - 5}{x - 3}$$

16. $\displaystyle\lim_{x \to 2^+} \frac{x - 7}{x - 2}$

17. $\displaystyle\lim_{x \to 5^+} \frac{6 - 2x}{x - 5}$

18. $\displaystyle\lim_{x \to -3^+} \frac{x + 1}{x + 3}$

19. $\displaystyle\lim_{x \to \infty} \frac{3x^2 - 9}{5x^2 + 8x + 2}$

20. $\displaystyle\lim_{x \to -\infty} \frac{3x + 9}{x^2 + 10x - 8}$

21. (*See Example 5*)

$$\lim_{x \to -\infty} \frac{5x + 7}{10x + 4}$$

22. $\displaystyle\lim_{x \to \infty} \frac{4x^2 + 3x - 9}{3x^2 + 2x - 5}$

23. $\displaystyle\lim_{x \to 1^+} \frac{x^2 - 4x + 3}{x^2 - 1}$

24. $\displaystyle\lim_{x \to 3^-} \frac{x^2 - x - 6}{2x^2 - 5x - 3}$

In Exercises 25 through 32, identify the vertical and horizontal asymptotes for each function and compute the appropriate limits, including the limit at each point of discontinuity of f. Draw an appropriate sketch interpreting each limit geometrically.

25. (*See Example 1*)

$$f(x) = \frac{3x + 2}{x + 5}$$

26. $f(x) = \dfrac{6}{x - 4}$

27. $f(x) = \dfrac{3x + 2}{x^2 + 4}$

28. $f(x) = \dfrac{x + 1}{2x + 10}$

29. (*See Examples 2 and 4*)

$$f(x) = \frac{x - 1}{x^2 - 3x + 2}$$

30. $f(x) = \dfrac{x}{x^2 + 3x}$

31. $f(x) = \dfrac{x^2 - 5x + 4}{x^2 - 3x - 4}$

32. $f(x) = \dfrac{x^2 - x - 6}{x^2 - 3x - 10}$

III

Compute each of the limits in Exercises 33 through 38 and draw a sketch interpreting the limit geometrically.

33. (*See Example 3*)

$$\lim_{x \to -3^+} \frac{1}{(x + 5)(x + 3)}$$

34. $\displaystyle\lim_{x \to 2^-} \frac{1}{(x + 3)(x - 2)}$

35. $\displaystyle\lim_{x \to -4^-} \frac{x - 2}{(x + 4)(x - 1)}$

36. $\displaystyle\lim_{x \to -1^-} \frac{x}{(x + 1)(x + 3)}$

37. $\displaystyle\lim_{x \to 2^-} \frac{x - 3}{(x - 2)(x + 5)}$

38. $\displaystyle\lim_{x \to 6^-} \frac{x - 2}{(x - 6)(x + 1)}$

Identify vertical and horizontal asymptotes for the functions in Exercises 39 through 48. For each function, sketch the behavior of the graph near each point of discontinuity, and indicate each asymptote by a dotted line.

39. $f(x) = \dfrac{1}{x^2}$

40. $f(x) = \dfrac{5}{x + 2}$

41. $f(x) = \dfrac{2x - 8}{x - 3}$

42. $f(x) = \dfrac{2x - 6}{x + 1}$

43. $f(x) = 1 + \dfrac{4}{x^2 + 1}$

44. $f(x) = \dfrac{6}{x^2 - 9}$

45. $f(x) = \dfrac{x^2 - 6x + 5}{x^2 - 3x + 2}$

46. $f(x) = \dfrac{1}{x^2 + x - 6}$

47. $f(x) = \dfrac{3}{x^2 + 4x}$

48. $f(x) = \dfrac{3x^2 - 16}{x^2 - 16}$

49. A company manufacturing computer chips has a daily cost in dollars given by $C(x) = 8x + 1200$, where x is the number of chips manufactured each day. What is the approximate average cost per chip for large-scale production?

50. If the cost of producing x folding chairs per week is given by $C(x) = 3x + 2170$, what is the approximate average cost per chair when a large number of chairs are produced each week?

51. With a weekly cost of producing x sets of drinking glasses given by $C(x) = 5x + 3200$, what is the approximate average cost per set of glasses when weekly production is very large?

11–4   GRAPHING: PUTTING IT ALL TOGETHER

In the first three sections of this chapter we saw the geometric significance of the first derivative, the second derivative, and asymptotes. In this section we show how to combine all of this information to draw an accurate graph of a function without a great deal of point plotting.

Our general **graphing strategy** is as follows:

1. Determine the domain of f and points of discontinuity. This is usually a good time to check for asymptotes. (Note that if the line $x = a$ is a vertical asymptote, then f cannot be continuous at a.)
2. Construct a sign chart for f'. This chart will be used to determine intervals on which f is increasing or decreasing and to find relative extrema.
3. If possible, construct a sign chart for f''. (Sometimes f'' will be so complicated that you cannot solve $f''(x) = 0$.) This chart will be used to determine intervals on which the graph of f is concave up or down and hence the points of inflection.
4. Evaluate $f(x)$ at all critical numbers, at all x such that $f''(x) = 0$, and (if they exist) at endpoints of the domain.

5. Check on the **consistency of the information** obtained in Steps 1–4. (For example, if the sign-of-f' chart shows that f has a relative maximum at c, the sign-of-f'' chart should not show $f''(c) > 0$.) If the information is consistent, go on to the next step; if not, find your error.
6. Plot the points obtained in Step 4, and fill in the curve using the sign charts of f' and f''. Show asymptotic behavior by using dotted lines, and show the behavior of f near its points of discontinuity.

You might find it easier to do Steps 5 and 6 simultaneously. We list them separately in order to call your attention to checking the consistency of your work.

In the examples that follow, we will not do all the steps involved in the sign analysis of f' and f''. Instead, we urge you to work through the details; refer to Section 2–4 and the first two sections of this chapter if you need further review.

EXAMPLE 1   (Compare Exercise 3)

Draw the graph of $f(x) = x^3 - 3x^2 - 9x + 2$.
SOLUTION

1. First note the domain is all x, and that f is continuous for all x. Thus the graph is connected and has no vertical asymptotes. Next, since $f(x)$ is a polynomial, the graph has no horizontal asymptotes.
2. $f'(x) = 3x^2 - 6x - 9$. Now analyze the sign of $f'(x)$.

$$3x^2 - 6x - 9 = 3(x^2 - 2x - 3) = 3(x - 3)(x + 1)$$

The cut points are $x = 3$ and $x = -1$, and the sign-of-f' chart is as follows:

Sign-of-f' + (−1) − (3) +

f is increasing on $(-\infty, -1)$ and on $(3, \infty)$, and f is decreasing on $(-1, 3)$.
3. $f''(x) = 6x - 6$. Set $f''(x) = 0$; the only cut point is $x = 1$.

Sign-of-f'' − (1) +

f is concave down on $(-\infty, 1)$ and concave up on $(1, \infty)$.
4. Evaluate $f(x)$ when

$$f'(x) = 0: \quad f(-1) = 7 \quad f(3) = -25$$
$$f''(x) = 0: \quad f(1) = -9$$

There are no endpoints.

FIGURE 11–36

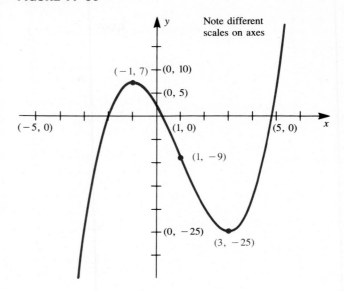

5. Note that the sign-of-f' chart tells us that f has a relative maximum at $x = -1$, so we expect $f''(-1)$ to be negative, which is what the sign-of-f'' chart shows. The similar information at $x = 3$ is also consistent. Furthermore, the sign-of-f' chart indicates that f is decreasing on $(-1, 3)$, and our evaluations in Step 4 showed $f(-1) > f(1) > f(3)$. All our information is consistent, and we now proceed to draw the graph.

6. See Figure 11–36.

EXAMPLE 2   *(Compare Exercise 19)*

Sketch the graph of $f(x) = x\sqrt{16 - x^2}$.

SOLUTION

1. The domain is restricted, since we must have $16 - x^2 \geq 0$; the domain is the interval $-4 \leq x \leq 4$. f is continuous everywhere on this interval, so the graph can have no vertical asymptotes. Because the domain is bounded, the graph can have no horizontal asymptotes.

2. $f'(x) = \sqrt{16 - x^2} + x \cdot \dfrac{1}{2}(16 - x^2)^{-1/2} \cdot (-2x)$

$= \sqrt{16 - x^2} + \dfrac{-x^2}{\sqrt{16 - x^2}}$

$= \dfrac{16 - x^2}{\sqrt{16 - x^2}} + \dfrac{-x^2}{\sqrt{16 - x^2}}$

$= \dfrac{16 - 2x^2}{\sqrt{16 - x^2}}$

f' does not exist at the endpoints, -4 and 4, but f' does exist on the open interval $(-4, 4)$. $f'(x) = 0$ is equivalent to $16 - 2x^2 = 0$; that is, $x^2 = 8$. The critical numbers for f in $(-4, 4)$ are $x = \sqrt{8}$ and $x = -\sqrt{8}$.

$$\text{Sign-of-}f' \qquad \begin{array}{ccccc} & - & + & - & \\ \hline & | & | & | & | \\ -4 & -\sqrt{8} & & \sqrt{8} & 4 \end{array}$$

Note that the chart includes only the interval $(-4, 4)$.
f is increasing on $(-\sqrt{8}, \sqrt{8})$; f is decreasing on $(-4, -\sqrt{8})$ and on $(\sqrt{8}, 4)$.

3. $f''(x) = \dfrac{-4x\sqrt{16 - x^2} - (16 - 2x^2)\dfrac{1}{2}(16 - x^2)^{-1/2}(-2x)}{(\sqrt{16 - x^2})^2}$

$= \dfrac{-4x\sqrt{16 - x^2} + \dfrac{x(16 - 2x^2)}{\sqrt{16 - x^2}}}{(\sqrt{16 - x^2})^2}$

$= \dfrac{-4x(16 - x^2) + x(16 - 2x^2)}{(\sqrt{16 - x^2})^3}$

$= \dfrac{x(-64 + 4x^2 + 16 - 2x^2)}{(\sqrt{16 - x^2})^3}$

$= \dfrac{x(2x^2 - 48)}{(\sqrt{16 - x^2})^3}$

We note that f'' does not exist at $x = 4$ and -4. (We actually already knew this, since f'' cannot exist at a point where f' does not exist.)

Next, set $f''(x) = 0$. A quotient equals 0 precisely when the numerator equals 0, so we set $x(2x^2 - 48) = 0$. The solutions to this equation are $x = 0$, $x = \sqrt{24}$, and $x = -\sqrt{24}$. But $\sqrt{24}$ and $-\sqrt{24}$ are not in the domain of f, so the only solution to $f''(x) = 0$ is $x = 0$.

$$\text{Sign-of-}f'' \qquad \begin{array}{ccc} & + & - \\ \hline & | & | \\ -4 & 0 & 4 \end{array}$$

f is concave up on $(-4, 0)$ and concave down on $(0, 4)$.
4. Evaluate $f(x)$ when

$$f'(x) = 0: \qquad f(-\sqrt{8}) = -\sqrt{8} \cdot \sqrt{8} = -8 \qquad f(\sqrt{8}) = 8$$
$$f''(x) = 0: \qquad f(0) = 0$$

Evaluation at the endpoints gives $f(-4) = 0$ and $f(4) = 0$.

FIGURE 11–37

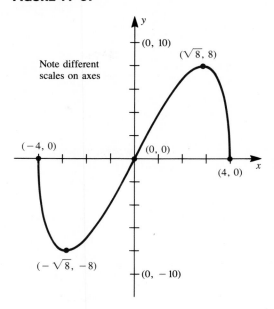

Note different scales on axes

5. The sign-of-f'' chart is consistent with the relative maximum and minimum indicated by the sign-of-f' chart. The evaluations have the correct magnitudes consistent with the information from the sign-of-f' chart, which indicates where f is increasing and where f is decreasing. (You should verify these statements as we did in Example 1.)
6. See Figure 11–37.

EXAMPLE 3 *(Compare Exercise 33)*

Draw the graph of

$$f(x) = \frac{3x^2 + 6}{x^2 - 4}$$

SOLUTION
1. The domain of f is all $x \neq \pm 2$;

$$f(x) = \frac{P(x)}{Q(x)}$$

where $P(x) = 3x^2 + 6$ and $Q(x) = x^2 - 4$. Since $Q(2) = 0$ and $P(2) \neq 0$, the line $x = 2$ is a vertical asymptote. Similarly, the line $x = -2$ is a vertical asymptote. Furthermore, the degree of both $P(x)$ and $Q(x)$ is the same, 2, so the graph has a horizontal asymptote. The ratio of the coefficients of x^2 is $\frac{3}{1} = 3$, so the line $y = 3$ is the horizontal asymptote.

2. $f'(x) = \dfrac{(x^2 - 4)(6x) - (3x^2 + 6)(2x)}{(x^2 - 4)^2}$

$= \dfrac{-36x}{(x^2 - 4)^2}$

f' does not exist when $x = 2$ or -2, and $f'(x) = 0$ when $x = 0$.

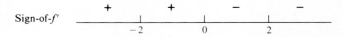

Sign-of-f'

f is increasing on $(-\infty, -2)$ and on $(-2, 0)$; f is decreasing on $(0, 2)$ and on $(2, \infty)$.

3. $f''(x) = \dfrac{-36(x^2 - 4)^2 - (-36x)[2(x^2 - 4)2x]}{(x^2 - 4)^4}$

$= \dfrac{-36(x^2 - 4) + 36x(4x)}{(x^2 - 4)^3}$

$= \dfrac{108x^2 + 144}{(x^2 - 4)^3}$

Again, f'' does not exist when $x = \pm 2$, and $f''(x) \neq 0$, since $108x^2 + 144$ is always positive.

Sign-of-f''
```
       +        −        +
 ————————|————————|————————
        −2        2
```

f is concave up on $(-\infty, -2)$ and on $(2, \infty)$; f is concave down on $(-2, 2)$.
4. The only evaluation we need is at the critical number $x = 0$; $f(0) = -\frac{3}{2}$.
5. The sign-of-f' chart shows a relative maximum at $x = 0$, which is consistent with the sign-of-f'' chart, which shows $f''(0) < 0$. Also $\displaystyle\lim_{x \to 2^+} f(x) = \infty$, which is consistent with f decreasing to the right of 2. You should check the consistency of the other limits.
6. See Figure 11–38.

EXAMPLE 4   *(Compare Exercise 27)*

Draw the graph of

$$f(x) = \frac{24x}{x^2 + 16}$$

SOLUTION
1. The function is defined and continuous for all x; hence there are no vertical asymptotes. To check for horizontal asymptotes, note that f is a quotient of polynomials with the degree of the denominator greater than the degree of the numerator, and so the x-axis is a horizontal asymptote.

FIGURE 11–38

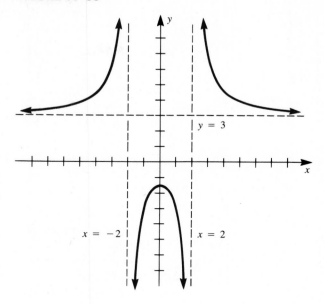

2. For ease of computation, write

$$\frac{24x}{x^2 + 16} \quad \text{as} \quad 24 \cdot \frac{x}{x^2 + 16}$$

Then

$$f'(x) = 24 \cdot \frac{(x^2 + 16) - x(2x)}{(x^2 + 16)^2}$$

$$= 24 \cdot \frac{16 - x^2}{(x^2 + 16)^2}$$

f' is defined for all x; $f'(x) = 0$ when $x = \pm 4$.

Sign-of-f'

$$\begin{array}{c c c} - & + & - \\ \hline & \!\!\!\!\!\!\!\!\!\!\!\!\!\!\!\!\!\! {\scriptstyle -4} & {\scriptstyle 4} \end{array}$$

3. $f''(x) = 24 \cdot \dfrac{-2x(x^2 + 16)^2 - (16 - x^2)[2(x^2 + 16)2x]}{(x^2 + 16)^4}$

$$= 24 \cdot \frac{-2x(x^2 + 16) - (16 - x^2)(4x)}{(x^2 + 16)^3}$$

$$= 24 \cdot \frac{x(-2x^2 - 32 - 64 + 4x^2)}{(x^2 + 16)^3}$$

$$= 24 \cdot \frac{x(2x^2 - 96)}{(x^2 + 16)^3}$$

$f''(x)$ exists for all x; $f''(x) = 0$ when $x = 0$ and when $2x^2 - 96 = 0$. $f''(x) = 0$ when $x = 0$, $\sqrt{48}$, and $-\sqrt{48}$.

$$
\begin{array}{c c c c}
 - & + & - & + \\
\end{array}
$$

Sign-of-f'' $-\sqrt{48}$ 0 $\sqrt{48}$

4. Evaluate $f(x)$ when

$$f'(x) = 0: \qquad f(-4) = \frac{-96}{32} = -3 \qquad f(4) = \frac{96}{32} = 3$$

$$f''(x) = 0: \qquad f(-\sqrt{48}) = \frac{-24\sqrt{48}}{64} \approx -2.60 \qquad f(0) = 0$$

$$f(\sqrt{48}) = \frac{24\sqrt{48}}{64} \approx 2.60$$

(The approximations for $f(-\sqrt{48})$ and $f(\sqrt{48})$ were computed with a calculator.)

There are no endpoints.

5. The evaluations and relative maximum and minimum from sign charts for f' and f'' are consistent. (Check this.)
6. See Figure 11–39.

FIGURE 11–39

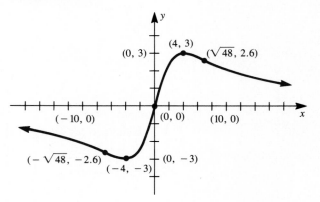

EXAMPLE 5 *(Compare Exercise 25)*

Draw the graph of $f(x) = x - 3\sqrt[3]{x}$.

SOLUTION

1. f is defined and continuous for all x; the graph of f has no asymptotes.

2. $f'(x) = 1 - x^{-2/3} = 1 - \dfrac{1}{x^{2/3}}$. f' does not exist for $x = 0$. Set $f'(x) = 0$; then $1 = \dfrac{1}{x^{2/3}}$ or $x^{2/3} = 1$. Cube both sides; $x^2 = 1$, so $x = \pm 1$.

Sign-of-f'

$$\begin{array}{ccccc} + & & - & & - & & + \\ \hline & -1 & & 0 & & 1 & \end{array}$$

3. $f''(x) = \frac{2}{3}x^{-5/3}$. f'' does not exist when $x = 0$; there are no solutions to $f''(x) = 0$.

Sign-of-f''

$$\begin{array}{ccc} - & & + \\ \hline & 0 & \end{array}$$

4. Evaluate $f(x)$ when

$$\begin{array}{lll} \text{No } f': & f(0) = 0 \\ f'(x) = 0: & f(-1) = 2 & f(1) = -2 \end{array}$$

5. The two sign charts and the evaluations are consistent. (Check this.)
6. See Figure 11–40.

FIGURE 11–40

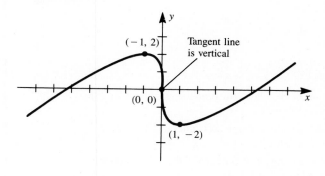

$(-1, 2)$

Tangent line is vertical

$(0, 0)$

$(1, -2)$

11-4 EXERCISES

I

Draw the graphs of the functions in Exercises 1 through 40, using the techniques of this section.

1. $f(x) = x^2 - 6x + 1$ 2. $f(x) = 7 + 2x - x^2$

3. (See Example 1)
   $f(x) = x^3 - 6x^2 - 15x + 4$

4. $f(x) = x^3 - 6x^2 + 7$

5. $f(x) = \frac{1}{4}x^4 - 6x^3 + 5$

6. $f(x) = x^4 - 6x^2 + 2$

7. $f(x) = 5 + 6x^2 - x^3$

8. $f(x) = 10 - 24x - 9x^2 - x^3$

9. $f(x) = (x + 3)^4 + 1$ 10. $f(x) = 6 - (x - 2)^4$

11. $f(x) = \sqrt{6 - x}$ 12. $f(x) = \sqrt{2x + 8}$

13. $f(x) = \sqrt{16 - x^2}$ 14. $f(x) = \sqrt{25 - x^2}$

15. $f(x) = \sqrt{x^2 - 16}$ 16. $f(x) = \sqrt{x^2 - 25}$

II

17. $f(x) = x\sqrt{x^2 + 16}$ 18. $f(x) = x\sqrt{x^2 + 8}$

19. (See Example 2)
    $f(x) = x\sqrt{18 - x^2}$ 20. $f(x) = x\sqrt{100 - x^2}$

21. $f(x) = x\sqrt{x + 9}$ 22. $f(x) = x\sqrt{6 - x}$

23. $f(x) = \frac{1}{8}x - \sqrt{x}$ 24. $f(x) = \sqrt{x} - \frac{x}{18}$

25. (See Example 5)
    $f(x) = 4 + x^{2/3}$ 26. $f(x) = 5 - \sqrt[3]{x}$

27. (See Example 4)
    $f(x) = \frac{4x}{x^2 + 1}$ 28. $f(x) = \frac{120}{x^2 + 12}$

29. $f(x) = \frac{x + 4}{x}$ 30. $f(x) = \frac{2x + 16}{x}$

31. $f(x) = \frac{6 - x}{x^2}$ 32. $f(x) = \frac{x + 3}{x^2}$

33. (See Example 3)
    $f(x) = \frac{1}{(x + 1)(x - 2)}$ 34. $f(x) = \frac{x}{x^2 - 9}$

35. $f(x) = \frac{x - 1}{x^2 + x - 2}$ 36. $f(x) = \frac{x + 3}{x^2 + x - 6}$

37. $f(x) = \frac{x^2}{x^2 + 1}$ 38. $f(x) = \frac{4x^2 + 7}{x^2 + 2}$

39. $f(x) = 6 - \frac{4}{x}$ 40. $f(x) = 8 + \frac{2}{x^2}$

III

41. If $C(x) = 3x + 5$ is a cost function, graph $AC(x)$, the average cost function.

42. Graph $AC(x)$, the average cost function, if the cost function is given by $C(x) = 1.5x + 4$.

43. Graph the average cost function if the cost function is given by $C(x) = \frac{1}{10}x^2 + 5x + 2$.

44. If the cost function is given by $C(x) = \frac{1}{40}x^2 + 3x + 8$, graph $AC(x)$, the average cost function.

In Exercises 45 through 52, draw the graph of a function that satisfies all the given properties, or state why some of the properties are inconsistent.

45. f is differentiable for all x; the critical numbers for f are $x = 1$ and $x = 4$.

Sign-of-f' $\quad \dfrac{\quad - \qquad + \qquad - \quad}{\qquad 1 \qquad\quad 4}$

$f''(2) = 0$ and $f''(6) = 0$

Sign-of-f'' $\quad \dfrac{\quad + \qquad - \qquad + \quad}{\qquad 2 \qquad\quad 6}$

$f(1) = -2, f(4) = 10, f(2) = 3, f(6) = 7$
The line $y = 3$ is a horizontal asymptote.

46. f is continuous for all x; $f'(-2)$ doesn't exist, $f'(3) = 0$, $f'(6) = 0$.

$f(-2) = -10, f(3) = 1, f(6) = 8$

47. f is continuous for all x.

The line $y = 5$ is a horizontal asymptote, and the line $x = 7$ is a vertical asymptote.

48. f is continuous for all x.

Sign-of-f' + -2 − 1 + 5 −

Sign-of-f'' − -1 + 3 −

$f(-2) = 7, f(1) = -3, f(5) = 2, f(-1) = 3$, and $f(3) = 6$

49. f is continuous for all x except $x = 1$.

Sign-of-f' − -2 + 1 +

The line $x = 1$ is a vertical asymptote; $f(-2) = 5$. The lines $y = 10$ and $y = -1$ are both horizontal asymptotes.

50. f is differentiable for all x except $x = -2$ and $x = 3$.

Sign-of-f' + -2 − 1 + 3 +

$\lim\limits_{x \to -2} f(x) = f(-2)$; the line $x = 3$ is a vertical asymptote.

51. f is continuous for all x.

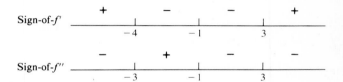

Sign-of-f'' − -3 + -1 − 3 −

52. f is continuous for all x.

Sign-of-f' − -3 − 1 + 5 +

Sign-of-f'' + -3 − -1 + 2 − 5 +

In Exercises 53 through 56, suppose f is a function with the given properties. Fill in each of the blanks that follow with TRUE if the statement *must* be true, FALSE if the statement *must* be false, or EITHER if the statement could be either true or false.

53. f is continuous for all x.

$f(-1) = -2, f'(-1) = 0, f''(-1) = 3$
$f(1) = 3, \quad f'(1) = 2, \quad f''(1) = 4$
$f(4) = 7, \quad f'(4) = 1, \quad f''(4) = 0$

(a) The point $(4, 7)$ is a point of inflection. _____
(b) f has a relative minimum at $x = -1$. _____
(c) f has a relative minimum at $x = 1$. _____
(d) f is increasing on the interval $[-1, 4]$. _____
(e) $\lim\limits_{x \to 1^+} f(x) = 3$. _____

54. f is continuous for all x except $x = 2$, and $f(2) = 3$.

Sign-of-f' + -1 − 2 − 4 +

Sign-of-f'' − 2 +

(a) f is increasing on the interval $(-\infty, -1)$.
_____

(b) f is decreasing on $(-1, 4)$. _____
(c) $\lim\limits_{x \to 2} f(x) = 3$. _____
(d) f has a relative maximum at $x = -1$.
_____

(e) $f(4) < 3$. _____

55. f is continuous for all x.

$f(-2) = -4, f'(-2) = 0, f''(-2) = -3$
$f(1) = 5, \qquad f'(1) = 0, \quad f''(1) = 0$
$f(7) = 6, \qquad f'(7) = -2, f''(7) = 4$

  (a) The point $(1, 5)$ is a point of inflection.
_____

  (b) f does not have a relative extreme value at
     $x = 1$. _____

  (c) f has a relative maximum at $x = 1$.
_____

  (d) The line $x = 3$ is a vertical asymptote.
_____

  (e) The line $y = 5$ is a horizontal asymptote.
_____

56. f is continuous for all $x \neq 3$; the line $x = 3$ is a vertical asymptote, and the line $y = 7$ is a horizontal asymptote.

Sign-of-f'
$$\overset{-}{} \quad \overset{-}{} \quad \overset{+}{} \quad \overset{-}{}$$
$$-5 \qquad -1 \qquad 3$$

Sign-of-f''
$$\overset{+}{} \quad \overset{-}{} \quad \overset{+}{} \quad \overset{+}{}$$
$$-5 \qquad -2 \qquad 3$$

  (a) $\lim\limits_{x \to -\infty} f(x) = 7$. _____

  (b) $\lim\limits_{x \to 3^-} f(x) = -\infty$. _____

  (c) The point $(-2, f(-2))$ is a point of inflection.
_____

  (d) $f(4) > f(7)$. _____

  (e) f has a relative minimum at $x = -1$.
_____

11–5 EXTREME VALUES

- *Existence of a Maximum and a Minimum*

- *Functions Defined on Closed and Bounded Intervals*

- *Functions with Only One Critical Number*

In the first two sections of this chapter we saw how the first and second derivatives determine the shape of a function's graph and how they can be used to find where a function has its relative extreme values. Frequently, however, applications require not just the relative extreme values of a function, but the function's maximum or minimum value over the whole domain. This section gives methods of finding the maximum and minimum value of a function. We concentrate in this section on developing the mathematical techniques that are used in applications. When we deal with applications in Sections 11–6 and 11–7, we can then concentrate on how to apply these techniques.

EXISTENCE OF A MAXIMUM AND A MINIMUM

The function whose graph is drawn in Figure 11–41 has a relative minimum when $x = -2$ and a relative maximum when $x = 3$ but does not have either a minimum value or a maximum value.

    Certain conditions often arise in applications, however, that guarantee that a function satisfying one of these conditions will have an extreme value. We will deal with two of these conditions, the first of which restricts the domain of the function to an interval of form $[a, b]$.

FIGURE 11-41

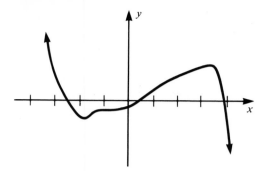

FUNCTIONS DEFINED ON CLOSED AND BOUNDED INTERVALS

A **closed and bounded interval** is an interval of form $[a, b]$. There is a theorem that guarantees that every continuous function whose domain is a closed and bounded interval has both a maximum value and a minimum value on that interval. We can take advantage of this theorem to simplify finding extreme values. To see how, suppose that f is continuous on $[a, b]$ and has its maximum value at c. If c is in the open interval (a, b), then $f(c)$ is a relative maximum, and so c is a critical number. If c is in $[a, b]$, but not in the open interval (a, b), then c is either a or b. Thus f has its maximum value either at a critical number or at one of the two endpoints a and b. Example 1 shows how these observations can quicken our computations.

EXAMPLE 1   *(Compare Exercise 1)*

If $f(x) = x^2 - 6x + 4$ for $-2 \le x \le 5$, find the maximum value of f.

SOLUTION   The restriction $-2 \le x \le 5$ means that the domain of the function is the interval $[-2, 5]$. The function is continuous, so the theorem assures us that both maximum and minimum values of f exist. Furthermore, the derivative of f exists for all x in $(-2, 5)$; we have $f'(x) = 2x - 6$. Setting $f'(x) = 0$, we find that the only critical number is $x = 3$.

The maximum value of f is either $f(3)$, $f(-2)$, or $f(5)$. To find out which one, we simply perform these three evaluations:

$$f(3) = -5 \qquad f(-2) = 20 \qquad f(5) = -1$$

The largest of these three numbers is 20, so the maximum value of f must be $f(-2) = 20$.

_____

The same reasoning that we used to find the maximum value of f also works to find the minimum value. Looking back at the end of Example 1, we can also say that the minimum value of f on $[-2, 5]$ is $f(3) = -5$. *(See Exercise 1)*

Theorem **Existence of Extreme Values**	If f is continuous on $[a, b]$, then both the maximum value of f and the minimum value of f occur when x is either a critical number or an endpoint.

This type of search for extreme values is sometimes referred to as the **candidates test.**

Theorem **The Candidates Test**	If f is continuous on an interval of the form $[a, b]$, find all the places where f could possibly have an extreme value (the critical numbers and the endpoints), and then evaluate the function at each of these points. These values are the candidates for the maximum and minimum. The greatest candidate is the maximum value of f on $[a, b]$, and the least candidate is the minimum.

CAUTION Remember the distinction between the maximum value of f and the number in the domain where f achieves its maximum.

EXAMPLE 2   *(Compare Exercise 11)*

Find the maximum and minimum values of f on the interval $[-2, 4]$ if $f(x) = 2x^3 - 3x^2 - 12x + 10$.

SOLUTION   The function is continuous on $[-2, 4]$ and $f'(x) = 6x^2 - 6x - 12$. Because $f'(x)$ exists for all x in $(-2, 4)$, the only critical numbers are solutions to $f'(x) = 0$.

Set

$$6x^2 - 6x - 12 = 0$$

and solve

$$x^2 - x - 2 = 0$$
$$(x - 2)(x + 1) = 0$$

The only critical numbers are $x = -1$ and $x = 2$. Now all we have to do is evaluate $f(-1)$ and $f(2)$ and then evaluate $f(-2)$ and $f(4)$ and compare these numbers. All the relevant information is displayed in the following table.

	CRITICAL NUMBERS		ENDPOINTS	
x	-1	2	-2	4
$f(x)$	17	-10	6	42

The maximum value of f is 42 when $x = 4$. The minimum value of f is -10 when $x = 2$.

EXAMPLE 3 *(Compare Exercise 21)*

Find the maximum and minimum values of f on the interval $-1 \le x \le 7$ if $f(x) = (2x - 6)^{2/3} + 5$.

SOLUTION

$$f'(x) = \frac{2}{3}(2x - 6)^{-1/3}(2)$$

$$= \frac{4}{3(2x - 6)^{1/3}}$$

There are no solutions to

$$\frac{4}{3(2x - 6)^{1/3}} = 0$$

The only critical number is $x = 3$ because $f'(3)$ is not defined. The candidates for maximum and minimum are $f(3), f(-1),$ and $f(7)$. $f(3) = 5; f(-1) = (-8)^{2/3} + 5 = (-2)^2 + 5 = 9;$ and $f(7) = (8)^{2/3} + 5 = 9$. The maximum value of f on $[-1, 7]$ is 9, and the minimum value is 5.

EXAMPLE 4 *(Compare Exercise 25)*

Find the extreme values of f on the interval $[0, 6]$ if $f(x) = x\sqrt{36 - x^2}$.

SOLUTION $f(x) = x(36 - x^2)^{1/2}$, so

$$f'(x) = (36 - x^2)^{1/2} + x\left(\frac{1}{2}\right)(36 - x^2)^{-1/2}(-2x)$$

$$= \sqrt{36 - x^2} - \frac{x^2}{\sqrt{36 - x^2}}$$

Thus $f'(x)$ exists for all x in $(0, 6)$. Next, $f'(x) = 0$ when

$$\sqrt{36 - x^2} = \frac{x^2}{\sqrt{36 - x^2}}$$

Cross-multiply to get

$$36 - x^2 = x^2$$
$$36 = 2x^2$$
$$18 = x^2$$
$$x = \pm\sqrt{18}$$

Reject $x = -\sqrt{18}$ because this number is not in the domain of f. Finally, we use the candidates test. The critical number is $\sqrt{18}; f(\sqrt{18}) = \sqrt{18}\sqrt{36 - 18} = \sqrt{18}\sqrt{18} = 18$. Evaluating f at the endpoints 0 and 6, we have

$$f(0) = 0 \quad \text{and} \quad f(6) = 0$$

If $f(x) = x\sqrt{36 - x^2}$ for $0 \le x \le 6$, the maximum value of f is 18; the minimum value of f is 0.

A model that assumes a linear relationship between price and demand lends itself to the candidates test.

EXAMPLE 5   *(Compare Example 33)*

Find the production level that will give a company its maximum revenue if the relationship between the price p and production level x is given by

$$p = -\frac{1}{40}x + 10$$

SOLUTION   Since x is production level, the application makes us assume that $x \geq 0$. And since p is price, we would also assume that $p \geq 0$. Since

$$p = -\frac{1}{40}x + 10$$

the inequality $p \geq 0$ is the same as

$$-\frac{1}{40}x + 10 \geq 0$$

Solving this inequality for x, we get $x \leq 400$. Thus x must satisfy $0 \leq x \leq 400$. The general expression for revenue is $R = x \cdot p$. In this case we can express R as a function of x by

$$R(x) = x\left(-\frac{1}{40}x + 10\right) = -\frac{1}{40}x^2 + 10x \qquad 0 \leq x \leq 400$$

R is continuous on the closed and bounded interval $[0, 400]$, so we can use the candidates test:

$$R'(x) = -\frac{1}{20}x + 10$$

is defined for all x in $(0, 400)$, so the only critical numbers will be solutions to

$$-\frac{1}{20}x + 10 = 0$$

$x = 200$ is the only critical number.

	CRITICAL NUMBER	ENDPOINTS	
x	200	0	400
$R(x)$	1000	0	0

The maximum revenue is 1000, and the best production level is $x = 200$.

FUNCTIONS WITH ONLY ONE CRITICAL NUMBER

Sometimes, an application forces you to try to find the extreme value of a function whose domain does not include both endpoints or whose domain is unbounded. Example 8 will show a typical problem of this sort. To explain how to handle this situation, we still assume that the function we are dealing with is continuous and that its domain is an interval. In this instance, no further conditions are assumed about the interval. Instead, we assume that the function has only one critical number. The following theorem tells how to handle this case.

Theorem
The One-Critical-Number Test

Suppose f is continuous on an interval and has only one critical number c in the interval

1. If $f(c)$ is a relative minimum, then $f(c)$ is the minimum value of f.
2. If $f(c)$ is a relative maximum, then $f(c)$ is the maximum value of f.

CAUTION   Be careful in applying this theorem—it requires that f have *exactly one* critical number. The theorem does *not* say that if $f(c)$ is the only relative maximum, then $f(c)$ is the maximum value of f. In fact, Example 2 gives a function f that has only one relative maximum, namely, $f(-1)$, but $f(-1)$ is not the maximum. Notice however that $x = -1$ is not the only critical number; $x = 2$ is another critical number for f. To use the one-critical-number test, you must make sure that f has a *total of only one critical number*.

EXAMPLE 6   *(Compare Example 13)*

Find the maximum value of f on $[-1, 5]$ if $f(x) = 14 + 24x + 3x^2 - x^3$.
SOLUTION $f'(x) = 24 + 6x - 3x^2$. Set $f'(x) = 0$ and solve:

$$24 + 6x - 3x^2 = 0$$
$$-8 - 2x + x^2 = 0$$
$$x^2 - 2x - 8 = 0$$
$$(x - 4)(x + 2) = 0$$

Be careful! The equation $24 + 6x - 3x^2 = 0$ has two solutions: $x = 4$ and $x = -2$, but -2 is not in the domain of the function; -2 is not in $[-1, 5]$. The function has only one critical number: $x = 4$. Also, $f''(x) = 6 - 6x$, so $f''(4) = 6 - 24 = -18 < 0$. Thus f has a relative maximum at $x = 4$, and $x = 4$ is the *only* critical number. Therefore f has its maximum value on $[-1, 5]$ when $x = 4$. The maximum value of f is $f(4) = 94$.

Frequently, there is more than one way to do a particular problem. For instance, you can check the answer to Example 6 by using the candidates test. The test that relies on f having only one critical number is especially useful when the domain of the function is not a closed and bounded interval and when you can easily compute $f''(c)$. We give two more examples in this section. The first is a straightforward computation, and the second is an application.

EXAMPLE 7 *(Compare Exercise 5)*

Find the extreme value of f on the interval $(0, \infty)$ if

$$f(x) = x + \frac{32}{x^2}$$

SOLUTION $f(x) = x + 32x^{-2}$, so $f'(x) = 1 - 64x^{-3} = 1 - \dfrac{64}{x^3}$; $f'(x)$ exists for all $x > 0$.

Set $f'(x) = 0$ and solve:

$$1 - \frac{64}{x^3} = 0$$

$$1 = \frac{64}{x^3}$$

$$x^3 = 64$$

$$x = 4 \qquad \text{is the only critical number}$$

Next, $f''(x) = 192x^{-4}$, so $f''(4) = \frac{192}{256} > 0$, and f has a relative minimum when $x = 4$. Since 4 is the only critical number, $f(4) = 6$ is the minimum value of f. Since there are no endpoints and no other critical number, f does not have a maximum value.

EXAMPLE 8 *(Compare Exercise 35)*

The Ace Trucking Company has data indicating that on a 300-mile trip, the cost of operating a truck that averages V miles per hour is $0.40 + (V/80)$ dollars per mile. The company pays its drivers $20 per hour. To minimize the total cost, which includes both labor and operating costs, at what speed should the trucks travel?

SOLUTION   The time spent traveling is $(300/V)$ hours, so the labor cost (in dollars) to the company is

$$(20)\left(\frac{300}{V}\right) = \frac{6000}{V}$$

The mileage cost (in dollars) of operating the truck is

$$300\left(0.40 + \frac{V}{80}\right) = 120 + \frac{300V}{80}$$

The total cost in dollars in terms of V is the sum of these two costs:

$$C(V) = \frac{6000}{V} + 120 + \frac{300V}{80}$$

and the domain is all $V > 0$. (We will rule out excessive speeds later, if necessary.) Note that we *cannot* use the candidate test to solve this problem because the domain is not of the form $[a, b]$.

$$C'(V) = -\frac{6000}{V^2} + \frac{300}{80} = -\frac{6000}{V^2} + \frac{15}{4}$$

$C'(V)$ exists for all V in the domain of C. To find the critical numbers, set

$$-\frac{6000}{V^2} + \frac{15}{4} = 0$$

and solve:

$$\frac{15}{4} = \frac{6000}{V^2}$$
$$V^2 = 1600$$

$V = \pm 40$; reject $V = -40$ because the domain requires $V > 0$. There is only one critical number: $V = 40$.

$$C''(V) = \frac{12000}{V^3} \qquad \text{so} \qquad C''(40) = \frac{12000}{(40)^3} > 0$$

$C''(40)$ is positive, so C has a relative minimum when $V = 40$. The cost is a relative minimum at 40 mph, and there is only one critical number, so the cost is minimized if the trucks average 40 mph.

11–5 EXERCISES

I

In Exercises 1 through 4, use the candidates test to find the maximum and minimum values of f on the given interval.

1. (*See Example 1*)
   $f(x) = x^2 - 4x + 1, -3 \le x \le 3$
2. $f(x) = x^2 + 2x - 3, -2 \le x \le 2$
3. $f(x) = -3x^2 + 6x - 5, -2 \le x \le 3$
4. $f(x) = -2x^2 + 8x + 3, -4 \le x \le 5$

In Exercises 5 through 8, find the minimum value of f on the given interval.

5. (*See Example 7*)
   $f(x) = x + \dfrac{9}{x}$, for $x > 0$
6. $f(x) = x + \dfrac{4}{x^2}$, for $x > 0$
7. $f(x) = 2x^2 + \dfrac{32}{x}$, for $x > 0$
8. $f(x) = x^2 + \dfrac{2}{x}$, for $x > 0$

II

In Exercises 9 through 14, find the maximum and minimum values of f on the given interval.

9. $f(x) = x^2 - 8x + 2$, $-2 \leq x \leq 3$

10. $f(x) = x^2 + 6x - 2$, $-1 \leq x \leq 4$

11. (*See Example 2*)
    $f(x) = x^3 - 6x^2 + 9x - 4$, $-1 \leq x \leq 2$

12. $f(x) = 4x^3 + 6x^2 - 24x + 5$, $-3 \leq x \leq 3$

13. (*See Example 6*)
    $f(x) = 6 + 24x + 3x^2 - x^3$, $0 \leq x \leq 5$

14. $f(x) = 2 + 21x + 9x^2 - x^3$, $-2 \leq x \leq 4$

In Exercises 15 through 20, find the maximum value of f on the indicated interval.

15. $f(x) = \dfrac{8}{2 + x^2}$, $-\infty < x < \infty$

16. $f(x) = \dfrac{6}{3 + x^2}$, $-\infty < x < \infty$

17. $f(x) = 3x + \dfrac{12}{x}$, for $x < 0$

18. $f(x) = -x^2 - \dfrac{16}{x}$, for $x > 0$

19. $f(x) = 1 - x^{2/3}$, $-\infty < x < \infty$

20. $f(x) = 7 - 6x^{2/3}$, $-\infty < x < \infty$

III

In Exercises 21 through 26, find maximum and minimum values of f on the given interval.

21. (*See Example 3*)
    $f(x) = (x^2 - 9)^{1/3}$, $-1 \leq x \leq 6$

22. $f(x) = (x^2 - 9)^{1/3}$, $-6 \leq x \leq 1$

23. $f(x) = (x^2 - 9)^{2/3}$, $-1 \leq x \leq 6$

24. $f(x) = (x^2 - 9)^{2/3}$, $-6 \leq x \leq 1$

25. (*See Example 4*)
    $f(x) = x\sqrt{16 - x^2}$, $0 \leq x \leq 4$

26. $f(x) = 2x\sqrt{25 - x^2}$, $0 \leq x \leq 5$

In Exercises 27 through 32, find an extreme value of f on the given interval, and identify whether the value is the maximum or minimum.

27. $f(x) = 4x + \dfrac{100}{x}$, $x > 0$

28. $f(x) = 4x + \dfrac{100}{x}$, $x < 0$

29. $f(x) = \dfrac{x^2 + 1}{x^2 + 4}$, $-\infty < x < \infty$

30. $f(x) = \dfrac{x^2 + 4}{x^2 + 1}$, $-\infty < x < \infty$

31. $f(x) = x - 3x^{1/3}$, for $x > 0$

32. $f(x) = x - 18\sqrt{x}$, for $x > 0$

33. (*See Example 5*) Find the production level that will give a company its maximum revenue if the relation between the price p and production level x is given by

$$p = -\frac{1}{50}x + 30$$

What is the corresponding price?

34. Find the production level that will give a company its maximum revenue if the relation between the price p and production level x is determined by the equation $x^2 + 25p^2 = 7200$.

35. (*See Example 8*) Suppose that the Ace Trucking Company in Example 8 finds that its dollar cost per mile is $0.40 + (V/80)$, no matter how long the trip. What is the most economical speed if the length of the trip is 500 miles (rather than 300 miles)?

36. The Ace Trucking Company in Example 8 finds that the dollar cost per mile for a new truck is $0.45 + (V/80)$. What is the most economical average speed for a new truck?

37. The Newton Trucking Company finds that its cost for operating a truck at V miles per hour is $0.35 + (V/100)$ dollars per mile, and this firm pays its drivers $25 per hour. What is the most economical average speed on a 300-mile trip?

38. What would be the most economical average speed for the Newton Trucking Company in Exercise 37 for a 500-mile trip? For a trip of M miles?

11–6 OPTIMIZATION IN APPLICATIONS

- *Getting Started*
- *A Six-Step Process*

The techniques of Sections 11–1, 11–2, and 11–5 showed you how to find the maximum and minimum values of a function when you already know the function. One of the major difficulties in applying mathematics, however, is the construction of the mathematical function that adequately represents, or models, the real-world problem to be solved. In short, a major difficulty is "getting started." These real world problems go by various names—applications, models, word problems, and even, in an attempt to reduce students' "math anxiety," story problems. Whatever they are called, they are important because life presents us with word problems; one seldom meets a function just sitting around waiting for someone to find its maximum value.

GETTING STARTED

The key to doing these problems is getting your paper dirty. You could get the impression from reading texts or listening to lectures that when the presentation of the solution begins, the writer or lecturer already knows what the answer is. Don't read or listen to the solutions as if they are finished products. Instead, think of a solution as a process; it is the way the problem is being attacked. The final answer is only one part of the solution. You shouldn't expect to know what the answer is before you write anything down. Some students don't give themselves a fair chance to do word problems because they don't view the solution process in a step-by-step manner. We have broken down the solution process into six steps. So that the steps themselves don't become too abstract, we begin by showing them in a concrete setting as we solve the following problem. We will give each general step and then show how it works in this particular problem.

THE SIX-STEP PROCESS

EXAMPLE 1 *(Compare Exercise 1)*

A university wants to build a rectangular patio next to the student union building. As part of its beautification program, the university will transplant some bushes and landscape three sides of the patio with these bushes. The student union building will serve as the fourth side of the rectangle. The university already has enough bushes to allow 800 feet for the three landscaped sides. What is the area of the largest patio the university can build without having to purchase more bushes?

SOLUTION

Step 1. Read through the whole problem. Then go back and find out what quantity the problem is asking you to maximize or minimize. (Be on the look out for question marks or words like "find" or "determine.") Write down what it is you are trying to find.

There are a lot of words in this problem (on purpose—we want to show you how to pick out essentials and how to effectively ignore the nonessentials). The question mark follows the last sentence. The question is "What is the area of the largest patio . . . ?" Therefore the answer will be in the form "The maximum area of the patio is. . . ."

Step 2. Write down a general formula or equation that represents the quantity to be maximized or minimized.

Here the question involves area, so we need some formula involving area. Read the problem again—do we want the area of a circle, a rectangle, a triangle, or what? The patio is to be a rectangle!

Area of rectangle = length × width

(or base × height, or some equivalent statement)

FIGURE 11–42

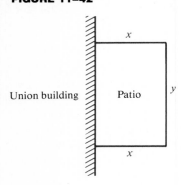

Step 3. Try to draw a picture or a chart representing the data in the problem. Introduce some letters that represent the variables in your formula from Step 2. Make sure the units used in the problem are consistent with each other.

For this problem we draw a rectangle. One side of the rectangle will be a building, so we indicate that in our drawing. Next, we use A to represent the area of the rectangle, x to represent the width of the rectangle, and y for the length. The unit of measurement in the problem was feet, so x and y are in feet. All units are feet or square feet. We now have $A = x \cdot y$, and we want to find the largest value of A. See Figure 11–42.

Step 4. Use information from the problem to express the quantity that you're looking for in terms of only one variable. (If you do this, you have then framed the problem in such a way that you can use the techniques developed earlier in this chapter to solve the problem.)

Here, we know that we have 800 feet of bushes to put around the three sides labeled x, y, and x. Thus $2x + y = 800$. We use this relation to solve for y: $y = 800 - 2x$. Next, we substitute this expression for y into our formula from Step 3:

$$A = x \cdot y = x(800 - 2x)$$
$$= 800x - 2x^2$$

We have a rule that expresses A in terms of x. Now we need the domain of the function. Because x represents width, we must have $x \geq 0$. Similarly, $y \geq 0$. Using $y = 800 - 2x$, we must have $800 - 2x \geq 0$ or $400 \geq x$. Thus the domain of the function is $0 \leq x \leq 400$.

Now we have completely determined a function of one variable, and we wish to maximize that function.

Step 5. Use calculus to maximize or minimize (whichever you're after) the function from Step 4.

Here, $A(x) = 800x - 2x^2$, so $A'(x)$ exists for all x, and $A'(x) = 800 - 4x$. Set

$$A'(x) = 800 - 4x = 0$$

and solve:

$$4x = 800$$
$$x = 200 \qquad \text{is the only critical number}$$

Because the domain of A is the closed and bounded interval $[0, 400]$, we can use the candidates test. Evaluating $A(x)$ at the endpoints, we have

$$A(0) = 0 \qquad \text{and} \qquad A(400) = 0$$

Evaluating $A(x)$ at the critical number, we have

$$A(200) = 800 \cdot 200 - 2(200)^2$$
$$= 160,000 - 80,000 = 80,000$$

Thus the maximum value of A occurs when $x = 200$.

Step 6. Answer the question. Use correct units. Ask yourself "Is my answer reasonable?"

The question does not ask for the dimensions of the patio; it asks for the area of the patio.

$$A(200) = 80,000$$

Answer: The maximum area of the patio is 80,000 sq ft.

We will go through this six-step process more briskly in the next example.

EXAMPLE 2 *(Compare Exercise 5)*

An apartment complex has 120 units. The manager can rent all 120 units if the rent is $280 per month. Some preliminary data indicate that for every $20 increase in the monthly rent, five units will become vacant. What rent should the manager charge to achieve the greatest revenue?

SOLUTION

Step 1. We want to maximize revenue.

Step 2. Revenue = (number of units rented) · (rent per apartment)

Step 3. Let R = revenue, x = number of units rented, and p = rental price per unit. All the units in the problem are dollars and dollars per month, so the units match. It is hard to draw a meaningful picture for this problem, but here is a table showing some data:

x	120	115	110
p	280	300	320

$R = x \cdot p$

Step 4. The problem states that if $\Delta p = 20$, then $\Delta x = -5$. Thus

$$\frac{\Delta p}{\Delta x} = \frac{20}{-5} = -4$$

is a constant; x and p are linearly related. If we treat p as a linear function of x, then the slope of the graph is -4. The problem also states that if $x = 120$, then $p = 280$. We use the point-slope equation of the line and then solve for p:

$$p - 280 = -4(x - 120)$$
$$p - 280 = -4x + 480$$
$$p = -4x + 760$$

(See the remark immediately following this example.)

$$R = x \cdot p \qquad \text{now becomes} \qquad R = x(-4x + 760)$$
$$= -4x^2 + 760x$$

x is the number of units rented, so $0 \le x \le 120$.

Step 5. Maximize $R = -4x^2 + 760x$, $0 \le x \le 120$. R is differentiable for all x in $(0, 120)$, and

$$R'(x) = -8x + 760$$

Set

$$-8x + 760 = 0$$

and solve:

$$-8x = -760$$
$$x = 95$$

The only critical value is $x = 95$.

Because there is only one critical number, we can use the second derivative test. $R''(x) = -8$, so $R''(95) = -8 < 0$. Thus $x = 95$ gives a relative maximum value to R. Since $x = 95$ is the only critical point, $x = 95$ gives the maximum value to R.

Step 6. The problem asked for the value of p that maximizes R; we have found the value of x that maximizes R. In Step 4 we found that

$$p = -4x + 760$$

so when $x = 95$,

$$p = -4(95) + 760 = -380 + 760 = 380$$

Answer: Profit will be maximized when the manager charges \$380 per month.

We would like to make some remarks about Step 4. You don't need to do this step exactly as we did. For instance, you could use two points from the chart and write

$$\frac{p - 280}{x - 120} = \frac{300 - 280}{115 - 120} = \frac{20}{-5} = -4$$

Then simplify:

$$\frac{p - 280}{x - 120} = -4$$

$$p - 280 = -4(x - 120)$$

$$p = -4x + 760$$

As another instance, you could compute $\dfrac{\Delta x}{\Delta p}$. Just remember to use the same variable on the top in both fractions:

$$\frac{120 - 155}{280 - 300} = \frac{x - 115}{p - 300}$$

$$\frac{-1}{4} = \frac{x - 115}{p - 300}$$

$$-1(p - 300) = 4(x - 115) = 4x - 460$$

$$p = -4x + 760$$

Or you could solve for x in terms of p and write the revenue as a function of p.

You may have noticed that Examples 1 and 2 presented us with the same situation in Step 5. In both cases there is only one critical number, and the domain is of the form $[a, b]$. In Example 1 we used the candidates test, which depends on the form of the interval. In Example 2 we found the maximum by a test that depends on the function having only one critical point. We also could have used the first derivative test in either example. Do not put yourself in a bind by thinking that there is only one correct way to do a problem. In fact, to stress to you that there is more than one correct way to attack a problem, and because so many applied problems are phrased similarly to the problem in Example 2, we would like to show you another way to solve this problem. The key phrase in the statement of the problem is "for every $20 increase in the monthly rent, five units will become vacant." This phrase suggests introducing a new variable for the number of such increases. Example 3 uses this solution to the same problem as given in Example 2.

EXAMPLE 3   *(Compare Exercise 5)*

An apartment complex has 120 units. The manager can rent all 120 units if the rent is $280 per month. Some preliminary data indicate that for every $20 increase in the monthly rent, five units will become vacant. What rent should the manager charge to achieve the greatest revenue?

SOLUTION   The first two steps are the same.

Step 1. We want to maximize revenue.

Step 2. Revenue = (number of apartments rented) · (rent per apartment)

Step 3. Let R = revenue, x = number of units rented, p = rental price per unit, and n = number of $20 increases in rent; n is the new variable.

	x	*p*
$n = 0$	120	280
$n = 1$	115	300
$n = 2$	110	320
⋮	⋮	⋮
$n = n$	$120 - 5n$	$280 + 20n$

Step 4. Because of the additional work done in Step 3, Step 4 is now easier; the one variable that we use is n:

$$R = (120 - 5n)(280 + 20n)$$
$$= 33{,}600 + 1000n - 100n^2$$

Since we must have $x \geq 0$, we also must have $120 - 5n \geq 0$, or $n \leq 24$.

Step 5. Maximize $R(n) = 33{,}600 + 1000n - 100n^2$, $0 \leq n \leq 24$. R is differentiable for all n and $R'(n) = 1000 - 200n$. Thus $R'(n) = 0$ when $n = 5$. For the sake of variety, instead of the one-critical-number-test that we used in Example 2, we use the candidates test:

$$R(0) = (120)(280) = 33{,}600$$
$$R(5) = (95)(380) = 36{,}100$$
$$R(24) = (0)(760) = 0$$

Thus $n = 5$ gives maximum revenue.

Step 6. $p = 280 + 20n$, so $p = 380$ when $n = 5$.

Answer. The profit will be maximized when the manager charges $380 per month.

EXAMPLE 4 *(Compare Exercise 11)*

The design department of a certain company has devised a new company logo.
The new logo has essentially a square shape, so the company will have to design
new boxes with a square front. The volume of the box must be 108 cubic inches.
Also, the boxes must have a bottom that is better made than the sides and top.
The bottom costs 10¢ per square inch, whereas the top and sides cost only 2¢ per
square inch. What are the dimensions of the box that minimize its cost?

SOLUTION

    Step 1. We want to minimize the cost of the box.

    Step 2. Volume of box = (length)(height)(depth); cost of a side = (cost
per square inch)(area in square inches); total cost = (cost of top) + (cost of
bottom) + (cost of four sides).

    Step 3. Draw a picture of a box. Let x = the length of the box, y = its
height, and z = its depth. See Figure 11–43. All the cost units are cents per
square inch, and all length units are inches, so the units match.

FIGURE 11–43

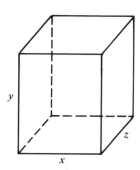

    Step 4. We need a cost function.

    The top and bottom of the box are the same size; they are x inches by z
inches. The cost of the top is $2xz$ cents. The cost of the bottom is $10xz$ cents. The
total cost of the top and bottom is $10xz + 2xz = 12xz$ cents.

    The front and back of the box are both x inches by y inches; each costs $2xy$
cents. The total cost for the front and back is $2xy + 2xy = 4xy$ cents.

    The other two sides of the box are both y inches by z inches; each costs $2yz$
cents. The total cost for these two sides is $4yz$ cents.

    Our first expression for the cost is

$$C = 12xz + 4xy + 4yz$$

    Next, we need to use some information in this particular problem to write
C as a function of one variable. The box must have a square front, so $x = y$. Now
we can eliminate y and write $C = 12xz + 4xx + 4xz = 16xz + 4x^2$.

    We have used one piece of information (a square front) to eliminate one
variable. But we still have C expressed in terms of x and z. We must use another
piece of information to solve for one of these variables in terms of the other. The
volume must be 108, so $xyz = 108$. Since $x = y$, we can write

$$xxz = 108$$
$$x^2z = 108$$

or

$$z = \frac{108}{x^2}$$

Now we can write C as a function of x:

$$C(x) = 16x\left(\frac{108}{x^2}\right) + 4x^2 = \frac{1728}{x} + 4x^2$$

The domain of C is all $x > 0$.

Step 5. Minimize C:

$$C'(x) = \frac{-1728}{x^2} + 8x$$

So $C'(x)$ exists for all $x > 0$. To find the critical numbers, set $C'(x) = 0$ and solve:

$$\frac{-1728}{x^2} + 8x = 0$$
$$-1728 + 8x^3 = 0$$
$$8x^3 = 1728$$
$$x^3 = 216$$
$$x = 6$$

We only have one critical number, and we use the second derivative test at $x = 6$. Note that we cannot use the candidates test.

$$C''(x) = \frac{3456}{x^3} + 8$$

so

$$C''(6) = \frac{3456}{216} + 8 > 0$$

C has a relative minimum at $x = 6$. Furthermore, C is continuous for $x > 0$ with only one critical number, which gives a relative minimum. Therefore the minimum of C occurs when $x = 6$.

Step 6. The problem asks for the dimensions of the least expensive box: $y = x$, so the sides are 6 inches by 6 inches.

$$z = \frac{108}{x^2} = \frac{108}{36} = 3$$

The depth of the box is 3 inches.

Answer. The front of the box is a 6-inch by 6-inch square; the depth of the box is 3 inches.

11-6 EXERCISES

1. (*See Example 1*) A farmer wishes to enclose a rectangular field with a fence. One side of the field is bounded by a straight river; this side of the field does not require fencing. What is the maximum area that the farmer can enclose with 4000 feet of fencing?

2. A rancher wishes to construct a pen to keep his pigs and chickens. The pen will be in the shape of a rectangle with a dividing fence down the middle parallel to one of the sides. What is the maximum total area that the rancher can enclose with 600 feet of fencing?

FIGURE 11–44

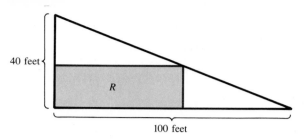

40 feet

R

100 feet

3. Find the dimensions of the rectangle R with the largest area that can be put inside a right triangle as in Figure 11–44. The legs of the triangle are 100 feet and 40 feet.

4. A rectangle must enclose 400 square inches. What are the dimensions of the rectangle that minimize its perimeter?

5. (*See Examples 2 and 3*) An airline company charges $400 regular one-way fare between New York and London in May. Its jumbo jets, with a capacity of 380 passengers, fly with an average of 300 passengers. It has been estimated that each $20 fare reduction attracts ten more passengers. What fare should be charged to maximize revenue?

6. An orange grove is being planted. The aim is to plant the number of trees that will yield the maximum number of oranges per acre. As the number of trees per acre increases, the average yield per tree decreases. Existing statistics for the area imply that a grove with 30 trees per acre will yield, on the average, 400 oranges per tree. The yield per tree will be reduced by approximately ten oranges for every additional tree per acre. Find the number of trees per acre that should be planted to give a maximum total yield per acre.

7. A restaurant is presently selling its special hamburger plate for $3.20. The restaurant sells 240 plates per day. For every 20¢ decrease in price, the restaurant can sell 30 more plates. What price should the restaurant charge to maximize its revenue?

8. A video rental store is now charging $3 per night to rent a movie and is renting 100 movies per night. The manager believes that for every decrease of 10¢ in the rental price, the store will rent five more movies. What rental price should the store charge to maximize its revenue?

9. A motel has 40 units and can rent every unit at the rate of $50 per day. Management knows that for every $5 increase in the daily rate, two fewer units will be rented.
   (a) What should the motel charge per day to maximize revenue?
   (b) What is the maximum revenue?
   (c) If the motel has fixed costs of $1400 per day and cleanup costs are an additional $10 per rented unit, what should the motel charge per day to maximize profit?
   (d) What is the motel's maximum profit?

10. A daily newspaper is currently charging subscribers $16 per month and has 42,000 subscribers. For every $1 increase in the monthly price, the paper will lose 3000 subscribers.
   (a) What should the newspaper charge per month to maximize its revenue?
   (b) What is the newspaper's maximum revenue?
   (c) The monthly fixed costs for publishing the newspaper are $400,000; also each paper costs $6 per month to print. How much should the newspaper charge to maximize profit?
   (d) What is the company's profit when it maximizes revenue?
   (e) What is the company's maximum profit?

11. (*See Example 4*) A closed box must have a volume of 9000 cubic inches. The bottom of the box will be twice as wide as it is long. Find the dimensions that will minimize the surface area of such a box.

12. An open box is to be made from a square piece of cardboard that is 12 inches on the side. Four equal squares will be cut from each corner of the cardboard, and then the sides will be folded up to form the box. What is the volume of the largest box that can be made in this way?

13. A company wants to install machinery that will occupy 1600 square feet of floor space. The machinery is to be arranged in a rectangle. Furthermore, there must be a 1-foot margin of free space on all four sides of the machinery. The company wants to use the least amount of floor space possible. What dimensions will require the least amount of floor space?

14. A man wishes to enclose 1000 square feet with fencing. He wants the enclosed area to be in the shape of a rectangle. The fencing along the side of the rectangle that faces the street will cost $4 per foot, and the fencing on the other three sides costs $1 per foot. What are the dimensions of the rectangle that minimize the man's total cost?

FIGURE 11–45

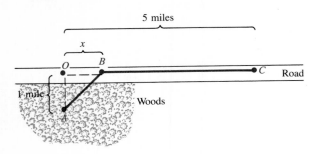

FIGURE 11–46

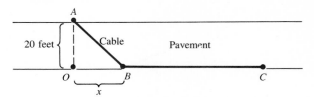

15. Susan's truck ran out of gasoline when she was in the woods. She can walk through the woods at 2 miles per hour, and once she gets to the road she can walk along the road at 4 miles per hour. Her path is from A to B to C as indicated in the sketch in Figure 11–45. The distance from A to 0 is 1 mile, the distance from 0 to C is 5 miles, and the distance from 0 to B is x miles. What value of x minimizes Susan's total time to get to the gasoline station? (Time $= \frac{\text{distance}}{\text{rate}}$ when rate is constant.)

16. A box is going to be built that must be 18 cubic feet. The bottom of the box will be a square and will cost 31¢ per square foot. The sides and top of the box will cost 6¢ per square foot. What are the dimensions of the most economical box?

17. An open box must have a volume of 640 cubic inches and a height of 10 inches. What are the dimensions of the box that minimize its surface area?

18. A cable connecting two switching stations, labeled A and C, is to be laid underground (see Figure 11–46). It costs $6 per foot to lay the cable under the pavement and $2 per foot to lay the cable from B to C. If the pavement is 20 feet wide and the distance from 0 to C is 100 feet, what value of x will minimize the total cost of the project?

19. The Mathematics Department uses 1000 boxes of chalk per year. The department finds that when it orders x boxes at a time, its total cost for purchasing and storage is 50¢ per box. The department has an additional fixed cost of $20 each time it places an order. How many boxes should the department order at a time to minimize its costs?

20. Suppose the department in Exercise 19 now finds that its costs for purchasing and storage are 40¢ per box but the fixed cost per order has increased to $36. Now what should be the size of the department's order?

11–7   APPLICATIONS TO BUSINESS AND ECONOMICS

- *Relation Between Average Cost and Marginal Cost*
- *Marginal Analysis of Profit*
- *Marginal Analysis and Changes in Cost*

In this section we introduce some general principles of economics and show how they may be justified by the use of calculus.

FIGURE 11–47

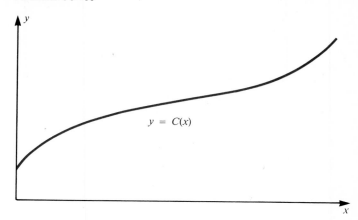

$y = C(x)$

RELATION BETWEEN AVERAGE COST AND MARGINAL COST

We saw in Section 11–2 that some cost functions are best modeled by a curve whose shape is shown in Figure 11–47.

Such a curve shows that, while costs increase with increased production, for small levels of production the cost curve is concave down; the marginal cost is decreasing because of efficiency. There is a point where the concavity of the graph changes, and the cost curve becomes concave up, reflecting the lack of efficiency. The marginal cost is increasing; more and more effort, and hence money, is needed to increase production. Such a cost curve is usually modeled by a third-degree polynomial. (This is why many of the cost functions that we use in this text are cubics.) That means that the marginal cost curve is a quadratic—it is the derivative of a cubic; $MC = C'$. The graph of the marginal cost then is a parabola. Since the marginal cost decreases and then increases, the parabola must open up. A typical marginal cost function is drawn in Figure 11–48.

FIGURE 11–48

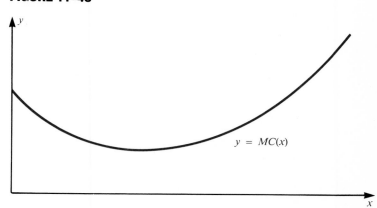

$y = MC(x)$

FIGURE 11-49

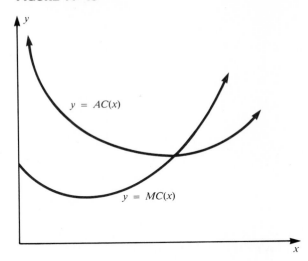

Now we look at the general shape of a typical average-cost function AC, where

$$AC(x) = \frac{C(x)}{x}$$

The average-cost function has the line $x = 0$ as a vertical asymptote (the average cost is very large when x is close to 0). Furthermore, because $C(x)$ is a cubic, for large x the average-cost function looks very much like a parabola. We now draw the average cost curve, AC, into Figure 11–48; we get Figure 11–49.

The figure is drawn so that it looks as if the two graphs cross where the average cost turns around. We look at a specific example.

EXAMPLE 1   *(Compare Exercise 1)*

A firm has modeled its cost C at different levels of production x by

$$C(x) = \frac{1}{2}x^3 - 8x^2 + 50x + 200 \qquad \text{for} \qquad x \geq 0$$

Find the production level that gives the smallest average cost, and compare $MC(x)$ and $AC(x)$ at that level.

SOLUTION

$$AC(x) = \frac{C(x)}{x}$$

$$= \frac{1}{2}x^2 - 8x + 50 + \frac{200}{x} \qquad \text{for} \qquad x > 0$$

To minimize AC, we first find $(AC)'$:

$$(AC)'(x) = x - 8 - \frac{200}{x^2}$$

$(AC)'(x)$ exists for all $x > 0$, so the only critical numbers for AC are where $(AC)'(x) = 0$. Set

$$x - 8 - \frac{200}{x^2} = 0$$

$$x^3 - 8x^2 - 200 = 0$$

This factors. (Don't panic! You will be given the factors when you need them in the exercises.)

$$x^3 - 8x^2 - 200 = (x - 10)(x^2 + 2x + 20)$$

Use of the quadratic formula shows that $x^2 + 2x + 20 = 0$ does not have any real solutions. Hence the only critical number for AC is $x = 10$:

$$AC(10) = \frac{1}{2}(10)^2 - 8(10) + 50 + \frac{200}{10} = 40$$

Now we compute $MC(10)$:

$$MC(x) = C'(x) = \frac{3}{2}x^2 - 16x + 50$$

and so

$$MC(10) = \frac{3}{2}(10)^2 - 16(10) + 50 = 40$$

Thus $AC(10) = MC(10)$. Figure 11–49 was accurate in this case. ∎

In fact, Figure 11–49 represents a general law of economics.

A Law of Economics   The marginal-cost curve cuts the average-cost curve at the lowest point of the average-cost curve.

Said another way,

Theorem   When AC is minimized, $MC(x) = AC(x)$.

To see why this theorem is true, we start with

$$AC(x) = \frac{C(x)}{x}$$

Next, look at the derivative of both sides, using the quotient rule on the right:

$$(AC)'(x) = \frac{x \cdot C'(x) - C(x) \cdot 1}{x^2}$$

$$= \frac{x \cdot C'(x) - C(x)}{x^2}$$

When AC has its minimum value, $(AC)'(x) = 0$. If $(AC)'(x) = 0$, then the numerator of $(AC)'(x) = 0$, so

$$x \cdot C'(x) - C(x) = 0$$
$$x \cdot C'(x) = C(x)$$

or, since $x \neq 0$,

$$C'(x) = \frac{C(x)}{x}$$

Because $C'(x) = MC(x)$ and $\dfrac{C(x)}{x} = AC(x)$, we have

$$MC(x) = AC(x)$$

Under the assumption that the cost curve has the general shape shown in Figure 11–47, AC has only one critical number. That critical number gives the minimum of AC and satisfies the equation $MC(x) = AC(x)$.

MARGINAL ANALYSIS OF PROFIT

Again, we refer to the typical curve used to describe cost as given in Figure 11–47. Because revenue is frequently the product of two numbers, (units sold) times (price per unit), the curve used to model revenue is frequently a piece of a parabola as shown in Figure 11–50.

FIGURE 11–50

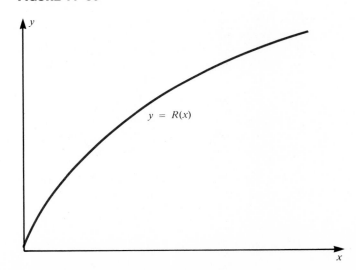

$y = R(x)$

FIGURE 11-51

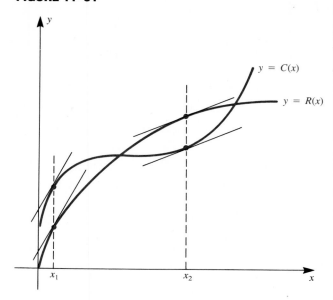

We now draw these two curves simultaneously; see Figure 11–51.

Notice the distinctive geometric feature that occurs at x_1 and x_2; the tangent lines to the two curves are parallel. Two lines are parallel if they have the same slope, and the slope of the tangent line is the derivative. Thus we must have $R'(x_1) = C'(x_1)$ and $R'(x_2) = C'(x_2)$.

The quantity $R(x) - C(x)$ is the profit, $P(x)$. (For some x, $C(x) > R(x)$, and the profit is negative; a negative profit is the same thing as a loss.) To find the maximum profit, you first find the critical numbers for P:

$$P(x) = R(x) - C(x)$$

so

$$P'(x) = R'(x) - C'(x)$$

The marginal profit equals the marginal revenue minus the marginal cost; $MP = MR - MC$. The critical numbers for P are where $P'(x) = 0$, but $P'(x) = 0$ precisely when $R'(x) = C'(x)$. Thus the maximum profit occurs when $MR(x) = MC(x)$.

Law of Economics   When the maximum profit occurs the marginal cost and the marginal revenue are equal.

In other words,

Theorem   When P has its maximum value, $MR(x) = MC(x)$.

Unfortunately, the minimum profit (that is, the maximum loss) also occurs when $MR = MC$. Figure 11–51 shows that $MR = MC$ at both x_1 and x_2. But with curves of this general shape, $P(x_1)$ is negative while $P(x_2)$ is positive. This leads to the following statement, often given as a general rule for optimizing profit: *To maximize profit, select the largest output at which marginal revenue equals marginal cost.* We do not present this statement as a law because it is not true for all cost and revenue functions. It is true under the general assumptions that led to Figure 11–51.

CAUTION Of course, to avoid an error in any particular case, you must either verify that the case satisfies these general assumptions or use the techniques for finding maxima developed earlier in this chapter.

The following example is typical.

EXAMPLE 2   *(Compare Exercise 5)*

A company produces x units of a certain product per day. The company models its daily cost by

$$C(x) = \frac{1}{150}x^3 - 3x^2 + 525x + 6000$$

The daily revenue function the company uses is given by

$$R(x) = -x^2 + 453x$$

Find the production level that maximizes the daily profit.

SOLUTION

$$MC(x) = \frac{1}{50}x^2 - 6x + 525$$

$$MR(x) = -2x + 453$$

Set

$$MC(x) = MR(x)$$

and solve:

$$\frac{1}{50}x^2 - 6x + 525 = -2x + 453$$

$$\frac{1}{50}x^2 - 4x + 72 = 0$$

Using the quadratic formula and a calculator, we get

$$x = \frac{-b \pm \sqrt{b^2 - 4ac}}{2a} = \frac{4 \pm \sqrt{16 - (288/50)}}{2(1/50)} = \frac{4 \pm 3.2}{1/25}$$

$$= 25[4 \pm 3.2] = 100 \pm 80 = 20 \text{ and } 180$$

Selecting the larger value of x tells us that the production level that maximizes profit for the company should be 180 units per day. We can check this conclusion by evaluating $P(x)$. We find that $P(20) = -6693\frac{1}{3}$ and $P(180) = 6960$. The company should indeed choose the production level of 180 units per day. ∎

Economists classify markets into various types. A **perfectly competitive market** is one in which there are many companies producing the same product. (For discussions of the other types of markets we refer you to a book such as Edwin Mansfield, *Economics, Principles, Problems and Decisions*, W. W. Norton and Company, 1977.) The price of the product is some constant determined by the open competitive market. No one buyer or seller is able to influence the price of the product. For example, products such as paper towels, nails, dishwashing detergent, refrigerators, and washing machines fall into this type of market.

Let p be the price of the product as determined by the open market. The revenue obtained from producing x items is $p \cdot x$. In this market the revenue function is given by

$$R(x) = p \cdot x \qquad \text{where } p \text{ is a constant}$$

With p a constant, the marginal revenue is

$$R'(x) = p$$

The optimum output in such a market is then ordinarily given by the largest value of x that satisfies

$$C'(x) = p$$

The following example illustrates this situation.

EXAMPLE 3 *(Compare Exercise 9)*

A company is manufacturing and selling refrigerators in a perfectly competitive market in which the price of a refrigerator is $600. The company is currently manufacturing 270 refrigerators per day. A management consulting firm has been given the task of determining whether an increase or a decrease in production would lead to increased profits. The firm has determined the cost function to be given by

$$C(x) = \frac{x^3}{120} - 4x^2 + 880x + 4250$$

where x is the number of refrigerators produced per day. What should the consulting firm recommend?

SOLUTION The marginal cost is

$$C'(x) = \frac{x^2}{40} - 8x + 880$$

The market price is $p = 600$.

The optimum output will satisfy the equation

$$C'(x) = p$$

$$\frac{x^2}{40} - 8x + 880 = 600$$

$$\frac{x^2}{40} - 8x + 280 = 0$$

Solving for x by using the quadratic formula, we have

$$x = \frac{-b \pm \sqrt{b^2 - 4ac}}{2a} = \frac{8 \pm \sqrt{(-8)^2 - 4(1/40)(280)}}{2(1/40)}$$

$$= \frac{8 \pm 6}{(1/20)} = 20[8 \pm 6] = 280 \quad \text{or} \quad 40$$

Selecting the larger number, we see that the optimum output should be 280 refrigerators per day. The management consulting firm should recommend that the company increase output from the present 270 refrigerators per day to 280 refrigerators per day.

_____∎

MARGINAL ANALYSIS AND CHANGES IN COST

How should a company react when its costs increase? There are two entirely different situations.

Case 1: Changes That Affect Fixed Cost. A company may find that the taxes on its property have increased or that a new labor contract will increase its fixed labor cost. Can the company pass any of these increased costs on to the consumer? *All other things being equal,* the surprising answer is *NO!* We have just seen that the optimum production strategy for a company is determined by analysis of its marginal revenue and marginal cost. The fixed cost is the constant term in the cost function. When you take the derivative of the cost function, the derivative of the fixed cost is 0. *Fixed cost does not affect the marginal cost function.* The solutions to $MR(x) = MC(x)$ are not affected by a change in fixed cost. Profits will be lowered, but the company's optimum production strategy does not change.

Of course, one of the things that makes economics so difficult is that "all other things being equal" never happens. The price-demand curve, and hence the formula for $R(x)$, will probably change because of inflation and other factors. The company may even decide to increase its advertising, thereby increasing the demand (it hopes), which in turn will allow the company to increase prices.

Case 2: Changes That Affect Variable Cost. Various plans for special taxes on gasoline have been proposed, and they continue to be debated. Generally, the proposals have two aims in mind: first, to collect more money for the government; second, to drive up the price of gasoline, thereby reducing the demand and so reducing the amount of oil that the United States imports. The tax levied on the producer in the form of a fixed amount per item produced is called an **excise tax.** We have seen that taxes affecting the fixed cost of a company do not affect production strategy. How does an excise tax, which increases the variable cost per item, affect optimum production strategy (*all other things being equal*)? Such a tax affects the whole industry. Our functions, or models, should not be the same in this situation as the ones we use for one small producer in a perfectly competitive market. Since the whole industry is affected, we treat the industry as if it were just one producer—a situation called a **monopoly.**

EXAMPLE 4   (*Compare Exercise 13*)

A company's revenue function is given by

$$R(x) = -\frac{1}{50}x^2 + 19x$$

and its cost function by

$$C(x) = 11x + 100$$

Determine the optimal output and the maximum profit.

EXAMPLE 5

If fixed costs increase from 100 to 120, what should the company's new production strategy be, and what will be its new profit?

EXAMPLE 6   (*Compare Exercise 13*)

If a tax of 2 per unit is imposed, what should the company's new production strategy be, and what will be its new profit?

SOLUTION TO EXAMPLE 4

$$MR(x) = R'(x) = -\frac{1}{25}x + 19$$
$$MC(x) = C'(x) = 11$$

Set $MR(x) = MC(x)$ and solve:

$$-\frac{1}{25}x + 19 = 11$$

$$-\frac{1}{25}x = -8$$

$$x = 200 \qquad \text{is the best production level}$$

$$P(200) = R(200) - C(200)$$

$$= -\frac{1}{50}(200)^2 + 19(200) - [11(200) + 100] = 700$$

The maximum profit is 700.

SOLUTION TO EXAMPLE 5   The new cost function is given by $C(x) = 11x + 120$. But $MC(x)$ still equals 11, and $MR(x)$ is also unaffected. The equation $MR(x) = MC(x)$ is still

$$-\frac{1}{25}x + 19 = 11$$

with solution

$$x = 200$$

The best production level for the company remains $x = 200$. Now $P(200) = 680$. The profit is lowered by the amount of the increase in the fixed cost, but the optimum production strategy is unchanged.

SOLUTION TO EXAMPLE 6 MR is still the same; $MR(x) = -\frac{1}{25}x + 19$. MC has been increased; $MC(x) = 13$. Solving $-\frac{1}{25}x + 19 = 13$, we get $x = 150$. The optimum production strategy is now $x = 150$, and the company should cut back on production. The new profit is

$$P(150) = -\frac{1}{50}(150)^2 + 19(150) - [13(150) + 100]$$

$$= 350$$

In Example 6, production must be cut back, and the profit will be reduced. If the production level was kept at $x = 200$, however, the new profit would be $P(200) = 300$. Staying with the old strategy would yield even less profit.

The last three examples dealt with the changes in production that an industry should make (or not make) in response to increased costs. As consumers, we are generally more interested in the pricing strategy of the company rather than its production strategy.

EXAMPLE 7 *(Compare Exercise 15)*

How is the price of the commodity in Examples 5 and 6 affected?
SOLUTION We assumed that

$$R(x) = -\frac{1}{50}x^2 + 19x$$

$$= x\left(-\frac{1}{50}x + 19\right)$$

$$= x \cdot p \qquad \text{where } p \text{ is price}$$

Hence we are assuming that the price is given by

$$p = -\frac{1}{50}x + 19$$

Thus in Example 4, when $x = 200$, the price $p = 15$. The change in fixed cost discussed in Example 5 did not affect the production level, x, and so the price is also unchanged. The change in variable costs in Example 6 caused the best production strategy for the industry to change from 200 to 150. At the new production level of 150 the new price is

$$p = -\frac{1}{50}(150) + 19 = 16 \qquad \text{per unit}$$

The price increased by 1.

Example 7 shows that the best strategy for the company is to pass half of the excise tax on to the consumer but to absorb half of the tax itself. This analysis runs counter to the belief that companies never have to bear the brunt of taxes and that they can always pass any tax on to the consumer. In some cases they may be able to do so, but in some cases they cannot.

11-7 EXERCISES

1. *(See Example 1)* Thompson Motor Company has calculated that the total cost of manufacturing x automobiles per day is

$$C(x) = \frac{x^3}{20} - 15x^2 + 3000x + 25{,}600$$

(a) What is the average-cost function for the company?
(b) Find the production level that minimizes the average cost of each car.
(c) What is that minimum average cost?
(d) Compare the marginal cost at this production level.
[*Hint:* Use $x^3 - 150x^2 - 256{,}000 =$
$(x - 160)(x^2 + 10x + 16{,}000)$]

2. The total cost of producing x units per week is

$$\frac{x^3}{8} - 29x^2 + 4000x + 14{,}400$$

(a) Determine the average-cost function.
(b) How many units per week would minimize the average cost of each item?
(c) Show that this occurs at the production level where average cost is equal to marginal cost.
[*Hint:* Use $x^3 - 116x^2 - 57{,}600 =$
$(x - 120)(x^2 + 4x + 480)$]

3. The total cost of manufacturing x items per day is

$$\frac{x^3}{4} - 49x^2 + 4{,}000x + 10{,}000$$

(a) Compute the average-cost and marginal-cost functions.
(b) Find the daily production that minimizes average cost per item.
(c) Show that when this occurs, the average cost is equal to marginal cost.
[*Hint:* $x^3 - 98x^2 - 20{,}000 = (x - 100)(x^2 + 2x + 200)$]

4. The total cost of manufacturing x units per day is

$$\frac{x^3}{200} - 2x^2 + 1000x + 9680$$

(a) Determine the average-cost and marginal-cost functions.
(b) Find the daily production that minimizes cost per unit.
(c) Show that this occurs when average cost is equal to marginal cost.
[*Hint:* $x^3 - 200x^2 - 968{,}000 = (x - 220)(x^2 + 20x + 4400)$]

5. (*See Example 2*) The cost and revenue functions of a manufacturing company are given by

$$C(x) = \frac{x^3}{180} - 4x^2 + 1000x + 4000$$

and

$$R(x) = -x^2 + 700x$$

Here, x is the number of units produced in one day. Determine the output that leads to maximum profit and also the maximum daily profit.

6. A company is operating with the cost and revenue functions given by

$$C(x) = \frac{x^3}{150} - 4x^2 + 2150x + 2700$$

and

$$R(x) = -x^2 + 1900x$$

Here, x is the number of units produced in one week. Determine the output that leads to the maximum weekly profit and the size of that profit.

7. The cost and revenue functions of a manufacturing company are given by

$$C(x) = \frac{x^3}{180} - 3x^2 + 1305x + 3500$$

and

$$R(x) = -x^2 + 1200x$$

where x is the number of units produced daily. The current daily production is 195 units. Will a change in the production rate lead to an increase in profits?

8. A company that manufactures motorboats is operating with weekly cost and revenue functions given by

$$C(x) = \frac{x^3}{120} - 6x^2 + 2360x + 4500$$

and

$$R(x) = -x^2 + 2000x$$

The current weekly output is 370 boats. Would a change in this output lead to increased profits?

9. (*See Example 3*) A company is manufacturing and selling a certain type of microcomputer for $400 in a perfectly competitive market. Its cost function is given by

$$C(x) = \frac{x^3}{270} - 2x^2 + 600x + 2420$$

where x is the number of computers manufactured in one week. The company is currently manufacturing 325 computers per week. Should it change its production rate?

10. A company manufactures a cooling fan that sells for $125 in a perfectly competitive market. The cost of manufacturing x fans per day is given by

$$C(x) = \frac{x^3}{240} - 4x^2 + 1000x + 3200$$

How many fans per day should be manufactured to realize maximum profit? What will that maximum profit be?

11. A company manufactures television sets in a perfectly competitive market. The price of a television set is $350. The cost for producing x sets per day is

$$C(x) = \frac{x^3}{150} - 3x^2 + 600x + 2750$$

How many sets per day should be manufactured to maximize profits?

12. A company operating in a perfectly competitive market has a daily cost for producing x units given by

$$C(x) = \frac{x^3}{180} - 2x^2 + 600x + 4500$$

The price of a unit, as determined by the market, is $495.
   (a) What should the daily output be to maximize profits?
   (b) What is the maximum daily profit that can be attained?

13. (*See Examples 4 and 6*) The weekly revenue and weekly cost of a manufacturing company are

$$R(x) = -2x^2 + 1620x$$

and

$$C(x) = 18x^2 + 60x + 2000$$

Here, x is the weekly output. A tax of $120 per unit is to be levied.
   (a) Determine the optimal output before the tax is imposed.
   (b) What is the optimal output after the tax has been imposed?

14. The weekly revenue and weekly cost functions of a manufacturing company are given by

$$R(x) = -x^2 + 1400x$$

and

$$C(x) = 14x^2 + 200x + 1000$$

Here, x is weekly output. A tax of $90 per unit is to be imposed.
   (a) Determine the optimal output before the tax is imposed.
   (b) What is the optimal output after the tax is imposed?

15. (*See Example 7*) Use the fact that the price p is given by

$$p = \frac{R(x)}{x}$$

to determine how the company in Exercise 13 will change its pricing strategy.

16. Use

$$p = \frac{R(x)}{x}$$

to determine how the company in Exercise 14 will change its pricing structure.

IMPORTANT TERMS

11-1
Increasing Functions
Decreasing Functions
Maximum Value
Minimum Value
Extreme Value
Relative Maximum Value
Relative Minimum Value
Relative Extreme Values
Critical Number
First Derivative Test

11-2
Concave Up
Concave Down
Second Derivative Test
Point of Inflection

11-3
Vertical Asymptote
Horizontal Asymptote
Limit at Infinity

$\lim\limits_{x \to \infty} f(x)$
Limit at Negative Infinity
$\lim\limits_{x \to -\infty} f(x)$
Infinite Limit
$\lim\limits_{x \to a^+} f(x) = \infty$
$\lim\limits_{x \to a^-} f(x) = \infty$
$\lim\limits_{x \to a^+} f(x) = -\infty$
$\lim\limits_{x \to a^-} f(x) = -\infty$

REVIEW EXERCISES

Find the maximum and minimum of each of the functions given in Exercises 1 through 10. Determine the intervals on which f is increasing. Indicate any points of inflection. Sketch a graph of f.

1. $f(x) = \dfrac{1}{x}, 2 \le x \le 5$

2. $f(x) = \dfrac{1}{x}, -6 \le x \le -\dfrac{1}{2}$

3. $f(x) = x^2 - 4x + 5, 0 \le x \le 5$

4. $f(x) = -2x^2 - 8x + 3, -1 \le x \le 3$

5. $f(x) = x + \dfrac{32}{x^2}, 1 \le x \le 8$

6. $f(x) = 2x + \dfrac{27}{x^2}, 1 \le x \le 6$

7. $f(x) = x^5 - 5x^4 + 2, -1 \le x \le 5$

8. $f(x) = x^4 - 4x^3 + 6, -1 \le x \le 4$

9. $f(x) = x + \sqrt{36 - x^2}, -6 \le x \le 0$

10. $f(x) = x + \sqrt{36 - x^2}, 0 \le x \le 6$

For each of the functions given in Exercises 11 through 18, find the intervals on which f is decreasing. Indicate all asymptotes. Sketch the graph of f, indicating any points of inflection.

11. $f(x) = x\sqrt{36 - x^2}$

12. $f(x) = (x - 8)^{1/3}$

13. $f(x) = \dfrac{1}{x^2 - 1}$

14. $f(x) = \dfrac{x}{x^2 - 1}$

15. $f(x) = \dfrac{x^2}{x^2 - 1}$

16. $f(x) = \dfrac{1}{x^2 + 6}$

17. $f(x) = \dfrac{x^2 - 1}{x - 1}$

18. $f(x) = \dfrac{x^2 - 9}{x + 3}$

19. If the sum of two positive numbers is 16, what is the maximum value of their product?

20. If the product of two positive numbers is 16, what is the minimum value of their sum?

21. (a) What is the minimum value of f if
$$f(x) = \frac{3x}{x^2 + 4}?$$
(b) What is the maximum value of f if
$$f(x) = \frac{3x}{x^2 + 4}?$$

22. A company's cost function for producing x items per day is given by
$$C(x) = \frac{x^2}{100} + 2x + 400$$
What level of production minimizes the average cost per item?

23. A ball is thrown straight up; its height (in feet) after t seconds is given by $h(t) = -16t^2 + 64t + 5$. What is the maximum height the ball reaches?

24. A company's price-supply equation is given by $4x + 3p = 120$. What price should the company charge to maximize its revenue?

25. A company's cost function is given by
$$C(x) = \frac{1}{3}x^3 + x^2 + 15x + 2$$
and its revenue is given by
$$R(x) = 4x^2 + 10x$$
What value of x maximizes the company's profit?

26. A rental company finds that the price it charges per day to rent an automobile is linearly related to the number of cars that it rents. If the company rents 40 cars when it charges $30 and rents 20 cars when it charges $35 per day, what rental fee will maximize the company's revenue?

27. A company manufacturing refrigerators is operating in a perfectly competitive market. The refrigerators are selling for $400, and the company's cost for producing x of these per week is

$$C(x) = \frac{x^3}{300} - x^2 + 436x + 3000$$

How many refrigerators should the company manufacture each week to maximize its profit?

28. A company is currently producing x items per week. Its revenue is given by

$$R(x) = 300x - x^2$$

and its cost is

$$C(x) = \frac{x^2}{10} + 80x + 200$$

What is the company's present optimal production strategy? How should the company change its production level if a new excise tax of 11 per unit is levied?

12
Exponential and Logarithmic Functions

12–1 EXPONENTIAL FUNCTIONS

- *Different Ways of Describing Change*
- *The Effect of Compounding*
- *Continuous Compounding and the Number e*
- *Exponential Functions and Their Graphs*

DIFFERENT WAYS OF DESCRIBING CHANGE

We have seen that the derivative is the mathematical tool used to describe the rate of change of a function. For example, if $A(t)$ is the amount of money an investment is worth t years after the investment is made, $A'(t)$ describes the rate of change of $A(t)$ in dollars per year. Similarly, if $P(t)$ is the population of a country at time t years, then $P'(t)$ describes the rate of change of the population in people per year. In general, if $y = f(x)$, then $f'(x)$ gives the rate of change of y per unit of x.

Often however, changes in the amount of an investment or changes in the population of a country are described not in terms of the actual *amount* of the change, but in terms of the *percentage* of the change. To see the distinction, suppose that two people, A and B, both invest money in an account that pays interest at the rate of 6% per year. Suppose that A invests $1000 and B invests $10,000. Let $A(t)$ be the amount of A's investment after t years, and similarly, let $B(t)$ be the amount of B's investment. After one year, A's investment is worth $1060, while B's is worth $10,600. Although the **percentage change** in the two amounts is the same, the *amount of change* in the two accounts is different. B's account has increased more than A's account; $B'(t) > A'(t)$. People use the word **"interest"** to mean both the actual amount of interest ($600 for B and $60 for A) and the rate of interest (6% for both A and B); you must determine by the context which is meant.

Many other real-world situations lend themselves to talking about change in terms of percentage rates—inflation, population growth, and radioactive decay are but a few. This chapter will develop the mathematical tools needed to deal with these situations. We will encounter new types of functions—ones that are not built by using polynomials or radicals. To show how these functions arise from real-world situations, we begin with a specific discussion about savings accounts.

THE EFFECT OF COMPOUNDING

We develop the theory in an example.

EXAMPLE 1   *(Compare Exercise 1)*

A person deposits $1000 in a savings account that pays an interest rate of 5%, compounded annually. Assuming no deposits or withdrawals, how much money will be in the account after four years?

SOLUTION   The **compounding period,** here one year, tells how often the interest amount is added to the savings account. Here, the account is worth a constant $1000 for a year, and then the bank adds 5% of $1000 (which is $50) to the account. [5% of 1000 = (0.05) · (1000).]

At the beginning of the second year the account is worth 1000 + 50 = 1050 dollars. At the end of the second year the bank adds 5% of $1050 to the account— during the second year the bank pays interest on the interest earned during the first year. This is what is meant by compounding. The interest added to the account at the end of the second year is 5% of $1050 = (0.05)($1050) = $52.50, so at the beginning of the third year the account is worth 1050 + 52.50 = 1102.50 dollars. We could continue in this manner to solve this particular problem, but we are going to want to solve other problems with different beginning investment amounts (here $1000), different interest rates (here 5%), and different compounding periods (here 1 year).

We leave this particular example now by replacing our particular numbers with letters. We hope to see more easily what is happening, and at the same time, to derive a formula for the more general case.

Let P = the beginning investment—the beginning *principal*.

Let r = the annual interest *rate*.

Let n = the *number* of compounding periods.

Let $A(n)$ = the *amount* in the account after n compounding periods.

The amount after one year is

$$A(1) = \underset{\text{principal}}{P} + \underset{+ \text{ interest}}{rP} = P(1 + r)$$

The amount after two years is

$$A(2) = \underset{\text{principal}}{P(1 + r)} + \underset{\text{interest}}{r(P(1 + r))} = P(1 + r)^2$$

The formula $A(2) = P(1 + r)^2$ can be obtained by factoring $P(1 + r)$ from the expression $P(1 + r) + r(P(1 + r)) = P(1 + r)(1 + r) = P(1 + r)^2$. It is easier, and more useful, to avoid this algebra by thinking for a bit about the first formula: $A(1) = P(1 + r)$. This formula says that you find the amount after one year by multiplying the amount you started with by the number $(1 + r)$. Now regard $P(1 + r)$ as the amount at the beginning of the second year; you find how much the account is worth one year from then by multiplying $P(1 + r)$ by the number $(1 + r)$. If you start the year with $P(1 + r)$ dollars, you will have $[P(1 + r)] \cdot (1 + r) = P(1 + r)^2$ when the year is over. Now regard $P(1 + r)^2$ as the beginning amount during the third year; the amount at the end of this year is $P(1 + r)^2$ multiplied by $(1 + r)$, or $P(1 + r)^3$.

$$A(3) = P(1 + r)^3$$

We can continue in this manner, establishing the formula

$$A(n) = P(1 + r)^n$$

Returning to our particular example, the amount after four years is

$$A(4) = 1000(1 + 0.05)^4 = 1000(1.05)^4 = (1000)(1.21551)$$
$$= 1215.51 \quad \text{dollars}$$

What happens for different compounding periods? For example, what if interest was added every six months (semiannually) rather than every year? Specifically, how much will be added after a six-month period if $1000 is invested at a 5% annual rate compounded semiannually? The bank does not pay 5% of the amount after only six months. In fact, what the bank does is pay the proportionate amount; after one half of a year, the bank pays one half of 5%, or $2\frac{1}{2}$%. The amount of interest paid is $2\frac{1}{2}$% of $1000 = (0.025)(1000) = \$25.00$. Remember that n is the number of compounding periods, so after six months, n is 1, and we have

$$A(1) = 1000 + \left(\frac{0.05}{2}\right)(1000) = 1000\left(1 + \frac{0.05}{2}\right)$$
$$= 1025 \quad \text{dollars}$$

We can go through the same argument that we went through in our first example to show that

$$A(2) = 1000\left(1 + \frac{0.05}{2}\right)^2 = 1050.62 \quad \text{dollars}$$

After one year the amount in the account would be $1050.62. After four years the amount would be (remember that there are now eight compounding periods)

$$A(8) = 1000\left(1 + \frac{0.05}{2}\right)^8 = 1218.40 \quad \text{dollars}$$

More frequent compounding has meant that the account is worth more after four years: $1218.40 compared to $1215.51.

If the compounding is done monthly, then the interest rate used in the formula is $\frac{0.05}{12}$. The amount after four years would be

$$A(48) = 1000\left(1 + \frac{0.05}{12}\right)^{48} = 1220.90 \quad \text{dollars}$$

We are now ready to state the general formula.

Compound Interest
Formula

If an initial principal P is invested in an account that pays interest at an annual rate r, compounded m times per year, the amount in the account after n compounding periods will be

Formula I $A(n) = P\left(1 + \dfrac{r}{m}\right)^n$

We can introduce the real variable t (the time expressed in years) in place of n (the number of compounding periods) by noticing that the (number of compounding periods) = (number of compounding periods per year) · (number of years). In symbols,

$$n = m \cdot t$$

We can now express $A(t)$ by the formula

Compound Interest Formula	**Formula II** $A(t) = P\left(1 + \dfrac{r}{m}\right)^{mt}$

CONTINUOUS COMPOUNDING AND THE NUMBER e

Some popular compounding periods are annually ($m = 1$), semiannually ($m = 2$), quarterly ($m = 4$), monthly ($m = 12$), and daily (m usually taken to be 360 or 365). Perhaps you have seen advertisements for "interest compounded continuously." What does that mean? There is no value of m that will give compounding instant by instant. However, we can imagine more frequent compounding than daily; the compounding period could be an hour ($m = 24 \cdot 365 = 8760$), a minute ($m = 8760 \cdot 60 = 525{,}600$), or a second ($m = 31{,}536{,}000$). We would then have to compute numbers of the form $(1 + (r/m))^{mt}$ for very large values of m.

We will avoid these horrendous computations because mathematicians have been able to prove an amazing theorem. Before presenting the general theorem, however, we need to examine a specific example, the case of $r = 1$ and $t = 1$. In other words, we want to look at numbers of the form $(1 + (1/m))^m$.

The following table evaluates the expression $(1 + (1/m))^m$ for various values of m.

m	1	10	100	1000	10,000	100,000
$\left(1 + \dfrac{1}{m}\right)^m$	2	2.59374	2.70481	2.71692	2.71815	2.71827

As m gets larger and larger, the expression $(1 + (1/m))^m$ gets closer and closer to a fixed number whose decimal expansion begins 2.7182818284590. . . . Because this decimal expansion does not repeat, we cannot write this number as a fraction. Like π, this number is irrational, and so we need special notation for this number. The letter that people use for this number is the English letter e. This is similar to using the Greek letter π to denote the number 3.14159265. . . . (This e notation is in honor of a distinguished mathematician, Leonard Euler (1707–1783), who obtained many results concerning this number and whose last name begins with the letter e.)

The number e occurs in so many applications that many calculators have a special button that enables you to compute e^r for various values of r.

The amazing theorem we referred to above follows.

Theorem   No matter what the value of r, as m gets larger and larger, the expression

$$\left(1 + \frac{r}{m}\right)^m$$

gets closer and closer to e^r. Using limit notation, we can write

$$\lim_{m \to \infty} \left(1 + \frac{r}{m}\right)^m = e^r$$

(For $r = 1$, note that $e^1 = e$.)

This theorem allows us to derive the formula to use for continuous compounding. By inserting a new pair of parentheses we can rewrite Formula II as

$$A(t) = P\left[\left(1 + \frac{r}{m}\right)^m\right]^t$$

We get closer and closer to the idea of continuous compounding by using more and more compounding periods, that is, by letting m get larger and larger. When m is a very large number, $(1 + (r/m))^m$ is very close to e^r. Thus when m is very large,

$$P\left[\left(1 + \frac{r}{m}\right)^m\right]^t \qquad \text{is close to} \qquad P[e^r]^t$$

All this lets us now write the formula that we use to model **continuous compounding.**

Formula for Continuous Compounding   If P dollars is invested at an annual interest rate of r, compounded continuously, then after t years the amount A is given by

Formula III $A(t) = P \cdot e^{rt}$

The next example compares the difference between continuous compounding and the annual and semiannual compounding discussed above.

EXAMPLE 2   *(Compare Exercise 17)*

If $1000 is invested at 5%, compounded continuously, how much is the investment worth after four years?

SOLUTION   We let $P = 1000$, $r = 0.05$, and $t = 4$ in Formula III, $A(t) = Pe^{rt}$. Then $A(4) = 1000e^{0.05(4)} = 1000e^{0.2}$. Using a calculator, we find that $e^{0.2} \approx 1.2214$, so $A(4) \approx 1000(1.2214) = 1221.40$ dollars ($\approx$ means approximately equal).

FIGURE 12–1

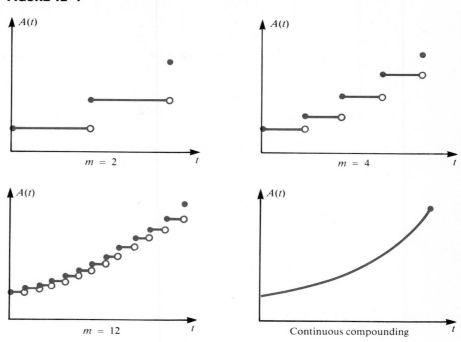

The graphs in Figure 12–1 show the growth of A for $m = 2$, $m = 4$, and $m = 12$ and for continuous compounding. Notice how the first three graphs "approach" the last graph as m gets larger.

Looking again at Formula III, $A(t) = Pe^{rt}$, we see that we have just encountered a new type of function; the variable t is in the **exponent.** Functions with a variable exponent are called exponential functions, and they are used in a wide variety of applications. The discussion so far has shown how one such function arises in a financial application; but before we go on to other applications, we will give you a quick review of exponential functions and their graphs. You might also want to review the material on exponents in Appendix A.

EXPONENTIAL FUNCTIONS AND THEIR GRAPHS

The **exponential functions** that we will look at are those of the form $f(x) = kb^{cx}$, where k and c are any two real numbers and b is a positive number. This is the form in Formula III, with $k = P$, $c = r$, and $b = e$. *The variable x is in the exponent.* The number b is called the **base,** and we require b to be positive so that we don't encounter complex numbers like $(-1)^{1/2} = \sqrt{-1}$.

We begin by letting k and c both equal 1 so that we are looking at functions of the form $f(x) = b^x$. We start with values of b that are more familiar than the number e.

EXAMPLE 3

Let $b = 1$. Graph $y = 1^x$.

SOLUTION The case of $b = 1$ is not very interesting because then $f(x) = 1^x = 1$ for all values of x.

The graph of 1^x is drawn in Figure 12–2.

FIGURE 12–2

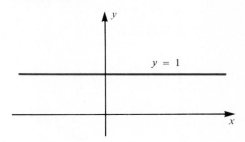

EXAMPLE 4 *(Compare Exercise 37)*

Let $b = 2$. Graph $y = 2^x$.

SOLUTION To see what the graph looks like, we computed the following table of values, plotted those points, and then drew a smooth curve through those points. The result is in Figure 12–3.

x	-5	-4	-3	-2	-1	0	1	2	3	4	5
$f(x) = 2^x$	0.03125	0.0625	0.125	0.25	0.5	1	2	4	8	16	32

FIGURE 12–3

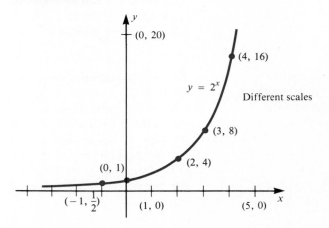

Notice the different scales on the x- and y-axes—the function 2^x grows very rapidly. (*See Exercise 47.*) Also notice that the entire graph lies above the x-axis. For negative values of x the values of 2^x are positive but small. When $x = -10$,

$$f(-10) = 2^{-10} = \frac{1}{2^{10}} \approx 0.00098$$

Our next example is closely related to $y = 2^x$.

EXAMPLE 5

Let $b = \dfrac{1}{2}$. Graph $f(x) = \left(\dfrac{1}{2}\right)^x$.

SOLUTION Again, we construct a table of values.

x	-5	-4	-3	-2	-1	0	1	2	3	4	5
$\left(\dfrac{1}{2}\right)^x$	32	16	8	4	2	1	0.5	0.25	0.125	0.0625	0.03125

The graph is given in Figure 12–4.

FIGURE 12–4

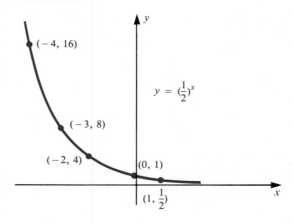

The tables in Examples 4 and 5 are very similar; the ordering is just reversed. The reason for this can be seen by rewriting $\frac{1}{2}$ as 2^{-1}. Then

$$\left(\frac{1}{2}\right)^x = (2^{-1})^x = 2^{-x}$$

Imagine the graph of $y = 2^x$ as a piece of wire that you can rotate around the y-axis (that is, imagine that the graph is like a weather vane that can pivot around the point $(0, 1)$). If you rotate the graph of $y = 2^x$ through a turn of 180 degrees, you get the graph of $y = (\frac{1}{2})^x = 2^{-x}$. The graphs are mirror images of each other.

These two graphs indicate the two general shapes of the graphs of exponential functions. If $f(x) = b^x$, then the graph of f goes through the point $(0, 1)$. If $b > 1$, then f is increasing, and its graph is similar to Figure 12–3. The larger the value of b, the steeper the shape of the curve. If $0 < b < 1$, then f is decreasing, and its graph is similar to Figure 12–4. The graphs of $y = (1/b)^x$ and $y = b^x$ are mirror images of each other.

The general shape of $y = kb^{cx}$ is very similar to the shape of $y = b^x$. (The exception is when k or c equals 0, in which case the graph is simply a horizontal line.) We note first that since b is positive, we know that b^c is also positive. There are four cases.

If $k > 0$, the graph of $y = kb^{cx}$ is similar to the graph of $y = (\frac{1}{2})^x$ when $0 < b^c < 1$, while the graph is similar to $y = 2^x$ when $b^c > 1$.

If $k < 0$, then the values of y must be negative, and the graphs are reflected across the x-axis.

The four cases are shown in Figure 12–5.

FIGURE 12–5

$k > 0$

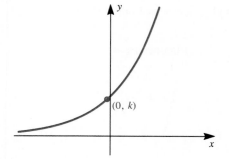

$k < 0$

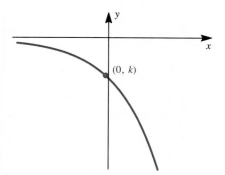

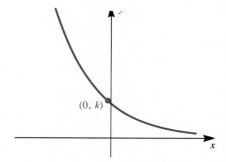

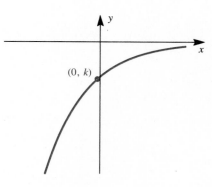

$b^c > 1$ $0 < b^c < 1$

Notice that the graph of $y = kb^{cx}$ goes through the point $(0, k)$ and does not meet the x-axis (unless $k = 0$).

Here is another specific example.

EXAMPLE 6 *(Compare Exercise 41)*

Let $k = 5$, $b = 2$, and $c = \frac{1}{4}$. Graph $y = 5 \cdot 2^{x/4}$

SOLUTION Note that $k > 0$ and $b^c = 2^{1/4} > 1$, so we can anticipate the general shape of the graph. The following table was constructed by using a calculator, and the values of y were rounded to the nearest tenth.

x	−5	−4	−3	−2	−1	0	1	2	3	4	5
y	2.1	2.5	3.0	3.5	4.2	5	5.9	7.1	8.4	10	11.9

The graph is shown in Figure 12–6.

FIGURE 12–6

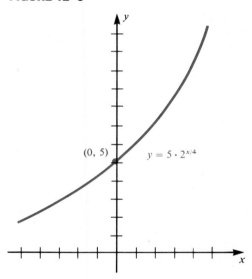

$(0, 5)$ $y = 5 \cdot 2^{x/4}$

EXAMPLE 7 *(Compare Exercises 23 and 27)*

Compare the graphs of $y = 2^{3x}$ and $y = 8^x$.

SOLUTION Because $2^{3x} = (2^3)^x = 8^x$, the graphs are identical. This example is to point out that the same function may have different forms.

EXAMPLE 8 *(Compare Exercise 31)*

Rewrite the function $f(x) = 3^{x+2}$ in the form $f(x) = k3^x$.

SOLUTION $3^{x+2} = 3^x \cdot 3^2 = 9 \cdot 3^x$. We see that $k3^x = 9 \cdot 3^x$ with $k = 9$, and so $3^{x+2} = 9 \cdot 3^x$.

We conclude this section by returning to the function that made us look at exponential functions in the first place.

EXAMPLE 9   *(Compare Exercise 39)*

Graph $y = e^x$.

SOLUTION   Remember that $e = 2.71828.\ .\ .$, so this graph will be very close to $y = (2.7)^x$. It will be "between" the graphs of $y = 2^x$ and $y = 3^x$.

x	-5	-4	-3	-2	-1	0	1	2	3	4	5
$y = e^x$	0.007	0.02	0.05	0.14	0.37	1	2.7	7.4	20.1	54.6	148.4

The graph is shown in Figure 12–7.

FIGURE 12–7

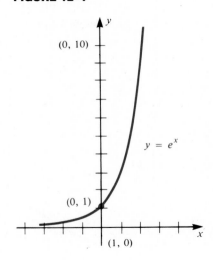

12–1   EXERCISES

I

1. *(See Example 1)* $1000 is invested at 6% interest, compounded annually.
  (a) How much is the investment worth after one year?
  (b) How much is the investment worth after two years?
  (c) How much is the investment worth after four years?

2. $1000 is invested at $7\frac{1}{2}$% interest, compounded annually.
  (a) How much is the investment worth after one year?
  (b) How much is the investment worth after three years?
  (c) How much is the investment worth after six years?

3. An investment is made at 8% interest, compounded annually. How much is the investment worth after three years if the original investment was:
   (a) $1000?
   (b) $2000?
   (c) $10,000?

4. $10,000 is invested at 8% interest. How much is the investment worth after one year if the compounding period is:
   (a) one year?
   (b) six months?
   (c) three months?

5. $10,000 is invested at 9% interest. How much is the investment worth after two years if the compounding period is:
   (a) one year?
   (b) three months?
   (c) one month?

In Exercises 6 through 11, evaluate and simplify.

6. $f(0)$ if $f(x) = e^x$

7. $f(1)$ if $f(x) = 16^{x/2}$

8. $g(0)$ if $g(x) = e^{-3x}$

9. $g(3)$ if $g(x) = 4^{x/2}$

10. $f(-1)$ if $f(x) = 3^x$

11. $f(-2)$ if $f(x) = 8^{x/3}$

12. $f(-3)$ if $f(x) = 16^{x/2}$

II

13. After how many years is $500 invested at 8% interest, compounded quarterly, worth $500(1.02)^{12}$?

14. What is the interest rate, compounded quarterly, if after one year a $1000 investment is worth $1000(1.03)^4$?

15. After four years, what is the value of a $1000 investment made at 6% interest, compounded semiannually? (*Hint:* Fill in the blanks: $1000(\underline{})^{\overline{}}$.)

16. After five years, what is the value of a $3000 investment made at 10% interest, compounded quarterly? ($3000(\underline{})^{\overline{}}$.)

17. (*See Example 2*) After how many years is $2000 invested at 6% interest, compounded continuously, worth $2000e^{0.12}$?

18. What is $2000 invested at 7% interest, compounded continuously, worth after eight years? ($2000e^{\overline{}}$.)

In Exercises 19 through 22, evaluate and simplify.

19. $f(2)$ if $f(x) = 5 \cdot 3^x$

20. $f(-1)$ if $f(x) = 6 \cdot 2^{3x}$

21. $f(0)$ if $f(x) = 7 \cdot 3^{x/2}$

22. $f(6)$ if $f(x) = 6 \cdot 4^{x/3}$

III

Find b in Exercises 23 through 26.

23. (*See Example 7*)
    $5^{2x} = b^x$

24. $9^{x/2} = b^x$

25. $3^{-2x} = b^x$

26. $16^{-x/2} = b^x$

Find c in Exercises 27 through 30.

27. (*See Example 7*)
    $2^{cx} = 8^x$

28. $9^{cx} = 3^x$

29. $5^{cx} = \left(\dfrac{1}{5}\right)^x$

30. $16^{cx} = \left(\dfrac{1}{2}\right)^x$

Find k in Exercises 31 through 34.

31. (*See Example 8*)
    $k4^x = 4^{x+2}$

32. $k2^x = 2^{x+5}$

33. $k3^x = 3^{x-2}$

34. $k5^x = 5^{x-3}$

In Exercises 35 through 42, sketch the graph of f.

35. $f(x) = 3^x;\ -3 \le x \le 3$

36. $f(x) = 3^{-x};\ -3 \le x \le 3$

37. (*See Example 4*)
    $f(x) = \left(\dfrac{1}{2}\right)2^x;\ -3 \le x \le 3$

38. $f(x) = 2 \cdot 2^x;\ -3 \le x \le 3$

39. (*See Example 9*)
    $f(x) = \dfrac{1}{2}e^x,\ -3 \le x \le 3$

40. $f(x) = e^{-x};\ -3 \le x \le 3$

41. (*See Example 6*)
    $f(x) = 2 \cdot 3^{x/2}$

42. $f(x) = -1 \cdot 2^x$

FIGURE 12–8

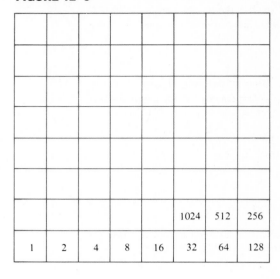

Number of grains of wheat in each square

43. (a) If $1000 is invested at 10% interest compounded quarterly, how much is the investment worth six years after it is made?
   (b) If the interest is compounded continuously, how much is the investment worth after six years?

44. If $1000 is invested at 7% interest, compounded continuously, how much is the investment worth three years after it is made?

45. American Bank offers investors 5.25% interest compounded continuously.
   (a) What is the equivalent interest if the compounding is yearly?
   (b) United Bank offers 5.3% interest compounded quarterly. Which bank should an investor use if the money isn't needed for a full year? Which bank should an investor use if she needs the money in 11 months?

46. A credit card advertises that it charges $1\frac{1}{2}$% interest per month, or 18% interest annually, since $18 = 1\frac{1}{2} \times 12$. What interest does a cardholder have to pay on a balance of $1000 if no payments are made for a year? What interest rate compounded annually is equivalent to $1\frac{1}{2}$% per month?

47. There is a folk tale that the game of chess was invented as an entry in a contest sponsored by a bored king who was looking for new amusements. The king was so pleased with the game that he offered the inventor anything the inventor would choose. The inventor asked for one grain of wheat in the square in the lower left-hand corner of the chess board; two grains in the square to the right of the first one; four grains in the next square, and so on (see Figure 12–8). The king thought the inventor should ask for more; after all there are thousands of grains of wheat in a single bushel. The king's country produced one trillion grains of wheat that year. Was the king able to give the inventor his wish?

48. Suppose your parents offer your kid brother the following choice for his allowance: $10 per week or 1¢ for the first week he keeps his room neat, 2¢ for the second week, 4¢ for the third week, and so on. The allowance will double every week that he keeps his room neat. What advice would you give your brother?

12–2 THE DERIVATIVE OF e^x

- *The Derivative of $f(x) = e^x$*
- *Use of the Chain Rule with Exponential Functions*

THE DERIVATIVE OF $f(x) = e^x$

We begin by recalling the definition of derivative as given in Chapter 9. The definition is

$$f'(x) = \lim_{\Delta x \to 0} \frac{f(x + \Delta x) - f(x)}{\Delta x}$$

We now use this definition to find the derivative of $f(x) = e^x$, but first we want to compute a limit that we will need along the way.

Theorem

$$\lim_{\Delta x \to 0} \frac{e^{\Delta x} - 1}{\Delta x} = 1$$

In other words, if Δx is close to 0, then $\dfrac{e^{\Delta x} - 1}{\Delta x}$ is close to 1.

To establish this limit, remember that the definition of e implies that if n is a large number, then $(1 + \frac{1}{n})^n$ is close to e. Now assume that n is a large number.

$$\left(1 + \frac{1}{n}\right)^n \approx e \qquad \text{(Now take the nth root of both sides)}$$

$$1 + \frac{1}{n} \approx e^{1/n} \qquad \text{(Let $\Delta x = \frac{1}{n}$; note that Δx is close to 0)}$$

$$1 + \Delta x \approx e^{\Delta x} \qquad \text{(Subtract 1 from both sides)}$$

$$\Delta x \approx e^{\Delta x} - 1 \qquad \text{(Divide by Δx)}$$

$$1 \approx \frac{e^{\Delta x} - 1}{\Delta x}$$

If $\Delta x \neq 0$, all these steps are reversible. Thus if Δx is a small positive number, then

$$\frac{e^{\Delta x} - 1}{\Delta x} \approx 1$$

The case of $\Delta x < 0$ can be handled by showing that if n is negative with $|n|$ large, then again

$$\left(1 + \frac{1}{n}\right)^n \approx e$$

that is, it is also true that

$$\lim_{n \to -\infty} \left(1 + \frac{1}{n}\right)^n = e$$

Thus $\Delta x \approx 0$ means

$$\frac{e^{\Delta x} - 1}{\Delta x} \approx 1$$

That is,

$$\lim_{\Delta x \to 0} \frac{e^{\Delta x} - 1}{\Delta x} = 1$$

We are now ready to establish the formula for the derivative of $f(x) = e^x$.

Theorem   If $f(x) = e^x$, then $f'(x) = e^x$.

The function $f(x) = e^x$ is its own derivative!

To see how this formula is obtained, we repeat the three-step process that we used in Chapter 9.

Step 1. Compute and simplify $f(x + \Delta x) - f(x)$:

$$f(x) = e^x, \text{ so } f(x + \Delta x) = e^{x + \Delta x}$$

Because $e^{a + b} = e^a e^b$, we can write $e^{x + \Delta x} = e^x e^{\Delta x}$. Thus

$$\begin{aligned}
f(x + \Delta x) - f(x) &= e^{x + \Delta x} - e^x \\
&= e^x e^{\Delta x} - e^x \\
&= e^x(e^{\Delta x} - 1)
\end{aligned}$$

Step 2. Divide the result of Step 1 by Δx. There's not much we can do in this step except write

$$\frac{e^x(e^{\Delta x} - 1)}{\Delta x} = e^x \left[\frac{e^{\Delta x} - 1}{\Delta x}\right]$$

Step 3. Compute the limit of the result from Step 2 as $\Delta x \to 0$. Notice that the factor e^x is independent of Δx. Therefore

$$\lim_{\Delta x \to 0} \left(e^x \frac{e^{\Delta x} - 1}{\Delta x}\right) = e^x \lim_{\Delta x \to 0} \frac{e^{\Delta x} - 1}{\Delta x} = e^x \cdot 1 = e^x$$

Notice that we just used

$$\lim_{\Delta x \to 0} \frac{e^{\Delta x} - 1}{\Delta x} = 1$$

Putting the three steps together, we find that if $f(x) = e^x$, then

$$f'(x) = e^x \lim_{\Delta x \to 0} \frac{e^{\Delta x} - 1}{\Delta x} = e^x \cdot 1$$
$$= e^x$$

which establishes the theorem.

Because the derivative gives the slope of a tangent line, the geometric interpretation of this formula is as follows: The slope of the line tangent to the graph of $y = e^x$ at any point P is the same as the second coordinate of P. More succinctly,

If $y = e^x$, then $y' = y$.

CAUTION This formula is very different from the formulas for derivatives that you have been using up to this point. In the previous chapters, every exponent was a number. When a function involves an exponent that is a fixed number, you use the power rule to compute the derivative. When the exponent is a variable, you must use a different formula. Be careful to keep the distinction between a constant exponent and a variable exponent. See Figure 12–9.

FIGURE 12–9

EXAMPLE 1 *(Compare Exercise 3)*

Find $f'(x)$ if $f(x) = x^3 + e^x$.

SOLUTION $f'(x) = 3x^2 + e^x$

We used two distinct formulas, the power rule formula for $\frac{d}{dx} x^3$ and the exponential rule formula for $\frac{d}{dx} e^x$.

Notice the use of different formulas in the following examples.

EXAMPLE 2 *(Compare Exercise 5)*

Find $f'(x)$ if $f(x) = x^2 e^x$.

SOLUTION   We must use the product rule:

$$\frac{d}{dx}(x^2 e^x) = e^x\left(\frac{d}{dx}\,x^2\right) + x^2\left(\frac{d}{dx}\,e^x\right)$$

$$= e^x \cdot 2x + x^2 \cdot e^x$$

$$f'(x) = 2xe^x + x^2 e^x$$

EXAMPLE 3 *(Compare Exercise 11)*

Find $f'(x)$ if $f(x) = \dfrac{e^x}{4x^3}$.

SOLUTION   Here we use the quotient rule:

$$f'(x) = \frac{4x^3\left(\dfrac{d}{dx}\,e^x\right) - e^x\left(\dfrac{d}{dx}\,4x^3\right)}{(4x^3)^2}$$

$$= \frac{4x^3 \cdot e^x - e^x \cdot 12x^2}{16x^6}$$

$$= \frac{4x^3 e^x - 12x^2 e^x}{16x^6}$$

Now simplifying, we get

$$= \frac{4x^2 e^x(x - 3)}{16x^6}$$

$$= \frac{e^x(x - 3)}{4x^4}$$

EXAMPLE 4 *(Compare Exercise 15)*

Find $f'(x)$ if $f(x) = (e^x - 4x)^3$.

SOLUTION   We can use the generalized power rule:

$$f(x) = (g(x))^k \qquad \text{with} \qquad g(x) = e^x - 4x \quad \text{and} \quad k = 3$$

$$f'(x) = k(g(x))^{k-1} \cdot g'(x), \qquad \text{and} \qquad g'(x) = e^x - 4$$

Hence

$$f'(x) = 3(e^x - 4x)^2(e^x - 4)$$

USE OF THE CHAIN
RULE WITH
EXPONENTIAL
FUNCTIONS

But what about an exponent other than x? For example, what is the derivative of e^{5x}? When the exponent is a function, you will have to use the chain rule, but first a reminder:

The Chain Rule Revisited. The **chain rule** says that

$$\frac{dy}{dx} = \frac{dy}{du} \cdot \frac{du}{dx}$$

We now show how the chain rule works with exponential functions.

EXAMPLE 5   *(Compare Exercise 7)*

If $f(x) = e^{5x}$, what is $f'(x)$?

SOLUTION   We let $y = e^{5x}$ and define the intermediary variable u by setting $u = 5x$ so that $y = e^u$. Then

$$\frac{dy}{du} = e^u \qquad \text{and} \qquad \frac{du}{dx} = 5$$

so

$$\frac{dy}{dx} = \frac{dy}{du} \cdot \frac{du}{dx}$$
$$= e^u \cdot 5$$
$$= e^{5x} \cdot 5 = 5e^{5x}$$
$$f'(x) = 5e^{5x}$$

The generalized power rule is a special form of the chain rule. When f has the form $f(x) = e^{g(x)}$, we are able to compute $f'(x)$ using another special form of the chain rule.

> *Theorem*   If $f(x) = e^{g(x)}$, then $f'(x) = e^{g(x)} \cdot g'(x)$.

To see this, we apply the chain rule to $y = e^{g(x)}$ by letting $u = g(x)$ so that $y = e^u$. Then

$$\frac{dy}{du} = e^u \qquad \text{and} \qquad \frac{du}{dx} = g'(x)$$

$$\frac{dy}{dx} = \frac{dy}{du} \cdot \frac{du}{dx}$$
$$= e^u \cdot g'(x)$$
$$= e^{g(x)} \cdot g'(x)$$

In Example 4, $g(x) = 5x$ and $g'(x) = 5$, so $f'(x) = e^{5x} \cdot 5 = 5e^{5x}$.

EXAMPLE 6 *(Compare Exercise 27)*

Find an equation of the line tangent to the curve $y = 4e^{3x}$ when $x = 2$.

SOLUTION To find the slope, we compute $\frac{dy}{dx}$. Since 4 is a constant,

$$\frac{d}{dx}(4e^{3x}) = 4\frac{d}{dx}e^{3x}$$
$$= 4(e^{3x} \cdot 3)$$
$$= 12e^{3x}$$

With $x = 2$ the slope of the tangent line is $12e^6$, and the value of y is $4e^6$, so the line has the equation

$$y - 4e^6 = 12e^6(x - 2)$$

CAUTION Sometimes the chain rule requires that the product rule must be used to compute $f''(x)$. *(See Example 7.)*

EXAMPLE 7 *(Compare Exercises 19 and 29)*

If $f(x) = e^{x^2}$, what is $f''(x)$?

SOLUTION
$$f'(x) = e^{x^2} \cdot 2x = 2xe^{x^2}$$

To compute $f''(x)$, we must use both the product rule and the chain rule. We use the product rule on $(2x)(e^{x^2})$ and, along the way, we must use the chain rule on e^{x^2}.

$$f''(x) = e^{x^2}(2) + 2x(e^{x^2} \cdot 2x) = 2e^{x^2} + 4x^2e^{x^2}$$

Sometimes you must use the chain rule more than once.

EXAMPLE 8 *(Compare Exercise 33)*

Find $f'(x)$ if $f(x) = (e^{x^2} + x)^3$.

SOLUTION First, use the generalized power rule form of the chain rule:

$$f'(x) = 3(e^{x^2} + x)^2 \cdot \frac{d}{dx}(e^{x^2} + x)$$
$$= 3(e^{x^2} + x)^2(e^{x^2} \cdot 2x + 1)$$

Notice the use of the chain rule in computing $\frac{d}{dx}e^{x^2}$:

$$= 3(e^{x^2} + x)^2(2xe^{x^2} + 1)$$

We can again use the first and second derivatives as tools to investigate how these new functions behave.

EXAMPLE 9 *(Compare Exercise 47)*

Sketch the graph of $f(x) = e^{2x}$.

SOLUTION   First, remember that e^{2x} is positive for all values of x, so the graph will be above the x-axis. Next, $f'(x) = e^{2x} \cdot 2 = 2e^{2x}$ is also positive for all x; thus f is increasing on $(-\infty, \infty)$. Finally, $f''(x) = 2e^{2x} \cdot 2 = 4e^{2x} > 0$, so the graph of f is concave up on $(-\infty, \infty)$.

To find the y-intercept, we compute $f(0) = e^{(2)(0)} = e^0 = 1$. See Figure 12–10 for the graph of $f(x) = e^{2x}$.

FIGURE 12–10

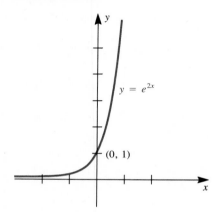

$y = e^{2x}$

$(0, 1)$

EXAMPLE 10   *(Compare Exercise 45)*

Let $f(x) = xe^{-2x}$, $0 \le x \le 3$.

(a) Find the maximum and minimum values of f.
(b) Sketch the graph of f.

SOLUTION   To compute $f'(x)$, we use the product rule on $(x)(e^{-2x})$ and must remember to use the chain rule when computing $\frac{d}{dx}e^{-2x}$. We have

$$f'(x) = e^{-2x}(1) + x(e^{-2x}(-2))$$
$$= e^{-2x} - 2xe^{-2x} \qquad \text{(Factor } e^{-2x})$$
$$= e^{-2x}(1 - 2x)$$

$f'(x)$ exists for all x, so the only critical numbers are solutions to $e^{-2x}(1 - 2x) = 0$. Since $e^{-2x} = 0$ has no solution, $x = \frac{1}{2}$ is the only critical number of f.

(a) The domain of f is a closed and bounded interval, so we use the candidates test:

$$f(0) = 0 \cdot 1 = 0 \qquad\qquad f(3) = 3e^{-6} = \frac{3}{e^6}$$

$$f\left(\frac{1}{2}\right) = \frac{1}{2}e^{-1} = \frac{1}{2e}$$

The last two evaluations are positive, so $f(0) = 0$ is the minimum value. Comparing the other two numbers, $\dfrac{1}{2e} \approx 0.184$ and $\dfrac{3}{e^6} \approx 0.007$, so the maximum value of f is $f(\frac{1}{2}) = \dfrac{1}{2e}$.

(b) When we plot the three points $(0, 0)$, $\left(\dfrac{1}{2}, \dfrac{1}{2e}\right)$, and $\left(3, \dfrac{3}{e^6}\right)$, we see that f is increasing on the interval $0 \leq x \leq \dfrac{1}{2}$ and is decreasing on the interval $\dfrac{1}{2} \leq x \leq 3$. (Check that the sign of f' gives the same information.)

Now we look at $f''(x)$ to determine concavity.

$$f'(x) = e^{-2x}(1 - 2x)$$

so

$$f''(x) = (1 - 2x)(-2e^{-2x}) + e^{-2x}(-2)$$
$$= e^{-2x}(-2 + 4x - 2) = e^{-2x}(4x - 4)$$

The sign-of-f'' chart is

Note that the domain restricts the chart to $0 < x < 3$. The graph is concave down on $(0, 1)$ and concave up on $(1, 3)$. The point $(1, f(1)) = \left(1, \dfrac{1}{e^2}\right)$ is a point of inflection. The graph is given in Figure 12–11.

FIGURE 12–11

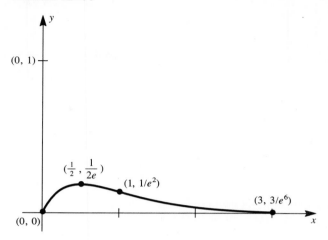

12-2 EXERCISES

I

Compute $f'(x)$ for Exercises 1 through 18.

1. $f(x) = 4e^x$

2. $f(x) = -7e^x$

3. (*See Example 1*)
$f(x) = x^3 - 2e^x$

4. $f(x) = 4x^2 + 5e^x$

5. (*See Example 2*)
$f(x) = x^3 e^x$

6. $f(x) = 2xe^x$

7. (*See Example 5*)
$f(x) = 6e^{3x}$

8. $f(x) = 3e^{-2x}$

9. $f(x) = 8e^{x/2}$

10. $f(x) = 12e^{x/4}$

11. (*See Example 3*)
$f(x) = \dfrac{x^3 + 2}{e^x}$

12. $f(x) = \dfrac{x^2 - 1}{3e^x}$

13. $f(x) = \dfrac{e^x + 2}{x^2}$

14. $f(x) = \dfrac{2e^x - 5}{x^3}$

15. (*See Example 4*)
$f(x) = (e^x - 7)^4$

16. $f(x) = (e^x + 7x^2)^3$

17. $f(x) = \sqrt{e^x + 1}$

18. $f(x) = \dfrac{1}{\sqrt{2e^x + 3}}$

II

Compute $f'(x)$ for Exercises 19 through 26.

19. (*See Example 7*)
$f(x) = 2x^3 e^{5x}$

20. $f(x) = 7x^2 e^{3x}$

21. $f(x) = (e^{4x} + 1)^3$

22. $f(x) = \sqrt{e^{2x} + 5}$

23. $f(x) = 3x^2 + xe^{-x}$

24. $f(x) = x^2 e^x - 4x$

25. $f(x) = (\sqrt{x^2 + 1})e^{4x}$

26. $f(x) = (3x + 1)^2 e^{5x}$

27. (*See Example 6*) What is an equation of the line tangent to the curve $y = e^{x/3}$ at the point whose first coordinate is 6?

28. What is an equation of the line tangent to the curve $y = e^{-2x}$ at the point whose first coordinate is 4?

III

Find $f''(x)$ for Exercises 29 through 32.

29. (*See Example 7*) **30.** $f(x) = e^{3x^2 - x}$
$f(x) = e^{x^2 + x}$

31. $f(x) = x^2 e^{4x}$ **32.** $f(x) = 2x^3 e^{-x}$

Find $f'(x)$ for Exercises 33 through 36.

33. (*See Example 8*) **34.** $f(x) = (e^{x^2} - 6x^3)^4$
$f(x) = \sqrt{e^{4x} + 5x}$

35. $f(x) = (x^2 + 1)e^{\sqrt{3x + 1}}$ **36.** $f(x) = \dfrac{5e^{(4x - 1)^2}}{(x^2 + 1)^3}$

37. What is an equation of the line tangent to the curve $y = e^{-x}$ at the point whose first coordinate is 4?

38. What is an equation of the line tangent to the curve $y = e^{x/3}$ at the point whose first coordinate is 8?

39. What are the critical numbers of $f(x) = x^2 e^{-x}$?

40. What are the critical numbers of $f(x) = xe^{x/3}$?

41. On what intervals is f decreasing if $f(x) = \dfrac{e^x}{x}$?

42. On what intervals is f decreasing if $f(x) = xe^x$?

43. What is the point of inflection on the curve $y = xe^{-x}$?

44. What is the point of inflection on the curve $y = xe^{x/2}$?

45. (*See Example 10*) Find the extreme values of $f(x) = xe^{x/2}$, $-4 \le x \le 4$.

46. Find the extreme values of $f(x) = x^2 e^x$, $-1 \le x \le 4$.

47. (*See Example 9*) Sketch the graph of $f(x) = xe^x$, $-5 \le x \le 5$.

48. Sketch the graph of $f(x) = xe^{-x}$, $-5 \le x \le 5$.

49. Use implicit differentiation to find an equation of the line tangent to the curve $y^2 e^x - ye^{4x} = 6$ at the point $(0, 3)$.

50. What is an equation of the line tangent to the curve $ye^{xy} = 2e^2$ at the point $(1, 2)$?

51. Show that the function $f(x) = 6e^{2x}$ satisfies the equation $y' = 2y$.

52. Show that every function of the form $f(x) = ke^{cx}$ satisfies the equation $y' = cy$.

53. The population of a colony of bacteria t minutes after an experiment starts is given by $P(t) = 5000e^{t/30}$. Two hours after the start of the experiment:
(a) how large is the colony?
(b) how fast is the colony growing?

54. If the amount of oil left in a well (in thousands of barrels) t months after pumping starts is given by $A(t) = 2500e^{-t/3}$, then:
(a) how much oil was there in the well when pumping began?
(b) how much oil remains after one year?
(c) at what rate is the oil being pumped out after one year?

12–3 THE NATURAL LOGARITHM FUNCTION

- *Doubling an Investment*
- *The Natural Logarithm Function*
- *Properties of ln x*
- *Solving Exponential Equations*

DOUBLING AN INVESTMENT

We return to our investigation of the situation in which someone invests $1000 at 5% compounded continuously. From the results of Section 12–1 we know that $A(t)$, the amount the investment is worth after t years, is given by $A(t) = 1000\, e^{0.05t}$ and that the graph of A looks like Figure 12–12.

FIGURE 12–12

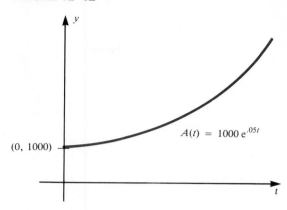

$A(t) = 1000\,e^{.05t}$

$(0, 1000)$

FIGURE 12–13

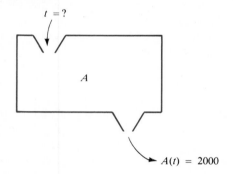

$t = ?$

A

$A(t) = 2000$

Up to now we have been using t as our independent variable and then determining $A(t)$. Now we would like to ask a slightly different question about this investment. We change our point of view and ask, "How long must we wait for the investment to be worth a certain amount?" To be specific, how long will it take for the investment to double? The time required for an investment to double is called the **doubling period.** Here we are asking: For what value of t is $A(t) = 2000$? In terms of the function machine we have the situation shown in Figure 12–13.

If the output is 2000, what is the input? We look at how this question can be interpreted graphically.

Normally, you would graph the function A by thinking of starting on the horizontal axis (the t-axis) and computing $A(t)$ (the height) and then plotting the point $(t, A(t))$. This time we're asking, "If you know the height of the point, what is its first coordinate?" Specifically, if the point is $(t, 2000)$, what is t?

FIGURE 12–14

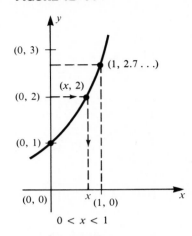

$$0 < x < 1$$

FIGURE 12–15

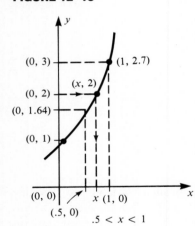

$$.5 < x < 1$$

To answer this question, we need to solve for t in the equation $1000e^{0.05t} = 2000$. Dividing both sides by 1000, we want to solve $e^{0.05t} = 2$. As an intermediate step, we change variables by letting $x = 0.05t$. Now, if we solve $e^x = 2$, then we can determine t by

$$t = \frac{x}{0.05} = 20x$$

The question can now be phrased, "What is the first coordinate of the point $(x, 2)$ on the graph $y = e^x$?"

We know that $e^0 = 1$ (which is below 2) and that $e^1 = e$ ($= 2.71. . .$, which is above 2), so x is somewhere between 0 and 1. See Figure 12–14.

To get a better idea of the value of x, we do some more evaluations. $e^{0.5} = 1.64. . .$, which is less than 2, so x is between 0.5 and 1.

We can continue in this manner, getting x to be about 0.7 ($e^{0.7} = 2.01. . .$). See Figure 12–15.

Because $t = 20x$, we have $t \approx (20)(0.7) = 14$. Here is the answer to our question: *It would take about 14 years for the investment to grow to $2000.*

THE NATURAL LOGARITHM FUNCTION

In the above example we wanted to solve the equation $e^x = 2$. If we ask how long it would take for the investment to triple, we would want to solve the equation $e^x = 3$. The general problem is to solve the equation $e^x = y$ for x when you know the value of y. If we know the output of $f(x) = e^x$, can we find the input? We want a function that "undoes" the exponential function; given the number e^x as input, this new function will return x to us. This function is so important that it has a special name—the **natural logarithm function.** (It is also called the logarithm function to the base e.) The term "natural" is used because the number e is forced on us by nature. Furthermore, nature does us a favor here because the calculus formulas for derivatives are simpler using base e than any other base.

CAUTION   It is not generally true that if you know the output of a function machine, then you can figure out what the input must have been. For example, if $f(x) = x^2$, and we know that the output is 9, there is no way of determining whether the input was 3 or -3. The key fact we are using is that *the graph of the exponential function is never at the same height twice*. A given value of y is the result of a unique input; if $e^c = e^d$, then $c = d$.

Definition **Natural Logarithm** **Function**	The natural logarithm function is written **ln** and is defined by $\qquad \ln B = A \qquad$ if and only if $\qquad e^A = B$

The definition of the natural logarithm involves two equations that are equivalent. To help us understand more fully the relationship between the natural logarithm function and the exponential function, we use these two equations to produce a third.

Equation (1) $\quad \ln B = A$

is equivalent to

Equation (2) $\quad e^A = B$

If we use Equation (2) to replace B by e^A in Equation (1), then Equation (1) becomes

Equation (3) $\quad \ln e^A = A$

We give some examples to show you how to use Equation (3) to perform some evaluations.

EXAMPLE 1   *(Compare Exercise 1)*

Compute $\ln e^2$.

SOLUTION   With $A = 2$, Equation (3) tells us that $\ln e^2 = 2$.   ∎

EXAMPLE 2   *(Compare Exercise 5)*

Compute $\ln \dfrac{1}{e}$.

SOLUTION   Rewrite $\dfrac{1}{e}$ as e^{-1}. Thus $\ln \dfrac{1}{e} = \ln e^{-1} = -1$.   ∎

If we replace A by x, then Equation (3) becomes $\ln e^x = x$. This equation now shows us that ln does exactly what we wanted it to do; given e^x as its input, ln gives us x as its output.

FIGURE 12–16

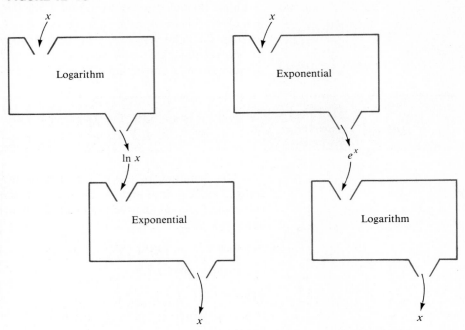

We use Equations (1) and (2) to produce another important equation. This time we use Equation (1) to replace A by $\ln B$ in Equation (2); we get

Equation (4) $e^{\ln B} = B$

When we replace B by x, Equation (4) becomes $e^{\ln x} = x$. Given $\ln x$ as input, the exponential function gives us x as output. The exponential and logarithm functions undo each other. See Figure 12–16.

In general, functions that "undo" each other are called inverse functions, but we will not pursue the general theory here. We do use this special relationship, however, to see what the graph of $y = \ln x$ looks like.

We proceed through a sequence of equivalent statements.

The point (B, A) is on the graph of $y = \ln x$

if and only if

$\ln B = A$

if and only if

$e^A = B$

if and only if

the point (A, B) is on the graph of $y = e^x$

FIGURE 12-17

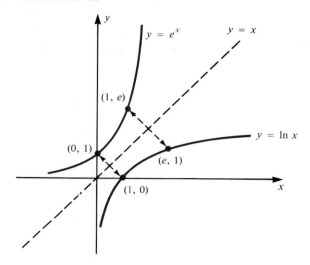

In summary, (B, A) is on the graph of $y = \ln x$ precisely when (A, B) is on the graph of $y = e^x$. See Figure 12–17.

If you rotate the plane about the dotted line $y = x$, the graph of $y = e^x$ will be rotated so that it lies exactly on top of the graph $y = \ln x$.

There are some important observations that we need to make about $\ln x$.

1. **The domain of the logarithm function is $(0, \infty)$.** The fact that e^x is never zero or negative means that $\ln x$ is defined only if x is positive.

Two special values of $\ln x$ are

2. **$\ln 1 = 0$, and**
3. **$\ln e = 1$.**

We were led to the natural logarithm function by trying to answer the question of when an exponential function would achieve a certain value. We return to this type of question with some examples that show how the ln function is used in applications.

EXAMPLE 3   *(Compare Exercise 35)*

Solve $e^x = 5$.

SOLUTION   Apply ln to both sides of the equation $e^x = 5$:

$$\ln e^x = \ln 5$$

We apply Equation (3) to the left-hand side: $\ln e^x = x$. Thus $x = \ln 5$.

EXAMPLE 4   *(Compare Exercise 47)*

How long will it take a $1000 investment to become worth $2000 at 8% interest, compounded continuously?

SOLUTION   The initial amount is $1000, and $r = 8\% = 0.08$, so

$$P(t) = 1000e^{0.08t}$$

We need to solve for t in the equation

$$2000 = 1000e^{0.08t}$$

Dividing by 1000, we get

$$2 = e^{0.08t}$$

Taking ln of both sides, we have

$$\ln 2 = \ln e^{0.08t}$$

Again we use Equation (3); $\ln e^{0.08t} = 0.08t$, so

$$\ln 2 = 0.08t$$

$$t = \frac{\ln 2}{0.08}$$

$$t = \frac{100 \ln 2}{8}$$

Using a calculator to approximate t, we have

$$t \approx \frac{(100)(0.6931)}{8} = 8.66. \ . \ .$$

Answer: The investment will be worth $2000 in about $8\frac{2}{3}$ years, or 8 years and 8 months.

We change the beginning principal in Example 5 but still ask how long it will take the investment to double.

EXAMPLE 5

How long will it take a $6000 investment to become worth $12,000 at 8% interest, compounded continuously?

SOLUTION   Solve for t in the equation

$$12,000 = 6000e^{0.08t} \qquad \text{(Divide by 6000)}$$

$$2 = e^{0.08t}$$

We just solved this equation in Example 4.

Answer: The investment will be worth $12,000 in approximately 8 years and 8 months.

Notice that the two examples have the same solution because

$$\frac{2000}{1000} = \frac{12,000}{6000} = 2$$

We can state a general principle: An amount invested at 8% interest, compounded continuously, will double in value in about 8 years and 8 months. Different interest rates will of course have different doubling periods, but all the different periods are independent of the size of the investment.

EXAMPLE 6   *(Compare Exercise 49)*

How long will it take an investment to double if the interest is 6%, compounded continuously?

SOLUTION   Let P be the initial amount invested. Then our model for $A(t)$ gives us

$$A(t) = Pe^{0.06t}$$

We want to know when $A(t) = 2P$, so we solve

$$2P = Pe^{0.06t} \qquad \text{(Divide by } P\text{)}$$
$$2 = e^{0.06t} \qquad \text{(Take ln of both sides)}$$
$$\ln 2 = \ln e^{0.06t} = 0.06t$$
$$t = \frac{\ln 2}{0.06} \approx 11.55$$

Answer: The investment will double in a little more than $11\frac{1}{2}$ years.

By changing the question slightly we discover the concept of **present value.** In the next example the amount of the investment is the unknown.

EXAMPLE 7   *(Compare Exercise 51)*

If we are going to need $2000 in three years, and we can make an investment that will earn $7\frac{1}{2}$% compounded continuously for three years, how large an investment must we make now?

SOLUTION   Again, let P be the initial amount invested. We know that $A(t) = Pe^{0.075t}$. When $t = 3$, we need the amount to be 2000, so the equation that we need to solve is

$$2000 = A(3)$$
$$2000 = Pe^{(0.075)(3)} = Pe^{0.225}$$

Dividing by $e^{0.225}$, we obtain

$$P = \frac{2000}{e^{0.225}} \approx \frac{2000}{1.252} \approx 1597 \quad \text{(to nearest unit)}$$

Answer: We should invest $1600 (rounded up to guarantee the result) now to have $2000 in three years.

Definition
Present Value

If the interest rate is R, compounded continuously, then the **present value**, PV, of $\$A$ to be received in t years is given by

$$PV = \frac{A}{e^{Rt}} = Ae^{-Rt}$$

The formula $A = Pe^{Rt}$ has four variables: A, P, R, and t. Solving for A or P, given the other three, does not involve logarithms; solving for R or t does. In the next example, R is the unknown, and so the solution involves logarithms.

EXAMPLE 8   *(Compare Exercise 55)*

If the present value of $\$10,000$ to be received in four years is $\$6703$, what is the rate of interest (compounded continuously) on the investment?

SOLUTION   Here we know A, P, and t in the formula $A = Pe^{Rt}$.

$$10,000 = 6703e^{4R}$$

$$\frac{10,000}{6703} = e^{4R}$$

Now we apply ln to both sides because the unknown is in the exponent. Remember that $\ln e^{4R} = 4R$.

$$\ln\left(\frac{10,000}{6703}\right) = 4R$$

$$R = \frac{1}{4}\ln\left(\frac{10,000}{6703}\right) \approx 0.100 = 10.0\%$$

Answer: The rate of interest is 10.0%

PROPERTIES OF ln x

We have stressed the special relationship between the ln function and the exponential function and have shown how the ln function enables us to solve equations that have a variable in an exponent.

Historically, logarithms were first introduced in the seventeenth century in a different setting. Their use became widespread because of the following properties that can be used to simplify calculations. We list these properties without proofs.

Arithmetic Properties
of the Logarithm

If p and q are positive, and m is any number, then:

1. $\ln(p \cdot q) = \ln p + \ln q$
2. $\ln\left(\frac{p}{q}\right) = \ln p - \ln q$
3. $\ln(p^m) = m \ln p$

Log tables became very important aids to computation, especially in navigation. It is ironic that the computational needs of modern navigation have made log tables obsolete. We now need to navigate at high speed in an ocean of space, rather than at low speed in an ocean of water. Modern navigational computations need to be done quickly and on board the spacecraft. These needs prompted the invention and miniaturization of calculators. If the only importance of logarithms were for calculations, they would be a thing of the past (like the slide rule). It is because logarithms and exponentials are so important *as functions in applications* using calculus that they still deserve our attention. We need them as functions to describe the behavior of real-world phenomena.

We conclude this section with some more examples using ln to solve exponential equations that can arise in applications.

SOLVING EXPONENTIAL EQUATIONS

We need to be able to solve equations, such as $18 = 2^x$, that involve a base other than e. To solve equations of this type requires use of Property 3 of the ln function listed above.

Theorem   If $p > 0$, then $\ln(p^m) = m \ln p$.

Proof. Rewrite p as $p = e^{\ln p}$. Thus $p^m = (e^{\ln p})^m = e^{m \ln p}$. Applying ln to both sides of $p^m = e^{m \ln p}$ gives

$$\ln p^m = \ln(e^{m \ln p})$$
$$= m \ln p$$

EXAMPLE 9   *(Compare Exercise 39)*

Solve for x if $20 = 2^{3x}$.

SOLUTION   Take ln of both sides:

$$\ln 20 = \ln 2^{3x} = 3x \ln 2 \qquad \text{(Here } m \text{ is the expression } 3x)$$

Next, divide by ln 2 to obtain

$$\frac{\ln 20}{\ln 2} = 3x$$

$$\frac{\ln 20}{3 \ln 2} = x$$

EXAMPLE 10   *(Compare Exercise 43)*

Solve for x if $42 = 3 \cdot 5^{2x}$.

SOLUTION   The simplest thing to do is to divide both sides by 3 as the first step:

$$14 = 5^{2x} \qquad \text{(Now take ln of both sides)}$$
$$\ln 14 = \ln 5^{2x}$$
$$\ln 14 = 2x \ln 5 \qquad \text{(Finally, divide by 2 ln 5)}$$
$$\frac{\ln 14}{2 \ln 5} = x$$

Using a calculator, we can approximate x by

$$\frac{2.639}{2(1.609)} \approx x$$
$$x \approx 0.8199$$

In the next section we will also see how Properties 1 and 2 of the ln function can be used to simplify the computation of $f'(x)$ when the expression $f(x)$ involves a complicated product or quotient.

12-3 EXERCISES

I

Simplify each of the expressions in Exercises 1 through 12.

1. *(See Example 1)*
$\ln e^3$

2. $\ln e^{1/2}$

3. $\ln e^{-4}$

4. $\ln e^{x/2}$

5. *(See Example 2)*
$\ln \dfrac{1}{e^2}$

6. $\ln \dfrac{1}{e^3}$

7. $\ln 1$

8. $\ln \sqrt{e}$

9. $e^{\ln 4}$

10. $e^{\ln (1/3)}$

11. $e^{\ln 5}$

12. $e^{\ln(x/3)}$

In Exercises 13 through 16 we use approximate values of the functions involved to emphasize that e^2, for example, is a number; $e^2 \approx 7.4$.

13. *(See Figure 12–17)* If $(2, 7.4)$ is on the graph of $y = e^x$, then what corresponding point is on the graph of $y = \ln x$?

14. If $(0.5, 1.6)$ is on the graph of $y = e^x$, then what corresponding point is on the graph of $y = \ln x$?

15. If $(4, 1.4)$ is on the graph of $y = \ln x$, then what corresponding point is on the graph of $y = e^x$?

16. If $(0.3, -1.20)$ is on the graph of $y = \ln x$, then what corresponding point is on the graph of $y = e^x$?

II

Simplify each of the expressions in Exercises 17 through 26.

17. $e^{2 \ln 3}$ *Hint:* First rewrite as $(e^{\ln 3})^2$

18. $e^{2 \ln 4}$

19. $e^{(1/2)\ln 9}$

20. $e^{-\ln 8}$

21. $e^{-\ln 2}$

22. $\ln(e^2 \cdot e^3)$

23. $(\ln e^2)(\ln e^3)$

24. $\ln\left(\dfrac{1}{e^2}\right)$

25. $\ln(e^4 \cdot e)$

26. $(\ln e^4)(\ln e)$

Solve for x in Exercises 27 through 34. Write the answer as an integer.

27. $40 = 5 \cdot 2^x$

28. $1 = 8 \cdot 2^x$

29. $16 = 2^x$

30. $\dfrac{1}{9} = 3^x$

31. $48 = 3 \cdot 2^{-x}$

32. $6 = 96 \cdot 2^{-x}$

33. $5 = 160 \cdot 2^{-x}$

34. $4 = 36 \cdot 3^{-x}$

III

Solve for x in Exercises 35 through 46. Write the answer using the natural logarithm function.

35. (*See Example 3*)
    $16 = e^{0.8x}$

36. $3 = e^{x/5}$

37. $10 = 40e^{-0.02x}$

38. $12 = 4e^{-0.3x}$

39. (*See Example 9*)
    $18 = 2^x$

40. $21 = 3^x$

41. $105 = 5^{2x}$

42. $37 = 4^{x/3}$

43. (*See Example 10*)
    $20 = 5 \cdot 3^x$

44. $18 = 2 \cdot 4^x$

45. $36 = 4 \cdot 3^{2x}$

46. $40 = 10 \cdot 2^{x/3}$

47. (*See Example 4*) $1000 is invested at 6% interest, compounded continuously. When will the investment be worth $3000?

48. If $2000 is invested at $7\frac{1}{4}$% interest, compounded continuously, when will the investment be worth $5000?

49. (*See Example 6*) How long will it take an investment earning 14% interest, compounded continuously, to double?

50. How long will it take an investment earning 7% interest, compounded continuously, to double?

51. (*See Example 7*) What is the present value of $10,000 to be received in five years if the interest earned will be $6\frac{1}{2}$% compounded continuously?

52. What is the present value of $5000 to be received in two years if the interest rate is 9.85% compounded continuously?

53. How much must be invested at 5% compounded continuously so that the investment is worth $20,000 after 30 years?

54. How much must be invested at 8% compounded continuously so that the investment will be worth $10,000 after six years?

55. (*See Example 8*) If an investment of $2000 is worth $2542.50 after three years, what is the rate of interest (continuously compounded) earned by the investment?

56. If an investment doubles every ten years, what is the interest rate (continuous compounding)?

57. If the population of the earth is growing at the rate of 2% compounded continuously, how long will it take the population to double?

58. If the population of the earth grows at the rate of 3%, compounded continuously, how long will it take the population to double?

12–4 THE DERIVATIVE OF ln x

- *The Derivative of ln x*

- *Use of the Chain Rule with the Logarithm Function*

We will not establish the formula for the derivative of $f(x) = \ln x$ by using the definition of the derivative. Instead, we use the relation between the functions $\ln x$ and e^x to first show that the natural logarithm function does indeed have a derivative and then to find the formula for this derivative.

Recall from Section 12–3 that if we let $g(x) = \ln x$ and $f(x) = e^x$, then g and f "undo" each other in the sense that $g(f(x)) = \ln e^x = x$ for all x in the domain of f, and $f(g(x)) = e^{\ln x} = x$ for all x in the domain of g. There is a general theorem that states that whenever f and g are two functions that have this relationship and f' exists and doesn't equal 0, then g' also exists. Because $f'(x) = e^x$, which is never equal to 0, this general theorem guarantees that the derivative of the natural logarithm exists. We now use the chain rule to establish the formula for this derivative.

THE DERIVATIVE
OF ln x

Theorem   If $g(x) = \ln x$, then $g'(x) = \dfrac{1}{x}$.

Remember that the domain of ln is $(0, \infty)$, so this formula is valid for $x > 0$.

To establish this theorem, we use a special case of the form of the chain rule given in the previous section. The formula we wish to use is

$$\text{if } h(x) = e^{g(x)}, \qquad \text{then} \qquad h'(x) = e^{g(x)} \cdot g'(x)$$

In particular, let $g(x) = \ln x$ so that $h(x) = e^{\ln x} = x$. We have

$$x = h(x) = e^{g(x)}$$

Now differentiate:

$$1 = h'(x) = e^{g(x)} \cdot g'(x)$$

Again, use $e^{g(x)} = e^{\ln x} = x$ so that

$$1 = x \cdot g'(x)$$

Solving for $g'(x)$, we have

$$g'(x) = \frac{1}{x}$$

EXAMPLE 1   *(Compare Exercise 3)*

Compute $f'(x)$ if $f(x) = x^3 \ln x$

SOLUTION   Using the product rule, we have

$$f'(x) = (\ln x)(3x^2) + (x^3)\left(\frac{1}{x}\right)$$

$$= 3x^2(\ln x) + x^2$$

EXAMPLE 2   *(Compare Exercise 13)*

Find $f'(x)$ if $f(x) = \dfrac{\ln x}{x^4}$.

SOLUTION   We must use the quotient rule:

$$f'(x) = \frac{x^4(1/x) - (\ln x)4x^3}{(x^4)^2}$$

$$= \frac{x^3 - (\ln x)4x^3}{x^8} = \frac{x^3(1 - 4 \ln x)}{x^8}$$

$$= \frac{1 - 4 \ln x}{x^5}$$

Next, we look at the composition of various functions with ln x and see how the chain rule applies in these cases.

EXAMPLE 3   *(Compare Exercise 5)*

Find $f'(x)$ if $f(x) = \ln(3x)$.

CAUTION   Remember that you must be precise when applying formulas, and this new differentiation formula gives only the derivative of ln x. You cannot conclude that $f'(x) = \dfrac{1}{3x}$. Computing the derivative of f in the form written above requires the use of the chain rule.

SOLUTION   We will remind you of the chain rule and show how it applies here, but first we do this example another way, by rewriting $f(x)$. We use the fact that

$$\ln(p \cdot q) = \ln p + \ln q$$

so with $p = 3$ and $q = x$,

$$\ln(3x) = \ln 3 + \ln x$$

Now we take the derivative of *f*:

$$\frac{d}{dx}(\ln 3x) = \frac{d}{dx}(\ln 3 + \ln x)$$

$$= \frac{d}{dx}(\ln 3) + \frac{d}{dx}(\ln x)$$

$$= 0 + \frac{1}{x}$$

$$= \frac{1}{x}$$

Answer: $f'(x) = \dfrac{1}{x}$

There are a few surprises in this computation (which is the real reason we did it). First, please observe that ln 3 is a constant, and so its derivative is 0. (Sometimes when first learning to find derivatives involving ln, students will write $\frac{1}{3}$ for the derivative of ln 3.) Second, the final result may also be surprising; ln x and ln $3x$ have the same derivative. This is due to the property of ln that allowed us to write ln $3x$ as ln 3 + ln x. You know that ln x and $(4 + \ln x)$ have the same derivative because the derivative of the constant 4 is 0. Remember that ln 3 is also a number, just as 4 is a number (ln 3 = 1.09861. . .).

EXAMPLE 4   *(Compare Exercise 11)*

If $f(x) = \ln(3x)$, compute $f'(x)$.

SOLUTION   This is the same function as in Example 3, but this time we do use the chain rule. The intermediate evaluation is $3x$; we let $u = 3x$ so that $y = \ln u$;

$$\frac{dy}{du} = \frac{1}{u} \qquad \text{and} \qquad \frac{du}{dx} = 3$$

Thus

$$f'(x) = \frac{dy}{dx} = \frac{dy}{du} \cdot \frac{du}{dx}$$

$$= \frac{1}{u} \cdot 3$$

Replace u by $3x$ so that the final answer is expressed in terms of x:

$$= \frac{1}{3x} \cdot 3 = \frac{1}{x}$$

Remember that you cannot get different answers by using different techniques; there may be more than one way to proceed through the computation, but the results must be the same.

EXAMPLE 5   *(Compare Exercise 37)*

If $f(x) = \ln x^3$, find $f'(x)$.

SOLUTION   This derivative can also be computed two different ways.

1. Use the chain rule with $u = x^3$ and $y = \ln u$;

$$\frac{dy}{du} = \frac{1}{u} \quad \text{and} \quad \frac{du}{dx} = 3x^2$$

$$f'(x) = \frac{1}{u} \cdot 3x^2 = \frac{1}{x^3} \cdot 3x^2 = \frac{3}{x}$$

$$f'(x) = \frac{3}{x}$$

2. We compute the derivative again, this time using a property of ln to rewrite $f(x) = \ln(x^3) = 3(\ln x)$. Thus

$$\frac{d}{dx} f(x) = \frac{d}{dx} 3(\ln x) = 3\frac{d}{dx}\ln x = 3 \cdot \frac{1}{x} = \frac{3}{x}$$

$$f'(x) = \frac{3}{x}$$

Once again, we have used two different techniques for computing $f'(x)$, and once again, the two techniques yield the same result.

EXAMPLE 6   *(Compare Exercise 23)*

If $g(x) = (\ln x)^3$, find $g'(x)$.

SOLUTION   You should contrast this example with Example 5; the order of the operations is very important. For instance, if we let $x = 2$, for the function in Example 5 we have $f(2) = \ln 2^3 = \ln 8 = 2.0794. \ldots$; while for the function in this example we have $g(2) = (\ln 2)^3 = (0.6931. \ldots)^3 = 0.3330. \ldots$

To compute $g'(x)$, we again have to use the chain rule, but now in the form of the generalized power rule because $g(x)$ is $(\ln x)$ raised to a power. Let $u = \ln x$; then $y = u^3$, and

$$g'(x) = \frac{dy}{dx} = \frac{dy}{du} \cdot \frac{du}{dx}$$

$$= 3u^2 \cdot \frac{1}{x}$$

$$= 3(\ln x)^2 \cdot \frac{1}{x}$$

$$= \frac{3(\ln x)^2}{x}$$

USE OF THE CHAIN
RULE WITH THE
LOGARITHM FUNCTION

We were able to give special forms of the chain rule for the generalized power rule and the exponential function, and we can again give a special case of the chain rule when f is of the form $f(x) = \ln(g(x))$.

---

*Special Form
of Chain Rule*

If $f(x) = \ln(g(x))$, then

$$f'(x) = \frac{1}{g(x)} \cdot g'(x)$$

$$= \frac{g'(x)}{g(x)}$$

This formula results from using the chain rule, with $y = f(x) = \ln(g(x))$, and setting $u = g(x)$. Then $y = \ln u$, so

$$\frac{dy}{du} = \frac{1}{u} \qquad \text{and} \qquad \frac{du}{dx} = g'(x)$$

$$f'(x) = \frac{dy}{dx} = \frac{dy}{du} \cdot \frac{du}{dx}$$

$$= \frac{1}{u} \cdot g'(x)$$

$$= \frac{1}{g(x)} \cdot g'(x) = \frac{g'(x)}{g(x)}$$

EXAMPLE 7   *(Compare Exercise 29)*

If $f(x) = \ln(x^3 + 4x)$, find $f'(x)$.

SOLUTION   We can use the special form of the chain rule, with $g(x) = x^3 + 4x$. Thus $g'(x) = 3x^2 + 4$, and

$$f'(x) = \frac{1}{x^3 + 4x} \cdot (3x^2 + 4)$$

$$= \frac{3x^2 + 4}{x^3 + 4x}$$

Use of this special form of the chain rule allows you to compute the derivative of $\ln(g(x))$ without having to go through the u substitution and so quickens your computation. To see this, go back and do Example 5 using this form. Use of this form also makes it easier to compute more complicated derivatives.

EXAMPLE 8   *(Compare Exercise 41)*

Find $f'(x)$ if $f(x) = [\ln(x^2 + x)]^3$.

SOLUTION $f(x)$ is of the form $(h(x))^3$, so first use the generalized power rule:

$$f'(x) = 3(h(x))^2 h'(x)$$

Now, compute $h'(x)$:

$$h(x) = \ln(g(x)) = \ln(x^2 + x)$$
$$h'(x) = \frac{2x + 1}{x^2 + x}$$

Putting the pieces together, we have

$$f'(x) = 3[\ln(x^2 + x)]^2\left(\frac{2x + 1}{x^2 + x}\right)$$

The next example also uses the chain rule twice.

EXAMPLE 9   *(Compare Exercise 45)*

If $f(x) = \ln(x + (x^2 + 1)^3)$, find $f'(x)$.

SOLUTION   Let $g(x) = x + (x^2 + 1)^3$. Then $g'(x) = 1 + 3(x^2 + 1)^2 \cdot 2x$. Note that the $2x$ is due to the chain rule used on $(x^2 + 1)^3$.

$$g'(x) = 1 + 6x(x^2 + 1)^2$$

Thus

$$f'(x) = \frac{g'(x)}{g(x)}$$
$$= \frac{1 + 6x(x^2 + 1)^2}{x + (x^2 + 1)^3}$$

The next example serves as a final reminder that sometimes the computation of $f'(x)$ will be easier if you can use the properties of the logarithm function to simplify the expression for $f(x)$ before differentiating.

EXAMPLE 10   *(Compare Exercise 49)*

Compute $f'(x)$ if $f(x) = \ln\sqrt{16x^3 + 2x}$.

SOLUTION   First rewrite $f(x)$, and use the $\ln p^m = m \ln p$ property.

$$f(x) = \ln(16x^3 + 2x)^{1/2} = \frac{1}{2}\ln(16x^3 + 2x)$$

Thus

$$f'(x) = \frac{1}{2}\frac{1}{16x^3 + 2x} \cdot (48x^2 + 2) = \frac{24x^2 + 1}{16x^3 + 2x}$$

The last example in this section reminds you of the techniques of curve sketching.

EXAMPLE 11   *(Compare Exercise 57)*

Sketch the graph of $f(x) = \ln(x^2 + 1)$.

SOLUTION   First note that $x^2 + 1 > 0$ for all x; thus $\ln(x^2 + 1)$ is defined for all x, and the domain of f is all real numbers. Next,

$$f'(x) = \frac{2x}{x^2 + 1}$$

so $f'(x) = 0$ only when $x = 0$. The sign-of-f' chart is as follows:

$$\text{Sign-of-}f' \qquad \underset{0}{\underline{\qquad - \qquad \overset{|}{} \qquad + \qquad}}$$

We now know that f is decreasing on $(-\infty, 0)$ and increasing on $(0, \infty)$. For concavity,

$$f''(x) = \frac{2(x^2 + 1) - 2x \cdot 2x}{(x^2 + 1)^2} = \frac{2(1 - x^2)}{(x^2 + 1)^2}$$

Thus $f''(x)$ will equal 0 only when $x = 1$ and when $x = -1$. The sign-of-f'' chart follows:

$$\text{Sign-of-}f'' \qquad \underline{\qquad - \qquad \underset{-1}{\overset{|}{}} \qquad + \qquad \underset{-1}{\overset{|}{}} \qquad - \qquad}$$

The graph of f is concave up on the interval $-1 < x < 1$ and is concave down on the intervals $(-\infty, -1)$ and $(1, \infty)$. The points $(-1, \ln 2)$ and $(1, \ln 2)$ are the points of inflection.

Using this information, we can draw the graph of f as shown in Figure 12–18.

FIGURE 12–18

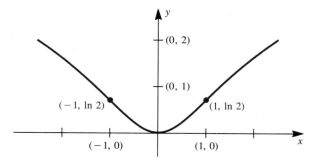

12–4   EXERCISES

I

Compute $f'(x)$ in Exercises 1 through 14.

1. $f(x) = x^2 + \ln x$
2. $f(x) = 7x^2 - 3\ln x$
3. (*See Example 1*)
$f(x) = x \ln x$
4. $f(x) = (x^2 + 1)\ln x$
5. (*See Example 3*)
$f(x) = \ln x + \ln 4$
6. $f(x) = (\ln 5)(\ln x)$
7. $f(x) = \dfrac{\ln x}{\ln 10}$
8. $f(x) = \dfrac{\ln x}{\ln 7}$

9. $f(x) = e^x \ln x$
10. $f(x) = x^2 \ln x$
11. (*See Example 4*)
$f(x) = \ln(6x)$
12. $f(x) = \ln(x/2)$
13. (*See Example 2*)
$f(x) = \dfrac{\ln x}{x}$
14. $f(x) = \dfrac{x}{\ln x}$

II

Compute $f'(x)$ in Exercises 15 through 32.

15. $f(x) = \ln(x^2 + 1)$
16. $f(x) = \ln(5x - 3)$
17. $f(x) = [\ln(x + 1)]^3$
18. $f(x) = \ln(x^2 + 3x)$
19. $f(x) = x \ln(3x - 8)$
20. $f(x) = \dfrac{\ln(5x - 1)}{3x^2}$
21. $f(x) = \dfrac{\ln(x^2 + 1)}{6x}$
22. $f(x) = 4x \ln(6x + 11)$

23. (*See Example 6*)
$f(x) = (\ln x)^4$
24. $f(x) = \ln x^5$
25. $f(x) = (\ln x)e^{5x}$
26. $f(x) = \ln(e^{2x} + 5)$
27. $f(x) = x^2(\ln 6)$
28. $f(x) = (\ln 4)^2$
29. (*See Example 7*)
$f(x) = \ln(x^2 - 3x + 1)$
30. $f(x) = \ln(x^3 - 9x)$
31. $f(x) = \ln(4x + 8)$
32. $f(x) = \ln(x + e^x)$

III

Compute $f'(x)$ in Exercises 33 through 52.

33. $f(x) = x \ln e^2$
34. $f(x) = e^{(\ln 4)x}$
35. $f(x) = e^{\ln x}$
36. $f(x) = x^{\ln e}$
37. (*See Example 5*)
$f(x) = \ln \sqrt{x}$
38. $f(x) = \ln(x^3 + 5x)$
39. $f(x) = \ln(3x + 1)^4$
40. $f(x) = \ln \sqrt{5x + 1}$
41. (*See Example 8*)
$f(x) = \sqrt{\ln(x^2 + 1)}$
42. $f(x) = [\ln(x^3 - 8)]^2$
43. $f(x) = [\ln(5x + 1)]^2$
44. $f(x) = e^{x^2}\ln(x^3 - 8x + 9)$
45. (*See Example 9*)
$f(x) = \ln(e^{2x} + \sqrt{4x + 10})$
46. $f(x) = \ln(e^{2x} + e^{4x})$
47. $f(x) = [\ln(x + e^{2x})]^3$
48. $f(x) = [\ln(x^2 + \sqrt{3x + 5})]^2$
49. (*See Example 10*)
$f(x) = \ln[(3x + 1)^2 \cdot (x^2 - 5x)]$

50. $f(x) = \ln \dfrac{5x^2 - 4x + 3}{6x^3 - 2x + 1}$
51. $f(x) = \ln \dfrac{1}{(x^3 - 2x)^2}$
52. $f(x) = \ln[(3x + 1)\sqrt{5x - 2}]$

Compute $f''(x)$ in Exercises 53 through 56.

53. $f(x) = x^2 \ln x$
54. $f(x) = x(\ln x)^2$
55. $f(x) = x \ln \sqrt{x + 1}$
56. $f(x) = x^2 e^{4x}$

57. (*See Example 11*) Sketch the graph of $f(x) = \ln(3x - 6)$.
58. Sketch the graph of $f(x) = (\ln x) - x$.
59. Find the maximum and the minimum of $f(x) = x \ln\left(\frac{1}{x}\right)$ on the interval $[\frac{1}{10}, 4]$.
60. Find the maximum and the minimum of $f(x) = \frac{\ln x}{x}$ on the interval $[\frac{1}{10}, 4]$.

12-5 APPLICATIONS OF EXPONENTIAL FUNCTIONS

We began this chapter by considering the problem of describing a rate of change when that rate is given in terms of the percentage of change rather than the amount of change. The particular situation we dealt with, continuously compounding interest, led us to look at the number e and exponential functions with base e. If y is such a function, then the particular relationship between y' and y makes exponential functions central to the solution of a wide variety of applications. We highlight this relationship by the following theorem.

Theorem   If $y = ke^{cx}$, then $y' = c \cdot y$.

Proof. If $y = ke^{cx}$, then

$$y' = \frac{d}{dx}(ke^{cx})$$

$$= k\frac{d}{dx}(e^{cx})$$

$$= ke^{cx} \cdot c$$

$$= y \cdot c$$

$$= cy$$

Thus

$$y' = cy$$

In words, *the rate of change of an exponential function is directly proportional to the value of the function.*

A typical application expresses this relationship by describing the rate of change as a percentage of the value of the function. For example, letting y represent the size of a population, we can translate the statement
    "The population is growing at the rate of 2%" to

"y' is 2% of y"

to

"$y' = 0.02y$"

Here, $c = 0.02$, so y is of the form $y = ke^{0.02t}$, where t is time.

An exponential function is the function to use when the rate of change is given in terms of percentage or, said another way, when the rate of change of the function is directly proportional to the value of the function. Thus when you want to describe population growth, inflation, unemployment statistics, the national debt, or any quantity for which the rate of change is given in terms of percentage, you should be using an exponential function as your model. We will do some examples showing these applications and then discuss further the implication of "exponential growth."

EXAMPLE 1 *(Compare Exercise 1)*

A certain city is growing at the continuous rate of 5%. If the population was 100,000 in 1980, what will it be in the year 2000?

SOLUTION Let us use $P(t)$ to denote the population at time t. The rate of change (growth) is 5% of the population (amount).

$$P'(t) = 0.05P(t)$$

We are using t instead of x and $P(t)$ instead of $f(x)$, but this equation tells us that $P(t)$ is of the form $P(t) = ke^{ct}$.

Notice that, in the expression $y' = cy$, the function was $y = ke^{cx}$. In this example, $c = 0.05$, and so we have

$$P(t) = ke^{0.05t}$$

NOTE *The number c in the expression $y' = cy$ is the coefficient of x in the expression $y = ke^{cx}$.*

To find k, we must use information about a particular value of y. Here, we need to use information about the size of the population at a particular time. When we are given data in this form, it is convenient to choose $t = 0$ to correspond to the year 1980. The convenience comes from the fact that if $P(t) = ke^{ct}$, then

$$P(0) = ke^{c \cdot 0} = ke^0 = k \cdot 1 = k$$

NOTE *The number k is the value of y when $x = 0$.*

If $t = 0$ corresponds to 1980, then the problem gives us the information that $P(0) = 100,000$, so $k = 100,000$. We can now write

$$P(t) = 100,000e^{0.05t}$$

The problem asks for the population in the year 2000, which is 20 years after 1980. The year 2000 corresponds to $t = 20$:

$$P(20) = 100,000e^{(0.05)(20)} = 100,000e^1$$
$$= 100,000e$$
$$\approx 271,828$$

It would be silly to calculate the population using more decimal places of e. In fact, it is not wise, in practice, to say much more than that this model predicts a population of a little over 270,000 in the year 2000.

———————■

EXAMPLE 2   *(Compare Exercise 5)*

If $1000 is invested in a trust fund in the year 2000, and the fund pays $5\frac{3}{4}\%$ interest, compounded continuously, how much will be in the fund: **(a)** after 100 years? **(b)** after 200 years?

SOLUTION   First, we invite you to guess the two answers; you might be surprised by the following computation. Let $A(t)$ be the amount the fund is worth t years after it is established; the continuous percentage growth rate tells us that $A(t)$ is of the form

$$A(t) = ke^{ct}$$

As in Example 1, the growth rate is c, and k is the initial amount. Here, $c = 5\frac{3}{4}\% = 0.0575$ and $k = 1000$, so $A(t) = 1000e^{0.0575t}$

(a) Setting $t = 100$, we have

$$
\begin{aligned}
A(100) &= 1000e^{(0.0575)(100)} \\
&= 1000e^{5.75} \\
&\approx (1000)(314.19) \\
&= 314{,}190
\end{aligned}
$$

After 100 years, the fund is worth $314,190.

Now that you know the answer to the first question, would you like to guess again at the second answer?

(b) We need to compute $A(200)$:

$$
\begin{aligned}
A(200) &= 1000e^{(0.0575)(200)} \\
&= 1000e^{11.5} \\
&\approx (1000)(98715.77) \\
&= 98{,}715{,}770
\end{aligned}
$$

After 200 years the fund is worth $98,715,770!

Exponential functions can grow very rapidly, as this example shows very dramatically. The amount of growth in the first 100 years is sizable, and we could all wish that one of our great-grandparents had created such a trust fund for us. The growth during the second hundred years is almost too much to believe. An investment of $1000 has grown to nearly $100 million. Imagine the social impact that an investment like that can have. Benjamin Franklin did, and he established such a fund that now, approximately 200 years after his death, provides scholarships for medical students. We should note that historically, a rate of $5\frac{3}{4}\%$ is a high rate of interest, and in the exercises you will see how small changes in the interest rate can affect the total amount, especially over a long period of time.

After the next two examples we explore different statements that people can make about the same data; growth at a constant percentage rate can lead to some interesting discussions.

Suppose the federal budget grows at the steady rate of 7% under two presidents, X and Y. Assume that the budget starts at $1000 billion under President X and that X is president for four years.

EXAMPLE 3   *(Compare Exercise 7)*

What will the budget be after four years?

SOLUTION   Let $B(t) =$ the budget (in billions of dollars) after t years. Percentage growth rate means that we should write

$$B(t) = ke^{ct}$$

Here, $k = 1000$ (units are billions of dollars) and $c = 0.07$. Using $t = 4$, we have

$$B(4) = 1000e^{(0.07)4} = 1000e^{0.28}$$
$$\approx 1323$$

After four years the budget is approximately \$1323 billion.

Now President Y takes over.

EXAMPLE 4   *(Compare Exercise 8)*

What will the budget be: **(a)** after three years of President Y's term? **(b)** after four years?

SOLUTION

(a) We continue letting $t = 0$ correspond to the beginning of President X's term, so to answer **(a)**, we use $t = 7$:

$$B(7) = 1000e^{(0.07)7} = 1000e^{0.49} \approx 1632$$

(b) With $t = 8$, we have

$$B(8) = 1000e^{(0.07)8} = 1000e^{0.56} \approx 1751$$

Now consider how these numbers can be debated. Under President X, the budget grew (in amount) a total of \$323 billion, for an average growth of about \$80 billion per year. Under President Y, the budget grew by $(1751 - 1632)$ billion $= \$119$ billion during the last year. Since $119 \approx (1\frac{1}{2})(80)$, some will claim that the budget is growing $1\frac{1}{2}$ times as fast under Y as it did under X! Yet remember that the percentage was a steady 7% under both presidents. Opponents of Y will talk about amounts; supporters of Y will talk about percentages. The effects of percentage growth rate on magnitudes are not well understood by the general public.

Sometimes, growth rates are given directly in terms of percentage; sometimes, the notion of doubling period (or half-life) is used. The presence of a doubling period also indicates that you should use an exponential function to model the real-world situation. We have seen that the number c represents the instantaneous percentage growth rate, and we now show how to find c when you are given a doubling period.

EXAMPLE 5   *(Compare Exercise 9)*

A certain bacteria colony doubles in size every 20 minutes. If 1000 bacteria are present at 1 P.M., how many will there be at 2:30 P.M. on the same day?

SOLUTION   Because the doubling time is given in minutes, we will measure time in minutes. We know how many bacteria are in the colony at 1 P.M., so we let $t = 0$ correspond to 1 P.M. We use $P(t)$ for the number of bacteria t minutes after 1 P.M.:

$$P(t) = ke^{ct}$$

and we must solve for k and c:

$$P(0) = 1000 \qquad \text{and so} \qquad k = 1000$$

$P(t)$ is of the form

$$P(t) = 1000e^{ct}$$

Furthermore, we are given that the population doubles in 20 minutes, so $P(20) = 2000$. By letting $t = 20$ in the expression $P(t) = 1000e^{ct}$, we have

$$P(20) = 1000e^{c(20)}$$

We set these two expressions for $P(20)$ equal to each other and then solve for c:

$$2000 = 1000e^{20c} \qquad \text{(Divide by 1000)}$$
$$2 = e^{20c} \qquad \text{(Take ln of both sides)}$$
$$\ln 2 = \ln e^{20c} = 20c \qquad \text{(Divide by 20)}$$
$$\frac{\ln 2}{20} = c \qquad (c \approx 0.0347)$$

We now have both k and c:

$$P(t) = 1000e^{[(\ln 2)/20]t}$$

To find the population at 2:30, we need to calculate $P(90)$:

$$P(90) = 1000e^{[(\ln 2)/20]90}$$
$$= 1000e^{[(9 \ln 2)/2]}$$
$$\approx 1000e^{3.119} \approx 22{,}627$$

The colony is over 22 times its original size.

Some applications deal not with growth, but rather with diminishing quantities. For example, psychologists may model retention rate of knowledge in terms of the percentage of the knowledge forgotten each week. The application that we will deal with here has to do with radioactive decay. Certain materials are called radioactive because they give off radiant energy. This is called radioactive decay.

One such element that exists in our atmosphere is Carbon-14 (C-14). Living animals and plants absorb the C-14 from the atmosphere, and because the supply is being replenished, the level of C-14 in living organisms remains constant. When the organism dies, however, the intake stops, and the amount of C-14 diminishes because of radioactive decay. We will let $R(t)$ be the measure of C-14 t years after the death of the organism. But we do not want to get too technical, so we will not worry about the units of $R(t)$. Scientists tell us that $R(0) = 15.3$ and that the half-life of C-14 is about 5730 years. The **half-life** of a radioactive substance is the amount of time it takes for half of the substance to decay. We use these numbers to find the formula for $R(t)$ in Example 6.

EXAMPLE 6

Find k and c for $R(t) = ke^{ct}$, where $R(t)$ is the amount of C-14 left t years after an organism dies.

SOLUTION $R(t) = ke^{ct}$ and $R(0) = 15.3$ tells us that $k = 15.3$, so

$$R(t) = 15.3e^{ct}$$

Now, a half-life of 5730 years means that

$$R(5730) = \frac{1}{2}R(0) = \frac{1}{2}(15.3) = 7.65$$

Also from the formula for $R(t)$,

$$R(5730) = 15.3e^{c5730}$$

We put these two expressions for $R(5730)$ equal to each other and solve for c:

$$7.65 = 15.3e^{c5730} \qquad \text{(Divide by 15.3)}$$

$$\frac{1}{2} = e^{5730c} \qquad \text{(Take ln of both sides)}$$

$$\ln\left(\frac{1}{2}\right) = 5730c \qquad \text{(Divide by 5730)}$$

$$c = \frac{\ln\left(\frac{1}{2}\right)}{5730} \qquad (\approx -0.000121)$$

We can use the fact that $\ln(\frac{1}{2}) = -\ln 2$ to write

$$R(t) = 15.3e^{[-(\ln 2)/5730]t}$$

Note that because R is a decreasing function, c must be negative. Notice also the similarity of the steps in Examples 5 and 6.

We can use this formula for $R(t)$ to determine the age of a fossil; this method is called **carbon dating.**

EXAMPLE 7   *(Compare Exercise 15)*

A piece of wood from the funeral boat of an Egyptian pharaoh was measured for C-14 radioactivity. The level was found to be 9.75. How long ago did this pharaoh die?

SOLUTION   The measurement tells us that $R(t) = 9.75$; we need to solve for t:

$$9.75 = 15.3e^{[-(\ln 2)/5730]t} \qquad \text{(Divide by 15.3)}$$
$$0.63725 = e^{[-(\ln 2)/5730]t} \qquad \text{(Take ln of both sides)}$$
$$\ln 0.63725 = [-(\ln 2)/5730]t$$
$$t = \frac{(5730)(\ln 0.63725)}{-\ln 2} \approx 3725$$

The pharaoh died about 3725 years ago.

This method of dating fossils was developed by Dr. Willard F. Libby of the University of Chicago in the late 1940s. He received a Nobel prize for this work in 1960. If you are interested in reading further about this method of dating fossils, we recommend *Radiocarbon Dating,* by Willard F. Libby, University of Chicago Press, 1955; and *Before Civilization,* by Colin Renfrew, Alfred A. Knopf, New York, 1973. The first book is Libby's original work; the second has a very readable discussion of carbon dating, including an appendix that discusses the assumptions made in the theory.

12-5   EXERCISES

1. *(See Example 1)* Property values in a certain suburb have been growing at a continuous rate of 5%. If the average house cost $80,000 in 1980, what would the average cost be in the year 2000?

2. If the average cost of a new automobile increases at the continuous rate of 6%, and if this average cost was $10,500 in 1985, what will the average cost be in 1995?

3. If the inflation rate in a certain country is 4%, continuously compounded, what would a person have to earn in 1995 just to stay even if the person's salary in 1990 was $20,000?

4. How would the answer to Exercise 3 change if the inflation rate was 8%?

5. *(See Example 2)* If $500 is invested in a trust fund paying interest at a continuous rate of 4%, how much will the fund be worth: **(a)** in 100 years? **(b)** in 200 years?

6. If $500 is invested in a trust fund that pays interest at a continuous rate of 3%, how much will the fund be worth: **(a)** after 100 years? **(b)** after 200 years?

7. *(See Example 3)* Suppose that a state government's budget grows at a continuous rate of 10%. If the budget is $20 billion when Governor A takes office, what will it be four years later?

8. *(See Example 4)* For the same state as in Example 6, if Governor B replaces A after four years, compare the growth of the budget during B's fourth year to the total growth under A.

9. *(See Example 5)* The population in a certain country is doubling every 20 years. If the country had 100 million people in 1950, how many will it have: **(a)** in 2000? **(b)** in 2050?

10. If the U.S. consumption of coal doubles every 30 years, and the United States consumed 600 million tons in 1980, how much will the United States consume in 2020?

11. Suppose that 500 bacteria are present in a wound at 1:00 P.M. and that the number of bacteria doubles every 30 minutes. Furthermore, medical attention should be given to the wound before the number of bacteria reaches 1,000,000. When is the latest that medical attention should be given to this wound?

12. A certain parasite invades a host's body, and the number of parasites doubles every 40 minutes. When the number of parasites is more than 300,000, the host dies. How long after the parasitic invasion will the host die?

13. The per-capita gross national product (GNP) of country A was $2000 in 1980 and was growing at a continuous rate of 8% per year.
    (a) When will the per-capita GNP of country A reach $6000?
    (b) The per-capita GNP of country B was $4400 in 1980 and was growing at a continuous rate of 5%. When will the per-capita GNP of country B reach $6000?
    (c) When will the per-capita GNP of country A equal that of country B?

14. Alice makes a high-risk investment of $3000; this investment earns 11% continuously compounded interest. Marti places her $5000 in a safer investment

that earns $7\frac{1}{2}\%$ continuously compounded. If the investments continue their respective yield, when will their investments be worth the same?

The results in Exercises 15 through 18 were obtained by measuring the radioactivity of samples. Determine the age of each sample; use 5730 years as the half-life of C-14.

15. (*See Example 7*) Wood from the foundation cribbing for a fortification wall in a mound at Alisher Huyuh, Turkey, if the present reading of $R(t) = 10.26$.

16. Wood from the floor of a central room in a large Hilani (palace) of the Syro-Hittite period in the city of Tayinat in northwest Syria, if the present reading of $R(t) = 11.17$.

17. Slab of wood from a roof beam of the tomb of Vizier Hemaka, contemporaneous with King Udimu, First Dynasty, in Sakkara, Egypt, if the present reading of $R(t) = 8.33$.

18. Lake mud from Neasham near Darlington in the extreme north of England, correlated directly with the last glacial stage, if the present reading of $R(t) = 3.96$.

12–6   BASES OTHER THAN *e*

- *Rewriting b^x*
- *The Derivative of $y = b^x$*
- *Logarithms with Bases Other Than e*
- *Rewriting $y = \log_b x$*
- *The Derivative of $y = \log_b x$*

In Section 12–1 we wrote the general form of an exponential function as kb^{cx}. Then we specialized to the case in which the base *b* was the special number *e*. In this section we show that in fact, every exponential function can be written by using base *e*. Further, we introduce logarithms to bases other than *e*, and show that they too can be written by using only the natural logarithm. The only exponential or logarithm functions that you really need are those whose base is *e*. However, because it may be more convenient in certain applications to use other bases, we derive the formulas for the derivatives of b^x and $\log_b x$.

REWRITING b^x

Let b be an arbitrary positive number. We write the equation $b^x = e^{cx}$ and solve for c. Take ln of both sides:

$$\ln b^x = \ln e^{cx}$$
$$x \ln b = cx$$
$$\ln b = c$$

We have found c. Now that we know what c is, we can rewrite b^x more directly. Since $b = e^{\ln b}$, we have

$$b^x = (e^{\ln b})^x = e^{(\ln b)x}$$

EXAMPLE 1   *(Compare Exercise 1)*

Express $f(x) = 2^x$, using base e.
SOLUTION $2 = e^{\ln 2}$, so $f(x) = 2^x = e^{(\ln 2)x} = e^{x \ln 2}$. It is customary to write $(\ln 2)x$ as $x \ln 2$ to avoid parentheses.

EXAMPLE 2   *(Compare Exercise 5)*

Express $f(x) = 2^{x/3}$, using base e.
SOLUTION   Again, $2 = e^{\ln 2}$, so $2^{x/3} = e^{(\ln 2)(x/3)}$. Thus $f(x) = e^{(x \ln 2)/3}$.

EXAMPLE 3   *(Compare Exercise 7)*

If $f(x) = 4 \cdot 3^x$, rewrite $f(x)$ using base e.
SOLUTION   We have to rewrite the base; here, $b = 3$ and $3 = e^{\ln 3}$.
Thus

$$4(3)^x = 4(e^{\ln 3})^x$$
$$= 4e^{x \ln 3} \qquad \text{(Exact form)}$$
$$\approx 4e^{1.0986x} \qquad \text{(Using the decimal approximation to } \ln 3)$$

THE DERIVATIVE
OF $y = b^x$

To find the derivative of $y = b^x$, we again rewrite the base. We have just seen that $b = e^{\ln b}$, so we write $y = (e^{\ln b})^x = e^{x \ln b}$. Now we use the chain rule to compute the derivative. The special form of the chain rule for an exponential function with base e was obtained in Section 12–2.

$$\text{If } f(x) = e^{g(x)}, \qquad \text{then} \qquad f'(x) = e^{g(x)} \cdot g'(x)$$

In this case, $g(x) = x \cdot \ln b$, and so $g'(x) = \ln b$. Remember that $\ln b$ is just a constant. We have the following:

$$\text{if } f(x) = e^{x \ln b}, \qquad \text{then} \qquad f'(x) = e^{x \ln b} \cdot \ln b$$

One further step can be made by going back to the original expression for $e^{x \ln b}$, namely, b^x.

Theorem   If $f(x) = b^x$, then $f'(x) = b^x \ln b$.

EXAMPLE 4   *(Compare Exercise 31)*

If $f(x) = 6^x$, what is $f'(x)$?
SOLUTION   Using $b = 6$, $f'(x) = 6^x \ln 6$.

For a more general exponent, if $f(x) = b^{g(x)}$, then $f(x) = e^{(\ln b)g(x)}$, and we have the following theorem.

Theorem   If $f(x) = b^{g(x)}$, then

$$f'(x) = e^{(\ln b)g(x)} \cdot \ln b \cdot g'(x)$$
$$= b^{g(x)} \cdot \ln b \cdot g'(x)$$

Notice that if $b = e$, then $\ln b = 1$, and we have the formulas for the derivative of e^x and $e^{g(x)}$, as before.

EXAMPLE 5   *(Compare Exercise 35)*

If $f(x) = 4^{x^2}$, what is $f'(x)$?
SOLUTION   Here, $b = 4$ and $g(x) = x^2$. Thus $g'(x) = 2x$, and we have $f'(x) = 4^{x^2}(\ln 4)2x$.

EXAMPLE 6   *(Compare Exercise 39)*

If $f(x) = 3 \cdot 5^{x^2 + x}$, find $f'(x)$.
SOLUTION   Here, $b = 5$ and $g(x) = x^2 + x$. The number 3 is simply a constant times $5^{x^2 + x}$.

$$f'(x) = (3 \cdot 5^{x^2 + x})(\ln 5)(2x + 1)$$

LOGARITHMS WITH BASES OTHER THAN e

If $b > 0$ ($b \neq 1$), we can now define the logarithm to the base b as the function that "undoes" b^x. Thus the function $\log_b x$ is related to b^x as the function $\ln x$ is related to e^x. Specifically,

$$\log_b M = N \qquad \text{if and only if} \qquad b^N = M$$

We now give you some examples to stress this definition and the relation between logarithms and exponentials. The examples will be done by using the definition of the logarithm.

EXAMPLE 7   *(Compare Exercise 11)*

What is $\log_2 8$?

SOLUTION   If we let $N = \log_2 8$, then $2^N = 8$, and we recognize that $N = 3$. Thus $\log_2 8 = 3$.

EXAMPLE 8   *(Compare Exercise 15)*

What is $\log_2(\frac{1}{8})$?

SOLUTION   We want B so that $2^B = \frac{1}{8}$; by "inspection," or "trial and error," $B = -3$. Thus $\log_2(\frac{1}{8}) = -3$.

EXAMPLE 9   *(Compare Exercise 23)*

What is $\log_2(-8)$?

SOLUTION   This expression is undefined; 2^N is always positive. The equation $2^N = -8$ has no solution.

CAUTION   As with the natural logarithm, the domain of any logarithm function is all positive numbers; $\log_b x$ may be negative, but x cannot be negative. Be sure that you understand the difference between Examples 8 and 9.

REWRITING $y = \log_b x$ As we mentioned, the traditional use of logarithms has been to aid in some calculations, and so a very commonly used logarithm is $\log_{10}$ (in fact, it is called the common logarithm). Often, all that is written is "log"; the base 10 is understood. With $\log_b$ notation the natural logarithm is the same as $\log_e$, but the natural logarithm is almost always written as "ln." Many calculators feature both a **log** and a **ln** button. We will show you how to compute $\log_b M$ for any base b using only the ln function.

$$N = \log_b M \qquad \text{means} \qquad b^N = M$$

Take ln of both sides of the equation $b^N = M$:

$$\ln b^N = \ln M$$
$$N \ln b = \ln M$$

Divide both sides by $\ln b$:

$$N = \frac{\ln M}{\ln b}$$

Remember that we began with $N = \log_b M$, so these two expressions for N give us the following theorem:

Theorem	$\log_b M = \dfrac{\ln M}{\ln b}$

Using the more common variable x in place of M, we have

$$\log_b x = \frac{\ln x}{\ln b}$$

EXAMPLE 10   *(Compare Exercise 17)*

What is $\log_3 81$?

SOLUTION   We compute $\log_3 81$ in two ways. First, we use the definition $\log_3 81 = N$, where $3^N = 81$. The number 81 was chosen for this example so that we can find the answer as an integer; $N = 4$.

Second, we use the conversion formula and compare results:

$$\log_3 81 = \frac{\ln 81}{\ln 3}$$

Our calculator gives $\ln 81 \approx 4.3944$. . . and $\ln 3 \approx 1.0986$. . . , and when we perform the division $(\ln 81)/(\ln 3)$ on our calculator, it gives the answer 4.

Of course, once we go to the calculator, we are dealing with approximations, and we were "lucky" to get exactly 4 as a result of our computations.

EXAMPLE 11   *(Compare Exercise 21)*

Find a numerical approximation to $\log_2 12$.

SOLUTION $\log_2 12 = N$ means $2^N = 12$, but we cannot solve this by inspection. We know that N is some number between 3 and 4 because $2^3 = 8$ is less than 12 but $2^4 = 16$ is larger than 12. The conversion formula gives us

$$\log_2 12 = \frac{\ln 12}{\ln 2}$$

Now, using the ln function on our calculator, we obtain

$$\frac{\ln 12}{\ln 2} \approx \frac{2.4849}{0.6931} \approx 3.585 \qquad \text{(Rounded to three places)}$$

THE DERIVATIVE OF $y = \log_b x$

To compute the derivative of $\log_b x$, rewrite $\log_b x$ as

$$\frac{\ln x}{\ln b} = \frac{1}{\ln b}\ln x$$

and remember that $\dfrac{1}{\ln b}$ is a constant. The derivative of $\ln x$ is simply $1/x$. Therefore, if

$$f(x) = \left(\frac{1}{\ln b}\right)\ln x, \quad \text{then} \quad f'(x) = \left(\frac{1}{\ln b}\right)\left(\frac{1}{x}\right) = \frac{1}{x\ln b}$$

Theorem   If $f(x) = \log_b x$, then $f'(x) = \dfrac{1}{x\ln b}$.

EXAMPLE 12   *(Compare Exercise 27)*

If $f(x) = \log_3 x$, find $f'(x)$.
SOLUTION   Using $b = 3$, we have

$$f'(x) = \frac{1}{x\ln 3}$$

The corresponding chain rule formula is

Theorem   If $f(x) = \log_b g(x)$, then $f'(x) = \dfrac{1}{\ln b}\dfrac{1}{g(x)} \cdot g'(x)$.

You can either learn this form directly or just remember to write

$$\log_b g(x) = \frac{\ln g(x)}{\ln b}$$

and use the chain rule when computing the derivative of $\ln g(x)$.

EXAMPLE 13   *(Compare Exercise 43)*

If $f(x) = \log_2(8x + 7)$, find $f'(x)$.
SOLUTION   We use the theorem with $b = 2$ and $g(x) = 8x + 7$. Thus $g'(x) = 8$, and

$$f'(x) = \left(\frac{1}{\ln 2}\right)\left(\frac{1}{8x + 7}\right) \cdot 8$$

$$= \frac{8}{(\ln 2)(8x + 7)}$$

12-6 EXERCISES

I

In Exercises 1 through 10, rewrite each function in the form $f(x) = ke^{cx}$ for some c and k.

1. (*See Example 1*)
   $f(x) = 3^x$

2. $f(x) = 10^x$

3. $f(x) = 9^{-x}$

4. $f(x) = \left(\dfrac{1}{2}\right)^x$

5. (*See Example 2*)
   $f(x) = 7^{x/2}$

6. $f(x) = 9^{x/3}$

7. (*See Example 3*)
   $f(x) = 5 \cdot 8^x$

8. $f(x) = 2 \cdot 10^x$

9. $f(x) = 7 \cdot 4^{x/3}$

10. $f(x) = 32^{x/6}$

II

In Exercises 11 through 16, what integer or fraction is represented by each expression?

11. (*See Example 7*)
    $\log_3 81$

12. $\log_5 25$

13. $\log_8 2$

14. $\log_{16} 4$

15. (*See Example 8*)
    $\log_3\left(\dfrac{1}{3}\right)$

16. $\log_2\left(\dfrac{1}{32}\right)$

In Exercises 17 through 26, rewrite each expression using the natural logarithm. Use a calculator with an ln button to find a decimal approximation.

17. (*See Example 10*)
    $\log_6 36$

18. $\log_{16} 2$

19. $\log_{25} 5$

20. $\log_8\left(\dfrac{1}{2}\right)$

21. (*See Example 11*)
    $\log_{10} 14$

22. $\log_5 30$

23. (*See Example 9*)
    $\log_2(-16)$

24. $\log_3(-9)$

25. $\log_{-3} 10$

26. $\log_{-4}(-8)$

In Exercises 27 through 34, find the derivative of each function.

27. (*See Example 12*)
    $f(x) = \log_2 x$

28. $f(x) = \log_{10} x$

29. $f(x) = x^2 \log_4 x$

30. $f(x) = 3x^5 \log_{10} x$

31. (*See Example 4*)
    $f(x) = 10^x$

32. $f(x) = 8^x$

33. $f(x) = 7^{x/2}$

34. $f(x) = 2^{x/3}$

III

In Exercises 35 through 50, find $f'(x)$.

35. (*See Example 5*)
    $f(x) = 16^{x^2}$

36. $f(x) = 9^{\sqrt{x}}$

37. $f(x) = 10^{\sqrt{4x + 1}}$

38. $f(x) = 3^{2x^2 + 5x}$

39. (*See Example 6*)
    $f(x) = 10 \cdot 3^{x^2 - 2x}$

40. $f(x) = 3 \cdot 2^{3x^2 - 1}$

41. $f(x) = 2^{2^x}$

42. $f(x) = 2^{x^2}$

43. (*See Example 13*)
    $f(x) = \log_3(4x - 2)$

44. $f(x) = \log_9(x^2 + 1)$

45. $f(x) = \log_4(2x^2 - 8)^3$

46. $f(x) = 3 \log_4(2x^2 - 8)$

47. $f(x) = [\log_4(x^2 - 9)]^3$

48. $f(x) = \sqrt{\log_{10}(3x + 1)}$

49. $f(x) = \log_x e$

50. $f(x) = \log_x 10$

IMPORTANT TERMS

12-1

Percentage Change

Interest

Compounding Period

Continuous Compounding

Number e

Exponent

Exponential Functions

Base

12-2

Derivative of f(x) = e^x

The Chain Rule with the Exponential Function

12-3

Doubling Period

Natural Logarithm Function

Relation Between ln x and e^x

Present Value

12-4

Derivative of f(x) = ln x

The Chain Rule with the Natural Logarithm Function

12-5

Percentage Growth Rate

Half-Life

Carbon Dating

12-6

Rewriting b^x

Derivative of f(x) = b^x

Rewriting log_b x

Derivative of f(x) = log_b x

The Chain Rule with General Exponential Functions

The Chain Rule with Logarithmic Functions

REVIEW EXERCISES

In Exercises 1 through 10, find $f'(x)$.

1. $f(x) = x^2 e^{3x}$

2. $f(x) = e^x \ln x$

3. $f(x) = \ln(x^2 + 1)$

4. $f(x) = \ln\sqrt{6x + 8}$

5. $f(x) = \sqrt{\ln(6x + 8)}$

6. $f(x) = \dfrac{x^2 + 1}{e^{3x}}$

7. $f(x) = [\ln(3x + 2)]^2$

8. $f(x) = e^{x^2} + 4x$

9. $f(x) = e^{\ln(2x)}$

10. $f(x) = e^2 + \ln 4$

11. Let $f(x) = x \ln x$.

   (a) Does f have a maximum value? If so, what is this maximum value?

   (b) Does f have a minimum value? If so, what is this minimum value?

12. Let $f(x) = \dfrac{x}{e^x}$.

   (a) On what interval(s) is f increasing?

   (b) What is the maximum value of f?

   (c) On what interval is the graph of f concave down?

   (d) Given that $\lim\limits_{x \to \infty} \dfrac{x}{e^x} = 0$, sketch the graph of f.

13. The population of a colony of bacteria growing in a test tube doubles every minute. After 30 minutes the test tube is full.

   (a) When was the test tube only half full?

   (b) What percentage of the test tube was occupied by the bacteria after 15 minutes?

14. A colony of a certain bacteria doubles in size every 17 minutes. How long will it take a colony to grow to:

   (a) 20 times its original size?

   (b) 100 times its original size?

   (c) 1000 times its original size?

15. Samples of basketry were taken from Lovelock Cave in Nevada. They had a C-14 reading of 12.4. Approximately how old were the baskets?

16. A recently discovered fossil has a C-14 reading of 2.3. Approximately how old is the fossil?

17. The population of a certain country is growing at the continuous rate of 3% per year, and the present population of the country is 25 million.

   (a) In how many years will the country have 100 million people?

   (b) How many people will the country have after 100 years?

18. If the earth has a human population of 5 billion, then what will be the earth's population in 100 years if the population is growing at the continuous rate of:
    (a) 1% per year?   (b) 2% per year?
    (c) 3% per year?

19. What is the present value of $15,000 to be received in three years if the rate of interest is $7\frac{1}{4}\%$ compounded continuously?

20. If you have $7000 to invest, and you can earn 9% interest per year continuously compounded, how long will you have to wait before your investment is worth $10,000?

21. An initial investment of $1000 is worth $1400 after four years. What is the continuous interest rate the investment was earning during these four years?

22. Country A had a per-capita GNP in 1988 that was $2500 and growing at the continuous rate of 7% per year. Country B had a per-capita GNP in 1988 that was $3400 and was growing at the continuous rate of $4\frac{1}{2}\%$ per year. When will the per-capita GNP of these countries be equal?

23. If $10,000 is invested at 8% interest, how much is the investment worth after 10 years if the compounding is done: (a) quarterly? (b) continuously?

24. If an investment pays 7% compounded continuously, then what rate would a second account have to pay to yield the same amount of interest if the second account is compounded annually?

25. A certain bank card charges interest at the rate of $1\frac{1}{2}\%$ per month. How much interest would a cardholder have to pay for the use of $1000 for one year? (Assume that no payments were made during the year.)

26. Determine an approximate decimal equivalent for:
    (a) $\left(1 + \dfrac{1}{1,000,000}\right)^{1,000,000}$
    (b) $\left(1 - \dfrac{1}{1,000,000}\right)^{1,000,000}$

13

The Integral

13-1 THE INDEFINITE INTEGRAL

- *From Marginal Cost to Total Cost*

- *Antiderivatives and Integral Notation*

- *Integration Formulas*

- *Fractional and Negative Exponents*

*I*N THE PREVIOUS FOUR chapters we studied one of the two major topics in calculus—the derivative. We turn now to the other major calculus topic—the integral.

FROM MARGINAL COST TO TOTAL COST

We have seen how to compute the derivative of a function f and how to use the derivative to analyze properties of f. For instance, if $P(x)$ represents the profit from selling x watches, we have seen how marginal analysis can show how many watches should be produced to maximize profit. Often, however, an application arises where the function isn't known to begin with, but what is known is the rate of change of the function. For example, if a company knows that it costs $17 to manufacture each wristwatch, then that knowledge implies that the cost function is defined by $C(x) = 17x + B$, where B represents the fixed costs. Using the language of marginal analysis, if $MC(x) = 17$, then $C(x) = 17x + B$. This example gives a simple application of a more general principle. If we know the marginal cost function, we know what the cost function looks like, except for an undetermined added constant term representing the fixed costs. The particular cost function is not completely known until the fixed costs are known. The two cost functions $C_1(x) = 17x + 109$ and $C_2(x) = 17x + 420$ have the same marginal cost function; $MC_1(x) = MC_2(x) = 17$. Furthermore, if f is any function with $f'(x) = 17$, then $f(x) = 17x + B$ for some constant B. This fact is part of a more general mathematical statement.

Theorem | If two functions f and g have the same derivative on some interval, then there is a constant B so that $f(x) = g(x) + B$ for all x in the interval.

In other words, if $f'(x) = g'(x)$ on some interval, then $f(x) - g(x)$ is a constant on that interval.

A geometric interpretation may help in understanding this theorem. We know from Chapter 4 that f' gives us knowledge about the shape of the graph of f. Thus if $f'(x) = g'(x)$ on some interval, the graphs of f and g have the same

FIGURE 13-1

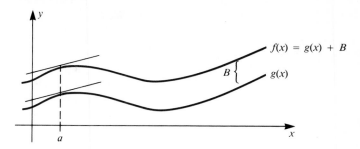

shape on this interval. The theorem says that these graphs are "parallel." For example, see Figure 13–1, where the graph of f is obtained by sliding the graph of g up B units:

$$f(x) = g(x) + B$$

Observe that $f'(x) = g'(x)$ means that the lines tangent to the graphs of f and g are parallel for every value of x (these tangents are drawn for $x = a$).

If $f'(x) = 17$, we are able to say that $f(x) = 17x + B$. We now address the problem of finding $f(x)$ if we start with a more complicated $f'(x)$.

EXAMPLE 1   *(Compare Exercise 1)*

If $f'(x) = 2x$, what is $f(x)$?

SOLUTION   We are looking for a function whose derivative is $2x$; one such function is $g(x) = x^2$. The theorem tells us that $f(x)$ must be of the form $f(x) = g(x) + B$. Thus $f(x)$ is of the form $f(x) = x^2 + B$. Note that we cannot determine a particular f; we can only determine $f(x)$ up to an additive constant.   ∎

ANTIDERIVATIVES AND INTEGRAL NOTATION

Definition
Antiderivative F is called an **antiderivative** of f if $F'(x) = f(x)$.

Referring to the previous example, we can now say that x^2 is an antiderivative of $2x$ and also, with $B = -9$, that $x^2 - 9$ is an antiderivative of $2x$. Furthermore, all antiderivatives of $2x$ are of the form $x^2 + B$. (The "anti" indicates that the process is going in the opposite direction from computing derivatives.) There is special mathematical notation for antiderivatives, just as the notations $f'(x)$ and dy/dx are used for derivatives. The notation will not single out a particular antiderivative, since B can be any number. The notation stands for *all* antiderivatives.

∫ *Notation*   The collection of all antiderivatives of f is written

$$\int f(x)dx$$

Thus $\int f(x)dx$ means the collection of all functions of the form $F(x) + B$, where $F'(x) = f(x)$. We write

$$\int f(x)dx = F(x) + B$$

We will also use another name for the collection of all antiderivatives of f.

Definition
Indefinite Integral $\int f(x)dx$ is called the **indefinite integral** of f.

We can now rephrase the result of Example 1 in the following way:

$$\int 2x \, dx = x^2 + B$$

There are historical reasons for this notation. The symbol ∫ is called an **integral sign.** This symbol is an elongated S, which is the first letter in the word "summation." We shall see later that there is a close connection between integrals and summations. The dx is called the **differential** and is also there for historical reasons. Furthermore, it proves very useful in actually computing antiderivatives, as we will see in Chapter 7. The $f(x)$ is called the **integrand;** the constant B is called the **additive constant of integration.** We have been using B to denote the constant term because our discussion began with a cost function C, and we didn't want to confuse the issue with several C's floating around. Generally, mathematicians use C, the first letter of the word constant, as the constant of integration. So $\int 2x \, dx = x^2 + C$. Finally, **antidifferentiation** is also called **integration.** We summarize as follows:

The indefinite integral of f, written $\int f(x)dx$, is the collection of functions of the form $F(x) + C$, where $F'(x) = f(x)$.

NOTE Before showing you some techniques that you can use to find antiderivatives, we wish to emphasize that we are now trying to find an *antiderivative* for a given function. Your skills in computing derivatives will still be very useful, however, because you can use these skills to check your answer. You can make sure that you have found the correct antiderivative by computing the derivative of your answer.

The point of Examples 2 through 5 is not to show how to compute indefinite integrals, but rather to emphasize the above note.

EXAMPLE 2   *(Compare Exercise 5)*

True or false: $\int \left(8x - \dfrac{6}{x^3} \right) dx = 4x^2 + \dfrac{3}{x^2} + C$?

SOLUTION   Here, $f(x) = 8x - \dfrac{6}{x^3}$ and $F(x) = 4x^2 + \dfrac{3}{x^2}$. Compute $F'(x)$. The derivative of $4x^2 + \dfrac{3}{x^2}$ is $8x - \dfrac{6}{x^3}$. TRUE.

EXAMPLE 3

True or false: $\int e^{3x}\, dx = \frac{1}{3}e^{3x} + C$?

SOLUTION   The derivative of $\frac{1}{3}e^{3x}$ is $\frac{1}{3}e^{3x} \cdot 3$ (remember the chain rule), which is e^{3x}. TRUE.

EXAMPLE 4

True or false: $\int (8x - 7)^3\, dx = \frac{1}{4}(8x - 7)^4 + C$?

SOLUTION   The derivative of $\frac{1}{4}(8x - 7)^4$ is $(\frac{1}{4})4(8x - 7)^3 \cdot 8 = 8(8x - 7)^3$. But $(8x - 7)^3 \neq 8(8x - 7)^3$. FALSE.

EXAMPLE 5

True or false: $\int 6x^2\, dx = 2x^3$?

SOLUTION   Although $2x^3$ is an antiderivative of $6x^2$, the answer to this example is FALSE. The correct answer is $2x^3 + C$.

INTEGRATION FORMULAS

Now we give some rules to help you actually compute the correct answers.

Power Rule for Integration   If p is a real number, $p \neq -1$, then

$$\int x^p\, dx = \frac{1}{p + 1}x^{p + 1} + C$$

To verify the power rule for integration, simply differentiate:

$$\frac{d}{dx}\left(\frac{1}{p + 1}x^{p + 1} + C \right) = x^p$$

EXAMPLE 6   *(Compare Exercise 11)*

Find $\int x^3 \, dx$.

SOLUTION   Here, $p = 3$:

$$\int x^3 \, dx = \frac{1}{3+1} x^{3+1} + C$$

$$= \frac{1}{4} x^4 + C$$

CAUTION   The case $p = -1$ is not covered by this rule. This rule can't work for $p = -1$ because then $1/(p+1)$ would be $1/[(-1)+1] = \frac{1}{0}$, and $\frac{1}{0}$ doesn't make sense. We will discuss $\int x^{-1} \, dx = \int \frac{1}{x} \, dx$ in the next section.

Our second rule for differentiation told us how to handle a constant times a function.

$$(c \cdot f)'(x) = cf'(x)$$

This rule gives us a corresponding integration rule:

Constant-Times Rule $\displaystyle\int c \cdot f(x) dx = c \cdot \int f(x) dx$

EXAMPLE 7   *(Compare Exercise 17)*

Find $\int 3x \, dx$.

SOLUTION

$$\int 3x \, dx = 3 \int x \, dx \qquad \text{(Constant-times rule)}$$

$$= 3\left(\frac{1}{2}x^2\right) + C \qquad \text{(Power rule)}$$

$$= \frac{3}{2}x^2 + C$$

Just as you learned to combine these two rules into one step when computing derivatives, you will also be able to combine them when computing integrals.

EXAMPLE 8   *(Compare Exercise 17)*

Find $\int 12x^2 \, dx$.

SOLUTION

$$\int 12x^2 \, dx = 12 \cdot \frac{1}{3}x^3 + C$$

$$= 4x^3 + C$$

The next two rules for finding derivatives had to do with sums and differences of functions; we follow that pattern again.

Sum Rule	$$\int [f(x) + g(x)]dx = \int f(x)dx + \int g(x)dx$$

The integral of the sum is the sum of the integrals.

Difference Rule	$$\int [f(x) - g(x)]dx = \int f(x)dx - \int g(x)dx$$

The integral of the difference is the difference of the integrals.

Again, you can check that these formulas are correct by differentiating.

EXAMPLE 9   *(Compare Exercise 19)*

Find $\int (9x^2 - 6)dx$.

SOLUTION

$$\int (9x^2 - 6)dx = \int 9x^2\, dx - \int 6\, dx$$
$$= \left(9 \cdot \frac{1}{3}x^3 + C_1\right) - (6x + C_2)$$
$$= 3x^3 - 6x + C_1 - C_2$$

where C_1 is the constant of integration associated with $\int 9x^2\, dx$ and C_2 is the constant associated with $\int 6\, dx$. The difference of two constants is constant, so we just write one constant of integration:

$$\int (9x^2 - 6)dx = 3x^3 - 6x + C$$

You need not write down constants like C_1 and C_2 when finding the antiderivative of a sum or difference. Just remember to include one constant at the end of the antiderivative.

EXAMPLE 10   *(Compare Exercise 21)*

Find $\int (5x^2 - 8x + 9)dx$.

SOLUTION

$$\int (5x^2 - 8x + 9)dx = \frac{5}{3}x^3 - 4x^2 + 9x + C$$

Of course, the power rule can be used with exponents that are fractions or that are negative, and we would like to make some helpful remarks about handling these types of exponents.

You might find it easier when dealing with fractions to notice that dividing by a fraction is the same as multiplying by its reciprocal; this will allow you to avoid an awkward computation.

EXAMPLE 11   *(Compare Exercise 25)*

Find $\displaystyle\int \frac{1}{\sqrt{x}}\, dx$.

SOLUTION   First, rewrite

$$\int \frac{1}{\sqrt{x}}\, dx = \int x^{-1/2}\, dx$$

Now we can see that $p = -\frac{1}{2}$, so $p + 1 = \frac{1}{2}$, and the reciprocal of $\frac{1}{2}$ is 2.

$$\int x^{-1/2}\, dx = 2x^{1/2} + C$$
$$= 2\sqrt{x} + C$$

CAUTION   We have two cautions if p is negative. First, be careful to add 1 to p. *(See Example 12.)* Second, be careful in handling the coefficient of x^p. *(See Example 13.)*

EXAMPLE 12   *(Compare Exercise 23)*

Find $\displaystyle\int \frac{1}{x^4}\, dx$.

SOLUTION   We have to rewrite the integrand so that we can apply the power rule:

$$\int \frac{1}{x^4}\, dx = \int x^{-4}\, dx$$

Here, $p = -4$, so $p + 1 = -3$ and $\dfrac{1}{p + 1} = -\dfrac{1}{3}$.

$$\int x^{-4}\, dx = -\frac{1}{3}x^{-3} + C$$

$$= -\frac{1}{3x^3} + C$$

CAUTION   *Don't* see the 4 and add the 1 to 4 and then paste on a minus sign:

$$\int x^{-4}\, dx \neq -\frac{1}{5}x^5 + C$$

EXAMPLE 13   *(Compare Exercise 29)*

Find $\int \dfrac{1}{7x^3}\,dx$.

SOLUTION   Again we rewrite the integrand:

$$\int \frac{1}{7x^3}\,dx = \int \frac{1}{7}x^{-3}\,dx$$

$$= \frac{1}{7}\left(-\frac{1}{2}x^{-2}\right) + C = -\frac{1}{14}x^{-2} + C$$

$$= -\frac{1}{14x^2} + C$$

CAUTION   Note that $\dfrac{1}{7x^3} = \dfrac{1}{7}x^{-3}$, not $7x^{-3}$. $\left(\text{In fact, } 7x^{-3} = \dfrac{7}{x^3}.\right)$ Be careful when rewriting the integrand.

The next two examples show that you might have to do some algebra to rewrite the integrand before finding the antiderivative.

EXAMPLE 14   *(Compare Exercise 33)*

Find $\int x^2(x + 5)\,dx$.

SOLUTION   We cannot apply the power rule to both factors; remember that the derivative of the product is *not* the product of the derivatives. Do the multiplication first, and then do the integration:

$$\int x^2(x + 5)\,dx = \int (x^3 + 5x^2)\,dx$$

$$= \frac{1}{4}x^4 + \frac{5}{3}x^3 + C$$

EXAMPLE 15   *(Compare Exercise 37)*

Find $\int \dfrac{x^3 - 9}{x^2}\,dx$.

SOLUTION   Again, do the indicated algebra first so that the integrand has the right form:

$$\int \frac{x^3 - 9}{x^2}\,dx = \int \left(\frac{x^3}{x^2} - \frac{9}{x^2}\right)dx$$

$$= \int (x - 9x^{-2})\,dx$$

$$= \frac{1}{2}x^2 - \left(\frac{9}{-1}\right)x^{-1} + C$$

$$= \frac{1}{2}x^2 + \frac{9}{x} + C$$

13-1 EXERCISES

I

Find the general expression for $f(x)$ in Exercises 1 through 4.

1. (See Example 1)
$f'(x) = x^3 - x + 5$

2. $f'(x) = \sqrt{x} - 6x$

3. $f'(x) = \dfrac{1}{x^5}$

4. $f'(x) = \dfrac{2}{3x^4}$

In Exercises 5 through 10, determine whether the equations are true or false.

5. (See Examples 2 through 5)
$$\int (2x + 1)^5 \, dx = \frac{1}{6}(2x + 1)^6 + C$$

6. $\displaystyle\int \sqrt{3x + 1} \, dx = \frac{2}{9}(3x + 1)^{3/2} + C$

7. $\displaystyle\int x(x + 1)^2 \, dx = \left(\frac{x^2}{2}\right)\frac{1}{3}(x + 1)^3 + C$

8. $\displaystyle\int \frac{1}{x^3} dx = \frac{1}{\frac{1}{4}x^4} + C$

9. $\displaystyle\int (x^2 - 4x + 3)dx = \frac{1}{3}x^3 - 2x^2 + 3x$

10. $\displaystyle\int e^{5x} \, dx = e^{5x} + C$

Compute the indefinite integrals in Exercises 11 through 22.

11. (See Example 6)
$\displaystyle\int x^4 \, dx$

12. $\displaystyle\int x^{-3} \, dx$

13. $\displaystyle\int x^{2/3} \, dx$

14. $\displaystyle\int \sqrt{x} \, dx$

15. $\displaystyle\int 14 \, dx$

16. $\displaystyle\int (4x^5 - 8)dx$

17. (See Examples 7 and 8)
$\displaystyle\int 3(x - 2)dx$

18. $\displaystyle\int 10x^4 \, dx$

19. (See Example 9)
$\displaystyle\int (6x^3 - 8x)dx$

20. $\displaystyle\int (9x^2 - 6x + 5)dx$

21. (See Example 10)
$\displaystyle\int (x^3 - x)dx$

22. $\displaystyle\int (x^5 - 4x^2 + x - 7)dx$

II

Compute the indefinite integrals in Exercises 23 through 32.

23. (See Example 12)
$\displaystyle\int \frac{1}{x^5} \, dx$

24. $\displaystyle\int \frac{6}{x^3} \, dx$

25. (See Example 11)
$\displaystyle\int \left(\sqrt{x} - \frac{2}{\sqrt{x}}\right)dx$

26. $\displaystyle\int x^{1/5} \, dx$

27. $\displaystyle\int \frac{4}{x^{1/3}} dx$

28. $\displaystyle\int 5\sqrt{x^3} \, dx$

29. (See Example 13)
$\displaystyle\int \left(\frac{1}{4x^3} - \frac{4}{x^2}\right)dx$

30. $\displaystyle\int \left(\frac{2}{3x^2} - \frac{1}{x^3}\right)dx$

31. $\displaystyle\int \left(\frac{1}{3\sqrt{x}} - \frac{x}{5}\right)dx$

32. $\displaystyle\int \left(\frac{9}{x^4} - \frac{1}{6\sqrt{x}}\right)dx$

III

Find the indefinite integrals in Exercises 33 through 44.

33. (*See Example 14*)
$$\int x(x-4)dx$$

34. $$\int x^2(x-3)dx$$

35. $$\int \sqrt{x}(x+3)dx$$

36. $$\int \sqrt{x}\left(x^2-\frac{1}{x}\right)dx$$

37. (*See Example 15*)
$$\int \frac{x^2-9}{x^2}dx$$

38. $$\int \frac{3x^2+4x}{x^5}dx$$

39. $$\int (x+1)(x+3)dx$$

40. $$\int (x^2+5)(x-2)dx$$

41. $$\int \frac{x^2-5x}{x}dx$$

42. $$\int \frac{x^3-8x+6}{x^3}dx$$

43. $$\int (\sqrt{x}+1)^2\,dx$$

44. $$\int \left(x^2+\frac{1}{x}\right)^2 dx$$

45. The Martin Company has a daily marginal revenue, when producing x sofas per day, given by $MR(x) = -6x + 200$. What is the company's revenue function? ($x = 0$ implies that $R = 0$.)

46. The marginal revenue of Sanders Supply, when manufacturing x display cases per week, is $R'(x) = -2x + 500$. What is the company's weekly revenue function?

47. A company's marginal cost function is given by
$$MC(x) = \frac{1}{2}x^2 - x + 2$$
where x is number of items produced weekly and the company's fixed costs are 11 per week. What is the company's weekly cost function?

48. The marginal cost function when manufacturing x medium trucks per week is given by
$$C'(x) = \frac{9x^2}{16} - 20x + 8000$$
The fixed cost is \$120,000 per week. What is the company's total cost function?

49. If the population in a congressional district was growing at a continuous rate of 5% per year and was 575,000 in the 1980 census, what was the population of that district in the 1990 census?

13–2 INTRODUCTION TO DIFFERENTIAL EQUATIONS

- *Differential Equations*
- *Particular Solutions to Differential Equations*
- *Solution of $y' = \dfrac{1}{x}$*
- *Antiderivatives of Exponential Functions*

DIFFERENTIAL EQUATIONS

A **differential equation** is simply an equation that has a derivative in it. For example, the equations
$$y' = 2x$$
$$y'' + 2y' - 3y = 0$$
and
$$f'(x) = -f(x)$$

are all differential equations. Differential equations arise in applications because it is sometimes possible to determine an equation involving the rate of change of a function without knowing what the function is to begin with. For example, we have seen how a production manager can know what the marginal cost function is and then use that knowledge to build the total cost function. For another example, you could know the rate at which you are paying off a car loan or a tuition loan without knowing exactly how much you still owe.

A **solution to a differential equation** is a function that satisfies the equation. For example, $y = e^{3x}$ is a solution to the differential equation $y' - 3y = 0$. To see this, first compute each term: $y' = 3e^{3x}$ and $3y = 3e^{3x}$. Next, substitute each expression into the equation. We have $3e^{3x} - 3e^{3x} = 0$, which is true. A given differential equation may have more than one solution. We have seen that $y = e^{3x}$ is one solution to $y' = 3y$, but $y = 5e^{3x}$ is also a solution. If $y = 5e^{3x}$, then $y' = 5e^{3x} \cdot 3 = 15e^{3x}$ and $3y = 3(5e^{3x}) = 15e^{3x}$, so $y' = 3y$ and $y' - 3y = 0$ is again true.

In the previous section we saw that $\int f(x)dx$ represents a collection of functions whose graphs are parallel. The problem of finding $\int f(x)dx$ can be viewed as solving a special form of differential equation—one of the form $y' = f(x)$.

EXAMPLE 1   *(Compare Exercise 1)*

Find all solutions to the differential equation

$$y' = 5x^2 - 3$$

SOLUTION   This problem is the same as finding $\int (5x^2 - 3)dx$. Any solution is an antiderivative of $5x^2 - 3$; so all solutions are of the form $y = \frac{5}{3}x^3 - 3x + C$ for some constant C.

PARTICULAR SOLUTIONS TO DIFFERENTIAL EQUATIONS

An application may demand finding a **particular solution** to a differential equation. There may be an additional condition the solution must satisfy, and this additional condition may determine a specific value for C.

EXAMPLE 2   *(Compare Exercise 43)*

The marketing research department tells us that if we increase the price of our soft drink, we will sell 50 fewer bottles per day for every penny that we increase the price. As managers of the soft drink company we want to know the precise price-demand equation. But before we can determine this equation, we need to know more information—we need to know how many bottles we can sell at a particular price. If the sales department tells us that we can sell 3500 bottles per day at a price of 30¢ per bottle, what is the price-demand equation for our soft drink?

SOLUTION   If y is the number of bottles we sell per day, and x is the price in pennies, then what the marketing research department has told us is that $dy/dx = -50$. Thus $y = -50x + C$. Now we use the information from the sales department. We substitute the values $y = 3500$ and $x = 30$ into the equation $y = -50x + C$ and obtain $3500 = (-50)(30) + C$, so $C = 5000$. Our particular price-demand equation is now fully determined; it is $y = -50x + 5000$.

EXAMPLE 3   *(Compare Exercise 17)*

Find the particular solution to $y' = x^2 + (18/x^3)$ that satisfies the added condition $y = 7$ when $x = 3$.

SOLUTION   We know that y must be an antiderivative of $x^2 + (18/x^3)$. First, we find the collection of all antiderivatives:

$$\int \left(x^2 + \frac{18}{x^3} \right) dx = \int (x^2 + 18x^{-3})dx$$

$$= \frac{1}{3}x^3 + 18\left(-\frac{1}{2} \right)x^{-2} + C$$

$$= \frac{1}{3}x^3 - \frac{9}{x^2} + C$$

Therefore y is of the form

$$y = \frac{1}{3}x^3 - \frac{9}{x^2} + C$$

Now we want to pick out a particular antiderivative from this collection. Let $x = 3$ and $y = 7$:

$$7 = \left(\frac{1}{3} \right)3^3 - \frac{9}{3^2} + C$$

$$7 = 9 - 1 + C$$

$$C = -1$$

Answer: $y = \dfrac{1}{3}x^3 - \dfrac{9}{x^2} - 1$

EXAMPLE 4   *(Compare Exercise 15)*

Find $y = f(x)$ if $f'(x) = x - 9\sqrt{x}$ and the point $(4, 10)$ is on the graph of f.

SOLUTION   First, find all antiderivatives of f:

$$\int (x - 9\sqrt{x})dx = \int (x - 9x^{1/2})dx$$

$$= \frac{1}{2}x^2 - 9\left(\frac{2}{3}\right)x^{3/2} + C$$

$$= \frac{1}{2}x^2 - 6x^{3/2} + C$$

The solution is of the form $f(x) = \frac{1}{2}x^2 - 6x^{3/2} + C$. The additional condition states that $(4, 10)$ is on the graph of f; that is, $f(4) = 10$. Substituting 10 for $f(x)$ and 4 for x in the equation

$$f(x) = \frac{1}{2}x^2 - 6x^{3/2} + C$$

we get

$$10 = \left(\frac{1}{2}\right)4^2 - 6(4^{3/2}) + C$$

Now, $4^2 = 16$ and $4^{3/2} = (4^{1/2})^3 = 2^3 = 8$, so we have

$$10 = 8 - 48 + C$$
$$C = 50$$

Answer: $y = \frac{1}{2}x^2 - 6x^{3/2} + 50.$

We will not go deeply into physics, but we would like to present an important application of antidifferentiation. We start with an equation due to Isaac Newton; the equation is $F = m \cdot a$, where F is force, m is mass, and a is acceleration. We will give only a very specific use of this equation. The force of the earth's gravity on an object becomes weaker the farther the object is from the earth. But if the distance from the earth doesn't change much, then we can assume that the force is constant. (You weigh only slightly less in an airplane at 30,000 feet than you do at ground level.) This means that the acceleration of an object falling to earth is a constant. Physicists are able to measure the acceleration due to gravity as 32 ft/sec². Acceleration is the rate of change of velocity. If we use $v(t)$ to denote the velocity at time t, then the differential equation can be written

$$a = \frac{dv}{dt} = -32$$

(We use a negative sign to indicate that when you drop a rock, it falls; its height decreases.)

EXAMPLE 5 *(Compare Exercise 37)*

A baseball is thrown straight up at an initial speed of 96 feet per second. What is the ball's velocity function?

SOLUTION The differential equation is $dv/dt = -32$, and so $v(t)$ has the form $v(t) = -32t + C$. The additional condition says that $v(0) = 96$. Let $v = 96$ and $t = 0$.

$$96 = -32 \cdot 0 + C$$
$$C = 96$$

The velocity function is given by $v(t) = -32t + 96$. ∎

The solution to Example 5 can itself be interpreted as a differential equation. If $h(t)$ represents the height of the ball at time t, then the velocity is the rate of change of $h(t)$:

$$v(t) = \frac{dh}{dt}$$

EXAMPLE 6 *(Compare Exercise 37)*

If a baseball is thrown straight up at a speed of 96 feet per second from a height of 6 feet, what is its height function?

SOLUTION From Example 5 we know that the baseball's velocity at time t is given by $v(t) = -32t + 96$.

$$\frac{dh}{dt} = v(t) = -32t + 96$$

so the general form for $h(t)$ is given by

$$h(t) = \int v(t)dt = \int (-32t + 96)dt$$
$$= -16t^2 + 96t + C$$

Here, if $t = 0$, then $h(0) = 6$:

$$6 = -16 \cdot 0^2 + 96 \cdot 0 + C \qquad \text{and} \qquad C = 6$$

The height function is given by $h(t) = -16t^2 + 96t + 6$. ∎

Newton's equation, $F = m \cdot a$, can be used to tell where the baseball is at every moment of its flight and also how fast the ball is going. What makes Newton's equation so important, however, is that the same principle applies to other bodies as well. Using this equation, if one knows the position and velocity of a particular body at a given moment and knows the forces acting on this body, then one can derive an equation that gives the position and velocity of the body for all time. Thus this differential equation can be used to derive the laws of planetary motion, predict solar and lunar eclipses, and guide our rockets through space.

The acceleration function is the derivative of the velocity function, which is the derivative of the position function. Examples 5 and 6 show how to compute $h(t)$ for a thrown rock when $h(0)$ and $h'(0)$ are given. We give another example that shows how to solve for a particular solution of a differential equation that involves the second derivative of the function. Such a differential equation is called a **second-order differential equation.**

EXAMPLE 7   *(Compare Exercise 33)*

Find the particular function that satisfies

$$f''(x) = 6x - \frac{4}{x^3}$$

and the additional conditions $f'(1) = 9$ and $f(2) = 12$.

SOLUTION   The general form for $f'(x)$ is given by

$$\begin{aligned}
f'(x) &= \int f''(x)dx \\
&= \int \left(6x - \frac{4}{x^3} \right) dx \\
&= \int (6x - 4x^{-3})dx \\
&= 3x^2 + 2x^{-2} + C_1
\end{aligned}$$

To solve for C_1, let $x = 1, f'(1) = 3 + 2 + C_1 = 5 + C_1$. We want $f'(1) = 9$; set $9 = 5 + C_1$ so $C_1 = 4$. We now know $f'(x)$:

$$f'(x) = 3x^2 + 2x^{-2} + 4$$

Next, the general form for $f(x)$ is given by

$$\begin{aligned}
f(x) &= \int f'(x)dx \\
&= \int (3x^2 + 2x^{-2} + 4)dx \\
&= x^3 - 2x^{-1} + 4x + C_2
\end{aligned}$$

To solve for C_2, we let $x = 2$:

$$f(2) = 8 - 1 + 8 + C_2 = 15 + C_2$$

We want $f(2) = 12 = 15 + C_2$, so $C_2 = -3$. The particular solution that we want is

$$f(x) = x^3 - \frac{2}{x} + 4x - 3$$

SOLUTION OF $y' = \dfrac{1}{x}$

Up to now, we have been using the specific formula

$$\int x^p \, dx = \frac{1}{p+1}x^{p+1} + C \qquad p \neq -1$$

The case $p = -1$ is special indeed. In Chapter 5 we showed that if $f(x) = \ln x$, then $f'(x) = 1/x$. The fact that $1/x$ is the derivative of $\ln x$ means that $\ln x$ is an antiderivative of $1/x$, so you might expect the formula to be

$$\int \frac{1}{x} \, dx = \ln x + C$$

But this formula is only "half right." Some special difficulties are caused by the domains of $\ln x$ and $1/x$; they are not the same; $\ln x$ is defined only when $x > 0$, while $1/x$ is defined for all $x \neq 0$.

$$\int \frac{1}{x} \, dx = \ln x + C \qquad \text{on the interval } (0, \infty)$$

But now we must find an antiderivative for $1/x$ on the interval $(-\infty, 0)$. If x is negative, then $-x$ is positive (although it doesn't *look* like it! Remember that x itself is negative), so $\ln(-x)$ is defined. We compute the derivative of $\ln(-x)$ using the chain rule. Let $u = -x$ so that $y = \ln u$:

$$\frac{dy}{dx} = \frac{dy}{du} \cdot \frac{du}{dx}$$

$$= \left(\frac{1}{u}\right)(-1)$$

$$= \left(\frac{1}{-x}\right)(-1) = \frac{1}{x}$$

If $x < 0$ and $y = \ln(-x)$, then $\dfrac{dy}{dx} = \dfrac{1}{x}$. Therefore

$$\int \frac{1}{x} \, dx = \ln(-x) + C \qquad \text{on the interval } (-\infty, 0)$$

The definition of absolute value allows us to combine the two cases ($x < 0$ or $x > 0$) into one formula. Remember that

if x is positive, $|x| = x$ and

if x is negative, $|x| = -x$.

The two formulas can now be combined; the derivative of $\ln|x|$ is $1/x$. Using this information in the opposite order, we have the formula for $\int 1/x \, dx$:

The Antiderivative of $\dfrac{1}{x}$

$$\int \frac{1}{x} \, dx = \ln |x| + C$$

EXAMPLE 8   *(Compare Exercise 19)*

If $\dfrac{dy}{dx} = \dfrac{1}{3x}$, find y.

SOLUTION

$$y = \int \frac{1}{3x}\,dx = \frac{1}{3}\int \frac{1}{x}\,dx$$

$$= \frac{1}{3}\ln|x| + C$$

CAUTION   Sometimes, the formula $\displaystyle\int \frac{1}{x}\,dx = \ln|x| + C$ is misused. In trying to compute $\displaystyle\int \frac{1}{3x}\,dx$, for instance, some people will write $\displaystyle\int \frac{1}{3x}\,dx = \ln|3x| + C$. But a careful use of the chain rule shows that this is not correct. If we let $g(x) = \ln|3x| + C$, then $g'(x) = \dfrac{1}{3x}\cdot 3$ (chain rule) $= \dfrac{1}{x}$, not $\dfrac{1}{3x}$. As you saw in the previous section, you must be careful with numbers in the denominator of the integrand.

The formula for $\int \ln x\,dx$ requires a certain technique for evaluating indefinite integrals that we will not encounter until Chapter 14. We can, however, proceed with a discussion of finding antiderivatives of exponential functions.

ANTIDERIVATIVES OF EXPONENTIAL FUNCTIONS

We will obtain the antiderivative of e^{ax} the same way that we found previous antiderivatives, by using the rule for derivatives in reverse. To find the derivative of e^{ax}, you multiply e^{ax} by a; to find the antiderivative of e^{ax}, you divide e^{ax} by a.

The Antiderivative of e^{ax}

$$\int e^{ax}\,dx = \frac{1}{a}e^{ax} + C$$

Check this formula by taking the derivative.

EXAMPLE 9   *(Compare Exercise 21)*

Find $\int e^{2x}\,dx$.

SOLUTION   Here, $a = 2$, so $\displaystyle\int e^{2x}\,dx = \frac{1}{2}e^{2x} + C$.

EXAMPLE 10 *(Compare Exercise 23)*

Find $\int \dfrac{1}{e^x} dx$.

SOLUTION Reminder: Do not be tempted to use logarithms just because the integral is a quotient. Instead, rewrite $1/e^x$ as e^{-x}, and apply the formula with $a = -1$:

$$\int \frac{1}{e^x} dx = \int e^{-x} dx = -e^{-x} + C = -\frac{1}{e^x} + C$$

We conclude with more examples using these two formulas.

EXAMPLE 11 *(Compare Exercise 27)*

Find $\int \left(x + \dfrac{1}{x^2} \right)^2 dx$.

SOLUTION Do the algebra first:

$$\left(x + \frac{1}{x^2} \right)^2 = x^2 + \frac{2}{x} + \frac{1}{x^4}$$

$$\int \left(x + \frac{1}{x^2} \right)^2 dx = \int \left(x^2 + \frac{2}{x} + x^{-4} \right) dx$$

$$= \frac{1}{3} x^3 + 2 \ln|x| - \frac{1}{3} x^{-3} + C$$

EXAMPLE 12 *(Compare Exercise 29)*

Find $\int \dfrac{u^2 - 2u - 1}{u} du$.

SOLUTION Again, perform the algebra first:

$$\frac{u^2 - 2u - 1}{u} = \frac{u^2}{u} - \frac{2u}{u} - \frac{1}{u}$$

$$= u - 2 - \frac{1}{u}$$

$$\int \frac{u^2 - 2u - 1}{u} du = \int \left(u - 2 - \frac{1}{u} \right) du$$

$$= \frac{1}{2} u^2 - 2u - \ln|u| + C$$

EXAMPLE 13

Find $\int \dfrac{1}{x^3}\, dx.$

SOLUTION   The purpose of this example is to emphasize that you shouldn't use ln as the antiderivative of every quotient. The answer to this example is *not* $\ln|x^3| + C$. Rewrite $\int \dfrac{1}{x^3}\, dx$ as $\int x^{-3}\, dx$. The exponent is -3, not -1, and you should use the power rule:

$$\int \frac{1}{x^3}\, dx = \int x^{-3}\, dx = -\frac{1}{2}x^{-2} + C$$

$$= -\frac{1}{2x^2} + C$$

CAUTION   Use $\ln|x|$ only as an antiderivative for x^{-1}.

EXAMPLE 14   *(Compare Exercise 31)*

Find $\int (e^x + e^{-x})^2\, dx.$

SOLUTION   First rewrite the integrand

$$(e^x + e^{-x})^2 = (e^x)^2 + 2e^x e^{-x} + (e^{-x})^2$$
$$= e^{2x} + 2 + e^{-2x}$$

Now

$$\int (e^x + e^{-x})^2\, dx = \int (e^{2x} + 2 + e^{-2x})\, dx$$

$$= \frac{1}{2}e^{2x} + 2x - \frac{1}{2}e^{-2x} + C$$

13-2   EXERCISES

I

Find the general solution for the differential equations given in Exercises 1 through 6.

1. *(See Example 1)*
$y' = 21x^2 - 14x + 8$

2. $y' = x^4 - 5x^2 - 9$

3. $\dfrac{dy}{dx} = 8x - \dfrac{1}{x}$

4. $\dfrac{dy}{dx} = \sqrt{x} + x$

5. $f'(x) = \dfrac{1}{3x^2} + \dfrac{8}{x}$

6. $f'(x) = x^3 + 4x$

In Exercises 7 through 14, determine whether the statement is true or false.

7. $y = \ln 7x$ is a solution to $y' = 1/x$.

8. $y = \ln x^3$ is a solution to $y' = 3/x$.

9. $y = (2x + 1)^3 + 5$ is a solution to $y' = 6(2x + 1)^2$.

10. $y = x^2 - 3$ is a solution to $y' = (1/3)x^3 - 3x + C$.

11. $y = 4\sqrt{x}$ is a solution to $y' = 1/(2\sqrt{x})$.

12. $y = x^3$ is a solution to $y' = 3x^2 + C$.

13. $y = 4e^{-x}$ is a solution to $y'' = y$.

14. $y = 5e^{2x}$ is a solution to $y'' = 20y$.

II

In Exercises 15 through 24, find the particular solution to each differential equation that satisfies the additional condition.

15. (*See Example 4*)
$f'(x) = 3x^2 + 6$ and $f(0) = 4$.

16. $f'(x) = 2x - 1$ and $f(1) = 3$.

17. (*See Example 3*)
$y' = x - (16/x^2)$ and $y = 2$ when $x = 8$.

18. $y' = 3\sqrt{x}$ and $y = 6$ when $x = 4$.

19. (*See Example 8*)
$\dfrac{dy}{dx} = 5 - \dfrac{1}{x}$ and $y = 8$ when $x = -1$.

20. $y' = 4 + (1/x)$ and $y = 9$ when $x = -1$.

21. (*See Example 9*)
$\dfrac{dy}{dx} = 8e^{2x}$ and $y = 14e^2$ when $x = 1$.

22. $y' = 4e^{-x}$ and $y = 6$ when $x = 0$.

23. (*See Example 10*)
$y' = \dfrac{1}{e^x}$ and $y = 3$ when $x = 0$.

24. $y' = \dfrac{4}{e^{2x}}$ and $y = 10$ when $x = 1$.

III

In Exercises 25 through 36, find the solution to each of the given differential equations and conditions.

25. Find the curve that satisfies $y' = 4x^2 + (1/x)$ and that goes through the point $(1, 8)$.

26. Find the curve that satisfies $y' = \sqrt{x}(x + 1)$ and that goes through the point $(4, 5)$.

27. (*See Example 11*)
What is $f(x)$ if $f'(x) = \left(x + \dfrac{1}{x}\right)^2$ and $f(1) = 7$?

28. Find $f(x)$ if $f'(x) = \left(2x + \dfrac{1}{x}\right)^2$ and $f(1) = 4$.

29. (*See Example 12*)
What is $f(x)$ if $f'(x) = \sqrt{x} + (3/x)$ and $f(1) = 5$?

30. Find $f(x)$ if $f'(x) = \dfrac{3x^2 - 4x + 1}{x^2}$ and $f(1) = 8$.

31. (*See Example 14*)
Find all solutions to $y' = (e^x + 1)^2$.

32. Find all solutions to $y' = \dfrac{e^{3x} + 1}{e^x}$.

33. (*See Example 7*) Find $f(x)$ if $f''(x) = 42x + 6$, $f'(0) = 4$, and $f(0) = 7$.

34. Find $f(x)$ if $f''(x) = 1/x^3$, $f'(1) = 8$, and $f(1) = -2$.

35. Find y if $y'' = 20$, $y' = 4$ when $x = 2$, and $y = 8$ when $x = 2$.

36. Find y if $y'' = 12$, $y' = 5$ when $x = 1$, and $y = 3$ when $x = 0$.

37. (*See Examples 5 and 6*) A baseball is thrown straight up with an initial speed of 60 feet per second from a height of 8 feet. Express the height, $h(t)$, of the ball as a function of time.

38. A ball is thrown straight up with an initial speed of 80 feet per second from a height of 5 feet.
    (a) Express the height of the ball t seconds after it is thrown.
    (b) What is the maximum height of the ball?
    (c) When does the ball return to its original height of 5 feet above the ground?

39. The driver of a car going 80 feet per second applies the brakes. The car's acceleration is given by $a(t) = -16 - 2t$ feet per second per second, where t is the number of seconds since the brakes were applied. (Note that the acceleration is negative because the car is slowing down; negative acceleration is sometimes called deceleration.)
    (a) Find $v(t)$, the velocity of the car after t seconds.
    (b) How fast is the car going one second after the brakes are applied?
    (c) When does the car come to a stop?
    (d) Find $s(t)$, the distance the car has traveled since the brakes were applied.
    (e) How far does the car travel before it stops?

40. A rock is thrown *down* from a bridge 84 feet above the river. The initial speed of the rock is 20 feet per second. If $h(t)$ is the height of the rock above the water t seconds after it is thrown, what is $h(t)$?

41. The marginal costs for a company have been estimated as being given by

$$MC(x) = \frac{x^2}{4} - 24x + 350$$

where x is the number of units manufactured per day. The present production level is $x = 6$, and daily costs at this level are 4000.
  (a) What is the company's cost function?
  (b) What is the company's fixed cost?

42. A company's marginal profit at a production level of x units per day is given by $MP(x) = 20 - \frac{1}{5}x$. If $x = 20$, the company breaks even.
  (a) What is the company's profit function?
  (b) What is the company's maximum possible profit?

43. (*See Example 2*) A company can sell 6200 candy bars per week at a price of 40¢ each. If the demand decreases by 80 candy bars per week for every penny increase in price, what is the price-demand equation for this company's candy bars?

44. An automobile manufacturer can sell 600,000 of a certain model if its base price is $15,000, but for every increase in price of $100 the company will lose 800 customers. What is the price-demand equation for this model of car?

13–3 THE DEFINITE INTEGRAL

- *Total Change of a Function*
- *The Definite Integral*

TOTAL CHANGE OF A FUNCTION

We introduced the derivative of a function as the instantaneous rate of change of that function. As a particular example, we saw that the velocity function is the derivative of the position function. Thus if we know the height function of a falling rock, we can determine the velocity function of the rock, $v(t) = h'(t)$.

In this chapter we are posing a different, although related, problem; the problem now is to find an *antiderivative* for a given function. The height function is an antiderivative for the velocity function. However, we have just seen that knowing $v(t)$ is not enough to completely determine $h(t)$. The height function depends on the initial height of the rock, which is completely independent of the rock's velocity. But knowing the velocity function over a period of time is enough to compute the distance traveled during this period.

EXAMPLE 1 (*Compare Exercise 49*)

How far does a rock travel in the third second after it is dropped?

SOLUTION We know from the previous section that $v(t) = -32t$ for a dropped rock (dropped means $v(0) = 0$). Now

$$h(t) = \int v(t)dt = \int -32t \, dt = -16t^2 + C$$

Thus $h(0) = -16 \cdot 0^2 + C = C$, so C is the height of the rock at time $t = 0$. This height is frequently written h_0 and is called the initial height; $h(t) = -16t^2 + h_0$. The height of the rock after two seconds is

$$h(2) = -64 + h_0$$

The height of the rock after three seconds is

$$h(3) = -144 + h_0$$

The total distance traveled during the time interval $2 \leq t \leq 3$ is the difference in the heights:

$$h(3) - h(2) = (-144 + h_0) - (-64 + h_0)$$
$$= -80 \quad \text{feet}$$

The h_0 terms subtracted out. The minus sign indicates that the height is less after three seconds than after two seconds; the rock has dropped 80 feet during the third second of its fall.

    The velocity function allows us to compute the total distance traveled—the total change in height—without knowing the specific height function.

    We now look at another example in which we need to compute the total change in a function over an interval.

EXAMPLE 2   *(Compare Exercise 47)*

A company that manufactures air conditioners has determined that its marginal cost function at the daily production level of x units is given by

$$MC(x) = \frac{x^2}{40} - 8x + 700$$

What will be the increase in the company's cost if production is raised from 120 units to 150 units per day?

SOLUTION   We are being asked to find the change in production cost, that is, $C(150) - C(120)$. The change in cost is independent of the fixed costs. Notice how this independence again shows up in the computations. The marginal cost function MC is the derivative of the cost function C. Said another way, the cost function C is an antiderivative of the marginal cost.

$$C(x) = \int MC(x)dx$$
$$= \int \left(\frac{x^2}{40} - 8x + 700\right)dx$$
$$= \frac{1}{40} \cdot \frac{1}{3}x^3 - 8 \cdot \frac{1}{2}x^2 + 700x + K$$
$$= \frac{x^3}{120} - 4x^2 + 700x + K$$

In this example, K represents the fixed costs. Thus

$$C(150) = \frac{150^3}{120} - 4(150)^2 + 700(150) + K$$
$$= 43125 + K$$

and

$$C(120) = \frac{120^3}{120} - 4(120)^2 + 700(120) + K$$
$$= 40800 + K$$

The increase in costs is

$$C(150) - C(120) = (43125 + K) - (40800 + K) = 2325$$

Notice that again the constant term is subtracted out. Costs will increase by $2325.

THE DEFINITE INTEGRAL

Now we analyze what was common to these two examples.

1. The problem was to find the total change in a function over an interval $[a, b]$. (The change in h over the interval $[2, 3]$ and the change in C over the interval $[120, 150]$.)
2. The function itself was not given, but the derivative of the function was given (velocity $= h'$, and marginal cost $= C'$).
3. To compute the desired answer, we needed an antiderivative of the given derivative. But because the total change is a difference of two values of the antiderivative $[h(3) - h(2)$ and $C(150) - C(120)]$, the total change is independent of the constant term of the antiderivative.

The first two steps are what you must recognize to solve problems like these; the actual solution of the problem occurs in Step 3: given f, find a function g that is an antiderivative of f, and then evaluate $g(b) - g(a)$.

The number obtained by the process of starting with a function f, finding an antiderivative g, and then evaluating $g(b) - g(a)$ has so many applications that it has its own name: the **definite integral.** The formal definition follows. We include the condition that f be continuous on $[a, b]$ because this condition guarantees that f does have an antiderivative g.

Definition
$\int_a^b f(x)\, dx$
(Definite Integral)

Let f be a continuous function on the interval $[a, b]$, and let g be an antiderivative of f on this interval. The **definite integral of f from a to b,** written $\int_a^b f(x)\, dx$, is the number $g(b) - g(a)$:

$$\int_a^b f(x)\,dx = g(b) - g(a)$$

The number b is called the **upper limit of the integral,** and a is called the **lower limit.** As with the indefinite integral, $\int f(x)dx$, the function f is called the integrand. Notice the similarity in notation between the indefinite integral and the definite integral, but remember the difference.

NOTE $\int f(x)dx$ is the collection of all antiderivatives of f—that is,
$\int f(x)dx$ is a family of functions.
$\int_a^b f(x)dx$ is a number.

In the definition of the definite integral, g is an antiderivative of f; that is, $g'(x) = f(x)$. We can now write the following:

Definition
Total Change of a Function on an Interval

The **total change of a function** g **on an interval** $[a, b]$ is given by the definite integral of its rate of change from a to b:

$$g(b) - g(a) = \int_a^b g'(x)\ dx$$

EXAMPLE 3   *(Compare Exercise 5)*

Find $\int_1^3 (x^2 + 4)dx$.

SOLUTION   First, find an antiderivative of $x^2 + 4$. The simplest is the one whose additive constant of integration is 0. Let $g(x) = \frac{1}{3}x^3 + 4x$. Now compute $g(3) - g(1)$:

$$g(3) = \frac{1}{3} \cdot 27 + 12 = 21$$

$$g(1) = \frac{1}{3} + 4 = 4\frac{1}{3}$$

$$g(3) - g(1) = 16\frac{2}{3}$$

$$\int_1^3 (x^2 + 4)dx = 16\frac{2}{3}$$

We now introduce a notation that allows us to compress the steps in the evaluation of $g(3) - g(1)$.

Notation $g(x)\big|_a^b = g(b) - g(a)$

EXAMPLE 4   *(Compare Exercise 1)*

Evaluate $(3x^2 - 5x)\big|_1^4$.

SOLUTION   Here, $g(x) = 3x^2 - 5x$, and we wish to compute $g(4) - g(1)$:

$$(3x^2 - 5x)\big|_1^4 = (3 \cdot 16 - 5 \cdot 4) - (3 \cdot 1 - 5 \cdot 1)$$
$$= 28 - (-2)$$
$$= 30$$

There is no calculus involved in Example 4; this notation is used simply to shorten the computations after you have found an antiderivative of f. We repeat Example 3 to show you how the computation is shortened.

EXAMPLE 3   *(Redone)*

Find $\int_1^3 (x^2 + 4)dx$.

SOLUTION

$$\int_1^3 (x^2 + 4)dx = \left(\frac{1}{3}x^3 + 4x\right)\bigg|_1^3$$
$$= (9 + 12) - \left(\frac{1}{3} + 4\right)$$
$$= 16\frac{2}{3}$$

The only step involving calculus is the first one, finding an antiderivative; the remaining steps just involve a special notation and evaluation.

We continue this section with more examples to let you become familiar with both the new notation and the definition of the definite integral. We will give more applications of the definite integral in the following sections.

EXAMPLE 5   *(Compare Exercise 23)*

Compute $\int_1^4 (x - \sqrt{x})dx$.

SOLUTION   First, we rewrite $\sqrt{x}$ as $x^{1/2}$ so we can use the integral power rule:

$$\int_1^4 (x - \sqrt{x})dx = \int_1^4 (x - x^{1/2})dx$$

Second, we find an antiderivative of $x - x^{1/2}$:

$$\int_1^4 (x - x^{1/2})dx = \left(\frac{1}{2}x^2 - \frac{2}{3}x^{3/2}\right)\bigg|_1^4$$

Now we do the evaluations:

$$= \left(\frac{1}{2} \cdot 16 - \frac{2}{3} \cdot 4^{3/2} \right) - \left(\frac{1}{2} - \frac{2}{3} \right)$$

$$= \left(8 - \frac{2}{3} \cdot 8 \right) - \left(\frac{-1}{6} \right)$$

$$= \frac{17}{6}$$

EXAMPLE 6   (*Compare Exercise 19*)

Compute $\displaystyle\int_1^5 \frac{1}{x}\, dx$

SOLUTION

$$\int_1^5 \frac{1}{x}\, dx = \ln|x| \,\Big|_1^5 \qquad \text{(Found an antiderivative)}$$

$$= \ln 5 - \ln 1 \qquad \text{(Computed } g(b) - g(a))$$

$$= \ln 5 \qquad\qquad \text{(Used } \ln 1 = 0)$$

CAUTION

$$\int_{-1}^5 \frac{1}{x}\, dx \neq \ln|x| \,\Big|_{-1}^5$$

because $\ln|x|$ is not an antiderivative of $1/x$ on the whole interval $[-1, 5]$. There is trouble at $x = 0$. The computation of $\int_a^b f(x)\,dx$ requires that f be continuous on $[a, b]$ and that you find g so that $g'(x) = f(x)$ for all x in $[a, b]$. Here, $f(x) = 1/x$ is not even defined for all x in $[-1, 5]$.

EXAMPLE 7   (*Compare Exercise 21*)

Compute $\int_0^3 e^{2x}\, dx$.

SOLUTION

$$\int_0^3 e^{2x}\, dx = \frac{1}{2} e^{2x} \,\Big|_0^3$$

$$= \frac{1}{2} e^6 - \frac{1}{2} e^0$$

$$= \frac{1}{2} e^6 - \frac{1}{2} \qquad \text{(Because } e^0 = 1)$$

The constant-times rule and the addition and subtraction rules for indefinite integrals carry over to definite integrals. We list these properties for emphasis.

**Properties of
the Definite Integral
Constant-Times**

1. $\int_a^b c \cdot f(x)dx = c \cdot \int_a^b f(x)dx$

Sum

2. $\int_a^b [f(x) + g(x)]dx = \int_a^b f(x)dx + \int_a^b g(x)dx$

Difference

3. $\int_a^b [f(x) - g(x)]dx = \int_a^b f(x)dx - \int_a^b g(x)dx$

EXAMPLE 8   *(Compare Exercise 39)*

Compute $\int_2^5 4e^x\, dx$.

SOLUTION

$$\int_2^5 4e^x\, dx = 4\int_2^5 e^x\, dx = 4\left(e^x \Big|_2^5\right)$$
$$= 4(e^5 - e^2)$$

EXAMPLE 9   *(Compare Exercise 37)*

Compute $\int_1^3 6x^2\, dx + \int_1^3 5\, dx$.

SOLUTION

$$\int_1^3 6x^2\, dx + \int_1^3 5\, dx = \int_1^3 (6x^2 + 5)dx$$
$$= (2x^3 + 5x)\Big|_1^3$$
$$= [2(27) + 5(3)] - [2(1) + 5(1)]$$
$$= 69 - 7 = 62$$

There is an important property of definite integrals that does not come directly from any property of indefinite integrals. This property comes from the observation that if c is between a and b, then the total change of a function over the interval $[a, b]$ is the sum of its change over the two intervals $[a, c]$ and $[c, b]$:

$$g(b) - g(a) = [g(b) - g(c)] + [g(c) - g(a)]$$

There is not a commonly agreed upon name for this property. We hope that the name we use helps you to remember what this property is.

The Gluing of Intervals Property	**4.** If $a < c < b$, then $$\int_a^c f(x)dx + \int_c^b f(x)dx = \int_a^b f(x)dx$$

If two intervals have an endpoint in common, you can "glue" them together and evaluate the definite integral over the whole interval.

The discussion of the definite integral $\int_a^b f(x)dx$ so far has involved only situations in which $a < b$. However, we could just as easily ask for the change in total costs if the production level goes from $x = 150$ to $x = 120$. Some applications may require the computation of $\int_a^b f(x)dx$ in cases other than $a < b$. There are exactly two such cases, $a = b$ and $a > b$. Our definition of definite integral leads us to the following two properties.

5. $\int_a^a f(x)dx = 0$
6. $\int_a^b f(x)dx = -\int_b^a f(x)dx$

In terms of the total change of f, these two properties are just what you expect. The first says that the total change of f on $[a, a]$ is 0. The second says that the change in f as x goes from a to b is the opposite of the change in f as x goes from b to a. Think about the change in costs as production goes from 120 to 150 compared to the change in costs as production goes from 150 to 120.

Using these properties, we can now show that the requirement $a < c < b$ in the gluing property (4) can be generalized.

7. Independent of the ordering of a, b, and c,
$$\int_a^c f(x)dx + \int_c^b f(x)dx = \int_a^b f(x)dx$$

EXAMPLE 10 *(Compare Exercise 29)*

Verify property (7) for $f(x) = 2x$, $a = -1$, $b = 2$, and $c = 3$.
SOLUTION We want to show that

$$\int_{-1}^2 2x \, dx = \int_{-1}^3 2x \, dx + \int_3^2 2x \, dx$$

First, $\int_{-1}^2 2x \, dx = x^2 \big|_{-1}^2 = 4 - (-1)^2 = 4 - 1 = 3$.

Second, $\int_{-1}^3 2x \, dx = x^2 \big|_{-1}^3 = 9 - 1 = 8$.

Third, $\int_3^2 2x \, dx = x^2 \big|_3^2 = 4 - 9 = -5$.

Finally, $3 = 8 + (-5)$ is true.

EXAMPLE 11   (*Compare Exercise 41*)

If $\int_1^3 f(x)dx = 4$ and $\int_1^5 f(x)dx = 11$, what is $\int_3^5 f(x)dx$?

SOLUTION   To use the gluing property, we must have the same number as the upper bound of one definite integral and the lower bound of the other definite integral. Here, the number that occurs in both integrals is 1, so we want 1 as the upper limit of one of the integrals. To accomplish this, note that

$$\int_3^1 f(x)dx = -\int_1^3 f(x)dx$$

Now we can write

$$\int_3^5 f(x)dx = \int_3^1 f(x)dx \quad + \int_1^5 f(x)dx$$

$$= -\int_1^3 f(x)dx + \int_1^5 f(x)dx$$

$$= -4 \qquad \quad + 11$$

$$= 7$$

13-3 EXERCISES

I

Compute the expressions in Exercises 1 through 4.

1. (*See Example 4*)
   $(2x^2 + x)|_{-1}^3$

2. $(x^3 - 3x^2 + x)|_{-1}^4$

3. $(\sqrt{x} - 4x)|_1^9$

4. $(x^{3/2} - x^{-1/2})|_4^{25}$

Compute the definite integrals in Exercises 5 through 12.

5. (*See Example 3*)
   $\int_1^3 (3x^2 - 4x + 1)dx$

6. $\int_2^5 (6x - 4)dx$

7. $\int_1^4 \sqrt{x}\, dx$

8. $\int_0^8 x^{1/3}\, dx$

9. $\int_2^5 \frac{1}{x^2}\, dx$

10. $\int_{-4}^{-1} \left(3x^2 - \frac{3}{x^2}\right)dx$

11. $\int_{-1}^4 3\, dx$

12. $\int_{-1}^4 -3\, dx$

13. Verify that $\int_1^3 x\, dx + \int_3^6 x\, dx = \int_1^6 x\, dx$ by computing all three definite integrals.

14. Verify that $\int_{-1}^2 4x\, dx + \int_{-1}^2 7\, dx = \int_{-1}^2 (4x + 7)dx$ by computing all three definite integrals.

II

Compute the expressions in Exercises 15 through 18.

15. $\ln x|_1^e$

16. $e^x|_0^{\ln 7}$

17. $\ln|x|\,|_{-4}^{-1}$

18. $e^{x/2}|_0^{\ln 16}$

Compute the definite integrals in Exercises 19 through 28.

19. (*See Example 6*)
    $\int_{-4}^{-1} \frac{1}{x}\, dx$

20. $\int_1^7 \frac{1}{x}\, dx$

21. (*See Example 7*)

$$\int_{-2}^{3} 4e^{-x}\, dx$$

22. $\int_{0}^{4} e^{3x}\, dx$

27. $\int_{2}^{8} \frac{1}{4x}\, dx$

28. $\int_{1}^{3} (5e^{-x/2})\, dx$

23. (*See Example 5*)

$$\int_{1}^{25} \left(\sqrt{x} - \frac{4}{\sqrt{x}} \right) dx$$

24. $\int_{0}^{64} (x^{1/3} - 2x^{1/2})\, dx$

Verify the equation $\int_{a}^{b} f(x)dx = \int_{a}^{c} f(x)dx + \int_{c}^{b} f(x)dx$ in Exercises 29 and 30 by computing all three definite integrals.

29. (*See Example 10*)
$f(x) = x^2$; $a = 2$, $b = 2$, $c = 4$

25. $\int_{0}^{5} (x^4 - 9x^2 + 2)\, dx$

26. $\int_{2}^{8} \frac{4}{x}\, dx$

30. $f(x) = x + 5$; $a = 5$, $b = 1$, $c = -2$

III

Evaluate the definite integrals in Exercises 31 through 36.

31. $\int_{0}^{\ln 8} e^{x/3}\, dx$

32. $\int_{1}^{4} \left(x^2 + \frac{3}{x} \right)^2 dx$

33. $\int_{-1}^{3} x(2x + 3)\, dx$

34. $\int_{1}^{5} \frac{6x^3 - 7x}{x}\, dx$

35. $\int_{1}^{3} \frac{6x^2 + 4x - 8}{x^2}\, dx$

36. $\int_{-3}^{1} (x + 2)(x - 4)\, dx$

In Exercises 37 through 40, use $\int_{1}^{3} f(x)dx = 7$ and $\int_{1}^{3} g(x)dx = -2$ to compute the given definite integral.

37. (*See Example 9*)

$$\int_{1}^{3} [f(x) + g(x)]dx$$

38. $\int_{1}^{3} -f(x)dx$

39. (*See Example 8*)

$$\int_{1}^{3} 2f(x)dx$$

40. $\int_{1}^{3} [2f(x) - 4g(x)]dx$

41. (*See Example 11*) If $\int_{1}^{4} f(x)dx = 10$

and $\int_{-2}^{4} f(x)dx = 11$, what is $\int_{-2}^{1} f(x)dx$?

42. If $\int_{2}^{6} f(x)dx = 11$ and $\int_{2}^{8} f(x)dx = -1$,

what is $\int_{6}^{8} f(x)dx$?

In Exercises 43 and 44, use $\int_{1}^{5} f(x)dx = 8$ and $\int_{-1}^{5} f(x)dx = 10$ to compute the given definite integral.

43. $\int_{5}^{1} f(x)dx$

44. $\int_{-1}^{1} f(x)dx$

45. If $\int_{2}^{5} f(x)dx = 6$, what is $\int_{2}^{5} (2f(x) + 5)dx$?

46. If $\int_{1}^{4} f(x)dx = 7$, what is $\int_{4}^{1} (2f(x) + 3)dx$?

47. (*See Example 2*) A car rental company has determined that its marginal cost is given by

$$MC(x) = \frac{x^2}{30} - 6x + 500$$

where x is the number of cars it has on hand for rental each week.
(a) How will the total cost change if the company increases its weekly supply of cars from 120 to 150 per week?
(b) How will the total cost change if the company decreases its weekly supply of cars from 120 to 90 per week?

48. The marginal cost of a company is given by

$$MC(x) = \frac{x^2}{40} - 10x + 52{,}000$$

where x is the number of units produced monthly. How will the total monthly cost of the company be affected if the company changes production level from 300 units per month to:
(a) 360 units per month?
(b) 270 units per month?

49. (*See Example 1*) A rock is thrown so that its velocity is given by $v(t) = -32t + 128$, where t is in seconds and $v(t)$ is in feet per second.
(a) How far does the rock travel in the first 2 seconds?
(b) What is its change in height from $t = 3$ seconds to $t = 5$ seconds?

50. The price of a certain microcomputer has been steadily declining. Let $P(t)$ be its price t months after it was introduced. Then $P'(t) = \frac{1}{4}t^2 - 5t - 24$. How much did the price drop during the first year?

51. When a clothing manufacturer produces x dresses per week, its marginal cost function is given by $MC(x) = \frac{x^2}{100} - 6x + 550$ and its marginal revenue function is given by $MR = 50$.
  (a) What is the change in profit if x increases from 480 to 500?
  (b) What is the change in profit if x increases from 480 to 510?

13–4 THE DEFINITE INTEGRAL AND AREA

- *Introduction*
- *Area and the Fundamental Theorem of Calculus*
- *Area Between Curves*
- *Application*

INTRODUCTION

One of the most important uses of the definite integral is to compute the area of certain figures. Thus the definite integral is important in solving some geometric questions. Furthermore, the area between two curves often turns out to represent some other physical quantity in applications. Later in this section, for instance, we will see how the area between the marginal revenue and the marginal cost curves can be interpreted in terms of profit. In the next section we will see further applications of area.

Before we can develop these interpretations, however, we need to start with a simpler area problem.

AREA AND THE FUNDAMENTAL THEOREM OF CALCULUS

Area Problem 1   If f is continuous on $[a, b]$ and $f(x) \geq 0$, what is the area of the region R bounded above by the graph of $y = f(x)$, bounded below by the x-axis, bounded on the left by the line $x = a$, and bounded on the right by the line $x = b$? See Figure 13–2.

One approach to this problem is to first approximate the region R with a region S that is the union of rectangles. Thus you can compute the area of S, and the area of $S \approx$ the area of R. The area of R is then defined as the limit of the areas of these approximating regions. We will return to this method in Section 13–6. Here we assume that R does have area, and we develop the solution to the

FIGURE 13–2

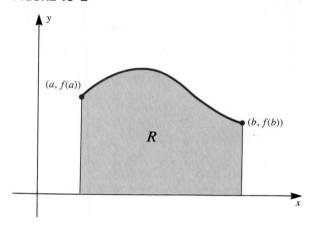

FIGURE 13–3

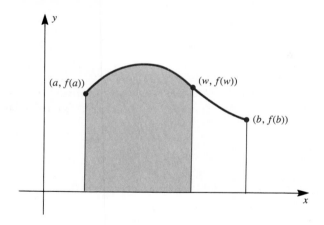

$A(w)$ = The area of the shaded region

area problem given by two famous mathematicians, Isaac Newton and Gottfried Leibniz, over 300 years ago. The key to their solution is to change the static problem of finding the area of one fixed region into the dynamic problem finding the area of a variable region. Following their idea, we introduce a new function $A(w)$, where for each number w in the interval $[a, b]$, $A(w)$ is the area of the portion of R that lies to the left of the line $x = w$. See Figure 13–3.

$A(w)$ is a function of w, and so it makes sense to ask about $A'(w)$, the rate of change of the area function. Newton and Leibniz discovered a relationship between the functions A and f that is so important that, in a slightly more general setting, it is called the **Fundamental Theorem of Calculus.** That relationship is

$$A'(w) = f(w)$$

FIGURE 13-4

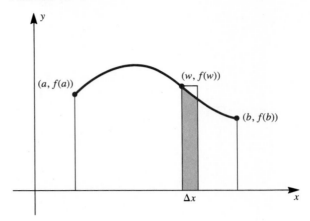

Area of shaded region $= \Delta A$
Area of rectangle $= f(w) \cdot \Delta x =$ height $\cdot$ base

When we remember that $f(w)$ is the height from the x-axis to the point $(w, f(w))$, we can interpret this relationship as follows:

The rate of change of the area function is the height function.

We can see this intuitively because ΔA, a small change in the area, is approximately $f(w) \cdot \Delta w$. See Figure 13-4.

$$\Delta A \approx f(w) \cdot \Delta w$$

means

$$\frac{\Delta A}{\Delta w} \approx f(w)$$

Now as $\Delta w \to 0$, $\dfrac{\Delta A}{\Delta w} \to A'(w)$, and so $A'(w) = f(w)$. Thus A is an antiderivative of f, and so

$$\int_a^b f(x)dx = A(b) - A(a)$$

From the definition of A as the area function we have $A(a) = 0$. Therefore

$$\int_a^b f(x)dx = A(b) = \text{area of } R$$

We have established the following theorem.

> *Theorem*
> **Answer to Area Problem 1**
>
> If f is continuous on $[a, b]$ with $f(x) \geq 0$, and if R denotes the region bounded above by the graph of $y = f(x)$, bounded below by the x-axis, bounded on the left by the line $x = a$, and bounded on the right by the line $x = b$, then
>
> $$\text{The area of } R = \int_a^b f(x)dx$$

This is a surprising and wonderful theorem. Derivatives were developed to describe rates of change and slopes of tangent lines. At first it would seem that this language would be useless in the computation of areas. The Fundamental Theorem of Calculus establishes the connection between computing area under a graph and finding antiderivatives.

We now turn to specific examples using this theorem, then to a more general area problem, and finally to how area can be used in applications. We will continue with more applications of area in the next section, and in Section 13–6 we will show how to define area independent of antiderivatives and how to approximate the definite integral when we cannot find an antiderivative for the integrand.

EXAMPLE 1   *(Compare Exercise 7)*

Verify that if $f(x) = 6x$ and $A(w)$ is the area of the region bounded above by the graph of f, below by the x-axis, on the left by the line $x = 0$, and on the right by the line $x = w$, then A is an antiderivative of f.

SOLUTION   Here, $A(w)$ is the area of the shaded region in Figure 13–5.

$$A(w) = \frac{1}{2} \cdot \text{base} \cdot \text{height} = \frac{1}{2} \cdot w \cdot 6w = 3w^2$$

Hence $A'(w) = 6w$, and since $f(w) = 6w$ also, we have

$$A'(w) = f(w)$$

Now we show how to compute these areas.

EXAMPLE 2   *(Compare Exercise 21)*

Find the area of R if R is the region bounded above by the graph of $y = x^2$, below by the x-axis, on the left by the line $x = -1$, and on the right by the line $x = 5$. (See Figure 13–6.)

FIGURE 13–5

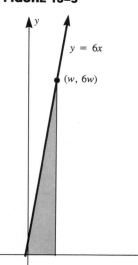

FIGURE 13–6

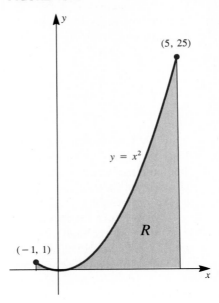

SOLUTION

$$\text{The area of } R = \int_{-1}^{5} x^2 \, dx = \frac{x^3}{3} \Big|_{-1}^{5}$$

$$= \frac{125}{3} - \frac{(-1)^3}{3}$$

$$= \frac{125}{3} + \frac{1}{3} = \frac{126}{3}$$

In this example the graph of $y = f(x)$ actually comes down and touches the x-axis, but $\int_{-1}^{5} x^2 \, dx$ gives the area of this region because $x^2 \geq 0$ on $[-1, 5]$. ∎

EXAMPLE 3   *(Compare Exercise 23)*

Find the area of the region bounded above by the graph of $y = \frac{1}{x}$ and below by the interval $[1, 3]$.

SOLUTION   We have shortened the formal terminology. The interval $[1, 3]$ is on the x-axis; its leftmost point is 1 and its rightmost point is 3. The region is shown in Figure 13–7. The area of the region is

$$\int_{1}^{3} \frac{1}{x} \, dx = \ln|x| \Big|_{1}^{3}$$

$$= \ln 3 - \ln 1$$

$$= \ln 3 - 0 \qquad \text{(Remember that } \ln 1 = 0\text{)}$$

$$= \ln 3$$

FIGURE 13–7

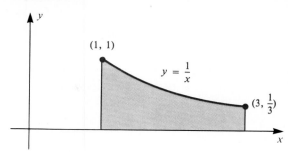

This example now gives us a geometric interpretation of logarithms; ln 3 is the area between the curve $y = 1/x$ and the x-axis from $x = 1$ to $x = 3$. Thus if we can find a numerical method of computing this area that doesn't involve antiderivatives, then we have a way to get a numerical approximation to ln 3, such as is found in tables; ln 3 ≈ 1.099. There is nothing special about the number 3. If b is any number larger than 1, the region shown in Figure 13–8 has area ln b.

FIGURE 13–8

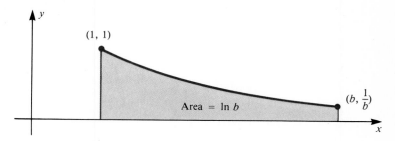

Therefore for $b > 1$ we have an important geometric formula for ln b that does not use exponents.

$$\ln b = \int_1^b \frac{1}{x}\,dx$$

(In fact, you should verify that this formula is valid for all $b > 0$.)
Using numerical techniques to approximate the area of this region would allow you to find the approximate value of ln b. Doing this for various values of b would then allow you to compute values of the natural logarithm function. (How *does* your calculator compute these values?)

AREA BETWEEN CURVES

Sometimes, applications force you to look at two curves, such as marginal revenue and marginal cost. The **area of a region between these two curves** and two vertical lines can be very significant. With this in mind we now look at the more general area problem of finding the area of a region between two curves.

Area Problem 2   If both f and g are continuous on $[a, b]$ with $f(x) \geq g(x)$, and R is the region bounded above by the graph of $y = f(x)$, bounded below by the graph of $y = g(x)$, bounded on the left by the line $x = a$, and bounded on the right by the line $x = b$, what is the area of R? See Figure 13–9.

FIGURE 13–9

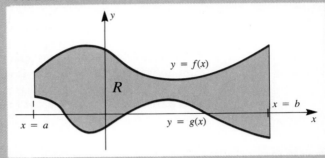

Again, we proceed by example. First we solve the problem in the special case $f(x) \geq g(x) \geq 0$.

EXAMPLE 4   *(Compare Exercise 27)*

Find the area of the region bounded by the graphs of $f(x) = 6 - x$ and $g(x) = x^2$ and by the lines $x = -2$ and $x = 1$.

SOLUTION   On the interval $[-2, 1]$, $f(x) \geq g(x) \geq 0$, and the region is shown in Figure 13–10 and is labeled R.

We can represent the area of R as one area minus another area, the area of S minus the area of T. See Figure 13–11.

FIGURE 13-10

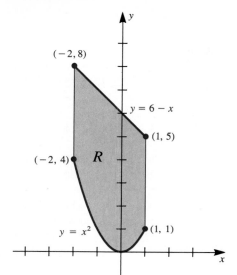

FIGURE 13-11

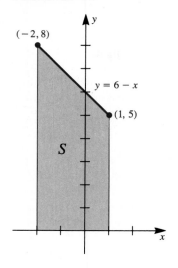

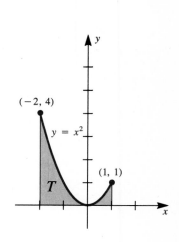

The area of R = the area of S − the area of T

$$= \int_{-2}^{1} f(x)\ dx - \int_{-2}^{1} g(x)\ dx = \int_{-2}^{1} (6 - x)\ dx - \int_{-2}^{1} x^2\ dx$$

$$= \int_{-2}^{1} (f(x) - g(x))\ dx = \int_{-2}^{1} (6 - x - x^2)dx$$

$$= \left(6x - \frac{1}{2}x^2 - \frac{1}{3}x^3 \right) \Big|_{-2}^{1}$$

$$= \left(6 - \frac{1}{2} - \frac{1}{3} \right) - \left(-12 - \frac{4}{2} - \left(-\frac{8}{3} \right) \right)$$

$$= \frac{33}{2}$$

Example 5 will show how to remove the requirement that $g(x) \geq 0$.

NOTE In Example 5 the lines $x = a$ and $x = b$ must be determined from the given functions.

EXAMPLE 5   *(Compare Exercise 39)*

Find the area of the region bounded above by the graph of $f(x) = x - 1$ and below by the graph of $g(x) = x^2 - 2x - 5$.

SOLUTION   The region is shown in Figure 13–12.

We must find the coordinates of P and Q. The two graphs meet at P and Q, so at these points we must have $f(x) = g(x)$. To find the x-coordinates of P and Q, we set $f(x) = g(x)$ and solve:

$$x - 1 = x^2 - 2x - 5$$
$$0 = x^2 - 3x - 4 = (x - 4)(x + 1)$$

The x-coordinates are $x = -1$ and $x = 4$. We redraw the region R in Figure 13–13, labeling P and Q and also labeling the lowest point of the region.

Now we shift the region R up 6 units to obtain the identically shaped region S. We chose 6 units so that S lies entirely above the x-axis, which allows us to compute the area of S using the techniques of Example 4. The new functions are $F(x) = f(x) + 6 = (x - 1) + 6 = x + 5$ and $G(x) = g(x) + 6 = (x^2 - 2x - 5) + 6 = x^2 - 2x + 1$. See Figure 13–14.

FIGURE 13–12

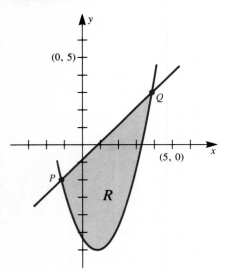

FIGURE 13–13

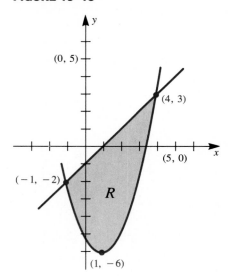

FIGURE 13–14

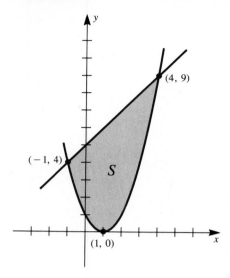

Now

The area of R = the area of S

$$= \int_{-1}^{4} (F(x) - G(x))dx$$

$$= \int_{-1}^{4} ((x + 5) - (x^2 - 2x + 1))dx$$

$$= \int_{-1}^{4} (-x^2 + 3x + 4)dx$$

$$= \left(-\frac{x^3}{3} + \frac{3}{2}x^2 + 4x\right)\Big|_{-1}^{4}$$

$$= \left(-\frac{64}{3} + \frac{3}{2} \cdot 16 + 16\right) - \left(\frac{1}{3} + \frac{3}{2} - 4\right)$$

$$= \frac{125}{6}$$

Repeating the calculation using $f(x)$ and $g(x)$ notation, we have

The area of $R =$ the area of S

$$= \int_{-1}^{4} (F(x) - G(x))dx$$

$$= \int_{-1}^{4} ((f(x) + 6) - (g(x) + 6))dx$$

$$= \int_{-1}^{4} (f(x) - g(x))dx$$

The general argument is similar. If R is the region bounded above by the graph of f, bounded below by the graph of g, bounded on the left by $x = a$, and bounded on the right by $x = b$, you can shift R up k units to a congruent region S, which lies entirely above the x-axis. Then

The area of $R =$ the area of S

$$= \int_{a}^{b} ((f(x) + k) - (g(x) + k))dx$$

$$= \int_{a}^{b} (f(x) + k + g(x) - k)dx$$

$$= \int_{a}^{b} (f(x) - g(x))dx$$

Once we have established this principle, we no longer go through the process of shifting R but use the final result directly.

Answer to Area Problem 2
Area Between Two Curves

If $f(x) \geq g(x)$ on the interval $[a, b]$, and if R is the region bounded above by $y = f(x)$, below by $y = g(x)$, on the left by the line $x = a$, and on the right by the line $x = b$, then

The area of $R = \int_{a}^{b} (f(x) - g(x))dx$

Finally, what if the curves cross so that $f(x) \geq g(x)$ on some subinterval and $f(x) \leq g(x)$ on another subinterval? In this case you must find where the graphs of f and g cross by solving the equation $f(x) = g(x)$. This will allow you to compute the area of the entire region as the sum of areas of subregions. The area of each smaller subregion is computed by using the above formula. Remember that *each integrand should be of the form (larger function − smaller function)*. Example 6 demonstrates how to do this.

NOTE Geometrically, the larger function is the one with the higher, or upper, graph; the smaller function is the one with the lower graph.

EXAMPLE 6   *(Compare Exercise 37)*

Find the area of the region bounded by the curves $y = 5 - x$ and $y = x^2 - 4x + 5$ and by the lines $x = 1$ and $x = 4$.

SOLUTION   The curves cross when

$$5 - x = x^2 - 4x + 5$$

Solving, we have

$$0 = x^2 - 3x$$
$$0 = x(x - 3)$$
$$x = 0, \qquad x = 3$$

The solution $x = 0$ does not concern us, since 0 is not in the interval $[1, 4]$. A quick sketch yields the shaded region of Figure 13-15.

The curves meet when $x = 3$. From $x = 1$ to $x = 3$, $y = 5 - x$ is the top boundary of the region, so

$$
\begin{aligned}
\text{Area I} &= \int_1^3 ((5 - x) - (x^2 - 4x + 5))\,dx \\
&= \int_1^3 (-x^2 + 3x)\,dx \\
&= \left(-\frac{1}{3}x^3 + \frac{3}{2}x^2 \right) \Big|_1^3 \\
&= \left(-\frac{27}{3} + \frac{27}{2} \right) - \left(-\frac{1}{3} + \frac{3}{2} \right) \\
&= \frac{10}{3}
\end{aligned}
$$

FIGURE 13-15

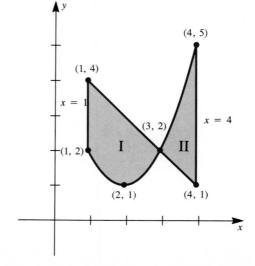

From $x = 3$ to $x = 4$, $y = x^2 - 4x + 5$ is on top, so

$$\text{Area II} = \int_3^4 ((x^2 - 4x + 5) - (5 - x))dx$$

$$= \int_3^4 (x^2 - 3x)dx$$

$$= \left(\frac{1}{3}x^3 - \frac{3}{2}x^2\right)\Big|_3^4$$

$$= \left(\frac{64}{3} - \frac{48}{2}\right) - \left(\frac{27}{3} - \frac{27}{2}\right)$$

$$= \frac{11}{6}$$

The total area is Area I + Area II = $\frac{10}{3} + \frac{11}{6} = \frac{31}{6}$.

NOTE Sometimes $g(x)$ is not explicitly given; if one of the boundaries of the region is the x-axis, then this is equivalent to saying that one of the functions is $g(x) = 0$ (which is the equation of the x-axis). To compute the area, you must find out where the graph of f crosses the x-axis. (*See Example 7.*)

EXAMPLE 7   (*Compare Exercise 35*)

Find the area of the region bounded by the lines $x = -1$ and $x = 3$, the x-axis, and the curve $y = x^2 - 4$.

SOLUTION   To see where the graph crosses the x-axis, set $f(x) = 0$ and solve:

$$f(x) = 0$$
$$x^2 - 4 = 0$$
$$x^2 = 4$$
$$x = \pm 2$$

Reject -2 because -2 is not in $[-1, 3]$. The curve crosses the x-axis at $x = 2$. The region is shaded in Figure 13–16.

The total area is area I plus area II. Because $y = x^2 - 4$ lies below the x-axis from $x = -1$ to $x = 2$,

$$\text{Area I} = \int_{-1}^2 (0 - (x^2 - 4))dx$$

$$= -\int_{-1}^2 (x^2 - 4)dx$$

$$= -\left(\frac{x^3}{3} - 4x\right)\Big|_{-1}^2$$

$$= -\left[\left(\frac{8}{3} - 8\right) - \left(\frac{-1}{3} - (-4)\right)\right]$$

$$= 9$$

FIGURE 13–16

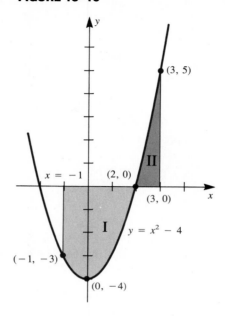

From $x = 2$ to $x = 3$, however, the curve lies above the x-axis, so

$$\text{Area II} = \int_{2}^{3} ((x^2 - 4) - 0)dx$$

$$= \int_{2}^{3} (x^2 - 4)dx$$

$$= \left(\frac{x^3}{3} - 4x\right) \Big|_{2}^{3}$$

$$= \left(\frac{27}{3} - 12\right) - \left(\frac{8}{3} - 8\right)$$

$$= \frac{7}{3}$$

The total area is $9 + \dfrac{7}{3} = \dfrac{34}{3}$.

We conclude with one application of area. For more applications, see Section 13–5.

APPLICATION

Let C be the daily cost function of a company, let R be its daily revenue function, and let x be the number of units it produces daily. Then its daily profit function P is given by

$$P(x) = R(x) - C(x)$$

and so

$$P'(x) = R'(x) - C'(x)$$

If production is increased from a units per day to b units per day, the change in profit is

$$P(b) - P(a) = \int_a^b P'(x)dx$$
$$= \int_a^b (R'(x) - C'(x))dx$$

If $R'(x) \geq C'(x)$, this last integral gives the area between the two curves over the interval $[a, b]$. See Figure 13–17.

FIGURE 13–17

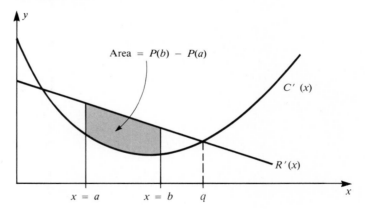

The shaded area in Figure 13–17 gives the increase in profit when production is increased from a units to b units. Let q be the largest production level where $R'(x) = C'(x)$, that is, where marginal revenue = marginal cost. As b moves to the right, the area of the shaded region increases until $b = q$. If the production level becomes bigger than q, then the curves cross on $[a, b]$. See Figure 13–18.

FIGURE 13-18

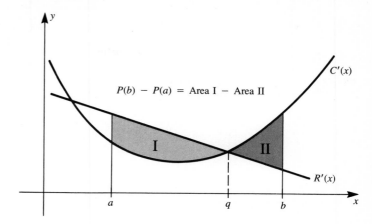

We have a geometric interpretation in terms of area. The change in profit remains

$$P(b) - P(a) = \int_a^b P'(x)dx = \int_a^b (R'(x) - C'(x))dx$$

$$= \int_a^q (R'(x) - C'(x))dx + \int_q^b (R'(x) - C'(x))dx$$

$$= \int_a^q (R'(x) - C'(x))dx - \int_q^b (C'(x) - R'(x))dx$$

$$= \text{Area I} - \text{Area II} < \text{Area I}$$

If b is larger than q, the total profit is less than when $b = q$.

We see again that with revenue and cost functions like those given in the above figures, the maximum profit will occur when the production level is the largest number x such that $R'(x) = C'(x)$. (*Compare Exercise 53*)

Often in applications, it is the marginal functions that are known first. Whenever $R'(x)$ and $C'(x)$ are so complicated that we cannot compute $\int_a^b (R'(x) - C'(x))\, dx$ by finding antiderivatives, this geometric interpretation gives us another method of computing profit. We can compute the profit by computing the area of a certain region.

13-4 EXERCISES

I

Compute each of the areas in Exercises 1 through 4 by
using formulas for the area of rectangles and triangles.
Then write a definite integral that gives the area, evaluate
the definite integral, and compare your answers.

1.

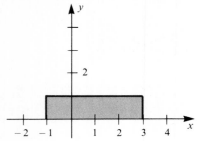

2.

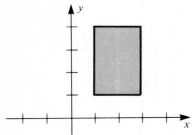

3.

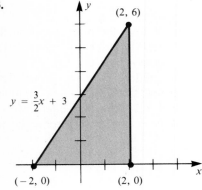

4.

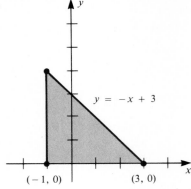

5. Find the area of the region between the graph of
$f(x) = 4$, the x-axis, and the vertical lines $x = -3$
and $x = 2$.

6. Find the area of the region between the graph of
$f(x) = 2x - 2$, the x-axis, and the vertical lines
$x = 1$ and $x = 6$.

7. (*See Example 1*) Let $A(w)$ be the area bounded above
by the graph of $f(x) = 4$, below by the x-axis, on the
left by the line $x = 2$, and on the right by the line
$x = w$. Use geometry to find a formula for $A(w)$ and
show that $A'(w) = f(w)$.

8. Let $A(w)$ be the area bounded above by the graph of
$f(x) = 3x$, below by the x-axis, on the left by the line
$x = 0$, and on the right by the line $x = w$. Use
geometry to find a formula for $A(w)$ and show that
$A'(w) = f(w)$.

II

In Exercises 9 through 14, compute the areas by geometry, using formulas for the area of rectangles and triangles. Then write a definite integral that gives the area, evaluate the definite integral, and compare your answers.

9.

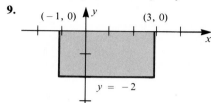

10.

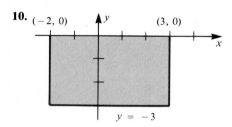

11.

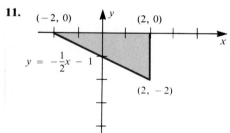

12.

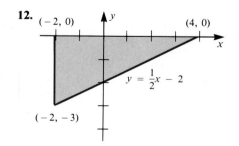

13.

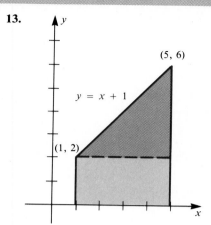

14.

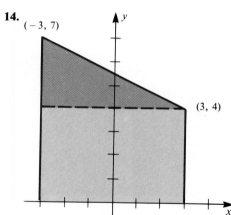

In Exercises 15 through 20, find the area of the indicated region.

15. The region between the graph of $f(x) = 2x - 1$, the x-axis, and the vertical lines $x = 2$ and $x = 7$.

16. The region between the graph of $f(x) = 5 - x$, the x-axis, and the vertical lines $x = -3$ and $x = 1$.

17. The region between the graph of $f(x) = -4$, the x-axis, and the vertical lines $x = 0$ and $x = 6$.

18. The region between the graph of $f(x) = 2x + 1$, the x-axis, and the vertical lines $x = -5$ and $x = -1$.

19. The region between the graph of $f(x) = 5 - 3x$, the x-axis, and the vertical lines $x = 2$ and $x = 6$.

20. The region between the graph of $f(x) = x - 9$, the x-axis, and the vertical lines $x = 3$ and $x = 5$.

Sketch each of the regions in Exercises 21 through 28 and use a definite integral to compute the area of the region.

21. (*See Example 2*) The region between the graph of $f(x) = x^2 - 2x + 1$, the x-axis, and the vertical lines $x = 0$ and $x = 3$.

22. The region between the graph of $f(x) = 4 - x^2$, the x-axis, and the vertical lines $x = -1$ and $x = 2$.

23. (*See Example 3*) The region between the graph of $f(x) = 2/x$, the x-axis, and the vertical lines $x = 2$ and $x = 10$.

24. The region between the graph of $y = -3/x$, the x-axis, and the vertical lines $x = 1$ and $x = 3$.

25. The region bounded above by the graph of $y = x^2 + 1$, bounded below by the graph of $y = x - 4$, and between the vertical lines $x = 1$ and $x = 3$.

26. The region bounded above by the graph of $y = 2x + 5$, bounded below by the graph of $y = 6 - x^2$, and between the vertical lines $x = 2$ and $x = 5$.

27. (*See Example 4*) The region bounded above by the graph of $y = x^3 + 2x^2 + 5x + 3$, below by the line $y = x + 2$, on the left by the y-axis, and on the right by the line $x = 2$.

28. The region bounded above by the graph of $y = 6 - x^2$, bounded below by the graph of $y = x^2 - 4$, and between the vertical lines $x = -2$ and $x = 1$.

29. Use geometry to find a formula for $A(w)$, the area of the region bounded on the left by the line $x = 3$, on the right by the line $x = w$, above by the graph of $f(x) = 4x$, and below by the x-axis. Show that $A'(w) = f(w)$.

30. Use geometry to find a formula for $A(w)$, the area of the region bounded above by the graph of $f(x) = 4x + 8$, below by the x-axis, on the left by the line $x = -2$, and on the right by the line $x = w$. Show that $A'(w) = f(w)$.

III

Use geometry to compute the area of the shaded regions in Exercises 31 through 34; then compute the area using definite integrals.

31.

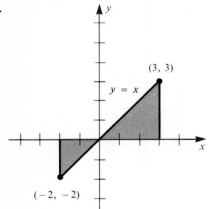

32.

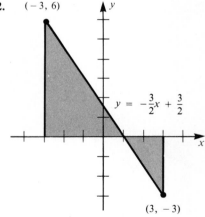

33.

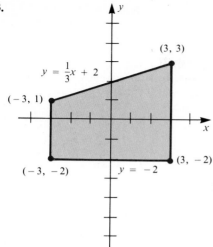

$y = \frac{1}{3}x + 2$

$(3, 3)$

$(-3, 1)$

$(-3, -2)$ $(3, -2)$

$y = -2$

34.

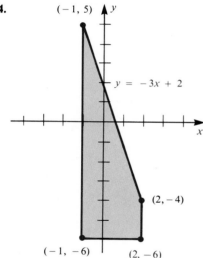

$(-1, 5)$

$y = -3x + 2$

$(2, -4)$

$(-1, -6)$ $(2, -6)$

In Exercises 35 through 42, sketch each region and find its area.

35. (*See Example 7*) The region between the *x*-axis, the graph of $y = 3x - 6$, and the vertical lines $x = 1$ and $x = 4$.

36. The region between the graph of $y = x^2 - 9$, the *x*-axis, and the vertical lines $x = 2$ and $x = 5$.

37. (*See Example 6*) The region between the graph of $y = x^2 + x + 2$, the line $y = 3x + 5$, and the vertical lines $x = -3$ and $x = 0$.

38. The region between the graph of $y = 9 - x^2$, the line $y - x = 7$, and the vertical lines $x = -2$ and $x = 2$.

39. (*See Example 5*) The region between the graphs of $y = x^2 - 6x + 7$ and $y = x - 3$.

40. The region between the graph of $y = x^2 + x - 5$ and the line $y = x + 4$.

41. The region between the graph of $y = x^3 + 3$ and the line $y = x + 3$.

42. The region between the graph of $y = x^3 + x + 1$ and the line $y = 5x + 1$.

43. Use properties of ln to show that the area under the curve $y = \frac{1}{x}$ and above the interval $[1, 4]$ is equal to the area under the same curve and above the interval $[2, 8]$.

44. Use properties of ln to show that the area under the curve $y = \frac{1}{x}$ and above the interval $[1, 5]$ is equal to the area under the same curve and above the interval $[3, 15]$.

45. Use properties of ln to show that the area under the curve $y = \frac{1}{x}$ and above the interval $[1, 3]$ is equal to the area under the same curve and above the interval $[\frac{1}{3}, 1]$.

46. Use properties of ln to show that the area under the curve $y = \frac{1}{x}$ and above the interval $[2, 8]$ is equal to the area under the same curve and above the interval $[\frac{1}{4}, 1]$.

47. Use properties of ln to show that the area under the curve $y = \frac{1}{x}$ and above the interval $[1, 9]$ is twice the area under the same curve and above the interval $[1, 3]$.

48. Use properties of ln to show that the area under the curve $y = \frac{1}{x}$ and above the interval $[\frac{1}{8}, 1]$ is three times the area under the same curve and above the interval $[1, 2]$.

In Exercises 49 through 52, use geometry to find $A(w)$, the area of the indicated region. Then show that $A'(w) = -f(w)$.

49. The region is bounded *below* by the graph of $f(x) = -10$, bounded *above* by the x-axis, bounded on the left by the line $x = 2$, and bounded on the right by the line $x = w$.

50. The region is bounded *below* by the graph of $f(x) = -6x$, bounded *above* by the x-axis, bounded on the left by the line $x = 0$, and bounded on the right by the line $x = w$.

51. The region is bounded above by the graph of $f(x) = 8x$, bounded below by the x-axis, bounded on the *right* by the line $x = 6$, and bounded on the *left* by the line $x = w$, $0 \le w \le 6$.

52. The region is bounded above by the graph of $f(x) = -4x$, below by the x-axis, on the *right* by the line $x = -1$, and on the *left* by the line $x = w$, $w \le -1$.

53. (*See Application*) A company's marginal cost is $MC(x) = x^2 - 20x + 300$, and its marginal revenue is $MR(x) = 276 - 6x$, where x is the number of units produced per day. The company is currently producing ten units per day.
   (a) What production level will maximize profit?
   (b) How much will the company's profit increase if the production level is changed to maximize profit?

54. A company's marginal cost function is given by $MC(x) = x^2 - 30x + 500$, and its marginal revenue function is given by $MR(x) = 480 - 9x$, where x is the weekly production. The company is currently producing 24 units per week.
   (a) What production level will maximize the company's profits?
   (b) How much will profit increase if production level is changed to maximize profit?

55. Find a formula for area R if R is the region bounded above by the x-axis, below by the graph of f, on the left by the line $x = a$, and on the right by the line $x = b$ (so $f(x) \le 0$ for all x in $[a, b]$).

13–5 APPLICATIONS OF AREA

- *Average Value of a Function*
- *Consumers' Surplus*
- *Producers' Surplus*
- *Flows and Accumulations*
- *The Gini Index*

In the last section we saw that the definite integral can be used to compute the area of a region that is bounded on the left and right by the vertical lines $x = a$ and $x = b$ and that is bounded above and below by the graphs of functions. Further, we saw that the change in profit can be interpreted as a certain area. We continue in this geometric vein, trying to obtain new insights into applications by viewing the problems geometrically.

AVERAGE VALUE OF A FUNCTION

When introducing the derivative, we used the concept of the average speed of a car over shorter and shorter intervals to provide us with some feeling for what "instantaneous rate of change" means. Integration is the opposite of differentiation. We now suppose that the odometer in our car is broken but that we can keep

FIGURE 13–19

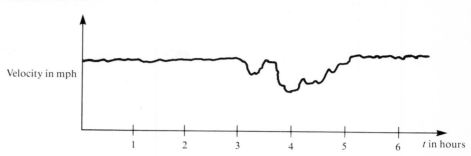

track of the velocity by looking at the speedometer. Let $t = 0$ correspond to the time we started our trip, and let $v(t)$ be our velocity at time t hours after we start. Suppose that during the fourth and fifth hours of our trip we were going through periods of construction and heavy traffic, so our speed on the highway varied considerably. The graph of $v(t)$ is drawn in Figure 13–19.

If we wanted to complain later about the difficulty of this trip, we would probably want to complain about our average speed during these two hours.

$$\text{Average speed} = \frac{\text{distance traveled}}{\text{elapsed time}}$$

We have seen earlier in this chapter that the distance travelled is $\int_3^5 v(t)dt;$ the total time is $5 - 3 = 2$. (Notice the limits of integration; for the first hour of our trip, $0 \leq t \leq 1$. The second hour corresponds to the interval $[1, 2]$; the third hour corresponds to the interval $[2, 3]$; the fourth hour corresponds to the interval $[3, 4]$; and the fifth hour corresponds to the interval $[4, 5]$. So the fourth and fifth hours correspond to $3 \leq t \leq 5$.) The average speed during this time is

$$\frac{\int_3^5 v(t)dt}{5 - 3}$$

We generalize this concept to any continuous function over an interval $[a, b]$.

Definition
**Average Value
of a Function
over an Interval**

The **average value of the function f over the interval $[a, b]$** is

$$\frac{1}{b - a} \int_a^b f(x)dx$$

We now interpret the average value of a function over $[a, b]$ geometrically and use area to see what this definition gives us in contexts other than average velocity.

FIGURE 13–20

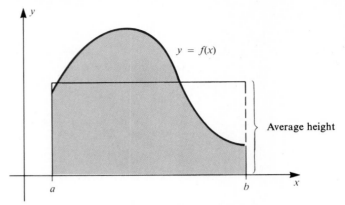

$$y = f(x)$$

Average height

a b x

Area of rectangle = Area of region under the curve

Let R be the region bounded above by the graph of $y = f(x)$, below by the x-axis, on the left by the line $x = a$, and on the right by the line $x = b$. If we let AVE stand for the average value of f on the interval $[a, b]$, we have

$$AVE = \frac{1}{b - a} \int_a^b f(x)dx$$

so

$$(AVE)(b - a) = \int_a^b f(x)dx = \text{area of } R$$

The average value of f is the average height of the graph of $y = f(x)$. The average height of the graph is that number which, when multiplied by the length of the interval, gives the area of R.

This idea is shown in Figure 13–20 and gives a geometric motivation for the definition of the average value of f on $[a, b]$ as

$$\frac{1}{b - a} \int_a^b f(x)dx$$

EXAMPLE 1   *(Compare Exercise 1)*

What is the average value of $f(x) = x^2$ on the interval $[-3, 3]$?
SOLUTION   First,

$$\int_{-3}^3 x^2 \, dx = \frac{x^3}{3} \Big|_{-3}^3$$

$$= \frac{27}{3} - \left(-\frac{27}{3}\right)$$

$$= 9 + 9$$

$$= 18$$

Next, the length of the interval, $b - a$, is $3 - (-3) = 6$. The average value of x^2 on $[-3, 3]$ is $\frac{18}{6} = 3$.

EXAMPLE 2 *(Compare Exercise 27)*

If the population (in millions) of a country is given by $P(t) = (43.2)e^{0.02t}$, where $t = 0$ corresponds to 1980 and t is in years, what was the average population of the country during the decade of the 1980s? (Notice that $P'(t) = 0.02P(t)$, so we are modeling a 2% growth rate.)

SOLUTION   The interval is $[0, 10]$, so the average population was

$$\frac{1}{10 - 0} \int_0^{10} (43.2)e^{0.02t} \, dt = \frac{1}{10}(43.2) \int_0^{10} e^{0.02t} \, dt$$

$$= 4.32\left(\frac{1}{0.02}e^{0.02t} \Big|_0^{10}\right)$$

$$= 216\left(e^{0.02t} \Big|_0^{10}\right)$$

$$= 216(e^{0.2} - e^0)$$

$$= 216(e^{0.2} - 1)$$

$$\approx 216(1.221 - 1)$$

$$\approx 47.8$$

The average population was about 47.8 million people.

CONSUMERS' SURPLUS

How do you quantify the individual satisfaction that comes when you've gotten a "good buy"? It's hard to do, but economists have a method for quantifying society's group satisfaction with certain price levels, and that method is called **consumers' surplus.** The explanation of how consumers' surplus is computed and what it means relies heavily on the interpretation of integrals as areas.

Suppose that the price-demand curve $p = D(x)$ of a certain commodity is given by

$$p = D(x) = 250 - \frac{x^2}{10^5}$$

Remember that x is the quantity of goods that can be sold at price p. It seems backwards to think of p as a function of x; as consumers, we usually think of demand as a function of price. The reason for viewing the relationship this way rests on the geometric interpretation of consumers' surplus that this viewpoint provides.

If the market price of this commodity is $160, then the corresponding value of x is 3000. Consumers will buy 3000 units at $160 each for a total cost to the consumers of $(3000)($160) = $480,000$. This number is represented by the shaded area in Figure 13–21.

FIGURE 13–21

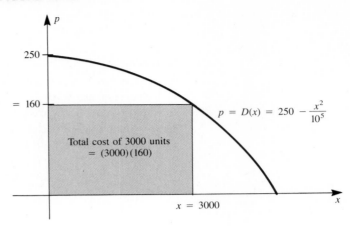

Presumably, the consumers who are willing to pay $220 for this good are even happier with the market price of $160 than are those consumers who are willing to pay $180. How can we measure this aggregate happiness? Economists call $D(x)$ the **value** of the xth unit purchased and define the **total value** of the 3000 units to the consumer by the equation

$$\text{Total value} = \int_0^{3000} D(x)\,dx$$

With $D(x) = 250 - \dfrac{x^2}{10^5}$ we have

$$\text{Total value} = \int_0^{3000} \left(250 - \frac{x^2}{10^5}\right) dx$$

$$= 250x - \frac{x^3}{3 \cdot 10^5} \Big|_0^{3000}$$

$$= 660{,}000$$

See Figure 13–22 for a geometric interpretation of the total value.

Next, the **consumers' surplus** is defined to be the total value minus the total cost. Here, the consumers' surplus is $660{,}000 - 480{,}000 = 180{,}000$. See Figure 13–23 for a geometric interpretation of this quantity.

Notice that the consumers' surplus is

$$\int_0^{3000} D(x)\,dx - \int_0^{3000} 160\,dx = \int_0^{3000} (D(x) - 160)\,dx$$

This now gives us a general formula for consumers' surplus.

FIGURE 13–22

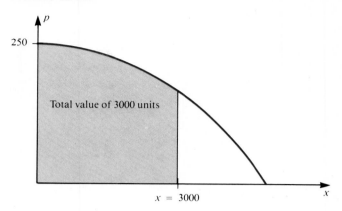

FIGURE 13–23

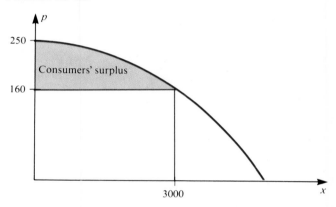

> *Definition*
> **Consumers' Surplus**
>
> If the market price is p_1 and the demand at that price is x_1, then the
>
> $$\text{consumers' surplus} = \int_0^{x_1} (D(x) - p_1)\, dx, \text{ where } D(x) = p \text{ is the price-}$$
>
> demand equation.

EXAMPLE 3   *(Compare Exercise 7)*

If $p = 250 - \dfrac{x^2}{10^5}$, what is the consumers' surplus when the market price is 90?

SOLUTION   (Before we begin the solution, we remark that consumers should be happier with a market price of 90 than with 160, so our answer should be greater than 180,000.)

To find x_1, substitute $p = 90$ into the demand-price equation and solve for x:

$$90 = 250 - \frac{x^2}{10^5}$$

$$-160 = -\frac{x^2}{10^5}$$

$$16{,}000{,}000 = x^2$$

$$x = 4000 \qquad \text{(Reject } x = -4000 \text{ because demand} \geq 0)$$

Thus $x_1 = 4000$ and $p_1 = 90$, so the

$$\text{Consumers' surplus} = \int_0^{4000} \left(250 - \frac{x^2}{10^5} - 90\right)dx$$

$$= \int_0^{4000} \left(160 - \frac{x^2}{10^5}\right)dx$$

$$= \left(160x - \frac{x^3}{3 \cdot 10^5}\right)\Big|_0^{4000}$$

$$= \left[(160)(4000) - \frac{4000^3}{3 \cdot 10^5}\right] - (0 - 0)$$

$$= 426{,}666.67$$

Consumers bought more items (4000 versus 3000) at a lower price (90 versus 160) and were more than twice as happy as measured by the consumers' surplus (426,666 versus 180,000).

PRODUCERS' SURPLUS

There is an analogous measure of the happiness of the producers, or suppliers, of the commodity; this measure is called the **producers' surplus.** While the consumers' surplus is computed by using the price-demand curve, we use a different curve, the price-supply curve, to compute the producers' surplus. The price-supply curve gives the relationship between p, the price, and x, the quantity that producers are willing to produce at price p. Again, we would normally think of x as a function of p, but economists like to graph the supply curve and the demand curve on the same axis because the intersection of these curves gives the **equilibrium price,** where supply equals demand. (*See Exercise 15.*) Thus we write $p = S(x)$ and notice that whereas the price-demand curve is decreasing, the price-supply curve is increasing (more goods are produced when the selling price is higher). Let p_1 be the selling price. The producers who would supply x amount of the commodity at a lower price $p = S(x)$ have a price "surplus" of $p_1 - S(x)$, the difference between the selling price and the price at which they would have supplied the commodity, that is, the price at which they are willing to sell the commodity. See Figure 13–24, where the total producers' surplus is represented by area of the shaded region.

FIGURE 13–24

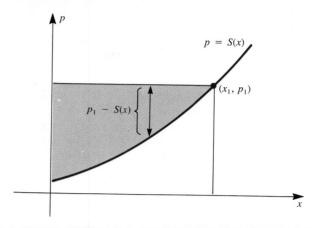

Let $p = S(x)$ be the price-supply equation. If p_1 is the selling price and x_1 is the amount of the commodity being produced, then the **producers' surplus** is $\int_0^{x_1} (p_1 - S(x))\, dx$.

EXAMPLE 4 *(Compare Exercise 11)*

If $S(x) = x^2 + 2x + 6$ and if the current selling price is 41, compute the producers' surplus.

SOLUTION We know that $p_1 = 41$, so we must find x_1. Since $S(x_1) = p_1$, to compute x_1, we set $S(x) = p_1$ and solve:

$$x^2 + 2x + 6 = 41$$
$$x^2 + 2x - 35 = 0$$
$$(x + 7)(x - 5) = 0$$
$$x = -7, \qquad x = 5$$

Reject $x = -7$, since $x_1 \geq 0$.

$$\text{Producers' surplus} = \int_0^5 (41 - (x^2 + 2x + 6))\, dx$$

$$= \int_0^5 (-x^2 - 2x + 35)\, dx$$

$$= -\frac{x^3}{3} - x^2 + 35x \Big|_0^5$$

$$= -\frac{125}{3} - 25 + 175 = \frac{325}{3}$$

The producers' surplus is $\frac{325}{3}$.

See Exercises 19 and 20 for another geometric interpretation of producers' surplus, which gives the following equivalent formula:

$$\text{Producers surplus} = p_1 x_1 - \int_0^{x_1} S(x)\,dx$$

FLOWS AND ACCUMULATIONS

Economists define investment as a flow of resources into the production of new capital. Capital here refers to inventory, equipment, and other resources of production of the firm. We use $K(t)$ to represent the total *capital* of a firm at time t (capital starts with c, but c is reserved for *cost* functions), and $I(t)$ to represent the amount of *investment* being made at time t. By definition, **investment flow** is the rate of change of capital:

$$I = \frac{dK}{dt}$$

This is analogous to any flow into (or out of) a container. For example, we can think of measuring the flow of gas into a balloon. The gas in the balloon corresponds to the total capital of the firm, and the flow of gas into or out of the balloon at time t corresponds to $I(t)$.

Firms may be able to project their investment flow over a period of time and then ask what the total change in capital will be. If the period of time is given by $a \le t \le b$, then the total change of capital over this interval is $K(b) - K(a)$. This total change of capital is called the **capital formation** for this period and is given by the definite integral of the flow function:

$$K(b) - K(a) = \int_a^b I(t)\,dt$$

EXAMPLE 5   *(Compare Exercise 21)*

Suppose that a company plans to increase its investment flow and has determined that the model that best suits its capabilities for the next 12 months is given by

$$I(t) = -\frac{1}{30}t^2 + t + 1$$

Here, the units of capital are millions of dollars, and t is measured in months. What will be the company's capital formation during the second quarter of this period?

SOLUTION   The capital formation for the entire 12-month period is the area under the curve

$$I(t) = -\frac{1}{30}t^2 + t + 1$$

over the interval [0, 12]. We have to be careful to choose the limits of integration that represent the second quarter.

Months

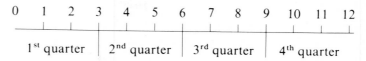

The capital formation for the second quarter is represented by the shaded region in Figure 13–25.

We can compute this area using the Fundamental Theorem of Calculus:

Capital formation = area

$$= \int_3^6 \left(-\frac{1}{30}t^2 + t + 1 \right) dt$$

$$= \left(-\frac{1}{90}t^3 + \frac{1}{2}t^2 + t \right) \Big|_3^6$$

$$= \left(-\frac{216}{90} + \frac{36}{2} + 6 \right) - \left(-\frac{27}{90} + \frac{9}{2} + 3 \right)$$

$$= 14.4$$

The company's capital will increase by $14.4 million.

FIGURE 13–25

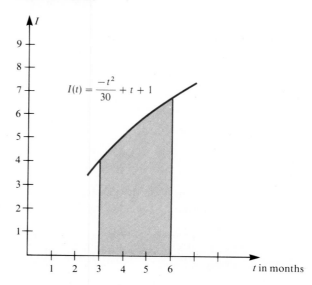

The importance of realizing that the capital formation can be viewed as area under a curve becomes even clearer when we cannot find an antiderivative for the function describing $I(t)$. For example, suppose the company decides that $I(t) = \sqrt{t^3 + 1}$ is a better model for its investment flow. This $I(t)$ does not have an antiderivative that can be expressed by using simple functions. Recognizing certain quantities as areas will allow you to use area-geometric computations to calculate an approximate value of

$$\int_a^b I(t)\,dt$$

As was mentioned at the beginning, this flow-accumulation model works with any flow problem, such as the population of a given political entity in terms of flow rate of people [(births + immigration) − (deaths + emigration)]; the trade balance of a country [exports − imports]; or the amount of water in a reservoir. Frequently, the flow function will be determined from data and will not have an antiderivative that can be found easily. Numerical techniques must be used in these cases.

THE GINI INDEX

The Lorenz curve for a given country is the graph of

$$F(x) = y \qquad 0 \le x \le 1$$

where $F(x) = y$ means that the lower $100x\%$ of the families (ranked by income) earned $100y\%$ of the total income. Thus $F(0.4) = 0.25$ would mean that the lower 40% of families earned 25% of the total income. (For a further discussion of Lorenz curves, see Appendix A.) The line of perfect equality is the line $y = x$. The area between this line and the Lorenz curve gives a measure of the income inequality of the country—the larger this area, the more the income distribution of the country deviates from perfect equality. The problem of comparing one country's income distribution to another country's is a difficult one. The difficulties come from gathering reliable data that are comparable. The measure that economists use for comparing the income distribution between various countries is called the **Gini index.** Referring to Figure 13–26, the Gini index for a given country is defined to be the ratio

$$\frac{\text{area of shaded region}}{\text{total area of lower triangle}}$$

Because the area of the lower triangle is $\frac{1}{2}$, the Gini index is twice the shaded area. If F is the income distribution for a given country (F is defined above), then

Definition
Gini Index   The Gini Index $= 2 \int_0^1 (x - F(x))\,dx$

FIGURE 13–26

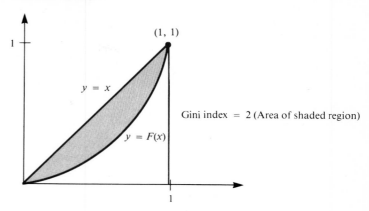

Gini index $= 2$ (Area of shaded region)

The function F is arrived at by finding the curve of a given type that best approximates the data collected. The type of curve that economists use arises in advanced statistics and is called a beta distribution. To keep our computations simple, we will use polynomial approximations to the data. We require that

$$F(0) = 0 \qquad \text{(0\% of population must earn 0\% of total income)}$$

and

$$F(1) = 1 \qquad \text{(100\% of population earns 100\% of total income)}$$

The data for the United States in 1971 is given in the table below. (It is a historical fact that the data varied *very* little in the U.S. for the period 1950–1983.)

PERCENTILE OF POPULATION	CUMULATIVE PERCENT OF TOTAL INCOME
0	0
20	5
40	15.8
60	32.3
80	55.4
100	100.0

The cubic $F(x) = 0.91x^3 - 0.25x^2 + 0.34x$ closely approximates this data (for example, $F(0.4) = 0.154$). Using this cubic, we get an approximation to the Gini index for the United States in 1971.

$$\text{The Gini index} = 2\int_0^1 (x - F(x))dx$$

$$= 2\int_0^1 (x - (0.91x^3 - 0.25x^2 + 0.34x))dx$$

$$= 2\int_0^1 (-0.91x^3 + 0.25x^2 + 0.66x)dx$$

$$= 2\left(\left(-\frac{0.91}{4}x^4 + \frac{0.25}{3}x^3 + \frac{0.66}{2}x^2\right)\Big|_0^1\right)$$

$$= 2\left(-\frac{0.91}{4} + \frac{0.25}{3} + \frac{0.66}{2}\right)$$

$$= 0.37$$

The actual Gini index computed by economists using a beta distribution is 0.39. Those of Brazil and Sweden are given in Exercises 25 and 26, respectively.

EXAMPLE 6 *(Compare Exercise 25)*

Use the function $F(x) = 1.95x^4 - 2.95x^3 + 2.08x^2 - 0.08x$ to approximate the Gini index for the United States in 1971. (This function is a fourth-degree polynomial that gives a good approximation to the data.)

SOLUTION

$$\text{The Gini index} = 2\int_0^1 (x - F(x))dx$$

$$= 2\int_0^1 (x - (1.95x^4 - 2.95x^3 + 2.08x^2 - 0.08x))dx$$

$$= 2\int_0^1 (-1.95x^4 + 2.95x^3 - 2.08x^2 + 1.08x)dx$$

$$= 2\left(\left(-\frac{1.95}{5}x^5 + \frac{2.95}{4}x^4 - \frac{2.08}{3}x^3 + \frac{1.08}{2}x^2\right)\Big|_0^1\right)$$

$$= 2\left(-\frac{1.95}{5} + \frac{2.95}{4} - \frac{2.08}{3} + \frac{1.08}{2}\right)$$

$$= 0.39$$

13-5 EXERCISES

In Exercises 1 through 6, compute the average value of each function on the given interval.

1. (*See Example 1*)
   $f(x) = x^2 - 2$ on $[-4, 4]$

2. $f(x) = 2x + 3$ on $[1, 6]$

3. $f(x) = e^{-x/2}$ on $[0, 4]$ 4. $f(x) = \sqrt{x}$ on $[4, 25]$

5. $f(x) = \dfrac{1}{x^3}$ on $[2, 6]$ 6. $f(x) = \dfrac{3}{x}$ on $[1, 6]$

7. (*See Example 3*) The consumer demand for a certain product is given by $p = 400 - 6x$. The market price is 190.
   (a) Determine how many units will be sold.
   (b) What is the total cost to the consumer of these units?
   (c) What is the total value to the consumer of these units?
   (d) What is the consumers' surplus?

8. For a certain product the consumer demand is given by $p = 510 - 8x$, and the market price is 110.
   (a) How many units will be sold at this price?
   (b) What is the total cost of these units to the consumer?
   (c) What is the total value of these units to the consumer?
   (d) What is the consumers' surplus?

9. For a certain product the consumer demand is given by $p = 300 - (x^2/10^5)$. The market price is 210.
   (a) How many units will be sold?
   (b) What is the total cost of these units to the consumer?
   (c) What is the total value of these units to the consumer?
   (d) What is the consumers' surplus?

10. If the consumer demand function is $p = 360 - (x^2/10^5)$ and the market price is 200, what is the consumers' surplus?

11. (*See Example 4*) The price-supply equation for a certain commodity is $p = 2 + \frac{x}{3}$, and the present market price is 62.
    (a) How many units will be produced at this price?
    (b) What is the producers' surplus?

12. The price-supply equation for a certain commodity is $p = 3 + \frac{x}{10}$, and the present market price is 8. What is the producers' surplus?

13. The price-supply equation for a certain commodity is $p = x^2 + 2x + 3$, and the present market price is 83. What is the producers' surplus?

14. The price-supply equation for a certain commodity is $p = x^2 + 4x + 6$, and the present market price is 51. What is the producers' surplus?

15. If the price-demand curve is given by $p = D(x) = 3 - \frac{x}{2}$ and the price-supply curve is given by $p = S(x) = 1 + \frac{x}{6}$, what is the equilibrium price, the price at which supply equals demand?

16. If the price-demand curve is given by $p = D(x) = 12 - \frac{x}{10}$ and the price-supply curve is given by
    $$p = S(x) = \frac{x + 24}{50}$$
    what is the equilibrium price?

17. The price-demand curve of a certain commodity is given by $p = D(x) = -x^2 - x + 71$, and the price-supply curve for the same commodity is $p = S(x) = x^2 + x + 11$.
    (a) Show that $D(x)$ is decreasing for $x \geq 0$, and interpret this in your own words.
    (b) Show that $S(x)$ is increasing for $x \geq 0$, and interpret this in your own words.
    (c) Find the equilibrium price.

18. If $p = D(x) = 256 - 3x - x^2$ is the price-demand equation for a given commodity, and $p = S(x) = x^2 + x + 16$ is its price-supply equation, then:
    (a) show that $D(x)$ is decreasing for $x \geq 0$, and interpret.
    (b) show that $S(x)$ is increasing for $x \geq 0$, and interpret.
    (c) find the equilibrium price.

19. This exercise develops an equivalent interpretation of producers' surplus. Let p_1 stand for the present market price and x_1 the amount of the commodity being produced (and sold) at this price.

(a) What significance does the number $x_1 \cdot p_1$ have to the producers?

(b) What significance does the number $\int_0^{x_1} S(x)dx$ have to the producers?

(c) Show that the producers' surplus, $\int_0^{x_1} (p_1 - S(x))dx$, is the same as

(the answer to part (a)) $-$ (the answer to part (b)).

20. This exercise asks for the geometric interpretation of the quantities developed in Exercise 19. In Figure 13–24:

(a) what region has area $x_1 \cdot p_1$?

(b) what region has area $\int_0^{x_1} S(x)dx$?

(c) what region has area $x_1 \cdot p_1 - \int_0^{x_1} S(x)dx$?

21. (*See Example 5*) The investment flow of a company during a given year is $I(t) = 30e^{t/20}$; capital is measured in thousands of dollars, and t is measured in months. What was the company's capital formation:

(a) during the second quarter of the year?

(b) during the third quarter?

22. The investment flow of a company during a given year is

$$I(t) = 6 + \frac{1}{2}t + \frac{1}{12}t^2$$

where capital is measured in millions of dollars and t is measured in months. What was the company's capital formation:

(a) during the third quarter?

(b) during the second half?

23. Oil is flowing out of a well at a rate of $12e^{-t/10}$ thousand gallons per year t years after it starts. How much oil flowed out of the well during the first 20 years of production?

24. Propane gas is flowing into a furnace at the rate of

$$10 + 2t - \frac{1}{6}t^2 \quad \text{cubic feet per hour}$$

t hours after it was started.

(a) How much gas is used during the first four hours?

(b) How much gas is used during the fifth hour?

25. (*See Example 6*) The income distribution for Brazil in 1972 is given by the following table.

PERCENTILE OF POPULATION	CUMULATIVE PERCENTAGE OF TOTAL INCOME
0	0
20	2.0
40	7.0
60	16.4
80	33.4
100	100

Source: W. van Ginneken and J. Park, eds., *Generating Internationally Comparable Income Distribution Estimates* (Geneva: International Labour Office, 1984).

The Gini index for Brazil in 1972 is 0.61.

(a) The curve $F(x) = 0.7x - 2.4x^2 + 2.7x^3$ is a good cubic approximation to the data. What is the approximation to the Gini index using this cubic?

(b) The curve $F(x) = 5.3x^4 - 7.7x^3 + 3.9x^2 - 0.5x$ is a good fourth-degree polynomial approximation to the data. What is the approximation to the Gini index obtained by using this fourth-degree polynomial?

26. The income distribution for Sweden in 1979 is given by the following table.

PERCENTILE OF POPULATION	CUMULATIVE PERCENTAGE OF TOTAL INCOME
0	0
20	7.2
40	20
60	37.4
80	62.8
100	100

Source: W. van Ginneken and J. Park, eds., *Generating Internationally Comparable Income Distribution Estimates* (Geneva: International Labour Office, 1984).

Sweden's Gini index for this data is 0.30.

(a) A good cubic fit to this data is given by $F(x) = 0.33x + 0.20x^2 + 0.47x^3$. What is the approximation to the Gini index given by this cubic?

(b) A good quartic fit to this data is given by
$F(x) = 0.20x + 0.95x^2 - 0.78x^3 + 0.63x^4$.
What is the approximation to the Gini index given by this quartic?

27. (*See Example 2*) One estimate of the world's population is given by $P(t) = 4.9e^{0.02t}$, with $t = 0$ corresponding to January 1, 1985. The units for $P(t)$ are billions of people, and t is in years.
   (a) Estimate the average population of the earth from January 1, 1985, to January 1, 1990.
   (b) Estimate the average population of the earth from January 1, 1990, to January 1, 1995.

28. The price, in dollars, of a typical three-bedroom house in a certain area from 1980 to 1985 is estimated by $P(t) = 300t^2 + 500t + 42,000$; t is years since 1980. What was the average price of such a house during this period?

29. The velocity of a decelerating train is given by

$$V(t) = 88 - 4t - \frac{1}{50}t^2$$

so that it comes to rest 20 seconds after the brakes are applied. V is measured in feet per second, and time, t, is in seconds.
   (a) What was the train's average speed during these 20 seconds?
   (b) What was its average speed during the first 10 seconds?

13–6 SUMMATION AND DEFINITE INTEGRALS

- *Approximation of Area*
- *Summations Using Integrals*
- *Volumes of Revolution (Optional)*

We have seen several applications of the definite integral and that the definite integral and the notion of area are closely related. In this section we look at this relationship again in three settings:

1. the concept of area can be used to approximate definite integrals by summations;
2. certain summations, in turn, can be approximated by definite integrals; and
3. the summation formulas themselves show how the definite integral can be used in the computation of other quantities, such as volume.

APPROXIMATION OF AREA

Although we have pointed to this section as a method of numerically approximating numbers, such as $\int_0^1 \sqrt{x^3 + 1}\, dx$, that cannot be computed using the Fundamental Theorem of Calculus, we start with a more familiar integrand so that you can compare results.

FIGURE 13–27

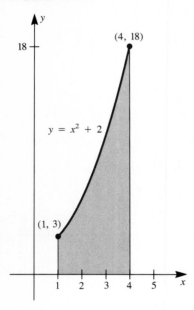

EXAMPLE 1   *(Compare Exercise 5)*

Find the area of the region bounded above by the curve $y = x^2 + 2$, below by the x-axis, on the left by the line $x = 1$, and on the right by the line $x = 4$. See Figure 13–27.

SOLUTION   We want the area of the shaded region in Figure 13–27. How would you have approached this problem if this had been the first problem presented in this course, before we had any notion of derivatives or antiderivatives? One way might be to carefully draw the region on lined graph paper and then to count the squares inside the region. This number would be too low, since there would be squares that would be partially inside and partially outside the region. You might then come up with some sort of estimation technique for the area of the region inside these squares.

This would be a good approach and is based on using the area of squares to estimate the area of a more complicated figure. The approximation technique that we will use is much like that outlined above. We will use rectangles instead of squares. Furthermore, we will not depend on lines already drawn on the paper but will draw our own rectangles. The bases of these rectangles will all lie on the x-axis, and for simplicity the bases will all be the same length. We want the bases to cover the interval $[1, 4]$ with no overlap. We start with three rectangles, so the length of each base is

$$\frac{4 - 1}{3} = 1$$

FIGURE 13–28

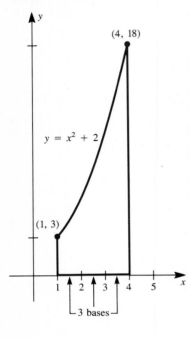

The bases are drawn in Figure 13–28.

Now we want to choose a height for each rectangle. For the first rectangle, if we use the height $f(1) = 3$, the top of the rectangle will be entirely inside the region; if we use the height $f(2) = 6$, the top of the rectangle will be entirely outside the region. If we pick some other number c between 1 and 2, the height $f(c)$ will be between 3 and 6. For this example we will choose as c the midpoint of the interval $[1, 2]$; let $c = 1.5$. The height of the first rectangle is $f(1.5) = (1.5)^2 + 2 = 4.25$. Similarly, for the next rectangle we use the height $f(2.5) = 8.25$; and for the last rectangle we use the height $f(3.5) = 14.25$. We let c_k stand for the midpoint of the base of the kth rectangle.

We now have a figure shaped like the one in Figure 13–29, a union of three rectangles.

The area of this figure is the sum of the areas of the rectangles:

$$\text{Sum of (height)(base)} = (4.25)(1) + (8.25)(1) + (14.25)(1)$$
$$= 26.75$$

If we used more rectangles with smaller bases and again used the value of f at the midpoint of each base as the height of the rectangle, then we would obviously get a better approximation. Doubling the number of rectangles to six, we would get a region like that shown in Figure 13–30.

FIGURE 13–29

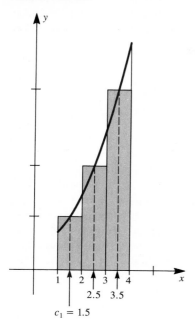

$c_1 = 1.5$

FIGURE 13–30

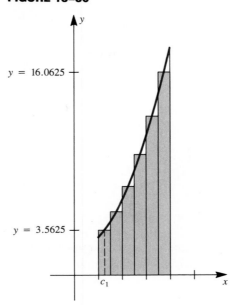

The following table computes the height of each rectangle.

BASE OF RECTANGLE	MIDPOINT OF BASE = c_k	HEIGHT OF GRAPH AT $x = c_k$	
[1, 1.5]	1.25	$f(1.25) = (1.25)^2 + 2$ =	3.5625
[1.5, 2]	1.75	$f(1.75) =$ =	5.0625
[2, 2.5]	2.25	$f(2.25) =$ =	7.0625
[2.5, 3]	2.75	$f(2.75) =$ =	9.5625
[3, 3.5]	3.25	$f(3.25) =$ =	12.5625
[3.5, 4]	3.75	$f(3.75) =$ =	16.0625

To find the area of the region in Figure 13–30, we compute, as before, the sum of the areas of the rectangles. Note that the length of each base is (the total length of the interval divided by the number of rectangles) $= \frac{3}{6} = 0.5$:

The sum of (height)(length of base) $= [(3.5625)(0.5) + (5.0625)(0.5)$
$+ (7.0625)(0.5) + (9.5625)(0.5)$
$+ (12.5625)(0.5) + (16.0625)(0.5)]$
$= 26.9375$

We have computed two approximations to the area of R; the first approximation was 26.75, and the second was 26.9375. To compare these approximations to the actual area, we compute that area by using the Fundamental Theorem of Calculus:

$$\text{Area of } R = \int_1^4 (x^2 + 2)\,dx = \left(\frac{x^3}{3} + 2x\right)\Big|_1^4$$

$$= \left(\frac{64}{3} + 8\right) - \left(\frac{1}{3} + 2\right)$$

$$= 27$$

The actual area is 27, so our approximations were pretty good.

In Section 13–4 we approached the Fundamental Theorem of Calculus by relying on your intuitive notion of area, but historically, people did not first begin to compute areas by using the definite integral. Calculus is only about 300 years old, yet the early Greeks had a formula for the area of a circle. The first approach to the problem of area was much like the approach we took in Example 1. That is, people first obtained approximations by regions whose area was known and then used a limiting process to determine the area of the desired region.

The procedure that we used in Example 1 can be generalized as follows: Suppose that f is a continuous function on $[a, b]$ and that $f(x) \geq 0$. Divide the interval $[a, b]$ into n subintervals, each of length $\frac{b-a}{n}$. Choose a number from each subinterval, say, c_1 from the first subinterval, c_2 from the second subinterval, . . . , c_k from the kth subinterval. Now compute the sum of the areas of all the rectangles with height $= f(c_k)$ and base $= \frac{b-a}{n}$. This sum is

$$f(c_1)\frac{b-a}{n} + f(c_2)\frac{b-a}{n} + \cdots + f(c_k)\frac{b-a}{n} + \cdots + f(c_n)\frac{b-a}{n}$$

Such a sum is called a **Riemann sum.** Then as n gets larger, these sums get closer to a fixed number A, no matter how the numbers c_k are chosen. This number A that these sums approach is the area of the region bounded above by the graph of f and below by the interval $[a, b]$.

Even more generally, the approximating rectangles need not all have the same length for their bases. We can let $\Delta x_k = $ base of the kth rectangle. Furthermore, we can drop the requirement that $f(x) \geq 0$. The following theorem is an alternative form of the Fundamental Theorem of Calculus.

Theorem
Fundamental Theorem of Calculus

Let f be continuous on the interval $[a, b]$. As the length of subintervals decreases, the Riemann sums

$$f(c_1)\Delta x_1 + f(c_2)\Delta x_2 + \cdots + f(c_n)\Delta x_n$$

all approach the same number, which is the definite integral $\int_a^b f(x)\,dx$.

We will return to the subject of numerical approximations in Section 14–5, but the point that we want to emphasize in this section is the relationship between the definite integral and Riemann sums. The method used in Example 1 is commonly called the **midpoint approximation** because of the method of selecting the height of each rectangle. The bases of the rectangles are all taken to have the same length; the interval $[a, b]$ is divided into n equal intervals, so the length of each is

$$\frac{b - a}{n}$$

The Midpoint Approximation Formula	If the interval $[a, b]$ is divided into n equal subintervals, each of length $(b - a)/n$, and if c_k is the midpoint of the kth interval, then $$\int_a^b f(x)dx \approx f(c_1)\frac{b - a}{n} + f(c_2)\frac{b - a}{n} + \cdots + f(c_n)\frac{b - a}{n}$$

We use the midpoint approximation method again in Example 2 to find a numerical approximation to ln 3.

EXAMPLE 2   *(Compare Exercise 17)*

Use the midpoint approximation method with $n = 4$ to approximate

$$\ln 3 = \int_1^3 \frac{1}{x} dx$$

SOLUTION   Recall that

$$\int_1^3 \frac{1}{x} dx = \ln|x| \Big|_1^3 = \ln 3 - \ln 1 = \ln 3$$

We are indeed computing a numerical approximation to ln 3. The interval $[a, b]$ is $[1, 3]$. With $n = 4$, each base has length

$$\frac{3 - 1}{4} = \frac{1}{2}$$

Thus the interval $[1, 3]$ is partitioned into four subintervals as follows:

c_k is the midpoint of the kth interval.

$$c_1 = 1.25 \qquad c_2 = 1.75 \qquad c_3 = 2.25 \qquad c_4 = 2.75$$

$f(x) = \dfrac{1}{x}$, so

$$f(c_1) = \frac{1}{1.25} \qquad f(c_2) = \frac{1}{1.75} \qquad f(c_3) = \frac{1}{2.25} \qquad f(c_4) = \frac{1}{2.75}$$

The sum of the areas of the rectangles is the sum of (height)(length of base)

$$= \left(\frac{1}{1.25}\right)\left(\frac{1}{2}\right) + \left(\frac{1}{1.75}\right)\left(\frac{1}{2}\right) + \left(\frac{1}{2.25}\right)\left(\frac{1}{2}\right) + \left(\frac{1}{2.75}\right)\left(\frac{1}{2}\right)$$

$$= \frac{1}{2.5} + \frac{1}{3.5} + \frac{1}{4.5} + \frac{1}{5.5}$$

$$\approx 0.4000 + 0.2857 + 0.2222 + 0.1818$$

$$\approx 1.0897 \qquad\qquad\qquad\qquad \text{(To four places)}$$

If the intermediate steps in a calculation are rounded to four places, it is generally a good idea to round off the final answer to three places. This gives us 1.090 as our approximation to ln 3. (In fact, the decimal expansion of ln 3 begins 1.0986. . . .)

Answer: ln 3 $\approx$ 1.090

You can find formulas that give bounds on the size of the error in approximating the definite integral by this method in texts that go more deeply into the theory of approximation methods.

SUMMATIONS USING INTEGRALS

The relationship between summations and integrals works both ways.

EXAMPLE 3   *(Compare Exercise 33)*

The number of people using a city's rapid transit system since it was modernized in 1985 is growing. Officials estimated that k years after the modernization was completed, $100(6k^2 + 500k + 6000)$ customers would use the system that year. This estimate means that in the first year, roughly

$$100(6 \cdot 1^2 + 500 \cdot 1 + 6000) = 650{,}600$$

customers used the system. In the second year, about

$$100(6 \cdot 2^2 + 500 \cdot 2 + 6000) = 702{,}400$$

customers used the system. If the official estimates are good, approximately how many customers will have used the modernized system by 1995?

SOLUTION   The answer can be computed by letting $N(k)$ be the number of customers in the kth year and then computing the sum

$$N(1) + N(2) + \cdots + N(10)$$

Notice that if we do something peculiar at this stage, we can start to get a quick method of approximating this number. We multiply each $N(k)$ by 1. Now the sum looks like

$$N(1) \cdot 1 + N(2) \cdot 1 + N(3) \cdot 1 + \cdots + N(10) \cdot 1$$

Multiplying each number by 1 makes this sum look like a summation that approximates an integral over the interval [0, 10] when the interval [0, 10] has been divided into ten subintervals each of length 1. This is not an approximation using the midpoint of each interval to evaluate the function, but here the right-hand endpoint of each interval is used. This summation is approximately

$$\int_0^{10} N(t)dt$$

We have replaced the variable k in the formula for N by the variable t:

$$\int_0^{10} N(t)dt = \int_0^{10} 100(6t^2 + 500t + 6000)dt$$

$$= 100\left[(2t^3 + 250t^2 + 6000t)\Big|_0^{10}\right]$$

$$= 100[2000 + 25,000 + 60,000]$$

$$= 8,700,000$$

The system will be used by about 8.7 million customers.

EXAMPLE 4   *(Compare Exercise 35)*

The annual payroll of a certain company has been growing at the continuous rate of 12%. At the beginning of 1984 the payroll was $450,000. What will be the total payroll expenditures for the company from the beginning of 1990 to the beginning of 1995?

SOLUTION   Let $P(t)$ be the payroll (in thousands of dollars) t years after January 1, 1984. We are given that $P'(t) = 0.12P(t)$ and that $P(0) = 450$. The function that we should use for $P(t)$ is $P(t) = 450e^{0.12t}$. The beginning of 1990 corresponds to $t = 6$, and the beginning of 1995 corresponds to $t = 11$. Thus this period corresponds to $6 \leq t \leq 11$.

$$\int_6^{11} 450e^{0.12t}\, dt = \left[450\left(\frac{1}{0.12}\right)e^{0.12t}\right]\Big|_6^{11}$$

$$= 3750e^{0.12t}\Big|_6^{11}$$

$$= 3750(e^{1.32} - e^{0.72})$$

$$\approx 3750(3.743 - 2.054)$$

$$\approx 6334 \quad \text{thousand dollars}$$

The company's payroll will total about $6.3 million during this period.

EXAMPLE 5   *(Compare Exercise 29)*

Suppose that you save $2000 per year in a retirement fund that pays 6% continuously compounded interest. You start saving at age 25. How much will your retirement fund be worth when you retire at age 65? (We suppose, for simplicity, that your contributions are made on January 1 of each year and that you retire on December 31.)

SOLUTION   Your first contribution to the fund earns interest for 40 years. The first $2000 will grow to $2000e^{(0.06)(40)}$ (using $A(t) = Pe^{Rt}$ with $P = 2000$, $R = 0.06$, and $t = 40$). The second $2000 is only in the account for 39 years; it will grow to $2000e^{(0.06)(39)}$. Your contribution of $2000 in the kth year will be in the fund for $(40 - k)$ years and will grow to $2000e^{(0.06)(40 - k)}$.

Instead of summing these 40 numbers, we proceed as we did in Example 3. Replace k by t and integrate. The total worth of the fund will be approximately

$$\int_0^{40} 2000e^{(0.06)(40 - t)}\, dt = 2000 \int_0^{40} e^{(0.06)(40 - t)}\, dt \quad \text{(Bring 2000 outside the integral; next multiply out in the exponent)}$$

$$= 2000 \int_0^{40} e^{2.4 - 0.06t}\, dt \quad \text{(Now use } e^{a - b} = e^a e^{-b})$$

$$= 2000 \int_0^{40} e^{2.4}e^{-0.06t}\, dt \quad \text{(Bring } e^{2.4} \text{ outside)}$$

$$= 2000e^{2.4} \int_0^{40} e^{-0.06t}\, dt \quad \text{(Integrate)}$$

$$= 2000e^{2.4}\left(-\frac{1}{0.06}\right)e^{-0.06t}\Big|_0^{40}$$

$$= 2000e^{2.4}\left(-\frac{100}{6}\right)(e^{-2.4} - e^0)$$

$$= 2000e^{2.4}\left(-\frac{100}{6}\right)(e^{-2.4} - 1)$$

$$= 2000e^{2.4}\left(\frac{100}{6}\right)(1 - e^{-2.4})$$

$$\approx 334{,}105.88$$

Answer: Your retirement fund will be worth about $334,000, over a third of a million dollars. You personally will have contributed $80,000, and you will have earned over $254,000 in interest.

VOLUMES OF REVOLUTION

The approximation

$$\int_a^b f(x)\, dx \approx f(c_1)\frac{b - a}{n} + \cdots + f(c_n)\frac{b - a}{n}$$

allows us to go from summations to definite integrals in all types of settings. One further geometric application is presented here. We derive the volume of a sphere

FIGURE 13–31

Semicircle

FIGURE 13–32

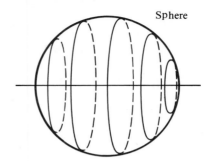
Sphere

whose radius is 4. The particular value 4 plays no special role, so you will be able to see how to derive the general formula for the volume of a sphere. The key to this approach is to think of a sphere as being the solid swept out by rotating a semicircle about the x-axis. See Figures 13–31 and 13–32.

The area of the semicircle can be approximated with rectangles (see Figure 13–33); and by rotating these rectangles we can arrive at an approximation to the volume of the sphere. See Figure 13–34.

FIGURE 13–33

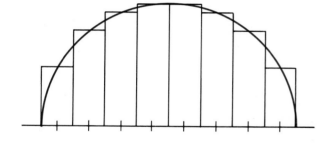

FIGURE 13–34

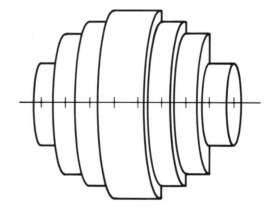

When you rotate a rectangle 360° about its base, you get a cylinder. The thickness of the cylinder is the length of the base of the rectangle, and the radius of the cylinder is the height of the rectangle. See Figure 13–35.

If L = (length of base of rectangle) and H = (height of rectangle), then the volume of the cylinder is $\pi H^2 \cdot L$.

FIGURE 13–35

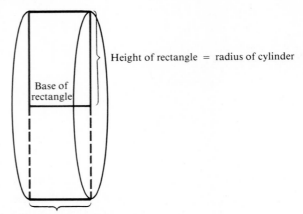

Height of rectangle = radius of cylinder

Base of rectangle

Thickness of cylinder = base of rectangle

Now, the original semicircle is the region under the curve $y = \sqrt{16 - x^2}$ over the interval $-4 \le x \le 4$. If we divide the interval into n equal subintervals, each will have length

$$L = \frac{4 - (-4)}{n} = \frac{8}{n}$$

If c_k is the midpoint of the kth interval, the height H of the kth rectangle will be

$$H = f(c_k) = \sqrt{16 - c_k^2}$$

Therefore the volume of the kth cylinder will be

$$\pi H^2 \cdot L = \pi(\sqrt{16 - c_k^2})^2 \left(\frac{8}{n}\right)$$

$$= \pi(16 - c_k^2)\left(\frac{8}{n}\right)$$

Summing all these volumes, we have

$$\pi(16 - c_1^2)\left(\frac{8}{n}\right) + \pi(16 - c_2^2)\left(\frac{8}{n}\right) + \cdots + \pi(16 - c_n^2)\left(\frac{8}{n}\right)$$

Remember that we got the 8 as $4 - (-4) = b - a$. Therefore this sum is approximately

$$\int_{-4}^{4} \pi(16 - x^2)dx = \pi \int_{-4}^{4} (16 - x^2)dx$$

We now compute this definite integral:

$$\pi \int_{-4}^{4} (16 - x^2)dx = \pi \left(16x - \frac{x^3}{3} \right) \Big|_{-4}^{4}$$

$$= \pi \left[\left(64 - \frac{64}{3} \right) - \left(-64 + \frac{64}{3} \right) \right]$$

$$= \pi \frac{256}{3}$$

In particular, the volume of a sphere whose radius is 4 inches is $\frac{256}{3}\pi$ cubic inches.

The general formula for a solid obtained by rotation of a region is obtained by similar considerations, replacing -4 by a, 4 by b, and $\sqrt{16 - x^2}$ by $f(x)$.

Volume Formula for a Solid of Revolution	If the region bounded above by the curve $y = f(x)$, below by the x-axis, on the left by the line $x = a$, and on the right by the line $x = b$ is rotated about the x-axis, then the **volume of the solid of revolution** is given by $$\text{Volume} = \pi \int_{a}^{b} [f(x)]^2 \, dx$$

EXAMPLE 6   *(Compare Exercise 27)*

Find the volume of the sphere of radius 5.

SOLUTION   Rotate the semicircle bounded above by $f(x) = \sqrt{25 - x^2}$ about the x-axis. See Figure 13–36.

$$\text{Volume} = \pi \int_{-5}^{5} (\sqrt{25 - x^2})^2 \, dx$$

$$= \pi \int_{-5}^{5} (25 - x^2)dx$$

$$= \pi \left(25x - \frac{x^3}{3} \right) \Big|_{-5}^{5}$$

$$= \pi \left[\left(125 - \frac{125}{3} \right) - \left(-125 + \frac{125}{3} \right) \right]$$

$$= \pi \frac{500}{3}$$

FIGURE 13–36

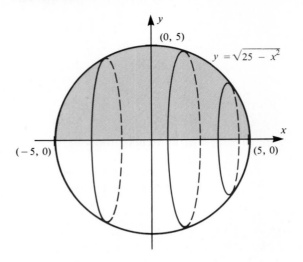

EXAMPLE 7   *(Compare Exercise 23)*

The inside of a soup bowl has a shape like that formed by rotating the curve
$y = \sqrt{x}$, $0 \le x \le 3$, about the x-axis. What is the volume of soup the bowl can
hold? See Figure 13–37.

FIGURE 13–37

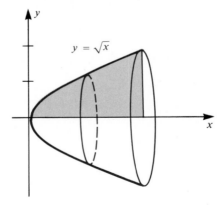

SOLUTION

$$\text{Volume} = \pi \int_0^3 (\sqrt{x})^2 \, dx$$

$$= \pi \int_0^3 x \, dx$$

$$= \frac{\pi}{2} x^2 \Big|_0^3$$

$$= \frac{9\pi}{2}$$

Answer: The volume is $9\pi/2$.

13-6 EXERCISES

I

In Exercises 1 through 6, use the midpoint approximation formula to approximate $\int_a^b f(x) \, dx$ with n giving the number of subintervals. Then evaluate each integral and compare your answers.

1. $\int_1^3 4 \, dx$ **(a)** $n = 2$ **(b)** $n = 4$

2. $\int_{-1}^2 2 \, dx$ **(a)** $n = 3$ **(b)** $n = 6$

3. $\int_0^3 2x \, dx$ **(a)** $n = 3$ **(b)** $n = 6$

4. $\int_0^4 x \, dx$ **(a)** $n = 4$ **(b)** $n = 8$

5. (*See Example 1*)   **(a)** $n = 2$ **(b)** $n = 4$
$\int_1^3 x^2 \, dx$

6. $\int_{-1}^2 x^2 \, dx$ **(a)** $n = 3$ **(b)** $n = 6$

II

In Exercises 7 through 11, use the midpoint formula to approximate $\int_a^b f(x) \, dx$ with n giving the number of subintervals to use in the approximation. Evaluate the integral and compare your answers.

7. $\int_1^3 (2x^2 - 3x) dx$ **(a)** $n = 2$ **(b)** $n = 4$

8. $\int_{-1}^5 (4 - 3x^2) dx$ **(a)** $n = 3$ **(b)** $n = 6$

9. $\int_1^5 \frac{1}{x^2} dx$ **(a)** $n = 2$ **(b)** $n = 4$

10. $\int_0^4 \sqrt{x} \, dx$ **(a)** $n = 4$ **(b)** $n = 8$

11. $\int_1^3 \frac{1}{x^3} dx$ **(a)** $n = 2$ **(b)** $n = 4$

In Exercises 12 through 14, approximate the summation by using the given integral.

12. $1 + 2 + 3 + 4 + \cdots + 100;$ $\int_0^{100} x \, dx$

13. $1^2 + 2^2 + 3^2 + \cdots + 60^2;$ $\int_0^{60} x^2 \, dx$

14. $1^3 + 2^3 + 3^3 + \cdots + 20^3;$ $\int_0^{20} x^3 \, dx$

Compute the volumes given by the integrals in Exercises 15 and 16.

15. $\pi \int_{-6}^6 (\sqrt{36 - x^2})^2 \, dx$ 16. $\pi \int_0^4 (x^2)^2 \, dx$

III

17. (*See Example 2*) Estimate ln 3 by approximating $\int_2^6 \frac{1}{x}\, dx$ with:

(a) $n = 4$.

(b) $n = 8$.

18. Estimate ln 3 by approximating $\int_3^9 \frac{1}{x}\, dx$ with:

(a) $n = 6$.

(b) $n = 12$. (*Compare results with Example 2.*)

19. (a) Estimate ln 4 by approximating $\int_1^4 \frac{1}{x}\, dx$ with:

(i) $n = 3$.   (ii) $n = 6$.

(b) Estimate ln 4 by approximating $\int_2^8 \frac{1}{x}\, dx$ with:

(i) $n = 6$.   (ii) $n = 12$.

20. (a) Estimate ln 9 by approximating $\int_1^9 \frac{1}{x}\, dx$ with $n = 8$.

(b) $\ln 9 = \ln 3^2 = 2 \ln 3 = 2 \int_1^3 \frac{1}{x}\, dx$. (*Compare your results in part (a) with twice the approximations to ln 3 obtained in Example 2.*)

21. Approximate $\int_0^2 \sqrt{x^2 + 1}\, dx$ with $n = 4$.

22. Approximate $\int_0^3 \frac{1}{\sqrt{x^2 + 1}}\, dx$ with $n = 6$.

In Exercises 23 through 28, find the volume of the solid obtained by rotating about the x-axis the region bounded above by $y = f(x)$, bounded below by the x-axis, and between the vertical lines $x = a$ and $x = b$.

23. (*See Example 7*)
$f(x) = x + 1, a = -1, b = 3$

24. $f(x) = \frac{1}{x}, a = 2, b = 5$

25. $f(x) = x^2 - 3, a = 2, b = 4$

26. $f(x) = \frac{1}{x^3}, a = \frac{1}{2}, b = 3$

27. (*See Example 6*) $f(x) = \sqrt{R^2 - x^2}, a = -R, b = R$. (This gives the formula for the volume of a sphere with radius R.)

28. $f(x) = \frac{R}{H} x, a = 0, b = H$. (This gives the formula for the volume of a cone with radius R and height H.)

29. (*See Example 5*) If $1000 is deposited into an account annually for 20 years, and the account pays 7% interest compounded continuously, what will the account be worth at the end of the 20 years?

30. If $1000 is deposited into an account annually for 10 years, and the account pays 7% interest compounded continuously, what will the account be worth at the end of the 10 years?

31. If $1000 is deposited into an account annually for 10 years, and the account pays 8% interest compounded continuously, what will the account be worth at the end of 10 years?

32. If $1000 is deposited into an account annually for 30 years, and the account pays 6% interest compounded continuously, what will the account be worth at the end of 30 years?

33. (*See Example 3*) The birth pattern of ducks in a certain park has been estimated to be approximated by the following formula: $N(t) = 3t^3 - 36t^2 + 108t + 750$, where t is time in years with $t = 0$ corresponding to 1980 and $N(t)$ is the number of births that took place at time t. Estimate the number of ducks born between 1982 and 1986.

34. A mining company estimates that the amount of phosphate it mines can be described by the following function: $W(t) = 4t^3 - 72t^2 + 420t + 7000$. Here, t is time measured in years from 1970, and the units of W are thousands of tons. The quantity mined at time t is $W(t)$. Estimate the quantity of phosphate mined between 1975 and 1985.

35. (*See Example 4*) A manufacturing company estimates that its costs at time t since 1975 are described by $C(t) = 3t^2 + 60t + 7000$. Time t is measured in years from 1975, and the units of C are thousands of dollars. Estimate the total costs incurred from 1977 to 1987.

36. The number of new automobiles sold at time t, on a worldwide basis since 1965, has been estimated to be described by $N(t) = 6t^2 + 72t + 9000$, where t is the time in years measured from 1965 and $N(t)$ is the number of cars in units of 100. Estimate the total number of new cars that were sold between 1969 and 1976.

IMPORTANT TERMS

13-1

Antiderivative

Indefinite Integral

∫ f(x) dx

Integral Sign

Differential

Integrand

Additive Constant of Integration

Antidifferentiation

Integration

13-2

Differential Equation

Solution to a Differential Equation

Particular Solution

Second-Order Differential Equation

Antiderivative of $\dfrac{1}{x}$

Antiderivative of e^{ax}

13-3

Total Change of a Function on an Interval

Definite Integral of f from a to b

$\int_a^b f(x)dx$

Upper Limit of Integration

Lower Limit of Integration

$f(x)\big|_a^b$

Gluing of Intervals Property for Definite Integrals

13-4

Fundamental Theorem of Calculus

ln b as a Definite Integral

Area Between Curves

13-5

Average Value of a Function on an Interval

Consumers' Surplus

Producers' Surplus

Investment Flow

Capital Formation

Gini Index

13-6

Approximating an Integral by a Summation

Riemann Sum

Fundamental Theorem of Calculus

Midpoint Approximation Formula

Approximating a Summation by an Integral

Volume of Revolution

REVIEW EXERCISES

Find the indicated indefinite integral in Exercises 1 through 10.

1. $\displaystyle\int \left(6x^2 + \frac{6}{x^2} \right) dx$

2. $\displaystyle\int \left(\sqrt{x} - \frac{1}{\sqrt{x}} \right) dx$

3. $\displaystyle\int \left(x^3 - \frac{1}{x} \right)^2 dx$

4. $\displaystyle\int \left(x + \frac{1}{x^2} \right)^2 dx$

5. $\displaystyle\int \frac{4x^2 + 8}{x} \, dx$

6. $\displaystyle\int \frac{6x - 4}{x^2} \, dx$

7. $\displaystyle\int (e^{6x} + e^{-4x}) dx$

8. $\displaystyle\int \frac{1}{e^{3x}} \, dx$

9. $\displaystyle\int (e^x + 4)^2 \, dx$

10. $\displaystyle\int (e^x + e^{-x}) dx$

Compute each of the definite integrals in Exercises 11 through 16.

11. $\displaystyle\int_1^9 (3\sqrt{x} + 4x - 1) dx$

12. $\displaystyle\int_{-2}^1 (9x^2 - 8x + 4) dx$

13. $\displaystyle\int_0^4 (e^{2x} - x) dx$

14. $\displaystyle\int_1^e \frac{1}{x} \, dx$

15. $\displaystyle\int_{\ln 3}^{\ln 8} e^x \, dx$

16. $\displaystyle\int_1^{e^5} \frac{1}{x} \, dx$

Verify the equations in Exercises 17 and 18 by evaluating each definite integral.

17. $\int_{-1}^{1} (6x^2 - 8x)dx + \int_{1}^{2} (6x^2 - 8x)dx = \int_{-1}^{2} (6x^2 - 8x)dx$

18. $\int_{2}^{1} (12x^2 - 4x)dx + \int_{1}^{3} (12x^2 - 4x)dx = \int_{2}^{3} (12x^2 - 4x)dx$

In Exercises 19 through 22, find the particular solution that satisfies the given differential equation and the additional condition or conditions.

19. $y' = 16x^3 - 12x + 9$, with $y = 4$ when $x = 1$

20. $y' = 6\sqrt{x} - 5$, with $y = 13$ when $x = 4$

21. $y'' = 12x - 2$, with $y' = 4$ and $y = 9$ when $x = 0$

22. $y'' = 18$, with $y' = 6$ and $y = 10$ when $x = 2$

23. From a height of 2 meters, a ball is thrown straight up into the air with a velocity of 30 meters per second; the deceleration due to gravity is -9.8 m/sec².
(a) What is the ball's velocity t seconds after it is thrown?
(b) What is the ball's height t seconds after it is thrown?

24. The marginal cost function for a company producing x hundred units per day is given by

$$MC(x) = \frac{1}{100}x^2 - 6x + 7000$$

How much will the company's daily costs increase if production is increased from 900 units per day to 1000 units?

25. A company's marginal cost function is given by $MC(x) = x^2 - 15x + 410$, and its marginal revenue function is given by $MR(x) = 390 - 3x$. The current level of production is $x = 8$.
(a) What level of production will maximize the profit?
(b) How much would the profit increase if the company changes to the level of production that you found as the answer to part (a)?

26. Find the area bounded by the line $y = 2x - 3$, the x-axis, the y-axis, and the line $x = 5$.

27. Find the area of the region bounded above by the curve $y = 3x^2 + 1$, below by the x-axis, on the left by the line $x = -1$, and on the right by the line $x = 2$.

28. Find the area bounded by the lines $y = 2x - 6$ and $y = 9 - x$ and the x-axis.

29. Find the area of the region bounded on the left by the line $x = -2$ and on the right by the line $x = 3$ and that lies between the two curves $y = x^2 + 4x + 2$ and $y = x^2 - 2x + 8$.

30. Find the area of the region between the curve $y = x^2 - x + 1$ and the line $y = 2x + 5$.

31. Find the area of the region between the curves $y = x^3 + 3x^2 - 2x + 5$ and $y = 4x^2 + 4x + 5$.

32. If the price-demand equation for a certain product is $p = 680 - 6x$ and the market price is 80, then what is the consumers' surplus?

33. If the price-supply equation for a certain commodity is given by $p = S(x) = x^2 + 4x + 20$ and the present price is 41, then:
(a) Show that $S(x)$ is increasing for $x \geq 0$.
(b) Compute the producers' surplus.

34. The price curves of a certain commodity are $p = \frac{1}{3}x^2 + 10x + 300$ and $p = 500 - \frac{2}{3}x^2$.
(a) Which is the reasonable choice for the price-demand curve?
(b) Which is the reasonable choice for the price-supply curve?
(c) What is the equilibrium price?
(d) If the actual market price is the equilibrium price, what is the consumers' surplus?
(e) If the actual market price is the equilibrium price, what is the producers' surplus?

35. What is the average value of $f(x) = \sqrt{x}$ on the interval $[0, 9]$?

36. What is the average value of the function

$$f(x) = \frac{x + 1}{x^2}$$

on the interval $[1, 6]$?

37. What is the Gini index for a country whose income distribution function is given by $F(x) = x^4 - 0.6x^3 + 0.3x^2 + 0.3x$?

38. Use the midpoint approximation formula to approximate $\int_{1}^{5} \frac{1}{x} dx$:
(a) with $n = 4$.
(b) with $n = 8$.

39. If $1000 is deposited into an account annually for 30 years and the account pays 6% interest, continuously compounded, what will the account be worth at the end of the 30 years?

40. The rate at which oil flows from a well t years after pumping starts is given by

$$R(t) = 50{,}000e^{-2t}$$

where R is in barrels per year.
   (a) How many barrels of oil were pumped from the well during the first four years of production?
   (b) How much oil was pumped during the third year?

14

Techniques of Integration

Integration by Substitution

Integration by Parts

Improper Integrals

Integration Using Tables

Numerical Approximations of Definite Integrals

14-1 INTEGRATION BY SUBSTITUTION

- *Introduction*
- *Method of Substitution*
- *Substitution and the Definite Integral*
- *Substitutions Involving Algebra*

INTRODUCTION

THE PROCESS OF FINDING an antiderivative of a given function is generally more difficult than the process of finding its derivative. Given a particular function f, if we recognize it as the sum, product, quotient, and composition of simpler functions, we can apply the corresponding rules of differentiation to compute the derivative of f. Applying these rules correctly requires care and practice, but at least there are rules to follow. So far, we have seen some rules of integration that parallel similar differentiation rules. We have three general rules regarding indefinite integrals:

Constant-times **1.** $\int c \cdot f(x)dx = c \cdot \int f(x)dx;$
Sum **2.** $\int [f(x) + g(x)]dx = \int f(x)dx + \int g(x)dx;$
Difference **3.** $\int [f(x) - g(x)]dx = \int f(x)dx - \int g(x)dx.$

And we have three rules for specific functions:

Power rule **4.** $\int x^n \, dx = \dfrac{1}{n+1}x^{n+1} + C, n \neq -1;$

5. $\int \dfrac{1}{x} \, dx = \ln|x| + C;$

6. $\int e^{ax} \, dx = \dfrac{1}{a}e^{ax} + C.$

Unfortunately, there is no antidifferentiation rule that corresponds to the quotient rule, and the rules that correspond to the chain rule and product rule are only of limited use. Indeed, there are functions, such as $f(x) = \sqrt{x^3 + 1}$, whose antiderivative cannot be written in simple terms. In fact, while mathematicians will talk about *rules* of differentiation, they use terms for antidifferentiation that don't carry the same guarantee of success—terms like "methods" or "techniques" of integration.

The method that we look at in this section is called "substitution" and corresponds to the chain rule. Because so many functions involve composition of simpler functions, this method must be used frequently. We start with two examples showing how substitution leads to a generalized power rule for integration, just as we had a generalized power rule for differentiation.

EXAMPLE 1

Find $\int \sqrt{5x + 1} \, dx$.

SOLUTION Rewriting the integrand, we have

$$\int \sqrt{5x + 1} \, dx = \int (5x + 1)^{1/2} \, dx$$

Now we try to find an antiderivative by using the power rule. Let $f(x) = \frac{2}{3}(5x + 1)^{3/2}$. Next, we check to see whether $f(x)$ is an antiderivative of $(5x + 1)^{1/2}$ by computing $f'(x)$:

$$f'(x) = \frac{2}{3} \cdot \frac{3}{2}(5x + 1)^{1/2} \cdot 5 \qquad \text{(Chain rule)}$$

$$= 1(5x + 1)^{1/2} \cdot 5 = 5\sqrt{5x + 1}$$

$$f'(x) = 5\sqrt{5x + 1} \neq \sqrt{5x + 1}$$

We are off by the factor of 5 that was forced into the computation by the chain rule. We were led to the generalized power rule for differentiation by substituting a single letter for the quantity to be raised to a power. We proceed here in the same manner. We have $5x + 1$ raised to a power, so we let $u = 5x + 1$. Then $\int(5x + 1)^{1/2} \, dx$ becomes $\int u^{1/2} \, dx$. But this last expression doesn't make sense. The variable in the integrand (here u) must match the variable following the d (here x). We must continue the substitution process and substitute an appropriate term for the dx.

To replace the dx, we use the formalism of differentials.

$$\text{If } u = f(x), \qquad \text{then} \qquad du = f'(x)dx.$$

Thus if $u = 5x + 1$, then $du = 5 \, dx$. Solving for dx, we have $\frac{1}{5} \, du = dx$. Next, we make the complete substitution:

$$\int (5x + 1)^{1/2} \, dx = \int u^{1/2}\left(\frac{1}{5} \, du\right) = \frac{1}{5} \int u^{1/2} \, du$$

Now we can use the power rule on $\frac{1}{5} \int u^{1/2} \, du$:

$$= \frac{1}{5}\left[\frac{2}{3} u^{3/2} + C\right]$$

$$= \frac{2}{15} u^{3/2} + C$$

As in using the chain rule, the last step is to rewrite the answer in terms of x. Since $u = 5x + 1$, we have

$$\frac{2}{15} u^{3/2} + C = \frac{2}{15}(5x + 1)^{3/2} + C$$

Finally, we have our answer:

$$\int (5x + 1)^{1/2}\, dx = \frac{2}{15}(5x + 1)^{3/2} + C$$

We check this answer:

If $f(x) = \frac{2}{15}(5x + 1)^{3/2}$, then

$$f'(x) = \frac{2}{15} \cdot \frac{3}{2}(5x + 1)^{1/2} \cdot 5 = (5x + 1)^{1/2}$$

       ■

Notice particularly how the substitution for the dx in the integration relates to the use of the chain rule in the differentiation. This is one of the important reasons that the expression dx occurs in the integral; it is a valuable tool in the method of substitution.

We go through the same procedure more succinctly in the next example.

EXAMPLE 2   *(Compare Exercise 1)*

Find $\int (6x - 8)^3\, dx$.

SOLUTION   We replace $6x - 8$ by a single variable. Let $u = 6x - 8$; then $du = 6\, dx$, so $\frac{1}{6}\, du = dx$. Substituting for both the integrand and the differential gives us

$$\int (6x - 8)^3\, dx = \int u^3\left(\frac{1}{6}\, du\right)$$

$$= \int \frac{1}{6}u^3\, du$$

$$= \frac{1}{24}u^4 + C$$

Resubstitute $6x - 4$ for u:

$$\int (6x - 8)^3\, dx = \frac{1}{24}(6x - 8)^4 + C$$

As we did in Example 1, you should check this answer by taking the derivative of $\frac{1}{24}(6x - 8)^4$.

       ■

We say that integration by substitution is the integration technique that corresponds to the chain rule because, just as we did with the chain rule, we are substituting a new variable u for a function of x. With this substitution we are writing

$$\int \left(\frac{dy}{dx}\right) dx = \int \left(\frac{dy}{du} \cdot \frac{du}{dx}\right) dx$$

$$= \int \left(\frac{dy}{du}\right)\left(\frac{du}{dx} \, dx\right) = \int \left(\frac{dy}{du}\right) du$$

We find this last integral in terms of u and then complete the process by substituting for u to end up with an expression in terms of x.

METHOD OF SUBSTITUTION

EXAMPLE 3 *(Compare Exercise 3)*

Find $\int 10x \sqrt{5x^2 + 1} \, dx$.

SOLUTION As with the chain rule, we look for a composition of functions, especially for a function raised to a power. Here, we have $\sqrt{5x^2 + 1} = (5x^2 + 1)^{1/2}$. So we start by letting $u = 5x^2 + 1$. Remember that $u = f(x)$ means $du = f'(x)dx$; here, $u = 5x^2 + 1$ means $du = 10x \, dx$. If we rewrite the original integral, then the substitution becomes clearer:

$$\int 10x \sqrt{5x^2 + 1} \, dx = \int \sqrt{5x^2 + 1}(10x \, dx)$$

$$= \int \sqrt{u} \, du$$

Now we integrate:

$$\int \sqrt{u} \, du = \int u^{1/2} \, du = \frac{2}{3}u^{3/2} + C$$

Finally, resubstitute $5x^2 + 1$ for u to end up with an expression in x:

$$\frac{2}{3}u^{2/3} + C = \frac{2}{3}(5x^2 + 1)^{3/2} + C$$

Answer: $\int 10x \sqrt{5x^2 + 1} \, dx = \frac{2}{3}(5x^2 + 1)^{3/2} + C$. (Check by computing the derivative of $\frac{2}{3}(5x^2 + 1)^{3/2}$.)

EXAMPLE 4   *(Compare Exercise 7)*

Find $\int (x^3 + 2)^4 x^2 \, dx$.

SOLUTION   Here, $x^3 + 2$ is raised to a power, so we let $u = x^3 + 2$; $(x^3 + 2)^4$ will become u^4. Next, compute du:

$$du = 3x^2 \, dx$$

We divide by 3 to isolate the $x^2 \, dx$:

$$\frac{1}{3} du = x^2 \, dx$$

Now we make those substitutions:

$$\int (x^3 + 2)^4 x^2 \, dx = \int u^4 \frac{1}{3} \, du$$

$$= \int \frac{1}{3} u^4 \, du \qquad \text{(Integrate } u^4\text{)}$$

$$= \frac{1}{15} u^5 + C \qquad \text{(Finally, resubstitute } u = x^3 + 2\text{)}$$

$$= \frac{1}{15}(x^3 + 2)^5 + C$$

Answer: $\int (x^3 + 2)^4 x^2 \, dx = \frac{1}{15}(x^3 + 2)^5 + C$. Check this answer by differentiating $\frac{1}{15}(x^3 + 2)^5$.

EXAMPLE 5   *(Compare Exercise 11)*

Find $\int xe^{x^2} dx$.

SOLUTION   The generalized power rule was not the only form of the chain rule that we used. We also had to use the chain rule when computing the derivative of $e^{f(x)}$. This integrand involves an expression of this form, so as with the chain rule, we replace the exponent by a single letter:

$$\text{let } u = x^2$$
$$du = 2x \, dx$$

so

$$\frac{1}{2} du = x \, dx$$

We have

$$\int xe^{x^2} dx = \int e^{x^2}(x \, dx)$$

Now we make the substitutions:

$$= \int e^u \left(\frac{1}{2} \, du \right)$$

$$= \int \frac{1}{2} \, e^u \, du$$

Now integrate:

$$= \frac{1}{2} e^u + C$$

Resubstituting, we have

$$= \frac{1}{2} e^{x^2} + C$$

Answer: $\int xe^{x^2} dx = \frac{1}{2} e^{x^2} + C$. Check this answer.

EXAMPLE 6 *(Compare Exercise 13)*

Find $\int \dfrac{2x + 3}{(x^2 + 3x + 6)^4} \, dx$.

SOLUTION The parentheses here again indicate composition. Let $u = x^2 + 3x + 6$, so $(x^2 + 3x + 6)^4$ becomes u^4, and $du = (2x + 3)dx$:

$$\int \frac{2x + 3}{(x^2 + 3x + 6)^4} \, dx = \int \frac{1}{(x^2 + 3x + 6)^4}(2x + 3) \, dx$$

$$= \int \frac{1}{u^4} \, du$$

(Remember that there is no quotient rule for antiderivatives; we must rewrite $1/u^4 = u^{-4}$.) Rewriting, we have

$$= \int u^{-4} \, du \qquad \text{(Now integrate)}$$

$$= \frac{-1}{3} u^{-3} + C$$

$$= \frac{-1}{3u^3} + C \qquad \begin{array}{l}\text{(Finally, resubstitute}\\ u = x^2 + 3x + 6)\end{array}$$

$$= \frac{-1}{3(x^2 + 3x + 6)^3} + C$$

Answer: $\int \dfrac{2x + 3}{(x^2 + 3x + 6)^4} \, dx = \dfrac{-1}{3(x^2 + 3x + 6)^3} + C$. Check the answer.

EXAMPLE 7   *(Compare Exercise 9)*

What is $\int \dfrac{4x}{x^2 + 6}\, dx$?

SOLUTION   This substitution is not immediately pointed out by parentheses or a radical or an exponent. But remember that we must rewrite quotients. Writing

$$\int \frac{4x}{x^2 + 6}\, dx = \int 4x(x^2 + 6)^{-1}\, dx$$

introduces the parentheses that can serve as an indicator of the substitution. Let

$$u = x^2 + 6$$

Then

$$du = 2x\, dx$$

We need to substitute for $4x\, dx$, so multiply by 2 and get

$$2\, du = 4x\, dx$$

$$\int 4x(x^2 + 6)^{-1}\, dx = \int u^{-1}\, 2\, du = 2 \int u^{-1}\, du$$

We cannot use the power rule with the exponent -1; the indefinite integral of u^{-1} is $\ln|u| + C$.

$$2 \int u^{-1}\, du = 2 \int \frac{1}{u}\, du$$
$$= 2 \ln|u| + C$$
$$= 2 \ln|x^2 + 6| + C$$

Answer: $\int \dfrac{4x}{x^2 + 6}\, dx = 2 \ln|x^2 + 6| + C$. Check the answer.

In the preceding example, because $x^2 + 6 > 0$ for all x, we could rewrite the expression $\ln|x^2 + 6|$ without using the absolute value bars as $\ln(x^2 + 6)$. But remember that the absolute value is necessary when integrating; in general,

$$\int \frac{1}{u}\, du = \ln|u| + C$$

A general pattern to look for is

$$\int \frac{f'(x)}{f(x)}\, dx$$

Example 8 shows how this pattern can involve an exponential function.

EXAMPLE 8 *(Compare Exercise 15)*

Find $\int \dfrac{e^{2x}}{e^{2x} - 5}\, dx$.

SOLUTION Again, we look to the denominator of the quotient. Let

$$u = e^{2x} - 5$$

Then

$$du = 2e^{2x}\, dx$$

Solving for $e^{2x}\, dx$, we have

$$\frac{1}{2}\, du = e^{2x}\, dx$$

$$\int \frac{1}{e^{2x} - 5}\, e^{2x}\, dx = \int \frac{1}{u}\, \frac{1}{2}\, du$$

$$= \frac{1}{2}\, \ln|u| + C$$

$$= \frac{1}{2}\, \ln|e^{2x} - 5| + C$$

Answer: $\int \dfrac{e^{2x}}{e^{2x} - 5}\, dx = \dfrac{1}{2}\, \ln|e^{2x} - 5| + C$. This time, the absolute value signs cannot be omitted. (Check the answer.)

EXAMPLE 9 *(Compare Exercise 17)*

Find $\int \dfrac{(8 + \ln x)^2}{x}\, dx$.

SOLUTION There is a quotient here, and after the last three examples you might anticipate the substitution $u = x$ because the denominator is x. One of the points of this example is that the substitution $u = x$ never does any good; all it does is change letters without simplifying the integral. In this case the substitution $u = x$ leads to $\int \dfrac{(8 + \ln u)^2}{u}\, du$, the same indefinite integral.

Here, $(8 + \ln x)$ is raised to a power, so we try

$$u = 8 + \ln x$$

Then

$$du = \frac{1}{x} dx$$

$$\int \frac{(8 + \ln x)^2}{x} dx = \int (8 + \ln x)^2 \frac{1}{x} dx$$

$$= \int u^2 \, du$$

$$= \frac{1}{3} u^3 + C$$

$$= \frac{1}{3} (8 + \ln x)^3 + C$$

Answer: $\int \frac{(8 + \ln x)^2}{x} dx = \frac{1}{3}(8 + \ln x)^3 + C$. (Check the answer.)

These examples have shown some general patterns to look for:

1. $\int [f(x)]^k f'(x) dx = \frac{1}{k+1} [f(x)]^{k+1} + C, \ k \neq -1;$

2. $\int \frac{f'(x)}{f(x)} dx = \ln |f(x)| + C;$ and

3. $\int e^{f(x)} \cdot f'(x) dx = e^{f(x)} + C$

In each of these integrals the substitution $u = f(x)$ leads to the following corresponding integrals:

1'. $\int u^k \, du = \frac{1}{k+1} u^{k+1} + C, \ k \neq -1;$

2'. $\int \frac{du}{u} = \ln |u| + C;$ and

3'. $\int e^u \, du = e^u + C.$

SUBSTITUTION AND THE DEFINITE INTEGRAL

You might have noticed that so far all our examples have been indefinite integrals. There is a reason for this; definite integrals are harder. When substituting into a definite integral, not only do you have to substitute for the integrand and the differential, you also have to substitute for the limits of integration.

EXAMPLE 10 (*Compare Exercise 21*)

Compute $\int_0^4 2x \sqrt{x^2 + 9}\, dx$.

SOLUTION First, we rewrite the integrand in preparation for the power rule:

$$\int_0^4 2x \sqrt{x^2 + 9}\, dx = \int_0^4 2x(x^2 + 9)^{1/2}\, dx$$

We let $u = x^2 + 9$, so $du = 2x\, dx$. Now the limits of integration must be taken care of. The 0 and the 4 are values of x. We must substitute the corresponding values of u, with $u = x^2 + 9$.

When $x = 0$, $u = 0^2 + 9 = 9$; replace the 0 with 9.

When $x = 4$, $u = 4^2 + 9 = 25$; replace the 4 with 25.

Substituting, we have $\int_0^4 \sqrt{x^2 + 9}(2x\, dx) = \int_9^{25} u^{1/2}\, du$. Now

$$\int_9^{25} u^{1/2}\, du = \frac{2}{3} u^{3/2} \Big|_9^{25}$$

$$= \frac{2}{3}(25)^{3/2} - \frac{2}{3}(9)^{3/2}$$

$$= \frac{2}{3}(5)^3 - \frac{2}{3}(3)^3$$

$$= \frac{250}{3} - \frac{54}{3} = \frac{196}{3}$$

Answer: $\int_0^4 2x\sqrt{x^2 + 9}\, dx = \frac{196}{3}$.

CAUTION Remember that $\int_0^4 2x\sqrt{x^2 + 9}\, dx$ is a number and that to keep equality throughout the computations, the limits of integration *must* be changed. Notice also that there was no final resubstitution; the answer does not involve a variable. We were asked not to find the family of antiderivatives, but to compute a number.

SUBSTITUTIONS INVOLVING ALGEBRA

Sometimes, the substitution leaves a variable left over even after taking care of the differential. In the above examples we saw how to handle the cases that involve the arithmetic of multiplying or dividing by constants. If there is still some of the original variable left over, go back to the substitution equation and see whether you can use that equation again.

EXAMPLE 11   *(Compare Exercise 27)*

Find $\int x\sqrt{x + 5}\, dx$.

SOLUTION   We let

$$u = x + 5$$
$$du = dx$$

Then $x\sqrt{x + 5}\, dx$ becomes $x\sqrt{u}\, du$, but there is an x left over. Go back to the original substitution (here, $u = x + 5$), and try to express this extra x in terms of u:

$$u = x + 5 \qquad \text{means} \qquad x = u - 5$$

Now

$$\int x\sqrt{x + 5}\, dx = \int (u - 5)\sqrt{u}\, du$$

$$= \int (u - 5)u^{1/2}\, du$$

Multiply through by $u^{1/2}$ to obtain

$$= \int u^{3/2} - 5u^{1/2}\, du$$

Now integrate:

$$= \frac{2}{5}u^{5/2} - \frac{10}{3}u^{3/2} + C$$

$$= \frac{2}{5}(x + 5)^{5/2} - \frac{10}{3}(x + 5)^{3/2} + C$$

Answer: $\int x\sqrt{x + 5}\, dx = \frac{2}{5}(x + 5)^{5/2} - \frac{10}{3}(x + 5)^{3/2} + C.$

EXAMPLE 12   *(Compare Exercise 29)*

Find $\int \dfrac{x^3}{x^2 + 9}\, dx$.

SOLUTION   As before, the denominator attracts our attention. Let

$$u = x^2 + 9$$
$$du = 2x\, dx$$
$$\frac{1}{2}du = x\, dx$$

$$\int \frac{x^3}{x^2 + 9}\, dx = \int \frac{1}{x^2 + 9}x^2(x\, dx)$$

$$= \int \frac{1}{u}x^2\left(\frac{1}{2}\, du\right)$$

This time, there is an x^2 left over. We go back to $u = x^2 + 9$ and solve for x^2:

$$x^2 = u - 9$$

Now our integral is

$$\int \frac{1}{u}(u - 9)\frac{1}{2}\,du = \frac{1}{2}\int \frac{u - 9}{u}\,du \qquad \text{(Divide } (u - 9) \text{ by } u)$$

$$= \frac{1}{2}\int \left(1 - \frac{9}{u}\right)du \qquad \text{(Now integrate)}$$

$$= \frac{1}{2}(u - 9\ln|u|) + C \qquad \text{(Resubstitute)}$$

$$= \frac{1}{2}(x^2 + 9 - 9\ln|x^2 + 9|) + C$$

Answer: $\displaystyle\int \frac{x^3}{x^2 + 9}\,dx = \frac{1}{2}(x^2 + 9 - 9\ln|x^2 + 9|) + C.$

14-1 EXERCISES

I

Evaluate the indefinite integrals in Exercises 1 through 20. Use the indicated substitution when given.

1. (*See Example 2*) $\int (5x + 1)^3\,dx$; let $u = 5x + 1$

2. $\int \sqrt{9x - 4}\,dx$; let $u = 9x - 4$

3. (*See Example 3*)
   $\int (2x^2 + 3x)^4(4x + 3)dx$; let $u = 2x^2 + 3x$

4. $\int (5x^3 + 4x)^5(15x^2 + 4)dx$; let $u = 5x^3 + 4x$

5. $\int 3(7u^2 + 3u - 2)^2(14u + 3)du$

6. $\int (x^3 - 3x^2 + 2)^3(3x^2 - 6x)dx$

7. (*See Example 4*) $\int (4x^3 - 6x)^3(2x^2 - 1)dx$

8. $\displaystyle\int \frac{4x}{x^2 - 3}\,dx$; let $u = x^2 - 3$

9. (*See Example 7*) $\displaystyle\int \frac{4}{4x - 3}\,dx$

10. $\displaystyle\int \frac{2x}{x^2 + 1}\,dx$

11. (*See Example 5*) $\int 2x^2 e^{x^3}\,dx$

12. $\int e^{6x}\,dx$

13. (*See Example 6*) $\displaystyle\int \frac{4x - 2}{\sqrt{x^2 - x + 5}}\,dx$

14. $\displaystyle\int \frac{12x - 2}{3x^2 - x + 4}\,dx$

15. (*See Example 8*) $\displaystyle\int \frac{e^x}{e^x - 7}\,dx$

16. $\displaystyle\int \frac{e^{4x}}{e^{4x} + 2}\,dx$

II

17. (*See Example 9*)

$$\int \frac{1}{x(1 + \ln x)^2} dx$$

18. $\int \frac{\sqrt{\ln x}}{x} dx$

19. $\int \frac{e^{1/x^2}}{x^3} dx$

20. $\int \frac{(\sqrt{x} + 6)^5}{\sqrt{x}} dx$

In Exercises 21 through 24, fill in the missing limits of integration, and then compute the definite integral.

21. (*See Example 10*)

$$\int_3^7 \frac{x}{x^2 - 4} dx = \int_-^- \frac{1}{2u} du, \text{ with } u = x^2 - 4$$

22. $\int_{-1}^5 x^2 \sqrt{x^3 + 9} \, dx = \int_-^- \frac{1}{3} \sqrt{u} \, du, \, u = x^3 + 9$

23. $\int_{-1}^3 xe^{x^2} dx = \int_-^- \frac{1}{2} e^u \, du$

24. $\int_0^1 (2x - 1)(3x^2 - 3x + 4)^3 \, dx = \int_-^- \frac{1}{3} u^3 \, du$

III

Find the indefinite integrals in Exercises 25 through 30.

25. $\int \frac{x}{e^{x^2}} dx$

26. $\int \frac{1}{x \ln x} dx$

27. (*See Example 11*)

$$\int x\sqrt{3x - 4} \, dx$$

28. $\int x\sqrt{5 - x} \, dx$

29. (*See Example 12*)

$$\int x^3(x^2 + 5)^3 \, dx$$

30. $\int \frac{4x^5}{x^3 + 10} dx$

Compute the definite integrals in Exercises 31 and 32.

31. $\int_0^5 \frac{2x^3}{x^2 + 1} dx$

32. $\int_4^{11} x\sqrt{x + 5} \, dx$

33. A company with fixed costs of $150 has modeled its marginal cost function by

$$MC(x) = x\sqrt{x^2 + 9}$$

What is the company's total cost function?

34. What is the area under the curve $y = xe^{x^2}$, above the x-axis, and bounded on the right by the line $x = 2$?

35. If a company's marginal production t hours after opening in the morning is

$$\frac{t}{\sqrt{t^2 + 1}} \qquad 0 \le t \le 8$$

what is its total volume of production over the eight-hour period?

36. A particle is moving with a velocity given by

$$V(t) = 6t\sqrt{t^2 + 16}$$

where V is given in feet per second and t is in seconds. How far does the particle travel during the interval $0 \le t \le 3$?

37. A company's marginal revenue is given by

$$MR(x) = \frac{20x}{x^2 + 1}$$

What would be the total change in revenue if x increased from 3 to 7?

14–2   INTEGRATION BY PARTS

The method of integration discussed in this section is called **integration by parts.** This technique is based on the product rule for differentiation. The formula to use looks almost silly in theory. It is in practice that its usefulness becomes apparent.

The product rule for differentiation states that

$$(f(x) \cdot g(x))' = g(x) \cdot f'(x) + f(x) \cdot g'(x)$$

We integrate both sides:

$$\int (f(x) \cdot g(x))' \, dx = \int [g(x) \cdot f'(x) + f(x) \cdot g'(x)] dx$$

$$= \int g(x) \cdot f'(x) dx + \int f(x) \cdot g'(x) dx$$

Now $\int (f(x) \cdot g(x))' \, dx = f(x) \cdot g(x) + C$ because $f(x) \cdot g(x)$ is an antiderivative of its derivative, $(f(x) \cdot g(x))'$. Using this to evaluate the left-hand side, we have

$$f(x) \cdot g(x) + C = \int g(x) \cdot f'(x) dx + \int f(x) \cdot g'(x) dx$$

Now subtract $\int g(x) \cdot f'(x) dx$ from both sides:

$$f(x) \cdot g(x) + C - \int g(x) \cdot f'(x) dx = \int f(x) \cdot g'(x) dx$$

We don't have to write $+ C$ anymore; the indefinite integral $\int g(x) \cdot f'(x) dx$ by itself indicates a family of functions that we know only up to an additive constant. If we change the order of the equation, we get the formula we want.

> *The Integration by Parts Formula* $\displaystyle \int f(x) \cdot g'(x) dx = f(x) \cdot g(x) - \int g(x) \cdot f'(x) dx$

Although this formula might not look very promising, examples will show that, in fact, integration by parts is a very useful technique. The idea is this: Try to recognize the integrand that you are given as the product of two functions, one of which you can integrate fairly easily; you will differentiate the other one. Call the one that you can integrate $g'(x)$, so its integral is $g(x)$. Apply this formula and hope that $\int g(x) \cdot f'(x) dx$ is an easier integral than the one you started with.

EXAMPLE 1 *(Compare Exercise 1)*

Find $\int x^2 \ln x\, dx$.

SOLUTION We factor the integral into two parts: $\ln x$ and x^2. We can integrate x^2; if $g'(x) = x^2$, then $g(x) = \frac{1}{3}x^3$. (We do not worry about $+ C$ until the *very* end.) The other part of the integrand in the formula is called $f(x)$; here, $f(x) = \ln x$, so $f'(x) = \frac{1}{x}$.

The parts formula

$$\int f(x) \cdot g'(x)dx = f(x) \cdot g(x) - \int g(x) \cdot f'(x)dx$$

now gives us

$$\int (\ln x)x^2\, dx = (\ln x)\left(\frac{x^3}{3}\right) - \int \frac{x^3}{3}\cdot\frac{1}{x}dx$$

We simplify $\dfrac{x^3}{x}$ to x^2 and continue:

$$= \frac{x^3 \ln x}{3} - \frac{1}{3}\int x^2\, dx$$

It worked! We can find $\int x^2\, dx$. Therefore

$$\int (\ln x)x^2\, dx = \frac{x^3 \ln x}{3} - \frac{1}{3}\left(\frac{1}{3}x^3\right) + C$$

(This is the last step, so we now include the $+ C$.)

Answer: $\displaystyle\int x^2 \ln x\, dx = \frac{x^3 \ln x}{3} - \frac{x^3}{9} + C.$

There is a change of notation that makes the integration by parts formula easier to remember and easier to use.

Denote $f(x)$ by u, so $f'(x)dx$ becomes du.

Denote $g'(x)dx$ by dv, so $g(x)$ is replaced by v.

The formula is now

$$\int u\, dv = uv - \int v\, du$$

We redo Example 1 so that you can see how this notation works.

EXAMPLE 1 (REDONE)

Find $\int x^2 \ln x\, dx$.

SOLUTION We integrate x^2 and differentiate $\ln x$, so

$$u = \ln x \qquad dv = x^2\, dx$$

$$du = \frac{1}{x}\, dx \qquad v = \frac{x^3}{3}$$

Using

$$\int u \, dv = uv - \int v \, du$$

we have

$$\int (\ln x)(x^2 \, dx) = (\ln x)\left(\frac{x^3}{3}\right) - \int \frac{x^3}{3} \cdot \frac{1}{x} \, dx$$

$$= \frac{x^3 \ln x}{3} - \frac{1}{9} x^3 + C, \qquad \text{as before.}$$

EXAMPLE 2 *(Compare Exercise 3)*

Find $\int x e^{3x} \, dx$.

SOLUTION We factor $x e^{3x}$ into parts, x and e^{3x}. We choose to differentiate the x and integrate the e^{3x}. (The other choice will be discussed after this solution.)
We let

$$u = x \qquad \text{and} \qquad dv = e^{3x} \, dx$$

Thus

$$du = dx \qquad \text{and} \qquad v = \frac{1}{3} e^{3x}$$

Then

$$\int u \, dv = uv - \int v \, du$$

becomes

$$\int x e^{3x} \, dx = x\left[\frac{1}{3} e^{3x}\right] - \int \frac{1}{3} e^{3x} \, dx$$

$$= \frac{x e^{3x}}{3} - \frac{1}{3} \int e^{3x} \, dx$$

Since $\int e^{3x} \, dx = \frac{1}{3} e^{3x} + C$, we conclude with

$$= \frac{x e^{3x}}{3} - \frac{e^{3x}}{9} + C$$

Answer: $\int x e^{3x} \, dx = \frac{x e^{3x}}{3} - \frac{e^{3x}}{9} + C.$

In discussing integration by substitution we were able to give you some things to look for that would suggest what the substitution might be: parentheses, radicals, and denominators. We can also give you some specific forms to watch for to use integration by parts. Knowledge of these forms comes from experience.

For instance, we look again at the integral of Example 2. How did we choose to treat xe^{3x} the way we did? What would happen if we switched the roles of e^{3x} and x? After all, we can integrate x very easily, too.

EXAMPLE 2 REVISITED

Find $\int xe^{3x}\,dx$.

ATTEMPT AT SOLUTION   This time, we let

$$u = e^{3x} \qquad \text{and} \qquad dv = x\,dx$$

Then

$$du = 3e^{3x} \qquad \text{and} \qquad v = \frac{x^2}{2}$$

and

$$\int u\,dv = uv - \int v\,du$$

becomes

$$\int xe^{3x}\,dx = e^{3x}\left(\frac{x^2}{2}\right) - \int \frac{3}{2}x^2e^{3x}\,dx$$

The new integral, $\frac{3}{2}\int x^2e^{3x}\,dx$, is not any simpler. In fact, it is more complicated than the one we started with, $\int xe^{3x}\,dx$. This choice of u and dv didn't work to get us a simpler integral. This choice of parts doesn't work. If in some problem your choice of u and dv leads to a more complicated integral than the one you started with, go back and try a different choice of parts.

Experience tells us that when confronted with an integral of the form $\int x^n e^{ax}\,dx$, where n is a positive integer, we let

$$u = x^n \qquad \text{and} \qquad dv = e^{ax}\,dx$$

Example 3 shows that this choice will help you to find the integral even if you have to be persistent.

EXAMPLE 3   *(Compare Exercise 5)*

Find $\int x^2e^{4x}\,dx$.

SOLUTION   The hint says let

$$u = x^2 \qquad \text{and} \qquad dv = e^{4x}\,dx$$

Then

$$du = 2x\,dx \qquad \text{and} \qquad v = \frac{1}{4}e^{4x}$$

and

$$\int u \, dv = uv - \int v \, du$$

becomes

$$\int x^2 e^{4x} \, dx = x^2 \frac{1}{4} e^{4x} - \int \frac{1}{4} e^{4x} 2x \, dx$$

$$= \frac{x^2 e^{4x}}{4} - \frac{1}{2} \int x e^{4x} \, dx$$

We can't evaluate this last integral immediately, but it is simpler than the one we started with, and the hint does say to be persistent. Remembering the successful solution to Example 2, we use parts again to find $\int x e^{4x} \, dx$.

Following the hint again, we let

$$u = x \qquad \text{and} \qquad dv = e^{4x} \, dx$$

$$du = dx \qquad\qquad v = \frac{1}{4} e^{4x}$$

$$\int u \, dv = uv - \int v \, du$$

becomes

$$\int x e^{4x} \, dx = x \frac{1}{4} e^{4x} - \int \frac{1}{4} e^{4x} \, dx$$

$$= \frac{x e^{4x}}{4} - \frac{1}{16} e^{4x} + C$$

Now we go back to our original problem. We had

$$\int x^2 e^{4x} \, dx = \frac{x^2 e^{4x}}{4} - \frac{1}{2} \left[\int x e^{4x} \, dx \right]$$

$$= \frac{x^2 e^{4x}}{4} - \frac{1}{2} \left[\frac{x e^{4x}}{4} - \frac{e^{4x}}{16} \right] + C$$

See the Note below regarding the $+ C$ term.

$$\text{Answer:} \int x^2 e^{4x} \, dx = \frac{x^2 e^{4x}}{4} - \frac{x e^{4x}}{8} + \frac{e^{4x}}{32} + C.$$

CAUTION Watch out for an arithmetic error when using parts twice. Notice that $-\frac{1}{2}$ must be multiplied through the whole expression for $\int x e^{4x} \, dx$.

NOTE We can write $+ C$ after completing the antidifferentiation. To find the integral, you find *one* antiderivative and then add the arbitrary constant term.

If k is a positive integer, you can also use integration by parts to compute integrals of the form

$$\int x^n (\ln x)^k \, dx$$

Let

$$u = (\ln x)^k \quad \text{and} \quad dv = x^n \, dx$$

This is what we did in Example 1 with $n = 2$ and $k = 1$. In the next example we show how this technique allows us to find the integral of $\ln x$.

EXAMPLE 4 *(Compare Exercise 7)*

Find $\int \ln x \, dx$.

SOLUTION   Following the hint with $n = 0$ and $k = 1$, we let

$$u = \ln x \quad \text{and} \quad dv = dx$$

Then

$$du = \frac{1}{x} \, dx \quad \text{and} \quad v = x$$

Applying

$$\int u \, dv = uv - \int v \, du$$

we have

$$\int \ln x \, dx = (\ln x)x - \int x \frac{1}{x} \, dx$$

$$= x \ln x - \int 1 \, dx$$

$$= x \ln x - x + C$$

Answer: $\int \ln x \, dx = x \ln x - x + C.$

EXAMPLE 5 *(Compare Exercise 9)*

Find $\int x(\ln x)^2 \, dx$.

SOLUTION   Following the hint with $n = 1$ and $k = 2$, we let

$$u = (\ln x)^2 \quad \text{and} \quad dv = x \, dx$$

$$du = 2(\ln x)\frac{1}{x} \, dx \qquad v = \frac{x^2}{2}$$

$$\int u \, dv = uv - \int v \, du$$

becomes

$$\int (\ln x)^2 x\, dx = (\ln x)^2 \frac{x^2}{2} - \int \frac{x^2}{2} 2(\ln x)\frac{1}{x}\, dx$$

$$= \frac{x^2(\ln x)^2}{2} - \int x \ln x\, dx$$

We use parts on $\int x \ln x\, dx$, following the same hint:

$$u = \ln x \qquad \text{and} \qquad dv = x\, dx$$

$$du = \frac{1}{x}\, dx \qquad\qquad v = \frac{x^2}{2}$$

$$\int x \ln x\, dx = \frac{(\ln x)x^2}{2} - \int \frac{x^2}{2} \frac{1}{x}\, dx$$

$$= \frac{(\ln x)x^2}{2} - \int \frac{x}{2}\, dx$$

$$= \frac{(\ln x)x^2}{2} - \frac{x^2}{4} + C$$

Returning to our original equation, we have

$$\int x(\ln x)^2\, dx = \frac{x^2(\ln x)^2}{2} - \left(\frac{x^2 \ln x}{2} - \frac{x^2}{4} \right) + C$$

$$= \frac{x^2(\ln x)^2}{2} - \frac{x^2 \ln x}{2} + \frac{x^2}{4} + C$$

EXAMPLE 6

Find $\int (x^2 - e^{-x})\, dx$.

SOLUTION Don't get "parts happy" and think that all integrals are now to be attacked by choosing u and dv.

$$\int (x^2 - e^{-x})dx = \frac{1}{3}x^3 - \frac{1}{-1}e^{-x} + C$$

$$= \frac{x^3}{3} + e^{-x} + C$$

14-2 EXERCISES

I

Use integration by parts to find the integrals in Exercises 1 through 4.

1. (*See Example 1*)

$$\int x \ln x \, dx$$

2. $$\int 4x^2 \ln x \, dx$$

3. (*See Example 2*)

$$\int xe^{5x} \, dx$$

4. $$\int 3xe^x \, dx$$

II

Use parts (repeat if necessary) in Exercises 5 through 10.

5. (*See Example 3*)

$$\int x^2 e^{2x} \, dx$$

6. $$\int x^3 e^{-x} \, dx$$

7. (*See Example 4*)

$$\int x^3 \ln x \, dx$$

8. $$\int x^5 \ln x \, dx$$

9. (*See Example 5*)

$$\int x^2 (\ln x)^2 \, dx$$

10. $$\int (\ln x)^2 \, dx$$

III

Find the indefinite integrals in Exercises 11 through 16. You might or might not have to use parts. You might have to use a substitution together with parts.

11. $$\int x^3 e^{x^2} dx$$ (*Hint:* Let $u = x^2$ and $dv = xe^{x^2}dx$)

12. $$\int \frac{x}{e^{4x}} \, dx$$

13. $$\int 4xe^{x^2} \, dx$$

14. $$\int x^2 (\ln x^2) \, dx$$

15. $$\int \frac{\ln x}{x^2} \, dx$$

16. $$\int \frac{\ln x}{x} \, dx$$

17. What is the area under the curve te^{-t} and above the interval $1 \le t \le 2$?

18. A company's marginal cost for producing x units is $MC(x) = x \ln[x + 1]$. What is the total change in its cost if production goes from eight units to ten units?

14-3 IMPROPER INTEGRALS

- *Unbounded Intervals*
- *Improper Integrals*
- *Applications*

UNBOUNDED INTERVALS

Suppose that a certain service business finds that its customers arrive at the average rate of 50 per hour and that the usual transaction takes four minutes. The business could be a bank, a cosmetics department, or a supermarket. The business must decide how many service personnel to hire so that there are enough to handle busy times. At the same time the business doesn't want to hire so many

FIGURE 14-1

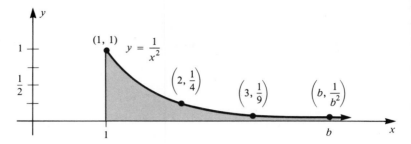

people that most of them are often idle. For example, the firm needs to know how likely it is that ten customers will need service all at once. The firm might ask questions like "What is the probability there will be more than 30 customers in 15 minutes?" or "If we hire six sales personnel, what is the probability that one of them will be idle for more than ten minutes at a time?"

These questions theoretically involve no upper bound on the number of customers or the length of time an employee is idle. To handle questions like these, the applied science of statistics frequently gets involved in **integrals over unbounded regions**—integrals that at first glance seem about as far removed from applications as possible. We approach the concept of integrating over unbounded regions by looking at some simple functions. Figure 14–1 gives the graph of $y = 1/x^2$ for $x \geq 1$.

If we can, we want to make sense of the question, "What is the area of the shaded region?" We start by just considering the area of that part of the region between $x = 1$ and $x = b$. That area is given by

$$\int_1^b \frac{1}{x^2}\, dx = -\frac{1}{x}\Big|_1^b = -\frac{1}{b} - \left(-\frac{1}{1}\right)$$

$$= 1 - \frac{1}{b}$$

No matter how far to the right you place b, the area of the region over $[1, b]$ is less than 1. For large values of b, $1 - \left(\dfrac{1}{b}\right)$ is very close to 1. As $b \to \infty$, the quantity

$$\left(1 - \frac{1}{b}\right) \to 1$$

$$\lim_{b \to \infty} \left(\int_1^b \frac{1}{x^2}\, dx\right) = \lim_{b \to \infty} \left(1 - \frac{1}{b}\right) = 1$$

These calculations lead us to say that the area of the shaded region in Figure 14–1 is 1. (*Compare Exercise 1*)

FIGURE 14–2

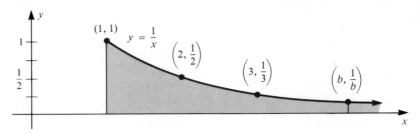

Now we look at another simple function, $y = \dfrac{1}{x}$, and ask the same question as we did with $y = \dfrac{1}{x^2}$. See Figure 14–2.

What is the area of the region bounded above by $y = \dfrac{1}{x}$, below by the x-axis, and on the left by the line $x = 1$, but unbounded on the right? Using the same approach as above, we first fix a number b and compute the area of that part of the region that is bounded on the right by the line $x = b$. This area is given by

$$\int_1^b \frac{1}{x}\, dx = \ln|x| \Big|_1^b$$

$$= \ln|b| - \ln|1| \qquad (b > 0 \text{ and } 1 > 0)$$

$$= \ln b - \ln 1 \qquad (\ln 1 = 0)$$

$$= \ln b$$

Again, the next step is to look at what happens as b grows arbitrarily large. But this time, $\lim_{b \to \infty} \ln b$ doesn't exist; as b grows arbitrarily large, so does $\ln b$. We conclude that the shaded region in Figure 14–2 does not have a finite area.

These two examples could play havoc with your intuition. First, it might seem "obvious" to many that an unbounded region cannot have a finite area. Second, it is hard to believe that there is that much difference in behavior between the region under $y = \dfrac{1}{x^2}$ and the region under $y = \dfrac{1}{x}$. These examples teach us that we must be very careful about jumping to "obvious" conclusions about unbounded regions.

EXAMPLE 1 *(Compare Exercise 1)*

Does the region bounded above by the graph $y = 1/x^4$, below by the x-axis, and on the left by the line $x = 2$ have a finite area or not?

SOLUTION The integral

$$\int_2^b \frac{1}{x^4}\,dx$$

gives the area of the part of this region that lies to the left of the line $x = b$. We compute the area of this subregion and then see what happens as $b \to \infty$.

$$\int_2^b \frac{1}{x^4}\,dx = -\frac{1}{3x^3}\bigg|_2^b = -\frac{1}{3b^3} + \frac{1}{24}$$

The area of this subregion is $\dfrac{1}{24} - \dfrac{1}{3b^3}$, and as $b \to \infty$, $\left(\dfrac{1}{24} - \dfrac{1}{3b^3}\right) \to \dfrac{1}{24}$.

Answer: The area of this unbounded region is $\dfrac{1}{24}$.

IMPROPER INTEGRALS

On the basis of these examples we now make the following definitions.

Definition
Improper Integral
$\int_a^\infty f(x)\,dx$

The integral $\int_a^\infty f(x)\,dx$ is called an **improper integral** (the upper limit of the integral is not a number), and we define

$$\int_a^\infty f(x)\,dx = \lim_{b \to \infty} \int_a^b f(x)\,dx$$

if this limit exists.

If $\lim\limits_{b \to \infty} \int_a^b f(x)\,dx$ exists, then we say that $\int_a^\infty f(x)\,dx$ is **convergent.**

If $\lim\limits_{b \to \infty} \int_a^b f(x)\,dx$ does not exist, then we say that $\int_a^\infty f(x)\,dx$ is **divergent.**

From our discussion above, we have

1. $\displaystyle\int_1^\infty \frac{1}{x^2}\,dx$ is convergent, while

2. $\displaystyle\int_1^\infty \frac{1}{x}\,dx$ is divergent.

EXAMPLE 2   *(Compare Exercise 9)*

Evaluate $\int_0^\infty e^{-2x}\, dx$ or determine that it is divergent.

SOLUTION   By definition,

$$\int_0^\infty e^{-2x}\, dx = \lim_{b \to \infty} \int_0^b e^{-2x}\, dx$$

Next, we compute the definite integral $\int_0^b e^{-2x}\, dx$:

$$\int_0^\infty e^{-2x}\, dx = \lim_{b \to \infty} \left[-\frac{1}{2} e^{-2x} \Big|_0^b \right]$$

$$= \lim_{b \to \infty} \left[-\frac{1}{2}(e^{-2b} - e^0) \right]$$

$$= \lim_{b \to \infty} \left[-\frac{1}{2}\left(\frac{1}{e^{2b}} - 1 \right) \right]$$

Now compute the limit. As $b \to \infty$, $e^{2b} \to \infty$, so $\dfrac{1}{e^{2b}} \to 0$. Thus

$$\lim_{b \to \infty} \left[-\frac{1}{2}\left(\frac{1}{e^{2b}} - 1 \right) \right] = -\frac{1}{2}(0 - 1) = \frac{1}{2}$$

Answer: $\displaystyle\int_0^\infty e^{-2x}\, dx$ is convergent, and $\displaystyle\int_0^\infty e^{-2x}\, dx = \frac{1}{2}$. ∎

NOTE Since $e^{-2x} \geq 0$ on $[0, \infty)$, we can interpret this integral geometrically; the region under the curve $y = e^{-2x}$, above the x-axis, and to the right of the y-axis has area $= \frac{1}{2}$.

EXAMPLE 3   *(Compare Exercise 15)*

Evaluate $\displaystyle\int_1^\infty \frac{1}{\sqrt{x}}\, dx$, or show that it is divergent. Interpret the answer geometrically.

SOLUTION   Using the definition, we write

$$\int_1^\infty \frac{1}{\sqrt{x}}\, dx = \lim_{b \to \infty} \int_1^b \frac{1}{\sqrt{x}}\, dx$$

$$= \lim_{b \to \infty} \int_1^b x^{-1/2}\, dx$$

$$= \lim_{b \to \infty} \left[2x^{1/2} \Big|_1^b \right]$$

$$= \lim_{b \to \infty} [2\sqrt{b} - 2]$$

But as $b \to \infty$, $\sqrt{b} \to \infty$ also, so this limit does not exist.

Answer: $\int_1^\infty \frac{1}{\sqrt{x}}\,dx$ diverges. The region bounded above by the curve $y = \frac{1}{\sqrt{x}}$, below by the x-axis, and on the left by the line $x = 1$ does not have finite area.

Next, we look at integrals over intervals of the form $(-\infty, b]$.

Definition
Improper Integral
$\int_\infty^b f(x)dx$

$$\int_{-\infty}^b f(x)dx = \lim_{a \to -\infty} \int_a^b f(x)dx, \text{ if this limit exists.}$$

As before, the improper integral is called *convergent* if it has a finite limit; otherwise, the integral is called *divergent*.

EXAMPLE 4   (*Compare Exercise 13*)

Evaluate $\int_{-\infty}^{-2} \frac{4}{x^5}\,dx$ or determine that the integral is divergent. Interpret the answer geometrically.

SOLUTION

$$\int_{-\infty}^{-2} \frac{4}{x^5}\,dx = \lim_{a \to -\infty} \int_a^{-2} \frac{4}{x^5}\,dx$$

$$= \lim_{a \to -\infty} \left(-\frac{1}{x^4}\Big|_a^{-2} \right)$$

$$= \lim_{a \to -\infty} \left(-\frac{1}{16} + \frac{1}{a^4} \right)$$

$$= -\frac{1}{16}$$

We have found that the integral is convergent. For the geometric interpretation we sketch the graph of $y = \frac{4}{x^5}$ for $-\infty < x \le -2$. See Figure 14–3.

If R is the region bounded above by the x-axis, below by the curve $y = \frac{4}{x^5}$, and on the right by the line $x = -2$, then the area of $R = \frac{1}{16}$. Note that the integral gives the negative of the area because $\frac{4}{x^5} < 0$ on the interval $(-\infty, -2]$.

FIGURE 14-3

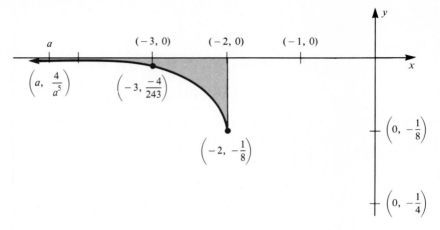

FIGURE 14-4

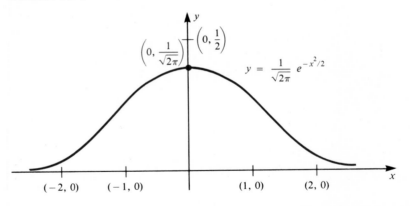

One of the most important curves in statistical applications is the **normal,** or bell-shaped, **curve.** See Figure 14–4, where the standard normal distribution curve is drawn.

The curve is the graph of the function

$$f(x) = \frac{1}{\sqrt{2\pi}} e^{-x^2/2}, \qquad -\infty < x < \infty$$

Areas of regions under this curve correspond to probabilities. To talk about the area under this curve, we have to extend our class of improper integrals. Notice that this function is defined for all real numbers; we will have to talk about integrals of functions defined over intervals that are unbounded in both directions.

Definition Improper Integral $\int_{-\infty}^{\infty} f(x)\,dx$	$\int_{-\infty}^{\infty} f(x)\,dx = \int_{-\infty}^{0} f(x)\,dx + \int_{0}^{\infty} f(x)\,dx$ if both the improper integrals on the right exist.

The terms convergent and divergent are used as before. Note that to discuss the convergence of $\int_{-\infty}^{\infty} f(x)\,dx$, you have to handle two different improper integrals separately.

EXAMPLE 5   *(Compare Exercise 7)*

Evaluate $\int_{-\infty}^{\infty} e^{-2x}\,dx$ or show that it is divergent.

SOLUTION   We consider $\int_{-\infty}^{0} e^{-2x}\,dx$ and $\int_{0}^{\infty} e^{-2x}\,dx$ separately. Example 2 tells us that $\int_{0}^{\infty} e^{-2x}\,dx = \frac{1}{2}$, so now we turn our attention to $\int_{-\infty}^{0} e^{-2x}\,dx$:

$$\int_{-\infty}^{0} e^{-2x}\,dx = \lim_{a \to -\infty} \int_{a}^{0} e^{-2x}\,dx$$

$$= \lim_{a \to -\infty} \left[-\frac{1}{2} e^{-2x} \Big|_{a}^{0} \right]$$

$$= \lim_{a \to -\infty} \left[-\frac{1}{2}(e^{0} - e^{-2a}) \right]$$

$$= \lim_{a \to -\infty} \left[-\frac{1}{2}(1 - e^{-2a}) \right]$$

$$= \lim_{a \to -\infty} \left[-\frac{1}{2} + \frac{1}{2} e^{-2a} \right]$$

To compute this limit, note that as $a \to -\infty$, $-2a \to +\infty$ (we use the $+$ for emphasis), so $e^{-2a} \to \infty$. Thus $\int_{-\infty}^{0} e^{-2x}\,dx$ diverges. Therefore $\int_{-\infty}^{\infty} e^{-2x}\,dx$ diverges also.

Answer: $\int_{-\infty}^{\infty} e^{-2x}\,dx$ diverges.

APPLICATIONS

EXAMPLE 6   *(Compare Exercise 23)*

Customers arrive at a certain service facility at the rate of 25 per hour. The probability that there will be a gap of six minutes or more between successive customers is given by the improper integral (6 minutes = $\frac{1}{10}$ hour)

$$\int_{1/10}^{\infty} 25 e^{-25t}\,dt$$

What is this probability?

SOLUTION

$$\int_{1/10}^{\infty} 25e^{-25t}\, dt = \lim_{b \to \infty} \int_{1/10}^{b} 25e^{-25t}\, dt$$

$$= \lim_{b \to \infty} \left[-e^{-25t} \Big|_{1/10}^{b} \right]$$

$$= \lim_{b \to \infty} \left[-e^{-25b} + e^{-2.5} \right]$$

$$= \lim_{b \to \infty} \left[\frac{1}{e^{2.5}} - \frac{1}{e^{25b}} \right]$$

$$= \frac{1}{e^{2.5}} \approx 0.082$$

The probability of waiting at least six minutes between customers is about 0.082.

Recall that in Chapter 6 we used definite integrals to approximate certain summations. We conclude this section with an application showing how improper integrals can be used to approximate "infinite summations."

A consulting firm in a certain city has estimated that 70¢ of every dollar earned in that city is spent within the city. This 70¢ then is earned within the city, so 70% of this amount will be spent within the city. This progression goes on indefinitely.

EXAMPLE 7 *(Compare Exercise 27)*

A company has a monthly payroll of $1,000,000. What is the total amount of income this payroll generates in the local community if 70¢ of every dollar earned in this community is spent in the community?

SOLUTION   First, there is the $1,000,000 generated directly by the company. But now we start to take the multiplier effect into account; 70% of this $1,000,000 is spent within the local community, thus generating another $700,000 of income. This $700,000 generates another 70% of $700,000 (that is, $490,000) of income, and so on. To find the total of all these amounts, we want to sum

$$1,000,000 + (0.7)(1,000,000) + (0.7)[(0.7)(1,000,000)] +$$
$$\cdots = 1,000,000[1 + 0.7 + (0.7)^2 + (0.7)^3 + \cdots]$$

There is a formula for this sum (which is called a geometric series), but we are interested here in approximating this sum by an integral. The variable in the summation is in the exponent, and so our integral is $1,000,000 \int_{0}^{\infty} (0.7)^t\, dt$. We compute

$$\int_0^\infty (0.7)^t \, dt = \lim_{b \to \infty} \int_0^b (0.7)^t \, dt$$

$$= \lim_{b \to \infty} \int_0^b e^{(\ln 0.7)t} \, dt$$

$$= \lim_{b \to \infty} \left[\frac{1}{\ln 0.7} e^{(\ln 0.7)t} \Big|_0^b \right]$$

$$= \lim_{b \to \infty} \left[\frac{1}{\ln 0.7} (e^{(\ln 0.7)b} - e^0) \right]$$

Now $e^0 = 1$, and because $\ln 0.7 < 0$ ($\ln 0.7 \approx -0.356675$), as $b \to \infty$, $e^{(\ln 0.7)b} \to 0$:

$$= \left(\frac{1}{\ln 0.7} \right)(0 - 1) = -\frac{1}{\ln 0.7}$$

$$\approx \frac{-1}{-0.356675}$$

$$\approx 2.8037$$

Remember to multiply by $1,000,000 to get the final answer. The total income generated in the local community by this company's monthly payroll is about $2.8 million.

14-3 EXERCISES

I

In Exercises 1 through 8, find the area of the given region or state "no finite area."

1. (*See Example 1*) The region under the curve $y = \dfrac{1}{x^3}$, above the x-axis, and to the right of the line $x = 1$.

2. The region under the curve $y = \dfrac{1}{\sqrt{x}}$, above the x-axis, and to the right of the line $x = 4$.

3. The region under the curve $y = e^{-x}$, above the x-axis, and to the right of the line $x = -2$.

4. The region under the curve $y = \dfrac{1}{x}$, above the x-axis, and to the right of the line $x = 100$.

5. The region under the curve $y = e^{2x}$, above the x-axis, and to the *left* of the line $x = 0$.

6. The region under the curve $y = \dfrac{1}{x^4}$, above the x-axis, and to the left of the line $x = -2$.

7. (*See Example 5*) The region under the curve e^{-x} and above the x-axis. (The region is unbounded on the left and on the right.)

8. The region under the curve $y = \dfrac{|x|}{x^2 + 1}$ and above the x-axis.

II

Compute the integrals in Exercises 9 through 22 or state that they are divergent. Give a geometric interpretation if possible.

9. (*See Example 2*)

$$\int_4^\infty e^{-x}\,dx$$

10. $\int_1^\infty e^x\,dx$

11. $\int_1^\infty \frac{1}{x^4}\,dx$

12. $\int_0^\infty \frac{1}{(x+2)^2}\,dx$

13. (*See Example 4*)

$$\int_{-\infty}^0 e^{4x}\,dx$$

14. $\int_{-\infty}^{-1} \frac{1}{x^2}\,dx$

15. (*See Example 3*)

$$\int_4^\infty \frac{1}{\sqrt{x}}\,dx$$

16. $\int_{-\infty}^{-4} \frac{1}{\sqrt{-x}}\,dx$

III

17. $\int_{-\infty}^{-1} \frac{1}{x}\,dx$

18. $\int_2^\infty \frac{2x}{(1+x^2)^2}\,dx$

19. $\int_0^\infty x^2 e^{-x^3}\,dx$

20. $\int_4^\infty x^{-3/2}\,dx$

21. $\int_{-\infty}^\infty x^{-4/3}\,dx$

22. $\int_{-\infty}^\infty \frac{2x}{(1+x^2)^3}\,dx$

23. (*See Example 6*) If customers arrive at a service facility at the rate of ten per hour, then the probability that there will be more than five minutes between successive customers is given by the improper integral

$$\int_{1/12}^\infty 10e^{-10t}\,dt$$

What is this probability?

24. A certain brand of refrigerator claims that its product lasts an average of ten years. Based on this claim, the probability that one of their refrigerators will last at least five years is given by

$$\frac{1}{10}\int_5^\infty e^{-t/10}\,dt$$

What is this probability?

25. The production of an oil well t years after it began production is given by $P(t) = 3e^{-t/6}$. What is the total production of this well?

26. The revenue produced from sales of a certain product t months after it was introduced is $R(t) = 10e^{-2t}$. What is the total revenue produced by this product?

27. (*See Example 7*) Suppose that a utility company gives its customers in a certain state rebates totaling $2 million and that 90% of any money earned in the state is spent in the state. How much money will be spent in the state as a result of these rebates?

14-4 INTEGRATION USING TABLES

Certain integrals occur frequently because they involve combinations of linear factors, quadratic factors, and square roots. These functions are commonly used to model real-world situations, and because integrals of this type occur so often, there are tables that contain their antiderivatives. We have included a rather limited table of such integrals to give you some practice in manipulating formulas. This table is printed inside the back cover. There are tables that are quite extensive; for instance, the 12th edition of the C.R.C. Standard Mathematical

Tables contains over 29 pages of integral formulas. The purpose here is to give you some practice in recognizing the correct formula to use and to demonstrate how to modify your particular integral so that you can use one of the integrals in the table. To use the table, search through the integrals on the left until you find an integrand that has the same *form* as yours; then evaluate the integral using the formula on the right.

CAUTION   Notice that the table, as is customary in such tables, does not include the additive constant term; you must remember to include it in your answer.

EXAMPLE 1   *(Compare Exercise 5)*

Evaluate the integral $\int \dfrac{x}{(3x + 2)^2}\, dx$, using the table inside the back cover.

SOLUTION   Looking through the integrals in the table, we find that integral 16 is the one we want. That integral is $\int \dfrac{x}{(ax + b)^2}\, dx$. Setting $a = 3$ and $b = 2$ gives our integral. The formula in the table is

$$\int \frac{x}{(ax + b)^2}\, dx = \frac{b}{a^2(ax + b)} + \frac{1}{a^2} \ln|ax + b|$$

Substituting $a = 3$ and $b = 2$ and remembering that the table does not include the additive constant, we get

$$\int \frac{x}{(3x + 2)^2}\, dx = \frac{2}{9(3x + 2)} + \frac{1}{9} \ln|3x + 2| + C$$

Sometimes, you must modify your integral somewhat to get it in the form that appears in the table.

EXAMPLE 2   *(Compare Exercise 3)*

Find $\int \dfrac{6x}{(3x + 2)^2}\, dx$.

SOLUTION   You will not find an integral of the form $\int \dfrac{cx}{(ax + b)^2}\, dx$. You must remember that

$$\int \frac{6x}{(3x + 2)^2}\, dx = 6 \int \frac{x}{(3x + 2)^2}\, dx$$

Now you can apply formula 16, as you did in Example 1:

$$\int \frac{6x}{(3x + 2)^2}\, dx = 6 \int \frac{x}{(3x + 2)^2}\, dx$$

$$= 6 \left[\frac{2}{9(3x + 2)} + \frac{1}{9} \ln|3x + 2| \right] + C$$

Sometimes, the table combines two formulas into one, especially when the only difference is a sign difference.

EXAMPLE 3   *(Compare Exercise 1)*

Find $\int \sqrt{x^2 - 9}\, dx$.

SOLUTION   This integral is a special case of integral 1, which is $\int \sqrt{x^2 \pm a^2}\, dx$. Here, we will let $a^2 = 9$ so that $a = 3$ and use the $-$ sign in the formula. The table gives

$$\int \sqrt{x^2 \pm a^2}\, dx = \frac{x}{2}\sqrt{x^2 \pm a^2} \pm \frac{a^2}{2} \ln\left|x + \sqrt{x^2 \pm a^2}\right|$$

With $a = 3$ and using $-$ in the four places where the formula has $\pm$, we have

$$\int \sqrt{x^2 - 9}\, dx = \frac{x}{2}\sqrt{x^2 - 9} - \frac{9}{2} \ln\left|x + \sqrt{x^2 - 9}\right| + C$$

Again, we show how you must sometimes do some arithmetic to modify your integral before you can apply the formula.

EXAMPLE 4   *(Compare Exercise 7)*

Find $\displaystyle\int \frac{1}{\sqrt{4x^2 + 25}}\, dx$.

SOLUTION   The closest integral in the table is number 2,

$$\int \frac{1}{\sqrt{x^2 \pm a^2}}\, dx$$

and we can choose the $+$ case.

The arithmetic here is a bit more complicated than it was in Example 2, but the idea is to write the integral so that the coefficient of x^2 is 1:

$$\sqrt{4x^2 + 25} = \sqrt{4\left(x^2 + \frac{25}{4}\right)} = \sqrt{4}\sqrt{x^2 + \frac{25}{4}}$$

$$= 2\sqrt{x^2 + \frac{25}{4}}$$

Therefore

$$\int \frac{1}{\sqrt{4x^2 + 25}}\, dx = \int \frac{1}{2\sqrt{x^2 + \frac{25}{4}}}\, dx$$

$$= \frac{1}{2}\int \frac{1}{\sqrt{x^2 + \frac{25}{4}}}\, dx$$

We have now manipulated our integral so that formula 2 can be used with $a^2 = \frac{25}{4}$. The table gives, choosing the $+$ sign,

$$\int \frac{1}{\sqrt{x^2 + a^2}}\, dx = \ln|x + \sqrt{x^2 + a^2}|$$

so

$$\int \frac{1}{\sqrt{4x^2 + 25}}\, dx = \frac{1}{2} \int \frac{1}{\sqrt{x^2 + \dfrac{25}{4}}}\, dx$$

$$= \frac{1}{2} \ln\left| x + \sqrt{x^2 + \frac{25}{4}} \right| + C$$

You should also notice the use of a^2 in the table. This is to indicate to you that the number appearing in that place in your particular integral must be positive. A constant that is not squared in the table may be positive or negative.

EXAMPLE 5 *(Compare Exercise 9)*

Find $\displaystyle\int \frac{1}{x(2x - 5)}\, dx$.

SOLUTION This integral exactly matches the form of integral 17,

$$\int \frac{1}{x(ax + b)}\, dx$$

with $a = 2$ and $b = -5$. Using $a = 2$ and $b = -5$ in

$$\int \frac{1}{x(ax + b)}\, dx = \frac{1}{b} \ln\left| \frac{x}{ax + b} \right| + C$$

gives

$$\int \frac{1}{x(2x - 5)}\, dx = \frac{-1}{5} \ln\left| \frac{x}{2x - 5} \right| + C$$

The following example illustrates that you might have to use algebra to rearrange the given integral into a form that is found in the table.

EXAMPLE 6   *(Compare Exercise 17)*

Evaluate $\int \dfrac{1}{4u^3 + 4u^2 + u}\, du$.

SOLUTION   The table does not contain any integral of this type. However, let us factor the denominator—all the denominators of the integrals in the table are in factored form.

$$\int \frac{1}{4u^3 + 4u^2 + u}\, du = \int \frac{1}{u(4u^2 + 4u + 1)}\, du$$

$$= \int \frac{1}{u(2u + 1)^2}\, du$$

We can now recognize this as the same form as integral 18,

$$\int \frac{1}{x(ax + b)^2}\, dx$$

Letting $a = 2$ and $b = 1$ and using the variable u in place of x, we can use formula 18,

$$\int \frac{1}{x(ax + b)^2}\, dx = \frac{1}{b(ax + b)} + \frac{1}{b^2} \ln \left| \frac{x}{ax + b} \right| + C$$

to get

$$\int \frac{1}{4u^3 + 4u^2 + u}\, du = \int \frac{1}{u(2u + 1)^2}\, du$$

$$= \frac{1}{2u + 1} + \ln \left| \frac{u}{2u + 1} \right| + C$$

As our final example, we point out that you must sometimes do a substitution to manipulate your integral into a form you can find in the table.

EXAMPLE 7   *(Compare Exercise 20)*

Find $\int \dfrac{e^x}{e^{2x} - 9}\, dx$.

SOLUTION $e^{2x} = (e^x)^2$ so $e^{2x} - 9 = (e^x)^2 - 9$. This denominator is of the form "something-squared-minus-something-squared," so we hope to use integral 10.

$$\int \frac{1}{x^2 - a^2}\, dx$$

Substitute $u = e^x$. Then $e^{2x} - 9 = (e^x)^2 - 9$ becomes $u^2 - 9$; Also, $u = e^x$ means that $du = e^x \, dx$. With these substitutions,

$$\int \frac{e^x}{e^{2x} - 9} \, dx = \int \frac{1}{u^2 - 9} \, du$$

Formula 10,

$$\int \frac{1}{x^2 - a^2} \, dx = \frac{1}{2a} \ln \left| \frac{x - a}{x + a} \right| + C$$

becomes, with $a^2 = 9$ so that $a = 3$ and u playing the role of x,

$$\int \frac{1}{u^2 - 9} \, du = \frac{1}{6} \ln \left| \frac{u - 3}{u + 3} \right| + C$$

Remember to back-substitute $u = e^x$ for the final answer:

$$\int \frac{e^x}{e^{2x} - 9} \, dx = \frac{1}{6} \ln \left| \frac{e^x - 3}{e^x + 3} \right| + C$$

14-4 EXERCISES

I

1. (*See Example 3*)
$\int \dfrac{1}{x^2 - 25} \, dx$

2. $\int \dfrac{x}{(x - 4)^2} \, dx$

3. (*See Example 2*)
$\int \dfrac{5}{36 - x^2} \, dx$

4. $\int \sqrt{x^2 + 100} \, dx$

5. (*See Example 1*)
$\int \dfrac{x}{(3x - 2)^2} \, dx$

6. $\int \dfrac{3}{x(x - 6)} \, dx$

7. (*See Example 4*)
$\int \sqrt{4x^2 + 100} \, dx$

8. $\int \dfrac{1}{3x^2 - 48} \, dx$

9. (*See Example 5*)
$\int \dfrac{6}{x(8 - 2x)} \, dx$

10. $\int \dfrac{5x}{12 - 3x} \, dx$

II

11. $\int \dfrac{6}{\sqrt{100 + 25x^2}} \, dx$

12. $\int \dfrac{\sqrt{3 + x^2}}{x} \, dx$

13. $\int \sqrt{(x + 2)^2 + 25} \, dx$

14. $\int \dfrac{1}{(x + 2)^2 - 9} \, dx$

15. $\int \sqrt{(2x + 1)^2 + 100} \, dx$

16. $\int \dfrac{e^{2x}}{4e^x + 5} \, dx$

17. (*See Example 6*)
$\int \dfrac{1}{x^2 + 3x} \, dx$

18. $\int \dfrac{x}{x^2 + 6x + 9} \, dx$

19. $\int \dfrac{3x}{x^2 - 4x + 4} \, dx$

20. (*See Example 7*)
$\int \dfrac{e^x}{e^x \sqrt{e^{2x} + 9}} \, dx$

III

21. $\displaystyle\int_0^4 \sqrt{x^2 + 9}\, dx$ **22.** $\displaystyle\int_3^6 \frac{dx}{\sqrt{4x^2 - 25}}$

23. What is the area under the curve

$$y = \frac{1}{x^2\sqrt{x^2 - 1}}$$

from $x = 2$ to $x = 4$?

24. What is the area under the curve

$$y = \frac{\sqrt{25 + 9x^2}}{4x}$$

from $x = 1$ to $x = 4$?

25. The marginal cost of producing x car stereos is given by

$$MC(x) = \frac{6x}{2x + 5}$$

How much do costs increase if the production level goes from $x = 10$ to $x = 20$?

26. A company purchased raw materials at the rate of $4\sqrt{x^2 + 25}$ tons on the xth day of the business month. What is the total they purchased during the first ten days of the business month?

14–5 NUMERICAL APPROXIMATIONS OF DEFINITE INTEGRALS

- *Introduction*
- *The Trapezoidal Rule*
- *Simpson's Rule*

INTRODUCTION

Sometimes you may encounter a definite integral in some applied problem, but you cannot find an antiderivative to help you compute the definite integral. For example, the function $f(x) = e^{-x^2}$ occurs in probability theory, but the number $\int_0^1 e^{-x^2} dx$ cannot be computed exactly, and people must rely on numerical techniques to approximate this number. This section will introduce you to two such techniques: the trapezoidal rule and Simpson's rule.

THE TRAPEZOIDAL RULE

In Section 13–6 we saw that we could use Riemann sums to approximate a definite integral, and the motivation for considering Riemann sums came from approximating a given region by the union of rectangles. The trapezoidal rule is so named because it is motivated by approximating a given region by the union of trapezoids. We will give you a specific example, followed by the general formula, and then another example.

EXAMPLE 1 *(Compare Exercise 1)*

Find a numerical approximation for ln 3.

SOLUTION We have seen that

$$\ln 3 = \int_1^3 \frac{1}{x}\, dx$$

FIGURE 14–5

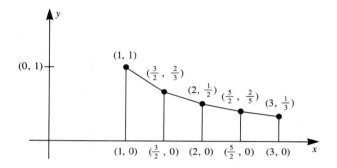

so our problem is to approximate this definite integral. We start by dividing the interval $[1, 3]$ into four equal subintervals. Each subinterval must have one fourth of the length of the entire interval; this length is $\frac{1}{4}(3 - 1) = \frac{1}{2}$. Therefore the four intervals are $[1, \frac{3}{2}]$, $[\frac{3}{2}, 2]$, $[2, \frac{5}{2}]$, and $[\frac{5}{2}, 3]$. Over each subinterval we construct a trapezoid so that the two sides of each trapezoid are the heights of the function at the endpoints of the interval. The top of the trapezoid is then the straight line joining these heights. See Figure 14–5.

The area of the trapezoid as shown in Figure 14–6 is

$$(\text{length of base}) \cdot (\text{average height}) = b \cdot \left(\frac{h_1 + h_2}{2} \right)$$

FIGURE 14–6

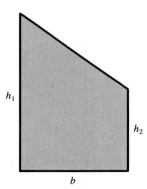

The sum of the areas of our four trapezoids is

$$\frac{1}{2}\left(\frac{f(1) + f(1.5)}{2}\right) + \frac{1}{2}\left(\frac{f(1.5) + f(2)}{2}\right) + \frac{1}{2}\left(\frac{f(2) + f(2.5)}{2}\right) + \frac{1}{2}\left(\frac{f(2.5) + f(3)}{2}\right)$$

$$= \frac{1}{2}\left(\frac{f(1)}{2} + \frac{f(1.5)}{2} + \frac{f(1.5)}{2} + \frac{f(2)}{2} + \frac{f(2)}{2} + \frac{f(2.5)}{2} + \frac{f(2.5)}{2} + \frac{f(3)}{2}\right)$$

$$= \frac{1}{2}\left(\frac{f(1)}{2} + f(1.5) + f(2) + f(2.5) + \frac{f(3)}{2}\right)$$

$$= \frac{1}{2}\left(\frac{1}{2} + \frac{2}{3} + \frac{1}{2} + \frac{2}{5} + \frac{1}{6}\right)$$

$$\approx 1.1167$$

We have $\ln 3 \approx 1.1167$. (In fact $\ln 3 = 1.0986.\ .\ .$, so there is an error of about 0.018 in this approximation. You will be asked in Exercise 10 to approximate $\ln 3$ using a larger value of n.)

The development of the general formula follows along the same lines that we used in Example 1. Note that, in general, when we subdivide $[a, b]$ into n equal subintervals, each of length $\frac{b-a}{n}$, then the endpoints of these subintervals are, reading from a to b,

$$x_0 = a,$$

$$x_1 = a + \frac{b-a}{n},$$

$$x_2 = x_1 + \frac{(b-a)}{n} = a + 2 \cdot \frac{b-a}{n},$$

$$x_3 = a + 3 \cdot \frac{b-a}{n}, \qquad \cdots,$$

$$x_k = a + k\frac{b-a}{n}, \qquad \cdots,$$

$$x_n = b$$

With this notation we can state the **trapezoidal rule.**

The Trapezoidal Rule	$\displaystyle\int_a^b f(x)\,dx \approx \frac{b-a}{n}\left(\frac{f(a)}{2} + f(x_1) + \ldots + f(x_{n-1}) + \frac{f(b)}{2}\right)$

The larger the value of n, the better the approximation.

We will leave to more advanced texts the discussion of how to estimate the size of the difference between the number $\int_a^b f(x)dx$ and the approximation to this number given by the trapezoidal rule.

EXAMPLE 2 *(Compare Exercise 3)*

Use the trapezoidal rule with $n = 5$ to approximate $\int_0^1 \sqrt{1 - x^2} \, dx$.

SOLUTION With $n = 5$ we have

$$\frac{b - a}{n} = \frac{1}{5} = 0.2$$

so the endpoints of the subintervals are

$$x_1 = a = 0, \qquad x_1 = 0.2, \qquad x_2 = 0.4, \qquad x_3 = 0.6,$$
$$x_4 = 0.8 \qquad \text{and} \qquad x_5 = b = 1$$

$f(0) = 1$, $f(0.2) = \sqrt{1 - 0.04} = \sqrt{0.96}$, $f(0.4) = \sqrt{0.84}$, $f(0.6) = \sqrt{0.64}$, $f(0.8) = \sqrt{0.36}$ and $f(1) = 0$. Thus

$$\int_0^1 \sqrt{1 - x^2} \, dx \approx 0.2\left(\frac{1}{2} + \sqrt{0.96} + \sqrt{0.84} + \sqrt{0.64} + \sqrt{0.36} + 0\right)$$

$$\approx 0.7593$$

In fact

$$\int_0^1 \sqrt{1 - x^2} \, dx = \frac{\pi}{4} \approx 0.7854$$

SIMPSON'S RULE

Riemann sums approximate $\int_a^b f(x)dx$ by using geometric figures whose "tops" are horizontal lines. The trapezoidal rule uses figures whose "tops" are straight lines between points on the graph of f. **Simpson's rule** uses geometric figures whose "tops" are pieces of parabolas. The procedure of subdividing $[a, b]$ into n equal subdivisions is the same as in the trapezoidal rule, so we again have the formula

$$x_k = a + k \cdot \frac{b - a}{n}$$

One further requirement for using Simpson's rule is that n *must be even*.

Simpson's Rule If n is an *even* counting number, then

$$\int_a^b f(x)dx \approx \frac{b - a}{3n}(f(a) + 4f(x_1) + 2f(x_2) + 4f(x_3) + 2f(x_4)$$
$$+ \ldots + 4f(x_{n - 1}) + f(b))$$

The larger the value of n, the better the approximation.

Note that the pattern of the coefficients is 1, 4, 2, 4, 2, 4, . . . , 2, 4, 1. If k is odd, then $f(x_k)$ is multiplied by 4. If k is even, $2 \leq k \leq n - 2$, then $f(x_k)$ is multiplied by 2; $f(a)$ and $f(b)$ are multiplied by 1.

EXAMPLE 3   *(Compare Exercise 11)*

Use $n = 4$ and approximate ln 3 using Simpson's rule. (Compare this computation with Example 1.)

SOLUTION

As in Example 1, the integral is again $\int_1^3 \frac{1}{x} \, dx$. We have

$$\frac{b - a}{n} = \frac{2}{4} = \frac{1}{2}$$

so the points are $x_0 = a = 1$, $x_1 = \frac{3}{2}$, $x_2 = 2$, $x_3 = \frac{5}{2}$, and $x_4 = b = 3$. The approximation is

$$\frac{2}{3 \cdot 4}\left(1 + 4 \cdot \frac{2}{3} + 2 \cdot \frac{1}{2} + 4 \cdot \frac{2}{5} + \frac{1}{3}\right) = 1.1000. \ . \ .$$

(Compare this approximation to the approximation using the trapezoidal rule with $n = 4$ from Example 1.)

EXAMPLE 4   *(Compare Exercise 9)*

Use $n = 5$ to approximate $\int_0^1 \sqrt{1 - x^2} \, dx$ with Simpson's rule. (Compare with Example 2.)

SOLUTION   This cannot be done; 5 is an odd integer. Simpson's rule requires an *even* integer.

EXAMPLE 5   *(Compare Exercise 13)*

Use Simpson's rule with $n = 8$ to approximate

$$\int_1^4 \frac{1}{1 + x^2} \, dx$$

SOLUTION   Here, $a = 1$, $b = 4$, and $n = 8$, so $\frac{b - a}{n} = \frac{3}{8}$. Therefore

$$x_0 = a = 1, \qquad x_1 = 1 + \frac{3}{8} = \frac{11}{8}, \qquad x_2 = \frac{14}{8},$$

$$x_3 = \frac{17}{8}, \qquad x_4 = \frac{20}{8}, \qquad x_5 = \frac{23}{8}, \qquad x_6 = \frac{26}{8},$$

$$x_7 = \frac{29}{8}, \qquad x_8 = \frac{32}{8} = 4 = b$$

Applying Simpson's rule, we have

$$\int_1^4 \frac{1}{1+x^2}\,dx \approx \frac{1}{3}\cdot\frac{3}{8}\left(\frac{1}{1+1^2} + 4\cdot\frac{1}{1+(11/8)^2} + 2\cdot\frac{1}{1+(14/8)^2}\right.$$

$$+ 4\cdot\frac{1}{1+(17/8)^2} + 2\cdot\frac{1}{1+(20/8)^2} + 4\cdot\frac{1}{1+(23/8)^2}$$

$$\left.+ 2\cdot\frac{1}{1+(26/8)^2} + 4\cdot\frac{1}{1+(29/8)^2} + \frac{1}{1+(4)^2}\right) \approx 0.54044$$

∎

14-5 EXERCISES

Use the trapezoidal rule with the indicated value of n to approximate the given definite integral in Exercises 1 through 8.

1. (*See Example 1*)

$$\int_1^3 \frac{1}{x}\,dx; n = 8$$

2. $\int_2^6 \frac{1}{x}\,dx; n = 8$

3. (*See Example 2*)

$$\int_0^1 \sqrt{1-x^2}\,dx; n = 8$$

4. $\int_0^1 \frac{1}{1+x^2}\,dx; n = 6$

5. $\int_0^2 \sqrt{x^3+1}\,dx; n = 6$

6. $\int_{-1}^4 \sqrt{x^2+1}\,dx; n = 5$

7. $\int_0^1 e^{-x^2}dx; n = 5$

8. $\int_1^3 \ln(x^2+1)dx; n = 5$

9. (*See Example 4*) For which of Exercises 1 through 8 could you also use Simpson's rule with the same value of n?

Use Simpson's rule with the given value of n to approximate the definite integrals in Exercises 10 through 18.

10. $\int_1^3 \frac{1}{x}\,dx; n = 6$

11. (*See Example 3*)

$$\int_2^6 \frac{1}{x}\,dx; n = 6$$

12. $\int_0^1 \frac{4}{1+x^2}\,dx; n = 6$

13. (*See Example 5*)

$$\int_0^1 \frac{4}{1+x^2}\,dx; n = 8$$

14. $\int_{-1}^1 2\sqrt{1-x^2}\,dx; n = 4$

15. $\int_{-1}^1 2\sqrt{1-x^2}\,dx; n = 6$

16. $\int_{-1}^1 2\sqrt{1-x^2}\,dx; n = 8$

17. $\int_0^1 e^{-x^2}dx; n = 4$

18. $\int_1^4 \ln(x^2+1)dx; n = 4$

19. (a) Estimate $\int_{-1}^3 (x^2-2x+5)dx$ using Simpson's rule with $n = 2$.

(b) Estimate $\int_{-1}^3 (x^2-2x+5)dx$ using Simpson's rule with $n = 4$.

(c) Evaluate $\int_{-1}^3 (x^2-2x+5)dx$ using antiderivatives.

20. (a) Estimate $\int_{-2}^4 (x^3+x)dx$ using Simpson's rule with $n = 2$.

(b) Estimate $\int_{-2}^4 (x^3+x)dx$ using Simpson's rule with $n = 4$.

(c) Evaluate $\int_{-2}^4 (x^3+x)dx$ using antiderivatives.

21. Find a calculus book (such as one for engineering or the physical sciences) that gives the error bound for Simpson's rule by going to the library or borrowing a friend's who is taking a more theoretical course. Look up the section on Simpson's rule and discuss the results of Exercises 19 and 20.

22. Use Simpson's rule to approximate ln 4 with:
   (a) $n = 2$ **(b)** $n = 4$ **(c)** $n = 6$

23. Use Simpson's rule to approximate ln 5 with:
   (a) $n = 2$ **(b)** $n = 4$ **(c)** $n = 6$

24. Sketch the graph of $y = \sqrt{1 - x^2}$. Remembering that the area of a circle of radius r is πr^2, show geometrically why

$$\int_0^1 \sqrt{1 - x^2}\, dx = \frac{\pi}{4}$$

IMPORTANT TERMS

14-1

Integration by Substitution

Change of the Limits of Integration for Definite Integrals

14-2

Integration by Parts

14-3

Unbounded Interval

Improper Integral

Convergent Integral

Divergent Integral

Normal Curve

14-4

Table of Integrals

14-5

Trapezoidal Rule

Simpson's Rule

REVIEW EXERCISES

Compute the integrals in Exercises 1 through 12 by using substitution, integration by parts, or both.

1. $\displaystyle\int x^2 e^{x^3}\, dx$

2. $\displaystyle\int \sqrt{3x + 4}\, dx$

3. $\displaystyle\int \frac{1}{5x + 8}\, dx$

4. $\displaystyle\int \frac{x}{e^x}\, dx$

5. $\displaystyle\int \frac{1}{x \ln x}\, dx$

6. $\displaystyle\int 2x^3 e^{x^2}\, dx$

7. $\displaystyle\int x \ln(3x)\, dx$

8. $\displaystyle\int x e^{(x + 1)}\, dx$

9. $\displaystyle\int x e^{(x^2 + 1)}\, dx$

10. $\displaystyle\int \sqrt{x} \ln x\, dx$

11. $\displaystyle\int x \ln x^2\, dx$

12. $\displaystyle\int x^2 \sqrt{x + 1}\, dx$

Evaluate each of the integrals in Exercises 13 through 16 or show that the integral is divergent.

13. $\displaystyle\int_1^\infty \frac{x}{1 + x^2}\, dx$

14. $\displaystyle\int_{-\infty}^{-1} \frac{1}{x^2}\, dx$

15. $\displaystyle\int_1^\infty \frac{1 + e^x}{e^{2x}}\, dx$

16. $\displaystyle\int_{-\infty}^\infty \frac{x^3}{(1 + x^4)^2}\, dx$

You may use the table of integrals to help you find the integrals in Exercises 17 through 21. You may also need to use substitution.

17. $\displaystyle\int \frac{1}{4x^2 - 100}\, dx$

18. $\displaystyle\int \frac{e^x}{e^{2x} - 4}\, dx$

19. $\displaystyle\int \frac{1}{\sqrt{x^2 + 2x + 10}}\, dx$
   (*Hint:* $x^2 + 2x + 10 = (x + 1)^2 + 9$)

20. $\displaystyle\int \frac{e^{2x}}{e^x + 5}\, dx$

21. $\displaystyle\int \frac{1}{x^2 + 6x}\, dx$

22. Use the trapezoidal rule to approximate
$$\int_1^4 \sqrt{x^2 - 1}\, dx \text{ with: (a) } n = 3; \text{ (b) } n = 6.$$

23. Use Simpson's rule to approximate $\displaystyle\int_0^1 e^{x^2} dx$ with $n = 4$.

24. **(a)** Use both the trapezoidal rule and Simpson's rule with $n = 6$ to approximate $\displaystyle\int_0^2 \sqrt{4 - x^2}\, dx$.

   (b) Use geometry to show $\displaystyle\int_0^2 \sqrt{4 - x^2}\, dx = \pi$, and then compare your answers from part (a) to π.

15

Calculus of Functions of Several Variables

15–1 FUNCTIONS OF SEVERAL VARIABLES

- *Introduction*
- *Applications*
- *Graphs of Functions of Two Variables*

INTRODUCTION

TO THIS POINT, THE functions that we have studied have all been functions of one variable. The function defined by $f(x) = 3x^2 + 2x - 4$, for example, is a function of the single variable x. We did see several applications, however, in which the function that we were analyzing really depended on more than one variable. For example, in the formula

$$\text{Revenue} = (\text{number of units sold}) \cdot (\text{price per unit})$$
$$R = x \cdot p$$

R depends on both x and p.

When discussing revenue, however, we generally assumed that there was a cost-demand curve that allowed us to solve for one of x or p in terms of the other. We could then express R as a function of one variable. In a perfectly competitive market, however, one firm's output will not affect the market price. Nevertheless, this market price might vary for other reasons. For that firm, x and p are independent variables.

Similarly, a company might launch an advertising campaign to raise the public's awareness of a new product. The company might want to measure the public's awareness, not just as a function of total amount spent on advertising, but also as a function of the expenditures on newspaper ads, billboards, radio, and television commercials. Consumer awareness would then be a function of several variables. To handle problems like these, we need to extend our mathematical vocabulary to include **functions of more than one variable.**

The general idea is the same; the only thing we are changing is the allowable input. For a function of two variables the input will be ordered pairs. See Figure 15–1.

We write the rule for evaluating $f(x, y)$ in a manner similar to that with one variable. For example, we can write

$$f(x, y) = 3x^2y + 4xy + y^3$$

Corresponding to each value of x and y, there will be a unique value of $f(x, y)$. For example, when $x = 1$ and $y = 2$, we get

$$f(1, 2) = 3(1)^2(2) + 4(1)(2) + (2)^3 = 22$$

Just as we wrote $y = f(x)$, we write $z = f(x, y)$. Thus we say that when $(x, y) = (1, 2)$, the value of z is 22. Here, x and y are two independent variables, and z is a function of these two variables.

FIGURE 15-1

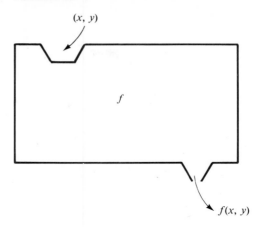

EXAMPLE 1 *(Compare Exercise 1)*

$$z = f(x, y) = 3x^2y + 4xy + y^3$$

(a) What is $f(-1, 3)$?
(b) What is z when $x = 2$ and $y = -1$?

SOLUTION

(a) $f(-1, 3) = 3(-1)^2(3) + 4(-1)(3) + (3)^3 = 24$.
(b) $f(2, -1) = 3(2)^2(-1) + 4(2)(-1) + (-1)^3 = -21$, so the value of z is -21 when $x = 2$ and $y = -1$.

Functions of three or more variables are handled in a similar manner. For example,

$$f(x, y, z) = 4xy - 2x^2z$$

is a function of the three variables, x, y, and z. If $x = 1$, $y = -2$, and $z = 3$, then

$$f(1, -2, 3) = 4(1)(-2) - 2(1)^2(3) = -8 - 6 = -14$$

EXAMPLE 2 *(Compare Exercise 3)*

If $w = f(x, y, z) = 2y - xz$:

(a) What is $f(-1, 3, 5)$?
(b) What is the value of w when $x = -2$, $y = 6$, and $z = 4$?

SOLUTION

(a) $f(-1, 3, 5) = 2 \cdot 3 - (-1)(5) = 6 + 5 = 11$.
(b) $f(-2, 6, 4) = 2 \cdot 6 - (-2)(4) = 12 + 8 = 20$. So $w = 20$ if $x = -2$, $y = 6$, and $z = 4$.

APPLICATIONS

Different products may use some of the same resources in their manufacture. For instance, both bread and doughnuts require flour. If a company manufactures both bread and doughnuts and decides to increase its production of bread, that increase in the demand for flour might allow the company's supplier of flour to raise the price of the flour, thereby raising the cost of manufacturing doughnuts. The costs of manufacturing these two products are interrelated.

EXAMPLE 3   *(Compare Exercise 13)*

The cost, in hundreds of dollars, to the company for manufacturing x thousand loaves of bread and y thousand dozen doughnuts is given by $C(x, y) = 6x + 7y + xy$. How much does it cost the company to manufacture 40,000 loaves of bread and 2000 dozen doughnuts?

SOLUTION   Here, $x = 40$ and $y = 2$, so

$$C(40, 2) = 6 \cdot 40 + 7 \cdot 2 + 40 \cdot 2$$
$$= 334$$

The company's manufacturing costs are $33,400.

The amount of a product that a company can manufacture depends upon how much labor and how much capital are devoted to the manufacture of this particular product. (Capital in this context includes buildings, machinery, and so on.) Economists can measure these expenditures in meaningful units, but for our purposes we will ignore the units and let x be the amount of labor used and y be the amount of capital. Often, the number of units produced is described by a function $f(x, y)$ of the type

$$f(x, y) = Cx^a y^{1-a}$$

where C and a are appropriate constants. This frequently used function is called a **Cobb-Douglas production function.**

EXAMPLE 4   *(Compare Exercise 17)*

Suppose that the manufacturing process of a company is described by the function

$$f(x, y) = 9x^{2/3}y^{1/3}$$

What is the number of units produced when 64 units of labor are used and 27 units of capital are invested?

SOLUTION   We get

$$f(64, 27) = 9(64)^{2/3}(27)^{1/3}$$
$$= 9(4)^2(3)$$
$$= 432$$

There will be 432 units produced.

FIGURE 15–2

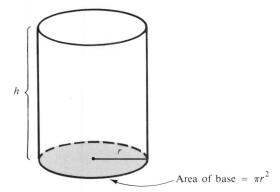

Area of base $= \pi r^2$

Geometric formulas can also be given in terms of several variables. For instance, the volume of a right circular cylinder is given by the area of the base times the height. See Figure 15–2.

If r is the radius of the base, then the area of the base is πr^2. If we let h be the height of the cylinder, then the volume V can be interpreted as a function of the two variables r and h:

$$V(r, h) = \pi r^2 h$$

EXAMPLE 5

Find the volume of a cylinder whose base has a radius 2 inches and whose height is 3 inches.

SOLUTION   When $r = 2$ and $h = 3$, the value of V is

$$V(2, 3) = \pi(2)^2 3 = 12\pi$$

The volume is 12π cubic inches.

GRAPHS OF FUNCTIONS OF TWO VARIABLES

We obtained insight into the behavior of a function of a single variable by looking at its graph, the set of points $(x, f(x))$. We called this graph the curve given by $y = f(x)$. A function of two variables has a graph in **three-dimensional space;** this graph is usually called a **surface.** We shall not go into a detailed discussion of graphs of functions of two variables. These graphs involve three dimensions and so are difficult to draw on a piece of two-dimensional paper. Furthermore, the graphs of functions of more than two variables involve more than three dimensions, and so our spatial intuition is of little use in this case. Nevertheless, we would like to have a few pictures available to help give you some insight into the geometric significance of the topics we will be discussing, such as partial rates of change and relative extreme values.

FIGURE 15–3

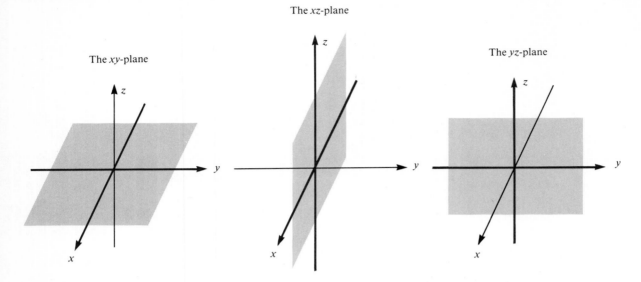

The *xy*-plane

The *xz*-plane

The *yz*-plane

With this aim in mind we introduce the concept of a three-dimensional co-ordinate system and illustrate how the graph of a function like $f(x, y) = x^2 + y^2$ is a surface in three-dimensional space.

A rectangular Cartesian coordinate system of three dimensions can be obtained by starting with a familiar Cartesian plane and putting a third axis through the origin perpendicular to the plane. The three axes, called the *x*-, *y*-, and *z*-axes, are at right angles to one another. Taken in pairs, these axes define planes called the **coordinate planes.** These planes are the *xy*-plane, the *xz*-plane, and the *yz*-plane as is shown in Figure 15–3.

As in the Cartesian plane, we introduce units of measurement along the axes. We can then locate a point, *P,* by knowing three coordinates that give the directed distance from the respective axes. In Figure 15–4, *P* would be described as the point with coordinates $(3, -1, 2)$.

Try to visualize the *yz*-plane as being the same as the plane of this page, and the *x*-axis is coming straight out at you. To locate $(3, -1, 2)$, you start at the origin $(0, 0, 0)$ and come straight out the *x*-axis three units $(x = 3)$, go left for one unit $(y = -1)$, and then go up two units $(z = 2)$.

Now consider the function $z = f(x, y)$, where

$$z = x^2 + y^2$$

The graph of this function is in three-dimensional space and consists of all those points (x, y, z), such that $z = x^2 + y^2$. For example, the point $(3, 4, 25)$ is on this graph. If we hold one variable fixed, we can use what we know about functions of one variable to get some idea of what the graph looks like. For instance, let's look at all points on the graph whose second coordinate is 0. The set of *all*

FIGURE 15–4

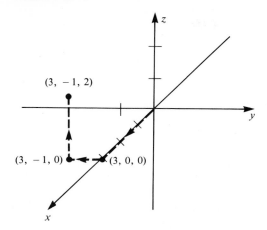

FIGURE 15–5

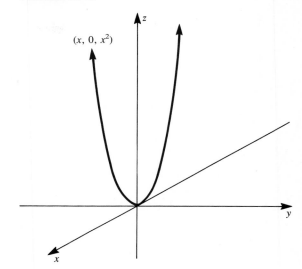

FIGURE 15–6

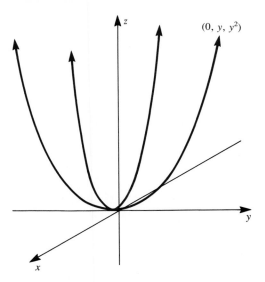

points for which $y = 0$ is the xz-plane, so the points on the graph with $y = 0$ will lie in the xz-plane. Turning now to the equation $z = x^2 + y^2$ and setting $y = 0$, we see that the equation becomes $z = x^2$, the equation of a parabola. The set of points $(x, 0, x^2)$ forms a parabola in the xz-plane. See Figure 15–5.

Next, we consider the points on the graph for which $x = 0$. These points will satisfy the equation $z = y^2$ and will form a parabola in the yz-plane. This is the set of points $(0, y, y^2)$. Figure 15–6 includes both parabolas. Sometimes, it is hard to visualize these graphs.

FIGURE 15–7

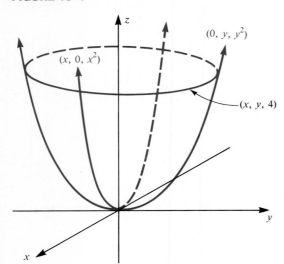

FIGURE 15–8

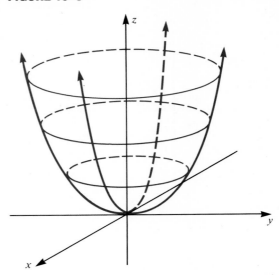

Next, we let z be constant; let us consider all the points on the graph for which $z = 4$. These points will satisfy the equation $4 = x^2 + y^2$, which is an equation of a circle. The set of points on the graph $z = x^2 + y^2$ with $z = 4$ is a circle of radius 2; the circle is four units above the xy-plane. This is the set of points $(x, y, 4)$ with $x^2 + y^2 = 4$. All three curves are drawn in Figure 15–7.

If we look at all points on this surface that are nine units high, then $z = 9$, and we would get a circle of radius 3. All cross sections of the surface parallel to the xy-plane will be circles.

Putting all this together, we find that the graph of $z = x^2 + y^2$ is a **paraboloid,** shown in Figure 15–8. The graph is like a bowl resting on the origin.

All functions of two variables, $z = f(x, y)$, that we shall discuss will have graphs consisting of smooth surfaces in three-dimensional space. In general, we can visualize the graph of such a function in the following manner. Let $(a, b, 0)$ be a point in the xy-plane, and let $f(a, b) = c$. Then $P = (a, b, c)$ is on the graph of $z = f(x, y)$. If $c > 0$, then P is c units above the point $(a, b, 0)$. If $c < 0$, then P is $|c|$ units below the point $(a, b, 0)$. If we plot all such points, we get a surface S, the graph of $f(x, y)$, as in Figure 15–9.

EXAMPLE 6   *(Compare Exercise 7)*

Sketch the graph of $z = x^2 + y^2 + 3$.

SOLUTION   If we let $g(x, y) = x^2 + y^2 + 3$, then $g(x, y) = f(x, y) + 3$, where $f(x, y) = x^2 + y^2$. The surface $z = g(x, y)$ lies three units above the surface $z = f(x, y)$; we obtain the graph of $z = x^2 + y^2 + 3$ by sliding the graph of $z = x^2 + y^2$ up a distance of three units. See Figure 15–10.

FIGURE 15-9

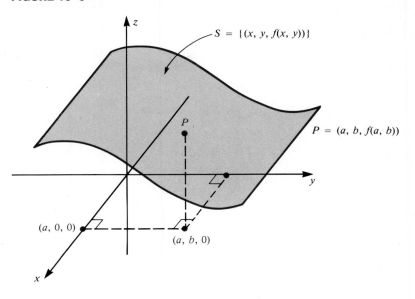

$S = \{(x, y, f(x, y))\}$

P

$P = (a, b, f(a, b))$

$(a, 0, 0)$

$(a, b, 0)$

FIGURE 15-10

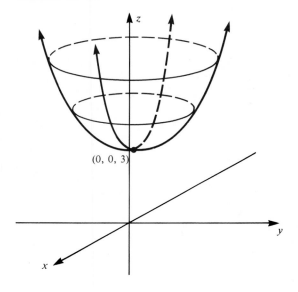

$(0, 0, 3)$

15–1 EXERCISES

I

In Exercises 1 through 6, determine the values of the functions at the given points.

1. (*See Example 1*) $f(x, y) = 4xy + 3$ at the point $(1, 2)$

2. $g(x, y) = 6x + 2y + x^3 + 4$ at $(3, 1)$

3. (*See Example 2*) $g(x, y, z) = x^2y + 4xz + y^3$ at $(-1, 2, 1)$

4. $f(x, y, z) = 2xyz - x^3 + 3y^2 + 4$ at $(0, 1, 2)$

5. $f(x, y) = 4ye^{x+2}$ at $(1, 2)$

6. $g(x, y) = x^2 \ln y - 4$ at $(3, 1)$

II

7. (*See Example 6*) Sketch the graph of $z = x^2 + y^2 - 2$.

8. Sketch the graph of $z = -x^2 - y^2 + 1$.

9. Sketch the locations of the following points in a coordinate system in three-dimensional space:

$$L = (1, 0, 0),$$
$$Q = (0, 3, 1),$$
$$M = (0, 0, 4),$$
$$R = (1, 2, 4),$$
$$N = (0, 2, 0),$$
$$S = (2, -1, 3),$$
$$P = (1, 2, 0).$$

10. Give an equation describing the set of all points in three-dimensional space that are:
    (a) in the yz-plane.
    (b) three units above the xy-plane.
    (c) a distance of five units from the origin.

11. Sketch the graph of the function $z = 3$ in three-dimensional space.

12. Sketch the graph of $z = y^2$ in three-dimensional space.

III

13. (*See Example 3*) A company manufactures two models of vans, A and B. The total cost of manufacturing x units of model A and y units of model B is

$$C(x, y) = \frac{x^3}{20} + \frac{y^3}{10} + 100x + 200y + 20xy$$

Determine the cost of manufacturing 40 units of model A and 100 units of model B.

14. A company sells two products, X and Y. The total revenue obtained on selling x units of X and y units of Y is given by

$$R(x, y) = -2x^2 + 500x - 4y^2 + 600y + 50xy$$

Compute the total revenue on selling 50 units of X and 40 units of Y.

15. The cost of quality control in a manufacturing line is a function of the numbers of inspections x and y made per week at two inspection points P and Q, respectively.

$$C(x, y) = 4x^2 + 2y^2 - 4y$$

Determine the cost if 20 inspections per week are made at point P, and 10 inspections per week are made at point Q.

16. There is a relationship between the number of units N of an item sold by a company and the amounts spent on television advertisements, x, and on newspaper advertisements, y. This relationship is

$$N(x, y) = 1600x + 1200y - 4x^2 - y^2$$

If $x = 500$ and $y = 800$, compute the anticipated sales.

In Exercises 17 and 18, f is the firm's Cobb-Douglas production, x is the number of units of labor, and y is the number of units of capital.

17. (*See Example 4*) What is the production when $x = 81$ and $y = 16$ if $f(x, y) = 10x^{1/4}y^{3/4}$?

18. What is the production when $x = 27$ and $y = 64$ if $f(x, y) = 7x^{1/3}y^{2/3}$?

15–2 **PARTIAL DERIVATIVES**

- *Definition of Partial Derivatives*
- *Higher-Order Partial Derivatives*
- *Geometry of Partial Derivatives*
- *Marginal Analysis in Several Variables*

DEFINITION OF PARTIAL DERIVATIVES

We used the derivative of a function of a single variable to talk about the rate of change of the function and to find relative maximum and minimum values of the function. We would like to carry over as much of the machinery of derivatives as possible to this new setting of several variables. Let us look at a specific example and see what we can do.

Suppose that a company produces two products whose costs of production are related, say, milk and cheese. Let x represent the amount of milk produced, and let y be the amount of cheese. The company is using

$$C(x, y) = \frac{x^3}{300} + \frac{y^3}{50} + 10x + 30y + 2xy$$

as its cost function and is currently manufacturing 30 units of milk and 10 units of cheese. The company's present costs are

$$C(30, 10) = 90 + 20 + 300 + 300 + 600 = 1310$$

What will happen if the amount of cheese produced is held fixed at $y = 10$ and the company varies the amount of milk produced? The function that gives the cost when $y = 10$ and x varies is

$$C(x, 10) = \frac{x^3}{300} + \frac{10^3}{50} + 10x + (30)(10) + 2 \cdot x \cdot 10$$

$$= \frac{x^3}{300} + 30x + 320$$

This is a function of one variable, and so we can take its derivative just as we did before:

$$\frac{d}{dx} C(x, 10) = \frac{x^2}{100} + 30$$

We now have a marginal cost function for x when $y = 10$. When $x = 30$, this marginal cost is

$$\frac{(30)^2}{100} + 30 = 39$$

Therefore if the company were to increase x from 30 to 31, *holding y constant at y = 10,* the company's costs would increase approximately 39 units, from 1310 to approximately 1349.

We could now ask the same kind of question, holding x fixed and letting y vary. When we hold one variable fixed and let the other one vary, all the rules of differentiation of a function of one variable still apply. So our strategy for dealing with rates of change of functions of several variables is to hold all but one variable fixed and use all the rules for derivatives of a function of one variable.

One thing that we must modify is our method of evaluating these rates of change. We don't want to have to plug in specific values of y first. We found formulas for $f'(x)$ so that we could find rates of change at any value of x. Similarly, we will want to know rates of change of functions of two variables at any production level (x, y). First, we must change notation. We will not be computing the derivative of $C(x, y)$. $C(x, y)$ is after all a function of two independent variables. The $\dfrac{dC}{dx}$ notation will be reserved for functions that depend on x alone.

Instead, the notation used is $\dfrac{\partial C}{\partial x}$, and this is called the **partial derivative of C with respect to x.** To see what this implies, we return to

$$C(x, y) = \frac{x^3}{300} + \frac{y^3}{50} + 10x + 30y + 2xy$$

Now think of y as some constant number whose specific value is unknown. To find $\dfrac{\partial C}{\partial x}(x, y)$, we compute the derivative of $C(x, y)$ with respect to x while holding y constant:

$$\frac{\partial C}{\partial x}(x, y) = \frac{x^2}{100} + 0 + 10 + 0 + 2y$$

Therefore

$$\frac{\partial C}{\partial x}(30, 10) = 9 + 10 + 20 = 39$$

as before.

For contrast we now find $\dfrac{\partial C}{\partial y}(x, y)$:

$$\frac{\partial C}{\partial y}(x, y) = 0 + \frac{3y^2}{50} + 0 + 30 + 2x$$

$$\frac{\partial C}{\partial y}(30, 10) = 6 + 30 + 60 = 96$$

If x is held fixed fixed at 30 and y is increased from 10 to 11, the total costs to the company will increase approximately 96 units, from 1310 to approximately 1406.

Although we do not have a derivative of $C(x, y)$, we do have two partial derivatives. The notation $C_x(x, y)$ is also widely used to mean the same as $\dfrac{\partial C}{\partial x}(x, y)$. Similarly, $C_y(x, y)$ means the same as $\dfrac{\partial C}{\partial y}(x, y)$. Since both notations are commonly used, you will need to be familiar with both, and we will use both.

In summary,

Definition
Partial Derivative

Let f be a function of two independent variables x and y. The **partial derivative of f with respect to x** is found by keeping y constant and differentiating with respect to x and is denoted by

$$\frac{\partial f}{\partial x} \quad \text{or} \quad f_x$$

The **partial derivative of f with respect to y** is computed by keeping x constant and differentiating with respect to y and is denoted by

$$\frac{\partial f}{\partial y} \quad \text{or} \quad f_y$$

EXAMPLE 1 *(Compare Exercise 1)*

If $f(x, y) = 4x^2y^3$, compute $\dfrac{\partial f}{\partial x}$ and $\dfrac{\partial f}{\partial y}$.

SOLUTION Keeping y constant and differentiating with respect to x, we have

$$\frac{\partial f}{\partial x}(x, y) = 4(2x)y^3$$
$$= 8xy^3$$

Keeping x constant and differentiating with respect to y, we have

$$\frac{\partial f}{\partial y}(x, y) = 4x^2(3y^2)$$
$$= 12x^2y^2$$

EXAMPLE 2 *(Compare Exercise 5)*

Compute f_x and f_y if $f(x, y) = 4x^2y^3 + e^{3xy^2}$

SOLUTION Holding y fixed and differentiating with respect to x, we have

$$f_x(x, y) = 8xy^3 + 3y^2e^{3xy^2}$$

Next, hold x fixed and differentiate with respect to y:

$$f_y(x, y) = 12x^2y^2 + 6xye^{3xy^2}$$

Notice that the chain rule carries over to several variables the same way the other differentiation rules do. In particular,

$$\text{if } f(x, y) = e^{g(x, y)}, \qquad \text{then} \qquad f_x(x, y) = e^{g(x, y)} \cdot g_x(x, y).$$

Example 3 shows another instance when the chain rule must be used.

EXAMPLE 3

Compute f_x and f_y if $f(x, y) = \ln(x^2 + 4y^3)$.

SOLUTION

$$f_x(x, y) = \frac{1}{x^2 + 4y^3} \, 2x = \frac{2x}{x^2 + 4y^3}$$

$$f_y(x, y) = \frac{1}{x^2 + 4y^3} \, 12y^2 = \frac{12y^2}{x^2 + 4y^3}$$

∎

Another commonly used notation parallels the $\dfrac{dy}{dx}$ notation used in the one variable case. If we let $z = f(x, y)$, then

$$\frac{\partial z}{\partial x} = \frac{\partial f}{\partial x} \qquad \text{and} \qquad \frac{\partial z}{\partial y} = \frac{\partial f}{\partial y}$$

EXAMPLE 4   *(Compare Exercise 3)*

Compute $\dfrac{\partial z}{\partial x}$ and $\dfrac{\partial z}{\partial y}$ for the function

$$z = 2x^2y^2 - 4xy + y^2$$

at the point $(1, 2)$.

SOLUTION   Holding y constant and differentiating with respect to x, we have

$$\frac{\partial z}{\partial x} = 4xy^2 - 4y$$

At the point $(1, 2)$, $\dfrac{\partial z}{\partial x}(1, 2) = 4(1)(2)^2 - 4(2) = 8$. Keeping x constant and differentiating with respect to y, we have

$$\frac{\partial z}{\partial y} = 4x^2y - 4x + 2y$$

At the point $(1, 2)$, $\dfrac{\partial z}{\partial y}(1, 2) = 4(1)^2(2) - 4(1) + 2(2) = 8$.

∎

These concepts can be extended to functions of more than two variables. If a function f depends on the three variables x, y, and z, then $\dfrac{\partial f}{\partial x}$ is obtained by differentiating f with respect to x, keeping y and z constant; $\dfrac{\partial f}{\partial y}$ and $\dfrac{\partial f}{\partial z}$ are defined analogously.

EXAMPLE 5   *(Compare Exercise 7)*

Find $\dfrac{\partial f}{\partial x}$, $\dfrac{\partial f}{\partial y}$, and $\dfrac{\partial f}{\partial z}$ for

$$f(x, y, z) = 2x^2yz - x^4z^3 + 2y^4$$

SOLUTION   Keeping y and z constant and differentiating with respect to x, we have

$$\frac{\partial f}{\partial x}(x, y, z) = 4xyz - 4x^3z^3$$

Keeping x and z constant, we have

$$\frac{\partial f}{\partial y}(x, y, z) = 2x^2z + 8y^3$$

Keeping x and y constant, we have

$$\frac{\partial f}{\partial z}(x, y, z) = 2x^2y - 3x^4z^2$$

EXAMPLE 6   *(Compare Exercise 9)*

If $w = \sqrt{x^2 + yz}$, find $\dfrac{\partial w}{\partial x}$, $\dfrac{\partial w}{\partial y}$, and $\dfrac{\partial w}{\partial z}$.

SOLUTION   Rewrite $w = (x^2 + yz)^{1/2}$. Now treat y and z as constants and differentiate with respect to x:

$$\frac{\partial w}{\partial x} = \frac{1}{2}(x^2 + yz)^{-1/2} \cdot (2x + 0) = \frac{x}{\sqrt{x^2 + yz}}$$

In a similar fashion,

$$\frac{\partial w}{\partial y} = \frac{1}{2}(x^2 + yz)^{-1/2}(0 + z) = \frac{z}{2\sqrt{x^2 + yz}}$$

and

$$\frac{\partial w}{\partial z} = \frac{1}{2}(x^2 + yz)^{-1/2}(0 + y) = \frac{y}{2\sqrt{x^2 + yz}}$$

HIGHER-ORDER PARTIAL DERIVATIVES

Remember that the second derivative was important in finding the relative extreme values of a given function of one variable. What is the analogous tool for functions of two or more variables? Notice that if f is a function of two variables, then so is $\dfrac{\partial f}{\partial x}$. Therefore, we can take partial derivatives of the function $\dfrac{\partial f}{\partial x}$, and keeping the terminology as familiar as possible, we say that a partial derivative of $\dfrac{\partial f}{\partial x}$ is a **second partial derivative of f.** Just as there are two partial derivatives of f, there are two partial derivatives of $\dfrac{\partial f}{\partial x}$. We have

$$\frac{\partial}{\partial x}\left(\frac{\partial f}{\partial x}\right) \qquad \text{and} \qquad \frac{\partial}{\partial y}\left(\frac{\partial f}{\partial x}\right)$$

Again, we introduce some less cumbersome notation:

$$\frac{\partial}{\partial x}\left(\frac{\partial f}{\partial x}\right) \quad \text{is written as} \quad \frac{\partial^2 f}{\partial x^2} \quad \text{or as} \quad f_{xx}$$

$$\frac{\partial}{\partial y}\left(\frac{\partial f}{\partial x}\right) \quad \text{is written as} \quad \frac{\partial^2 f}{\partial y\,\partial x} \quad \text{or as} \quad f_{xy}$$

Similarly,

$$\frac{\partial}{\partial x}\left(\frac{\partial f}{\partial y}\right) = \frac{\partial^2 f}{\partial x\,\partial y} = f_{yx}$$

and

$$\frac{\partial}{\partial y}\left(\frac{\partial f}{\partial y}\right) = \frac{\partial^2 f}{\partial y^2} = f_{yy}$$

EXAMPLE 7   *(Compare Exercise 11)*

Let $f(x, y) = 3x^2 + 4xy^3 + 5y$. Find $\dfrac{\partial^2 f}{\partial x^2}$, $\dfrac{\partial^2 f}{\partial y\,\partial x}$, $\dfrac{\partial^2 f}{\partial x\,\partial y}$, and $\dfrac{\partial^2 f}{\partial y^2}$.

SOLUTION   First, we have to find $\dfrac{\partial f}{\partial x}$ and $\dfrac{\partial f}{\partial y}$:

$$\frac{\partial f}{\partial x}(x, y) = 6x + 4y^3$$

$$\frac{\partial f}{\partial y}(x, y) = 12xy^2 + 5$$

To get $\dfrac{\partial^2 f}{\partial x^2}$, we differentiate $\dfrac{\partial f}{\partial x}$ with respect to x:

$$\frac{\partial^2 f}{\partial x^2}(x, y) = \frac{\partial}{\partial x}(6x + 4y^3) = 6$$

To find $\dfrac{\partial^2 f}{\partial y\,\partial x}$, differentiate $\dfrac{\partial f}{\partial x}$ with respect to y:

$$\frac{\partial^2 f}{\partial y\,\partial x}(x, y) = \frac{\partial}{\partial y}(6x + 4y^3) = 12y^2$$

Next, find $\dfrac{\partial^2 f}{\partial x\,\partial y}$ by differentiating $\dfrac{\partial f}{\partial y}$ with respect to x:

$$\frac{\partial^2 f}{\partial x\,\partial y}(x, y) = \frac{\partial}{\partial x}(12xy^2 + 5) = 12y^2$$

Finally,

$$\frac{\partial^2 f}{\partial y^2}(x, y) = \frac{\partial}{\partial y}(12xy^2 + 5) = 24xy$$

Observe that in Example 8, $\dfrac{\partial^2 f}{\partial y\,\partial x}$ and $\dfrac{\partial^2 f}{\partial x\,\partial y}$ are the same. This is no accident; there is a theorem guaranteeing that if either $\dfrac{\partial^2 f}{\partial x\,\partial y}$ or $\dfrac{\partial^2 f}{\partial y\,\partial x}$ is continuous, then they both are continuous, and further, that $\dfrac{\partial^2 f}{\partial x\,\partial y} = \dfrac{\partial^2 f}{\partial y\,\partial x}$. Because of this theorem, we didn't stress the ordering of $\partial x\,\partial y$ or $\partial y\,\partial x$ when writing the second partials. The ordering makes a theoretical difference but not a practical difference for all the functions that we will encounter. (Although there are functions for which $\dfrac{\partial^2 f}{\partial x\,\partial y} \neq \dfrac{\partial^2 f}{\partial y\,\partial x}$.)

One can continue taking partial derivatives of higher order than 2, just as we did in the case of a single variable. We will not do so here however.

GEOMETRY OF PARTIAL DERIVATIVES

The derivative of a function of one variable has a geometrical interpretation; $f'(x)$ is the slope of the line tangent to the graph at the point $(x, f(x))$. A partial derivative of a function of two variables also has a geometrical interpretation as the slope of a tangent line. We illustrate this geometrical interpretation in terms of the function $f(x, y) = x^2 + y^2$. From the previous section we know that the graph of this function looks like Figure 15–11.

FIGURE 15–11

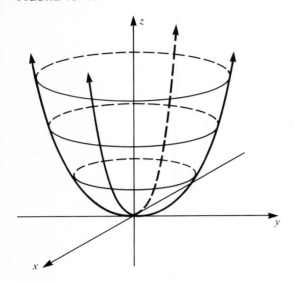

FIGURE 15–12

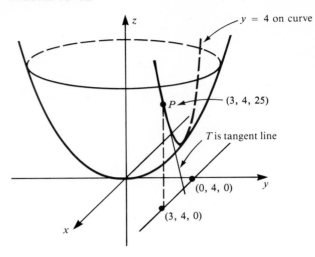

The partial derivatives of this function are

$$f_x(x, y) = 2x \qquad \text{and} \qquad f_y(x, y) = 2y$$

Consider the point P on the graph above $(3, 4, 0)$. The third coordinate of P is

$$f(3, 4) = z = 3^2 + 4^2 = 25$$
$$P = (3, 4, 25)$$

The corresponding partial derivatives are

$$f_x(3, 4) = 2 \cdot 3 = 6 \qquad \text{and} \qquad f_y(3, 4) = 2 \cdot 4 = 8$$

We now give geometrical significance to the two numbers 6 and 8. See Figure 15–12.

Consider the curve on the surface, passing through P, that lies in a plane parallel to the xz-plane. On such a curve, all the points have the same second coordinate, namely, $y = 4$. Points on this curve are of the form $(x, 4, z)$, and the change in z is with respect to x only. $f_x(x, 4)$ is the slope in the plane $y = 4$ of the line tangent to this curve at an arbitrary point $(x, 4, z)$. Therefore $f_x(3, 4) = 6$ tells us that the slope of the line tangent to the curve at the point P is 6. We label this tangent line T in Figure 15–12.

Similarly, $f_y(3, 4)$ is the slope of the line that is tangent to the surface at P and that lies in the plane through P parallel to the yz-plane. See Figure 15–13.

A general picture is given in Figure 15–14.

Let C be the curve on the surface through P that lies in the plane $y = b$ parallel to the xz-plane. The slope of the tangent T to this curve at P is $f_x(a, b)$.

FIGURE 15–13

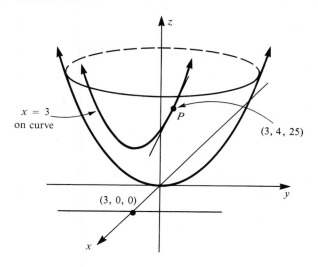

$x = 3$
on curve

P

$(3, 4, 25)$

$(3, 0, 0)$

FIGURE 15–14

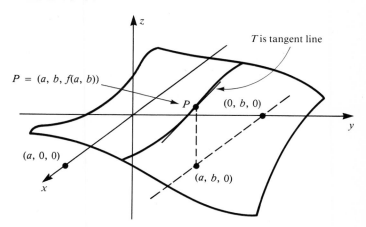

T is tangent line

$P = (a, b, f(a, b))$

P $(0, b, 0)$

$(a, 0, 0)$

$(a, b, 0)$

MARGINAL ANALYSIS IN SEVERAL VARIABLES

In the case of a single variable the slope of the tangent line is the rate of change of the function. We have just seen that we can carry over to several variables this geometric relation between slope and rate of change. Now we see how marginal analysis can also be carried over to functions of more than one variable. We introduced the class of **Cobb-Douglas production functions** in the preceding section; they are functions of the type

$$f(x, y) = Cx^a y^{1-a}$$

where C and a are appropriate constants.

Generally, x is the amount of labor, and y is the amount of capital. The functions $\dfrac{\partial f}{\partial x}$ and $\dfrac{\partial f}{\partial y}$ are called the **marginal productivity of labor** and the **marginal productivity of capital,** respectively. $\dfrac{\partial f}{\partial x}$ and $\dfrac{\partial f}{\partial y}$ evaluated at a point (x, y) are interpreted as follows: $\dfrac{\partial f}{\partial x}(x, y)$ is approximately the additional output obtained on raising labor from x to $(x + 1)$ units, while capital is held constant at y units. $\dfrac{\partial f}{\partial y}(x, y)$ is approximately the additional output obtained on raising capital from y to $(y + 1)$ units, while labor is held constant at x units.

EXAMPLE 8   *(Compare Exercise 25)*

If a company's production function is given by

$$f(x, y) = 9x^{2/3}y^{1/3}$$

find the marginal productivities of labor and capital when $x = 64$ and $y = 27$.

SOLUTION

$$\frac{\partial f}{\partial x}(x, y) = 9\left(\frac{2}{3}\right)x^{-1/3}y^{1/3} = \frac{6y^{1/3}}{x^{1/3}}$$

$$\frac{\partial f}{\partial y}(x, y) = 9\left(\frac{1}{3}\right)x^{2/3}y^{-2/3} = \frac{3x^{2/3}}{y^{2/3}}$$

When $x = 64$ and $y = 27$, we get

$$\frac{\partial f}{\partial x}(64, 27) = \frac{6(27)^{1/3}}{(64)^{1/3}} = \frac{6(3)}{4} = \frac{9}{2}$$

$$\frac{\partial f}{\partial y}(64, 27) = \frac{3(64)^{2/3}}{(27)^{2/3}} = \frac{3(16)}{9} = \frac{16}{3}$$

Therefore raising labor by one unit from 64 to 65 while maintaining capital at 27 units would increase output by about $4\frac{1}{2}$ units. On the other hand, raising capital by one unit, from 27 to 28, while maintaining the level of labor at 64 units would increase output by approximately $5\frac{1}{3}$ units. ∎

15–2   EXERCISES

I

1. *(See Example 1)* If $f(x, y) = x^2 + 3xy$, compute $\dfrac{\partial f}{\partial y}$ and $\dfrac{\partial f}{\partial x}$.

2. If $f(x, y) = x^2y - y^3$, compute $\dfrac{\partial f}{\partial y}$ and $\dfrac{\partial f}{\partial x}$.

3. *(See Example 4)* If $z = 5x^2y^2 + 2y$, compute $\dfrac{\partial z}{\partial y}$ and $\dfrac{\partial z}{\partial x}$.

4. Compute $\dfrac{\partial z}{\partial y}$ and $\dfrac{\partial z}{\partial x}$ for $z = e^{4x} + yx^3$.

5. (*See Example 2*) If $f(x, y) = \dfrac{x}{x^2 + y^2}$, compute f_x and f_y.

6. If $f(x, y) = x \ln |y|$, compute f_x and f_y.

7. (*See Example 5*) If $f(x, y, z) = \dfrac{x^2 y}{z^3}$, compute $\dfrac{\partial f}{\partial x}, \dfrac{\partial f}{\partial y}$, and $\dfrac{\partial f}{\partial z}$.

8. If $f(x, y, z) = e^x + y^2$, compute $\dfrac{\partial f}{\partial x}, \dfrac{\partial f}{\partial y}$, and $\dfrac{\partial f}{\partial z}$.

9. (*See Example 6*) For $w = \ln|xy + yz^2|$, compute $\dfrac{\partial w}{\partial x}, \dfrac{\partial w}{\partial y}$, and $\dfrac{\partial w}{\partial z}$.

10. Compute $\dfrac{\partial w}{\partial x}, \dfrac{\partial w}{\partial y}$, and $\dfrac{\partial w}{\partial z}$ if $w = xy^2z^3$.

II

Compute $\dfrac{\partial f}{\partial y}, \dfrac{\partial f}{\partial x}, \dfrac{\partial^2 f}{\partial x^2}, \dfrac{\partial^2 f}{\partial y\, \partial x}, \dfrac{\partial^2 f}{\partial x\, \partial y}$, and $\dfrac{\partial^2 f}{\partial y^2}$ for each of the functions in Exercises 11 through 18. Observe that $\dfrac{\partial^2 f}{\partial y\, \partial x} = \dfrac{\partial^2 f}{\partial x\, \partial y}$ for these functions.

11. (*See Example 7*) $f(x, y) = 2x^3 y$

12. $f(x, y) = x^2 + 2y^2$

13. $f(x, y) = 2x^2 y - 3xy^2$

14. $f(x, y) = 4x^2 y - 3x^3 - y^4 + 2$

15. $f(x, y) = 2e^{x^2 + y}$

16. $f(x, y) = x^2 \ln(xy)$

17. $f(x, y) = 2x + e^{x^2 y}$

18. $f(x, y) = y \ln(x^2 + 3y)$

Calculate f_x, f_y, f_{xx}, f_{yy}, and f_{xy} at the point p for each of the functions in Exercises 19 through 24.

19. $f(x, y) = x^2 y;\ p = (2, 3)$

20. $f(x, y) = 3x^2 + 2xy;\ p = (1, 1)$

21. $f(x, y) = xy - 4xy^3;\ p = (-1, 0)$

22. $f(x, y) = 4xy^2 - xy + 2;\ p = (1, 2)$

23. $f(x, y) = x \ln(xy);\ p = (e, 1)$

24. $f(x, y) = x^2 e^{(x^2 - y^2)};\ p = (2, 3)$

III

25. (*See Example 8*) The manufacturing process of a company is described by the Cobb-Douglas production function $f(x, y) = 10x^{1/4} y^{3/4}$.
    (a) Determine the number of units manufactured when 16 units of labor are used and 625 units of capital are invested.
    (b) Find the marginal productivity of labor and the marginal productivity of capital.
    (c) What are the values of these marginal functions when 16 units of labor and 625 units of capital are being used?
    (d) What is the approximate change in the production level if the use of labor is increased from 16 units to 17 units while the level of capital used is held constant at 625 units?
    (e) What is the approximate change in the production level if the number of units of labor is held constant at 16, but the amount of capital used is *decreased* from 625 units to 624 units?

26. A company manufactures two products, X and Y. The total cost incurred from manufacturing x units of X and y units of Y is

$$C(x, y) = \frac{x^3}{900} + \frac{y^3}{600} + 60x + 40y + 20xy$$

    (a) What is the total cost of manufacturing 90 units of X and 120 units of Y?
    (b) Compute $\dfrac{\partial C}{\partial x}$ (the marginal cost of X) and $\dfrac{\partial C}{\partial y}$ (the marginal cost of Y).
    (c) Evaluate $\dfrac{\partial C}{\partial x}(90, 120)$ and $\dfrac{\partial C}{\partial y}(90, 120)$.
    (d) What will be the approximate change in costs if the company increases the production of X from 90 units to 91 while holding the production of Y fixed at 120?
    (e) What is the approximate change in production costs if the company *decreases* the production of Y from 120 units to 118 units while holding the production of X fixed at 90 units?

27. The total revenue function of a company that sells x units of trash compactors and y units of garbage disposals is

$$R(x, y) = -3x^2 + 400x - 2y^2 + 500y$$

(a) What is the total revenue if $x = 10$ and $y = 15$?

(b) Compute $\dfrac{\partial R}{\partial x}$ and $\dfrac{\partial R}{\partial y}$.

(c) Evaluate $\dfrac{\partial R}{\partial x}(10, 15)$ and $\dfrac{\partial R}{\partial y}(10, 15)$.

(d) How will the company's revenue change if x increases from 10 to 11 while y remains 15?

(e) How will the company's revenue change if y decreases from 15 to 14 while x remains 10?

15–3 MAXIMA AND MINIMA OF FUNCTIONS OF TWO VARIABLES

- *Extreme Values and Critical Points*

- *The Second Derivative Test for a Function of Two Variables*

- *An Application*

Derivatives helped us find relative extreme values of a function of one variable. In this section we will see how partial derivatives help us to find relative extreme values for a function of two variables. We will restrict our discussion here to nice functions of two variables. "Nice" means that all the second-order partial derivatives exist and are continuous. We stay with two variables for simplicity. There are analogous methods for functions of more than two variables, but these methods are more complicated.

EXTREME VALUES AND CRITICAL POINTS

A function f has a **relative maximum** at the point (a, b) if $f(a, b) \geq f(x, y)$ for all points (x, y) "near" (a, b). A **relative minimum** is defined analogously. We can visualize maxima and minima of functions of two variables geometrically, as shown in Figure 15–15. This time the graph gives you more than the outline of a mountain; now you can see the whole mountain.

Again, by letting only one coordinate vary at a time, we try to see how much of our knowledge of a single variable we can apply to several variables. We begin by holding the second variable fixed and supposing that $f(a, b)$ is a relative maximum. Then $f(a, b) \geq f(x, y)$ for all (x, y) near (a, b); this in turn implies that $f(a, b) \geq f(x, b)$ for all x near a. Therefore $f(x, b)$ has a relative maximum when $x = a$. We know from the calculus of a single variable that this means that $\dfrac{\partial f}{\partial x}(a, b) = 0$. Similarly, $f(a, y)$ will have a relative maximum when $y = b$, so $\dfrac{\partial f}{\partial y}(a, b) = 0$. Geometrically, the highest point on a north-south trail across the

FIGURE 15–15

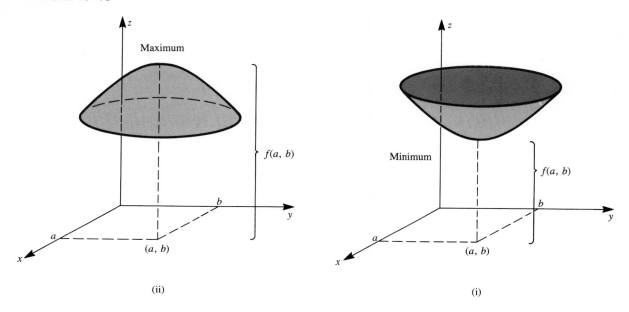

(ii)   (i)

top of a mountain will be at the top of the mountain, and the same is true of an east-west trail. Since relative extrema occur when both partial derivatives equal 0, we make a definition similar to the one we made in the one variable case.

Definition
Critical Point

The point (a, b) is called a **critical point** of the function f if both
$$\frac{\partial f}{\partial x}(a, b) = 0 \text{ and } \frac{\partial f}{\partial y}(a, b) = 0$$

EXAMPLE 1   *(Compare Exercise 1)*

Find the critical points of the function defined by

$$f(x, y) = x^2 + 2y^2 - 2x + 8y + 12$$

SOLUTION

$$f_x(x, y) = 2x - 2$$
$$f_y(x, y) = 4y + 8$$

We must have both $2x - 2 = 0$ and $4y + 8 = 0$. The first equation tells us that $x = 1$, and the second says that $y = -2$. There is only one critical point, $(1, -2)$.

EXAMPLE 2   *(Compare Exercise 3)*

Find the critical points of

$$f(x, y) = 2x^3 - 3x^2 + 12y^2 - 12xy - 18x + 10$$

SOLUTION

$$f_x(x, y) = 6x^2 - 6x - 12y - 18$$
$$f_y(x, y) = 24y - 12x$$

At the critical point, the two equations $f_x = 0$ and $f_y = 0$ must be true simultaneously. We have to solve the system of equations

$$6x^2 - 6x - 12y - 18 = 0 \qquad (1)$$
$$24y - 12x = 0 \qquad (2)$$

From equation (2) we have $24y = 12x$ or $y = \frac{1}{2}x$. We substitute $\frac{1}{2}x$ for y in equation (1), getting

$$6x^2 - 6x - 12\left(\frac{1}{2}x\right) - 18 = 0$$
$$6x^2 - 12x - 18 = 0$$
$$x^2 - 2x - 3 = 0$$
$$(x - 3)(x + 1) = 0$$

The solutions are $x = 3$ and $x = -1$. Since $y = \frac{1}{2}x$, when $x = 3$, $y = \frac{3}{2}$; and when $x = -1$, $y = -\frac{1}{2}$.
The two critical points are $(3, \frac{3}{2})$ and $(-1, -\frac{1}{2})$.

      ■

The relation between the critical points of f and the points where f has a relative extreme value is the same for functions of several variables as it is for functions of one variable. The critical points are the candidates for finding relative extrema, but (a, b) may be a critical point for f even though $f(a, b)$ is not a relative extreme value.

EXAMPLE 3

Show that $f(x, y) = 2 - (x - 1)^2 + (y - 3)^2$ does not have a relative extreme value at its critical point.

SOLUTION

$$f_x(x, y) = -2(x - 1) \qquad \text{and} \qquad f_y(x, y) = 2(y - 3)$$

$f_x = 0$ when $x = 1$, and $f_y = 0$ when $y = 3$. The point $(1, 3)$ is the only critical point, and we now show that f does not have a relative extreme value at $(1, 3)$. First, $f(1, 3) = 2$. Next, if $(x, 3)$ is close to $(1, 3)$ but not equal to $(1, 3)$, then $f(x, 3) = 2 - (x - 1)^2 < 2$; so $f(1, 3) = 2$ cannot be a relative minimum. Furthermore, if $(1, y)$ is close to $(1, 3)$ but not equal to $(1, 3)$, then $f(1, y) = 2 + (y - 3)^2 > 2$; so $f(1, 3) = 2$ cannot be a relative maximum.
The only critical point of f is $(1, 3)$ and f does not have a relative extreme value at $(1, 3)$:

      ■

FIGURE 15–16

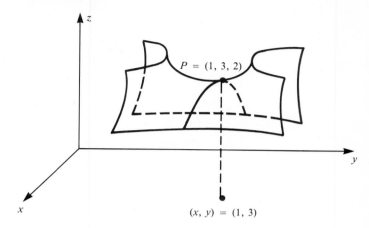

Figure 15–16 shows what the graph of f looks like. As we saw in Example 3, $f(x, 3)$ has a relative maximum when $x = 1$, but $f(1, y)$ has a relative minimum when $y = 3$. The graph of f bends up in one direction and down in the other. The graph of f is shaped somewhat like a saddle above $(1, 3)$, so the point $(1, 3)$ is called a **saddle point** of the function.

The task of classifying critical points is more complicated in the several variable case than it was with just one variable, as is seen in the second derivative test for two variables.

THE SECOND DERIVATIVE TEST FOR A FUNCTION OF TWO VARIABLES

Theorem
Second Derivative Test for a Function of Two Variables
	Let (a, b) be a critical point.
	Define
	
	$$M(x, y) = f_{xx}(x, y)f_{yy}(x, y) - [f_{xy}(x, y)]^2$$
	
	1. If $M(a, b) > 0$, then $f(a, b)$ is a relative extreme value.
	    (i) If $f_{xx}(a, b) < 0$, then $f(a, b)$ is a relative maximum.
	    (ii) If $f_{xx}(a, b) > 0$, then $f(a, b)$ is a relative minimum.
	2. If $M(a, b) < 0$, then $f(a, b)$ is neither a relative maximum nor a relative minimum.
	3. If $M(a, b) = 0$, this test gives no information.

Case 1 indicates (i) a relative maximum or (ii) a relative minimum as illustrated in Figure 15–15.

Case 2 indicates a saddle-shaped graph as in Figure 15–16.

Definition	If (a, b) is a critical point and if $M(a, b) < 0$, then (a, b) is called a
Saddle Point	**saddle point** of f.

In case 3, that is, if $M(a, b) = 0$, we have to resort to other techniques to find out whether (a, b) is a maximum or a minimum. This text will not go further into case 3.

The following examples show how this test works.

EXAMPLE 4   *(Compare Exercise 7)*

Find the relative maxima and minima of

$$f(x, y) = x^2 + 2y^2 - 2x + 8y + 12$$

SOLUTION   This is the same function as in Example 1. The first partial derivatives are

$$f_x(x, y) = 2x - 2 \quad \text{and} \quad f_y(x, y) = 4y + 8$$

We have already seen that there is only one critical point, namely, $(1, -2)$. Now we use the second derivatives to determine whether this critical point leads to a relative maximum or minimum value of f. The second derivatives are

$$f_{xx}(x, y) = 2, \quad f_{yy}(x, y) = 4, \quad f_{xy}(x, y) = 0$$

These functions are all constant, so

$$M(1, -2) = (2)(4) - (0)^2 = 8$$

$M(1, -2) > 0$, so part 1 of the test says that $f(1, -2)$ *is* a relative extremum. Now we find out which kind:

$$f_{xx}(1, -2) = 2$$

$f_{xx}(1, -2) > 0$, so (ii) tells us that f has a relative minimum at the point $(1, -2)$. This minimum value is

$$f(1, -2) = (1)^2 + 2(-2)^2 - 2(1) + 8(-2) + 12 = 3$$

EXAMPLE 5   *(Compare Exercise 13)*

Find the relative maxima and minima of

$$f(x, y) = 2x^3 - 3x^2 + 12y^2 - 12xy - 18x + 10$$

SOLUTION   This is the function from Example 2. We already have

$$f_x(x, y) = 6x^2 - 6x - 12y - 18$$
$$f_y(x, y) = 24y - 12x$$

and two critical points, $(3, \frac{3}{2})$ and $(-1, -\frac{1}{2})$. Next

$$f_{xx}(x, y) = 12x - 6$$
$$f_{xy}(x, y) = -12$$

and

$$f_{yy}(x, y) = 24$$

1. Test $(3, \frac{3}{2})$:

$$f_{xx}\left(3, \frac{3}{2}\right) = 30, \qquad f_{xy}\left(3, \frac{3}{2}\right) = -12, \qquad f_{yy}\left(3, \frac{3}{2}\right) = 24$$

$$M\left(3, \frac{3}{2}\right) = (30)(24) - (-12)^2$$
$$= 720 - 144 = 576 > 0$$

Thus $f(3, \frac{3}{2})$ is a relative extremum. Next $f_{xx}(3, \frac{3}{2}) = 30 > 0$, so $f(3, \frac{3}{2})$ is a relative minimum.

2. Test $(-1, -\frac{1}{2})$:

$$f_{xx}\left(-1, -\frac{1}{2}\right) = -18, \qquad f_{xy}\left(-1, -\frac{1}{2}\right) = -12,$$

$$f_{yy}\left(-1, -\frac{1}{2}\right) = 24$$

$$M\left(-1, -\frac{1}{2}\right) = (-18)(24) - (-12)^2$$
$$= -432 - 144 = -576 < 0$$

We are in case 2, and there is no need to do any more calculation. $f(-1, -\frac{1}{2})$ *is not* a relative extreme value.

AN APPLICATION

Generally speaking, the demand for a certain commodity and the price of that commodity are related. Moreover, that relationship often involves other factors. For example, the demand for a certain company's computers will depend not only on the price of the computer, but also on the price that the company charges for supporting services and software.

EXAMPLE 6 *(Compare Exercise 15)*

Suppose that a firm charges x for its computer and y for a certain package of programs, where x and y are in thousands of dollars. The firm estimates its revenue function as

$$R(x, y) = -2x^2 + 40x - 4y^2 + 48y$$

Find the values of x and y which lead to the maximum revenue for the company.

SOLUTION   The partial derivatives of R are

$$R_x(x, y) = -4x + 40 \qquad \text{and} \qquad R_y(x, y) = -8y + 48$$

The critical points must simultaneously satisfy the equations

$$-4x + 40 = 0 \qquad \text{and} \qquad -8y + 48 = 0$$

There is a single critical point, $x = 10$, $y = 6$. Now we use the second derivative test at this critical point. The second derivatives are

$$R_{xx}(x, y) = -4, \qquad R_{yy}(x, y) = -8, \qquad R_{xy}(x, y) = 0$$

Next, evaluate $M(10, 6)$:

$$M(10, 6) = (-4)(-8) - (0)^2 = 32$$

Therefore $M(10, 6) > 0$, and R does have a relative extreme value at $(10, 6)$. Furthermore, $R_{xx}(10, 6) = -4 < 0$, so R has a relative maximum at $x = 10$, $y = 6$.

There is no "single critical point test" for several variables as there was in the one-variable situation. However, it is true that if a function has the form $f(x, y) = ax^2 + bx + cy^2 + dy + e$ with both a and c negative, then the relative maximum is in fact the maximum value of the function. So in this case we can conclude that the company will maximize its revenue by charging $10,000 for the computer and $6000 for its software.

15–3 EXERCISES

I

Find the critical points for the functions defined in Exercises 1 through 6.

1. (*See Example 1*) $f(x, y) = x^2 + y^2 + 3$

2. $f(x, y) = 2x^2 + y^2 + 2x$

3. (*See Example 2*) $f(x, y) = x^2 + xy + y^2$

4. $f(x, y) = 3xy - x^2 - y^2$

5. $f(x, y) = 4x^3 + y^2 - 12x^2 - 36x$

6. $f(x, y) = x^2 - 2x + xy$

II

Find the critical points for each function defined in Exercises 7 through 14. Then use the second derivative test to determine whether the function has a relative extreme value at the critical point. If f does have a relative extremum, determine whether it is a relative maximum or minimum.

7. (*See Example 4*) $f(x, y) = x^2 + 2y^2 - 4x + 4y - 3$

8. $f(x, y) = -2x^2 - 2xy - y^2 + 4x + 2y$

9. $f(x, y) = x^2 - xy + y^2 + 2x + 2y + 3$

10. $f(x, y) = x^2 + xy + y^2 - 4x - 5y$

11. $f(x, y) = y^3 + x^2 - 6xy + 3x + 6y - 7$

12. $f(x, y) = x^3 + 3x^2 + y^2 - 4y + 3$

13. (*See Example 5*) $f(x, y) = 2x^3 + 2x^2 - 6xy + 3y^2 - 4x + 5$

14. $f(x, y) = 2x^4 + y^4 - x^2 - 2y^2$

III

15. (*See Example 6*) A company manufactures two products, X and Y, each affecting the demand and supply of the other. Let x be the price of X, and let y be the price of Y. The demand D for product X depends on both x and y and is given by

$$D(x, y) = -x^2 + 20x - 6y^2 + 60y + 550$$

Determine the prices x and y that maximize this demand D.

16. A firm produces two products, X and Y, each affecting the supply of the other. The supply S for product X is the following function of the prices, x of X and y of Y.

$$S(x, y) = -2x^2 + 400x - y^2 + 480y + 700$$

Find the prices x and y that maximize the supply of X.

17. A manufacturing company produces two items, X and Y. When its resources are divided between producing x units of X and y units of Y, then its daily profit function is given by

$$P(x, y) = -x^2 + 300x - 2y^2 + 400y + 8000$$

Determine the daily production of items X and Y that leads to maximum profit.

18. The U.S. Postal Service puts a limit to the size of a package that can be sent by mail. The sum of the length and girth of the package must be less than or equal to 100 inches. Determine the dimensions of the box with the largest volume that can be sent by mail.

19. The number of shutdowns N (either intentional or due to malfunctions) of a certain machine in an industrial plant is a function of the number of replacements made of two components X and Y. If x replacements of X and y replacements of Y are made per month, the number of shutdowns is

$$N(x, y) = 2x^3 - 12x^2 + 2y^3 - 18y^2 + 290$$

How many replacements of each component should be made per month to minimize the number of shutdowns?

20. A company plans to manufacture large rectangular storage containers. These containers are to have a volume of 1250 cubic feet. The cost of the material to be used is \$4 per square foot for the base, \$2 per square foot for the sides, and \$1 per square foot for the top. Find the dimensions of the container that will minimize cost.

15–4 LAGRANGE MULTIPLIERS

- *Introduction to Constraints*
- *The Method of Lagrange Multipliers for f(x, y)*
- *The Method of Lagrange Multipliers for f(x, y, z)*

INTRODUCTION TO CONSTRAINTS

In the previous section we introduced the second derivative test for functions of two variables and used this test to determine the relative maxima and minima of such functions. Now we change the problem somewhat; in this section we will show how to find the maximum or minimum of a function of x and y when these two variables are subject to a certain **constraint.** For example, we discussed earlier in this chapter the Cobb-Douglas production function, $f(x, y) = Cx^a y^{1-a}$, where C and a are constants. This function is used by economists to model the amount of a good produced when x units of labor and y units of capital go into the process.

Naturally, any manufacturer has only limited resources and must decide how to allocate these resources between labor and capital. This limitation on resources is an example of what is called a **constraint on x and y.**

Specifically, suppose that the manufacturing process of a company is described by

$$f(x, y) = 9x^{2/3}y^{1/3}$$

and that each unit of labor costs $200 and each unit of capital costs $300. Then x units of labor cost $200x$, and y units of capital cost $300y$. If $90,000 is available for production, then the company must operate under the constraint $200x + 300y = 90,000$. The company will want to find the values of x and y that maximize $f(x, y) = 9x^{2/3}y^{1/3}$, subject to the constraint $200x + 300y - 90,000 = 0$.

We will solve this particular problem in Example 2 but will begin with an easier problem. The method used to solve this type of problem, the method of **Lagrange multipliers,** is named after a French mathematician, Joseph Louis Lagrange, and introduces a new variable, traditionally represented by λ (lambda), the Greek letter corresponding to the letter L. (Notice that Lagrange's last name begins with L.) We will demonstrate the method in Example 1 and then give the general procedure.

EXAMPLE 1   *(Compare Exercise 1)*

Find the extreme values of $f(x, y) = x^2 + y^2$, subject to the constraint $x + 2y = 10$.

SOLUTION   First, rewrite the constraint as $x + 2y - 10 = 0$. Second, define a new function F by

$$F(x, y, \lambda) = f(x, y) + \lambda(x + 2y - 10)$$
$$= x^2 + y^2 + \lambda(x + 2y - 10)$$

Third, compute the partial derivatives of this new function F. In this case we have

$$\frac{\partial F}{\partial x}(x, y, \lambda) = 2x + \lambda$$

$$\frac{\partial F}{\partial y}(x, y, \lambda) = 2y + 2\lambda$$

$$\frac{\partial F}{\partial \lambda}(x, y, \lambda) = x + 2y - 10$$

Fourth, set each of these derivatives equal to zero and solve the corresponding system of equations. Here, we have the system

$$2x + \lambda = 0 \qquad (1)$$
$$2y + 2\lambda = 0 \qquad (2)$$
$$x + 2y - 10 = 0 \qquad (3)$$

The procedure that we use to solve this particular system is a general procedure that you will be able to use in further problems.

Solve equations (1) and (2) for λ. From (1),

$$\lambda = -2x$$

and from (2),

$$\lambda = -y$$

Set these expressions for λ equal to each other,

$$-y = -2x$$

and solve for either x or y. Here, we solve for y:

$$y = 2x$$

Now we have y in terms of x, so we substitute $2x$ for y in equation (3). This gives us an equation that only involves x, so we can solve for x:

$$x + 2(2x) - 10 = 0$$
$$5x - 10 = 0$$
$$x = 2$$

To find y, we go back to the expression for y in terms of x. We had $y = 2x$, so when $x = 2$, $y = 4$.

The solutions to this system of equations give us the candidates for the extreme values of f. Here, we have only one candidate: $(x, y) = (2, 4)$.

Now, $f(2, 4) = 4 + 16 = 20$. But how do we know whether this is a minimum or maximum value of f? If we evaluate $f(x, y)$ at some other point that satisfies the constraint $x + 2y - 10 = 0$, the point $(10, 0)$, for example, we see that $f(10, 0) = 100$, so 20 cannot possibly be the maximum. But we cannot evaluate the function everywhere; we must try to analyze the situation. If (x, y) is such that $|x|$ or $|y|$ is large, then $f(x, y) = x^2 + y^2$ is also large. Therefore $f(x, y)$ does have a minimum on the line whose equation is $x + 2y - 10 = 0$, the constraint equation.

Answer: Subject to the constraint $x + 2y - 10 = 0$, $f(x, y) = x^2 + y^2$ does not have a maximum value; the minimum value of $f(x, y)$ is $f(2, 4) = 20$.

We now outline the general method for finding the extreme values of f, subject to some constraining equation.

THE METHOD OF LAGRANGE MULTIPLIERS FOR $f(x, y)$

The Method of Lagrange Multipliers for $f(x, y)$

To find the relative extreme values of f under a constraint:

1. Rewrite the constraint in the form $g(x, y) = 0$.
2. Define a new function F by

$$F(x, y, \lambda) = f(x, y) + \lambda g(x, y)$$

3. Compute $\dfrac{\partial F}{\partial x}, \dfrac{\partial F}{\partial y}$, and $\dfrac{\partial F}{\partial \lambda}$.

4. Set these partial derivatives equal to 0 and solve that system of equations. The solutions to this system together with points where any of these partial derivatives fail to exist give you the points where f will have its extrema, subject to the constraint.
5. Finally, analyze the function and the constraint to determine whether the functional value is a maximum, a minimum, or neither.

Thus the points (x, y, λ) that satisfy the system

$$\frac{\partial F}{\partial x} = 0, \qquad \frac{\partial F}{\partial y} = 0, \qquad \text{and} \qquad \frac{\partial F}{\partial \lambda} = 0$$

play the same role as critical points; they tell you where to look for extreme values.

Also, notice that the equation

$$\frac{\partial F}{\partial \lambda}(x, y, \lambda) = 0$$

is the same equation as the constraint, $g(x, y) = 0$. Finally, we review the way in which we solved the system of equations

$$\frac{\partial F}{\partial x} = 0, \qquad \frac{\partial F}{\partial y} = 0, \qquad \text{and} \qquad \frac{\partial F}{\partial \lambda} = 0$$

We solved for λ in equations (1) and (2). Equating these expressions for λ gave us an equation involving only x and y. We used that equation to express y in terms of x (sometimes of course, you may wish to express x in terms of y) and substituted that expression into equation (3), giving us an equation involving only x. We solved this equation for x and then found the corresponding values of y.

We return to the problem of maximizing production that led us into the discussion of Lagrange multipliers.

EXAMPLE 2 *(Compare Exercise 11)*

Maximize $9x^{2/3}y^{1/3}$, subject to the constraint $200x + 300y = 90,000$.

SOLUTION The function f is given by $f(x, y) = 9x^{2/3}y^{1/3}$, and we rewrite the constraint as $g(x, y) = 200x + 300y - 90,000 = 0$.

Next, define

$$F(x, y, \lambda) = 9x^{2/3}y^{1/3} + \lambda(200x + 300y - 90,000)$$

Now we compute the partial derivatives of F:

$$\frac{\partial F}{\partial x}(x, y, \lambda) = 9\left(\frac{2}{3}\right)x^{-1/3}y^{1/3} + 200\lambda = 6x^{-1/3}y^{1/3} + 200\lambda$$

$$\frac{\partial F}{\partial y}(x, y, \lambda) = 9\left(\frac{1}{3}\right)x^{2/3}y^{-2/3} + 300\lambda = 3x^{2/3}y^{-2/3} + 300\lambda$$

$$\frac{\partial F}{\partial \lambda}(x, y, \lambda) = 200x + 300y - 90,000$$

Setting these derivatives equal to zero gives the following system:

$$6x^{-1/3}y^{1/3} + 200\lambda = 0 \qquad (1)$$
$$3x^{2/3}y^{-2/3} + 300\lambda = 0 \qquad (2)$$
$$200x + 300y - 90,000 = 0 \qquad (3)$$

Solving equation (1) for λ gives

$$200\,\lambda = -6x^{-1/3}y^{1/3}$$

$$\lambda = \frac{-3}{100}x^{-1/3}y^{1/3}$$

Solving equation (2) for λ gives

$$300\,\lambda = -3x^{2/3}y^{-2/3}$$

$$\lambda = \frac{-1}{100}x^{2/3}y^{-2/3}$$

Equating these expressions for λ, we have

$$\frac{-3}{100}x^{-1/3}y^{1/3} = \frac{-1}{100}x^{2/3}y^{-2/3}$$

Multiplying both sides by $-100x^{1/3}y^{2/3}$ gives

$$3y = x$$

This time, we have x in terms of y; substituting $3y$ for x in equation (3) gives

$$200(3y) + 300y - 90,000 = 0$$
$$900y = 90,000$$
$$y = 100$$

Since $x = 3y$, the corresponding value of x is 300.

One candidate for maximizing production is $(x, y) = (300, 100)$. Furthermore, notice that other critical points are introduced into this example because $\dfrac{\partial F}{\partial x}$ does not exist when $x = 0$, and $\dfrac{\partial F}{\partial y}$ does not exist when $y = 0$. Referring to the constraint $200x + 300y - 90,000 = 0$, $y = 300$ when $x = 0$, and $x = 450$ when $y = 0$.

$$f(0, 300) = 0$$
$$f(300, 100) = 9(300)^{2/3}100^{1/3}$$
$$f(450, 0) = 0$$

Moreover, the physical constraints from the application also require that both $x \geq 0$ and $y \geq 0$. Production will be maximized when the company uses 300 units of labor and 100 units of capital. At \$200 per unit for labor and \$300 per unit for capital, the resources of \$90,000 should be distributed as follows: \$60,000 for labor and \$30,000 for capital.

THE METHOD OF LAGRANGE MULTIPLIERS FOR $f(x, y, z)$

The method of Lagrange multipliers can also be used with functions of more than two variables. We will give an example showing how it works for three variables. The procedure is essentially unchanged.

The Method of Lagrange Multipliers for $f(x, y, z)$

Let $f(x, y, z)$ be a function, subject to the constraint $g(x, y, z) = 0$. Define a new function $F(x, y, z, \lambda)$ by

$$F(x, y, z, \lambda) = f(x, y, z) + \lambda g(x, y, z)$$

Solve the system of equations

$$\frac{\partial F}{\partial x} = 0, \qquad \frac{\partial F}{\partial y} = 0, \qquad \frac{\partial F}{\partial z} = 0, \qquad \frac{\partial F}{\partial \lambda} = 0$$

The values of x, y, and z that give maxima or minima of f subject to the constraint are among the simultaneous solutions of these equations together with the values for which any partial derivative fails to exist.

The technique for solving the system

$$\frac{\partial F}{\partial x} = 0, \qquad \frac{\partial F}{\partial y} = 0, \qquad \frac{\partial F}{\partial z} = 0, \qquad \frac{\partial F}{\partial \lambda} = 0$$

is slightly more complicated than in the previous examples. We solve for λ in each of the three equations

$$\frac{\partial F}{\partial x} = 0, \qquad \frac{\partial F}{\partial y} = 0, \qquad \text{and} \qquad \frac{\partial F}{\partial z} = 0$$

Next, these expressions for λ are used *in pairs* to write first y and then z in terms of x. These expressions for y and z are then substituted into the equation $\dfrac{\partial F}{\partial \lambda} = 0$ to give an equation involving only x. We solve this equation for x and then go back and find the corresponding values of y and z.

EXAMPLE 3 *(Compare Exercise 9)*

Find the minimum value of the function

$$f(x, y, z) = 10xy + 4xz + 6yz$$

subject to the constraint $xyz = 240$, where x, y, and z are all positive.

SOLUTION Applications frequently require that the variables be positive, and we will show at the end of the solution that this requirement is necessary here in order that f have a minimum. We construct the function

$$F(x, y, z, \lambda) = 10xy + 4xz + 6yz + \lambda(xyz - 240)$$

The partial derivatives of F are

$$F_x(x, y, z, \lambda) = 10y + 4z + \lambda(yz)$$
$$F_y(x, y, z, \lambda) = 10x + 6z + \lambda(xz)$$
$$F_z(x, y, z, \lambda) = 4x + 6y + \lambda(xy)$$
$$F_\lambda(x, y, z, \lambda) = xyz - 240$$

We now must solve the following system:

$$10y + 4z + \lambda(yz) = 0 \qquad (1)$$
$$10x + 6z + \lambda(xz) = 0 \qquad (2)$$
$$4x + 6y + \lambda(xy) = 0 \qquad (3)$$
$$xyz - 240 = 0 \qquad (4)$$

Solving equations (1), (2), and (3) for λ, we get, respectively,

$$\lambda = -\frac{10y + 4z}{yz}$$

$$\lambda = -\frac{10x + 6z}{xz}$$

$$\lambda = -\frac{4x + 6y}{xy}$$

The constraint, $xyz = 240$, means that x, y, and $z \neq 0$, so we have no problems with the denominators possibly being equal to 0. We now equate the first two expressions for λ:

$$-\frac{10y + 4z}{yz} = -\frac{10x + 6z}{xz}$$

Cross-multiply:

$$-(10xyz + 4xz^2) = -(10xyz + 6yz^2)$$
$$4xz^2 = 6yz^2$$
$$4x = 6y$$
$$y = \frac{2x}{3}$$

We have solved for y in terms of x. Next, equate the first and third expressions for λ:

$$-\frac{10y + 4z}{yz} = -\frac{4x + 6y}{xy}$$

Again, cross-multiply:

$$-(10xy^2 + 4xyz) = -(4xyz + 6y^2z)$$
$$10xy^2 = 6y^2z$$
$$10x = 6z$$
$$z = \frac{5x}{3}$$

Having arrived at expressions for y and z in terms of x, substitute them into equation (4). We get

$$(x)\left(\frac{2x}{3}\right)\left(\frac{5x}{3}\right) - 240 = 0$$

$$\frac{10x^3}{9} = 240$$

$$10x^3 = 2160$$

$$x^3 = 216$$

$$x = 6$$

Since $y = \frac{2x}{3}$ and $z = \frac{5x}{3}$, we have $x = 6$, $y = 4$, and $z = 10$; and

$$f(6, 4, 10) = 10 \cdot 6 \cdot 4 + 4 \cdot 6 \cdot 10 + 6 \cdot 4 \cdot 10 = 720$$

To see that 720 is the minimum of f for x, y, and z, all positive, we use the constraint $xyz = 240$ to write $z = \frac{240}{xy}$. Next, rewrite $10xy + 4xz + 6yz$ as

$$10xy + 4x\left(\frac{240}{xy}\right) + 6y\left(\frac{240}{xy}\right) = 10xy + \frac{960}{y} + \frac{1440}{x}$$

If xy is large, then the corresponding value of f will be large because of the $10xy$ term. If xy is small, then at least one of the terms, $\frac{960}{y}$ or $\frac{1440}{x}$, will be large. Therefore, f must have a minimum at $(6, 4, 10)$. This function behaves like the function

$$h(x) = x + \frac{1}{x}$$

in the one-variable case, which also indicates why we restricted the domain to x, y, and z positive. If we let $x > 0$ but both y and $z < 0$, f does not have a minimum value.

_____■

Exercise 19 shows how a function involving three variables, under constraint, can arise in practice and how for the problem to be meaningful, all three variables must be positive.

We complete this section by mentioning that some applications may involve more than one constraint. For example, you might want to find the extreme values of a function f subject to two constraints, $g(x, y, z) = 0$ and $h(x, y, z) = 0$. To do this, construct a function F that involves two Lagrange multipliers, λ and μ, one for each constraint. Define

$$F(x, y, z, \lambda, \mu) = f(x, y, z) + \lambda g(x, y, z) + \mu h(x, y, z)$$

If all the partial derivatives exist, then the values of x, y, and z that yield maxima or minima of f are among the solutions of the system of five equations,

$$\frac{\partial F}{\partial x} = 0, \qquad \frac{\partial F}{\partial y} = 0, \qquad \frac{\partial F}{\partial z} = 0, \qquad \frac{\partial F}{\partial \lambda} = 0,$$

$$\text{and} \quad \frac{\partial F}{\partial \mu} = 0$$

The algebraic manipulation involved in solving such a system is more involved than the ones we have discussed, but the basic method is the same.

15-4 EXERCISES

In Exercises 1 through 10, find the maximum or minimum value of the given function under the given constraint.

1. (*See Example 1*) Minimum value of $x^2 + 4y^2 + 6$, subject to $x - 4y = 9$

2. Maximum value of $x^2 + xy - 3y^2$, subject to $x + 2y = 4$

3. Maximum value of $8x - x^2 + 4y - y^2$, subject to $x + y = 8$

4. Maximum value of $x^2 - y^2$, subject to $2x + y = 6$

5. Minimum value of $3x^2 + y^2 + 3xy - 60x - 32y + 504$, subject to $x + y = 10$

6. Maximum value of $12xy - 3x^2 - y^2$, subject to $x + y = 16$

7. Minimum value of $6x^2 + 5y^2 - xy$, subject to $2x + y = 24$

8. Maximum and minimum values of $4x + 3y$, subject to $x^2 + y^2 - 9 = 0$

9. (*See Example 3*) Minimum value of $x^2 + y^2 + z^2$, subject to $x + 2y + 4z - 21 = 0$

10. Maximum value of x^2yz subject to $x + y + z = 16$, $x > 0$, $y > 0$, $z > 0$

11. (*See Example 2*) A manufacturing process is described by the Cobb-Douglas function

$$f(x, y) = 10x^{1/4}y^{3/4}$$

where x is the units of labor, y is the units of capital, and \$60,000 is available for production. How many units of labor and how many units of capital should be used to maximize production if each unit of labor costs \$100 and each unit of capital costs \$200?

12. The profit that a company makes from employing workers x hours at regular time and y hours at overtime per day is estimated to be described by the function

$$p(x, y) = 6xy + \frac{x^2}{2} - 2y^2$$

The company has a rule that employees who work overtime cannot work more than a total of nine hours in any day. How should regular time and overtime be divided to ensure maximum profit?

13. A company manufactures refrigerators at two plants, X and Y, and sells the refrigerators at a town Z. The cost of manufacturing and transporting x refrigerators from X to Z and y refrigerators from Y to Z is

$$C(x, y) = 2x^2 + 4y^2 - xy$$

Town Z wants 126 refrigerators. How many should come from X and how many from Y?

14. A company manufactures a certain product on two production lines. The total daily profit on manufacturing x items on the one line and y items on the other is $20xy - 2x^2 - y^2$. The company wants to produce 92 items per day. How many items should it manufacture on each line?

15. The cost of quality control in a manufacturing line is a function of the numbers of inspections x and y made per week at two points, X and Y:

$$C = 4x^2 + 2y^2 - 4y$$

Safety regulations require that 22 inspections be made each week. How many inspections should be made at each location to minimize cost?

16. A company manufactures a certain product on two separate production lines, X and Y. The profit realized on producing x units on line X and y units on line Y is

$$P = 20x + 16y - 2x^2 - y^2$$

The company wants to manufacture 64 units per week. How many should be produced on each line to maximize profit?

17. The relationship between the number of units N of an item sold and the amounts x and y (in dollars) spent on two advertising media is given by

$$N = 1600x + 1200y - 4x^2 - y^2$$

If $20,000 is available to spend on advertising, how should this be distributed between the media to maximize sales?

18. A company uses two types of communication equipment. The total cost of using x of one type and y of the other type is

$$C = 4x^2 + y^2 - 4xy$$

If $x + y = 6$, how should the distribution of the equipment be allocated to minimize cost?

19. To construct a free-standing garage, a construction company charges $5.00 per square foot for walls, $3.00 per square foot for the ceiling, and $4.00 per square foot for the floor. These costs include both labor and material and allow for all the required doors and windows. What are the dimensions of the largest garage (in terms of volume) that can be built for $9000?

15–5 MULTIPLE INTEGRALS

- *Iterated Integrals*
- *The Double Integral*
- *Volume*
- *Average Value of f(x, y)*

So far in this chapter, we have introduced functions of several variables, shown how to compute partial derivatives, and discussed the problem of finding extreme values, both with and without constraints. Remembering how we developed the calculus for functions of a single variable, you might have anticipated this section's topic: **multiple integrals.** Just as we did for functions of one variable, we will avoid the *theory* of integration, treating only the "nice" cases and concentrating on the computational aspects.

ITERATED INTEGRALS   If f is a function of two variables, x and y, then you can compute $\dfrac{\partial f}{\partial x}$ by treating y as a constant and differentiating with respect to x. Similarly, you can compute $\int f(x, y)\, dx$ by treating y as a constant and antidifferentiating with respect to x.

EXAMPLE 1   *(Compare Exercise 1)*

Find $\int (6x^2 + y - 2xy)\, dx$.

SOLUTION

$$\int (6x^2 + y - 2xy)\, dx = 2x^3 + xy - x^2y + g(y)$$

NOTE   Rather than $+ C$, we have written $+ g(y)$, where $g(y)$ denotes an expression that involves only constants and y, but not x. We mean by $g(y)$ the most general expression so that $\dfrac{\partial g}{\partial x} = 0$. Recall that $\int f(x)dx$ is the family of all functions whose derivative is $f(x)$. Similarly, $\int f(x, y)dx$ is the family of all functions whose partial derivative with respect to x is $f(x, y)$.

We can also treat y as the variable and x as a constant.

EXAMPLE 2   *(Compare Exercise 3)*

Find $\int (6x^2y - e^{xy})dy$.

SOLUTION

$$\int (6x^2y - e^{xy})dy = 3x^2y^2 - \frac{1}{x}e^{xy} + h(x)$$

Next, we introduce the definite integral, which is evaluated in the same manner as with functions of one variable. There is a difference in the answer however; $\int_a^b f(x)dx$ is a number, while $\int_a^b f(x, y)dx$ is, in general, an expression in y. The common aspect is that neither involves x.

EXAMPLE 3   *(Compare Exercise 5)*

Compute $\int_1^3 (12xy^2 - 4x + 2y)dx$.

SOLUTION

$$\int_1^3 (12xy^2 - 4x + 2y)\, dx = (6x^2y^2 - 2x^2 + 2xy)\Big|_1^3$$
$$= (54y^2 - 18 + 6y) - (6y^2 - 2 + 2y)$$
$$= 48y^2 + 4y - 16$$

Notice that, as was the case in evaluating definite integrals involving a function of one variable, you need to find only one particular antiderivative to perform the evaluation.

EXAMPLE 4

Compute $\int_{-1}^{2} (x^2 - 6y + 5)\,dy$.

SOLUTION

$$\int_{-1}^{2} (x^2 - 6y + 5)dy = (x^2 y - 3y^2 + 5y)\Big|_{-1}^{2}$$
$$= (2x^2 - 12 + 10) - (-x^2 - 3 - 5)$$
$$= 3x^2 + 6$$

We are now in a position to evaluate an expression such as

$$\int_{1}^{2} \int_{2}^{4} (3x^2 + 2xy)dx\,dy$$

which is called an **iterated integral.** This expression stands for two integrals, the inner integral being computed first. The brackets are commonly omitted, but better notation might be

$$\int_{1}^{2} \left(\int_{2}^{4} (3x^2 + 2xy)dx \right) dy$$

EXAMPLE 5 *(Compare Exercise 9)*

Compute $\int_{1}^{2} \int_{2}^{4} (3x^2 + 2xy)dx\,dy$.

SOLUTION Performing the inside integration first, we have

$$\int_{2}^{4} (3x^2 + 2xy)dx = (x^3 + x^2 y)\Big|_{2}^{4}$$
$$= (4^3 + 4^2 y) - (2^3 + 2^2 y)$$
$$= 56 + 12y$$

Thus the inner evaluation gives us $56 + 12y$. Our next evaluation is

$$\int_{1}^{2} (56 + 12y)dy = (56y + 6y^2)\Big|_{1}^{2}$$
$$= (112 + 24) - (56 + 6)$$
$$= 74$$

Therefore

$$\int_{1}^{2} \int_{2}^{4} (3x^2 + 2xy)dx\,dy = 74$$

The iteration can be done in either order.

EXAMPLE 6   *(Compare Exercise 13)*

Evaluate $\int_0^3 \int_{-1}^2 (4y + 6x^2y)dy\,dx$.

SOLUTION   First,

$$\int_{-1}^2 (4y + 6x^2y)dy = (2y^2 + 3x^2y^2)\Big|_{-1}^2$$

$$= (8 + 12x^2) - (2 + 3x^2)$$

$$= 6 + 9x^2$$

Second,

$$\int_0^3 (6 + 9x^2)dx = (6x + 3x^3)\Big|_0^3$$

$$= (18 + 81) - (0 + 0)$$

$$= 99$$

Therefore

$$\int_0^3 \int_{-1}^2 (4y + 6x^2y)dy\,dx = 99$$

THE DOUBLE INTEGRAL

Example 6 asked you to evaluate

$$\int_0^3 \int_{-1}^2 (4y + 6x^2y)dy\,dx$$

Notice that Example 7 has the same function for the integrand but that the order of integration has been reversed.

EXAMPLE 7   *(Compare Exercise 17)*

Evaluate $\int_{-1}^2 \int_0^3 (4y + 6x^2y)dx\,dy$.

SOLUTION   This time, the first computation is

$$\int_0^3 (4y + 6x^2y)dx = (4yx + 2x^3y)\Big|_0^3$$

$$= (12y + 54y) - (0 + 0)$$

$$= 66y$$

Next,

$$\int_{-1}^2 66y\,dy = 33y^2\Big|_{-1}^2$$

$$= 132 - 33$$

$$= 99$$

The answers to Examples 6 and 7 are the same. This situation is not unique.

In general, if $f(x, y)$ is continuous,

$$\int_a^b \int_c^d f(x, y)dy\, dx = \int_c^d \int_a^b f(x, y)dx\, dy$$

This independence of the order of integration allows us to make the following definition. We let R denote the rectangle $\{(x, y)$ with $a \le x \le b$ and $c \le y \le d\}$. (See Figure 15–17.) For the type of functions that we are considering, we can define the **double integral of f over the rectangle R** to be the number obtained as either iterated integral. This common number is written $\iint_R f$.

FIGURE 15–17

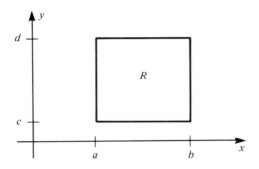

EXAMPLE 8   (Compare Exercise 17)

Evaluate $\iint_R f$ where $R = \{(x, y)$ with $2 \le x \le 4$ and $1 \le y \le 2\}$ and $f(x, y) = 3x^2 + 2xy$.

SOLUTION   We can evaluate $\iint_R f$ as

$$\int_1^2 \int_2^4 (3x^2 + 2xy)dx\, dy$$

This iterated integral was found to be equal to 74 in Example 5. Therefore we have $\iint_R f = 74$.

VOLUME

We have shown how to compute a double integral by using an iterated integral, and we now discuss the geometric interpretation of double integrals. Suppose that $f(x, y) \ge 0$ for all points (x, y) in a rectangle R. Then the graph of f is a surface lying above the xy-plane, as shown in Figure 15–18.

FIGURE 15–18

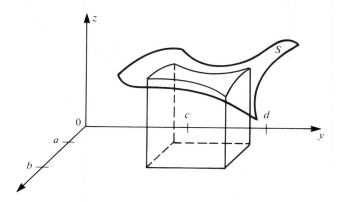

There is a three-dimensional solid bounded above by the graph of f and below by the rectangle R. The volume of this solid is $\iint\limits_{R} f$. We will not go into a rigorous discussion of the theory of volumes; in fact, we restrict our discussion to **volumes of solids** bounded below by a rectangle in the xy-plane and above by the graph of a function.

EXAMPLE 9   *(Compare Exercise 21)*

Determine the volume of the solid under the graph of $f(x, y) = 3x^2 + 2y$ and having as base the rectangle R defined by $1 \leq x \leq 2$, $2 \leq y \leq 4$.

SOLUTION   The volume will be given by the iterated integral

$$
\int_{2}^{4} \int_{1}^{2} (3x^2 + 2y)dx \, dy = \int_{2}^{4} \left(\int_{1}^{2} (3x^2 + 2y)dx \right) dy
$$

$$
= \int_{2}^{4} \left((x^3 + 2xy) \Big|_{1}^{2} \right) dy
$$

$$
= \int_{2}^{4} [(8 + 4y) - (1 + 2y)]dy
$$

$$
= \int_{2}^{4} (7 + 2y)dy
$$

$$
= (7y + y^2) \Big|_{2}^{4}
$$

$$
= (28 + 16) - (14 + 4)
$$

$$
= 26
$$

The volume under the surface and above the given rectangular region is 26.

Volume plays the same role in discussing functions of two variables that area does in the case of one variable. For example, if $f(x, y)$ is the amount of money spent on leisure activities as a function of age (x) and income (y), volumes can be used to compare total amounts spent by different groups. Furthermore, statistics and decision-making theory use probability distributions that depend on more than one variable. In this case the double integral over a rectangle R gives the probability that the two variables lie inside the rectangle. The double integral is also closely connected to double summations, and we saw in Chapter 13 that the connection between summations and the definite integral leads to various applications of the integral. However, we will not pursue these topics here. Our aim is simply to give you a brief introduction to double integrals and their evaluation. We conclude with an application that shows how applications of the double integral can closely parallel some of the applications of the definite integral that we saw.

AVERAGE VALUE OF $f(x, y)$

The double integral is used to define the **average value of a function over a rectangular region** in a natural extension of the definition of the average value of a function of a single variable. For purposes of our picture we again assume that $f(x, y) \geq 0$ over R, so the graph of f will be as shown in Figure 15–19.

Geometrically, you can think of $f(x, y)$ as the height from the point (x, y) to the surface S. We are interested in the average value of all such heights. Denote this average height by H. The area of R is $(b - a)(d - c)$. We call H the average height if the volume of the box having base R and height H is equal to the volume of the solid below the graph and over R. Therefore

$$(\text{Area of } R) \times H = \text{volume under the surface}$$

$$(b - a)(d - c) \times H = \int_c^d \int_a^b f(x, y)dx \, dy$$

$$H = \frac{1}{(b - a)(d - c)} \int_c^d \int_a^b f(x, y)dx \, dy$$

FIGURE 15–19

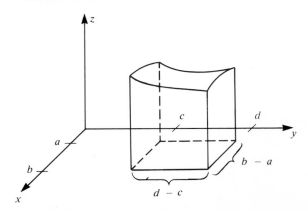

Definition	**The average value of $f(x, y)$,** denoted H, over a region $a \le x \le b$,
Average Value of $f(x, y)$ on a Rectangle	$c \le y \le d$, is given by

$$H = \frac{1}{(b - a)(d - c)} \int_c^d \int_a^b f(x, y)dx \, dy$$

EXAMPLE 10   *(Compare Exercise 25)*

Compute the average value of a function $f(x, y) = 4x^3y$ over the region $0 \le x \le 1, 2 \le y \le 4$.

SOLUTION   We get

$$H = \frac{1}{(1 - 0)(4 - 2)} \int_2^4 \int_0^1 4x^3y \, dx \, dy$$

$$= \frac{1}{2} \int_2^4 \left(\int_0^1 4x^3y \, dx \right) dy$$

$$= \frac{1}{2} \int_2^4 \left(x^4y \Big|_0^1 \right) dy$$

$$= \frac{1}{2} \int_2^4 y \, dy = \frac{1}{2} \left(\frac{y^2}{2} \Big|_2^4 \right)$$

$$= \frac{1}{2}(8 - 2)$$

$$= 3$$

The average value of the function over this region is 3.

15–5   EXERCISES

I

Do the antidifferentiation indicated in Exercises 1 through 4.

1. *(See Example 1)*

$$\int (12x^3y - 6x) \, dy$$

2. $\int (12x^3y - 6x) \, dx$

3. *(See Example 2)*

$$\int \frac{x}{y} \, dy$$

4. $\int \frac{x}{y} \, dx$

Evaluate the given expression in Exercises 5 through 8.

5. *(See Example 3)*

$$\int_1^4 (10xy + 2x - 4y)dx$$

6. $\int_1^4 (10xy + 2x - 4y)dy$

7. $\int_{-1}^2 (6x^2y + 7 - 4x)dy$

8. $\int_{-1}^2 (6x^2y + 7 - 4x)dx$

II

In Exercises 9 through 16, evaluate the given integrals.

9. (*See Example 5*)

$$\int_0^1 \int_0^1 4xy \, dx \, dy$$

10. $\int_1^2 \int_0^2 2x \, dx \, dy$

11. $\int_0^1 \int_2^3 (x + y - 4) dx \, dy$

12. $\int_1^3 \int_0^2 (8x + 4y) dx \, dy$

13. (*See Example 6*)

$$\int_0^4 \int_1^5 (6x^2y + 2x) dy \, dx$$

14. $\int_{-1}^2 \int_0^1 (12x^3y^2 - 6x^2y) dy \, dx$

15. $\int_{-1}^1 \int_2^4 (3y^2 + 4y^3) dx \, dy$

16. $\int_0^1 \int_0^2 e^{x+y} \, dx \, dy$

III

Compute $\iint_R f$ two different ways for the function f and the region R given in Exercises 17 through 20.

17. (*See Examples 7 and 8*) $f(x, y) = x^2 - y^2$, $-1 \le x \le 3, 1 \le y \le 2$

18. $f(x, y) = 4x - 8y, 1 \le x \le 4, -1 \le y \le 1$

19. $f(x, y) = \dfrac{x}{y}, 1 \le x \le 3, 1 \le y \le e$

20. $f(x, y) = 4ye^{2x}, 1 \le x \le 2, 1 \le y \le 2$

In each of Exercises 21 through 24, compute the volume of the region that is under the graph of the given function and that has the given rectangle as its base.

21. (*See Example 9*) $f(x, y) = 2x + 4y, 1 \le x \le 3$, $0 \le y \le 2$

22. $f(x, y) = 4xy + 6y^2, 0 \le x \le 1, 1 \le y \le 3$

23. $f(x, y) = 3x^2 + 6xy^2, 1 \le x \le 2, -2 \le y \le 3$

24. $f(x, y) = 6x^2y + 2y, -2 \le x \le 1, 0 \le y \le 4$

In each of Exercises 25 through 28, determine the average value of the given function over the given region.

25. (*See Example 10*) $f(x, y) = 4xy, 0 \le x \le 2$, $0 \le y \le 2$

26. $f(x, y) = 4xy + 6, 0 \le x \le 2, 0 \le y \le 2$ (Discuss your answer in the light of your answer to Exercise 25.)

27. $f(x, y) = 3x^2 + 6xy^2, 0 \le x \le 3, -1 \le y \le 3$

28. $f(x, y) = 3y^2 - 4x^3, 1 \le x \le 2, 0 \le y \le 4$

IMPORTANT TERMS

15-1

Function of More Than One Variable

Cobb-Douglas Production Function

Three-Dimensional Space

Surface

Coordinate Planes

Paraboloid

15-2

Partial Derivative

Second Partial Derivatives

Marginal Productivity of Labor

Marginal Productivity of Capital

15-3

Relative Maximum

Relative Minimum

Critical Point

Saddle Point

Second Derivative Test for a Function of Two Variables

15-4

Constraint

Extreme Value of f, Subject to a
*   Constraint on x and y*

Method of Lagrange Multipliers

15-5

Iterated Integrals

Double Integral

Reversing the Order of Integration

Volume of Solid

Average Value of f(x, y) over a
*   Rectangle*

REVIEW EXERCISES

For each of the functions given in Exercises 1 through 8, compute $f(x, y)$, $\dfrac{\partial f}{\partial x}$, $\dfrac{\partial f}{\partial y}$, $\dfrac{\partial^2 f}{\partial x^2}$, $\dfrac{\partial^2 f}{\partial y^2}$, and $\dfrac{\partial^2 f}{\partial x \, \partial y}$ at the indicated point p.

1. $f(x, y) = x^2 + y^3 - 4xy^2; p = (1, -2)$

2. $f(x, y) = \dfrac{y}{x^2 + 1}; p = (-1, 4)$

3. $f(x, y) = e^{xy^2}; p = (0, 2)$

4. $f(x, y) = \ln(x^2 + y^4); p = (2, -1)$

5. $f(x, y) = \dfrac{x}{y}; p = (-4, 2)$

6. $f(x, y) = \sqrt{x^2 + y^3}; p = (1, 2)$

7. $f(x, y) = x\sqrt{y^2 + 9}; p = (2, 4)$

8. $f(x, y) = e^{(x - 2y)}; p = (3, 1)$

Find the critical points for each of the functions given in Exercises 9 through 12. Then use the second derivative test to determine whether f has a relative maximum, a relative minimum, or neither at each critical point.

9. $f(x, y) = x^2 - y^2 - 6x - 4y + 20$

10. $f(x, y) = x^2 + y^3 - 6xy$

11. $f(x, y) = x^3 + y^3 - 6xy$

12. $f(x, y) = x^2 + y^2 + 8xy - 18x - 12y + 10$

Use the method of Lagrange multipliers in Exercises 13 through 16.

13. Find the maximum and the minimum of $f(x, y) = 6x + 8y$ if (x, y) must be on the circle $x^2 + y^2 = 25$.

14. Find the minimum $f(x, y) = x^2 + y^2$, subject to the constraint $xy = 4$.

15. Find the maximum of $f(x, y, z) = xyz$, subject to the constraint $2x + y + z = 6$ and x, y, and z are all positive.

16. Find the minimum of $f(x, y, z) = 3xy + xz + 2yz$, subject to the constraint $xyz = 6$ and x, y, and z must all be positive.

Compute the iterated integrals in Exercises 17 through 20.

17. $\displaystyle\int_{-1}^{2} \int_{0}^{3} (x^2 - yx)dy \, dx$

18. $\displaystyle\int_{0}^{9} \int_{1}^{4} \sqrt{xy} \, dx \, dy$

19. $\displaystyle\int_{-1}^{3} \int_{0}^{1} yxe^{x^2} \, dx \, dy$

20. $\displaystyle\int_{1}^{4} \int_{2}^{5} \frac{1}{x + y} \, dx \, dy$

21. What is the area under the surface $z = x^2 + y^2$ and above the rectangle $-1 \le x \le 2, 0 \le y \le 3$?

Appendix A
Review Topics

*T*HIS APPENDIX CONTAINS BASIC algebra topics that are necessary for the materials in this book. You are encouraged to study those topics for which you need review and skip those topics with which you are familiar.

A–1   PROPERTIES OF REAL NUMBERS

- *The Real Number Line*
- *The Arithmetic of Real Numbers*

THE REAL NUMBER LINE

The most basic numbers in our study of mathematics are the **natural numbers,**

$$1, 2, 3, 4, \ldots$$

These are, in fact, the numbers that we use to count. They can be represented graphically as points on a line, as in Figure A–1.

FIGURE A–1

Begin with a starting point on the line, which we label 0 (called zero), and a convenient unit scale. Starting at 0, mark off equal lengths to the right. These marks represent 1, 2, 3, ...

We can mark off lengths in the opposite direction from 0 and let them represent numbers, the negatives of the natural numbers. (See Figure A–2.) This collection of numbers represented by the marks on the line is written

$$\ldots, -5, -4, -3, -2, -1, 0, 1, 2, 3, 4, 5, \ldots$$

and is called the set of **integers.** Zero is neither positive nor negative.

FIGURE A–2

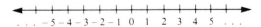

Other numbers, the **fractions,** can be represented with points between the integers. In Figure A–3, point *A,* halfway between 1 and 2, represents $1\frac{1}{2}$; point *B,* one quarter of the way from 3 to 4, represents $3\frac{1}{4}$. Point *C* is three quarters of the way from -4 to -5, so it represents $-4\frac{3}{4}$. These numbers together with the integers are called **rational numbers.**

FIGURE A–3

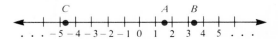

All these points can be expressed in terms of finite or infinite **decimals.** Point *A* is the point 1.5, *B* the point 3.25, and *C* the point −4.75. Every rational number can be expressed either as a decimal that terminates, such as *A, B,* and *C* above, or as a decimal that repeats infinitely. For example, $5\frac{1}{3}$ is a rational number that can be written in decimal form as 5.333 . . . ; the 3 repeats endlessly.

There are, however, certain numbers called **irrational numbers** that do not have any pattern of repetition in their decimal form. One such number is $\sqrt{2}$. Its decimal form is 1.414213. . . .

The set of all rational and irrational numbers is called the set of **real numbers.** One way to visualize the set of real numbers is to think of each point on the line as a real number.

THE ARITHMETIC OF REAL NUMBERS

There are four useful operations on the set of real numbers: addition, subtraction, multiplication, and division. The following table summarizes several rules that govern these operations.

In all the rules, the denominator is *never* zero.

Rule		*Example*
Division by zero is not allowed.		5/0 and 0/0 have no meaning.

Rules of Operations		*Examples*
$a + b = b + a$	Numbers can be added in either order.	$4 + 9 = 9 + 4$
$ab = ba$	Numbers can be multiplied in either order.	$3 \times 11 = 11 \times 3$
$ab + ac = a(b + c)$	A common number can be factored from each term in a sum.	$12a + 15b = 3(4a + 5b)$

Rules of Signs		*Examples*

Here we let *a* and *b* be positive numbers.

$-a = (-1)a$	The negative of a number *a* is the product $(-1)a$.	$-12 = (-1)12$
$-(-a) = a$		$-(-7) = 7$
$(-a)b = a(-b) = -ab$	The product of a positive and a negative number is a negative number.	$(-4)8 = -32$
		$5(-3) = -15$
$(-a)(-b) = ab$	The product of two negative numbers is a positive number.	$(-2)(-7) = 14$
$(-a) + (-b) = -(a + b)$	The sum of two negative numbers is a negative number.	$(-4) + (-5) = -9$
$\dfrac{-a}{b} = \dfrac{a}{-b}$	Division using a positive and a negative number is a negative number.	$\dfrac{-18}{3} = -6$
$\quad = -\left(\dfrac{a}{b}\right)$		$\dfrac{22}{-11} = -2$

Arithmetic of Fractions

$$\frac{ac}{bc} = \frac{a}{b}$$

The value of a fraction is unchanged if both the numerator and the denominator are multiplied or divided by the same number.

$$\frac{a}{b} + \frac{c}{b} = \frac{a + c}{b}$$

To add two fractions with the same denominators, add the numerators and keep the same denominator.

$$\frac{a}{b} + \frac{c}{d} = \frac{ad}{bd} + \frac{bc}{bd}$$

$$= \frac{ad + bc}{bd}$$

To add two fractions with different denominators, convert them to fractions with the same denominators by multiplying the numerator and denominator of each fraction by the denominator of the other.

$$\frac{a}{b} \times \frac{c}{d} = \frac{ac}{bd}$$

To multiply two fractions, multiply their numerators and multiply their denominators.

$$\frac{a}{b} \div \frac{c}{d} = \frac{a}{b} \times \frac{d}{c} = \frac{ad}{bc}$$

To divide by a fraction, invert the divisor and multiply.

Division may also be written in the form

$$\frac{\left(\dfrac{a}{b}\right)}{\left(\dfrac{c}{d}\right)} = \frac{a}{b} \div \frac{c}{d}$$

$$= \frac{a}{b} \times \frac{d}{c} = \frac{ad}{bc}$$

$$\frac{a}{b} = \frac{c}{d} \text{ if and only if } ad = bc$$

Examples

$$\frac{10}{15} = \frac{2}{3}$$

$$\frac{7}{4} = \frac{14}{8}$$

$$\frac{5}{3} + \frac{2}{3} = \frac{7}{3}$$

$$\frac{3}{7} + \frac{2}{5}$$

$$= \frac{3(5)}{7(5)} + \frac{7(2)}{7(5)}$$

$$= \frac{3(5) + 7(2)}{7(5)}$$

$$= \frac{15 + 14}{35}$$

$$= \frac{29}{35}$$

$$\frac{3}{4} \times \frac{6}{11} = \frac{18}{44} = \frac{9}{22}$$

$$\frac{2}{3} \div \frac{5}{8} = \frac{2}{3} \times \frac{8}{5}$$

$$= \frac{16}{15}$$

$$\frac{\left(\dfrac{5}{3}\right)}{\left(\dfrac{4}{7}\right)} = \frac{5}{3} \div \frac{4}{7}$$

$$= \frac{5}{3} \times \frac{7}{4}$$

$$= \frac{35}{12}$$

$$\frac{3}{7} = \frac{9}{21} \text{ because } 3(21) = 7(9)$$

$$\frac{5}{9} \neq \frac{3}{4} \text{ because } 5(4) \neq 9(3)$$

A–1 EXERCISES

Evaluate the expressions in Exercises 1 through 49.

1. $(-1)13$

2. $(-1)(-7)$

3. $-(-23)$

4. $(-10)(-4)$

5. $(-5)(6)$

6. $(-2)(-4)$

7. $5(-7)$

8. $(-6) + (-11)$

9. $-(7 - 2)$

10. $\dfrac{-10}{5}$

11. $\dfrac{21}{-3}$

12. $\dfrac{5 \times 3}{7 \times 3}$

13. $(-4) + (-6)$

14. $(-3)(-2)$

15. $(-4)2$

16. $\dfrac{4}{9} + \dfrac{2}{9}$

17. $\dfrac{5}{3} + \dfrac{4}{3}$

18. $\dfrac{4}{11} - \dfrac{2}{11}$

19. $\dfrac{12}{5} - \dfrac{3}{5}$

20. $\dfrac{6}{10} - \dfrac{13}{10}$

21. $\dfrac{2}{3} + \dfrac{3}{4}$

22. $\dfrac{5}{8} - \dfrac{1}{3}$

23. $\dfrac{5}{6} - \dfrac{7}{4}$

24. $\dfrac{5}{12} - \dfrac{1}{6}$

25. $\dfrac{2}{5} + \dfrac{1}{4}$

26. $(-3) + 6$

27. $\dfrac{4}{7} - \dfrac{3}{5}$

28. $\dfrac{2}{3} \times \dfrac{4}{5}$

29. $\dfrac{\left(\dfrac{3}{4}\right)}{\left(\dfrac{9}{8}\right)}$

30. $\dfrac{3}{8} + \dfrac{2}{5}$

31. $\dfrac{\left(\dfrac{2}{7}\right)}{\left(\dfrac{4}{5}\right)}$

32. $\left(\dfrac{4}{3}\right)\left(\dfrac{6}{7}\right)$

33. $\left(\dfrac{1}{3}\right)\left(\dfrac{1}{5}\right)$

34. $6 \times (-3)$

35. $\dfrac{2}{5} \times \dfrac{4}{3}$

36. $\left(-\dfrac{2}{3}\right)\left(\dfrac{1}{9}\right)$

37. $\left(-\dfrac{3}{5}\right)\left(-\dfrac{4}{7}\right)$

38. $\dfrac{4}{5} \div \dfrac{2}{15}$

39. $\dfrac{3}{11} + \dfrac{1}{3}$

40. $\dfrac{\left(-\dfrac{4}{9}\right)}{\left(\dfrac{5}{2}\right)}$

41. $\dfrac{5}{7} \div \dfrac{15}{28}$

42. $\dfrac{\left(\dfrac{4}{9}\right)}{\left(\dfrac{16}{3}\right)}$

43. $\dfrac{5}{8} \div \dfrac{1}{3}$

44. $\left(\dfrac{1}{2} - \dfrac{1}{3}\right)\left(\dfrac{5}{7}\right)$

45. $\left(\dfrac{3}{4} + \dfrac{1}{5}\right) \div \left(\dfrac{2}{9}\right)$

46. $5(4a + 2b)$

47. $-2(3a + 11b)$

48. $2(a - 3b)$

49. $-5(2a + 10b)$

A–2 SOLVING LINEAR EQUATIONS

Numerous disciplines including science, technology, social sciences, business, manufacturing, and government find mathematical techniques essential in day-to-day operations. They depend heavily on mathematical equations that describe conditions or relationships between quantities.

In an equation such as

$$4x - 5 = 7$$

the symbol x, called a **variable**, represents an arbitrary, an unspecified, or an unknown number just as "John Doe" and "Jane Doe" often denote an arbitrary, unspecified, or unknown person.

The equation $4x - 5 = 7$ may be true or false depending on the choice of the number x. If we substitute the number 3 for x in

$$4x - 5 = 7$$

both sides become equal, and we say that $x = 3$ is a **solution** of the equation. If 5 is substituted for x, then both sides are *not* equal, so $x = 5$ is *not* a solution.

It might help a sales representative to know that the expression $0.20x + 11$ describes the daily rental of a car. Furthermore, the solution of the equation $0.20x + 11 = 40$ answers the question "You paid \$40 for car rental, how many miles did you drive?" Solutions of equations can sometimes help one to make a decision or give needed information.

One basic procedure for solving an equation is to obtain a sequence of equivalent equations with the goal of isolating the variable on one side of the equation and the appropriate number on the other side.

The following two operations help to isolate the variable and find the solution.

1. The same number may be added to or subtracted from both sides of an equation.
2. Both sides of an equation may be multiplied or divided by a nonzero number.

Either of these operations yields another equation that is equivalent to the first, in other words, a second equation that has the same solution as the first.

EXAMPLE 1   *(Compare Exercise 3)*

Solve the equation $3x + 4 = 19$.

SOLUTION   We begin to isolate x by subtracting 4 from both sides:

$$3x + 4 - 4 = 19 - 4$$
$$3x = 15$$

Next, divide both sides by 3:

$$\frac{3x}{3} = \frac{15}{3}$$
$$x = 5 \quad \text{is the solution}$$

We can check our answer by substituting $x = 5$ into the original equation.

$$3(5) + 4 = 15 + 4 = 19$$

so the solution checks.

EXAMPLE 2   *(Compare Exercise 7)*

Solve $4x - 2 = 2x + 12$.

SOLUTION

$$4x - 2 = 2x + 12 \qquad \text{(First, add 2 to both sides)}$$
$$4x - 2 + 2 = 2x + 12 + 2$$
$$4x = 2x + 14 \qquad \text{(Next, subtract } 2x \text{ from both sides)}$$
$$4x - 2x = 2x + 14 - 2x$$
$$2x = 14 \qquad \text{(Now divide both sides by 2)}$$
$$x = 7$$

Check: $4(7) - 2 = 28 - 2 = 26$ (left-hand side) and $2(7) + 12 = 14 + 12 = 26$ (right-hand side), so it checks.

EXAMPLE 3   *(Compare Exercise 9)*

Solve $7x + 13 = 0$.

SOLUTION

$$7x + 13 = 0 \qquad \text{(Subtract 13 from both sides)}$$
$$7x = -13 \qquad \text{(Divide both sides by 7)}$$
$$x = -\frac{13}{7}$$

The above examples all use **linear equations**.

Definition
Linear Equation

A **linear equation in one variable**, x, is an equation that can be written in the form

$$ax + b = 0 \qquad \text{where} \qquad a \neq 0$$

A **linear equation in two variables**, x and y, is an equation that can be written in the form

$$y = ax + b \qquad \text{where} \qquad a \neq 0$$

EXAMPLE 4   *(Compare Exercise 13)*

Solve $\dfrac{3x - 5}{2} + \dfrac{x + 7}{3} = 8$.

SOLUTION   We show two ways to solve this. First, use rules of fractions to combine the terms on the left-hand side:

$$\frac{3x - 5}{2} + \frac{x + 7}{3} = 8 \qquad \text{(Convert fractions to the same denominator)}$$

$$\frac{3(3x - 5)}{6} + \frac{2(x + 7)}{6} = 8 \qquad \text{(Now add the fractions)}$$

$$\frac{3(3x - 5) + 2(x + 7)}{6} = 8$$

$$\frac{9x - 15 + 2x + 14}{6} = 8$$

$$\frac{11x - 1}{6} = 8 \qquad \text{(Now multiply both sides by 6)}$$

$$11x - 1 = 48$$

$$11x = 49$$

$$x = \frac{49}{11}$$

An alternative, and simpler, method is the following:

$$\frac{3x - 5}{2} + \frac{x + 7}{3} = 8$$

Multiply through by 6 (the product of the denominators):

$$3(3x - 5) + 2(x + 7) = 48$$

$$9x - 15 + 2x + 14 = 48$$

$$11x - 1 = 48$$

$$11x = 49$$

$$x = \frac{49}{11}$$

EXAMPLE 5   *(Compare Exercise 17)*

A car rental company charges \$0.21 per mile plus \$10 per day for car rental. Thus the daily fee is represented by the equation

$$y = 0.21x + 10$$

where x is the number of miles driven and y is the daily fee.

(a) Determine the rental fee if the car is driven 165 miles during the day.
(b) Determine the rental fee if the car is driven 420 miles during the day.
(c) The rental fee is \$48.64. Find the number of miles driven.

SOLUTION

(a) $x = 165$, so $y = 0.21(165) + 10 = 44.65$. The fee is \$44.65.
(b) $x = 420$, so $y = 0.21(420) + 10 = 98.2$. The fee is \$98.20.
(c) $y = 48.64$, so x is the solution of the equation

$$0.21x + 10 = 48.64$$
$$0.21x = 48.64 - 10$$
$$0.21x = 38.64$$
$$x = \frac{38.64}{0.21} = 184$$

The car was driven 184 miles.

A-2 EXERCISES

Determine which of the following values of x are solutions to the equations in Exercises 1 and 2. Use $x = 1, 2, -3, 0, 4,$ and -2.

1. $2x - 4 = -10$

2. $3x + 1 = x + 5$

Solve the equations in Exercises 3 through 16.

3. *(See Example 1)*
$2x - 3 = 5$

4. $-4x + 2 = 6$

5. $4x - 3 = 5$

6. $7x - 4 = 0$

7. *(See Example 2)*
$7x + 2 = 3x + 4$

8. $2x - 4 = -5x + 2$

9. *(See Example 3)*
$12x + 21 = 0$

10. $5 - x = 8 + 3x$

11. $3(x - 5) + 4(2x + 1) = 9$

12. $6(4x + 5) + 7 = 2$

13. *(See Example 4)*
$\dfrac{2x + 3}{3} + \dfrac{5x - 1}{4} = 2$

14. $\dfrac{4x + 7}{6} + \dfrac{2 - 3x}{5} = 5$

15. $\dfrac{12x + 4}{2x + 7} = 4$

16. $\dfrac{x + 1}{x - 1} = \dfrac{3}{4}$

17. (*See Example 5*) U-Drive-It Rental Company charges $0.20 per mile plus $112 per week for car rental. The weekly rental fee for a car is represented by the linear equation

$$y = 0.20x + 112$$

where x is the number of miles driven and y is the weekly rental charge.

(a) Determine the rental fee if the car is driven 650 miles during the week.

(b) Determine the rental fee if the car is driven 1500 miles.

(c) The weekly rental fee is $302. How many miles was the car driven?

18. Joe Cool has a summer job selling real estate in a subdivision development. He receives a base salary of $100 per week plus $50 for each lot sold. Therefore, the equation

$$y = 50x + 100$$

represents his weekly income, where x is the number of lots sold.

(a) What is his weekly income if he sells seven lots?

(b) What is his weekly income if he sells 15 lots?

(c) If he receives $550 one week, how many lots did he sell?

19. A Girl Scout troop collects aluminum cans for a project. The recycling center weighs the cans in a container that weighs eight pounds, so the Scouts are paid according to the equation

$$y = 0.42(x - 8)$$

where x is the weight in pounds given by the scale and y is the payment in dollars.

(a) How much money do the Girl Scouts receive if the scale reads 42 pounds?

(b) How much do they receive if the scale reads 113 pounds?

(c) The Scouts received $22.26 for one weekend's collection. What was the reading on the scale?

20. The tuition and fees paid by students at a local junior college is given by the equation

$$y = 27x + 85$$

where x is the number of hours enrolled and y is the total cost of tuition and fees ($85 fixed fees and $27 per hour tuition).

(a) How much does a student pay who is enrolled in 13 hours?

(b) A student who pays $517 is enrolled in how many hours?

A–3 COORDINATE SYSTEMS

We have all seen a map, a house plan, or a wiring diagram that shows information recorded on a flat surface. Each of these uses some notation that is unique to the subject to convey the desired information. In mathematics we often use a flat surface called a **plane** to draw figures and locate points. We place a reference system in the plane to record and communicate information accurately. The standard mathematical reference system consists of a horizontal and a vertical line (called **axes**). These two perpendicular axes form a **Cartesian,** or **rectangular, coordinate system.** They intersect at a point called the **origin.**

We name the horizontal axis the **x-axis,** and we name the vertical axis the **y-axis.** The origin is labeled O.

Two numbers are used to describe the location of a point in the plane, and they are recorded in the form (x, y). For example, $x = 3$ and $y = 2$ for the point $(3, 2)$. The first number, 3, called the **x-coordinate** or **abscissa,** represents the horizontal distance from the y-axis to the point. The second number, 2, called the **y-coordinate** or **ordinate,** represents the vertical distance measured from the

FIGURE A–4

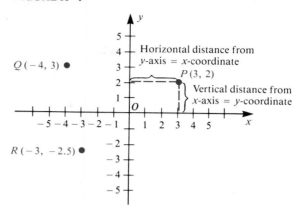

x-axis to the point. The point (3, 2) is shown as point P in Figure A–4. Points located to the right of the y-axis have positive x-coordinates; points to the left have negative x-coordinates. The y-coordinate is positive for points located above the x-axis and negative for those located below.

Figure A–4 shows other examples of points in this coordinate system: Q is the point $(-4, 3)$, and R is the point $(-3, -2.5)$. The origin O has coordinates $(0, 0)$.

Figure A–5 shows the points $(-3, 2)$, $(-4, -2)$, $(1, 1)$, and $(1, -2)$ plotted on the Cartesian coordinate system.

FIGURE A–5

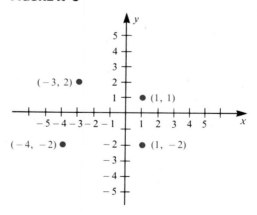

FIGURE A–6

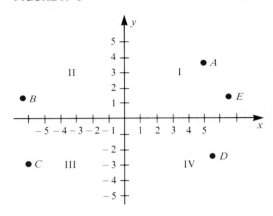

The coordinate axes divide the plane into four parts called **quadrants.** The quadrants are labeled I, II, III, and IV as shown in Figure A–6. Point *A* is located in the first quadrant, *B* in the second quadrant, *C* in the third, and *D* in the fourth. Points *A* and *E* lie in the same quadrant.

René Descartes (1596–1650), a French philosopher-mathematician, invented the Cartesian coordinate system. His invention of the coordinate system is one of the outstanding ideas in the history of mathematics because it combined algebra and geometry in a way that enables us to use algebra to solve geometry problems and to use geometry to clarify algebraic concepts.

A–3 EXERCISES

1. The following are the coordinates of points in a rectangular Cartesian coordinate system. Plot these points.

   $(-5, 4), (-2, -3), (-2, 4), (1, 5), (2, -5)$

2. What are the coordinates of the points *P, Q, R,* and *S* in the coordinate system in Figure A–7?

3. Locate the following points in a Cartesian coordinate system:

   $(-2, 5), (3, -2), (0, 4), (-2, 0), (\frac{7}{2}, 2),$
   $(\frac{2}{3}, \frac{9}{4}), (-4, -2), (0, -5), (0, -2), (-6, -3)$

4. Give the coordinates of *A, B, C, D, E,* and *F* in the coordinate system shown in Figure A–8.

FIGURE A–7

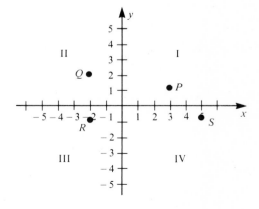

FIGURE A–8

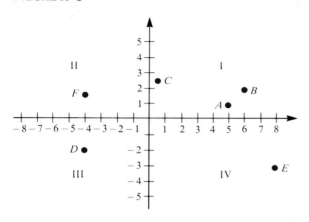

5. Note that all points in the first quadrant have positive *x*-coordinates and positive *y*-coordinates. What are the characteristics of the points in:
   (a) the second quadrant?
   (b) the third quadrant?
   (c) the fourth quadrant?

6. For each case shown in Figure A–9, find the property that the points have in common.

7. An old map gives these instructions to find a buried treasure: Start at giant oak tree. Go north 15 paces, then east 22 paces to a half-buried rock. The key to the treasure chest is buried at the spot that is 17 paces west and 13 paces north of the rock. From the place where the key is buried, go 32 paces west and 16 paces south to the location of the buried treasure. Use a coordinate system to represent the location of the oak tree, the rock, the key, and the treasure.

FIGURE A–9

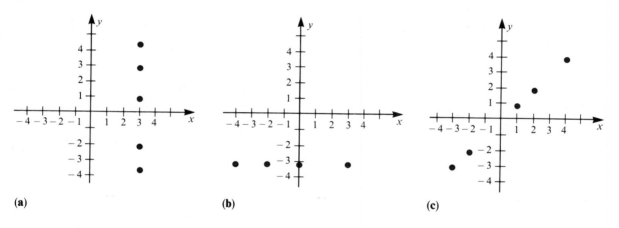

(a)   (b)   (c)

A–4   LINEAR INEQUALITIES AND INTERVAL NOTATION

- *Solving Inequalities*
- *Interval Notation*

We frequently use inequalities in our daily conversation. They may take the form "Which store has the lower price?" "Did you make a higher grade?" "Our team scored more points." "My expenses are greater than my income." Statements such as these basically state that one quantity is greater than another. Statements using the terms "greater than" or "less than" are called **inequalities.** Our goal is to solve inequalities. First, we give some terminology and notation.

The symbol $<$ means "less than," and $>$ means "greater than." Just remember that each of these symbols points to the smaller quantity. The notation $a > b$ and $b < a$ have exactly the same meaning. We may interpret the definition of $a > b$ in three equivalent ways. At times, one may be more useful than the other, so choose the most appropriate one.

Definition $a > b$	If a and b are real numbers, the following statements have the same meaning. **(a)** $a > b$ means that a lies to the right of b on a number line. **(b)** $a > b$ means that there is a positive number p such that $a = b + p$. **(c)** $a > b$ means that $a - b$ is a positive number p.

The positive numbers lie to the right of zero on a number line, and the negative numbers lie to the left.

We will also use the symbols $<$ (less than), $\geq$ (greater than or equal to), and $\leq$ (less than or equal to).

Definition $a < b, a \geq b, a \leq b$	$a < b$ means $b > a$. $a \geq b$ means $a = b$ or $a > b$. $a \leq b$ means $a = b$ or $a < b$.

EXAMPLE 1   *(Compare Exercise 1)*

The numbers 5, 8, 17, -2, -3, and -15 are plotted on a number line in Figure A–10. Notice the following.

FIGURE A–10

1. **(a)** 17 lies to the right of 5.
   (b) $17 = 5 + 12$
   (c) $17 - 5 = 12$
   Each of these three statements is equivalent to saying that $17 > 5$.
2. $8 > -3$ because $8 - (-3) = 8 + 3 = 11$ (by part (c)).
3. $-2 > -15$ because $-2 = -15 + 13$ (by part (b) where $p = 13$). ∎

SOLVING INEQUALITIES

By the **solution** of an inequality like

$$3x + 5 > 23$$

we mean the value or values of x that make the statement true. The method for solving inequalities is similar to that for solving equations. We want to operate on an inequality in a way that gives an equivalent inequality but that enables us to determine the solution.

Here are some simple examples of useful properties of inequalities.

EXAMPLE 2

1. Since $18 > 4$, $18 + 6 > 4 + 6$, that is, $24 > 10$ (6 added to both sides).
2. Since $23 > -1$, $23 - 7 > -1 - 7$, that is, $16 > -8$ (7 subtracted from both sides).
3. Since $6 > 2$, $4(6) > 4(2)$, that is, $24 > 8$ (both sides multiplied by 4).
4. Since $10 > 3$, $-2(10) < -2(3)$, that is, $-20 < -6$ (both sides multiplied by -2).

CAUTION   The inequality symbol reverses when we multiply each side by a negative number.

5. Since $-15 > -21$, $\dfrac{-15}{3} > \dfrac{-21}{3}$, that is, $-5 > -7$ (both sides divided by 3.)
6. Since $20 > 6$, $\dfrac{20}{-2} < \dfrac{6}{-2}$, that is, $-10 < -3$ (both sides divided by -2.)

CAUTION   The inequality symbol reverses when dividing each side by a negative number.

These examples illustrate basic properties that are useful in solving inequalities.

Properties of Inequalities

For real numbers a, b, and c the following properties are true.

1. Adding a number to both sides of an inequality leaves the direction of the inequality unchanged.

    If $a > b$, then $a + c > b + c$.

2. Subtraction of a number from both sides of an inequality leaves the direction of the inequality unchanged.

    If $a > b$, then $a - c > b - c$.

3. Multiply both sides of an inequality by a nonzero number:

    (a) If $a > b$ and c is positive, then $ac > bc$.

    (b) If $a > b$ and c is negative, then $ac < bc$. (Notice the change from $>$ to $<$.)

4. Divide both sides of an inequality by a nonzero number:

    (a) If $a > b$ and c is positive, then $\dfrac{a}{c} > \dfrac{b}{c}$.

    (b) If $a > b$ and c is negative, then $\dfrac{a}{c} < \dfrac{b}{c}$. (Notice the change from $>$ to $<$.)

Note: All these properties hold if $>$ is replaced by $<$ and vice versa or if $>$ is replaced by $\geq$ and $<$ is replaced by $\leq$.

We use these properties to solve an inequality, that is, to find the values of x that make the inequality true. In general, we proceed by finding equivalent inequalities that will eventually isolate x on one side of the inequality and the appropriate number on the other side.

EXAMPLE 3   *(Compare Exercise 3)*

Solve the inequality $3x + 5 > 14$.

SOLUTION   Begin with the given inequality:

$$3x + 5 > 14 \qquad \text{(Next, subtract 5 from each side)}$$
$$3x > 9 \qquad \text{(Now divide each side by 3)}$$
$$x > 3$$

All values of x greater than 3 make the inequality true. This solution can be graphed on a number line as shown in Figure A–11. The empty circle indicates that $x = 3$ is omitted from the solution, and the heavy line indicates the values of x that are included in the solution.

FIGURE A–11

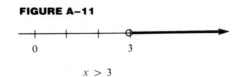

$x > 3$

EXAMPLE 4 *(Compare Exercise 9)*

Solve the inequality $5x - 17 > 8x + 14$ and indicate the solution on a graph.

SOLUTION Start with the given inequality:

$$5x - 17 > 8x + 14 \qquad \text{(Now add 17 to both sides)}$$
$$5x > 8x + 31 \qquad \text{(Now subtract } 8x \text{ from both sides)}$$
$$-3x > 31 \qquad \text{(Now divide both sides by } -3)$$
$$x < -\frac{31}{3} \qquad \text{(This reverses the inequality symbol)}$$

The solution consists of all x to the left of $-\frac{31}{3}$. See Figure A–12.

FIGURE A–12

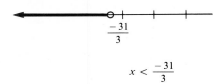

$$x < \frac{-31}{3}$$

EXAMPLE 5 *(Compare Exercise 13)*

Solve and graph $2(x - 3) \le 3(x + 5) - 7$.

SOLUTION

$$2(x - 3) \le 3(x + 5) - 7 \qquad \text{(First perform the indicated multiplications)}$$
$$2x - 6 \le 3x + 15 - 7$$
$$2x - 6 \le 3x + 8 \qquad \text{(Now add 6 to both sides)}$$
$$2x \le 3x + 14 \qquad \text{(Subtract } 3x \text{ from both sides)}$$
$$-x \le 14 \qquad \text{(Multiply both sides by } -1)$$
$$x \ge -14$$

Since the solution includes -14 and all numbers greater, the graph shows a solid circle at -14 (see Figure A–13).

FIGURE A–13

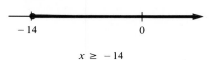

$$x \ge -14$$

The next example illustrates a problem that involves two inequalities.

EXAMPLE 6   *(Compare Exercise 17)*

Solve and graph $3 < 2x + 5 \leq 13$.

SOLUTION   This inequality means both $3 < 2x + 5$ *and* $2x + 5 \leq 13$. Solve it in a manner similar to the preceding examples except that you try to isolate the x in the middle.

Begin with the given inequality:

$$3 < 2x + 5 \leq 13 \qquad \text{(Subtract 5 from all parts of the inequality)}$$
$$-2 < 2x \leq 8 \qquad \text{(Divide each part by 2)}$$
$$-1 < x \leq 4$$

The solution consists of all numbers between -1 and 4, including 4 but not including -1. The graph of the solution (see Figure A–14) shows an empty circle at -1 because -1 is not a part of the solution. It shows a solid circle at 4 because 4 is a part of the solution. The solid line between -1 and 4 indicates that all numbers between -1 and 4 are included in the solution.

FIGURE A–14

$$-1 < x \leq 4$$

INTERVAL NOTATION

The solution of an inequality can be represented by yet another notation, the **interval notation.** Identify the portion of the number line that represents the solution of an inequality by its endpoints; brackets or parentheses indicate whether or not the endpoint is included in the solution. A parenthesis indicates that the endpoint is not included, and a bracket indicates that the endpoint is included. For example, the notation $(-1, 4]$ means $-1 < x \leq 4$ and indicates the set of all numbers between -1 and 4 with -1 excluded and 4 included in the set. The notation $(-1, 4)$ means $-1 < x < 4$ and indicates that both -1 and 4 are excluded from the set.

The notation $(-1, \infty)$ denotes $x > -1$, the set of all numbers greater than -1. The symbol ∞ denotes infinity and indicates that there is no upper bound to the interval.

Table A–1 shows the variations of the interval notation.

TABLE A–1

INEQUALITY NOTATION		INTERVAL NOTATION		GRAPH OF INTERVAL
General	*Example*	*General*	*Example*	
$a < x < b$	$-1 < x < 4$	(a, b)	$(-1, 4)$	
$a \leq x < b$	$-1 \leq x < 4$	$[a, b)$	$[-1, 4)$	
$a < x \leq b$	$-1 < x \leq 4$	$(a, b]$	$(-1, 4]$	
$a \leq x \leq b$	$-1 \leq x \leq 4$	$[a, b]$	$[-1, 4]$	
$x < b$	$x < 4$	$(-\infty, b)$	$(-\infty, 4)$	
$x \leq b$	$x \leq 4$	$(-\infty, b]$	$(-\infty, 4]$	
$a < x$	$-1 < x$	(a, ∞)	$(-1, \infty)$	
$a \leq x$	$-1 \leq x$	$[a, \infty)$	$[-1, \infty)$	

EXAMPLE 7   *(Compare Exercise 25)*

Solve $1 \leq 2(x - 5) + 3 < 5$.

SOLUTION

$$1 \leq 2(x - 5) + 3 < 5 \qquad \text{(Multiply to remove parentheses)}$$
$$1 \leq 2x - 10 + 3 < 5$$
$$1 \leq 2x - 7 < 5 \qquad \text{(Add 7 throughout)}$$
$$8 \leq 2x < 12 \qquad \text{(Divide through by 2)}$$
$$4 \leq x < 6$$

The solution consists of all values of x in the interval $[4, 6)$, and the graph is shown in Figure A–15.

FIGURE A–15

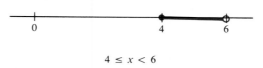

$$4 \leq x < 6$$

EXAMPLE 8   *(Compare Exercise 31)*

The total points on an exam given by Professor Passmore are 20 points plus 2.5 points for each correct answer. A total score in the interval [70, 80) is a C. If Scott made a C on the exam, how many questions did he answer correctly?

SOLUTION   The score on an exam is given by $20 + 2.5x$, where x is the number of correct answers. Therefore the condition for a C is

$$70 \leq 20 + 2.5x < 80$$

Solve for x to obtain the number of correct answers:

$$70 \leq 20 + 2.5x < 80$$
$$50 \leq 2.5x < 60$$
$$\frac{50}{2.5} \leq x < \frac{60}{2.5}$$
$$20 \leq x < 24$$

In this case, only whole numbers make sense, so Scott got 20, 21, 22, or 23 correct answers.

A–4 EXERCISES

I

1. (*See Example 1*) The following inequalities are of the form $a > b$. Verify the truth or falsity of each one by the property that $a > b$ means $a - b$ is a positive number.
   (a) $9 > 3$ (b) $4 > 0$ (c) $-5 > 0$
   (d) $-3 > -15$ (e) $\frac{5}{6} > \frac{2}{3}$

2. Plot the numbers 10, 2, 5, -4, 3, and -2 on a number line. Verify the truth or falsity of each of the following by using the property that $a > b$ if a lies to the right of b.
   (a) $10 > 5$ (b) $-4 > 2$ (c) $10 > 2$
   (d) $5 > 10$ (e) $-4 > -2$ (f) $-2 > -4$

Solve the inequalities in Exercises 3 through 8. State your solution using inequalities.

3. (*See Example 3*)   4. $12 > 1 - 5x$
   $3x - 5 < x + 4$

5. $5x - 22 \leq 7x + 10$ 6. $13x - 5 \leq 7 - 4x$

7. $3(2x + 1) < 9x + 12$ 8. $14 - 5x \geq 6x - 15$

Solve the inequalities in Exercises 9 through 20. Graph the solution.

9. (*See Example 4*)   10. $3x + 2 < 2x - 3$
   $3x + 2 \leq 4x - 3$

11. $6x + 5 < 5x - 4$ 12. $78 < 6 - 3x$

13. (*See Example 5*) $3(x + 4) < 2(x - 3) + 14$

14. $4(x - 2) > 5(2x + 1)$

15. $3(2x + 1) < -1(3x - 10)$

16. $-2(3x + 4) > -3(1 - 6x) - 17$

17. (*See Example 6*) $-16 < 3x + 5 < 22$

18. $124 > 5 - 2x \geq 68$

19. $14 < 3x + 8 < 32$

20. $-9 \leq 3(x + 2) - 15 < 27$

Solve the inequalities in Exercises 21 through 26. Give the solution in interval form.

21. $3x + 4 \leq 1$ 22. $5x - 7 > 3$

23. $-7x + 4 \geq 2x + 3$ 24. $-3x + 4 < 2x - 6$

25. (*See Example 7*)   26. $16 > 2x - 10 \geq 4$
    $-45 < 4x + 7 \leq -10$

II

Solve the inequalities in Exercises 27 through 30.

27. $\dfrac{6x + 5}{-2} \geq \dfrac{4x - 3}{5}$ **28.** $\dfrac{2x - 5}{3} < \dfrac{x + 7}{4}$ **29.** $\dfrac{2}{3} < \dfrac{x + 5}{-4} \leq \dfrac{3}{2}$ **30.** $\dfrac{3}{4} < \dfrac{7x + 1}{6} < \dfrac{5}{2}$

III

31. (*See Example 8*) Professor Tuff computes a grade on a test by $35 + 5x$, where x is the number of correct answers. A grade in the interval $[75, 90)$ is a B. If a student receives a B, how many correct answers were given?

32. A professor computes a grade on a test by $25 + 4x$, where x is the number of correct answers. A grade in the interval $[70, 79]$ is a C. What number of correct answers can be obtained to receive a C?

33. On a final exam, any grade in the interval $[85, 100]$ was an A. The professor gave three points for each correct answer and then adjusted the grades by adding 25 points. If a student made an A, how many correct answers were given?

34. A sporting goods store runs a special on jogging shoes. The manager expects to make a profit if the number of pairs of shoes sold, x, satisfies $32x - 4230 > 2x + 480$. How many pairs of shoes need to be sold to make a profit?

A–5 POLYNOMIAL ARITHMETIC

- *Addition and Subtraction of Polynomials*
- *Multiplication of Polynomials*
- *Factoring Polynomials*
- *Factoring Polynomials of Degree 2*
- *Solving Quadratic Equations*
- *The Quadratic Formula*
- *Rational Expressions*

ADDITION AND SUBTRACTION OF POLYNOMIALS

Expressions like $2x + 6$ and $4x^3 - 7x + 9$ are called polynomials. The general form of a polynomial is

$$a_n x^n + a_{n-1} x^{n-1} + \cdots + a_1 x + a_0$$

where n is a positive integer and $a_n, a_{n-1}, \ldots, a_1, a_0$ are real numbers; if $a_n \neq 0$, then the polynomial is said to be of degree n. Thus $3x^2 + 8x + 4$ is a polynomial of degree 2, and $5x^4 + 3x^2 + 2x + 2$ is a polynomial of degree 4.

We add polynomials by adding the coefficients of equal powers of x.

EXAMPLE 1   *(Compare Exercise 1)*

Add the polynomials $2x^2 + 8x + 4$ and $5x^4 + 3x^2 + 2x + 2$.

SOLUTION   We group terms involving corresponding powers of x together, starting with the highest power:

$$(2x^2 + 8x + 4) + (5x^4 + 3x^2 + 2x + 2)$$
$$= 5x^4 + 2x^2 + 3x^2 + 8x + 2x + 4 + 2$$
$$= 5x^4 + 5x^2 + 10x + 6$$

EXAMPLE 2   *(Compare Exercise 7)*

Simplify $2(4x^4 + 3x^2 + 2x - 1) - 5(2x^4 - 3x^2 + 2x + 5)$

SOLUTION   Multiply each term in parentheses by the number outside. We get

$$2(4x^4 + 3x^2 + 2x - 1) - 5(2x^4 - 3x^2 + 2x + 5)$$
$$= 8x^4 + 6x^2 + 4x - 2 - 10x^4 + 15x^2 - 10x - 25$$
$$= 8x^4 - 10x^4 + 6x^2 + 15x^2 + 4x - 10x - 2 - 25$$
$$= -2x^4 + 21x^2 - 6x - 27$$

MULTIPLICATION OF POLYNOMIALS

EXAMPLE 3   *(Compare Exercise 15)*

Perform the multiplication $(4x + 3)(2x^2 + 3x - 4)$.

SOLUTION   The second polynomial is multiplied by every term in the first polynomial:

$$(4x + 3)(2x^2 + 3x - 4) = 4x(2x^2 + 3x - 4) + 3(2x^2 + 3x - 4)$$
$$= 8x^3 + 12x^2 - 16x + 6x^2 + 9x - 12$$
$$= 8x^3 + 12x^2 + 6x^2 - 16x + 9x - 12$$
$$= 8x^3 + 18x^2 - 7x - 12$$

EXAMPLE 4   *(Compare Exercise 17)*

Perform the following multiplication:

$$(3x^2 - 4x + 2)(2x^2 + 5x - 3)$$

SOLUTION   By multiplying the second polynomial by every term in the first polynomial we get

$$(3x^2 - 4x + 2)(2x^2 + 5x - 3)$$
$$= 3x^2(2x^2 + 5x - 3) - 4x(2x^2 + 5x - 3) + 2(2x^2 + 5x - 3)$$
$$= 6x^4 + 15x^3 - 9x^2 - 8x^3 - 20x^2 + 12x + 4x^2 + 10x - 6$$
$$= 6x^4 + 15x^3 - 8x^3 - 9x^2 - 20x^2 + 4x^2 + 12x + 10x - 6$$
$$= 6x^4 + 7x^3 - 25x^2 + 22x - 6$$

FACTORING POLYNOMIALS

The reverse of multiplying polynomials is called **factoring polynomials.** You use factoring when you start with a polynomial and want to express it as a product of simpler polynomials, that is, polynomials of lower degree. In some circumstances you may need to multiply polynomials, while at other times you may need to go in the opposite direction, to factor polynomials.

EXAMPLE 5 *(Compare Exercise 19)*

Factor $2x^2 + 4x$.

SOLUTION First we look for a common factor in the coefficients. We see that 2 is a common factor, and we can write

$$2x^2 + 4x = 2(x^2 + 2x)$$

Next, look to see whether some power of x is a common factor. Here, x is a factor, and we can write

$$2x^2 + 4x = 2x(x + 2)$$

EXAMPLE 6 *(Compare Exercise 21)*

Factor $8x^3 - 16x^2$.

SOLUTION

$$8x^3 - 16x^2 = 8(x^3 - 2x^2)$$

Next, x^2 can also be factored out:

$$8x^3 - 16x^2 = 8x^2(x - 2)$$

FACTORING POLYNOMIALS OF DEGREE 2

Given a polynomial of the type $ax^2 + bx + c$, we want to express it in terms of factors, $(px + q)(rx + s)$, if possible. Notice that when we multiply $(px + q)(rx + s)$, we get $(pr)x^2 + (ps + qr)x + qs$. Therefore we want numbers p, q, r, and s such that

$$pr = a$$
$$qs = c$$
$$ps + qr = b$$

Use trial and error to find p, q, r, and s.

EXAMPLE 7   *(Compare Exercise 23)*

Factor $x^2 + 5x + 6$.

SOLUTION   We want to find p, q, r, and s such that

$$x^2 + 5x + 6 = (px + q)(rx + s)$$

On comparison with the preceding notation we see that $a = 1$, $b = 5$, and $c = 6$. The three conditions on p, q, r, and s become

$$pr = 1$$
$$qs = 6$$
$$ps + qr = 5$$

The first condition suggests that $p = r = 1$. The second condition suggests that $q = 3$, $s = 2$. We see that these values satisfy the third condition, $ps + qr = (1)(2) + (3)(1) = 5$. Thus

$$x^2 + 5x + 6 = (x + 3)(x + 2)$$

EXAMPLE 8   *(Compare Exercise 27)*

Factor $12x^2 + 4x - 5$.

SOLUTION   Let $12x^2 + 4x - 5 = (px + q)(rx + s)$
The conditions on p, q, r, and s are

$$pr = 12$$
$$qs = -5$$
$$ps + qr = 4$$

If we try $p = 4$ and $r = 3$ in the first equation and $q = 5$ and $s = -1$ in the second equation, we find that $ps + qr = -4 + 15 = 11$. The third equation is not satisfied. This combination will not do.

However, $p = 6$ and $r = 2$ in the first equation and $q = 5$ and $s = -1$ in the second lead to $ps + qr = -6 + 10 = 4$. The third equation is satisfied. This is a correct set of values. We get

$$12x^2 + 4x - 5 = (6x + 5)(2x - 1)$$

You should check the answers to Examples 7 and 8 by multiplying the factors. This will help you to see how the conditions on p, q, r, and s are obtained.

SOLVING QUADRATIC EQUATIONS

A quadratic equation is an equation of the form $ax^2 + bx + c = 0$, where $a \neq 0$. If $ax^2 + bx + c$ can be factored, with

$$ax^2 + bx + c = (px + q)(rx + s)$$

then the equation becomes

$$(px + q)(rx + s) = 0$$

This gives

$$px + q = 0 \qquad \text{or} \qquad rx + s = 0$$

Therefore

$$x = -\frac{q}{p} \qquad \text{or} \qquad -\frac{s}{r}$$

EXAMPLE 9   *(Compare Exercise 33)*

Solve the equation $12x^2 + 4x - 5 = 0$.

SOLUTION   We saw in the previous example that $12x^2 + 4x - 5$ can be factored as

$$12x^2 + 4x - 5 = (6x + 5)(2x - 1)$$

The solutions are given by

$$(6x + 5)(2x - 1) = 0$$
$$6x + 5 = 0 \qquad \text{or} \qquad 2x - 1 = 0$$
$$x = -\frac{5}{6} \qquad \text{or} \qquad x = \frac{1}{2}$$

THE QUADRATIC FORMULA

We now introduce a method that can always be used to solve a quadratic equation, whether or not you can successfully factor the polynomial.

The solutions to the quadratic equation $ax^2 + bx + c = 0$ are given by the **quadratic formula:**

$$x = \frac{-b \pm \sqrt{b^2 - 4ac}}{2a}$$

EXAMPLE 10   *(Compare Exercise 37)*

Solve the quadratic equation $2x^2 + 7x + 3 = 0$.

SOLUTION   We have that $a = 2$, $b = 7$, $c = 3$. Using the above formula, we get

$$x = \frac{-7 \pm \sqrt{7^2 - 4(2)(3)}}{2(2)} = \frac{-7 \pm \sqrt{49 - 24}}{4}$$

$$= \frac{-7 \pm \sqrt{25}}{4} = \frac{-7 \pm 5}{4}$$

The two solutions are

$$\frac{-7 + 5}{4} \quad \text{and} \quad \frac{-7 - 5}{4}$$

$$= \frac{-2}{4} \quad \text{and} \quad \frac{-12}{4}$$

$$= \frac{-1}{2} \quad \text{and} \quad -3$$

EXAMPLE 11   *(Compare Exercise 41)*

Solve the quadratic equation

$$3x^2 - 2x + 4 = 0$$

SOLUTION   For this equation, $a = 3$, $b = -2$, and $c = 4$. The quadratic formula gives

$$x = \frac{-(-2) \pm \sqrt{(-2)^2 - 4(3)(4)}}{2(3)} = \frac{2 \pm \sqrt{4 - 48}}{6}$$

$$= \frac{2 \pm \sqrt{-44}}{6}$$

But there is no real number that corresponds to $\sqrt{-44}$. We say that no real solution exists. Whenever the number under the radical sign in the quadratic formula is negative, there is no real solution.

RATIONAL EXPRESSIONS

An algebraic fraction, one whose numerator and denominator are polynomials, is called a **rational function.** Examples of rational functions are

$$\frac{1}{x} \qquad \frac{2x - 3}{4x^2 + 2x + 1} \qquad \frac{x^4 + 2x}{4x + 3}$$

The rules for working with these expressions are similar to those that apply to ordinary fractions. We summarize some of the important rules. Let $P, Q, R,$ and S be polynomials.

$$\text{Addition: } \frac{P}{Q} + \frac{R}{Q} = \frac{P + R}{Q} \qquad (Q \neq 0)$$

$$\text{Subtraction: } \frac{P}{Q} - \frac{R}{Q} = \frac{P - R}{Q} \qquad (Q \neq 0)$$

$$\text{Multiplication: } \frac{P}{Q} \cdot \frac{R}{S} = \frac{PR}{QS} \qquad (Q \neq 0, S \neq 0)$$

$$\text{Division: } \frac{P}{Q} \div \frac{R}{S} = \frac{PS}{QR} \qquad (Q \neq 0, S \neq 0, R \neq 0)$$

In addition to the above rules, the numerator and denominator of a rational expression can both be multiplied by a polynomial. This rule proves to be useful in simplifying sums of rational expressions:

$$\frac{P}{Q} = \frac{PR}{QR} \qquad (Q \neq 0, R \neq 0)$$

EXAMPLE 12 *(Compare Exercise 47)*

Simplify

$$\frac{x^2 + 3x}{4x + 2} + \frac{3x^3 - 2x + 1}{4x + 2}$$

SOLUTION Using the rule for addition, we get

$$\frac{x^2 + 3x}{4x + 2} + \frac{3x^3 - 2x + 1}{4x + 2} = \frac{x^2 + 3x + 3x^3 - 2x + 1}{4x + 2}$$

$$= \frac{3x^3 + x^2 + 3x - 2x + 1}{4x + 2}$$

$$= \frac{3x^3 + x^2 + x + 1}{4x + 2}$$

EXAMPLE 13 *(Compare Exercise 55)*

Simplify

$$\frac{(x + 1)(x + 2)}{x^2 + 1} \div \frac{3(x + 2)}{4x}$$

given that $x + 2 \neq 0$ and $x \neq 0$.

SOLUTION Apply the rule for division:

$$\frac{(x + 1)(x + 2)}{x^2 + 1} \div \frac{3(x + 2)}{4x} = \frac{(x + 1)(x + 2)}{x^2 + 1} \cdot \frac{4x}{3(x + 2)}$$

$$= \frac{(x + 1)(x + 2)4x}{3(x^2 + 1)(x + 2)}$$

At this stage we can simplify by dividing both the numerator and denominator by the $(x + 2)$ factor as in the case of ordinary fractions. We get

$$\frac{(x + 1)(x + 2)}{x^2 + 1} \div \frac{3(x + 2)}{4x} = \frac{4x(x + 1)}{3(x^2 + 1)}$$

EXAMPLE 14   *(Compare Exercise 59)*

Simplify

$$\frac{x^2 + 3}{x} + \frac{x - 1}{x + 1}$$

SOLUTION   The common denominator is $x(x + 1)$. Multiply both the numerator and denominator of the first expression by $(x + 1)$ and the numerator and denominator of the second expression by x. We get

$$\frac{x^2 + 3}{x} + \frac{x - 1}{x + 1} = \frac{(x^2 + 3)(x + 1)}{x(x + 1)} + \frac{x(x - 1)}{x(x + 1)}$$

$$= \frac{(x^2 + 3)(x + 1) + x(x - 1)}{x(x + 1)}$$

$$= \frac{x^2(x + 1) + 3(x + 1) + x^2 - x}{x(x + 1)}$$

$$= \frac{x^3 + x^2 + 3x + 3 + x^2 - x}{x(x + 1)}$$

$$= \frac{x^3 + 2x^2 + 2x + 3}{x(x + 1)}$$

A–5 EXERCISES

Add the polynomials in Exercises 1 through 6.

1. *(See Example 1)*
   $2x^3 + 3x - 1$ and $5x^2 - 3x + 2$

2. $3x^2 - 2x + 3$ and $5x^2 + 2x + 1$

3. $4x^3 - 2x^2 + 3$ and $2x^2 - 5x + 2$

4. $7x^4 - 2x + 3$ and $-4x^3 - 5x + 2$

5. $5x^3 - 2x^2 + 3x + 2$ and $-4x^3 - 5x^2 + 5$

6. $7x^4 - 2x^2 - 3x + 6$ and $-3x^3 - 4x^2 - x + 2$

Simplify the expressions in Exercises 7 through 12.

7. *(See Example 2)*   8. $4x - 2(x - 1) - 6$
   $4(x + 2) - 3$

9. $5x - 2 + 3(2 - x)$

10. $3(x - 2) + 4(2x + 3) - (2x - 1)$

11. $-2(3x + 2) + 6x - 4(x + 3)$

12. $2(x + 3) - 3(5 - x)$

Perform the multiplications in Exercises 13 through 18.

13. $(x + 2)(x - 3)$ 14. $(2x - 1)(x + 3)$

15. *(See Example 3)*
    $(3x^2 + 2x - 1)(x + 3)$

16. $(3x - 2)(x^3 - 4x^2 + 2x - 1)$

17. *(See Example 4)*
    $(2x^2 - x + 1)(2x^3 + 2x + 1)$

18. $(-x^2 + 2x + 4)(x^2 - 2x + 1)$

Factor the polynomials in Exercises 19 through 32.

19. *(See Example 5)*   20. $x^3 - 3x^2 + 4x$
    $x^2 + 3x$

21. *(See Example 6)*   22. $6x^3 - 3x^2$
    $2x^3 - 4x^2$

23. *(See Example 7)*   24. $x^2 - 3x - 10$
    $x^2 + 6x + 5$

25. $x^2 + x - 6$ **26.** $x^2 - 7x + 12$

27. (*See Example 8*)   **28.** $3x^2 + 2x - 5$
$\quad\,2x^2 + x - 6$

29. $4x^2 + 4x - 3$ **30.** $6x^2 - 7x - 5$

31. $4x^2 - 11x + 6$ **32.** $6x^2 - x - 15$

Solve the equations in Exercises 33 through 36 by factoring.

33. (*See Example 9*)   **34.** $x^2 + 7x + 10 = 0$
$\quad\,x^2 + 2x - 3 = 0$

35. $2x^2 - x - 3 = 0$ **36.** $2x^2 + 9x + 10 = 0$

Solve the equations in Exercises 37 through 46 by using the quadratic formula or state that there are no real solutions.

37. (*See Example 10*)   **38.** $6x^2 - x - 1 = 0$
$\quad\,2x^2 - x - 3 = 0$

39. $4x^2 - 11x = 3$ **40.** $10x^2 - x = 2$

41. (*See Example 11*)   **42.** $3x^2 - 2x + 5 = 0$
$\quad\,x^2 + 2x + 3 = 0$

43. $4 + 9x - 9x^2 = 0$ **44.** $6 - x + x^2 = 0$

45. $1 + x - 2x^2 = 0$ **46.** $7 - x - x^2 = 0$

Perform the operations in Exercises 47 through 66.

47. (*See Example 12*)   **48.** $\dfrac{x+2}{x^2-3} + \dfrac{2x+4}{x^2-3}$
$\quad\dfrac{x^2+2}{x-1} + \dfrac{x-3}{x-1}$

49. $\dfrac{2x-3}{x+2} - \dfrac{3x-3}{x+2}$ **50.** $\dfrac{4x+1}{x-1} \cdot \dfrac{x}{3x+2}$

51. $\dfrac{5x-1}{2x+1} \cdot \dfrac{3x+2}{4x-1}$ **52.** $\dfrac{4x+3}{2x+3} \cdot \dfrac{x}{3x^2-x+2}$

53. $\dfrac{2x+3}{4x-1} \cdot \dfrac{5}{2x+3}$ **54.** $\dfrac{5x-1}{2x} \div \dfrac{3x}{2}$

55. (*See Example 13*)   **56.** $\dfrac{4x}{3x+2} \div \dfrac{5x^2+2}{4x^2-3}$
$\quad\dfrac{4x+3}{5x-1} \div \dfrac{4x}{2x+1}$

57. $\dfrac{2x-3}{4} \cdot \dfrac{2x}{7}$ **58.** $\dfrac{3x-1}{4} \div \dfrac{3x-2}{2x}$

59. (*See Example 14*)   **60.** $\dfrac{5}{x+2} + \dfrac{7x+3}{x}$
$\quad\dfrac{2}{x} + \dfrac{4}{x-1}$

61. $\dfrac{5x-1}{x-1} + \dfrac{4x+2}{x+1}$ **62.** $\dfrac{5x}{2} - \dfrac{7}{x-1}$

63. $\dfrac{4x+3}{5x-1} - \dfrac{2x+1}{x}$ **64.** $\dfrac{3x-1}{x+1} + \dfrac{x+2}{2x+5}$

65. $\dfrac{5}{x} + \dfrac{7}{x^2}$ **66.** $\dfrac{5x}{2x^2-3} + \dfrac{2x-1}{x}$

A–6 EXPONENTS

- *Positive Integer Exponents*
- *Other Integer Exponents*
- *Fractional Exponents*

Most people seem to remember that **exponents** stand for "repeated multiplication," and they have little problem computing 2^3: $2^3 = 2 \cdot 2 \cdot 2 = 8$. This explanation of exponents, however, does not extend to expressions like 2^0, 2^{-3}, and $2^{1/5}$. You can't multiply 2 times itself $\frac{1}{5}$ times, for example. There are also rules for manipulating exponents—rules like $2^3 \cdot 2^2 = 2^5$ and $(2^3)^2 = 2^6$ that cause some trouble, especially when the exponents are not positive integers. We will start with the notion of "repeated multiplication" and show what the rules for combining exponents must be when the exponents are positive integers. Then the meaning that we attach to, say, 2^{-3}, is motivated by a desire to keep these exponent rules the same no matter what the exponent is. If you have trouble handling exponents, we hope to encourage you to think about the meaning of the rules in a very concrete setting.

POSITIVE INTEGER EXPONENTS

In this *one* case we do think of the exponent as a symbol meaning "repeated multiplication." Thus $3^4 = 3 \cdot 3 \cdot 3 \cdot 3 = 81$; $b^n = b \cdot b \cdot \ldots \cdot b$ (n times). Now we establish the two main rules for positive integers and then introduce other types of numbers as exponents so that *the rules stay the same*.

How can we simplify $b^n \cdot b^k$? Think concretely—how can we simplify $4^3 \cdot 4^2$? $4^3 = 4 \cdot 4 \cdot 4$, and $4^2 = 4 \cdot 4$, so

$$4^3 \cdot 4^2 = (4 \cdot 4 \cdot 4)(4 \cdot 4) = 4 \cdot 4 \cdot 4 \cdot 4 \cdot 4 = 4^5$$

Note that the new exponent 5 is the sum of the exponents 2 and 3. This example shows us the rule for simplifying $b^n \cdot b^k$.

Rule 1 $b^n \cdot b^k = b^{n+k}$

EXAMPLE 1   *(Compare Exercise 5)*

Simplify $7^5 \cdot 7^3$.
SOLUTION
$$7^5 \cdot 7^3 = 7^{5+3} = 7^8$$

Next, how can we simplify $(b^n)^k$? Again, let's look at a concrete example with $b = 4$, $n = 3$, and $k = 2$. $(4^3)^2 = 4^3 \cdot 4^3 = (4 \cdot 4 \cdot 4)(4 \cdot 4 \cdot 4) = 4^6$, and $6 = 2 \cdot 3$, so we know what Rule 2 must be.

Rule 2 $(b^n)^k = b^{n \cdot k}$

EXAMPLE 2   *(Compare Exercise 9)*

Simplify $(7^5)^3$.
SOLUTION
$$(7^5)^3 = 7^{5 \cdot 3} = 7^{15}$$

OTHER INTEGER EXPONENTS

We want Rule 1 and Rule 2 to be true for all possible exponents n and k, so we extend the meaning of exponents to numbers that are not positive integers. But when we do, we can no longer explain the exponent as "repeated multiplication." Furthermore, as we allow more kinds of exponents, we must introduce some restrictions on b.

First, let's try to define 2^0. We want Rule 1 to hold, so we want $2^3 \cdot 2^0 = 2^{3+0} = 2^3$. Multiplying by 2^0 does not change the value of 2^3, so 2^0 must equal 1.

Definition
Zero Exponent   If $b \neq 0$, $b^0 = 1$.

With this definition we know that Rule 1 is always satisfied. What about Rule 2? We compute $(b^n)^0$ and b^{n0} separately. If we let $c = b^n$, then $(b^n)^0 = c^0 = 1$. Also, $b^{(n \cdot 0)} = b^0 = 1$. Thus $(b^n)^0 = 1 = b^{n \cdot 0}$, and Rule 2 holds.

Next we want to define b^n when n is a negative integer. What do we want 2^{-3} to mean? If Rule 1 is still to hold, we must have $2^3 \cdot 2^{-3} = 2^{3+-3} = 2^0 = 1$. So 2^{-3} is the reciprocal of 2^3.

Definition
Negative Exponent   If n is a positive integer and $b \neq 0$, $b^{-n} = \dfrac{1}{b^n}$.

This definition also keeps Rule 2 valid.

EXAMPLE 3   *(Compare Exercise 17)*

Simplify $(4^{-2})^3$.
SOLUTION

$$(4^{-2})^3 = 4^{-6} = \frac{1}{4^6}$$

We have defined negative exponents so that the rules still work. Remembering how the rules work can help you to remember what negative exponents mean. Thus

$$\frac{2^4}{2^3} = (2 \cdot 2 \cdot 2 \cdot 2) \div (2 \cdot 2 \cdot 2) = 2 = 2^{4-3} = 2^4 \cdot 2^{-3}$$

might help you to remember $2^{-3} = \dfrac{1}{2^3}$.

FRACTIONAL EXPONENTS

Next we would like to see what **fractional exponents** should mean. We know that $4 = 4^1 = 4^{3/3}$. If we want Rule 2 to remain valid, we have $4 = 4^{3/3} = (4^{1/3})^3$. Thus $4^{1/3} \cdot 4^{1/3} \cdot 4^{1/3} = 4$, and $4^{1/3}$ is called the cube root of 4.

Definition
nth root of b, b > 0

If $b > 0$ and n is a positive integer, then $b^{1/n}$ is called the **nth root of b** and is the positive number c such that $c^n = b$. More briefly, if n, b, and c are positive, then $b^{1/n} = c$, where $c^n = b$.

Notation
$\sqrt[n]{b}$

The (positive) square root of b, $b^{1/2}$, can also be written as $\sqrt{b}$; if n is a positive integer greater than 2, then $b^{1/n}$ can also be written as $\sqrt[n]{b}$.

EXAMPLE 4   *(Compare Exercises 25, 27, and 29)*

Compute: **(a)** $\sqrt{25}$; **(b)** $\sqrt[3]{8}$; **(c)** $81^{1/4}$.
(a) $\sqrt{25} = 5$ (*Note:* $\sqrt{25}$ means 5, not ± 5)
(b) $\sqrt[3]{8} = 2$
(c) $81^{1/4} = 3$

With this definition for $b^{1/n}$, we extend the definition to all rational numbers k/n by making sure that Rule 2 still holds.

Definition

If $b > 0$, $b^{k/n} = (b^{1/n})^k = (b^k)^{1/n}$

EXAMPLE 5   *(Compare Exercises 31 and 37)*

Compute: **(a)** $32^{3/5}$; **(b)** $64^{-2/3}$.
SOLUTION
(a) $32^{3/5} = (32^{1/5})^3 = ((2^5)^{1/5})^3 = 2^3 = 8$.

(b) $64^{-2/3} = (64^{1/3})^{-2} = ((4^3)^{1/3})^{-2} = 4^{-2} = \dfrac{1}{4^2} = \dfrac{1}{16}$

REMARK Note that $b > 0$ was required in the general definition of nth root. The reason for this restriction is that the square root, fourth root, or any even root of a negative number is not a real number. For example, $\sqrt{-4}$ is not a real number because $c^2 = -4$ has no real solution. However, we can solve $c^3 = -8$ with $c = -2$. Therefore if $b < 0$ and n is odd, we have the following definition.

Definition
nth Root of b, b < 0, n Odd

If $b < 0$ and n is a positive odd integer, then $b^{1/n}$ is called the nth root of b and is the negative number c such that $c^n = b$. More briefly, if n is odd with b and c negative, then $b^{1/n} = c$, where $c^n = b$.

EXAMPLE 6   *(Compare Exercises 39 and 41)*

Compute: **(a)** $\sqrt{-16}$; **(b)** $(-32)^{1/5}$.

SOLUTION

(a) $(-16)^{1/2}$ is not defined.

(b) $(-32)^{1/5} = (-2^5)^{1/5} = -2$.

A–6   EXERCISES

Simplify the expressions in Exercises 1 through 52.

1. 5^2

2. 4^3

3. 8^1

4. 6^0

5. *(See Example 1)* $3^2 \cdot 3^4$

6. $2^4 \cdot 2^3$

7. $x \cdot x^6$

8. $y^2 \cdot y^5$

9. *(See Example 2)* $(3^2)^4$

10. $(8^3)^2$

11. $(x^2)^3$

12. $(y^3)^3$

13. 3^{-1}

14. 5^{-2}

15. 3^{-3}

16. 10^{-4}

17. *(See Example 3)* $(2^{-2})^3$

18. $(3^{-1})^4$

19. $(x^{-2})^2$

20. $(x^{-1})^3$

21. $(5^2)^{-1}$

22. $(3^2)^{-2}$

23. $(x^2)^{-1}$

24. $(x^3)^{-1}$

25. *(See Example 4a)* $\sqrt{36}$

26. $\sqrt{81}$

27. *(See Example 4b)* $16^{1/2}$

28. $9^{1/2}$

29. *(See Example 4c)* $\sqrt[3]{27}$

30. $\sqrt[4]{16}$

31. *(See Example 5a)* $8^{2/3}$

32. $16^{3/2}$

33. $32^{1/5}$

34. $16^{3/4}$

35. $(\sqrt{6})^4$

36. $(\sqrt[3]{8})^2$

37. *(See Example 5b)* $32^{-1/5}$

38. $8^{-2/3}$

39. *(See Example 6a)* $\sqrt{-9}$

40. $(-4)^{1/2}$

41. *(See Example 6b)* $(-8)^{1/3}$

42. $\sqrt[3]{-27}$

43. $(-27)^{2/3}$

44. $(-32)^{3/5}$

45. $-\sqrt{81}$

46. $5^2 \cdot 5^{-3}$

47. $3^4 \cdot 3^{-2}$

48. $x^{-1} \cdot x^2$

49. $(-8)^{-1/3}$

50. $(-27)^{-2/3}$

51. $-(9^{-1/2})$

52. $-(16^{-1/4})$

A–7   FUNCTIONS

- *Introduction*
- *Evaluation of a Function*
- *Domain*
- *Applications*

INTRODUCTION

You are the manager in charge of the toy department of Meyer's Department Store in Kansas City, and your buyer has just sent you a memo saying that the hottest toy for the fall will be Burpy-Baby. The buyer has ordered a large shipment, so you have to sell the Cuddle-Me dolls you have on hand to make room for this new shipment. Naturally, you want to make as much money on your present stock as possible, but you have some decisions to make. If you keep your prices as high as they are now, you will make a good profit on each doll sold, but you won't sell very many. Furthermore, you will have to take a loss on all the ones you don't sell. On the other hand, if you lower the price too much, you will suffer a loss even if you sell all the dolls you have on hand. How do you decide what price to charge so that you make as much money as possible?

Calculus can help you to answer this question. In fact, calculus will give you mathematical tools that will enable you to answer questions not only about the relationship between selling price and profit, but also about the relationship between any two quantities when one depends on the other. Mathematicians have developed a type of shorthand that uses letters for dealing with quantities like these and with the relationship between them. To use this shorthand, let x stand for the selling price of the Cuddle-Me's, and let y stand for the profit. Mathematicians use the word *function* to express the dependence of y on x. Thus y is a function of x; the profit is a function of the selling price. This statement is condensed even further by using the single letter f to stand for the phrase "a function of," and writing $y = f(x)$. The expression $y = f(x)$ is read "y equals f of x" and means that y is a function of x.

Suppose, using our example, you determine that if you sell the Cuddle-Me's for \$15 each, your total profit will be \$130. You can express that information in function notation by writing $130 = f(15)$. Similarly, the expression $125 = f(16)$ would mean that a price of \$16 would result in a total profit of \$125. Notice that a higher price may mean fewer sales and hence may mean a smaller total profit.

To clarify the concept of function it may be helpful to think of a function as a machine that takes a certain number x as input and produces the number $f(x)$ as the output (Figure A–16).

In general, the set of values that are allowed as input into the function is called *the domain of the function*. The set of values that result as the output is called *the range of the function*.

We can now give a more formal description of a function.

Definitions
**Function,
Domain,
and Range**   A **function** f is a relationship between two sets A and B such that every element a in A is related to a unique element b of B. We express this relationship by the equation $f(a) = b$. The number b is called the **value** of f at a. A is called the **domain** of f, and B is called the **range** of f.

FIGURE A–16

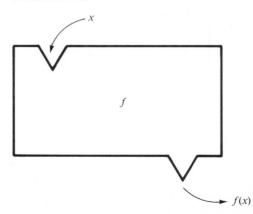

**EVALUATION
OF A FUNCTION**

Generally, there is some rule or formula that tells you how to compute the output in terms of the input. For instance, instead of writing "the function that squares a number and subtracts 6 from that result," we write "the function defined by $f(x) = x^2 - 6$." The equation $f(x) = x^2 - 6$ is called *the rule for evaluating the function* or, more simply, the **rule of the function.** Here are some examples to help you become familiar with this notation.

EXAMPLE 1 *(Compare Exercise 19)*

What is the rule for evaluating the function—the machine—that multiplies the input by 3 and then adds 5 to this result?

SOLUTION   Let x stand for the input to the function; the rule would be

$$f(x) = 3x + 5$$

We continue to use the function defined by $f(x) = 3x + 5$ in order to demonstrate some evaluations. Letting $x = 2$, we have $f(2) = 3 \cdot 2 + 5$; $f(2) = 11$. We say the value of f at $x = 2$ is 11. To evaluate f at $x = 6$, we have $f(6) = 3 \cdot 6 + 5 = 23$. Similarly, $f(0) = 3 \cdot 0 + 5 = 5$, and $f(-4) = 3(-4) + 5 = -7$.

EXAMPLE 2   *(Compare Exercise 1)*

If f is the function defined by $f(x) = 4 - 2x^2$, find each of the following values of f:

(a) $f(1)$ **(b)** $f(3)$ **(c)** $f(-5)$

SOLUTION

(a) Replacing the "x" by "1" in the rule, we have

$$f(1) = 4 - 2(1)^2 = 4 - 2 = 2$$
$$f(1) = 2$$

(b)
$$f(3) = 4 - 2(3)^2 = 4 - 2 \cdot 9 = 4 - 18 = -14$$
$$f(3) = -14$$

(c)
$$f(-5) = 4 - 2(-5)^2 = 4 - 2 \cdot 25 = 4 - 50 = -46$$
$$f(-5) = -46$$

Often, the function rule is written without the $f(x)$ notation by just showing how the value of y depends on the value of x. We shall do Example 2 again, using this alternate notation.

EXAMPLE 3   *(Compare Exercise 3)*

If $y = 4 - 2x^2$, what is y when:

(a) $x = 1$?   **(b)** $x = 3$?   **(c)** $x = -5$?

SOLUTION   Using the computations from Example 2:

(a) $y = 2$ if $x = 1$.
(b) $y = -14$ if $x = 3$.
(c) $y = -46$ if $x = -5$.

The relationship between profit and price, for example, is usually expressed by a formula such as $y = -x^2 + 26x - 35$, where y stands for the profit and x for the price. Later, we will show how these formulas are obtained. Right now we concentrate on how to read them. (In fact, this is the formula that gives the profit in our doll example.)

EXAMPLE 4   *(Compare Exercise 25)*

Using $y = -x^2 + 26x - 35$, find the profit y for the various prices $x = 16$, $x = 10$, $x = -3$.

SOLUTION   When $x = 16$,

$$y = -(16)^2 + 26(16) - 35$$
$$= -256 + 416 - 35$$
$$= 125$$

When $x = 10$,

$$y = -(10)^2 + 26(10) - 35$$
$$= -100 + 260 - 35$$
$$= 125$$

Notice that different selling prices may yield the same total profit. When $x = 16$, the profit per doll is greater than when $x = 10$, but fewer dolls are sold at the higher price.
When $x = -3$,

$$y = -(-3)^2 + 26(-3) - 35$$
$$= -9 - 78 - 35$$
$$= -122$$

(See the discussion following Example 9)

CAUTION   Be careful computing with negative numbers; it's easy to make a mistake with the signs.

The computations in the next chapter will demand a good understanding of functional notation. So that you can better concentrate on the meaning of those computations, we give more examples that stress the mechanics of functional evaluation.

EXAMPLE 5 *(Compare Exercise 43)*

If $f(x) = 3x + 7$, what is:

(a) $f(a)$?
(b) $f(t)$?
(c) $f(x + t)$?

SOLUTION
(a) Replacing x by a as the input, we have $f(a) = 3a + 7$.
(b) Replacing x by t, we have $f(t) = 3t + 7$.
(c) Using $x + t$ as the input, we have $f(x + t) = 3(x + t) + 7 = 3x + 3t + 7$.

The evaluations $f(a)$ and $f(t)$ were meant to warm you up for $f(x + t)$. The rule states that $f(\text{input}) = 3 \cdot (\text{input}) + 7$, no matter how the input is expressed, by x, a, t, or even $x + t$.

CAUTION There is no distributive law for functional evaluations; in general, $f(x + t) \neq f(x) + f(t)$. We saw that $f(x + t) = 3x + 3t + 7$; but on the other hand, $f(x) + f(t) = (3x + 7) + (3t + 7) = 3x + 3t + 14$.

EXAMPLE 6 *(Compare Exercise 47)*

If $f(x) = 2x^2 - x$, what is $f(3 + h)$?
SOLUTION Replacing x by $3 + h$, we have

$$
\begin{aligned}
f(3 + h) &= 2(3 + h)^2 - (3 + h) \\
&= 2(9 + 6h + h^2) - 3 - h \\
&= 18 + 12h + 2h^2 - 3 - h \\
&= 15 + 11h + 2h^2
\end{aligned}
$$

CAUTION You must compute $(3 + h)^2$, not $3^2 + h^2$. We encourage use of parentheses to help you remember this. Also, parentheses help to make sure that you write $-(3 + h) = -3 - h$. Without parentheses the attempt to write $f(3 + h)$ could look like $2 \cdot 3 + h^2 - 3 + h$, which could be interpreted to mean $6 + h^2 - 3 + h$, or $h^2 + h + 3$.

DOMAIN

EXAMPLE 7 *(Compare Exercise 7)*

If $f(x) = \dfrac{x + 2}{x - 3}$, what is the domain of the function?

SOLUTION If $x = 3$ then $x - 3 = 0$; this means that you cannot compute $f(3)$; 5 divided by 0 doesn't make sense. Thus 3 is not in the domain of this function. Every other number can be substituted for x, so the domain of this function is all real numbers except 3—all $x \neq 3$.

CAUTION If $f(x)$ is a quotient, then the domain of f never includes numbers that make the denominator of the quotient equal to zero. *You can never divide by 0.*

EXAMPLE 8

What is the domain of f if $f(x) = \sqrt{x}$?

SOLUTION   The domain of the square root function is all $x \geq 0$; a negative number does not have a real square root. Using interval notation, we can write the domain as $[0, \infty)$.

EXAMPLE 9   *(Compare Exercise 9)*

What is the domain of f if $f(x) = \sqrt{x - 5}$?

SOLUTION   If x is in the domain of f, then $x - 5$ cannot be negative; the domain of f is all x such that $x - 5 \geq 0$, that is, all $x \geq 5$. The domain of f is $[5, \infty)$.

Notice that in Example 4, even caring about the value of y when $x = -3$ is rather silly, since this would represent your profit if you paid people \$3 for each Cuddle-Me they carried out of your store. The corresponding value $y = -122$ would represent a "profit" of $-\$122$, which is the same as a loss of \$122. It would seem reasonable in this example to require that the selling price be greater than or equal to 0; that is, don't allow negative numbers as input. Letting $x = 0$ would correspond to giving the dolls away, but maybe you would do that for public relations or to attract people into your store rather than just throwing the dolls away. This restriction on the domain is indicated by explicitly giving the domain at the same time the formula for $f(x)$ is given. For example, we could indicate that the selling price of the dolls can't be negative by writing $f(x) = -x^2 + 26x - 35$, $x \geq 0$. If the domain is given explicitly, be careful that you don't try to evaluate the function outside its domain.

EXAMPLE 10   *(Compare Exercise 39)*

If f is defined by $f(x) = 3x^2 + 5x - 2$, $2 \leq x \leq 7$, what are $f(3)$, $f(1)$, and $f(2)$?

SOLUTION $f(3) = 40$, as you expect, but $f(1)$ is not defined; 1 is not in the domain of this function. The domain is only those numbers from 2 to 7 inclusive. Because 2 is in the domain, we can use the rule to compute $f(2)$; $f(2) = 20$.

APPLICATIONS

So far, we have used only the letter f to denote a function, but there's no need to be so restrictive. Indeed, you will run into applications later in which you will want to talk about three functions in the same problem—the cost function, the revenue function, and the profit function. It would certainly be confusing to use the same letter to represent all three! Likewise, you might want to use different letters for your variables. For example, if you are interested in representing the cost of a telephone call in terms of the call's length, you might want to name the function C (for cost), and you could let the input variable be t (for time) as in the next example.

NOTE Notice how the particular application determines the domain of the function.

EXAMPLE 11   *(Compare Exercise 51)*

You want to call home on a pay telephone that charges 25¢ to place the call and 65¢ per minute to talk.

(a) Express the cost in dollars as a function of the length of the call.
(b) What does an eight-minute call cost?
(c) What is the cost of a one-hour call?
(d) How long can you talk for $10?

SOLUTION
(a) Let t stand for the length of the call in minutes, and let $C(t)$ be the cost of the call. Then $C(t) = 0.65t + 0.25$, $t \geq 0$.
(b) $C(8) = (0.65)8 + 0.25 = 5.45$, so the cost of an eight-minute call is $5.45.
(c) $C(60) = 39.25$, so the cost of a one-hour call is $39.25. Be careful with the units; time must be expressed in minutes.
(d) To answer this question, we need to solve the equation $C(t) = 10$. Using the formula for $C(t)$, we have

$$0.65t + 0.25 = 10$$
$$0.65t = 9.75$$
$$t = 15$$

You can talk for 15 minutes.

EXAMPLE 12   *(Compare Exercise 53)*

If a newspaper sells for 30¢, express the publisher's daily revenue in terms of the number of newspapers sold daily.

SOLUTION   We let x be the number of newspapers sold daily and R be the daily revenue in dollars. We can write $R(x) = 0.30x$, $x \geq 0$.

EXAMPLE 13

A salesman's monthly salary is $500 plus 4% of his sales for the month.

(a) Express his monthly salary as a function of his total sales for the month.
(b) What must his sales be in order to earn a monthly salary of $2000?

SOLUTION

(a) Let S be his monthly salary in dollars and x be his sales, also in dollars, for the month. Then

$$S(x) = 500 + 0.04x \qquad x \geq 0$$

(b) We must solve the equation $S(x) = 2000$:

$$500 + 0.04x = 2000$$
$$0.04x = 1500$$
$$4x = 150,000$$
$$x = 37,500$$

His total sales for the month must be $37,500.

A-7 EXERCISES

I

1. (*See Example 2*) Let $f(x) = 3x + 7$. Evaluate each of the following:

   (a) $f(2)$ (b) $f(-4)$ (c) $f\left(\dfrac{1}{3}\right)$

2. If $f(x) = 6x - 5$, evaluate:

   (a) $f(-2)$ (b) $f(3)$ (c) $f\left(\dfrac{1}{2}\right)$

3. (*See Example 3*) If $y = 7 - 2x$, determine y when:

   (a) $x = 4$ (b) $x = -3$ (c) $x = \dfrac{5}{2}$

4. If $f(x) = 9 - 3x$, determine y when:

   (a) $x = 5$ (b) $x = 4$ (c) $x = \dfrac{10}{3}$

In Exercises 5 through 18, find the domain of the function given by each rule for evaluating $f(x)$.

5. $f(x) = 7x + 5$

6. $f(x) = 5x - 6x^2$

7. (*See Example 7*)

   $f(x) = \dfrac{3}{x - 9}$

8. $f(x) = \dfrac{7}{x + 5}$

9. (*See Example 9*)
   $f(x) = \sqrt{x - 8}$

10. $f(x) = \sqrt{x + 5}$

11. $f(x) = \sqrt{2x + 6}$

12. $f(x) = \sqrt{x - 4}$

13. $f(x) = \sqrt[3]{16 - 2x}$

14. $f(x) = \sqrt[3]{4 - x}$

15. $f(x) = \dfrac{6}{x^2 + 4}$

16. $f(x) = \sqrt{x^2 + 9}$

17. $f(x) = x^2, \; -1 \leq x \leq 5$

18. $f(x) = \dfrac{1}{x + 4}, \; 2 \leq x \leq 8$

II

In Exercises 19 through 24, write a rule for evaluating a function that performs the given operations on the input.

19. (*See Example 1*) The function squares the input.

20. The function subtracts 8 from the input.

21. The function multiplies the input by 3 and then adds 2 to the result.

22. The function adds 2 to the input and then multiplies the result by 3.

23. The function squares the input and then subtracts 9 from the result.

24. The function subtracts 4 from the input and then squares the result.

Perform each evaluation as indicated in Exercises 25 through 28.

25. (*See Example 4*) If $f(x) = 9x^2 - 3x + 7$, evaluate
(a) $f(4)$ (b) $f(-2)$ (c) $f\left(\dfrac{1}{3}\right)$

26. If $f(x) = 8x^2 - 6x + 5$, evaluate
(a) $f(3)$ (b) $f(-3)$ (c) $f\left(\dfrac{1}{2}\right)$

27. If $f(x) = \sqrt{x + 9}$, evaluate
(a) $f(7)$ (b) $f(-5)$ (c) $f(-25)$

28. If $f(x) = \sqrt{2x + 10}$, evaluate
(a) $f(13)$ (b) $f(-5)$ (c) $f(-7)$

In Exercises 29 through 34, find the domain of the function given by each of the following rules.

29. $f(x) = \dfrac{3x - 6}{x^2 - 9}$ **30.** $f(x) = \dfrac{5x + 10}{x^2 - 4}$

31. $f(x) = \dfrac{x^2 - 4}{x^2 - 2x - 3}$ **32.** $f(x) = \dfrac{x^2 - 16}{x^2 - 2x + 1}$

33. $f(x) = \dfrac{3x + 5}{\sqrt{x - 4}}$ **34.** $f(x) = \dfrac{x - 7}{\sqrt{x + 3}}$

III

In Exercises 35 through 38, find the domain of f.

35. $f(x) = \sqrt{x^2 - 1}$ **36.** $f(x) = \sqrt{x^2 - x - 6}$

37. $f(x) = \sqrt{2 - x - x^2}$ **38.** $f(x) = \dfrac{5}{\sqrt[3]{x - 8}}$

Perform each evaluation as indicated in Exercises 39 through 49.

39. (*See Example 10*) If $f(x) = 5x + 6$, $-2 \le x \le 3$, evaluate:
(a) $f(2)$ (b) $f(-2)$ (c) $f(4)$

40. If $f(x) = 2x - 4$, $1 \le x \le 5$, evaluate:
(a) $f(0)$ (b) $f(5)$ (c) $f(6)$

41. If $f(x) = x^2 + 1$, $-1 \le x < 4$, evaluate:
(a) $f(3)$ (b) $f(-3)$ (c) $f(4)$

42. If $f(x) = -x^2 - 2x + 6$, $-3 < x \le 3$, evaluate:
(a) $f(2)$ (b) $f\left(-\dfrac{5}{2}\right)$ (c) $f(-4)$

43. (*See Example 5*) If $f(x) = 3x + 7$, evaluate:
(a) $f(w)$ (b) $f(x + 2)$

44. If $f(x) = 5x - 8$, evaluate:
(a) $f(u)$ (b) $f(x - 3)$

45. If $f(x) = 4 - 7x$, evaluate:
(a) $f(x + 3)$ (b) $f(x - 3)$

46. If $f(x) = 5 - 4x$, evaluate:
(a) $f(x + 2)$ (b) $f(x - 2)$

47. (*See Example 6*) If $f(x) = x^2 - 4x$, evaluate:
(a) $f(2 + h)$ (b) $f(x + h)$

48. If $f(x) = 3x - 2x^2$, evaluate:
(a) $f(x + t)$ (b) $f(3 + t)$

49. If $f(x) = 2x^2 - 4x + 5$, evaluate:
(a) $f(3 + h)$ (b) $f(x + w)$

50. Catherine has a summer job selling magazine subscriptions by telephone. She makes $4 per hour plus $2.50 for every customer she gets to subscribe to the magazine. She works six hours every day.
(a) Express her daily salary in dollars as a function of the number of subscriptions she sells.
(b) How many magazine subscriptions must she sell to make $44 in one day?

51. (*See Example 11*) Herb is going to an amusement park that costs $3 for admission and $0.50 for each ride.
(a) Express Herb's total expenses (in dollars) as a function of the number of rides he takes.
(b) What will it cost Herb to go to the park and ride eight rides?
(c) How many rides can he take with $10 to spend?

52. The cost of a classified advertisement in the college newspaper is 40¢ plus 3¢ per word.
(a) Express the cost of an advertisement as a function of the number of words in the ad.
(b) How much does an ad that is 15 words long cost?
(c) How many words are there in an advertisement that costs $1.00?

53. (*See Example 12*) The pep squad of South County High School wants to raise money by selling candy bars for $2.50 each.
   (a) Express the revenue as a function of the number of candy bars the members of the squad sell.
   (b) The squad needs a revenue of $400 just to meet expenses. How many candy bars must the members sell to meet their expenses?

54. Shoshona pulls into a gasoline station that is selling unleaded gasoline for $1.25 per gallon.
   (a) Express her total cost as a function of the number of gallons of unleaded gasoline she buys.
   (b) What will six gallons of gasoline cost her?
   (c) If she has $10 to spend, how many gallons of gasoline can she buy?

55. Express the area of a circle as a function of its radius.

56. Express the area of a circle as a function of its circumference.

57. Express the volume of a cube as a function of the length of one of the edges.

58. Express the surface area of a cube as a function of the length of one of the edges.

A–8 NONLINEAR FUNCTIONS AND THEIR GRAPHS

- *Quadratic Functions*
- *Lorenz Curves*
- *Higher-Degree Polynomials*
- *Functions Defined Piecewise*

One of the goals of a calculus course is to give the student the ability to sketch a graph of a function accurately and quickly. In Chapter 11 we see how to identify a few crucial points to plot and then how to use these points to fill in the rest of the curve without having to plot additional points. There are some functions, however, whose graphs can be drawn without using calculus. In this section we introduce several different types of functions and their graphs.

QUADRATIC FUNCTIONS

> *Definition*
> **Quadratic Function, Parabola**
>
> A function is called a **quadratic function** if its rule can be written $f(x) = ax^2 + bx + c$ with $a \neq 0$; its graph is called a **parabola.**

Quadratic functions are often used to describe revenue, or income, from sales because the revenue is obtained as the product of two variables; revenue equals the sales price per item times the number of items sold. A Girl Scout who sells 40 boxes of cookies at $3 per box has a revenue of $120. In general, if a seller sells x items at a price of p per item, the seller's revenue is $x \cdot p$.

| *Definition* **Revenue** | The revenue R from selling x items at a price p per item is given by $$R = x \cdot p$$ |

In most cases there is a relationship between x and p. If the price per item is low, the seller may be able to sell a large number of items. But as the seller raises the price, the demand for the item goes down. Economists often assume that demand is linearly related to price. This relation may be expressed by an equation like $x = 180 - 3p$. If we let R stand for revenue, then $R = x \cdot p = (180 - 3p)p$, or $R = 180p - 3p^2$. R is a quadratic function of p, with $a = -3$, $b = 180$, and $c = 0$.

NOTE If demand and price are related by a linear equation, then the revenue can be expressed as a quadratic function of either the price or the demand.

EXAMPLE 1   *(Compare Exercise 1)*

The number of television sets a store can sell in a month, x, is related to the price, p, by the linear equation $x = 200 - \frac{1}{5}p$.

(a) What will be the revenue from TV sales if the price is \$250 per set?
(b) More generally, if the price is the variable p, express the revenue R as a function of p.

SOLUTION

(a) When $p = 250$, $x = 200 - \frac{1}{5}(250) = 150$; the store will sell 150 sets. 150 sets at \$250 per set produces a revenue R of $(150)(250) = 37,500$ dollars per month.

(b) In general, $R = x \cdot p$. Substituting $x = 200 - \frac{1}{5}p$ gives
$$R = [200 - \tfrac{1}{5}p] \cdot p = 200p - \tfrac{1}{5}p^2$$

The manager in charge of television sales might be interested in knowing what price will produce the largest revenue. To find this price, we need to look at the general shape of parabolas. The graph of $f(x) = ax^2 + bx + c$, a parabola, has the general shape of a bowl that either opens upward or downward. If $a > 0$, the parabola opens upward; if $a < 0$, it opens downward (Figure A–17).

The vertex is the point where the parabola changes direction. If $a > 0$, the vertex is the lowest point on the graph; if $a < 0$, the vertex is the highest point on the graph. The first coordinate of the vertex is given by $x = -b/(2a)$. You may have seen this result derived in an algebra course by a method called "completing the square." Later, you will be able to derive this result easily using calculus.

We could also give a formula for the y-coordinate of the vertex, but the fewer formulas to be memorized the better. Once you have the x-coordinate, $-b/(2a)$, simply evaluate $f(-\frac{b}{2a})$ to find the y-coordinate.

FIGURE A–17

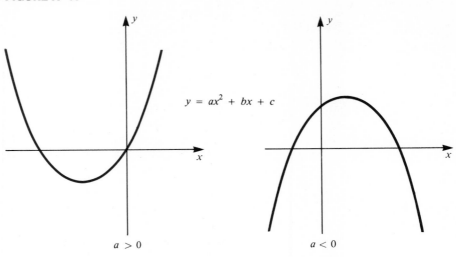

$$y = ax^2 + bx + c$$

$a > 0$ $a < 0$

FIGURE A–18

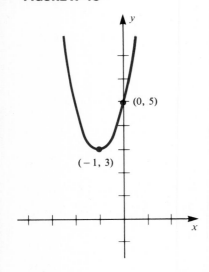

$(0, 5)$

$(-1, 3)$

EXAMPLE 2 *(Compare Exercise 7)*

Sketch a rough graph of $f(x) = 2x^2 + 4x + 5$.

SOLUTION Here $a = 2$, $b = 4$, and $c = 5$. Because $a > 0$, the parabola opens up. (*Compare Exercise 3.*) The x-coordinate of the vertex is

$$\frac{-b}{2a} = \frac{-4}{2 \cdot 2} = -1$$

The y-coordinate is $f(-1) = 2 - 4 + 5 = 3$. Therefore, the vertex is the point $(-1, 3)$. We can now sketch a rough graph of this parabola, as shown in Figure A–18.

                                                 ▮

If we wanted a more accurate picture, we could plot a few more points. Usually when sketching a parabola, you should plot the vertex and the points where the parabola meets the axes. We indicate this requirement for the graph by leaving out the word "rough."

EXAMPLE 3 *(Compare Exercise 11)*

Sketch the graph of $f(x) = -2x^2 + 4x + 6$.

SOLUTION Here $a = -2$, $b = 4$, and $c = 6$. Since $a < 0$, the parabola opens down. The x-coordinate of the vertex is $-b/(2a) = -4/-4 = 1$; the y-coordinate is $f(1) = 8$. The vertex is the point $(1, 8)$. To find the point where the parabola crosses the y-axis, we set $x = 0$ and evaluate $f(0)$; $f(0) = 6$. The point $(0, 6)$ is on the graph. In general, the y-intercept is simply the constant term c.

Finding the x-intercepts is not as easy. This time we know the value of y and are looking for the value of x that satisfies $f(x) = y$. In this instance, we want $y = 0$ and need to solve

$$-2x^2 + 4x + 6 = 0 \qquad \text{(Divide by } -2)$$
$$x^2 - 2x - 3 = 0 \qquad \text{(Now factor)}$$
$$(x - 3)(x + 1) = 0$$
$$x = 3 \qquad \text{and} \qquad x = -1$$

The parabola meets the x-axis at the points $(-1, 0)$ and $(3, 0)$. We can now draw Figure A–19.

FIGURE A–19

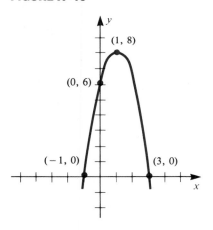

<table>
<tr><td>Definition</td><td rowspan="2">The solutions to the equation $f(x) = 0$ are called the zeros of the function.</td></tr>
<tr><td>Zeros of a Function</td></tr>
</table>

So using the last example, the zeros of the function $f(x) = -2x^2 + 4x + 6$ are the numbers $x = -1$ and $x = 3$.

CAUTION When solving the equation $f(x) = 0$, we were able to employ the technique of dividing both sides of the equation by -2. You are *not* allowed to divide the function by -2. The function $y = -2x^2 + 4x + 6$ is *not* the same as the function $y = x^2 - 2x - 3$. There is a difference between *solving* an equation and writing the rule for *evaluating* the function.

If you cannot factor $ax^2 + bx + c$, you can find the solutions to $ax^2 + bx + c = 0$ by using the **quadratic formula,** which gives the solution in the form

$$x = \frac{-b \pm \sqrt{b^2 - 4ac}}{2a}$$

EXAMPLE 4   (*Compare Exercise 17*)

Let $f(x) = 2x^2 - 8x - 5$.

(a) What are the zeros of f?
(b) Draw the graph of f.

SOLUTION

(a) We use the quadratic formula to find the zeros with $a = 2$, $b = -8$ and $c = -5$:

$$x = \frac{-(-8) \pm \sqrt{(-8)^2 - 4(2)(-5)}}{2(2)}$$

$$= \frac{8 \pm \sqrt{64 + 40}}{4}$$

$$= \frac{8 \pm \sqrt{104}}{4} \qquad\qquad (\sqrt{104} = \sqrt{4 \cdot 26} = 2\sqrt{26})$$

$$= \frac{8 \pm 2\sqrt{26}}{4} \qquad\qquad \text{(Divide the numerator and denominator by 2)}$$

$$= \frac{4 \pm \sqrt{26}}{2} \qquad \text{or}$$

$$= 2 \pm \frac{\sqrt{26}}{2}$$

The zeros of f are $2 + \dfrac{\sqrt{26}}{2}$ and $2 - \dfrac{\sqrt{26}}{2}$.

(b) The x-coordinate of the vertex is $-b/(2a) = -(-8)/(2 \cdot 2) = 2$. The y-coordinate is $f(2) = 2(2)^2 - 8(2) - 5 = -13$. The vertex is the point $(2, -13)$. $f(0) = -5$, so the y-intercept is -5, and the point $(0, -5)$ is on the graph.

The x-intercepts are $2 + \sqrt{26}/2$ and $2 - \sqrt{26}/2$. The parabola crosses the x-axis at the points $(2 + \sqrt{26}/2, 0)$ and $(2 - \sqrt{26}/2, 0)$.

The graph is shown in Figure A–20.

FIGURE A–20

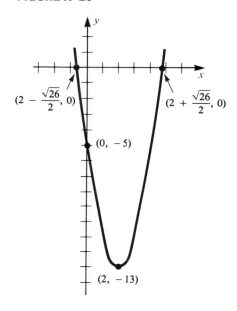

Notice that the x-intercepts are

$$\frac{-b}{2a} + \frac{\sqrt{b^2 - 4ac}}{2a}$$

and

$$\frac{-b}{2a} - \frac{\sqrt{b^2 - 4ac}}{2a}$$

The x-intercepts are the same distance from $-b/(2a)$, the first coordinate of the vertex. In Example 3 the intercepts were two units away from 1 (Note that $1 + 2 = 3$ and $1 - 2 = -1$). In Example 4 the intercepts were $\sqrt{26}/2$ units away from 2. These are examples of symmetry. Parabolas are symmetric about the vertical line through the vertex. This means that at any height, the distances d_1 and d_2 in Figure A–21 are the same.

FIGURE A–21

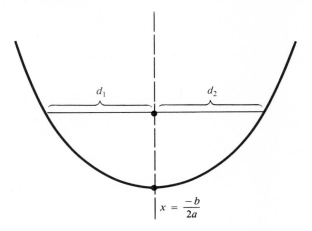

$$x = \frac{-b}{2a}$$

EXAMPLE 5   *(Compare Exercise 15)*

Refer to Figure A–20. What is the other point whose second coordinate is -5?
SOLUTION   We redraw the graph, and label the other point P. The point P and
$(0, -5)$ are the same height, so they are the same distance from the vertical line
through the vertex. See Figure A–22. The point $(0, -5)$ is two units to the left
of the vertical line through the vertex; $d_1 = 2$. Hence $d_2 = 2$ also. P is two units
to right of the vertical line; $P = (4, -5)$.

FIGURE A–22

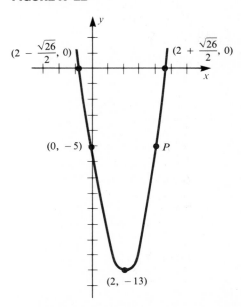

EXAMPLE 6   *(Compare Exercise 21)*

Let $f(x) = 2x^2 + 4x + 5$. What are the zeros of f?

SOLUTION   Again use the quadratic formula, this time with $a = 2$, $b = 4$, and $c = 5$:

$$x = \frac{-4 \pm \sqrt{4^2 - 4 \cdot 2 \cdot 5}}{2 \cdot 2}$$

$$= \frac{-4 \pm \sqrt{-24}}{4}$$

Since $\sqrt{-24}$ is not a real number, the function has no real zeros. The graph of $f(x) = 2x^2 + 4x + 5$ never crosses the x-axis. See Figure A–18.

We now look at a particular application of graphing.

LORENZ CURVES

Economists, sociologists, and political scientists are especially interested in the distribution of wealth within a given country. The curves used to study this distribution are called **Lorenz curves;** they are the graphs of wealth distribution functions. This general class of curves can also be used to measure other concentrations of wealth or power, but let us deal with a specific example before explaining their general use.

We start by explaining the meaning of a wealth distribution function. There are various measures of wealth; our example will deal with gross family income. For every number x in $[0, 1]$, define $W(x)$ to be the percentage of a country's total income earned by the lower $100x\%$ of the families when families are ranked by income. Thus $W(0.3) = 0.2$ would mean that the lower 30% of families (in terms of income) earn 20% of the nation's total income. Every such function must satisfy two conditions:

$W(0) = 0$ (the lower 0% of population earn 0% of the income) and

$W(1) = 1$ (100% of the population accounts for 100% of the income).

Thus every Lorenz curve goes through the origin, $(0, 0)$, and the point $(1, 1)$. The graph of a typical Lorenz curve looks like that shown in Figure A–23.

If income were distributed perfectly equally, then the lower $100x\%$ of the population would account for $100x\%$ of the income. The wealth distribution function would be $W(x) = x$. The graph of this function is called the line of perfect equality, and its graph is shown in Figure A–24.

For purposes of comparison, economists often draw the line of perfect equality on the same graph as the Lorenz curve for a specific country, as in Figure A–25.

The area of the shaded region has particular economic significance. We show how to compute this area and talk more about its significance in Chapter 6. Note that the Lorenz curve always lies under the line of perfect equality because $W(x) \leq x$ for all x, $0 \leq x \leq 1$.

We look now at a Lorenz curve and show you how to read its graph in two ways.

FIGURE A–23

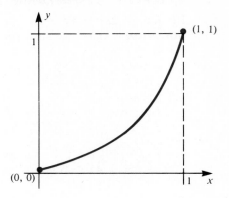

FIGURE A–24

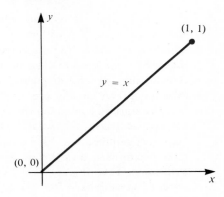

FIGURE A–25

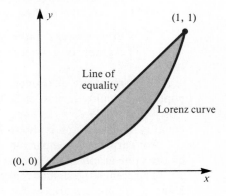

EXAMPLE 7 *(Compare Exercise 37)*

The Lorenz curve for a certain country can be approximated by

$$W(x) = 0.75x^2 + 0.25x$$

(a) What percent of the total income is earned by the lower 20% of the families?

(b) What percent of the total income is earned by the upper 20% of the families?

(c) Solve $W(x) = 0.5$ and interpret.

SOLUTION

(a) Compute $W(0.2)$.

$$W(0.2) = 0.75(0.04) + (0.25)(0.2)$$
$$= 0.03 + 0.05 = 0.08$$

The lowest 20% of the families earn 8% of the total income.

(b) Remember that $W(x)$ gives the percentage income for the *lower* $100x\%$ of the families. We first must compute the income earned by the lower 80% of the families, $W(0.8) = 0.75(0.64) + 0.25(0.8) = 0.68$. The lower 80% of the families earn 68% of the total income, so the upper 20% must earn the rest, or 32%.

(c) To solve $W(x) = 0.5$, set

$$
\begin{aligned}
0.75x^2 + 0.25x &= 0.5 & \text{(Multiply by 100)}\\
75x^2 + 25x &= 50 & \text{(Divide by 25)}\\
3x^2 + x &= 2 \\
3x^2 + x - 2 &= 0 \\
(3x - 2)(x + 1) &= 0 \\
\end{aligned}
$$

$$x = \frac{2}{3} \qquad x = -1$$

Reject $x = -1$ because $x = -1$ is not in the domain of W.

Thus $W(\frac{2}{3}) = 0.5$. Since $\frac{2}{3} = 66\frac{2}{3}\%$, we have the following interpretation: The lowest $66\frac{2}{3}\%$ of families account for 50% of the total income.

_____

We look at the results of Example 7 geometrically. The graph of $y = 0.75x^2 + 0.25x$ is shown in Figure A–26. The arrows indicate the two different ways the graph is used. To answer questions (a) and (b), you start with a value of x and find the corresponding value of y. To answer question (c), you start with the value of $y = 0.5$ and follow the arrow to the correct value of x.

Lorenz curves are also used to measure other concentrations of wealth or power. For example, you can determine how monopolistic a given industry is by defining a monopoly function:

$M(x) = y$ if the lower $100x\%$ of the companies in the industry produce $100y\%$ of the total output of that industry.

FIGURE A–26

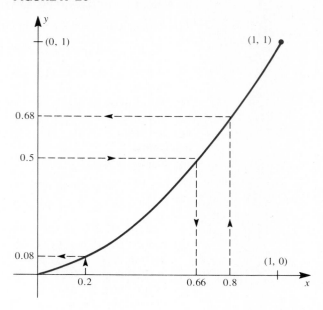

HIGHER-DEGREE POLYNOMIALS

Generally speaking, functions that arise in applications are constructed to approximate some data. The person choosing which function to use to model the real situation should be familiar with the general behavior of different types of functions. The function chosen should have properties found in the application. For example, here is a table giving data for family incomes in Brazil in 1972.

PERCENTILE OF POPULATION	PERCENTILE OF INCOME
0	0
20	2
40	7
60	16.4
80	33.4
100	100

Source: W. van Ginneken and J. Park, eds., *Generating Internationally Comparable Income Distribution Estimates* (Geneva: International Labour Office, 1984).

Figure A–27 shows these data points plotted and also shows the parabola that best approximates these points. ("Best" here is meant in a technical sense from advanced statistics.) You don't need to worry about how this parabola was constructed, but it obviously has at least one undesirable characteristic. The graph

FIGURE A–27

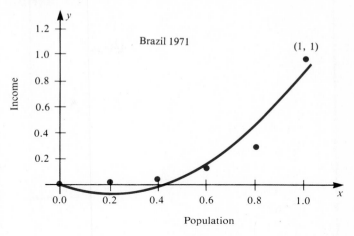

Population

Best parabola
$$W(x) = 1.6x^2 - 0.6x$$

FIGURE A–28

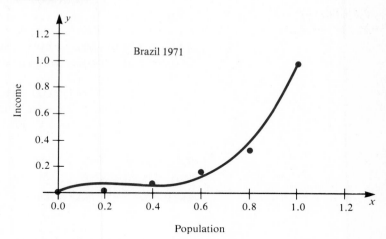

Population

Best cubic
$$W(x) = 2.7x^3 - 2.4x^2 + .7x$$

FIGURE A–29

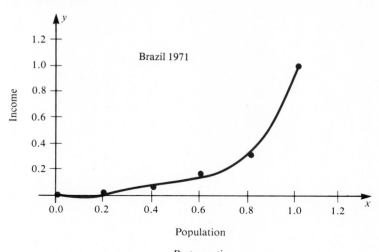

Population

Best quartic
$$W(x) = 5.3x^4 - 7.7x^3 + 3.9x^2 - .5x$$

goes below the x-axis. It looks as if the lower 20% of the families accounted for a negative percentage of the total income! Compare with Figure A–28, which shows the best fit to the data by a third-degree polynomial, and Figure A–29, which shows the best fit by a fourth-degree polynomial. These curves seem to describe reality better. Different situations may call for different types of functions.

We deal with the general problem of graphing polynomials of degree greater than 2 in Chapter 11. Here we simply ask you to plot some points, and then draw a "smooth" curve through them.

EXAMPLE 8   *(Compare Exercise 25)*

Sketch the graph of $y = x^3 - 6x^2 + 9x + 2$.

SOLUTION   We make a table of values:

x	−1	0	1	2	3	4
$f(x) = x^3 - 6x^2 + 9x + 2$	−14	2	6	4	2	6

A sketch of the curve using these points is found in Figure A–30.

FIGURE A–30

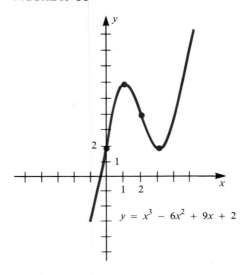

$$y = x^3 - 6x^2 + 9x + 2$$

FUNCTIONS DEFINED PIECEWISE

Sometimes the rule for evaluating $f(x)$ depends on the value of x. Such functions often arise in business applications, for example, because many businesses give discount rates for large orders.

EXAMPLE 9 *(Compare Exercise 27)*

A print shop makes copies at a rate of 5¢ per page if 1200 or fewer copies are ordered. If more than 1200 copies are ordered, the charge is only 4¢ per page. Describe the cost function and draw its graph.

SOLUTION Let x be the number of hundreds of copies ordered, and let $C(x)$ be the cost in dollars of x pages. We write the rule for $C(x)$ as

$$C(x) = \begin{cases} 5x & \text{if } 0 \le x \le 12 \\ 4x & \text{if } x > 12 \end{cases}$$

Thus if $x = 8$, then $C(8) = 5 \cdot 8 = 40$; the charge for 800 copies is $40. If $x = 20$, we use the rule $C(20) = 4 \cdot 20 = 80$. The charge for 2000 copies is $80.

The graph of C is given in Figure A–31. Notice that the scale used on the y-axis is different from the scale used on the x-axis. This is often necessary in applications.

This graph is another example in which in reality the application would require that x can only have a finite number of values but we draw the graph through other points to get a better picture. Note that the second piece of the graph

FIGURE A–31

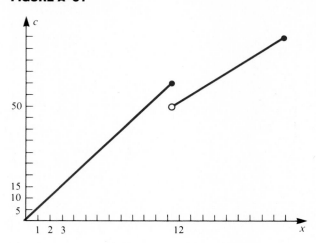

has an empty dot for its left-hand point; this signifies that the point, which is (12, 48), is not on the graph. The solid dot above it at (12, 60) indicates that (12, 60) is on the graph.

This graphical notation is also used in the next example, which again shows that a function may have a graph that is not connected.

EXAMPLE 10   (*Compare Exercise 41*)

A cosmetics company has studied public awareness of its product. The awareness was measured on a scale of 0 to 5, with 0 indicating that consumers were not aware of the product and 5 meaning that consumers were very aware of the product. The company found that after running a TV commercial, it could put general consumer awareness at 5 but that awareness dropped off linearly. Four days after the commercial, consumer awareness was at the 3 level. The company decided to run the commercial every four days. If t measures time in days after the original commercial, and $A(t)$ is consumer awareness, the company found that the awareness function was given by

$$A(t) = \begin{cases} -\dfrac{1}{2}t + 5 & 0 \leq t < 4 \\[2mm] -\dfrac{1}{2}t + 7 & 4 \leq t < 8 \\[2mm] -\dfrac{1}{2}t + 9 & 8 \leq t < 12 \end{cases}$$

Graph the awareness function.

FIGURE A–32

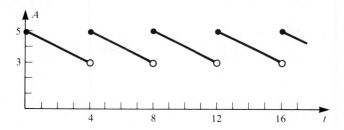

SOLUTION The graph is assembled in stages. First we graph the line segment $A(t) = -\frac{1}{2}t + 5$ that is above the interval $0 \le t \le 4$. Then, because this rule is used only for $0 \le t < 4$ in the actual graph, we delete the endpoint (4, 3) of this segment by drawing an empty dot for this point. Next we draw the line segment $A(t) = -\frac{1}{2}t + 7$ above $4 \le t \le 8$ and repeat the empty dot drawing process for the point (8, 3). Repeating this procedure, we obtain Figure A–32.

The last function that we look at in these examples is the **absolute value function.** While students generally have no problem evaluating the absolute value of any specific number, sometimes the general rule for evaluation does give trouble. We use the notation $|x|$ to mean the **absolute value of x.** If $x \ge 0$, then $|x|$ is x. If $x < 0$, then $|x|$ has the opposite sign from x. To change the sign of a number, you multiply it by -1.

Thus if $x < 0$, $|x| = (-1) \cdot x = -x$. This is the part of the rule that causes difficulty; $-x$ looks negative because it has that minus sign in front of it. But remember that we started with "if $x < 0$," so x itself is negative, and $-x$ is positive!

Definition **Absolute Value**	The **absolute value of x,** written $|x|$, is defined by $$|x| = \begin{cases} x & \text{if } x \ge 0 \\ -x & \text{if } x < 0 \end{cases}$$

EXAMPLE 11 *(Compare Exercise 30)*

Graph $f(x) = |x|$.

SOLUTION The graph is given in Figure A–33. Notice that the graph is connected; the point (0, 0) is not drawn with an empty dot because (0, 0) is on the graph.

FIGURE A–33

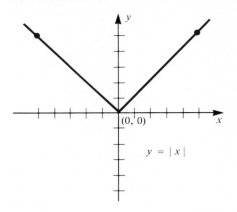

$$y = |x|$$

A–8 EXERCISES

I

1. (*See Example 1*) If $R = x \cdot p$ and $x = 300 - \frac{1}{6}p$, express R as a function of p.

2. If $R = x \cdot p$ and $x = 400 - p^2$, express R as a function of p.

3. (*See Example 2*) If $y = 5x^2 - 9x + 2$, does the parabola open down or up?

4. If $y = -2x^2 + 10x + 3$, does the parabola open down or up?

5. If $y = 5 + 4x - 6x^2$, does the parabola open down or up?

6. If $y = -8x - 7 + 2x^2$, does the parabola open down or up?

7. (*See Example 2*) What is the vertex of the parabola $y = x^2 - 6x + 7$?

8. What is the vertex of the parabola $y = -2x^2 + 8x + 9$?

9. What is the vertex of the parabola $y = x^2 + 4x - 7$?

10. What is the vertex of the parabola $y = -3x^2 - 12x + 10$?

II

11. (*See Example 3*) Sketch the graph of $f(x) = x^2 - 4x + 5$.

12. Sketch the graph of $y = 9 - x^2$.

13. Sketch the graph of $y = 3 - 2x - x^2$.

14. Sketch the graph of $y = 2x^2 - 3x - 2$.

15. (*See Example 5*) A certain parabola has vertex $(3, 7)$. The point $(5, 13)$ is on the parabola. What other point on the parabola has 13 for its y-coordinate?

16. A certain parabola has vertex $(-3, -5)$. The point $(1, 11)$ is on the parabola. What other point on the parabola has 11 for its y-coordinate?

17. (*See Example 4*) What are the zeros of $f(x) = 6x^2 + 7x - 20$?

18. What are the zeros of $f(x) = 3x^2 + 5x + 7$?

19. What are the zeros of $f(x) = 4 + 8x - 3x^2$?

20. What are the zeros of $f(x) = -5x^2 + x + 2$?

21. (*See Example 6*) What are the zeros of $f(x) = x^2 + 2x + 5$?

22. What are the zeros of $f(x) = x^2 + x - 5$?

III

Graph each of the functions defined in Exercises 23 through 36.

23. $f(x) = x^2 - x - 7$

24. $f(x) = x^2 + 2x - 5$

25. (*See Example 8*) $f(x) = x^3 - 3x^2 + 2x$

26. $f(x) = x^3 + 3x^2 - 9x + 1$

27. (*See Example 9*) $f(x) = \begin{cases} 2x + 1 & x \le 1 \\ 3 - x & x > 1 \end{cases}$

28. $f(x) = \begin{cases} x^2 & x \le 2 \\ 4 & x > 2 \end{cases}$

29. $f(x) = \begin{cases} 3x + 1 & x < 2 \\ 9 - x & x \ge 2 \end{cases}$

30. (*See Example 11*)

$$f(x) = |x - 3| = \begin{cases} x - 3 & x - 3 \ge 0 \\ -(x - 3) & x - 3 < 0 \end{cases}$$

31. $f(x) = |x + 5|$

32. $f(x) = |2x + 1|$

33. $f(x) = \sqrt{x^2}$

34. $f(x) = \sqrt{(x - 1)^2}$

35. $f(x) = |x^2 - 1|$

36. $f(x) = |x^2 - 4|$

37. (*See Example 7*) A certain country's Lorenz curve is given by

$$W(x) = \frac{2}{3}x^2 + \frac{1}{3}x$$

(a) What percent of the total income does the lower 30% of the families account for?

(b) What percent of the total income does the upper 10% of the families account for?

(c) Solve $W(x) = \frac{1}{3}$ and interpret.

38. A certain country's Lorenz curve is given by

$$W(x) = 0.8x^2 + 0.2x$$

(a) What percent of the total income does the lower 50% of the families account for?

(b) What percent of total income does the upper 75% of the families account for?

(c) The lower x percent of the families account for 60% of the income. Solve for x.

39. A certain country's Lorenz curve is given by $W(x) = 0.6x^2 + 0.4x$.

(a) What percent of the total income does the lower 30% of the families earn?

(b) What percent of the total income does the upper 30% of the families earn?

(c) Solve $W(x) = 0.6$ and interpret.

40. The wealth distribution curve of a certain country is $W(x) = 0.82x^2 + 0.18x$.

(a) What percent of the total income is earned by the lowest quarter of the families?

(b) What percent of the total income is earned by this country's "middle class," that is, by those families whose incomes rank above the lowest 25% and below the top 25%?

(c) What percent of the total income is earned by the top 25% of the families?

(d) Solve $W(x) = 0.4$ and interpret.

41. (*See Example 10*) The manager of the meat department likes to have at least 20 lb of hamburger on hand at all times but never more than 80 lb. The store sells 30 lb of hamburger per hour, so the meat department replenishes its supply of hamburger every two hours. The manager starts the morning with 80 lb of hamburger. If $A(t)$ is the amount of hamburger on hand t hours after opening, express the rule for $A(t)$, $0 \le t \le 8$.

42. The camera department in a drug store is open every day of the week. The department starts July 1 with 300 rolls of film and sells 40 rolls of film per day. The department receives 280 fresh rolls of film at start of the day on July 8, 15, 22, and 29. Express the number of rolls of film the department has on hand at the beginning of the day as a function of the date, $1 \le t \le 31$.

43. A copying service charges 5¢ per copy for the first 20 copies and 4¢ per copy for each additional copy.

(a) Express the total cost as a function of the number of copies made.

(b) How much does it cost to have 50 copies made?

(c) How many copies can you have made for $3.00?

44. If $R = x \cdot p$ and $x = 300 - \frac{1}{6}p$, express R as a function of x.

45. If $R = x \cdot p$ and $x = 400 - p^2$, express R as a function of x.

46. Let $R = x \cdot p$ and suppose that $3x + 2p = 600$.
   (a) Express R as a function of x.
   (b) Express R as a function of p.

47. If the demand and price of an item are linearly related and a price of \$20 means that the demand is 40 items per week while a price of \$25 means the demand is 30 items per week, then:
   (a) find an equation relating the price and the weekly demand.

   (b) express the weekly revenue as a function of the price.
   (c) express the weekly revenue as a function of the weekly demand.

48. Express the area of a rectangle in terms of its width if the total perimeter of the rectangle is 40 meters.

49. Express the perimeter of a rectangle as a function of its width if the rectangle has an area of 30 square centimeters.

IMPORTANT TERMS

A-1
Natural Numbers
Integers
Rational Numbers
Irrational Numbers
Real Numbers

A-2
Variable
Solution
Linear Equation

A-3
Cartesian Coordinate System
Rectangular Coordinate System
Origin
x-Axis
y-Axis
x-Coordinate

Absicssa
y-Coordinate
Ordinate
Quadrants

A-4
>, <, ≥, ≤
Properties of Inequalities
Interval Notation

A-5
Polynomial Arithmetic
Addition and Multiplication of Polynomials
Factoring Polynomials
Quadratic Formula
Rational Function

A-6
Exponents
Zero Exponent

Negative Exponent
Fractional Exponent
nth Root of b

A-7
Function
Domain
Range
Rule of a Function
Value of a Function

A-8
Quadratic Function
Parabola
Revenue
Zeros of a Function
Quadratic Formula
Lorenz Curve
Piecewise Defined Functions
Absolute Value of x

CHAPTER 1

SECTION 1-1,   PAGE 5

1. $y = 15x + 20$ **3. (a)** \$23.75   **(b)** \$14.25   **5. (a)** $f(1) = 1$ **(b)** $f(-2) = -11$ **(c)** $f(\frac{1}{2}) = -1$
(d) $f(a) = 4a - 3$ **7. (a)** $f(5) = \frac{6}{4} = \frac{3}{2}$ **(b)** $f(-6) = \frac{5}{7}$ **(c)** $f(0) = -1$ **(d)** $f(2c) = \frac{(2c + 1)}{(2c - 1)}$
9. (a) $f(5) = 390$ calories, $f(2.5) = 195$ calories, $f(6.4) = 499.2$ calories   **(b)** 9.5 ounces   **11. (a)** 540 calories
(b) 83.3 minutes   **13.** $f(x) = 1.25x + 25$ ($x =$ number of hamburgers)   **15.** $f(x) = 0.80x$ ($x =$ regular price)
17. $f(x) = 0.60x + 12$ ($x =$ number of miles)   **19.** $f(x) = 3500x + 5,000,000$ ($x =$ number of students)
21. $f(x) = 0.88x$ ($x =$ list price)   **23. (a)** 13,500 sq. feet   **(b)** $f(125) = 3750$ sq. ft.   **(c)** \$7800   **(d)** 530 feet

SECTION 1-2,   PAGE 20

1.

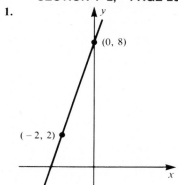

3.

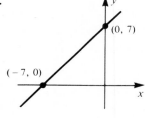

5.

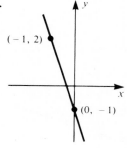

7. $m = 7, b = 22$ **9.** $m = -\frac{2}{5}, b = 6$ **11.** $m = -\frac{2}{5}, b = \frac{3}{5}$ **13.** $m = \frac{1}{3}, b = 2$
15. $m = 1$ **17.** $-\frac{4}{3}$ **19.** $y = -2$ **21.** $y = 0$
23.

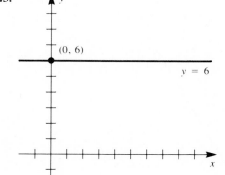

25.

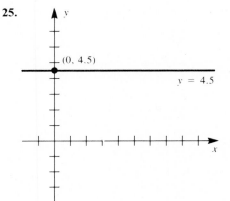

27. $x = 3$ **29.** $x = 10$

31.

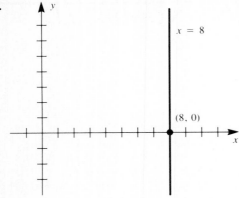

33.

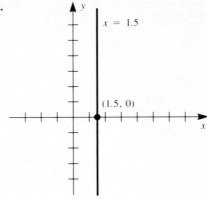

35. $y = 4x + 3$ **37.** $y = -x + 6$ **39.** $y = \frac{1}{2}x$ **41.** $y = -4x + 9$ **43.** $x - 2y = -3$ **45.** $y = 7x - 2$

47. $x - 5y + 21 = 0$

49. $y = (\frac{1}{3})x + \frac{1}{3}$

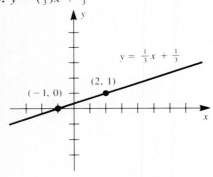

51. $y = 2x$

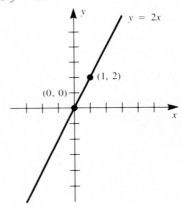

53. $y = 4$

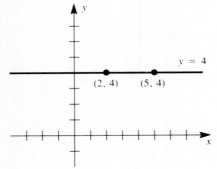

55. x-intercept $= 3$, y-intercept $= -5$

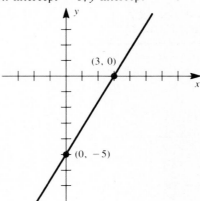

57. x-intercept $= 12.5$, y-intercept $= -5$

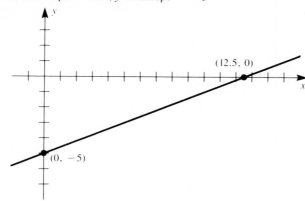

59. $m_1 = 1$, $m_2 = 1$; lines parallel   **61.** No, the slopes are $\frac{6}{4}$ and $\frac{6}{5}$.   **63.** Parallel, both slopes are 6.
65. Not parallel, slopes are $\frac{1}{2}$ and -2.   **67.** $y = 3x + 8$ **69.** $5x + 7y = 56$ **71.** $y = -4$ **73.** $\frac{11}{3}$
75. (a) $y = -3x + 238$ (b) 238 pounds   **77.** $c = \frac{7}{5}x + 640$ **79.** (a) -6 (b) $\frac{3}{4}$ (c) $\frac{21}{4}$ (d) -15
81. $5x + 6y = 54$ **83.** $y = 3.5x + 185$ (x = number of years since 1980, y = value)
85. $y = 0.078x + 5.00$ (x = kilowatt-hours used, y = amount of bill)   **87.** (a) 4   (b) -3 (c) $\frac{2}{3}$ (d) $-\frac{1}{2}$
(e) $-\frac{2}{3}$ (f) 0   **89.** $y = 0.11x + 22$

SECTION 1–3,   PAGE 31

1. (a) \$10,040   (b) 223   (c) unit cost $=$ \$43, fixed cost $=$ \$2300 per week   **3.** (a) Fixed cost $=$ \$400 per day, unit
cost $=$ \$3   (b) $C(600) =$ \$2200, $C(1000) =$ \$3400   **5.** (a) $R(x) = 32x$ (b) $R(78) =$ \$2496   (c) 21 pairs
7. (a) $R(x) = 3.39x$ (b) $R(834) =$ \$2827.26   **9.** (a) $C(x) = 57x + 780$ (b) $R(x) = 79x$ (c) 36 (rounded)
11. $C(x) = 4x + 500$; cost of 800 units $=$ \$3700   **13.** (a) $C(x) = 2x + 200$ (b) \$200   (c) \$2
15. (a) $C(x) = 649x + 1500$ (b) $R(x) = 899x$ (c) $C(37) =$ \$25,513   (d) $R(37) =$ \$33,263   (e) six computers
17. (a) $BV = -50x + 425$ (b) \$50   (c) $BV(3) =$ \$275   **19.** (a) $BV = -1575x + 9750$ (b) \$1575
(c) $BV(2) =$ \$6600, $BV(5) =$ \$1875   **21.** Sales greater than 2159   **23.** Mileage less than 1400 miles
25. At least 2154   **27.** $C(x) = 12.65x + 2140$ **29.** (a) 183   (b) 368   (c) 264   **31.** (a) $R(x) = 35x$
(b) \$43,330   (c) 17   **33.** (a) $y = -1425x + 18,450$ (b) \$1425   (c) \$18,450   **35.** (a) $R(x) = 12x$
(b) $C(x) = 6.5x + 1430$ **37.** (a) $R(x) = 22.50x$ (b) $C(x) = 16.7x + 1940$ (c) 335

CHAPTER 1 REVIEW
EXERCISES,   PAGE 35

1. (a) 16   (b) 2   (c) 12.5   (d) $\frac{7b - 3}{2}$ **3.** 22   **5.** (a) \$4.20   (b) 2.75 pounds   **7.** (a) $f(x) = 29.95x$
(x = number of pairs bought)   (b) $f(x) = 1.25x + 40$ (x = number of people)

9.

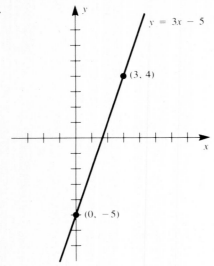

(a)

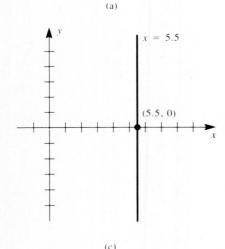

(c)

(b)

(d)

11. (a) $m = -2, b = 3$ (b) $m = \frac{2}{3}, b = -4$ (c) $m = \frac{5}{4}, b = \frac{3}{2}$ (d) $m = -\frac{6}{7}, b = -\frac{5}{7}$ **13.** (a) $-\frac{6}{5}$
(b) 3   (c) 2.5   **15.** (a) $y = -0.75x + 5$ (b) $y = 8x - 3$ (c) $y = -2x + 9$ (d) $y = 6$
(e) $y = -\frac{1}{6}x + \frac{23}{6}$ (f) $x = -2$ (g) $4x - 3y = -13$ **17.** (a) $y = 2$ (b) $x = -4$ (c) $x = 5$ (d) $y = 6$
19. No, one has slope $\frac{12}{7}$ and the other $\frac{2}{3}$.   **21.** No, the slope of the line through two points is $-\frac{8}{11}$. Slope of the given line
is $-\frac{8}{4} = -2$.   **23.** No, slopes are 1 and $\frac{3}{2}$.   **25.** $C(x) = 36x + 12,800$ **27.** (a) \$4938   (b) 655
29. (a) $R(x) = 11x$ (b) $C(x) = 6.50x + 675$ (c) 150 shirts   **31.** $R(x) = 19.50x, C(x) = 12.3x + 2628$, break-
even volume $= 365$ **33.** (a) $BV = -2075x + 17,500$ (b) \$2075   (c) \$7125   **35.** $BV = -296x + 1540$
37. Line is $4x - 5y = -37, k = 5$ **39.** $V = -2100x + 12,000$ **41.** $C(x) = 0.67x + 480$ **43.** When the sales
exceed \$20,000.   **45.** $k = 26$ **47.** \$1015

CHAPTER 2

SECTION 2–1,   PAGE 52

1. $(2, 3)$ **3.** $(-3, 0)$ **5.** $(-3, -15)$ **7.** $(5, 3)$ **9.** $(6, -8)$ **11.** $(\frac{7}{2}, 4)$ **13.** $(\frac{2}{3}, -\frac{5}{3})$
15. $(-2.5, -12.5)$ **17.** $(6, -1)$ **19.** $(\frac{5}{2}, -3)$ **21.** $(-2, 3)$ **23.** $(-14, 19)$ **25.** $(-2.4, 5.1)$
27. $(0.06, 0.13)$ **29.** No solution   **31.** Infinite number of solutions of the form $(k, 0.2 - 0.8k)$
33. Infinite number of solutions of the form $(4 + 6k, k)$ **35.** $(4, 3)$ **37.** $(30, 10)$ **39.** $(15, 8)$ **41.** $(25, 85.50)$
43. 2.5 oranges, 3.25 apples   **45.** 43 nickels and 122 dimes   **47.** 600 gallons of 20% acid and 240 gallons of 55% acid
49. 905 at Ennis and 595 at McGregor   **51.** 60 lb peanuts and 20 lb cashews   **53.** 11 cases of Golden Punch and 14
cases of Light Punch   **55.** 62 chopped beef and 53 sausage   **57.** $23,500 at 7.4%, $26,500 at 8.8%
59. Federal = $38,000, state = $8000

SECTION 2–2,   PAGE 71

1. $(3, 2)$ **3.** $(2, -1)$ **5.** $(2, -1, 2)$ **7.** $(7, 5, 3)$ **9.** $(3, 1, 2)$ **11. (a)** 2, 3, 6, 11   **(b)** (2, 3) location

(c) 4, 0, 9   **13.** $\begin{bmatrix} 5 & -2 \\ 3 & 1 \end{bmatrix} \begin{bmatrix} 5 & -2 & | & 1 \\ 3 & 1 & | & 7 \end{bmatrix}$ **15.** $\begin{bmatrix} 1 & 1 & -1 \\ 3 & 4 & -2 \\ 2 & 0 & 1 \end{bmatrix} \begin{bmatrix} 1 & 1 & -1 & | & 14 \\ 3 & 4 & -2 & | & 9 \\ 2 & 0 & 1 & | & 7 \end{bmatrix}$

17. $\begin{bmatrix} 1 & 5 & -2 & 1 \\ 1 & -1 & 2 & 4 \\ 6 & 3 & -11 & 1 \\ 5 & -3 & -7 & 1 \end{bmatrix} \begin{bmatrix} 1 & 5 & -2 & 1 & | & 12 \\ 1 & -1 & 2 & 4 & | & -5 \\ 6 & 3 & -11 & 1 & | & 14 \\ 5 & -3 & -7 & 1 & | & 22 \end{bmatrix}$

19.
$$5x_1 + 3x_2 = -2$$
$$-x_1 + 4x_2 = 4$$
21.
$$5x_1 + 2x_2 - x_3 = 3$$
$$-2x_1 + 7x_2 + 8x_3 = 7$$
$$3x_1 + x_3 = 5$$
23.
$$3x_1 + 2x_3 + 6x_4 = 4$$
$$-4x_1 + 5x_2 + 7x_3 + 2x_4 = 2$$
$$x_1 + 3x_2 + 2x_3 + 5x_4 = 0$$
$$-2x_1 + 6x_2 - 5x_3 + 3x_4 = 4$$

25. $\begin{bmatrix} 1 & 2 & -4 & | & 6 \\ 4 & 2 & 5 & | & 7 \\ 1 & -1 & 0 & | & 4 \end{bmatrix}$ **27.** $\begin{bmatrix} 1 & 3 & 2 & | & -4 \\ 0 & -7 & -1 & | & 13 \\ 0 & -6 & -10 & | & 19 \end{bmatrix}$ **29.** $\begin{bmatrix} 1 & -3 & 2 & | & -6 \\ 0 & 1 & -2 & | & 4 \\ 0 & 4 & 3 & | & 8 \end{bmatrix}$

31. $(1, 1)$ **33.** $(5, 2)$ **35.** $(\frac{3}{2}, -\frac{5}{2})$ **37.** $(3, 1, 2)$ **39.** $(9, -4, 2)$ **41.** $(4, -3, -1)$ **43.** $(3, 0, 2)$
45. $(0, 4, 2)$ **47.** $(5, -4, 1)$ **49.** $(4, 1, -3, 2)$ **51.** $(1, 2, 3, 4)$

53. x_1 = number cases of Regular
x_2 = number cases of Premium
x_3 = number cases of Classic
$$4x_1 + 4x_2 + 5x_3 = 316$$
$$5x_1 + 4x_2 + 2x_3 = 292$$
$$x_1 + 2x_2 + 3x_3 = 142$$

55. x_1 = number of tickets sold to students
x_2 = number of tickets sold to faculty
x_3 = number of tickets sold to public
$$3x_1 + 5x_2 + 8x_3 = 2542$$
$$x_1 = 3x_2$$
$$2x_1 = x_3$$

57. x_1 = number shares of X
x_2 = number shares of Y
x_3 = number shares of Z
$$44x_1 + 22x_2 + 64x_3 = 20,480$$
$$42x_1 + 28x_2 + 62x_3 = 20,720$$
$$42x_1 + 30x_2 + 60x_3 = 20,580$$

59. Two of Portfolio I, three of Portfolio II, two of Portfolio III   **61.** Stock A: $22,000, Stock B: $3,000, Stock C:
$15,000   **63.** 540 high school students, 1230 college students, 680 adults.   **65.** 24 cases of Regular, 35 cases of
Premium, and 16 cases of Classic   **67.** 123 students, 41 faculty, 246 general public   **69.** 90 shares of X, 140 shares of
Y, 210 shares of Z

SECTION 2-3,   PAGE 88

1. Reduced echelon form   **3.** Not reduced echelon form. The leftmost nonzero entry in row 2 is not a 1.
5. Not reduced echelon form. The leading 1 in row 3 is to the left of the leading 1 in row 2.   **7.** Not reduced echelon form. The columns containing the leading 1's of rows 3 and 4 have other nonzero entries.   **9.** Not reduced echelon form. The leftmost nonzero entry in row 2 is not a 1.

11. $\begin{bmatrix} 1 & 0 & 1 & 4 \\ 0 & 1 & 2 & 3 \\ 0 & 0 & 1 & 2 \end{bmatrix}$
13. $\begin{bmatrix} 1 & 3 & 4 & -1 \\ 0 & 4 & 3 & 4 \\ 0 & 0 & 6 & 2 \end{bmatrix}$
15. $\begin{bmatrix} 1 & 4 & 2 & 4 & 5 \\ 0 & 0 & 3 & 1 & 2 \\ 0 & 0 & 0 & 2 & 3 \\ 0 & 0 & 0 & 0 & 6 \end{bmatrix}$

17. $\begin{bmatrix} 1 & 0 & 2 & 3 \\ 0 & 1 & 4 & 4 \\ 0 & 0 & 0 & 5 \\ 0 & 0 & 0 & 0 \end{bmatrix}$
19. $\begin{bmatrix} 1 & 0 & 0 & \frac{5}{4} \\ 0 & 1 & 0 & -\frac{3}{2} \\ 0 & 0 & 1 & -\frac{1}{4} \end{bmatrix}$
21. $\begin{bmatrix} 1 & 0 & 0 & \frac{22}{13} \\ 0 & 1 & 0 & 0 \\ 0 & 0 & 1 & -\frac{12}{13} \end{bmatrix}$
23. $\begin{bmatrix} 1 & 0 & 0 & 0 & \frac{5}{3} \\ 0 & 1 & 0 & -\frac{1}{7} & \frac{10}{21} \\ 0 & 0 & 1 & \frac{2}{7} & \frac{8}{21} \end{bmatrix}$

25. $x_1 = 2$
$x_2 + 2x_3 = 3$
$x_4 = -1$
Solution $x_1 = 2$
$x_2 = 3 - 2r$
$x_3 = r$
$x_4 = -1$

27. $x_1 + 2x_3 + 2x_5 = -1$
$x_2 + 4x_3 + 3x_5 = 2$
$x_4 + 4x_5 = 1$
Solution $x_1 = -1 - 2r - 2s$
$x_2 = 2 - 4r - 3s$
$x_3 = r$
$x_4 = 1 - 4s$
$x_5 = s$

29. $x_1 + 2x_3 = 2$
$x_2 - 3x_3 = 1$
$x_4 = 3$
Solution $x_1 = 2 - 2r$
$x_2 = 1 + 3r$
$x_3 = r$
$x_4 = 3$

31. $x_1 + 2x_2 + x_4 = 4$
$x_3 + 3x_4 = -1$
$x_5 = 3$
$x_6 = 2$
Solution $x_1 = 4 - 2r - s$
$x_2 = r$
$x_3 = -1 - 3s$
$x_4 = s$
$x_5 = 3$
$x_6 = 2$

33. No solution   **35.** $x_1 = 4$, $x_2 = -\frac{1}{2}$, $x_3 = -\frac{3}{2}$ **37.** $x_1 = -32 - 2r$
$x_2 = 45 + r$
$x_3 = r$
$x_4 = 16$

39. No solution   **41.** No solution   **43.** $x_1 = -59 + 11x_3$ **45.** $x_1 = 3 + x_3 + x_4$
$x_2 = 23 - 5x_3$ $x_2 = 6 + x_3 + x_4 - x_5$

47. No solution   **49.** No solution   **51.** $(2, -3)$ **53.** $(-5, 2)$ **55.** $(2, 1, 3)$ **57.** No solution
59. No solution   **61.** $(\frac{9}{2}, -\frac{5}{2}, 0, \frac{1}{2})$ **63.** $(-9, 6, 2, 1)$
65. $x_1 = -2x_2 + 3x_3 - x_5 + 3x_6$
$x_4 = -2x_5 - x_6$
67. \$15,000 in stocks, \$18,000 in bonds, \$12,000 in money markets
69. $x_1 = $ minutes jogging
$x_2 = $ minutes playing handball
$x_3 = $ minutes riding bike
$x_1 = 2x_3$
$x_2 = 60 - 3x_3$
Celia may ride bike from zero through 20 minutes, jog twice that time, and play handball the rest of the 60 minutes.

SECTION 2–4,   PAGE 98

1.

	Alpha	Beta
Salvation Army	50	65
Boy's Club	85	32
Girl Scouts	68	94

3.

	Joe	Jane	Judy
Checking	12	11	5
Savings	15	18	8
Safe deposit	8	9	21

5. 2×2 **7.** 3×3 **9.** 3×1 **11.** 2×3 **13.** 2×1 **15.** 2×2 **17.** Not equal   **19.** Equal

21. Not equal   **23.** $\begin{bmatrix} 3 & 3 & 2 \\ 7 & 4 & 3 \end{bmatrix}$ **25.** $\begin{bmatrix} 2 \\ 58 \end{bmatrix}$ **27.** Not possible   **29.** $\begin{bmatrix} 6 & 5 & 8 \\ 5 & 1 & 3 \\ 5 & -3 & 4 \end{bmatrix}$ **31.** $\begin{bmatrix} 12 & 3 \\ 6 & 15 \end{bmatrix}$

33. $\begin{bmatrix} 20 \\ 15 \\ 5 \\ 10 \end{bmatrix}$ **35.** $[-12 \quad 6 \quad -15]$ **37.** $\begin{bmatrix} 0 & 0 \\ 0 & 0 \end{bmatrix}$ **39. (a)** $2A = \begin{bmatrix} 2 & 4 \\ 6 & 0 \end{bmatrix}$, $3B = \begin{bmatrix} -3 & 6 \\ 3 & 3 \end{bmatrix}$, $-2C = \begin{bmatrix} 0 & -2 \\ -2 & -8 \end{bmatrix}$

(b) $A + B = \begin{bmatrix} 0 & 4 \\ 4 & 1 \end{bmatrix}$, $B + A = \begin{bmatrix} 0 & 4 \\ 4 & 1 \end{bmatrix}$, $A + C = \begin{bmatrix} 1 & 3 \\ 4 & 4 \end{bmatrix}$, $B + C = \begin{bmatrix} -1 & 3 \\ 2 & 5 \end{bmatrix}$

(c) $A + 2B = \begin{bmatrix} -1 & 6 \\ 5 & 2 \end{bmatrix}$, $3A + C = \begin{bmatrix} 3 & 7 \\ 10 & 4 \end{bmatrix}$, $2A + B - C = \begin{bmatrix} 1 & 5 \\ 6 & -3 \end{bmatrix}$

41.

	I	II	III
PC	23	17	20
Print	19	22	11
Disk	151	151	105

43. $x = 3$ **45.** $x = \frac{17}{8}$

47.

	A	B	C
Small	5.4	9.2	6.7
Regular	7.5	11.3	5.0
Giant	6.3	9.3	7.0

49.

	Sulphur dioxide	Nitric oxide	Particulate matter
Fairfield	2760	1080	1680
Tyler	3120	1380	1992

51.

	Average
A	89.7
B	68.0
C	75.3
D	82.0
E	75.7

SECTION 2–5,   PAGE 107

1. 14   **3.** 12   **5.** 14   **7.** \$6.25   **9.** $\begin{bmatrix} -5 & 11 \\ 0 & 14 \end{bmatrix}$ **11.** $\begin{bmatrix} 30 & 2 \\ 39 & -3 \end{bmatrix}$ **13.** $\begin{bmatrix} 14 & 6 \\ 16 & -1 \end{bmatrix}$ **15.** $\begin{bmatrix} 10 \\ 20 \end{bmatrix}$

17. $\begin{bmatrix} 7 & 4 \\ 0 & 5 \\ 22 & 14 \end{bmatrix}$ **19.** $\begin{bmatrix} -12 & 4 & -3 \\ -14 & 22 & 5 \\ 6 & 14 & 9 \end{bmatrix}$ **21.** $\begin{bmatrix} 2 & 3 \\ 8 & 7 \end{bmatrix}$ **23.** Not possible   **25.** Not possible

27. Not possible   **29.** $AB = \begin{bmatrix} 1 & 8 \\ -1 & 2 \end{bmatrix}$, $BA = \begin{bmatrix} 3 & 10 \\ -1 & 0 \end{bmatrix}$ **31.** $AB = \begin{bmatrix} -3 & 10 \\ -2 & 5 \end{bmatrix}$, $BA = \begin{bmatrix} -1 & 2 \\ -4 & 3 \end{bmatrix}$

33. $AB = \begin{bmatrix} 6 & 2 & 13 \\ -11 & -6 & -4 \end{bmatrix}$, BA not possible   **35.** $AB = [27 \quad 38]$, BA not possible   **37.** $[39 \quad 91]$

39. $\begin{bmatrix} 5 & 37 & \frac{5}{2} & 29 & 20 \\ 7 & 59 & \frac{31}{2} & 53 & 52 \\ 11 & 31 & -\frac{1}{2} & 9 & 11 \\ 25 & 113 & \frac{17}{2} & 103 & 65 \end{bmatrix}$ **41.** $\begin{bmatrix} 11 & 9 \\ 10 & 19 \end{bmatrix}$ **43.** $\begin{bmatrix} 1 & 2 \\ 3 & 1 \end{bmatrix}$ **45.** $\begin{bmatrix} 1 & 2 & 3 \\ 4 & -1 & 0 \\ 2 & 1 & 7 \end{bmatrix}$

47. $\begin{bmatrix} 3x + y \\ 2x + 4y \end{bmatrix}$ **49.** $\begin{bmatrix} x_1 + 2x_2 - x_3 \\ 3x_1 + x_2 + 4x_3 \\ 2x_1 - x_2 - x_3 \end{bmatrix}$ **51.** $\begin{bmatrix} x_1 + 3x_2 + 5x_3 + 6x_4 \\ -2x_1 + 9x_2 + 6x_3 + x_4 \\ 8x_1 + 17x_3 + 5x_4 \end{bmatrix}$

53. $\begin{bmatrix} 4 & 5.5 \\ 1 & 2 \end{bmatrix} \begin{bmatrix} 300 \\ 450 \end{bmatrix} = \begin{bmatrix} 3675 \\ 1200 \end{bmatrix}$; 3675 assembly hours, 1200 checking hours   **55.** $\begin{bmatrix} 114 & 85 \\ 118 & 84 \\ 116 & 86 \end{bmatrix} \begin{bmatrix} 60 \\ 140 \end{bmatrix} = \begin{bmatrix} 18{,}740 \\ 18{,}840 \\ 19{,}000 \end{bmatrix}$

57. $\begin{bmatrix} 0.5 & 1.5 & 0.5 & 1.0 & 1.0 \\ 0 & 1.0 & 1.0 & 3.0 & 2.0 \end{bmatrix} \begin{bmatrix} 500 & 0.2 & 0 & 129 \\ 0 & 0.2 & 0 & 0 \\ 1560 & 0.32 & 1.7 & 6 \\ 0 & 0 & 0 & 0 \\ 460 & 0 & 0 & 0 \end{bmatrix} = \begin{matrix} A & B_1 & B_2 & C \\ \begin{bmatrix} 1490 & 0.56 & 0.85 & 67.5 \\ 2480 & 0.52 & 1.70 & 6.0 \end{bmatrix} & & & \begin{matrix} \text{I} \\ \text{II} \end{matrix} \end{matrix}$

SECTION 2–6,   PAGE 123

1. $25^{-1} = 0.04$, $\left(\frac{2}{3}\right)^{-1} = \frac{3}{2}$, $(-5)^{-1} = -\frac{1}{5}$, $0.75^{-1} = 1.333$, $11^{-1} = \frac{1}{11}$ **3.** Yes, $AB = I$ **5.** No, $AB \neq I$

7. Yes, $AB = I$ **9.** $\begin{bmatrix} -5 & 2 \\ 3 & -1 \end{bmatrix}$ **11.** $\begin{bmatrix} 3 & -2 \\ -4 & 3 \end{bmatrix}$ **13.** $\begin{bmatrix} -\frac{5}{4} & \frac{9}{4} & \frac{3}{4} \\ 3 & -6 & -1 \\ -\frac{3}{4} & \frac{7}{4} & \frac{1}{4} \end{bmatrix}$ **15.** $\begin{bmatrix} -\frac{7}{5} & -\frac{8}{5} & \frac{13}{5} \\ \frac{3}{10} & \frac{1}{5} & -\frac{1}{5} \\ \frac{1}{10} & \frac{2}{5} & -\frac{2}{5} \end{bmatrix}$

17. No inverse   **19.** No inverse   **21.** No inverse   **23.** $\begin{bmatrix} \frac{3}{2} & -\frac{1}{2} \\ -2 & 1 \end{bmatrix}$ **25.** $\begin{bmatrix} -\frac{3}{7} & \frac{5}{7} & -\frac{11}{7} \\ \frac{2}{7} & -\frac{1}{7} & -\frac{2}{7} \\ \frac{2}{7} & -\frac{1}{7} & \frac{5}{7} \end{bmatrix}$

27. (a) $\left[\begin{array}{ccc|c} 3 & 4 & -5 & 4 \\ 2 & -1 & 3 & -1 \\ 1 & 1 & -1 & 2 \end{array}\right]$ **(b)** $\begin{bmatrix} 3 & 4 & -5 \\ 2 & -1 & 3 \\ 1 & 1 & -1 \end{bmatrix}$ **(c)** $\begin{bmatrix} 3 & 4 & -5 \\ 2 & -1 & 3 \\ 1 & 1 & -1 \end{bmatrix} \begin{bmatrix} x_1 \\ x_2 \\ x_3 \end{bmatrix} = \begin{bmatrix} 4 \\ -1 \\ 2 \end{bmatrix}$

29. (a) $\left[\begin{array}{cc|c} 4 & 5 & 2 \\ 3 & -2 & 7 \end{array}\right]$ **(b)** $\begin{bmatrix} 4 & 5 \\ 3 & -2 \end{bmatrix}$ **(c)** $\begin{bmatrix} 4 & 5 \\ 3 & -2 \end{bmatrix} \begin{bmatrix} x \\ y \end{bmatrix} = \begin{bmatrix} 2 \\ 7 \end{bmatrix}$ **31.** $\begin{bmatrix} 1 & 3 \\ 2 & -1 \end{bmatrix} \begin{bmatrix} x_1 \\ x_2 \end{bmatrix} = \begin{bmatrix} 5 \\ 6 \end{bmatrix}$

33. $\begin{bmatrix} 1 & 2 & -3 & 4 \\ 1 & 1 & 0 & 1 \\ 3 & 2 & 1 & 2 \end{bmatrix} \begin{bmatrix} x_1 \\ x_2 \\ x_3 \\ x_4 \end{bmatrix} = \begin{bmatrix} 0 \\ 5 \\ 4 \end{bmatrix}$ **35.** No inverse   **37.** $\begin{bmatrix} \frac{1}{9} & \frac{1}{3} & \frac{5}{9} \\ \frac{1}{3} & 0 & -\frac{1}{3} \\ -\frac{2}{9} & \frac{1}{3} & -\frac{1}{9} \end{bmatrix} \begin{bmatrix} 2 \\ 0 \\ 1 \end{bmatrix} = \begin{bmatrix} \frac{7}{9} \\ \frac{1}{3} \\ -\frac{5}{9} \end{bmatrix}$

39. $\begin{bmatrix} x_1 \\ x_2 \\ x_3 \\ x_4 \end{bmatrix} = \begin{bmatrix} -\frac{1}{4} & \frac{3}{4} & \frac{5}{12} & -\frac{1}{12} \\ 0 & -1 & -\frac{1}{3} & \frac{2}{3} \\ \frac{1}{4} & \frac{1}{4} & \frac{1}{4} & -\frac{1}{4} \\ \frac{3}{4} & -\frac{1}{4} & -\frac{7}{12} & -\frac{1}{12} \end{bmatrix} \begin{bmatrix} 4 \\ 6 \\ 3 \\ 9 \end{bmatrix} = \begin{bmatrix} 4 \\ -1 \\ 1 \\ -1 \end{bmatrix}$

41. $\begin{bmatrix} -16 & 4 & -13 \\ 5 & -1 & 4 \\ -12 & 3 & -10 \end{bmatrix} \begin{bmatrix} 1 \\ 5 \\ 2 \end{bmatrix} = \begin{bmatrix} -22 \\ 8 \\ -17 \end{bmatrix}$

$\begin{bmatrix} 16 & 4 & -13 \\ 5 & -1 & 4 \\ -12 & 3 & -10 \end{bmatrix} \begin{bmatrix} -1 \\ 3 \\ 1 \end{bmatrix} = \begin{bmatrix} 15 \\ -4 \\ 11 \end{bmatrix}$

$\begin{bmatrix} -16 & 4 & -13 \\ 5 & -1 & 4 \\ -12 & 3 & -10 \end{bmatrix} \begin{bmatrix} 0 \\ 1 \\ 2 \end{bmatrix} = \begin{bmatrix} -22 \\ 7 \\ -17 \end{bmatrix}$

43. $\begin{bmatrix} -5 & 2 \\ 3 & -1 \end{bmatrix} \begin{bmatrix} 3 \\ 8 \end{bmatrix} = \begin{bmatrix} 1 \\ 1 \end{bmatrix}$

$\begin{bmatrix} -5 & 2 \\ 3 & -1 \end{bmatrix} \begin{bmatrix} 4 \\ 9 \end{bmatrix} = \begin{bmatrix} -2 \\ 3 \end{bmatrix}$

$\begin{bmatrix} -5 & 2 \\ 3 & -1 \end{bmatrix} \begin{bmatrix} 3 \\ 7 \end{bmatrix} = \begin{bmatrix} -1 \\ 2 \end{bmatrix}$

45. (a) $32x$ = mg of vitamin C in food A
$24y$ = mg of vitamin C in food B
$900x$ = iu of vitamin A in food A
$425y$ = iu of vitamin A in food B
so $32x + 24y$ = total mg of vitamin C
$900x + 425y$ = total iu of vitamin A
$\begin{bmatrix} 32 & 24 \\ 900 & 425 \end{bmatrix} \begin{bmatrix} x \\ y \end{bmatrix} = \begin{bmatrix} 32x + 24y \\ 900x + 425y \end{bmatrix} = \begin{bmatrix} b_1 \\ b_2 \end{bmatrix}$
gives total vitamin C in row 1 and total vitamin A in row 2.

(b) $\begin{bmatrix} 32 & 24 \\ 900 & 425 \end{bmatrix} \begin{bmatrix} 3.2 \\ 2.5 \end{bmatrix} = \begin{bmatrix} 162.4 \\ 3942.5 \end{bmatrix} \begin{matrix} C \\ A \end{matrix}$
162.4 mg of vitamin C and 394.2 iu of vitamin A

(c) $\begin{bmatrix} 32 & 24 \\ 900 & 425 \end{bmatrix} \begin{bmatrix} 1.5 \\ 3.0 \end{bmatrix} = \begin{bmatrix} 120 \\ 2625 \end{bmatrix}$
120 mg of C and 2625 iu of A

(d) $\begin{bmatrix} -0.053125 & 0.003 \\ 0.1125 & -0.004 \end{bmatrix} \begin{bmatrix} 107.2 \\ 2315 \end{bmatrix} = \begin{bmatrix} 1.25 \\ 2.8 \end{bmatrix}$
1.25 units of A and 2.80 units of B

(e) $\begin{bmatrix} -0.053125 & 0.003 \\ 0.1125 & -0.004 \end{bmatrix} \begin{bmatrix} 104 \\ 2575 \end{bmatrix} = \begin{bmatrix} 2.2 \\ 1.4 \end{bmatrix}$
2.2 units of food A and 1.4 units of food B

47. (a) 340 children and 560 adults
(b) 435 children and 565 adults
(c) 110 children and 640 adults

SECTION 2–7,   PAGE 135

1. Let x_1 = farmer's income
x_2 = carpenter's income
x_3 = tailor's income
$x_1 = x_3$
$x_2 = 0.75x_3$
If we let $x_3 = \$8000$, then the farmer's income is \$8000, the carpenter's is \$6000, and the tailor's is \$8000.

3. $x_1 = \frac{5}{3}x_3$
$x_2 = \frac{5}{6}x_3$
If $x_3 = \$6000$, then $x_1 = \$10,000$, $x_2 = \$5000$.

5. $\begin{bmatrix} 2.16 \\ 4.8 \end{bmatrix}$ **7.** $\begin{bmatrix} 3.06 \\ 2.90 \\ 1.40 \end{bmatrix}$ **9.** $\begin{bmatrix} 1.4 & 0.6 \\ 0.4 & 1.6 \end{bmatrix}$ **11.** $\begin{bmatrix} \frac{12}{9} & \frac{1}{9} \\ \frac{3}{18} & \frac{19}{18} \end{bmatrix} \begin{bmatrix} 15 \\ 12 \end{bmatrix} = \begin{bmatrix} 21.3 \\ 15.17 \end{bmatrix}$

13. $(I - A)^{-1} = \begin{bmatrix} \frac{4}{3} & \frac{2}{3} \\ \frac{1}{2} & \frac{3}{2} \end{bmatrix}$, $D = \begin{bmatrix} 6 \\ 12 \end{bmatrix}$, output $= \begin{bmatrix} 16 \\ 21 \end{bmatrix}$, $D = \begin{bmatrix} 18 \\ 6 \end{bmatrix}$, output $= \begin{bmatrix} 28 \\ 18 \end{bmatrix}$, $D = \begin{bmatrix} 24 \\ 12 \end{bmatrix}$, output $= \begin{bmatrix} 40 \\ 30 \end{bmatrix}$

15. $(I - A)^{-1} = \begin{bmatrix} 1.25 & 0.625 & 0.625 \\ 0 & 2 & 1 \\ 0 & 1 & 3 \end{bmatrix}$, $D = \begin{bmatrix} 4 \\ 8 \\ 8 \end{bmatrix}$, output $= \begin{bmatrix} 15 \\ 24 \\ 32 \end{bmatrix}$, $D = \begin{bmatrix} 0 \\ 8 \\ 16 \end{bmatrix}$, output $= \begin{bmatrix} 15 \\ 32 \\ 56 \end{bmatrix}$, $D = \begin{bmatrix} 8 \\ 24 \\ 8 \end{bmatrix}$,

output $= \begin{bmatrix} 30 \\ 56 \\ 48 \end{bmatrix}$ **17.** Internal demand $\begin{bmatrix} 5.6 \\ 5.0 \end{bmatrix}$, consumer demand $\begin{bmatrix} 2.4 \\ 5.0 \end{bmatrix}$ **19.** Internal demand $\begin{bmatrix} 21.6 \\ 64.8 \\ 36.0 \end{bmatrix}$,

consumer demand $\begin{bmatrix} 14.4 \\ 7.2 \\ 0 \end{bmatrix}$

CHAPTER 2 REVIEW
EXERCISES,   PAGE 137

1. $(\frac{1}{4}, \frac{17}{8})$ **3.** $(6, -4)$ **5.** $(2, 0, \frac{1}{3})$ **7.** $(-6, 2, -5)$ **9.** No solution   **11.** $(-k, 1 - k, k)$

13. $x_1 = -56 + 29x_4$
$x_2 = 23 - 12x_4$
$x_3 = -13 + 8x_4$

15. $x_1 = \frac{1}{2}(6 + x_3)$, $x_2 = \frac{1}{3}(2 + 4x_3)$ **17.** $x = \frac{3}{4}$ **19.** $\begin{bmatrix} -3 & -2 \\ 6 & 7 \end{bmatrix}$ **21.** $\begin{bmatrix} 11 & -3 \\ 7 & -1 \\ 3 & 0 \end{bmatrix}$ **23.** $[3]$

25. Not possible   **27.** $\begin{bmatrix} -\frac{5}{2} & 3 \\ \frac{7}{2} & -4 \end{bmatrix}$ **29.** $\begin{bmatrix} -2 & -6 & 15 \\ 0 & -1 & 2 \\ 1 & 2 & -5 \end{bmatrix}$ **31.** $\begin{bmatrix} 6 & 4 & -5 & | & 10 \\ 3 & -2 & 0 & | & 12 \\ 1 & 1 & -4 & | & -2 \end{bmatrix}$ **33.** $\begin{bmatrix} 1 & 0 & -\frac{3}{5} & 0 \\ 0 & 1 & \frac{9}{5} & 0 \\ 0 & 0 & 0 & 1 \end{bmatrix}$

35. 23 field goals, 13 free throws   **37.** \$20,000 in bonds and \$30,000 in stocks   **39.** 120 shares of High-Tech and 68 shares of Big Burger   **41.** 630 dolls at plant A and 270 at plant B   **43.** The growth function is $y = \frac{400}{3}x + 5400$, where x is the number of years measured from today (when the population is 5400). The population expected 15 years from now is 7400.

CHAPTER 3
SECTION 3–1,   PAGE 149

1. $(1, -1)$, $(3, 1)$, and $(2, 3)$ are solutions.

3.

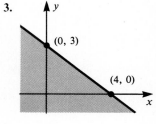

5.

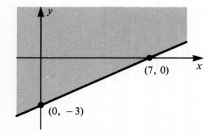

7.

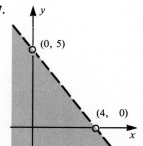

9.

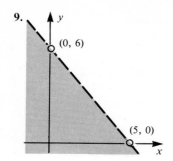

11.

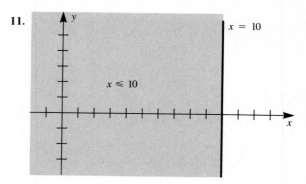

$x = 10$

$x \leq 10$

13.

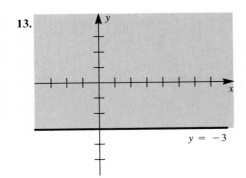

$y = -3$

15.

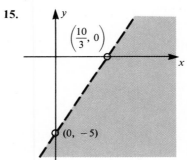

$\left(\dfrac{10}{3}, 0\right)$

$(0, -5)$

17.

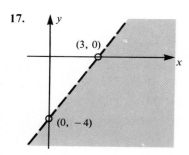

$(3, 0)$

$(0, -4)$

19.

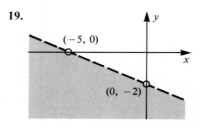

$(-5, 0)$

$(0, -2)$

21. $x =$ number of air conditioners, $y =$ number of fans $3.2x + 1.8y \leq 144$

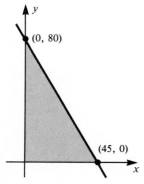

$(0, 80)$

$(45, 0)$

23. **(a)** $4x + 6y \geq 500$ $x =$ number of members, $y =$ number of pledges
(b)

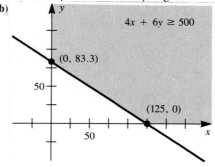

$4x + 6y \geq 500$

$(0, 83.3)$

50

$(125, 0)$

50

25. x = number of TV ads, y = number of newspaper ads
x and y must satisfy $900x + 830y \leq 75{,}000$
The graph is

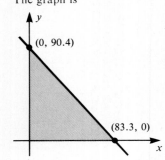

27. Let x = number of acres of strawberries
y = number of acres of tomatoes
$$9x + 6y \leq 750$$

29. Let x = number of days at Glen Echo
y = number of days at Speegleville Road
  (a) $200x + 300y \geq 2400$ (paperback)
  (b) $300x + 200y \geq 2100$ (hardback)

SECTION 3–2,   PAGE 156

1.

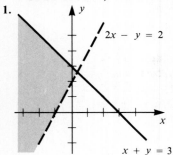

3.

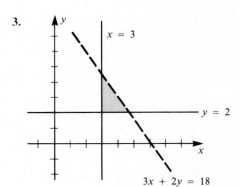

5.

7.

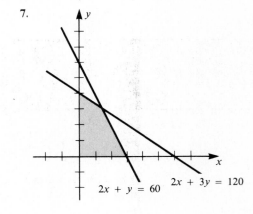

9.

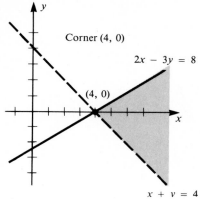

Corner (4, 0)

$2x - 3y = 8$

(4, 0)

$x + y = 4$

11.

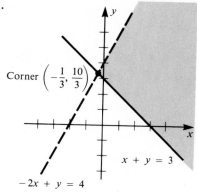

Corner $\left(-\frac{1}{3}, \frac{10}{3}\right)$

$x + y = 3$

$-2x + y = 4$

13.

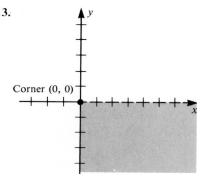

Corner (0, 0)

15.

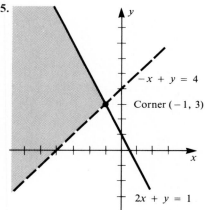

$-x + y = 4$

Corner $(-1, 3)$

$2x + y = 1$

17. No feasible region.

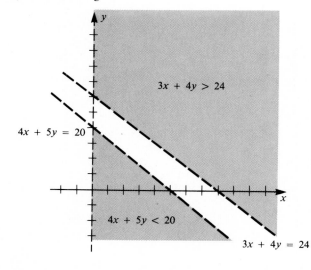

$3x + 4y > 24$

$4x + 5y = 20$

$4x + 5y < 20$

$3x + 4y = 24$

19. No feasible region.

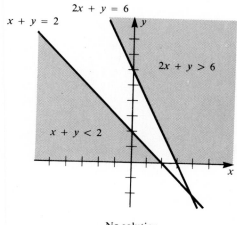

$2x + y = 6$

$x + y = 2$

$2x + y > 6$

$x + y < 2$

No solution

21.

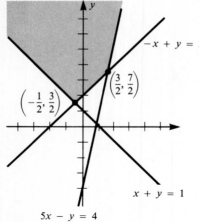

$-x + y = 2$

$\left(\dfrac{3}{2}, \dfrac{7}{2}\right)$

$\left(-\dfrac{1}{2}, \dfrac{3}{2}\right)$

$x + y = 1$

$5x - y = 4$

Corners $\left(\dfrac{3}{2}, \dfrac{7}{2}\right)$ and $\left(-\dfrac{1}{2}, \dfrac{3}{2}\right)$

23. Corners $\left(-\dfrac{2}{3}, \dfrac{14}{3}\right)$, $\left(\dfrac{1}{7}, \dfrac{10}{7}\right)$, $(-1, -2)$, $\left(-\dfrac{8}{5}, \dfrac{14}{5}\right)$

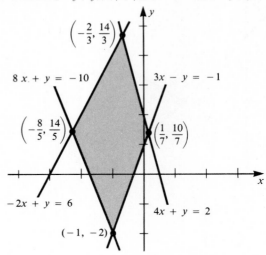

$\left(-\dfrac{2}{3}, \dfrac{14}{3}\right)$

$8x + y = -10$ $3x - y = -1$

$\left(-\dfrac{8}{5}, \dfrac{14}{5}\right)$ $\left(\dfrac{1}{7}, \dfrac{10}{7}\right)$

$-2x + y = 6$

$4x + y = 2$

$(-1, -2)$

25.

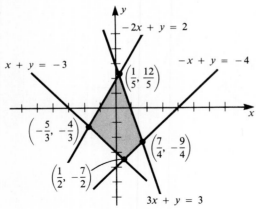

$-2x + y = 2$

$x + y = -3$ $-x + y = -4$

$\left(\dfrac{1}{5}, \dfrac{12}{5}\right)$

$\left(-\dfrac{5}{3}, -\dfrac{4}{3}\right)$

$\left(\dfrac{7}{4}, -\dfrac{9}{4}\right)$

$\left(\dfrac{1}{2}, -\dfrac{7}{2}\right)$

$3x + y = 3$

Corners $\left(\dfrac{1}{5}, \dfrac{12}{5}\right)$, $\left(\dfrac{7}{4}, -\dfrac{9}{4}\right)$, $\left(\dfrac{1}{2}, -\dfrac{7}{2}\right)$, $\left(-\dfrac{5}{3}, -\dfrac{4}{3}\right)$

27. Let x = ounces of High Fiber, y = ounces Corn Bits
$0.25x + 0.02y \geq 0.40$
$0.04x + 0.10y \geq 0.25$

29. Let x = number of student tickets,
     y = number of adult tickets
$x + y \geq 500$
$3x + 8y \geq 2500$

31. Let x = number correct, y = number wrong
$x + y \geq 60$
$4x - y \geq 200$

SECTION 3-3,   PAGE 172

1. Let x = number of style A, y = number of style B
$x + 2y \leq 110$ (labor restriction)
$x +\ \ y \leq\ \ 80$ (space restriction)
$x \geq 0, y \geq 0$
Maximize $z = 50x + 40y$

3. At $(0, 9)$, $z = 108$
At $(4, 3)$, $z = 116$
At $(5, 0)$, $z = 100$
At $(0, 0)$, $z =\ \ \ 0$
So maximum z is 116 at $(4, 3)$

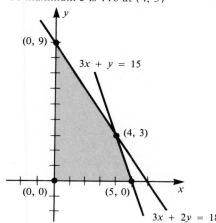

5. 66 at $(4, 15)$ **7.** 32 at $(16, 0)$ **9.** 343.5 at $(16.5, 15)$ **11.** 630 at $(18, 9)$ **13.** $z = 28{,}200$ at $(75, 30)$
15. 52 at $(8, 4)$ **17.** 66 at $(6, 12)$ **19.** Maximum z is 380 at $(10, 6)$. Minimum z is 40 at $(2, 0)$ **21.** Max $z =$
245 at $(40, 7.5)$. Min $z = 90$ at $(0, 15)$ **23.** Maximum z is 90 at $(3, 5)$, $(0, 10)$ and all points on the line segment
between   **25.** Maximum $z = 176.4$ at $(10.8, 24)$ **27.** Min $z = 500$ at $(40, 30)$ and $(60, 20)$ and all points on the line
segment joining these points.   **29.** Maximum $z = 26$ at $(8, 2)$ **31.** No feasible solution   **33.** Maximum z is 30.4 at
$\left(\dfrac{14}{5}, \dfrac{2}{5} \right)$

35. Let x = number of Standard VCR
$\ \ \ \ \ \ \ \ y$ = number of Deluxe VCR
Maximize $z = 39x + 26y$, subject to
$\ \ 8x +\ \ \ 9y \leq\ \ 2200$
$115x + 136y \leq 18{,}000$
$x \geq 35, y \geq 0$

37. Let x = number shipped to A
$\ \ \ \ \ \ \ \ y$ = number shipped to B
Minimize $z = 13x + 11y$, subject to
$x + y \geq 250$
$x \leq 110$
$y \leq 147$
$x \geq 0, y \geq 0$

39. Let x = number of cartons of regular
$\ \ \ \ \ \ \ \ y$ = number of cartons of diet
Maximize $z = 0.15x + 0.17y$, subject to
$x + 1.20y \leq 5400$
$x + y \leq 5000$
$x \geq 0, y \geq 0$

41. Let x = number of desk lamps
$\ \ \ \ \ \ \ \ y$ = number of floor lamps
Maximize $z = 2.65x + 3.15y$, subject to
$0.8x + 1.0y \leq 1200$
$4x + 3y \leq 4200$
$x \geq 0, y \geq 0$
Maximum profit is \$3828.75 for 375 desk lamps and
900 floor lamps.

43. Let x = number acres for cattle
y = number acres for sheep
Maximize $z = 30x + 32y$, subject to
$x + y \leq 1000$
$2x + 8y \leq 3200$
$x \geq 0, y \geq 0$
Maximum profit is $30,400 using 800 acres for cattle and 200 acres for sheep.

47. Let x = number of standard gears
y = number of heavy duty gears
Minimize $z = 15x + 22y$, subject to
$8x + 10y \geq 12,000$
$3x + 10y \geq 8400$
$x \geq 0, y \geq 0$
Minimum cost = $24,528 for 720 standard and 624 heavy duty gears.

51. Maximum profit is $790 with 3000 cartons of Regular and 2000 cartons of Diet

55. Let x = number of days at Glen Echo plant
y = number of days at Speegleville plant
Minimize $z = x + y$, subject to
$200x + 300y \geq 2400$
$300x + 200y \geq 2100$
Minimum number of days is nine with three at Glen Echo and six at Speegleville.

45. Let x = amount of food I
y = amount of food II
Minimize $z = 0.03x + 0.04y$, subject to
$0.4x + 0.6y \geq 10$
$0.5x + 0.2y \geq 7.5$
$0.06x + 0.04y \geq 1.2$
$x \geq 0, y \geq 0$
Minimum cost is $0.72 for 16 grams of food I and 6 grams of food II.

49. Let x = number of SE
y = number of LE
Minimize $z = 2700x + 2400y$, subject to
$16,000x + 20,000y \leq 160,000$
$x + y \geq 9$
$x \geq 0, y \geq 0$
Minimum operating costs = $23,100 per year for five SE and four LE.

53. Let x = number of square feet of type A
y = number of square feet of type B
(a) Minimize $z = x + 0.25y$, subject to
$x + y \geq 4000$
$0.80x + 1.20y \leq 4500$
$x \geq 0, y \geq 0$
Minimum conductance = 1562.50 BTU with 750 square feet of type A and 3250 square feet of type B.
(b) Minimize $z = 0.80x + 1.20y$, subject to
$x + y \geq 4000$
$x + 0.25y \leq 2200$
$x \geq 0, y \geq 0$
Minimum cost is $4160 with 1600 square feet of type A and 2400 square feet of type B.

57. (a) The maximum value of z is 100 at (8, 5) and (10, 0), so it is maximum at all points on the line segment between. The slope of that line is $m = -\frac{5}{2}$. The slope of the objective function is also $-\frac{5}{2}$.

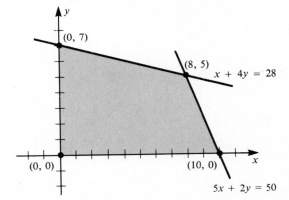

(b) The maximum value of z is 180 at (12, 20) and (24, 10) and all points on the line segment joining them. The slope of that line is $-\frac{5}{6}$, the same as the objective function.

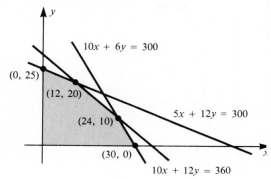

(c) The minimum value of z is 300 at (6, 16) and (24, 4) and all points between that are on $2x + 3y = 60$ (its slope is $-\frac{2}{3}$). The slope of $10x + 15y = 300$ is also $-\frac{2}{3}$.

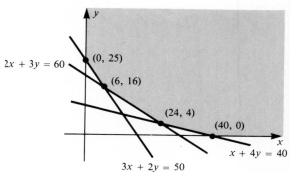

(d) The maximum value of z is 2400 at (0, 100) and (60, 75) and all points between that are on the line $5x + 12y = 1200$. The slope of this line is $-\frac{5}{12}$, the same as the slope of $10x + 24y = 2400$.

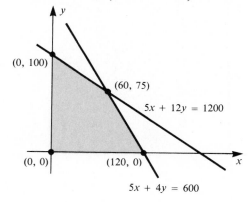

**CHAPTER 3 REVIEW
EXERCISES,   PAGE 178**

1.

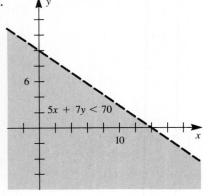

$5x + 7y < 70$

(a)

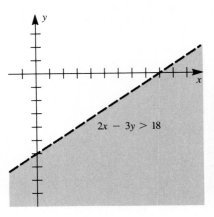

$2x - 3y > 18$

(b)

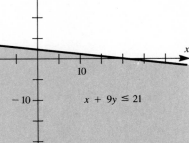

$x + 9y \leq 21$

(c)

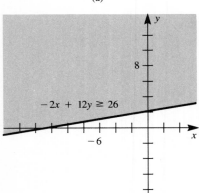

$-2x + 12y \geq 26$

(d)

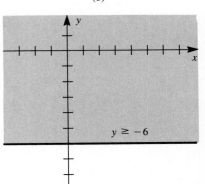

$y \geq -6$

(e)

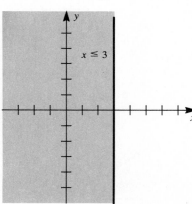

$x \leq 3$

(f)

3. Corners are $(-9, -5)$, $(-1, -5)$, and $(3, -1)$.

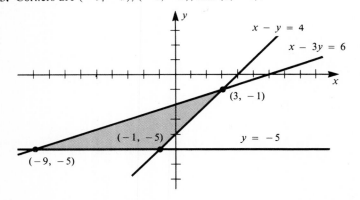

$x - y = 4$

$x - 3y = 6$

$(3, -1)$

$(-1, -5)$

$y = -5$

$(-9, -5)$

5. Corners are $(-4, 2)$, $(4, 8)$, $(5, 0)$, and $(-2, 0)$.

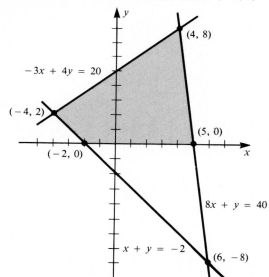

7. Corners are $(-\frac{4}{3}, -\frac{2}{3})$, $(0, 2)$, $(2, 2)$, and $(2, 1)$.

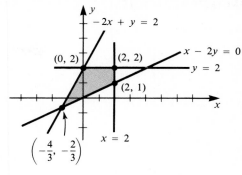

9. Maximum z is 22 at $(2, 3)$.   **11. (a)** Minimum z is 34 at $(2, 6)$.   **(b)** Minimum z is 92 at $(2, 6)$, $(8, 1)$ and points in between.   **13.** Maximum $z = 290$ at $(20, 30)$.

15. (a) $65x + 105y \le 1500$

(b)

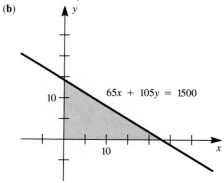

17. Let x = number adult tickets

   y = number children tickets

   $x + y \le 275$

   $4.50x + 3.00y \ge 1100$

   $x \ge 0, y \ge 0$

19. 640 bars of standard and 280 bars of premium yield a revenue of $85,600.

CHAPTER 4
SECTION 4–1, PAGE 190

1. Maximize $[50 \quad 80]\begin{bmatrix} x_1 \\ x_2 \end{bmatrix}$, subject to $\begin{bmatrix} 7 & 15 \\ 3 & 14 \end{bmatrix}\begin{bmatrix} x_1 \\ x_2 \end{bmatrix} \leq \begin{bmatrix} 30 \\ 56 \end{bmatrix}$ and $\begin{bmatrix} x_1 \\ x_2 \end{bmatrix} \geq \begin{bmatrix} 0 \\ 0 \end{bmatrix}$

3. Maximize $[42 \quad 26 \quad 5]\begin{bmatrix} x_1 \\ x_2 \\ x_3 \end{bmatrix}$, subject to $\begin{bmatrix} 13 & 4 & 23 \\ 4 & 15 & 7 \\ 3 & -2 & 32 \end{bmatrix}\begin{bmatrix} x_1 \\ x_2 \\ x_3 \end{bmatrix} \leq \begin{bmatrix} 88 \\ 92 \\ 155 \end{bmatrix}$ and $\begin{bmatrix} x_1 \\ x_2 \\ x_3 \end{bmatrix} \geq \begin{bmatrix} 0 \\ 0 \\ 0 \end{bmatrix}$

5. $\begin{aligned} 2x_1 + 3x_2 + s_1 &= 9 \\ x_1 + 5x_2 + s_2 &= 16 \end{aligned}$

7. $\begin{aligned} x_1 + 7x_2 - 4x_3 + s_1 &= 150 \\ 5x_1 + 9x_2 + 2x_3 + s_2 &= 435 \\ 8x_1 - 3x_2 + 16x_3 + s_3 &= 345 \end{aligned}$

9. $\begin{aligned} 2x_1 + 6x_2 + s_1 \quad\quad\quad\quad &= 9 \\ x_1 - 5x_2 \quad + s_2 \quad\quad\quad &= 14 \\ -3x_1 + x_2 \quad\quad + s_3 \quad &= 8 \\ -3x_1 - 7x_2 \quad\quad\quad\quad + z &= 0 \end{aligned}$

11. $\begin{aligned} 6x_1 + 7x_2 + 12x_3 + s_1 &= 50 \\ 4x_1 + 18x_2 + 9x_3 + s_2 &= 85 \\ x_1 - 2x_2 + 14x_3 + s_3 &= 66 \\ -420x_1 - 260x_2 - 50x_3 + z &= 0 \end{aligned}$

13. $\begin{bmatrix} 4 & 5 & 1 & 0 & 0 & 10 \\ 3 & 1 & 0 & 1 & 0 & 25 \\ -3 & -17 & 0 & 0 & 1 & 0 \end{bmatrix}$

15. $\begin{bmatrix} 16 & -4 & 9 & 1 & 0 & 0 & 128 \\ 8 & 13 & 22 & 0 & 1 & 0 & 144 \\ 5 & 6 & -15 & 0 & 0 & 1 & 225 \\ -20 & -45 & -40 & 0 & 0 & 0 & 0 \end{bmatrix}$

17. Let x_1 = number of cartons of screwdrivers, x_2 = number of cartons of chisels, x_3 = number of cartons of putty knives.

$\begin{bmatrix} 3 & 4 & 5 & 1 & 0 & 0 & 2200 \\ 15 & 12 & 11 & 0 & 1 & 0 & 8500 \\ -5 & -6 & -5 & 0 & 0 & 1 & 0 \end{bmatrix}$

19. x_1 = number ounces of salad, x_2 = number ounces of potato, x_3 = number ounces steak.

$\begin{bmatrix} 20 & 50 & 56 & 1 & 0 & 0 & 1000 \\ 1.5 & 3.0 & 2.0 & 0 & 1 & 0 & 35 \\ -0.5 & -1.0 & -9.0 & 0 & 0 & 1 & 0 \end{bmatrix}$

21. $\begin{bmatrix} 0.75 & 0.50 & 0.15 & 1 & 0 & 0 & 0 & 2320 \\ 0.25 & 0.25 & 0.60 & 0 & 1 & 0 & 0 & 1380 \\ 0 & 0.25 & 0.25 & 0 & 0 & 1 & 0 & 700 \\ -0.25 & -0.25 & -0.32 & 0 & 0 & 0 & 1 & 0 \end{bmatrix}$

23. $\begin{bmatrix} 4 & 3 & 2 & 1 & 0 & 0 & 0 & 4900 \\ 1 & 2 & 4 & 0 & 1 & 0 & 0 & 2200 \\ 0.1 & 0.2 & 0.3 & 0 & 0 & 1 & 0 & 210 \\ -6 & -7 & -9 & 0 & 0 & 0 & 1 & 0 \end{bmatrix}$

25. $\begin{bmatrix} 4 & 2 & 1 & 1 & 0 & 0 & 0 & 120 \\ 3 & 2 & 1 & 0 & 1 & 0 & 0 & 80 \\ 1 & 1 & 0.5 & 0 & 0 & 1 & 0 & 40 \\ -400 & -250 & -160 & 0 & 0 & 0 & 1 & 0 \end{bmatrix}$

SECTION 4–2, PAGE 205

1. $x_1 = 8$, $x_2 = 0$, $s_1 = 0$, $s_2 = 10$
x_1, s_2 basic; x_2, s_1 nonbasic

3. $x_1 = 0$, $x_2 = 86$, $x_3 = 0$, $s_1 = 54$, $s_2 = 0$, $s_3 = 39$
x_2, s_1, s_3 basic; x_1, x_3, s_2 nonbasic

5. Pivot element = 4 in row 1, column 2 **7.** Pivot element = 4 in row 2, column 3 **9.** Pivot element = either 4 in row 2, column 2 or 5 in row 3, column 2 **11.** Pivot element = either 8 in row 2, column 2, or 6 in row 1, column 3

13. Pivot element = 4 in row 2, column 1

15. Pivot element = 1 in row 2, column 1

$\begin{bmatrix} 0 & -1 & 1 & -2 & 0 & 0 & 0 \\ 1 & 2 & 0 & 1 & 0 & 0 & 6 \\ 0 & 1 & 0 & -2 & 1 & 0 & 8 \\ 0 & 5 & 0 & 4 & 0 & 1 & 24 \end{bmatrix}$

17. Pivot element on -3 in row 3

$\begin{bmatrix} \frac{14}{3} & \frac{29}{3} & 0 & 1 & 0 & \frac{4}{3} & 0 & -270 \\ -\frac{7}{3} & -\frac{34}{3} & 0 & 0 & 1 & -\frac{8}{3} & 0 & 580 \\ \frac{1}{3} & \frac{1}{3} & 1 & 0 & 0 & -\frac{1}{3} & 0 & 130 \\ 0 & -40 & 0 & 0 & 0 & -10 & 1 & 3900 \end{bmatrix}$

19. $x_1 = 6$, $x_2 = 4$, $s_1 = 0$, $s_2 = 0$, $z = 16$ **21.** $x_1 = 1$, $x_2 = 2$, $s_1 = 0$, $s_2 = 0$, $z = 14$ **23.** $x_1 = 180$, $x_2 = 0$,
$z = 1440$ **25.** $x_1 = 0$, $x_2 = 100$, $x_3 = 50$, $z = 22{,}500$ **27.** $x_1 = 0$, $x_2 = 75$, $x_3 = 15$, $z = 450$ **29.** $z = 2610$
at $(168, 0, 6)$ **31.** $x_1 = 24$, $x_2 = 0$, $z = 792$ **33.** $x_1 = 20$, $x_2 = 20$, $x_3 = 20$, $z = 1200$ **35.** $x_1 = 62.5$,
$x_2 = 75$, $x_3 = 35$, $z = 1700$ **37.** 316.67 screwdrivers, 312.5 chisels, 0 putty knives, maximum profit \$3,458.33
39. 30 notepads, 0 loose-leaf paper, 120 spiral notebooks, profit \$1,740
41. Initial tableau:

$$\begin{bmatrix} 0.80 & 0.75 & 0.50 & 1 & 0 & 0 & 0 & 255 \\ 0.20 & 0.20 & 0.40 & 0 & 1 & 0 & 0 & 80 \\ 0 & 0.05 & 0.10 & 0 & 0 & 1 & 0 & 15 \\ \hline -1.00 & -1.10 & -1.20 & 0 & 0 & 0 & 1 & 0 \end{bmatrix}$$

43. Initial tableau:

$$\begin{bmatrix} 600 & 500 & 300 & 1 & 0 & 0 & 0 & 39{,}500 \\ 300 & 300 & 200 & 0 & 1 & 0 & 0 & 22{,}500 \\ 100 & 200 & 400 & 0 & 0 & 1 & 0 & 16{,}500 \\ \hline -4.4 & -4.8 & -5.2 & 0 & 0 & 0 & 1 & 0 \end{bmatrix}$$

Maximum profit is \$380 with 100 lb Early Riser, 200 lb After Dinner, and 50 lb Deluxe

Maximum revenue = \$380 for 25 lb TV mix, 40 lb Party mix, and 15 lb Dinner mix

45. Initial tableau:

$$\begin{bmatrix} 4 & 2 & 1 & 1 & 0 & 0 & 0 & 124 \\ 3 & 1 & 1 & 0 & 1 & 0 & 0 & 81 \\ 1 & 1 & 0.5 & 0 & 0 & 1 & 0 & 46 \\ \hline -400 & -250 & -160 & 0 & 0 & 0 & 1 & 0 \end{bmatrix}$$

Maximum revenue = \$14,110 for 16 Majestic, 27 Traditional, and 6 Wall Clocks

SECTION 4–3, PAGE 214

1. (a) $17, 3, -33, 6, 0$ **(b)** $(0, 0), (2, 2), (2, 1), (2, 3)$ **(c)** $(2, 3)$ **3.** $40, 26, 0, 13$
5.

Point	s_1	s_2	s_3	Point on boundary	Point in feasible region
$(5, 10)$	15	32	18	no	yes
$(8, 10)$	12	14	-3	no	no
$(5, 13)$	0	29	0	yes	yes
$(11, 13)$	-6	-7	-42	no	no
$(10, 12)$	0	0	-29	no	no
$(15, 11)$	0	-29	-58	no	no

7. (i) (a) $(0, 0, 900, 2800, 0)$ **(ii) (a)** $(180, 0, 0, 1360, 540)$ **(iii) (a)** $(100, 200, 0, 0, 700)$
  (b) $x_1 = 0$, $x_2 = 0$ **(b)** $x_2 = 0$ **(b)** $5x_1 + 2x_2 = 900$
  $5x_1 + 2x_2 = 900$ $8x_1 + 10x_2 = 2800$

9. (a) $\frac{36}{7}$ **(b)** 6

SECTION 4–4, PAGE 234

1. Minimum $z = -200$ at $(0, 40)$ **3.** Minimum $z = -158$ at $\left(0, 2, \frac{56}{3}\right)$ **5.** Maximum $z = 60$ at $(12, 0)$

7. Maximum $z = 14$ at $\left(0, \frac{28}{5}, \frac{14}{5}\right)$ **9.**

$$\begin{bmatrix} 8 & 12 & 7 & 1 & 0 & 0 & 0 & 171 \\ -5 & -14 & -8 & 0 & 1 & 0 & 0 & -172 \\ 2 & 9 & 13 & 0 & 0 & 1 & 0 & 174 \\ \hline -20 & -35 & -28 & 0 & 0 & 0 & 1 & 0 \end{bmatrix}$$

11. Maximum $z = 1050$ at $(70, 0)$ **13.** Maximum $z = 21$ at $(3, 5)$ **15.** Maximum $z = 5000$ at $(50, 0, 150)$

17.
$$\begin{bmatrix} 5 & 8 & 1 & 0 & 0 & 180 \\ -3 & -6 & 0 & 1 & 0 & -127 \\ \hline 11 & 20 & 0 & 0 & 1 & 0 \end{bmatrix}$$
     19. Minimum $z = 35$ at $(15, 20)$ **21.** Minimum $z = 30$ at $(5, 0, 10)$

23.
$$\begin{bmatrix} 8 & 10 & 1 & 0 & 0 & 0 & | & 80 \\ -2 & 5 & 0 & 1 & 0 & 0 & | & 10 \\ 2 & -5 & 0 & 0 & 1 & 0 & | & -10 \\ \hline -3 & 1 & 0 & 0 & 0 & 1 & | & 0 \end{bmatrix}$$

25. Maximum $z = 300$ at $(4, 14)$ **27.** Maximum $z = 266$ at $(13, 24, 9)$

29. Minimum $z = 360$ at $(8, 12)$ **31.** Minimum $z = 240$ at $(20, 0, 4)$

33.
$$\begin{bmatrix} 1 & 4 & 3 & 1 & 0 & 0 & 0 & 0 & | & 124 \\ -2 & -10 & -5 & 0 & 1 & 0 & 0 & 0 & | & -295 \\ 6 & 1 & 3 & 0 & 0 & 1 & 0 & 0 & | & 100 \\ -6 & -1 & -3 & 0 & 0 & 0 & 1 & 0 & | & -100 \\ \hline -7 & -7 & -3 & 0 & 0 & 0 & 0 & 1 & | & 0 \end{bmatrix}$$

35. Maximum $z = 120$ at $(10, 15)$ **37.** Maximum $z = 640$ at $(0, 18, 8)$ **39.** Minimum $z = 166$ at $(14, 8)$

41. Minimum $z = 63$ at $(\frac{5}{2}, \frac{5}{2}, 9)$ **43.** Minimum $z = 191$ at $(2, 35, 0)$ **45.** Minimum $z = 472$ at $(10, 12, 8)$

47. Initial tableau:
$$\begin{bmatrix} -1 & -1 & 1 & 0 & 0 & 0 & | & -100 \\ 4 & 5 & 0 & 1 & 0 & 0 & | & 800 \\ -90 & -120 & 0 & 0 & 1 & 0 & | & -10,800 \\ \hline 70 & 80 & 0 & 0 & 0 & 1 & | & 0 \end{bmatrix}$$
Minimum cost = \$7600 at 40 Custom and 60 Executive

49. Initial tableau:
$$\begin{bmatrix} -1 & -1 & -1 & 1 & 0 & 0 & 0 & 0 & | & -6,600 \\ 20 & 25 & 15 & 0 & 1 & 0 & 0 & 0 & | & 133,000 \\ 1 & 3 & 2 & 0 & 0 & 1 & 0 & 0 & | & 13,600 \\ 8 & 10 & 15 & 0 & 0 & 0 & 1 & 0 & | & 73,000 \\ \hline -6 & -9 & -6 & 0 & 0 & 0 & 0 & 1 & | & 0 \end{bmatrix}$$

Maximum profit = \$46,800 at 2000 of item A, 2400 of item B, and 2200 of item C

51. Maximum profit is \$47,040 at 2080 of item A, 2000 of item B, and 2760 of item C.

53. x_1 = minutes jogging, x_2 = minutes playing handball, x_3 = minutes swimming.

(a) Initial tableau:
$$\begin{bmatrix} 1 & 0 & -1 & 1 & 0 & 0 & 0 & 0 & | & 0 \\ -1 & 0 & 1 & 0 & 1 & 0 & 0 & 0 & | & 0 \\ 2 & -1 & 0 & 0 & 0 & 1 & 0 & 0 & | & 0 \\ -13 & -11 & -7 & 0 & 0 & 0 & 1 & 0 & | & -660 \\ \hline 1 & 1 & 1 & 0 & 0 & 0 & 0 & 1 & | & 0 \end{bmatrix}$$
Minimum time is 60 minutes using all 60 minutes playing handball.

(b) Initial tableau:
$$\begin{bmatrix} 1 & 0 & -1 & 1 & 0 & 0 & 0 & 0 & | & 0 \\ -1 & 0 & 1 & 0 & 1 & 0 & 0 & 0 & | & 0 \\ 2 & -1 & 0 & 0 & 0 & 1 & 0 & 0 & | & 0 \\ 1 & 1 & 1 & 0 & 0 & 0 & 1 & 0 & | & 90 \\ \hline -13 & -11 & -7 & 0 & 0 & 0 & 0 & 1 & | & 0 \end{bmatrix}$$
Maximum of 990 calories used by using all 90 minutes playing handball.

SECTION 4–5,   PAGE 245

1. Maximum $z = 210$ at $(5, 9)$, $(10, 4)$ and points between.   **3.** Maximum $z = 40$ at $(5, 5, 2.5)$, $(\frac{20}{3}, \frac{20}{3}, 0)$ and points between.   **5.** An unbounded feasible region because all entries in column 1 become negative after pivoting
7. An unbounded feasible region because all entries in column 2 become negative after pivoting
9. Pivoting leads to a row with a negative entry in the last column and all other entries in the row are not negative. Thus there is no feasible solution.   **11.** Pivoting leads to a row with a negative entry in the last column and all other entries in the row are not negative. Thus there is no feasible solution.   **13.** Unbounded   **15.** Pivoting leads to a row with a negative entry in the last column and all other entries in the row are not negative. Thus there is no feasible solution.
17. Pivoting leads to a row with a negative entry in the last column and all other entries in the row are not negative. Thus there is no feasible solution.   **19.** No feasible solution   **21.** Maximum $z = 360$ at $(\frac{115}{8}, \frac{215}{24}, 25)$, $(30, 10, 0)$ and points between.   **23.** Minimum $z = 51$ at $(\frac{51}{4}, \frac{15}{2}, 3)$, $(24, 0, 3)$ and points between.   **25.** Unbounded   **27.** Let $x =$ number of Petite dryers and $y =$ number of Deluxe dryers.
Maximize $z = 5x + 6y$ subject to $x + 2y \leq 3950$
$$4x + 3y \leq 9575$$
$$y \geq 2000$$
$$x \geq 0, y \geq 0$$

Initial tableau:

$$\begin{bmatrix} 1 & 2 & 1 & 0 & 0 & 0 & | & 3950 \\ 4 & 3 & 0 & 1 & 0 & 0 & | & 9575 \\ 0 & -1 & 0 & 0 & 1 & 0 & | & -2000 \\ -5 & -6 & 0 & 0 & 0 & 1 & | & 0 \end{bmatrix}$$

Pivoting leads to a row with a negative entry in the last column and all other entries nonnegative. Therefore there is no solution.

SECTION 4–6,   PAGE 256

1. $\begin{bmatrix} 2 & 4 \\ 1 & 0 \\ 3 & 2 \end{bmatrix}$ **3.** $\begin{bmatrix} 4 & 1 & 6 & 2 \\ 3 & 8 & -7 & 4 \\ 2 & -2 & 1 & 6 \end{bmatrix}$ **5. (a)** $\begin{bmatrix} 6 & 5 & | & 30 \\ 8 & 3 & | & 42 \\ \hline 25 & 30 & | & 1 \end{bmatrix}$ **(b)** $\begin{bmatrix} 6 & 8 & | & 25 \\ 5 & 3 & | & 30 \\ \hline 30 & 42 & | & 1 \end{bmatrix}$

(c) $\begin{bmatrix} 6 & 8 & 1 & 0 & 0 & | & 25 \\ 5 & 3 & 0 & 1 & 0 & | & 30 \\ \hline -30 & -42 & 0 & 0 & 1 & | & 0 \end{bmatrix}$ **7. (a)** $\begin{bmatrix} 22 & 30 & | & 110 \\ 15 & 40 & | & 95 \\ 20 & 35 & | & 68 \\ \hline 500 & 700 & | & 1 \end{bmatrix}$ **(b)** $\begin{bmatrix} 22 & 15 & 20 & | & 500 \\ 30 & 40 & 35 & | & 700 \\ \hline 110 & 95 & 68 & | & 1 \end{bmatrix}$

(c) $\begin{bmatrix} 22 & 15 & 20 & 1 & 0 & 0 & | & 500 \\ 30 & 40 & 35 & 0 & 1 & 0 & | & 700 \\ \hline -110 & -95 & -68 & 0 & 0 & 1 & | & 0 \end{bmatrix}$

9. Initial tableau for dual problem:

$$\begin{bmatrix} 1 & 2 & 1 & 0 & 0 & | & 4 \\ 1 & 1 & 0 & 1 & 0 & | & 3 \\ \hline -8 & -14 & 0 & 0 & 1 & | & 0 \end{bmatrix}$$

Minimum $z = 30$ at $(6, 2)$

11. Initial tableau for dual problem:

$$\begin{bmatrix} 3 & 1 & 0 & 1 & 0 & 0 & 0 & | & 10 \\ 1 & 1 & 4 & 0 & 1 & 0 & 0 & | & 16 \\ 6 & 0 & 1 & 0 & 0 & 1 & 0 & | & 20 \\ \hline -9 & -9 & -12 & 0 & 0 & 0 & 1 & | & 0 \end{bmatrix}$$

Minimum $z = 108$ at $(6, 3, 0)$

13. Initial tableau for dual problem:

$$\begin{bmatrix} 1 & 3 & 3 & 1 & 0 & 0 & 0 & 8 \\ 1 & 1 & 6 & 0 & 1 & 0 & 0 & 5 \\ 1 & 3 & 8 & 0 & 0 & 1 & 0 & 12 \\ -37 & -81 & -216 & 0 & 0 & 0 & 1 & 0 \end{bmatrix}$$

Minimum $z = 279$ at $(18, 27, 0)$

15. Initial tableau:

	y_1	y_2	x_1	x_2	w	
	800	280	1	0	0	22,000
	500	150	0	1	0	12,000
	−28,000	−9000	0	0	1	0

Dallas 15 days; New Orleans 32 days; cost $714,000

CHAPTER 4 REVIEW EXERCISES,   PAGE 258

1. $6x_1 + 4x_2 + 3x_2 + s_1 = 220$
$x_1 + 5x_2 + x_3 + s_2 = 162$
$7x_1 + 2x_1 + 5x_3 + s_3 = 139$

3. $6x_1 + 5x_2 + 3x_3 + 3x_4 + s_1 = 89$
$7x_1 + 4x_2 + 6x_3 + 2x_4 + s_2 = 72$

5. $10x_1 + 12x_2 + 8x_3 + s_1 = 24$
$7x_1 + 13x_2 + 5x_3 + s_2 = 35$
$-20x_1 - 36x_2 - 19x_3 + z = 0$

7. $3x_1 + 7x_2 + s_1 = 14$
$9x_1 + 5x_2 + s_2 = 18$
$x_1 - x_2 + s_3 = 21$
$-9x_1 - 2x_2 + z = 0$

9. $x_1 + x_2 + x_3 + s_1 = 15$
$2x_1 + 4x_2 + x_3 + s_2 = 44$
$-6x_1 - 8x_2 - 4x_3 + z = 0$

11. (a) 6 in Row 2, Column 2
(b) 5 in Row 2, Column 4
(c) 3 in Row 2, Column 3

13. (a) $x_1 = 0, x_2 = 80, s_1 = 0, s_2 = 42, z = 98$ **(b)** $x_1 = 73, x_2 = 42, x_3 = 15, s_1 = 0, s_2 = 0, s_3 = 0, z = 138$

15. (a)
$$\begin{bmatrix} 11 & 5 & 3 & 1 & 0 & 0 & 0 & 142 \\ -3 & -4 & -7 & 0 & 1 & 0 & 0 & -95 \\ 2 & 15 & 1 & 0 & 0 & 1 & 0 & 124 \\ -3 & -5 & -4 & 0 & 0 & 0 & 1 & 0 \end{bmatrix}$$

(b)
$$\begin{bmatrix} 7 & 4 & 1 & 0 & 0 & 28 \\ -1 & -3 & 0 & 1 & 0 & -6 \\ 14 & 22 & 0 & 0 & 1 & 0 \end{bmatrix}$$

(c)
$$\begin{bmatrix} 1 & 2 & 7 & 1 & 0 & 0 & 0 & 90 \\ 8 & 4 & 3 & 0 & 1 & 0 & 0 & 100 \\ -5 & -1 & -6 & 0 & 0 & 1 & 0 & -75 \\ -1 & -3 & -5 & 0 & 0 & 0 & 1 & 0 \end{bmatrix}$$

17. (a)
$$\begin{bmatrix} -6 & -4 & -1 & 1 & 0 & 0 & 0 & 0 & -40 \\ -1 & -2 & -5 & 0 & 1 & 0 & 0 & 0 & -36 \\ 5 & 1 & 3 & 0 & 0 & 1 & 0 & 0 & 30 \\ -5 & -1 & -3 & 0 & 0 & 0 & 1 & 0 & -30 \\ 1 & 3 & 9 & 0 & 0 & 0 & 0 & 1 & 0 \end{bmatrix}$$

(b)
$$\begin{bmatrix} -15 & -8 & 1 & 0 & 0 & 0 & 0 & -120 \\ 10 & 12 & 0 & 1 & 0 & 0 & 0 & 120 \\ 15 & 5 & 0 & 0 & 1 & 0 & 0 & 75 \\ -15 & -5 & 0 & 0 & 0 & 1 & 0 & -75 \\ -5 & -12 & 0 & 0 & 0 & 0 & 1 & 0 \end{bmatrix}$$

(c)
$$\begin{bmatrix} 14 & 9 & 1 & 0 & 0 & 0 & 0 & 126 \\ -10 & -11 & 0 & 1 & 0 & 0 & 0 & -110 \\ -5 & 1 & 0 & 0 & 1 & 0 & 0 & 9 \\ 5 & -1 & 0 & 0 & 0 & 1 & 0 & -9 \\ 3 & 2 & 0 & 0 & 0 & 0 & 1 & 0 \end{bmatrix}$$

19. $x_1 = 13, x_2 = 0, x_3 = 4, z = 47$ **21.** Unbounded feasible region, no solution
23. $x_1 = 60, x_2 = 132, x_3 = 0, z = 456$

25. (a) x_3 **(b)** x_2 **27.** $\begin{bmatrix} 3 & 4 & 5 \\ 1 & 0 & 7 \\ -2 & 6 & 8 \end{bmatrix}$ $\begin{bmatrix} 4 & -5 \\ 3 & 0 \\ 2 & 12 \\ 1 & 9 \end{bmatrix}$

29. Minimum $z = 64$ at $(0, 6, 1)$ and $(0, 8, 0)$ and points between   **31.** Maximum $z = 92$ at $(4, 4, 3)$

33. Maximum $z = 22$ at $(2, 3, 1)$ **35.** Unbounded   **37.** $x_1 = 6$, $x_2 = 4$, $x_3 = 2$, $z = 252$

39. Maximum $z = 1050$ at $(30, 60)$ **41.** $x_1 = 0.75$, $x_2 = 2.75$, $z = 4.25$

43.
$$\begin{bmatrix} 3 & 2.5 & 3.5 & 1 & 0 & 0 & 3200 \\ 26 & 20 & 22 & 0 & 1 & 0 & 18{,}000 \\ -7.50 & -9 & -11 & 0 & 0 & 1 & 0 \end{bmatrix}$$

CHAPTER 5

SECTION 5–1,   PAGE 269

1. (a) True   **(b)** False   **(c)** False   **(d)** False   **(e)** True   **(f)** True   **(g)** False   **(h)** True   **(i)** False
(j) True   **3.** $\{M, i, s, p\}$ **5.** $\{16, 18, 20, \ldots\}$ **7.** $A \neq B$ **9.** $A = B$ **11.** $A \neq B$ **13.** Subset
15. Not a subset   **17.** Is a subset   **19.** Is a subset   **21. (a)** $\emptyset, \{-1\}, \{2\}, \{4\}, \{-1, 2\}, \{-1, 4\}, \{2, 4\}, \{-1, 2, 4\}$
(b) $\emptyset, \{4\}$ **(c)** $\emptyset, \{-3\}, \{5\}, \{6\}, \{8\}, \{-3, 5\}, \{-3, 6\}, \{-3, 8\}, \{5, 6\}, \{5, 8\}, \{6, 8\}, \{-3, 5, 6\}, \{-3, 5, 8\}, \{-3, 6, 8\},$
$\{5, 6, 8\}, \{-3, 5, 6, 8\}$ **23.** Empty   **25.** Not empty   **27.** Empty   **29.** Empty   **31.** Empty   **33.** $\{2, 1, 7, 4, 6\}$
35. $\{a, b, c, x, y, z, d\}$ **37.** $\{9, 12\}$ **39.** $\{1, 2, 3\}$ **41.** $\{1, 2, 3, 6, 9\}$ **43.** $\{2, 3\}$ **45.** $\emptyset$ **47.** $\{1, 2, 3, 6\}$
49. $\{1, 2, 3, 6, 9\}$ **51.** $\{13, 22, 33, \ldots\}$ **53.** $\{1, 2, 3, 4\}$ **55. (a)** $\subset$ **(b)** Neither   **(c)** $=$ **(d)** Neither
(e) $\subset$ **57.** $A \cap B = \{x \mid x$ is an integer that is a multiple of $35\}$ **59.** Disjoint   **61.** Not disjoint
63. $A \cap B =$ set of students at Miami Bay U who are taking both finite math and American history.

SECTION 5–2,   PAGE 279

1. $\{17, 18, 19\}$ **3.** $\{11, 12, 13\}$ **5. (a)** $\{-1, 0, 12\}$ **(b)** $\{1, 12, 13\}$ **(c)** $\{12\}$ **(d)** $\{-1, 0, 1, 12, 13\}$
7. (a) 10   **(b)** 5   **(c)** 4   **(d)** 11   **9.** 180   **11.** 7   **13.** 19   **15. (a)** $\{f, g, i, j, m\}$ **(b)** $\{f, g, h, i, j, k, l, m\}$
(c) $\emptyset$ **(d)** $\{h, k, l\}$ **(e)** $\{f, g, i, j, m\}$ **17.** 35   **19. (a)** 42   **(b)** 60   **(c)** 84   **(d)** 57   **(e)** 39   **(f)** 81
(g) 15   **(h)** 15   **(i)** 81   **21. (a)** 35   **(b)** 9   **(c)** 6   **(d)** 38   **(e)** 38   **(f)** 12
23.

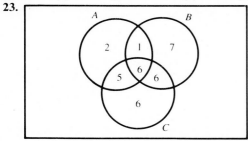

25. 225   **27. (a)** 14   **(b)** 24   **(c)** 38   **(d)** 44   **29. (a)** 8   **(b)** 27   **(c)** 4   **(d)** 31   **31. (a)** 21   **(b)** 10
(c) 8   **(d)** 56   **(e)** 29   **(f)** 62   **33. (a)** 42   **(b)** 9   **(c)** 44   **(d)** 24   **35. (a)** 28   **(b)** 9   **(c)** 20
(d) 7   **37.** 69   **39.** $n(A \cup B)$ must be at least as large as $n(A)$.   **41. (a)** 30   **(b)** 20   **43.** This information
accounts for only 133 students.   **45. (a)** 0   **(b)** $\emptyset$

SECTION 5-3,   PAGE 289

1.

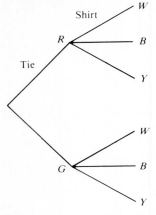

3.

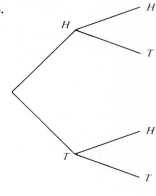

5. 180   **7.** 45   **9.** 42   **11.** 28   **13. (a)** 169   **(b)** 28,561   **15.** 24   **17.** 90   **19.** 4096
21. 8,000,000   **23. (a)** 625   **(b)** 120   **25. (a)** 17,576,000   **(b)** 11,232,000
27.

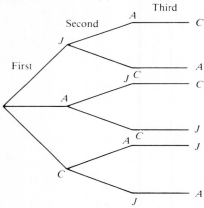

29. (a) 210   **(b)** 30   **(c)** 60   **(d)** 60   **(e)** 180   **31.** 384   **33.** 144   **35. (a)** 360   **(b)** 750
37. 1440   **39.** 128   **41.** There are 26 × 26 = 676 choices of a first and last initial. This is not enough for all of 750 people to have different pairs of initials.
43.

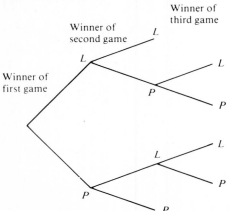

SECTION 5–4,   PAGE 299

1. 6   **3.** 120   **5.** 720   **7.** 840   **9.** 95,040   **11.** 360   **13.** 970,200   **15.** 840   **17.** 120   **19.** 2520
21. 336   **23. (a)** 5040   **(b)** 210   **25.** 6   **27.** 9240   **29. (a)** 24   **(b)** 840   **31.** 210   **33.** 120   **35.** 24
37. (a) 24   **(b)** 64   **39.** 658,627,200   **41.** 20,160   **43.** 120   **45. (a)** 10,080   **(b)** 34,650   **(c)** 151,200
(d) 151,200   **47. (a)** 35   **(b)** 21   **49. (a)** 35   **(b)** 35   **(c)** 70   **51.** 5040   **53.** 19,656   **55. (a)** $n(n-1)$
(b) $n(n-1)(n-2)$ **(c)** n **(d)** $n(n-1)(n-2)(n-3)(n-4)$ **57.** 1,423,656   **59.** 32,760   **61. (a)** 120
(b) 362,880   **(c)** 24   **63. (a)** 35   **(b)** 56

SECTION 5–5,   PAGE 309

1. 15   **3.** 286   **5.** 126   **7.** 1   **9.** $\{a, b\}, \{a, c\}, \{a, d\}, \{b, c\}, \{b, d\}, \{c, d\}$ **11.** $\{a, b, c, d\}, \{a, b, c, e\}, \{a, b, d, e\},$
$\{a, c, d, e\}, \{b, c, d, e\}$ **13.** 15   **15.** 455   **17. (a)** 35   **(b)** 840   **19.** 5600   **21.** 4200   **23.** 249   **25.** 55
27. 181   **29.** 826   **31.** 187,200   **33.** 27,720   **35.** 35   **37.** 15,504   **39. (a)** $\{$Alice$\}, \{$Bianca$\}, \{$Cal$\},$
$\{$Dewayne$\}$ **(b)** $\{$Alice, Bianca$\}, \{$Alice, Cal$\}, \{$Alice, Dewayne$\}, \{$Bianca, Cal$\}, \{$Bianca, Dewayne$\}, \{$Cal, Dewayne$\}$
(c) $\{$Alice, Bianca, Cal$\}, \{$Alice, Bianca, Dewayne$\}, \{$Alice, Cal, Dewayne$\}, \{$Bianca, Cal, Dewayne$\}$ **(d)** $\{$Alice, Bianca,
Cal, Dewayne$\}$ **(e)** $\emptyset$ **(f)** 16   **41.** 24   **43. (a)** 11,760   **(b)** 6885   **45.** 31

SECTION 5–6,   PAGE 317

1. 369,600   **3.** 35   **5.** 1260   **7.** 15   **9.** 1680   **11.** 168,168   **13.** 17,153,136   **15.** 630,630   **17.** 3150

19. 252   **21.** 17,153,136   **23.** 280   **25.** 5775   **27.** 3,783,780   **29.** 840,840   **31.** $\dfrac{22!}{3!(2!)^3 4!(4!)^4}$ **33.** 1260

35. $\dfrac{50!}{10!(5!)^{10}}$

**CHAPTER 5 REVIEW
EXERCISES,   PAGE 319**

1. (a) True   **(b)** False   **(c)** False   **(d)** False   **(e)** True   **(f)** False   **(g)** True   **(h)** False   **(i)** True
(j) False   **(k)** True   **(l)** False   **(m)** True   **(n)** False   **(o)** False   **3. (a)** Equal   **(b)** Not equal   **(c)** Equal
5. 14   **7.**

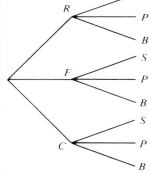

9. (a) 6,760,000   **(b)** 3,276,000   **11.** 3003   **13.** 3,121,200   **15.** 1440   **17. (a)** 990   **(b)** 1331
19. 6300   **21. (a)** 2730   **(b)** 455   **(c)** 10,100   **(d)** 175,560   **(e)** 6   **(f)** 120   **(g)** 560   **(h)** 69,300
23. This information yields only 58 people.   **25. (a)** 20   **(b)** 6   **(c)** 23   **27.** 280   **29.** 10
31. (a) 8000   **(b)** 6840   **33.** $C(15, 4)C(20, 4)C(25, 3)C(11, 1)$ **35.** 15,120   **37.** 26,334   **39. (a)** 1680
(b) 126   **(c)** 5040   **(d)** 1   **(e)** 24   **(f)** 35   **(g)** 1680   **41.** 142,500   **43.** 14   **45.** 210   **47.** $\emptyset, \{$red$\},$
$\{$white$\}, \{$blue$\}, \{$red, white$\}, \{$red, blue$\}, \{$white, blue$\}, \{$red, white, blue$\}$ **49.** 5040   **51.** 85   **53. (a)** 120   **(b)** 20
(c) 10,080   **55.** 85,765,680   **57.** 92,400

CHAPTER 6

SECTION 6-1,   PAGE 331

1. (a) {T, F}   **(b)** All letters of alphabet   **(c)** {1, 2, 3, 4, 5, 6}   **(d)** {HHH, HHT, HTH, THH, HTT, THT, TTH, TTT}   **(e)** {Mon, Tue, Wed, Thurs, Fri, Sat, Sun}   **(f)** {GC win, GC lose, GC tie} or {BC win, BC lose, BC tie}   **(g)** {A, B, C, D, F} or the grades 0–100   **(h)** {Susan Leah, Susan Dana, Susan Julie, Leah Dana, Leah Julie, Dana Julie}   **(i)** {1, 2, . . . , 30, 31} or {Mon., Tue., Wed., . . . , Sun.}   **(j)** List of students or {male, female}   **3. (a)** Valid   **(b)** Valid   **(c)** Not valid   **(d)** Not valid   **(e)** Valid   **(f)** Not valid   **(g)** Valid   **(h)** Not valid   **(i)** Not valid   **5. (a)** .3   **(b)** .6   **(c)** 0.8   **(d)** 1.0   **7. (a)** .47   **(b)** .53   **9. (a)** .21   **(b)** .43   **(c)** .64   **(d)** .27   **11.** $P(A) = .2$, $P(B) = .3$, $P(C) = .4$, $P(D) = .1$ **13.** $P(A) = .55$, $P(B) = .20$, $P(C) = .25$ **15.** $P(\text{Miniburger}) = \frac{140}{800} = .175$, $P(\text{Burger}) = \frac{345}{800} = .431$, $P(\text{Big Burger}) = \frac{315}{800} = .394$ **17.** $P(\text{Below 40}) = \frac{16}{180} = .089$, $P(40-49) = \frac{270}{1800} = .150$, $P(50-55) = \frac{1025}{1800} = .569$, $P(\text{over 55}) = \frac{345}{1800} = .192$ **19. (a)** .46   **(b)** .54   **(c)** .55   **21. (a)** $\frac{4}{52} = .0769$ **(b)** $\frac{8}{52} = .538$ **(c)** $\frac{1}{4} = .25$ **(d)** $\frac{1}{2} = .50$

SECTION 6-2,   PAGE 340

1. $\frac{4}{15} = .267$ **3.** $\frac{5}{8} = .625$ **5.** $\frac{1}{6}$ **7.** $\frac{45}{136} = .331$ **9.** $\frac{1}{221} = .0045$ **11. (a)** $\frac{5}{9} = .555$ **(b)** 0   **(c)** 1   **13.** $\frac{3}{4}$ **15.** $\frac{594}{1330} = \frac{297}{665} = .447$ **17. (a)** $\frac{1}{1365}$ **(b)** $\frac{44}{1365} = .032$ **(c)** $\frac{22}{91} = .242$ **(d)** $\frac{22}{91} = .242$ **19. (a)** $\frac{15}{728} = .021$ **(b)** $\frac{15}{364} = .041$ **21. (a)** $\frac{1}{70} = .014$ **(b)** $\frac{3}{35} = .086$ **23.** .1   **25.** $\frac{5}{9} = .555$ **27. (a)** $\frac{1}{120}$ **(b)** $\frac{1}{10}$ **29.** $\frac{48}{143} = .336$ **31. (a)** $\frac{6}{28} = .214$ **(b)** $\frac{3}{28} = .107$ **(c)** $\frac{10}{28} = .357$ **33. (a)** $\frac{5}{14} = .357$ **(b)** $\frac{9}{14} = .643$ **35. (a)** $\frac{4}{5} = .80$ **(b)** $\frac{1}{5} = .20$ **37. (a)** $\frac{8}{65} = .123$ **(b)** $\frac{28}{195} = .144$ **(c)** $\frac{2}{91} = .022$ **39.** $\frac{324}{570} = .568$ **41. (a)** $\frac{1}{4}$ **(b)** $\frac{1}{16}$ **43. (a)** $\frac{1}{6}$ **(b)** $\frac{1}{2}$ **45.** 50   **47.** $\frac{1}{15}$ **49. (a)** $\frac{1}{24}$ **(b)** $\frac{1}{18}$ **(c)** $\frac{1}{60}$

SECTION 6-3,   PAGE 352

1. $E \cup F = \{1, 2, 3, 4, 5, 7, 9\}$, $E \cap F = \{1, 3\}$, $E' = \{2, 4, 6, 8, 10\}$ **3.** $E \cup F$ is the set of students passing English or not passing chemistry. $E \cap F$ is the set of students passing English and not passing chemistry. E' is the set of students at State U not passing English.   **5.** $\frac{2}{5}$ **7.** .3   **9.** .7   **11.** Yes   **13.** No   **15.** Yes   **17. (a)** $\frac{1}{270,725}$ **(b)** $\frac{2}{270,725}$ **19.** $\frac{4}{10}$ **21. (a)** $\frac{21}{22} = .955$ **(b)** $\frac{37}{44} = .841$ **23.** $1 - \frac{[C(46, 3)]}{[C(50, 3)]} = \frac{221}{980} = .226$ **25. (a)** $\frac{120}{400} = .3$ **(b)** $\frac{220}{400} = .55$ **(c)** $\frac{55}{400} = .1375$ **(d)** $\frac{285}{400} = .7125$ **27. (a)** $\frac{4}{35}$ **(b)** $\frac{20}{35}$ **29.** .81   **31.** .51   **33. (a)** .90   **(b)** .10   **35. (a)** .84   **(b)** .16   **37. (a)** .5   **(b)** $\frac{1}{3}$ **(c)** .5   **(d)** $\frac{2}{3}$ **39.** Mutually exclusive   **41.** Mutually exclusive   **43. (a)** $\frac{5}{6}$ **(b)** $\frac{1}{6}$ **(c)** $\frac{1}{2}$ **(d)** $\frac{1}{3}$ **(e)** $\frac{1}{3}$ **45. (a)** $\frac{1}{10}$ **(b)** $\frac{1}{10}$ **(c)** $\frac{1}{2}$ **(d)** $\frac{1}{2}$ **(e)** $\frac{1}{2}$ **(f)** $\frac{8}{10}$ **(g)** $\frac{9}{10}$ **47.** $\frac{16}{52}$ **49.** .49   **51.** 10%   **53.** $\frac{2}{3}$ **55. (a)** $P(E)$ is the probability of going to a state university. $P(E) = .4$. $P(F)$ is the probability of attending a private university. $P(F) = .6$. $P(G)$ is the probability of attending a large university. $P(G) = .5$. $P(H)$ is the probability of attending a small university. $P(H) = .5$.   **(b)** $P(E')$ is the probability of not attending a state university. $P(E') = .6$ **(c)** $P(E \cup G)$ is the probability of attending a state university or a large university. $P(E \cup G) = .6$ **(d)** $P(F' \cap H)$ is the probability of attending a small state university, $P(F' \cap H) = .1$ **57.** .97

SECTION 6-4,   PAGE 362

1. (a) $\frac{3}{4}$ **(b)** $\frac{1}{2}$ **3. (a)** $\frac{16}{45}$ **(b)** $\frac{7}{24}$ **(c)** $\frac{9}{16}$ **5. (a)** $\frac{3}{8}$ **(b)** $\frac{7}{10}$ **7.** $P(K|F) = \frac{1}{10}$ $P(F|K) = 1$ **9. (a)** $\frac{7}{15}$ **(b)** $\frac{3}{10}$ **(c)** $\frac{3}{14}$ **11.** $P(E|F) = \frac{3}{7}$ $P(F|E) = \frac{1}{2}$ **13.** $P(E|F) = .60$ $P(F|E) = .40$ **15. (a)** $\frac{4}{9} = .444$ **(b)** $\frac{4}{15} = .267$ **17. (a)** .082   **(b)** .523   **(c)** .292   **(d)** .177   **(e)** .400   **(f)** .440   **19.** $(\frac{4}{52})(\frac{4}{51}) = \frac{4}{663} = .006$ **21. (a)** $(\frac{4}{52})(\frac{4}{52}) = \frac{1}{169}$ **(b)** $\frac{1}{16}$ **(c)** $\frac{1}{4}$ **23.** $\frac{2}{55}$ **25.** $\frac{15}{91}$ **27.** $\frac{9}{1024}$ **29. (a)** $\frac{16}{225}$ **(b)** $\frac{12}{225}$ **31. (a)** $\frac{16}{375}$ **(b)** $\frac{1}{27}$ **33. (a)** .555   **(b)** .35   **(c)** .40   **(d)** .378   **(e)** .588   **35.** $\frac{2}{10}$ **37.** $\dfrac{C(24, 9)C(16, 3)}{C(40, 12)}$ **39.** $\frac{152}{897} = .169$ **41.** $\dfrac{C(15, 2)C(20, 2)C(10, 2)C(5, 2)}{C(50, 8)}$ **43. (a)** $\dfrac{C(4, 1)C(48, 12)}{C(52, 13)}$ **(b)** $\dfrac{C(4, 4)C(48, 9)}{C(52, 13)}$ **(c)** $\dfrac{C(48, 13)}{C(52, 13)}$

45. Given: $P(\text{forged}) = .0001$, $P(\text{postdated}) = .05$, $P(\text{postdated}|\text{forged}) = .80$

Since $P(\text{postdated}|\text{forged}) = \dfrac{P(\text{postdated and forged})}{P(\text{forged})}$

$$.80 = \dfrac{x}{.0001}$$

$$x = .00008$$

$$P(\text{forged}|\text{postdated}) = \dfrac{.00008}{.05} = .0016$$

47. $.27$ **49. (a)** $\frac{1}{3}$ **(b)** $\frac{1}{3}$ **(c)** $\frac{2}{3}$ **51. (a)** $\frac{1}{60}$ **(b)** $\frac{1}{10}$ **(c)** 0 **(d)** $\frac{1}{10}$ **(e)** $\frac{1}{10}$ **(f)** $\frac{3}{5}$ **53. (a)** $\frac{1}{10}$

(b) $\frac{8}{10}$ **(c)** $\frac{9}{10}$ **55.** $\frac{91}{204}$ **57.** If $E \subset F$, then $E \cap F = E$, so $P(E|F) = \dfrac{P(E \cap F)}{P(F)} = \dfrac{P(E)}{P(F)}$

59. If $E \subset F$, then $F \cap E = E$. Then $P(F|E) = \dfrac{P(F \cap E)}{P(E)} = \dfrac{P(E)}{P(E)} = 1$

SECTION 6–5,   PAGE 378

1. (a) Not mutually exclusive. Independent because $P(E \cap F) = P(E)P(F) = \frac{1}{16}$.   **(b)** Not mutually exclusive. Dependent because $P(E \cap F) \neq P(E)P(F)$.   **(c)** Not mutually exclusive. Independent because $P(E|F) = .5 = P(E)$. **(d)** Mutually exclusive. Dependent because $P(E \cap F) = 0 \neq P(E)P(F) = \frac{1}{16}$.   **(e)** Mutually exclusive. Dependent because $P(E \cap F) = 0 \neq P(E)P(F) = \frac{1}{12}$.   **(f)** Mutually exclusive. Independent because $P(E \cap F) = 0 = P(E)P(F)$. **3.** $P(E)P(F) = .15 = P(E \cap F)$. Independent   **5.** $P(E)P(F) = .21 \neq P(E \cap F)$. Dependent   **7. (a)** No. A ring may have both a diamond and a ruby.   **(b)** Yes. $P(E \cap F) = \frac{1}{4}$. $P(E)P(F) = (\frac{1}{2})(\frac{1}{2}) = \frac{1}{4}$ **9.** $P(\text{A grade})P(\text{SAT} > 550)$ $= (.15)(.20) = .03 \neq .10 = P(\text{A grade} \cap \text{SAT} > 550)$. Dependent   **11.** $\frac{12}{49}$ **13.** $\frac{1}{20}$ **15. (a)** $.06$ **(b)** $.56$ **(c)** $.38$ **17. (a)** $.24$ **(b)** $.04$ **19. (a)** $.65$ **(b)** $.68$ **(c)** $.76$ **21. (a)** $.92$ **(b)** $.52$ **23.** $.93$ **25.** $P(F) = \frac{12}{52}$, $P(G) = \frac{4}{52}$, $P(G|F) = \frac{4}{12}$, $P(F|G) = 1$. F and G are not independent because $P(F) \neq P(F|G)$ **27.** $\frac{1}{864}$ **29. (a)**

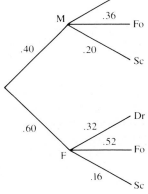

(b) $.456$ **(c)** $.176$ **(d)** No, $P(E \cap F) = .312$ and $P(E)P(F) = .2736$ **31.** $P(F) = \frac{1}{2}$, $P(G) = \frac{3}{13}$, $P(F \cap G) = \frac{6}{26}$, $P(F)P(G) = P(F \cap G)$. Independent   **33. (a)** $(.5)^{12} = .000244$ **(b)** $(.9)^{12} = .282$ **35.** $\frac{1}{5}$ **37.** If E and F are mutually exclusive, $P(E \cap F) = 0$. If $P(E) \neq 0$ and $P(F) \neq 0$, then $P(E)P(F) \neq 0$, so $P(E \cap F) \neq P(E)P(F)$, which makes E and F dependent.

SECTION 6–6,   PAGE 388

1.

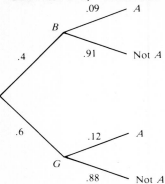

.09 — A

B

.4   .91 — Not A

.6   .12 — A

G

.88 — Not A

3. (a) .777   **(b)** .923   **5. (a)** $P(E_1 \cap F) = \frac{1}{6}$, $P(E_2 \cap F) = \frac{1}{12}$, $P(E_3 \cap F) = \frac{1}{12}$ **(b)** $\frac{1}{3}$ **(c)** $P(E_1|F) = \frac{1}{2}$, $P(E_3|F) = \frac{1}{4}$ **7.** .522   **9.** .686   **11. (a)** .057   **(b)** .340   **(c)** .604

13. (a)

$\frac{3}{5}$

I

$\frac{4}{10}$ — R   .24

$\frac{6}{10}$ — G   .36

$\frac{2}{5}$

II

$\frac{5}{12}$ — R   .167

$\frac{7}{12}$ — G   .233

(b) $P(R|I) = .4$, $P(R \cap I) = .24$, $P(R) = .407$ **(c)** $P(I|R) = .590$

15. .290

17. (a)

$\frac{5}{9}$

W

$\frac{1}{10}$ — W from I $P = \frac{5}{90}$

$\frac{3}{10}$ — W not from I $P = \frac{15}{90}$

$\frac{6}{10}$ — Black $P = \frac{30}{90}$

$\frac{4}{9}$

B

$\frac{3}{10}$ — W not from I $P = \frac{12}{90}$

$\frac{7}{10}$ — Black $P = \frac{28}{90}$

(b) $P(I|W) = \dfrac{5/90}{32/90} = \frac{5}{32}$ **19.** .991

21. (a) $P(\text{Under 25}|\text{Accident}) = .18$

(b) $P(\text{Over 50}|\text{Accident}) = .30$

(c) $P(\text{Accident}|\text{Under 25}) = \dfrac{P(\text{Accident})P(\text{Under 25}|\text{Accident})}{P(\text{Under 25})} = .225$

23. (a) $P(\text{Fraud}) = P(\text{Exceeds})P(\text{Fraud}|\text{Exceeds})$
$+ P(\text{Not exceeds})P(\text{Fraud}|\text{Not exceeds})$
$= .11(.20) + .89(.03) = .0487$

(b) $P(\text{Exceeds}|\text{Fraud}) = \dfrac{.022}{.0487} = .452$

25. $P(A|\text{Defective}) = .171, P(B|\text{Defective}) = .086, P(C|\text{Defective}) = .628, P(D|\text{Defective}) = .114$ **27.** .324

29. .294

SECTION 6–7,   PAGE 399

1. .0154   **3.** .0486   **5.** .00122   **7.** .0701   **9.** .2344   **11.** .00045   **13.** .0879

15.   **17.** .2048   **19.** .1406   **21.** .00804

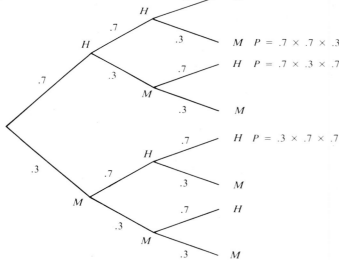

The probability of 2 hits and 1 miss is $3 (.7 \times .7 \times .3) = .441$

23. No sixes .4823, 1 six .3858, 2 sixes .1157, 3 sixes .0154, 4 sixes .00077   **25.** .2344

27. .2458   **29.** .2765   **31.** .0425   **33.** .1209   **35.** .0355   **37.** .3633   **39. (a)** .0439   **(b)** .0547

(c) .0547   **41. (a)** .1975   **(b)** .3951   **(c)** .2963   **(d)** .0988   **(e)** .0123   **43.** .0080   **45.** .5906   **47.** .1663

SECTION 6–8,   PAGE 412

1. (a) Transition   **(b)** Not transition   **(c)** Not transition   **(d)** Transition   **3. (a)** 10%   **(b)** .6   **(c)** .9

(d) 40%   **5. (a)** .4   **(b)** .8   **(c)** .3   **7.** [.675   .325]   **9.** $M_1 = [.282$ $.718], M_2 = [.32616$ $.67384]$

11. $M_1 = [.175$ $.375$ $.450], M_2 = [.1800$ $.4075$ $.4125]$ **13.** $\begin{bmatrix} \frac{2}{3} & \frac{1}{3} \end{bmatrix} \begin{bmatrix} .6 & .4 \\ .8 & .2 \end{bmatrix} = \begin{bmatrix} \frac{2}{3} & \frac{1}{3} \end{bmatrix}$

15. $\begin{bmatrix} \frac{13}{28} & \frac{15}{28} \end{bmatrix} \begin{bmatrix} .25 & .75 \\ .65 & .35 \end{bmatrix} = \begin{bmatrix} \frac{13}{28} & \frac{15}{28} \end{bmatrix}$

17.
$$MT = [.25 \quad .33 \quad .42]$$
$$(MT)T = [.259 \quad .323 \quad .418]$$
$$((MT)T)T = [.2577 \quad .3233 \quad .419]$$
$$T^3 = \begin{bmatrix} .249 & .345 & .406 \\ .242 & .386 & .372 \\ .276 & .260 & .464 \end{bmatrix}$$
$$[.3 \quad .3 \quad .4]T^3 = [.2577 \quad .3233 \quad .419]$$

19. $x = .4$ **21.** Next year, 42% contribute 58% do not. In two years, 40.2% contribute.   **23.** [.6 .4], [.38 .62], [.314 .686], [.2942 .7058], [.28826 .71174], [.286478 .713522], [.2859434 .7140566] It appears to be approaching [.285 .714]. The steady state matrix is actually $[\frac{2}{7} \quad \frac{5}{7}]$.   **25.** $[\frac{4}{17} \quad \frac{10}{17} \quad \frac{3}{17}]$ **27.** $[\frac{18}{57} \quad \frac{29}{57} \quad \frac{10}{57}]$ **29.** $[\frac{7}{29} \quad \frac{16}{29} \quad \frac{6}{29}]$

31. $[\frac{10}{11} \quad \frac{1}{11}]$ **33.** $[\frac{3}{11} \quad \frac{4}{11} \quad \frac{4}{11}]$

35.

	To				
	1	2	3	4	5
From 1	0	$\frac{1}{2}$	0	0	$\frac{1}{2}$
2	$\frac{1}{2}$	0	$\frac{1}{2}$	0	0
3	0	$\frac{1}{2}$	0	$\frac{1}{2}$	0
4	0	0	$\frac{1}{2}$	0	$\frac{1}{2}$
5	$\frac{1}{2}$	0	0	$\frac{1}{2}$	0

37. $\frac{1}{4}$ red, $\frac{1}{2}$ pink, $\frac{1}{4}$ white   **39. (a)** .06   **(b)** .05   **(c)** .80   **(d)** .04

CHAPTER 6 REVIEW EXERCISES,   PAGE 416

1. No   **3.** $\frac{146}{360} = .406$ **5.** $\frac{17}{30}$ **7.** $\frac{1}{22}$ **9.** $\frac{16}{52} = \frac{4}{13}$ **11.** $\frac{1}{32}$ **13. (a)** $\frac{3}{4}$ **(b)** $\frac{13}{66}$ **15. (a)** $\frac{3}{13}$ **(b)** $\frac{10}{13}$

17. .3456   **19.** No, $P(F)P(G) = (\frac{20}{52})(\frac{4}{52})$, $P(F \cap G) = \frac{4}{52}$ **21. (a)** $\frac{1}{1296}$ **(b)** $\frac{24}{1296}$ **(c)** $\frac{1}{72}$ **23. (a)** .036

(b) .196   **(c)** .084   **25. (a)** .290   **(b)** .234   **27. (a)** 0   **(b)** $\frac{1}{30}$ **(c)** $\frac{1}{15}$ **(d)** $\frac{1}{2}$ **(e)** $\frac{7}{30}$ **29.** $\frac{2}{13} = .1538$

31. .0171   **33. (a)** 12   **(b)** 12   **35. (a)** .06   **(b)** .09   **37. (a)** .536   **(b)** .162   **(c)** .488   **(d)** .436

39. $P(\text{Belt not used}) = \frac{94}{192} = \frac{47}{96}$
$P(\text{Injuries}) = \frac{80}{192} = \frac{5}{12}$
$P(\text{Belt not used and injuries}) = \frac{66}{192} = \frac{11}{32}$
$\frac{47}{96} \times \frac{5}{12} \neq \frac{11}{32}$, so the events are dependent.

CHAPTER 7
SECTION 7–1,   PAGE 432

1. (a) 2   **(b)** 3   **(c)** 4   **(d)** 2   **(e)** 1

3.

Category	Frequency
85–99	7
100–114	8
115–129	13
130–144	7
145–159	5

5. (a) 67   **(b)** 19   **(c)** 22   **(d)** Cannot determine   **(e)** 40   **(f)** Cannot determine

7.

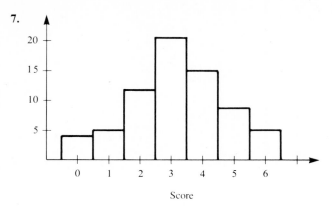

Score

9.

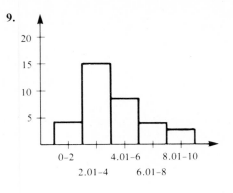

11.

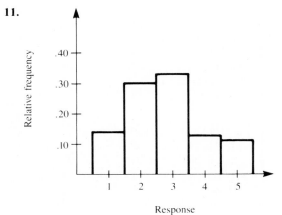

Response

13.

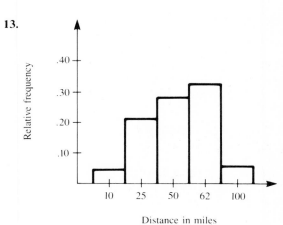

Distance in miles

15.

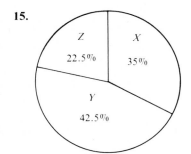

Brand of coffee preferred

17.

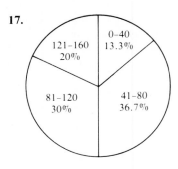

Concentration of ozone

19.

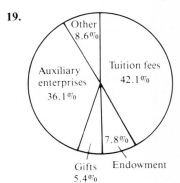

Income of Old Main University

21.

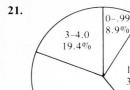

GPA of Tech students

23.

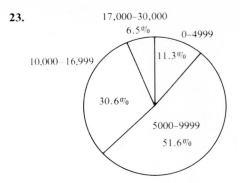

Family incomes in Dogpatch

SECTION 7–2,   PAGE 441

1. 6   **3.** 3.9   **5.** 0.667   **7.** 4.825   **9.** 77.5   **11.** 85.07 mph   **13.** 9   **15.** 23   **17.** 11.5   **19.** 72
21. 5   **23.** 1 and 5   **25.** No mode   **27.** 73.83   **29.** 0.780   **31.** 11.19   **33.** 76   **35.** $138.40
37. Mean = $3.965, median = $3.95   **39. (a)** 5   **(b)** 2   **(c)** 2   **(d)** 2   **41.** 82   **43.** $25,538.46
45. $29,644.44   **47.** It is 82 or larger   **49.** $1.30   **51. (a)** It is 7.4, 3 more than 4.4   **(b)** It is 10 more than 4.4
(c) It is 2 × 4.4 = 8.8   **(d)** It is 6 × 4.4   **(e)** When a constant is added to each score, it increases the mean by that
constant. When each score is multiplied by a constant, the mean is multiplied by that constant.   **53.** 2.97

SECTION 7–3,   PAGE 454

1. Mean = 16, variance = 15.5, $\sigma = \sqrt{15.5} = 3.94$ **3.** Mean = 9, variance = 10.4, $\sigma = \sqrt{10.4} = 3.22$
5. Mean = 35, variance = 266.2, $\sigma = 16.32$ **7.** Mean = −2, variance = 11.67, $\sigma = 3.42$ **9.** Mean = 4.5,
variance = 21.75, standard deviation = 4.66   **11.** Mean = 3.5, variance = 2.15, standard deviation = 1.47
13. Mean = 3.62, variance = .0455, standard deviation = .213   **15.** Mean = 16.6, variance = 52.84, $\sigma = 7.269$
17. Mean = 18.26, standard deviation = 4.17   **19.** Mean = 31, standard deviation = 3.12   **21. (a)** 1.25
(b) $-\frac{10}{16} = -0.625$ **(c)** 0   **(d)** 176   **(e)** 146   **23. (a)** For lathe I, $\sigma = 0.00346$. For lathe II, $\sigma = 0.00210$.
(b) Lathe II is more consistent because σ is smaller.   **25. (a)** Six 3's, one 2, and one 4.   **(b)** Four 2's, no 3's, and four
4's   **(c)** No because the largest possible value of the sum of squared deviations is 8, for which $\sigma = 1$.   **27.** 34 out of
110   **29.** 31   **31.** For the score of 86, $z = 1.75$. For the score of 82, $z = 1.67$, so the score of 86 is better.   **33.** The
z-score for the runner was 1. The z-score for the cyclist was 1.67. The runner's time was one z-score higher (slower) than the
mean, and the cyclist's time was 1.67 z-scores above the mean (slower). So the runner had the better performance.

SECTION 7–4,   PAGE 464

1.

Outcome	X
HHH	3
HHT	2
HTH	2
THH	2
TTH	1
THT	1
HTT	1
TTT	0

3.

Outcome	X
Ann, Betty	2
Ann, Jason	1
Ann, Tom	1
Betty, Jason	1
Betty, Tom	1
Jason, Tom	0

5. 0, 1, 2, 3   **7. (a)** 0, 1, 2, 3, 4   **(b)** 0, 1, 2, 3   **9. (a)** Discrete
(b) Continuous   **(c)** Continuous   **(d)** Discrete   **11. (a)** Continuous   **(b)** Discrete   **(c) (i)** Discrete
(ii) Continuous   **(iii)** Discrete   **13.** Yes

15.

X	P(X)
0	$\frac{1}{8}$
1	$\frac{3}{8}$
2	$\frac{3}{8}$
3	$\frac{1}{8}$

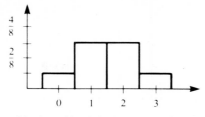

Number of heads in three tosses of a coin

17.

X	P(X)
3	$\frac{1}{5}$
4	$\frac{1}{5}$
5	$\frac{2}{5}$
6	$\frac{1}{5}$

19.

X	P(X)
0	$\frac{8}{75}$
1	$\frac{49}{75}$
2	$\frac{13}{75}$
3	$\frac{4}{75}$
4	$\frac{1}{75}$

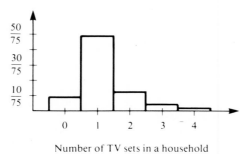

Number of TV sets in a household

21.

X	P(X)
1	.3
2	.2
3	.2
4	.1
5	.2

23. (a) 1, 2, 3, 4, . . .   **(b)** Discrete

25.

X	No.
0	15
1	30
2	10

27.

X	P(X)
0	3/14
1	8/14
2	3/14

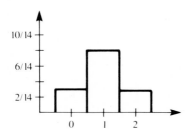

Number of men selected

29.

X	P(X)
0	7/15
1	7/15
2	1/15

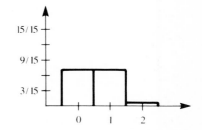

Number of defective components

31. (a)

X	P(X)
0	$\frac{6}{15}$
1	$\frac{8}{15}$
2	$\frac{1}{15}$

(b)

X	P(X)
0	$\frac{2}{3}$
1	$\frac{1}{3}$

33.

X	P(X)
0	.4096
1	.4096
2	.1536
3	.0256
4	.0016

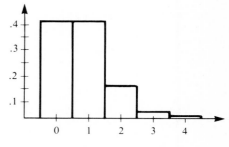

Number of correct answers

35.

X	$P(X)$
0	$\frac{343}{1728} = .198$
1	$\frac{735}{1728} = .425$
2	$\frac{525}{1728} = .304$
3	$\frac{125}{1728} = .072$

37.

X	No.
0	1
1	2
2	3

39. (a) Weight of shoppers   **(b)** Shirt size, suit size, etc.   **(c)** Shoe size   **(d)** Number of cavities

41. 1, 2, 3, 4, . . .

43.

X	$P(X)$
2	$\frac{3}{7}$
3	$\frac{2}{7}$
4	$\frac{6}{35}$
5	$\frac{3}{35}$
6	$\frac{1}{35}$

45.

X	$P(X)$
1	$\frac{1}{2}$
2	$\frac{1}{4}$
3	$\frac{1}{4}$

47.

X	$P(X)$
0	.160
1	.192
2	.648

SECTION 7–5,   PAGE 474

1. 12.8   **3.** 325   **5.** \$5.00   **7. (a)** \$0.50   **(b)** \$1.50   **9. (a)** \$227.50   **(b)** \$28,437.50
11. $\mu = 131, \sigma^2(X) = 1049$ $\sigma(X) = 32.39$ **13.** $\mu = 34, \sigma(X) = 24.98$

15.

X	$P(X)$
0	$\frac{11}{21}$
1	$\frac{44}{105}$
2	$\frac{2}{35}$

Expected number of defective $= 0.53$

17. Venture A has an expected value of \$23,000, and venture B \$28,000, so B is the better risk.   **19.** .55
21. (a) $\mu = 2.7$ **(b)** $\sigma = 1.487$ **23. (a)** \$2.40   **(b)** \$3.20   **25. (a)** \$15.95   **(b)** \$2,392,500

SECTION 7–6,   PAGE 492

1. -3.0 **3.** 0.05   **5.** 2.65   **7.** 0.1915   **9.** 0.0987   **11.** 0.3643   **13.** 0.2734   **15.** 17.72%   **17.** 14.80%
19. 39.25%   **21.** 49.81%   **23.** 0.7888   **25.** 0.9722   **27.** 48.44%   **29.** 29.60%   **31.** 0.6255   **33.** 0.7855
35. 0.0968   **37.** 0.0082   **39.** 38.98%   **41.** 13.36%   **43.** 0.4953   **45.** 0.3413   **47.** 0.4649   **49.** 0.7888
51. 0.2417   **53.** 0.2039   **55.** 0.1360   **57.** 0.4207   **59.** 0.3174   **61.** 44.30%   **63.** 65.54%   **65.** 30.85%
67. 94.52%   **69.** 1.41   **71.** 1.08   **73.** 1.70   **75. (a)** 21.19%   **(b)** 0.2119   **77. (a)** .0977   **(b)** .2033
(c) .3256   **79. (a)** 478   **(b)** 16   **(c)** 64   **81. (a)** 86   **(b)** 92   **83. (a)** 0.5468   **(b)** 0.1555   **(c)** 0.5000,
0.7422   **(d)** 352 or higher   **(e)** .1079   **85.** .621   **87.** .0359   **89. (a)** .2417   **(b)** .1934   **(c)** .1452
(d) .0968   **(e)** .0484   **(f)** .0242   **(g)** .0049

SECTION 7–7,   PAGE 507

1.

X	$P(X)$
0	.1681
1	.3602
2	.3087
3	.1323
4	.0284
5	.0024

3.

X	$P(X)$
0	.0778
1	.2592
2	.3456
3	.2304
4	.0768
5	.0102

5.

X	$P(X)$
0	.4823
1	.3858
2	.1157
3	.0154
4	.0008

7.

X	P(X)
0	.0625
1	.2500
2	.3750
3	.2500
4	.0625

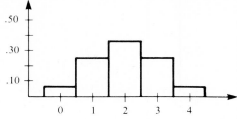

Number of heads in
four tosses of a coin

9.

X	P(X)
0	.0256
1	.1536
2	.3456
3	.3456
4	.1296

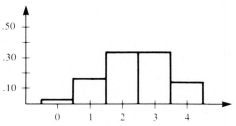

Number of times an
odd number is drawn

11. $C(90, 40)(0.4)^{40}(0.6)^{50}$ **13.** $C(75, 35)(0.25)^{35}(0.75)^{40}$ **15.** $\mu = 20$, $\sigma^2(X) = 12$, $\sigma(X) = 3.46$
17. $\mu = 312$, $\sigma^2(X) = 149.76$, $\sigma(X) = 12.24$ **19.** $\mu = 37.6$, $\sigma^2(X) = 34.592$, $\sigma(X) = 5.88$ **21.** $np = 35$, $nq = 15$,
so the normal is a good estimate.   **23.** $np = 36$, $nq = 4$, so normal distribution is not a good estimate.
25. $np = 12.5$, $nq = 12.5$, so normal distribution is a good estimate   **27.** (a) .0377   (b) .0118   (c) .0805
29. $\mu = 6$, $\sigma = 1.90$ (a) .5704   (b) .8132   (c) .3040   **31.** $\mu = 8$, $\sigma = 2$ (a) .8944   (b) .9599
(c) .2266   **33.** $\mu = 7.2$, $\sigma = 2.24$ (a) .8485   (b) .9292   (c) .2236   **35.** (a) .9830   (b) .0008
(c) .0162   **37.** .5167   **39.** .4041   **41.** .1493   **43.** .9357   **45.** .9265   **47.** (a) 47   (b) .3745

SECTION 7–8,   PAGE 515
1. 0.560, 0.719   **3.** 0.193, 0.407   **5.** 0.149, 0.451   **7.** 0.451, 0.549   **9.** (a) 0.403, 0.497   (b) 0.394, 0.506
11. (a) 0.218, 0.342   (b) 0.236, 0.324   **13.** 0.757 to 0.863   **15.** 0.434 to 0.646   **17.** (a) 9604   (b) 16,641
19. 156   **21.** $p = .6$ with bounds 0.504 to 0.696   **23.** 40.3% to 45.7%

**CHAPTER 7 REVIEW
EXERCISES,   PAGE 518**

1.

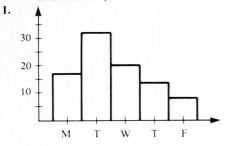

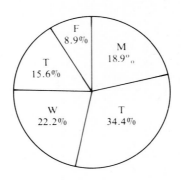

New accounts

3. (a) 6   **(b)** 10.5   **(c)** 2   **5.** 2.64   **7.** 26   **9.** 0, 1, 2, 3   **11.** 2.85   **13.** 2.67   **15.** .0227

17.

X	$P(X)$
0	.3164
1	.4219
2	.2109
3	.0469
4	.0039

19. (a) .6368   **(b)** .0009   **(c)** .1669   **21.** 81st percentile

23.

X	$P(X)$
1	.025
2	.200
3	.4625
4	.2688
5	.0438

25.

X	Number of outcomes
0	10
1	30
2	15
3	1

27.

X	Number of ways x can occur
1	1
2	1
3	4

29. 11.238   **31. (a)** 0.070   **(b)** 0.0466   **(c)** 0.02   **33.** 0.575 to 0.892

CHAPTER 8

SECTION 8–1,   PAGE 529

1. $66.00   **3.** $90.00   **5.** $31.66   **7.** $I = \$18.00$, $A = \$318.00$ **9.** $120.00   **11.** $52.50   **13.** $116.38
15. $660.00   **17.** $860   **19.** 6.5%   **21.** 8.5%   **23.** $3024   **25.** $7478.25   **27.** $1607.14
29. Discount = $138.75, PR = $1711.25   **31.** Discount = $94.58, PR = $390.42   **33.** $1050
35. $3750 annually, $22,500 total   **37. (a)** $750   **(b)** $54,000   **39.** 3 years   **41.** 3 months   **43.** $650
45. Interest = $150.00, principal = $29.95   **47.** 9.3%   **49.** $6576.73   **51.** $39,175.26   **53.** Simple interest =
$8.67, $8.78 = simple discount   **55.** 10.53%   **57.** 10.1% discount is $104.52, 10.3% simple interest is $103.00, so
simple interest is better.   **59.** $49.5 billion   **61.** $225,000   **63.** $16,000 payments, $320,000 total   **65.** $982,500
67. 7.2%   **69.** $1,988,125

SECTION 8–2,   PAGE 540

1. (a) 1.225043   **(b)** 1.1040808   **(c)** 1.0613636   **(d)** 1.071225   **(e)** 1.1925186   **(f)** 1.1314082   **3. (a)** 7.5%
(b) 3.75%   **(c)** 1.25%   **5. (a)** $6944.85   **(b)** $2444.85   **7. (a)** $55,287.88   **(b)** $24,287.88   **9. (a)** $6554.00
(b) $1554.00   **11.** $900.41   **13.** $1965.65   **15. (a)** $15,972.00   **(b)** $16,081.20   **(c)** $16,138.68
17. $18,061.10   **19.** $483.48   **21.** $720.74   **23.** $34.08   **25.** $10,299.68   **27.** $2020.87   **29.** 6.09%
31. 12 years   **33.** 6 years   **35.** 10%   **37.** 11.5 years   **39.** $281.48   **41.** Ken had $1575.84, and Barb had
$1575.03, so Ken had $0.81 more   **43.** 8.8% compound semiannually has an effective rate of 8.9936%, while 8.6%
compounded quarterly has an effective rate of 8.8813%, so 8.8% is better.   **45.** 9.2% compounded quarterly is better
because its effective rate is 9.522%.   **47.** 10% compounded quarterly is better because its effective rate is 10.38%.
49. 42,665   **51.** $26,115.30   **53.** 8%   **55.** 6%   **57.** $16,000 lump sum. The other will be worth $15,919.80
59. About 14 years   **61.** $162,135.87

SECTION 8–3,   PAGE 547

1.
First deposit	$798.60
Second deposit	726.00
Third deposit	660.00
Fourth deposit	600.00
Total	$2784.60

3. (a) 18.59891   **(b)** 29.77808   **(c)** 14.19203   **(d)** 19.59863   **(e)** 12.68250   **5.** $402,064.32   **7.** $6074.34
9. $4,403.80   **11.** $119,112.32   **13.** $15,117.66   **15.** $546.67   **17.** $438.52   **19.** $724.87   **21.** $3869.93
23. $764.73   **25.** $2697.35   **27.** $4802.44   **29.** $306.72   **31.** $59,889.95   **33.** $20,969.37   **35.** $34,365.00
37. About 9%   **39. (a)** $14,486.56   **(b)** $1158.92   **41.** $3812.16   **43.** $198.88   **45.** $13,597.20

SECTION 8–4,   PAGE 558

1. 12.84926   **3.** 10.83777   **5.** $23,885.20   **7.** $12,263.57   **9.** $5734.96   **11.** $5029.62   **13.** $2400.00
15. $15,000   **17.** $1476.14   **19.** $3207.36   **21.** $13,077.68   **23.** $194.97   **25.** $167.29
27. (a) $297,270.00   **(b)** $222,270   **29. (a)** $850.00 interest, $20.96 principal   **(b)** $261,288.00   **31.** $46,576.21
33. $7600   **35.** $574.49   **37.** $91,285.50   **39.** $564.88   **41.** $1326.61   **43.** $9634.67   **45.** $201.36
47. $1076.74

CHAPTER 8 REVIEW
EXERCISES,   PAGE 560

1. $90.00   **3.** $960.00   **5.** $1350.00   **7.** Discount = $1530, proceeds = $6970   **9.** $1125.20   **11.** Nine years
13. 6.09%   **15.** 26.824%   **17.** 18% compounded quarterly is better because its effective rate is 19.25%.
19. (a) $10,099.84   **(b)** $2099.84   **21. (a)** $9043.65   **(b)** $4043.65   **23.** $17,496   **25.** $33,648.51
27. 19 quarters or 4.75 years   **29.** $2189.94   **31.** $5637.09   **33.** $7546.73   **35.** $7605.47   **37.** $138,059.00
39. $3736.28   **41.** $4037.82   **43.** $33,648.51   **45.** Five years   **47.** $301.39   **49.** $1,234.04
51. $736,265.12   **53.** $17,706.09   **55.** $2434.91   **57.** $3680.77   **59.** $9619.48   **61.** $955.02

CHAPTER 9
SECTION 9–1,   PAGE 574

1. (a) -7 **(b)** -7 **3. (a)** $\frac{1}{2}$ **(b)** $\frac{1}{2}$ **(c)** $\frac{1}{2}$ **5. (a)** 6   **(b)** 4   **(c)** $4 + \Delta x$ **7. (a)** 0   **(b)** 0
(c) $2a - 4 + \Delta x$ **9. (a)** $\frac{1}{9}$ **(b)** $\frac{1}{5}$ **11. (a)** -0.9 (dollars per year)   **(b)** -1.0 (dollars per year)
(c) -0.8 (dollars per year)   **13. (a)** $128 + 16\Delta t$ ft/sec   **(b)** 128 ft/sec   **15. (a)** 390 feet
(b) $390 + 250\Delta t + 40(\Delta t)^2$ feet   **(c)** $250 + 40\Delta t$ ft/sec   **(d)** 250 ft/sec   **17.** 24   **19.** 2   **21.** 2   **23.** -1
25. $\dfrac{-3}{4}$ **27.** m **29.** 0 (dollars per item)   **31. (a)** 17 (dollars per item)   **(b)** 17 (dollars per item)
(c) 17 (dollars per item)   **33.** $1000 per year

SECTION 9-2, PAGE 588

1. 4   **3.** 6   **5.** −5   **7.** $\frac{-4}{3}$ **9.** 5   **11.** 17   **13.** 5   **15.** −3   **17.** 1   **19.** Does not exist   **21.** 0
23. 7   **25.** 30   **27. (a)** 22   **(b)** −7   **29. (a)** 3   **(b)** 81   **31.** 10   **33.** 36   **35.** 2   **37.** 5   **39.** 6
41. $\frac{1}{6}$ **43.** $\frac{-1}{16}$ **45.** 10   **47.** $\frac{1}{4}$ **49.** Not a number   **51.** 0   **53.** 0   **55.** Not a number   **57.** 1

SECTION 9-3, PAGE 600

1. (a) 1   **(b)** 3   **(c)** Does not exist   **(d)** 2   **(e)** No   **3. (a)** 4   **(b)** 4   **(c)** 4   **(d)** 4   **(e)** Yes   **5. (a)** 1
(b) 4   **(c)** Does not exist   **(d)** 4   **(e)** No   **7. (a)** 5   **(b)** 6   **(c)** Does not exist   **(d)** 5   **(e)** No   **(f)** 9
(g) 9   **(h)** 9   **(i)** 9   **(j)** Yes   **9. (a)** 5   **(b)** 7   **(c)** No   **11.** Yes, $B = -3$ **13. (a)** −1   **(b)** 1
(c) Does not exist   **(d)** 1   **(e)** 1   **(f)** 1
15.

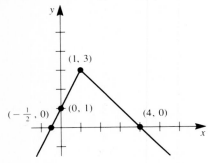

17.

19. No   **21. (a)** $C(x) = \begin{cases} 0.8x & 0 \le x \le 10 \\ 8 + 0.75(x - 10) & 10 < x \end{cases}$ **(b)** Yes

SECTION 9-4, PAGE 610

1. [6, 7] and [−2, −1] are two such intervals   **3.** [3, 4] and [−2, −1] are two such intervals   **5.** $x > 3$
7. $x \le -2$ **9.** $-2 \le x \le 3$ **11.** Solution is 1.748 . . . , so any number in [1.55, 1.94] will do.
13. Solution is 4.344 . . . , so any number in [4.15, 4.50] will do.   **15.** Solution is 4.713 . . . , so any number in
[4.52, 4.90] will do.   **17.** All $x < \dfrac{-1}{2}$ and all $x > 4$ **19.** $-4 \le x \le 2$ **21.** $2 - 2\sqrt{3} \le x \le 2 + 2\sqrt{3}$
23. Solution is 2.156 . . .   **25.** Solution is −0.433. . . .   **27.** Solution is 7.368 . . .   **29.** All $x < -5$
and all $x \ge \dfrac{-14}{3}$ **31.** $-2 < x < 2$ and $x \ge 4$ **33.** $-4 \le x < 0$ **35.** $-9 < x \le -6$ **37.** $x < 6$
39. 140 units per week   **41.** Up to 9 hours   **43. (a)** 144 feet   **(b)** 80 feet   **(c)** Ball hits the ground in 6 seconds
45. $0 \le t \le \dfrac{100 + \sqrt{10384}}{32}$, $0 \le t \le 6.309$ (to three decimal places)

SECTION 9-5, PAGE 623

1. (a) $\dfrac{-1}{x^2}$ **(b)** $\dfrac{-1}{x^2}$ **(c)** $\dfrac{-1}{x^2}$ **(d)** $\dfrac{-1}{x^2}$ **3.** $y - 10 = 6(x - 3)$ **5.** $y - \dfrac{1}{10} = -\dfrac{1}{100}(x - 1)$
7. (a) $f'(x) = 2x - 8$ **(b)** $\dfrac{dy}{dx} = 2x - 8$ **9.** 4   **11.** $y + \dfrac{1}{2} = -\dfrac{1}{4}(x + 2)$ **13.** $y = 4(x - 3)$
15. (a) $x = -2$, (vertical tangent); $x = 2$, (discontinuity); $x = 3$, (corner)   **(b)** (2, 0) and (3, −2)   **(c)** 0   **(d)** 2
(e) 2   **(f)** 0   **(g)** 0 and 1

17. (a) $\displaystyle \lim_{\Delta x \to 0} \frac{|3 + \Delta x - 3| - 0}{\Delta x} = \lim_{\Delta x \to 0} \frac{|\Delta x|}{\Delta x}$; does not exist.   **(b)** Yes

19. $\displaystyle \lim_{\Delta x \to 0} \frac{\sqrt{9 + \Delta x} - 3}{\Delta x} = \lim_{\Delta x \to 0} \frac{(\sqrt{9 + \Delta x} - 3)(\sqrt{9 + \Delta x} + 3)}{\Delta x(\sqrt{9 + \Delta x} + 3)}$

$\displaystyle = \lim_{\Delta x \to 0} \frac{(9 + \Delta x) - 9}{\Delta x(\sqrt{9 + \Delta x} + 3)} = \lim_{\Delta x \to 0} \frac{\Delta x}{\Delta x(\sqrt{9 + \Delta x} + 3)}$

$\displaystyle = \lim_{\Delta x \to 0} \frac{1}{\sqrt{9 + \Delta x} + 3} = \frac{1}{\sqrt{9} + 3} = \frac{1}{6}$

21. $\displaystyle \lim_{\Delta x \to 0} \frac{(a + \Delta x)^2 - a^2}{\Delta x} = \lim_{\Delta x \to 0} \frac{2a\Delta x + (\Delta x)^2}{\Delta x} = \lim_{\Delta x \to 0} (2a + \Delta x) = 2a$

23. $\displaystyle \lim_{\Delta x \to 0} \frac{\dfrac{1}{a + \Delta x + 4} - \dfrac{1}{a + 4}}{\Delta x} = \lim_{\Delta x \to 0} \frac{a + 4 - (a + \Delta x + 4)}{(\Delta x)(a + \Delta x + 4)(a + 4)}$

$\displaystyle = \lim_{\Delta x \to 0} \frac{-\Delta x}{\Delta x(a + \Delta x + 4)(a + 4)} = \lim_{\Delta x \to 0} \frac{-1}{(a + \Delta x + 4)(a + 4)} = \frac{-1}{(a + 4)^2}$

25. (a) $\displaystyle \lim_{\Delta x \to 0} \frac{\Delta x^{1/3}}{\Delta x} = \lim_{\Delta x \to 0} \frac{1}{\Delta x^{2/3}}$; does not exist.   **(b)** Yes   **(c)**

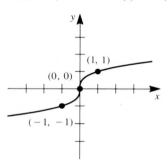

(d) Figure 2–28   **27. (a)** Use one-sided limits to compute $\displaystyle \lim_{\Delta x \to 0} \frac{f(3 + \Delta x) - f(3)}{\Delta x}$. The right-hand limit is -1; the left-hand limit is 2; the limit does not exist.   **(b)** Yes   **(c)** Figure 2–26   **29.** Both left- and right-hand limits are 2; $f'(1) = 2$.

CHAPTER 9 REVIEW EXERCISES,   PAGE 625

1. 0   **3.** 6   **5.** 2   **7.** 0   **9.** 3   **11.** $\dfrac{-5}{2}$ **13.** $\dfrac{1}{4}$ **15.** $5x + 8$ **17. (a)** 0   **(b)** -2 **(c)** 3

19. $f'(1) = 6$ **21.** $f'(4) = \dfrac{1}{2}$ **23.** $y - 6 = 3(x - 4)$ **25. (a)** No   **(b)** Yes   **27. (a)** 3   **(b)** 4

(c) Does not exist   **29. (a)** 5   **(b)** 5   **(c)** 5   **31. (a)** Yes   **(b)** No   **(c)** No   **33. (a)** Yes   **(b)** Yes

(c) Yes   **35. (a)** 1   **(b)** 2   **37. (a)** -1 **(b)** Does not exist   **39.** $-1, 1, 2, 4, 5$ **41. (a)** 6   **(b)** 8   **(c)** 8

(d) No; $\displaystyle \lim_{x \to 4} C(x)$ does not exist   **43.** Yes, $M = 6$ **45.** Yes, $B = 18$ **47.** $f'(a) = \dfrac{1}{2\sqrt{a}}$ **49.** $f'(x) = 2x + 3$

51. $x < 0$ and $x \geq \dfrac{1}{5}$ **53.** $x \leq 2 - 2\sqrt{2}$ and $x \geq 2 + 2\sqrt{2}$ **55.** $0 < x < 9$ **57.** $\dfrac{-11}{2} \leq x < -1$ and $x > 2$

59. Any number within 0.1 of 2.748 . . .   **61.** Any number within 0.1 of 80   **63.** $x > 5\sqrt{56} - 30 = 7.416$ . . . (to three decimal places)   **65.** for x in the interval $[32, 246]$

CHAPTER 10

SECTION 10-1,   PAGE 638

1. $f'(x) = 5x^4$ **3.** $f'(x) = -4x^{-5} = \dfrac{-4}{x^5}$ **5.** $f'(x) = \dfrac{4}{3}x^{1/3}$ **7.** $f'(x) = \dfrac{5}{2}x^{3/2} = \dfrac{5}{2}\sqrt{x^3}$

9. $f'(x) = 40x^3$ **11.** $\dfrac{dy}{dx} = 6x$ **13.** $\dfrac{dy}{dx} = \dfrac{-9}{x^2} = -9x^{-2}$ **15.** $\dfrac{dy}{dx} = 30x^2 + \dfrac{5}{2}x^{-1/2} = 30x^2 + \dfrac{5}{2\sqrt{x}}$

17. $\dfrac{dy}{dx} = -30x^{-3} + 2x = \dfrac{-30}{x^3} + 2x$ **19.** $\dfrac{dy}{dx} = 20x - 4$ **21.** $f'(x) = 12x^2 + 5$ **23.** $f'(x) = 12x - 4$

25. $f'(x) = 27x^2 - 6x^{-4} = 27x^2 - \dfrac{6}{x^4}$ **27.** $f'(x) = 7x^{-1/2} - 48x^{-5}$ **29.** $\dfrac{dy}{dx} = 9x^2 - 5x^{-1/2} = 9x^2 - \dfrac{5}{\sqrt{x}}$

31. $\dfrac{dy}{dx} = 20x - 16x^{-3} = 20x - \dfrac{16}{x^3}$ **33.** $\dfrac{dy}{dx} = 4x^{-1/2} + 16 = \dfrac{4}{\sqrt{x}} + 16$

35. $\dfrac{dy}{dx} = \dfrac{9}{2}x^{-1/2} + 10x^{-3} = \dfrac{9}{2\sqrt{x}} + \dfrac{10}{x^3}$ **37.** $f'(x) = -\dfrac{2}{4}x^{-3} - \dfrac{1}{2}x^{-1/2} = \dfrac{-1}{2x^3} - \dfrac{1}{2\sqrt{x}}$

39. $f'(x) = \dfrac{-3}{5}x^{-2} - \dfrac{12}{7}x^{-3} = \dfrac{-3}{5x^2} - \dfrac{12}{7x^3}$ **41.** $g'(t) = \dfrac{-8}{5}t^{-3} - \dfrac{5}{3} = \dfrac{-8}{5t^3} - \dfrac{5}{3}$

43. $g'(x) = 9 - 2x^{-1/2} - \dfrac{9}{5}x^{-4} = 9 - \dfrac{2}{\sqrt{x}} - \dfrac{9}{5x^4}$ **45.** $f(x) = 3\sqrt{x}; f'(x) = \dfrac{3}{2\sqrt{x}}$

47. $f(x) = x^2 + 2 + \dfrac{1}{x^2}; f'(x) = 2x - \dfrac{2}{x^3}$ **49.** $g(t) = \dfrac{t^2}{3t} + \dfrac{6}{3t} = \dfrac{t}{3} + \dfrac{2}{t}; g'(t) = \dfrac{1}{3} - \dfrac{2}{t^2}$

51. (a) $R'(x) = 2000 - \dfrac{1}{2}x; C'(x) = 720; P' = R' - C' = 1280 - \dfrac{1}{2}x$ **(b)** $MR(600) = 1700$; the monthly revenue
is increasing at the rate of \$1700 per system. $MC(600) = 720$; the monthly cost is increasing at the rate of \$720 per system.
$MP(600) = 980$; the monthly profit is increasing at the rate of \$980 per system.   **53.** $y - 8 = -6(x + 1)$
55. 24 ft/sec

SECTION 10-2,   PAGE 649

1. $f'(x) = (7x)3 + (3x)7 = 42x$ **3.** $f'(x) = (x^3)0 + (3x^2)9 = 27x^2$ **5.** $f'(x) = \sqrt{x}(1) + x\left(\dfrac{1}{2\sqrt{x}}\right) = \dfrac{3}{2}\sqrt{x}$

7. $f'(x) = \dfrac{3x^2 - 6x^2}{x^4} = \dfrac{-3}{x^2}$ **9.** $f'(x) = \dfrac{12\sqrt{x} - 6\sqrt{x}}{4x} = \dfrac{3}{2\sqrt{x}}$ **11.** $f'(x) = \dfrac{-1}{x^2}$ **13.** $f'(x) = \dfrac{16x}{64} = \dfrac{x}{4}$

15. $f'(x) = (x^2 + 9)(3x^2 - 4) + (x^3 - 4x + 1)(2x)$ **17.** $f'(x) = \left(x - \dfrac{1}{x}\right)\left(1 - \dfrac{1}{x^2}\right) + \left(x + \dfrac{1}{x}\right)\left(1 + \dfrac{1}{x^2}\right)$

19. $f'(x) = \left(x^4 - 7x + \dfrac{1}{x}\right)(2x + 3) + (x^2 + 3x)\left(4x^3 - 7 - \dfrac{1}{x^2}\right)$

21. $f'(x) = \dfrac{-7}{(x-2)^2}$ **23.** $f'(x) = \dfrac{(x^3 - 7x)(2x + 4) - (x^2 + 4x)(3x^2 - 7)}{(x^3 - 7x)^2}$

25. $f'(x) = \dfrac{(x^3 - 5)(6x - 9) - (3x^2 - 9x + 2)(3x^2)}{(x^3 - 5)^2}$

27. $f'(x) = \dfrac{(x^3 - 9)[(x + 2)(2x - 8) + (x^2 - 8x)(1)] - [(x^2 - 8x)(x + 2)](3x^2)}{(x^3 - 9)^2}$

29. $f'(x) = \dfrac{[(x + 2)(x^2 + 7)](3) - (3x + 7)[(x^2 + 7)(1) + (x + 2)(2x)]}{(x + 2)^2(x^2 + 7)^2}$ **31.** $y + 6 = -3(x - 4)$

33. $y + 6 = -18(x + 1)$ **35.** $y - 24 = 20(x - 1)$ **37.** $A' = h \cdot w' + w \cdot h' = (16)(2) + (25)(3) = 107$. Area
is increasing at rate of 107 square inches per minute.   **39.** $A' = h \cdot w' + w \cdot h' = (6)\left(\dfrac{1}{2}\right) + (7)(-1) = -4$. Area is

decreasing at rate of 4 square inches per minute.   **41.** $A' = \frac{1}{2}(h \cdot b' + b \cdot h') = \frac{1}{2}(9 \cdot 2 + 16 \cdot 6) = 57$. Area is
increasing at rate of 57 square inches per minute.   **43.** $(f \cdot g)'(2) = g(2) \cdot f'(2) + f(2)g'(2) = 6 \cdot 3 + 7 \cdot 4 = 46$
45. $\left(\dfrac{f}{g}\right)'(1) = \dfrac{g(1)f'(1) - f(1)g'(1)}{g(1)^2} = \dfrac{2 \cdot 4 - 7 \cdot 3}{4} = \dfrac{-13}{4}$ **47. (a)** $R(p) = \dfrac{-4}{3}p^2 + 40p$

(b) $MR(p) = \dfrac{-8}{3}p + 40$ **(c)** $MR(12) = 8$; revenue is increasing at the rate of \$8 per dollar.

(d) $MR(21) = -16$; revenue is decreasing at the rate of \$16 per dollar.   **49. (a)** $MC(x) = \dfrac{1}{10}x^2 + 2x + 100$

(b) $AC(x) = \dfrac{1}{30}x^2 + x + 100 + \dfrac{9500}{x}$ **(c)** $MAC(x) = (AC)'(x) = \dfrac{1}{15}x + 1 - \dfrac{9500}{x^2}$

SECTION 10-3,   PAGE 659

1. (a) $f(g(x)) = 4x^2 + 10x + 4$ **(b)** $g(f(x)) = 2x^2 + 6x + 1$ **3. (a)** $f(g(x)) = \sqrt{9x + 25}$

(b) $g(f(x)) = 9\sqrt{x} + 25$ **5.** $\dfrac{dy}{dx} = 5(x^3 - 4x)^4(3x^2 - 4)$ **7.** $\dfrac{dy}{dx} = \dfrac{1}{2}(9x + 16)^{-1/2} \cdot 9 = \dfrac{9}{2\sqrt{9x + 16}}$

9. $\dfrac{dy}{dx} = 3(3x^2 + 8)^2 \cdot 6x = 18x(3x^2 + 8)^2$ **11.** $\dfrac{dy}{dx} = \dfrac{1}{2}(4x + 9)^{-1/2} \cdot 4 = \dfrac{2}{\sqrt{4x + 9}}$

13. $f'(x) = 3(x^2 - 9x + 5)^2(2x - 9)$ **15.** $f'(x) = \dfrac{1}{2}(16x - 4)^{-1/2} \cdot 16 = \dfrac{8}{\sqrt{16x - 4}}$

17. $\dfrac{dy}{dx} = -30(4x + 1)^{-4} \cdot 4 = \dfrac{-120}{(4x + 1)^4}$ **19.** $\dfrac{dy}{dx} = -12(3x + 1)^{-4} \cdot 3 = \dfrac{-36}{(3x + 1)^4}$

21. $f'(x) = \sqrt{4x + 9} + x \cdot \dfrac{1}{2}(4x + 9)^{-1/2} \cdot 4 = \dfrac{6x + 9}{\sqrt{4x + 9}}$

23. $f'(x) = (6x - 4)^2 3(7x - 8)^2 \cdot 7 + (7x - 8)^3 2(6x - 4) \cdot 6 = (6x - 4)(7x - 8)^2(210x - 180)$

25. $f'(x) = \dfrac{(8x + 10)[3(x^2 + 1)^2 \cdot 2x] - (x^2 + 1)^3(8)}{(8x + 10)^2} = \dfrac{(x^2 + 1)^2[40x^2 + 60x - 8]}{(8x + 10)^2}$

27. $f'(x) = \dfrac{(x^2 - 4)^2 3 - (3x + 1)[2(x^2 - 4)(2x)]}{(x^2 - 4)^4} = \dfrac{(x^2 - 4)(-9x^2 - 4x - 12)}{(x^2 - 4)^4} = -\dfrac{9x^2 + 4x + 12}{(x^2 - 4)^3}$

29. $f'(x) = 5(3x + (2x + 1)^3)^4(3 + 3(2x + 1)^2 \cdot 2)$ **31.** $f'(x) = 3(7x + \sqrt{3x + 1})^2\left(7 + \dfrac{3}{2\sqrt{3x + 1}}\right)$

33. $y - 5 = \dfrac{1}{5}(x - 4)$ **35.** $y - 180 = 217.2(x - 3)$ **37.** $D(7) = 1331$; seven weeks after the beginning of the
advertising campaign, the weekly demand is 1331. $D'(7) = 49.5$; seven weeks after the beginning of the advertising
campaign, the weekly demand is increasing at the rate of 49.5 per week.   **39.** $R(2) = 4$; $R'(2) = \dfrac{5}{4}$. After two years the
yearly revenue is \$4 million and is increasing at the rate of \$1.25 million per year.

SECTION 10-4,   PAGE 664

1. $f'''(x) = 0$ **3.** $g'''(t) = 6$ **5.** $f''''(x) = \dfrac{-120}{x^5}$ **7.** $f'''(x) = 1620(3x + 1)^2$ **9.** $f'''(x) = 192(8x + 4)^{-5/2}$

11. $g'''(x) = \dfrac{-240}{(2x + 1)^4}$ **13.** $y'' = 6(x^2 + 1)^2 + 24x^2(x^2 + 1)$ **15.** $y'' = \dfrac{6}{\sqrt{6x^2 - 8}} - \dfrac{36x^2}{(\sqrt{6x^2 - 8})^3}$

17. $y'' = \dfrac{-18}{(x^2 + 1)^4} + \dfrac{144x^2}{(x^2 + 1)^5}$ **19.** $y'' = \dfrac{-120}{(3x^2 + 9)^6} + \dfrac{4320x^2}{(3x^2 + 9)^7}$

21. $f''(x) = \dfrac{2}{\sqrt{2x^2 + 1}} - \dfrac{4x^2}{(\sqrt{2x^2 + 1})^3}$; $f''(2) = \dfrac{2}{27}$

23. (a) $C(150) = 192,200$ **(b)** $MC(150) = 2740$; the daily cost is increasing at the rate of \$2740 per unit.
(c) $MC'(150) = 25$; the marginal cost is increasing at the rate of \$25 per unit.   **25. (a)** 56 feet above the ground
(b) -96 feet per second   **(c)** -32 (feet per second) per second

SECTION 10-5,   PAGE 671

1. Explicitly   3. Implicitly   5. Implicitly   7. $y = \frac{2}{3}(x + 5) + 1$ 9. $y = \frac{3x - 7}{x + 1}$

11. $y = \frac{10}{x + 3}$ 13. $y = \frac{-9x}{x^2 + x - 5}$ 15. $y' = \frac{-x}{y}$ 17. $y' = \frac{-5}{12y + 2}$

19. $y' = \frac{8x - 2xy}{x^2 + 3y^2}$ 21. $y' = \frac{12xy - 6x}{2y - 6x^2}$ 23. $y' = \frac{6y^2 + 9}{12y^2 - 12xy + 3}$ 25. $y' = \frac{y - y^2}{2y^3 + x}$

27. $y' = \frac{1 - y}{x + 3y^2}$. Now $\frac{1 - y}{x + 3y^2} = \frac{y - y^2}{xy + 3y^3} = \frac{y - y^2}{(x - y^3) + 3y^3} = \frac{y - y^2}{2y^3 + x}$

29. $y + 1 = 6(x - 2)$ 31. $y + 4 = \frac{3}{4}(x - 3)$ 33. $C = -77; y + 2 = \frac{69}{104}(x - 3)$ 35. (a) 50

(b) $\frac{-1}{8}$ (c) -8

SECTION 10-6,   PAGE 678

1. $2x\frac{dx}{dt} + 2y\frac{dy}{dt} = 0$ 3. $\frac{dx}{dt} + 2\frac{dy}{dt} = 0$ 5. $6x\frac{dx}{dt} - \frac{dx}{dt} + 4y\frac{dy}{dt} = 0$ 7. $\frac{dy}{dt} = \frac{1}{2}$ 9. $\frac{dy}{dt} = -\frac{3}{14}$

11. $2x\frac{dx}{dt} + 2y\frac{dy}{dt} = 0; \frac{dy}{dt} = \frac{3}{2}$ 13. $2\frac{dx}{dt} + 3\frac{dy}{dt} = 0; \frac{dy}{dt} = -\frac{8}{3}$ 15. $2x\frac{dx}{dt} - \frac{1}{2\sqrt{y}}\frac{dy}{dt} = 0; \frac{dy}{dt} = 120$

17. $\frac{dy}{dt} = -15$ 19. $\frac{dy}{dt} = 48$ 21. 52 mph   23. $\frac{dx}{dt} = \frac{-45}{160}$; the demand is decreasing at the rate of 281.25 shirts

per year.   25. $\frac{dy}{dt} = \frac{110}{4}$; y is increasing at a rate of $27\frac{1}{2}$ rentals per week.

SECTION 10-7,   PAGE 688

1. $dy = 15x^2\, dx$ 3. $dy = \frac{x}{\sqrt{x^2 + 1}}\, dx$ 5. $dy = \frac{-1}{2(\sqrt{x})^3}\, dx$ 7. $dy = (24x^2 - 4)dx$ 9. $dy = 10$

11. $dy = \frac{24}{1000}$ 13. $dy = 30$ 15. $\Delta y \approx dy = 1$ 17. $\Delta y \approx dy = \frac{1}{200}$ 19. $\sqrt[3]{29} \approx 3\frac{2}{27}$

21. $\sqrt{23} \approx 4\frac{4}{5}$ 23. $\sqrt{52} \approx 7\frac{3}{14}$ 25. $\sqrt[3]{61} \approx 3\frac{15}{16}$ 27. (a) The approximate cost is $21.
(b) The actual cost is $21.01.   (c) The approximation is within 0.048% of the actual cost.
29. (a) Revenue is increased by approximately $120.   (b) Revenue is decreased by approximately $120.   31. (a) 6.45
(b) 5.7   33. We can guess that $x = 6$ is an approximate solution; this is the x-intercept of the line through (4, 10) with
slope -5.   35. 1.85

CHAPTER 10 REVIEW
EXERCISES,   PAGE 690

1. $f'(x) = \frac{x}{\sqrt{x^2 + 1}}$ 3. $f'(x) = \frac{(x^3 - 4x)2x - (x^2 + 1)(3x^2 - 4)}{(x^3 - 4x)^2}$
5. $f'(x) = (5x + 1)^3 \cdot 2(7x + 4) \cdot 7 + (7x + 4)^2 \cdot 3(5x + 1)^2 \cdot 5$
7. $f'(x) = 4(3x + \sqrt{5x + 1})^3\left(3 + \frac{5}{2\sqrt{5x + 1}}\right)$ 9. $y'' = \frac{48}{x^5}$

11. $\frac{dy}{dx} = \frac{3 - y}{x + 2y}$ 13. $y - 72 = 35.25(x - 3)$ 15. $y - 3 = \frac{4}{3}(x + 4)$ 17. (a) 0.54 mile

(b) 0.39 mile per minute, or 23.4 miles per hour   (c) 0.16 (mile per minute) per minute   19. $\frac{dy}{dt} = -1.05$

21. $dy = \frac{-37}{(2x - 5)^2}\, dx$ 23. $\sqrt[3]{10} \approx 2\frac{1}{6}$ 25. $MP(x) = MR(x) - MC(x) = \sqrt{x^2 + 4x} - 6\sqrt{x} - 5$

27. $\frac{dR}{dt} = 1775$; the revenue is increasing at the rate of $1775 per week.   29. $20\frac{1}{3}$

CHAPTER 11
SECTION 11–1,   PAGE 706

1. (a) 4   **(b)** -2 **(c)** -1 and 3   **(d)** 2   **(e)** $-1, 0, 2, 3$ **(f)** $(-3, -1)$ and $(2, 3)$ **(g)** $(-1, 0)$, $(0, 2)$ and $(3, 5)$ **3.** $x = \frac{1}{3}$ **5.** $x = 2$ and 1   **7.** $(-\infty, \frac{4}{5})$ **9.** $(-\infty, -2)$ and $(4, \infty)$ **11.** $f(\frac{4}{5}) = -\frac{29}{5}$ is a relative maximum   **13.** $f(-2) = \frac{46}{3}$ is a relative maximum and $f(4) = -\frac{62}{3}$ is a relative minimum
15. $x = \frac{-2}{3}$ and $x = 1$ **17.** $x = -4$ **19.** $(-\infty, -2)$ and $(0, 1)$ **21.** $(-\infty, 3)$

23. Increasing on $(2, \infty)$, decreasing on $(-\infty, 2)$ **25.** Increasing on $(-\infty, \frac{5}{2})$, decreasing on $(\frac{5}{2}, \infty)$

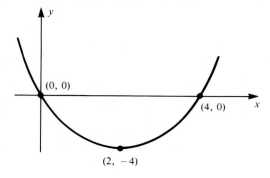

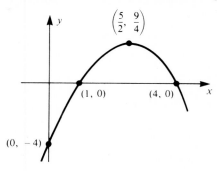

27. Increasing on $(-\frac{5}{2}, \infty)$, decreasing on $(-\infty, -\frac{5}{2})$; $f(\frac{-5}{2}) = -\frac{49}{4}$ is a relative minimum

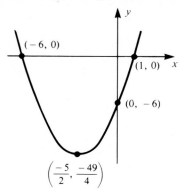

29. Increasing on $(-\infty, 0)$ and $(4, \infty)$, decreasing on $(0, 4)$; $f(0) = 2$ is a relative maximum; $f(4) = -30$ is a relative minimum

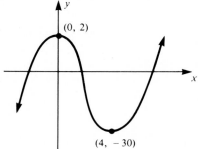

31. Increasing on $(-\infty, \infty)$; no relative extremum

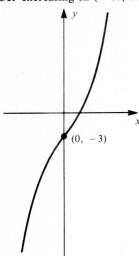

$(0, -3)$

33. Increasing on $(-\infty, 8)$ and $(8, \infty)$; no relative extremum

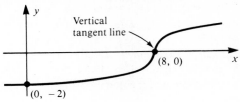

Vertical tangent line

$(8, 0)$

$(0, -2)$

35. Increasing on $(-3, \infty)$, decreasing on $(-\infty, -3)$; $f(-3) = -28$ is a relative minimum

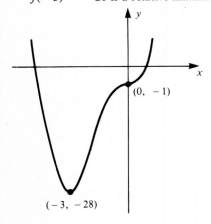

$(0, -1)$

$(-3, -28)$

37. Increasing on $(-3, 0)$, decreasing on $(0, 3)$; $f(0) = 3$ is a relative maximum

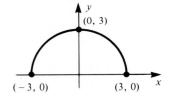

$(0, 3)$

$(-3, 0)$ $(3, 0)$

39. Decreasing on $(-\infty, 0)$ and $(0, 2)$, increasing on $(2, 4)$ and $(4, \infty)$; $f(2) = -4^{1/3}$ is a relative minimum

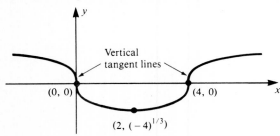

Vertical tangent lines

$(0, 0)$ $(4, 0)$

$(2, (-4)^{1/3})$

41. Decreasing on $(-6, -4)$, increasing on $(-4, \infty)$; $f(-4) = -8$ is a relative minimum

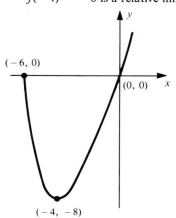

43. Increasing on $(-\infty, 2)$, decreasing on $(2, 3)$; $f(2) = 8$ is a relative maximum

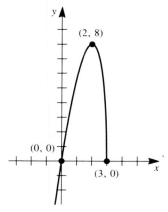

45. (a) $0 < t < 20$ **(b)** 240 **47. (a)** $0 < t < 3$ **(b)** 150 feet   **(c)** When $t = 3$ **49. (a)** Never
(b) $0 < x < 40$ **(c)** 21 **(d)** 21; they are equal.   **51. (a)** The marginal profit function is positive on I.
(b) The profit function is increasing on I.

SECTION 11–2,   PAGE 721

1. $(-5, -3)$, $(0, 2)$, and $(3, 5)$ **3.** The points $(-3, 2)$, $(0, 3)$, $(2, 2)$, and $(3, 1)$ **5.** Relative minimum at $x = \frac{2}{7}$
7. Relative maximum at $x = 3$ **9.** Relative maximum at $x = -5$; relative minimum at $x = 2$
11. Relative minimum at $x = -1$ and $x = 2$; relative maximum at $x = 0$ **13.** Relative maximum at $x = -\frac{1}{3}$;
relative minimum at $x = \frac{1}{3}$ **15.** Concave up on $(-\infty, \infty)$, no points of inflection   **17.** Concave down on $(-\infty, 2)$,
concave up on $(2, \infty)$; $(2, -2)$ is the point of inflection.   **19.** Concave up on $(-\infty, \frac{2}{3})$, concave down on $(\frac{2}{3}, \infty)$;
$(\frac{2}{3}, -\frac{82}{27})$ is the point of inflection.   **21.** Concave up on $(-\infty, -3)$ and $(2, \infty)$, concave down on $(-3, 2)$. The points of
inflection are $(-3, -325)$ and $(2, -100)$.   **23.** Concave up on $(-\infty, 0)$, concave down on $(0, \infty)$; no points of inflection
25. Concave up on $(-\infty, -\frac{1}{2})$ and on $(0, \infty)$, concave down on $(-\frac{1}{2}, 0)$. Point of inflection is $(-\frac{1}{2}, 3)$
27. Concave up on $(-\infty, 5)$, concave down on $(5, \infty)$; $(5, 2)$ is a point of inflection.
29. (a) Increasing on $(-\infty, \infty)$ **(b)** Concave up on $(4, \infty)$; concave down on $(-\infty, 4)$
(c)

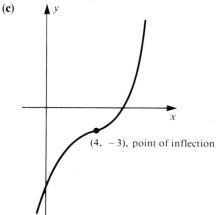

$(4, -3)$, point of inflection

31. (a) Increasing on $(-\infty, -3)$ and $(1, \infty)$, decreasing on $(-3, 1)$ **(b)** Concave down on $(-\infty, -1)$, concave up on $(-1, \infty)$ **(c)**

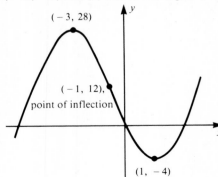

33. (a) Decreasing on $(0, 1)$, increasing on $(1, \infty)$ **(b)** Concave up on $(0, \infty)$
(c)

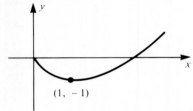

35. (a) Increasing on $(-\infty, 2)$, decreasing on $(2, \infty)$ **(b)** Concave down on $(-\infty, \infty)$
(c)

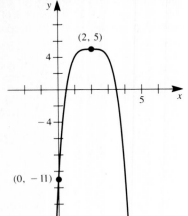

37. **(a)** Increasing on $(-\sqrt{3}, 0)$ and $(\sqrt{3}, \infty)$, and decreasing on $(-\infty, -\sqrt{3})$ and $(0, \sqrt{3})$
(b) Concave up on $(-\infty, -1)$ and $(1, \infty)$, concave down on $(-1, 1)$
(c)

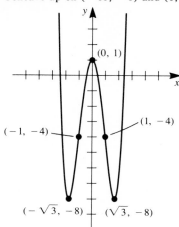

39. **(a)** $x = 400$ **(b)** $0 < x < 400$ **41.** **(a)** $0 < x < 140 + \sqrt{19{,}860} = 280.925\ldots$ **(b)** R has a relative maximum when $x = 140 + \sqrt{19{,}860}$ **(c)** $x = 140$ **43.** **(a)** For all $t > 0$ **(b)** $0 < t < 2$ **(c)** 2 days
45. Relative minimum when $x = 4$, relative maximum when $x = 50$ **47.** $(-6, -1)$ and $(1, 4)$

SECTION 11–3,   PAGE 738
1. V.A. is the line $x = 6$; H.A. is the line $y = 1$.   **3.** V.A.'s are the lines $x = 3$ and $x = -3$; H.A. is the line $y = 0$.

5. V.A.'s are the lines $x = -3$ and $x = 4$; H.A. is the line $y = 0$.   **7.** V.A. is the line $x = -2$; H.A. is the line $y = \dfrac{4}{5}$.

9. No V.A.; H.A. is the line $y = 0$.   **11.** No H.A.; V.A.'s are the lines $x = 2$ and $x = -2$.   **13.** No asymptotes

15. ∞

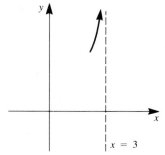

17. $-\infty$

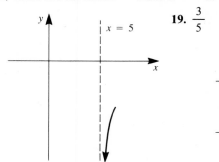

19. $\dfrac{3}{5}$

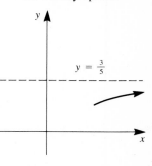

21. $\dfrac{1}{2}$

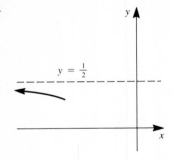

23. -1

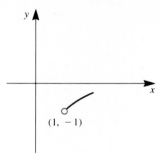

25. V.A. is $x = -5$; $\displaystyle\lim_{x \to -5^+} f(x) = -\infty$; $\displaystyle\lim_{x \to -5^-} f(x) = \infty$; H.A. is $y = 3$; $\displaystyle\lim_{x \to \infty} f(x) = 3 = \lim_{x \to -\infty} f(x)$

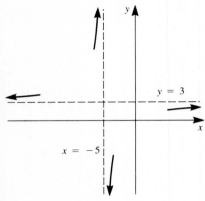

27. No V.A.; the x-axis is a H.A.; $\displaystyle\lim_{x \to \infty} f(x) = 0 = \lim_{x \to -\infty} f(x)$

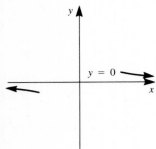

29. $\lim\limits_{x \to 1} f(x) = -1$, so the line $x = 1$ is not a V.A.; the line $x = 2$ is a V.A.; $\lim\limits_{x \to 2^+} f(x) = \infty$; $\lim\limits_{x \to 2^-} f(x) = -\infty$; the x-axis is a H.A.; $\lim\limits_{x \to \infty} f(x) = \lim\limits_{x \to -\infty} f(x) = 0$

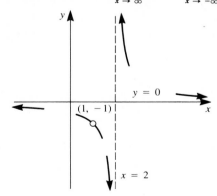

31. $\lim\limits_{x \to 4} f(x) = \frac{3}{5}$, so the line $x = 4$ is not a V.A.; the line $x = -1$ is a V.A. because $\lim\limits_{x \to -1^+} f(x) = -\infty$, also $\lim\limits_{x \to -1^-} f(x) = \infty$. The line $y = 1$ is a H.A. because $\lim\limits_{x \to \infty} f(x) = \lim\limits_{x \to -\infty} f(x) = 1$

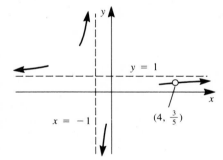

33. ∞

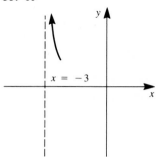

35. $-\infty$

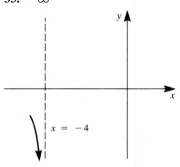

37. ∞

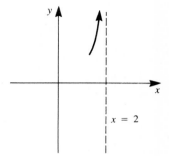

39. Line $x = 0$ is a vertical asymptote.
Line $y = 0$ is a horizontal asymptote.

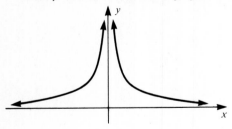

41. Line $x = 3$ is a vertical asymptote.
Line $y = 2$ is a horizontal asymptote.

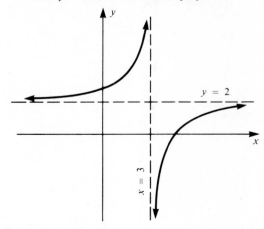

43. Line $y = 1$ is a horizontal asymptote.

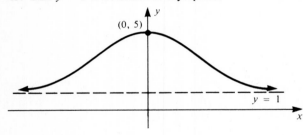

45. Line $x = 2$ is a vertical asymptote.
Line $y = 1$ is a horizontal asymptote.

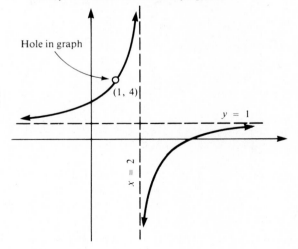

47. The y-axis and the line $x = -4$ are vertical asymptotes.
The x-axis is a horizontal asymptote.

49. About \$8 per chip.

51. About \$5 per set.

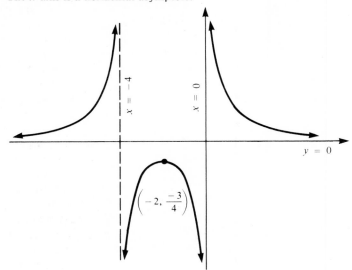

SECTION 11–4,   PAGE 748

1.

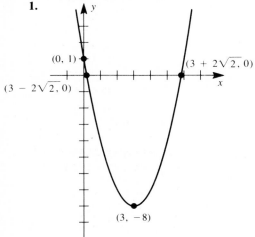

3.

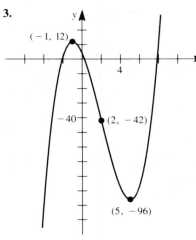

5.

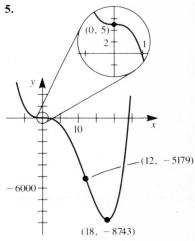

7.

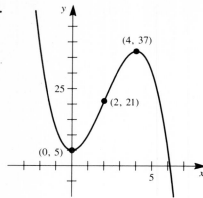

9.

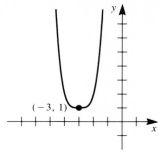

11.

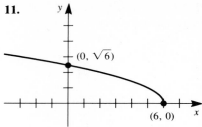

13.

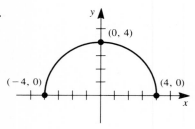

15.

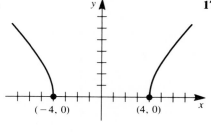

17.

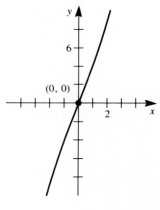

19.

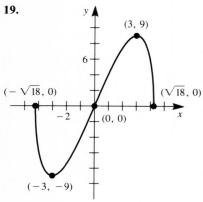

21.

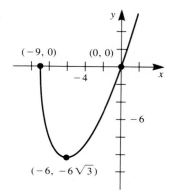

23.

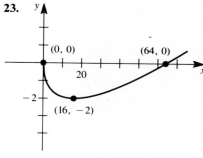

25.

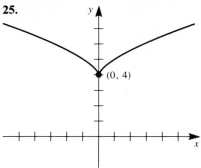

27.

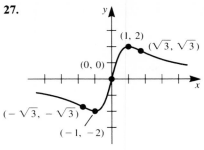

29.

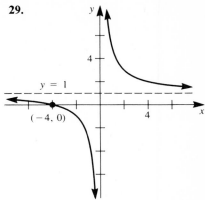

31.

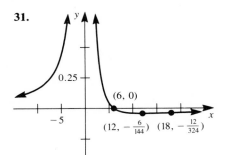

33.

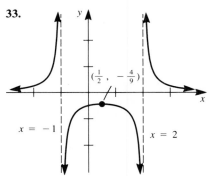

35.

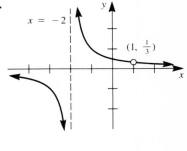

37.

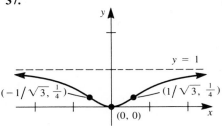

39.

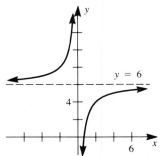

41.

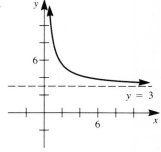

43.

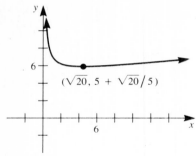

$(\sqrt{20}, 5 + \sqrt{20}/5)$

45.

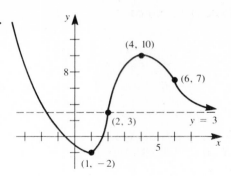

(4, 10)

(6, 7)

(2, 3)

$y = 3$

5

(1, −2)

47. No such graph; if the line $x = 7$ is a vertical asymptote, then f is not continuous at $x = 7$.

49.

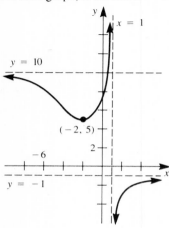

$x = 1$

$y = 10$

(−2, 5)

−6

2

$y = −1$

51.

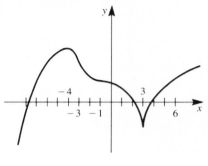

−4

−3 −1

3

6

53. (a) Either   **(b)** True   **(c)** False   **(d)** Either   **(e)** True   **55. (a)** Either   **(b)** Either   **(c)** True
(d) False   **(e)** Either

SECTION 11–5,   PAGE 757

1. Max. is 22, min. is −3   **3.** Max. is −2, min. is −29   **5.** Min. is 6   **7.** Min. is 24   **9.** Max. is 22, min. is −13
11. Max. is 0, min. is −20   **13.** Min. is 6, max. is 86   **15.** Max. is 4   **17.** Max. is −12   **19.** Max. is 1
21. Max. is 3, min. is $(-9)^{1/3}$ **23.** Min. is 0, max. is 9   **25.** Min. is 0, max. is 8   **27.** Min. is 40, no max.
29. Min. is $\dfrac{1}{4}$, no max.   **31.** Min. is −2, no max.   **33.** $x = 750$, $p = 15$ **35.** 40 mph   **37.** 50 mph

SECTION 11–6,   PAGE 766

1. 2,000,000 square feet   **3.** Height: 20 feet, base: 50 feet   **5.** $500   **7.** $2.40   **9. (a)** $75   **(b)** $2250 per day
(c) $80   **(d)** $560 per day   **11.** Base is 15″ by 30″, height is 20″   **13.** Machinery is in a square 40′ on each side;
total floor space is a 42′ by 42′ square.   **15.** $\sqrt{\dfrac{1}{3}}$, or 0.577. . . mile   **17.** Base is a 8″ by 8″ square.
19. 200 boxes

SECTION 11-7,   PAGE 779

1. (a) $AC(x) = \dfrac{x^2}{20} - 15x + 3000 + \dfrac{25,600}{x}$ **(b)** $x = 160$ **(c)** average cost is \$2040   **(d)** $MC(160) = 2040$

3. (a) $AC(x) = \dfrac{x^2}{4} - 49x + 4000 + \dfrac{10,000}{x}$; $MC(x) = \dfrac{3x^2}{4} - 98x + 4000$ **(b)** $x = 100$

(c) $AC(100) = MC(100) = 1700$ **5.** $x = 300$; $P(300) = \$26,000$ **7.** Yes; increase production to 210 units per day.
9. Decrease to 300 per week.   **11.** 250 sets per day   **13. (a)** $x = 39$;   **(b)** $x = 36$ **15.** When $x = 39$, $p = 1542$; after tax with $x = 36$, $p = 1548$.

CHAPTER 11 REVIEW EXERCISES,   PAGE 782

1. Maximum is $\frac{1}{2}$; minimum is $\frac{1}{5}$; f is decreasing on (2, 5).

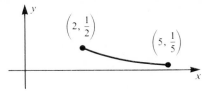

3. Maximum is 10; minimum is 1; f is increasing on (2, 5).

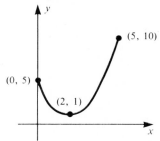

5. Maximum is 33; minimum is 6; f is increasing on (4, 8).

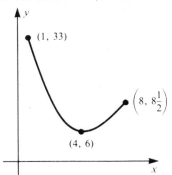

7. Maximum is 2; minimum is -254; f is increasing on $(-1, 0)$ and $(4, 5)$; $(3, -160)$ is a point of inflection.

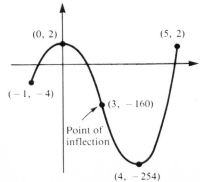

9. Maximum is 6; minimum is -6; f is increasing on $(-6, 0)$.

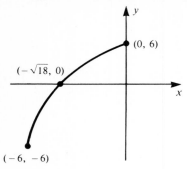

11. f is decreasing on $(-6, -\sqrt{18})$ and on $(\sqrt{18}, 6)$; $(0, 0)$ is a point of inflection.

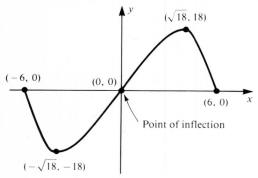

13. f is decreasing on $(0, 1)$ and on $(1, \infty)$.

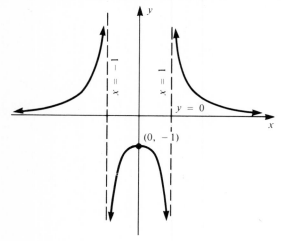

15. f is decreasing on $(0, 1)$ and on $(1, \infty)$.

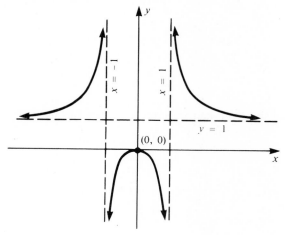

17.

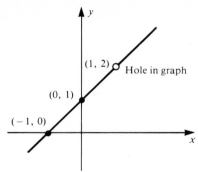

(1, 2) Hole in graph
(0, 1)
(−1, 0)

19. 64   **21. (a)** Minimum $= -\frac{3}{4}$ **(b)** Maximum $= \frac{3}{4}$ **23.** 69 ft   **25.** $x = 5$ **27.** 180 refrigerators per week

CHAPTER 12
SECTION 12–1,   PAGE 796

1. (a) $1060   **(b)** $1123.60   **(c)** $1262.47   **3. (a)** $1259.71   **(b)** $2519.42   **(c)** $12,597.12   **5. (a)** $11,881

(b) $11,948.31   **(c)** $11,964.13   **7.** $f(1) = 4$ **9.** $g(3) = 8$ **11.** $f(-2) = \dfrac{1}{4}$ **13.** 3 years

15. $1000(1.03)^8$ **17.** 2 years   **19.** $f(2) = 45$ **21.** $f(0) = 7$ **23.** $b = 25$ **25.** $b = \dfrac{1}{9}$ **27.** $c = 3$

29. $c = -1$ **31.** $k = 16$ **33.** $k = \dfrac{1}{9}$

35.

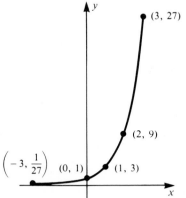

(3, 27)
(2, 9)
$\left(-3, \dfrac{1}{27}\right)$ (0, 1)   (1, 3)

37.

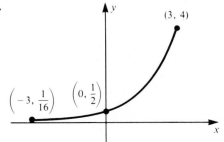

(3, 4)
$\left(-3, \dfrac{1}{16}\right)$ $\left(0, \dfrac{1}{2}\right)$

39.

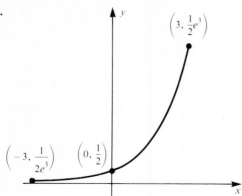

.41.

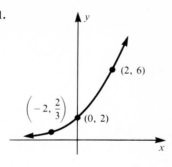

43. (a) $1808.72   **(b)** $1822.11   **45. (a)** 5.39%   **(b)** United Bank, its interest is equivalent to 5.4% yearly rate; American Bank, because she would not receive any interest during the last two months at United Bank.   **47.** The king could fill only 39 squares. The 64th square *alone* would require over 9,000,000,000,000,000,000 grains of wheat!

SECTION 12–2, PAGE 807

1. $4e^x$ **3.** $3x^2 - 2e^x$ **5.** $3x^2e^x + x^3e^x = e^x[x^3 + 3x^2]$ **7.** $18e^{3x}$ **9.** $4e^{x/2}$ **11.** $-\dfrac{x^3 - 3x^2 + 2}{e^x}$

13. $\dfrac{xe^x - 2e^x - 4}{x^3}$ **15.** $4(e^x - 7)^3e^x$ **17.** $\dfrac{e^x}{2\sqrt{e^x + 1}}$ **19.** $2x^2e^{5x}(5x + 3)$ **21.** $12(e^{4x} + 1)^2e^{4x}$

23. $6x + e^{-x} - xe^{-x}$ **25.** $\dfrac{x}{\sqrt{x^2 + 1}}e^{4x} + 4e^{4x}\sqrt{x^2 + 1}$ **27.** $y - e^2 = \dfrac{1}{3}e^2(x - 6)$

29. $f'(x) = (2x + 1)e^{(x^2 + x)}; f''(x) = 2e^{(x^2 + x)} + (2x + 1)^2e^{(x^2 + x)}$

31. $f'(x) = 2xe^{4x} + 4x^2e^{4x} = e^{4x}(4x^2 + 2x); f''(x) = e^{4x}(16x^2 + 16x + 2)$ **33.** $f'(x) = \dfrac{4e^{4x} + 5}{2\sqrt{e^{4x} + 5x}}$

35. $f'(x) = 2xe^{\sqrt{3x + 1}} + \dfrac{3(x^2 + 1)}{2\sqrt{3x + 1}}e^{\sqrt{3x + 1}}$ **37.** $y - \dfrac{1}{e^4} = \dfrac{-1}{e^4}(x - 4)$ **39.** $x = 0, x = 2$

41. On $(-\infty, 0)$ and $(0, 1)$ **43.** $\left(2, \dfrac{2}{e^2}\right)$ **45.** Maximum value $= 4e^2$, minimum value $= \dfrac{-2}{e}$

47.

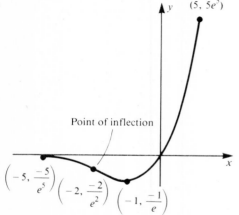

49. $y - 3 = \dfrac{3}{5}x$ **51.** $(6e^{2x})' = 12e^{2x} = 2(6e^{2x})$ **53. (a)** About 272,990 bacteria

(b) About 9100 bacteria per minute

SECTION 12–3,   PAGE 818

1. 3   **3.** -4 **5.** -2 **7.** 0   **9.** 4   **11.** 5   **13.** $(7.4, 2)$ **15.** $(1.4, 4)$ **17.** 9   **19.** 3

21. $\dfrac{1}{2}$ **23.** 6   **25.** 5   **27.** 3   **29.** 4   **31.** -4 **33.** 5   **35.** $\dfrac{5 \ln 16}{4}$ **37.** $50 \ln 4$ **39.** $\dfrac{\ln 18}{\ln 2}$

41. $\dfrac{\ln 105}{2 \ln 5}$ **43.** $\dfrac{\ln 4}{\ln 3}$ **45.** 1   **47.** In $\dfrac{50 \ln 3}{3}$ years, a little over 18 years and 3 months

49. $\dfrac{50 \ln 2}{7}$ years, slightly less than 5 years   **51.** $\dfrac{\$10,000}{e^{0.325}}$, or approximately \$7225.27   **53.** $\dfrac{\$20,000}{e^{1.5}} \approx \$4462.60$

55. 8%   **57.** $50 \ln 2$ years, a little bit less than 35 years

SECTION 12–4,   PAGE 827

1. $f'(x) = 2x + \dfrac{1}{x}$ **3.** $1 + \ln x$ **5.** $\dfrac{1}{x}$ **7.** $\dfrac{1}{x \ln 10}$ **9.** $e^x \ln x + \dfrac{e^x}{x}$ **11.** $\dfrac{1}{x}$ **13.** $\dfrac{1 - \ln x}{x^2}$

15. $\dfrac{2x}{x^2 + 1}$ **17.** $3[\ln(x + 1)]^2\left(\dfrac{1}{x + 1}\right)$ **19.** $\ln(3x - 8) + \dfrac{3x}{3x - 8}$ **21.** $\dfrac{12x^2 - 6(x^2 + 1)\ln(x^2 + 1)}{36x^2(x^2 + 1)}$

23. $\dfrac{4(\ln x)^3}{x}$ **25.** $\dfrac{1}{x}e^{5x} + 5(\ln x)e^{5x}$ **27.** $2(\ln 6)x$ **29.** $\dfrac{2x - 3}{x^2 - 3x + 1}$ **31.** $\dfrac{4}{4x + 8}$ **33.** 2

35. 1   **37.** $\dfrac{1}{2x}$ **39.** $\dfrac{12}{3x + 1}$ **41.** $[\ln(x^2 + 1)]^{-1/2}\left[\dfrac{x}{x^2 + 1}\right]$ **43.** $\dfrac{10 \ln(5x + 1)}{5x + 1}$

45. $\dfrac{1}{e^{2x} + \sqrt{4x + 10}}\left[2e^{2x} + \dfrac{4}{2\sqrt{4x + 10}}\right]$ **47.** $3[\ln(x + e^{2x})]^2\left(\dfrac{1}{x + e^{2x}}\right)(1 + 2e^{2x})$

49. $\dfrac{6}{3x + 1} + \dfrac{2x - 5}{x^2 - 5x}$ **51.** $\dfrac{-2(3x^2 - 2)}{(x^3 - 2x)}$ **53.** $f'(x) = 2x(\ln x) + x; f''(x) = 2(\ln x) + 3$

55. $f'(x) = \dfrac{1}{2}\ln(x + 1) + \dfrac{x}{2(x + 1)}$

$f''(x) = \dfrac{1}{2(x + 1)} + \dfrac{1}{2(x + 1)^2}$

57.

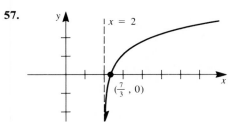

59. Maximum is $f\left(\dfrac{1}{e}\right) = \dfrac{1}{e}$, minimum is $f(4) = 4 \ln \dfrac{1}{4}$

SECTION 12–5,   PAGE 834

1. \$217,462   **3.** \$24,428   **5. (a)** \$27,299   **(b)** \$1,490,479   **7.** Approximately \$29.84 billion
9. (a) 565 million   **(b)** 3200 million, or 3.2 billion   **11.** Within 5 hours and 30 minutes   **13. (a)** After 13.7 years
(b) After 6.2 years   **(c)** After 26.3 years   **15.** About 3300 years old   **17.** About 5000 years old

SECTION 12–6,   PAGE 841

1. $e^{x \ln 3}$ **3.** $e^{-x \ln 9}$ **5.** $e^{(x \ln 7)/2}$ **7.** $5e^{x \ln 8}$ **9.** $7e^{((\ln 4)/3)x}$ **11.** 4   **13.** $\dfrac{1}{3}$ **15.** -1 **17.** $\dfrac{\ln 36}{\ln 6} = 2$

19. $\dfrac{\ln 5}{\ln 25} = \dfrac{1}{2}$ **21.** $\dfrac{\ln 14}{\ln 10} \approx 1.146$ **23.** Not defined   **25.** Not defined   **27.** $\dfrac{1}{x \ln 2}$ **29.** $2x \log_4 x + \dfrac{x}{\ln 4}$

31. $(\ln 10)10^x$ **33.** $\left(\dfrac{\ln 7}{2}\right)7^{x/2}$ **35.** $2x(\ln 16)16^{x^2}$ **37.** $\dfrac{4 \ln 10}{2\sqrt{4x+1}}10^{\sqrt{4x+1}}$

39. $10(2x-2)(\ln 3)3^{x^2-2x}$ **41.** $(\ln 2)^2 2^{(2^x)}2^x$ **43.** $\dfrac{4}{(\ln 3)(4x-2)}$ **45.** $\dfrac{12x}{(\ln 4)(2x^2-8)}$

47. $3[\log_4(x^2-9)]^2\left[\dfrac{2x}{(\ln 4)(x^2-9)}\right]$ **49.** $\dfrac{-1}{x(\ln x)^2}$

CHAPTER 12 REVIEW
EXERCISES, PAGE 842

1. $f'(x) = 2xe^{3x} + 3x^2 e^{3x}$ **3.** $f'(x) = \dfrac{2x}{x^2+1}$ **5.** $\dfrac{6}{2\sqrt{\ln(6x+8)}(6x+8)}$ **7.** $\dfrac{6\ln(3x+2)}{3x+2}$ **9.** 2

11. (a) No maximum value   **(b)** Minimum value is $f\left(\dfrac{1}{e}\right) = \dfrac{-1}{e}$ **13. (a)** After 29 minutes   **(b)** 0.003%

15. About 1737 years old   **17. (a)** About 46 years   **(b)** About 502 million   **19.** $12,068   **21.** About 8.4%
23. (a) $22,080   **(b)** $22,255   **25.** About $195

CHAPTER 13
SECTION 13–1, PAGE 854

1. $f(x) = \dfrac{1}{4}x^4 - \dfrac{1}{2}x^2 + 5x + C$ **3.** $f(x) = \dfrac{-1}{4x^4} + C$ **5.** False   **7.** False   **9.** False   **11.** $\dfrac{1}{5}x^5 + C$

13. $\dfrac{3}{5}x^{5/3} + C$ **15.** $14x + C$ **17.** $\dfrac{3}{2}x^2 - 6x + C$ **19.** $\dfrac{3}{2}x^4 - 4x^2 + C$ **21.** $\dfrac{1}{4}x^4 - \dfrac{1}{2}x^2 + C$

23. $\dfrac{-1}{4x^4} + C$ **25.** $\dfrac{2}{3}x^{3/2} - 4\sqrt{x} + C$ **27.** $6x^{2/3} + C$ **29.** $\dfrac{-1}{8x^2} + \dfrac{4}{x} + C$ **31.** $\dfrac{2}{3}\sqrt{x} - \dfrac{x^2}{10} + C$

33. $\dfrac{1}{3}x^3 - 2x^2 + C$ **35.** $\dfrac{2}{5}x^{5/2} + 2x^{3/2} + C$ **37.** $x + \dfrac{9}{x} + C$ **39.** $\dfrac{1}{3}x^3 + 2x^2 + 3x + C$

41. $\dfrac{1}{2}x^2 - 5x + C$ **43.** $\dfrac{1}{2}x^2 + \dfrac{4}{3}x^{3/2} + x + C$ **45.** $R(x) = -3x^2 + 200x$

47. $C(x) = \dfrac{1}{6}x^3 - \dfrac{1}{2}x^2 + 2x + 11$ **49.** Approximately 948,000

SECTION 13–2, PAGE 864

1. $y = 7x^3 - 7x^2 + 8x + C$ **3.** $y = 4x^2 - \ln|x| + C$ **5.** $f(x) = \dfrac{-1}{3x} + 8\ln|x| + C$ **7.** True   **9.** True

11. False   **13.** True   **15.** $f(x) = x^3 + 6x + 4$ **17.** $y = \dfrac{1}{2}x^2 + \dfrac{16}{x} - 32$ **19.** $y = 5x - \ln|x| + 13$

21. $y = 4e^{2x} + 10e^2$ **23.** $y = \dfrac{-1}{e^x} + 4$ **25.** $y = \dfrac{4}{3}x^3 + \ln|x| + \dfrac{20}{3}$ **27.** $f(x) = \dfrac{1}{3}x^3 + 2x - \dfrac{1}{x} + \dfrac{17}{3}$

29. $f(x) = \dfrac{2}{3}x^{3/2} + 3\ln|x| + \dfrac{13}{3}$ **31.** $y = \dfrac{1}{2}e^{2x} + 2e^x + x + C$ **33.** $f(x) = 7x^3 + 3x^2 + 4x + 7$

35. $y = 10x^2 - 36x + 40$ **37.** $h(t) = -16t^2 + 60t + 8$ **39. (a)** $v(t) = -t^2 - 16t + 80$

(b) 63 feet per second   **(c)** After 4 seconds   **(d)** $s(t) = -\dfrac{1}{3}t^3 - 8t^2 + 80t$ **(e)** $170\frac{2}{3}$ feet

41. (a) $C(x) = \dfrac{1}{12}x^3 - 12x^2 + 350x + 2314$ **(b)** 2314   **43.** $p = -80x + 9400$, where p is the price in pennies

SECTION 13-3,   PAGE 874

1. 20   **3.** -30 **5.** 12   **7.** $\dfrac{14}{3}$ **9.** $\dfrac{3}{10}$ **11.** 15   **13.** $\dfrac{8}{2} + \dfrac{27}{2} = \dfrac{35}{2}$ **15.** 1   **17.** $-\ln 4$ **19.** $-\ln 4$

21. $\dfrac{-4}{e^3} + 4e^2$ **23.** $\dfrac{152}{3}$ **25.** 260   **27.** $\dfrac{1}{4}\ln 4$ **29.** $0 = \dfrac{56}{3} - \dfrac{56}{3}$ **31.** 3   **33.** $\dfrac{92}{3}$ **35.** $\dfrac{20}{3} + 4\ln 3$

37. 5   **39.** 14   **41.** 1   **43.** -8 **45.** 27   **47.** (a) Increase by 9000   (b) Decrease by 7200   **49.** (a) 192 ft
(b) 0 ft; same height

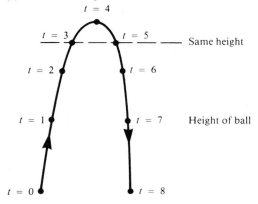

51. (a) Increases by $773\frac{1}{3}$ (b) Increases by 570

SECTION 13-4,   PAGE 892

1. $4 \cdot 1 = 4;\ \displaystyle\int_{-1}^{3} 1\,dx = 4$ **3.** $\left(\dfrac{1}{2}\right)(4)(6) = 12;\ \displaystyle\int_{-2}^{2}\left(\dfrac{3}{2}x + 3\right)dx = 12$ **5.** $\displaystyle\int_{-3}^{2} 4\,dx = 20$

7. $A(w) = 4(w - 2);\ A'(w) = 4 = f(w)$

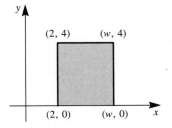

9. Area $= 2 \cdot 4 = 8 = \displaystyle\int_{-1}^{3} - (-2)dx$

11. Area $= \dfrac{1}{2}(4)(2) = 4;\ \displaystyle\int_{-2}^{2} -\left(-\dfrac{1}{2}x - 1\right)dx = 4$ **13.** Area $= 4 \cdot 2 + \dfrac{1}{2}(4)(4) = 16;\ \displaystyle\int_{1}^{5} (x + 1)dx = 16$

15. $\displaystyle\int_{2}^{7} (2x - 1)dx = 40$ **17.** $\displaystyle\int_{0}^{6} -(-4)dx = 24$ **19.** $\displaystyle\int_{2}^{6} - (5 - 3x)dx = 28$

21. $\int_0^3 (x^2 - 2x + 1)dx = 3$

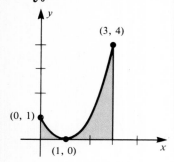

23. $\int_2^{10} \frac{2}{x}\, dx = 2 \ln 5$

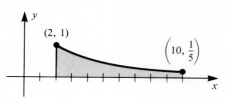

25. $\int_1^3 [(x^2 + 1) - (x - 4)]dx = \frac{44}{3}$

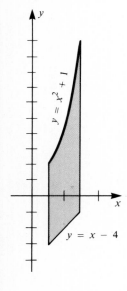

27. $\int_0^2 [(x^3 + 2x^2 + 5x + 3) - (x + 2)]dx = \frac{58}{3}$

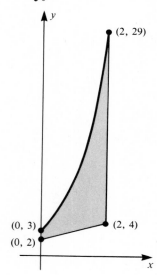

29. $A(w) = 12(w - 3) + \dfrac{1}{2}(w - 3)(4w - 12) = 2w^2 - 18$; $A'(w) = 4w = f(w)$

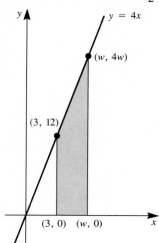

31. Area $= \dfrac{1}{2}(2)(2) + \dfrac{1}{2}(3)(3) = \dfrac{13}{2}$; $\displaystyle\int_{-2}^{0} -x\,dx + \int_{0}^{3} x\,dx = \dfrac{4}{2} + \dfrac{9}{2} = \dfrac{13}{2}$

33. Area $= (3)(6) + \dfrac{1}{2}(6)(2) = 24$; $\displaystyle\int_{-3}^{3}\left(\dfrac{1}{3}x + 2\right) - (-2)\,dx = 24$

35. $\displaystyle\int_{1}^{2} -(3x - 6)\,dx + \int_{2}^{4} (3x - 6)\,dx = \dfrac{15}{2}$

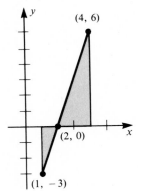

37. $\int_{-3}^{-1} [(x^2 + x + 2) - (3x + 5)]dx + \int_{-1}^{0} (3x + 5) - (x^2 + x + 2)dx = \dfrac{32}{3} + \dfrac{5}{3} = \dfrac{37}{3}$

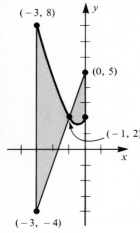

(-3, 8)

(0, 5)

(-1, 2)

(-3, -4)

39. $\int_{2}^{5} ((x - 3) - (x^2 - 6x + 7))dx = \int_{2}^{5} (-x^2 + 7x - 10)dx = 4.5$

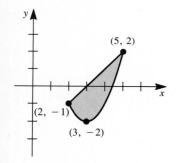

(5, 2)

(2, -1)

(3, -2)

41. $\int_{-1}^{0} (x^3 + 3) - (x + 3)dx + \int_{0}^{1} (x + 3) - (x^3 + 3)dx = \dfrac{1}{4} + \dfrac{1}{4} = \dfrac{1}{2}$

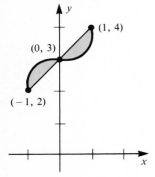

(1, 4)

(0, 3)

(-1, 2)

43. $\int_1^4 \dfrac{1}{x}\, dx = \ln|x| \Big|_1^4 = \ln 4 - \ln 1 = \ln 4$

$\int_2^8 \dfrac{1}{x}\, dx = \ln|x| \Big|_2^8 = \ln 8 - \ln 2 = \ln \dfrac{8}{2} = \ln 4$

45. $\int_1^3 \dfrac{1}{x}\, dx = \ln 3;\ \int_{1/3}^1 \dfrac{1}{x}\, dx = \ln 1 - \ln \dfrac{1}{3} = -\ln \dfrac{1}{3} = -\ln 3^{-1} = \ln 3$

47. $\int_1^9 \dfrac{1}{x}\, dx = \ln 9 = \ln 3^2 = 2\ln 3;\ \int_1^3 \dfrac{1}{x}\, dx = \ln 3$

49. $A(w) = 10(w - 2)$
$A'(w) = 10 = -f(w)$

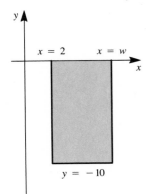

51. $A(w) = (6w - 8w) + \frac{1}{2}(6 - w)(48 - 8w)$
$\qquad\quad = 144 - 4w^2$
$A'(w) = -8w$

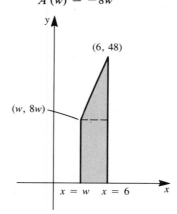

53. (a) $x = 12$ (b) $17\frac{1}{3} = \int_{10}^{12} MR(x) - MC(x)\, dx$ **55.** $A = \int_a^b -f(x)\, dx$, or $A = -\int_a^b f(x)\, dx$

SECTION 13–5,   PAGE 909

1. $\dfrac{10}{3}$ **3.** $\dfrac{1}{4}\left(2 - \dfrac{2}{e^2}\right) = \dfrac{1}{2} - \dfrac{1}{2e^2}$ **5.** $\dfrac{1}{4} \cdot \dfrac{1}{9} = \dfrac{1}{36}$ **7.** (a) 35   (b) 6650   (c) 10,325   (d) 3675

9. (a) 3000   (b) 630,000   (c) 810,000   (d) 180,000   **11.** (a) 180   (b) 5400   **13.** $405\frac{1}{3}$ **15.** $p = 1.5$

17. (a) $D'(x) = -2x - 1$, which is negative if $x \geq 0$; greater demand means lower prices.   (b) $S'(x) = 2x + 1 > 0$ for $x \geq 0$; more units will be available at higher prices.   (c) $p = 41$ **19.** (a) It is their total income.   (b) It is the total value of the goods to the producers.   (c) $\int_0^{x_1} (p_1 - S(x))\, dx = \int_0^{x_1} p_1\, dx - \int_0^{x_1} S(x)\, dx = p_1 x_1 - \int_0^{x_1} S(x)\, dx$

21. (a) $600(e^{6/20} - e^{3/20})$ thousand dollars $\approx \$112,800$ (b) $600(e^{9/20} - e^{6/20})$ thousand dollars $\approx \$131,000$
23. $120(1 - e^{-2})$ thousand gallons $\approx 103,760$ gallons   **25.** (a) 0.55   (b) 0.63

27. (a) $\dfrac{1}{5}[245(e^{0.1} - 1)] \approx 5.15$ (billion)   (b) $\dfrac{1}{5} \cdot 245(e^{0.2} - e^{0.1}) \approx 5.7$ (billion)   **29.** (a) $45\frac{1}{3}$ ft/sec
(b) $67\frac{1}{3}$ ft/sec

SECTION 13-6, PAGE 923

1. (a) 8 **(b)** 8 **3. (a)** 9 **(b)** 9 **5. (a)** 8.5 **(b)** 8.625 **7.** $\int_1^3 (2x^2 - 3x)dx = \dfrac{16}{3} = 5\dfrac{1}{3}$ **(a)** 5

(b) 5.25 **9.** $\int_1^5 \dfrac{1}{x^2}\,dx = \dfrac{4}{5}$ **(a)** 0.625 **(b)** 0.735 **11.** $\int_1^3 \dfrac{1}{x^3}\,dx = \dfrac{4}{9} = 0.444\ldots$ **(a)** 0.360 **(b)** 0.417

13. $\int_0^{60} x^2\,dx = 72{,}000$; actual sum is 73,810 **15.** 288π **17. (a)** 1.0898 **(b)** 1.0963 **19. (a) (i)** 1.35

(ii) 1.377 **(b) (i)** 1.377 **(ii)** 1.384 **21.** 2.949 **23.** $\dfrac{64\pi}{3}$ **25.** $\dfrac{522\pi}{5}$ **27.** $\dfrac{4}{3}\pi R^3$ **29.** $\approx \$43{,}645$

31. $\approx \$15{,}319$ **33.** 3192 **35.** \$75,920,000

CHAPTER 13 REVIEW EXERCISES, PAGE 925

1. $2x^3 - \dfrac{6}{x} + C$ **3.** $\dfrac{1}{7}x^7 - \dfrac{2}{3}x^3 - \dfrac{1}{x} + C$ **5.** $2x^2 + 8\ln|x| + C$ **7.** $\dfrac{1}{6}e^{6x} - \dfrac{1}{4}e^{-4x} + C$

9. $\dfrac{1}{2}e^{2x} + 8e^x + 16x + C$ **11.** 204 **13.** $\dfrac{1}{2}(e^8 - 17)$ **15.** 5 **17.** $4 + 2 = 6$

19. $y = 4x^4 - 6x^2 + 9x - 3$ **21.** $y = 2x^3 - x^2 + 4x + 9$ **23. (a)** $v(t) = -9.8t + 30$
(b) $h(t) = -4.9t^2 + 30t + 2$ **25. (a)** 10 **(b)** $5\frac{1}{3}$ **27.** 12 **29.** 39 **31.** $21\frac{1}{12}$
33. (a) $S'(x) = 2x + 4 > 0$ for $x \geq 0$ **(b)** 36 **35.** 2 **37.** 0.40 **39.** \$84,160.79

CHAPTER 14

SECTION 14-1, PAGE 941

1. $\dfrac{1}{20}(5x + 1)^4 + C$ **3.** $\dfrac{1}{5}(2x^2 + 3x)^5 + C$ **5.** $(7u^2 + 3u - 2)^3 + C$ **7.** $\dfrac{1}{24}(4x^3 - 6x)^4 + C$

9. $\ln|4x - 3| + C$ **11.** $\dfrac{2}{3}e^{x^3} + C$ **13.** $4(x^2 - x + 5)^{1/2} + C$ **15.** $\ln|e^x - 7| + C$ **17.** $-(1 + \ln x)^{-1} + C$

19. $-\dfrac{1}{2}e^{1/x^2} + C$ **21.** $\int_5^{45} \dfrac{1}{2u}\,du = \dfrac{1}{2}(\ln 45 - \ln 5) = \ln 3$ **23.** $\int_1^9 \dfrac{1}{2}e^u\,du = \dfrac{1}{2}(e^9 - e)$ **25.** $-\dfrac{1}{2}e^{-x^2} + C$

27. $\dfrac{2}{45}(3x - 4)^{5/2} + \dfrac{8}{27}(3x - 4)^{3/2} + C$ **29.** $\dfrac{1}{10}(x^2 + 5)^5 - \dfrac{5}{8}(x^2 + 5)^4 + C$ **31.** $25 - \ln 26$

33. $C(x) = \dfrac{1}{3}(x^2 + 9)^{3/2} + 141$ **35.** $\sqrt{65} - 1$ **37.** $10(\ln 50 - \ln 10) = 10\ln 5$

SECTION 14-2, PAGE 950

1. $\dfrac{1}{2}x^2\ln x - \dfrac{1}{4}x^2 + C$ **3.** $\dfrac{1}{5}xe^{5x} - \dfrac{1}{25}e^{5x} + C$ **5.** $\dfrac{1}{2}x^2e^{2x} - \dfrac{1}{2}xe^{2x} + \dfrac{1}{4}e^{2x} + C$ **7.** $\dfrac{1}{4}x^4\ln x - \dfrac{1}{16}x^4 + C$

9. $\dfrac{1}{3}x^3(\ln x)^2 - \dfrac{2}{9}x^3\ln x + \dfrac{2}{27}x^3 + C$ **11.** $\dfrac{1}{2}x^2e^{x^2} - \dfrac{1}{2}e^{x^2} + C$ **13.** $2e^{x^2} + C$ **15.** $-\dfrac{1}{x}\ln x - \dfrac{1}{x} + C$

17. $\dfrac{2}{e} - \dfrac{3}{e^2}$

SECTION 14-3,   PAGE 959

1. $\dfrac{1}{2}$ **3.** e^2 **5.** $\dfrac{1}{2}$ **7.** No finite area   **9.** e^{-4}; this is the area of the region under the curve $y = e^{-x}$, bounded

below by the x-axis and bounded on the left by the line $x = 4$.   **11.** $\dfrac{1}{3}$; this is the area of the region above the x-axis,

under the curve $y = \dfrac{1}{x^4}$, and bounded on the left by the line $x = 1$.   **13.** $\dfrac{1}{4}$; this is the area of the region above the x-

axis, under the curve $y = e^{4x}$, and bounded on the right by the y-axis.   **15.** This integral diverges; the region that is above

the x-axis, under the curve $y = \dfrac{1}{\sqrt{x}}$, and bounded on the left by the line $x = 4$ does not have finite area.   **17.** Diverges

19. $\dfrac{1}{3}$ **21.** Diverges   **23.** 0.435   **25.** 18   **27.** Approximately \$17 million (The first \$2 million is not *spent* in the

state; the initial amount spent is \$1.8 million.)

SECTION 14-4,   PAGE 965

1. $\dfrac{1}{10} \ln \left| \dfrac{x-5}{x+5} \right| + C$ **3.** $\dfrac{-5}{12} \ln \left| \dfrac{x-6}{x+6} \right| + C$ **5.** $\dfrac{-2}{9(3x-2)} + \dfrac{1}{9}\ln|3x-2| + C$

7. $x\sqrt{x^2+25} + 25 \ln|x + \sqrt{x^2+25}| + C$ **9.** $\dfrac{3}{4} \ln \left| \dfrac{x}{8-2x} \right| + C$ **11.** $\dfrac{6}{5} \ln|x + \sqrt{x^2+4}| + C$

13. $\dfrac{x+2}{2} \sqrt{(x+2)^2+25} + \dfrac{25}{2} \ln|x+2 + \sqrt{(x+2)^2+25}| + C$

15. $\dfrac{1}{2}\left[\dfrac{2x+1}{2}\right]\sqrt{(2x+1)^2+100} + 25 \ln|2x+1 + \sqrt{(2x+1)^2+100}| + C$ **17.** $\dfrac{1}{3} \ln \left| \dfrac{x}{x+3} \right| + C$

19. $3\left[\dfrac{-2}{x-2} + \ln|x-2|\right] + C$ **21.** $10 + \dfrac{9}{2}(\ln 9 - \ln 3)$ **23.** $\dfrac{\sqrt{15}}{4} - \dfrac{\sqrt{3}}{2}$ **25.** $30 - \dfrac{15}{2} \ln 45 + \dfrac{15}{2} \ln 25$

SECTION 14-5,   PAGE 971
1. 1.10321   **3.** 0.772455   **5.** 3.25989   **7.** 0.744368   **9.** Exercises 1, 2, 3, 4, and 5   **11.** 1.09894
13. 3.14159   **15.** 3.05202   **17.** 0.746855   **19.** (a) $21\frac{1}{3}$ (b) $21\frac{1}{3}$ (c) $21\frac{1}{3}$
21. Simpson's rule is exact for polynomials of degree 2.   **23.** (a) 1.68889   (b) 1.62220   (c) 1.61311

CHAPTER 14 REVIEW
EXERCISES,   PAGE 972

1. $\dfrac{1}{3}e^{x^3} + C$ **3.** $\dfrac{1}{5} \ln|5x+8| + C$ **5.** $\ln|\ln x| + C$ **7.** $\dfrac{x^2}{2} \ln(3x) - \dfrac{x^2}{4} + C$ **9.** $\dfrac{1}{2}e^{(x^2+1)} + C$

11. $\dfrac{x^2}{2} \ln x^2 - \dfrac{x^2}{2} + C$ **13.** Divergent   **15.** $\dfrac{1}{2e^2} + \dfrac{1}{e}$ **17.** $\dfrac{1}{40} \ln \left| \dfrac{x-5}{x+5} \right| + C$

19. $\ln|(x+1) + \sqrt{x^2+2x+10}| + C$ **21.** $\dfrac{1}{6} \ln \left| \dfrac{x}{x+6} \right| + C$ **23.** 1.46371

CHAPTER 15
SECTION 15–1,   PAGE 982

1. 11   **3.** 6   **5.** $8e^3$

7.

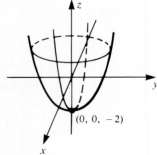

$(0, 0, -2)$

9.

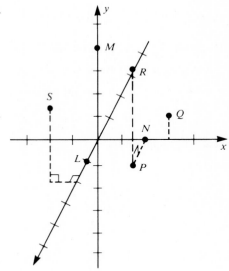

11.

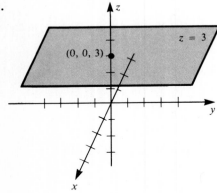

$z = 3$

$(0, 0, 3)$

13. 207,200   **15.** 1760   **17.** 240

SECTION 15-2,   PAGE 992

1. $\frac{\partial f}{\partial x}(x, y) = 2x + 3y; \frac{\partial f}{\partial y}(x, y) = 3x$ **3.** $\frac{\partial z}{\partial y} = 10x^2y + 2; \frac{\partial z}{\partial x} = 10xy^2$

5. $f_x(x, y) = \frac{y^2 - x^2}{(x^2 + y^2)^2}; f_y(x, y) = \frac{-2xy}{(x^2 + y^2)^2}$

7. $\frac{\partial f}{\partial x}(x, y, z) = \frac{2xy}{z^3}; \frac{\partial f}{\partial y}(x, y, z) = \frac{x^2}{z^3}; \frac{\partial f}{\partial z}(x, y, z) = -\frac{3x^2y}{z^4}$

9. $\frac{\partial w}{\partial x} = \frac{y}{xy + yz^2}; \frac{\partial w}{\partial y} = \frac{x + z^2}{xy + yz^2}; \frac{\partial w}{\partial z} = \frac{2yz}{xy + yz^2}$

11. $\frac{\partial f}{\partial x}(x, y) = 6x^2y; \frac{\partial f}{\partial y}(x, y) = 2x^3; \frac{\partial^2 f}{\partial y \partial x}(x, y) = 6x^2; \frac{\partial^2 f}{\partial x \partial y}(x, y) = 6x^2; \frac{\partial^2 f}{\partial x^2}(x, y) = 12xy; \frac{\partial^2 f}{\partial y^2}(x, y) = 0$

13. $\frac{\partial f}{\partial x}(x, y) = 4xy - 3y^2; \frac{\partial f}{\partial y}(x, y) = 2x^2 - 6xy; \frac{\partial^2 f}{\partial y \partial x}(x, y) = 4x - 6y; \frac{\partial^2 f}{\partial x \partial y}(x, y) = 4x - 6y; \frac{\partial^2 f}{\partial x^2}(x, y) = 4y;$

$\frac{\partial^2 f}{\partial y^2}(x, y) = -6x$

15. $\frac{\partial f}{\partial x}(x, y) = 4xe^{x^2 + y}; \frac{\partial f}{\partial y}(x, y) = 2e^{x^2 + y}; \frac{\partial^2 f}{\partial y \partial x}(x, y) = 4xe^{x^2 + y}; \frac{\partial^2 f}{\partial x \partial y}(x, y) = 4xe^{x^2 + y};$

$\frac{\partial^2 f}{\partial x^2}(x, y) = 4e^{x^2 + y} + 8x^2e^{x^2 + y}; \frac{\partial^2 f}{\partial y^2}(x, y) = 2e^{x^2 + y}$

17. $\frac{\partial f}{\partial x}(x, y) = 2 + 2xye^{x^2y}; \frac{\partial f}{\partial y}(x, y) = x^2e^{x^2y}; \frac{\partial^2 f}{\partial y \partial x}(x, y) = 2xe^{x^2y} + 2x^3ye^{x^2y}; \frac{\partial^2 f}{\partial x \partial y}(x, y) = 2xe^{x^2y} + 2x^3ye^{x^2y};$

$\frac{\partial^2 f}{\partial x^2}(x, y) = 2ye^{x^2y} + 4x^2y^2e^{x^2y}; \frac{\partial^2 f}{\partial y^2}(x, y) = x^4e^{x^2y}$

19. $f_x(2, 3) = 12; f_y(2, 3) = 4; f_{xy}(2, 3) = 4; f_{xx}(2, 3) = 6; f_{yy}(2, 3) = 0$
21. $f_x(-1, 0) = 0; f_y(-1, 0) = -1; f_{xy}(-1, 0) = 1; f_{xx}(-1, 0) = 0; f_{yy}(-1, 0) = 0$

23. $f_x(e, 1) = 2; f_y(e, 1) = e; f_{xy}(e, 1) = 1; f_{xx}(e, 1) = \frac{1}{e}; f_{yy}(e, 1) = -e$ **25. (a)** 2500

(b) The marginal productivity of labor $= f_x(x, y) = \frac{5}{2}x^{-3/4}y^{3/4}$. The marginal productivity of capital $= f_y(x, y) = \frac{15}{2}x^{1/4}y^{-1/4}$.

(c) $f_x(16, 625) = \frac{1250}{32}; f_y(16, 625) = 3$ **(d)** Production will increase by approximately $\frac{1250}{32}$ units.   **(e)** Production will

decrease by approximately 3 units.   **27. (a)** 10,750   **(b)** $\frac{\partial R}{\partial x}(x, y) = -6x + 400; \frac{\partial R}{\partial y}(x, y) = -4y + 500$

(c) $\frac{\partial R}{\partial x}(10, 15) = 340; \frac{\partial R}{\partial y}(10, 15) = 440$ **(d)** Revenue will increase by approximately 340 units.   **(e)** Revenue will

decrease by approximately 440 units.

SECTION 15-3,   PAGE 1000

1. $(0, 0)$ **3.** $(0, 0)$ **5.** $(-1, 0)$ and $(3, 0)$ **7.** f has a relative minimum at $(2, -1)$.

9. f has a relative minimum at $(-2, -2)$.   **11.** f has a relative minimum at $\left(\frac{27}{2}, 5\right)$ and a saddle point at $\left(\frac{3}{2}, 1\right)$.

13. f has a relative minimum at $(1, 1)$ and a saddle point at $\left(-\frac{2}{3}, -\frac{2}{3}\right)$.   **15.** $x = 10, y = 5$

17. $x = 150, y = 100$ **19.** 4 replacements for x, 6 replacements for y

SECTION 15-4,   PAGE 1009

1. $\frac{111}{5}$ **3.** 18   **5.** 203   **7.** 612   **9.** 21   **11.** 150 units of labor; 225 units of capital

13. 81 from X, 45 from Y   **15.** 7 inspections at X, 15 at Y   **17.** \$4040 on X, \$15,960 on Y
19. Base is 20.7 feet by 20.7 feet, height is 14.5 feet (to nearest tenth)

SECTION 15–5,   PAGE 1017

1. $6x^3y^2 - 6xy + f(x)$ **3.** $x \ln|y| + f(x)$ **5.** $63y + 15$ **7.** $9x^2 - 12x + 21$ **9.** 1   **11.** -1 **13.** 1600
15. 4   **17.** 0   **19.** 4   **21.** 32   **23.** 140   **25.** 4   **27.** 30

**CHAPTER 15 REVIEW
EXERCISES,   PAGE 1019**

1. $f(1, -2) = -23; f_x(1, -2) = -14; f_y(1, -2) = 28; f_{xx}(1, -2) = 2; f_{yy}(1, -2) = -20; f_{xy}(1, -2) = 16$
3. $f(0, 2) = 1; f_x(0, 2) = 4; f_y(0, 2) = 0; f_{xx}(0, 2) = 16; f_{yy}(0, 2) = 0; f_{xy}(0, 2) = 4$

5. $f(-4, 2) = -2; f_x(-4, 2) = \dfrac{1}{2}; f_y(-4, 2) = 1; f_{xx}(-4, 2) = 0; f_{yy}(-4, 2) = -1; f_{xy}(-4, 2) = -\dfrac{1}{4}$

7. $f(2, 4) = 10; f_x(2, 4) = 5; f_y(2, 4) = \dfrac{8}{5}; f_{xx}(2, 4) = 0; f_{yy}(2, 4) = \dfrac{18}{125}; f_{xy}(2, 4) = \dfrac{4}{5}$

9. $(3, -2)$ is a saddle point.   **11.** $(0, 0)$ is a saddle point; f has a relative minimum at $(2, 2)$.

13. Maximum is 50; minimum is -50 **15.** 4   **17.** $\dfrac{9}{4}$ **19.** $2e - 2$ **21.** 36

APPENDIX A
SECTION A–1,   PAGE 1025

1. -13 **3.** 23   **5.** -30 **7.** -35 **9.** -5 **11.** -7 **13.** -10 **15.** -8 **17.** 3   **19.** $\frac{9}{5}$ **21.** $\frac{17}{12}$
23. $-\frac{11}{12}$ **25.** $\frac{13}{20}$ **27.** $-\frac{1}{35}$ **29.** $\frac{2}{3}$ **31.** $\frac{5}{14}$ **33.** $\frac{1}{15}$ **35.** $\frac{8}{15}$ **37.** $\frac{12}{35}$ **39.** $\frac{20}{33}$ **41.** $\frac{4}{3}$ **43.** $\frac{15}{8}$
45. $\frac{171}{40}$ **47.** $-6a - 22b$ **49.** $-10a - 50b$

SECTION A–2,   PAGE 1029

1. -3 **3.** 4   **5.** 2   **7.** $\frac{1}{2}$ **9.** $-\frac{7}{4}$ **11.** $\frac{20}{11}$ **13.** $\frac{15}{23}$ **15.** 6   **17.** (a) \$242   (b) \$412   (c) 950 miles
19. (a) \$14.28   (b) \$44.10   (c) 61 lb

SECTION A–3,   PAGE 1032

1.

3.

5. (a) x-coordinate is negative, y-coordinate is positive.   (b) x- and y-coordinates are both negative.
(c) x-coordinate is positive, y-coordinate is negative.

7.

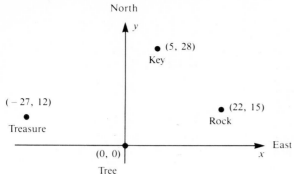

North

y

● (5, 28)
Key

(−27, 12)
●
Treasure

● (22, 15)
Rock

East

(0, 0)
Tree

x

SECTION A–4,   PAGE 1040

1. (a) $9 - 3$ is a positive number 6, so true.   (b) $4 - 0$ is a positive number 4, so true.   (c) $-5 - 0$ is not a positive number, so false.   (d) $-3 - (-15)$ is a positive number 12, so true.   (e) $\frac{5}{6} - \frac{2}{3}$ is a positive number $\frac{1}{6}$, so true.
3. $x < \frac{9}{2}$ **5.** $x \geq -16$ **7.** $x > -3$

9. ●————→   5

11. ←————○   −9

13. ←————————○   −4

15. ←————○ $\frac{7}{9}$

17. ○————○   −7 $\frac{17}{3}$

19. ○————○   2   8

21. $(-\infty, -1]$ **23.** $(-\infty, \frac{1}{9}]$ **25.** $(-13, -\frac{17}{4}]$ **27.** $x \leq -\frac{1}{2}$ **29.** $[-11, -\frac{23}{3})$ **31.** 8, 9, or 10
33. 20, 21, 22, 23, 24, or 25

SECTION A–5,   PAGE 1048

1. $2x^3 + 5x^2 + 1$ **3.** $4x^3 - 5x + 5$ **5.** $x^3 - 7x^2 + 3x + 7$ **7.** $4x + 5$ **9.** $2x + 4$ **11.** $-4x - 16$
13. $x^2 - x - 6$ **15.** $3x^3 + 11x^2 + 5x - 3$ **17.** $4x^5 - 2x^4 + 6x^3 + x + 1$ **19.** $x(x + 3)$ **21.** $2x^2(x - 2)$
23. $(x + 5)(x + 1)$ **25.** $(x + 3)(x - 2)$ **27.** $(2x - 3)(x + 2)$ **29.** $(2x - 1)(2x + 3)$

31. $(4x - 3)(x - 2)$ **33.** $x = -3, 1$ **35.** $x = \frac{3}{2}, -1$ **37.** $x = \frac{1 \pm \sqrt{1 + 24}}{4}, x = \frac{3}{2}, -1$

39. $x = \frac{11 \pm \sqrt{121 - 4(4)(-3)}}{8}, x = \frac{11 \pm 13}{8}, x = 3, \frac{-1}{4}$ **41.** $x = \frac{-2 \pm \sqrt{-8}}{2}$. There are no real solutions.

43. $x = \frac{-9 \pm \sqrt{81 - 4(-9)(4)}}{-18}, x = \frac{-9 \pm 15}{-18}, x = \frac{-1}{3}, \frac{4}{3}$

45. $x = \frac{-1 \pm \sqrt{1 - 4(-2)(1)}}{-4}, x = \frac{-1 \pm 3}{-4}, x = \frac{-1}{2}, 1$

47. $\frac{x^2 + x - 1}{x - 1}$ **49.** $\frac{-x}{x + 2}$ **51.** $\frac{(5x - 1)(3x + 2)}{(2x + 1)(4x - 1)}$ **53.** $\frac{5}{4x - 1}$ **55.** $\frac{(4x + 3)(2x + 1)}{4x(5x - 1)}$ **57.** $\frac{x(2x - 3)}{14}$

59. $\frac{6x - 2}{x(x - 1)}$ **61.** $\frac{9x^2 + 2x - 3}{(x - 1)(x + 1)}$ **63.** $\frac{-6x^2 + 1}{x(5x - 1)}$ **65.** $\frac{5x + 7}{x^2}$

SECTION A–6,   PAGE 1053

1. 25   **3.** 8   **5.** $3^6 = 729$ **7.** x^7 **9.** $3^8 = 6561$ **11.** x^6 **13.** $\frac{1}{3}$ **15.** $\frac{1}{27}$ **17.** $2^{-6} = \frac{1}{64}$
19. $x^{-4} = \frac{1}{x^4}$ **21.** $5^{-2} = \frac{1}{25}$ **23.** $x^{-2} = \frac{1}{x^2}$ **25.** 6   **27.** 4   **29.** 3   **31.** 4   **33.** 2   **35.** 36   **37.** $\frac{1}{2}$
39. Not defined   **41.** -2 **43.** 9   **45.** -9 **47.** 9   **49.** $\frac{-1}{2}$ **51.** $\frac{-1}{3}$

SECTION A–7,   PAGE 1060

1. (a) $f(2) = 13$ (b) $f(-4) = -5$ (c) $f\left(\dfrac{1}{3}\right) = 8$ **3.** (a) $y = -1$ (b) $y = 13$ (c) $y = 2$

5. All real numbers   **7.** All $x \neq 9$ **9.** All $x \geq 8$; $[8, \infty)$ **11.** All $x \geq -3$; $[-3, \infty)$ **13.** All real numbers
15. All real numbers   **17.** $-1 \leq x \leq 5$; $[-1, 5]$ **19.** $f(x) = x^2$ **21.** $f(x) = 3x + 2$ **23.** $f(x) = x^2 - 9$

25. (a) $f(4) = 139$ (b) $f(-2) = 49$ (c) $f\left(\dfrac{1}{3}\right) = 7$ **27.** (a) $f(7) = 4$ (b) $f(-5) = 2$

(c) $f(-25)$ is not defined   **29.** All $x \neq 3, -3$ **31.** All $x \neq 3, -1$ **33.** All $x > 4$, $(4, \infty)$ **35.** All $x \geq 1$ and
all $x \leq -1$ **37.** $-2 \leq x \leq 1$ **39.** (a) $f(2) = 16$ (b) $f(-2) = -4$ (c) $f(4)$ is not defined
41. (a) $f(3) = 10$ (b) $f(-3)$ is not defined   (c) $f(4)$ is not defined   **43.** (a) $f(w) = 3w + 7$
(b) $f(x + 2) = 3x + 13$ **45.** (a) $f(x + 3) = -7x - 17$ (b) $f(x - 3) = -7x + 25$
47. (a) $f(2 + h) = h^2 - 4$ (b) $f(x + h) = (x + h)^2 - 4(x + h) = x^2 + (2h - 4)x + h^2 - 4h$
49. (a) $f(3 + h) = 2h^2 + 8h + 11$ (b) $f(x + w) = 2(x + w)^2 - 4(x + w) + 5$ **51.** (a) $f(x) = 3 + 0.5x$
(b) \$7   (c) 14 rides   **53.** (a) $R(x) = 2.5x$ (b) 160 bars   **55.** $A = \pi r^2$ **57.** $V = x^3$

SECTION A–8,   PAGE 1078

1. $R(p) = (300 - \frac{1}{6}p)p = 300p - \frac{1}{6}p^2$ **3.** Up; $5 > 0$ **5.** Down; $-6 < 0$ **7.** $(3, -2)$ **9.** $(-2, -11)$

11.

13.

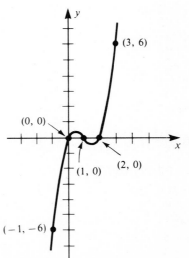

15. $(1, 13)$ **17.** $\dfrac{-7 \pm \sqrt{49 + 480}}{12} = \dfrac{-7 \pm 23}{12} = \dfrac{-5}{2}$ and $\dfrac{4}{3}$ **19.** $\dfrac{-8 \pm \sqrt{64 + 48}}{-6} = \dfrac{-8 \pm 4\sqrt{7}}{-6} = \dfrac{4 + 2\sqrt{7}}{3}$

and $\dfrac{4 - 2\sqrt{7}}{3} \approx 3.097$ and -0.431 **21.** No real zeros

23.

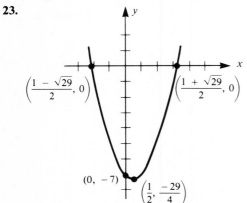

25.

27.

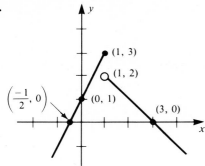

29.

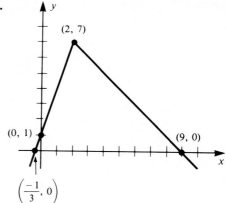

31.

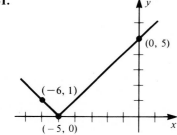

33.

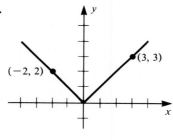

35.

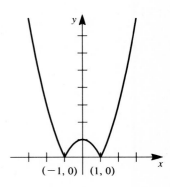

37. (a) 16%   **(b)** 16%   **(c)** $x = \frac{1}{2}$. Interpretation: The lowest 50% of families account for $33\frac{1}{3}$% of the total income.

39. (a) 17.4%   **(b)** 42.6%   **(c)** $x = \dfrac{-2 + \sqrt{40}}{6} \approx 0.721$. Interpretation: The lowest 72% of the families earn

approximately 60% of the income.

41. $A(t) = \begin{cases} 80 - 30t & 0 \le t < 2 \\ 80 - 30(t - 2) & 2 \le t < 4 \\ 80 - 30(t - 4) & 4 \le t < 6 \\ 80 - 30(t - 6) & 6 \le t < 8 \end{cases}$

43. (a) $C(x) = \begin{cases} 0.05x & 0 \le x \le 20 \\ 1 + 0.04(x - 20) & 20 < x \end{cases}$ **(b)** \$2.20   **(c)** 70 copies   **45.** $R = x\sqrt{400 - x}$

47. (a) $2p + x = 80$ **(b)** $R = 80p - 2p^2$ **(c)** $R = -\frac{1}{2}x^2 + 40x$ **49.** $P = 2w + \frac{60}{w}$

GLOSSARY

A

ABSCISSA (p. 1030)
The x-coordinate.

ABSOLUTE VALUE OF x (p. 1077)
$|x| = x$ if $x \geq 0$, $|x| = -x$ if $x < 0$.

ACCELERATION (p. 664) Word often used in interpretating the second derivative.

ADDITION OF MATRICES (p. 94)
Two matrices of the same size are added by adding corresponding entries of the two given matrices.

ADDITION OF POLYNOMIALS (p. 1041) Polynomials are added by adding the coefficients of equal powers of x.

ADDITIVE CONSTANT OF INTEGRATION (p. 848) If $g'(x) = f(x)$, then $\int f(x)\, dx = g(x) + C$; C is called the additive constant of integration.

AMORTIZATION (p. 552) The amortization method is a way to repay interest-bearing debt by a series of equal periodic payments. Each payment pays all the interest for that time period and repays part of the principal.

AMOUNT OF AN ANNUITY (p. 524)
The value of all payments plus all accumulated interest. It is also called the future value.

AMOUNT OF A SIMPLE INTEREST LOAN (p. 544) The total paid by the borrower; the principal plus interest. *Future value* is another term for amount.

ANNUAL DEPRECIATION (p. 29)
The decrease in the value of an item that occurs in one year.

ANNUITY (p. 543) A series of equal payments paid at equal time intervals.

ANTIDERIVATIVE (p. 847)
If $g'(x) = f(x)$, then g is called an antiderivative of f.

ANTIDERIVATIVE OF $1/x$ (p. 861)
$\int (1/x)\, dx = \ln |x| + C$.

ANTIDERIVATIVE OF e^{ax} (p. 862)
$\int e^{ax}\, dx = (1/a)e^{ax} + C$.

ANTIDIFFERENTIATION (p. 848)
The process of finding an antiderivative for a function.

APPROXIMATING AN INTEGRAL BY A SUMMATION (p. 914)
If f is continuous on $[a, b]$, then $\int_a^b f(x)\, dx$ can be approximated by $(f(c_1) + f(c_2) + \cdots + f(c_n))$ $(b - a)/n$, where c_i is some point in the ith subinterval of length $(b - a)/n$ from a to b.

APPROXIMATING A SUMMATION BY AN INTEGRAL (p. 916) A technique to approximate a sum of the form $f(1) + f(2) + \cdots + f(n)$ by $\int_0^n f(x)\, dx$.

AREA BETWEEN CURVES (p. 886)
If $f(x) \geq g(x)$ on $[a, b]$, then the area bounded above by the graph of f, below by the graph of g, on the left by the line $x = a$, and on the right by the line $x = b$ is given by $\int_a^b (f(x) - g(x))\, dx$.

AUGMENTED MATRIX (p. 61)
A matrix that represents a system of equations. It includes the numbers on the right-hand side of the equations as well as the coefficients of a linear system.

AVERAGE COST FUNCTION (p. 647)
The cost of producing x items divided by the number of items: $AC(x) = C(x)/x$.

AVERAGE RATE OF CHANGE (p. 565)
The average rate of change of the function f on the interval $[a, b]$ is $(f(b) - f(a))/(b - a)$.

AVERAGE VALUE OF A FUNCTION ON AN INTERVAL (p. 897)
The average value of f on $[a, b]$ is $1/(b - a) \int_a^b f(x)\, dx$.

AVERAGE VALUE OF $f(x, y)$ OVER A RECTANGLE (p. 1017)
$1/(\text{area of } R) \iint_R f$, where R is the rectangle.

B

BASE (p. 791) In the expression b^x the number b is called the base.

BASIC FEASIBLE SOLUTION (p. 196)
A feasible solution of a linear programming problem with k of the variables (except z) set to zero and with none of the slack variables or x's negative.

BASIC SOLUTION (pp. 194–195)
If a linear programming problem has k x's in the constraints, then a basic solution is obtained by setting k variables (except z) to zero and solving for the others.

BASIC VARIABLE (p. 198) The variables in a basic feasible solution of a linear programming problem that remain after the nonbasic variables have been set to zero.

BAYES' RULE (p. 384) Let E_1 and E_2 be mutually exclusive events whose union is the sample space. F is an event with $P(F) \neq 0$. Then, $P(E_1|F) = P(E_1 \cap F)/P(F)$.

BERNOULLI EXPERIMENT (p. 392)
The experiment is repeated a fixed number of times. Each trial has only two possible outcomes: success and failure. The possible outcomes are exactly the same for each trial. The probability of success remains the same for each trial. The trials are

independent. Only the number of successes is of interest, not the order in which they occur.

BICONDITIONAL (p. 616)
A statement of the form "p if and only if q."

BINOMIAL DISTRIBUTION (p. 496)
The probability distribution of a Bernoulli experiment of n repeated trials. The random variable X is the number of successes in n trials. The probabilities in the distribution are the probabilities of x successes in n trials.

BISECTION METHOD (p. 604)
A method for approximating the zeros of a continuous function.

BOOK VALUE (p. 29)   The value of an item after the depreciation has been deducted from the cost.

BOUNDARY OF A FEASIBLE REGION (p. 153)   The lines (or planes) that bound a feasible region. They are determined by the inequalities of the system of inequalities.

BOUNDED FEASIBLE REGION (p. 162)
A feasible region that has definite finite bounds.

BREAK-EVEN ANALYSIS (p. 27)   An analysis to determine the sales volume at which the revenues equal costs.

BREAK-EVEN POINT (p. 27)   The point (sales and revenue) at which costs equal revenues.

C

CANDIDATES TEST (p. 752)   The maximum and minimum values of a continuous function on an interval $[a, b]$ are among the numbers $f(a)$, $f(b), f(c_1), f(c_2), \ldots$, where the c_1, $c_2, \ldots$ are the critical numbers.

CAPITAL FORMATION (p. 904)
The total change in capital in a given period.

CARBON DATING (p. 833)   The process of determining the age of a fossil from its amount of C-14.

CARTESIAN COORDINATE SYSTEM (p. 1030)   The system for locating points in the plane by their coordinates (x, y).

CHAIN RULE (p. 654)   If $h(x)$ $= g(f(x))$, then $h'(x) = g'(f(x)) \cdot$ $f'(x)$, or $dy/dx = (dy/du)(du/dx)$.

CHAIN RULE WITH EXPONENTIAL FUNCTION (p. 803)   If $f(x) = e^{g(x)}$, then $f'(x) = e^{g(x)} \cdot g'(x)$.

CHAIN RULE WITH GENERAL EXPONENTIAL FUNCTIONS (p. 837)
If $f(x) = b^{g(x)}$, then $f'(x) = b^{g(x)} (\ln b)$ $g'(x)$.

CHAIN RULE WITH GENERAL LOGARITHMIC FUNCTIONS (p. 840)
If $f(x) = \log_b g(x)$, then $f'(x)$ $= g'(x)/(g(x) \ln b)$.

CHAIN RULE WITH NATURAL LOGARITHM FUNCTION (p. 824)
If $f(x) = \ln (g(x))$, then $f'(x)$ $= g'(x)/g(x)$.

CHANGE OF LIMITS OF INTEGRATION FOR DEFINITE INTEGRALS (p. 938)   If $u = g(x)$, then $\int_a^b f(g(x)) \, g'(x) \, dx = \int_{g(a)}^{g(b)} f(u) \, du$.

CHANGE OF SIGN (p. 603)   If f is defined on an interval I and there are two numbers x_1 and x_2 in I with $f(x_1) > 0$ and $f(x_2) < 0$, then we say that f changes sign on I.

CLOSED AND BOUNDED INTERVAL (p. 751)   An interval of the form $[a, b]$; a continuous function has both a maximum value and a minimum value on such an interval.

CLOSED MODEL (p. 126)   In a closed model of an economy the industries in the system produce and use all the items among themselves.

COBB-DOUGLAS PRODUCTION FUNCTION (p. 976)   A function of the form $f(x, y) = Cx^a y^{1-a}$, where C and a are appropriate constants.

COEFFICIENT MATRIX (p. 61)
A matrix formed by using only the coefficients of a system of linear equations.

COLUMN MATRIX (p. 59)   An array composed of a single column of numbers.

COMBINATION (p. 302)
A combination is a subset of a set in which repetitions are not allowed and the order in which elements are arranged is not significant.

COMPLEMENT (p. 273)   The complement of a set A is the set of all elements in the universe that are not in A.

COMPOSITION OF FUNCTIONS (p. 652)   Successive evaluation of two functions, as in $f(g(x))$.

COMPOUND EVENTS (p. 343)   An event formed from two or more events.

COMPOUNDING PERIOD (p. 787)
How often interest is added to an account.

COMPOUND INTEREST (p. 531)
Interest is computed at specified periods of time, and the interest is added to the principal. This new total becomes the principal for the next time period.

CONCAVE DOWN (p. 710)   The graph of f is concave down on an interval I if $f''(x) < 0$ for all x in I.

CONCAVE UP (p. 710)   The graph of f is concave up on an interval I if $f''(x) > 0$ for all x in I.

CONDITIONAL PROBABILITY (p. 356)
The probability of an event E is sought. A related event F occurs, giving reason to change the sample space. The conditional probability of E given that the event F occurred is the probability of E taking into consideration the change brought about by F.

CONSISTENCY OF INFORMATION (p. 740)   The information obtained about behavior of f from (1) asymptotes, (2) sign-of-f', and (3) sign-of-f'' must be consistent.

CONSTANT-TIMES RULE (p. 632)   If $g(x) = c \cdot f(x)$, then $g'(x) = c \cdot f'(x)$.

CONSTRAINT (p. 1001) (Calculus) A condition that the variables being studied must satisfy, usually of the form $g(x, y) = C$ or $g(x, y, z) = C$.

CONSTRAINTS (p. 158) (Linear Programming) The restrictions imposed on a linear programming problem by a system of inequalities.

CONSUMER DEMAND MATRIX (p. 131) A matrix representing the amount of goods available to consumers.

CONSUMERS' SURPLUS (p. 899) The quantity $\int_0^{x_1} (D(x) - p_1) \, dx$, where the market price is p_1, the demand is x_1, and $D(x) = p$ is the price-demand equation.

CONTINUOUS AT A POINT (p. 596) A function f is continuous at c if $\lim_{x \to c} f(x) = f(c)$.

CONTINUOUS COMPOUNDING (p. 790) The phrase used when the interest is added onto an account instantaneously.

CONTINUOUS DATA (p. 426) For two different values of the data, all values between them are permissible values for the data.

CONTINUOUS ON AN INTERVAL (p. 598) A function f is continuous on an interval I if the function is continuous at each number in I.

CONTINUOUS VARIABLE (p. 459) A variable that represents continuous values of the data.

CONVERGENT INTEGRAL (p. 953) An improper integral with a finite value.

COORDINATE PLANES (p. 978) The three planes in three space of the form $x = 0$, $y = 0$, or $z = 0$; the yz-, xz-, and xy-coordinate planes, respectively.

CORNERS OF A FEASIBLE REGION (p. 153) The points in the feasible region where two boundaries meet.

COST-VOLUME FUNCTION (p. 25) A function that relates the number of items produced to the cost of production. The linear cost-volume function is of the form $C(x) = ax + b$, where a is the unit cost and b is the fixed cost.

CRITICAL NUMBER (p. 697) The number c in the domain of f is called a critical number of f if either $f'(c) = 0$ or $f'(c)$ does not exist.

CRITICAL POINT (p. 995) The point (a, b) is a critical point of $f(x, y)$ if both $\partial f/\partial x \, (a, b) = 0$ and $\partial f/\partial y \, (a, b) = 0$.

CUT POINT (p. 607) A point c is a cut point of the inequality $f(x) \leq 0$, $f(x) < 0, f(x) \geq 0$, or $f(x) > 0$ if $f(c) = 0$ or if f is not continuous at c.

D

DECREASING FUNCTION (p. 695) f is decreasing if whenever $x_1 < x_2$, then $f(x_1) > f(x_2)$.

DEFINITE INTEGRAL OF f FROM a TO b (p. 868) The number $g(b) - g(a)$, where $g'(x) = f(x)$ on the interval $[a, b]$.

DEPRECIATION (p. 29) The decline in value of an item over a period of time.

DERIVATIVE (p. 571) The derivative of f at a, written $f'(a)$, is given by $f'(a) = \lim_{\Delta x \to 0} f(a + \Delta x) - f(a)/\Delta x$.

DERIVATIVE OF A CONSTANT (p. 630) If $f(x) = c$, then $f'(x) = 0$.

DERIVATIVE OF A LINEAR FUNCTION (p. 572) If $f(x) = mx + b$, then $f'(x) = m$.

DERIVATIVE OF $f(x) = b^x$ (p. 837) If $f(x) = b^x$, then $f'(x) = b^x \ln b$.

DERIVATIVE OF $f(x) = e^x$ (p. 800) If $f(x) = e^x$, then $f'(x) = e^x$.

DERIVATIVE OF $f(x) = \ln x$ (p. 820) If $f(x) = \ln x$, then $f'(x) = 1/x$.

DERIVATIVE OF $f(x) = \log_b x$ (p. 840) If $f(x) = \log_b x$, then $f'(x) = 1/(x \ln b)$.

DIAGONAL LOCATIONS (p. 65) The $(1, 1)$, $(2, 2)$, etc. locations in a matrix.

DIFFERENCE RULE (p. 636) If $h(x) = f(x) - g(x)$, then $h'(x) = f'(x) - g'(x)$.

DIFFERENTIAL (p. 685) If $y = f(x)$, then $dy = f'(x) \, dx$ is called the differential of y.

DIFFERENTIAL (p. 848) The dx in the integral, $\int f(x) \, dx$.

DIFFERENTIAL EQUATION (p. 855) An equation involving derivatives.

DIFFERENTIATION (p. 622) The process of computing $f'(x)$, given $f(x)$.

DISCOUNT RATE (p. 526) The fee for borrowing money in a simple discount loan. It is usually expressed as a percentage of the principal per year.

DISCRETE DATA (p. 426) The values of the data are exact, and for two different values there are some values between them that are not permissible values for the data.

DISCRETE VARIABLE (p. 459) A variable that can take on only discrete values.

DISJOINT SETS (p. 269) Two sets are disjoint if their intersection is empty; the sets have no elements in common.

DIVERGENT INTEGRAL (p. 953) An improper integral that does not have a finite value.

DOMAIN (p. 1054) The set A in the definition of function. If f is a function, the domain of f is the set of all numbers a such that $f(a)$ is defined.

DOT PRODUCT (p. 102) The dot product of a matrix row and a matrix column is a number obtained by multiplying the first numbers from both the row and column, then the second numbers from both, etc., then adding the results.

DOUBLE INTEGRAL (p. 1014) An integral of the form $\iint_R f$.

DOUBLING PERIOD (p. 809)   The time required for a quantity growing at an exponential rate to double.

DUAL PROBLEM (p. 247)   A matrix of the constraints (with no slack variables) and objective function of a standard minimum problem is transposed. This transposed matrix is interpreted as the matrix (without slack variables) of a standard maximum problem. The solution of the original problem is obtained from the solution of the resulting standard maximum problem.

E

EFFECTIVE RATE (p. 538)   The effective rate of an annual interest rate r compounded m times per year is the simple interest rate that produces the same amount of interest per year as the compound interest.

ELEMENT OF A MATRIX (p. 59)   The numbers in the array that form a matrix.

ELEMENT OF A SET (p. 265)   One of the objects in a set.

ELIMINATION METHOD (p. 41)   This method determines the solution to a system of equations by systematically eliminating a variable from some of the equations. This is done in a way that produces a simpler system of equations having the same solution as the original system.

EMPIRICAL PROBABILITY (p. 330)   The probability assigned to each outcome is the fraction of time (relative frequency) the outcome occurs.

EMPTY SET (p. 267)   A set that contains no elements.

EQUALITY CONSTRAINT (p. 223)   A constraint that is an equation.

EQUALLY LIKELY (p. 334)   Each outcome in a sample space has the same probability of occurring as any other outcome.

EQUAL MATRICES (p. 93)   The matrices are the same size, and corresponding entries are equal.

EQUAL SETS (p. 266)   Two sets are equal if they consist of exactly the same elements.

EQUATION OF TANGENT LINE (p. 614)   The equation of the line tangent to the graph of f at $(a, f(a))$, which can be written $y - f(a) = f'(a)(x - a)$.

EQUILIBRIUM (MARKOV PROCESS) (p. 406)   Another term for the steady state of a Markov process.

EQUILIBRIUM PRICE (p. 51)   The price at which the amount of a commodity willingly supplied is equal to the amount willingly demanded.

EQUIVALENT AUGMENTED MATRICES (p. 62)   Two augmented matrices are equal if one augmented matrix is obtained from a second by a series of row operations.

EQUIVALENT SYSTEMS (p. 43)   Two systems of linear equations are equivalent if they have exactly the same solutions.

ERROR BOUNDS (p. 510)   Limits above and below the proportion of a sample. The limits are $p + E$ and $p - E$, where $E = Z \times SE$ and Z is the z-score associated with the specified confidence level.

EVENT (p. 326)   A subset of outcomes.

EXCISE TAX (p. 777)   The tax levied on the producer of an item in the form of a fixed amount per item produced.

EXISTENCE OF THE LIMIT (p. 592) $\lim\limits_{x \to c} f(x) = L$ if and only if both $\lim\limits_{x \to c^-} f(x) = L$ and $\lim\limits_{x \to c^+} f(x) = L$.

EXPECTED VALUE (p. 468)   If a random variable X has the values $x_1, x_2, \ldots, x_n$ and corresponding probabilities $p_1, p_2, \ldots, p_n$, then the expected value of X, $E(X)$, is $p_1 x_1 + p_2 x_2 + \cdots + p_n x_n$.

EXPERIMENT (p. 325)   An activity or phenomenon under study or consideration.

EXPLICITLY DEFINED FUNCTION (p. 666)   A function defined by an equation $y = f(x)$.

EXPONENT (p. 791)   In the expression b^x the x is called the exponent; it is the power to which b is raised.

EXPONENTIAL FUNCTION (p. 791)   A function for which the exponent is a variable.

EXTREME VALUE (p. 696)   If $f(c)$ is either a maximum value or a minimum value, then $f(c)$ is called an extreme value.

EXTREME VALUE OF f, SUBJECT TO A CONSTRAINT ON x AND y (p. 1002)   A value of the function f, say, $f(a, b)$, such that $f(a, b) \geq f(x, y)$ or $f(a, b) \leq f(x, y)$ for all (x, y) that satisfy the constraint.

F

FACTORIAL (p. 296) n-factorial ($n!$) is the product of the integers 1, 2, 3, $\ldots, n$.

FACTORING POLYNOMIALS (p. 1043)   The process of writing a given polynomial as the product of other polynomials.

FEASIBLE REGION (p. 152)   The solution set of a system of inequalities.

FINAL TABLEAU (p. 200)   The simplex tableau that contains no negative numbers in the bottom row. This tableau gives the solution to a linear programming problem.

FIRST DERIVATIVE TEST (p. 698)
The test using a change of sign of the derivative at critical numbers to determine relative extrema.

FRACTIONAL EXPONENT (p. 1052)
When the exponent is a fraction; $b^{p/q} = (b^{1/q})^p$.

FREQUENCY DISTRIBUTION (p. 423)
Another term for frequency table.

FREQUENCY TABLE (p. 423)
A table that summarizes data by grouping the data in categories and reporting the number of observations in each category.

FUNCTION (pp. 2, 1054)
A relationship between two sets A and B such that every element a in A is related to a unique element b of B.

FUNCTION OF MORE THAN ONE VARIABLE (p. 974)   A function of two or more variables; can be written as $f(x, y)$ or $f(x, y, z)$, etc.

FUNDAMENTAL COUNTING PRINCIPLE (p. 286)   Given two activities, A_1 and A_2, that can be performed in N_1 and N_2 different ways, respectively, the total number of ways in which A_1 followed by A_2 can be performed is $N_1 \times N_2$.

FUNDAMENTAL THEOREM OF CALCULUS (pp. 877, 914)   If f is continuous and $g'(x) = f(x)$, then $\int_a^b f(x)\, dx = g(b) - g(a)$.

FUTURE VALUE OF AN ANNUITY (p. 544)   The value of all payments plus all accumulated interest. It is also called the amount.

FUTURE VALUE OF A SIMPLE INTEREST LOAN (p. 524)   The total paid by the borrower; the principal plus interest. *Amount* is another term for future value.

FUTURE VALUE OF COMPOUND INTEREST (p. 532)   The total value at the end of a specified number of compound periods. It is the original principal plus the interest accumulated over all the compound periods.

G

GAUSS-JORDAN METHOD (pp. 58, 65)
A matrix technique used to solve a system of linear equations. The procedure involves a series of row operations on an augmented matrix.

GENERALIZED POWER RULE (p. 657)
If $h(x) = (f(x))^k$, then $h'(x) = k(f(x))^{k-1} \cdot f'(x)$.

GINI INDEX (p. 906)   The quantity $2\int_0^1 (x - F(x))\, dx$, where F is the income distribution of a given country.

GLUING OF INTERVALS PROPERTY FOR DEFINITE INTEGRALS (p. 873)
$\int_a^b f(x)\, dx = \int_a^c f(x)\, dx + \int_c^b f(x)\, dx$.

GRAPH (pp. 7, 9)   The set of points (x, y) in the plane that satisfy the equation $y = f(x)$.

GRAPHING STRATEGY (p. 739)
A general six-step process for graphing a function based on analysis of asymptotes, sign-of-f', and sign-of-f''.

GROUPED DATA (p. 437)   Scores are combined into categories, and the frequency of that category is given.

H

HALF-LIFE (p. 833)   The time period required for an amount that is decreasing exponentially to become half of what it was.

HALF PLANES (p. 143)   The area of a plane that lies on one side of a line.

HIGHER-ORDER DERIVATIVES (p. 661)
General term referring to second derivative, third derivative, etc.

HISTOGRAM (p. 425)   A histogram is a visual display of a frequency table. Each category is represented by a bar, and the height of the bar indicates the frequency of the category.

HOLE IN THE GRAPH (p. 596)
What occurs in a graph when $\lim_{x \to c} f(x) \neq f(c)$.

HORIZONTAL ASYMPTOTE (p. 754)
The line $y = b$ is a horizontal asymptote if either $\lim_{x \to \infty} f(x) = b$ or $\lim_{x \to -\infty} f(x) = b$.

HORIZONTAL LINE (pp. 13, 20)
A line with slope $m = 0$ and whose graph is a horizontal line. Its equation is of the form $y = b$.

I

IDENTITY MATRIX (p. 111)
A square matrix with ones on the diagonal and zeros elsewhere.

IMPLICIT DIFFERENTIATION (p. 667)
A process used to compute dy/dx when y is defined implicitly as a function of x.

IMPLICITLY DEFINED FUNCTION (p. 666)   An equation that defines y as a function of x in a form other than $y = f(x)$.

IMPROPER INTEGRAL (p. 953)   An integral such that either the integrand is unbounded or the interval of integration is unbounded.

INCONSISTENT SYSTEM (p. 47)
A system of equations that has no solution.

INCREASING FUNCTION (p. 695)
f is increasing if whenever $x_1 < x_2$, then $f(x_1) < f(x_2)$.

INDEFINITE INTEGRAL OF f (p. 848)
The collection of all antiderivatives of f.

INDEPENDENT EVENTS (p. 367)
E and F are independent if $P(E) = P(E|F)$, or $P(F) = P(F|E)$, or $P(E \cap F) = P(E)P(F)$.

INFINITE LIMIT (p. 726) f has an infinite limit at c if either $\lim f(x) = \infty$ or $\lim f(x) = -\infty$.

INITIAL BASIC SOLUTION (p. 196)
The basic solution in the first step of a linear programming problem. All x's are set to zero, then the values of the other variables are found.

INITIAL STATE MATRIX (p. 404)
A row matrix that shows the probability of the Markov process being in each possible state at the beginning of the process.

INPUT-OUTPUT MATRIX (p. 128)
A matrix that describes the interdependence of industries.

INPUT-OUTPUT MODEL (p. 126)
A model used to analyze the interdependence of industries in an economic situation.

INSTANTANEOUS RATE OF CHANGE (pp. 570, 571)   The instantaneous rate of change of f at a is $\lim\limits_{\Delta x \to 0}$ $(f(a + \Delta x) - f(a))/\Delta x$.

INTEGERS (p. 1022)   The natural numbers, their negatives, and 0; . . . , $-3, -2, -1, 0, 1, 2, 3, \ldots$.

INTEGRAL SIGN (p. 848)
The symbol $\int$.

INTEGRAND (p. 848)   In the integral $\int f(x)\, dx$, $f(x)$ is called the integrand.

INTEGRATION (p. 848)   Another word for antidifferentiation.

INTEGRATION BY PARTS (p. 943)
$\int u\, dv = uv - \int v\, du$.

INTEGRATION BY SUBSTITUTION (p. 933)   If $u = g(x)$, then $\int f(g(x)) \cdot g'(x)\, dx = \int f(u)\, du$.

INTEREST (p. 786)   Interest can refer both to the percentage being added to an amount and to the actual amount added.

INTEREST RATE (p. 522)   The fee for borrowing money. It is usually expressed as a percentage of the principal per year.

INTERMEDIATE VALUE THEOREM (p. 603)   If f is continuous on the interval $[a, b]$ and if M is any number between $f(a)$ and $f(b)$, then the equation $f(x) = M$ has a solution in (a, b); that is, there is a number c in (a, b) with $f(c) = M$.

INTERNAL DEMAND MATRIX (p. 131)
A matrix representing the amount of goods consumed internally by industries in producing their products.

INTERSECTION (p. 268)   The intersection of two sets, A and B, is the set of all elements contained in both A and B.

INTERVAL NOTATION (p. 1039)
Using brackets or parentheses to denote a particular type of interval.

INVERSE MATRIX (p. 113)
B is the inverse of a matrix A if $AB = BA = I$.

INVESTMENT FLOW (p. 904)
The rate of change of capital.

IRRATIONAL NUMBER (p. 1023)
A number that is not the quotient of integers; a number with a nonrepeating decimal.

ITERATED INTEGRAL (p. 1011)   An integral of the form $\int_a^b (\int_c^d f(x, y)\, dx)\, dy$.

J

JUMP IN THE GRAPH (p. 593)
Behavior of graph when $x = c$ if $\lim\limits_{x \to +} f(x) \neq \lim\limits_{x \to c^-} f(x)$.

L

LEFT-HAND LIMIT (p. 591)   The number L is called the left-hand limit of f at c if $f(x)$ is near L whenever x is near c and less than c; we write $\lim\limits_{x \to c^-} f(x) = L$.

LIMIT AT INFINITY (p. 725)   The limit of $f(x)$ as x approaches infinity is L if $f(x)$ is close to L whenever x is a large number; we write $\lim\limits_{x \to \infty} f(x) = L$.

LIMIT AT NEGATIVE INFINITY (p. 725)   The limit of $f(x)$ as x approaches negative infinity is L if $f(x)$ is close to L whenever x is a negative number with $|x|$ large; we write $\lim\limits_{x \to -\infty} f(x) = L$.

LIMIT OF A FUNCTION (p. 576)
The limit of a function f as x approaches c is the number L if the values of $f(x)$ are close to L whenever x is close to, but not equal to, c.

LINEAR APPROXIMATION (p. 683)
Using the tangent line at $(a, f(a))$ to approximate $f(x)$ for values of x near a.

LINEAR FUNCTION (p. 9)
A function whose defining equation can be written $f(x) = mx + b$.

LINEAR PROGRAMMING (p. 157)
A procedure that determines the maximum (or minimum) value of a linear function within the feasible region of a system of inequalities.

ln b AS A DEFINITE INTEGRAL (p. 881) $\ln b = \int_1^b (1/x)\, dx$.

LORENZ CURVE (pp. 906, 1069)
The curve used to study the distribution of wealth in a given country.

LOWER LIMIT OF INTEGRATION (p. 869)   The number a in the expression $\int_a^b f(x)\, dx$.

M

MAIN DIAGONAL OF MATRIX (p. 112)
The diagonal running from the upper left corner to the lower right corner of a matrix.

MANY SOLUTIONS TO A SYSTEM (p. 48)   Many different sets of numbers, each forming a solution to a system of equations.

MARGINAL (p. 637)   Rate of change of; in calculus, marginal means derivative of. For example, the marginal cost function is the derivative of the cost function.

MARGINAL COST (p. 594)   The cost of the next item; the derivative of the cost function.

MARGINAL COST FUNCTION (p. 594) $MC(x)$, the derivative of the cost function. $MC(x) = C'(x)$.

MARGINAL PRODUCTIVITY OF LABOR AND CAPITAL (p. 992)   If $f(x, y)$ is a productivity function with x the number of units of labor and y the number of units of capital, then $\partial f/\partial x$ is called the marginal productivity of labor and $\partial f/\partial y$ is called the marginal productivity of capital.

MARGINAL REVENUE FUNCTION (p. 638) $MR(x)$, the derivative of the revenue function: $MR(x) = R'(x)$.

MARKOV CHAIN (p. 406) A sequence of experiments with the following properties. (1) The experiment has a finite number of discrete outcomes, called states. The experiment is always in one of these states. (2) With each additional trial the experiment can move from its present state to any other state or remain in the same state. (3) The probability of going from one state to another on the next trial depends only on the present state and not on past states.

MATRIX (p. 59)   A rectangular array of numbers.

MATRIX MULTIPLICATION (p. 104) The product AB is a matrix obtained by taking dot products of rows from matrix A and columns of matrix B. The (i, j) entry of the product is the dot product of row i from A and column j from B.

MATURITY VALUE OF A SIMPLE DISCOUNT LOAN (p. 526)   The amount the borrower is required to pay at the end of the loan. It is the same as the principal.

MAXIMIZE AN OBJECTIVE FUNCTION (p. 160)   Find a point in the feasible region that yields the maximum value of the objective function.

MAXIMUM STANDARD PROBLEM (p. 183)   A linear programming problem in which (a) the objective function is to be maximized; (b) all the constraints are $\leq$ inequalities; (c) the constants to the right of the inequalities are nonnegative.

MAXIMUM VALUE (p. 696) $f(c)$ is the maximum value of f if $f(c) \geq f(x)$ for all x.

MEAN (p. 435)   A measure of central tendency obtained by adding the numbers in the set and dividing by how many numbers are added.

MEAN OF A BINOMIAL DISTRIBUTION (p. 400)   If n is the number of trials and p is the probability of success, the mean is $\mu = np$.

MEASURE OF CENTRAL TENDENCY (p. 435)   A number that represents a typical or central number of a set of data.

MEASURE OF DISPERSION (p. 446) A number that gives an indication of how closely data tend to cluster around the mean. Some measures used are variance and standard deviation.

MEDIAN (p. 438)   The value of the middle item after the data have been arranged in order. When there is an even number of items, the mean of the two middle items is the median.

METHOD OF LAGRANGE MULTIPLIERS (p. 1004)   Analyzing the function $F(x, y, \lambda) = f(x, y) - \lambda g(x, y)$ to find the extreme values of f subject to the constraint g.

MIDPOINT APPROXIMATION FORMULA (p. 915) $\int_a^b f(x)\, dx \approx (f(c_1) + \cdots + f(c_n))\, (b - a)/n$, where $[a, b]$ is divided into n equal subintervals and c_i is the midpoint of the ith subinterval.

MINIMIZE OBJECTIVE FUNCTION (p. 160)   Find a point in the feasible region that yields the minimum value of the objective function.

MINIMUM VALUE (p. 696) $f(c)$ is the minimum value of f if $f(c) \leq f(x)$ for all x.

MIXED CONSTRAINTS (p. 216) Constraints that include two or more constraints of the type $\geq$, $\leq$, or $=$.

MODE (p. 440)   The number in a set of data that occurs most often.

MONOPOLY (p. 777)   An industry controlled by just one producer.

MULTIPLE OPTIMAL SOLUTIONS (p. 169)   More than one point in a feasible region yields an optimal solution to a linear programming problem.

MULTIPLE SOLUTION (p. 240) The optimal solution to a linear programming problem occurs at more than one point.

MULTIPLICATION OF POLYNOMIALS (p. 1042)   Two polynomials are multiplied by multiplying each term of the first by each term of the second.

MULTIPLICATION RULE (p. 359) E and F are events in a sample space. The multiplication rule states that $P(E \cap F) = P(E)P(F|E)$.

N

NATURAL LOGARITHM FUNCTION (p. 811)   Written ln x, the natural logarithm function is the logarithm function whose base is e.

NATURAL NUMBERS (p. 1022)   The numbers 1, 2, 3, 4, ...

NEGATIVE EXPONENT (p. 1051) When the exponent is negative; if t is positive, then $b^{-t} = 1/b^t$.

NEXT STATE (p. 401)   When a transition is made in a Markov process, it goes from the present state to the next state.

NO FEASIBLE SOLUTION (p. 242)
There is no feasible region for the system of inequalities of a linear programming problem. Hence there is no feasible solution to the problem.

NONBASIC VARIABLE (p. 198)
The variables that are set to zero in a basic feasible solution of a linear programming problem.

NONEXISTENCE OF DERIVATIVE (p. 621)   The derivative of f is not defined at c if (1) the graph has a corner, a sharp change of direction, at $(c, f(c))$, or (2) f is not continuous at c, or (3) the graph has a vertical tangent line at $(c, f(c))$.

NORMAL CURVE (p. 476)   A bell-shaped curve that represents the distribution of a continuous variable. The curve is symmetric about the mean, and the mean, median, and mode coincide. It is the graph of the function $f(x) = 1/\sqrt{2\pi}\, e^{-x/2}$.

NORMAL DISTRIBUTION (p. 476)   A continuous distribution of data whose graph is a normal curve. Many sets of data such as heights of females, scores on standardized tests, and reaction times to a medication are represented by a normal distribution.

NO SOLUTION (SYSTEM OF EQUATIONS) (p. 85)   There is no set of numbers that forms a solution to a system of equations.

nTH ROOT OF b (p. 1052)
The number c such that $c^n = b$.

NUMBER e (p. 789)   The number e is $\lim\limits_{n \to \infty} (1 + (1/n))^n$.

O

OBJECTIVE FUNCTION (p. 158)   A linear function of the form $z = a_1x_1 + a_2x_2 + \cdots + a_nx_n$ in a linear programming problem. The objective function is to be maximized or minimized.

ONE-CRITICAL-NUMBER TEST (p. 755)   Suppose f is continuous on an interval I and has only one critical number c in I; it follows that (1) if $f(c)$ is a relative minimum, then $f(c)$ is the minimum value of f on I, and (2) if $f(c)$ is a relative maximum, then $f(c)$ is the maximum value of f on I.

OPEN MODEL (p. 129)   In an open model of an economic system the industries in the system produce greater quantities of the commodities than they consume themselves. This is also called a production model.

OPTIMAL SOLUTION (p. 160)
A point in the feasible region that yields the maximum (or minimum) value of the objective function.

ORDERED PARTITION (p. 313)
The subsets of a partition are selected on the basis of a certain order or according to a different characteristic for each subset.

ORDINARY ANNUITY (p. 543)   An ordinary annuity is an annuity with periodic payments made at the end of each period.

ORDINATE (p. 1030)
The y-coordinate.

ORIGIN (p. 1030)   The point $(0, 0)$ in the Cartesian coordinate system.

OUTCOME (p. 325)   The result of an experiment.

OUTPUT MATRIX (p. 131)   A matrix representing the amount of goods produced by industries.

P

PARABOLA (p. 1062)   The graph of a quadratic function.

PARALLEL LINES (p. 18)   Two lines are parallel if they have the same slope or if they are both vertical lines.

PARAMETER (p. 49)   When a system of linear equations has an infinite number of solutions, some of the variables can be expressed in terms of another variable or variables, called a parameter.

PARAMETRIC FORM OF A SOLUTION (p. 49)   When many solutions to a system exist, the numbers in a solution can be represented in terms of an arbitrary value called the parameter.

PARTIAL DERIVATIVE (p. 985)   The derivative of a function with respect to one of its variables, holding the other variables constant.

PARTICULAR SOLUTION TO A DIFFERENTIAL EQUATION (p. 856)
A function that satisfies both the different equation and some additional condition or conditions.

PARTITION (p. 313)   A set S is partitioned into nonempty subsets if every pair of subsets is disjoint and the union of the subsets is S.

PAYMENT PERIOD OF AN ANNUITY (p. 543)   The time between successive payments.

PERCENTAGE CHANGE (p. 786)
Used when the change is described not in terms of the actual amount of change, but as a percentage of the original amount.

PERCENTAGE GROWTH (p. 828)
When the rate of change is a percentage of the amount; when $y' = ky$.

PERCENTILE (p. 453)   A measure of position giving the percent of scores that are the same as or less than the score measured.

PERFECTLY COMPETITIVE MARKET (p. 775)   A market in which many companies are producing the same product and no one company can influence the price of the product.

PERIODIC INTEREST RATE (p. 532)
The interest rate per time period used in computing compound interest. It is usually the annual rate divided by the number of compound periods per year.

PERIODIC PAYMENT OF AN ANNUITY (p. 543) The amount of each annuity payment.

PERMUTATION (p. 292) A permutation is an arrangement of elements from a set in which repetitions of elements are not allowed and the order in which the elements are arranged is significant.

PERMUTATION WITH IDENTICAL OBJECTS (p. 297) A permutation with some of the objects identical so that an interchange of two identical objects produces no new arrangement.

PHASE I (p. 219) When a negative constant appears in the rightmost column of an initial simplex tableau and the basic solution is not feasible, the tableau must be modified so that the basic solution is feasible. This step is called Phase I. This step is done by selecting a row with a negative entry in the last column and using another negative entry in that row as a pivot element.

PHASE II (p. 219) When the modifications in Phase I produce a tableau with basic feasible solutions, then the usual simplex method is carried out. This is called Phase II.

PIECEWISE DEFINED FUNCTION (p. 1075) A function such that the rule for evaluating $f(x)$ depends on the value of x.

PIE CHART (p. 425) A visual representation of a frequency table. A circle is cut into pie-shaped pieces. Each piece represents a category of data, and the size of the piece indicates the proportion of data that fall in that category.

PIVOT COLUMN (p. 197) The column in the simplex tableau that contains the pivot element. It is the column with the most negative entry in the bottom row.

PIVOT ELEMENT (p. 196) The element common to the pivot row and pivot column.

PIVOT ROW (p. 197) The row in the simplex tableau that contains the pivot element. The row is determined by dividing the constant in the last column by the corresponding number in the pivot column. The smallest nonnegative ratio determines the pivot row.

POINT OF INFLECTION (p. 716) The point $(a, f(a))$ is a point of inflection if the graph of f is concave up on one side of $(a, f(a))$ and concave down on the other side.

POINT-SLOPE FORMULA (pp. 17 20) The equation of a line in terms of a given slope and point. It is of the form $y - y_1 = m(x - x_1)$, where m is the given slope and (x_1, y_1) is the given point on the line.

POLYNOMIAL ARITHMETIC (p. 1041) Adding, subtracting, multiplying, or dividing polynomials.

POWER RULE (p. 631) If $f(x) = x^k$, then $f'(x) = kx^{k-1}$.

PREMISE OF AN ARGUMENT (p. 621) A given statement in a proof.

PRESENT STATE (p. 401) The current state of a Markov process.

PRESENT VALUE OF A (p. 815) The amount that must be invested now to receive A in t years.

PRESENT VALUE OF A LOAN (p. 522) The amount of money received by the borrower in a loan.

PRESENT VALUE OF AN ANNUITY (p. 549) A lump sum payment invested at compound interest that yields the same total amount over a period of time as an annuity with equal periodic payments made over the same time frame.

PRESENT VALUE OF COMPOUND INTEREST (p. 537) The present value of an amount due at a specified time is the principal that must be invested now to accumulate the amount due.

PRINCIPAL (p. 522) The amount of money borrowed in a loan.

PROBABILITY ASSIGNMENT (p. 327) A sample space is given a probability assignment when (a) each outcome is assigned a probability, (b) each probability is a number in the interval from 0 to 1 (0 and 1 may be used as probabilities), and (c) the sum of probabilities of all the simple outcomes is 1.

PROBABILITY DISTRIBUTION (p. 459) If a random variable X has the values $x_1, x_2, \ldots, x_n$, then a probability distribution $P(X)$ is a rule that assigns a probability $P(x_i)$ to each value x_i. More specifically, $0 \le P(x_i) \le 1$ and $P(x_1) + P(x_2) + \cdots + P(x_n) = 1$.

PROBABILITY STATE MATRIX (p. 402) A row matrix that shows, for each state in a Markov process, the probability the process is in that state.

PROCEEDS (p. 526) The amount the borrower receives in a simple discount loan. The formula is $PR = M - Mdt$.

PRODUCERS' SURPLUS (p. 902) The quantity $\int_0^{x_1} (p_1 - S(x))\, dx$, where the market price is p_1, the demand is x_1, and $S(x) = p$ is the price-supply equation.

PRODUCTION MODEL (p. 129) In a production model of an economic system the industries in the system produce greater quantities of the commodities than they consume themselves. This is also called an open model.

PRODUCT RULE (p. 640) If $h(x) = f(x) \cdot g(x)$, then $h'(x) = g(x) \cdot f'(x) + f(x) \cdot g'(x)$.

PROPERTIES OF INEQUALITIES (p. 1033) (1) If the same quantity is added to or subtracted from both sides of an inequality, the inequality remains unchanged. (2) If both sides of an inequality are multiplied or divided by a positive number, the inequality remains unchanged. (3) If both sides of an inequality are multiplied or divided by a negative number, the inequality reverses.

Q

QUADRANTS (p. 1032)   The four regions of the plane separated by the x- and y-axes.

QUADRATIC FORMULA (pp. 1045, 1066)   The formula that gives the solutions to the equation $ax^2 + bx + c = 0$; $x = (-b \pm \sqrt{b^2 - 4ac})/2a$.

QUADRATIC FUNCTION (p. 1062) A function whose rule can be written $f(x) = ax^2 + bx + c$ with $a \neq 0$.

QUOTIENT RULE (p. 644)   If $h(x) = f(x)/g(x)$, then $h'(x) = (g(x) \cdot f'(x) - f(x) \cdot g'(x))/[g(x)]^2$.

R

RANDOM SELECTION (p. 337) A selection process in which the selections are equally likely.

RANDOM VARIABLE (p. 457)   A rule that assigns a number to each outcome of an experiment.

RANGE (pp. 2, 1054)   The set B in the definition of function; the set of all numbers b such that $b = f(a)$ for some a in the domain of f.

RANK (p. 452)   A measure of position; the position occupied by a number after all numbers are placed in order.

RATIONAL FUNCTION (p. 1046) The quotient of two polynomials.

RATIONAL NUMBER (p. 1022)   A number of the form p/q, where p and q are integers; a number with a repeating decimal.

REAL NUMBER (p. 1023)   A rational or an irrational number.

RECTANGULAR COORDINATE SYSTEM (p. 1030)   The same as Cartesian coordinate system.

REDUCED ECHELON FORM (p. 75) A matrix in which the rows consisting of all zeros are grouped at the bottom of the matrix, the leftmost nonzero number in a row is a 1, a leftmost 1 of a row is to the right of the leftmost 1 of the previous row, and all elements above and below a leftmost 1 are zeros.

REDUCED SAMPLE SPACE (p. 358) In computing the conditional probability $P(E|F)$, F becomes the sample space. It is called the reduced sample space.

REGULAR MATRIX (p. 410)   A transition matrix of a Markov process is regular if some power of the matrix has only positive entries.

RELATED RATES (p. 673)   The rates of change of two quantities that are themselves related by some equation.

RELATION BETWEEN ln x AND e^x (pp. 811, 820) $\ln(e^x) = x = e^{\ln x}$.

RELATIVE EXTREME VALUE (p. 697) $f(c)$ is a relative extreme value if $f(c)$ is either a relative maximum or relative minimum value.

RELATIVE MAXIMUM OF A FUNCTION OF TWO VARIABLES (p. 994) $f(a, b)$ is a relative maximum if $f(a, b) \geq f(x, y)$ for all (x, y) near (a, b).

RELATIVE MAXIMUM VALUE (p. 696) $f(c)$ is a relative maximum value of f if there is an open interval (a, b) in the domain of f with c in (a, b) and $f(c) \geq f(x)$ for all x in (a, b).

RELATIVE MINIMUM OF A FUNCTION OF TWO VARIABLES (p. 994) $f(a, b)$ is a relative minimum if $f(a, b) \leq f(x, y)$ for all (x, y) near (a, b).

RELATIVE MINIMUM VALUE (p. 696) $f(c)$ is a relative minimum value of f if there is an open interval (a, b) in the domain of f with c in (a, b) and $f(c) \leq f(x)$ for all x in (a, b).

REPLACEMENT PRINCIPLE (p. 580) If f and g are two functions with $f(x) = g(x)$ for all x near c, $x \neq c$, and if $\lim_{x \to c} g(x) = L$, then $\lim_{x \to c} f(x) = L$ also.

REVENUE FUNCTION (p. 26)   A function that relates the number of items sold to the revenue obtained. The linear revenue function is of the form $R(x) = cx$, where c is the unit price.

REVERSING THE ORDER OF INTEGRATION (p. 1014)   Rewriting $\int_a^b \int_c^d f(x, y)\, dx\, dy$ as $\int_c^d \int_a^b f(x, y)\, dy\, dx$, or vice versa.

REWRITING b^x (p. 836) $b^x = e^{x \ln b}$.

REWRITING LOG$_b$ x (p. 838) $\log_b x = \ln x/\ln b$.

RIEMANN SUM (p. 914)   A sum of the form $f(c_1)\, \Delta x_1 + f(c_2)\, \Delta x_2 + \cdots + f(c_n)\, \Delta x_n$, where c_i is in the ith subinterval from a to b and Δx_i is the length of the ith interval; this sum approximates $\int_a^b f(x)\, dx$.

RIGHT-HAND LIMIT (p. 592)   The number L is called the right-hand limit of f at c if $f(x)$ is near L whenever x is near c and greater than c; we write $\lim_{x \to c^+} f(x) = L$.

ROW MATRIX (p. 59)   An array composed of a single row of numbers.

ROW OPERATIONS (p. 62) Operations on the rows of a matrix that lead to the solution to a system of equations. The operations are: interchange two rows, multiply or divide a row by a nonzero constant, multiply a row by a constant and add it to another row.

RULE OF A FUNCTION (pp. 2, 1055) The rule that determines the number in the range that is assigned to a number in the domain of the function.

S

SADDLE POINT (p. 998) The point (a, b) is a saddle point if (a, b) is a critical point but $f(a, b)$ is not a relative extreme value.

SAMPLE SPACE (p. 325) The set of all possible outcomes of an experiment.

SCALAR MULTIPLICATION (p. 96) Each entry in a matrix is multiplied by a number called a scalar.

SECOND DERIVATIVE (p. 660) The derivative of the derivative, written f''.

SECOND DERIVATIVE TEST (p. 712) If $f'(c) = 0$ and if (a) $f''(c) > 0$, then $f(c)$ is a relative minimum, (b) $f''(c) < 0$, then $f(c)$ is a relative maximum.

SECOND DERIVATIVE TEST FOR A FUNCTION OF TWO VARIABLES (p. 997) If (a, b) is a critical point with $M(a, b) \neq 0$, then this test can be used to determine whether $f(a, b)$ is a relative maximum, a relative minimum, or neither.

SECOND-ORDER DIFFERENTIAL EQUATION (p. 860) A differential equation that involves the second derivative.

SECOND PARTIAL DERIVATIVE (p. 988) The partial derivative of a partial derivative.

SET (p. 264) A collection of objects.

SIGN-OF-f (p. 605) A chart showing $+$ if $f(x) > 0$ and $-$ if $f(x) < 0$.

SIMPLE DISCOUNT (p. 526) In a simple discount loan the interest is deducted from the principal at the time the loan is made, so the borrower receives less than the principal.

SIMPLE INTEREST (p. 522) The fee paid for the use of money. The fee is based on a specified percent per year of the loan. The formula is $I = Prt$.

SIMPLE OUTCOME (p. 325) An element from a sample space.

SIMPLEX TABLEAU (p. 188) A matrix formed by the constraints and objective function of a linear programming problem.

SIMPSON'S RULE (p. 969) $\int_a^b f(x)\, dx \approx (b - a)/3n\ (f(a) + 4f(x_1) + 2f(x_2) + \cdots + 4f(x_{n-1}) + f(b))$, where n is even and $x_k = a + k\,((b - a)/n)$.

SINKING FUND (p. 546) Money accumulated to provide a specified amount A at some future date. It is an annuity with the periodic payments that yield a future value equal to A.

SIX-STEP PROCESS FOR SOLVING WORD PROBLEMS (p. 759) A procedure, broken down into six steps, for setting up and solving word problems.

SIZE OF MATRIX (p. 93) The number of rows and columns of a matrix.

SLACK VARIABLE (p. 185) Variables with nonnegative values that are used to convert an inequality to an equation.

SLOPE (pp. 10, 11, 20) The slope of a line is the number m when the equation of the line is written $y = mx + b$; also $m = (y_2 - y_1)/(x_2 - x_1)$, where (x_1, y_1) and (x_2, y_2) are any two points on the line.

SLOPE OF A TANGENT LINE (p. 614) The slope of the line tangent to the graph of f at the point $(a, f(a))$ is $f'(a)$, the derivative of f at a.

SOLUTION (p. 1026) A number that satisfies an equation or inequality.

SOLUTION OF A SYSTEM OF EQUATIONS (p. 40) A set of numbers, one number for each variable in a system of equations, that makes all equations in the system true.

SOLUTIONS TO A SYSTEM OF LINEAR INEQUALITIES (p. 40) The set of points that satisfy all inequalities in a system of inequalities.

SOLUTION TO A DIFFERENTIAL EQUATION (p. 856) A function that satisfies the equation.

SQUARE MATRIX (p. 93) A matrix with the same number of rows as the number of columns.

STANDARD DEVIATION (p. 447) A number that measures the dispersion of data around the mean. It is the square root of the variance.

STANDARD DEVIATION OF A BINOMIAL DISTRIBUTION (p. 499) If n is the number of trials and p is the probability of success, the standard deviation is $\sigma(X) = \sqrt{np(1 - p)} = \sqrt{npq}$.

STANDARD DEVIATION OF A RANDOM VARIABLE (p. 473) The standard deviation, $\sigma(X) = \sqrt{\text{variance }(X)}$.

STANDARD ERROR (p. 510) Let n be the sample size and let p be the proportion that respond favorably. The standard error of the proportion is $SE = \sqrt{(p(1 - p))/n}$.

STANDARD MINIMUM PROBLEM (p. 183) A linear programming problem is standard minimum if (a) the objective function is to be minimized, (b) all inequalities are $\geq$, and (c) the constants to the right of the inequalities are nonnegative.

STATE (MARKOV PROCESS) (p. 401) A category, situation, outcome, or position that a process can occupy at any given time. The states are disjoint and cover all possible outcomes of a Markov experiment.

STEADY STATE (MARKOV PROCESS) (p. 406) When there is no change in a Markov process from one state to the next, the process has reached a steady state.

STRAIGHT-LINE DEPRECIATION (p. 29) The depreciation of an item is assumed to follow a straight line; the amount of depreciation is the same each year.

SUBSET (p. 267)   A set B is a subset of A if every element in B is also an element of A.

SUCCESSES (p. 335)   When seeking the probability of an event, an outcome in the event is called a success.

SUM RULE FOR DERIVATIVES (p. 634)   If $h(x) = f(x) + g(x)$, then $h'(x) = f'(x) + g'(x)$.

SUPPLY AND DEMAND (p. 51) Supply is the amount of a commodity that is available to the consumer. Demand is the amount of a commodity bought by consumers.

SURFACE (p. 977)   A two-dimensional figure in three-dimensional space; the graph of a function.

SYSTEM OF EQUATIONS (p. 40) A set of two or more equations.

T

TABLE OF INTEGRALS (p. 960) Used to evaluate integrals.

TANGENT LINE (p. 614)   The line tangent to the graph of f at the point $(a, f(a))$ is the line through $(a, f(a))$ with slope $f'(a)$.

THREE-DIMENSIONAL SPACE (p. 977) The set of all triples (x, y, z), where x, y, and z are real numbers.

THREE-STEP PROCESS FOR COMPUTING THE INSTANTANEOUS RATE OF CHANGE (p. 571)   Method for computing $\lim_{\Delta x \to 0} (f(a + \Delta x) - f(a))/\Delta x$.

TOTAL CHANGE OF A FUNCTION ON AN INTERVAL (p. 869)   The difference $g(b) - g(a)$, where $g'(x)$ is the rate of change of a function on the interval $[a, b]$.

TRANSITION MATRIX (p. 402) A matrix representing a Markov process. The (i, j) entry is the probability that the process moves from state i to state j.

TRANSPOSE OF A MATRIX (p. 248) The transpose of a matrix is another matrix obtained by using the first row of the given matrix as the first column of the transpose. The second row, etc., become the second column, etc., of the transpose.

TRAPEZOIDAL RULE (p. 968) $\int_a^b f(x)\, dx \approx (b - a)/n\, (f(a)/2 + f(x_1) + \cdots + f(x_{n-1}) + f(b)/2)$, where $x_k = a + k\,((b - a)/n)$.

TREE DIAGRAM (p. 284) A diagram showing all the different ways in which a sequence of activities can be performed.

TRIAL (p. 325)   Each observation or repetition of an experiment is a trial.

U

UNBOUNDED FEASIBLE REGION (p. 170)   A feasible region with some part that extends indefinitely.

UNBOUNDED INTERVAL (p. 951) An interval of the form (a, ∞), $[a, \infty)$, $(-\infty, b)$, $(-\infty, b]$, or $(-\infty, \infty)$.

UNBOUNDED SOLUTION (p. 240) The feasible region of a linear programming problem is unbounded, and the objective function is unbounded. There is no maximum value to the objective function.

UNION (p. 274)   The union of two sets, A and B, is the set whose elements are from A, from B, or from both.

UNIQUE SOLUTION (p. 88)   There is exactly one set of numbers that forms a solution to a system of equations.

UNIVERSE (p. 271)   Sets under discussion come from a restricted set that is determined by the context. This restricted set is the universe from which the sets come.

UNORDERED PARTITION (p. 316) The subsets of a partition are selected with no regard for the order of selection.

UPPER LIMIT OF INTEGRATION (p. 869)   The number b in the expression $\int_a^b f(x)\, dx$.

V

VALUE OF A FUNCTION (p. 1054) If $f(a) = b$, then b is called the value of f at a.

VARIABLE (p. 1026)   A quantity that varies, usually represented by a letter such as t, x, or y.

VARIANCE (p. 447)   A number that measures the dispersion of data around the mean.

VARIANCE OF A BINOMIAL DISTRIBUTION (p. 499)   If n is the number of trials and p is the probability of success, the variance $\sigma^2(X) = np(1 - p) = npq$.

VARIANCE OF A RANDOM VARIABLE (p. 473)   If a random variable X has the values $x_1, x_2, \ldots, x_n$, corresponding probabilities $p_1, p_2, \ldots, p_n$, and expected value μ, then $\sigma^2(X) = p_1(x_1 - \mu)^2 + p_2(x_2 - \mu)^2 + \cdots + p_n(x_n - \mu)^2$.

VENN DIAGRAM (p. 271) A diagram used to represent a universe, sets, and their relationship. A rectangle represents the universe, and circles represent sets.

VERTICAL ASYMPTOTE (p. 727) The line $x = a$ is a vertical asymptote if at least one of the following is true: (1) $\lim_{x \to a^+} f(x) = \infty$, (2) $\lim_{x \to a^-} f(x) = \infty$, (3) $\lim_{x \to a^+} f(x) = -\infty$, or (4) $\lim_{x \to a^-} f(x) = -\infty$.

VERTICAL LINE (pp. 14, 20)   A line whose equation can be written $x = k$; a line parallel to the y-axis; a line with no slope.

VOLUME OF A SOLID (p. 1015)   If $f(x, y) \geq 0$ for all (x, y) in a rectangle R, the volume of the solid bounded above by the graph of f and below by the rectangle R is $\iint_R f$.

VOLUME OF REVOLUTION (p. 918)
The volume obtained by revolving a region about an axis.

X

x-AXIS (p. 1030)   The set of points $(x, 0)$ in the Cartesian coordinate system; the horizontal axis.

x-COORDINATE (p. 1030)   The directed distance of a point from the y-axis; the first coordinate of (x, y).

Y

y-AXIS (p. 1030)   The set of points $(0, y)$ in the Cartesian coordinate system; the vertical axis.

y-COORDINATE (p. 1030)   The directed distance of a point from the x-axis; the second coordinate of (x, y).

y-INTERCEPT (pp. 10, 20)   The y-coordinate of the point where the y-axis meets the graph of a function 0, that is, $f(0)$.

Z

ZERO EXPONENT (p. 1051)   When the exponent equals 0; $b^0 = 1$ if $b \neq 0$.

ZEROS OF A FUNCTION (p. 1065)
The solutions to the equation $f(x) = 0$.

z-SCORE (p. 453)   The number of standard deviations a score lies from the mean. It is computed by $z = (x - \mu)/\sigma$.

Special Symbols

Δx (p. 569)   Delta x, the change in x.

dy/dx AND d/dx $f(x)$ (p. 622)   Other notations for $f'(x)$, the derivative of f at x.

$f(x)\big|_a^b$ (p. 869)   Shorthand notation for $f(b) - f(a)$.

$f'(x)$ (p. 619)   The derivative of f at x; $f'(x) = \lim_{\Delta x \to 0} (f(x + \Delta x) - f(x))/\Delta x$.

$f'(a)$ (p. 571)   The derivative of f at a.

$>, <, \geq, \leq$ (p. 1034)   Greater than, less than, greater than or equal to, less than or equal to, respectively.

$\int f(x)\ dx$ (p. 848)   The indefinite integral of f.

$\int_a^b f(x)\ dx$ (p. 868)   The definite integral of f from a to b.

$\lim_{x \to a^-} f(x) = -\infty$ (p. 727)   The limit of $f(x)$ as x approaches a from the left is negative infinity if $f(x)$ is a negative number with $|f(x)|$ large whenever x is close to a and $x < a$.

$\lim_{x \to a^-} f(x) = \infty$ (p. 727)   The limit of $f(x)$ as x approaches a from the left is infinity if $f(x)$ is a large number whenever x is close to a and $x < a$.

$\lim_{x \to a^+} f(x) = -\infty$ (p. 727)   The limit of $f(x)$ as x approaches a from the right is negative infinity if $f(x)$ is a negative number with $|f(x)|$ large whenever x is close to a and $x > a$.

$\lim_{x \to a^+} f(x) = \infty$ (p. 727)   The limit of $f(x)$ as x approaches a from the right is infinity if $f(x)$ is a large number whenever x is close to a and $x > a$.

$\lim_{x \to -\infty} f(x)$ (p. 725)   The limit of f as x approaches negative infinity (see *Limit at Negative Infinity*).

$\lim_{x \to \infty} f(x)$ (p. 725)   The limit of f as x approaches infinity (see *Limit at Infinity*).

$\lim_{\Delta x \to 0} (f(a + \Delta x) - f(a))/\Delta x$ (p. 571)   The derivative of f at a; the instantaneous rate of change of f at a.

INDEX

FORMULAS FROM GEOMETRY

AREA OF A TRIANGLE:

$$A = \frac{1}{2} \text{ base} \cdot \text{height}$$

$$= \frac{1}{2} b \cdot h$$

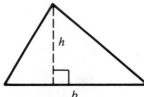

AREA OF A TRAPEZOID:

$$A = \frac{1}{2} (\text{sum of heights}) \cdot \text{base}$$

$$= \frac{1}{2} (h_1 + h_2) \cdot b$$

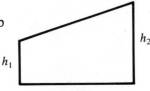

AREA OF A RECTANGLE:

$$A = \text{base} \cdot \text{height}$$
$$= b \cdot h$$

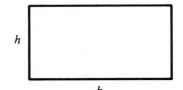

VOLUME OF A SPHERE:

$$V = \frac{4}{3} \pi (\text{radius})^3$$

$$= \frac{4}{3} \pi R^2$$

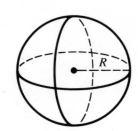

AREA OF A CIRCLE:

$$A = \pi \cdot (\text{radius})^2$$
$$= \pi R^2$$

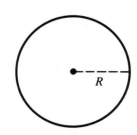

VOLUME OF A CYLINDER:

$$V = (\text{area of base}) \cdot \text{height}$$
$$= \pi R^2 \cdot h$$

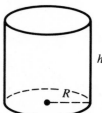